A Review of the Events of 1985

The 1986 World Book Year Book

The Annual Supplement to The World Book Encyclopedia

World Book, Inc.

a Scott Fetzer company

Chicago London Sydney Toronto

Staff

Publisher
William H. Nault

Editor in Chief
Robert O. Zeleny

Editorial Staff
Executive Editor
A. Richard Harmet

Managing Editor
Wayne Wille

Associate Editor
Sara Dreyfuss

Senior Editors
David L. Dreier
Barbara A. Mayes
Jay Myers
Rod Such

Contributing Editors
Robie Liscomb
Karin C. Rosenberg
Darlene R. Stille

Research Editor
Irene B. Keller

Index Editor
Claire Bolton

Statistical Editor
Tom Klonoski

Editorial Assistant
Ethel Matthews

Art Staff
Executive Art Director
William Hammond

Art Director
Roberta Dimmer

Senior Artist
Nikki Conner

Artists
Alice F. Dole
Alexandra Kalantzis
Lucy Smith

Photography Director
John S. Marshall

Senior Photographs Editor
Sandra M. Ozanick

Photographs Editor
Geralyn Swietek

Research Services
Director
Mary Norton

Researchers
Rebecca Chekouras
David Shannon

Library Services
Mary Kayaian, Head
Susan O'Connell

Cartographic Services
H. George Stoll, Head

Product Production
Executive Director
Peter Mollman

Director of Manufacturing
Joseph C. LaCount

Director of Pre-Press
Jerry Stack

Production Control Manager
Barbara Podczerwinski

Assistant Product Manager
Madelyn Krzak

Film Separations Manager
Alfred J. Mozdzen

Research and Development Manager
Henry Koval

Printed in the United States of America.
ISBN 0-7166-0486-8
ISSN 0084-1439
Library of Congress Catalog Card Number: 62-4818

Preface

The following people have something in common—economist Franco Modigliani, tennis players Kevin Curren and Martina Navratilova, Chicago student Walter Polovchak, and some of the 21 workers at Hantscho, Incorporated, Mount Vernon, N.Y., who shared a lottery jackpot. What do they have in common? All of them are written about in Year on File articles in this edition of THE YEAR BOOK—Modigliani in "Nobel Prizes," Curren and Navratilova in "Tennis," and Polovchak and the workers in "Newsmakers." But, more than that, all of them were born elsewhere and, for one reason or another, moved to the United States.

Immigrants founded the United States, and waves of immigrants have continued to settle in America—in search of economic opportunity or for political or religious freedom. For many immigrants, the Statue of Liberty in New York Harbor has been a welcoming symbol. But 100 years of exposure to the weather and to millions of visitors left the statue badly in need of repair. A Special Report on page 50, "Restoring Lady Liberty," details what has been done to ready the statue for its centennial celebration in 1986.

But most of the latest wave of immigrants do not see the Statue of Liberty as they arrive. They enter on the U.S. West Coast from Asia or cross the southern border from Latin America. Some arrive legally, some illegally. Another Report, "The New New Americans" on page 66, examines this controversial wave.   WAYNE WILLE

Contents

A tear-out page of cross-reference tabs for insertion in THE WORLD BOOK ENCYCLOPEDIA appears after page 16.

Contributors

Contributors not listed on these pages are members of THE WORLD BOOK YEAR BOOK editorial staff.

Adachi, Ken, B.A., M.A.; Literary Critic, *The Toronto Star.* [CANADIAN LITERATURE]

Adams, Nicholas, Ph.D; Chairman, Department of Art and Architecture, Lehigh University. [WORLD BOOK SUPPLEMENT: RUDOLPH, PAUL]

Alexiou, Arthur G., B.S.E.E., M.S.E.E.; Assistant Secretary, Intergovernmental Oceanographic Commission. [OCEAN]

Andrews, Peter J., B.A., M.S.; Free-Lance Writer; Biochemist. [CHEMISTRY]

Apseloff, Marilyn Fain, B.A., M.A.; Assistant Professor of English, Kent State University. [LITERATURE FOR CHILDREN]

Barber, Peggy, B.A., M.L.S.; Associate Executive Director-Communications, American Library Association. [AMERICAN LIBRARY ASSOCIATION; LIBRARY]

Beatty, J. Kelly, B.S., M.S.; Senior Editor, *Sky & Telescope.* [Special Report: A NEW ERA IN SPACE]

Becker, William H., Ph.D.; Professor of History, George Washington University. [WORLD BOOK SUPPLEMENT: IACOCCA, LEE]

Beckwith, David C., A.B., M.S., J.D.; National Correspondent, *Time* magazine. [COURTS; CRIME; PRISON; SUPREME COURT OF THE UNITED STATES; SUPREME COURT OF THE UNITED STATES (Close-Up)]

Bednarski, P. J., Entertainment Media Business Reporter, *Chicago Sun-Times.* [RADIO; TELEVISION]

Benjamin, Gerald, A.B., M.A., Ph.D.; Professor of Political Science, State University of New York, New Paltz College. [WORLD BOOK SUPPLEMENT: CUOMO, MARIO MATTHEW]

Berman, Howard A., M.H.L.; Rabbi, Chicago Sinai Congregation. [JEWS AND JUDAISM]

Biggar, Jeanne C., B.S., M.S., Ph.D.; Associate Professor of Sociology, University of Virginia. [POPULATION]

Blackadar, Alfred K., A.B., Ph.D.; Professor of Meteorology, The Pennsylvania State University. [WEATHER]

Borklund, Elmer W., A.B., M.A., Ph.D.; Professor of English, Pennsylvania State University. [WORLD BOOK SUPPLEMENT: HUGHES, TED]

Bradsher, Henry S., A.B., B.J.; Foreign Affairs Analyst; Author. [ASIA and Asian Country Articles]

Breslin, Paul, Ph.D.; Associate Professor of English, Northwestern University. [POETRY]

Brown, Kenneth, former Editor, *United Kingdom Press Gazette.* [EUROPE and European Country Articles]

Bukro, Casey, B.S.J., M.S.J.; Environment Writer, *Chicago Tribune.* [ENVIRONMENTAL POLLUTION]

Campbell, Robert, B.A., M.S., M. Arch.; Architect and Critic. [ARCHITECTURE; Special Report: ARCHITECTURE'S NEW LOOK]

Campion, Owen F., B.A.; Editor in Chief, *The Tennessee Register.* [ROMAN CATHOLIC CHURCH]

Cawthorne, David M., Reporter, *The Journal of Commerce.* [Transportation Articles]

Cormier, Frank, B.S.J., M.S.J.; former White House Correspondent, Associated Press. [U.S. Government Articles]

Cormier, Margot, B.A., M.S.; Free-Lance Writer. [U.S. Government Articles]

Cromie, William J., B.S.; Executive Director, Council for the Advancement of Science Writing. [SPACE EXPLORATION; Special Report: RESTORING LADY LIBERTY]

Cviic, Chris, B.A., B.S.; Eastern European Specialist, *The Economist.* [Eastern European Country Articles; RUSSIA (Close-Up)]

Datre, Donna M., B.A.; Public Information Manager, Toy Manufacturers of America, Incorporated. [GAMES AND TOYS]

DeFrank, Thomas M., B.A., M.A.; Correspondent, *Newsweek* magazine. [ARMED FORCES]

Dent, Thomas H., Executive Director, The Cat Fanciers' Association, Inc. [CAT]

Dertouzos, Michael L., B.S., M.S., Ph.D.; Director, M.I.T. Laboratory for Computer Science, Massachusetts Institute of Technology. [WORLD BOOK SUPPLEMENT: COMPUTER, PERSONAL]

Dewey, Russell A., B.A., Ph.D.; Assistant Professor of Psychology, Georgia Southern College. [PSYCHOLOGY]

DiCesare, Annmaria B., B.A.; Director of Information Services, Magazine Publishers Association. [MAGAZINE]

Duffy, Robert R., National Affairs Writer, *The Toronto Star.* [TORONTO]

El-Hawary, M. E., B.Eng., Ph.D.; Professor of Electrical Engineering, Technical University of Nova Scotia. [WORLD BOOK SUPPLEMENT: ELECTRIC POWER]

Ellis, Barbara W., B.A., B.S.; Editor/Publications Director, *American Horticulturist.* [GARDENING]

Esseks, J. Dixon, A.B., A.M., Ph.D.; Associate Professor of Political Science, Northern Illinois University. [AFRICA and African Country Articles]

Evans, Larry, B.A.; Syndicated Chess Columnist. [WORLD BOOK SUPPLEMENT: CHESS]

Evans, Sandra, B.S.J.; Staff Writer, *The Washington Post.* [WASHINGTON, D.C.]

Farr, David M. L., M.A., D.Phil.; Professor of History, Carleton University, Ottawa. [CANADA; Canadian Province Articles; MULRONEY, M. BRIAN; SAUVÉ, JEANNE M.; TRUDEAU, PIERRE ELLIOTT]

Fisher, Robert W., B.A., M.A.; Senior Economist, U.S. Bureau of Labor Statistics. [LABOR]

Fitzgerald, Mark, B.A.; Midwest Editor, *Editor & Publisher* magazine. [NEWSPAPER; PUBLISHING]

Francis, Henry G., B.S.; Executive Editor, American Contract Bridge League. [BRIDGE]

Fuchs, Lawrence H., Ph.D.; Chair, American Studies Department, Brandeis University. [Special Report: THE NEW NEW AMERICANS]

Gatty, Bob, President, Gatty Communications, Incorporated. [FOOD]

Goldhaber, Judith Shally, B.A.; Editor/Writer, Lawrence Berkeley Laboratory, University of California. [Special Report: DOOMSDAY FOR THE DINOSAURS]

Goldner, Nancy, B.A.; Dance Critic, *The Philadelphia Inquirer.* [DANCING]

Goldstein, Jane, B.A.; Director of Publicity, Santa Anita Park. [HORSE RACING]

Gordon, Margaret T., B.S.J., M.S.J., Ph.D.; Director, Center for Urban Affairs and Policy Research, and Professor, Medill School of Journalism, Northwestern University. [CITY]

Gould, William, B.A.; Civil Servant, Central Office of Information, Her Majesty's Government, London. [ENGLAND]

Graham, Jarlath J., A.B.; Vice President and Director of External Relations, Crain Communications Incorporated. [ADVERTISING]

Grigadean, Jerry, B.S., M.Mus., Ph.D.; Writer and Producer, Grigadean Productions. [POPULAR MUSIC]

Guyot, James F., B.A., A.M., Ph.D.; Professor of Political Science and Public Administration, City University of New York. [WORLD BOOK SUPPLEMENT: BURMA]

Hannan, Patrick, B.A.; Producer/Presenter, British Broadcasting Corporation. [WALES]

Harakas, Stanley Samuel, B.A., B.D., Th.D.; Professor of Christian Ethics, Holy Cross Greek Orthodox School of Theology. [EASTERN ORTHODOX CHURCHES]

Haverstock, Nathan A., A.B.; Director, The Latin American Service. [LATIN AMERICA and Latin-American Country Articles]

Herreid, Clyde Freeman, II, A.B., M.Sc., Ph.D.; Professor of Biological Sciences, State University of New York at Buffalo. [ZOOLOGY]

Higgins, James V., B.A.; Automotive Industry Reporter, *The Detroit News.* [AUTOMOBILE]

Hillgren, Sonja, B.J., M.A.; Farm Editor, United Press International. [FARM AND FARMING]

Hunzeker, Jeanne M., D.S.W.; Associate Professor of Social Welfare, Southern University at New Orleans. [CHILD WELFARE]

Jacobi, Peter P., B.S.J., M.S.J.; Professor of Journalism, Indiana University. [CLASSICAL MUSIC]

Johanson, Donald C., B.S., M.A., Ph.D.; Director, Institute of Human Origins. [ANTHROPOLOGY]

Joseph, Lou, B.A.; Senior Medical Writer, Hill and Knowlton. [DENTISTRY]

Kind, Joshua B., B.A., Ph.D.; Professor of Art History, Northern Illinois University. [VISUAL ARTS]

Kisor, Henry, B.A., M.S.J.; Book Editor, *Chicago Sun-Times.* [LITERATURE]

Kitchen, Paul, B.A., B.L.S.; Executive Director, Canadian Library Association. [CANADIAN LIBRARY ASSOCIATION]

Knapp, Elaine Stuart, B.A.; Editor, Council of State Governments. [STATE GOVERNMENT]

Koenig, Louis W., B.A., M.A., Ph.D., L.H.D.; Professor of Government, New York University. [CIVIL RIGHTS]

Kolgraf, Ronald, B.A., M.A.; Publisher, *Computer & Electronics Marketing.* [MANUFACTURING]

Kuersten, Joan, B.A.; Editor/Writer, National PTA. [NATIONAL PTA]

Kushma, David W., B.A., M.A.; City-County Bureau Chief, *Detroit Free Press.* [DETROIT]

Langdon, Robert, Executive Officer, Pacific Manuscripts Bureau, Australian National University. [NEW CALEDONIA; PACIFIC ISLANDS]

Larsen, Paul A., P.E., B.S., Ch.E.; Member: American Philatelic Society; Collectors Club of Chicago; Fellow, Royal Philatelic Society, London; past President, British Caribbean Philatelic Study Group. [STAMP COLLECTING]

Lawrence, Al, A.B., M.Ed., M.A.; Associate Director, United States Chess Federation. [CHESS]

Lawrence, Richard, B.E.E.; Reporter, International Economic Affairs, *The Journal of Commerce.* [INTERNATIONAL TRADE]

Lesko, Leonard H., A.B., M.A., Ph.D.; Professor of Egyptology, University of California, Berkeley. [WORLD BOOK SUPPLEMENT: EGYPT, ANCIENT; TUTANKHAMEN]

Levy, Emanuel, B.A.; Editor/Publisher, *Insurance Advocate.* [INSURANCE]

Lieberthal, Kenneth G., A.B., M.A., Ph.D.; Professor of Political Science, Research Associate of Center for Chinese Studies, University of Michigan. [Special Report: CHINA AFTER MAO: CHARTING A NEW COURSE]

Litsky, Frank, B.S.; Sports Writer, *The New York Times.* [Sports Articles]

Locher, Dick, B.A.; Editorial Cartoonist, *Chicago Tribune.* [DEATHS (Close-Up)]

Maki, John M., B.A., M.A., Ph.D.; Professor Emeritus, University of Massachusetts. [JAPAN]

Mandile, Tony, Free-Lance Writer. [FISHING; HUNTING]

Maran, Stephen P., B.S., M.A., Ph.D.; Senior Staff Scientist, National Aeronautics and Space Administration-Goddard Space Flight Center. [ASTRONOMY]

Mariani, John F., B.A., M.A., Ph.D.; Contributing Editor, *Millimeter Magazine.* [WORLD BOOK SUPPLEMENT: DE NIRO, ROBERT; LANG, FRITZ; LEAN, SIR DAVID]

Martin, Lee, Associate Editor/Columnist, Miller Magazines. [COIN COLLECTING]

Marty, Martin E., Ph.D.; Fairfax M. Cone Distinguished Service Professor, University of Chicago. [PROTESTANTISM; RELIGION]

Mather, Ian J., M.A.; Defense Correspondent, *The Observer,* London. [GREAT BRITAIN; IRELAND; NORTHERN IRELAND]

Maugh, Thomas H., II, Ph.D.; Science Writer, *Los Angeles Times.* [BIOCHEMISTRY]

McCarron, John F., M.S.J.; Urban Affairs Editor, *Chicago Tribune.* [CHICAGO]

McDermott, Vincent, B.F.A.; M.A., Ph.D.; Associate Professor of Music, Lewis and Clark College. [WORLD BOOK SUPPLEMENT: GLASS, PHILIP]

Merina, Victor, A.A., B.A., M.S.; Staff Writer, *Los Angeles Times.* [LOS ANGELES]

Miller, J. D. B., M.Ec., M.A.; Professor of International Relations, Australian National University, Canberra. [AUSTRALIA]

Miller, Jonathan, Publisher, *Space Today.* [COMMUNICATIONS]

Moores, Eldridge M., B.S., Ph.D.; Professor of Geology, University of California at Davis. [GEOLOGY]

Morgan, Ann Lee, B.A., M.A., Ph.D.; Assistant Editor, *New Art Examiner.* [WORLD BOOK SUPPLEMENT: DINE, JIM; ROSENQUIST, JAMES ALBERT]

Moritz, Owen, B.A.; Urban Affairs Editor, New York *Daily News.* [NEW YORK CITY]

Morris, Bernadine, B.A., M.A.; Chief Fashion Writer, *The New York Times.* [FASHION]

Newcomb, Eldon H., A.B., A.M., Ph.D.; Professor and Chairman, Department of Botany, University of Wisconsin-Madison. [BOTANY]

Oatis, William N., former United Nations Correspondent, Associated Press. [UNITED NATIONS]

Pankhurst, Richard, B.Sc., Ph.D.; Librarian, Royal Asiatic Society of London. [WORLD BOOK SUPPLEMENT: ETHIOPIA]

Perkins, Kenneth J., Ph.D.; Associate Professor of History, University of South Carolina. [WORLD BOOK SUPPLEMENT: ALGERIA]

Pollock, Steve, B.A.; Managing Editor, *Popular Photography.* [PHOTOGRAPHY]

Priestaf, Iris, Ph.D.; Geographer/Water Resources Specialist, David Keith Todd Consulting Engineers Incorporated. [WATER]

Raloff, Janet, B.S.J., M.S.J.; Policy/Technology Editor, *Science News.* [Special Report: NUCLEAR POWER AT THE CROSSROADS]

Reinken, Charles, B.B.A., M.A.; Associate Editor and Columnist, *The Houston Post.* [HOUSTON]

Ross, Lynn L., Member, Board of Directors, Lighthouse for the Blind; Free-Lance Writer. [Special Report: HOW SCIENCE IS SAVING SIGHT]

Rotberg, Robert I., A.B., M.P.A., D.Phil.; Professor of Political Science and History, Massachusetts Institute of Technology. [WORLD BOOK SUPPLEMENT: TUTU, DESMOND]

Rowse, Arthur E., I.A., M.B.A.; Associate Editor, Washington Letter, *U.S. News & World Report.* [CONSUMERISM; SAFETY]

Scott, Douglas D., B.A., M.A., Ph.D.; Chief, Rocky Mountain Division of the Midwest Archaeological Center, National Park Service. [ARCHAEOLOGY (Close-Up)]

Shand, David A., B.C.A., B.Com.; Chief Director, State Audit Office of Victoria, Melbourne, Australia. [NEW ZEALAND]

Shapiro, Howard S., B.S.; Deputy New Jersey Editor, *The Philadelphia Inquirer.* [PHILADELPHIA]

Shearer, Warren W., B.A., M.A., Ph.D., J.D.; Partner, Thorpe & Shearer, Attorneys at Law; former Chairman, Department of Economics, Wabash College. [ECONOMICS]

Spencer, William, A.B., A.M., Ph.D.; Writer; Professor Emeritus of History, Florida State University. [MIDDLE EAST and Middle Eastern Country Articles; North Africa Country Articles]

Stasio, Marilyn, B.A., M.A.; Theater Critic, *New York Post.* [THEATER]

Swanton, Donald W., B.S., M.S., Ph.D., M.B.A.; Chairman, Department of Finance, Roosevelt University. [BANK; STOCKS AND BONDS]

Taylor, Doreen, Free-Lance Journalist, Writer, and Broadcaster, Scotland. [SCOTLAND]

Taylor, Michael J. H., Author and Editor. [WORLD BOOK SUPPLEMENT: AIRSHIP]

Thompson, Ida, A.B., M.S., Ph.D.; Associate Research Professor, Center for Coastal and Environmental Studies, Rutgers University. [PALEONTOLOGY]

Toch, Thomas, B.A.; Research Associate, Carnegie Foundation for the Advancement of Teaching. [EDUCATION]

Tuchman, Janice Lyn, B.S., M.S.; Senior Editor, *Engineering News-Record.* [BUILDING AND CONSTRUCTION]

Van Camp, Leonard W., M.M.E., D.M.A.; Director of Choral Activities, Southern Illinois University at Edwardsville. [WORLD BOOK SUPPLEMENT: LEVINE, JAMES]

Vesley, Roberta, A.B., M.L.S.; Library Director, American Kennel Club. [DOG]

Voorhies, Barbara, B.S., Ph.D.; Professor and Chair, Department of Anthropology, University of California at Santa Barbara. [ARCHAEOLOGY]

Walter, Eugene J., Jr., B.A.; Editor in Chief, *Animal Kingdom* magazine, and Curator of Publications, New York Zoological Society. [CONSERVATION; ZOOS]

Weininger, Jean, A.B., M.S., Ph.D.; Research Fellow, Department of Nutritional Sciences, University of California at Berkeley. [NUTRITION]

Whitaker, Donald R., A.B.; Industry Economist, National Marine Fisheries Service. [FISHING INDUSTRY]

White, Thomas O., B.S., Ph.D.; University Lecturer in Physics, Cambridge University, Cambridge, England. [PHYSICS]

Wilkinson, Sylvia, B.A., M.A.; Contributing Editor, *Auto Week.* [WORLD BOOK SUPPLEMENT: AUTOMOBILE RACING]

Windeyer, Kendal, President, Windeyer Associates, Montreal, Canada. [MONTREAL; WORLD BOOK SUPPLEMENT: GARNEAU, MARC]

Wolff, Howard, B.S.; Managing Editor, *Electronics Week.* [COMPUTER; ELECTRONICS]

Woods, Michael, B.S.; Science Editor, *The Toledo Blade.* [Energy, Mining, and Health Articles]

Wuntch, Philip, B.A.; Film Critic, *Dallas Morning News.* [MOTION PICTURES; MOTION PICTURES (Close-Up)]

The Year
in Brief

1981
1982
1983
1984
1985

A short essay captures the spirit
of 1985, and a month-by-month
listing highlights some of the
year's significant events.

See page 13.

The Year in Brief

A review of some of the major trends and events that touched many of our lives during 1985.

In September 1985, one of the largest gatherings of world leaders in history attended the 40th anniversary session of the United Nations (UN) General Assembly in New York City. Those from the Western Hemisphere included United States President Ronald Reagan, Canada's Prime Minister Brian Mulroney, and Nicaragua's President Daniel Ortega. From Asia came Prime Minister Yasuhiro Nakasone of Japan, Prime Minister Rajiv Gandhi of India, and President M. Zia-ul-Haq of Pakistan. Great Britain's Prime Minister Margaret Thatcher was there from Europe, as were Italy's Prime Minister Bettino Craxi and West Germany's Chancellor Helmut Kohl. Prime Minister Shimon Peres of Israel attended. And there were dozens of others.

Jaime de Piniés of Spain was confirmed as Assembly president. In accepting the post, De Piniés told the Assembly that "the United Nations is now in the midst of a crisis." He said that the UN "has

Tens of thousands of rock fans jam John F. Kennedy Stadium in Philadelphia in July for Live Aid—a concert for Africa's starving millions.

10

not lived up to the hopes vested in it when it was founded." Indeed, during the anniversary celebration, the 159 UN member nations failed to agree on a declaration stating the organization's accomplishments and objectives.

The nations that won World War II founded the UN in 1945 primarily, as stated in the preamble of the UN Charter, "to save succeeding generations from the scourge of war, which twice in our lifetime has brought untold sorrow to mankind . . . ."

The scourge of war was still bringing sorrow in 1985. International wars raged in Afghanistan, Kampuchea, and Iran and Iraq. There were civil wars in Central America, the Philippines, and several African nations. Lebanon, South Africa, and Northern Ireland seethed with hatred and violence. Political terrorism, a "close cousin" of open warfare, was increasing.

Yet, in 1985, as in all the other years since the founding of the UN, the world was spared the most terrible of conflicts—a nuclear war. It is virtually impossible to assess the role of the UN in preventing war between the nuclear powers. But at the very least, the UN has provided an alternative to the battlefield—an international forum, a setting for verbal warfare, a way to win hearts and minds without shedding blood.

Another means of keeping the lid on the pressure cooker of superpower tensions has been the summit conference—a meeting of world leaders. Summit conferences date back at least to the World War II "Big Three" talks among the leaders of the Allies—U.S. President Franklin D. Roosevelt, Great Britain's Prime Minister Winston Churchill, and the Soviet Union's Premier Joseph Stalin.

Until 1985, Reagan was the only U.S. President since Roosevelt not to have participated in a summit conference with a Soviet leader—partly because of frequent changes in leadership in the Kremlin. The Soviet Union changed leaders three times between 1981, when Reagan took office, and the spring of 1985. All three changes resulted from the death of elderly men at the Soviet helm. Leonid I. Brezhnev died in November 1982 at the age of 75 and was replaced by 68-year-old Yuri V. Andropov, who died in February 1984. Andropov's successor, Konstantin U. Chernenko, died in March 1985, when he was 73 years old.

After Chernenko's death, the Soviets finally got a relatively young leader, 54-year-old Mikhail S. Gorbachev. The day after Gorbachev assumed office, Reagan told reporters that he would welcome the chance to meet Gorbachev in the "cause of world peace." On July 2, U.S. officials disclosed that the two leaders would meet on November 19 and 20 in Geneva, Switzerland, scene of ongoing arms talks between U.S. and Soviet negotiators.

At the summit, Reagan and Gorbachev discussed a wide range of issues, including nuclear arms, human rights, and regional conflicts. The two leaders remained in substantial disagreement over the ma-

Lights blaze at United Nations (UN) Headquarters in New York City, *left,* announcing the 40th anniversary in 1985 of the UN, an organization founded primarily to prevent war. Mikhail S. Gorbachev, leader of the Soviet Union, and President Ronald Reagan of the United States meet in Geneva, Switzerland, in November, *below,* in an effort to promote peace.

jor issues that separate their two nations, but they agreed to cultural exchanges and said that they would encourage their arms negotiators to arrange a 50 per cent reduction in nuclear weapons. The two leaders also agreed to meet again.

Hijackings by Middle East terrorists took a heavy toll of lives in 1985. On June 14, Lebanese Shiite Muslims hijacked a Trans World Airlines jet shortly after take-off from Athens, Greece, and demanded that Israel release more than 700 Lebanese prisoners. On June 15, the hijackers beat a 23-year-old U.S. Navy diver, Robert D. Stethem, and then shot him to death. The hijackers freed more than 100 passengers but held 39 as hostages until June 30. On July 1, the Israeli Cabinet decided to free 300 of the Lebanese prisoners but denied that the move was part of a deal with the hijackers.

Four Palestinians on October 7 seized the Italian cruise ship *Achille Lauro* off the coast of Egypt. The next day, they murdered Leon Klinghoffer, a 69-year-old American confined to a wheelchair. On October 9, they surrendered in Egypt in exchange for a pledge of safe conduct out of the country. An Egyptian jet carried the hijackers out of Egypt on October 10, but U.S. fighter planes forced the jet to land at Sigonella, Sicily, where the hijackers were arrested.

On November 23, four hijackers believed to be Palestinians seized the same jet shortly after it took off from Athens and forced it to land in Malta. Egyptian commandos stormed the plane on Novem-

Lebanese gunmen seize a TWA jet, *top,* in June, taking hostages who are held for up to 16 days. In October, officials escort Marilyn Klinghoffer from the Italian cruise ship *Achille Lauro, above,* site of her husband's murder by Palestinian terrorists.

ber 24, killing three of the hijackers. A total of 60 people died either before or during the battle.

During 1985, Middle Eastern leaders struggled with the problem underlying the acts of terrorism—the continuing conflict between Israel and its Muslim neighbors. Israel's Prime Minister Peres, addressing the UN General Assembly on October 21, presented a plan for settling the conflict. He repeated Israel's official policy that direct peace talks should be held between Israel and Jordan or a Jordanian-Palestinian delegation. But he added that an international conference could help get the talks going—"if deemed necessary."

Another long-standing struggle between peoples intensified in 1985. South Africa's official policies of *apartheid,* or racial segregation, came under intense pressure in that nation and abroad. A pattern of violence that had begun in black residential townships in 1984 continued into 1985. In July, the government imposed emergency rule in 36 of the nation's 265 court districts.

In the United States and other Western nations, some foes of apartheid advocated the imposition of strong economic sanctions against South Africa. Other foes argued that sanctions would harm the nation's blacks—the very people they were meant to benefit. A middle course prevailed. On September 9, Reagan ordered mild trade and financial sanctions against South Africa. The next day, 11 West European nations agreed on moderate economic, cultural, and military sanctions.

On September 29, 91 South African business leaders signed full-

A financially exhausting conflict between striking British coal miners, *left,* and the government ended in March after miners had been off the job for nearly a year. Racial conflict took a heavy toll of lives throughout 1985 in South Africa. Blacks who died in August disturbances are buried in a mass funeral, *below.*

page ads in South African newspapers calling for the end of apartheid. On October 24, State President Pieter Willem Botha announced the end of emergency rule in six districts, saying it had been effective in restoring order in those areas. Violence continued, however, and in November, South Africa imposed sweeping restrictions on local and foreign journalists, including the barring of television crews, photographers, and radio reporters from covering unrest in parts of the nation still under emergency rule.

Another long-standing problem in Africa—famine caused by drought—continued in 1985. Aid poured into Ethiopia and other affected countries—more than $100 million by way of an unlikely source: rock musicians and their fans. In 1984, Band Aid, a collection of British pop music stars led by Bob Geldof, produced a recording, "Do They Know It's Christmas?," to raise funds for famine victims. The record quickly became a hit, earning more than $11-million in 1984 and 1985. In January 1985, a group of U.S. pop stars gathered to record a song and video, "We Are the World," for famine relief. Released in March, the two productions were instant hits, eventually raising $45 million. The biggest famine-relief effort came on July 13, with the Live Aid concert—a day-long telethon

Natural disasters took a heavy toll of lives in 1985. They included two earthquakes in September that toppled tall buildings in Mexico City, *above right,* and killed more than 7,000 people. In November, a volcanic eruption in Colombia triggered mud slides and floods, *right,* killing 25,000 people.

16

Here are your

1986 YEAR BOOK
Cross-Reference Tabs

For insertion in your WORLD BOOK

Each year, THE WORLD BOOK YEAR BOOK adds a valuable dimension to your WORLD BOOK set. The Cross-Reference Tab System is designed especially to help youngsters and parents alike *link* THE YEAR BOOK's new and revised WORLD BOOK articles, its Special Reports, and its Close-Ups to the related WORLD BOOK articles they update.

How to Use These Tabs

First, remove this page from THE YEAR BOOK. Begin with the top Tab, AIRSHIP.

Turn to the A volume of your WORLD BOOK set and find the first page of the AIRSHIP article. Moisten the gummed Tab and affix it to that page.

Your WORLD BOOK set may not contain an article with the same name as every Tab. COMPUTER, PERSONAL is an example. Put that Tab in the C volume in its proper alphabetical sequence.

A heavy police guard at a soccer stadium in Brussels, Belgium, failed to prevent a riot during a championship match between British and Italian teams in May. Thirty-eight people died in the riot.

organized by Geldof. Live performances in Philadelphia and London were broadcast via satellite to about 1.5 billion people throughout the world. Live Aid generated more than $50 million in pledges.

In addition to the drought that caused famine in Africa, three natural disasters claimed thousands of lives in 1985. On May 24 and 25, tidal waves killed at least 10,000 people in Bangladesh. On September 19 and 20, earthquakes in Mexico City and other parts of Mexico killed more than 7,000. The year's worst disaster occurred in Colombia on November 13. Molten material from beneath Earth's crust boiled up through a natural passageway inside a volcano named Nevado del Ruiz and struck the volcano's huge icecap. A tremendous amount of ice melted, triggering mud slides that killed about 25,000 people.

Another type of disaster, accidental rather than natural, occurred on August 12. In the worst single-aircraft accident in history, a Japan Air Lines plane struck Mount Osutaka, 70 miles northwest of Tokyo, killing 520 people.

A new enemy of humanity continued to gain ground in 1985. By the end of the year, acquired immune deficiency syndrome (AIDS) had infected an estimated 15,000 Americans and had killed half of them, including actor Rock Hudson.

An old enemy of humanity surfaced—literally—in June. Bones dug up in Brazil were identified as the remains of Nazi war criminal Josef Mengele, the "Angel of Death." Mengele had been wanted for the torture and murder of inmates at a German concentration camp during World War II.

Several countries were hit by major strikes by workers in 1985. In March and April, hundreds of Danes struck for shorter hours and higher pay. In April, some 17,000 blacks struck South African gold mines. The government fired them but later gave them back their jobs. In May, a strike of civil servants almost brought commerce to a halt in Sweden. In September, Bolivia declared a state of siege in an attempt to end a nationwide strike protesting tough economic measures imposed by the government.

In Great Britain, a nationwide coal strike that had lasted nearly a year finally ended on March 5, when members of the National Union of Mineworkers went back to work. Two days earlier, the union had voted to return to the mines without a settlement. The strike cost an estimated $3.1 billion.

A riot that occurred during a sports event also was costly to Britain. On May 29, violence erupted in a soccer stadium in Brussels, Belgium, while an English team was playing a squad from Italy. A section of the British crowd attacked Italian spectators, causing 38 deaths. As a result of the riot, organizations that govern soccer banned English teams from European competition.

But sports also had its moments of glory in 1985. On September 11, player-manager Pete Rose of the Cincinnati Reds baseball team lined a single into left field for the 4,192nd base hit of his career, breaking a record set by Ty Cobb in 1928. On July 7, Boris Becker of West Germany propelled a tennis ball into a service court in front of Kevin Curren of the United States. The ball ticked off Curren's racquet, propelling the 17-year-old Becker into the record books as the youngest player ever to win the men's singles tournament at Wimbledon, England.

Youth was served in chess as well.   On November 9, Gary Kas-

Sports heroes of 1985 included the Cincinnati Reds' Pete Rose, *below right,* who broke Ty Cobb's career record for base hits, and William (the Refrigerator) Perry of the Chicago Bears, *below,* a defensive player who was also very big on offense.

parov of the Soviet Union defeated a fellow Soviet, world champion Anatoly Karpov. At 22 years of age, Kasparov became the youngest world champion in chess history.

And there were other events that helped to make 1985 the year that it was. A comet arrived from beyond the orbit of Neptune, and Tennessee announced that it had landed the Saturn. Two baseball teams from the "show me" state showed 'em—and the players from Kansas City went as far as they could go. And Sylvester Stallone—with *Rambo* and *Rocky IV*—showed 'em that he had gone a long way beyond the original *Rocky*.

At the beginning of 1985, Coke was "it." In April, "it" became something else. And by July, "it" was "them."

In 1985, undersea explorers achieved a long-sought goal by finding the luxury liner *Titanic* in chilly waters at the bottom of the Atlantic Ocean, and a titanic defensive lineman called "The Refrigerator" found fame by finding various ways to cross a football goal line, chilling his opponents' hopes for victory. A film named *Back to the Future* proved to be a cool present for its producers, and 21 men produced a lottery ticket and split a lot of cold cash.

All in all, 1985 was the kind of year the billions of men and women and children who share this planet have become used to—filled with tragic moments and happy ones, significant events and those of little importance. THE EDITORS

For details about 1985:
The Year on File section—which begins on page 172—describes events of 1985 according to the country, field, or general subject area in which they occurred. The Chronology, which starts on page 20, lists major events month by month.

A new soft-drink formula, *top left,* met with only modest success in 1985, but two time-tested formulas for motion-picture success worked extremely well—science fiction mixed with a love story in *Back to the Future, top right;* and a blend of war action and individual heroism in *Rambo, above.*

Jan. 26

Jan. 21

Jan. 20

January

		1	2	3	4	5
6	7	8	9	10	11	12
13	14	15	16	17	18	19
20	21	22	23	24	25	26
27	28	29	30	31		

2   **Rafael Hernández Colón** takes office as governor of Puerto Rico.
United States President Ronald Reagan and Japanese Prime Minister Yasuhiro Nakasone agree on new trade talks aimed at increasing U.S. exports to Japan.

7-8   **U.S. Secretary of State George P. Shultz** and Soviet Foreign Minister Andrei A. Gromyko hold preliminary arms talks in Geneva, Switzerland.

8   **Reagan announces** that Secretary of the Treasury Donald T. Regan and White House Chief of Staff James A. Baker III will exchange jobs.
Vietnamese forces overrun Ampil, one of the largest Kampuchean resistance camps.

10   **Daniel Ortega** takes office as president of Nicaragua.
Reagan names three new Cabinet leaders—Secretary of Energy Donald Paul Hodel to succeed William P. Clark as secretary of the interior, John S. Herrington to replace Hodel, and William J. Bennett to succeed Terrel H. Bell as secretary of education.

12   **France declares** a state of emergency in its South Pacific territory of New Caledonia because of riots between islanders seeking independence and French settlers.

13   **An express train derails** in Ethiopia, killing at least 428 people in one of the worst train wrecks in history.

15   **Tancredo de Almeida Neves,** a moderate, is chosen by an electoral college to become Brazil's first civilian president since 1964. He dies on April 21 without taking office.
The Supreme Court of the United States rules that public school officials may search students they suspect are breaking a law or school rule.

20   **The San Francisco 49ers** win Super Bowl XIX, defeating the Miami Dolphins 38-16.
Israel begins to withdraw its troops from Lebanon.

21   **Reagan** takes the oath of office for his second term as President in a public inauguration, following a private ceremony on January 20.

24   **Former Israeli Defense Minister Ariel Sharon** loses a libel suit against *Time* magazine.

24-27   **The space shuttle *Discovery*** carries out a secret military mission, during which it launches a spy satellite to eavesdrop on Soviet communications.

26   **Pope John Paul II** arrives in Venezuela for the start of a 12-day tour of Venezuela, Ecuador, Peru, and Trinidad and Tobago.

29   **Premier Richard Hatfield** of New Brunswick, Canada, is acquitted on a charge of marijuana possession.

Feb. 7

Feb. 20

Feb. 5-7

February

					1	2
3	4	5	6	7	8	9
10	11	12	13	14	15	16
17	18	19	20	21	22	23
24	25	26	27	28		

1   **Paul G. Kirk, Jr.,** is elected chairman of the Democratic Party.

4   **New Zealand forbids** a United States warship to dock without assurance that it does not carry nuclear weapons.

5   **Spain reopens** its border—closed since 1969—with the British colony of Gibraltar.

5-7   **Australian Prime Minister Robert Hawke** visits the United States.

6   **President Reagan,** in his State of the Union message, calls for a "second American revolution" and urges tax simplification, reduced domestic spending, and a continuing military build-up.

7   **Four Polish secret-police officers** are convicted and sentenced to prison for the 1984 kidnapping and murder of pro-Solidarity priest Jerzy Popieluszko.

8   **South Korean opposition leader** Kim Dae Jung returns safely to Seoul after more than two years in the United States but is manhandled by police and confined to his home.

Vernon A. Walters is nominated to succeed Jeane J. Kirkpatrick as United States ambassador to the United Nations.

12   **Canadian Defense Minister Robert Carman Coates** resigns after reports that he visited a West German striptease club.

15   **Chess officials** halt the world championship match between titleholder Anatoly Karpov and challenger Gary Kasparov after 48 games.

17   **General William C. Westmoreland** drops his $120-million libel suit against CBS Inc.
Surgeons at Humana Hospital Audubon in Louisville, Ky., perform the world's third artificial-heart implant on a human being.

18   **South Korea's President Chun Doo Hwan** reorganizes his cabinet after a new opposition party makes surprising gains in parliamentary elections on February 12.

20   **British Prime Minister Margaret Thatcher** addresses the United States Congress and praises Reagan's defense policies.
Kuwaiti voters elect a bloc of leftists to the National Assembly in voting that reflects widespread discontent with the government.

23   **The Senate confirms** Edwin Meese III as attorney general of the United States more than a year after he was first nominated by Reagan.

24   **Libyan leader Muammar Muhammad al-Qadhafi,** in a speech transmitted to a Chicago meeting of the Nation of Islam, calls on black Americans to quit the military and fight for independence.

25-26   **The United States dollar** soars to record highs against the British pound, the French franc, and the Italian lira.

21

March 17-18

March 10

March

					1	2
3	4	5	6	7	8	9
10	11	12	13	14	15	16
17	18	19	20	21	22	23
24	25	26	27	28	29	30
31						

1   **Julio María Sanguinetti** takes office as Uruguay's first civilian president since the 1970's.

4-10   **U.S. Vice President George H. W. Bush** visits famine-stricken Sudan, Niger, and Mali.

5   **British coal miners** return to work after nearly a year on strike, the longest in British history.
The Canadian dollar drops to a record low against the U.S. dollar.

10   **Soviet leader Konstantin U. Chernenko,** 73, dies of lung, heart, and liver disease. His funeral, shown above, is on March 13.

11   **Mikhail S. Gorbachev** succeeds Chernenko in the Soviet Union's most powerful post—general secretary of the Central Committee of the Communist Party.

15   **Ohio Governor Richard F. Celeste** closes all state-insured savings and loan associations in his state to stem a run on deposits.
Raymond J. Donovan resigns as U.S. secretary of labor to defend himself against fraud and larceny charges.

17-18   **Reagan and Canadian Prime Minister Brian Mulroney,** meeting in Quebec City, Canada, agree to appoint special envoys to seek ways to combat acid rain.

18   **American Broadcasting Companies (ABC)** announces that it will be bought by Capital Cities Communications Incorporated for $3.5-billion, the first time a major television network has ever been sold.

20   **William E. Brock III** is nominated to succeed Donovan as secretary of labor.

24   **A U.S. Army major** on a reconnaissance mission in East Germany is shot and killed by a Soviet guard.

25   *Amadeus,* a film about Austrian composer Wolfgang Amadeus Mozart, wins the Academy Award for best picture. One of the film's stars—F. Murray Abraham, shown above—wins the Oscar for best actor.

27   **Bernhard H. Goetz** is indicted on charges of attempted murder for shooting four teen-agers whom he believed to be threatening him in New York City in December 1984.
The U.S. Supreme Court limits the right of police to use deadly force against fleeing suspects.

28   **Japan announces** that it will increase automobile exports to the United States by about 24 per cent over the next year.
Congress gives final approval to release $1.5 billion to build 21 new MX missiles.

30   **Christos Sartzetakis** takes office as president of Greece, succeeding Constantine Karamanlis, who resigned on March 10.

31   **El Salvador's** moderate Christian Democratic Party wins a majority in elections for the National Assembly.

April 9

April 23

April 1

April

	1	2	3	4	5	6
7	8	9	10	11	12	13
14	15	16	17	18	19	20
21	22	23	24	25	26	27
28	29	30				

1   **Villanova University** wins the National Collegiate Athletic Association men's basketball championship, beating Georgetown University 66-64.

6   **Sudanese President Gaafar Mohamed Nimeiri** is overthrown by a military coup.

9   **Jewel Companies, Incorporated,** closes its Melrose Park, Ill., dairy and removes milk from its stores after the dairy is linked to an outbreak of salmonella poisoning.

     A federal appeals court reinstates a $2-million jury verdict that *The Washington Post* libeled the president of Mobil Oil Corporation in 1979.

11   **Albania's leader Enver Hoxha,** 76, dies of complications brought on by heart failure.

12   **The space shuttle *Discovery*** lifts off with a crew of seven, including Senator Edwin Jacob (Jake) Garn (R., Utah).

13   **Ramiz Alia** succeeds Hoxha in Albania's most powerful post—first secretary of the Communist Party.

14   **Alan García Pérez,** a center-left candidate, wins the most votes in Peru's presidential election but falls short of an outright majority. He is declared president-elect on June 1 after the runner-up withdraws.

15   **Marvelous Marvin Hagler** keeps the middleweight boxing championship by defeating Thomas Hearns.

     South Africa announces that it will repeal laws forbidding interracial sex and marriage.

     Nigeria orders about 700,000 illegal aliens, mainly Ghanaians, to leave by May 10.

18   ***The Adoration of the Magi*** by Italian Renaissance painter Andrea Mantegna sells for $10.4 million, the highest price ever paid for a painting at auction.

21   **Brazil's President-elect Neves** dies without ever taking office after a series of operations for an intestinal ailment. José Sarney, who has been standing in for Neves, is formally installed as president on April 22.

22   **The United States and Israel** sign an agreement to eliminate all trade barriers between the two nations by 1995—the first free-trade pact in U.S. history.

23   **The Coca-Cola Company** announces that it will change the formula for Coke to give it a new taste, touching off protests by old-Coke lovers, shown above.

24   **Pope John Paul II** names 28 new cardinals, including Archbishops John J. O'Connor of New York City and Bernard F. Law of Boston.

26   **The Soviet Union** and its Eastern European allies extend their Warsaw Pact military treaty for 20 years.

28   **United Press International** files for bankruptcy.

May 5

May 13

May 29

May

			1	2	3	4
5	6	7	8	9	10	11
12	13	14	15	16	17	18
19	20	21	22	23	24	25
26	27	28	29	30	31	

1   **Reagan** imposes a ban on trade with Nicaragua and bars Nicaraguan aircraft and ships from the United States.

The House of Representatives seats Frank McCloskey (D., Ind.) after declaring him the winner by four votes over Republican Richard D. McIntyre in the closest congressional election in history, held on Nov. 6, 1984.

2-4   **An economic summit conference** in Bonn, West Germany, is attended by leaders of Canada, France, Great Britain, Italy, Japan, the United States, and West Germany.

5   **Reagan places wreaths** at Bergen-Belsen concentration camp and at a German military cemetery in Bitburg, West Germany—shown above—to honor victims of the Holocaust and World War II.

7   **The Diablo Canyon nuclear power plant** in California begins commercial operation after years of public protest against its location near a major earthquake fault.

12   **Illinois Governor James R. Thompson** commutes the sentence of Gary E. Dotson,

imprisoned since 1979 for raping Cathleen Crowell Webb, who said in March 1985 that the rape never happened.

13   **Philadelphia police** bomb a house occupied by a radical group called MOVE, who were resisting eviction, and the bomb starts a fire that kills 11 people and destroys 61 nearby houses.

The General Electric Company pleads guilty to defrauding the U.S. government on a missile contract and is fined $1.04 million.

14   **Maryland Governor Harry R. Hughes,** to halt a run on deposits, imposes a $1,000 monthly withdrawal limit on accounts at privately insured savings and loans.

15   **Sinn Féin,** the political wing of the outlawed Irish Republican Army, runs for the first time in town council elections in Northern Ireland and wins about 12 per cent of the vote.

17   **United Airlines pilots** strike over a plan to pay newly hired pilots lower salaries. The strikers return to work on June 17.

20   **Radio Martí,** a U.S. government radio service, begins broadcasting to Cuba.

21   **A California teacher** gives birth to seven babies, one of them stillborn, in the largest multiple birth recorded in the United States. Three of the babies die within days of birth, but three leave the hospital in the fall.

24-25   **A cyclone and tidal wave** kill at least 10,000 people in Bangladesh.

29   **A bloody riot** in which British soccer fans storm Italian fans leaves 38 people dead at a match in Brussels, Belgium.

30   **The Edmonton Oilers** win professional hockey's Stanley Cup, defeating the Philadelphia Flyers four games to one.

June 11

June 14

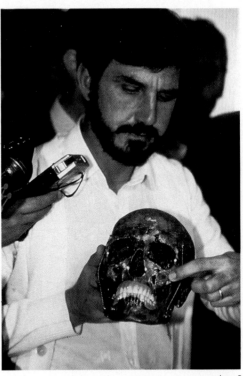

June 6

June

						1
2	3	4	5	6	7	8
9	10	11	12	13	14	15
16	17	18	19	20	21	22
23	24	25	26	27	28	29
30						

2 **R. J. Reynolds Industries, Incorporated,** and Nabisco Brands, Incorporated, announce that they will merge.

4 **The U.S. Supreme Court** overturns an Alabama law authorizing a period of silence "for meditation or voluntary prayer" in public schools.

6 **Brazilian police** exhume the remains of a man reported to be fugitive Nazi war criminal Josef Mengele at a cemetery in Embu, Brazil. On June 21, American, Brazilian, and West German scientists confirm that the remains, shown above, are Mengele's.

9 **The Los Angeles Lakers** win the National Basketball Association championship, defeating the Boston Celtics four games to two.

10 **Claus von Bülow,** a Danish-born socialite, is acquitted in Providence, R.I., in a second trial of trying to murder his wealthy wife. The first trial, in 1982, resulted in a conviction that was overturned on technical grounds.

11 **Indian Prime Minister Rajiv Gandhi** arrives in Washington, D.C., for a four-day visit, during which he addresses Congress, above.

12 **Spain and Portugal** sign a treaty admitting them to the European Community (EC or Common Market) as of Jan. 1, 1986.

14 **Arab hijackers** seize a TWA jetliner near Athens, Greece. They free more than 100 passengers but murder 1 American and hold 39 others hostage in Beirut, Lebanon, until June 30.

Argentina's President Raúl Alfonsín freezes wages and prices, and replaces Argentina's peso with a new monetary unit, the austral.

19 **Gunmen kill** 13 people, including 6 Americans, at two sidewalk cafes in El Salvador.

20 **Quebec Prime Minister René Lévesque** resigns as head of the Parti Québécois.

23 **An Air-India jetliner** crashes in the Atlantic Ocean off Ireland, killing all 329 people on board in one of history's worst air disasters.

24 **Former Prime Minister Francesco Cossiga** of Italy is elected the nation's president.

25 **Prime Minister Mário Soares** of Portugal resigns after the Social Democrats quit his two-party coalition government in an economic dispute.

26 **The U.S. Supreme Court** overturns a Connecticut law that gave employees the right not to work on the Sabbath day of their choice.

David Peterson, a Liberal, is sworn in as premier of Ontario, succeeding Frank Miller, whose Progressive Conservative Party lost its legislative majority in May elections.

July 20

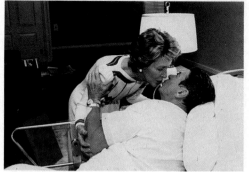

July 13

July 7

1   **The U.S. Supreme Court** rules that public school systems may not send teachers into parochial schools to provide remedial or enrichment instruction.

2   **Soviet Foreign Minister Gromyko** is elected to his nation's presidency, chairman of the Supreme Soviet Presidium.

7   **Boris Becker,** 17, of West Germany becomes the youngest tennis player ever to win the Wimbledon men's singles championship.

10   *Rainbow Warrior,* a ship owned by the Greenpeace environmental group, sinks in Auckland, New Zealand, after two bombs explode on its hull. France admits on September 22 that its agents sank the ship.
The Coca-Cola Company says it will bring back original-formula Coke in addition to the new version introduced in April.

11   **China's President Li Xiannian** arrives in Vancouver, B.C., on a visit to Canada and the United States.

13   **Reagan undergoes surgery** to remove a cancerous tumor from his large intestine.
Live Aid, the biggest rock concert in history, raises more than $50 million for African famine relief with performances in London and Philadelphia televised worldwide.

15-27   **The United Nations Decade for Women** conference meets in Nairobi, Kenya.

19   **A dam bursts** at an artificial lake near Stava, Italy, sending a flood through the town and killing at least 232 people.
A New Hampshire high school teacher, Sharon Christa McAuliffe, is chosen to be what the National Aeronautics and Space Administration (NASA) calls the "first citizen observer" on a space shuttle flight, scheduled for January 1986.

20   **Divers find** the wreck of a Spanish ship that sank off Florida in 1622 carrying hundreds of silver bars and other treasure.
South Africa declares a state of emergency because of increasing racial violence.

21   **About 8,500 steelworkers,** protesting an 18 per cent cut in wages and benefits, walk off their jobs at Wheeling-Pittsburgh Steel Corporation in the first major U.S. steel strike since 1959. The strike lasts until October 28.

24   **India's Prime Minister Gandhi** signs a pact with the main Sikh political party, led by Harchand Singh Longowal, to ease tension in the Punjab.

27   **Uganda's President Milton Obote** is overthrown by a military coup. Lieutenant General Tito Okello Lutwa is sworn in as the new leader on July 29.

29   **GM announces** that it will build the world's largest automobile plant to manufacture its new Saturn car near Spring Hill, Tenn.

Aug. 12

Aug. 22

August

				1	2	3
4	5	6	7	8	9	10
11	12	13	14	15	16	17
18	19	20	21	22	23	24
25	26	27	28	29	30	31

5 **Víctor Paz Estenssoro,** a moderate, is elected president of Bolivia.

6-7 **Major-league baseball players** strike for two days because of a dispute over pensions and salary arbitration.

7 **Journalists** in Great Britain stop news broadcasts for 24 hours to protest the British Broadcasting Corporation's cancellation of a documentary about Northern Ireland.

8-19 **Pope John Paul II** makes a 12-day tour of seven African countries.

9 **A federal judge** in Norfolk, Va., convicts Arthur J. Walker of helping pass U.S. military secrets to the Soviet Union as part of a spy ring. The ring allegedly included Walker's nephew and a family friend and was run by his brother John A. Walker, Jr., who pleads guilty on October 28.

11 **Toxic gas** escapes from a Union Carbide Corporation plant in Institute, W.Va., sending about 135 people to hospitals for treatment of eye, throat, and lung irritation.

12 **A Japanese jumbo jet** crashes in central Japan, killing 520 people in the worst single-plane accident ever.

14 **Vietnam** returns what may be the remains of 26 American soldiers killed in the Vietnam War.

19 **Former Teamsters Union President** Roy L. Williams is sentenced to 10 years in prison for trying to bribe a U.S. senator.

20 **Sikh gunmen** assassinate India's leading moderate Sikh politician, Harchand Singh Longowal.
Canada's Prime Minister Mulroney shuffles his cabinet.

21 **The A. H. Robins Company,** manufacturer of the Dalkon Shield birth control device, files for bankruptcy to gain protection from lawsuits filed against it.

22 **Three winning tickets—** one of them shared by 21 co-workers, shown above—divide a New York state lottery jackpot of $41-million, the largest in U.S. history.

25 **Samantha Smith,** a Maine schoolgirl who toured the Soviet Union in 1983 as the guest of Soviet leader Yuri V. Andropov, is killed in a plane crash with seven other people.

27 **The Nigerian army** overthrows military ruler Muhammadu Buhari.
The U.S. Department of Defense cancels the U.S. Army's Sergeant York antiaircraft gun because of poor performance.
Cook County Circuit Judge Richard F. LeFevour, the highest-ranking judge convicted of judicial corruption in the federal Greylord probe in Illinois, is sentenced to 12 years in prison.

29 **Reagan orders a** 15-month pay freeze for federal civil servants.

27

Sept. 1

Sept. 19-20

September

1	2	3	4	5	6	7
8	9	10	11	12	13	14
15	16	17	18	19	20	21
22	23	24	25	26	27	28
29	30					

1   **A joint U.S.-French expedition** finds the wreck of the liner *Titanic*, which sank in 1912 in the Atlantic Ocean off Canada.

2   **Britain's Prime Minister Thatcher** shuffles her Cabinet.

     Hurricane Elena roars ashore in Mississippi, causing four deaths and about $543 million in damage.

4   **A federal appeals court** overturns a 1983 order that Washington state give comparable pay for jobs of comparable worth.

9   **Thai government troops** crush a coup attempt by a group of military officers.

10   **Leftist rebels** kidnap the eldest daughter of El Salvador's President José Napoleón Duarte. She is released unharmed in a complex prisoner exchange on October 24.

11   **Pete Rose** of the Cincinnati Reds gets his 4,192nd career hit to break the major-league baseball record set by Ty Cobb in 1928.

     A NASA spacecraft relays data from Comet Giacobini-Zinner in the first direct probe of a comet in history.

19-20   **Two devastating earthquakes** jolt western and central Mexico, causing more than 7,000 deaths.

22   **Farm Aid,** a benefit concert in Champaign, Ill., organized by singer Willie Nelson, raises about $7 million to help U.S. farmers.

23   **The U.S. dollar** plunges more than 4 per cent in value against other major currencies, the largest one-day drop since 1973, after the United States and four other nations announce a joint effort to lower its value.

23-25   **Two senior Canadian cabinet ministers** resign—Fisheries Minister John Allen Fraser after it was learned that he authorized the sale of rancid tuna, and Communications Minister Marcel Masse because of an investigation of his campaign spending. Masse is reinstated in November after the investigation clears him.

26-27   **Hurricane Gloria** pounds the Eastern United States, causing 16 deaths and about $210-million in damage.

27   **The Federal Aviation Administration** announces that it fined American Airlines $1.5 million for aircraft-maintenance violations, the largest fine in aviation history.

     Philip Morris Companies agrees to buy General Foods Corporation for $5.8 billion.

28   **President Nicolás Ardito Barletta Vallarina** of Panama resigns and is replaced by Eric Arturo Delvalle.

29   **Pierre Marc Johnson** is elected leader of the Parti Québécois, replacing Quebec's Prime Minister Lévesque.

30   **Margaret M. Heckler,** U.S. secretary of health and human services, is asked by Reagan to become ambassador to Ireland.

Oct. 27

Oct. 7

October

		1	2	3	4	5
6	7	8	9	10	11	12
13	14	15	16	17	18	19
20	21	22	23	24	25	26
27	28	29	30	31		

1   **Israeli planes** attack the Palestine Liberation Organization headquarters near Tunis, Tunisia, killing 61 Palestinians and 12 Tunisians in retaliation for the killing of 3 Israelis in Cyprus in September.

2   **Actor Rock Hudson,** 59, dies in Beverly Hills, Calif., 10 weeks after announcing that he suffered from acquired immune deficiency syndrome (AIDS).

3-7   **The space shuttle** *Atlantis* carries out a secret military mission on its maiden voyage.

6   **Portugal's centrist Social Democratic Party** defeats the ruling Socialist Party in elections but fails to win a majority in Parliament.

7   **A mud slide** kills as many as 150 people in Ponce, Puerto Rico.
Four Palestinian guerrillas hijack the Italian cruise ship *Achille Lauro* with more than 400 people aboard in the Mediterranean Sea. The hijackers surrender in Egypt on October 9 after killing one American passenger.

10   **U.S. fighter planes** intercept an Egyptian airliner carrying the four Palestinian hijackers and force it to land in Sigonella, Italy, near Catania, where the hijackers are arrested.

13   **Belgium's ruling center-right coalition** adds to its majority in parliament in elections.
Donald Getty is elected leader of Alberta's Progressive Conservative Party. He takes office as premier on November 1, succeeding Peter Lougheed, who resigned.

14   **A wall collapses** in the Welland Canal, part of the St. Lawrence Seaway linking Lakes Erie and Ontario, closing the seaway until November 7.

16   **The United Auto Workers** strike Chrysler Corporation in the United States and Canada. The Canadians return to work on October 21, and U.S. auto workers end their strike a week later.

22-23   **Warsaw Pact leaders** hold a summit meeting in Sofia, Bulgaria.

24   **Iceland's President** Vigdis Finnbogadottir joins women employees and housewives in a 24-hour strike to protest male privilege.

25   **Argentina** declares a state of siege to combat a wave of political bombings and threats.

27   **The Kansas City Royals** win the World Series, defeating the St. Louis Cardinals four games to three.
Robbers steal nine impressionist paintings, including five by Claude Monet and two by Pierre Auguste Renoir, from Paris' Marmottan Museum.
Tanzanian voters elect Ali Hassan Mwinyi to succeed President Julius K. Nyerere.

27-29   **Hurricane Juan** causes eight deaths and more than $1 billion in damage in Louisiana.

Nov. 9

Nov. 13

Nov. 19-20

November

					1	2
3	4	5	6	7	8	9
10	11	12	13	14	15	16
17	18	19	20	21	22	23
24	25	26	27	28	29	30

3   **Argentina's ruling party,** the center-left Radical Civic Union, adds one seat to its majority in the House of Deputies in midterm elections.

4   **Vitaly Yurchenko,** a high-ranking Soviet intelligence officer who defected to the West in July, tells reporters that he never defected but instead was kidnapped by American agents. He leaves the United States on November 6 to return to Russia.

5   **Many big-city mayors** in the United States win reelection, including Edward I. Koch of New York City, Coleman A. Young of Detroit, and Kathryn J. Whitmire of Houston.
West Virginia suffers its worst floods ever, and 45 people are killed in a storm that deluges that state as well as Maryland, North Carolina, Pennsylvania, and Virginia.

6   **Polish leader Wojciech Jaruzelski** appoints Zbigniew Messner to replace him as Council of Ministers chairman but retains the powerful post of Communist Party first secretary.

7   **Reagan nominates** former Indiana Governor Otis R. Bowen to succeed Heckler as secretary of health and human services.
Colombian troops storm the Palace of Justice in Bogotá, freeing about 50 hostages and ending a two-day siege by leftist guerrillas that leaves about 100 people dead, including 11 judges.

9   **Prince Charles and Diana,** Princess of Wales, arrive in Washington, D.C., on their first visit together to the United States.
Gary Kasparov, 22, becomes the youngest world champion in the history of chess, defeating titleholder Anatoly Karpov.

13   **A volcanic eruption** in Colombia triggers mud slides and floods that kill about 25,000 people.

15   **Great Britain and Ireland** sign a landmark agreement giving Ireland an advisory role in governing Northern Ireland for the first time since Ireland was divided into two countries in 1920.

19-20   **Reagan and Soviet leader Gorbachev** hold a summit meeting in Geneva, Switzerland.

21-22   **Hurricane Kate** strikes Florida and Georgia, causing seven deaths and $1 billion in damage.

23   **Arab terrorists** hijack an EgyptAir jetliner shortly after it leaves Athens, Greece, and force it to Malta. Egyptian commandos storm the plane the next day, but 60 people die before and during the assault.

24   **Pope John Paul II** opens a synod of bishops in Vatican City to review reforms adopted in 1965 by Vatican Council II.
José Azcona Hoyo of the Liberal Party is elected president of Honduras.

Dec.1

December

1	2	3	4	5	6	7
8	9	10	11	12	13	14
15	16	17	18	19	20	21
22	23	24	25	26	27	28
29	30	31				

1 *Atlantis* **astronauts** build a 45-foot (13.7-meter) metal tower in the shuttle's open cargo bay to practice techniques that will be used to build a permanent space station.

2 **Quebec's Liberal Party** defeats the Parti Québécois in provincial elections. Liberal leader Robert Bourassa becomes prime minister of Quebec on December 12.

A three-judge Philippine court acquits armed forces chief General Fabian C. Ver and 25 other defendants of charges in the 1983 assassination of opposition leader Benigno S. Aquino, Jr.

4 **National Security Adviser Robert C. McFarlane** resigns, and Reagan appoints John M. Poindexter to replace him.

The National Cancer Institute in Bethesda, Md., announces a promising but experimental new cancer treatment that uses the body's own white blood cells to attack tumors.

7 **Yelena G. Bonner**—wife of Soviet dissident Andrei D. Sakharov, who staged three hunger strikes to win permission for her to leave the Soviet Union—arrives in the United States for medical treatment.

8 **Marco Vinicio Cerezo Arévalo,** a moderate, is elected Guatemala's first civilian president since 1970.

The Organization of Petroleum Exporting Countries, meeting in Geneva, Switzerland, agrees to abandon its fixed price for oil.

9 **An Argentine court** sentences former Presidents Jorge Rafael Videla and Roberto Eduardo Viola to life and 17 years in prison, respectively, for their part in the kidnapping and murder of about 9,000 people during the late 1970's.

11 **Congress** approves landmark legislation ordering a balanced federal budget by 1991. Reagan signs the bill into law on December 12.

General Electric Company agrees to acquire RCA Corporation for $6.28 billion in cash, the largest merger outside the petroleum industry in U.S. history.

12 **A chartered jet** carrying U.S. military personnel crashes in Gander, Canada, killing all 248 soldiers and 8 crew members aboard.

16 **The Dow Jones Industrial Average** climbs to a record high of 1,553.10.

27 **Terrorists** hurl grenades and fire guns at El Al Israel Airlines counters in Rome and Vienna, Austria, killing 15 people and wounding 121. Four of the terrorists also die.

31 **Great Britain** officially withdraws from the UN Educational, Scientific and Cultural Organization, saying that the agency is inefficient and "harmfully politicized."

Special Reports

1981
1982
1983
1984
1985

Eight articles give special treatment to subjects of current importance and lasting interest.

See "Restoring Lady Liberty," page 60.

By J. Kelly Beatty

A New Era
in Space

The space shuttle has made space flight
seem almost routine, and it may also
have opened a new economic frontier.

Sunlight glinted from the wings of the giant jet transport plane as it eased onto the long concrete runway of the John F. Kennedy Space Center in Cape Canaveral, Fla. But what caught the eye's attention on this day in July 1985 was the transport's unique cargo. Perched atop the plane in piggyback fashion was a 74-ton winged spacecraft named *Columbia*, returning to the cape after an 18-month stay in California for upgrading and repair. *Columbia* was joining three similar spacecraft at the Kennedy Space Center. *Challenger* sat on the center's launch pad, *Discovery* was taking on a trio of satellites in one area of the center's Orbiter Processing Facility, and in another area stood *Atlantis*, the newest and last orbiter to be added to the space shuttle system.

July 14, 1985, was a significant day in the history of the United States space program. It was the first time that all four space shuttle orbiters—the entire fleet, as now planned—were together at the same time and in the same place. Their combined presence marked the completion of the Space Transportation System, the official name for the shuttle program, after nearly 13 years of design and development involving tens of thousands of engineers, scientists, and technicians and a cost of $13.1 billion.

The space shuttle is a key part of a new era in the space age. In this new era, outer space is no longer a place for only exploration or scientific experiment. It is now also a place to live and work. It is an economic frontier with a vast potential for new products. Today, the Soviet Union and the United States are no longer the only spacefaring nations, for a number of other nations are claiming their place in space. Finally, it is an era in which space is increasingly becoming a military arena.

All these developments have been influenced by the successful performance of the space shuttle. In the five years since *Columbia* first thundered aloft on April 12, 1981, the orbiters have figured prominently in a number of impressive feats, such as the first free-floating spacewalk by an astronaut, the first repair of a satellite in space, and the first retrieval and return to Earth of a malfunctioning satellite. With the shuttle, the sight of astronauts at work—equipped with tool caddies—has become commonplace.

The space shuttle has made it easier for people with a wide variety of backgrounds and skills to go into space. The early astronauts were all military-trained test pilots, but these new space travelers—known as *mission specialists*—have included engineers, physicians, scientists, and even a United States senator. Thanks to the shuttle, the daring space missions undertaken 25 years ago by former test pilots now seem almost routine.

Getting to and from space routinely was really the whole point of the space shuttle when the program was conceived in the early 1970's by the U.S. National Aeronautics and Space Administration (NASA). So NASA designed a space vehicle that takes off like a rocket and lands like an airplane. Except for an external fuel tank, it is entirely reusable. The shuttle's planners felt it would be less

The author:
J. Kelly Beatty covers U.S. and international space activities for *Sky & Telescope* magazine. He is the principal editor of *The New Solar System,* and writes frequently about space policy and exploration.

The U.S. space program entered a new era with the space shuttle, the first reusable spacecraft that takes off like a rocket, *left,* and lands like a plane, *above.*

costly to operate in the long run than expensive rockets that can be used only once.

Because the shuttle is a relatively economical method of placing satellites in orbit, NASA's biggest customer to date has been the communications industry. Since the shuttle program went into service, it has launched more than a dozen communications satellites for private industry, other countries, and the U.S. military.

NASA officials also saw the shuttle as an opportunity to open space to business ventures. They hoped that such ventures eventually would earn more money than it cost to operate the shuttle, thus actually producing revenue for the nation.

Some of these ventures, which take advantage of the vacuum and near-weightless conditions available only in space, have already produced useful results. In July 1985, NASA announced the first sale of a space-made product—microscopic plastic spheres manufactured during several shuttle flights. The perfect size and roundness of these spheres will be used as measurement standards in a variety of industries. The spheres are perfectly round because they were made in the low gravity of space. On Earth, gravity would have distorted their shape during the manufacturing process.

"This material is the first of what we expect will be a long line of products to carry the made-in-space label," said James M. Beggs, NASA's administrator. Indeed, some experts think space manufacturing may become a $25-billion-a-year business by the year 2000. Among the products that can be made in space are new drugs for

The space shuttle is in many ways a business venture. Its huge cargo bay enables it to carry large payloads into space, plus an astronaut crew. An astronaut at work in the bay, *above,* stands near the remote manipulator arm used to launch satellites into orbit.

Working and living in space means learning how to recover a malfunctioning satellite, *above,* and how to adapt to conditions of weightlessness, *right.*

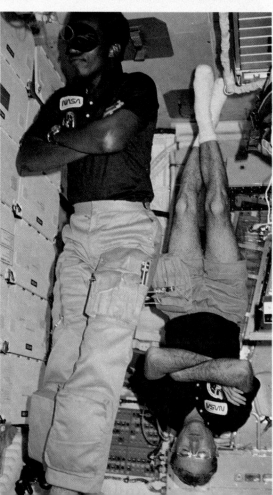

fighting disease, crystals for use in the electronics industry, lighter and stronger metals, and glass for a wide variety of uses.

Businesses are not yet racing to place *payloads* (cargo) aboard the space shuttle, however. NASA has been unable to deliver the dependable, frequent service that was promised when Congress and President Richard M. Nixon approved the program in 1972.

The original plan for the shuttle called for nearly 500 flights by the end of 1991, with a peak rate of 60 flights per year. During the shuttle's decade-long development, however, NASA exceeded its budget by as much as 20 per cent because of technical problems with the shuttle's engines and other components that resulted in a production delay of two years. To save money, NASA trimmed the number of orbiters to be built from five to four. NASA now realizes that a more realistic goal will be about 24 shuttle flights per year by 1989 and a total of perhaps 125 flights by the end of 1991.

With fewer flights, NASA has been unable to lower the prices it charges its customers for launching satellites. A typical satellite launch by shuttle cost $25 million in 1985. With more flights earning more money for the shuttle program, NASA could afford to reduce launching costs for its satellite customers who share in the cost of maintaining the orbiters. But without the additional flights, these lower costs have not materialized.

Another factor in NASA's declining expectations has been competition from abroad, specifically from the Ariane program developed by the European Space Agency (ESA). The ESA, founded in 1975, is an association of 13 nations—Austria, Belgium, Denmark, France, Great Britain, Ireland, Italy, the Netherlands, Norway, Spain, Sweden, Switzerland, and West Germany—that once existed in the shadow of NASA. But the ESA became a formidable competitor with the development of the Ariane rockets, which are launched from the Kourou Space Center in French Guiana. A corporation called Arianespace Incorporated, created in 1980 and owned by the French government and several European banks and corporations, is responsible for selling the services of the Ariane rockets.

Arianespace, which calls itself "the first commercial space carrier," has won more than $1 billion in contracts to launch satellites—business that otherwise might have gone to the shuttle. Between 1981 and 1985, the Ariane program put 12 satellites into orbit.

With its ability to launch its own satellites, the ESA shed much of its earlier dependence on NASA, which formerly provided launching services for the European agency. The two space agencies still cooperate with each other, as when the ESA-built Spacelab flew inside the orbiter *Columbia*'s cargo bay in November 1983, but increasingly the ESA ventures out on its own. The ESA now builds its own *remote-sensing* satellites, which use sophisticated sensing devices and cameras to provide information about Earth's natural resources. For example, these satellites can detect geologic formations that might

Science in a Spacelab

The European-built Spacelab, *right,* fits snugly inside the shuttle's cargo bay. Spacelab makes possible a variety of scientific experiments and studies in the fields of astronomy, Earth observations, life sciences, materials science, and space plasma physics, as shown below. Spacelab's scientists take advantage of the unique conditions of weightlessness in space, panoramic views of Earth, and a view of the universe free of Earth's obscuring atmosphere to perform studies that cannot be done on Earth.

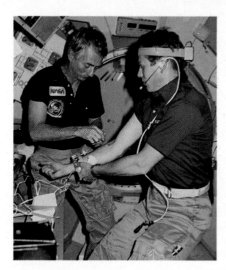

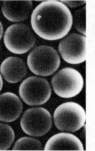 

Materials science creates new products such as microscopic plastic beads, *left,* that are perfectly round, unlike those made on Earth, *far left,* where gravity distorts the shape.

Life science experiments include taking blood, *above,* for studies that seek to determine how the human body adapts to conditions of weightlessness in space.

Space plasma physics—the study of electrified gases called plasmas trapped in Earth's magnetic field, *above*—may yield important clues about Earth's weather.

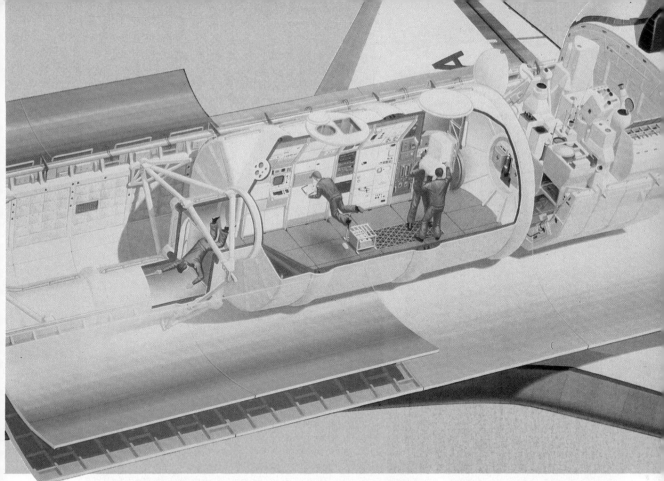

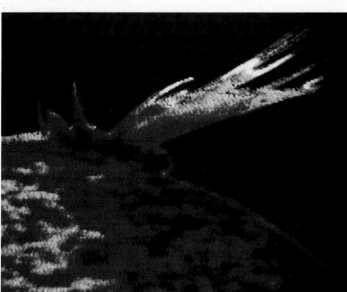

Earth observations, *above,* are uniquely suited to Spacelab with its sweeping, picture-window view of the planet and its resources.

Astronomers on board Spacelab can view solar eruptions, *above,* free of the distortions of Earth's atmosphere. Spacelab makes an ideal astronomical observatory for that reason.

yield significant new oil and natural gas discoveries, and land areas that might be ripe for agriculture. In addition, in July 1985, the ESA launched its first deep-space probe, called *Giotto*, which was to fly by Halley's Comet in March 1986.

Other nations have also jumped into the growing space business. The situation is similar to the 1500's, when several European countries followed Spain's lead in the exploration of the New World, motivated by the New World's economic promise and the desire to maintain national prestige. Similar motivations are broadening membership in the "space club," noted a July 1985 study by the Office of Technology Assessment, an advisory agency of the U.S. Congress. The study found that a growing number of countries are developing their own space-launching capabilities in order to be independent technologically, to gain any economic benefits from the commercial and scientific use of outer space, and to acquire the prestige of being known as a "space power."

In addition to the ESA, the Soviet Union, and the United States, Japan has developed an ambitious and aggressive space program. Between 1970 and 1985, Japan launched 19 satellites on its own. In 1986, it plans to launch a series of remote-sensing and communications satellites, using a number of its own powerful rockets to carry these satellites into orbit. In January and August 1985, Japan launched its first interplanetary spacecraft. One, known as *Sakigake* (Japanese for *pioneer*), was a test spacecraft, formerly known as *MS-T5*. The other, formerly known as *Planet A* but later renamed *Suisei* (Japanese for *comet*), was to fly within 60,000 miles of Halley's Comet.

Since 1970, China has successfully launched 16 spacecraft—mainly test satellites. In 1984, the Chinese Academy of Space Technology put its first communications satellite into orbit. In April 1985, Chinese space officials announced that they, too, have rockets for hire.

Meanwhile, India continues to push forward with its rockets and satellites. Since 1980, the In-

The space shuttle faced its first commercial competitor when the European Space Agency developed the Ariane rocket, *left,* lifting off from the Kourou Space Center in French Guiana.

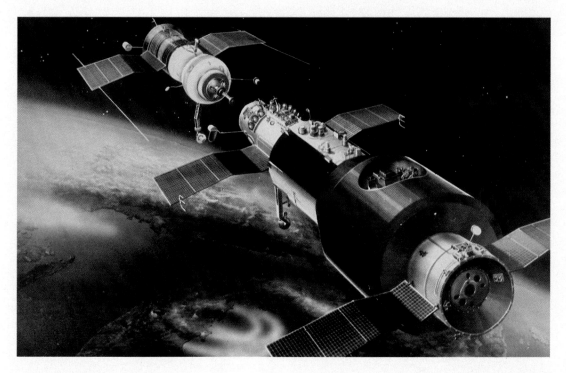

dian Space Research Organization has used its own rockets to launch three satellites into orbit. Mexico, Indonesia, Canada, Brazil, and Australia now have communications satellites in orbit, though they do not yet have the ability to launch their own satellites. The Soviet Union does not compete with the United States for commercial space launches such as these. One of the Soviet Union's most successful space programs is its manned space station.

NASA can also look forward to competition from private companies. Private enterprises in the United States, notably Space Services Incorporated of America, based in Houston, and Starstruck, Incorporated, of Redwood City, Calif., have attempted to cash in on the lucrative trade of building, launching, and servicing space-bound payloads. In September 1982, Space Services successfully tested its Conestoga 1 rocket, a small version of the booster rocket it will eventually use to put a payload into space.

All of this means that for the first time the success of a NASA project depends more on its acceptance in the market place than on its technical or scientific accomplishments. In this respect, the shuttle represents a new departure for NASA.

NASA was created on Oct. 1, 1958, in response to the Soviet Union's 1957 launch of the first artificial satellite, *Sputnik 1*. In the late 1950's, the United States already had a military rocket program, but President Dwight D. Eisenhower and Congress determined that space exploration should be a peaceful, civilian activity. Consequently, they created a powerful new space agency from an existing,

Competition of a different sort—mainly political and military—comes from the Soviet Union, which developed the *Salyut* space station, drawing *above.* The space station is linked to Earth by the *Soyuz* spacecraft, upper left. In 1984, Soviet cosmonauts set a record stay in space of 237 days on board *Salyut 7,* which is used for various scientific and technical experiments and for unspecified military studies.

The Spacefaring Nations

The Soviet Union and the United States no longer have an exclusive hold on the exploration of outer space. Although the two space superpowers retain a sizable lead, a number of other nations have joined the "space club" by using their own rockets to launch spacecraft. Between 1957 and 1984, the currently active members of the "space club" recorded the following number of successful launches:

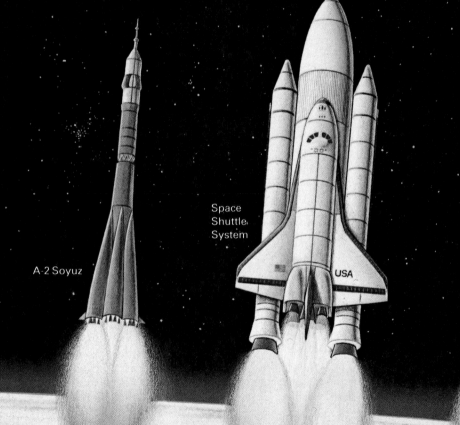

A-2 Soyuz

Space
Shuttle
System

USA

N-1

Soviet Union
1,733

Japan
27

United States
848

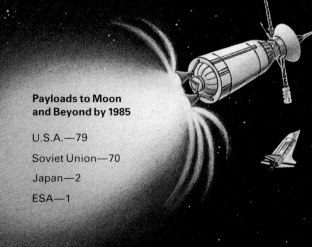

**Payloads to Moon
and Beyond by 1985**

U.S.A.—79

Soviet Union—70

Japan—2

ESA—1

CSL-2
FB-1

Ariane 1

SLV-3

**China
14**

**European Space Agency
9**

**India
3**

well-established scientific and engineering organization known as the National Advisory Committee for Aeronautics. Six days after NASA was pronounced "open for business" came the go-ahead for Project Mercury, the first U.S. program to put astronauts in space. After Mercury came the Gemini and Apollo programs. Apollo's goal was to put an astronaut on the moon, and it succeeded on July 20, 1969, when astronaut Neil A. Armstrong became the first person to walk on the moon. But after the last Apollo flight in 1975, NASA did not send anyone into space until the first shuttle flight in 1981.

Since NASA was established, many factors have shaped U.S. space policy, including the quest for scientific discovery, the testing of new technology, and the need to maintain national prestige and remain at the forefront of a new frontier. But in recent years, U.S. space planners have also become increasingly preoccupied with military concerns. In 1982, the U.S. armed forces for the first time in 22 years began to spend more money on space activities than NASA did. In the fiscal year of 1986, for example, the funds allocated for military space projects were about twice the $7.5 billion earmarked for civilian programs. About $4 billion was spent to develop a jet-launched rocket to attack and destroy satellites in space, a system that was tested successfully on Sept. 13, 1985. Another $2.75 billion was budgeted for research for President Ronald Reagan's contro-versial Strategic Defense Initiative, commonly known as "Star Wars"—a project designed to shield the United States from nuclear missiles by stationing armed orbiting satellites as sentinels. Shuttle flights have been used to test the feasibility of "Star Wars."

The original legislation creating NASA drew a clear line between military and civilian space programs and required NASA to make public the results of its explorations. The planned frequent use of the space shuttle for military payloads, however, has clouded NASA's role as a civilian agency. In January 1985, for example, *Discovery* blasted off from Cape Canaveral with a Department of Defense (DOD) satellite aboard, under strict security, including a press-information blackout. For the first time since the space age began, American citizens were not officially told what their astronauts did while in orbit, though leaks to the press revealed that *Discovery* carried a spy satellite capable of eavesdropping on Soviet radio communications. The inaugural flight of the orbiter *Atlantis*, from Oct. 3 to 7, 1985, again under strict security, launched two communications satellites for the DOD. Through 1990, roughly one-fourth of all shuttle flights will involve secret defense activities. In fact, U.S. military projects scheduled for the shuttle during this period outnumber those of any other group—including NASA.

In contrast, no clear distinction between civilian and military programs has *ever* existed in the Soviet Union, though in October 1985, the Soviet Union announced the creation of its first civilian space agency. From the outset, that country's space activities have been

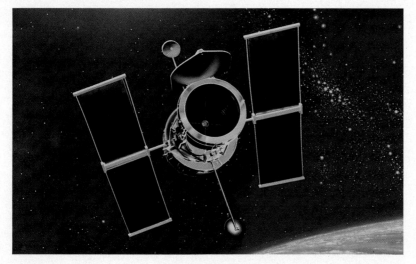

Although much attention is focused on the economic potential of the space shuttle, the shuttle continues to play a key role in space science programs. In 1986, the shuttle will launch the *Hubble Space Telescope,* shown *left* in an artist's drawing, an orbiting observatory that will enable astronomers to see nearly to the edge of the universe.

cloaked in secrecy, and details of even its purely scientific endeavors are rarely given. Military programs had a great deal to do with the Soviet Union's early successes in space. Ironically, the Soviet Union's technological backwardness was responsible for its success. During the 1950's, Soviet engineers developed a series of large rockets to deliver nuclear warheads over great distances. Their power and carrying capacity dwarfed the rockets under construction in the United States. Because of its more advanced technology, the United States had succeeded in *miniaturizing* (making smaller) its warheads and so did not need large and powerful rockets. The Soviet Union's powerful rockets, however, gave it a commanding lead in the early years of space exploration, enabling it to place the first satellite in space in 1957 and the first human being in orbit in 1961.

In sheer numbers, the Soviet Union has been quite successful in its exploration of space. From 1957 through 1984, it boosted 2,020 payloads into orbit, twice as many as the United States. Most of these carried the name *Cosmos,* a catchall designation for experimental, military, and other spacecraft.

A long-standing feature of the Soviet space program has been its series of *Salyut* space stations, the first of which reached orbit in 1971. Scores of cosmonauts have visited these stations, including one crew that stayed a record 237 days in space aboard *Salyut 7* in 1984. *Salyut 7,* the latest in the series of space stations, is about 50 feet long and weighs 42,000 pounds. It is used for scientific, technical, and unspecified military studies.

Until recently, the Soviet Union's space science missions have not been as impressive as those of the United States. Most of its interplanetary missions failed during the 1960's. Since then, however, the Soviet Union has sent a number of successful probes to explore Venus. Several Soviet spacecraft have mapped the planet's terrain

from space, sampled its atmosphere, and photographed its landscape. The Soviet Union also collected samples of the moon and returned them to Earth with automated spacecraft, and it sent spacecraft to intercept Halley's Comet in March 1986. The Soviet Union's future plans include sending robot craft to the moon, to Mars and its satellites, and to an area where asteroids orbit between Mars and Jupiter, known as the *asteroid zone.*

Although the United States did not send a probe to Halley's Comet, it continues to maintain its leadership in space science missions. In September 1985, a NASA spacecraft relayed data from Comet Giacobini-Zinner in the first direct probe of a comet in history. By the end of 1985, the U.S. spacecraft *Voyager 2* had returned the first close-up photographs of the giant planet Uranus. In 1986, NASA plans to launch *Galileo,* an interplanetary spacecraft that will probe the atmosphere of Jupiter. NASA has also announced plans to send probes to Venus and Mars within the next five years.

Perhaps the most dramatic event in U.S. space science is the planned 1986 launch of the *Hubble Space Telescope,* an orbiting telescope that will expand our vision to near the edge of the universe. Orbiting beyond the interference of Earth's atmosphere, which blocks light from distant astronomical objects, the space telescope is expected to result in the most sweeping advances in astronomy since the Italian astronomer Galileo made the first practical use of a telescope to observe the heavens in the 1600's.

The space telescope will enable astronomers to look back in time to the earliest stages of the universe. Meanwhile, U.S. space policymakers are looking to the future. On Jan. 25, 1984, President Reagan unveiled a key component of that future when he announced that NASA would undertake the development of a permanent space station to be occupied continuously by visiting astronauts. Echoing a similar commitment made by President John F. Kennedy to the Apollo program in the early 1960's, Reagan directed NASA to build the space station within a decade, and he extended an open invitation to other nations to participate in the new venture.

The Soviet Union has also announced plans to build a permanent space station, along with a reusable shuttle craft to deliver and retrieve crews of cosmonauts. Soviet space officials have not announced a timetable for completion of their permanent space station, but they appear to have a considerable head start on the United States.

As presently imagined, the U.S. space station will consist of a number of interlocking modules carried into orbit by the space shuttle. Some of the modules will be made by other countries and some by NASA's industrial contractors. Circling about 300 miles above Earth, the station will measure hundreds of feet in length and width, making it easily visible from Earth at night. The crew will conduct scientific experiments and manufacture new products that are impossible to make on Earth due to gravity. The space station could also be used as a departure point for trips to other parts of the solar system because rockets fired from the station will not have to expend the vast amounts of fuel needed to escape Earth's gravity.

Future plans for space call for even greater adventures. Scientists and engineers are now studying the exact requirements for missions to other worlds. They are laying the groundwork for men and women to live on the moon and to journey to Mars early in the next century. Trips such as these are no longer simply the visions of science-fiction writers.

Once solely the domain of U.S. and Soviet craft, outer space is now within the technological grasp not only of many nations but also of private corporations. Hundreds, and maybe even thousands, of people now living will experience the thrill of rocketing away from Earth during their lifetime. Space is now more accessible than ever before, and we have barely begun to harness its potential.

By William J. Cromie

Restoring Lady Liberty

An ambitious restoration project for the
Statue of Liberty should ensure the survival
of this symbol of freedom and promise.

We stood on the scaffolding more than 300 feet above New York Harbor, looking down on the crown of the Statue of Liberty. It was a rare view that let us appreciate the majesty—and the deterioration—of a monument that has symbolized the United States for 100 years. Liberty's upraised right arm, opposite us, was streaked with black stains and pocked with holes. Missing from her hand was the famous torch she holds aloft. It was so badly corroded that it had to be removed to prevent it from falling off. Through the opening in the torch handle, we could see that the framework of iron bars supporting Liberty's hollow copper shell was also badly corroded. Leaking rain water and a chemical reaction had caused such corrosion throughout the 151-foot 1-inch statue.

Rain began to soak us, and wind shook the aluminum scaffolding that has encased the statue during a major restoration effort. Begun in 1983, the work is scheduled for completion in time for a gala national celebration on July 3, 1986. As construction foreman Anthony J. Anello and I rode down the front of the statue on an elevator built on the scaffolding, we could see black marks and holes all over Liberty's gown.

"Coal tar," Anello said, motioning to the black streaks with his head. "The inside of the skin and the iron framework were coated with it as a waterproofing measure. But over the years, the tar seeped through the seams between the copper plates that make up the outer skin and through holes where rivets holding the plates together popped out."

The Statue of Liberty, erected in 1886, was showing her age. The extensive renovation will not only restore but also enhance her beauty and the experience of visiting her.

Anello and I took shelter from the rain in a workshop near the base of the monument. There, we watched French craftsmen, experts in a metalworking technique called *repoussé* (pronounced *ruh poo SAY*), create a new flame. Placing thin copper sheets in molds, the workers tapped the sheets with special hammers until the copper curved into the intricate shapes of a licking flame.

The scene reminded me of photographs from the 1800's showing French workers using the same technique to sculpture the entire statue. In fact, Liberty's current restoration has much in common with the statue's original construction. The French initiated both efforts—the first to honor 100 years of American independence, the second as a gesture of concern over the condition of the statue after 100 years of exposure to wind, pollution, and millions of visitors.

The idea for the statue was first proposed in 1865 at a dinner party given by Édouard-René Lefebvre de Laboulaye, a French historian and politician. Laboulaye, who admired Americans and their struggle for freedom, suggested that France and the United States cooperate to erect a colossal monument to liberty. At the dinner was a 31-year-old sculptor, Frédéric Auguste Bartholdi, whose imagination caught fire with the idea. At first, few people shared the two men's enthusiasm. Nevertheless, in 1871, with Laboulaye's encouragement, Bartholdi toured the United States to promote the project. Although he failed to arouse much American support, Bartholdi found a site—Bedloe's Island in New York Harbor (renamed Liberty Island in 1956). On the island was Fort Wood, built in the shape of an 11-pointed star in the early 1800's to defend New York City against naval attack. Bartholdi decided that the fort would make an excellent base for the monument.

Enthusiasm for the project lagged in France until 1875, when the establishment of a new government and constitution put the French in a mood to celebrate liberty. Finally that year, the French-American Union was established to raise funds for the statue and oversee construction.

Fund-raising progressed slowly, however. By the United States centennial in 1876, Bartholdi had finished only the statue's right forearm and torch. They were displayed at the Centennial Exposition in Philadelphia, then at Madison Square Park in New York City. By 1878, Bartholdi had completed Liberty's head, using his mother, Auguste-Charlotte, as the model for the face.

To create the statue, Bartholdi worked with a series of models. The final model consisted of 300 full-sized plaster sections. Workers in the Paris shop of Gaget, Gauthier, and Company built wooden molds in the shape of each of these plaster sections. Then repoussé workers laid thin sheets of copper—only $3/32$ inch thick—inside the molds and hammered the metal into shape. The statue's skin consists of 300 such sheets, connected with copper rivets.

To support the 151-foot 1-inch copper shell against the winds of New York Harbor, the project's first engineer, Eugène Viollet-le-

The author:
William J. Cromie is executive director of the Council for the Advancement of Science Writing.

52

Duc, proposed filling it with masonry and sand. Viollet-le-Duc died in 1879, however, and Bartholdi replaced him with Alexandre Gustave Eiffel, a French engineer. Then 47 years old, Eiffel had not yet designed the famous tower in Paris that bears his name.

Eiffel took a different approach to support the statue. He designed a central *pylon* or tower—an iron "backbone" 97 feet tall, consisting of four vertical columns connected by horizontal and diagonal bracing. Extending from the pylon is a framework of iron bars. From this framework extend flat bars of lighter iron that almost reach the skin. These bars, in turn, connect to a network of 1,800 flat, curved, and twisted bars, called the *armature,* that follow the shape of the copper plates making up Liberty's gown, body, torch, and crown. The bars, which all have different shapes, were ingeniously set in U-shaped copper fittings called *saddles,* which were riveted to the skin.

"This system allows Liberty to breathe," explains Richard S. Hayden of Swanke Hayden Connell Architects, the New York City firm selected to oversee the architectural part of the restoration. "As the temperature rises and falls and winds blow, the 'Lady' expands, contracts, sways, and twists. Eiffel's brilliant design permits the skin to move independently of its rigid support and so to accommodate the structural stresses produced by these movements."

Eiffel's ingenious system, however, had a built-in flaw that almost became Liberty's downfall. When iron and copper touch in the presence of a conductor, such as water or moisture in the air, electric

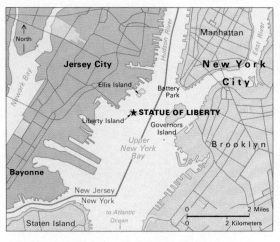

Towering majestically over Liberty Island in Upper New York Bay, the Statue of Liberty dominates the entrance to New York Harbor. The base of the statue is old Fort Wood, built in the shape of an 11-point star in the early 1800's to defend New York City against naval attack.

currents pass between them. Over time, this process causes the iron to corrode.

Eiffel tried to prevent this by separating the iron armature from the copper saddles with pads of leather and asbestos. Over the years, these pads deteriorated. Rain water leaking into the statue, the humid air of New York Harbor, and even the exhaled breath of visitors caused the armature to corrode and swell.

Some of the corroded bars pulled the copper saddles away from the skin, tearing out rivets. The resulting holes let in more rain water, aggravating the problem.

No one suspected this would happen when France presented the completed statue, officially called *Liberty Enlightening the World*, to Levi P. Morton, the U.S. minister to France, in Paris on July 4, 1884. After the presentation, workers disassembled the 450,000-pound statue and packed it into 214 mammoth crates. The crates were carried aboard the French naval ship *Isère* to New York City, arriving in June 1885.

Meanwhile, the United States struggled with the problem of a pedestal on which to mount the statue. Congress had agreed in 1877 to accept the statue and donate the site on Bedloe's Island on the condition that the money for the pedestal be contributed by the public. The construction of the 89-foot-tall pedestal, designed by American architect Richard Morris Hunt, began in 1884, but a lack of funds soon halted the project.

Then, in 1885, Joseph Pulitzer, the owner and editor of two news-

papers, *The World* in New York City and the *St. Louis Post-Dispatch*, entered the picture. Pulitzer urged everyone—rich and poor—to contribute, and he promised to print the name of everyone who did in his newspapers. His campaign raised $100,000, bringing the total of American contributions to $270,000. This paid for a pedestal faced with granite and backed with what was then the largest block of concrete in the world. For the statue itself, the French had collected the equivalent of $400,000.

The statue and pedestal finally were dedicated on Oct. 28, 1886, at ceremonies presided over by President Grover Cleveland. The U.S.S. *Despatch*, with the President aboard, led a fleet of 300 ships that sailed past the monument. An estimated 1 million people onshore and on boats watched and cheered.

Bartholdi's beautiful figure faces east toward Europe because, in the sculptor's mind, it represented the light of liberty, nurtured in the New World, streaming back to guide the way for the Old World. The statue also thrilled millions of immigrants who arrived in increasing numbers in the late 1800's and early 1900's. For them, it symbolized freedom from oppression and the promise of a better life. A bronze plaque affixed to the pedestal in 1903 recognizes this with the words of a poem by Emma Lazarus: " 'Give me your tired, your poor, / Your huddled masses yearning to breathe free . . . . I lift my lamp beside the golden door!' "

The idea for Liberty's restoration began with Philippe Vallery-Radot, a French philanthropist, who had read of holes and corro-

The Statue of Liberty

The enormous copper statue stands on Liberty Island in Upper New York Bay. Its official name is *Liberty Enlightening the World*. France gave the statue to the United States in 1884 as a symbol of the ideal of liberty shared by the people of both countries. The statue also became a symbol of freedom and opportunity for millions of immigrants entering the United States through the immigration station on nearby Ellis Island. Each year, about 2 million people visit the Statue of Liberty.

Frédéric Auguste Bartholdi, Liberty's sculptor

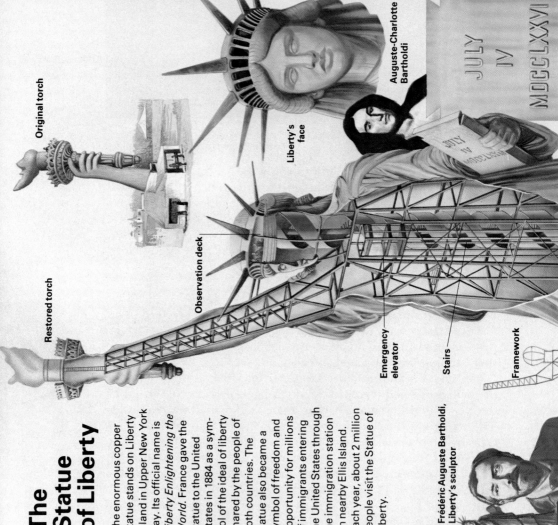

Restored torch

Original torch

Observation deck

Liberty's face

Auguste-Charlotte Bartholdi

Emergency elevator

Stairs

Framework

JULY
IV

MDCCLXXVI

The restored torch, which follows more faithfully the original design, measures 21 feet from bottom to top. At night, the shiny surface of its gilded flame reflects light from 16 powerful electric lamps located around the torch's rim.

The original torch was displayed at the Centennial Exposition in Philadelphia in 1876. For a fee of 50 cents, visitors could climb a ladder inside the arm to the balcony. The money raised in this way was used to help fund the construction of the rest of the statue in Paris.

The observation deck in the crown gives visitors a magnificent view of New York City and New York Harbor. It is 246 feet high, has 25 windows, and can hold about 20 people.

Liberty's face was modeled after the features of Auguste-Charlotte Bartholdi, the sculptor's mother. The nose is 4½ feet long, and each eye is 2½ feet across.

Frédéric Auguste Bartholdi, Liberty's sculptor, designed the statue, chose its site, and supervised its construction in Paris. Bartholdi also spent a great deal of time and energy promoting the project in France and the United States. His other works include statues of the French soldier and statesman the Marquis de Lafayette and of George Washington, both in New York City.

Alexandre Gustave Eiffel, the brilliant French engineer who later created the Eiffel Tower in Paris, designed the framework that supports Liberty's 100-ton copper skin. The unique iron and steel tower enables the statue to withstand fierce winds.

The pedestal was designed by American architect Richard Morris Hunt. Made of granite and concrete, it stands 154 feet high. When completed, its foundation was the world's largest concrete structure. The pedestal houses the American Museum of Immigration.

The inspiration for the Statue of Liberty came from Édouard-René Lefebvre de Laboulaye, a French legal scholar. He envisioned the statue as a monument to U.S. independence. The figure of Liberty holds a tablet inscribed with the date of the Declaration of Independence in Roman numerals.

Mother of Exiles is the name given to the statue in "The New Colossus," a poem by American poet Emma Lazarus. In the poem, the statue welcomes immigrants seeking freedom and opportunity in the United States. A bronze tablet inscribed with the poem was installed in the pedestal in 1903.

A model of the statue stands on a small island in the Seine River, just downstream from the Eiffel Tower in Paris. This model, about one-fourth the size of the original Statue of Liberty, was given to France in 1885 by U.S. citizens living in Paris.

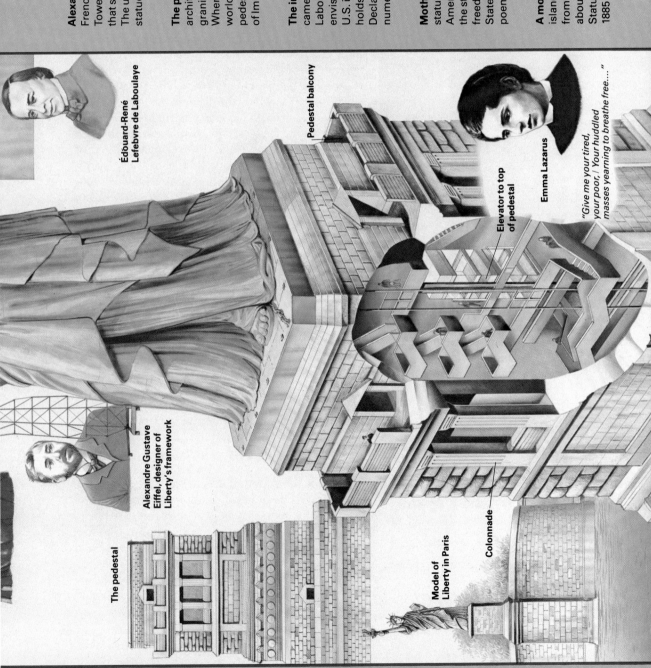

Édouard-René Lefebvre de Laboulaye

Pedestal balcony

The pedestal

Alexandre Gustave Eiffel, designer of Liberty's framework

Elevator to top of pedestal

Emma Lazarus

"Give me your tired, / your poor, / Your huddled masses yearning to breathe free...."

Colonnade

Model of Liberty in Paris

Scaffolding encases Liberty from base to torch during a major renovation effort to ensure the survival of the 100-year-old monument, which has welcomed millions of immigrants to the United States.

sion found on the statue. Organizing a group of engineers, architects, and other interested people, Vallery-Radot in 1981 formed the French-American Committee for the Restoration of the Statue of Liberty. The committee joined with the U.S. National Park Service, which took charge of the statue in 1924 when it became a national monument, to conduct a thorough inspection of the structure.

Advised of the serious problems that the inspection revealed, President Ronald Reagan on May 18, 1982, organized the Statue of Liberty-Ellis Island Centennial Commission. The restoration effort was expanded to include nearby Ellis Island, an immigration station where more than 12 million people entered the United States from 1892 to 1954, when the facility was closed. Reagan named Lee A. Iacocca, chairman of Chrysler Corporation, to head the commission. Charged with the restoration and future maintenance of both the statue and the buildings on Ellis Island, the commission formed the Statue of Liberty-Ellis Island Foundation to raise the necessary $230-million—$62 million for restoration of the statue and $168 million for work on Ellis Island.

About half of the needed money was contributed by corporations, foundations, and service organizations. Much of the remainder came from individuals and employee groups responding to fund-raising letters. "The most highly valued contribution came from schoolchildren," says foundation President William May. "By July 1985, they had added more than $3 million to the restoration effort."

The restoration work began in 1983. The exterior of the statue required a minimum amount of work, according to Thierry W. Despont, a French-born New York City architect who worked with both the foundation and the French-American Committee. The restoration team carefully inspected the statue's skin and measured its thickness with sound waves to determine whether corrosion had thinned the already thin plates.

"Despite stains on the exterior, the skin has remained in good condition," Despont says. "Originally the deep-brown color of a penny, the outside gradually aged to its present light-green hue.

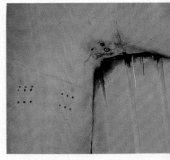

Liberty's right hand and arm, streaked with coal tar that seeped from inside the statue and pocked with holes from missing rivets, testify to the damage caused by 100 years of exposure to the elements.

This patina [a film on the surface that is a result of mild corrosion] protects the copper, and we decided not to change it."

The restorers did remove the accumulation of dirt, coal tar, and bird droppings. They also washed the exterior of the statue. Finally, they replaced missing rivets with new ones colored to match the statue's patina. This work was relatively minor, compared with replacing Liberty's torch and her corroded armature.

The solid copper flame originally was designed to be lit by external lamps. But one week before the dedication, portholes were cut into the copper and lamps were placed inside.

When Bartholdi first saw the flame, he complained that it was so dim that it resembled a "glowworm." To increase its brightness, more portholes and a skylight were cut into the plates. In 1916, American sculptor Gutzon Borglum, who later became famous for carving the huge stone portraits of U.S. Presidents on Mount Rushmore in South Dakota, replaced most of the flame's copper with amber glass panes. Unfortunately, these windows were not sealed properly, causing the leaks and corrosion that threatened to topple the torch. In addition, 100 years of wear and neglect had colored the flame's remaining copper greenish-black.

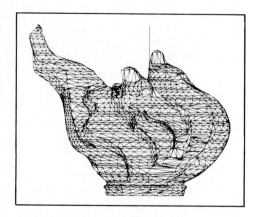

Liberty's badly corroded torch and flame are carefully lifted from the statue's hand on July 4, 1984, *left.* To create a new flame, the restorers first made a plaster model based on measurements obtained from a computer analysis, *above,* of old photographs of the original flame. Metal sheets fitted against the plaster model, *below,* provided molds to fashion the new flame.

The National Park Service decided to restore the torch according to Bartholdi's original design. Bartholdi's drawings of the statue, however, were destroyed in a fire that swept through Gaget and Gauthier's workshop in the early 1900's. So restorers turned to old photographs and a computer technique called photogrammetry to verify the original design. The repoussé workers used the measurements obtained in this way to construct their molds. Finally, the flame was plated with gold.

Replacing the corroded armature and saddles—one-third of which had pulled away from the copper skin—turned out to be the most difficult and complex task of the restoration. When the workers began to remove the iron ribs, they found that much of the asbestos between the iron and copper skin remained intact. Because asbestos is linked with lung cancer and other health problems, workers had to wear face masks, carry their own air supply, and take other safety precautions.

The restorers next had to find a replacement for the corroded iron. "After testing dozens of materials, including plastics, we decided on stainless steel because it will not react with copper or significantly change the weight or stiffness of the statue," explains Philip Kleiner of Lehrer/McGovern, Incorporated, construction managers on the project.

To prevent the skin from buckling or ripping while the supports were replaced, workers removed only a few bars at a time from several different sections of the statue. They moved the bars to the workshop on Liberty Island, where another team used a large hydraulic press and hammers to duplicate their curves and twists in stainless steel heated to a workable softness. The new bars were then *annealed* (heated and cooled quickly) to strengthen them. The following morning, workers installed the new bars. Despite the difficulty of the process, workers replaced 50 to 60 bars each week. New copper saddles took the place of the old saddles.

The restoration team found the worst corrosion in Liberty's upraised arm, where water had leaked down from the torch. Here, too, they replaced the ribs and saddles.

But the arm was plagued with another problem, the origin of which is something of a puzzle. Liberty's head is not on straight. Instead of sitting directly over the central pylon, as Eiffel planned, the head is about 2 feet off-center, toward the right arm. Liberty's upraised arm also is positioned improperly. As a result, the bracing for the right shoulder is not as strong as it should be.

Some experts believe that the statue was reassembled incorrectly in New York City in 1886. John C. Robbins, a historical architect with the National Park Service, insists, however, that it was changed in Paris.

"The most reasonable scenario," declares chief architect Hayden, "is that when Bartholdi first saw the completed statue, he was dissatisfied with it and moved the shoulder and head. Although the change is not logical from an engineering point of view, the statue looks perfectly proportioned from every angle."

The National Park Service decided not to change the position of the head and arm. "Our feeling was that the present structure tells a significant story about the statue so we should not change it," says Robbins. "We chose to add new bracing and to reinforce the existing framework in the shoulder."

While all this was going on, other workers struggled with the problem of removing seven layers of paint from the inside of the copper skin and from the iron framework. This was done to restore the inside to its original appearance. "We thought of using chemical paint removers on the skin," explains engineer Larry Bellante, a technical adviser. "But the inside of the statue is like a poorly ventilated chimney and has no emergency exits. So we ruled out chemicals because of the health hazard and danger of explosion. We also considered blasting off the paint. However, we were afraid that sand and other abrasives that are traditionally used for this might damage the thin skin."

Noting that ice can be used to remove old chewing gum from surfaces, Robbins and Frances Gale, a preservationist at Columbia University in New York City, suggested freezing the paint off. The restorers tried dry ice, but that didn't work. Then they experimented with liquid nitrogen cooled to a temperature of −350°F. To everyone's surprise, the supercold spray caused the paint to become brittle, crack, and fall off.

The view downward from inside Liberty at about waist level reveals the statue's ingenious iron skeleton. From a central tower, a framework of straight iron bars extending outward connects with curved bars that follow the contours of Liberty's copper skin.

But the liquid nitrogen did not remove the layer of coal tar under the paint. "We were now next to the skin and increasingly concerned about damaging or thinning it," Bellante explains. "We unsuccessfully tried a lot of abrasives until Victor Strauss, one of the painters, came up with the idea of blasting the coal tar with bicarbonate of soda." The suggestion startled everyone. "A coarser grade than that used in the home is used for industrial cleaning, but no one, as far as we knew, had employed it on such a massive scale. The soda worked, but it gave us problems. We had to find a way to keep it from filling the statue with clouds of dust. Also, it absorbed moisture and tended to clog up the blasting nozzles. But once we worked out methods to use dryers and to vacuum up the debris, baking soda did the job smoothly and efficiently."

Neither the baking soda nor the liquid nitrogen would remove the layers of paint from the iron framework. Liberty's skeleton is stouter than her skin, so blasting off the paint with *corundum* (sand-like aluminum oxide) seemed feasible. The aluminum oxide worked, but it also filled the interior with grit and lead from the paint, creating a health hazard for the workers. The restorers solved this problem by putting the blasting nozzles inside vacuum-cleaner hoses, which sucked up the grit and old paint as it was blasted off. For added safety, the workers wore protective clothing and helmets and carried their own supply of fresh air.

The next problem was how to repaint the iron framework without filling the statue with explosive paint fumes. The solution, engineers realized, involved using water-based paint, which contains no flam-

A worker compares a corroded iron bar—one of 1,800 curved bars in Liberty's framework—with its stainless steel replacement.

Illuminated by the fireworks of a Fourth of July celebration, the Statue of Liberty remains a thrilling symbol of American democracy and freedom.

mable solvents. After painting the framework, the restorers coated it with a special material from which graffiti can be easily removed.

The newly restored statue is scheduled to be unveiled on the night of July 3, 1986, and celebrated with official ceremonies on July 4. A new lighting system, turned on by the President of the United States, will illuminate the darkened statue section by section. The unveiling will kick off a week of celebrations, featuring brilliant fireworks displays, the world's tallest sailing ships, and naval vessels from more than 60 countries. On October 28, the presidents of the United States and France plan to reenact the original dedication ceremony.

The public will get its first look at the restored statue on July 5. Visitors will enter the monument through doors in the walls of old Fort Wood, just as they did before the restoration. After that, the experience will be completely different.

"In pre-restoration times," Hayden says, "visitors stood in line in cramped spaces and looked at blank walls. Then they rode up through the pedestal in a closed elevator, traveling through 40 per cent of the height of Liberty without seeing anything."

After the restoration, visitors will be able to explore two museums in the pedestal—scheduled to open on July 5, 1986—which graphically tell the stories of the statue and of Ellis Island. They will then board a double-decked, glass elevator—the highest hydraulic elevator in the United States.

As the elevator ascends through the nine-story pedestal, lights inside the elevator car will dim while lights outside increase in brightness. "People will see the huge crossbeams, recessed into the concrete, which anchor the 15-story statue above them. Along with feeling the grandeur of the space, this will allow visitors to begin to understand how the statue works," says Hayden.

The elevator will discharge passengers near the top of the pedestal, where they will be able to go out onto a colonnade and a balcony for a spectacular view of Manhattan and New York Harbor. Sightseers will also get a good view of Ellis Island, about 1 mile to the north. It is scheduled to be completely restored by 1992.

Visitors will then walk up several flights of stairs to the foot of the statue, where they will be able to see another awesome sight. Thanks to the removal of a ceiling, the installation of a new observation level, and improved lighting, "visitors will be able to stand at Liberty's feet and see up as far as her neck," architect Despont says. The National Park Service considered a variety of ideas to make it easier to climb the double staircase that spirals up through the central pylon. But, Robbins explains, "Letters that we received convinced us that the hard climb is what people remember most vividly—even more than the view from the crown. Therefore, we decided to stay true to history and not change this experience."

It will be a more pleasant experience, however. Before the restoration, visitors trudged up a gloomy staircase surrounded by a stout metal safety cage, beyond which they saw little more than shadows. On hot summer days, temperatures climbed above 120°F., and the build-up of carbon dioxide made the poorly ventilated interior very uncomfortable. Lack of heating made the climb a chilling ordeal in winter.

In the restored statue, the metal of the cage is to be replaced by one made of laminated tempered glass. Tired climbers will be able to step off on rest platforms. New cooling, heating, and ventilation systems will make the climb more comfortable, as well as protect the restored interior.

Changes on the outside will be less noticeable. From a distance, Liberty's green gown will look the same, but it will be cleaner and fresher up close. The most striking difference will be the flame. On a sunny day it will shine with reflected sunlight and will be visible from a much greater distance than was the old flame. At night, external spotlights will turn the flame into a brilliant beacon.

Architects and engineers expect the restored statue to last much longer than another 100 years. "The gold on the flame may not survive that long, but the copper skin and iron and steel framework should last several centuries," Despont believes. Hayden, who expects the statue to stand for 1,000 years, reflects that "in 1986, *Liberty Enlightening the World* is a monument to engineering and architecture as well as to hope and freedom. In the future, it also will become one of the most important archaeological monuments in history."

For further reading:

Allen, Frederick. "Saving the Statue." *American Heritage,* June/July 1984.
Bell, James B., and Abrams, Richard I. *In Search of Liberty: The Story of the Statue of Liberty and Ellis Island.* Doubleday, 1984.
Liberty: The Story and the Dream. National Geographic, 1985.

By Lawrence H. Fuchs

The New New Americans

The unusual makeup of the present wave of immigration is generating concerns—some old, some new—about the future of the United States as a melting pot.

Children in an elementary school in Ventura, Calif., began a school day in October 1985 by rising from their seats, putting their hands over their hearts, and reciting, *"Prometo lealtad a la bandera de los Estados Unidos de América,"* a Spanish rendition of "I pledge allegiance to the flag of the United States of America."

That evening, across the country in Fall River, Mass., a young Kampuchean refugee couple watched a cooking program on television to improve their English and to learn about American foods. "I want to live in a liberties country," the woman told a visitor.

And that night, dozens of Mexicans seeking jobs and a better life slipped across the border into Texas. Many of them would eventually return to Mexico, but others would remain in the United States as illegal immigrants.

Such scenes have raised the questions of how well the United States can function as a *melting pot*—a place where immigrants quickly adopt the mainstream culture—and how illegal immigration should be controlled. Each scene is part of a larger picture that evokes a particular concern.

■ Some 3½ million children like those in Ventura are enrolled in *bilingual education* programs, in which the classroom language changes gradually from the students' native language to English. Many Americans wonder whether many of these children will fail to learn English and will be disadvantaged as adults because the melting pot is not allowed to work as it once did.

■ Kampucheans and other Asian immigrants speak languages, practice religions, and follow traditions that, until recently, were virtually unknown in the United States. Many Americans wonder whether these newcomers, in spite of their efforts to adopt American ways, are too alien for the melting pot.

■ No one is sure how many people enter the United States illegally. Many Americans fear the number is so large that the Southern border states soon will be overrun by millions of Hispanics living outside the law, taking jobs away from U.S. citizens, and wanting nothing to do with the melting pot.

These concerns have generated a variety of reactions. There have been calls for new approaches to bilingual education. The U.S. Congress has debated—but has not passed—legislation to stem the tide of illegal immigration. And some critics want to cut the rate of legal immigration as well.

The concerns about immigrants are not new to the United States. Americans have worried about immigrants since the earliest days of the republic. And, except for illegal immigration, most concerns about immigrants have been virtually identical throughout the nation's history.

Beginning in the 1600's, immigrants from many European countries settled in what would become the original 13 states. Most of the colonists were English, so by 1700 the English culture became dominant. Non-English immigrants and their descendants spoke English and behaved generally like English people. One notable exception were German settlers in Pennsylvania, who retained their language and culture throughout the 1700's. In 1751, the American statesman Benjamin Franklin complained that, by insisting on speaking German, these immigrants might "Germanize us instead of [our] Anglifying them."

Since Franklin's time, three great waves of immigration have reached the nation's shores. The first, which lasted from 1831 until 1870, was made up of more than 7 million people. Sixty-four per cent of them were German or Irish. They were attracted by America's good farmland, its plentiful jobs, and its political and religious freedom.

The author:
Lawrence H. Fuchs is chairman of the American Studies Department at Brandeis University in Waltham, Mass.

Many English-speaking Americans resented the Germans' loyalty to their own language and culture. The Irish immigrants were feared and disliked, in large part because of religious differences. Most U.S. citizens were Protestants, while almost all Irish immigrants were Roman Catholics. Many Protestants thought the Irish were unfit for U.S.-style self-government because the Roman Catholic Church was governed by a strong central authority over which ordinary parishioners had no control. So vicious was anti-Catholic feeling that gangs of Protestant toughs frequently attacked Catholic churches and convents in the mid-1800's.

Earlier settlers also scorned the Irish newcomers because their extreme poverty and lack of education resulted in high rates of tuberculosis, alcoholism, and crime. *Nativists*—people who opposed immigration and easy naturalization—feared for the future of the United States. They wrote articles filled with statistics on the criminal activity of foreign-born Irish people and their children.

Hostility toward Germans and Irish was extensive long after the end of the first wave of immigrants, even though the nation needed them to open vast lands for settlement, to gouge the earth for coal and iron, to work in rapidly developing mills, and to build cities and railroads. Many native-born Americans—whose own ancestors had, of course, been immigrants themselves—continued to feel that German immigrants and their descendants were not complete Americans. German-Americans saw nothing wrong with speaking German in public and listening to a band in a beer garden on Sundays, but the nativists felt otherwise. So outraged was the *Chicago Tribune* in the 1870's that it argued for a strict enforcement of a law requiring beer gardens and other businesses to close on Sundays to prevent "the German conquest of the city." But as the descendants of German, Irish, and other immigrants from northwestern Europe intermarried and otherwise melted in the pot, hostility waned.

Meanwhile, the second wave of immigrants arrived, generating fresh concerns. This wave lasted from 1891 through 1914, and was made up of 17 million people, who—like the immigrants of the first wave—sought economic opportunities.

The chief source of concern about these immigrants was that most of them came from Greece, Hungary, Italy, Poland, Portugal, Russia, and Spain. Many were Jewish. Also in the second wave were Chinese, Filipinos, Japanese, and West Indians. Just as the Irish and Germans had appeared to native-born Americans to be more foreign than English Protestant immigrants, so did the new immigrants appear to be more foreign than the previous arrivals. Unlike the Irish, the vast majority of the newcomers spoke no English. Unlike the Germans, most of them were not fair-skinned. Poor and without skills, they settled in congested urban ghettos, where they were accused of being criminal and diseased. The Chinese were despised as more suited to opium addiction and gambling than to U.S. citizenship. Italians often were labeled as criminals. Anti-Semitism kept Jews out of many kinds of businesses and many colleges and universities. In 1908, New York City's police commissioner charged that 85 per cent of the city's criminals were foreign and that 50 per cent of them were Jews. Despite these attacks, the melting process continued, and the second-wave immigrants and their descendants contributed greatly to every aspect of American life.

The Americanization of the turn-of-the-century immigrants and their descendants, however, changed the meaning of "melting pot." The term came to signify not the complete disappearance of all the immigrants' old ways, but the sharing of many of them within the framework of an American identity. Today, ethnic traditions— dances, foods, holidays, religious practices, and family customs—are celebrated as part of the American heritage.

In earlier decades, such traditions drew the fire of nativists, who believed they threatened the American way of life. Reflecting nativist sentiment, Congress passed laws restricting the immigration of certain nationalities. The Chinese Exclusion Act of 1882, for example, barred Chinese laborers, and in 1917 immigration from Asia was curtailed to a trickle. A 1924 law placed an annual ceiling of 150,000 on immigration, except for wives and the unmarried children of U.S. citizens, and established the *national-origins system* of quotas. The government assigned each country an annual quota for immigration, based upon estimates of the ethnic composition of the U.S. population in 1890, sharply reducing immigration from Asia and from eastern and southern Europe. The quotas for countries in northern and western Europe amounted to 82 per cent of the total number assigned. For nations in southern and eastern Europe, the share was 16 per cent; and for the remainder of the world, just 2 per cent.

Following the end of World War II in 1945, President Harry S. Truman criticized the national-origins system. He saw it as a rejection of first President George Washington's view that the United States should remain "an asylum to the oppressed and needy of the earth" and as a turning away from the ideals of equality and cultural pluralism.

Presidents Dwight D. Eisenhower, John F. Kennedy, and Lyndon B. Johnson echoed Truman's criticism. By the mid-1960's, Congress was ready to liberalize immigration policy. Under Johnson's prodding, Congress in 1965 changed the national-origins system and assigned the entire Western Hemisphere an annual limit of 120,000. Each country in the Eastern Hemisphere received a ceiling of 20,000, with an overall limit of 170,000 for that hemisphere. A 1976 law made the regulations the same for both hemispheres, giving each nation a limit of 20,000. Two years later, Congress established an annual world ceiling of 290,000 (reduced to 270,000 after the passage of the Refugee Act of 1980) and retained equal limits for

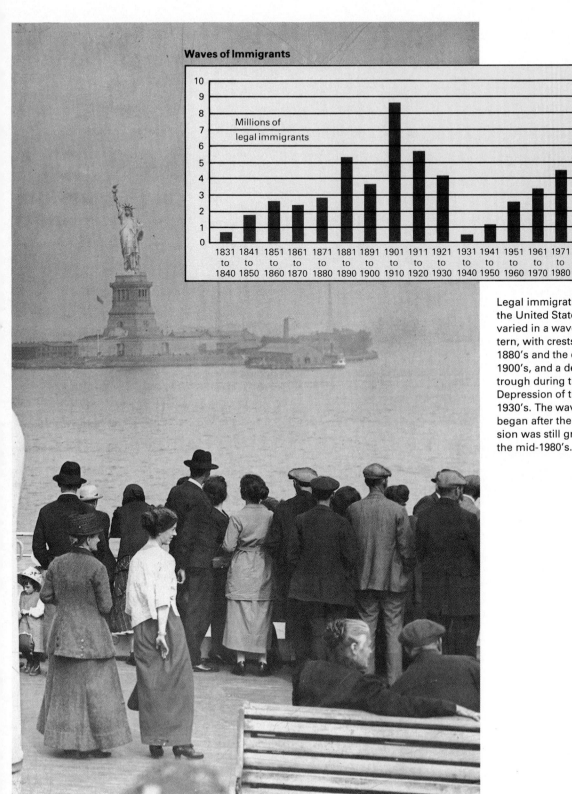

Waves of Immigrants

Millions of legal immigrants

| 1831 to 1840 | 1841 to 1850 | 1851 to 1860 | 1861 to 1870 | 1871 to 1880 | 1881 to 1890 | 1891 to 1900 | 1901 to 1910 | 1911 to 1920 | 1921 to 1930 | 1931 to 1940 | 1941 to 1950 | 1951 to 1960 | 1961 to 1970 | 1971 to 1980 | 1981 to 1984 |

Legal immigration to the United States has varied in a wavelike pattern, with crests in the 1880's and the early 1900's, and a deep trough during the Great Depression of the 1930's. The wave that began after the depression was still growing in the mid-1980's.

A Changing Pattern

Europe and Canada have supplied the United States with the vast majority of its legal immigrants. But immigration-reform laws passed in 1965 and 1976 have allowed a massive influx of newcomers from lands south of the border and from Asia.

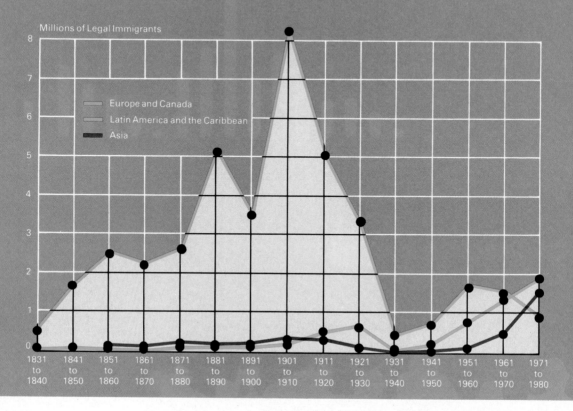

Millions of Legal Immigrants

— Europe and Canada
— Latin America and the Caribbean
■ Asia

each country. Spouses, minor children, and parents of U.S. citizens continued to be admitted without limit.

These laws along with others providing for refugee admissions were major causes of the third wave of immigration, which began in the late 1960's and was still going strong at the end of 1985. Since 1978, the average annual legal immigration to the United States has been more than 550,000.

The ethnic composition of the third wave of immigrants differs sharply from those of the previous waves. A major difference is the heavy influx from Asia—a result of the vast increases in the quotas for Asian nations and of the ongoing warfare in Southeast Asia. Since 1980, Asia has accounted for about 50 per cent of the legal immigrants; Latin America, about 25 per cent; and Europe, only about 10 per cent.

Another new element in the third wave has been a growth in illegal immigration. The rate of illegal immigration is not known, but

Where Immigrants Come from and Where They Settle

About two-thirds of the legal immigrants who have arrived in the United States since 1975* have settled in just six states. The three groupings of newcomers shown account for 97 per cent of the legal immigration.

Europe and Canada:
634,000 immigrants

Leading sources:
Great Britain 106,000
Canada 91,000
Portugal 60,000
Soviet Union 54,000
Germany, East and
West 51,000

Latin America and the Caribbean:
1,522,000 immigrants

Leading sources:
Mexico 481,000
Cuba 198,000
Dominican
Republic 138,000
Jamaica 129,000
Colombia 71,000

Asia:
1,726,000 immigrants

Leading sources:
Philippines 316,000
Vietnam 269,000
South Korea 247,000
China and
Taiwan 218,000
India 165,000

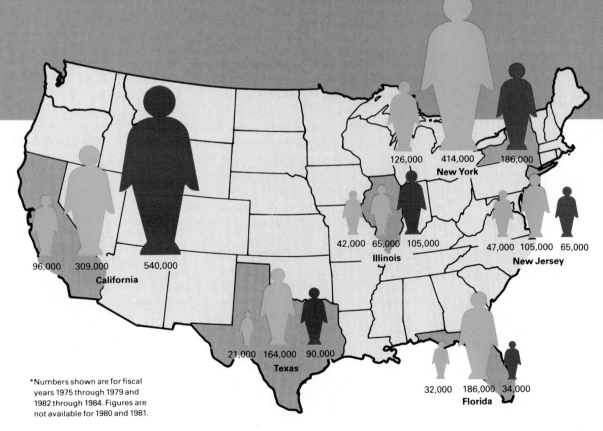

126,000 414,000 186,000
New York

42,000 65,000 105,000
Illinois

47,000 105,000 65,000
New Jersey

96,000 309,000 540,000
California

21,000 164,000 90,000
Texas

32,000 186,000 34,000
Florida

*Numbers shown are for fiscal years 1975 through 1979 and 1982 through 1984. Figures are not available for 1980 and 1981.

Vietnamese registering at an immigration office, *right,* and Mexicans waiting to cross the United States border illegally, *opposite page,* represent major segments of the current wave of newcomers.

experts estimate no fewer than 3 million and no more than 6 million illegal aliens are in the United States. Probably 75 per cent of the illegal aliens in the United States are from the Western Hemisphere. Most are from Mexico. A majority work at jobs that require little or no skill. Among the remainder are students, tourists, and even business people who stayed after their visas expired. A Swedish car salesman, an English legal secretary, a Dutch medical technician, a Canadian journalist, a Filipino clerk, a businessman from Hong Kong—all may be illegal aliens.

The two groups of immigrants—legal and illegal—raise separate concerns. The major area of concern over legal immigrants may be the language issue. This issue raises anxieties because Spanish-speaking immigrants, like the German immigrants before them, constitute a large group; and many members of this group want to retain their ancestral language. Opposition to such newcomers has been most intense in areas such as Dade County, Florida, where large numbers of Cubans quickly achieved an unusual degree of political and economic strength. Today, Spanish is the language of commerce in large sections of Miami and nearby cities in Dade County.

Another major concern is that immigrants and refugees will take jobs away from American workers. Still another fear is that many newcomers will not take jobs at all, but will become a burden on the welfare system.

Despite these concerns, the hostility toward legal immigrants is not as great as in former eras. This may be partly because current U.S. immigration policies favor family reunification. About three-fourths of all legal immigrants are close relatives of U.S. citizens or of aliens who are registered as permanent residents. In addition,

every legal immigrant must pass 33 qualifying tests. For example, even a spouse of a U.S. citizen will not be admitted if he or she is severely retarded mentally, has an infectious communicable disease, has a chronic dependence on alcohol, suffers from a psychotic disorder, has been convicted of a serious crime, or is likely to become dependent on welfare. Such restrictions contrast sharply with immigration policy in the 1700's and much of the 1800's, when tens of thousands of English paupers and felons immigrated to the United States.

Another explanation is the decline in racism in the United States, partly as a result of the World War II fight against the racist policies of Nazism, and partly because of the civil rights movement in the United States in the 1960's and 1970's. Finally, most Americans have come to accept ethnic diversity, and many celebrate it as part of the American way of life.

Most of today's concern about immigration is focused on illegal aliens. Labor leaders charge that they are taking jobs away from Americans and lowering wages and other standards of employment such as hours and work rules. There also are complaints that many of them are bringing health problems and social ills such as criminal behavior into the United States.

In spite of such complaints, many Americans favor doing nothing to curtail the flow of illegal aliens. They believe that the vast major-

Some immigrant children, such as these Vietnamese-speaking youngsters in Mississippi, receive special language training to help them shift from their native tongues to English.

ity of such people work at jobs that Americans will not take, and that the aliens are generally hard-working and healthy.

The Chamber of Commerce of the United States and employers associations agree with this view. They say that, because Americans would not take certain jobs now held by illegal aliens, shutting off the flow of illegal aliens would harm U.S. economic growth. Americans would take some such jobs if the pay were increased, the organizations claim. But employers would pass the wage hikes along to their customers, resulting in higher prices for the consumer.

In previous years, especially during the two world wars, legal foreign workers contributed substantially to the U.S. economy. The United States imported large numbers of such workers to do jobs for which it was thought Americans were unavailable. They worked on farms, in factories, and in service businesses such as restaurants. Beginning in 1942, Mexican farm workers called *braceros* received temporary permits to work in the United States for specified employers. The end of the bracero program in 1964 and the setting of numerical limits on immigration from countries in the Western Hemisphere in 1976 contributed to a substantial increase in illegal immigration across the southern border. Mexicans were determined to go to the United States for jobs, regardless of the law.

Illegal aliens crossing this border face great dangers. Robbery, rape, extortion, and even murder are not unusual. Sometimes *coyotes*—smugglers of human beings—abandon their charges, as they did in July 1980 when 12 Salvadorans died in the Arizona desert from lack of food and water.

For most who make the journey, however, the benefits of work in the United States far outweigh the risks of illegal entry. One study revealed that Salvadorans who earned an average hourly wage of 95 cents in their own country made $3.77 per hour in the United States. Other studies show that many illegal aliens make more than

A notice near voting booths in San Francisco, *below left,* and a street sign in Boston, *below,* are examples of official efforts to accommodate adult immigrants who read other languages more easily than English.

Migrant workers harvest a crop in California. Many fruit and vegetable pickers in the United States are Mexicans who enter the country illegally, work during the harvesting season, and return to Mexico until the next year.

that. Many illegal aliens earn enough to send money back home for their families.

Congress became so concerned with the problems of immigration, particularly the illegal influx, that in 1978 it created a Select Commission on Immigration and Refugee Policy to gather information about immigrants, examine immigration and refugee policy, and recommend policy changes. The commission—made up of four senators, four members of the House of Representatives, four Cabinet members, and four individuals not associated with the federal government—was headed by Theodore M. Hesburgh, a Roman Catholic priest, president of the University of Notre Dame, and former chairman of the Commission on Civil Rights, an independent agency of the U.S. government.

The Select Commission held regional hearings in 12 cities throughout the United States, conducted 24 sessions with expert witnesses, analyzed all existing research on immigration, and contracted for 22 research projects. In addition, the commission staff visited many areas where immigration is a major concern. In March 1981, the commission filed a 13-volume report and more than 100 recommendations, providing an estimate of the number of illegal

Legal immigrants work in a wide variety of occupations, ranging from grocer, *top left,* to physician, *top right,* to taxi driver, *above.* Illegal aliens also have such diverse jobs.

aliens, conclusions about how they affect the U.S. job market, and findings concerning the social consequences of their illegal position.

The number of illegal aliens residing permanently in the United States had been in dispute. Estimates had ranged as high as 12 million, a figure used by Leonard Chapman, a former commissioner of the Immigration and Naturalization Service. With the help of three officials from the Bureau of the Census, the commission reported that in 1978 the number was "almost certainly below 6 million, and maybe substantially less, possibly only 3.5 [million] to 5 million." In June 1985, a panel commissioned by the National Academy of Sciences said that the number was 2 million to 4 million in 1980, and that there is no indication of rapid growth since then.

The Select Commission concluded that illegal aliens have some negative effect on the U.S. job market. They sometimes displace American workers, especially in factories and service businesses, where most aliens work. The report also indicated that illegal aliens depress wages and working standards in some U.S. localities and in some sections of the economy.

In spite of these findings, the commission concluded that the major reason for curtailing illegal immigration is not economic, but social. The illegality of the aliens' presence breeds further illegality, according to the commission. Some illegal aliens are so afraid of coming to the attention of law enforcement officials that they fail to report serious health problems or crimes committed against them, and they do not send their children to school. Studies show that their fear of detection prevents them from entering mainstream American life as lawfully admitted immigrants and refugees do. Illegal aliens are not as likely to learn English, upgrade their skills or education, or contribute to society except as low-level workers.

To stem the tide of illegal immigration, the commission recom-

A display of national flags, *above,* and a traditional Romanian dance, *above right,* at a folk festival in Chicago express the ethnic diversity of the United States, a nation of immigrants.

mended *sanctions*, or penalties, against employers who hire illegal aliens. Once the sanctions and other law enforcement measures took effect, the government would allow illegal aliens who entered the United States before a specific date to apply for legal status.

The idea of employer sanctions was not new, but the U.S. Senate had never approved of it. Following the commission's recommendation, however, the Senate in 1983 passed immigration-reform legislation that included employer sanctions. In 1984, both houses of Congress passed such legislation—named the Simpson-Mazzoli bill after its chief sponsors, Senator Alan K. Simpson (R., Wyo.) and Representative Romano L. Mazzoli (D., Ky.) The two houses failed to reconcile the differences between their respective versions of the bill, however, so the bill died.

Public opinion surveys consistently show that most American people, including U.S. citizens of Hispanic background, support the use of sanctions to curtail illegal immigration. Many Mexican-American leaders, however, opposed employer sanctions. They claimed that employers would discriminate against people who look and sound foreign, rather than risk penalties for hiring illegal aliens. But advocates of the Simpson-Mazzoli bill said that the measure provided strong protection against discrimination.

Other groups lobbying against sanctions included the Chamber of Commerce of the United States and agricultural organizations representing employers who depend on foreign labor. Some groups argued that many agricultural employers would have to go out of business if sanctions were implemented effectively.

Civil liberties organizations opposed sanctions on the grounds that they might lead to the establishment of a national work-eligibility system. Every individual authorized to work in the United States would be assigned an identification number. Opponents said that the numbers might form the basis of a national databank containing personal information on workers.

The amnesty provision of the Simpson-Mazzoli bill also drew fire. One criticism was that such amnesty would reward aliens who had broken the law. Some people also said that the welfare claims made by newly legalized aliens and their relatives would be too costly for certain states and localities.

In May 1985, Simpson introduced a simpler bill that focused sharply on stepped-up enforcement, including employer sanctions, and a more limited form of amnesty. In September, the Senate passed an amended version of Simpson's bill, including a provision for the seasonal importation of 350,000 foreign workers each year to work for growers of perishable fruits and vegetables.

Meanwhile, the House considered a similar measure sponsored by Representative Peter W. Rodino, Jr. (D., N.J.). This bill was expected to reach the House floor in 1986.

Some critics say that the solution to the problem of illegal immigration lies in neither beefed-up enforcement nor amnesty. They claim that the problem will continue as long as there is a great disparity in economic opportunity between the United States and other countries, such as Mexico. These critics say that economic development of the poorer countries is the only realistic, long-range approach to curbing illegal immigration.

Whether or not the illegal alien problem has reached crisis proportions is a matter of dispute. Representatives of organized labor say it has; employer groups disagree. But experts generally acknowledge that a severe recession in the United States could lead to a roundup of illegal aliens like the one that took place in the 1950's, when more than 1 million Mexicans were deported. Such an event may never occur again. Nonetheless, the growth of a large and easily exploited group of workers living apart from the mainstream American culture is inconsistent with the American way of life. Most Americans seem to agree with President Ronald Reagan that the United States should continue to serve as a land of opportunity for lawfully admitted immigrants and as a haven of liberty for refugees. There also seems to be a growing consensus that, while the front door must stay open, stronger attempts must be made to close the back door. But the question remains: How?

For further reading:

Cafferty, Pastora S., and Chiswick, Barry R. *The Dilemma of American Immigration: Beyond the Golden Door*. Transaction Books, 1983.

Crewdson, John. *The Tarnished Door*. Times Books, 1983.

Fallows, James. "Immigration: How It's Affecting Us." *The Atlantic*, November 1983.

"Immigrants" (special section). *Time*, July 8, 1985.

Kessner, Thomas, and Caroli, Betty B. *Today's Immigrants, Their Stories: A New Look at the Newest Americans*. Oxford University Press, 1982.

By Janet Raloff

Nuclear Power at the Crossroads

A drop in energy demand has weakened the U.S. nuclear power industry. Safety and cost concerns threaten its recovery.

Peering out of his clear plastic face mask, a technician grasps a small metal pipe and begins to cut it with a hacksaw. Normally, he would not find the task difficult, but thick gloves hamper his labor. Like the rest of the special garments that completely cover his body, the gloves protect him from the radiation around him. He is one of dozens of technicians dismantling the historic Shippingport Atomic Power Station in southwestern Pennsylvania, the plant where commercial nuclear power was born in 1957.

The Three Mile Island plant near Harrisburg, Pa., was the scene of a 1979 accident that raised questions about the safety of nuclear power.

Glossary

The author:
Janet Raloff is policy/technology editor of *Science News* magazine.

Shippingport produced electricity for nearly 25 years until its retirement in October 1982. Now, as the first commercial reactor ever dismantled, it serves as a teaching tool. The United States Department of Energy (DOE) is using the project to learn how to safely take apart and bury a reactor, and to determine how long certain reactor parts last.

Even with the highly radioactive materials, such as fuels, already removed, the dismantling project, which began in September 1985, is an enormous task. Before it is completed in about 1990, the plant's steel reactor vessel—a tanklike container 35 feet high, 10½ feet in diameter, and weighing 218 tons—will be encased in concrete and hoisted out of the plant. A barge will carry the reactor vessel down the Ohio and Mississippi rivers, through the Panama Canal, and up the Pacific Coast for burial as low-level radioactive waste at the DOE's Hanford nuclear-storage facility near Richland, Wash. The project will cost more than $98 million.

Meanwhile, just a stone's throw from the dismantling project, other workers are building a new nuclear power plant in Shippingport. This facility, called Beaver Valley 2, is expected to cost $3.9-billion. More than 30 such plants were under construction in the United States in mid-1985.

Since Shippingport began operating in December 1957, more than 90 U.S. reactors have gone into commercial service. By mid-1985, nuclear power plants were generating about 15 per cent of the nation's electricity.

The world nuclear picture

Many other countries use nuclear power extensively. The nations that rely most heavily on it are France, with almost 65 per cent of its electricity coming from nuclear reactors; Belgium, at around 50 per cent; and Finland and Sweden, at more than 40 per cent. Japan gets 23 per cent of its electricity from nuclear plants; Great Britain, 18 per cent; and Canada, 12 per cent. In the mid-1980's, about 340 nuclear plants throughout the world generated about 7 per cent of the global supply of electricity.

The number of reactors continues to grow. Sixty-four reactors were scheduled to go into commercial operation between June 30, 1985, and the beginning of 1988, according to the American Nuclear Society (ANS), an association of scientists and engineers employed in the nuclear industry.

This growth will soon slow substantially, however, especially in the United States, where not one new nuclear plant has been ordered since 1978. By 1985, in fact, 112 plants ordered over the preceding 17 years had been canceled, including some on which construction had already begun. So the dismantling of Shippingport may be more symbolic of the U.S. nuclear industry than the construction of Beaver Valley 2.

A major reason for the slowdown has been a sharp and unex-

The historic Shippingport, Pa., nuclear power plant, the first built solely to generate electricity, produced power from 1957 until its retirement in 1982. Now, technicians are taking it apart and will ship it to a burial site.

pected reduction in the growth of demand for electricity over the past 10 years. And a major cause of this reduction was the oil crisis of the 1970's. In 1973, several oil-producing nations raised the prices of their fuels and cut production. The resulting shortages and higher prices led to widespread conservation of all types of energy.

There is little indication that the growth of demand will return to pre-1973 levels in the near future. But even if the growth of demand is slow, power companies will eventually have to build new plants to meet new demand, and to replace old plants.

The need for new facilities may not lead to a recovery of the nuclear power industry, however. Utility companies may decide to build coal-fired plants because nuclear power has two major drawbacks: unresolved safety issues and skyrocketing costs.

Today, nuclear power in the United States is at a crossroads. If the industry resolves the safety and cost issues in the next few years, it may eventually move into the dominant position in the field of electric power generation. But if these problems remain unresolved, the industry may fade as nuclear plants wear out.

Nuclear plants and safety

What makes a nuclear plant so potentially dangerous is the radioactivity it could release into the environment. A nuclear plant cannot blow up like a bomb. But if highly radioactive gases or contaminated particles of dust and debris escaped from a plant, people could become exposed to dangerous levels of radiation. The source of the radioactivity is the plant's fuel—a solid substance containing certain atoms, typically uranium atoms, that *fission*, or split, to produce heat. The reactor uses this heat to produce steam that runs a turbine connected to an electric generator.

A Smaller Slice of a Smaller Pie

In 1985, the United States consumed only about two-thirds as much electricity as predicted in a 1974 government report. Nuclear power made only half as large a contribution as predicted.

Estimate made in 1974: 3.614 trillion kilowatt-hours

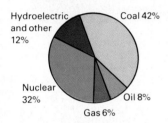

Hydroelectric and other 12%

Coal 42%

Nuclear 32%

Oil 8%

Gas 6%

Estimate made in mid-1985: 2.331 trillion kilowatt-hours

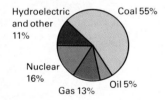

Hydroelectric and other 11%

Coal 55%

Nuclear 16%

Gas 13%

Oil 5%

Source: U.S. Department of Energy.

Fission takes place in the *core*, housed in the reactor vessel. The core contains a pool of water into which extend *fuel rods*—cylinders about 12 feet long. In each rod is a stack of fuel pellets. Individual pellets are about half an inch in diameter and half an inch long.

To begin the fission process, the fuel is bombarded with subatomic particles called *neutrons*. About 3 per cent of the uranium in the core is composed of a type of atom that fissions easily when it absorbs a neutron. This splitting produces two smaller atoms, which typically are radioactive. As it splits, the uranium atom also ejects one or more neutrons.

The neutrons expelled as one atom fissions are absorbed by other atoms in the fuel and the water. More uranium atoms split, each ejecting two or more neutrons, creating a nuclear *chain reaction* that produces a tremendous amount of heat.

Reactor operators regulate core temperature by controlling the rate of fission. They do this with *control rods* made of a material that absorbs neutrons. These rods fit among the fuel rods in the core, and slide into or out of the core to change the fission rate. For instance, if the fission process is too slow, producing too little heat, some of the control rods will be withdrawn from the core, increasing the flow of neutrons and thereby boosting the intensity of the chain reaction.

Two types of reactors

The two main types of nuclear plants in the United States are *boiling water reactors* (*BWR's*) and *pressurized water reactors* (*PWR's*). In a BWR, the core boils water to produce steam for the turbine. In a PWR, the core heats water past its normal boiling point. This water is under high pressure, however, so it does not boil. Instead, it circulates to a device called a steam generator. There, it transfers heat through the walls of its pipes to a supply of low-pressure water circulating inside other pipes. The low-pressure water boils to produce the steam for the turbines.

Water that circulates through the core of a BWR or a PWR becomes radioactive. Many other substances also become radioactive as a reactor operates, but the materials that must be contained are the water, the radioactive atoms created by fission, and the fuel.

Engineers have designed nuclear power plants to prevent these substances from escaping. The reactor vessel's steel walls are at least 6 inches thick. Surrounding the reactor vessel is another steel vessel. And around both is a reinforced-concrete *containment building* with walls at least 3 feet thick.

Instruments within each plant record critical temperatures, pressures, water levels, and other factors affecting safety. These instruments feed information to control systems that can adjust the plant's operations or even shut the plant down if a key factor such as core temperature strays from normal. Lights flash and buzzers sound whenever unusual events occur. These alarm systems alert reactor

The World's Nuclear Energy Plants

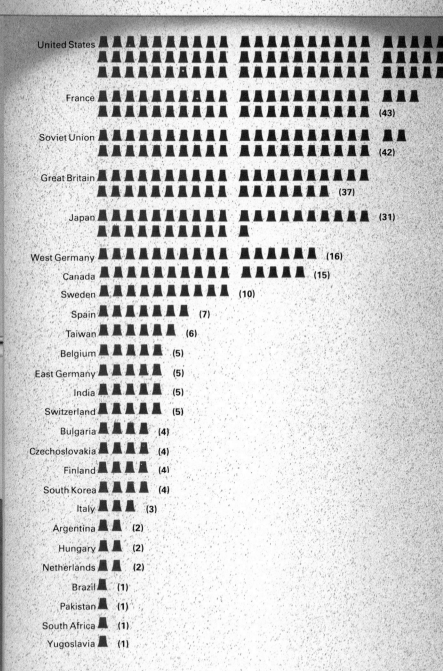

Country	Plants
United States	(86)
France	(43)
Soviet Union	(42)
Great Britain	(37)
Japan	(31)
West Germany	(16)
Canada	(15)
Sweden	(10)
Spain	(7)
Taiwan	(6)
Belgium	(5)
East Germany	(5)
India	(5)
Switzerland	(5)
Bulgaria	(4)
Czechoslovakia	(4)
Finland	(4)
South Korea	(4)
Italy	(3)
Argentina	(2)
Hungary	(2)
Netherlands	(2)
Brazil	(1)
Pakistan	(1)
South Africa	(1)
Yugoslavia	(1)

On June 30, 1985, there were 342 commercial nuclear power plants in operation in 26 countries.

Source: American Nuclear Society.

operators—who oversee the largely automatic plant operations from a radiation-shielded area—to potential problems.

The BWR's and PWR's used throughout the United States have been designed to contend with the most severe types of nuclear accidents imaginable—those involving a loss of coolant. By *coolant*, engineers mean the water that removes heat from the core.

Loss-of-coolant accidents can cause core meltdowns. If, for example, a broken pipe allowed so much leakage that coolant no longer covered the core, the fuel would overheat. If the fuel became hot enough to melt, it would run onto the vessel floor and eventually melt its way through the bottom of the vessel. The fuel could melt through the concrete floor of the containment building and

How a Nuclear Reactor Works

A nuclear reactor converts heat generated by nuclear fission in uranium fuel into electricity. A pressurized water reactor, the most common type in the United States, heats water kept under high pressure by a device called a pressurizer. Pressurized water can be heated beyond its normal boiling point without actually boiling. The extremely hot water is pumped to a steam generator, where its heat boils a supply of low-pressure water, producing steam. The steam drives a turbine connected to an electric generator. Steam leaving the turbine turns back into water, aided by a separate supply of cool water pumped from a cooling tower.

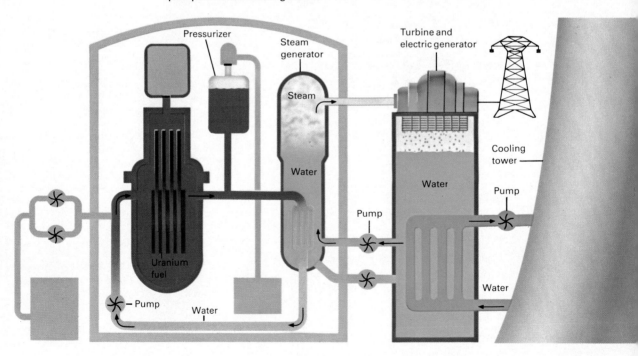

into the earth—the so-called *China syndrome*. In addition, if the containment building were not cooled properly, so much pressure would build up that the building would crack.

To prevent this chain of events, a reactor has *emergency core cooling systems (ECCS's)*, which are designed to flood the core with water whenever the coolant level becomes too low. In a severe accident, another safety system automatically inserts control rods into the core, stopping fission. But even when there is no fission, the core can heat up because of the radioactivity of the fuel, so the core must always be covered.

The ECCS's and other safety equipment have made severe accidents unlikely. They are not impossible, however. The crippled

Preventing the Escape of Radioactivity

A pressurized water reactor has numerous barriers and devices to prevent radioactive substances from escaping into the environment in case of an accident. Most of the devices shown below are designed to go into action if there is a break in the piping that carries water between the uranium fuel and the steam generator. Without safety equipment, this water, which becomes radioactive during normal operation of the reactor, would escape. Fuel then would overheat and eventually melt, releasing other radioactive materials. Other safety devices, including an emergency pump that can feed water to the steam generator, serve as backups to the main equipment.

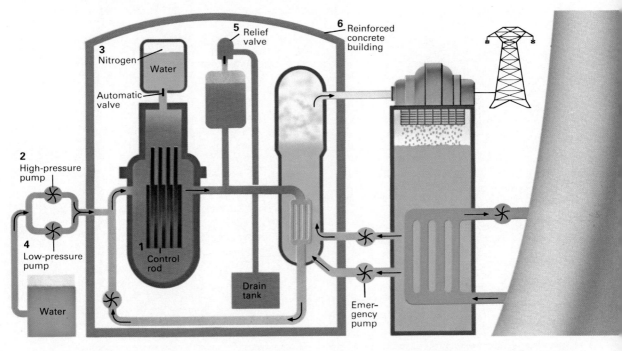

(1) Control rods would plunge into the uranium fuel, halting nuclear fission.

(2) A high-pressure pump would add water if the break were small.

(3) Pressurized nitrogen would force in water if the break were large.

(4) A low-pressure pump would start if even more water were needed.

(5) A relief valve would open if the pressure became too high.

(6) A reinforced concrete building would hold gas and spilled water and fuel.

Three Mile Island (TMI) 2 plant, a PWR near Harrisburg, Pa., stands as proof that severe accidents can happen.

About 4 A.M. on March 28, 1979, a series of unusual events at TMI stopped the circulation of the low-pressure water that turns to steam in the steam generator. The blockage prevented the water from carrying heat away from the steam generator, so the coolant was unable to transfer a normal amount of heat. As a result, the coolant became hotter and hotter. As the coolant's temperature climbed, its pressure increased. A relief valve then opened automatically to relieve some of the pressure—and remained stuck open. The stuck valve permitted much of the coolant to escape from the core, initiating a dreaded loss-of-coolant accident. The reactor's operators did not know that the relief valve was stuck, so the emergency actions they took did not prevent much of the fuel from melting. It took almost a week to bring the accident under control. Experts estimate that it will take until 1988 to clean up the crippled reactor.

TMI 1, the other reactor at the site, was shut down for refueling when the accident occurred. The two reactors were virtual "twins," so the TMI 2 accident cast doubts on the safety of TMI 1. As a result, TMI 1 remained idle for more than six years. After a long legal battle that went all the way to the Supreme Court of the United States, TMI 1 was restarted on Oct. 3, 1985.

The nuclear industry, in arguing that nuclear power is safe, points out that there was no major release of radiation at TMI and

The Radioactivity Around Us
Ordinary objects and activities expose individuals in the United States to much more radioactivity than do commercial nuclear power plants, the facilities that produce their fuel, and used fuel rods that are in storage.

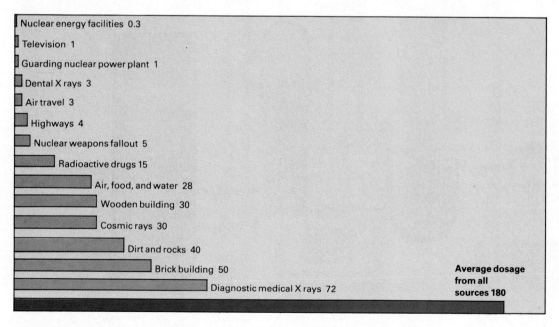

Nuclear energy facilities 0.3
Television 1
Guarding nuclear power plant 1
Dental X rays 3
Air travel 3
Highways 4
Nuclear weapons fallout 5
Radioactive drugs 15
Air, food, and water 28
Wooden building 30
Cosmic rays 30
Dirt and rocks 40
Brick building 50
Diagnostic medical X rays 72
Average dosage from all sources 180

Annual dosage from various sources in millirems (units of radiation absorption)

Source: Atomic Industrial Forum, Incorporated.

no measurable health impact on the environment. Moreover, the nuclear industry and the Nuclear Regulatory Commission (NRC)—the federal agency that regulates the industry—believe that all nuclear plants are safer today than they were in 1979 because of changes made in reactor management and operation as a result of the TMI accident.

Other groups, however, doubt strongly that nuclear plants are safe enough. One such organization is the Union of Concerned Scientists (UCS), a public-interest group based in Cambridge, Mass. In February 1985, the UCS published a report pointing to numerous *generic issues*, problems that affect either all nuclear reactors or large groups of reactors, such as all PWR's.

Typical of these generic issues is *equipment qualification.* A 1971 law requires that the NRC certify all major nuclear safety equipment as qualified to withstand the conditions expected in a severe accident. In 1982, however, the NRC estimated that only 6.6 per cent of such equipment had been certified. And as of November 1985, that agency still had not forced utilities to have previously unqualified equipment certified.

Nonetheless, the NRC reported in June 1985 that "existing plants pose no undue risk to public health and safety . . . because of severe accident risk." One NRC commissioner, James K. Asselstine, dissented from the NRC opinion. He said that, in arriving at the conclusion that no undue risk to public health and safety exists, the NRC had accepted that there was a substantial risk of core-meltdown accidents in existing reactors.

Asselstine was referring to calculations disclosed by the NRC in April 1985. One of these calculations determined the likelihood of a core-melt accident much more severe than the TMI accident, but causing no immediate deaths. The NRC found that the chance of such an accident occurring in the United States over a 20-year period might be 45 in 100—in other words, there might be close to a 50 per cent risk of such an accident. In fact, Asselstine said, because of uncertainties about some of the assumptions used in those calculations, the risk could be anywhere from 6 to 99 per cent.

Used fuel rods also a safety issue

Not all of nuclear power's radioactive hazards are associated with the plants themselves. The fission process in an operating plant consumes uranium fuel at a rate requiring the replacement of one-fourth to one-third of the fuel rods every 12 to 18 months. The rods that are removed add to a growing store of nuclear wastes that will remain radioactive for hundreds of thousands of years.

A 1,000-megawatt plant—a size typical of new U.S. facilities—discards about 34 tons of rods each year. According to the DOE, U.S. utilities had accumulated more than 13,000 tons of these wastes by the end of 1985. And because the DOE has not determined how or where it will permanently dispose of these hazardous wastes, used

Nuclear Waste Disposal

The pictures below show how the United States may eventually dispose of used fuel rods, which are highly radioactive. At the end of 1985, the government had not yet implemented a disposal plan, so rods were stored temporarily in water, usually near the reactors where they

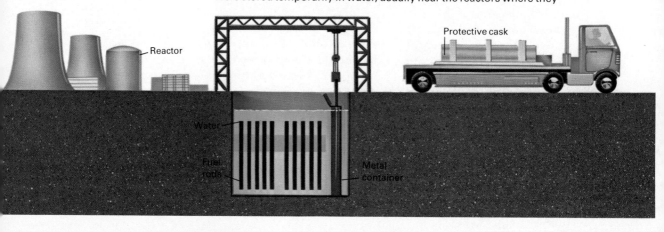

Reactor

Protective cask

Water

Fuel rods

Metal container

Temporary Storage in Water

Loading a Shipping Cask

had been used. One plan being tested calls for transferring rods to a metal container and transporting the container in a protective cask to a deep tunnel. There, the container would be lowered into a hole in the tunnel floor, sealed, and covered.

Circular Seals Covering Buried Containers

Dirt and rocks

Seal   Hole

The Accumulation of Used Fuel Rods
While the United States government debates various plans for the disposal of used fuel rods, this highly radio-active material is accumulating at temporary storage sites and will continue to do so.

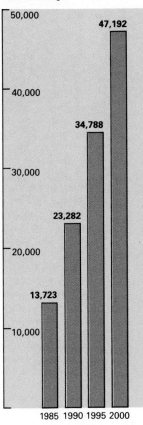

Tons in storage

50,000	
	47,192
40,000	
	34,788
30,000	
	23,282
20,000	
13,723	
10,000	

1985 1990 1995 2000

Walkaway Reactors: A Second Chance for Nuclear Power?

Pressurized water reactors (PWR's) and boiling water reactors (BWR's) have been standard for commercial nuclear reactors—but not because reactor engineers thought they represented the safest possible design. According to Alvin M. Weinberg, director of the Institute of Energy Analysis in Oak Ridge, Tenn., designers have known all along that PWR's and BWR's were susceptible to core-meltdown accidents. Weinberg says these reactors were chosen for their low cost and compactness, even though that compactness worked against their safety.

Today, increasing concern over the likelihood of a core-melt accident threatens the future of the nuclear power industry, so interest in building inherently safe reactors is growing. Sometimes called *walkaway reactors*, these plants are designed to be so safe that plant operators could ignore them—virtually walk away from them if an accident occurred—without risking a core-melt accident or a major release of radioactivity into the environment.

At least three strong contenders are under development in this walkaway class. The best known is the Process Inherent Ultimately Safe (PIUS) reactor being developed by the Swedish firm ASEA-ATOM.

PIUS resembles a conventional PWR. Pressurized water—called *coolant*—picks up heat generated by fission in the core and carries it to a steam generator. There, another supply of water absorbs heat and turns into steam. The core, the steam generator, the piping between them, and the pump that circulates water through this piping are located inside a huge vessel that is filled with cold water. Pipes penetrate this vessel only at the top. As a result, there is almost no chance any core water will leak out, uncovering the fuel.

In addition, through a clever bit of engineering, the hot water circulating between PIUS' core and steam generator is kept from mixing with the surrounding pool of cold water, except in an accident. If an accident interrupted the normal flow of hot water, cold water would enter the hot water circuit. The cold water contains a quantity of boron, a substance that readily absorbs neutrons. The fission process that produces most of a reactor's heat depends upon the flow of neutrons in the core. When the pool water reached the core, the boron would absorb flowing neutrons, quickly stopping fission.

The second walkaway reactor, known as the Pebble-Bed Reactor, uses hot helium gas rather than water as its coolant. Also known as a high-temperature gas reactor (HTGR), it has two major safety features. First, unlike the coolant in a PWR, the HTGR's helium coolant cannot become radioactive. Second, the fuel is embedded in graphite, which would absorb more heat during a severe accident than would the core water of a PWR. The HTGR's temperature would rise slowly even if helium flow through the core were interrupted. When the temperature reached a certain level, fission would stop automatically. The graphite would continue to absorb heat generated by radioactivity in the core and would safely conduct heat to the environment, according to the HTGR's developer, Hochtemperatur-Reaktorbau of Mannheim, West Germany.

The third walkaway device, the integral fast reactor (IFR), would use liquid sodium as the coolant. The core, the coolant circuit, and other major equipment would be submerged in a pool of coolant.

If the flow in the coolant circuit were interrupted, the pool would absorb large amounts of heat from the core without much of a rise in temperature. Even after the reactor shut down, convection in the pool would keep sodium circulating through the core, removing heat.

A second safety feature is a fortunate by-product of design, according to Charles E. Till, head of reactor research at Argonne National Laboratory outside Chicago. If core temperature rose so much that there was a risk of a fuel meltdown, it would be desirable to terminate fission by removing the fuel from the core automatically. It just happens, Till says, that at a temperature near the fuel's melting point, the fuel would pop up and out of the core.

Each cylindrical fuel element fits loosely within a slightly longer cylindrical rod. Inside the rod, a little extra sodium surrounds the fuel element. Sodium boils at a much lower temperature than the melting point of the fuel. So when the sodium inside the rod boiled, sodium vapor would launch the fuel element up the rod and out of the core.

The IFR belongs to a class of experimental reactors called *breeders*, which transform nonfissionable uranium into fissionable plutonium as they operate. By doing so, they actually produce more fuel than they consume. [J. R.]

Checking Heat Build-Up

Simple devices and design features would prevent the core from overheating rapidly if an accident interrupted the normal flow of coolant in a walk-away reactor.

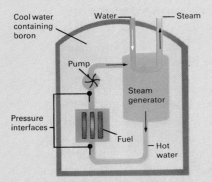

The Process Inherent Ultimately Safe Reactor has devices called pressure interfaces that would allow cool water to flood the core.

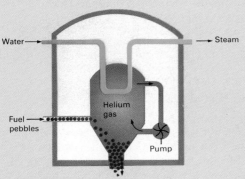

The Pebble-Bed Reactor uses fuel embedded in graphite spheres that would absorb tremendous amounts of heat.

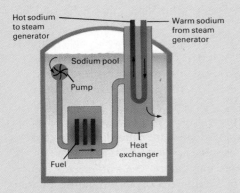

The Integral Fast Reactor would contain a large pool of sodium that would absorb much heat from the core.

rods are now stored temporarily in large pools of water, usually near the reactors from which they were removed. The water keeps them cool.

Some critics say that the NRC should not approve any additional nuclear plants until the DOE finds an acceptable method of disposing of these wastes permanently. The DOE believes that science can develop technologies and find safe disposal sites to protect the environment from contamination by these wastes for at least 50,000 years. One proposal suggests that used rods be placed inside steel cylinders and buried in solid rock far under the surface of the earth.

A harder problem than determining how to bury such wastes will be finding a community that will accept them. Every time the DOE mentions a place under consideration as a burial site, state and local governments take legal action to block storage of the wastes in their area.

Cost may decide nuclear's future

Although the issues of waste disposal and plant operating safety are extremely important, most energy analysts believe that the cost issue may decide nuclear energy's future.

Utilities divide their electric power plants into three categories: *base-load*, *intermediate-load*, and *peaking*. Utilities run base-load plants continuously to meet their customers' basic year-round needs. Power companies bring on or shut down intermediate-load plants to accommodate seasonal variations in demand. In the summer months, for example, utilities bring on intermediate-load plants to meet the extra demand for electricity to run air conditioners. Peaking plants are used to meet demand surges for periods lasting from about one hour to one day, such as the hottest days of summer when most customers want to use high-wattage appliances.

Most base-load plants are coal-fired or nuclear because coal and uranium are cheaper than the other two major fuels—oil and natural gas. Coal-fired and nuclear plants take a long time to reach their full power, however, so they are not built for peaking loads. Coal-fired plants—but not nuclear plants—are economical for intermediate loads.

Today, most utilities still see coal-fired and nuclear plants as their only affordable options for future base-load power needs. Coal-fired plants may turn out to be more affordable than nuclear plants, however, even though uranium is cheaper than coal.

Nuclear power once was cheaper than electricity produced by coal-fired plants. According to economist Charles Komanoff, an independent consultant who specializes in analysis of energy costs, nuclear plants that were finished in the late 1960's and early 1970's generate electricity for 1.5 cents per kilowatt-hour (kwh) today. Coal-fired plants of the same period produce electricity for about 2 cents per kwh.

By the mid-1970's, construction costs and interest rates paid on money borrowed to build power plants had increased so much that nuclear power lost its advantage. Coal-fired and nuclear plants built during the mid-1970's produce comparably priced electricity today. A recent survey conducted by the Atomic Industrial Forum, the nuclear-industry trade association, showed that coal and nuclear plants in service among its member utilities during 1983 provided electricity at the same average cost, 3.5 cents per kwh.

Power produced by the extremely expensive nuclear plants that went into operation after 1983, however, costs much more. Komanoff says that electricity from new nuclear plants will average 15 cents per kwh, compared with 5 to 7 cents per kwh for power from new coal-fired plants.

Coal a greater safety risk?

Some experts argue that the United States should not let costs alone dictate a decision to reject the nuclear option. Physicist Alvin M. Weinberg, director of the Institute of Energy Analysis in Oak Ridge, Tenn., cites a safety issue in arguing against the selection of coal-fired plants on the basis of costs. He points out that several scientists who analyzed the health risks posed by various energy sources concluded that "nuclear power poses a lesser risk to human health than does coal, its main competitor." As of mid-1985, not one member of the general public had been killed by the generation of nuclear power in the United States. The same cannot be said of power produced by coal.

Among researchers who have attempted to assess coal's impact are Daniel Deudney and Christopher Flavin of Worldwatch Institute in Washington, D.C. (Worldwatch is a nonprofit organization that studies uses of Earth's resources.) In a 1983 study on energy resources, Deudney and Flavin reported that in the United States each year, 50,000 people die prematurely from air pollution due to the burning of coal. Most of these deaths are caused by lung cancer and respiratory diseases such as pneumonia and emphysema.

The ultimate justification for maintaining nuclear energy, however, is the danger of carbon dioxide (CO_2) accumulating in the atmosphere from burning coal and other fossil fuels, says Weinberg. This gas absorbs energy that radiates upward from Earth and then reradiates part of this energy back to the surface. In this way, some of Earth's radiation is trapped, warming the surface. This warming action is similar to the heating process in a greenhouse, so the action is known as the *greenhouse effect*. Many scientists fear that increasing the amount of CO_2 in the atmosphere could cause a global warming on Earth. This warming could alter the climate, wipe out some agriculture, and partially melt the polar icecaps so that the oceans would cover large parts of many coastal areas.

Some people believe the industrialized world may be able to reduce its reliance on coal while it simultaneously weans itself off nuclear power. The Worldwatch Institute researchers would prefer, from an environmental standpoint, to see greater use made of renewable energy sources such as sunlight, wind, flowing water, and hot subsurface rocks. Today, these sources can produce electricity economically in small plants, particularly in rural, developing countries. According to an August 1985 report issued by the U.S. Office of Technology Assessment, however, they are not likely to challenge coal or uranium soon as energy sources for large plants in industrialized nations.

Physicist James M. Mackenzie of the UCS in Cambridge believes, however, that many utilities may be able to put off building large plants until one of the alternative sources can mount a strong challenge. Through conservation, he claims, the need for new, large plants can be delayed for years. When the need finally does arise, the choices may no longer be limited to coal and uranium. Mackenzie looks for strong competition from *photovoltaic cells*, crystals that convert sunlight directly to electric current.

The utilities may not have to wait for long, according to physicist Paul D. Maycock, former head of the DOE's photovoltaic research office and now a photovoltaic-energy analyst. Photovoltaic cells soon will be cost-competitive in California, he forecasts, if that state continues to grant tax credits for solar-power facilities.

What if U.S. utilities do turn away from nuclear power? According to Weinberg, the nuclear industry may not get new orders for major plants for another 10 to 20 years, but that long dry spell need not kill the industry. Weinberg sees it as only a period of hibernation and believes that the nuclear industry could come back stronger than ever if it uses the time to create a new breed of reactor—one that is invulnerable to large-scale core damage.

Studies at Weinberg's Institute of Energy Analysis in Tennessee suggest that such reactors are possible. Now, he says, it is up to somebody to build one—and perhaps eventually to lead nuclear power to a triumphant turn at the crossroads.

For further reading:

Hawkes, Nigel. *Nuclear Power*. Watts, 1984.
Kiefer, Irene. *Nuclear Energy at the Crossroads*. Atheneum, 1982.
Pringle, Laurence. *Nuclear Power: From Physics to Politics*. Macmillan, 1979.

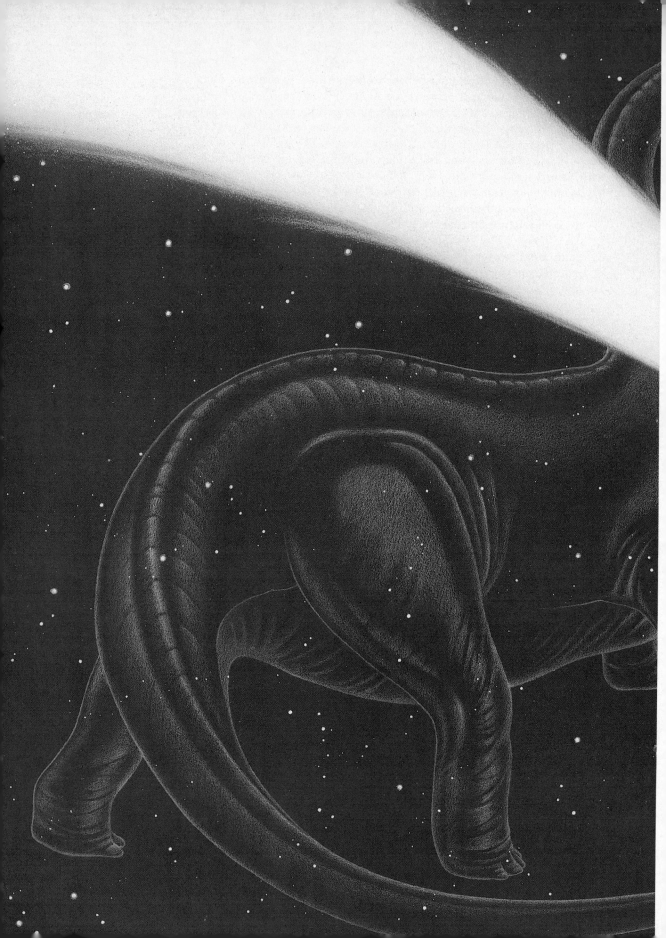

By Judith Shally Goldhaber

Doomsday for the Dinosaurs

Tantalizing evidence suggests that the collision of a comet or asteroid with Earth sealed the dinosaurs' fate.

On the day the ball of fire fell from the sky, the dinosaurs were lords of Earth and had been for nearly 140 million years. The planet they ruled was a paradise, with a gentle climate, an abundance of living creatures, and a lush vegetation of trees and flowering plants.

The time was 65 million years ago. The ball of fire was a comet or asteroid perhaps 6 miles in diameter. It tore a hole in the atmosphere as it hurtled earthward. Slamming into the ground or the sea at a speed of up to 30,000 miles per hour, it turned solid rock to liquid and gas, digging a crater 15 to 20 miles deep and about 100 miles wide. A gigantic cloud of dust and molten rock was thrown up into the atmosphere. As the cloud spread around Earth, it blocked out much of the sun's heat and light for several months. In the cold and darkness, many plants and the animals that depended on them for food died out. Deprived of their prey, many meat-eaters soon followed.

According to one bold theory, that scenario explains one of the most fascinating scientific mysteries of all time: What killed the dinosaurs? Of course, when the dinosaurs died out, they did not go alone. In the mass extinction that occurred 65 million years ago, nearly 70 per cent of all species of plants and animals on Earth vanished. But for many people, the death of the dinosaurs has remained the most intriguing part of that disaster.

The theory that the impact of a comet or asteroid was the dinosaurs' agent of doom was proposed in 1979 by a team of scientists headed by Nobel Prize-winning physicist Luis W. Alvarez of the Lawrence Berkeley Laboratory at the University of California, Berkeley, and his son Walter Alvarez, a professor of geology and geophysics at Berkeley. The theory has stirred up a great deal of scientific debate, in part because it challenges current thinking about the nature of evolution and extinction. The theory has also stimulated considerable research attempting to confirm or refute it. Perhaps its most controversial offshoot is the idea that mass extinctions may occur in a regular cycle and that the cause of this cycle may be found beyond Earth—perhaps beyond the solar system.

A puzzling end

The author:
Judith Shally Goldhaber is an editor and writer at the Lawrence Berkeley Laboratory at the University of California, Berkeley.

People have been puzzling over the disappearance of the dinosaurs since the first dinosaur fossils were identified in the 1840's. Because no one knows for sure whether dinosaurs were warm-blooded or cold-blooded, there has been plenty of speculation. Some scientists and popular writers blamed the dinosaurs' extinction on their size, arguing that it hampered their movements. Others claimed the animals' brains were too small, making them slow to adapt to environmental changes. Still others maintained that plant-eating dinosaurs starved because they could not eat the flowering plants that appeared toward the end of their reign. Some scientists even theorized that mammals ate the dinosaurs' eggs.

By the mid-1970's, the most widely accepted explanation was that a worldwide drop in temperatures at the end of the Cretaceous Period—the geologic period that lasted from 225 million to 65 million years ago—sealed the dinosaurs' fate. Unprotected by feathers or fur and too big to hide in caves, the large reptiles could not withstand the cold. Scientists were unsure, however, what caused this drop in temperatures.

These theories fit nicely with the prevailing scientific belief that *natural selection* and *gradualism* could account for all the biological changes that occurred as life evolved on Earth. Natural selection is the process by which organisms best suited to their environment become the ones most likely to survive and leave descendants. Gradualism is the idea that major evolutionary changes, such as the appearance of new species, are the result of many small changes accumulating over time. These theories, proposed in the 1800's, replaced earlier beliefs that biological changes occurred as the result of sudden cataclysms, such as floods and volcanic eruptions.

Alvarez and his colleagues were not the first modern scientists to link a mass extinction with a catastrophic event. But they were the first to offer solid evidence to back their claim. Interestingly, this evidence was a surprise discovery.

The evidence in the clay

The first clue was in rock samples brought back to California in 1977 by Walter Alvarez, who had spent the summer near Gubbio, Italy, studying beds of limestone to learn more about how mountains are formed. The limestone beds near Gubbio are particularly interesting because in the rock layers there, scientists can clearly see the boundary that marks the end of the Cretaceous Period, when the dinosaurs became extinct, and the beginning of the Tertiary Period that followed. In many areas of the world, the boundary between geologic periods is blurred or missing because of erosion or other geologic processes. Near Gubbio, however, a thin layer of dark clay, about half an inch wide, separates the limestone laid down during the two periods. This clay layer also contains evidence of a mass extinction. Below the layer are many fossils of tiny shelled sea creatures called *foraminifera*. Above the layer, there are none.

Luis Alvarez suggested that by studying the amount of certain elements in the limestone and clay, he and Walter could determine how long it took these layers to form. He based his suggestion on the knowledge that a rain of material from space—a kind of cosmic dust—falls to Earth at the rate of about 100,000 tons per year. This extraterrestrial dust can be detected by the amount of certain metallic elements, such as iridium, in it. These elements are rare in Earth's crust because they alloy with iron and sank deep into the planet while it was still molten, about 4½ billion years ago. They are more plentiful in extraterrestrial bodies, such as asteroids and comets, that have not formed iron cores.

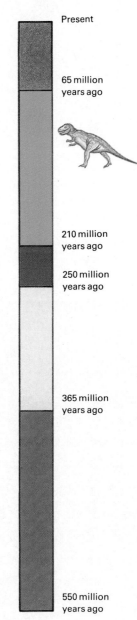

The Great Dyings
At least five times in Earth's history, at the dates shown below, large numbers of species died out suddenly. During the Cretaceous extinction 65 million years ago, nearly 70 per cent of all species, including the dinosaurs, vanished.

Present

65 million years ago

210 million years ago

250 million years ago

365 million years ago

550 million years ago

101

Death by Meteor

According to one theory, dinosaurs died out when a huge meteor collided with Earth 65 million years ago, *above left.* The impact raised a giant cloud of dust and molten rock, *above center,* that blanketed Earth, plunging the world into a period of darkness and cold that killed many plant and animal species, including the dinosaurs, *above right.* Luis Alvarez, at left *below,* and his son Walter, at right, proposed the theory after finding high levels of iridium, an element rare on Earth but plentiful in meteors, in 65-million-year-old rock.

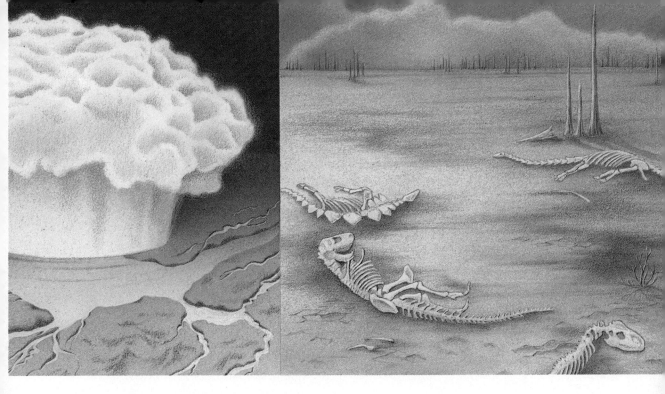

The Alvarezes recruited nuclear chemists Frank Asaro and Helen Michel, also of the Lawrence Berkeley Laboratory, to subject the Gubbio rock samples to neutron activation analysis. Scientists using this technique can detect concentrations of rare elements as small as one part per hundred billion. When Asaro and Michel analyzed the concentrations of 28 elements in the samples, they found something remarkable. The clay layer contained high amounts of iridium—about 600 times more than the limestone layers immediately above and below. Further analysis of the Gubbio clay showed that the level of iridium matched that found in meteorites. These findings suggested that the iridium had entered the clay as the result of a meteorite impact, not as the result of any process occurring on Earth.

The scientists then examined two other sites where there is a clear sequence of rocks marking the Cretaceous-Tertiary boundary. At both sites, one in Denmark and one in New Zealand, they found a similar clay layer with a high concentration of iridium, indicating that the iridium at Gubbio was not a local phenomenon.

To Luis Alvarez, the conclusion—though startling—was clear. A formidable intruder—a giant asteroid or comet—had struck Earth at the end of the Cretaceous Period and left its iridium footprints in clay around the world. Originally, the Alvarez team suggested that the darkness caused by the airborne dust and ash following the impact may have lasted several years. Later, after studying how volcanic ash and dust circulate in the atmosphere, they revised their estimate downward to several months of darkness.

When Alvarez and his colleagues published their theory in 1980, other scientists initially reacted with skepticism. Some scientists suggested that the iridium had an earthly origin. For example, geolo-

Clues in the Clay

A thin layer of clay, *right,* indicated by arrow, laid down 65 million years ago, holds evidence of a meteor impact with Earth. The evidence includes high levels of iridium; shocked quartz grains, *below,* with a pattern of grooves found at sites of meteor impacts; and particles of soot, *below right,* which may have resulted from fire storms ignited by the impact.

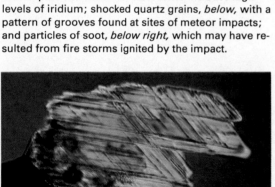

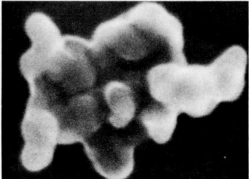

gists Charles B. Officer and Charles L. Drake of Dartmouth College in Hanover, N.H., argued that the iridium in the clay layer may have come from a series of intense volcanic eruptions that blasted iridium-rich material from deep within Earth into the atmosphere. They based their argument on the discovery of high levels of iridium in particles emitted by the Kilauea volcano in Hawaii. Officer and Drake also contended that the iridium was not deposited over a short time but over a period lasting from 10,000 to 100,000 years. Other scientists suggested that the iridium built up gradually as sediments accumulated to form the clay layer.

Some scientists pointed out that although Earth's surface is pockmarked with meteor craters, earth scientists have not found one that is 65 million years old. The Berkeley team countered that the crater in question is probably on the ocean floor, which covers more than 70 per cent of Earth's surface. Moreover, they pointed out, 20 per cent of the ocean floor that existed 65 million years ago has been destroyed by movements of the huge plates making up Earth's outer crust. Therefore, even if such a crater once existed, there is a chance it could never be found.

Other scientists argued that even if there was an impact, it had little or nothing to do with the extinction of the dinosaurs. For example, paleobiologist William A. Clemens, a colleague of the Alvarezes at Berkeley and a well-known authority on dinosaurs, believes that the giant reptiles became extinct *before* the end of the Cretaceous Period. He points out that the last dinosaur bone at the Hell Creek Formation—several hundred feet of sediment deposited by ancient streams in eastern Montana—was found 6 feet below the iridium layer. According to Clemens, the gap indicates that the dinosaurs had died out at least 25,000 years before the iridium was deposited. The Alvarez team, however, argues that the gap reflects only the scarcity of dinosaur bones.

An even stronger objection made by Clemens and other scientists is that many animal species, including nearly all other reptiles, survived the Cretaceous extinction. "If you're hypothesizing a worldwide catastrophe of such vast dimensions," Clemens says, "the lights going out all over the world, how do you explain the fact that the mammals—as well as crocodiles, turtles, virtually all of the reptiles except the dinosaurs—survived it? In fact, they came through the Cretaceous-Tertiary boundary almost unchanged." Clemens feels that advocates of the impact theory place too much importance on mathematical data—for example, the number of fossil species found in a particular rock layer—and too little on ecological and biological questions.

Still other opponents of the impact theory continue to support the idea that the Cretaceous extinction resulted from a worldwide lowering of temperatures. For example, paleontologist Steven M. Stanley of Johns Hopkins University in Baltimore examined the record of marine fossils for the Cretaceous extinction and reported that many species disappeared from the oceans gradually, not suddenly. In addition, he found that many more tropical species died out than did cold-water species. Stanley argues that if worldwide temperatures had fallen, cold-water species would have been able to migrate

The meteor that many scientists believe collided with Earth 65 million years ago would have dug a crater many times larger than Great Meteor Crater in Arizona, *below,* which measures about 4,150 feet across and 570 feet deep. Some studies of the ages of meteor craters suggest a cycle of formation that parallels the 26-million-year extinction cycle reported for the fossil record. But other studies contradict these findings.

Some organisms that became extinct 65 million years ago, such as *Micula decussata, top,* a type of minute algae, disappeared suddenly. Others, such as the rudists, *above,* reef-building mollusks that grew up to 3 feet tall, had begun to die out earlier. This suggests that factors other than a meteor impact, such as climate changes, may have been responsible for some extinctions at that time.

toward the equator, where temperatures would have been warm enough for these species to survive. Tropical species would have had no refuge.

Supporting evidence

Despite such criticism, the impact theory has become increasingly accepted, chiefly because evidence continues to grow. By 1985, researchers had found high concentrations of iridium in 74 of the 75 places around the world, including several on the ocean floor, where the Cretaceous-Tertiary boundary is complete. Additional evidence came in 1983 from geochemist Karl K. Turekian and geologist Jean-Marc Luck of Yale University in New Haven, Conn. They reported that the ratio of isotopes of the heavy metal osmium in the clay layer from the Cretaceous-Tertiary boundary matched that found in meteorites, not that found in most Earth rocks.

Scientists studying the clay layer have also found other supporting evidence in the form of *microtektites*. These are tiny, glassy spheres believed to form from rock melted by the heat of a meteorite impact. During the impact, the microtektites are carried aloft into the atmosphere, then deposited around the world.

The discovery in 1984 of "shocked" quartz crystals in the clay layer from the Cretaceous-Tertiary boundary by scientists of the United States Geological Survey in Denver further bolstered the case for the impact theory. These crystals, which had been found only around meteor craters or the sites of underground nuclear explosions, show a pattern of grooves that appear only if the quartz is subjected to great pressure, such as during a meteorite impact.

In October 1985, a team of chemists from the University of Chicago, headed by Edward Anders, reported finding soot in the clay layer at sites in Denmark, New Zealand, and Spain. The chemists theorized that the soot resulted from worldwide fire storms ignited by a meteorite. The fire storms created a global cloud of soot that blocked sunlight even more effectively than the dust cloud could have done. Other scientists, however, argued that the fires could have been caused by lightning.

The Alvarez team's iridium findings at the Cretaceous-Tertiary boundary triggered a search for iridium at the extinction boundaries of other geologic periods. Scientists soon reported finding high levels of the rare element at a number of other boundaries, both earlier and later than the Cretaceous-Tertiary boundary. Some of these reports have not been confirmed, and others are being challenged. Nevertheless, it began to seem possible that—as the Alvarezes had suggested in their original paper—impacts might be responsible for more than one mass extinction. They assumed, however, that even if such catastrophes had occurred more than once in Earth's history, they were irregular events.

Then, in 1984, paleontologists David M. Raup and J. John Sepkoski, Jr., of the University of Chicago reported discovering what appeared to be a pattern of extinctions in the fossil record. Raup and Sepkoski analyzed the fossil record of 567 of the 3,500 families of marine animals that lived during the past 250 million years. They found that extinctions seemed not to occur at a random rate but instead seemed to occur more often at certain times. Furthermore, they reported that these periods of extinction happened about every 26 million years.

Raup and Sepkoski's findings triggered a new flurry of activity. Because no known earthly biological or geologic process could account for such a cycle, scientists sought an explanation in the skies. Two teams of researchers—astronomers Michael R. Rampino and Richard B. Stothers of the Goddard Institute for Space Studies in New York City, and Walter Alvarez and physicist Richard A. Muller of Berkeley—independently suggested that the reported extinction cycle might be reflected in the ages of meteor craters on Earth. And,

Extinctions Cycle
An analysis of the fossil record of marine organisms that became extinct during the past 250 million years by paleontologists David M. Raup, at left in photo, and J. John Sepkoski, Jr., at right, of the University of Chicago revealed an apparent pattern of mass extinctions. The scientists reported finding eight definite and four possible periods of mass extinction roughly 26 million years apart, *below.*

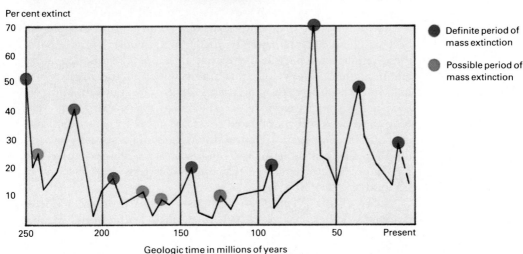

Per cent extinct

● Definite period of mass extinction

● Possible period of mass extinction

Geologic time in millions of years

indeed, both teams reported evidence of an apparent cycle of crater formation that paralleled the extinction cycle.

But what could trigger these periodic impacts? Three theories—Nemesis, Planet X, and a molecular cloud theory—were proposed. Two teams of scientists—physicist Daniel P. Whitmire of the University of Southwestern Louisiana in Lafayette and Albert A. Jackson IV of Computer Sciences Corporation in Houston; and Muller, astrophysicist Marc Davis of Berkeley, and astronomer Piet Hut of the Institute for Advanced Study in Princeton, N.J.—speculated that the sun might have a small, dim companion star. They suggested that this star, which became known as Nemesis, follows an elongated orbit around the sun that takes it through the Oort cloud every 26 million to 30 million years. The Oort cloud is a mass of comets thought to surround the solar system at a distance of up to 10 trillion miles from the sun. According to this theory, the gravitational pull of Nemesis disturbs the orbits of the comets, sending some of them hurtling toward Earth.

Whitmire and physicist John J. Matese, also of Southwestern Louisiana, suggested that the comet storms were caused by Planet X, an as-yet-undiscovered 10th planet with an unusual orbit. They contended that every 28 million years, Planet X's orbit takes it through a belt of comets orbiting the sun at the edge of the solar system. Whitmire and Matese speculated that the gravitational pull of the planet would knock comets off their normal path and send some of them crashing toward Earth.

Rampino and Stothers suggested that comet showers might be triggered by the bobbing motion of the solar system as it passes through molecular clouds in the *central plane of the Galaxy*, an imaginary two-dimensional layer that divides the Galaxy horizontally.

Theories under attack

By early 1985, however, these theories, including Raup and Sepkoski's original ideas, were coming under increasing attack. Several scientists, including Antoni Hoffman of the Lamont-Doherty Geological Observatory in Palisades, N.Y., criticized Raup and Sepkoski for excluding from their study any family of organisms that did not become completely extinct. The dissenting scientists argued that if these families are included, the cycle of extinctions disappears. In addition, they pointed out that uncertainties in the fossil record make it difficult to determine precise dates for extinctions and geologic periods and, therefore, to establish a precise extinction cycle. Raup and Sepkoski reevaluated the fossil record for all 3,500 marine families and again reported finding a 26-million-year cycle.

Other scientists attacked the reports of a parallel cycle of crater formation. They contended that too few craters were included in the studies.

As far as the Nemesis theory was concerned, some scientists doubted whether a star with such an elongated orbit would retain a stable orbit for so many million years. They argued that Nemesis would soon be pulled off course by other stars and planets.

Critics also cast doubt on the Planet X theory. Astrophysicist Scott D. Tremaine of the Massachusetts Institute of Technology in Cambridge calculated that even if Planet X existed, it would not be massive enough to jostle many comets from their orbits.

The Rampino-Stothers dust-cloud theory also came in for criticism, with scientists arguing that the Galaxy's molecular clouds are not dense enough near the central plane to disturb the comets in the Oort cloud. In addition, researchers pointed out that the solar system is now close to the central plane and Earth is not being bombarded with comets.

Acceptance and doubt

As a result of all this controversy, most scientists remain skeptical about the theory that extinctions occur in regular cycles. They believe that the case—though enticing—is unproven. The Alvarezes' idea that an asteroid or comet crashed into Earth 65 million years ago has more widespread support. While acknowledging the strong evidence for an impact, however, some scientists still question the link between such a catastrophe and the death of the dinosaurs. Perhaps the impact 65 million years ago really did wipe out these huge creatures. Perhaps it was only the last straw for animals already in decline, doomed by changes in climate. Perhaps the collision triggered environmental changes that actually caused the dinosaurs' death. Or perhaps the impact had little or nothing at all to do with their demise.

The scientific community seems to agree on only one point. If meteor impacts are responsible for some mass extinctions, scientists may have to reexamine some of their ideas about evolution. As evolutionary biologist Stephen Jay Gould of Harvard University in Cambridge has noted, mammals coexisted with dinosaurs for millions of years without getting much of a foothold. "Mammals didn't outcompete dinosaurs," he says. "In fact, they evolved at the same time as dinosaurs, and they lived for 100 million years as small creatures in the nooks and crannies of an ecological sphere dominated by dinosaurs. Had some external force not intervened 65 million years ago to wipe out dinosaurs and clear away enough space so that mammals could take over, the world would still be dominated by dinosaurs . . . and we wouldn't be here."

For further reading:

Angier, Natalie. "Did Comets Kill the Dinosaurs? A Bold New Theory About Mass Extinctions." *Time,* May 6, 1985.
"The Great Dyings," *Discover,* May 1984.
Pringle, Laurence. *Dinosaurs and People: Fossils, Facts, and Fantasies.* Harcourt, 1978.

By Kenneth G. Lieberthal

China After Mao: Charting a New Course

Nearly 10 years after Mao's death, China has departed radically from the policies of the "Great Helmsman," and the result is a startlingly different nation.

In February 1985, a government reception in Beijing (Peking), China's capital, honored that nation's 10 "outstanding young entrepreneurs"—that is, people who started successful businesses. Top Communist Party leaders turned out to sing the praises of these business leaders, who were also spotlighted in the national press and on television. Yet, just 10 years ago, the financial activities of these young men would have landed most of them in jail. The Beijing reception reflected the sharp changes that China has experienced since the death in 1976 of China's leader Mao Zedong (Mao Tsetung in the traditional Wade-Giles spelling).

Mao, one of history's greatest revolutionaries, led the Chinese Communist Party during nearly 30 years of military struggle until the Communists came to power in 1949. Known as the "Great Helmsman," he virtually dominated Chinese politics for another 27 years until his death. But, despite his forceful personality and sharp political skills, Mao had trouble putting his revolutionary ideals into practice once he became the head of the political system that ruled the world's most populous country.

Mao sought to control Chinese society, often ruthlessly. During the land reform that followed the 1949 revolution, rich landlords were killed by the thousands. But for those who accepted Communist rule, Mao sought to create a largely egalitarian society—one in which people were nearly equal in income and privilege despite differences in their work and education. He was no believer in Western-style democracy, but he wanted government officials to remain close to the common people. He sought to avoid an elitist society in which government officials and other members of a privileged upper class drove around in limousines, for example, while most Chinese could not afford bicycles for transportation.

In 1966, Mao launched a movement called the Cultural Revolution in pursuit of his egalitarian vision. Communist Party leaders who opposed Mao and the Cultural Revolution were designated "enemies" and became targets of propaganda campaigns that aroused people to white-hot anger. Some of Mao's opponents were treated harshly and were forced to spend months in poor villages, hauling water and feeding pigs. The Cultural Revolution continued in fits and starts until Mao's death 10 years later—a period that the Chinese government now officially calls "the 10 years of disaster."

Mao turned to China's students to lead the political battles of the Cultural Revolution. In June 1966, Mao called off all elementary, secondary, and university classes and encouraged students with the slogan, "To Rebel Is Justified!" Even after the schools and universities gradually reopened, Cultural Revolution reforms lowered entrance and examination requirements and challenged the teachers' traditional authority. In the early 1970's, for example, a university student named Zhang Tiemin became a national hero when he turned in a blank examination paper to challenge examinations as fostering elitism. Through such misguided policies, the opportunity to educate a whole generation of young people was lost. As China emerged from the Cultural Revolution, it remained a poor and relatively backward nation.

The Cultural Revolution produced widespread chaos. The Chinese government has estimated that the lives of some 100 million people were severely disrupted. Many suffered either false arrests or beatings. Many were driven to suicide. Society was torn apart at the seams, and people began to lose confidence in the Communist Party and its leaders.

Mao died on Sept. 9, 1976. A month later, his radical wife, Jiang Qing (Chiang Ching), and her top supporters, who had risen to prominence during the Cultural Revolution, were arrested by other Communist leaders in a coup. Two years elapsed, however, before the new leadership's policies moved China in a new direction.

The most powerful architect of the new policies was Deng Xiaoping (Teng Hsiao-p'ing). Deng was born in 1904 and became a Communist in the 1920's while he was a student in France. A smart, tough politician, Deng became a close colleague of Mao during the Communists' guerrilla war in the 1930's. Early in the Cultural Revolution, however, Mao turned against Deng and removed him from his offices, calling him "the number-two person in authority taking the capitalist road." Deng returned to power in 1973 but was deposed again in 1976 by the group headed by Jiang. In 1977, after Jiang's arrest, he regained his authority. At the end of 1978, Deng persuaded the Communist Party Central Committee, which determines China's political leadership, to make China's top priority the

The author:
Kenneth G. Lieberthal is a professor of political science at the University of Michigan in Ann Arbor and a research associate at the university's Center for Chinese Studies.

112

achievement of the *Four Modernizations*—the rapid modernization of agriculture, industry, science and technology, and national defense.

Deng's Four Modernizations differed profoundly in their approach and consequences from Mao's Cultural Revolution. Where Mao stressed serving the nation's Communist goals through class struggle and self-sacrifice, Deng emphasized rapid economic development based on material rewards. Mao, for example, opposed pay bonuses for productive workers, while Deng supported such measures. Since 1978, Deng and his political allies have tried to raise China's standard of living by increasing individual and cultural freedom, opening China to the outside world, and using the talents of China's intellectuals to the fullest.

Three new social policies have improved the lives of numerous Chinese since 1978. First, the government announced that many things it once supervised no longer had any political significance— including how young people style their hair, what clothes they wear, and the kind of music they prefer. The results are startling for peo-

China

China is the world's third-largest country in land area and the most heavily populated, with more than 1 billion people.

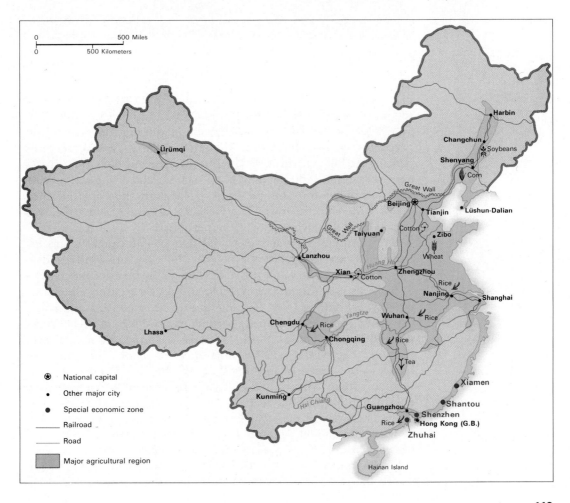

113

ple who knew China under Mao. For example, Taiwan's latest love songs are heard on tape throughout China. And in 1984, the Communist Youth League—an organization of young people being prepared for membership in the Communist Party—sponsored disco dancing at Beijing's historic Temple of Heaven, built for China's emperors in the 1400's. Under Mao, such social dancing was prohibited, and only a few political songs, particularly those that glorified Mao's leadership, such as "The East Is Red" and "Sailing the Seas Depends on the Helmsman," were permitted.

Second, the government declared that people should try to become rich, a radical shift for people who were previously told to sacrifice for the party and the state. Today, the typical Chinese tries to make as much money as possible and uses it to live well. Consequently, everything from clothing and music to housing and major consumer goods has gradually become more stylish, of higher quality, and more plentiful. Since 1978, for example, the annual production of television sets has multiplied 12 times. The output of bicycles—the principal means of transportation in China's cities—has more than tripled, and electric fan production has increased nearly eightfold. China remains an extremely poor country, however. The average personal income per year is under $400, and close to 400 million peasants still lack electricity. But the standard of living has risen, and some Chinese have begun to live quite well.

Finally, and of great importance, the government largely abandoned the practice of labeling people according to their class back-

Since the Communist revolution of 1949, Mao Zedong and Deng Xiaoping have had the greatest impact on Chinese society, though their policies differed radically. During the Cultural Revolution of the 1960's, *left,* Mao was idolized and even likened to the rising sun, but in the late 1970's Deng, *above,* brought China back down to earth.

ground—that is, whether they were descended from working-class, peasant, landlord, or capitalist families. Under that system, a "bad" class label—a landlord or capitalist family background, for example—often led to beatings, imprisonment, and social isolation. Many such people were killed or committed suicide, and most others lived in fear. These labels, moreover, passed from one generation to the next. Thus, the abolition of this system ended an official policy of severe discrimination against tens of millions of citizens.

The new policies also brought significant cultural changes. Under Mao, the government strictly controlled writers and artists. Only works of art that conformed to the Communist Party's policies were allowed. Writers, for example, were expected to create heroic characters who exemplified Communist virtues and made great sacrifices for the state. Characters who opposed Communist goals were to be portrayed in an unfavorable light. Authors accused of deviating from those policies were criticized and prohibited from publishing. Many were beaten and imprisoned.

Since the Cultural Revolution ended, cultural policy has zigged and zagged. Open opposition to official policy still lands writers in immediate and serious trouble. But in December 1984, the government announced that restrictions would be eased, and the number and diversity of books, motion pictures, plays, and operas have increased enormously since then.

Most Chinese have only recently had the opportunity to watch television and to see Western films, such as *The Sound of Music, Kra-*

mer vs. Kramer, and *On Golden Pond*. After I settled my hotel bill during a recent visit to China, a young cashier whispered, "May the Force be with you," an obvious reference to the movie *Star Wars*.

Such changes in social and cultural life reflect Deng's efforts to reform China. Most of his initiatives, however, have centered on the crucial economic and political spheres.

About 800 million of China's more than 1 billion people live in the countryside. Despite this enormous work force, inadequate agricultural production has remained a major drawback to China's economic growth. About 70 per cent of the industries that produce consumer goods use agricultural products as raw materials. For example, the clothing industry requires cotton. But from 1949 to 1978, agricultural output in China barely kept pace with the increase in population. Consequently, a shortage of raw materials made it difficult for consumer-goods industries to grow, and many products became scarce.

Beginning in 1979, China's government drastically revised agricultural policy. Mao's policy had organized peasants into large collective farms called *communes*. The government dictated what crops they would grow and held down their incomes by setting low prices for agricultural products. The post-Mao leaders under Deng Xiaoping made three major changes in agriculture. First, they paid the peasants 20 to 50 per cent more for their produce. Second, the government shifted production back to the family, rather than make people work in communes. Finally, it allowed the peasants more freedom to choose what they would grow. After selling a fixed annual quota of grain to the government, peasants were permitted to sell the remainder of their produce on the open market. These reforms fundamentally changed Mao's agricultural policy.

The new farm policies produced spectacular results. Throughout the early 1980's, output increased at nearly double its previous rate, faster than anyone thought possible. For example, grain production, including rice and wheat, increased 30 per cent between 1978 and 1984, while cotton production tripled during the same period. Although China is still far from agricultural abundance, it has ceased being a major grain importer and, in 1983, no longer had to import cotton. In fact, China now ranks second only to the United States as a cotton exporter.

China's new leadership has had a more difficult time trying to carry out economic reforms in the cities. The urban economy is far more complex and less well understood than the rural economy. Nevertheless, Deng's goal of reducing the number of activities directly managed by the government has had some success. Today, people are permitted to set up small private businesses, which are owned either individually or collectively by several people. These businesses are mainly in such services as small tailor shops, streetside barbershops, shoe repair stalls, and sidewalk restaurants. Before the

After Mao's death, new
policies fashioned
by Deng Xiaoping
stressed the improve-
ment of living stand-
ards and an opening up
to the West. As a result,
many families now
have TV sets and other
modern appliances, *be-
low,* and Western
clothes are modeled at
fashion shows, *left.*

In the countryside, China's new policies called for ending collective farming. Peasants can now grow crops on their own land, *above,* and sell them on the free market, *right,* rather than turn all their produce over to the state at a fixed price. These policies have enriched many peasants and ushered in an era of growth in agriculture.

Cultural Revolution, about 1 million small businesses existed in China. After Mao discouraged such activities, the number of such businesses dropped to about 190,000. The new policies under Deng, however, encouraged the growth of such businesses. By June 1985, 36 million people were working in the private sector. Some of these new businesses have been highly successful, and a few of their owners have become rich.

The new policies have also brought changes in China's state-run factories. Today, the heads of large firms are allowed to fire unproductive workers. Increasingly, workers' incomes are determined by how well they do their jobs. Deng has sought greater use of economic rewards for productive workers and economic penalties for inefficient ones. These policies have reversed Mao's teachings that all work was of equal value and that rewarding good work was uncommunist. The state-run factories have been put under pressure to produce profits, not just goods.

Another major economic reform was the *open-door* policy that opened China to foreign investment. During the 1960's and early 1970's, China refused all foreign loans and investments in an attempt to achieve self-sufficiency. Under the new open-door policy, China has invited foreign businesses to set up shop within its borders. In 1979, the government designated four areas along China's eastern seaboard as *special economic zones*, areas where foreign investors can operate using Chinese labor without many of the restrictions that apply elsewhere. In 1984, China named 14 coastal cities as additional such areas. And many billboards in these cities that once were covered with Maoist political slogans now carry colorful advertisements for such consumer items as Seiko watches and Sony radios. Most foreign investment to date has been poured into an enormous effort to find oil off the Chinese coast, but many other ventures, including several Western-style hotels, have been built with foreign assistance. China's foreign trade has also grown rapidly, from about $13 billion in 1976 to more than $40 billion in 1984.

Despite the government's efforts to increase the efficiency of China's industry, little had been accomplished by 1985. Three major obstacles have stood in the way. First, the prices for goods in China generally fail to reflect scarcity, quality, or production costs. For example, China is short of energy, but government subsidies keep energy prices artificially low. This has encouraged industry to squander energy rather than adopt expensive energy-saving technologies. Price reform, however, is politically difficult because it could cause severe inflation.

Second, critical shortages have held back the entire economy. The two most pressing deficiencies are in energy and transportation. China produces enough electricity to run only 80 per cent of its industry at any one time, so thousands of factories must shut down

China's economic reforms created special economic zones to attract foreign investment. A luxury hotel, *left,* in Shenzhen (Shen-chen), one such zone, is modeled after Western resorts to make foreign travelers feel at home.

In China's cities, new policies have encouraged the growth of small, privately owned businesses, such as a new fast-food restaurant in Beijing (Peking), *opposite page.* Benefiting from reforms that also encourage consumer spending, shoppers eye the latest electronic gear at a Shanghai store, *below.*

for hours each week. The transport system has many bottlenecks, and this too contributes to the energy problem. China burns coal for most of its power, but a shortage of rail lines and modern highways hampers the transport of coal to industrial users.

Third, China still lacks the talented and well-trained people needed to make its reforms work. Under Mao, for example, the directors of large firms were chosen for their ability to carry out government orders. Now, however, directors of these same firms must be able to increase efficiency and make a profit. These goals require different skills, and many of the old-style directors are not equal to the challenge.

The astonishing thing about these breathtaking social, cultural, and economic changes is that they are occurring in a country where political power is still monopolized by the Communist Party. It is remarkable that the party could admit to making such serious errors and then oversee such fundamental reforms. This complete reversal of policy shows how disillusioned the current party leaders became with the system that Mao created. Nevertheless, changes on this scale inevitably rearrange power within the political system, and thus produce opposition and tension as some people benefit from the reforms while others do not.

Many of the people who prosper in China now are the same people who suffered under Mao. In

Since Mao's death, China, the world's most populous country, has sought to control population growth. A billboard, *right,* urges couples to have only one child.

YOU SHENG YOU YU ZH N NG ZHONG HUA

122

the countryside, a new group of relatively wealthy peasants has emerged. In the cities, those with higher education, foreign connections, or business skills have flourished. Inevitably, the new reforms have created resentment among those who benefited from the Cultural Revolution or who have been unable to find a niche in the new scheme of things, such as those young people who missed a chance for an education during the Cultural Revolution.

The roles and power of aging officials have also changed, breeding resentment among some. Deng, who was 81 in 1985, has recognized the need to bring younger people into the government, turning over key posts to more youthful individuals. In a sweeping leadership change in September 1985, 131 top Communist Party leaders, mostly aging officials, resigned to give way to younger leadership. Between 1979 and 1985, some 900,000 party and government officials had been forcefully retired. Deng also implemented this policy in the powerful military officer corps, where many of the elderly peasant generals who brought the Communists to power in

China's reforms can be a mixed blessing. The economic growth they helped to spur brought an increase in industrial pollution, and construction of new homes and factories takes up valuable land, *above,* once used for farming.

1949 were forced to retire in favor of younger men with more technical training. Many resisted this forced retirement.

Political changes have also weakened some of the bureaucracies that grew powerful during the Cultural Revolution. For example, China's army had become involved in almost all aspects of society, including the management of factories. But Deng's government directed the army to concentrate on its military duties and to reduce its personnel of more than 4 million by 25 per cent. The military budget—as a percentage of national income—has declined steadily over the last 10 years. Other bureaucrats, such as full-time Communist Party officials and propagandists who directed the publication of party newspapers and magazines, saw their authority weakened by similar changes.

The reforms have also brought problems, which is not surprising in the world's most highly populated country—a society so complex that almost every success creates entirely new problems in its wake. For example, the improved standard of living for peasants, brought about by the reforms, has resulted in a building boom in peasant housing. But the building boom has taken up scarce farmland, complicating efforts to increase food production. Although China is the world's third-largest country, only about 13 per cent of the land can be cultivated. Mountains and extremely dry conditions make most of China unsuitable for agriculture. Consequently, a housing boom that takes up farmland can pose a serious problem.

Another of the reform policies—the removal of farms from collective management and the return to the family farm—has made it more difficult to implement the birth control campaign that China believes is necessary. The campaign, which seeks to hold population

A billboard carries the slogan, "Race to the year 2000," reflecting the urgency of the Chinese government's drive to transform China into a powerful, modern nation by the end of the century.

growth below 12 million people per year, encourages couples to have only one child. The new family-farm policy, however, has made that limit unpopular because peasants want larger families to help them produce more on their family plots. Yet limiting the size of families is critically important because otherwise China may one day be unable to feed or find employment for its mushrooming population.

Finally, urban economic reforms have produced inflation and corruption, along with increasing signs of moral decay. Prostitution, black markets in foreign currencies, and other shady activities—sharply curtailed during Mao's era—appear to be spreading rapidly in an atmosphere that seems to encourage doing whatever is necessary to make money.

There might be a strong reaction against some of these excesses after Deng dies. Then, a political struggle to determine his successor will begin. Officials who lost power under the reforms might use these problems to discredit the reformers during the succession struggle. In 1985, it was impossible to predict what final balance would be struck, partly because the result will depend on how much longer Deng lives and how successful he is in controlling inflation and other problems while carrying out his reforms.

The outcome will be important on an international level because it will determine the terms on which more than a fifth of humankind will deal with the rest of the world. If China modernizes rapidly, its East Coast regions will develop a labor pool of some 300 million skilled but low-paid workers who will provide stiff competition to other Asian countries, including Japan, South Korea, and Singapore. As China becomes increasingly powerful, it will pose a greater challenge to the United States and other Western nations. Although relations between China and the West have improved, China and the United States frequently take opposite sides on issues in the United Nations General Assembly. China voted against the United States 86 per cent of the time during the 1984 General Assembly session. Also, China has long championed the interests of the developing nations of the Third World in opposition to those of the industrialized West. But a return to the radical, unstable political climate that existed during Mao's last years would be a far more disruptive force in the world. That kind of China would rather promote revolution in other countries than seek peaceful solutions to global problems.

Since Mao's death, China has embarked on an exciting new path. Its ultimate direction remains both vitally important and disturbingly uncertain.

For further reading:

Bernstein, Richard. *From the Center of the Earth*. Little, Brown, 1982.
Butterfield, Fox. *China: Alive in the Bitter Sea*. Times Books, 1982.
Mathews, Jay and Linda. *One Billion*. Random House, 1983.
Schell, Orville. *To Get Rich Is Glorious*. Pantheon, 1984.

By Robert Campbell

Architecture's New Look

Post-Modernists are enlivening our cities with buildings that are colorful, fanciful, and in touch with the past.

Preceding pages: The AT&T Building (1984) in New York City, designed by architects Philip Johnson and John Burgee, is one of the monuments of the Post-Modern movement. The top of the office tower is suggestive of English Chippendale furniture of the 1700's.

One of the latest additions to the New York City skyline is a 37-story office building clad with pink granite. The features that distinguish the structure from other high-rise buildings in that part of midtown Manhattan are its base and its top. The huge entryway, which includes an 80-foot-high arch flanked by a row of massive rectangular columns, is patterned—in greatly enlarged form—after the Pazzi Chapel, a Renaissance structure in Florence, Italy. The building's summit, constructed in the shape of a *split pediment*—a low triangle with a round opening at the peak—recalls English Chippendale furniture of the 1700's. All these elements combine to create an aura of grandeur that has little to do with the building's primary function—providing office space for telephone company employees.

This remarkable skyscraper, designed by New York City architect Philip Johnson with his partner, John Burgee, is the new headquarters of the American Telephone and Telegraph Company (AT&T) completed in 1984. When Johnson and AT&T announced plans for the building in 1978, they created a stir among architects in the United States. For the first time in many years, a major American corporation had rejected Modernism, the "glass box" style that had dominated architectural circles for decades. And, perhaps even more noteworthy, Johnson had been one of Modern architecture's most ardent advocates. His break with Modernism signaled the coming of age of a new movement, which by 1978 had already been recognized and given the name Post-Modernism. Johnson's appearance on the cover of *Time* magazine in January 1979 holding a model of the planned AT&T Building can be taken as the moment when Post-Modernism emerged into the mainstream of American culture.

Like most labels in the history of art and architecture, Post-Modernism is an umbrella word that covers many different trends. But those trends have one thing in common: They are all rebelling, in some way, against Modernism. In reaction to Modern architecture's insistence on boxlike forms and unadorned surfaces, a Post-Modern building is likely to have a fanciful shape, ornamentation, and bright colors. It is likely, also, to resemble buildings of the past. Post-Modern architects commonly borrow design elements from buildings of bygone eras, sometimes even copying details exactly, and they often combine many historical styles in one building. To give their creations a traditional look, Post-Modernists use many long-established materials, including stone, brick, and wood. In other cases, new materials mimic the old. An epoxy-based stucco, for instance, can be shaped to resemble stonework, but is cheaper and easier to work with than stone.

As well as looking to the past, Post-Modern architects may adopt design ideas from popular culture, such as advertising, current trends in art, or highway commercial strips with their fast-food restaurants and discount stores. In short, a building by a Post-Modern architect is likely to be more unusual and elaborate than a building designed in accord with the principles of Modernism.

The author:
Robert Campbell is an architect and writer living in Cambridge, Mass.

Simple shapes and extensive use of steel and glass mark the Modern style. The Seagram Building (1958) in New York City, *left,* by Ludwig Mies van der Rohe and Philip Johnson, and Le Corbusier's Unité d'Habitation (1952) in Marseille, France, *below,* are classics. Modernism still has many followers, such as I. M. Pei, designer of the National Gallery of Art East Building (1978) in Washington, D.C., *bottom.*

A 1962 house near Philadelphia designed by Robert Venturi, *above,* features the boldly sloping roof and large chimney typical of houses of the 1800's, such as Stratford Hall, *left,* Virginia birthplace of Civil War General Robert E. Lee.

The Modernist movement, which got its start in Europe during the early 1900's, was a style that completely rejected the past. According to those who shaped Modernism's principles, the buildings of this century should not resemble the buildings of any earlier period. Instead, they should be "functional," and Modern architects adhered to the rule that "form follows function." What that meant was that the architect was expected to study carefully the uses, or functions, to which a building would be put and arrive at a design that would fit those uses perfectly. Instead of designing, for example, a library that resembled a Renaissance palace and then somehow stuffing desks and bookshelves into it, the architect was supposed to organize the interior functions first and then design the building around them. Because ornamentation was considered non-functional, it was frowned upon.

In designing buildings, the architect was also expected to study technology and to take advantage of the efficiencies of machine-produced materials and mechanized construction methods. Modernism was an outgrowth of the machine age, a new era in which the "old-fashioned" ways of previous centuries were no longer considered valid. According to the wisdom of the day, buildings themselves should be machinelike in their clean lines and ease of use. One of Modernism's greatest masters, the Swiss-French architect Charles Édouard Jeanneret-Gris—who went by the professional name Le Corbusier—proclaimed in fact that "a house is a machine for living in."

The three guiding principles of the Modernist movement—functional design, lack of ornamentation, and industrial methods of construction—resulted in a particular kind of building. A Modern building was simple, even boxlike, in appearance and was made of contemporary materials, such as steel-reinforced concrete and new kinds of steel and glass. Modern buildings, Le Corbusier predicted in the 1920's, would be the salvation of the world's cramped, overcrowded cities. He envisioned urban areas with large buildings set well apart from one another in sunny parklands. The Modern architect would provide all that free space by making buildings tall and narrow rather than low and spread out. In the late 1940's, Le Corbusier designed a now-famous apartment complex in Marseille, France, that embodied those ideas. The gray, rectangular high-rise, which he called simply Unité d'Habitation—loosely translated, *communal dwelling*—became the model for thousands of multilevel apartment buildings and urban redevelopment projects in many countries.

In the 1950's, Modernism took hold throughout the world in a building boom unprecedented in human history. By then, Modern

Despite its boxy shape, the Lang House (1974) in Washington, Conn., designed by Robert A. M. Stern, is Post-Modern in several respects: its thin stucco construction, bright color, and ornamentation around doors and windows, all of which give it the look of a stage set.

architecture was commonly referred to as the International Style. That name came from the title of a book cowritten in 1932 by Philip Johnson that defined and named the architectural trend that was soon to become the dominant style in both Europe and the United States.

Modernism's chief practitioner in the postwar United States was the German-born architect Ludwig Mies van der Rohe, who immigrated to the United States in 1938 to escape Adolf Hitler's Nazi regime. Mies van der Rohe—or Mies, as he is usually called—settled in Chicago, where he designed the campus buildings of the Illinois Institute of Technology and some of the high-rises that line the city's lakefront. Mies's motto was *Less Is More*, by which he meant that the simpler a building is, the stronger it will look. He and Johnson collaborated on the Seagram Building (1958) in New York City, an amber-glass office tower that is considered a classic of Modern architecture. The building has the kind of spare elegance Mies admired and advocated.

Mies died in 1969, four years after Le Corbusier. The departure of those two giants of Modernism came at a time when the world was becoming increasingly disillusioned with Modern architecture. In the United States especially, people were disturbed by the rate of change in their cities, as sweeping urban renewal programs demolished whole neighborhoods and replaced them with unfamiliar Modernist buildings. In a reaction to this disturbing trend, the residents of many American cities persuaded government agencies to designate numerous older buildings and neighborhoods as historical, thus preventing them from being razed. The people were saying—in an ever-louder voice—that they preferred the traditional city, with its well-defined streets and squares, to the open city of towers, freeways, and parks imagined by Le Corbusier and others.

Michael Graves's Portland Building (1983) in Portland, Ore., *below,* features vertical design elements reminiscent of the *pilasters*—columns set into a wall—often used in classical and Renaissance architecture, such as those in the Pazzi Chapel in Florence, Italy, *left.* The lobby of the new AT&T Building, *opposite page,* is based directly on this chapel. The statue, symbolizing communications, came from the old AT&T headquarters.

Architects were forced to take notice. Thus, by stimulating a new appreciation for the architecture and urban landscape of the past, the preservation movement made a key contribution to the rise of Post-Modernism.

Meanwhile, architectural critics were turning their guns on Modernism. The opening round was fired in a 1966 book entitled *Complexity and Contradiction in Architecture* by Philadelphia architect Robert Venturi, the most important early theorist of Post-Modernism. In a mockery of Mies's motto, Venturi declared, "Less is a bore." Venturi argued that buildings should be complicated and visually stimulating, not simple and abstract. Rather than breaking with the past, he said, buildings should incorporate traditional shapes and details that remind us of older buildings, because such mental associations give meaning to architecture.

A house near Philadelphia that Venturi designed for his mother exemplifies his ideas. It suggests many dwellings of the 1800's in its ornamental trim, large chimney, symmetrical design, and steeply sloping roof. The use of such elements—a clear departure from the featureless walls, lack of symmetry, and flat roof of the typical Modern house—is based on the idea that there is a visual "language" of architecture that everybody understands. In this language, gabled roofs, chimneys, and other features traditionally associated with houses say "house." Abstract Modern buildings, contended Venturi, don't say anything.

Venturi also attacked the idea of functionalism. He argued that because most buildings are adapted to new functions many times during their lifetime, it makes little sense to design them for one specific use. According to Venturi, if a building designed to be, say, a courthouse can be converted into a marvelous library (as was later done, in 1967, with the Jefferson Market Courthouse in New York City), doubt is cast on the whole notion of functional design.

Venturi's sentiments were echoed by other theorists, and by the 1970's Post-Modernism was becoming an established trend. A key event in the growth of the movement was a four-month exhibit that opened in October 1975 at the Museum of Modern Art in New York City. The subject of the exhibit was "The Architecture of the École des Beaux-Arts," a famous school of art and architecture in Paris that flourished in the 1800's and against which the founders of Modernism rebelled.

For the museum, long a temple of Modernism, to suddenly look favorably on the classical beaux-arts tradition signaled clearly to architects that the winds of change were blowing. Those winds blew stronger in 1977 with the publication of *The Language of Post-Modern Architecture* by British architect and author Charles A. Jencks. Jencks, whose opinions are widely noted in the architectural profession, declared flatly that Modernism was dead.

By that time, many architects were designing buildings that were

The Humana Building (1985) in Louisville, Ky., *opposite page,* designed by Michael Graves, is clad with pink granite, a traditional material commonly used by Post-Modernists. The main office tower sits on an eight-story base that helps the building to fit in with the scale of other buildings on the street. Exterior design elements, such as the curving structure near the top, are references to the mills and bridges of Louisville.

Charles W. Moore combined Gothic elements with a tile floor like those of California's many Spanish missions in his design for St. Matthew's Church (1983) in Pacific Palisades, Calif.

distinctly Post-Modern. Among them was Robert A. M. Stern of New York City, perhaps the first prominent architect to employ deliberate historical references in his work. In 1974, for example, he created a two-story stucco house in Washington, Conn., that is reminiscent of various architectural sources, including the house designs of Robert Adam, a Scottish architect of the 1700's.

But the central figure of the Post-Modern movement, at least in the United States, has been Philip Johnson. His conversion to the new movement was especially important in light of his earlier devotion to Modernism. Johnson was a follower of Mies, with whom he collaborated on the Seagram Building. Even as they worked on that project, however, Johnson was growing bored with Modernism. He began experimenting with designs for buildings, usually art museums, that resembled Greek temples. With the AT&T Building, his break with Modernism was complete.

Since the late 1970's, Johnson and John Burgee have designed dozens of major Post-Modernist buildings, all as different from one another as possible, deriving their shapes and forms in a free and even whimsical manner from various styles of the past. Johnson defends his creations on the grounds that variety is the spice of architecture as well as of life.

Other prominent Post-Modernists in the United States include Michael Graves of Princeton University in New Jersey, Charles W. Moore of the University of Texas in Austin, Stanley Tigerman and Helmut Jahn of Chicago, and Frank O. Gehry of Los Angeles. To look at the sum of their work is to be reminded once more that Post-Modernism comprises many different styles of architecture.

Graves is considered by many in the profession to be the most daring and influential of the Post-Modernists. His Portland Building, an office building in Portland, Ore., completed in 1983, is essentially a box, but a lavishly decorated one. Its giant surface elements borrow heavily from architectural history. For example, the broad vertical stripes on each face of the building resemble the *pilasters*—flat rectangular columns set into a wall—that were a common feature of classical and Renaissance architecture. Graves's Humana Building in Louisville, Ky., which opened in 1985, carries Post-Modern ideas into a more three-dimensional form. The base of the pink-granite building is just eight stories high, in keeping with the Post-Modernist interest in maintaining the continuity of the traditional street. The main part of the office tower, rising to a height of 27 stories, incorporates architectural references to the

The work of Stanley Tigerman often includes visual jokes. The facade of the building he designed for the Anti-Cruelty Society (1980) in Chicago resembles the face of a dog.

mills and bridges of Louisville. Many of Graves's other buildings hark back to the geometric art deco style of the 1920's and 1930's, one of several historical styles that Post-Modern architects find especially appealing.

Moore has been a continuing force in Post-Modernism for 20 years, working with a number of other architects to create buildings that are often witty, playful, and theatrical. Some of his best-known designs are in California, including Kresge College (1974) at the University of California at Santa Cruz and Sea Ranch Condominiums (1965), overlooking the Pacific Ocean north of San Francisco. Kresge College, with its angled pathways and expanses of colorfully painted wood, resembles a stylized Mediterranean village. Sea Ranch—all dark wood and pitched roofs—recalls the mining shacks of the 1849 gold rush. Moore's St. Matthew's Church (1983) in Pacific Palisades, Calif., combines wooden ornamentation reminiscent of Gothic architecture with a tile floor like those of California's Spanish missions.

Where Moore's designs tend to be whimsical, those of Stanley Tigerman are often deliberate visual jokes. Tigerman, who in the 1970's led a revolt among younger Chicago architects against the dominance of Miesian ideas in that city, designs vivid, usually small buildings that sometimes suggest faces and body parts. He designed a building for Chicago's Anti-Cruelty Society (1980), for example, whose entrance facade resembles the face of a dog.

The most prolific of American Post-Modernists is German-born Helmut Jahn, who has dozens of large buildings throughout the

The large expanses of glass and steel in Helmut Jahn's State of Illinois Center (1985) in Chicago, *opposite page,* are typical of Modern architecture, but the building's striking shape and use of color are distinctly Post-Modern. The spectacular interior, *left,* contains office space set around a vast atrium.

United States to his credit. Jahn favors a bold, glittery, jazzy, and angular style that often makes his buildings look like glass-skinned versions of art deco office towers such as New York City's Empire State Building (1931). His newest work, the mammoth State of Illinois Center in Chicago, completed in 1985, wraps a bold sloping curve of steel and colored-glass panels around a vast interior atrium.

Frank O. Gehry derives his inspiration not from the architecture of the past but rather from the contemporary art scene. He often works with "junk art" materials, such as chain link fencing and metal siding, to create buildings that have the jumbled vitality of a highway commercial strip. His California Aerospace Museum (1984) in Los Angeles announces its function by means of an actual airplane mounted on the facade.

Prominent Post-Modernists outside the United States include Ricardo Bofill of Spain, who has built apartment houses in France in the form of vast, traditional palaces made of concrete; and James Stirling of Great Britain, whose Arthur M. Sackler Museum (1985)

Frank O. Gehry often seeks a sense of vitality by letting parts of his buildings appear to collide almost randomly with each other. For example, the walls and columns in the interior of his California Aerospace Museum (1984) in Los Angeles, *below right,* intersect at many angles. The exterior of the museum, *right,* has a jet plane mounted on the facade.

Post-Modernists borrow ideas from many past eras. James Stirling drew from various sources, including the temples of ancient Egypt, such as the Temple of Karnak, *left,* in designing the cartoonlike columns that adorn his Arthur M. Sackler Museum (1985) in Cambridge, Mass., *above.*

at Harvard University in Cambridge, Mass., has an entrance facade with cartoonlike columns inspired by various sources, including ancient Egyptian temples. One of the movement's rising stars is Hans Hollein of Austria, winner of the 1985 Pritzker Architecture Prize, the profession's equivalent of the Nobel Prize. Hollein is a master at creating exquisite and unexpected details. The interior of a travel agency he designed in Vienna in 1978, for example, is given an exotic touch with stylized metal palm trees.

Despite the growing influence of these and other Post-Modernists—including several Japanese architects whose work recently began to attract international attention—the obituaries for Modernism have been premature. A number of architects in the United States and elsewhere have continued to develop the Modern style and have adopted certain materials frequently used by Post-Modernists, notably marble veneer. Among the best known of the die-hard Modernists is the Chinese-born American architect I. M. Pei of New York City, designer of many notable buildings, including the East Building (1978) of the National Gallery of Art in Washington, D.C. The East Building, though far from being a simple box, is decidedly modern in its angular expanses of unadorned marble and concrete. Other American architects who have remained committed to Modernism include Richard Meier, also of New York City, whose High Museum of Art (1983) in Atlanta, Ga., is another stark-white showpiece of the Modern style.

Still other architects defy easy categorization as either Modernists or Post-Modernists, since their work contains design elements used by both camps. Those stylistic labels are thus helpful only up to a point in thinking about architecture. Specifically, we must avoid the simplistic view that Modern buildings are "bad" and Post-Modern ones "good," with hybrid buildings falling somewhere in-between. Good buildings can be constructed in any style, and there are some fine examples of Modern architecture—just as there are some not-

Hans Hollein is famed for the many exquisite details he employs in his designs, such as the stylized palm trees that grace this travel agency (1978) he designed in Vienna, Austria.

so-fine Post-Modern designs. Post-Modernism has, in fact, come in for its own share of criticism. It is often deplored as too much a visual art that tends to ignore the practical aspects of design, resulting in many buildings that are dazzling to look at but difficult to live or work in. The movement's detractors have compared Post-Modern works to Disneyland, calling them theatrical and frivolous, more like stage design than real architecture. Post-Modernists themselves have been accused of feeding the national media's hunger for novelty—for new styles and new architectural "stars." Lastly, Post-Modernism is sometimes regarded as a reactionary and self-indulgent retreat from the sterner, more honest ideals that animated the Modern movement.

There is some truth to those charges. Nonetheless, the Post-Modern movement has probably been a necessary corrective to Modernism's excesses—the blank walls and dismal concrete "plazas" that city dwellers have found so alienating. Furthermore, by bringing back respect for our architectural heritage, Post-Modernism has reawakened an understanding that buildings are not just containers for everyday functions; they are also physical records of the societies that erected them. Think how much less we would know about the past if, throughout history, important buildings had been torn down as soon as another architectural fashion came along.

Post-Modernism has also revived interest in the principle of *contextualism*, the idea that a building should fit comfortably into its context, or surroundings. Because of Modern architecture's disregard for contextualism, Modernist structures frequently seem at odds with neighboring buildings. This conflict has detracted from the architectural coherence that our cities once had. Post-Modernists are trying to reverse that trend and, in the process, to bring back the dynamic street life that has always made cities so exciting.

Post-Modernism, once considered controversial, is now well established and is moving into the mainstream of architectural theory and practice. Despite its growing dominance, however, Post-Modernism is not, strictly speaking, replacing Modernism. Rather, it is merging with Modernism in a stylistic blending that will ultimately produce a new kind of architecture—a style for tomorrow.

For further reading:

"Doing Their Own Thing." *Time*, Jan. 8, 1979.
Jencks, Charles A. *The Language of Post-Modern Architecture.* Rizzoli, 1977.
Portoghesi, Paolo. *After Modern Architecture.* Rizzoli, 1982.
Safdie, Moshe. "Private Jokes in Public Places." *The Atlantic*, December 1981.
Venturi, Robert. *Complexity and Contradiction in Architecture.* Rev. ed. Museum of Modern Art, 1977.
"What Is the Focus of Post-Modern Architecture?" *American Artist*, December 1981.

By Lynn L. Ross

How Science Is Saving Sight

Medical research has made great strides
in treating eye disorders, including
many that once led to blindness.

A few days after birth, Catherine is wheeled into the operating room. An examination has revealed that she was born with *cataracts*, a clouding of the lens of the eye. The cataracts must be removed, or the infant will be unable to see. After the baby has been anesthetized, the surgeon makes a tiny incision in one eye and opens the lens capsule. The doctor then uses a needlelike "hose" to carefully wash the cloudy tissue out of the eye, leaving a clear visual pathway. After both eyes have been operated on, Catherine is fitted with special contact lenses for infants, which will enable her to see almost normally.

At a nearby doctor's office, 62-year-old Mr. Davis is being treated for a form of *glaucoma*, a build-up of fluid pressure within the eye that can result in blindness. He sits in a chair with his head held immobile, staring into a laser instrument. Opposite Mr. Davis, a physician peers into a binocular eyepiece and focuses the instrument on the man's left eye. A moment later, firing short pulses of blue-green laser light into the eye, the doctor opens the drainage channel for the fluid. The doctor next focuses on the patient's right eye and repeats the procedure. Later that day, Mr. Davis is on his way home, his glaucoma relieved.

Patients of all ages are benefiting from recent advances in *ophthalmology*, the medical specialty concerned with problems of the eye. In the past 20 years, research in ophthalmology has achieved explosive progress in treating eye disorders, including many conditions that

Opposite page: A laser beam strikes a patient's eye. The laser has become a valuable tool in the treatment of several eye disorders.

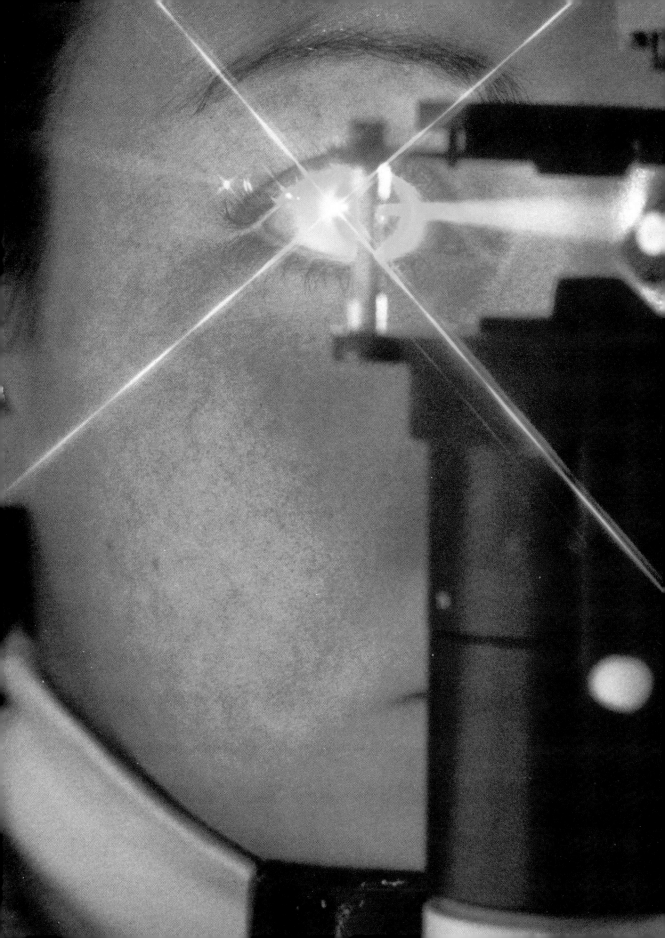

once doomed their victims to blindness. New surgical techniques, laser therapy, safer and more effective drugs, and other innovations have given eye doctors an unprecedented ability to preserve sight.

This rapid progress is good news for many people. At least 11 million people in the United States suffer from seriously impaired vision that is not correctable with glasses, and 6 million new cases of eye disease occur each year. Not everyone can be helped, of course. Some 500,000 Americans are legally blind, a number that will no doubt continue to grow until medical science has unraveled all the mysteries of the eye, one of nature's most incredible creations.

The anatomy of the eye

The human eye is a roughly spherical organ about 1 inch in diameter. The white of the eye, called the *sclera*, makes up about five-sixths of the eyeball's outer covering. The other one-sixth is the *cornea*, a tough, transparent "dome" at the front of the eye that focuses incoming light rays. Light enters the interior of the eye through the *pupil*, a variable-sized opening at the center of the *iris*, the colored part of the eye. Behind the pupil is the *lens*, which bends light rays still further. The lens continually changes shape to focus on objects at varying distances from the eye. Images are projected onto the *retina*, a thin layer of tissue attached to the inside wall of the eye. The retina is made up of millions of light-sensitive cells. Nerve fibers connected to these cells join at the back of the eyeball to form the *optic nerve*, a "cable" that carries visual information to the brain. The area of the retina that gives us sharp central vision is the *macula lutea* or *macula*, a small, round spot near the center of the retina. Other parts of the retina are responsible for *peripheral*, or side, vision. The *fovea centralis*, a tiny pit within the macula, is the point of sharpest vision. The spaces within the eye are filled with two clear substances, the *aqueous humor* and *vitreous humor*. The aqueous humor, a watery fluid that bathes and nourishes the cornea and lens, is continuously secreted into the chamber between those two structures. The jellylike vitreous humor fills the interior of the eyeball and maintains its shape.

The eye can be afflicted with a multitude of serious disorders, but the three most common ones are cataracts, glaucoma, and diseases of the retina. No matter how bad a cataract becomes, surgery can nearly always restore eyesight, but glaucoma and certain retinal conditions can lead to permanent blindness if left untreated. The key to a successful solution of these and many other visual disorders is early detection. Ophthalmologists therefore stress the importance of periodic eye examinations, especially after age 40, to catch eye disorders in their early stages.

Cataracts are somewhat of a puzzle. Researchers have not yet determined exactly why cataracts develop, though they have found that most types of cataracts are caused by changes in the chemical composition of the lens. The most common form of cataracts, called

The author:
Lynn L. Ross is a free-lance writer and former manager of media information for the American Academy of Ophthalmology in San Francisco.

senile cataracts, are a result of the aging process. These usually occur in people over 60, though they can develop as early as age 40. Injury to the eye, as well as various illnesses, can lead to a clouding of the lens at any age. The cataracts that are sometimes present in newborn infants such as Catherine result from either a hereditary defect or an infection that the mother contracted during pregnancy.

Two of every 100 people in the United States will be treated for cataracts at some time in their life. The only remedy for a cataract is surgical removal of the lens. Currently, more than 700,000 Americans undergo such surgery each year, a number that will increase steadily as the average age of the U.S. population continues to rise. Modern instruments and techniques have greatly reduced the dangers of cataract removal. Just 10 years ago, cataract surgery was performed in a hospital operating room, and the patient was required to remain hospitalized for up to a week. Now, such surgery can be done in as little as 30 to 40 minutes in an outpatient setting.

The most common operation for cataracts is *extracapsular extraction*. In this procedure, the surgeon leaves the rear *capsule*, or membrane, of the lens in place to maintain the basic anatomy of the eye. The rest of the lens is removed through an incision in the white of the eye, either by forcing it out by pressure applied to the outside of the eye or washing it out with a small stream of water. In a variation of this procedure, called *phacoemulsification*, the surgeon uses an ultrasound needle—an instrument that emits high-frequency sound waves—to break the lens into tiny bits. As the lens disintegrates, the fragments are drawn out of the eye through a suction tube.

Once the biological lens has been removed, the patient must use an artificial lens to regain sharp vision. Many patients prefer simply to wear eyeglasses or a contact lens, but about half a million people each year are now choosing to have a plastic *intraocular lens* implanted in the eye. The lens is usually inserted into the space behind the iris that had been occupied by the natural lens.

Glaucoma and its treatment

Glaucoma, one of the leading causes of blindness in the United States, affects about 2 per cent of the population over the age of 35. The fluid build-up within the eye—like Mr. Davis'—results when the channel for drainage of the aqueous humor becomes blocked. The resulting pressure can damage the optic nerve. Initially, this causes small blind spots to develop, usually in peripheral vision. Because glaucoma victims are seldom aware of these blind areas until considerable optic nerve damage has occurred, early diagnosis is essential in preventing permanent vision loss.

The most common type of glaucoma—called *open-angle glaucoma* or *chronic simple glaucoma*—is caused when the tissue meshwork leading to the drainage channel collapses and prevents fluid from passing through. Most adult glaucoma patients have this form of the disease. *Angle-closure glaucoma* or *acute congestive glaucoma* occurs

Glossary

Age-related macular degeneration (AMD): A condition marked, in its most serious form, by the growth of new blood vessels into the macula.

Amblyopia: Reduced vision in one eye, often caused by strabismus.

Cataract: A clouding of the eye's natural lens.

Cornea: A transparent "dome" over the front of the eye that helps focus light rays.

Diabetic retinopathy: An eye disease, associated with diabetes, that causes the growth of abnormal blood vessels in the retina.

Glaucoma: A build-up of fluid pressure in the eye.

Intraocular lens: A plastic lens that replaces the eye's natural lens after removal of a cataract.

Macula: The area of the retina that is responsible for sharp central vision.

Myopia (near-sightedness): Fuzzy distance vision caused by light rays coming into focus before they reach the retina.

Radial keratotomy: A surgical treatment for myopia in which cuts are made in the cornea to change its curvature.

Retina: A tissue of light-sensitive cells covering the inside of the eye.

Scatter photocoagulation: A laser treatment for diabetic retinopathy in which hundreds of burns are made on the retina.

Strabismus: An imbalance in the muscles controlling eye movement, resulting in two different visual images being sent to the brain.

Parts of the Eye

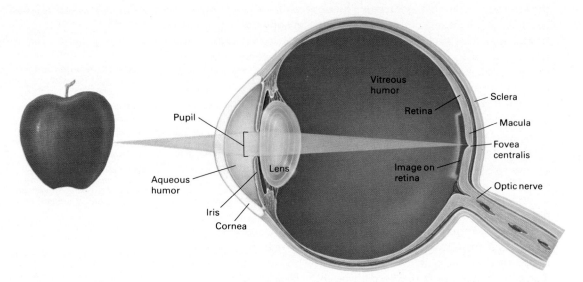

Labels on diagram:
Vitreous humor
Pupil
Sclera
Retina
Macula
Fovea centralis
Aqueous humor
Lens
Image on retina
Optic nerve
Iris
Cornea

The white *sclera* and the colored *iris* form the outer covering of the eye. The transparent *cornea* protects the iris and focuses light rays, which enter the eye through the *pupil,* an opening in the iris. The *lens* bends light rays further and focuses them on the *retina,* a layer of light-sensitive cells. The point of sharpest focus is the *fovea centralis,* a tiny pit within an area called the *macula.* The retina is connected to the brain by the *optic nerve.* A fluid called *aqueous humor* bathes the lens and iris; a clear substance called *vitreous humor* fills the interior of the eyeball.

when the iris presses against the lens, trapping the aqueous humor near its source above the front of the lens. This causes a fluid build-up in that part of the eye. The increased pressure pushes the root of the iris against the drainage meshwork, further closing off the flow of aqueous humor. The sudden rise in fluid pressure produces such symptoms as blurred vision, severe pain, and nausea. Angle-closure glaucoma usually leads to complete blindness within a few days if it is not treated. Another form of the disease, *congenital glaucoma*, results when drainage openings in the eye do not function normally at birth.

During the past 15 years, medical science has made phenomenal advances in the treatment of glaucoma. The use of computers in diagnosis and the development of new drugs and laser surgery have all helped to make glaucoma a highly treatable disease.

Instruments that measure pressure within the eye are the primary means of detecting glaucoma, but computers are playing an increasingly important role in diagnosing the extent of the disease. By sorting through thousands of bits of information from specialized diagnostic instruments, the computer can give the ophthalmologist an instant description of a glaucoma patient's level of vision. The computer analysis reveals exactly how clear and sharp the patient's eyesight is at every point in the entire field of vision. This information helps the doctor to decide whether to continue treating the patient with medication or to advise surgery.

Chronic glaucoma is usually treated with drugs that lessen the production of aqueous humor in the eye or increase its flow out of the eye. The major development in drug therapy in recent years has been the introduction of beta-blockers, substances that are most commonly used to moderate heart rate in cardiac patients. These drugs act to decrease the production of aqueous humor and can be applied in eye drops. Beta-blockers have proved effective in reducing pressure in the eye without producing the undesirable side effects, such as headaches or blurred vision, often caused by other glaucoma drugs. When used as eye medications, beta-blockers rarely affect the heart or respiratory system, except in patients with asthma. Nevertheless, most ophthalmologists are exercising caution in prescribing beta-blockers for any glaucoma patient.

In addition to their presumed lack of side effects, beta-blockers have the further advantage of long-lasting action. The patient must apply the drug just twice a day, compared with four times a day for conventional glaucoma medications. Even twice daily may be too often to suit many patients, who frequently neglect to use their eye drops. The solution for some patients has been Ocusert, a tiny wafer that fits under the eyelid and releases a drug at a steady rate for about a week. Unfortunately, not all patients can tolerate this device, so researchers have been trying to develop longer-lasting eye drops. In April 1985, the U.S. Food and Drug Administration approved a gel containing pilocarpine, a drug that has been used for years to treat glaucoma. The gel, which can be applied at bedtime, reduces pressure in the eye for 24 hours.

The increasing use of lasers

In many cases of glaucoma, particularly angle-closure glaucoma, the drainage channels in the eye must be reopened. This can be done in several ways, including conventional surgery. Increasingly, however, ophthalmologists are using lasers to treat glaucoma. A laser is a device that produces a narrow and intense beam of light. It does this by exciting the atoms of a crystal, gas, or other substance, causing them to release light energy of a single wavelength. This "needle of light" enables the ophthalmologist to alter tissues without having to cut into the eye.

To treat open-angle glaucoma, the surgeon focuses the laser beam on the tissue meshwork that carries the aqueous humor out of the eye. The laser's pulsating bursts of light, each lasting no more than a thousandth of a second, make small burns at carefully selected points. The burns apparently cause the meshwork to contract, which opens up the drainage spaces within it.

Laser treatment has almost completely replaced conventional surgery for the correction of angle-closure glaucoma. The ophthalmologist burns a hole through the iris, creating a new drainage channel.

Lasers have also proved effective for stopping abnormal changes in the blood vessels of the retina. One such condition, *diabetic retinopathy*, a disorder in which these tiny vessels weaken and break down, is the leading cause of blindness in the United States among adults between the ages of 20 and 64. Some 5,000 Americans lose

Treating Cataracts

A cataract, a clouding of the eye's lens, reduces the amount of light transmitted to the retina. The only treatment for a cataract is surgical removal. The rear capsule, or membrane, of the lens is usually left in place to maintain the structure of the eye. An artificial lens—often a surgically implanted intraocular lens (as shown *below*)—must substitute for the natural lens.

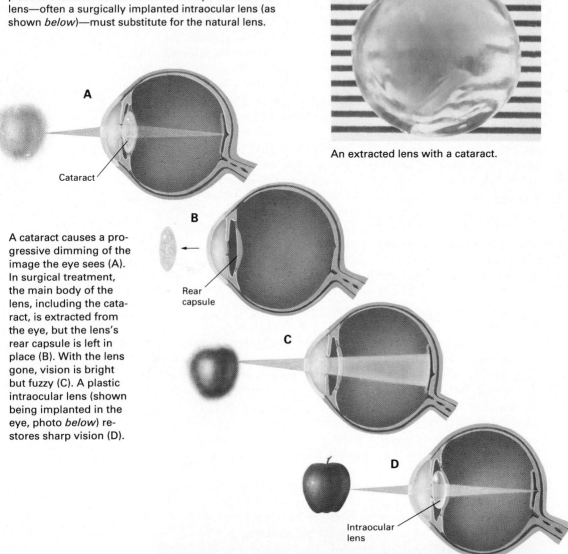

An extracted lens with a cataract.

A

Cataract

A cataract causes a progressive dimming of the image the eye sees (A). In surgical treatment, the main body of the lens, including the cataract, is extracted from the eye, but the lens's rear capsule is left in place (B). With the lens gone, vision is bright but fuzzy (C). A plastic intraocular lens (shown being implanted in the eye, photo *below*) restores sharp vision (D).

B

Rear capsule

C

D

Intraocular lens

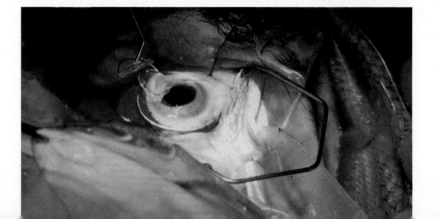

their sight each year as a result of diabetic retinopathy. As its name implies, this condition is associated with diabetes, a chronic disease that disrupts the body's ability to use and store sugar. The longer a person has suffered from diabetes, the more likely it becomes that he or she will develop retinopathy.

In the early stages of retinopathy, the weakened blood vessels may leak fluid or blood, or become enlarged in some places. Occasionally, the leaking fluid and blood damage or scar the retina, causing blurred vision. Oftentimes, however, these changes produce no noticeable symptoms. In later stages of the disease, new blood vessels, associated with fibrous bands of scar tissue, develop. These changes may pull on the retina until it detaches from the back of the eye. The new blood vessels are fragile and sometimes rupture, spilling blood into the vitreous humor and clouding eyesight. Blood vessels may even grow on the iris and cause a form of glaucoma.

A laser technique known as *scatter photocoagulation* has become the standard treatment for diabetic retinopathy. In this procedure, the ophthalmologist uses an argon laser to make 500 to 1,000 tiny burns across most of the retina. The sheer number of burns produces changes in the retina that cause the abnormal blood vessels to dry up. The burns result in some loss of vision, but rarely enough to bother the patient.

Laser therapy cannot be used to treat all retinopathy patients, however. If the vitreous humor is too clouded by blood, the doctor must perform a conventional surgical operation called a *vitrectomy*.

Using an operating microscope, a surgeon repairs a detached retina. Because the structures of the eye are so small and delicate, most eye surgery is done with the aid of this device.

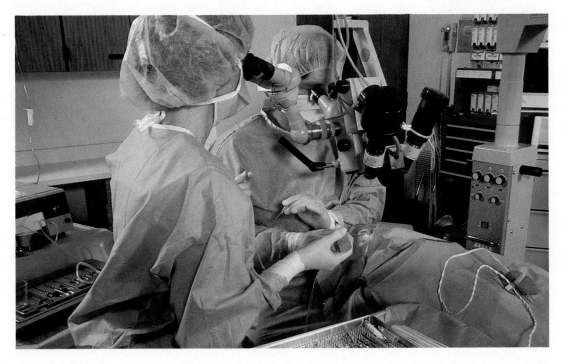

The Laser—A Powerful Weapon in the Battle to Save Sight

Laser instruments, such as the one shown at the right, have become a valuable tool for the treatment of glaucoma—excessive fluid pressure within the eye—and certain diseases of the retina. The physician focuses on the patient's eye through a binocular eyepiece and fires short bursts of laser light at the trouble spots. The procedure, conducted in an office setting, takes just 15 to 20 minutes.

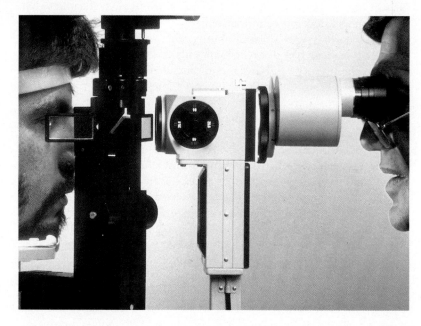

Open-Angle Glaucoma
The most common form of glaucoma is open-angle glaucoma, in which the tissue meshwork leading to the drainage channel for aqueous humor collapses. Laser burns cause the meshwork to contract, opening the spaces within it.

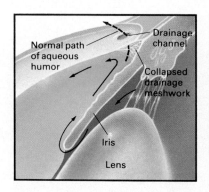

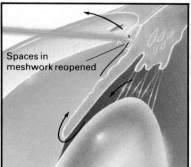

Angle-Closure Glaucoma
In angle-closure glaucoma, the iris presses against the lens, trapping the aqueous humor. The laser beam burns through the iris, creating a new drainage route for the fluid.

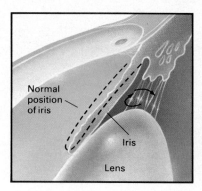

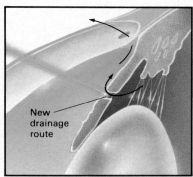

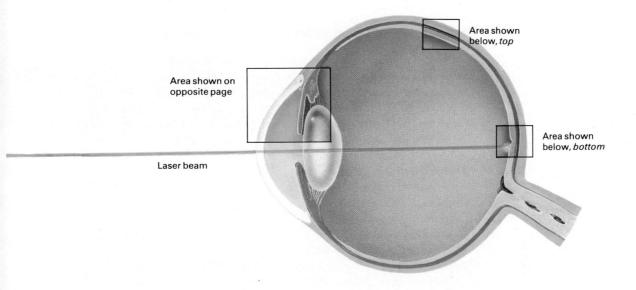

Area shown below, *top*

Area shown on opposite page

Area shown below, *bottom*

Laser beam

Diabetic Retinopathy

Diabetic retinopathy, a disease associated with diabetes, causes weak blood vessels to grow and rupture in the retina. Hundreds of laser burns made across the retina cause these vessels to dry up.

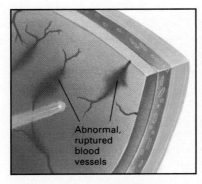

Abnormal, ruptured blood vessels

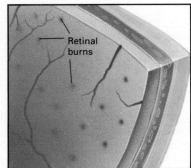

Retinal burns

Age-Related Macular Degeneration (AMD)

AMD, a deterioration of the macula caused by aging, has several forms. In its most serious form, new blood vessels grow beneath the macula and leak fluid and blood. Laser burns destroy the abnormal vessels.

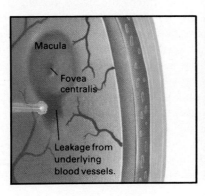

Macula

Fovea centralis

Leakage from underlying blood vessels.

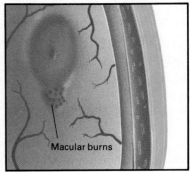

Macular burns

This procedure involves removing the vitreous humor from the eye and replacing it with a clear artificial solution. About 70 per cent of the patients who undergo a vitrectomy gain improved eyesight.

Macular degeneration afflicts many older people

Among nondiabetics, the most common problem affecting the retina is *age-related macular degeneration* (AMD), a deterioration of the macula caused by the aging process. About one-third of the approximately 60 million Americans over the age of 50 have some degree of AMD. In the great majority of cases, the disorder is limited to the formation of yellowish round spots called *drusen* that appear in a scattered pattern in the macula. Drusen, researchers believe, are a slowly growing accumulation of waste material that some people's eyes can no longer properly eliminate.

In most instances, drusen do not lead to any appreciable loss of vision. But each year, some 100,000 people in the United States with this condition develop further problems, usually a form of macular degeneration called *atrophic AMD* or "dry" AMD. This disease causes the atrophy, or withering, of small areas of the macula. No way has yet been found to reverse or halt this process. Fortunately, atrophic AMD generally causes only a mild impairment of vision.

Another 14,000 Americans a year are affected by a more serious type of macular degeneration called *choroidal neovascularization* or "wet" AMD. This condition is marked by a sudden growth of new blood vessels in the *choroid,* the tissue layer underlying the retina. In the early stages of the disease, these vessels leak fluid and blood, causing the retina to blister and pull away from the wall of the eye. This produces distortions in sight: Straight lines appear wavy, and objects look blurred and distorted. Finally, blood-vessel growth in the macula causes scarring, resulting in blank spots at the center of vision.

If diagnosed early enough, about two-thirds of the people suffering from wet AMD can be successfully treated with laser therapy. The ophthalmologist focuses the beam of a laser on the abnormal blood vessels and destroys them. But this must be done before the blood vessels have begun to grow into the center of the macula. When the laser burns the blood vessels, it also destroys the portion of the retina into which the vessels are growing. If the vessels have entered the fovea centralis, the laser in most cases cannot be used because it would wipe out central vision. Wet AMD progresses so rapidly that many cases are not diagnosed until they are too far along to be treated. Of patients who have had the disease for six months, only about 10 per cent can be helped.

Although many eye conditions are serious, sight-threatening disorders, a few vision problems are usually more annoying than dangerous. One of the most prevalent of these nuisance conditions is *myopia* (near-sightedness). A near-sighted person can see nearby objects sharply but is unable to focus on objects in the distance. In

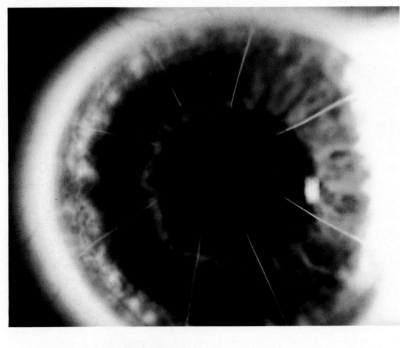

Correcting Myopia with Surgery

Myopia, or near-sightedness, is usually caused by the eyeball being too long from front to back. Light rays then come into focus before they reach the retina, resulting in fuzzy vision (A). In a controversial new surgical procedure called radial keratotomy, cuts are made around the periphery of the cornea (B). This weakens the cornea, allowing fluid pressure within the eye to partially flatten its surface. The change in curvature causes light rays to focus on the retina, restoring sharp vision (C). After the surgery, tiny slits can be seen on the cornea, *left*.

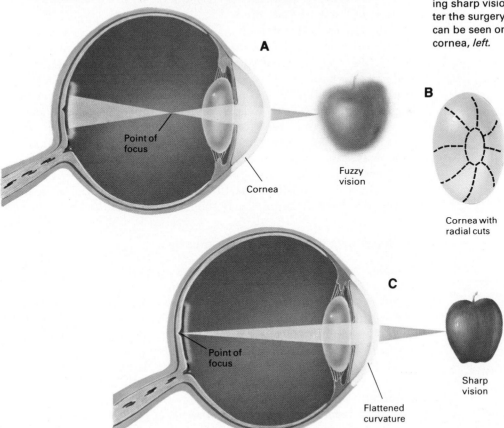

A

Point of focus

Cornea

Fuzzy vision

B

Cornea with radial cuts

C

Point of focus

Flattened curvature

Sharp vision

severe cases, anything more than a few feet away is hopelessly fuzzy. Myopia usually results from the eyeball being too long from front to back, causing light rays from distant objects to come into focus before they reach the retina. Eyeglasses or contact lenses can correct this problem by changing the angle of the incoming light rays, thereby shifting the point of focus onto the retina.

Radial keratotomy—controversial cure

Since the late 1970's, thousands of near-sighted people seeking to avoid wearing glasses or contact lenses have undergone a controversial surgical operation called *radial keratotomy*. This technique, developed in the Soviet Union, corrects myopia by altering the shape of the cornea. With an exquisitely sharp diamond-bladed knife, the surgeon makes eight or more cuts, like the spokes of a wheel, around the periphery of the cornea. This weakens the cornea and allows the normal fluid pressure inside the eye to partially flatten the cornea's curvature. Radial keratotomy is a fairly simple procedure, but it requires great precision: The depth of the cuts must be accurate to within a few thousandths of a millimeter for the operation to succeed. If the cuts are too shallow, they will have little effect. If the cuts are too deep, aqueous humor will leak from the eye, and the eye may become infected.

Although radial keratotomy has clearly benefited many patients with myopia, particularly those whose near-sightedness is not too severe, the procedure has some drawbacks. For one thing, its outcome cannot be accurately predicted, and thus it often does not result in 20/20 vision. Moreover, the cuts sometimes cause glare in bright light for several months after the operation, and the patient may have fluctuating vision for two years or more. Perhaps the most important consideration, though, is the possibility of such complications as scarring, glaucoma, or infection. Since 1981, the procedure has been under study by the National Eye Institute, an agency of the U.S. Department of Health and Human Services. The final verdict on radial keratotomy may still be several years away.

Drug corrects imbalance in eye muscles

Ophthalmologists are also evaluating new solutions to other eye disorders. For example, they are testing an experimental drug called Oculinum for the treatment of *strabismus*, a misalignment of the eyes that affects about 4 per cent of the children in the United States. Strabismus is caused by improperly balanced eye muscles. For both eyes to focus on an object, all six muscles of each eye must work together in a coordinated manner with the corresponding muscles of the other eye. If this does not happen, the brain receives a different image from each eye. The brain quickly learns to ignore the image from the "wandering," or weaker, eye and to see the image from the correctly aligned eye. If strabismus is not remedied in the first few years of life, it can lead to permanently reduced vision in the misaligned eye, a condition known as *amblyopia*.

Amblyopia is treated by placing a patch over the normal eye, thus forcing the problem eye to work harder. Many patients, however, need an operation to adjust the tension in the muscles of the wandering eye. Ophthalmologists hope that Oculinum will cure many cases of strabismus that ordinarily would require surgery. The drug is a weak solution of botulinus toxin, the bacterial poison that causes botulism, a severe form of food poisoning. When injected in minute quantities into overly tight eye muscles, the drug has no poisonous effect on the body, but it causes the eye muscles to relax and stretch. The opposing muscles, which are not injected with the drug, then tighten to take up the slack, restoring balance to the eye. Unfortunately, the patient must receive additional injections of the drug every two to four months—perhaps on a lifelong basis.

What the future holds

New drugs for treating other eye conditions will come from research on the body's biochemistry. Scientists are painstakingly working out the thousands of biochemical reactions that take place in the human body and learning why they sometimes go awry, causing disease. Once the abnormal changes that lead to eye disorders such as retinal degeneration are understood, it should be possible to design drugs that will prevent or reverse those processes. And because so many diseases originate in our genes, the science of genetics is sure to play a large role in preventing visual disorders.

Further advances in surgical technology will also improve the prospects for many eye patients. One new development may be the use of *microwaves* (high-frequency electromagnetic waves) in eye surgery. A handheld microwave "scalpel," introduced recently in Japan, cuts to a depth of just 1 to 2 millimeters, leaving underlying tissue unaffected. Heat generated by the microwaves instantly seals severed blood vessels.

Today, research on the causes and treatment of eye disorders is more intensive than ever before. Much of this research is a highly cooperative effort involving hundreds of physicians and scientists at many institutions, working together toward common goals. Their labors are certain to bring untold medical advances. Meanwhile, ophthalmologists continue to emphasize preventive eye care. Early detection and treatment is still the greatest factor in saving sight.

For further reading:

Langone, John. "Cataracts: Behind the Clouded Lens." *Discover*, February 1984.

Manber, Malcolm M. "Can Surgery Cure Myopia?" *The New York Times Magazine*, Dec. 6, 1981.

Michelson, Paul E. *Insight into Eyesight*. Nelson-Hall, 1981.

A Year in Perspective

1881
1889
1882
1884
1885

THE YEAR BOOK casts a backward glance at the furors, fancies, and follies of yesteryear. The coincidences of history that are revealed offer substantial proof that the physical world may continually change, but human nature—with all its inventiveness, amiability, and even perversity—remains fairly constant, for better or worse, throughout the years.

See page 164.

By Sara Dreyfuss

The Past That Helped Shape Our Present

Rebellions in Canada and Sudan ended in 1885, and inventors developed new products that have changed modern life.

Innovations of 1885 that have had a great impact on modern life include—*clockwise from lower right*—the motorcycle, invented by Gottlieb Daimler; the founding of AT&T, which operated telephone offices such as the one shown; Karl Benz's pioneer gasoline automobile; rabies vaccine, developed by Louis Pasteur; and the first skyscraper, Chicago's Home Insurance Building.

161

General Charles G. Gordon of Great Britain died defending Sudan's capital of Khartoum against al-Mahdi's forces in January 1885.

The author:
Sara Dreyfuss is Associate Editor of THE WORLD BOOK YEAR BOOK.

In one of those strange coincidences with which history abounds, two men with great personal magnetism—each hailed as a savior—led uprisings that ended in 1885. The revolts took place on opposite sides of the world, one in Sudan in Africa and the other in what is now Saskatchewan, Canada.

In Sudan, a Muslim holy man named Muhammad Ahmed had proclaimed in 1881 that he was *al-Mahdi* (the Guide), the leader whom the Muslims expected to come and establish a reign of righteousness. He gathered a large group of followers who strictly observed the teachings of Islam and wore ragged clothing to show their disdain for worldly wealth. They revered al-Mahdi so greatly that they collected his bathwater in small bottles and kept it to ward off evil.

At that time, Egypt controlled Sudan. Al-Mahdi charged that the Egyptians were not fit to rule devout Muslims, and he led an uprising against them, gaining control of several areas by 1884. Great Britain, which had occupied Egypt in 1882, became worried about the safety of an Egyptian garrison commanded by British officers in Khartoum, Sudan's capital. The British government sent General Charles G. Gordon, an experienced officer who had served in Sudan, to evacuate the garrison.

Gordon arrived in Khartoum in February 1884. The next month, before Gordon could evacuate more than a few hundred people, al-Mahdi arrived with an army of 30,000 troops and laid siege to the city. Gordon had only 8,000 Egyptian soldiers, but he strengthened Khartoum's defenses, sent repeatedly for reinforcements, and settled in to hold the city as long as possible.

The British government, which wanted to reduce military expenditures, hesitated over Gordon's pleas for help. Food ran short in the besieged city, and the people ate rats to stay alive. Gordon continually promised his troops that reinforcements would arrive. Eventually, he ordered every male over 8 years old to help defend the city. In a moving letter to his friend Lord Wolseley, Gordon wrote, "How many times have we written asking for reinforcements . . . and no answer came! Men's hearts become weary of delay. While you are eating and drinking and resting in good beds, we and those with us, soldiers and servants, are watching night and day . . . ."

Finally, in August 1884, the public outcry for Gordon's rescue persuaded the British government to organize a relief force. Having decided to help Gordon—"grudgingly, after an almost criminal delay," commented *The Atlantic Monthly*—the government spared no expense. It appointed Wolseley, one of Britain's top generals, to lead the expedition. He had 800 special boats built to negotiate waterfalls on the Nile River and employed 400 *voyageurs* (French-Canadian canoeists) to navigate. Wolseley even hired Thomas Cook, the head of a famous travel agency, to arrange the expedition.

Delay after delay occurred. The rescue party's steamers ran out of coal, and the group could not obtain enough camels for the final leg of the journey across the desert. The advance unit finally reached Khartoum on Jan. 28, 1885, only to find that the city had fallen two days earlier. Al-Mahdi's followers had killed Gordon and delivered his head to their leader's tent.

The news of Gordon's death brought a huge outburst of grief in Britain. The British observed a day of national mourning, and Parliament voted that a monument to Gordon be erected in London's Trafalgar Square. "All the civilized world mourns . . . the loyal Christian soldier, Gordon," reported *Frank Leslie's Illustrated Newspaper*. Along with the grief came renewed anger at the delay. *The Times* of London remarked, "Everything has been done that could be done to add to the risks of defeat. Advice has been spurned, time wasted, and opportunity lost."

By autumn 1885, al-Mahdi's forces controlled Sudan, though al-Mahdi had died of typhus in June. His successor ruled Sudan until 1898, when British and Egyptian troops reconquered it.

On the other side of the world, the leader of the Saskatchewan Rebellion was, like al-Mahdi, regarded by his followers as a savior. This man, Louis Riel, became known as the messiah of the *métis* (people of mixed French and Indian descent). *Leslie's* newspaper said, "He gives out that he is the High Priest, Prophet, Messiah, etc. . . . He is the American El Mahdi."

The métis were the descendants of early French traders who married Indian women and led lives that borrowed from both cultures. They hunted buffalo and raised crops on Canada's vast western prairie. By the 1880's, English-speaking settlers began to move into the prairie and take land from the French-speaking métis, who held no legal title to their farms.

Muhammad Ahmed, a Muslim holy man who called himself *al-Mahdi* (the Guide), led a successful uprising in 1885 against the Egyptian rulers of Sudan.

The Canadian government, though it acknowledged that the métis had a claim to the land they worked, was slow to survey their holdings and slower still to issue official deeds. When surveyors finally arrived, they ignored the arrangement of métis farms, which had been laid out on the old French plan of strips reaching back from the riverfronts. Instead, the surveyors insisted on dividing the land into square sections. Valentin Végreville, a Roman Catholic priest in Batoche, a village in central Saskatchewan, complained to the government: "These inflexible limits, right-lines and parallels will traverse fields, pass through houses, cut off farm houses from the fields connected with them . . . . What deplorable results must flow from all this!"

The métis repeatedly petitioned the government for sensible surveys, legal titles to their lands, and a voice in their own affairs. But their appeals received little attention, and they turned in desperation to Louis Riel. A métis himself, Riel had been banished from Canada after leading a successful métis revolt in Manitoba in 1869 and 1870. In 1884, a group led by a métis hunter named Gabriel Dumont rode to Montana, where Riel was teaching Indian children

Grover Cleveland's 1885 inauguration as President of the United States is celebrated with fireworks near the new Washington Monument, *above,* and an inaugural ball, *top left;* and the new President is besieged by jobseekers, *top right.*

at a mission school. Dumont's group persuaded Riel to come to Saskatchewan to take up their cause.

Riel made powerful speeches urging the métis to stand up for their rights. On March 16, 1885, he told a métis audience that "God will draw His hand over the face of the sun" to show support for them. As if by magic, the sky darkened and a shadow moved across the sun. Few métis could read, but Riel was well educated and had seen a prediction of a partial solar eclipse for that day.

A few days later, Riel helped the métis form a provisional government with Dumont as head of the army. Riel sent an ultimatum to the North-West Mounted Police at Fort Carlton, Saskatchewan, threatening to attack the fort if they did not surrender. The Mounties did not wait for an attack but marched out to meet the rebels at nearby Duck Lake. Like other frontier people, the métis were skilled riders and sharpshooters. They surrounded the Mounties, inflicted heavy casualties, and forced them to retreat.

The defeat of the famous Mounties stunned Canada and aroused the government to quick action. It assembled a force of nearly 8,000 troops to crush the revolt. During Riel's first rebellion in 1869-1870, the army had taken weeks to march to Manitoba and put down the uprising. This time, the government turned to the new Canadian Pacific Railway, Canada's uncompleted coast-to-coast railroad.

The Canadian Pacific was teetering on the edge of bankruptcy and begging for a government-backed loan. Its general manager,

William C. Van Horne, saw his chance to prove the railroad's value to Canada and thus win financial support. He promised the government that he would move soldiers and supplies to the scene in 11 days. The railroad had several gaps, so Van Horne organized shuttles of horse-drawn sleighs to carry the troops between segments of track. He met his deadline, and the grateful Canadian Parliament approved loans and other financial aid to complete the railroad.

In May, the government troops attacked Batoche, which had become the rebels' main stronghold, with an army that outnumbered the métis by more than 3 to 1. The rebels' ammunition ran so low that they had to retrieve spent bullets from the battlefield at night to reload their rifles the next day. After the bullets ran out, they fired nails, pebbles, and even metal buttons. The métis surrendered after four days. Dumont escaped to the United States, where he eventually became a star of Buffalo Bill's Wild West show. Riel gave himself up and was charged with high treason.

At Riel's trial, his lawyers tried to prove him not guilty by reason of insanity. Historians disagree on whether Riel was sane. He firmly believed that God had chosen him to save the métis from destruction. He also claimed that he was a prophet and a descendant of the Biblical King David. A physician who examined Riel reported, "He suffers under hallucinations on political and religious subjects, but on other points I believe him to be quite sensible and can distinguish right from wrong."

Railroads fill the news in the spring of 1885. Canadian troops rest while the new Canadian Pacific Railway, *above left,* carries them west in April to crush the Saskatchewan Rebellion. In March, the Noble Order of the Knights of Labor stops a train, *above,* during a successful strike against railroads owned by financier Jay Gould.

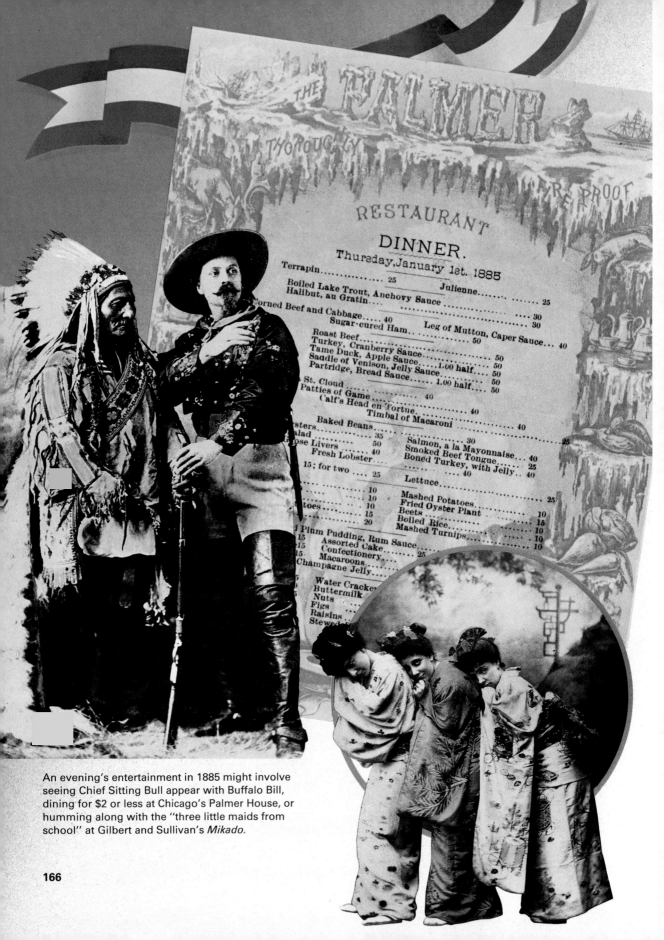

THE PALMER

THOROUGHLY FIRE PROOF

RESTAURANT

DINNER.

Thursday, January 1st, 1885

Terrapin.............. 25   Julienne........ 25
Boiled Lake Trout, Anchovy Sauce
Halibut, au Gratin................ 30
Corned Beef and Cabbage..... 40   30
Sugar-cured Ham............ Leg of Mutton, Caper Sauce... 40
                          50
Roast Beef......................... 50
Turkey, Cranberry Sauce............ 50
Tame Duck, Apple Sauce........1.00 half.. 50
Saddle of Venison, Jelly Sauce....... 50
Partridge, Bread Sauce......1.00 half.... 50
St. Cloud.................... 40
Patties of Game.........
Calf's Head en Tortue....... 40
                  Timbal of Macaroni........ 40
        Baked Beans.....
Oysters............. 35   30
Salad..........   Salmon, a la Mayonnaise... 40   25
Goose Livers....... 50   Smoked Beef Tongue... 25
Fresh Lobster...   Boned Turkey, with Jelly.. 40
15; for two 25
                          Lettuce.
.... 10
.... 10   Mashed Potatoes........... 25
Potatoes...... 10   Fried Oyster Plant
.... 15   Beets............ 10
.... 20   Boiled Rice........ 15
                          Mashed Turnips....... 10
d Plum Pudding, Rum Sauce.....   10
.15   Assorted Cake.....
.15   Confectionery..... 25
.15   Macaroons.....
Champagne Jelly.....
                  Water Cracker
                  Buttermilk
                  Nuts
                  Figs
                  Raisins
                  Stewed

An evening's entertainment in 1885 might involve seeing Chief Sitting Bull appear with Buffalo Bill, dining for $2 or less at Chicago's Palmer House, or humming along with the "three little maids from school" at Gilbert and Sullivan's *Mikado*.

166

Riel himself protested efforts to brand him insane. In a dramatic speech to the jury, he declared, "I acted reasonably and in self-defense, while the Government, my aggressor, . . . acted madly and wrong." The court found Riel guilty and sentenced him to death.

Prime Minister John A. Macdonald rejected appeals from French Canadians to spare Riel's life, saying, "He shall hang though every dog in Quebec bark in his favour." Riel was hanged on Nov. 16, 1885, in Regina, Sask. When news of the execution reached Montreal, Que., the largest French-Canadian city, it exploded with angry demonstrations. A huge crowd marched to the main square with a banner reading, "Riel, the Martyr and Hero" and hanged a dummy representing Macdonald. The death of the métis leader left a legacy of hostility between French- and English-speaking Canadians that undermined Canadian unity for generations.

Meanwhile, on November 7, just nine days before Riel met his death, the Canadian Pacific Railway was finally completed. The westward line met the eastward line at Craigellachie, B.C. A crowd of workers watched as one of the railroad's directors drove the last spike, which General Manager Van Horne had insisted should be ordinary iron, not silver or gold. Van Horne's speech also reflected his love of simplicity: "All I can say is that the work has been done well in every way."

Sharpshooter Annie Oakley, who joined Buffalo Bill's Wild West show in 1885, tries a trick shot over her shoulder.

While Canada struggled with the Saskatchewan Rebellion, the United States entered a new era with the inauguration on March 4, 1885, of Grover Cleveland, the first Democratic President since the Civil War. His election represented a protest against the corruption that had plagued Republican administrations since the war, and the American people looked to Cleveland for a fresh start.

Like other newly elected Presidents, Cleveland was besieged by jobseekers. He told a reporter, "I go to bed after a long day with the feeling that I must be the meanest man in the world, for I seem to say only 'no.' "

Cleveland tried to steer a middle course between reformers, who called for a clean sweep of the civil service system, and Democratic politicians, who hungered for jobs after nearly 25 years out of power. He more than doubled the number of workers who held government jobs through the merit system. But many reform-minded Republicans who had crossed party lines to support Cleveland were displeased because Democrats got the best jobs.

After a business slump in 1884, economic growth in the United States resumed in 1885. Many new businesses were established, including some that are major companies today. The American Telephone and Telegraph Company (AT&T), which became the largest communications firm in the world, was chartered in New York state on March 3, 1885. The Burroughs Corporation, a leading office products company, got its start that year in St. Louis when a young bank clerk named William S. Burroughs patented his first adding

Births of notable persons in 1885 included:

Berg, Alban (1885–1935), Austrian composer who worked with a 12-tone musical scale.

Bohr, Niels (1885–1962), Danish physicist whose theory of the atom became the foundation of modern nuclear physics.

Durant, Will (1885–1981), American historian best known for his 11-volume series *The Story of Civilization.*

Kern, Jerome (1885–1945), American composer who wrote such famous songs as "Ol' Man River" and "Smoke Gets in Your Eyes."

Klemperer, Otto (1885–1973), German-born orchestra conductor.

Lardner, Ring (1885–1933), American writer best known for his humorous short stories.

Lawrence, D. H. (1885–1930), British writer who examined male-female relationships in such novels as *Women in Love* (1920) and *Lady Chatterley's Lover* (1928).

Lewis, Sinclair (1885–1951), American author whose novel *Main Street* (1920) satirizes small-town life.

Morton, Jelly Roll (Ferdinand Joseph Morton) (1885–1941), American pianist and composer who claimed he invented jazz.

Patton, George S., Jr. (1885–1945), U.S. Army general during World War II.

Pound, Ezra L. (1885–1972), American poet best known for his epic *Cantos.*

machine. The first issue of *Good Housekeeping* magazine was published on May 2 by Clark W. Bryan, a Massachusetts newspaper editor. Early issues of the magazine had no illustrations but provided a lively mixture of household hints, recipes, fashion advice, puzzles, quiz games, poetry, and fiction. John Meyenberg, a Swiss-born inventor, manufactured the first evaporated milk on June 25 in Highland, Ill. The company he founded, the Helvetia Milk Condensing Company, became the Pet Milk Company (now Pet, Incorporated).

Other business innovations of 1885 are also commonplace today. Marshall Field & Company, a Chicago department store, opened the first bargain basement, where it sold inexpensive fabrics, household linens, and clothing advertised as "Specially Attractive Bargains." The U.S. Post Office established special delivery service on March 3, 1885, but the service was slow to win customers. *The Nation* commented in October 1885, "People generally continue to rely upon the telegraph or the private-messenger service for the transmission of any message where haste is essential, rather than take their chances at the hands of the postal authorities."

Of all the new products introduced in 1885, the gasoline engine has had the biggest impact on modern life. Karl Benz and Gottlieb Daimler, two German engineers working independently, designed and built internal-combustion engines that were basically the same as those used in automobiles today. Daimler powered a bicycle with his engine, creating the first motorcycle, while Benz installed his in a three-wheeled carriage that became one of the first gasoline-powered automobiles. The 1885 Benz had many features that a modern driver would find familiar, including electric ignition, a water-cooled engine, and a carburetor to mix vaporized fuel and air. The car's top speed of only 8 miles per hour did not save Karl Benz from having what was probably history's first automobile accident. During a public demonstration of his car in 1885, he forgot to steer and ran the vehicle into a brick wall.

The American labor movement, still in its infancy in 1885, achieved one of its first major successes that year. In March, a group called the Noble Order of the Knights of Labor led a strike against railroads owned by financier Jay Gould to protest a 10 per cent cut in pay. Gould had once said, "I can hire one half of the working class to kill the other half." But in 1885 he had financial problems and could not afford a lengthy strike, so he restored the workers' wages. "No such victory," exclaimed the St. Louis *Chronicle*, "has ever been secured in this or any other country." The successful strike set off a stampede to join the Knights. Within a year, the organization's membership shot up from about 100,000 to more than 700,000.

Higher education made many advances in 1885, with a number of colleges and universities being founded by churches, other private organizations, states, and wealthy individuals. Railroad builder

Leland Stanford founded Stanford University in California that year, endowing it with more than $20 million plus land for a campus. "It is Senator Stanford's intention to make this institution the best in this country or Europe," said *Leslie's*. Other colleges and universities established that year included the University of Arizona in Tucson; Arizona State University in Tempe; Bryn Mawr College in Bryn Mawr, Pa.; Georgia Institute of Technology in Atlanta; Goucher College in Towson, Md.; and Macalaster College in St. Paul, Minn.

The world's first skyscraper, the Home Insurance Building, was completed in Chicago in 1885. The architect, William Le Baron Jenney, gave the building a frame of iron and steel, and walls that hung like curtains on the frame. Although the Home Insurance Building stood only 10 stories high, it was the first tall building supported entirely by a skeletonlike metal frame instead of by thick walls—which is why architects consider it the first skyscraper. It was demolished in 1931.

The distinction of being the world's tallest structure belonged to the new Washington Monument in Washington, D.C., which was dedicated on Feb. 21, 1885. The great stone shaft, rising 555 feet 5⅛ inches, could be seen for miles. The tip of the monument consisted of 100 ounces of aluminum, the largest and costliest block of the new metal ever cast. The aluminum cap was so unusual that it was displayed at Tiffany's jewelry store in New York City before being installed. People went to Tiffany's to jump over the tip so that they could say they had leaped over the top of the world's tallest building. Despite its height, the Washington Monument aroused little enthusiasm. *Leslie's* called it "the unsightly pile on the Potomac," and *Harper's New Monthly Magazine* said, "The huge shaft is in itself a rather meaningless memorial of a great man."

Louis Pasteur, a brilliant French chemist, created his own memorial with a medical breakthrough that was to save the lives of thousands of children. On a hot July day in 1885, a 9-year-old German boy named Joseph Meister was bitten 14 times by a rabid dog. The boy's doctors believed they could do nothing except wait for him to die of rabies, a deadly disease spread by the bite of infected animals. The boy's parents went to Pasteur, who had developed a vaccine that prevented rabies in animals, and begged him to save their son. Pasteur hesitated to use his treatment on a human being, but he finally agreed. After 13 daily injections and weeks of anxious waiting, the vaccine proved successful. The boy remained well, and Pasteur became a medical hero to the world.

Pasteur's vaccine got another trial in November, when six children in Newark, N.J., were bitten by a dog that was foaming at the mouth. Their physician had closely followed Pasteur's research and cabled the scientist in Paris. The reply came: "If you think there is danger, send children immediately.—PASTEUR."

Deaths of notable persons in 1885 included:

Billings, Josh (Henry Wheeler Shaw) (1818–1885), American humorist and essayist.

Cooper, Anthony Ashley (1801–1885), Earl of Shaftesbury, British social reformer who worked for better treatment of the poor and the insane.

Damrosch, Leopold (1832–1885), Prussian-born orchestra conductor who founded the New York Symphony Society.

Gordon, Charles G. (1833–1885), British military leader who died defending Khartoum, Sudan's capital.

Grant, Ulysses S. (1822–1885), general who led the Union Army to victory in the Civil War and later became 18th President of the United States.

Hugo, Victor M. (1802–1885), French poet, playwright, and novelist who was a leading figure in French romanticism.

Jackson, Helen Hunt (1830–1885), American author whose most famous novel, *Ramona* (1884), dramatized the plight of American Indians.

McClellan, George B. (1826–1885), Union Army general during the Civil War.

McCloskey, John Cardinal (1810–1885), Roman Catholic archbishop of New York City who was responsible for building St. Patrick's Cathedral.

Vanderbilt, William H. (1821–1885), American railroad executive.

Jumbo the elephant, the largest animal in captivity, lies near the railroad track in Ontario, Canada, where a freight train killed him in September 1885.

The Newark doctor began a drive to raise money to send his little patients to Paris. *Leslie's* reported, "The spontaneous generosity of the people of Newark and elsewhere made his task an easy one, even the Sunday-schools of the city contributing to the fund." The children sailed for France in early December. By January 1886, Pasteur pronounced them cured. *Leslie's* added, "They may, in Pasteur's opinion, safely report to New Jersey, and, if they choose, get bitten by mad dogs without further danger."

Without radio, television, or motion pictures, most entertainment in 1885 was provided by live performers. People flocked to theaters, opera houses, and music halls. One of the year's greatest successes was *The Mikado*, a new operetta by Sir William S. Gilbert and Sir Arthur S. Sullivan, which opened at London's Savoy Theatre on March 14. The operetta, set in Japan, poked fun at officials who try to assume too much authority. *Harper's* said, "The whole world goes and laughs at *The Mikado*, and goes constantly and with unflagging delight."

The Boston Pops Orchestra was founded that year to provide summer jobs for musicians from the Boston Symphony Orchestra. The Pops presented concerts of light classical and popular music, and its performances remain a beloved summertime tradition 100 years later.

Another show-business success was Buffalo Bill's Wild West show. Its founder and star, William F. Cody, steadily added new attractions to his troupe. In 1885, he hired an Ohio farm girl named Annie Oakley as a sharpshooter. She could shoot a cigarette from her husband's lips or hit a dime tossed into the air. But Cody's most sensational addition that year was Sitting Bull, the Sioux chief whose warriors had defeated Lieutenant Colonel George A. Custer in the Battle of the Little Bighorn in 1876. The chief signed on for $50 a week, much of which he gave to children who hung around the show. Sitting Bull gave Annie Oakley a nickname that stuck to her ever afterward. Watching the petite sharpshooter, who stood only 5 feet tall, he repeatedly exclaimed "*Watanya cicilia*," Sioux words meaning Little Sure Shot.

P. T. Barnum's circus lost one of its star attractions in 1885. Jumbo the elephant, the largest animal in captivity at more than 11 feet tall, was killed by a railroad train in Canada near St. Thomas, Ont., on September 15. Jumbo's keeper was leading him along the track to load him into his railroad car when a speeding freight train rounded a curve and hit the animal. "The king of elephants has met with a sudden and untimely death," *Leslie's* said. *Scientific American* commented, "He made many friends, who will mourn with his disconsolate keeper over his untimely fate." Barnum told reporters, "The loss is tremendous," but the master showman made use of Jumbo even in death. For the next two seasons, carts bearing the elephant's skeleton and stuffed hide led Barnum's circus parade, followed by trained elephants holding black-bordered cloths in their trunks and wiping their eyes.

Many literary masterpieces were published in 1885, including *Germinal* by French writer Émile Zola, a novel about the life of coal miners. Among the other noteworthy books of the year were two children's classics by British writers—Robert Louis Stevenson's *A Child's Garden of Verses*, a collection of poems written from a child's point of view, and H. Rider Haggard's *King Solomon's Mines*, a story about a search for the legendary lost treasure of the Biblical King Solomon. Probably the greatest book of the year was Mark Twain's *Adventures of Huckleberry Finn*, which was not published in the United States until 1885 though it had come out the previous year in Great Britain. It describes the adventures of the runaway boy Huck and the escaped slave Jim as they travel by raft down the Mississippi River. Trustees of the public library in Concord, Mass., banned the novel from their shelves because they believed it was morally damaging for young people. Twain was delighted at the publicity, which he called "a rattling tiptop puff." "They have expelled *Huck* from their library as 'trash suitable only for the slums,' " he said. "That will sell 25,000 copies for us sure." Despite praise from critics for *Huckleberry Finn*, efforts to ban the book have continued through the years. Many parent groups have found it racially offensive and tried to remove it from school libraries.

Another book that ran into trouble with censors in 1885 was a new translation of *The Arabian Nights* by the British explorer Sir Richard Francis Burton. *The Arabian Nights*, a collection of folk tales from the Middle East and Asia, includes the adventures of Aladdin, Ali Baba, and Sinbad, as well as some bawdy stories. "The fact is, this book, the greatest literary curiosity of the age, is unfit for publication," *Leslie's* declared in December 1885. A judge in Cairo, Egypt, reached the same conclusion 100 years later. In May 1985, the judge ruled the book obscene and ordered more than 3,000 copies destroyed. He proved once again that, as President Harry S. Truman said, "The only thing new in the world is the history you don't know."

The Year
on File

Contributors to THE WORLD BOOK YEAR BOOK report on the major developments of 1985. The contributors' names appear at the end of the articles they have written, and a complete roster of contributors, listing their professional affiliations and the articles they have written, is on pages 6 and 7.

A quiz on some events of 1985 as reported in various Year on File articles appears on pages 174 and 175.

Articles in this section are arranged alphabetically by subject matter. In most cases, the article titles are the same as those of the articles in THE WORLD BOOK ENCYCLOPEDIA that they update. The numerous cross-references (in **bold type**) guide the reader to a subject or information that may be in some other article or that may appear under an alternative title. "See" and "See also" cross-references appear within and at the end of articles to direct the reader to related information elsewhere in THE YEAR BOOK. "In WORLD BOOK, see" references point the reader to articles in the encyclopedia that provide background information to the year's events reported in THE YEAR BOOK.

See "Latin America," page 373.

The Year
on File Quiz

THE YEAR BOOK presents a quiz on some events of 1985 as reported in various articles in the Year on File. Answers appear on page 527.

1. In a January ruling, the Supreme Court of the United States said school officials may take what action with students whom they suspect of violating laws or school rules?

2. Why did Vice President George H. W. Bush become acting President for nearly eight hours on July 13?

3. In July, a New Hampshire high-school teacher named Sharon Christa McAuliffe was chosen for what unusual honor?

4. The man below broke one of the oldest records in professional baseball in September. Who is he, and what record did he break?

5. Where did a cyclone and tidal wave kill at least 10,000 people in May?

6. What is the name of the newest U.S. space shuttle, which made its first flight in October?

7. What two young West German athletes in April and July won major tournaments never before won by athletes from their country?

8. In February, Edwin Meese III won Senate confirmation in a post to which he was first nominated more than a year ago. What was the post?

9. Why did women from more than 150 nations go to Nairobi, Kenya, in July?

10. A grueling world championship contest was called off in February after 48 games that lasted nearly five months, only to resume in September and end in November. What championship was it, and who won?

11. What is Live Aid?
    a. A beverage used to replenish body fluids and salts lost during exercise.
    b. A rock concert that raised millions of dollars for African famine relief.
    c. The virus that causes acquired immune deficiency syndrome (AIDS).

12. Tancredo de Almeida Neves, elected in January as president of Brazil, never took office. Why not?

13. Two former Navy officers who are brothers, a Navy seaman who is one officer's son, and a family friend were arrested in May and June on what charges?

14. The first free-trade pact in U.S. history, signed in April, will eliminate tariffs between the United States and what other nation by 1995?

15. The remains of the man scientists believe to be Nazi war criminal Josef Mengele were found in what country?

16. In April, drinking milk turned out to be bad for the health of about 18,000 people in Illinois and neighboring states. Why?

17. In May, Representative Frank McCloskey (D., Ind.) took his seat in the House. What was unusual about his election?

18. What is Radio Martí?

19. In April, the Soviet Union and its Eastern European allies extended for 20 years a military treaty that they signed in a Polish town in 1955. What is the treaty called?

20. Match the locations on the left below with the descriptions on the right.

New Caledonia	research center in Japan
Tsukuba	island in the South Pacific
Johannesburg	town in West Germany
Bitburg	state in India
Punjab	city in South Africa

21. Why were English soccer teams barred in June from international competition?

22. What U.S. action in October caused Egyptian President Hosni Mubarak to demand a public apology from President Ronald Reagan?

23. What caused the fire in Philadelphia in May that killed 11 people and destroyed 61 houses?

24. Who is Yelena G. Bonner?

25. What household appliance was also the nickname of a professional athlete who made headlines in the fall of 1985?

26. The Italian and Tunisian officials shown below in February are signing a peace treaty marking the official end of what war?

27. Why is this Austrian wine being tested?
28. What is the austral?
29. What 1985 motion picture made the most money at the box office?
30. Did the Supreme Court of the United States uphold or overturn the following state laws:
    a. An Alabama law authorizing a period of silence "for meditation or voluntary prayer" in public schools.
    b. A Connecticut law giving employees the right not to work on the Sabbath day of their choice.
    c. Michigan and New York laws sending public school teachers to provide remedial and enrichment instruction in parochial schools.
31. What major city in August passed a law banning discrimination against victims of AIDS?
32. It is not unusual for congressmen to travel at government expense, so what was out of the ordinary about a government-sponsored trip that Senator Edwin Jacob (Jake) Garn (D., Utah) took in April?
33. Peru's new President Alan García Pérez startled the financial world with a bold statement at his inauguration in July. What did he say?
34. What noted actor died in October, 10 weeks after announcing that he had AIDS?
35. What major city in July approved a zoning law that limits the height, size, and number of buildings that can be erected downtown?
36. Who is the carpenter in the striped shirt?

37. What young British couple made headlines in November on their first visit together to the United States?
38. When is the renovation of the Statue of Liberty scheduled to be completed?
39. Why was Amy Carter, daughter of former President Jimmy Carter, arrested in April?
40. What caused the governor of Ohio to close state-insured thrift institutions for several days in March, and the governor of Maryland in May to impose a limit on withdrawals from privately insured thrift accounts?
41. What United States company said in April that it would change the taste of its product for the first time in 99 years?
42. Who is this singer, who ended her opera career in January by performing Aïda, the role that made her a star 25 years ago?

43. What superpower in March 1985 got its third new leader since 1982?
44. What country was struck by two killer earthquakes in two days in September?
45. The first products manufactured in space went on sale in July. What were they?
46. In March, it was announced that Portugal and Spain would become the 11th and 12th members of what organization?
47. In January, violence erupted on two islands usually considered tropical paradises—one in the Caribbean and one in the South Pacific. What are the two islands, and what was the cause of unrest on each?
48. January and February brought to an end two court cases in which military leaders sued news media for libel. Who were the military leaders, whom were they suing, and what happened in their cases?
49. A major manufacturer announced in July that it would build a plant near Spring Hill, Tenn., to produce the Saturn, its first new brand name since the 1920's. Who is the manufacturer, and what is Saturn?
50. Interest in sunken treasure soared as a result of what discovery in July?

ABRAHAM, F. MURRAY

ABRAHAM, F. MURRAY (1939?-   ), won the Academy of Motion Picture Arts and Sciences Award for best actor on March 25, 1985. The award honored his performance in *Amadeus* as Antonio Salieri, a composer of the 1700's who was Wolfgang Amadeus Mozart's rival. The part was Abraham's first starring role in a motion picture.

Fahrid Murray Abraham was born in El Paso, Tex., of Syrian and Italian parents. He began acting in high school. He won a drama scholarship to the University of Texas in El Paso but left after two years to pursue an acting career in Los Angeles. In 1965, he moved to New York City.

Abraham played supporting roles in a number of Broadway and off-Broadway productions, including *The Man in the Glass Booth* (1968), *Little Murders* (1969), and *The Ritz* (1975). In 1979, he won his first starring role on Broadway—portraying a man who is a bumbler by day and a great lover by night—in *Teibele and Her Demon*.

Abraham played his first major role in a motion picture as Omar the gangster in the 1983 remake of *Scarface*. His other film credits include *The Sunshine Boys* (1975), *The Prisoner of Second Avenue* (1975), *All the President's Men* (1976), *The Ritz* (1976), and *Serpico* (1976). He also has appeared in several television shows.

Abraham married Kate Hannan in 1962. They have a daughter and a son.   Barbara A. Mayes

ADVERTISING. The advertising/marketing event of 1985 in the United States concerned the decision by the Coca-Cola Company to change its formula for Coke. The soft-drink giant, celebrating its 99th anniversary in 1985, announced the taste change in New York City on April 23. Details of the new formula were not released, but the general impression was that the new Coke was sweeter and less carbonated than the old version.

Coca-Cola reportedly budgeted $100 million for advertising and promotion of the new product during its first year. Throughout May and June, Coke ran an aggressive ad campaign claiming that the new Coke tasted better than its archrival, Pepsi-Cola. Pepsi's advertising, in turn, mocked the change. One Pepsi commercial boasted, "In the showdown between the colas, one fact stands clear: One cola's changed and one cola's chosen."

The taste change brought angry reaction and organized protests by people who preferred the old Coke. Within a few weeks of the announcement, several groups sprang up whose purpose was to force the Coca-Cola Company to bring back the original formula. On July 10, the company suddenly announced that it would revive the old formula and market it under the name Coca-Cola Classic. The company continued offering the new Coke also, thus satisfying devotees of both formulas. Marketing analysts speculated that the Coca-Cola Company, in a masterly marketing move, may have intended all along to reintroduce the original formula—though Coke officials denied it. In any case, the company emerged with a new product and a great deal of publicity. See FOOD (Close-Up).

Alcohol and Tobacco Marketing. Various groups lobbied Congress in 1985 to ban celebrity endorsements of beer and wine in radio and television advertisements. The groups argued that such celebrity endorsements glamorized drinking and helped lead to such problems as alcoholism and drunken driving. Since the 1950's, the U.S. Department of the Treasury's Bureau of Alcohol, Tobacco and Firearms has barred active athletes from appearing in beer or wine ads. The proposed change, however, would extend this ban to retired athletes and other celebrities. At year's end, Congress had not acted on the matter.

In April, the U.S. Federal Trade Commission (FTC) ruled that there was no need for it to regulate alcoholic beverage marketing practices. The decision came in response to petitioners concerned that certain marketing practices encouraged alcohol abuse.

In December, the American Medical Association (AMA) called for a ban on all cigarette advertising. Federal law has banned broadcast cigarette ads

"UHHH...THIS WEEK IT'S AEROBICS."

WE'RE WAITING TO HEAR YOUR LATEST EXCUSE FOR NOT GIVING BLOOD.
It better be a dilly. Because we've heard them all. From "I just got back from Monaco" to "I gave 6 months ago." It's all too easy to chicken out from doing something that's so important and worthwhile. Knowing that you helped save a life is a feeling that's worth more than the few minutes out of your day it takes to give blood. Please, don't chicken out.

EXCUSES DON'T SAVE LIVES. BLOOD DOES.

American Red Cross ✚

"Don't chicken out—give blood," is the message of this public service ad prepared by the Ad Council for the 1985 American Red Cross campaign.

since 1971. The AMA proposal would extend the ban to print and billboard advertising.

Advertising Statistics. In July, Robert J. Coen, senior vice president and director of forecasting for McCann Erickson, Incorporated, a New York City advertising agency, estimated that spending on advertising in the United States in 1985 would be $95.9 billion—up 9.1 per cent from 1984.

According to an annual study conducted by *Advertising Age* magazine, U.S. advertising agencies' worldwide gross income increased by 17.3 per cent in 1984 to $7.23 billion on billings of $49.36-billion. For the fifth consecutive year, Young & Rubicam led all other U.S. ad agencies in worldwide income, with a gross income of $480.1 million on an estimated $3.2 billion in billings. In addition, the agency regained its former status as the world's largest ad agency—based on its 1984 gross income. It bumped Dentsu, Incorporated, of Tokyo into second place with $468.4 million in gross income on $3.48 billion in billings. Dentsu had occupied the top spot since 1973. In third place was Ted Bates Worldwide, with $424.4 million in income on $2.84 billion in billings.

Advertisers. In 1984, Procter & Gamble Company (P & G) spent an estimated $872 million on ads—more than any other U.S. company. Other top advertisers in 1984 were General Motors Corporation in second place with $764 million; Sears Roebuck & Company third with $747 million; Beatrice Companies, Incorporated, fourth with $680 million; and R. J. Reynolds Industries, Incorporated, fifth with $678 million.

When the figures have been counted for 1985, however, P & G may find itself ousted from its usual top spot. With company mergers occurring at a furious pace, the advertising budget of one of the new combined companies may well surpass that of P & G. For example, Reynolds and Nabisco Brands, Incorporated, announced in June that they would merge. Had they merged in 1984, their combined advertising budget would have been $1.01 billion—far outstripping that of P & G and making the new company the first in history to top $1 billion in advertising expenditures in a year.

Ad Agency Mergers. Advertising agencies were not immune to merger fever in 1985. In June, the largest merger in the history of advertising was announced—between D'Arcy MacManus Masius Worldwide and Benton & Bowles, Incorporated, both of New York City. The resulting company, D'Arcy Masius Benton & Bowles, had $2.4 billion in worldwide billings. Another merger, scheduled for January 1986, will join Bozell & Jacobs, Incorporated, with Kenyon & Eckhardt, Incorporated, both of New York City, forming Bozell, Jacobs, Kenyon & Eckhardt.   Jarlath J. Graham

In WORLD BOOK, see ADVERTISING.

AFGHANISTAN. The war between forces of the Soviet Union occupying Afghanistan and the Afghan *mujahedeen* (fighters for the faith) moved toward its sixth anniversary in December 1985, with little change in the positions of the two sides and no progress toward a peace settlement. The Soviet-backed government of Revolutionary Council President Babrak Karmal claimed several times during 1985 to have scored important victories over the mujahedeen, notably the capture in July of the strategic Panjshir Valley north of Kabul. Government forces also claimed to have destroyed villages on the Afghanistan-Pakistan border used as transfer points on the guerrilla supply route. But each time the mujahedeen struck back.

In August, during a major escalation of the war, the mujahedeen besieged the border town of Khost. Soviet-Afghan forces launched a counteroffensive to relieve the town and close the border in Paktia province. Soviet forces relieved Khost in September but suffered heavy casualties and failed to seal the frontier.

Mujahedeen Coordination. Although there was little likelihood that the mujahedeen could defeat the vastly superior Soviet forces, improved training and organization and better weapons enabled them to mount large-scale operations. Coordination among mujahedeen groups also improved measurably. On April 7, rebel groups based in Peshawar, Pakistan, formed a united resistance front. The group's leader, Gulbuddin Hekmatyar, said the front would seek recognition as the legitimate Afghan government from the Organization of the Islamic Conference—an organization of Muslim countries—and the United Nations (UN). In August, the front arranged the first Soviet-mujahedeen prisoner exchange.

In the meantime, the Soviet Union rejected all attempts at outside mediation. Talks between United States and Soviet negotiators, the first since the 1979 invasion, got nowhere. UN negotiator Diego Cordovez opened a fourth round of negotiations between Afghan and Pakistani representatives in June but made little progress toward a political settlement.

Government Affairs. In July, the Karmal government convened the first *Loya Jirga* (national tribal assembly) held since the 1978 Communist revolution in an effort to gain public support. But many tribal leaders refused to attend.

The Karmal government also sponsored local elections in July. But the mujahedeen alliance called the elections a fraud and urged Afghan voters not to participate. In December, the government appointed five non-Communists to important posts. Many of the new officials had strong tribal connections.   William Spencer

See also ASIA (Facts in Brief Table). In WORLD BOOK, see AFGHANISTAN.

AFRICA

The famine crisis, which spread in 1984 to more than one-third of the countries in Africa, moderated considerably in 1985 as rains came to many areas of the continent. The bloody civil disorders that erupted in South Africa in late 1984, however, continued without letup. Nor was there much progress toward ending the long-standing civil wars in Angola, Chad, Ethiopia, and Mozambique. Military coups changed the governments of Nigeria and Uganda, while in Tanzania a new president was selected through peaceful elections.

Famine. At the beginning of 1985, the United Nations (UN) Food and Agriculture Organization (FAO) identified 21 African countries as suffering severe food shortages: Angola, Botswana, Burkina Faso (formerly Upper Volta), Burundi, Cape Verde, Chad, Ethiopia, Kenya, Lesotho, Mali, Mauritania, Morocco, Mozambique, Niger, Rwanda, Senegal, Somalia, Sudan, Tanzania, Zambia, and Zimbabwe. The food deficits resulted primarily from a prolonged drought. But there were other causes as well, including low government-set prices for agricultural products, which discouraged farmers from increasing their output, and inadequate transportation systems—sometimes made worse by military conflicts—that prevented food from getting to needy people.

Virtually all the starving countries needed food donations to help make up their agricultural shortfalls. In Ethiopia, for example, about 6.2 million people received foreign food assistance each month between December 1984 and August 1985. The United States government was the largest single contributor of famine relief, providing some $1.3 billion in assistance to African nations in the fiscal year ending Sept. 30, 1985.

The Rains Come at Last. The terrible drought finally broke in most parts of Africa in mid-1985. Harvests were good in many countries, including Niger, Somalia, Tanzania, and Zimbabwe, and the FAO predicted that only six countries—Angola, Botswana, Ethiopia, Lesotho, Mozambique, and Sudan—would continue to need relief assistance on a large scale. In those six nations, however, the total number of famine victims was still tragically high—an estimated 21.4 million.

Racial Violence in South Africa. The wave of violent demonstrations begun by blacks in September 1984 against the racial policies of the South

Mourners near Uitenhage, South Africa, carry the coffins of 27 blacks who were killed in clashes with police to burial grounds in April.

African government continued throughout 1985. According to official counts, about 1,000 black people had died in clashes with police—and, often, with other blacks—by year-end. The initial cause of the discord was government-imposed rent increases black tenants believed were unfair. But demonstrations against the rent hikes soon evolved into a general protest against *apartheid*, the white-imposed system of racial segregation.

On September 12, a committee appointed by South Africa's State President Pieter Willem Botha recommended that the government eliminate the so-called pass laws, which prohibit the presence of blacks in white-dominated urban areas except as temporary workers authorized to live in nearby black townships. And on September 30, Botha announced tentative plans for political reform that would allow blacks for the first time to elect representatives to the central government. Botha implied, however, that the white minority would continue to control the government.

Namibia. The United States encouraged negotiations between South Africa and Angola over the future of Namibia (formerly called South West Africa), a territory administered by South Africa that borders Angola. South Africa insisted that the approximately 25,000 Cuban troops stationed in Angola had to be sent home before it would agree to a cease-fire with Namibian nationalist guerrillas and to UN-supervised elections in Namibia. The negotiators seemed to be making progress toward satisfying South Africa's demand. In late May, however, Angola terminated the talks after South African commandos were apprehended near an Angolan oil installation.

Rather than hold internationally supervised elections in Namibia, South Africa on June 17 appointed an interim government for the territory. But the Namibian political movement with the largest following, the South West Africa People's Organization (SWAPO), was excluded from the new government because it backed the guerrillas.

Civil Wars persisted in Angola and Mozambique, and the governments of those two countries accused South Africa of aiding their rebel adversaries. After repeated denials of those charges, South Africa admitted in late September that it had provided military supplies to both the Mozambique National Resistance (MNR) movement and to its counterpart in Angola, the National Union for the Total Independence of Angola (UNITA). In return, the rebels helped to keep border areas of their countries from being used as military bases by South African black nationalists.

Guerrilla wars also continued against the central governments of Chad, Ethiopia, and Uganda.

A policeman in Beida, Sudan, forces hungry villagers back with a whip in July as they push toward a grain shipment from the Save the Children Fund.

Beside leaders of Niger and Tanzania, UN Secretary-General Javier Pérez de Cuéllar, right, opens a meeting on African famine in March in Geneva.

France, aided by the leaders of Congo, Gabon, and Mali, tried to arrange a negotiated settlement between the warring factions in Chad, but those efforts proved fruitless. In Uganda, military leaders who overthrew President Milton Obote in a July coup asked the main rebel force, the National Resistance Army (NRA), to lay down its arms and join the new government. The two sides signed a peace agreement on December 17. In Ethiopia, rebels in Eritrea and Tigre provinces continued military operations against the government.

Mali Attacks Burkina Faso. On December 25, Burkina Faso said several of its villages had been attacked by troops and planes from Mali. This was the latest incident in a 25-year border dispute between the two former French colonies. The two nations signed a cease-fire pact on December 30.

Military Coups. The coup in Uganda was the fifth since that country became independent in 1962. The army officers who seized control of government charged that President Obote had favored members of his own ethnic group and brutally suppressed political opposition. The NRA claimed, however, that the new government's leaders were biased toward their own ethnic groups.

On August 27, Nigeria experienced its fifth coup since gaining independence in 1960. A group of military officers deposed Nigeria's head of state, Major General Muhammadu Buhari, on the grounds that Buhari had failed to revive the nation's economy and had violated the human rights of hundreds of citizens. On December 20, the new government announced that it had foiled an attempted coup and arrested many military officers, including three senior army generals, charged with plotting the coup.

Coups also failed in Guinea, Comoros, and Liberia. In Guinea, Colonel Diarra Traore seized the radio station in the capital, Conakry, on the night of July 4 and announced the formation of a new government. Although supported by police units, Traore and his followers were captured later that night by military forces loyal to President and Prime Minister Lansana Conté, who was in Togo at the time. Traore had been second-in-command in the April 1984 coup that brought Conté to power and had served as Conté's prime minister, but he was demoted to minister of education in December 1984. In the days following the attempted coup, about 200 people were arrested.

As in Guinea, the abortive coup in Comoros—a nation of several small islands off the east coast of Africa—occurred when the president was out of the country. On March 8, members of President Ahmed Abdallah Abderemane's presidential guard mutinied, but loyal troops suppressed the uprising.

Facts in Brief on African Political Units

Country	Population	Government	Monetary Unit*	Foreign Trade (million U.S. $) Exports†	Imports†
Algeria	22,611,000	President Chadli Bendjedid; Prime Minister Abdelhamid Brahimi	dinar (4.7 = $1)	11,163	10,395
Angola	8,256,000	President José Eduardo dos Santos	kwanza (29.9 = $1)	1,600	1,500
Benin	4,135,000	President Mathieu Kerekou	CFA franc (383.4 = $1)	304	590
Bophuthatswana	1,300,000	President & Prime Minister Lucas Mangope	rand (2.7 = $1)	no statistics available	
Botswana	1,118,000	President Quett K. J. Masire	pula (2 = $1)	673	554
Burkina Faso (Upper Volta)	7,083,000	National Council of Revolution President Thomas Sankara	CFA franc (383.4 = $1)	57	288
Burundi	4,759,000	President Jean-Baptiste Bagaza	franc (111 = $1)	148	187
Cameroon	9,826,000	President Paul Biya	CFA franc (383.4 = $1)	886	1,112
Cape Verde	326,000	President Aristides Pereira; Prime Minister Pedro Pires	escudo (88.9 = $1)	1.6	68
Central African Republic	2,625,000	National Recovery Committee President & Prime Minister André-Dieudonné Kolingba	CFA franc (383.4 = $1)	115	137
Chad	5,129,000	President Hissein Habré	CFA franc (383.4 = $1)	78	99
Ciskei	660,000	President Lennox Sebe	rand (2.7 = $1)	no statistics available	
Comoros	468,000	President Ahmed Abdallah Abderemane; Prime Minister Ali Mroudjae	CFA franc (383.4 = $1)	18	19
Congo	1,784,000	President Denis Sassou-Nguesso; Prime Minister Ange Edouard Poungui	CFA franc (383.4 = $1)	1,066	806
Djibouti	299,000	President Hassan Gouled Aptidon; Prime Minister Barkat Gourad Hamadou	franc (149.9 = $1)	108	179
Egypt	47,968,000	President Hosni Mubarak; Prime Minister Ali Lotfy	pound (1 = $1.23)	3,215	10,274
Equatorial Guinea	289,000	President Teodoro Obiang Nguema Mbasogo; Prime Minister Cristino Seriche Bioko	ekuele (383.4 = $1)	17	41
Ethiopia	33,468,000	Provisional Military Administrative Council & Council of Ministers Chairman Mengistu Haile-Mariam	birr (2 = $1)	416	942
Gabon	1,034,000	President Omar Bongo; Prime Minister Léon Mébiame	CFA franc (383.4 = $1)	1,975	853
Gambia	733,000	President Sir Dawda Kairaba Jawara	dalasi (3.4 = $1)	66	87
Ghana	13,892,000	Provisional National Defense Council Chairman Jerry John Rawlings	cedi (54.6 = $1)	2,029	2,534
Guinea	5,889,000	President and Prime Minister Lansana Conté	syli (22.3 = $1)	537	403
Guinea-Bissau	873,000	President João Bernardo Vieira; Vice President Paulo Correia	peso (169.5 = $1)	9	57
Ivory Coast	9,775,000	President Félix Houphouët-Boigny	CFA franc (383.4 = $1)	2,591	1,314
Kenya	21,415,000	President Daniel T. arap Moi	shilling (14.6 = $1)	1,804	1,519
Lesotho	1,556,000	King Moshoeshoe II; Prime Minister Leabua Jonathan	loti (2.7 = $1)	24	426
Liberia	2,261,000	President Samuel K. Doe	dollar (1 = $1)	429	415
Libya	3,834,000	Leader of the Revolution Muammar Muhammad al-Qadhafi; General People's Committee Chairman (Prime Minister) Mohamed el Zarouk Ragab	dinar (1 = $3.38)	10,056	8,079

*Exchange rates as of Dec. 1, 1985, or latest available data. †Latest available data.

Country	Population	Government	Monetary Unit*	Foreign Trade (million U.S. $) Exports†	Imports†
Madagascar	10,284,000	President Didier Ratsiraka; Prime Minister Désiré Rakotoarijaona	franc (526.9 = $1)	296	387
Malawi	7,229,000	President H. Kamuzu Banda	kwacha (1.7 = $1)	293	279
Mali	8,189,000	President Moussa Traoré	CFA franc (383.4 = $1)	167	344
Mauritania	1,687,000	President Maaouiya Ould Sidi Ahmed Taya	ouguiya (76.9 = $1)	294	194
Mauritius	1,064,000	Governor General (vacant); Prime Minister Aneerood Jugnauth	rupee (14.1 = $1)	373	472
Morocco	24,192,000	King Hassan II; Prime Minister Mohammed Karim-Lamrani	dirham (9.7 = $1)	2,171	3,911
Mozambique	14,470,000	President Samora Moisés Machel	metical (41.7 = $1)	120	581
Namibia (South West Africa)	1,187,000	Administrator-General Willie van Niekerk	rand (2.7 = $1)	no statistics available	
Niger	6,703,000	Supreme Military Council President Seyni Kountché; Prime Minister Hamid Algabid	CFA franc (383.4 = $1)	368	438
Nigeria	94,278,000	President Ibrahim Babangida	naira (1 = $1.08)	11,317	13,440
Rwanda	6,299,000	President Juvénal Habyarimana	franc (93.5 = $1)	124	197
São Tomé and Príncipe	90,000	President Manuel Pinto da Costa	dobra (42.7 = $1)	9	20
Senegal	6,700,000	President Abdou Diouf	CFA franc (383.4 = $1)	543	1,039
Seychelles	67,000	President France Albert René	rupee (6.8 = $1)	2.8	81
Sierra Leone	4,013,000	President Joseph S. Momoh	leone (6 = $1)	148	166
Somalia	6,797,000	President Mohamed Siad Barre	shilling (37.4 = $1)	41	466
South Africa	33,185,000	State President Pieter Willem Botha	rand (2.7 = $1)	17,348	16,234
Sudan	22,177,000	Transitional Military Council Chairman Abdul Rahman Mohamed el Hassan Suwar El-Dahab; Prime Minister Jazzuli Dafalla	pound (2.5 = $1)	790	1,800
Swaziland	668,000	Queen Regent Ntombi; Prime Minister Prince Bhekimpi Dlamani	lilangeni (2.7 = $1)	272	351
Tanzania	23,122,000	President Ali Hassan Mwinyi; Prime Minister Joseph Warioba	shilling (16.2 = $1)	370	782
Togo	3,093,000	President Gnassingbe Eyadéma	CFA franc (383.4 = $1)	253	237
Transkei	2,335,000	President Kaiser Matanzima; Prime Minister George Matanzima	rand (2.7 = $1)	no statistics available	
Tunisia	7,413,000	President Habib Bourguiba; Prime Minister Mohamed Mzali	dinar (1 = $1.28)	1,794	3,174
Uganda	15,144,000	Military Council Chairman and Head of State Tito Okello Lutwa; Prime Minister Abraham Waligo	shilling (992 = $1)	380	509
Venda	343,000	President Patrick Mphephu	rand (2.7 = $1)	no statistics available	
Zaire	33,972,000	President Mobutu Sese Seko; Prime Minister Kengo wa Dondo	zaire (50.2 = $1)	1,003	676
Zambia	6,987,000	President Kenneth David Kaunda; Prime Minister Kebby Musokotwane	kwacha (5.7 = $1)	652	730
Zimbabwe	9,064,000	President Canaan Banana; Prime Minister Robert Gabriel Mugabe	dollar (1.6 = $1)	1,088	959

On November 12, rebel soldiers in Liberia tried to overthrow President Samuel K. Doe. Leading the coup attempt was a former army commander, Brigadier General Thomas Quiwonkpa. The general had been one of the leaders of the April 1980 coup that put Doe in power, but Doe dismissed him from government office in 1983. Quiwonkpa's followers succeeded in capturing the three radio stations in the capital city, Monrovia. By the next day, however, the stations were back in government hands, and most of the fighting had ended. Quiwonkpa was captured on November 15 and reportedly was executed the same day.

Elections. Quiwonkpa may have decided to attempt a coup because of controversy over the results of Liberia's national elections, held on October 15. By the official ballot count, Doe was elected president with 51 per cent of the vote, while his party won large majorities in both houses of the national legislature. Three opposition parties accused Doe of rigging the election, refused to take their seats in the legislature, and vowed to contest the election results in court.

Zimbabwe held parliamentary elections in late June and early July. Although the governing party of Prime Minister Robert Gabriel Mugabe increased its parliamentary majority, Mugabe was disappointed with the election because large numbers of both black and white voters had cast their ballots for opposition candidates. Mugabe had wanted near unanimous support so that he could amend the Constitution and establish a one-party socialist state.

Tanzania, a one-party state since 1964, held its national elections on Oct. 27, 1985. The winning—and only—candidate for the presidency was Ali Hassan Mwinyi, the chosen successor of Julius K. Nyerere, who had been president for 21 years. Mwinyi is a former teacher and onetime president of Zanzibar Island, which is part of Tanzania.

The Organization of African Unity (OAU) held its 21st annual summit conference from July 18 to 20 in Addis Ababa, Ethiopia. In the meeting's most important resolution—the Addis Ababa Economic Declaration—the OAU proclaimed that most African countries are near "economic collapse." The declaration blamed that state of affairs on "an unjust and inequitable [worldwide] economic system," compounded by natural disasters—notably the lengthy drought that was just then coming to an end. The resolution conceded, however, that "some domestic policy shortcomings" have also contributed to the continent's problems, and it pledged African nations to increase their expenditures on agriculture.

A preliminary draft of the declaration contained a paragraph expressing "profound gratitude to the international community" for its assistance in dealing with the African famine crisis. But that passage was deleted in the final draft of the declaration, which instead asked for more aid.

Among other resolutions passed was a warning to the United States not to assist the rebels in the Angolan civil war. The delegates issued that warning in response to legislation approved on July 11 by the U.S. Congress repealing a 1976 ban on such intervention. The OAU also adopted a resolution urging Western governments and businesses to impose economic sanctions on South Africa to protest that country's racial policies.

Pope John Paul II made a 12-day journey through Africa from August 8 to 19, visiting seven countries: Togo, Ivory Coast, Cameroon, the Central African Republic, Zaire, Kenya, and Morocco. During a Mass attended by about 250,000 people in Lubumbashi, Zaire, the pope called for a more equitable distribution of the world's wealth. In Nairobi, Kenya, he closed the 43rd International Eucharistic Congress, the first such meeting held in black Africa.   J. Dixon Esseks

See also the various African country articles. In WORLD BOOK, see AFRICA.

AGRICULTURE. See FARM AND FARMING.
AIR FORCE. See ARMED FORCES.
AIR POLLUTION. See ENVIRONMENTAL POLLUTION.
AIRPORT. See AVIATION.
ALABAMA. See STATE GOVERNMENT.
ALASKA. See STATE GOVERNMENT.

ALBANIA changed leaders in 1985, but its foreign and domestic policies remained unchanged. Enver Hoxha, 76, first secretary of the Communist Party and the country's ruler since 1944, died on April 11. He was succeeded by Ramiz Alia, 59, who since November 1982 had been official head of state as president of the Presidium of the People's Assembly (parliament). See ALIA, RAMIZ.

Alia had been in line to succeed Hoxha since the mysterious death of Prime Minister Mehmet Shehu in December 1981. On Feb. 28, 1985, Albania's major Communist Party newspaper reported that Shehu had been "liquidated." The government had claimed previously that he had committed suicide. On March 1, however, an Albanian Embassy official in Vienna, Austria, maintained that Shehu had not been killed but only liquidated politically.

Alia did not change many party or government personnel. A major change occurred in July, however, when Alia appointed Pirro Kondi to replace Foto Çami as Communist Party secretary in Tiranë, the nation's capital.

The West. Alia continued Hoxha's policy of closer economic relations with Western Europe. Jean-Michel Baylet, France's secretary of state for foreign relations, visited Albania in September with a delegation that included 20 business people and 34 journalists. In October, Albania and Italy signed an agreement to trade more goods with each other.

In January, Albania opened a pass on the main highway between Greece and parts of Albania that are heavily inhabited by ethnic Greeks. That same month, Albania and Greece signed a new trade pact and an agreement under which a Greek firm will build a $7-million chromium-processing plant in Albania.

Albania and West Germany resumed talks about the possibility of establishing diplomatic relations. In November, a large delegation of West German business people visited Albania.

Relations with Yugoslavia remained strained because of the ongoing dispute about the status of ethnic Albanians living in Kosovo, a province of the Republic of Serbia, which is part of Yugoslavia. Alia denied responsibility for agitation in Kosovo aimed at upgrading the province to a republic within Yugoslavia.

Economic Troubles. Albanian farms suffered losses from a severe summer drought. Alia admitted that there were problems in the oil industry, which, with the gas industry, accounts for 60 per cent of the country's exports. But Albania claimed that oil production during the first eight months of 1985 exceeded the official quota.   Chris Cviic

See also EUROPE (Facts in Brief Table). In WORLD BOOK, see ALBANIA.

Donald Getty waves to supporters in October after being elected leader of Alberta's Progressive Conservatives. He became premier on November 1.

ALBERTA. Donald Ross Getty was sworn in as premier of this oil-rich province on Nov. 1, 1985. Getty, an oil industry executive and former provincial energy minister, became premier as a result of winning an election for leader of Alberta's Progressive Conservative Party (PC) on October 13. He succeeded Peter Lougheed, who retired from both these posts. See GETTY, DONALD ROSS.

Lougheed retired in 1985 after serving as Alberta's premier for 14 years. During his political career, Lougheed rebuilt the PC from a party with no seats in Alberta's Legislative Assembly to one with 75 of the 79 seats. Lougheed emerged as the spokesman for the West in demanding a larger role in the Canadian federation. Lougheed's greatest achievement was the creation of the Alberta Heritage Savings Trust Fund—a $14-billion fund accumulated from oil and gas revenues and used for a variety of projects in the province. (All monetary amounts in this article are Canadian dollars, with $1 = U.S. 72 cents as of Dec. 31, 1985.) Getty, also a strong supporter of Alberta's interests, was expected to continue Lougheed's policies and to stress agricultural development.

Budget. The 1985-1986 provincial budget, announced on March 25, showed about $10 billion in spending and a deficit of about $250 million. Government spending was increased for education and tourism and decreased for health care.

The budget included plans to spend about $1.6-billion in investment income from the Heritage Savings Trust Fund.

Bank Failures. In early September 1985, the Canadian Commercial Bank of Edmonton failed. This was the first bank failure in Canada since 1923. At the end of the month, the Northland Bank of Calgary also failed. The banks had suffered financially from risky real estate and energy loans. The federal government promised to reimburse all depositors.

Other Developments. On July 20, an Alberta court found James Keegstra, a former high school social studies teacher in Eckville, Alta., guilty of willfully promoting hatred of Jews. He had taught that there is an international Jewish conspiracy that controls banks, politicians, and the news media. Keegstra, who was fined $5,000, planned to appeal the ruling.

Publishing history was made in Alberta in September with the appearance of *The Canadian Encyclopedia,* a three-volume, 2,089-page reference work devoted to information pertaining to Canada past and present. The Alberta provincial government provided $6 million in capital and loan guarantees for the publishing project, and it also donated a set of the encyclopedia to every school and library in Canada.   David M. L. Farr

In WORLD BOOK, see ALBERTA.

ALGERIA. President Chadli Bendjedid visited the United States in April 1985 on the first official U.S. visit by an Algerian head of state since that country became independent in 1962. Relations between the United States and Algeria remained cool, however, chiefly because of U.S. support for Morocco, which was fighting Algerian-backed guerrillas in Western Sahara. Nevertheless, since 1983, the two countries had been increasingly drawn together by a common opposition to Libya and by Algeria's role as a mediator in several Middle East hostage crises.

Regional Developments. Algeria continued its efforts to strengthen North African unity. In May, Algeria signed a pact with Mauritania fixing their border. In August, Algeria invoked a 1983 friendship treaty with Tunisia to offer military aid against a possible invasion by Libya after Libya expelled about 21,000 Tunisian workers.

Elections. Algeria's slow move toward democracy advanced another step early in 1985 with the election of local and provincial assemblies. The voter turnout was a record 80 per cent. In January, Bendjedid launched a national debate on the 1976 National Charter, which forms the basis for Algeria's socialist system.

Fundamentalist Trials. The first major trial of Islamic fundamentalists charged with antigovern-

ment activity ended in April with 31 people receiving 3- to 12-year prison terms. Several religious leaders were also given 3-year terms for making what the government said were inflammatory speeches in mosques. In August, a fundamentalist group raided a police barracks, killing five policemen in what they called a "war against foreign cultural infiltration."

The Economy. The 1985-1989 development plan was approved by the National Assembly in February. It projects a 7.5 per cent annual growth rate, the creation of 900,000 new jobs, and investments of $110 billion. The country's economic performance between 1980 and 1984 suggested that the new targets could be met. During that period, Algeria had a 6 per cent growth rate.

Bendjedid's main goals were to expand private industry and reduce government control of the economy; diversify Algeria's industry, which is highly dependent on oil and gas production; and reduce Algeria's reliance on food imports by increasing food production. In an effort to stimulate agriculture, the government began in June to lease undeveloped cropland to farmers. Under the program, farmers will own the land in five years if they improve production. William Spencer

See also AFRICA (Facts in Brief Table). In the WORLD BOOK SUPPLEMENT section, see ALGERIA.

Algerian President Chadli Bendjedid meets with President Ronald Reagan in April on the first official U.S. visit by an Algerian leader since 1962.

ALIA, RAMIZ (1925-   ), became leader of Albania as first secretary of the Albanian Party of Labor, the nation's Communist Party, on April 13, 1985. He succeeded Enver Hoxha, who died on April 11. Alia had been in line to succeed Hoxha since November 1982, when Alia became head of state officially, as chairman of the Presidium (administrative committee) of the People's Assembly (parliament). See ALBANIA.

Ramiz Alia (pronounced *rah MEEZ uh LEE ah*) was born on Oct. 18, 1925. According to the Albanian government, he was born in Shkodër, a city in northern Albania. During World War II, Alia was active in the resistance movement against Italy and Germany. He became a lieutenant colonel and political instructor in the Communist force that gained control of the country in 1944.

From 1946 until 1955, Alia led Albania's youth organization, except for a brief stint in the Party of Labor's propaganda department in 1948. He also joined the party's Central Committee in 1948. In 1958, he became a full-time adviser on Communist doctrine for the Central Committee. He joined the Politburo, the party's ruling group, as a nonvoting member in 1956 and became a full member in 1961.

Alia's wife, Semiramis, is dean of the natural science faculty at Tiranë University. The Alias are believed to have at least two children.   Jay Myers

AMERICAN LIBRARY ASSOCIATION (ALA). Chicago, home city of the ALA, was the site of the association's 104th annual conference, held from July 6 to 11, 1985. More than 13,600 librarians, library trustees, exhibitors, and friends of libraries attended the meeting. The conference honored former ALA Executive Director Robert Wedgeworth, who resigned in 1985 to become dean of the Columbia University School of Library Service in New York City. Thomas J. Galvin, dean of the University of Pittsburgh School of Library and Information Science, was appointed to succeed Wedgeworth as the ALA's executive director. Beverly P. Lynch, librarian of the University of Illinois at Chicago and ALA vice president, took office as the new ALA president. Regina U. Minudri, director of the Berkeley (Calif.) Public Library, was elected ALA vice president and president-elect.

Promoting Libraries and Reading. To support the literacy campaign it launched in 1984, the ALA chose the theme "A Nation of Readers" for National Library Week, held from April 14 to 20, 1985. The association promoted Library Week with colorful posters featuring comedian Bill Cosby, ballet dancer Mikhail Baryshnikov, singer Bette Midler, and rock star Sting that were displayed in libraries throughout the United States.

U.S. Adopts Library Symbol. In 1982, the ALA developed a national library symbol for use on highway signs. The symbol—a stylized drawing of a reader with a book—has been used in several states. In March 1985, it was adopted by the Federal Highway Administration as a general-information sign for U.S. highways.

Service Awards. World Book, Incorporated, funds two $5,000 World Book-ALA Goals Awards each year to advance the development of library service in the United States. One of the 1985 grants went to the Library Instruction Round Table—a section of the ALA consisting of volunteers throughout the nation who are involved with helping people learn to use libraries. The ALA Commission on Pay Equity, together with the ALA's Committee on the Status of Women in Librarianship and Office for Library Personnel Resources Advisory Committee, received a Goals Award for an ALA institute on pay equity.

Children's Books. The 1985 Newbery Medal for the most distinguished contribution to American children's literature published in 1984 was awarded to Robin McKinley, author of *The Hero and the Crown*. Illustrator Trina Schart Hyman won the 1985 Caldecott Medal for the best children's picture book for the illustrations in *Saint George and the Dragon*.   Peggy Barber

See also CANADIAN LIBRARY ASSOCIATION; LIBRARY; LITERATURE FOR CHILDREN. In WORLD BOOK, see AMERICAN LIBRARY ASSOCIATION.

ANGOLA. On July 29, 1985, the Marxist government of Angola's President José Eduardo dos Santos launched an offensive against strongholds of the nation's main rebel movement, the National Union for the Total Independence of Angola (UNITA). UNITA has been waging a guerrilla war since 1975, when a coalition of UNITA and Dos Santos' party, the Popular Movement for the Liberation of Angola, broke apart.

On Sept. 18, 1985, the government's offensive succeeded in capturing the UNITA-held town of Cazombo in eastern Angola, near the border with Zaire. Those government forces then turned south to join a government column attacking a UNITA base at Mavinga in southeastern Angola. That battle ended on September 29 with government forces retreating.

The Soviet Union assisted the government's offensive by providing tanks, warplanes, and other supplies, and UNITA leader Jonas Savimbi charged that Soviet officers had directed the military operation. On September 20, South Africa's government admitted supplying war materials to UNITA, which controlled much of the border between Angola and South African-administered Namibia. In return for South African aid, UNITA had apparently agreed to prevent Namibian nationalist guerrillas from infiltrating into Namibia from bases in southern Angola.

South African troops on guard against guerrillas patrol the
border between Angola and South African-administered Namibia.

Namibian Independence Talks. Earlier in the
year, South Africa, Angola, and the United States
discussed the issue of granting independence to
Namibia. The negotiators made progress in meeting South Africa's requirement that an estimated
25,000 Cuban troops stationed in Angola had to
return to Cuba before South Africa would withdraw its military forces from Namibia. The negotiations continued until late May, when Angola
terminated them after foiling a South African
commando raid on an Angolan oil installation in
the northwestern district of Cabinda.

Congress Angers Angola. On July 13, the Dos
Santos government canceled bilateral talks with
the United States—also aimed at reaching a settlement with South Africa—following the passage of
a foreign-aid bill two days earlier by the U.S.
House of Representatives. The bill included a provision repealing a nine-year-old prohibition on U.S.
aid to UNITA and other rebels fighting Angola's
central government. Dos Santos was particularly
disturbed that the Administration of President
Ronald Reagan had supported the repeal of the
ban. On October 2, Representative Claude D. Pepper (R., Fla.) introduced a bill that would provide
$27 million in aid to UNITA.   J. Dixon Esseks

See also AFRICA (Facts in Brief Table). In
WORLD BOOK, see ANGOLA.

ANIMAL. See CAT; DOG; ZOOLOGY; ZOOS.

ANTHROPOLOGY. Scientists from around the
world gathered in Johannesburg, South Africa,
from Jan. 27 to Feb. 4, 1985, for a conference celebrating the 60th anniversary of the discovery of
the Taung skull. The Taung skull—found in
1924—was the first truly ancient *hominid* fossil
ever found. (Hominids include human beings and
our closest human and prehuman ancestors.)
Among those attending the meeting was Raymond
A. Dart, who found the skull—that of a child—
near Taung, South Africa. Dart was then an anatomy teacher at the University of the Witwatersrand in Johannesburg.

Dart named his specimen *Australopithecus africanus* (the southern ape of Africa) and suggested
that it represented a creature between apes and
human beings. Other scientists vehemently disagreed, and the Taung child's position as a hominid remained controversial for nearly 30 years
until other australopithecine fossils were found.

The scientists attending the conference in 1985
agreed that *Australopithecus* was indeed a human
ancestor. But the agreement stopped there.

For a variety of reasons, scientists have been unable to establish a precise geological age for the
Taung fossil. Some researchers believe the fossil is
at least 2 million years old, while others estimate
its age at closer to 3 million years. At the meeting,
geologist John Vogel of the Council for Scientific

and Industrial Research in Pretoria, South Africa, reported that by using radioactive dating methods, he arrived at an age of 1 million years. Other scientists at the conference disputed his finding.

The biological age of the Taung fossil was also a bone of contention at the meeting. Dart had concluded that the skull was that of a child about 6 years of age because the first permanent molars were beginning to erupt—an event that occurs at about that age in modern human beings. Anthropologist Tim Bromage of University College in London reported, however, that his study of the skull's facial bones suggests that the Taung child died between the ages of 2.7 and 3.7 years. If Bromage is correct, our early ancestors may have matured faster than do modern human beings.

Scientists attending the conference also argued about the position of *A. africanus* in human evolution. In the past, most anthropologists believed that this species was the common ancestor of two later groups of hominids. One group included *Australopithecus robustus*, a vegetarian species that became extinct about 1 million years ago. The second group eventually gave rise to *Homo sapiens*, the species to which modern human beings belong.

This version of human evolution was challenged in 1978 with the discovery of a new type of aus-

tralopithecine named *Australopithecus afarensis*. Some scientists, including its codiscoverer, anthropologist Donald C. Johanson of the Institute of Human Origins in Berkeley, Calif., consider *A. afarensis* to be the common ancestor of all later hominids. In their view, *A. africanus* was an ancestor of only *A. robustus* and other members of that group and not of *Homo sapiens*.

Other scientists, including anthropologist Henry M. McHenry of the University of California, Davis, contend that *A. afarensis* was an ancestor of *A. africanus*, from which the two groups then developed. Anatomist Phillip V. Tobias of Witwatersrand and some other scientists argue that *A. afarensis* is merely a variation of *A. africanus*.

Earliest Higher Primate. In August 1985, a team of scientists led by anthropologist Russell L. Ciochon of the State University of New York in Stony Brook reported the discovery of a lower-jaw fragment from a creature that the scientists believe may be the ancestor of all later *anthropoids* (a group of primates that includes apes, monkeys, and human beings). Estimated to be from 40 million to 44 million years old, the fossil—a piece of jawbone about 2 inches (5 centimeters) long with two teeth—was found in Burma. Ciochon suggests that the animal, named *Amphipithecus mogaungensis*, weighed from 15 to 20 pounds (6.8 to 9 kilo-

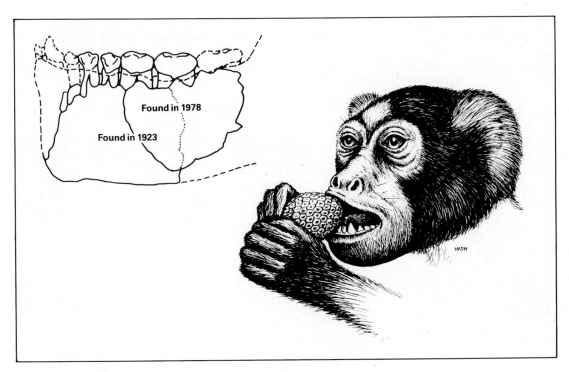

A partial lower jaw, whose discovery was reported in August 1985, may have belonged to the earliest higher primate, *reconstructed at right*.

grams), was about 2½ to 3 feet (76 to 91 centimeters) tall, lived in the trees, and ate fruit.

Ciochon and his colleagues contend that *Amphipithecus* was a bridge between the anthropoids and the lower primates, such as lemurs and tarsiers, from which they developed. Ciochon also suggests that the find indicates that anthropoids arose first in Asia, then migrated over land bridges into Africa. Since the late 1960's, *Aegyptopithecus*, a 33-million-year-old fossil primate found in Africa, has been considered the most likely ancestor of anthropoids. Other scientists dispute Ciochon's interpretations, arguing that there is not enough fossil evidence to clearly identify *Amphipithecus* as an anthropoid.

Chinese *Homo Erectus*. In September, Chinese archaeologists announced the discovery in Liaoning province of major portions of a *Homo erectus* skeleton estimated to be 200,000 years old. *Homo erectus* is the hominid species thought to have developed into *Homo sapiens*. The find consisted of the entire skull except for the lower jaw, several arm and hand bones, some vertebrae, part of the pelvis, and some foot bones. The discovery promises to add substantially to knowledge about *Homo erectus* in China.   Donald C. Johanson

See also ARCHAEOLOGY. In WORLD BOOK, see ANTHROPOLOGY; PREHISTORIC PEOPLE.

ARCHAEOLOGY. In an article published in March 1985, archaeologist E. James Dixon of the University of Alaska in Fairbanks reviewed evidence challenging the long-held belief that the earliest Americans arrived in North America from Asia and then spread southward. The new evidence suggests that the earliest Americans arrived first in South America and then migrated northward.

During the Pleistocene Epoch—a geological period that lasted from 1¾ million to 10,000 years ago—the sea level was much lower than it is today. A huge land bridge, believed to have been 1,000 miles (1,600 kilometers) wide, linked Asia with North America where the Bering Strait now exists. Scientists have long believed that the earliest Americans were hunting bands from Asia that crossed this land bridge in pursuit of game, particularly mammoths.

In recent years, however, some scientists have reported findings that challenge this view. For example, geologic and botanical evidence suggests that the Bering Land Bridge was bleak and cold between 30,000 and 14,000 years ago, when most scientists believe the human migrations occurred. Such a dry, windswept tundra would have had too little vegetation to support large herds of mammoths and other grazing animals. In addition, scientists have not found firm archaeological evi-

Ruins found near Diyarbakir, Turkey, in June are of a 10,000-year-old building that is among the earliest examples of formal architecture discovered.

Taking a New Look at Custer's Last Stand

A devastating grass fire has given archaeologists an unusual opportunity to investigate one of the most intriguing mysteries in United States military history: What really happened at the Battle of the Little Bighorn? There, in a legendary battle on June 25, 1876, a large force of Sioux and Cheyenne Indians wiped out Lieutenant Colonel George Armstrong Custer of the U.S. Army and all the men under his direct command. Since the fire, which occurred in 1983, investigators armed with metal detectors, trowels, and computers have searched the Montana site of Custer's Last Stand. In 1985, they reported evidence that both confirms and challenges historical accounts of the battle.

In June 1876, Custer led the 650-man Seventh Cavalry Regiment into the valley of the Little Bighorn River to find Sioux and Cheyenne Indians who refused to move from their lands in the Black Hills onto reservations. After finding the Indians' camp on June 25, Custer ordered an immediate attack, divided his troops into three groups, and rode off with one group of 212 men.

Too late, he discovered that he was facing a force of as many as 4,000 warriors, probably the largest gathering of Indian warriors in Western history. Although 350 of the soldiers in the other two groups survived, Custer and all the men in his unit were killed.

The details of the battle have remained shrouded in mystery. Most Indian accounts of the fighting came to light only years afterward, and most of these stories as well as accounts by survivors of Custer's regiment were conflicting.

Then in August 1983, a raging prairie fire destroyed most of the thick buffalo grass covering the hills and gullies of the battlefield, which is now administered by the National Park Service as a memorial to the soldiers who fought in the Indian Wars. At the request of the privately financed Custer Battlefield Historical and Museum Association, the Park Service agreed to allow a group of professional and amateur archaeologists to search the fire-stripped battlefield for artifacts.

The archaeologists swept the area with metal detectors and dug trenches and shallow pits. They turned up more than 5,000 artifacts, including bullets, cartridge cases, buttons, spurs, horseshoes, arrowheads, and bones. The position of each find was carefully recorded on a three-dimensional grid, and then the information was fed into a computer. The computer was used to analyze the data. For instance, cartridge cases were sorted by type, which told archaeologists whether they were fired by soldiers or Indians. This analysis helped the archaeologists determine the positions of both groups during the fight. The investigators also examined the microscopic markings left on fired cartridge cases that can be used to identify a particular gun. This enabled the archaeologists to determine how many individual guns were used in the battle and trace the movement of the Indians and troops during the fighting.

This information, combined with historical accounts, has given archaeologists a much clearer picture of Custer's last battle. One of the most significant discoveries was that Custer really did make a last stand. He spread his men in a broad V-shaped pattern, stationing himself at the point of the V at the top of a small hill. Also, contrary to belief, the Indians were well armed. In addition to bows and arrows, they carried several hundred firearms, including many repeating rifles. In contrast, Custer's men carried Army-issue single-shot weapons. The ferocious battle lasted only about an hour. A few of the soldiers along the sides of the V fought their way to Custer on the hill. But in the end, they all died.

The evidence also lays to rest the idea that Custer and his men committed suicide to avoid capture. Nor did Custer's Last Stand become a rout. He and his men died holding their positions.

Many mysteries about the battle still remain. But the new archaeological evidence has helped solve some of the puzzles about a battle that has enthralled many Americans for more than 100 years. Douglas D. Scott

An archaeologist digs into a burial site at the Custer battlefield in Montana. A shoe, right, and human bones, left, were found at the site.

dence in Alaska indicating that human beings using stone tools lived there earlier than 11,000 years ago, 4,000 years after mammoths probably became extinct.

Other scientists have pointed out that the oldest known archaeological sites where both mammoth bones and stone spearpoints have been found are in southwestern North America. In addition, some archaeological sites in South America, such as Monte Verde in south-central Chile, are at least as old as, and may even be older than, sites in North America. According to Dixon, this evidence—along with the geologic and botanical evidence—suggests that the earliest Americans may have reached South America first, by boat from Asia, then spread northward.

South American Mummies. The discovery in Chile of the oldest known mummies was reported in October 1985 by pathologist Marvin J. Allison of the University of Tarapacá in Arica, Chile. Found in 1983 near Arica in an ancient cemetery that was in use about 6000 B.C., the 96 mummies are 3,000 years older than the oldest Egyptian mummies.

The mummies were buried over a 3,000-year period. During the burial rites, each corpse was carefully skinned with a pelican beak used as a knife. The internal organs and major muscles were removed, and the body was dried by filling it with hot coals and ashes. The body cavity was then filled with wool, feathers, grass, and a variety of other materials.

Autopsies of the mummies revealed that many of the men had chronic ear infections, which the scientists believe were caused by diving for shellfish. Many of the women had leg deformities, which were attributed to spending long hours squatting while cleaning and preparing the fish. Allison believes that the bodies were not buried immediately but instead were displayed in groups, perhaps to help bring good hunting and fishing to the people of the community.

Maya Discovery. Ornate jewelry found in August 1985 with a Maya skeleton from the late 1400's suggests that the Maya had greater contact with the Aztecs than had been thought. Experts have long believed that the Maya were isolated from the Aztecs, then the most powerful group in Mexico and Central America.

The skeleton was discovered near Corozal, Belize, by archaeologists Arlen F. Chase and Diane Z. Chase of the University of Central Florida in Orlando. The skeleton—that of a Maya leader—was adorned with elaborate jewelry, including gold ear ornaments inlaid with turquoise and jade. Because the ornaments were similar to those worn by Aztec nobility, the Chases concluded that the Maya leader was someone of great importance who may have exchanged royal gifts with Aztec nobles.

Stone Age Finds. The discovery of a spectacular cache of objects more than 9,000 years old was revealed in April 1985, when the objects went on display in Israel. The objects, which include the oldest cloth fragments and painted mask ever found, were discovered in 1983 in a cave near the Dead Sea. Also found in the cave were carved figures; wooden and bone tools; stone, clay, and wooden beads; and a human skull adorned with asphalt.

Underwater Finds. In July, adventurer Mel Fisher discovered off Key West, Fla., the wreckage of the Spanish galleon *Nuestra Señora de Atocha*, which sank in 1622, and what may be the biggest cache of sunken treasure ever found (see OCEAN). In September, a team of American and French scientists found the hulk of the British luxury liner *Titanic*, which sank in 1912 (see OCEAN [Close-Up]).

In October, the recovery of a ship's bell used to chime the watches confirmed the identity of the *Whydah*, a pirate ship found in July 1984 off Cape Cod, Mass. The ship is apparently the first pirate wreck ever identified and salvaged. The *Whydah*, which sank on Feb. 17, 1717, was carrying a treasure estimated to be worth hundreds of millions of dollars.   Barbara Voorhies

In WORLD BOOK, see ARCHAEOLOGY; INDIAN, AMERICAN; MAYA.

ARCHITECTURE. The event in 1985 with the greatest long-term significance for architecture in the United States was probably the enactment, in July, of the much-debated San Francisco Downtown Plan. The plan is the first attempt by a major U.S. city to limit construction of large buildings. Supporters of the new law argued that oversized buildings, especially office towers, were destroying the city's special charm. The law limits new construction downtown each year to 950,000 square feet (88,300 square meters) of floor area—about the size of one large office tower.

Especially controversial are the San Francisco plan's artistic guidelines. They state that new buildings should be light in color, should be made of solid materials rather than glass, should feature ornamentation and detail, and should have a tapered rather than a flat top. Some opponents described these rules as an attempt to enforce Post-Modern architecture by legislation. Post-Modernism is an architectural movement that involves the use of ornamentation and details borrowed from both historical styles and contemporary popular culture (in the Special Reports section, see ARCHITECTURE'S NEW LOOK).

Philadelphia Lifts Limit. While San Francisco moved to restrain growth, Philadelphia tried to stimulate it by lifting a long-standing limit on building height. Since the 1800's, a Philadelphia

A 1982 museum in Mönchengladbach, West Germany, is the masterpiece of Austria's Hans Hollein, winner of the 1985 Pritzker Architecture Prize.

tradition banned any building taller than the statue of the city's founder, Quaker leader William Penn, atop City Hall, 548 feet (167 meters) above street level. The height limit appeared in the code of the city's redevelopment authority. Removal of the limit permitted construction to begin in May on One Liberty Place, an office-hotel complex designed by German-born American architect Helmut Jahn. The tallest part of the complex will rise 935 feet (285 meters).

New Buildings that opened in 1985 included the Humana Building in Louisville, Ky., completed in March and designed by a leading Post-Modern architect, Michael Graves of Princeton University in New Jersey. The Humana is a 27-story office tower made of marble and granite in shades of pink and red. Graves gave it an elaborate sculptured shape that stands in marked contrast to the simple boxlike office buildings of the Modern style. The Humana Building's rich materials, elaborate profile, and classical symmetry recall the skyscrapers of the art deco period of the 1920's and 1930's, such as the Chrysler Building and the Empire State Building in New York City.

The beautiful Transco Tower in Houston, by the New York City firm of John Burgee Architects with Philip Johnson, also recalls art deco skyscrapers. The Transco Tower, however, is built of shimmering reflective glass.

Another notable Post-Modern building is the Arthur M. Sackler Museum at Harvard University in Cambridge, Mass., designed by the British architect James Stirling, which opened in October. The museum's striking entrance, framed by two huge columns and false stonework made of stucco, seems to mock its own pretensions.

Post-Modern, too, is the Hood Museum of Art at Dartmouth College in Hanover, N.H., by Charles W. Moore and Centerbrook Architects, which opened in September. Parts of the building respond in appearance to two dramatically different structures on either side.

The Ordway Music Theatre in St. Paul, Minn., by Benjamin Thompson of Cambridge, is a copper-sheathed wood building with a welcoming warmth that defied the frigid weather at its January opening. The State of Illinois Center by Jahn, which opened in May in Chicago, has a sloping, curved shape that contrasts sharply with the boxlike buildings surrounding it.

Overseas, the most noteworthy building of 1985 was the Hong Kong and Shanghai Banking Corporation in Hong Kong, by British architect Norman R. Foster. The tower's exposed steel frame gives it a look of having been assembled from an erector set.

Awards. The Pritzker Prize, architecture's equivalent of the Nobel Prize, went to Austria's Hans

Hollein, known for his luxurious small shops and, more recently, for the Municipal Museum (1982) in Mönchengladbach, West Germany. The Gold Medal of the Royal Institute of British Architects was awarded to British architect Richard Rogers, codesigner of the Georges Pompidou National Center for Art and Culture (1977) in Paris. The Gold Medal of the American Institute of Architects (AIA) went posthumously to William Wayne Caudill, founder of the large international firm of CRS Incorporated. The AIA's Twenty-Five-Year Award, given annually to a building at least 25 years old that has proved its merit, was given to the General Motors Technical Center (1955) in Warren, Mich., designed by the Finnish-born American architect Eero Saarinen.

Controversy erupted over a proposal by Graves, announced in May 1985, for a 10-story addition to the Whitney Museum of American Art in New York City. Graves's design involved gutting the building, a 1966 landmark by Hungarian-born American architect Marcel Breuer.

The National Building Museum opened in October in the former U.S. Pension Building in Washington, D.C., whose interior was newly renovated. The museum is the only one in the United States devoted to building design.   Robert Campbell

In WORLD BOOK, see ARCHITECTURE.

ARGENTINA. A tense political drama unfolded in Argentina in 1985 as three former heads of military juntas—Generals Jorge Rafael Videla, Roberto Eduardo Viola, and Leopoldo Galtieri—and some of their subordinates went on trial on April 22 for human rights abuses. They were charged with murder, torture, and kidnapping in the disappearance of an estimated 9,000 people during the military juntas' campaign against left wing guerrillas in the late 1970's. General Galtieri was also being tried for his handling of the 1982 Falkland Islands war, which Argentina lost to Great Britain.

On December 9, a six-judge tribunal found five of the defendants guilty, including Videla and Viola. Videla was given the maximum sentence of life imprisonment. Viola was sentenced to 17 years in prison. Galtieri was acquitted but was still being held on charges relating to the war. The verdicts were believed to be the first time in Latin America that civilians had punished military leaders for human rights abuses.

The trial's conclusion was likely to bolster the popularity of Argentine President Raúl Alfonsín, who already was enjoying the success of his far-reaching programs of economic reform. On June 14, Alfonsín announced a freeze on wages and prices, an end to the long-standing practice of

Wearing masks to symbolize those who disappeared under military rule, Argentines demonstrate in May during the trial of former junta leaders.

printing new money to cover government spending, and the creation of a new currency, the austral, to replace the Argentine peso.

In announcing the program, Alfonsín called it "a battle plan" and told Argentines that they would have to become accustomed to living in a "wartime economy." The enemy, he said, was rampant inflation, which reached an annual rate of 1,010 per cent in May. To avoid public panic and wide-scale bank withdrawals, Alfonsín ordered a bank holiday immediately after his address.

Alfonsín had been careful to set the stage. On February 18, he accepted the resignations of Economics Minister Bernardo Grinspun, whose economic program was not working, and Enrique García Vazquez, president of the Central Bank. The new economics minister was Juan Vital Sourrouille, an academic who had earlier served as planning secretary.

In the Political Arena, Alfonsín kept his opponents off balance. He was helped by disunity in the Justicialist Liberation Front, the party established by long-time dictator Juan Domingo Perón. On February 4, Perón's widow, Isabel, confirmed bitter divisions within the party by resigning as its head.

On March 7, Alfonsín took a further step in bringing the military under control by appointing Air Force Chief of Staff Teodoro Guillermo Waldner the armed forces chief of staff, a post traditionally reserved for an army general. With an officer personally loyal to him in command, Alfonsín felt secure enough to leave the country to visit President Ronald Reagan in Washington, D.C., on March 19 and 20. He addressed a joint session of the United States Congress and stressed the need for support within the hemisphere of the principle of nonintervention in the affairs of other nations. This was a reminder that shortly after he assumed power, Argentina stopped supporting rebels fighting against the Sandinista regime in Nicaragua.

Economic Aid. In June, the U.S. Treasury announced that agreement had been reached on a 12-nation, $483-million loan to help Argentina repay overdue interest on its estimated foreign debt of $48 billion. The United States contributed $150 million of the total, and 11 other nations, including Brazil and Venezuela, provided the balance.

By October, the economic program appeared to be working, with inflation in Argentina running at 1.9 per cent—its lowest level in more than a decade. In congressional elections on November 3, Alfonsín's party, the Radical Civic Union, led with 44 per cent of the vote.   Nathan A. Haverstock

See also LATIN AMERICA (Facts in Brief Table). In WORLD BOOK, see ARGENTINA.

ARIZONA. See STATE GOVERNMENT.

ARKANSAS. See STATE GOVERNMENT.

ARMED FORCES. A summit meeting between United States President Ronald Reagan and Soviet leader Mikhail S. Gorbachev took place on Nov. 19 and 20, 1985, in Geneva, Switzerland. Although both leaders insisted they wanted peace, no concrete steps toward arms reduction were taken. See PRESIDENT OF THE UNITED STATES.

The U.S. Defense Build-Up. In June, Reagan ordered an aging Poseidon-missile submarine dismantled to comply with ceilings set by the unratified 1979 Strategic Arms Limitation Talks (SALT II) agreement with the Soviet Union. Nevertheless, an aggressive build-up of U.S. military strength continued in 1985. Research proceeded on Reagan's Strategic Defense Initiative, the so-called "Star Wars" program designed to destroy incoming missiles in space. Development went ahead on a single-warhead intercontinental ballistic missile (ICBM) and on a "stealth" bomber that could escape detection by enemy air defenses. But Congress cut by half Reagan's plan to install 100 MX missiles in underground silos.

Terrorists Intercepted. On October 10, an EgyptAir jet carrying four Palestinian terrorists was intercepted by U.S. Navy F-14 Tomcat jet fighters from the aircraft carrier *Saratoga* in international airspace south of the Greek island of Crete. The jet was forced to land at an air base

The beam from a high-powered laser tears apart a stationary target in a September test conducted as part of the U.S. "Star Wars" defense program.

"At last! A weapons system absolutely impervious to attack:
It has components manufactured in all 435 congressional districts!"

operated jointly by Italy and the North Atlantic Treaty Organization (NATO) at Sigonella, Italy, near Catania. The terrorists had been sought by the United States government for the murder of an American passenger aboard the Italian cruise ship *Achille Lauro*, which they hijacked on October 7. The Egyptian government had guaranteed the hijackers safe passage despite demands that they be turned over to Italy or the United States for prosecution. The daring interception was carried out without a shot being fired.

A Series of Espionage Cases shook the Pentagon in 1985. In May, retired Navy warrant officer John A. Walker, Jr., was charged with spying for the Soviet Union. Also charged with espionage were Walker's son, Michael, a seaman on the aircraft carrier *Nimitz*; Walker's brother, Arthur, a retired Navy lieutenant commander; and a friend, retired Navy radio operator Jerry A. Whitworth. Pentagon officials said that John Walker may have passed secrets to the Soviets for more than a decade. As a result of the security breach, the Navy said in June it would reduce by one-half the personnel with access to classified information.

In August, a jury found Arthur Walker guilty of espionage, and in November he was sentenced to life imprisonment. Government officials announced in October that John Walker had agreed to plead guilty in return for a reduced sentence

for his son. As part of the agreement, Walker was to provide an account of the information his spy ring had turned over to the Soviet Union.

A Navy enlisted man was among several men charged in July with smuggling parts of F-14 jet fighters to Iran. An Army lieutenant colonel was arrested in August on charges of conspiring to ship antitank missiles to Iran. A Navy civilian counterintelligence analyst was arrested in November. He was suspected of spying for Israel. With these cases providing impetus, Congress passed an amendment to a military authorization bill allowing the death penalty for military personnel convicted of peacetime espionage. Reagan signed the bill into law on November 8.

A U.S. Army Officer was shot and killed in East Germany on March 24 while on a reconnaissance mission near a Soviet military installation. The officer, Major Arthur D. Nicholson, Jr., had been photographing a Soviet military building when a Soviet sentry shot him. Nicholson had been a member of a U.S. military mission stationed in Potsdam, East Germany, as part of a 1947 agreement that allowed American, Soviet, British, and French military observers on both sides of the Iron Curtain. The Soviets claimed Nicholson had entered an unauthorized area. United States officials said he was operating in an unrestricted zone and termed his death cold-blooded murder.

Defense Budget. On Feb. 4, 1985, Reagan submitted a $277.5-billion defense-budget request to Congress for the 1986 fiscal year beginning Oct. 1, 1985. The budget proposal was $31.2 billion higher than fiscal 1985 outlays and reflected an 8.3 per cent increase after adjustment for inflation. It included huge jumps in funding for major weapons systems for the fourth consecutive year.

The budget request was viewed as excessive on Capitol Hill. Although Congress approved funds for all major weapons programs, the defense appropriations bill passed in December reduced the increase in total defense spending.

In Conventional Weapons Developments, the Pentagon canceled production of the Army's Sergeant York air defense gun in August. Secretary of Defense Caspar W. Weinberger admitted that the weapon's poor performance did not justify projected additional costs of $3 billion. The Army had already spent $1.8 billion on the gun. Congress in July agreed to allow the Pentagon to produce chemical weapons after a 16-year moratorium.

More Instances of Waste, fraud, and abuse within the armed forces fueled the debate over whether the nearly $1 trillion spent by the Pentagon during Reagan's first term had produced a more effective military force. Such prominent defense contractors as General Dynamics Corporation and General Electric Company (GE) were accused of overcharging the Pentagon. GE pleaded guilty on May 13 to defrauding the government on a missile contract and was fined $1.04 million. It was disclosed that same month that a California naval air station had purchased $659 ashtrays from Grumman Aerospace Corporation for several aircraft. Such scandals prompted Reagan to create an independent commission in July to examine the military procurement system. On December 2, a federal grand jury indicted General Dynamics on charges of trying to defraud the Pentagon of millions of dollars to cover the company's losses on a 1978 defense contract. Also indicted were four of the company's current or former officials, including James M. Beggs, director of the National Aeronautics and Space Administration.

The Senate Armed Services Committee issued a sharply critical report on the state of the armed forces on October 16. The study claimed that a drastic reorganization of the military, including the abolition of the Joint Chiefs of Staff, was necessary to eliminate interservice rivalries and mismanagement, which endangered the Pentagon's ability to wage war. "If we have to fight tomorrow," said Senator Barry Goldwater (R., Ariz.), who chaired the committee, "these problems will cause Americans to die unnecessarily. Even more, they may cause us to lose the fight."

Responding to the committee, Secretary of Defense Weinberger said in November that he op-

A soldier at Fort Ord, California, scales a cliff as part of the Army's training for its new smaller and faster-moving light infantry divisions.

posed any attempt to abolish the Joint Chiefs. Interservice rivalries, he said, were "simply not the case with the chiefs with whom I have worked." On November 20, the House of Representatives voted 383 to 27 to strengthen the authority of the chairman of the Joint Chiefs of Staff.

A Chartered Plane carrying 248 U.S. soldiers crashed near Gander, Canada, on December 12, killing everyone aboard. The soldiers were returning to Fort Campbell, Kentucky, from duty in a Middle East peacekeeping force. The crash raised questions about Pentagon supervision of commercial aircraft used to transport troops.

Personnel. All the military services met their recruitment and reenlistment objectives for 1985. An improvement in the nation's economic climate and a decline in the number of young people of recruitment age forced the Pentagon to increase incentives for reenlistment, however.

Pentagon officials said in October that all members of the armed forces would be tested for exposure to acquired immune deficiency syndrome (AIDS). Personnel found to have the disease were to be issued a medical discharge.   Thomas M. DeFrank

In WORLD BOOK, see the articles on the branches of the armed forces.

ARMY. See ARMED FORCES.

ART. See ARCHITECTURE; CLASSICAL MUSIC; DANCING; LITERATURE; POETRY; VISUAL ARTS.

ASIA

Asia made slow progress toward raising the living standards of its people during 1985 amid a number of setbacks and economic problems. Continuing wars left millions of people living in refugee camps, but some regional cooperation efforts were expanded.

Continued Economic Growth in most Asian countries improved generally low living standards, though improvements did little to eliminate wide gaps between the region's few pockets of prosperity and its many areas of near-starvation. Many countries found, however, that their economies were growing at slower rates than in the early 1980's. Because population growth remained high, in many places the increased output of food and industrial goods was barely enough to keep up with the growing number of consumers.

Food production was an Asian success story, but one that brought problems with it. Bad weather caused agricultural problems in only a few areas during 1985. Political conditions significantly hindered farming in Afghanistan and Kampuchea, which were racked by guerrilla wars. But in general, crops were good. China and India, the continent's two most populous countries, both in-

The funeral procession of Queen Rambhai Barni,
the wife of Thailand's last absolute ruler,
passes the royal palace in Bangkok in April.

Malaysia and Thailand were hard-hit by a collapse of the international market for tin. The world price for sugar dropped below production costs, hurting a number of countries. In the Philippines, Communist guerrillas gained supporters among farmers who were impoverished by low prices for sugar cane.

Asia's exporters of manufactured goods also faced difficulties. The largest Asian exporter, Japan, was so successful that foreign resentment against its trade policies grew. Meanwhile, smaller, newly industrialized countries such as Singapore and South Korea saw their economic miracles fade. The main reason was a reduced demand for their goods in the West, where the boom of the early 1980's was slowing. Singapore, one of the most spectacular economic growth stories of the 1970's, suffered a slight decline in gross national product. In Hong Kong, South Korea, and Taiwan, the accustomed economic expansion failed to materialize. The very success of all four in achieving prosperity through industrialization began to work against them. Their people earned higher wages, which pushed up costs and allowed other, poorer countries to undercut them.

Automation took some Asian jobs. United States firms had opened electronics plants during the 1970's in Indonesia, Malaysia, and other Asian countries to take advantage of their cheap labor. But by 1985, some of these plants were being closed as robots made production even cheaper in the United States.

Wars in Asia were fought internally during 1985, only occasionally lapping across borders. No two Asian countries came to open war. The largest conflicts were guerrilla resistances in Afghanistan and Kampuchea to regimes imposed by outside powers—the Soviet Union and Vietnam.

Local separatist movements fought the governments of Indonesia in western New Guinea, of Sri Lanka in Tamil ethnic areas, and of India in several regions. In Burma, the army scored victories against Karen separatists.

Conflicts between neighboring countries included skirmishes between Indian and Pakistani patrols along a disputed border in India's Jammu and Kashmir state. Chinese and Vietnamese troops also fought occasional border skirmishes.

The conflicts left millions of sad, bewildered, and impoverished refugees. Some 3 million refugees from Afghanistan had fled to Pakistan, and another 1 million to Iran. Thousands of Kampucheans huddled along the border of Thailand. Some 40,000 Tamils camped in India to escape Sri Lanka's troubles. Between 15,000 and 20,000 Karens fled from Burma into Thailand. The "boat people" who had flooded out of Vietnam during the late 1970's continued to trickle across the South China Sea in 1985.

creased their grain exports. Indonesia, the world's largest rice importer in 1981, attained self-sufficiency in rice in 1985 with a growing surplus. But Indonesia's success cut the income of farmers in Thailand, the world's largest rice exporter, who lost a major market when Indonesia stopped buying their grain.

One reason for the slowdown in economic growth was a drop in the prices Asian countries earned for the raw materials that they exported.

Facts in Brief on Asian Countries

Country	Population	Government	Monetary Unit*	Foreign Trade (million U.S. $) Exports†	Imports†
Afghanistan	14,292,000	Revolutionary Council President Babrak Karmal; Prime Minister Sultan Ali Keshtmand	afghani (50.5 = $1)	680	940
Australia	15,924,000	Governor General Sir Ninian Martin Stephen; Prime Minister Robert Hawke	dollar (1.5 = $1)	23,769	23,424
Bangladesh	104,663,000	President Hussain Muhammad Ershad	taka (27.5 = $1)	934	2,042
Bhutan	1,451,000	King Jigme Singye Wangchuck	Indian rupee (11.8 = $1) & ngultrum (no data available)	17	58
Brunei Darussalam	235,000	Sultan Sir Muda Hassanal Bolkiah	dollar (2 = $1)	3,386	728
Burma	40,069,000	President U San Yu; Prime Minister U Maung Maung Kha	kyat (7.8 = $1)	310	239
China	1,076,900,000	Communist Party General Secretary Hu Yaobang; Communist Party Deputy Chairman Deng Xiaoping; President Li Xiannian; Premier Zhao Ziyang	yuan (3.17 = $1)	24,831	25,950
India	778,434,000	President Zail Singh; Prime Minister Rajiv Gandhi	rupee (11.8 = $1)	8,294	13,215
Indonesia	168,057,000	President Suharto; Vice President Umar Wirahadikusumah	rupiah (1,099 = $1)	21,903	13,882
Iran	46,466,000	President Ali Khamenei; Prime Minister Hosein Musavi-Khamenei	rial (84.7 = $1)	19,414	11,539
Japan	120,931,000	Emperor Hirohito; Prime Minister Yasuhiro Nakasone	yen (202 = $1)	169,700	136,176
Kampuchea (Cambodia)	6,365,000	People's Revolutionary Party Secretary General & Council of State President Heng Samrin (Coalition government: President Norodom Sihanouk; Vice President Khieu Samphan; Prime Minister Son Sann)	riel (4 = $1)	no statistics available	
Korea, North	20,543,000	President Kim Il-song; Premier Yi Chong-ok	won (1 = $1.06)	1,400	1,500
Korea, South	41,446,000	President Chun Doo Hwan; Prime Minister Shinyong Lho	won (847 = $1)	29,244	30,634
Laos	3,895,000	President Souphanouvong; Prime Minister Kayson Phomvihan	kip (35 = $1)	52	125
Malaysia	15,880,000	Paramount Ruler Tunku Mahmood Iskandar Al-Haj Ibni Almarhum Sultan Ismail; Prime Minister Mahathir bin Mohamed	ringgit (2.4 = $1)	16,487	14,068
Maldives	183,000	President Maumoon Abdul Gayoom	rupee (7 = $1)	23	61
Mongolia	1,952,000	People's Great Khural Presidium Chairman Jambyn Batmonh; Council of Ministers Chairman Sodnom Dumaagiyn	tughrik (3.3 = $1)	436	655
Nepal	16,856,000	King Birendra Bir Bikram Shah Dev; Prime Minister Lokendra Bahadur Chand	rupee (18.2 = $1)	100	473
New Zealand	3,315,000	Governor General Sir Paul Reeves; Prime Minister David R. Lange	dollar (2 = $1)	5,517	6,195
Pakistan	102,836,000	President M. Zia-ul-Haq; Prime Minister Mohammed Khan Junejo	rupee (15.7 = $1)	2,558	5,853
Papua New Guinea	3,506,000	Governor General Sir Kingsford Dibela; Prime Minister Paias Wingti	kina (1 = $1.01)	915	966
Philippines	57,214,000	President Ferdinand E. Marcos; Prime Minister César E. A. Virata	peso (18.5 = $1)	5,274	6,432
Russia	281,057,000	Communist Party General Secretary Mikhail S. Gorbachev; Supreme Soviet Presidium Chairman Andrei A. Gromyko; Council of Ministers Chairman Nikolai I. Ryzhkov	ruble (1 = $1.31)	91,649	80,624
Singapore	2,601,000	President Wee Kim Wee; Prime Minister Lee Kuan Yew	dollar (2.1 = $1)	24,070	28,667
Sri Lanka	16,660,000	President J. R. Jayewardene; Prime Minister R. Premadasa	rupee (27 = $1)	1,467	1,869
Taiwan	19,862,000	President Chiang Ching-kuo; Prime Minister Sun Yun-hsuan	new Taiwan dollar (37 = $1)	30,400	21,600
Thailand	53,754,000	King Bhumibol Adulyadej; Prime Minister Prem Tinsulanonda	baht (25 = $1)	7,414	10,398
Vietnam	60,826,000	Communist Party General Secretary Le Duan; National Assembly Chairman Nguyen Huu Tho; Prime Minister Pham Van Dong	dong (9.75 = $1)	652	1,550

*Exchange rates as of Dec. 1, 1985, or latest available data.   †Latest available data.

Kampuchean refugees gather in Khao Ta Ngoc, Thailand, where they fled to avoid fighting between Vietnamese occupation forces and Kampuchean guerrillas.

International Negotiations tried to end some of the conflicts. The United Nations sponsored indirect talks between Afghanistan—advised by the Soviet Union—and Pakistan. Two rounds of these talks in 1985 failed to fix a timetable for a Soviet troop withdrawal from Afghanistan.

China and the Soviet Union continued meetings that brought agreement on expanded trade ties but failed to resolve political and military issues. China insisted that better relations with Moscow depended on a reduction of Soviet troops near its border, a Soviet withdrawal from Afghanistan, and a halt to Soviet aid for Vietnam's war in Kampuchea. The Soviets refused to discuss these conditions. India tried to mediate an end to Sri Lanka's ethnic strife, but success was not in sight.

One negotiating success was achieved by Burma and Bangladesh. They completed marking their 123-mile (197.9-kilometer) border and on August 12 formally accepted a map of the official line. India and China in November held another round of negotiations on their Himalayan border. A dispute about it had led to a limited war between the two countries in 1962, and agreement remained elusive. Despite the border argument, India and China signed an agreement on Nov. 23, 1985, to expand trade with each other.

A future political change caused new anxiety in 1985. Great Britain had agreed with China in 1984 that the British colony of Hong Kong would be transferred to Chinese control in 1997 but would retain its own laws for another 50 years. Both countries formally ratified that agreement on May 27, 1985. Soon after, Chinese leader Peng Zhen—a member of the Communist Party Politburo and chairman of China's parliament—said that China's parliament, rather than Hong Kong courts, should have the final word on Hong Kong's legal status. This worried many residents of the colony, who wanted more self-government.

Britain, meanwhile, began to introduce democracy to Hong Kong. On September 26, it conducted the first colonywide elections. Voters chose 24 members of the Legislative Council, which also had 32 members appointed by the governor.

Peng Zhen said that Macao as well as Hong Kong should be ready for reunification with China in 1997. Macao, a Portuguese colony on China's coast, had not been the subject of any agreement.

Regional Cooperation. The 30th anniversary of the Asia-Africa Conference, the first big meeting of newly independent and developing countries, was celebrated in April 1985. Delegates from more than 80 countries and national liberation movements met in Bandung, the Indonesian resort where leaders of 29 African and Asian nations had gathered in 1955. That meeting laid the foundation for the nonaligned movement. At the

201

1985 gathering, tensions over such issues as Afghanistan and Kampuchea kept the delegates from agreeing on anything beyond economic development and disarmament.

The Association of Southeast Asian Nations (ASEAN)—Brunei, Indonesia, Malaysia, the Philippines, Singapore, and Thailand—made new efforts to find a solution to Kampuchea's troubles. Foreign ministers of the six countries on February 11 appealed to nations friendly toward the Kampuchean resistance movement to supply the rebels with weapons. On July 13, ASEAN foreign ministers ended a meeting that discussed a possible diplomatic settlement to the conflict in Kampuchea. Both Vietnam and its puppet government in Kampuchea rejected the ASEAN proposals.

A new regional group, the South Asian Association for Regional Cooperation, held its first summit meeting on December 7 and 8 in Dhaka, Bangladesh. The members were Bangladesh, Bhutan, India, the Maldives, Nepal, Pakistan, and Sri Lanka. Foreign ministers of the seven nations met in Thimphu, Bhutan, on May 13 and 14 to plan the summit. They agreed on expanding economic cooperation but could not settle on a common trade and industrial policy. Political suspicions limited the chances for a well-integrated organization. The smaller nations, which all together have less than one-third India's population and only about one-fourth as much wealth, feared that India might use the association to dominate them.

Asia's Leadership remained basically unchanged. The only reported coup attempt, in Thailand on September 9, quickly failed. On September 2, Wee Kim Wee became president of Singapore, a largely ceremonial post. Prime Minister Lee Kuan Yew holds the real governing power. Wee succeeded Devan Nair, who resigned on March 27 because of alcoholism.

Three Indochinese leaders died during the year. Xuan Thuy, a vice chairman of Vietnam's National Assembly, died in Hanoi on June 18. He had headed the North Vietnamese team that negotiated in Paris with United States officials during the Vietnam War. Phoumi Nosavan, a leader of anti-Communist forces in Laos in the early 1960's and briefly prime minister in 1962, died in Thailand on Nov. 3, 1985. Former Kampuchean President Lon Nol—who overthrew Prince Norodom Sihanouk in 1970—died in Fullerton, Calif., on Nov. 17, 1985. Lon had fled to the United States after the Communist Khmer Rouge ousted him in 1975.   Henry S. Bradsher

See also the various Asian country articles. In the Special Reports section, see CHINA AFTER MAO: CHARTING A NEW COURSE. In the WORLD BOOK SUPPLEMENT section, see BURMA. In WORLD BOOK, see ASIA.

ASTRONOMY. On Sept. 11, 1985, the *International Cometary Explorer* (*ICE*) flew through the tail of Comet Giacobini-Zinner, marking the first visit of a spacecraft to a comet. *ICE*, a National Aeronautics and Space Administration (NASA) spacecraft, passed 8,000 kilometers (5,000 miles) behind the solid nucleus, or core, of the comet. The comet was about 71 million kilometers (44 million miles) from Earth at the time of the encounter.

Hundreds of microscopic particles of dust from the comet struck *ICE* at estimated impact speeds of 21 kilometers (13 miles) per second, but the spacecraft suffered no apparent damage. This finding encouraged scientists concerned about possible damage to spacecraft from dust bombardment during the missions to Halley's Comet in 1986 (see Close-Up).

Since the 1950's, astronomers have believed that comets are "dirty snowballs," frozen mixtures of ice and dust. When warmed by the sun, the ices vaporize into a gas and release dust trapped inside the ice layers. The gas and dust spread out to make the *coma*, or head of the comet, and stream away in the direction opposite the sun to form the comet's long, shining tail.

Instruments Aboard *ICE* revealed three major new findings about comets and their structure. The first was the unexpected discovery of *pickup ions*—heavy, electrically charged gas molecules. Pickup ions are not usually seen in interplanetary space, but *ICE* began detecting them when it was still 1.6 million kilometers (1 million miles) from the comet. They appeared to be coming from the sun and moving toward the comet. This phenomenon puzzled scientists at first because they were sure that the pickup ions consisted of molecules shed by the comet itself.

The scientists concluded that the heavy molecules left the comet while they were still electrically neutral. Unlike ions, neutral molecules are not confined by magnetic fields in the comet. Consequently, these neutral molecules escaped in all directions and at great distances. As the escaping molecules drifted away at low speed, they were struck by ultraviolet light from the sun, which converted them to positively charged ions.

Once charged, the molecules were subject to electrical forces exerted by the *solar wind*, a continuous stream of electrically charged subatomic particles ejected from the sun at supersonic speeds. The solar wind accelerated the charged ions to speeds reaching about 800 kilometers (500 miles) per second and swept some of them back toward the comet, so that they appeared to be coming from the sun and moving toward the comet in directed beams. The term *pickup* indicates that the ions were swept up by the solar wind, much as debris is carried off by a raging river that has overflowed its banks.

The second major finding concerned a vast, thick bullet-shaped structure, invisible on photographs, that surrounds and precedes the comet as it flies through space, much as the bow wave of a fast motorboat plows ahead of the boat as it speeds across the water. Third, *ICE* found that the structure of the comet's ion tail, composed of electrified gas, was threaded with a magnetic field shaped like a hairpin. Magnetic field lines are bent around the head of the comet and continue along each side of the ion tail with opposite polarity. The magnetic hairpin confines the ionized molecules, causing them to flow away from the comet's head in the characteristic narrow shape of a comet tail. *ICE* also discovered that the ion tail is relatively cool, about one-fifth the temperature of the solar wind.

Meteorite Origins. In April 1985, mathematician Jack Wisdom of the Massachusetts Institute of Technology in Cambridge reported findings that help answer two questions: Where is the missing material from the Kirkwood gaps, and where do meteorites come from? Between the orbits of Mars and Jupiter, thousands of asteroids revolve around the sun, each with a slightly different orbital period—that is, each asteroid follows a different path that requires a different period of time to complete. But certain orbital periods in this asteroid belt are missing, as though asteroids with such periods were removed from their orbits. The missing orbital periods came to be known as the *Kirkwood gaps*, after their discovery by American astronomer Daniel Kirkwood in 1866. Astronomers have long thought that the missing asteroids were thrown out of their orbits by gravitational disturbances from the planet Jupiter, but no one had presented a satisfactory explanation for what happened to the asteroids once they were removed.

Using new mathematical calculations, Wisdom proved that asteroids from the gaps were ejected into new orbits that crossed the path of Mars, where gravitational tugs exerted by Mars sent them on into still different orbits. Wisdom's calculations showed that some of the asteroids are ejected into orbits that cross the path of Earth. Asteroids are continually colliding with one another, and these collisions create smaller fragments called meteoroids. It now seems that most meteorites, which are meteoroids that have landed on Earth, represent material that was originally ejected from the Kirkwood gaps.

Black Hole. Astronomers suspect that black holes of immense mass may lurk at the centers of many galaxies, including our own. (Black holes are objects so dense that their powerful gravity prevents even light from escaping.) Evidence for this theory was reported in May and June 1985 by two groups of observers. In May, a team of astrono-

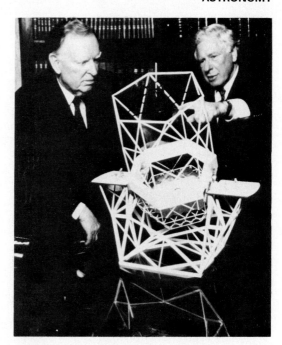

Officials examine a model of the Keck optical telescope, the world's largest, to be built atop Mauna Kea, an extinct volcano in Hawaii.

mers led by Kwok-Yung Lo of the California Institute of Technology in Pasadena announced that the strong radio signals from the center of our own Milky Way galaxy come from a region that is barely larger in diameter than the orbit of Saturn, about 1.4 billion kilometers (870 million miles) across, which is almost infinitesimal on the scale of the Galaxy as a whole. Such a concentrated source of radio signals is consistent with theories describing a supermassive black hole.

In June, a group of infrared astronomers led by Charles H. Townes of the University of California, Berkeley, reported that gas located about 5.5 *light-years* from the center of the Milky Way is orbiting the center at a speed of 110 kilometers (68 miles) per second. (A light-year is the distance light travels in one year, about 9.5 trillion kilometers or 5.9 trillion miles.) The speed of the orbiting gas indicates the existence of something massive at the center of the Galaxy because the greater the central mass, the higher the speed of orbiting matter. The masses of stars that can be seen in the region of the galactic center, however, do not appear to be sufficient to account for the speed of the orbiting gas. This seems to indicate the presence at the center of our Galaxy of a black hole having about 4 million times the mass of our sun. Stephen P. Maran

See also Space Exploration. In World Book, see Astronomy.

A Close Encounter with Halley's Comet

One of the longest-running sequels in the history of sky watching drew attention to the heavens during 1985 and 1986. Halley's Comet made its 30th recorded appearance, giving most people a rare, once-in-a-lifetime opportunity to see it.

This most famous of comets comes around on an average of every 77 years and has been doing so since at least 240 B.C., the first time its appearance was recorded. The last time Halley's Comet appeared in the sky was 1910.

Halley's Comet travels on an *elliptical* (oval-shaped) path that takes it just beyond the orbit of Neptune, about 3 billion miles (4.8 billion kilometers) from the sun at its farthest point. Halley's Comet traveled past Earth in November 1985, rounded the sun in February 1986, and will pass close to Earth again in April 1986 as it heads back out to the outer reaches of the solar system.

Astronomers have identified approximately 1,000 comets, but Halley's Comet is particularly famous for several reasons. First, its relatively large size and close approaches to Earth have made it easy to see with the naked eye, unlike many comets that can be seen only with large telescopes. Second, Halley's Comet was the first comet to have its return predicted. Astronomers once thought comets traveled in straight lines and were seen once and never again. But in 1705, English astronomer Edmond Halley (pronounced *HAL ee* or possibly *HAWL ee*) claimed that a comet he observed in 1682 was the same one that appeared in 1531 and 1607, and he predicted it would return in 1758. When it did, the comet was named after him.

Halley's Comet is famous, too, for its association with historic events. It was visible in 1066 when William, Duke of Normandy, invaded England. William's Norman troops took the comet as a sign of good luck for them and bad luck for King Harold, the last Anglo-Saxon king of England, who was killed by the Normans at the Battle of Hastings that year. The comet's supposed role is depicted in a scene from the famous Bayeux Tapestry, which was commissioned by William to commemorate the Norman conquest. The scene shows a comet hovering above King Harold, who looks upset. According to legend, Halley's Comet foretold the death of the Roman general Marcus Agrippa in 12 B.C., the revolt of Jerusalem in A.D. 66, and the defeat of Attila the Hun in A.D. 451.

Superstitious beliefs about Halley's Comet persisted during the comet's 1910 return, despite the best efforts of scientists to calm fears. Many people were convinced that the end of the world was at hand and expected the comet to collide with Earth, though astronomers noted that at its closest approach, Halley's Comet would be 15 million miles (24 million kilometers) away.

Most people in the United States, however,

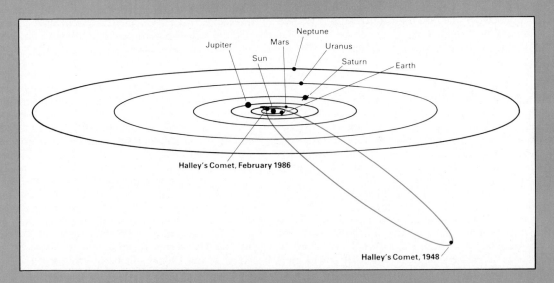

Halley's Comet follows an *elliptical* (oval-shaped) path through the solar system that brought it closest to the sun in February 1986.

greeted the comet's 1910 arrival calmly. The comet became a social, as well as a celestial, phenomenon. Advertisers made the comet seem almost domestic, using its appearance as a theme to market soaps, perfume, fountain pens, and custard or to sell comet socks and comet vests. A composer was inspired to create "Halley's Comet Rag," and manufacturers churned out tons of comet memorabilia. In New York City, hostesses held rooftop parties so that their guests could observe the comet while sipping "comet cocktails."

In 1910, the most advanced instrument available to astronomers was the 60-inch (152-centimeter) telescope at Mount Wilson Observatory in southwestern California. In 1986, a fleet of four crewless spacecraft, launched by various nations, was expected to fly past the comet in March, obtaining the most detailed close-up views of a comet ever achieved. A fifth crewless spacecraft will monitor the comet from afar. And on Earth, the International Halley Watch, a worldwide organization of professional and amateur astronomers, planned to use telescopes and other scientific instruments to observe the comet.

During a single week in March 1986, when the spacecraft were to fly past Halley's Comet, astronomers expected to learn more about comets than scientists have learned in all of the 2,226 years since Halley's Comet was first recorded. They hoped to make the first visual sighting of a comet's nucleus, analyze its makeup, and determine if comets can shed light on the origin of the solar system.

Since 1950, most astronomers have believed that comets are "dirty snowballs," mixtures of ice and dust and various chemical compounds such as ammonia and methane. Many astronomers think that comets formed at the same time as the solar system, about 4½ billion years ago, and have remained unchanged since then.

When a comet travels in the outer reaches of the solar system, far from the sun, it is a small frozen body, irregular in size. This frozen lump of ice and dust is known as the *nucleus*. Astronomers have estimated that the nucleus of Halley's Comet is 2.5 to 6 miles (4 to 10 kilometers) in diameter. But no one has actually seen the nucleus of a comet because a comet grows warmer as it approaches the sun, and its outermost ices are released as a gas that forms a huge cloud, known as the *coma*, around the nucleus. The coma makes it impossible to see the nucleus. The coma may grow as large as 60,000 to 600,000 miles (100,000 to 1 million kilometers) in diameter.

The closer the comet gets to the sun, the more material it loses. As the ices turn into gas,

dust particles trapped within the ices are released, and the gas and dust stream away to form the comet's *tail*. These streams of dust and electrically charged gas are pushed away from the nucleus by solar forces, so the tail always points away from the sun. A comet's tail can range in length from 620,000 to 6.2 million miles (1 million to 10 million kilometers).

Comets have been called frauds because their long tails and enormous comas make them seem immense, but actually they are among the smallest objects in the solar system. According to astronomer Andrew G. Fraknoi of the Astronomical Society of the Pacific in San Francisco, "If you took millions of miles of the tail, you could stuff it in a suitcase and still have room left over for a change of underwear."

Some of the spacecraft sent to fly past Halley's Comet were to collect and analyze samples of the dust streaming from the nucleus and perhaps provide the first glimpses of the nucleus. The probes belong to the European Space Agency (ESA), an association of 11 Western European countries; Japan; and the Soviet Union. The United States did not send a spacecraft to Halley's Comet, but a space shuttle mission scheduled for March 1986 was equipped with telescopes to observe the comet from above Earth's atmosphere.

The Soviet Union launched its two probes, *Vega 1* and *Vega 2*, in December 1984. The probes were launched early because they traveled by way of Venus. After dropping off scientific instruments to probe Venus' atmosphere and study the planet's surface, the two spacecraft journeyed on to rendezvous with Halley's Comet.

The ESA's *Giotto* spacecraft—which was named after the Italian artist Giotto, who depicted a comet as the Star of Bethlehem in a fresco painted in the 1300's—was to come closest to the comet, approaching to within 300 miles (480 kilometers) of the nucleus. Finally, two Japanese spacecraft were to study the comet, one from a much greater distance.

Although astronomers seemed likely to enjoy their best views ever of a comet, many people in the Northern Hemisphere faced disappointment. Some astronomers thought that Halley's Comet would not put on much of a show this time around. At its closest point to Earth in April 1986, it was to be 39 million miles (63 million kilometers) away, and the best view would be from the Southern Hemisphere. Also, astronomers warned that people in cities might be unable to see the comet due to the glare of city lights. For many people, television seemed likely to provide the best view of the comet, which will not be back until 2061.   Rod Such

Two whales flounder on the shore near Newcastle, Australia, where a herd of more than 60 whales swam ashore in June. Only 21 survived.

AUSTRALIA. The Labor Party government of Australia's Prime Minister Robert Hawke maintained firm political control during 1985. The opposition Liberal Party elected John Howard party leader on September 5, replacing Andrew Peacock, who resigned the post. Howard, who served as treasurer in the government of Malcolm Fraser, made his reputation in the field of economic policy.

In the only state election of 1985, the Labor Party government of Premier John Cain was reelected in Victoria on March 2. On October 3, Sir Brian Murray resigned as governor of Victoria after it was revealed that he had accepted free airline tickets. Victoria celebrated its 150th anniversary in October, highlighted by a visit from the Prince and Princess of Wales.

A judge on Australia's High Court, the country's highest judicial body, was found guilty on July 5 of attempting to pervert the course of justice. The judge, Justice Lionel K. Murphy, allegedly had tried to influence the decision of a lower court. On September 3, the Supreme Court of New South Wales sentenced Murphy to 18 months in jail. He was freed on bail, however, and appealed the conviction in November. His appeal was upheld, and a retrial was ordered.

The Economy. Australia's economy was troubled by continued deficits in the national budget and in overseas trade. Inflation for the fiscal year ending in June 1985 was 6.7 per cent, compared with 6.5 per cent for the previous year. The overall number of jobs increased, but the unemployment rate remained above 8 per cent.

Treasurer Paul Keating announced on February 27 that 16 foreign banks would be allowed to begin operations in Australia. The banks, from eight countries, were selected from among 42 applicants. Keating estimated that this action would create 4,500 jobs in Australia within five years.

On August 20, Keating presented the federal budget for fiscal year 1985-1986. It provided for spending of $69 billion. It anticipated a growth rate of 4.5 per cent and a $1.8-billion reduction of the budget deficit to $4.9 billion. (All monetary amounts in this article are Australian dollars, with $1 = U.S. 68 cents as of Dec. 31, 1985.)

On September 4, the government and the Australian Council of Trade Unions agreed to a two-year extension of wage and price restraints. This encouraged hopes for a continued low level of labor disputes.

The Labor government on June 4 proposed a 12.5 per cent sales tax on most goods and services to reduce the income tax and eliminate some tax cheating. The proposal was discussed by leaders of government, business, labor, and community groups at a tax summit in Canberra, Australia's capital, in July. These representatives agreed on the need for taxation reform but objected to the sales tax. On September 19, the government announced a reduction in the income tax for 1986 and 1987. No sales tax was imposed, but capital gains and employee benefits were to be taxed and the corporate income tax increased.

Australia's trade deficit for the fiscal year ending in June 1985 was $1.3 billion. The total balance-of-payments deficit, including international financial transactions, reached a record $10.74 billion. Australia's exports grew by about 20 per cent, but imports increased about 30 per cent.

Exports of sugar, beef, and wheat suffered from low prices on the world market. On July 16, the Bureau of Agricultural Economics estimated that the net value of farm production in Australia would be 22 per cent below the 1984 level.

The government attributed some of the beef industry's trouble to competition in foreign markets from subsidized farm exports from the European Community (EC). In September, the EC promised that it would not sell subsidized agricultural products at discount prices in Asian markets.

Coal was Australia's most successful mineral export in 1985. Australia is the world's largest exporter of coal, with Japan as its biggest market.

Increasing inflation and the trade deficit led to a fall in the value of the Australian dollar. The Australian dollar decreased in value from about U.S. 83 cents in January to about U.S. 65 cents in May and ended the year at U.S. 68 cents. This weakening of the currency made Australian exports more attractive during the latter part of the year, but demand for imports remained high.

Foreign Affairs were dominated by issues of nuclear weapons and the ANZUS military alliance among Australia, New Zealand, and the United States. The Hawke government declared its support for the alliance in spite of New Zealand's refusal to allow nuclear-armed warships in its ports. On February 6, during a visit to the United States, Hawke announced that Australia would not allow U.S. planes to use bases in Australia to monitor tests of the American MX missile. On February 28, he said Australia would not share with New Zealand any intelligence gained from the United States. Hawke said, however, that it was not the business of his government to put pressure on New Zealand. Australia and New Zealand announced on April 3 that they would continue to conduct joint military exercises.

On August 6, Australia and seven other nations of the 13-nation South Pacific Forum signed a treaty declaring the South Pacific a nuclear-free zone. The pact, signed at a meeting on Rarotonga in the Cook Islands, prohibits the manufacture, use, testing, or stockpiling of nuclear weapons in the area controlled by the signing countries. The agreement allows the passage of nuclear-armed or nuclear-powered vessels through the region, but it leaves to individual countries the decision of whether to give such vessels port privileges.

In related developments, the Australian government objected to French nuclear weapons testing at Mururoa Atoll in the Pacific Ocean. It also condemned the July 10 bombing by French secret service agents in New Zealand waters of the *Rainbow Warrior*, a ship owned by the Greenpeace environmental group.

Other Developments. In January, Helen Williams was appointed secretary of the Department of Education. Williams, a long-time officer of the agency, is the first woman to head a federal government department.

On October 26, the government returned ownership of Ayers Rock in the Northern Territory to the Mutitjulus, an Aborigine people. The rock, a sacred site for the Mutitjulus and Australia's greatest tourist attraction, will be leased back to the government for continued use as a national park.

On Australia Day, January 26, Lois O'Donoghue, an Aborigine, was named Australian of the Year. This honor came in recognition of her contribution as special adviser on Aboriginal housing.

In Western Australia, preparations were underway for the America's Cup yacht race to be held near Perth in 1987.   J. D. B. Miller

See also ASIA (Facts in Brief Table); NEW ZEALAND. In WORLD BOOK, see AUSTRALIA.

AUSTRIA suffered from a costly wine scandal in 1985. On July 11, West Germany announced that it had seized thousands of bottles of imported Austrian wine because large amounts of the beverage had been poisoned with diethylene glycol, a chemical used in automobile antifreeze. Adding the chemical sweetened the wine, enabling merchants to raise its price.

Austrian police arrested four wine manufacturers from the major winegrowing area of Burgenland on July 20. On July 23, the farmers' union called for the resignation of Agriculture Minister Günther Haiden, charging that his department had not checked wine properly and had not acted quickly enough when the contamination was first discovered in April. By September 1, Austrian police had arrested 40 manufacturers, merchants, and chemists. The sale of Austrian wines was banned in a number of countries, including France, Great Britain, and the United States.

Haiden refused to resign and promised new legislation for the wine industry. He made good on his promise, submitting a bill that would establish a system of inspections to prevent the addition of improper substances to wine. On October 24, the day the bill was due for a vote, angry winegrowers blockaded the parliament building in protest. The growers handed in a petition, then left. Parliament proceeded to pass the bill.

A health technician in West Berlin in July tests wine imported from Austria after a contaminant was found in some of that country's wine.

War Criminal. On January 25, the three main political parties demanded the resignation of Defense Minister Friedhelm Frischenschlager for welcoming Nazi war criminal Walter Reder to Austria the previous day. Reder, an Austrian, had flown to Austria immediately after his release from prison in Italy. He had been sentenced in 1951 to a life term for leading a massacre in an Italian village during World War II. In 1980, however, an Italian court had shortened his sentence. Frischenschlager met Reder at Graz, shook his hand, and accompanied him in an Austrian military plane to Baden, a town near Vienna.

On January 29, Chancellor Fred Sinowatz recalled Frischenschlager from a visit to Egypt to explain his behavior to the cabinet. The minister apologized to the cabinet for his "false estimation of the situation." Sinowatz accepted the apology and said he would resign if Frischenschlager left the government. On February 1, however, parliament gave the defense minister a vote of confidence, 98 to 80.

Economy Boosted. Austria's 1984 economic upswing continued in 1985. Manufacturing and mining largely accounted for a 3 per cent growth in the gross domestic product, the value of goods and services produced in the country. Kenneth Brown

See also EUROPE (Facts in Brief Table). In WORLD BOOK, see AUSTRIA.

AUTOMOBILE. In 1985, an unusually eventful year for the automobile industry, total United States sales of new cars and trucks rose to a record 15.6 million units. Cut-rate financing, generally good economic times, and a variety of new models contributed to the boom.

Sales performance, however, did not seem as important as three other developments. They were the large-scale movement of Japanese automobile manufacturers into U.S. assembly operations; multibillion-dollar business ventures outside the auto industry by major U.S. automakers; and the establishment of a new line of low-priced cars made up entirely of imports.

Record Sales. Although auto industry analysts generally agreed that 1985 was the peak of the current auto-sales cycle, there was no evidence that the industry would soon lapse into a major recession. A high level of consumer confidence and a favorable outlook for inflation and gasoline prices promised another good year in 1986.

It was clear, however, that the best years for U.S. automakers were in the past. The overall sales record of 15.6 million cars and trucks set in 1985 was slightly better than the previous high of 15.42 million in 1978. But although total sales by U.S. automakers in 1985 reached 12.03 million cars and trucks—a 5.2 per cent increase over 1984—domestic sales were down 8.1 per cent from the 1978 record of 13.09 million units. Foreign carmakers posted the biggest gains, selling 3.58 million vehicles, up 17 per cent from 1984 and 53 per cent over 1978's 2.34 million.

Japanese Challenge. In March, Japan announced it would continue to restrict auto imports to the United States after a four-year voluntary restraint program expired in April. Japanese automakers, however, were allowed to increase the number of cars shipped by 24 per cent. Nevertheless, demand for Japanese cars in the United States continued to outrun supplies.

As a result, Japanese automakers decided the only way to substantially increase car sales in the United States was to begin producing cars there. In March, Nissan Motor Company began building cars at its truck plant in Smyrna, Tenn. Honda Motor Company continued work on a major expansion of its car assembly plant in Marysville, Ohio, and announced it would manufacture some auto engines in the United States instead of importing them. Mazda Motor Manufacturing (U.S.A.) Corporation broke ground in Flat Rock, Mich., in May for an automobile-assembly plant.

In October, Mitsubishi Motors Corporation and Chrysler Corporation announced plans for a joint auto plant in central Illinois. And in December, Toyota Motor Corporation announced it would build auto assembly plants near Georgetown, Ky., and in Cambridge, Ontario, in Canada.

Diversification. Most economists and auto industry analysts agreed that Japanese expansion came at the expense of U.S. manufacturers. The Big Three automakers—Ford Motor Company, Chrysler, and General Motors Corporation (GM)—appeared to agree that their future growth in the automobile industry was limited. Each company moved aggressively into other businesses.

In June, GM bought the Hughes Aircraft Company for an estimated $5.1 billion. In purchasing Hughes—one of the world's chief defense, electronics, and telecommunications firms—GM gained entry into several new high-technology, high-growth industries.

In August, Ford paid $493 million for First Nationwide Financial Corporation, the ninth largest U.S. savings and loan association, and in October, Ford bought Sperry New Holland, Sperry Corporation's farm implement division, for $330 million.

Diversification spending at Chrysler exceeded $1 billion in 1985. Chrysler bought Gulfstream Aerospace Corporation for $640 million and E. F. Hutton Credit Corporation for $125 million in June, and spent $405 million for FinanceAmerica, the consumer credit operation of BankAmerica Corporation, in October.

General Motors executives in January stand by a model of the Saturn, a new subcompact car that will be produced at a new plant in Tennessee.

The president of Mazda Motor Manufacturing (U.S.A.) breaks ground in a Shinto ceremony for a new plant in Flat Rock, Mich., in May.

The goals in each case were to enter new areas with growth potential and to obtain sources of earnings outside the notoriously cyclic auto business. Industry executives were convinced that a steadier flow of earnings during the inevitable slumps in car sales would help support stock prices and corporate credit ratings.

Planning for the Future. But the carmakers did not ignore their core business. Investments in new car and truck development and in new factories remained at record levels, far exceeding the sums spent for diversification. Each of the Big Three companies insisted that its most important task was to prepare its automotive operations for intensified global competition.

GM followed through by creating Saturn Corporation, a wholly owned subsidiary with $5 billion in assets, to produce, in the United States, profitable small cars that could compete with efficiently manufactured imports. After receiving bids from 35 states eager to host Saturn's $3.5-billion manufacturing complex, which was expected to create more than 6,000 jobs, the company announced in July that it had selected Spring Hill, Tenn., as the plant site. The Saturn will be the first new brand name from GM since the 1920's.

Saturn officials gambled that by relying on new, highly automated production techniques and a new contract with the United Automobile Workers that cut labor costs, they could keep a major share of small-car production from going overseas.

Ford's Project Alpha had a similar goal. The project was designed to investigate every aspect of car manufacturing to increase efficiency. Ford executives said their findings probably would be applied to ongoing car and truck programs rather than focused on a single car line or plant.

Chrysler also initiated a small-car-manufacturing study—Project Liberty. The project's goal was to produce a highly efficient small car while reducing manufacturing costs by $2,000 per vehicle.

A New Class. Saturn, Alpha, and Liberty concentrated on the family subcompact market. With base prices of about $5,500 to $6,000, that market had served as the industry's bottom line.

But that changed quickly with the introduction of a new entry-level vehicle—the Yugo, a car smaller than the Escort. Built in Yugoslavia, the Yugo entered the U.S. market with a base price just under $4,000. Public reaction was favorable.

Future cars in the Yugo class were expected from Japan, South Korea, Spain, Brazil, and Italy. Auto industry analysts predicted that they would capture no more than 5 per cent of the overall U.S. car market. But the analysts also expected that they would open the entire small-car market to the most intense price competition in recent memory. James V. Higgins

In WORLD BOOK, see AUTOMOBILE.

AUTOMOBILE RACING. Al Unser, Sr., and Darrell Waltrip won the two most important United States automobile-racing series of 1985. The deciding margin for each came in his season's last race.

The 46-year-old Unser, of Albuquerque, N. Mex., narrowly defeated his 23-year-old son, Al Unser, Jr., in the Championship Auto Racing Teams (CART) series of 15 races for Indianapolis-type cars. Waltrip, of Franklin, Tenn., overtook Bill Elliott of Dawsonville, Ga., in the National Association for Stock Car Racing (NASCAR) series of 28 races for late-model sedans.

CART. The championship was decided on November 9 in Miami, Fla. Al Unser, Sr., started that race three points ahead of his son and had to finish not more than one place behind him to become the U.S. champion. As it turned out, the son finished third in the race and the father fourth, so the father won the series, 151 points to 150.

The most important race for these cars was the Indianapolis 500 on May 26. On May 11, the first day of time trials, Scott Brayton of Coldwater, Mich., set a one-lap record of 214.199 miles per hour (mph) or 344.720 kilometers per hour (kph). Duane (Pancho) Carter, Jr., of Brownsburg, Ind., won the pole position with a four-lap average of 212.583 mph (342.119 kph). Of the 33 starters, 30 were powered by British Cosworth V-8 engines.

Brayton and Carter used Buick V-6 turbo engines, but despite their trial runs, neither did well in the race. Brayton finished 30th because his engine failed after 19 laps, and Carter was last because his engine's oil pump failed after six laps.

Danny Sullivan of Louisville, Ky., a former New York City taxi driver, won, beating Mario Andretti of Nazareth, Pa., by 2.47 seconds. Sullivan's average speed was 152.982 mph (246.201 kph).

NASCAR. Elliott, in a Ford Thunderbird, won 10 of the first 20 races. He also earned a $1-million bonus by winning three of the four major races in the series—the Daytona 500 on February 17 in Daytona Beach, Fla.; the Winston 500 on May 5 in Talladega, Ala.; and the Southern 500 on September 1 in Darlington, S.C. Had he also won the World 600 on May 26 in Charlotte, N.C., he would have earned another $1-million bonus. Instead, Waltrip won, and Elliott finished 18th.

Although Waltrip won only 3 races to Elliott's 11, Waltrip had more high finishes and thus earned more points. He led Elliott for the series championship by 4,141 points to 4,121 entering the final race of the year on November 17 in Riverside, Calif. Waltrip won the championship when he finished seventh, well ahead of Elliott. Elliott's consolation was more than $2 million in prize money, a one-year record for the sport.

Danny Sullivan, left, spins out of control, narrowly avoiding the concrete wall, during the Indianapolis 500 in May, which he went on to win.

Formula One. The World Drivers' Championship was decided in 16 Grand Prix races in Australia, Brazil, Canada, several European countries, the United States, and South Africa. The Formula One cars are lighter, less powerful versions of the open-cockpit, no-fender Indianapolis cars.

In 1985, Alain Prost of France won the championship comfortably with 76 points to 53 for second-place Michele Alboreto of Italy in a Ferrari. Prost, in a McLaren-TAG-Porsche, won five Grand Prix races: Brazil in April, Monaco in May, Great Britain in July, Austria in August, and Italy in September. In the North American races, Alboreto won the Canadian Grand Prix on June 16 in Montreal, Que., and Keke Rosberg of Finland, in a Williams-Honda, won the U.S. Grand Prix on June 23 in Detroit.

Other Races. A Porsche 956 driven by John Winter and Klaus Ludwig of West Germany and Paolo Barilla of Italy won the 24 Hours of Le Mans, held on June 15 and 16 in France. At age 53, Don Garlits of Ocala, Fla., won the world and U.S. titles for top-fuel dragsters and set a record of 268.01 mph (431.32 kph). Other leading U.S. drivers included Al Holbert of Warrington, Pa., in grand touring (GT) races and Willy T. Ribbs of San Jose in the Trans-Am series.   Frank Litsky

In the WORLD BOOK SUPPLEMENT section, see AUTOMOBILE RACING.

AVIATION. Airline crashes and safety issues dominated aviation news in 1985. The United States airline industry did well financially in spite of major strikes, and the number of passengers increased over 1984 levels. Passenger traffic for the first eight months of 1985 was 13 per cent above the level for 1984. Airline stocks rose in value more than 20 per cent over the first nine months of 1985, fueled by sales and mergers of major airline companies.

Crashes and Air Safety. The International Civil Aviation Organization reported that 2,089 people died during 1985 as a result of civil aviation accidents—the highest death toll in aviation history. There was no simple explanation for the great increase. Some of the crashes appeared to be due to mistakes by pilots, mechanics, or air-traffic controllers. Others seemed to have been caused by such factors as bad weather, mechanical failure, and even sabotage.

On January 1, an Eastern Airlines Boeing 727 slammed into a mountain in Bolivia, killing 29 people. On June 23, an Air-India Boeing 747 crashed off the coast of Ireland, killing all 329 people on board. Evidence pointed to terrorist sabotage as the cause of the crash. A Delta Air Lines Lockheed L-1011 Tristar crashed at Dallas-Fort Worth International Airport on August 2, killing 137 people. The worst single-plane accident in history occurred in Japan on August 12, when a Japan Air Lines Boeing 747 crashed into Mount Osutaka, near Tokyo, killing 520 people. Mechanical failure or faulty repair work was suspected as the cause of the accident. On August 22, an engine on a British Airtours Boeing 737 burst into flames on take-off from Manchester Airport in England. The resulting fire killed 55 people. On December 12, a chartered jet carrying U.S. military personnel home from the Middle East crashed in Gander, Canada. All 248 soldiers and 8 crew members aboard were killed.

A United States Department of Transportation (DOT) report critical of the safety-enforcement program of the Federal Aviation Administration (FAA) was made public in August. The report concluded that the program was too slow in issuing safety rules, suffered from poor communication, was too decentralized, and applied and interpreted safety rules inconsistently. On September 19, Secretary of Transportation Elizabeth Hanford Dole announced that the FAA would begin hiring 500 additional aircraft-safety inspectors and about 1,000 additional air-traffic controllers.

On September 27, American Airlines agreed to pay $1½ million in fines for violating FAA regulations on aircraft safety, maintenance, and inspection. This was the largest fine ever paid by a commercial airline for violating federal standards.

Strikes. On February 28, the Transport Workers Union struck Pan American World Airways (PanAm). The union, representing mechanics, baggage handlers, and food-service workers, wanted to win back wage concessions granted in previous years. The strike ended on March 27 with the union accepting further concessions in wages and work rules. Similar agreements were reached at about the same time between PanAm and unions for the pilots and flight attendants.

On May 17, the Air Line Pilots Association struck United Airlines. A major issue was United's attempt to establish a two-tier pay scale, lowering the pay level of newly hired pilots. On June 17, the pilots returned to work under an agreement that included a two-tier pay scale.

Airline Sales and Mergers. On April 22, PanAm agreed to sell its Pacific Ocean operations to United Airlines for about $715 million. President Ronald Reagan approved the sale in November. The sale gave PanAm needed cash to modernize its aging fleet of planes. PanAm will continue to fly to Latin America, Europe, Africa, the Middle East, and India from New York City; Miami, Fla.; and Washington, D.C. At the completion of the deal, United, already the largest U.S. domestic airline, also became a major international carrier.

People Express Airlines in October agreed to buy Frontier Airlines and in December agreed to

Members of the Air Line Pilots Association walk the picket line during a strike against United Airlines that lasted from mid-May to mid-June.

buy Britt Airways. In addition, Muse Air Corporation was purchased in June by its main competitor, Southwest Air Lines.

International Aviation Agreements. In April, the United States and Poland signed an agreement to resume commercial flights between the two countries. The United States and the Soviet Union reached a similar agreement in November. In both cases, flights had been suspended since the Polish government declared martial law in 1981.

In November, Japan, the Soviet Union, and the United States announced an agreement to improve emergency communications for airliners over the North Pacific. The agreement grew out of talks following the shooting down of a Korean Air Lines plane by the Soviets in 1983.

Aircraft Sales. McDonnell Douglas Corporation in January announced that it had received orders for 12 of its new MD-87 aircraft and would begin commercial production of the plane. The MD-87, a smaller version of the MD-80 twin-jet, seats 109 to 130 passengers. In April, McDonnell Douglas agreed to sell 26 MD-82 jetliners to China.

The Boeing Company announced plans for its new 747-400, an advanced version of the 747, in May. The West German airline Lufthansa ordered 10 Boeing 737-300 aircraft in June with an option to buy 10 more. It also ordered 40 new aircraft from Airbus Industrie of France. In November,

United Airlines announced that it had ordered 110 Boeing 737-300 jets and up to 6 Boeing 747-200B aircraft. In December, All Nippon Airways, Japan Air Lines, and United Parcel Service of America, Incorporated, placed orders for up to 101 aircraft from Boeing.

Skyjackings. At least three Arabs hijacked a TWA jetliner carrying 153 people shortly after take-off from Athens, Greece, on June 14 and ordered the plane flown to Beirut, Lebanon. The terrorists murdered an American passenger and demanded the release of more than 700 Arabs held in Israeli prisons. On June 24, Israel released some of its prisoners. On June 30, the hijackers released the last passengers and crew members held hostage. Shortly thereafter, Israel began to release the remaining Arab prisoners.

Terrorists hijacked an EgyptAir jetliner en route from Athens to Cairo, Egypt, on November 23 and forced it to land in Valletta, Malta. The hijackers killed 2 passengers before Egyptian commandos stormed the plane on November 24. During the attack, 58 people, including at least 2 hijackers, were killed. The terrorists were believed to belong to a splinter group of the Palestine Liberation Organization.   David M. Cawthorne

See also TRANSPORTATION. In the WORLD BOOK SUPPLEMENT section, see AIRSHIP. In WORLD BOOK, see AVIATION.

AWARDS AND PRIZES given in 1985 included:

Arts Awards

ACADEMY OF MOTION PICTURE ARTS AND SCIENCES. "Oscar" Awards: **Best Picture,** *Amadeus.* **Best Actor,** F. Murray Abraham, *Amadeus.* **Best Actress,** Sally Field, *Places in the Heart.* **Best Supporting Actor,** Haing S. Ngor, *The Killing Fields.* **Best Supporting Actress,** Dame Peggy Ashcroft, *A Passage to India.* **Best Director,** Milos Forman, *Amadeus.* **Best Original Screenplay,** Robert Benton, *Places in the Heart.* **Best Screenplay Adaptation,** Peter Shaffer, *Amadeus.* **Best Cinematography,** Chris Menges, *The Killing Fields.* **Best Film Editing,** Jim Clark, *The Killing Fields.* **Best Original Score,** Maurice Jarre, *A Passage to India.* **Best Original Song Score,** Prince, *Purple Rain.* **Best Original Song,** Stevie Wonder, "I Just Called to Say I Love You." **Best Foreign Language Film,** *Dangerous Moves* (Switzerland). See ABRAHAM, F. MURRAY; FIELD, SALLY.

AMERICAN ACADEMY AND INSTITUTE OF ARTS AND LETTERS. Gold Medal in Music, Leonard Bernstein. **Gold Medal in Poetry,** Robert Penn Warren.

AMERICAN DANCE FESTIVAL. Samuel H. Scripps-American Dance Festival Award, Alwin Nikolais, choreographer.

AMERICAN INSTITUTE OF ARCHITECTS. Gold Medal, William Wayne Caudill (posthumous).

AMERICAN MUSIC AWARDS. Pop-Rock Awards: **Favorite Female Vocalist,** Cyndi Lauper. **Favorite Male Vocalist,** Lionel Richie. **Favorite Duo or Group,** Daryl Hall and John Oates. **Favorite Single,** "Dancing in the Dark," Bruce Springsteen. **Favorite Album,** *Purple Rain,* Prince. **Favorite Female Video Artist,** Cyndi Lauper. **Favorite Male Video Artist,** Lionel Richie. **Favorite Video,** "Hello," Lionel Richie. **Black Music Awards: Favorite Female Vocalist,** Tina Turner. **Favorite Male Vocalist,** Lionel Richie. **Favorite Duo or Group,** Pointer Sisters. **Favorite Single,** "When Doves Cry," Prince. **Favorite Album,** *Purple Rain,* Prince. **Favorite Video,** "Hello," Lionel Richie. **Favorite Female Video Artist,** Tina Turner. **Favorite Male Video Artist,** Lionel Richie. **Country Music Awards: Favorite Female Vocalist,** Barbara Mandrell. **Favorite Male Vocalist,** Kenny Rogers. **Favorite Duo or Group,** Alabama. **Favorite Single,** "Islands in the Stream," Kenny Rogers and Dolly Parton. **Favorite Album,** *Eyes That See in the Dark,* Kenny Rogers. **Favorite Video,** "A Little Good News," Anne Murray. **Favorite Female Video Artist,** Anne Murray. **Favorite Male Video Artist,** Willie Nelson.

CANNES INTERNATIONAL FILM FESTIVAL. Golden Palm Grand Prize, *When Father Was Away on Business* (Yugoslavia). **Best Actor,** William Hurt, *Kiss of the Spider Woman* (Brazil). **Best Actress,** Cher, *Mask* (United States); Norma Aleandro, *The Official Story* (Argentina). **Best Director,** André Techine, *Rendez-Vous* (France). **Special Jury Prize,** *Birdy* (United States). **Jury Prize,** *Colonel Redl* (Hungary, Austria, and West Germany). **Special Jury Prize for Artistic Creation,** *Mishima* (United States).

HYATT FOUNDATION. Pritzker Architecture Prize, Hans Hollein, Austria, for lifetime work.

JOHN F. KENNEDY CENTER FOR THE PERFORMING ARTS. Honors, Merce Cunningham, dancer and choreographer; Irene Dunne, actress; Bob Hope, comedian; Alan Jay Lerner and Frederick Loewe, songwriters; Beverly Sills, opera singer.

MACDOWELL COLONY. Edward MacDowell Medal, American painter Robert Motherwell.

NATIONAL ACADEMY OF RECORDING ARTS AND SCIENCES. Grammy Awards: Record of the Year, "What's Love Got to Do with It?," Tina Turner. **Album of the Year,** *Can't Slow Down,* Lionel Richie. **Song of the Year,** "What's Love Got to Do with It?," Graham Lyle and Terry Britten, composers. **Best New Artist,** Cyndi Lauper. **Producer of the Year (Nonclassical),** David Foster;

Lionel Richie and James Anthony Carmichael (tie). **Best Pop Vocal Performance, Female,** "What's Love Got to Do with It?," Tina Turner. **Male,** "Against All Odds (Take a Look at Me Now)," Phil Collins. **Duo or Group with Vocal,** "Jump (For My Love)," Pointer Sisters. **Instrumental,** "Ghostbusters," Ray Parker, Jr. **Best Rock Vocal Performance, Female,** "Better Be Good to Me," Tina Turner. **Male,** "Dancing in the Dark," Bruce Springsteen. **Duo or Group with Vocal,** *Purple Rain,* Prince and the Revolution. **Instrumental,** "Cinema," Yes. **Best Rhythm and Blues Vocal Performance, Female,** "I Feel for You," Chaka Khan. **Male,** "Caribbean Queen (No More Love on the Run)," Billy Ocean. **Duo or Group with Vocal,** "Yah Mo B There," James Ingram and Michael McDonald. **Instrumental,** *Sound-System,* Herbie Hancock. **Best Rhythm and Blues Song,** "I Feel for You," Prince, composer. **Best Jazz Fusion Performance,** *First Circle,* Pat Metheny Group. **Best Country Vocal Performance, Female,** "In My Dreams," Emmylou Harris. **Male,** "That's the Way Love Goes," Merle Haggard. **Duo or Group with Vocal,** "Mama He's Crazy," The Judds. **Instrumental,** "Wheel Hoss," Ricky Skaggs. **Best Country Song,** "City of New Orleans," Steve Goodman, composer. **Best Jazz Vocal Performance,** *Nothin' But the Blues,* Joe Williams. **Best Jazz Instrumental Performance, Solo:** *Hot House Flowers,* Wynton Marsalis. **Group,** *New York Scene,* Art Blakey and The Jazz Messengers. **Big Band,** *88 Basie Street,* Count Basie & His Orchestra. **Best Classical Album,** *Amadeus,* Neville Marriner, conductor. **Best Classical Orchestra Performance,** *Prokofiev: Symphony No. 5 in B Flat, Op. 100,* Leonard Slatkin, conductor. **Best Opera,** *Bizet: Carmen,* Lorin Maazel, conductor. **Best Classical Choral Performance,** *Brahms: A German Requiem,* Margaret Hillis, conductor. See SPRINGSTEEN, BRUCE; TURNER, TINA.

NATIONAL ACADEMY OF TELEVISION ARTS AND SCIENCES. Emmy Awards: Best Comedy Series, "The Cosby Show." **Best Actor in a Comedy Series,** Robert Guillaume, "Benson." **Best Actress in a Comedy Series,** Jane Curtin, "Kate & Allie." **Best Supporting Actor in a Comedy Series,** John Larroquette, "Night Court." **Best Supporting Actress in a Comedy Series,** Rhea Perlman, "Cheers." **Best Drama Series,** "Cagney & Lacey." **Best Actor in a Drama Series,** William Daniels, "St. Elsewhere." **Best Actress in a Drama Series,** Tyne Daly, "Cagney & Lacey." **Best Supporting Actor in a Drama Series,** Edward James Olmos, "Miami Vice." **Best Supporting Actress in a Drama Series,** Betty Thomas, "Hill Street Blues." **Best Drama or Comedy Special,** *Do You Remember Love?* **Best Limited Series,** "The Jewel in the Crown." **Best Variety Program,** *Motown Returns to the Apollo.*

NATIONAL SOCIETY OF FILM CRITICS AWARDS. Best Film, *Ran.* **Best Actor,** Jack Nicholson, *Prizzi's Honor.* **Best Actress,** Vanessa Redgrave, *Wetherby.* **Best Director,** John Huston, *Prizzi's Honor.*

NEW YORK DRAMA CRITICS CIRCLE AWARDS. Best New Play, *Ma Rainey's Black Bottom,* August Wilson.

NEW YORK FILM CRITICS CIRCLE AWARDS. Best Film, *Prizzi's Honor.* **Best Actor,** Jack Nicholson, *Prizzi's Honor.* **Best Actress,** Norma Aleandro, *The Official Story.* **Best Supporting Actor,** Klaus Maria Brandauer, *Out of Africa.* **Best Supporting Actress,** Anjelica Huston, *Prizzi's Honor.* **Best Director,** John Huston, *Prizzi's Honor.* **Best Screenplay,** Woody Allen, *The Purple Rose of Cairo.* **Best Cinematography,** David Watkin, *Out of Africa.*

ANTOINETTE PERRY (TONY) AWARDS. Drama: Best Play, *Biloxi Blues.* **Best Actor,** Derek Jacobi, *Much Ado About Nothing.* **Best Actress,** Stockard Channing, *Joe Egg.* **Best Featured Actor,** Barry Miller, *Biloxi Blues.* **Best Featured Actress,** Judith Ivey, *Hurlyburly.* **Best Director,** Gene Saks, *Biloxi Blues.* **Musical: Best Musical,** *Big River.* **Best Featured Actor,** Ron Richardson, *Big River.* **Best Featured Actress,** Leilani Jones, *Grind.* **Best Director,** Des McAnuff, *Big River.* **Best Book,** William Hauptman, *Big River.* **Best**

Score, Roger Miller, *Big River*. **Best Reproduction of a Play or Musical,** *Joe Egg*.

UNITED STATES GOVERNMENT. National Medal of Arts, Elliott Carter, composer; Dorothy Chandler, patron of the arts; Ralph Ellison, author; José Ferrer, actor; Martha Graham, dancer and choreographer; Hallmark Cards, sponsor of the "Hallmark Hall of Fame" television series; Lincoln E. Kirstein, ballet director; Paul Mellon, patron of the arts; Louise Nevelson, sculptor; Leontyne Price, opera singer; and Alice Tully, patron of the arts.

Journalism Awards

AMERICAN SOCIETY OF MAGAZINE EDITORS. See Magazine.

LONG ISLAND UNIVERSITY. George Polk Memorial Awards: National Reporting, Robert Parry, Associated Press, for articles about Central Intelligence Agency handbooks advising Nicaraguan rebels on the use of assassination. **Local Reporting,** Ellen Whitford, *The* (Norfolk) *Virginian-Pilot*, for exposing a clinic that performed false abortions on women who were not pregnant. **Foreign Reporting,** Mark Fineman, *The Philadelphia Inquirer*, for coverage of events in India. **Environmental Reporting,** Tom Harris and Jim Morris, *The Sacramento* (Calif.) *Bee*, for a study of toxic-waste disposal at U.S. military installations. **Medical Reporting,** William R. Ritz and John Aloysius Farrell, *The Denver Post*, for a series on defective anesthesia equipment. **Special Interest Reporting,** Lois R. Ember, *Chemical and Engineering News*, for an analysis of U.S. government statements about biological warfare. **News Photography,** Ozier Muhammad, *Newsday* (Long Island, N.Y.), for a picture of a starving Ethiopian child. **Magazine Reporting,** John Vinocur, *The New York Times Magazine*, for an article about Paraguay. **Foreign Television Reporting,** Michael Buerk, British Broadcasting Company, and Mohammed Amin, VisNews, London, for reporting on the Ethiopian famine. **National Television Reporting,** Alex Kotlowitz, Kwame Holman, and Susan Ades, "The MacNeil/Lehrer NewsHour," for a report on opponents of abortion. **Local Television Reporting,** Rick Nelson and Joe Collum, KPRC-TV, Houston, for a series on home-improvement swindles. **Special Award,** Amnesty International, for its reports on human rights. **Career Award,** sports broadcaster Red Barber.

THE SOCIETY OF PROFESSIONAL JOURNALISTS, SIGMA DELTA CHI. Sigma Delta Chi Distinguished Service Awards, Newspaper Awards: General Reporting, Circulation More than 100,000, Dolly Katz, *Detroit Free Press*, for a series about inept and unethical physicians; **General Reporting, Circulation Less than 100,000,** Betsy August, Tom Dubocq, and J. P. Faber, *The Miami* (Fla.) *News*, for a series about Christopher Wilder's cross-country killing spree; **Editorial Writing,** Jonathan Freedman, *The* (San Diego) *Tribune*, for editorials urging reform of U.S. immigration laws; **Washington Correspondence,** Larry Eichel, *The Philadelphia Inquirer*, for a series on the 1984 presidential election; **Foreign Correspondence,** Charles T. Powers, *Los Angeles Times*, for a series on the problems confronting African nations; **News Photography,** Viorel Florescu, *The Bridgeport Post* and *The Telegram*, both in Bridgeport, Conn., for photographs of a shooting victim; **Editorial Cartooning,** Mike Lane, *The* (Baltimore) *Evening Sun*, for a cartoon depicting Israeli leader Ariel Sharon and U.S. General William C. Westmoreland reacting to American news media; **Public Service in Newspaper Journalism, Circulation More than 100,000,** *Fort Worth* (Tex.) *Star-Telegram* for a series on design flaws in U.S. Army helicopters; **Public Service in Newspaper Journalism, Circulation Less than 100,000,** *The* (Winter Haven, Fla.) *News-Chief* for a series on the need to screen teaching applicants for criminal records. **Magazine Awards: Magazine Reporting,** Eric Harrison, *The Philadelphia Inquirer*, for a series in the newspaper's Sunday magazine on life

F. Murray Abraham and Sally Field in 1985 won Academy Awards as best actor and best actress for *Amadeus* and *Places in the Heart,* respectively.

in a housing project; **Public Service in Magazine Journalism,** *Life,* for an article on sexual abuse of children. **Radio Awards: Radio Reporting,** CBS News-Radio for Richard Wagner's on-the-scene reporting of the death of a *Newsweek* photographer in El Salvador; **Public Service in Radio Journalism,** WCBS-Radio, New York City, for a documentary on questionable measures used by the New York Police Department to combat drug abuse; **Editorializing on Radio,** KCBS-Radio, San Francisco, for editorials urging reforms in the use of animals in medical research. **Television Awards: Television Reporting,** WVEC-TV, Norfolk, Va., for coverage of an explosion that resulted from the collision of a tanker truck and a garbage truck; **Public Service in Television Journalism, Stations in the Top 50 Markets,** KPRC-TV, Houston, for a documentary on medical malpractice in area hospitals; **Public Service in Television Journalism, Stations in Markets 51 to 209,** WOI-TV, Ames, Iowa, for a documentary on the problems of American farmers; **Editorializing on Television,** Van Carter, KTIV-TV, Sioux City, Iowa, for an editorial urging that a single criminal justice center be built instead of the two expensive centers proposed. **Research About Journalism:** Robert W. Desmond, *Tides of War: World News Reporting 1931-1945.*

UNIVERSITY OF GEORGIA. George Foster Peabody Broadcasting Awards, KNX Newsradio, Los Angeles, for a report on the influx of illegal aliens into southern California; WAFX Radio, Fort Wayne, Ind., for *D-Day: 40 Years Later;* Brigham Young University, Provo, Utah, for a radio series based on stories by science-fiction writer Ray Bradbury; WNYC AM/83, New York City, for the children's series "Small Things Considered"; KFGO, Fargo, N. Dak., for coverage of a blizzard that struck the station's area; WFMT, Chicago, and Ray Nordstrand for their contributions to fine arts radio; "The Protestant

Tina Turner and Lionel Richie carry off five Grammy Awards in February—three Grammys for Turner, including Record of the Year, and two for Richie.

Hour," produced by the Protestant Radio and Television Center, Atlanta, Ga., for 40 years of outstanding religious programming; KDFW-TV, Dallas, for a series investigating the emergency medical services of the Dallas Fire Department; WMAQ-TV, Chicago, for a series about excessive spending for study commissions by the Illinois state legislature; WDVM-TV, Washington, D.C., for reports examining a medical clinic operating without a license; WCAX-TV, Burlington, Vt., for a look into variation in the length of hospital stays for patients undergoing routine surgery; American Broadcasting Companies (ABC) for *Heartsounds,* a television drama about the triumph of love over illness; WNET/Thirteen, New York City, for "Heritage: Civilization and the Jews," which traced 3,000 years of Jewish history; KGW-TV, Portland, Ore., for a series about how the Rajneesh religious group has affected local elections and community life; WCCO Television, Minneapolis, Minn., for a documentary about Vietnam under Communism; ABC News Closeup for *To Save Our Schools, to Save Our Children,* an inquiry into problems of education in the United States; "Frontline," for overall excellence in documentary television programming; WNET/Thirteen, New York City, for *The Brain,* a documentary about the human mind; CBS Entertainment for the historical miniseries "George Washington"; WCVB, Boston, for *Somerville High,* an examination of daily life in a typical urban high school; National Broadcasting Company and MTM Enterprises for "St. Elsewhere"; Central Independent Television, Great Britain, for *Seeds of Despair,* a report on the famine in Ethiopia; Showtime for "Faerie Tale Theatre," a television series retelling classic fairy tales; Turner Broadcasting System, Atlanta, for "Cousteau/Amazon," a documentary about the Amazon River of South America; Ted Koppel, "Nightline," for news commentary; "The Roger Rosenblatt Essays" on "The MacNeil/Lehrer NewsHour"

for news commentary; "A Walk Through the 20th Century with Bill Moyers," produced by the Corporation for Entertainment and Learning, New York City; Granada Television, Great Britain, for "The Jewel in the Crown," a dramatic series depicting the last years of the British Empire in India; Roone Arledge, ABC, New York City, for contributions to television news and sports.

Literature Awards

ACADEMY OF AMERICAN POETS. Lamont Poetry Selection, *Victims of the Latest Dance Craze,* Cornelius Eady. **Walt Whitman Award,** *Bindweed,* Christianne Balk.

AMERICAN LIBRARY ASSOCIATION. See AMERICAN LIBRARY ASSOCIATION.

ASSOCIATION OF AMERICAN PUBLISHERS. American Book Awards: Fiction, *White Noise,* Don DeLillo; **Nonfiction,** *Common Ground: A Turbulent Decade in the Lives of Three American Families,* J. Anthony Lukas; **First Work of Fiction,** *Easy in the Islands,* Bob Shacochis.

CANADA COUNCIL. Governor General's Literary Awards, English-Language: Fiction, *The Engineer of Human Souls,* Josef Skvorecky. **Poetry,** *Celestial Navigation,* Paulette Jiles. **Drama,** *White Biting Dog,* Judith Thompson. **Nonfiction,** *The Private Capital: Ambition and Love in the Age of Macdonald and Laurier,* Sandra Gwyn. **French-Language: Fiction,** *Agonie,* Jacques Brault. **Poetry,** *Double Impression,* Nicole Brossard. **Drama,** *Ne blâmez jamais les Bédouins,* René-Daniel Dubois. **Nonfiction,** *Le XXe siècle: Histoire du catholicisme québécois,* Jean Hamelin and Nicole Gagnon.

CANADIAN LIBRARY ASSOCIATION. See CANADIAN LIBRARY ASSOCIATION.

COLUMBIA UNIVERSITY. Bancroft Prizes in American History, Suzanne Lebsock, *The Free Women of Petersburg:*

Status and Culture in a Southern Town, 1784-1860; Kenneth Silverman, *The Life and Times of Cotton Mather.*

INGERSOLL FOUNDATION. Ingersoll Prizes: T. S. Eliot Award for Creative Writing, Romanian-born French playwright Eugène Ionesco. **Richard M. Weaver Award for Scholarly Letters,** American sociologist Robert Nisbet.

NATIONAL BOOK CRITICS CIRCLE. National Book Critics Circle Awards: Fiction, *Love Medicine,* Louise Erdrich. **General Nonfiction,** *Weapons and Hope,* Freeman Dyson. **Biography,** *Dostoevsky: The Years of Ordeal, 1850-1859,* Joseph Frank. **Poetry,** *The Dead and the Living,* Sharon Olds. **Criticism,** *Twentieth Century Pleasures: Prose on Poetry,* Robert Hass.

PEN AMERICAN CENTER. Faulkner Award, *The Barracks Thief,* Tobias Wolff.

Nobel Prizes. See NOBEL PRIZES.

Public Service Awards

AMERICAN INSTITUTE FOR PUBLIC SERVICE. Thomas Jefferson Awards, James A. Baker III, U.S. secretary of the treasury; Linda Barker, Seattle, for work with crime victims; Trevor Ferrell, social worker who helped the homeless in Philadelphia; Betty Ford, former first lady; Lee A. Iacocca, chairman of Chrysler Corporation; Frank B. McGlone, Littleton, Colo., physician who helped the elderly; Arturo Montoya, Tucson, Ariz., for service to the Yaqui Indian community; Jean Kennedy Smith, New York City, for bringing arts programs to the disabled; Mary Beth Tober, Johnson City, Tenn., for combating alcoholism and drug abuse among teen-agers.

ALBERT EINSTEIN PEACE PRIZE FOUNDATION. Albert Einstein Peace Prize, Willy Brandt, former chancellor of West Germany, for his efforts for world peace.

NATIONAL ASSOCIATION FOR THE ADVANCEMENT OF COLORED PEOPLE. Spingarn Medal, Bill Cosby, American entertainer.

THE TEMPLETON FOUNDATION. Templeton Prize for Progress in Religion, Sir Alister C. Hardy, British marine biologist.

UNITED STATES GOVERNMENT. Presidential Medal of Freedom, Count Basie, jazz musician (posthumous); Jacques-Yves Cousteau, undersea explorer; Jerome Holland, civil rights leader; Sidney Hook, philosopher and educator; Jeane J. Kirkpatrick, former U.S. representative to the United Nations; George M. Low, educator (posthumous); Frank Reynolds, television news anchorman (posthumous); S. Dillon Ripley, former secretary of the Smithsonian Institution; Frank Sinatra, singer; James Stewart, actor; Mother Teresa, founder of the Missionaries of Charity religious order; Albert Coady Wedemeyer, U.S. Army general; Charles E. Yeager, test pilot.

Pulitzer Prizes

JOURNALISM. Public Service, *Fort Worth* (Tex.) *Star-Telegram* for a series on design flaws in U.S. Army helicopters. **General News Reporting,** Thomas Turcol, *The* (Norfolk) *Virginian-Pilot* and *Ledger-Star,* for a series exposing questionable financial practices by a local economic development official. **Investigative Reporting,** Lucy Morgan and Jack Reed, *St. Petersburg* (Fla.) *Times,* for a series examining the financial dealings of a local sheriff; and William K. Marrimow, *The Philadelphia Inquirer,* for a series revealing attacks on innocent people by city police dogs. **Explanatory Journalism,** Jon Franklin, *The* (Baltimore) *Evening Sun,* for a series on the new science of molecular psychiatry. **Specialized Reporting,** Randall Savage and Jackie Crosby, *Macon* (Ga.) *Telegraph and News,* for their investigation of academics and athletics at two Georgia universities. **National Reporting,** Thomas J. Knudson, *The Des Moines* (Iowa) *Register,* for a series on the occupational hazards of farming. **International Reporting,** Josh Friedman, Dennis Bell, and Ozier Muhammad, *Newsday*

(Long Island, N.Y.) for their series on the famine in Africa. **Feature Writing,** Alice Steinbach, *The* (Baltimore) *Sun,* for a story about a blind child's world. **Commentary,** Murray Kempton, *Newsday.* **Criticism,** Howard Rosenberg, *Los Angeles Times.* **Editorial Cartooning,** Jeff MacNelly, *Chicago Tribune.* **Editorial Writing,** Richard Aregood, *Philadelphia Daily News.* **Spot News Photography,** Santa Ana, Calif., *Register* for coverage of the 1984 Summer Olympics. **Feature Photography,** Stan Grossfeld, *The Boston Globe,* for photographs of famine victims and illegal immigrants; and Larry C. Price, *The Philadelphia Inquirer,* for photographs of El Salvador and Angola.

LETTERS. Biography, *The Life and Times of Cotton Mather,* Kenneth Silverman. **Drama,** *Sunday in the Park with George,* Stephen Sondheim and James Lapine. **Fiction,** *Foreign Affairs,* Alison Lurie. **General Nonfiction,** *"The Good War": An Oral History of World War II,* Studs Terkel. **History,** *Prophets of Regulation,* Thomas K. McCraw. **Poetry,** *Yin,* Carolyn Kizer.

MUSIC. Music Award, *Symphony, RiverRun,* Stephen Albert. **Special Citation,** William H. Schuman.

Science and Technology Awards

COLUMBIA UNIVERSITY. Louisa Gross Horwitz Prize, Donald D. Brown, Carnegie Institution of Washington, and Mark S. Ptashne, Harvard University.

GAIRDNER FOUNDATION. Gairdner Foundation International Awards, Stanley Cohen, Vanderbilt University School of Medicine; Paul C. Lauterbur, State University of New York at Stony Brook; Raymond U. Lemieux, University of Alberta, Canada; Mary F. Lyon, Medical Research Council, Great Britain; Mark S. Ptashne, Harvard University; Charles Yanofsky, Stanford University.

ALBERT AND MARY LASKER FOUNDATION. Albert Lasker Basic Medical Research Award, Michael S. Brown and Joseph L. Goldstein, University of Texas Health Science Center at Dallas. **Albert Lasker Clinical Medical Research Award,** Bernard Fisher, University of Pittsburgh School of Medicine. **Public Service Awards,** Lane W. Adams, chief executive officer, American Cancer Society; newspaper columnist Ann Landers.

ROYAL SOCIETY OF CANADA. Thomas W. Eadie Medal, Elvie L. Smith, Pratt & Whitney Canada Limited. **McLaughlin Medal,** Herbert H. Jasper, Université de Montreal. **Willet G. Miller Medal,** William S. Fyfe, University of Western Ontario. **Rutherford Memorial Medal in Chemistry,** Stephen C. Wallace, University of Toronto. **Rutherford Memorial Medal in Physics,** John C. Simpson, University of Guelph. **Henry Marshall Tory Medal,** Keith U. Ingold, National Research Council of Canada.

UNITED STATES GOVERNMENT. National Medal of Science, Howard L. Bachrach, U.S. Department of Agriculture; Paul Berg, Stanford University; E. Margaret Burbridge, University of California at San Diego; Maurice Goldhaber, Brookhaven National Laboratory; Herman H. Goldstine, American Philosophical Society; William R. Hewlett, Hewlett-Packard Company; Roald Hoffmann, Cornell University; Helmut E. Landsberg, University of Maryland; George M. Low, Rensselaer Polytechnic Institute (posthumous); Walter H. Munk, University of California at San Diego; George C. Pimentel, University of California at Berkeley; Frederick Reines, University of California at Irvine; Wendel L. Roelofs, Cornell University; J. Robert Schrieffer, University of California at Santa Barbara; Isadore M. Singer, Massachusetts Institute of Technology (M.I.T.); John G. Trump, M.I.T.; and Richard N. Zare, Stanford University.

UNIVERSITY OF SOUTHERN CALIFORNIA. Tyler Prize for Environmental Achievement, Bruce N. Ames, University of California at Berkeley; and the Organization for Tropical Studies.

Sara Dreyfuss

BAHAMAS. See LATIN AMERICA.

BAHRAIN. See MIDDLE EAST.

BAKER, JAMES ADDISON, III (1930-) became United States secretary of the treasury on Feb. 3, 1985. Baker, who had been President Ronald Reagan's chief of staff since 1981, exchanged jobs with Treasury Secretary Donald T. Regan. Baker was considered a skilled negotiator with Congress.

Baker was born on April 28, 1930, in Houston. He graduated in 1952 from Princeton University in New Jersey and earned a law degree in 1957 at the University of Texas in Austin. He then entered the practice of corporate law in Houston.

In 1970, Baker helped George H. W. Bush—who later became Vice President of the United States—in his campaign for the U.S. Senate. Although Bush lost that race, Baker showed considerable talent as a political organizer. In 1976, he served as campaign chairman in President Gerald R. Ford's unsuccessful bid for a new term in the White House. In 1980, Baker helped to guide Reagan to his victory over President Jimmy Carter. Reagan then chose Baker as his chief of staff.

Baker's first wife, Mary, died in 1970. In 1973, he married Susan Garrett Winston, who had also been widowed. They have eight children, including seven from previous marriages.　　David L. Dreier

See also CABINET, UNITED STATES.

BALLET. See DANCING.

BANGLADESH suffered a devastating cyclone on May 24 and 25, 1985. The storm roared up the Bay of Bengal and pushed a wall of water across low-lying islands created by silt from the Ganges and Brahmaputra rivers. Such storms ravage the coastal islands every 5 to 10 years, but the population density in Bangladesh is so great that landless farmers continue to settle on the islands, which are extremely fertile.

The lack of land records or established villages in the area made it difficult to calculate the storm's toll. President Hussain Muhammad Ershad, who supervised relief operations, estimated the number of dead at 5,000 to 10,000. International aid officials said at least 15,000 people died.

The Economy. The natural disaster in May ensured Bangladesh's continued need for foreign aid in 1985. The country used $1.34 billion in aid in the fiscal year ending on June 30. Its economy grew at a rate of 3.8 per cent in that year, down from 4.5 per cent the previous year. Western aid-giving countries promised $1.68 billion in assistance for the year beginning July 1, 1985.

Flirting with Democracy. Ershad continued throughout 1985 to try to establish an elective political system to replace his army-based government. But he refused to end martial law, and opposition politicians would not accept his plans for

An umbrella provides the only shelter for a Bangalee woman in May after a cyclone and tidal wave destroyed the Bay of Bengal island where she lived.

parliamentary elections held under continued martial law.

On March 1, Ershad banned all political activities and called a *referendum* (direct vote) on his rule, to be held on March 21. The government said that 72 per cent of eligible voters went to the polls and that 94 per cent of the ballots supported Ershad. Foreign observers estimated, however, that the turnout was only 25 to 30 per cent.

Elections for chairmen of the 460 rural municipal organizations that link Bangladesh's 60,000 villages were held on May 16 and 20. The Janadal Party, founded by Ershad in 1983, claimed to have won 40 per cent of the chairmanships. This eclipsed the two main political parties, the Awami League and the Bangladesh National Party.

Ershad lured some National Party members into his cabinet as he expanded the group in July and August to dilute its military makeup with civilian politicians. The president then broadened his political base by launching a coalition called the National Front that included the Janadal Party and elements from opposition political groups.

Ershad announced on September 12 that he would allow "indoor politics" beginning October 1 but no outdoor rallies. He said national elections might be held in early 1986.   Henry S. Bradsher

See also ASIA (Facts in Brief Table). In WORLD BOOK, see BANGLADESH.

BANK. In 1985, the Federal Reserve System (Fed) applied fairly strong monetary stimulation to the United States economy, but the economy continued to grow slower than in 1983 and 1984. The Fed stimulates the economy—expands the money supply—by furnishing banks with additional reserves, which the banks can use to make new loans.

Money and Inflation. The basic measure of the money supply is called *M1*. It consists of currency in the hands of the public plus checking accounts, NOW accounts, and Super NOW's. M1 began 1985 at $562 billion, hit $614 billion in August, and ended the year at $625 billion. Its rate of growth, only 5.7 per cent for all of 1984, doubled to 11.4 per cent for the first half of 1985 but slowed to about 5 per cent for the second half.

M1 is considered "money to spend." The broader measure of the money supply, M2, also includes "money to hold" in savings accounts, certificates of deposit, money market mutual funds, and money market deposit accounts. M2 began the year at $2.189 trillion and rose at 8.7 per cent per year until the end of June when it reached $2.473 trillion. It then grew at 7.2 per cent to end November at $2.547 trillion.

In 1984, the U.S. gross national product (GNP)—the value of all goods and services produced—had grown at an unusually high 4.6 per

cent in real terms—that is, after adjustment for inflation. But its real rate of growth fell to 2.4 per cent for 1985. When money grows at a much higher rate than real GNP, a rise in inflation usually follows because the number of dollars to be spent has increased faster than the volume of goods and services to spend them on. In the 12-month period ending in June 1985, however, the Consumer Price Index (CPI), a common measure of inflation, rose only 3.7 per cent, down from 4.2 per cent in the previous 12-month period.

Interest Rates. As the rate of inflation falls, so do interest rates. The three-month Treasury-bill (T-bill) rate, which had briefly climbed above 16 per cent in 1981, began 1985 at 7.8 per cent and peaked during the first week of March at 8.7 per cent. It fell to 6.8 per cent in the last week of June, hovered between 6.9 per cent and 7.2 per cent during the second half of the year, and ended the year at 7.1 per cent. The prime rate, which banks announce as the rate they charge their best corporate customers, started the year at 10.8 per cent and dropped steadily to 9.5 per cent by the last week in June. This was the first time since 1978 that the prime had fallen to single-digit levels.

Long-term interest rates are usually higher than short-term rates, reflecting the greater risk of changes in bond prices or in the purchasing power of money over the longer period. The spread between the five-year Treasury-bond rate and the three-month T-bill rate, which remained between 3.5 and 4.0 per cent during 1983 and 1984, narrowed to about 3.0 per cent in 1985, representing lowered expectations of inflation.

Real interest rates—the short-term rates minus the rate of inflation—remained at a fairly high 4 per cent in 1985, compared with an average of 2.5 per cent since 1900. The high real rates reflected continued strong demand for business loans and continued heavy borrowing by the Department of the Treasury to finance the federal deficit.

Bank Failures. A post-World War II record for bank failures—120—was set again in 1985. Defaults continued on energy loans made when it seemed the price of oil would continue to rise forever. And loans to foreign countries were still being rescheduled to avoid default, as most of the rest of the world lagged behind the United States in economic growth. Conditions eased late in 1985, however, as the U.S. dollar fell more than 20 per cent against other currencies. The lower dollar made it easier to pay off loans in dollar denominations.

The big news in U.S. bank failures in 1985 came from unexpected directions. The Farm Credit System reported itself near collapse in September, and two state deposit-insurance schemes fell apart.

The Farm Credit System, the largest agricultural lender in the United States, consists of 37

Bank customers line up for the reopening of an Ohio savings and loan association on March 23, after an eight-day closing to stem a run on deposits.

main banks and their affiliates. Until the third quarter of 1985, it had not reported a loss since the 1930's. In 1984, the system recorded a profit of $441 million. But from July through September of 1985, it reported a loss of $522.5 million, and it was expected to charge off losses of up to $2-billion by early 1986. As 1985 ended, Congress agreed to bail out the system. It extended a line of credit to the system but also tightened control of the system's banks.

The most dramatic banking events of the year were the closing of privately insured savings and loan associations (S&L's) in Ohio and Maryland. Most depository institutions have their deposits insured by the Federal Deposit Insurance Corporation (FDIC) or the Federal Savings and Loan Insurance Corporation (FSLIC). At the beginning of 1985, however, S&L's in five states belonged to private, state-sponsored deposit-insurance plans.

Toward the end of 1984, rumors began to circulate about problems at E.S.M. Government Securities Incorporated in Fort Lauderdale, Fla., and on March 4, 1985, E.S.M. collapsed. The Home State Savings Bank in Cincinnati, Ohio, was a large customer of E.S.M. and had bought many government bonds still in the possession of E.S.M. When some of those bonds could not be found, Home State depositors rushed to withdraw their money, and Home State collapsed on March 9.

Home State's deposits were insured by the Ohio Deposit Guarantee Fund, which paid out $40 million of its total assets of $136 million to Home State depositors. The next week, the 70 other Ohio S&L's insured by the fund began to experience runs, even though the Ohio legislature voted to add another $90 million to the insurance pool. Finally, on March 15, Ohio Governor Richard F. Celeste closed all state-insured S&L's. By March 22, when they began to reopen, the S&L's that remained healthy were switching to the FSLIC.

In May, the drama was repeated in Maryland when the Old Court Savings and Loan Association of Baltimore closed after a run on its deposits, and Maryland Governor Harry R. Hughes ordered withdrawals at all 102 state-insured S&L's limited to $1,000 per account per month. Maryland S&L's also switched to the FSLIC.

The superiority of federal insurance lies not in its larger asset pool, but rather in the ultimate guarantor of federally insured deposits, the Federal Reserve System. With its ability to create reserves, the Fed will never run out of money, and thus it can prevent a recurrence of the wave of bank failures that swept the United States during the 1930's.   Donald W. Swanton

See also ECONOMICS. In WORLD BOOK, see BANK.

BARBADOS. See LATIN AMERICA.

BASEBALL. For dramatic pennant races and an exciting World Series and for history making by some of the game's long-time stars, the 1985 baseball season ranked high. The Kansas City Royals provided much of the drama. They entered the final week of the regular season one game behind the California Angels in the American League's Western Division. They won three of four games from California and took the division. Then, in the American League championship series, Kansas City fell behind the Toronto Blue Jays, 3 games to 1. They won the next three games and the pennant. In the World Series, the Royals fell behind the St. Louis Cardinals, 3 games to 1. Then they won the next three games and the series.

All four division races were undecided until the final week of the regular season. Three were decided on the next-to-last day of the season. Those close races stirred high interest among fans and helped the major leagues set a regular-season attendance record of 46,838,819.

In the American League, Kansas City finished 1 game ahead of California in the West. Toronto finished 2 games ahead of the New York Yankees in the Eastern Division. In the National League, St. Louis won in the East by 3 games over the New York Mets. The Los Angeles Dodgers won in the West by 5½ games over the Cincinnati Reds.

Milestones. On September 11, Pete Rose, Cincinnati's 44-year-old player-manager, made the 4,192nd hit of his major-league career. He thus broke the career record for hits set by Ty Cobb of the Detroit Tigers in 1928. See ROSE, PETE.

On July 11, 38-year-old Nolan Ryan of the Houston Astros became the first pitcher to record 4,000 career strikeouts. On August 4, 39-year-old Rod Carew of California became the 16th player to reach 3,000 career hits; and on the same day, 40-year-old Tom Seaver of the Chicago White Sox became the 17th pitcher to win 300 games in his career. On October 6, the final day of the regular season, Phil Niekro of the Yankees became the 18th 300-game winner. At 46, Niekro was the oldest player in the major leagues.

Youth made its impact, too. At the age of 20, Dwight Gooden of the Mets became the youngest pitcher to win 20 games in a season and the youngest to win the Cy Young Award. He led the major leagues in victories (24), earned-run average (1.53), and strikeouts (268). In the National League, he also led in innings pitched (276⅔) and complete games (16). Vince Coleman, who failed to make the Cardinals in spring training, was called up early in the season and stole 110 bases, a record for a major-league rookie.

Play-Offs. The league championships, which had formerly been decided by the best three of five games, were extended to four of seven in 1985. Kansas City reached the American League play-offs for the sixth time in 10 years, Toronto for the first time in the club's nine-year history.

Toronto was favored and had the lead in games until Kansas City won the last three by scores of 2-0, 5-3, and 6-2. George Brett, Kansas City's third baseman, was voted the Most Valuable Player of the play-offs.

In the National League, the Mets led the Eastern Division by one game with three weeks remaining. Two weeks later, St. Louis led by four games, and the Cardinals went on to win. In the West, Los Angeles started the season with an 18-21 record but then rallied behind its pitchers.

In the play-offs, Los Angeles won the first two games. St. Louis won the next four and the pennant. In the final game, St. Louis was one out from defeat when first baseman Jack Clark's three-run home run provided a 7-5 victory. The Most Valuable Player of the play-offs was St. Louis shortstop Ozzie Smith.

World Series. St. Louis' speed and power were expected to dominate Kansas City's strong young pitching in the all-Missouri World Series. St. Louis started strongly, winning two games in Kansas City, 3-1 and 4-2. Kansas City won the third game, 6-1, behind Bret Saberhagen's pitching.

St. Louis won the fourth game 3-0. The end seemed near. No team had ever lost the first two

Pete Rose of the Cincinnati Reds gets his 4,192nd career hit on September 11 in Cincinnati, breaking Ty Cobb's record.

Final Standings in Major League Baseball

American League

Eastern Division

	W.	L.	Pct.	G.B.
Toronto Blue Jays	99	62	.615	
New York Yankees	97	64	.602	2
Detroit Tigers	84	77	.522	15
Baltimore Orioles	83	78	.516	16
Boston Red Sox	81	81	.500	18½
Milwaukee Brewers	71	90	.441	28
Cleveland Indians	60	102	.370	39½

Western Division

	W.	L.	Pct.	G.B.
Kansas City Royals	91	71	.562	
California Angels	90	72	.556	1
Chicago White Sox	85	77	.525	6
Minnesota Twins	77	85	.475	14
Oakland Athletics	77	85	.475	14
Seattle Mariners	74	88	.457	17
Texas Rangers	62	99	.385	28½

Offensive Leaders

Batting Average—Wade Boggs, Boston	.368
Runs Scored—Rickey Henderson, New York	146
Home Runs—Darrell Evans, Detroit	40
Runs Batted In—Don Mattingly, New York	145
Hits—Wade Boggs, Boston	240
Stolen Bases—Rickey Henderson, New York	80

Leading Pitchers

Games Won—Ron Guidry, New York	22
Win Average—Ron Guidry, New York (22–6)	.786
Earned Run Average (162 or more innings)—Dave Stieb, Toronto	2.48
Strikeouts—Bert Blyleven, Minnesota	206
Saves—Dan Quisenberry, Kansas City	37

Awards*

Most Valuable Player—Don Mattingly, New York
Cy Young—Bret Saberhagen, Kansas City
Rookie of the Year—Ozzie Guillen, Chicago
Manager of the Year—Bobby Cox, Toronto

National League

Eastern Division

	W.	L.	Pct.	G.B.
St. Louis Cardinals	101	61	.623	
New York Mets	98	64	.605	3
Montreal Expos	84	77	.522	16½
Chicago Cubs	77	84	.478	23½
Philadelphia Phillies	75	87	.463	26
Pittsburgh Pirates	57	104	.354	43½

Western Division

	W.	L.	Pct.	G.B.
Los Angeles Dodgers	95	67	.586	
Cincinnati Reds	89	72	.553	5½
Houston Astros	83	79	.512	12
San Diego Padres	83	79	.512	12
Atlanta Braves	66	96	.407	29
San Francisco Giants	62	100	.383	33

Offensive Leaders

Batting Average—Willie McGee, St. Louis	.353
Runs Scored—Dale Murphy, Atlanta	118
Home Runs—Dale Murphy, Atlanta	37
Runs Batted In—Dave Parker, Cincinnati	125
Hits—Willie McGee, St. Louis	216
Stolen Bases—Vince Coleman, St. Louis	110

Leading Pitchers

Games Won—Dwight Gooden, New York	24
Win Average—Orel Hershiser, Los Angeles (19–3)	.864
Earned Run Average (162 or more innings)—Dwight Gooden, New York	1.53
Strikeouts—Dwight Gooden, New York	268
Saves—Jeff Reardon, Montreal	41

Awards*

Most Valuable Player—Willie McGee, St. Louis
Cy Young—Dwight Gooden, New York
Rookie of the Year—Vince Coleman, St. Louis
Manager of the Year—Whitey Herzog, St. Louis

*Selected by Baseball Writers Association of America.

games at home and still won the World Series. In the 81 previous World Series, only four teams had rallied from a 3-1 deficit.

Kansas City had to win the last three games, and it did. It took the fifth game, 6-1. In the sixth game; St. Louis was three outs away from winning when a controversial call by umpire Don Denkinger ruled the leadoff batter safe at first base. Later, with the bases loaded, pinch hitter Dane Iorg hit a two-run single, and Kansas City won the game, 2-1. Kansas City won the seventh and deciding game, 11-0, on Saberhagen's five-hit pitching.

Strike. Major-league owners, attempting to negotiate a new basic agreement with the players, said industry losses would reach $155 million by 1988 unless changes were made. The players' union disputed the projected losses and rejected the owners' proposal to restrict salary arbitration.

On August 6, the players went on strike. On August 7, a five-year agreement was reached that tightened salary arbitration, abolished the free-agent draft and compensation, and provided for owner contributions of $196 million over six years in pensions and other benefits.

Drugs. In May 1985, seven men were indicted in Pittsburgh, Pa., on charges of selling drugs to major-league players. In September, seven current and former players testified under immunity from prosecution that they had purchased drugs from these men. The players included such stars as infielder Keith Hernandez of the Mets and outfielder Dave Parker of Cincinnati.

Hall of Fame. Hoyt Wilhelm and Lou Brock were voted into the National Baseball Hall of Fame in Cooperstown, N.Y., by veteran baseball writers. Wilhelm holds the major-league record for appearing in the most games as a relief pitcher—1,018. During a 21-year career, from 1952 to 1972, he played for six major-league teams. In 1974, outfielder Brock stole 118 bases, still a National League record. In 19 seasons from 1961 to 1979, mostly with St. Louis, he compiled 3,023 hits, a .293 batting average, and the career record for stolen bases with 938. The veterans' committee elected outfielder Enos Slaughter and shortstop Floyd (Arky) Vaughan to the Hall of Fame. Vaughan had a .318 career batting average with Pittsburgh and the Brooklyn Dodgers from 1932 to 1948. Slaughter played from 1938 to 1959, mostly with the Cardinals, and had a .300 career batting average.

In March, Commissioner of Baseball Peter Ueberroth reinstated Willie Mays and Mickey Mantle, Hall of Fame center fielders, to organized baseball. They had been barred by then-Commissioner Bowie Kuhn after they accepted public-relations jobs with gambling casinos. Frank Litsky

In WORLD BOOK, see BASEBALL.

BASKETBALL. Villanova University was the upset winner of the 1985 National Collegiate Athletic Association (NCAA) championship tournament. The Los Angeles Lakers, who had never defeated the Boston Celtics in a National Basketball Association (NBA) final, finally did and became the professional champion.

College Men. Georgetown University, winner of the NCAA championship in 1984, was ranked first in the 1985 preseason polls of the Associated Press and United Press International. When the regular season ended, Georgetown had a won-lost record of 30-2 and again was ranked first.

Georgetown led a field of 64 teams, up from 53 in 1984, into the NCAA championship tournament. The four regional champions were Georgetown, Memphis State, St. John's of New York City, and Villanova.

In the national semifinals on March 30 in Lexington, Ky., Georgetown was considered the favorite and Villanova the long shot. Georgetown defeated St. John's, 77-59, and Villanova upset Memphis State, 52-45. Georgetown was a 9½-point favorite over Villanova in the championship game on April 1 in Lexington because of its 17-game winning streak, tenacious defense, and superior manpower. In addition, Villanova had lost 10 games during the regular season, including 2 to Georgetown.

During the 1985 championship game, however, Villanova's players seldom missed a shot, and the team won, 66-64. Its field-goal average of 78.6 per cent (22 of 28 shots) was the best ever in an NCAA final. Villanova held Patrick Ewing, Georgetown's 7-foot (213-centimeter) all-America center, to 14 points and 5 rebounds.

The consensus all-America team comprised Ewing, Chris Mullin of St. John's, Wayman Tisdale of Oklahoma, Keith Lee of Memphis State, Johnny Dawkins of Duke, and Xavier McDaniel of Wichita State.

UCLA defeated Indiana, 65-62, on March 29 in New York City in the final of the National Invitation Tournament.

College Women. In the NCAA women's tournament, Texas—ranked first during the regular season with a 27-2 record—was eliminated in an early round. In the final of the 32-team tournament on March 31 in Austin, Tex., Old Dominion defeated Georgia, 70-65. Cheryl Miller, a Southern California junior, was named Player of the Year.

NBA Season. The six-month regular season from October 1984 to April 1985 eliminated seven teams from NBA play-off berths. The best records during the regular season were compiled by the Celtics (63-19) and the Lakers (62-20). The Lakers won their division by 20 games, the Milwaukee Bucks won theirs by 13, the Celtics by 5, and the Denver Nuggets by 4.

The 1984-1985 College Basketball Season

College Tournament Champions

NCAA (Men) Division I: Villanova University (Villanova, Pa.)
    Division II: Jacksonville State (Alabama)
    Division III: North Park (Illinois)
NCAA (Women) Division I: Old Dominion (Virginia)
    Division II: California State Polytechnic-Pomona
    Division III: Scranton (Pennsylvania)
NAIA (Men): Fort Hays State (Kansas)
    (Women): Southwestern Oklahoma State
NIT: University of California at Los Angeles
Junior College (Men): Dixie (Utah)
    (Women): Connors State (Oklahoma)

College Champions

Conference	School
Atlantic Coast	Georgia Tech—North Carolina—North Carolina State (tie; regular season)
	Georgia Tech (conference tournament)
Atlantic Ten	West Virginia (regular season)
	Temple (conference tournament)
Big East	St. John's (regular season)
	Georgetown (conference tournament)
Big Eight	Oklahoma*
Big Sky	Nevada-Reno*
Big Ten	Michigan
East Coast	Bucknell (regular season)
	Lehigh (conference tournament)
Eastern College Athletic-North	Canisius—Northeastern (tie; regular season)
	Northeastern (conference tournament)
Eastern College Athletic-Metro	Marist (regular season)
	Fairleigh Dickinson (conference tournament)
Eastern College Athletic-South	Navy—Richmond (tie; regular season)
Gulf Star	Southeastern Louisiana
Ivy League	Pennsylvania
Metro	Memphis State*
Metro Atlantic	Iona*
Mid-American	Ohio*
Mid-Continent	Cleveland State (regular season)
	Eastern Illinois (conference tournament)
Mid-Eastern	North Carolina A & T*
Midwestern City	Loyola*
Missouri Valley	Tulsa (regular season)
	Wichita State (conference tournament)
Ohio Valley	Tennessee Tech (regular season)
	Middle Tennessee (conference tournament)
Pacific Coast Athletic	Nevada-Las Vegas*
Pacific Ten	Washington—Southern California (tie)
Southeastern	Louisiana State (regular season)
	Auburn (conference tournament)
Southern	Tennessee-Chattanooga (regular season)
	Marshall (conference tournament)
Southland	Louisiana Tech*
Southwest	Texas Tech*
Southwestern Athletic	Alcorn State (regular season)
	Southern (conference tournament)
Sun Belt	Virginia Commonwealth*
Trans America Athletic	Georgia Southern (regular season)
	Mercer (conference tournament)
West Coast Athletic	Pepperdine
Western Athletic	Texas-El Paso (regular season)
	San Diego State (conference tournament)

*Regular season and conference tournament champions.

National Basketball Association Standings

Eastern Conference
Atlantic Division

	W.	L.	Pct.	G.B.
Boston Celtics	63	19	.768	
Philadelphia 76ers	58	24	.707	5
New Jersey Nets	42	40	.512	21
Washington Bullets	40	42	.488	23
New York Knicks	24	58	.293	39

Central Division

Milwaukee Bucks	59	23	.720	
Detroit Pistons	46	36	.561	13
Chicago Bulls	38	44	.463	21
Cleveland Cavaliers	36	46	.439	23
Atlanta Hawks	34	48	.415	25
Indiana Pacers	22	60	.268	37

Western Conference
Midwest Division

Denver Nuggets	52	30	.634	
Houston Rockets	48	34	.585	4
Dallas Mavericks	44	38	.537	8
San Antonio Spurs	41	41	.500	11
Utah Jazz	41	41	.500	11
Kansas City Kings	31	51	.378	21

Pacific Division

Los Angeles Lakers	62	20	.756	
Portland Trail Blazers	42	40	.512	20
Phoenix Suns	36	46	.439	26
Los Angeles Clippers	31	51	.378	31
Seattle SuperSonics	31	51	.378	31
Golden State Warriors	22	60	.268	40

Individual Leaders
Scoring

	G.	F.G.	F.T.	Pts.	Avg.
Bernard King, New York	55	691	426	1,809	32.9
Larry Bird, Boston	80	918	403	2,295	28.7
Michael Jordan, Chicago	82	837	630	2,313	28.2
Purvis Short, Golden State	78	819	501	2,186	28.0
Alex English, Denver	81	939	383	2,262	27.9
Dominique Wilkins, Atlanta	81	853	486	2,217	27.4
Adrian Dantley, Utah	55	512	438	1,462	26.6

Rebounding

	G.	Tot.	Avg.
Moses Malone, Philadelphia	79	1,031	13.1
Bill Laimbeer, Detroit	82	1,013	12.4
Buck Williams, New Jersey	82	1,005	12.3
Akeem Olajuwon, Houston	82	974	11.9

Ed Pinckney of Villanova defends against Georgetown's Patrick Ewing as Villanova wins the NCAA basketball championship in April.

As expected, the Lakers and the Celtics advanced to the play-off finals. During the play-offs, the Lakers defeated the Phoenix Suns (3 games to 0), the Portland Trail Blazers (4-1), and Denver (4-1). The Celtics defeated the Cleveland Cavaliers (3-1), the Detroit Pistons (4-2), and the Philadelphia 76ers (4-1).

That set up the ninth meeting between the Lakers and the Celtics in the history of the play-off championships. The Celtics had defeated the Lakers in the previous eight contests, including the championship final in 1984.

This time, in an often-physical series, the Lakers won, 4 games to 2. They won the deciding game by a score of 111-100 on June 9 in Boston, the first time the Celtics had lost a championship on their home court. Kareem Abdul-Jabbar, the Lakers' 7-foot 2-inch (218-centimeter) center, scored 29 points in the final game and was voted the Most Valuable Player in the play-offs. This was the 16th NBA season for the 38-year-old Abdul-Jabbar.

In all-star voting, Abdul-Jabbar made only the second team. Moses Malone of Philadelphia was the first-team center. Also on the first team were Larry Bird of Boston and Bernard King of the New York Knicks at forward, and Earvin (Magic) Johnson of the Lakers and Isiah Thomas of Detroit at guard. For the second straight year, Bird was voted regular season Most Valuable Player.

The Rookie of the Year was Michael Jordan, the Chicago Bulls' 6-foot 6-inch (198-centimeter) guard. His exciting play helped the Bulls increase their attendance at home by 87 per cent. Fan interest in Jordan also helped total NBA attendance rise 4.9 per cent to 10,506,355, a record.

Financially, the NBA was healthier than in previous years. Television ratings—indicating the size of the audience for televised NBA games—rose 2 per cent. NBA Commissioner David J. Stern reported that 15 teams showed a profit at the end of the season. In 1982, 13 of the NBA's 23 teams were in serious financial trouble.   Frank Litsky

See also EWING, PATRICK. In WORLD BOOK, see ABDUL-JABBAR, KAREEM; BASKETBALL.

BECKER, BORIS (1967-   ), won the men's singles at the All England Lawn Tennis Championships in the London suburb of Wimbledon on July 7, 1985. The 17-year-old Becker was the first German, the first nonseeded player, and the youngest player ever to win that event. He defeated Kevin Curren of the United States, 6-3, 6-7, 7-6, 6-4, in the final match. See TENNIS.

Becker was born in 1967 in Leimen, West Germany, near Heidelberg, to Elvira Becker and architect Karl-Heinz Becker.

Becker was unheralded—if not virtually unknown—outside tennis circles prior to Wimbledon. He entered the tournament ranked 20th in the world, but his victory won him international recognition.

Becker's style of play also attracted a following. His forceful, often overpowering, serve earned him the nickname "Boom Boom," and his habit of diving to the ground to return difficult shots, rolling in the grass and dirt, delighted the crowd.

Becker followed his Wimbledon victory with a victory over Aaron Krickstein of the United States on Aug. 4, 1985, in Hamburg, West Germany, that helped West Germany defeat the United States for the first time in Davis Cup competition. But a month later, Becker was defeated in an early round of the United States Open.   Rod Such

BELGIUM. A riot at Heysel Stadium in Brussels on May 29, 1985, forced an early national election and almost toppled the coalition government. Thirty-eight fans died after a concrete wall collapsed during a riot at the European Cup soccer championship game between Liverpool of Great Britain and Juventus of Turin, Italy. Most of those killed were Italians. The riot began when a section of the British crowd charged Italian spectators. As the Italians fled, the wall collapsed.

After the dead and wounded were removed, the match continued. The decision to continue was criticized, but officials said they feared more violence if they canceled the game.

A report published by a commission of inquiry on July 6 said British fans who carried out the "murderous charge" were chiefly responsible for the disaster but that a series of Belgian "oversights and deficiencies" played a major role. The report formed the basis of a no-confidence motion that threatened to bring down the government.

Saved by Liberals. A two-day debate in Parliament ended on July 13 with Liberals, who are members of the coalition, supporting the government's handling of the soccer match. As the vote was taken in the House of Representatives, all members of opposition parties walked out. An emergency Cabinet meeting held on July 16 failed

Belgium's Prime Minister Wilfried A. E. Martens, speaking in Parliament in March, wins approval of a plan to place United States cruise missiles in Belgium.

to end the disagreement between Liberal and Christian Social members of the coalition, so Prime Minister Wilfried A. E. Martens offered the government's resignation. King Baudouin I refused to accept it, however. On July 18, Martens announced that a general election planned for December 8 would take place on October 13. In the election, his coalition increased its majority in Parliament by four seats. On November 28, Martens formed a new coalition that was only slightly different from the previous government.

Parliament Dissolved. During the summer, a rift developed over the control of education. On one side was the Christian Social Party of the Dutch-speaking Flemings, led by Martens. On the other was the Christian Social Party of the French-speaking Walloons. The rift became so deep that the king dissolved Parliament on September 2. The government ruled by decree until October 13.

"Yes" to Missiles. On March 15, Martens said Belgium should keep its promise to the North Atlantic Treaty Organization (NATO) by allowing installation of 16 cruise missiles. Parliament approved the installation on March 20.   Kenneth Brown

See also EUROPE (Facts in Brief Table). In WORLD BOOK, see BELGIUM.

BELIZE. See LATIN AMERICA.

BENIN. See AFRICA.

BENNETT, WILLIAM JOHN (1943-   ), took the oath of office as the third United States secretary of education on Feb. 6, 1985, replacing Terrel H. Bell, who resigned on Dec. 31, 1984. Bennett, a conservative Democrat, had served since December 1981 as chairman of the National Endowment for the Humanities. In that position, he aroused controversy by refusing to set hiring goals for women and minorities. A believer in strict academic standards, the new secretary was expected to exert pressure on the states to institute tougher certification requirements for teachers.

Bennett was born in New York City on July 31, 1943. After graduating in 1965 from Williams College in Williamstown, Mass., he earned a doctorate in philosophy at the University of Texas in Austin and a law degree at Harvard Law School in Cambridge, Mass.

Bennett taught philosophy at several institutions, including the University of Texas, Boston University, and the University of Wisconsin in Madison. In 1976, he was named executive director of the National Humanities Center in Research Triangle Park, N.C. From 1979 through 1981, he was president of the center.

In May 1982, Bennett married Mary Elayne Glover. They have one son.   David L. Dreier

See also CABINET, UNITED STATES; EDUCATION.

BHUTAN. See ASIA.

BIOCHEMISTRY. Researchers at Harvard Medical School in Boston reported in September that they had discovered a protein that promotes the formation of blood vessels. The scientists said their finding may lead to new treatments for heart disease, cancer, and other diseases in which blood vessels play a major role.

The researchers discovered the protein—which they named angiogenin, from the Greek words for *vessel* and *produce*—in human cancer tissue. Later, they also found it in normal cells. They determined that the substance, even in extremely tiny concentrations, causes tissue to immediately begin generating new blood vessels. The investigators located the gene that carries the instructions for producing the protein, and they reconstructed the gene in the laboratory. That achievement will make it possible to manufacture the protein in large quantities.

Artificially administered angiogenin could be of great benefit to the victims of heart disease by causing new blood vessels to grow in the heart. In addition, it may be possible to help cancer patients by interfering with the action of naturally occurring angiogenin. Cancerous tumors cannot grow until they have established their own blood supply, a process that presumably requires angiogenin. If a tumor could be denied the protein, its growth would probably be halted.

Earlier in the year, in April, scientists at Collagen Corporation of Palo Alto, Calif., announced that they had isolated two proteins that trigger the formation of a tough, flexible substance called *cartilage*. The proteins stimulate a particular kind of cell to form cartilage, most of which the body gradually converts to bone.

The discoveries by the Boston and Palo Alto research teams raised hopes that growth-promoting proteins will eventually be found for all types of body tissue. Such proteins might usher in a new age of medicine in which patients could grow new limbs or organs to replace ones lost to injury or disease.

Monoclonal Antibodies. Scientists have expressed great hopes for treating cancer with *monoclonal antibodies*, laboratory-produced copies of antibodies against specific cells, bacteria, and viruses. Investigators have been trying to produce monoclonal antibodies that will seek out and bind to cancer cells. The cells would then be killed by the antibodies themselves or by drugs or radioactive substances attached to the antibodies.

Researchers at Stanford University in California reported in July that treatment with monoclonal antibodies produced a disappearance of lymphoma, cancer of the lymph glands, in 1 of 11 patients and improvement in 4 others. None of the patients had been helped by conventional therapy. In August, physicians at Johns Hopkins Hospital

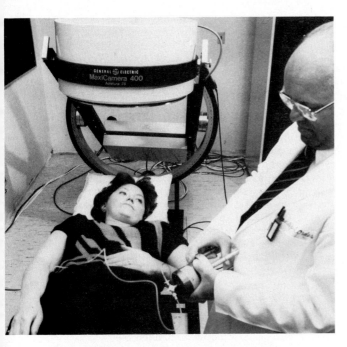

A patient at Johns Hopkins Hospital in Baltimore receives laboratory-made antibodies, an experimental treatment for advanced liver cancer.

peroxide dismutase, a substance that reduces damage to tissues deprived of blood flow, in artery blockage, for example; *epidermal growth factor*, a substance that stimulates the healing of wounds and may be useful in the treatment of burns and stomach ulcers; and *factor VIII*, a blood-clotting protein that is absent in the blood of most *hemophiliacs* (persons whose blood does not clot properly).

Vaccines. Investigators are also using genetic engineering techniques to produce *antigens*—protein molecules normally found on the surfaces of disease-causing viruses and bacteria. Because these laboratory-produced antigens stimulate the immune system but cannot cause illness, they can be used in a vaccine. In May, scientists at Genentech, Incorporated, of South San Francisco, Calif., reported that they had used antigens to protect guinea pigs against herpes infections.

Also in May, a team of researchers at five institutions in the United States reported that they had used genetic engineering to produce antigens from the parasite that causes the most severe form of malaria. These antigens may enable scientists to develop a malaria vaccine. Thomas H. Maugh II

In WORLD BOOK, see BIOCHEMISTRY.

BIOLOGY. See BIOCHEMISTRY; BOTANY; ENVIRONMENTAL POLLUTION; OCEAN; PALEONTOLOGY; ZOOLOGY.

BLINDNESS. See HANDICAPPED.

BOATING. The owners of a major United States yacht, preparing for the America's Cup races, unveiled a radical change in 1985. The yacht, *Courageous III*, won yachting's most treasured trophy in 1974 and 1977 with a conventional keel, but the remodeled version has a new vortex winged keel. The Australian sloop *Australia II* had a revolutionary keel with two winged appendages when it won the cup in 1983. Australia's defense of the cup was scheduled for 1987 off Perth, Australia.

Of the 24 syndicates that once indicated they would challenge for the cup, 18 remained—10 from the United States, 2 from France, 2 from Italy, 2 from Canada, 1 from Great Britain, and 1 from New Zealand. The number was expected to fall sharply by October 1986, when the trials to choose a challenger begin off Perth.

Other Yachting. The major U.S. competition of 1985 was the Southern Ocean Racing Conference's annual six-race series. More than 70 yachts sailed in some or all of the six races off Florida and the Bahamas in January and February 1985.

The overall winner was *Smiles*, a J-41 owned and sailed by Charlie Scott of Annapolis, Md. In Class 1, for the largest boats, the winner was *Boomerang*, an 80-foot (24-meter) vessel owned and sailed by George Coumantaros of New York City.

Powerboating. From June to September 1985, the unlimited hydroplanes, the fastest and the

in Baltimore reported what they termed "the first effective treatment" for advanced liver cancer. They treated 104 patients with monoclonal antibodies linked to radioactive elements. Seven patients had no sign of cancer at the end of the therapy, and 50 other patients showed marked improvement.

Anxiety Peptide. Investigators at the National Institute of Mental Health in Bethesda, Md., reported in February that they had isolated from rat and human brain tissues a *peptide* that increases anxiety. A peptide is a string of amino acids, the building blocks of proteins. Interestingly, the peptide was found because of its shape. It binds to the same brain cell *receptors*—molecules that serve as a sort of mooring point—that bind the tranquilizers Valium and Librium, even though its effect is opposite to that produced by those drugs. The scientists are now looking for ways to counteract the peptide.

New Products. Many new biological products for human use were produced by genetic engineering techniques in 1985. (Genetic engineering is the insertion of genes from one organism into the genetic material of another. A genetically engineered organism produces the proteins that its newly acquired genes carry the instructions for making.) The new products, most of which were being tested in clinic patients, included *human su-*

most powerful of all powerboats, held their nine-race series. *Miller American*, driven by Chip Hanauer of Seattle, won five races and took the series championship.

On July 27, in qualifying for the Budweiser Columbia Cup in Kennewick, Wash., *Miller American* set a world record of 153.061 miles per hour (mph), or 246.328 kilometers per hour (kph). The next day, *Miller American* won the race and established three more records—143.190 mph (230.442 kph) for a 2½-mile (4-kilometer) lap; 131.259 mph (211.241 kph) for a 12½-mile (20-kilometer) heat; and 129.399 mph (208.248 kph) for a 37½-mile (60-kilometer) race.

The American Power Boat Association conducted a seven-race series from May to November 1985 for various U.S. offshore powerboat championships. The greatest attention went to the superboats, which were 35 to 50 feet (11 to 15 meters) long.

Howard Quam of Chicago won the first two superboat races in *Active Cat*, a 38-foot (12-meter) catamaran driven by two 700-horsepower (522-kilowatt) MerCruiser engines. Al Copeland of Metairie, La., won the next four and the title. Copeland's boat was *Popeye's/Diet Coke*, a 50-foot (15-meter) Cougar powered by four 750-horsepower (559-kilowatt) MerCruiser engines.   Frank Litsky

In WORLD BOOK, see BOATING; SAILING.

BOLIVIA. On Aug. 6, 1985, Víctor Paz Estenssoro, candidate of the Revolutionary Nationalist Movement, was sworn in for the fourth time as Bolivia's president. In the elections on July 14, none of the 18 candidates received a majority of the popular vote, and Paz Estenssoro trailed Hugo Banzer Suárez, candidate of the right wing Nationalist Democratic Action Party. By law, Bolivia's Congress decided the winner, and on August 5, it selected Paz Estenssoro as president after a bitter session.

Paz Estenssoro faced the formidable task of bringing Bolivia's rampaging inflation under control. By August 1985, inflation was running at an average annual rate of more than 14,000 per cent. On August 29, Paz Estenssoro announced a wage freeze and other harsh economic measures. In response, labor leaders called a general strike on September 4. On September 19, the government declared a state of siege and rounded up 150 labor leaders. On October 3, the labor unrest ended when Bolivian tin and silver miners returned to work. The government lifted the state of siege on December 18.   Nathan A. Haverstock

See also LATIN AMERICA (Facts in Brief Table); PAZ ESTENSSORO, VÍCTOR. In WORLD BOOK, see BOLIVIA.

BOOKS. See CANADIAN LITERATURE; LITERATURE; LITERATURE FOR CHILDREN; POETRY; PUBLISHING.

BOTANY. In October 1985, botanists said they had confirmed the long-held theory that roots of plants grow toward water—a response called *hydrotropism*. Previous attempts to prove the theory had always been hampered by the effects of gravity on plant roots. The scientists—at Wake Forest University in Winston-Salem, N.C., and the Bionetics Corporation at the John F. Kennedy Space Center in Cape Canaveral, Fla.—studied a *mutant* (genetically changed) pea called *Ageotropum*. *Ageotropum* has an unusual property that made it especially useful for this research: Its roots do not respond to gravity when it is grown in darkness. Instead, the investigators found, when the plant was kept in a dark, humid environment, its roots always grew toward an area of greater moisture.

The scientists showed that *Ageotropum* roots sense water by means of the root cap, a covering of cells on the tip of the root. After the researchers removed a root's cap, the root continued to grow but no longer could find its way to water.

Preserving Endangered Plants. Botanists estimate that more than 3,000 species of wild plants native to the United States—10 per cent of all plant species in the continental United States and 40 to 50 per cent of the species native to Hawaii—are threatened with extinction. To ensure the survival of those plants, a group of 18 botanical gar-

A botanist at Morton Arboretum near Chicago carries seedlings of a new variety of elm tree that is resistant to Dutch elm disease.

dens in 14 states joined forces in 1985 to establish the Center for Plant Conservation, headquartered at Harvard University's Arnold Arboretum in Boston. Botanists at the affiliated gardens will participate by collecting threatened species in their respective regions. The botanists will grow the plants in a protected environment or preserve the plants' seeds for future cultivation.

New Class of Regulatory Molecules? In September, biochemists at the University of Colorado in Boulder reported evidence that fragments of molecules from a plant's cell walls may act as regulators of many of the plant's life processes, such as growth and flowering. The scientists explained that the fragments arise from complex molecules called *polysaccharides*, which make up the walls of plant cells. Polysaccharides are composed of a variety of small molecules linked into long chains.

The investigators found that short sections of a polysaccharide chain can be released from a plant cell wall. They named these short fragments *oligosaccharins*. Oligosaccharins, even in extremely low concentrations, apparently act as important triggering signals in a plant's cells. Each particular kind of oligosaccharin may produce a specific response—for example, the development of leafy shoots or flowers. Eldon H. Newcomb

In WORLD BOOK, see BOTANY.

BOTSWANA. See AFRICA.

BOURASSA, ROBERT (1933-), became Quebec's prime minister for a second time on Dec. 12, 1985, as a result of a landslide victory for his Liberal Party in elections on December 2. Ousted from power was the Parti Québécois (PQ), which had governed since defeating Bourassa's previous administration in 1976. See QUEBEC.

Bourassa was born on July 14, 1933, in Montreal. He received a bachelor's degree from Collège Jean-de-Brébeuf in Montreal in 1953 and studied law at the University of Montreal, graduating in 1956. He received a master's degree in politics and economics from Oxford University in England in 1959 and a master's in fiscal and financial law from Harvard University in Cambridge, Mass., in 1960. From 1960 to 1963, he taught economics at the University of Ottawa in Ontario.

Bourassa was first elected to Quebec's legislature, the National Assembly, in 1966. He became leader of Quebec's Liberal Party in January 1970 and was elected prime minister of Quebec in April of that year. He lost his seat in the Assembly in the PQ electoral victory of 1976.

From 1976 to 1982, Bourassa taught at universities in Belgium, Canada, France, and the United States. He was reelected Liberal leader in 1983.

Bourassa married the former Andrée Simard. They have a son and a daughter. Robie Liscomb

In WORLD BOOK, see QUEBEC.

BOWEN, OTIS RAY (1918-), a physician and former governor of Indiana, took office as secretary of health and human services under President Ronald Reagan on Dec. 13, 1985. Bowen succeeded Margaret M. Heckler, who resigned in October to become ambassador to Ireland.

Bowen was born on Feb. 26, 1918, in Richland Center, Ind. He grew up in Indiana, living in various towns where his father, a teacher, found work. Bowen graduated from Indiana University in Bloomington in 1939 and went on to earn a medical degree from the Indiana University School of Medicine in 1942. After serving in the U.S. Army Medical Corps from 1943 to 1946, during World War II, he returned to Indiana to practice medicine in Bremen.

In 1956, following four years as Marshall County coroner, Bowen was elected to the Indiana House of Representatives. He served as a state representative for 14 years.

Running on a platform of reducing property taxes, Bowen was elected governor by an overwhelming margin in 1972. He was reelected in 1976.

In 1981, Bowen accepted a teaching position at Indiana University School of Medicine. That same year, his first wife, Elizabeth, with whom he had four children, died. Bowen married Rose Mary Hochstetler in late 1981. David L. Dreier

BOWLING. Mike Aulby of Indianapolis, Marshall Holman of Medford, Ore., and Mark Williams of Beaumont, Tex., won the three major bowling tournaments for men on the 1985 Professional Bowlers Association (PBA) tour.

In previous years, Aulby won a total of six tournaments. In 1985, he won six more. The most important was the $235,000 PBA championship held in Toledo, Ohio, from March 3 to 9. Aulby, a left-hander, defeated his brother-in-law Steve Cook of Roseville, Calif., in the final, 253-211.

In the $200,000 United States Open, held from February 3 to 9 in Venice, Fla., Holman scored a 233-205 victory over Wayne Webb of Indianapolis in the final. Holman, who also won the U.S. Open in 1981, became the first man to win it twice.

In 1984, Williams almost quit after being on the tour for four years, but he decided to stay on. In 1985, he won the $200,000 Tournament of Champions, held from April 15 to 20 in Akron, Ohio. He overwhelmed Bob Handley of Pompano Beach, Fla., 191-140, in the final as Handley left four open frames.

The PBA Tour comprised 35 major tournaments—16 in the winter, 12 in the spring and summer, and 7 in the fall. Almost all of the finals were televised nationally by network or cable broadcasters, and prize money for the national and regional tournaments exceeded $6.25 million.

BOXING

Aulby, with $201,200, and Pete Weber of St. Louis, Mo., with $174,536, became the largest one-year earners in PBA tour history. The highest previous earnings for a full year was Earl Anthony's $164,735 in 1981.

Aulby's victories, in addition to the PBA championship, came in Union City, Calif., in January; Garden City, N.Y., in April; Denver in June; Las Vegas, Nev., in July; and Glendale Heights, Ill., in November. Williams and Webb each won two tournaments in two weeks.

Women. Among the many young stars on the Ladies Pro Bowlers Tour was 22-year-old Aleta Sill, a left-hander from Cocoa, Fla. In 1984, she set women's one-season records for victories with five and earnings with $81,452. In 1985, she led in earnings with $52,655 for the 14 tournaments. She also shared attention with two older bowlers—38-year-old Patty Costello of Scranton, Pa., and 35-year-old Pat Mercatanti of Yardley, Pa.

Costello, who had not won in four years, captured tournaments in Rockford, Ill., in June and Fairhaven, Mass., in August and raised her career victory total to 23, a women's record. Mercatanti, who had never won in seven years on the tour, took the women's U.S. Open, held from April 28 to May 4 in Topeka, Kans. She defeated Nikki Gianulias of Vallejo, Calif., 214-178.   Frank Litsky

In WORLD BOOK, see BOWLING.

BOXING. Boxing's most dramatic moment of 1985 came on September 21 in Las Vegas, Nev., when Michael Spinks of St. Louis, Mo., won the International Boxing Federation's (IBF) heavyweight title from Larry Holmes. Spinks became the first light heavyweight to defeat a heavyweight champion in this century. And in so doing, he prevented Holmes from surpassing the perfect 49-0 professional record of Rocky Marciano, heavyweight champion from 1952 to 1956.

The year began with boxing's governing bodies recognizing three world heavyweight champions. Holmes of Easton, Pa., was recognized by the IBF; Pinklon Thomas of Wyncotte, Pa., by the World Boxing Council (WBC); and Greg Page of Louisville, Ky., by the World Boxing Association (WBA).

For the public, the real champion was Holmes, who won the WBC heavyweight title in 1978 but then resigned it in 1983 and soon went to the IBF. In 1985, at the age of 35, Holmes's skills were diminishing. He took many hard punches in knocking out David Bey of Philadelphia in 10 rounds on March 15 in Las Vegas, and when he outpointed Carl (The Truth) Williams of New York City in 15 rounds on May 20 in Reno, Nev.

Those bouts were Holmes's 19th and 20th title defenses and raised his professional record to 48-0. He hoped to tie Marciano's record by beat-

World Champion Boxers
World Boxing Association

Division	Champion	Country	Date won
Heavyweight	Greg Page	U.S.A.	1984
	Tony Tubbs	U.S.A.	April '85
Junior heavyweight	Piet Crous	South Africa	1984
	Dwight Muhammad Qawi	U.S.A.	July '85
Light heavyweight	Michael Spinks	U.S.A.	1981
Middleweight	Marvelous Marvin Hagler	U.S.A.	1980
Junior middleweight	Mike McCallum	Jamaica	1984
Welterweight	Donald Curry	U.S.A.	1983
Junior welterweight	Gene Hatcher	U.S.A.	1984
	Ubaldo Sacco	Argentina	July '85
Lightweight	Livingstone Bramble	U.S. Virgin Islands	1984
Junior lightweight	Rocky Lockridge	U.S.A.	1984
	Wilfredo Gomez	Puerto Rico	May '85
Featherweight	Eusebio Pedroza	Panama	1978
	Barry McGuigan	N. Ireland	June '85
Junior featherweight	Victor Callejas	Puerto Rico	1984
Bantamweight	Richard Sandoval	U.S.A.	1984
Junior bantamweight	Khaosal Galaxy	Thailand	1984
Flyweight	Santos Laciar	Argentina	1982
Junior flyweight	Francisco Quiroz	Dom. Rep.	1984
	Joey Olivo	U.S.A.	April '85
	Yoo Myong-Woo	South Korea	Dec. '85

World Boxing Council

Division	Champion	Country	Date won
Heavyweight	Pinklon Thomas	U.S.A.	1984
Cruiserweight	Carlos DeLeon	Puerto Rico	1983
	Alfonzo Ratliff	U.S.A.	June '85
	Bernard Benton	U.S.A.	Sept. '85
Light heavyweight	Michael Spinks	U.S.A.	1983
	J. B. Williamson	U.S.A.	Dec. '85
Middleweight	Marvelous Marvin Hagler	U.S.A.	1980
Super welterweight	Thomas Hearns	U.S.A.	1982
Welterweight	Milton McCrory	U.S.A.	1983
	Donald Curry	U.S.A.	Dec. '85
Super lightweight	Billy Costello	U.S.A.	1984
	Lonnie Smith	U.S.A.	Aug. '85
Lightweight	José Luis Ramirez	Mexico	1984
	Hector Camacho	Puerto Rico	Aug. '85
Super featherweight	Julio Cesar Chavez	Mexico	1984
Featherweight	Azumah Nelson	Ghana	1984
Super bantamweight	Juan Meza	Mexico	1984
	Lupe Pintor	Mexico	Aug. '85
Bantamweight	Alberto Davila	U.S.A.	1983
	Daniel Zaragoza	Mexico	June '85
	Miguel Lora	Colombia	Aug. '85
Super flyweight	Jiro Watanabe	Japan	1984
Flyweight	Sot Chitalada	Thailand	1984
Light flyweight	Jung-Koo Chang	South Korea	1983

ing Spinks, who held the WBA and WBC light-heavyweight titles. Holmes was heavily favored, but Spinks won a unanimous decision. Later, Spinks relinquished his IBF, WBA, and WBC light-heavyweight titles to concentrate on the heavyweight division.

Other Divisions. Middleweight champion Marvelous Marvin Hagler of Brockton, Mass., and welterweight Donald Curry of Fort Worth, Tex., were the only champions recognized by all the major governing bodies. In a fierce fight, Hagler kept his title with a knockout of Thomas Hearns of Detroit on April 15 in Las Vegas. Curry knocked out Milton McCrory in December for the undisputed welterweight title.

Livingstone Bramble of the United States Virgin Islands, who took Ray (Boom Boom) Mancini's WBA lightweight title in 1984, kept it in the 1985 rematch by outpointing Mancini of Youngstown, Ohio, on February 16 in Reno. In August, Mancini retired from boxing at age 24.

Alexis Arguello of Nicaragua, winner of three world titles, started a comeback in 1985 at the age of 33 because he was broke. He had retired a millionaire after 1982 and 1983 defeats at the hands of Aaron Pryor of Miami, Fla.   Frank Litsky

In WORLD BOOK, see BOXING.

BOY SCOUTS. See YOUTH ORGANIZATIONS.

BOYS CLUBS. See YOUTH ORGANIZATIONS.

BRAZIL. Brazilians mourned the death on April 21, 1985, of Tancredo de Almeida Neves, the man they had elected their first civilian president after 20 years of military dictatorship. The 75-year-old president-elect underwent the first of a series of operations on his inauguration day. Too ill to take the oath of office, Neves languished in the hospital while José Sarney, his elected vice president, was sworn in as acting president on March 15 (see SARNEY, JOSÉ).

After Neves died, hundreds of thousands of Brazilians paid their final respects. The man who had stirred passionate hopes for a democratic future was buried with the sash of the office in which he never served.

New President. On April 22, a special session of the Congress meeting in Brasília, the capital, confirmed Sarney as Brazil's president. Ironically, during most of his political career, Sarney had been a political opponent of Neves, who chose Sarney as his running mate to attract opposition votes.

Sarney, the former head of the promilitary Social Democratic Party, sought to broaden the base of his support once in office. The splintering of the five political parties that existed when the military left power benefited Sarney. During 1985, these parties broke up into squabbling factions. Some 25 new—and generally small—political par-

Tancredo de Almeida Neves, left, and José Sarney celebrate in January after an electoral college chooses them as president and vice president of Brazil.

ties emerged during the year. Most represented the ambitions of individual politicians rather than broadly based constituencies.

Labor Unrest was widespread in the first half of 1985. Brazil's metalworkers went out on strike on April 11, seeking higher wages and a shorter workweek. The strike paralyzed automobile and automotive-parts production in industrial São Paulo state. A negotiated settlement was reached on June 3. Sarney won praise for refusing to use a law passed under the previous military government that permitted him to decree an end to the strike in the national interest.

Sarney was faced with a wave of strikes by postal workers, teachers, doctors, nurses, transportation workers, airline employees, and farmworkers. A wave of riots also broke out in the jails of populous São Paulo state to protest overcrowded conditions. About 22,000 prisoners were being held in jails that were built to accommodate half ·that number. In one of the most dramatic protests, prisoners in the Belo Horizonte city jails held a death lottery to draw attention to overcrowded conditions. Sixteen inmates were either hanged or beaten to death by fellow prisoners after drawing lots.

As the year progressed, opposition to Sarney's administration united around two well-known figures on the political scene—former President

Jânio Quadros and Leonel Brizola, governor of the state of Rio de Janeiro. Observers credited Sarney with a clever political move, however, when he backed a constitutional amendment that gives Brazilian voters the power to elect their next president directly. The amendment, passed in May, denied Sarney's opponents a popular issue.

Technology Advances. Brazil continued to make progress toward achieving the status of a major power. On January 17, Brazil's first commercial nuclear reactor—years behind schedule and at several times its projected cost—went into operation. Located in São Paulo state, it was built by Westinghouse Electric Corporation.

On February 8, the European Space Agency launched a communications satellite for Brazil. The Canadian-built satellite is capable of handling 12,000 telephone calls at once.

Brazil's $5.5-billion trade surplus for the first six months of the year indicated that the nation would be able to meet its interest payments, despite a foreign debt of some $103 billion. On July 4, the government announced spending reductions to meet conditions for obtaining further assistance from the International Monetary Fund, a United Nations agency. Nathan A. Haverstock

See also LATIN AMERICA (Facts in Brief Table). In WORLD BOOK, see BRAZIL.

BRIDGE. See BUILDING AND CONSTRUCTION.

BRIDGE. The United States won the Bermuda Bowl, the world championship of team contract bridge, at São Paulo, Brazil, on Nov. 2, 1985. The Americans defeated Austria for their sixth straight Bermuda Bowl victory.

The U.S. team consisted of partners Robert Hamman and Robert Wolff of Dallas and two California partnerships—Chip Martel of Davis and Lew Stansby of Castro Valley; and Hugh Ross of Oakland and Peter Pender of Forestville.

Great Britain kept the Venice Cup, the women's world team championship, defeating the United States on November 1 in São Paulo. The British partners were Nicola Smith and Pat Davies, Sally Horton and Sandra Landy, and Gillian Scott-Jones and Michelle Brunner.

Barry Crane of Los Angeles, one of the world's most successful bridge players, was killed by unknown attackers in his apartment in July. Crane won more than 35,000 master points in American Contract Bridge League competition, nearly 12,000 more than his closest challenger.

Special events throughout the world commemorated the 60th birthday of contract bridge in November. The game was first played under rules devised by American yachtsman Harold S. Vanderbilt on a cruise in the Panama Canal on Nov. 1, 1925. Henry G. Francis

In WORLD BOOK, see BRIDGE.

BRITISH COLUMBIA. Premier William R. Bennett affirmed in 1985 that three years of reduced government spending by his Social Credit Party administration had succeeded in controlling the province's budget deficit. The 1985-1986 budget, introduced on March 14, called for spending of $9-billion with a deficit of $890 million—down from $907 million in 1984-1985. (All monetary amounts in this article are Canadian dollars, with $1 = U.S. 72 cents as of Dec. 31, 1985.) The budget also cut corporate taxes in an effort to revive the flagging economy. Building projects for Vancouver, including the construction of the site for Expo 86—the 1986 world's fair—and a rapid transit line, required massive government borrowing.

Pay Cuts. In January, unions representing 15,000 construction workers in Vancouver accepted 30 per cent wage cuts, a longer workweek, and lower overtime payments in an effort to preserve their jobs. The unemployment rate in the province remained about 15 per cent in 1985.

School Board Dispute. The provincial government in May dismissed nine elected trustees of the Vancouver School Board—the province's largest—because they had refused to comply with legislation imposing financial restraint. The government appointed a trustee to cut the budget and reduce the number of teachers.

Forest Fires. The summer of 1985 brought the most costly outbreak of forest fires in British Columbia's history. In mid-July, 6,000 fire fighters were attempting to quell 800 forest fires burning at various points in the province. A budget of $46 million to fight forest fires was depleted before midsummer, by which time most of the blazes had been brought under control.

Indian Blockade. In October, the British Columbia government lifted a six-year-old ban on logging in some areas of the South Moresby region of the Queen Charlotte Islands, off the Pacific Coast. This action angered the approximately 2,000 Haida Indians living on the islands, who had filed claim to ownership of the islands with the Canadian federal government in 1983.

The Haida set up a blockade in late October, successfully keeping loggers from cutting trees on Lyell Island. More than 50 Haida were arrested and charged with obstruction. A number were sentenced to short jail terms. In December, the federal minister of Indian affairs arranged a meeting between representatives of the Haida and the provincial government. The Haida called off the blockade while negotiations were held. No settlement had been announced by year's end.

Football. On November 24, the British Columbia Lions won the Grey Cup, the championship of Canadian professional football. They defeated the Hamilton Tiger-Cats 37 to 24. David M. L. Farr

In WORLD BOOK, see BRITISH COLUMBIA.

BROCK, WILLIAM EMERSON, III (1930-   ) became United States secretary of labor on April 29, 1985, replacing Raymond J. Donovan, who resigned on March 15. Brock began meeting ·with union leaders to improve the relationship between organized labor and the Administration of President Ronald Reagan. Another of Brock's top priorities was reformation of the Occupational Safety and Health Administration, which critics charged was not adequately protecting workers.

Brock was born on Nov. 23, 1930, in Chattanooga, Tenn. He graduated in 1953 from Washington and Lee University in Lexington, Va., and served as a Navy supply officer from 1953 to 1956.

After several years as an executive with the Brock Candy Company, which his grandfather founded, Brock in 1962 became the first Republican in more than 40 years to be elected to Congress from Tennessee's Third District. Eight years later, after serving four terms in the House of Representatives, he was elected to the Senate.

Brock was named Republican Party national chairman in 1977, a post he held until 1981. In that year, Reagan appointed him U.S. trade representative.

Brock's wife, Laura, with whom he had four children, died on Dec. 30, 1985.   David L. Dreier

See also CABINET, UNITED STATES.

BRUNEI. See ASIA.

BUILDING AND CONSTRUCTION. Construction growth in the United States slowed in 1985 after two years of solid gains. Spending for new construction reached a record $313 billion in 1984—an increase of 12 per cent over 1983 after adjustment for inflation—and the total for 1985 was expected to be roughly the same. In the first six months of 1985, $157 billion in new construction was completed.

In 1983 and 1984, the expanding U.S. economy stimulated private construction, and the federal government spent heavily to repair the nation's aging *infrastructure* (public works, such as highways, bridges, and sewer systems). Those forces, combined with stable construction costs, produced real growth in the building industry. In 1985, however, economic uncertainties, foreign competition, proposed tax reform measures, and attempts to cut the federal deficit put a damper on some types of construction.

Government Construction. In fiscal 1985, which ended on September 30, federal outlays included $50 billion in construction-related expenditures—15 per cent more than in fiscal 1984. Of that amount, $26.4 billion was for grants and loans.

The government spent heavily in 1985 on military facilities and the construction and repair of roads. Military building has grown rapidly since 1981, when the Administration of President Ronald Reagan began its program of increasing U.S. military power. Spending on roads has also increased in recent years, a trend that began with the passage of the Surface Transportation Assistance Act of 1982. That law included an increase of 5 cents per gallon (3.8 liters) in the federal gasoline tax, as well as higher taxes on truckers, for highway construction and maintenance.

Private Building. Most segments of U.S. industry did little major building in 1985, but the automotive industry was a notable exception. The highlight of the year was Detroit-based General Motors Corporation's announcement in July that it would construct a $3.5-billion manufacturing complex—one of the world's largest automobile plants—in Spring Hill, Tenn., to produce its new line of Saturn automobiles. Also in 1985, Chrysler Corporation started preparing the site for a $500-million technical center north of Detroit, and Mazda Motor Corporation of Japan began building a manufacturing plant in Flat Rock, Mich., in May.

Power-plant construction since 1984 has suffered one of the few real downswings in the building industry. The dollar value of work completed was down 10 per cent in 1984 from 1983 and was expected to slide even further by the end of 1985. The major reason for the slump is that the rate of growth in the demand for electricity has declined by more than 50 per cent since 1973 as a result of energy conservation. Because utility companies expect that trend to continue, they have signed few contracts for new power plants since 1980. In the Special Reports section, see NUCLEAR POWER AT THE CROSSROADS.

Office-building construction began to level off in 1985 after a prolonged boom. Office vacancy rates—soaring to almost 25 per cent in some cities, such as Miami, Fla.; San Diego; and Houston—dampened many developers' enthusiasm for erecting office buildings. Some economists believed the market had been artificially buoyed by the Economic Recovery Tax Act of 1981, which allows businesses to write off the cost of a new building in as little as 15 years.

Construction of Housing picked up in late 1985 after a slump earlier in the year. By the end of September, work had begun on a total of 1,321,800 units, compared with 1,372,000 units for the same period in 1984—a decline of just 4 per cent.

The shortage of affordable housing for low-income families became a national issue in 1985. Most low-income housing erected during the past few years has been financed by developers and nonprofit groups, who use tax-exempt bonds, accelerated depreciation, and other tax breaks to bring costs into line. In 1985, however, the Reagan Administration's tax reform package proposed eliminating such tax breaks, a threat that threw these private builders into a tailspin. But in October, the Ways and Means Committee of the House of Representatives voted to limit, rather than abolish, the use of tax-exempt bonds.

Building Costs. Continuing a two-year trend, construction costs rose only slightly in 1985. One of the factors moderating cost increases was a glut in the worldwide oil market, which kept fuel prices stable. Low to moderate wage increases for construction workers and modest price hikes on building materials also helped to hold down construction costs.

Worker Safety. In the fall, the U.S. Department of Labor's Occupational Safety and Health Administration (OSHA) announced that it was intensifying its inspections of construction sites that include trench digging. OSHA said the fatality rate was much higher in trench construction than in other kinds of construction.

Lessons from Mexico Quake. The devastating earthquake that jolted Mexico City on September 19 had at least one positive result—it added to the knowledge of how severe earthquakes affect buildings. Earthquake engineers gathered data from strong-motion instruments, and they think they documented the phenomenon of *resonance*, or magnification of an earthquake's destructive power. Like an opera singer's high note that causes a glass to vibrate and shatter, the force of an earthquake can be magnified on buildings of a certain height and stiffness. Buildings in Mexico City between 7 and 20 stories in height suffered severe damage and often collapsed. The natural period of such buildings—the amount of time it took the buildings to sway back and forth—was apparently close to the vibration time of the earthquake, causing the buildings to shake especially violently.

Engineers Found Negligent. A Missouri administrator ruled in November that two St. Louis structural engineers were guilty of negligence in connection with a 1981 accident at a Kansas City hotel that killed 113 people. The engineers—Jack D. Gillum and Daniel M. Duncan—designed an elevated walkway at the Hyatt Regency Hotel. On July 17, 1981, the walkway collapsed and fell onto a crowd of people. The Missouri licensing board for architects and architectural engineers will use the official's ruling to decide whether to suspend or revoke the two engineers' licenses.

Waterway Completed. After 14 years of construction, the Tennessee-Tombigbee Waterway in Mississippi was officially opened on June 1, 1985. The 234-mile (377-kilometer) channel links the Tennessee and Tombigbee rivers, giving ship traffic on the Tennessee River a more direct route to the Gulf of Mexico. Janice Lyn Tuchman

In WORLD BOOK, see BUILDING CONSTRUCTION; CANAL.

BULGARIA suffered serious economic problems and political turbulence in 1985. In March, the government announced that severe winter weather had disrupted supplies of coal and electricity, retarding industrial output. Production fell short of official goals in 30 areas, including phosphate, cement, soda ash, tiles, and harvesting machines. In the first six months of 1985, industrial production grew by only 2.4 per cent, compared with 3.8 per cent in the first half of 1984.

Bulgaria rationed electricity throughout 1985. A long summer drought caused the government to turn off entire hydroelectric systems.

The grain harvest was well below the 1984 figure. Certain foods became scarce. On October 1, the government hiked some prices drastically. Industrial firms paid 58 per cent more for electricity; private households, 41 per cent more. The price of natural gas and diesel fuel went up by 35 per cent.

The government made three major appointments to economic management posts. In May, Todor Bozhinov, minister of energy and raw materials, became minister of supply, a new position. In October, Ivan Iliev replaced Stanish Bonev as deputy prime minister and head of the planning commission. Iliev had led the planning commission from 1973 to 1977. Chudomir Alexandrov

Bulgarian airline official Sergei Ivanov Antonov stands in a cage in May during his trial in Rome on charges of plotting to kill the pope.

was put in charge of a special energy commission. Since January 1984, Alexandrov has been a member of the Politburo, the policymaking body of the Communist Party.

Bulgaria's family code went into force on July 1, 1985. The code provides financial incentives for Bulgarians to have more children. Bulgaria's birth rate is one of the lowest in Europe.

Ethnic Troubles. In February, Bulgaria became embroiled in a bitter dispute with Turkey about the treatment of the 800,000 Turkish-surnamed individuals living in Bulgaria. Turkey charged that Bulgaria was forcing some of these people to change from Turkish names to Bulgarian ones in preparation for the Bulgarian census in December 1985. Bulgaria admitted that such changes were taking place but said they resulted from the "spontaneous" wish of some Turkish-surnamed citizens to return to their Bulgarian roots. Some of the 800,000 are *Pomaks,* descendants of ethnic Bulgarians who embraced Islam and adopted Turkish names during the 500 years of Turkish rule of Bulgaria.   Chris Cviic

See also EUROPE (Facts in Brief Table). In WORLD BOOK, see BULGARIA.

BURMA. See ASIA. In the WORLD BOOK SUPPLEMENT section, see BURMA.

BURUNDI. See AFRICA.

BUS. See TRANSIT; TRANSPORTATION.

BUSH, GEORGE H. W. (1924-   ), 43rd Vice President of the United States, made history on July 13, 1985, when he served as acting President for about eight hours. Before undergoing abdominal surgery that day, President Ronald Reagan signed letters temporarily transferring his power to Bush. Reagan reclaimed power after the surgery. See CONSTITUTION OF THE UNITED STATES.

It became clear in 1985 that Bush intended to seek the presidency in 1988. He formed a political action committee, hired campaign professionals, and made appearances at political events. On June 23, Bush attended his party's Midwest Leadership Conference in Grand Rapids, Mich.

The Vice President also traveled widely abroad. On March 13, while in Moscow to attend funeral services for Soviet leader Konstantin U. Chernenko, he met with Mikhail S. Gorbachev, who succeeded Chernenko. Earlier in March, Bush toured the drought-stricken African countries of Niger, Mali, and Sudan and then gave an address at the United Nations conference on African famine relief, held in Geneva, Switzerland. During the year, Bush also visited Brazil, Honduras, and Grenada. He went to Western Europe in June and China in October.   Frank Cormier and Margot Cormier

In WORLD BOOK, see BUSH, GEORGE H. W.

BUSINESS. See BANK; ECONOMICS; LABOR; MANUFACTURING.

CABINET, UNITED STATES. President Ronald Reagan's Cabinet underwent major changes in 1985. Several Cabinet members departed and were replaced, presidential counselor Edwin Meese III became United States attorney general, and two Cabinet members switched jobs.

In February, the Senate confirmed William J. Bennett, chairman of the National Endowment for the Humanities, as secretary of education; Energy Secretary Donald P. Hodel as secretary of the interior; and John S. Herrington, White House personnel director, as Hodel's successor in the Department of Energy. The previous secretaries of education and the interior—Terrel H. Bell and William P. Clark—both resigned to return to private life.

Also in February, Meese received Senate confirmation, 63 to 31, as attorney general. Meese's appointment had been held up for more than a year due to a variety of charges.

In April, the Senate confirmed William E. Brock III, a former Republican senator from Tennessee, as secretary of labor. Brock succeeded Raymond J. Donovan, who resigned in March after being indicted on fraud and larceny charges.

Stockman and Heckler Resign. David A. Stockman, director of the Office of Management and Budget, resigned on August 1 to join a New York City investment banking firm. Stockman was succeeded by James C. Miller III, former chairman of the Federal Trade Commission.

On October 1, Reagan announced that Margaret M. Heckler, secretary of health and human services, had agreed to leave her Cabinet post and become ambassador to Ireland. The President denied reports that Heckler was being forced out of the Cabinet at the urging of some members of the White House staff. On November 7, Reagan nominated former Indiana Governor Otis R. Bowen to succeed Heckler. The Senate confirmed the appointment, 93 to 2, on December 12.

Trading Places. In January, Reagan announced that White House Chief of Staff James A. Baker III and Treasury Secretary Donald T. Regan were switching jobs, at their request. In April, Reagan increased the power of Baker, Regan, and Attorney General Meese through a reorganization that reduced the seven Cabinet councils to two—an Economic Policy Council that would set national and international economic policy and a Domestic Policy Council that would develop domestic policy. The restructuring allowed Baker, Regan, and Meese to oversee virtually all of the Administration's domestic and economic policies.   David L. Dreier

In WORLD BOOK, see CABINET.

CALIFORNIA. See LOS ANGELES; STATE GOV'T.

CAMBODIA. See KAMPUCHEA.

CAMEROON. See AFRICA.

CAMP FIRE. See YOUTH ORGANIZATIONS.

CANADA

Canadians in 1985 seemed hesitant to pass judgment on the performance of Prime Minister Brian Mulroney and his Progressive Conservative Party (PC) government during its first year in office. With 211 of the 282 seats in the House of Commons filled with his supporters in 1985, Mulroney was in a position to initiate major policy changes. But he proved to be a cautious leader, anxious to hold the support of a broad spectrum of voters and regions. Polling in December showed that both the PC and the Liberal Party commanded the confidence of 38.5 per cent of voters who had decided what party to support, compared with 22 per cent for the New Democratic Party. Other parties claimed the remaining 1 per cent. The PC continued to lead in the West and the Atlantic Provinces, with the Liberals ahead in Ontario and Quebec.

Western Accord. The new government's principal accomplishments were in the economic field. On March 28, representatives of the federal government and Canada's three major Western oil-producing provinces—Alberta, British Columbia, and Saskatchewan—signed an agreement called the Western Accord. The agreement provided for decontrol of the price of Canadian oil, effective June 1. At the same time, the federal government agreed to remove certain taxes and royalties on oil and natural gas—a move long demanded by Alberta and the other Western provinces.

On October 30, Patricia Carney, minister of energy, mines, and resources, announced that generous grants to help reimburse oil company drilling costs in remote northern and offshore regions would be phased out, to be replaced by a 25 per cent tax credit. Carney also announced the end of a controversial provision by which the federal government could buy 25 per cent of any successful oil and gas find in northern lands. Although the government had never exercised this option, the provision had been bitterly attacked by oil companies in Canada and the United States.

Another agreement between Western provinces and the federal government set up a new system for natural gas prices. According to this pact, announced on October 31, the Western provinces would be allowed to sell gas to the United States at market prices. Previously, the export price of natural gas was not allowed to exceed the price of gas delivered to Toronto, Ont. In addition, the price of natural gas sold within Canada was to be gradually deregulated over a 12-month period.

Atlantic Accord. Another energy agreement, the Atlantic Accord, was signed by Mulroney and Newfoundland Premier Brian Peckford on February 11. The Atlantic Accord gave Newfoundland equal representation with the federal government on a management board, allowing the province a greater say in controlling the manner of developing offshore resources. The area covered by the agreement includes rich oil and natural gas deposits off the Newfoundland coast. Under the accord, the province also is allowed to tax the offshore resources as if they were on land.

Parliament. The first session of the 33rd Parliament ended on June 28, 1985, when the summer recess was called. It had been in session since Nov. 5, 1984. A total of 49 bills were adopted; the majority were routine housekeeping measures dating from the previous administration. The Mulroney government was expected to introduce more of its own measures during the second session of Parliament, which began on Sept. 9, 1985.

In what was probably the most important legislation of the government's first parliamentary session, the Foreign Investment Review Agency (FIRA) was scrapped. The agency had been created by the Liberals in 1973 to screen foreign investments and to determine whether they were of "significant benefit" to Canada. The FIRA had never been popular with Canadian business and was detested by business in the United States—the source of most of Canada's investment from abroad. On June 30, 1985, the FIRA was replaced by Investment Canada, an agency charged with encouraging new investment, whether from home or abroad. It also was to advise the government on proposed acquisitions of major Canadian companies by businesses from other countries. The new agency had limited screening powers in such culturally sensitive areas as communications.

During the summer, Parliament moved to redress a long-standing grievance of Indians who had lost their native status. Under a provision of the 114-year-old Indian Act, Indian women lost their Indian status when they married non-Indians. In losing this status, they also lost the right to live on reserves, participate in tribal affairs, and receive certain government benefits. In 1985, Parliament amended the act to remove this provision. Parliament also struck down provisions that denied Indian status to any Indian who registered to vote, worked outside the reserve, joined the armed forces, or sent his or her children to a non-Indian school. Indian groups had opposed the changes, arguing that the government had no right to decide who was or was not an Indian.

The Charter of Rights and Freedoms, Canada's bill of rights, went into effect on April 17. Its im-

Canada's Prime Minister Brian Mulroney and U.S. President Ronald Reagan chat during their "Shamrock Summit" in the city of Quebec in March.

The Ministry of Canada*
In order of precedence

Martin Brian Mulroney, prime minister
George Harris Hees, minister of veterans affairs
Duff Roblin, leader of the government in the Senate
Charles Joseph Clark, secretary of state for external affairs
Flora Isabel MacDonald, minister of employment and immigration
Erik H. Nielsen, deputy prime minister and minister of national defence
John Carnell Crosbie, minister of justice and attorney general of Canada
Roch LaSalle, minister of public works
Donald Frank Mazankowski, minister of transport
Elmer MacIntosh MacKay, minister of national revenue
Arthur Jacob Epp, minister of national health and welfare
Sinclair McKnight Stevens, minister of regional industrial expansion
John Wise, minister of agriculture
Ramon John Hnatyshyn, president of the Queen's Privy Council for Canada (government House leader)
David Edward Crombie, minister of Indian affairs and northern development
Robert R. de Cotret, president of the Treasury Board
Perrin Beatty, solicitor general of Canada
Michael Halcombe Wilson, minister of finance
Jack Burnett Murta, minister of state (tourism)
Harvie Andre, associate minister of national defence
Otto John Jelinek, minister of state (fitness and amateur sport; multiculturalism)
Thomas Edward Siddon, minister of fisheries and oceans
Charles James Mayer, minister of state (Canadian Wheat Board)
William Hunter McKnight, minister of labour
Walter Franklin McLean, minister of state (immigration)
Thomas Michael McMillan, minister of the environment
Patricia Carney, minister of energy, mines, and resources
André Bissonnette, minister of state (small businesses)
Benoît Bouchard, secretary of state of Canada
Andrée Champagne, minister of state (youth)
Michel Côté, minister of consumer and corporate affairs
James Francis Kelleher, minister for international trade
Robert E. Layton, minister of state (mines)
Marcel Masse, minister of communications
Barbara Jean McDougall, minister of state (finance)
Gerald S. Merrithew, minister of state (forestry)
Monique Vézina, minister for external relations
Stewart McInnes, minister of supply and services
Frank Oberle, minister of state for science and technology

*As of Dec. 31, 1985.

Premiers of Canadian Provinces

Province	Premier
Alberta	Donald Getty
British Columbia	William R. Bennett
Manitoba	Howard Pawley
New Brunswick	Richard B. Hatfield
Newfoundland	Brian Peckford
Nova Scotia	John Buchanan
Ontario	David Peterson
Prince Edward Island	James M. Lee
Quebec	Robert Bourassa
Saskatchewan	Grant Devine

Commissioners of Territories

Northwest Territories	John H. Parker
Yukon Territory	Douglas Bell

plementation had been delayed three years after the adoption of the new Canadian constitution to allow time for federal and provincial governments to make the changes necessary to bring their laws into compliance with the charter. But by 1985, only 7 of the 10 provinces had taken or were about to take the necessary steps. The province of Quebec, which had never recognized the federal charter, had implemented its own Charter of Rights in 1976.

Cabinet Changes. There were four resignations from the 40-member Mulroney cabinet in 1985—all politically embarrassing. On February 12, Minister of National Defence Robert Carman Coates resigned following criticism of a visit he had made several months before to a bar featuring nude dancers near a Canadian Armed Forces base in West Germany. Mulroney called his minister's action an error in judgment and said that there had been no risk of Canada's security involved. On February 27, Deputy Prime Minister Erik H. Nielsen was given the additional post of minister of national defense, replacing Coates.

The next minister to resign was John A. Fraser of British Columbia, minister of fisheries and oceans. A public outcry brought about his resignation on September 23 after it became known that he had allowed 1 million cans of tainted tuna from a New Brunswick plant to go to market despite objections from fisheries inspectors. He was replaced on November 20 by Thomas Edward Siddon, who had been minister of state for science and technology. Frank Oberle became the new minister of state for science and technology.

Minister of Communications Marcel Masse resigned on September 25 while a complaint that he had not reported all his election expenses in 1984 was being investigated. Masse had been a strong Quebec voice within the Mulroney cabinet. In late November, he was cleared of all wrongdoing in the matter by a police investigation, and he returned to his cabinet post on November 30.

Minister of State for Transport Suzanne Blais-Grenier resigned her cabinet post on December 31 after protesting a government decision to allow the closing of a Montreal oil refinery, eliminating more than 300 jobs. Blais-Grenier, who had also served as environment minister, had been criticized for cutting environmental programs and for her extravagant expense accounts.

There was a minor cabinet shuffle on August 20 in which nine ministers changed jobs. One new face, from Nova Scotia, entered the cabinet when Stewart McInnes became minister of supply and services.

Canada's Economy showed robust growth in income and employment during 1985. Automobile sales were a key factor in determining the brisk tempo of economic activity, being far above production levels in August and September. Consumer demand for other products, together with spending on plants and equipment, were other components of economic growth.

Canada's trade performance, which had been strong for several years, showed signs of faltering in 1985. The trade surplus, however, was predicted at $1 billion in October, bolstered by sales of automobiles and auto parts. (All monetary amounts in this article are Canadian dollars with $1 = U.S. 72 cents as of Dec. 31, 1985.) The gross national product (GNP)—the total of all goods and services produced—was expected to reach $449-billion. Economic growth, adjusted for inflation, was 4 per cent during the first half of 1985 and 6 per cent during the third quarter. The unemployment rate was 10.2 per cent in November, down from 11.2 per cent at the beginning of the year. Inflation remained under control, with an annual rate of 4 per cent as of November. Interest rates showed an almost continuous decline from 1984 levels. The influential Bank of Canada lending rate stood at 8.7 per cent in late October 1985.

The basis for limiting Japanese auto imports into Canada was changed by an understanding reached with Japan on July 3. For 1985, imports were kept under 18 per cent of the anticipated Canadian car market. This formula gave Japanese automakers a chance to increase their sales as long as demand for vehicles in Canada remained strong. Three Asian car manufacturers—Honda Motor Company and Toyota Motor Corporation of Japan and Hyundai Motor Company of South Korea—announced in 1985 that they would build car assembly plants in Canada.

Two small banks, both based in Alberta, collapsed in September—the first bank failures in Canada for 62 years. The Canadian Commercial Bank of Edmonton had been given a bailout package of $255 million in March by the federal and Alberta governments and six large banks. This did not restore the needed confidence among depositors, however. The Northland Bank of Calgary was the other bank that failed—a victim of unsound loans made to petroleum companies and other businesses during the recession of the early 1980's. The federal government promised to reimburse depositors in the two banks—assistance that was expected to amount to $900 million.

The Budget and Taxes. Finance Minister Michael Halcombe Wilson introduced his first budget on May 23. It called for reduced spending and slightly increased revenues for the fiscal year that began April 1, 1985. These actions, he estimated, would lead to a decline of about $1.1 billion in the level of the deficit he had predicted in November 1984. Still, the deficit was likely to be $33.8 billion on expenditures of $105 billion. The finance minister's budget raised income and consumer taxes,

Canada, Provinces, and Territories Population Estimates

	1984	1985
Alberta	2,340,600	2,348,800
British Columbia	2,865,100	2,892,500
Manitoba	1,058,100	1,069,600
New Brunswick	714,200	719,200
Newfoundland	579,000	580,400
Northwest Territories	49,500	50,900
Nova Scotia	872,100	880,700
Ontario	8,946,900	9,066,200
Prince Edward Island	125,600	127,100
Quebec	6,541,500	6,580,700
Saskatchewan	1,008,800	1,019,500
Yukon Territory	22,100	22,800
Canada	**25,123,500**	**25,358,400**

City and Metropolitan Population Estimates

	Metropolitan Area June 1, 1984, estimate	City 1981 Census
Toronto	3,140,500	599,217
Montreal	2,865,900	980,354
Vancouver	1,331,000	414,281
Ottawa-Hull	756,600	
Ottawa		295,163
Hull		56,225
Edmonton	687,500	532,246
Calgary	619,700	592,743
Winnipeg	603,500	564,473
Quebec	589,100	166,474
Hamilton	554,400	306,434
St. Catharines-Niagara	307,500	
St. Catharines		124,018
Niagara Falls		17,010
Kitchener	298,400	139,734
London	290,100	254,280
Halifax	285,900	114,594
Windsor	247,900	192,083
Victoria	242,000	64,379
Regina	173,400	162,613
Oshawa	166,900	117,519
Saskatoon	165,100	154,210
St. John's	160,100	83,770
Sudbury	148,800	91,829
Chicoutimi-Jonquière	138,700	
Chicoutimi		60,064
Jonquière		60,354
Thunder Bay	121,700	112,486
Saint John	115,500	80,521
Trois-Rivières	114,000	50,466

imposing a special surtax of up to 10 per cent for 18 months on individuals earning more than $30,000. Corporation taxes were also increased, as were federal sales taxes, the gasoline tax, and excise taxes on various items.

On December 4, Wilson announced the government's long-awaited plan for a minimum personal income tax. Under the plan, which took effect on Jan. 1, 1986, some Canadians would pay federal taxes of 24 per cent on taxable incomes between $45,000 and $50,000 a year.

Free Trade was a prominent topic at the "Shamrock Summit"—so called because the two leaders, both of Irish descent, met on St. Patrick's Day—between Prime Minister Mulroney and President

Federal Spending in Canada

Estimated Budget for Fiscal 1986*

	Billions of dollars †
Transfer payments:	
To other levels of government:	
Health insurance	6.5
Post-secondary education	2.3
Fiscal transfer payments	5.4
Canada assistance plan	3.9
Other	1.8
To persons:	
Old age security, guaranteed income supplement, and spouse's allowance	12.5
Government's contribution to unemployment insurance	2.6
Family allowances	2.5
Other	1.7
Subsidies:	
Petroleum incentive payments	1.6
Other	1.8
Other transfer payments:	
Foreign aid	1.3
Regional industrial expansion	1.0
Indians and Inuit	1.0
Job creation projects of employment and immigration	0.4
Other	2.2
Public debt charges	25.5
Payments to Crown corporations:	
Canada Mortgage and Housing Corporation	1.5
Canadian Broadcasting Corporation	0.8
VIA Rail Canada Inc.	0.6
Canada Post Corporation	0.4
Other	1.3
Operating and capital expenditures:	
National defense	9.4
Other departments and agencies	14.5
Total	**102.5**

*April 1, 1985, to March 31, 1986.
†Canadian dollars; $1 = U.S. 72 cents as of Dec. 1, 1985.

Spending Since 1980

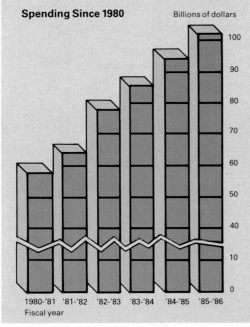

Billions of dollars

Fiscal year: 1980-'81, '81-'82, '82-'83, '83-'84, '84-'85, '85-'86

Source: Treasury Board of Canada.

Reagan at Quebec City, Que., on March 17 and 18. The two leaders instructed officials to resolve what they called "specific impediments to trade" between the two countries. Reagan assured Mulroney that he would resist protectionist moves that might hurt trade with Canada.

A royal commission on the future of the Canadian economy, appointed by Prime Minister Pierre Elliott Trudeau in 1982, strongly recommended in September that Canada make a "leap of faith" by negotiating free trade with the United States. A joint committee of Canada's House of Commons and Senate also reported in favor of beginning trade discussions with the U.S. government.

On September 26, Mulroney sent a message to Reagan that he wished to begin negotiations. At an October meeting between Canada's Secretary of State for External Affairs Charles Joseph (Joe) Clark and U.S. Secretary of State George P. Shultz, Shultz said talks could begin early in 1986.

North American Air Defense. The Canadian government gave its permission for the United States to conduct cruise missile tests over northern Canada in late February. At the "Shamrock Summit" in March, Mulroney and Reagan signed a $1.5-billion plan to improve the North American radar warning system.

Acid Rain. On the issue of acting to control air pollution and other environmental damage caused by acid rain, the March "Shamrock Summit" led to no direct action. Instead, Prime Minister Mulroney and President Reagan agreed to refer the question for further study to two former public officials. Ontario Premier William G. Davis, who had resigned his post a month before, and Andrew L. (Drew) Lewis, Jr., formerly Reagan's transportation secretary, were assigned to report on the question, especially its political dimensions, before the next meeting of the President and the prime minister in 1986.

On December 17, the government of Ontario announced a program to sharply cut sulfur dioxide pollution—a major cause of acid rain. It ordered four large sources of the pollution to reduce emissions of the chemical from present levels of 1.9 million metric tons (2 million short tons) per year to 665,000 metric tons (733,000 short tons).

Northwest Passage. The continuing uncertainty over the legal status of the Northwest Passage between Canada's Arctic islands came up again in the summer of 1985. In 1970, Canada had claimed pollution-control jurisdiction to protect the fragile Arctic environment. At the time, the United States had contended that the Arctic Ocean north of North America constituted international waters. During early August 1985, the United States Coast Guard icebreaker *Polar Sea* made a successful voyage through the ice-clogged Northwest Passage. The Mulroney government

Scandals led to the resignations of two cabinet ministers in September, Marcel Masse, left, and John A. Fraser, right, but Masse was reinstated in November.

did not protest the trip. Canadians who felt their country's claim to sovereignty in these Arctic waters was being challenged criticized the governments of both countries.

On September 10, the Canadian government issued a statement on the North, pointing to evidence of Soviet submarine activity in the Arctic seas as well as the *Polar Sea* voyage. External Affairs Minister Clark announced the government's intention to class the waters around Canada's Arctic islands as "internal" waters under Canadian ownership according to international law. The new Arctic boundaries would go into effect on Jan. 1, 1986. Clark expressed the hope that Canada and the United States could cooperate in the Arctic for their joint defense—but only on the basis of Canadian jurisdiction over the islands and the channels between them.

Sanctions Against South Africa. The Canadian government took a strong stand against South Africa's official policy of racial segregation—called *apartheid*—in 1985. On July 6, after violent demonstrations in South Africa against apartheid, External Affairs Minister Clark imposed trade sanctions on South Africa that included banning the export of computers and electronic equipment to South African government agencies, discouraging the sale of South African gold coins in Canada,

and terminating contracts to process uranium ore from Namibia, a territory seeking independence from South Africa.

At the Commonwealth Heads of Government meeting in the Bahamas during mid-October, Prime Minister Mulroney played a key role in working out a compromise representing a Commonwealth position on South Africa. The compromise, approved by all 49 members of the Commonwealth, banned government loans to South Africa, threatened to limit the importation of South African gold coins, and ended government funding for trade missions to South Africa.

On October 23, in his first address to the United Nations, Mulroney expressed Canada's strongest stand to date against South African apartheid. In threatening total sanctions and the ending of diplomatic relations, Mulroney went beyond what any other Western leader had said on the subject.

Facts in Brief: Population: 25,358,400. Government: Governor General Jeanne M. Sauvé; Prime Minister M. Brian Mulroney. Monetary unit: the Canadian dollar. Value of foreign trade (in U.S. dollars): exports, $86,817,000,000; and imports, $73,999,000,000.   David M. L. Farr

See also the Canadian provinces articles; CANADIAN LIBRARY ASSOCIATION (CLA); CANADIAN LITERATURE; MULRONEY, M. BRIAN; SAUVÉ, JEANNE M.; TRUDEAU, PIERRE ELLIOTT.

CANADIAN LIBRARY ASSOCIATION (CLA), released a study in June 1985 assessing the legal limits to freedom of expression. The study warned that libraries, by providing easy access to books and magazines that some groups might find morally objectionable, could be found guilty of circulating obscene material. The CLA advised libraries to put such material in restricted areas.

Copyright Law. In June, CLA representatives appeared before a parliamentary subcommittee that is preparing legislation to revise the Copyright Act, passed in 1924. Libraries have long been concerned about whether the amount of photocopying of library materials is fair to the authors and publishers of those materials, and thus legally permissible. The CLA asked the subcommittee to address that question.

UNESCO. Throughout 1985, the CLA urged the Canadian government to continue participating in the United Nations Educational, Scientific and Cultural Organization (UNESCO). Some of UNESCO's member countries have expressed dissatisfaction with its operations, and the United States and Great Britain have dropped out of the organization. Citing the agency's accomplishments in promoting literacy, culture, and scientific knowledge, the CLA asked the government to work within the organization to bring about whatever reforms are necessary.

Annual Meeting. Some 1,500 delegates attended the CLA's annual conference, in Calgary, Alta., from June 13 to 18, 1985. Beth Miller, special collections librarian at the University of Western Ontario in London, assumed office as president of the association, succeeding Judith McAnanama, chief of the Hamilton, Ont., Public Library.

Awards. The CLA awarded three scholarships in 1985: the Howard V. Phalin-World Book Graduate Scholarship in Library Science to Claudia Douglas of Calgary; the H. W. Wilson Scholarship to Patricia Bennett of Millgrove, Ont.; and the CLA-Elizabeth Dafoe Scholarship to Suzanne Lucier of Ottawa, Ont.

The CLA Outstanding Service to Librarianship Award winner in 1985 was Mary E. P. Henderson, former dean of library science at the University of Alberta in Edmonton. The Grolier Award for Research in School Librarianship went to Ganga Dakshinamurti of Winnipeg, Man., and the CLA Research and Development Award was shared by Jacqueline McDonald and Frances Nowakowski, both of Halifax, N.S. Artist Ian Wallace received the Amelia Frances Howard-Gibbon Illustrator's Award for his illustrations in *Chin Chiang and the Dragon's Dance* (Groundwood Books), and author Jean Little received the CLA Book of the Year for Children Award for *Mama's Going to Buy You a Mockingbird* (Penguin Books).   Paul Kitchen

In WORLD BOOK, see CANADIAN LIBRARY ASSN.

CANADIAN LITERATURE enjoyed a productive year in 1985, highlighted by the publication of *The Canadian Encyclopedia.* This three-volume, 2,089-page reference work consisted of some 8,000 entries written by 2,500 contributors. Rich in detail, the work brought Canada's past and present to life and displayed a sensitivity to the people and ideas that helped fashion the nation.

Fiction. The outstanding work of Canadian fiction in 1985 was Robertson Davies' *What's Bred in the Bone,* a many-layered novel that explored questions of art and predestination through the life of a Canadian painter. Margaret Atwood, another internationally recognized novelist, contributed *The Handmaid's Tale,* a novel that speculated about the emotional and physical subjugation of women in a future society. Morley Callaghan's allegorical *Our Lady of the Snows* told of a woman's descent into the tawdry world of nighttime Toronto. Brian Moore brought historical detail to life in *Black Robe,* a narrative about a Canadian Jesuit's crisis of faith during the 1600's.

Other noteworthy novels included Paul Quarrington's *The Life of Hope,* Janette Turner Hospital's *Borderline,* and Ann Ireland's *A Certain Mr. Takahashi.* The best first novel of 1985 was *Wales' Work* by Robert Walshe, a stylish satire of the publishing world. Anthony Hyde's *The Red Fox* was a compelling thriller that earned more than $1 million in sales and foreign rights before publication. But the best mystery novel of the year was Eric Wright's *Death in the Old Country.*

The short-story genre, in which Canadians excel, was represented by Neil Bissoondath's *Digging Up the Mountains;* Marian Engel's *The Tattooed Woman;* Keath Fraser's *Foreign Affairs;* Mavis Gallant's *Overhead in a Balloon: Stories of Paris;* Hugh Hood's *August Nights;* Bharati Mukherjee's *Darkness;* and Jane Rule's *Inland Passage.*

Biographies and Memoirs. Two books that provoked lively controversy in 1985 were Elspeth Cameron's *Irving Layton,* a biography of a major Canadian poet that combined scholarship and scandal, and the poet's own memoir, *Waiting for the Messiah,* a self-promoting account of Layton's adolescence and early marriages.

Farley Mowat's *My Discovery of America* was a vigorous account of the popular writer's well-publicized encounter with United States bureaucracy (see NEWSMAKERS OF 1985). Albert and Theresa Moritz' *Leacock* shed new light on the famous Canadian humorist Stephen Butler Leacock. Two other books with important literary associations were *Letters of a Lifetime,* the correspondence of Susanna Moodie, a Canadian novelist and poet of the 1800's; and the first volume of *The Selected Journals of Lucy Maud Montgomery,* author of *Anne of Green Gables* (1908). George Ignatieff's *The Making of a Peacemonger* traced his life from his child-

Popular Canadian writer Farley Mowat stays at home and writes *My Discovery of America* after he was denied entry into the United States in April.

hood in czarist Russia to his later work as a high-ranking Canadian diplomat.

Many books in 1985 took up the subject of court proceedings and imprisonment. The sensational trial of Wilbert Colin Thatcher inspired Maggie Siggins' *A Canadian Tragedy* and Garrett and Leslie Wilson's *Deny, Deny, Deny.* Thatcher, a former member of the Saskatchewan legislature, was convicted of murdering his ex-wife in 1984. Thatcher himself produced *Backrooms,* the story of his political career, written in prison after his conviction. In *A Minute at a Time,* Michael Harris told the story of Donald Marshall, imprisoned 11 years for a crime he did not commit. Roger Caron, a former convict and winner of a Governor General's Literary Award, wrote *Bingo!,* an account of the 1971 riots in Kingston Penitentiary in Ontario.

History and Politics. Peter C. Newman's *Company of Adventurers* was a well-researched, sweeping, and lively chronicle of the Hudson's Bay Company and the role of its merchant princes in the exploration and commercial development of western Canada. Several books marked the 100th anniversary of an uprising against the Canadian government led by Louis Riel. Among them was *Voices of the Rebellion* by Rudy Wiebe and Bob Beale. Barry Broadfoot's *The Veterans' Years* was an oral history of the experiences of soldiers after they returned to Canada from World War II battlefields.

Richard Gwyn wrote about the problems of U.S.-Canadian relationships in *The 49th Paradox,* and a former secretary of state of Canada, John Roberts, contributed *Agenda for Canada.* Jean Chrétien's *Straight from the Heart* was a best-selling biography that traced his rise to power in Canada's Liberal Party. *Personal Letters of a Public Man,* edited by Thad McIlroy, provided yet another view of John Diefenbaker, one of Canada's most colorful prime ministers.

Poetry. New collections by Lorna Crozier, Robert Kroetsch, Erin Mouré, Susan Musgrave, P. K. Page, and Phyllis Webb demonstrated the diversity and energy of Canadian poetry. *The New Canadian Poets,* edited by Dennis Lee, brought together the work of poets who have emerged since 1970. *The Contemporary Canadian Poem Anthology,* edited by George Bowering, provided yet another perspective on Canadian verse.

Business and Finance. Books published in this category in 1985 included Rod McQueen's *Ri$$$ky Business,* an investigation of Canada's insurance industry, and *A Matter of Trust,* a study of banks that administer trusts, by Patricia Best and Ann Shortell. *The Money Rustlers* by Paul Grescoe and David Cruise examined entrepreneurs of western Canada.

Other Books. A timely book in this period of cuts in government support for cultural activities was George Woodcock's *Strange Bedfellows,* which assessed government policies toward the arts.

The status of women in Canadian society was the topic of several books. Isabel Bassett's *The Bassett Report* analyzed the social repercussions of women in the work force. Susan Crean's *Newsworthy* examined the careers of successful women journalists. Sylvia Bashevkin's *Toeing the Lines* studied the reasons why women have failed to reach the top in the Canadian political structure. *Women Against Censorship,* edited by Varda Burstyn, examined the dilemma of pornography versus freedom of expression. Anne Collins' *The Big Evasion* dealt with abortion issues.

Art and Photography. The most popular art book of 1985 was *The World of Robert Bateman,* a collection of wildlife paintings by the successful artist. The late Roloff Beny's last photographs were featured in *The Romance of Architecture.* Grace Deutsch and Avanthia Swan edited a book of photographs entitled *Canada Coast to Coast.* Joel Russ and Lou Lynn examined Canadian examples of *Contemporary Stained Glass.* Patricia Pierce edited *Canada: The Missing Years,* a collection of forgotten photographs taken from 1895 to 1924. George Woodcock joined with artist Toni Onley to produce *Walls of India.*   Ken Adachi

See also AWARDS AND PRIZES; LITERATURE. In WORLD BOOK, see CANADIAN LITERATURE.

CAPE VERDE. See AFRICA.

CARTER, JAMES EARL, JR. (1924-   ), the 39th President of the United States, in 1985 continued his relationship with former President Gerald R. Ford, the Republican he defeated in the 1976 presidential election. Carter and Ford took part in an April 1985 conference on American-Soviet relations at the Carter Center at Emory University in Atlanta, Ga. In January, their wives, Rosalynn Carter and Betty Ford, took part in a program on "Women in a Changing World" at American University in Washington, D.C.

In his book *The Blood of Abraham*, published in April, Carter cited the 1978 Camp David accords between Egypt and Israel as the major achievement of his presidency. He contended that under President Ronald Reagan, "the [Middle East] peace process has come to a screeching halt."

Carter and his wife traveled to Greece, Turkey, and Nepal and, for the second summer in a row, spent a week in New York City helping renovate low-income housing. The Carters' daughter, Amy, 17, was arrested in Washington, D.C., on April 8 while demonstrating against South Africa's racial policies. She was arrested for marching too close to the South African Embassy. In August, Amy started her freshman year at Brown University in Providence, R.I.   Frank Cormier and Margot Cormier

In WORLD BOOK, see CARTER, JAMES EARL, JR.

Former President Jimmy Carter works with two other volunteers to renovate housing for the poor on New York City's Lower East Side in July.

CAT. A major breakthrough in feline health occurred in early 1985 with the introduction of a vaccine against feline leukemia virus. Prior to Leukocell vaccine, developed by Norden Laboratories, Incorporated, a division of SmithKline Beckman Corporation of Philadelphia, there was no protection against the virus, which was estimated to kill about 1½ million cats a year in the United States.

Cats continued to grow in popularity as pets. The Market Research Corporation of America estimated in 1985 that there were 23.4 million cat-owning households in the United States in 1984, with a total of almost 49 million cats. Registrations of purebred cats rose to 55,000, according to the Cat Fanciers' Association, Incorporated.

The 1985 National Best Cat was Grand Champion Charoe's Rosetta of Comarro, a red Persian female bred by Roe Alexander of Park Ridge, Ill., and owned by Marcia and Ron Collins of Downers Grove, Ill. Grand Champion Rambo's Rocky Mountain Sunrise, a red-and-white Persian male bred and owned by Jim and Anne Rambo and Judy Hamilton, all of Atlanta, Ga., claimed the title of National Best Kitten. Rose and Peter Peise of New Hyde Park, N.Y., were the breeders and owners of the Best Altered Cat, Champion and Grand Premier Harborhill's Aragorn, a copper-eyed white Persian.   Thomas H. Dent

In WORLD BOOK, see CAT.

CAVACO SILVA, ANÍBAL (1939-   ), a Social Democrat, became prime minister of Portugal on Nov. 6, 1985, succeeding Mário Soares, a Socialist. Cavaco Silva had been elected leader of the Social Democrats in May 1985, when that party and the Socialists were partners in the coalition governing Portugal. A disagreement over labor and agricultural policies caused the Social Democrats to leave the coalition in June, triggering national elections on October 6. The Social Democrats defeated the Socialists in the election but did not win enough seats in Parliament for a majority.

Cavaco Silva was born July 15, 1939, in Boliqueime, Portugal. He earned a bachelor's degree in finance from the Higher Institute of Economic and Financial Sciences in Lisbon. After obtaining a doctorate in economics from York University in England in 1973, Cavaco Silva pursued an academic career, eventually becoming a professor of economics at Catholic University in Lisbon. He served briefly as Portugal's minister of finance and planning in 1980.

Cavaco Silva is a strong advocate of free enterprise. He has called for the sale of many of Portugal's government-owned businesses.

The new prime minister's wife, Maria Alves, is a professor of language and Portuguese culture at Catholic University. The couple have a son and a daughter, both students.   Jay Myers

CENSUS. On Jan. 1, 1986, the population of the United States stood at about 240.4 million, about 2.1 million, or 0.9 per cent, more than a year earlier. In April 1985, the U.S. Bureau of the Census reported that between 1980 and 1984 the black population of the United States increased at a faster rate than the population as a whole, rising 6.7 per cent to 28.6 million. On July 1, 1984, the median age—meaning that half the population was older and half younger—was 31.2 years, up from 30.9 years in 1983.

Single-Parent Families. In May 1985, the Census Bureau reported a continued rise in the number of single-parent families. As of March 1984, 25.7 per cent of U.S. families with children had only one parent, up from 21.5 per cent in 1980. In 1970, the figure was 12.9 per cent. In 1984, the rate of single-parent families among whites was 20.1 per cent; among blacks, 59.2 per cent.

Government Payrolls at state and local levels increased between 1977 and 1982, the Census Bureau said in January 1985, though the overall rise was lower than the growth rate for the U.S. labor force as a whole. State payrolls rose 7.2 per cent to 3.74 million during the five-year period, and local government employment increased 1.4 per cent to 9.25 million. The number of federal workers was unchanged at 2.85 million. Overall, government employees represented 15.9 per cent of the civilian labor force in 1982, down from 16.8 per cent in 1977. In August 1985, however, the bureau reported that by October 1984 full-time and part-time civilian employment in the federal government had increased to 2.94 million, chiefly because of hiring by the Department of Defense and the U.S. Postal Service.

Aid, Income. The Census Bureau said in April that 47 per cent of all U.S. nonfarm households had received benefits from at least one government program, such as social security, Medicare, Medicaid, food stamps, welfare assistance, or unemployment compensation, during the first three months of 1984. A Census Bureau study released in July 1985 showed that between 1980 and 1983 the wealthiest U.S. families—those with after-tax incomes above $29,763—increased their share of income to 42 per cent of all after-tax income, up from 40.6 per cent in 1980. This top-income group was the only group to increase its share of total after-tax income during that period.

Participation Campaign. In 1985, the Census Bureau began a public relations campaign to persuade Americans to participate in the 1990 census. Between the early 1950's and late 1970's, the number refusing to answer surveys by the bureau more than doubled.   Frank Cormier and Margot Cormier

See also POPULATION; WELFARE. In WORLD BOOK, see CENSUS; POPULATION.

CENTRAL AFRICAN REPUBLIC. See AFRICA.

CHAD continued to be severely divided in 1985, as its seemingly endless civil war dragged on. Forces of the Libyan-backed rebel movement, led by former Chadian President Goukouni Weddeye, occupied the northern third of Chad. Allied with Weddeye's troops were a number of separate antigovernment guerrilla groups that operated in southern Chad. Those forces, calling themselves *codos* (commandos), fought several large but indecisive battles in January and April with the army of Hissein Habré, Chad's current president. On April 1, three other rebel groups announced an alliance opposed to both Weddeye and Habré.

France and three African countries—Congo, Gabon, and Mali—tried to arrange a negotiated settlement among Chad's political factions. Guy Penne, France's presidential adviser on foreign affairs, met on March 8 with Weddeye's representatives in Libreville, the capital of Gabon. Penne proposed that a peace conference be held outside Chad, an idea that was seconded by Gabon's President Omar Bongo and Congo's President Denis Sassou-Nguesso. On April 1, the president of Mali, Moussa Traoré, succeeded in bringing Habré and Weddeye together for a brief meeting in Mali's capital, Bamako. After that, however, no further progress was made.   J. Dixon Esseks

See also AFRICA (Facts in Brief Table). In WORLD BOOK, see CHAD.

CHEMISTRY. In September 1985, polymer scientist Ioannis V. Yannas of the Massachusetts Institute of Technology (M.I.T.) in Cambridge announced that he and his colleagues had *regenerated* nerves in mice—that is, they had caused severed nerves in mice to grow healthy tissue across gaps of nearly ¾ inch (19 millimeters). The research offers hope that one day scientists will develop a way to repair human nerves damaged by accidents and disease.

In their research, the M.I.T. scientists first packed tubes made of silicon with a *polymer* (a chainlike molecule) taken from cowhide or shark cartilage. Next, they cut through nerves in the legs of anesthetized mice, creating the gaps. Finally, they connected the ends of the nerves to opposite ends of the tubes. In six weeks, the nerves grew together, breaking down the polymer chemically as they grew. The new nerve tissue appeared normal and contained blood vessels.

The scientists also caused nerves to grow through unpacked tubes, but the new nerve tissue was 40 to 110 times narrower than the tissue that grew through the packed tubes, and it developed no blood vessels.

Cold Cure? In April 1985, chemist Guy Diana of Sterling-Winthrop Research Institute in Rensselaer, N.Y., reported the development of new compounds that may someday be used to cure the common cold. There are 120 known forms of *rhinovirus*, the virus responsible for most colds. This wide variety of forms is one of the reasons why no one has yet developed a cure for the cold.

A rhinovirus, like most viruses, is made up of genetic material and a protein coating. When a rhinovirus infects a mucous membrane cell, the genetic material separates from the coating. The genetic material then uses raw materials in the cell to produce more rhinoviruses.

The new compounds, oxazolylphenylisoxazoles, prevent the genetic material from separating from the coating. Preventing separation stops the virus from reproducing and so stops the infection.

In laboratory tests, the new compounds worked against 34 of the 40 rhinoviruses tested. In tests with cell samples and laboratory mice, the compounds also worked against poliovirus—which causes poliomyelitis—and enterovirus, which dwells in the intestine and sometimes causes diseases of the nervous system. These viruses were stopped in mice that were fed the new compounds, indicating that compounds eventually developed for human beings might be taken in the form of pills, capsules, or drops.

The compounds seem safe. Mice that received up to 50 times the dosage that may be recommended for human beings showed no ill effects.

Markers Mark Criminals. In September 1985, research chemist Bruce Budowle of the Federal Bureau of Investigation (FBI) National Academy at Quantico, Va., announced that FBI researchers have developed a new method of analyzing blood that helps identify criminals. The new method, called *ultra-thin gel isoelectric focusing*, enables investigators to perform 5 to 10 tests on a single drop of blood. The tests identify at least three important *markers*—blood proteins that vary from individual to individual.

When markers in blood connected with a crime do not match those of a suspect, he or she is likely to be innocent. But as more markers do match, the evidence against a suspect becomes stronger.

To determine what markers are present in a drop of blood, the blood is placed on a special gelatin and then subjected to an electric field. The resulting reactions lock even extremely similar proteins onto different places on the gelatin. Each place is characteristic of a certain marker.

The new method is up to 10 times faster than conventional methods of blood analysis. In addition, it is more precise. For example, the method revealed 10 variations of one marker. Scientists had known of only 3 variations of that marker previously. Each new marker or new variation enables investigators to narrow the field of suspects. In 1985, the FBI began using three markers in their investigations. They expected to be using five by the beginning of 1986.

Nuclear Poison? Following a nuclear war, the chemical contamination of air, water, and soil could be as severe a long-term health hazard as radioactive fallout, according to chemists at the University of Colorado in Boulder. In April 1985, John Birks said that he and Johannes Staehelin estimated the amounts of asbestos, polychlorinated biphenyls (PCB's), and other dangerous compounds currently in use, and then calculated what their concentrations would be after nuclear explosions redistributed them. The chemists also considered the chemical products of the thousands of fires that would be ignited in a nuclear war.

The researchers' results showed that nuclear explosions in the Northern Hemisphere would scatter thousands of chemicals, including many chlorine compounds that are poisonous and can cause birth defects, genetic mutations, and cancer. The concentrations of the dangerous chemicals would be so low that the chemicals would not kill many people immediately. The long-term effects of the chemicals would be extremely harmful, however. Natural poisons such as those produced by the decay of animals and plants also would threaten survivors of the nuclear blasts, because the explosions would reduce the amounts of natural chemicals called oxidants that counteract such poisons under normal conditions.   Peter J. Andrews

In WORLD BOOK, see CHEMISTRY.

CHESS. Gary Kasparov of the Soviet Union captured the world championship of chess from his countryman Anatoly Karpov on Nov. 9, 1985. The two contestants played a total of 72 games in two matches, the first of which began in Moscow on Sept. 10, 1984. On Feb. 15, 1985, after a record 48 games—including 40 draws—World Chess Federation President Florencio Campomanes stopped the match and declared it void. The score stood at 5 wins to 3 in favor of Karpov, but Karpov was obviously tiring. (Stamina is a major factor in a long chess match.) Kasparov had won two games in a row, and Karpov had not won since game 27.

A second match began on September 3, with play limited to 24 games. Karpov stood to retain the title if the match ended in a tie. Kasparov won the 24th game to capture the championship. He won 5 games in this match, Karpov won 3, and there were 16 draws.

Countdown for 1986. Even as Kasparov and Karpov dueled, the two-year cycle of events that produces challengers for both the world championship and women's world championship ground on. Soviets Artur Yusupov, Rafael Vaganian, and Andrei Sokolov tied for first at the candidates' tournament, which ended on November 3 in Montpellier, France. These three players and the fourth-place winner, Jan Timman of the Netherlands, earned the right to proceed to world championship semifinal matches. The eventual survivor of these matches will challenge the champion in September 1986.

In the Women's Interzonal Tournament, held in Havana, Cuba, and ending on July 24, 1985, Nana Alexandria, Marta Litanskaya, Irina Levitina, and Lidia Semenova—all of the Soviet Union—and Pia Cramling of Sweden won the right to advance to the women's candidates' matches. The winner will meet Women's World Champion Maya Chiburdanidze in 1986.

Younger Players. In a match that ended on Jan. 27, 1985, in Foxborough, Mass., British champion Nigel Short, 19, the world's youngest grand master, defeated United States champion Lev Alburt of New York City. In September, Maxim Dlugy, 19, of New York City, won the World Junior Championship in the United Arab Emirates.

Hunter College Elementary School of New York City won the U.S. elementary school team chess championship in 1985. Orange Grove Junior High School of Tucson, Ariz., again won the championship for the eighth grade and below, while Martin Junior High School of Crossville, Tenn., took the championship for the ninth grade and below. Stuyvesant High School of New York City won the high school chess championship.   Al Lawrence

In the WORLD BOOK SUPPLEMENT section, see CHESS.

Wearing a Chinese army cap, Chicago Mayor Harold Washington visits the Great Wall in September during a tour of China.

CHICAGO. Although 1985 was not an election year in Chicago, politics influenced almost every aspect of civic life. The so-called Council Wars raged on between Mayor Harold Washington, elected the city's first black mayor in 1983, and the white majority of the City Council, led by Alderman Edward R. Vrdolyak.

The City Council continued to block mayoral appointments to politically sensitive posts, but under pressure from the public and the media, the council confirmed the mayor's choices for many lesser boards and commissions. The mayor's position was further strengthened by a court-ordered remap of the city's 50 *wards* (districts) to increase the representation of the city's black and Hispanic populations. Under the new ward boundaries, a special election in seven predominantly black and Hispanic wards scheduled for March 1986 will likely provide Washington with three or more new council allies, perhaps enough to give him equal strength with the Vrdolyak bloc. In 1985, 21 council members backed Washington, while 29 were in the Vrdolyak bloc.

On Dec. 22, 1985, the City Council adopted a record city budget of $2.1 billion.

Economy. The city continued to lose manufacturing jobs at the rate of 10,000 per year, but vigorous growth in the service and financial industries indicated that Chicago's economy was changing rather than declining. A private study released in August concluded that Chicago was riding the crest of a $10-billion office-construction boom.

Trials. Two very different sorts of legal proceedings dominated Chicago courtroom news in 1985: clemency hearings for convicted rapist Gary E. Dotson, and the trial of several Cook County judges accused of taking bribes.

In a highly publicized clemency hearing in May, Dotson's alleged victim, Cathleen Crowell Webb, said she had lied in 1977 when she accused Dotson of raping her. After the hearing, Illinois Governor James R. Thompson said Dotson had been proved guilty "beyond reasonable doubt" in 1979 but had served more time in prison than the average for a rapist convicted in Illinois. So on May 12, 1985, Thompson commuted Dotson's sentence from 25 years to the 6 years he had already served.

On December 18, 22 more indictments—for a total of 50—were handed down in Operation Greylord, a federal probe of the Cook County Circuit Court. The investigation claimed its mightiest victim on July 13 with the conviction of Judge Richard F. LeFevour, the court's presiding judge. See COURTS.

World's Fair. Chicago's plan to hold a world's fair in 1992 collapsed because of lack of support in the Illinois legislature. Michael Madigan,

Speaker of the House of Representatives, delivered the killing blow on June 20 when he opposed continued state funding for the Chicago World's Fair 1992 Authority. Madigan cited a study that showed the $1-billion event would likely result in a deficit of at least $50 million.

Public Buildings. On May 6, Governor Thompson dedicated the State of Illinois Center in downtown Chicago. The huge Post-Modernist structure quickly became a top tourist attraction; but it was also the butt of jokes concerning its often unreliable air-conditioning system and its $170-million price tag—twice the amount originally budgeted.

Cost overruns also plagued a new addition to McCormick Place, the lakefront convention center. In June, McCormick Place officials said they needed another $60 million in state funds to finish the project, originally expected to cost $252 million. The state legislature approved the extra funds in November, but only after the center's governing board and director were removed.

Teachers' Strike. On September 2, the Chicago Teachers Union voted to strike for the third time in three years. The strike ended two days later when the teachers accepted a new contract providing for a 6 per cent pay hike in 1985 and a possible 3 per cent raise in 1986.   John F. McCarron

See also CITY. In WORLD BOOK, see CHICAGO.

CHILD WELFARE. As of mid-October 1985, 204 children in the United States aged 12 or under had contracted acquired immune deficiency syndrome (AIDS), a disease that destroys the immune system and makes the victim vulnerable to a form of cancer, a number of serious infections, and possible brain damage. Most children who develop AIDS, which is caused by a virus, have had prolonged contact with a family member who has the disease or is at high risk for getting it, or have received blood from an adult later diagnosed as an AIDS victim.

Children with AIDS were a growing problem for the child welfare system in 1985, particularly children in foster care. Some of the children who developed AIDS or related immune deficiencies were already in foster homes. In other cases, children waiting for foster placement have been at risk for contracting AIDS because a parent has the disease. Foster-care agencies are concerned about the risk to health of the foster parents—and about the possibility of lawsuits if any of those parents catch AIDS from a child in their care.

Childhood Suicide. The suicide rate of children aged 5 to 14 rose from about 4 per 1 million children in 1979 to more than 5 per 1 million in 1982, according to the National Center for Health Statistics in Hyattsville, Md. But many authorities think

Photos of missing children appear on cartons of milk sold in Chicago, one of several U.S. cities that started such programs in 1985.

the actual figure is much higher. Officials who investigate the deaths of young children are faced with confusing evidence that often causes them to reach a verdict of accident rather than suicide. The fact that children usually do not write suicide notes compounds this difficulty.

Missing Children. After the U.S. Department of Health and Human Services said in 1983 that 1.5 million children are reported missing each year in the United States, that figure became widely accepted. Many law enforcement officials, however, have questioned the government estimate. They say that most "missing" children are located within hours, often found wandering near home or staying with a friend. Also, many children of divorced parents are found to have been taken away by the parent who does not have legal custody of the child. Daniel G. Mascaro, director of the state program for missing children in Illinois, said in 1985 that the number of children in the United States who are abducted each year by strangers probably does not exceed 6,000. The number of children who run away from home is undoubtedly much higher, but the Society for Young Victims in Newport, R.I., said even that figure is probably only in the tens of thousands. Jeanne M. Hunzeker

In WORLD BOOK, see CHILD WELFARE.

CHILDREN'S BOOKS. See LITERATURE FOR CHILDREN.

CHILE. The military government of President Augusto Pinochet Ugarte responded to growing pressures at home and from abroad on June 16, 1985, by announcing an end to the state of siege that he imposed in November 1984. The military authorities, however, retained many of the measures imposed under the state of siege, including the right to impose curfews at night and hold people in jail for five days without filing charges.

The lifting of some repressive measures was due partly to pressure from the United States government. The Administration of President Ronald Reagan had expressed its opposition to further World Bank loans to Chile until Chile demonstrated progress toward ending human rights abuses. On June 18, two days after Pinochet lifted the stage of siege, the United States voted in favor of a $55-million World Bank loan to Chile.

Human Rights Case. On March 30, three leading Communist Party members were found murdered on the outskirts of Santiago. The victims were Manuel Guerrero, president of the Teachers' Association in Santiago; José Manuel Parada, member of a Roman Catholic human rights organization; and Santiago Nattino Allende, an illustrator. Despite laws prohibiting free assembly, some 15,000 Chileans braved arrest to attend funeral ceremonies for the three victims on April 1.

From that moment on, Chileans followed closely the activities of Judge José Cánovas Robles, a special prosecutor charged with conducting an inquiry into the murders. The judge's careful investigation, which he carried as far as the political situation allowed, made him a national hero. Cánovas' handling of the case encouraged Chileans to believe justice could be restored, not only in the matter of the three murders, but conceivably also with respect to thousands of human rights violations during 12 years of military rule.

The judge's investigation revealed deep divisions within the top echelons of Chile's armed forces. Using information supplied by dissident officers, the judge indicted two policemen and forced the resignation on August 2 of General César Mendoza, head of the paramilitary national police force, after 14 policemen under his command were implicated in the murders. The judge also pressured the government into disbanding the national police force's intelligence unit, and he jailed seven policemen in a related kidnapping case.

Protests Continued. From September 1 to 7, 10 people were killed in antigovernment riots that demanded an end to military rule and the restoration of democracy. A protest on September 4 was the largest in a year. Nathan A. Haverstock

See also LATIN AMERICA (Facts in Brief Table). In WORLD BOOK, see CHILE.

CHINA made sweeping leadership changes in 1985. Deng Xiaoping (Teng Hsiao-p'ing in the traditional Wade-Giles spelling), China's dominant political figure, engineered the leadership changes. Deng wanted to replace the aging, poorly educated generation that had established Communist power in 1949 with younger, better-educated officials.

Many revolutionary leaders had assumed they held lifetime jobs. The government charged that numerous older officials had become lazy, arrogant, and corrupt. To weed them out, it prosecuted more than 20,000 members of the Communist Party for corruption and other crimes.

Seeking Better-Trained Leaders. A plan adopted by the Communist Party in 1983 called for the selection of 1,000 people in their 40's and 50's for a "third echelon" of leaders, behind the first echelon of veterans such as Deng, who turned 81 in 1985, and the second echelon of slightly younger men such as Communist Party General Secretary Hu Yaobang, who was 70.

The party sought "well-educated, enterprising, professionally competent [people] who have a strong sense of responsibility." It barred from selection officials who had risen to prominence during the Cultural Revolution, a period from 1966 to 1976 when leftist radicals tried to restore China to a revolutionary path.

A model shows a traditional Chinese gown in January at an exhibition of Chinese goods in Tokyo, part of China's effort to promote foreign trade.

The Standing Committee of the National People's Congress, China's parliament—which is completely controlled by the Communist Party—announced on June 18, 1985, the appointment of nine new cabinet ministers. All were in their 40's or 50's and had some higher education. The Chinese news media emphasized that, in relation to the men they replaced, the new ministers had "comparatively profound professional knowledge."

On the Provincial Level, party and government changes that began in 1982 had by late 1985 retired more than 1 million officials. There was a shortage of trained people to take their place, partly because of school closures during the Cultural Revolution. China's universities were closed from 1966 to 1970, and the entire educational system was disrupted. Officials in 1985 said China had 710,000 trained economists and expert managers but would need 8 million by the year 2000.

Between 1982 and 1985, the average age of provincial party leaders, governors, and mayors dropped from 64 to 53. The proportion with college educations rose from 20 to 60 per cent. In June 1985, Wan Shaofen, an attorney in Jiangxi (Kiangsi) Province, became the first woman to head a provincial party organization.

At the same time that personnel changes were being made, Communist Party and government bureaucracies on the provincial level were also being streamlined. The number of official posts was reduced 34 per cent.

On the National Level, personnel changes peaked on September 16 with the retirement of 10 of the 24 members of the Communist Party's Politburo, the country's top policymaking body, and the appointment of 6 new full members on September 24. The Politburo members submitted their resignations at a meeting of the party's Central Committee, which consists of 340 leading party members—210 full members and 130 alternates. At the same meeting, 64 Central Committee members also resigned. From the party's Central Advisory Commission, a consultant group made up of party elders, 37 stepped down. Another 30 officials resigned from the Central Discipline Inspection Commission, which investigates wrongdoing by party members.

Nine men who left the Politburo had military backgrounds, and some had opposed Deng's efforts to reduce the cost and political influence of the army. The Politburo's only woman, Deng Yingchao, the widow of Premier Zhou Enlai (Chou En-lai), also retired. Defense Minister Zhang Aiping and several other military leaders were among the 64 who stepped down from the Central Committee.

The Central Committee meeting was followed by a national conference of the Communist Party, held from September 18 to 23 by 992 delegates.

Such conferences are unusual—the last one was held in 1955. The 1985 conference elected 91 new full and alternate members to the Central Committee, 56 new Advisory Commission members, and 31 members to the discipline commission.

The Central Committee met again on Sept. 24, 1985, and named six new full Politburo members. The new members included Hu Qili, 56 years old, an English-speaking engineer. Informed Chinese believed he might succeed Hu Yaobang at the party congress scheduled for 1987. Another new Politburo member was Li Peng, 57, a Soviet-trained engineer and foster son of the late Premier Zhou. Rumors had Li in line to succeed Premier Zhao Ziyang in 1987.

Trouble with Economic Reforms. The government admitted in 1985 that economic reforms adopted in 1984 to reduce government control over the economy had caused problems. These included overly rapid growth in industry. Manufacturing output increased 23 per cent in the first half of 1985 instead of a targeted 8 per cent growth for the whole year, thus tying up money in stockpiles of goods that were not immediately needed. Industrial and commercial construction soared 44 per cent instead of the planned 1.1 per cent. Consumer prices rose unevenly as the government freed more goods from price controls.

The party conference in September adopted a new five-year economic development plan, for 1986-1990. The plan called for a 25 per cent increase in the production of consumer goods.

China's longer goal was to quadruple output from 1980 to the year 2000 by an average annual growth rate of 5 per cent. If efforts to control population growth were successful, this would result in an average income of $800 per person in the year 2000. A study by the World Bank, an agency of the United Nations, said China had "a good chance" of achieving this goal.

In July, China revealed a financial scandal on Hainan (Hai-nan) Island. The government had made the island a duty-free port and given it other special privileges to encourage its development. Island officials unlawfully used about $1.5-billion in loans to buy imported cars, trucks, and luxury goods. They then resold the goods on the mainland without paying customs duties, making huge profits.

China's *special economic zones*—coastal areas that offer low taxes and other special advantages to attract foreign investment—failed to develop as hoped. The government left open the 4 original zones established in 1979, but it halted development on 10 others added in 1984.

Military Cutbacks. Party leader Hu Yaobang announced on April 19 that about 1 million troops would be cut from China's armed forces, which numbered about 4 million. Deng had long com-

plained that the armed forces suffered from "bloating, laxity, conceit, extravagance, and inertia." The government also overhauled the military command structure.

Relations with Other Countries. Relations between China and the Soviet Union improved slightly during 1985. On July 10 in Moscow, Vice Premier Yao Yilin signed an agreement to double trade between the two countries from $1.8 billion in 1985 to $3.5 billion by 1990. The two countries later agreed to exchange visits of their foreign ministers, the first since 1960.

Three United States Navy ships were scheduled to dock at Shanghai in May. But in April, General Secretary Hu Yaobang said Washington had promised that the ships would not carry nuclear armaments. United States officials, who had refused to make such promises to New Zealand or other close allies, denied making such a pledge and canceled the visit. This incident chilled slowly developing military ties between the United States and China. In October, however, the U.S. Congress cleared the way for the first governmental military sales to China. It authorized a $98-million deal to modernize Chinese artillery ammunition production.

On July 23, China and the United States signed an agreement on cooperation in peaceful uses of

Shoppers in Beijing (Peking) stock up on canned goods on May 9, a day before prices soar as China relaxes price controls in 23 major cities.

nuclear power, tentatively made when President Ronald Reagan visited China in 1984. Some U.S. senators held up ratification of the agreement while questioning whether China was violating its pledge not to help other countries develop nuclear weapons. But the Senate approved the pact on November 21.

On November 22, Larry Wu-Tai Chin, a former employee of the U.S. Central Intelligence Agency, was arrested on charges of spying for China. Intelligence officials said Chin had given China top-secret information for more than 30 years.

Hostility to Foreigners who had been brought in by China's efforts to attract foreign investment flared up on May 19, 1985. After Hong Kong beat China in a soccer match in Beijing (Peking), Chinese soccer fans attacked foreigners near the stadium. Initially, the police did not interfere, but later they arrested more than 100 people. Five youths who took part in the riot received prison terms ranging from 4 months to 2½ years.

An American businessman, Richard S. Ondrik, was sentenced on August 13 to 18 months' imprisonment and a fine of about $52,000 for negligently starting a fire that killed 10 people in April at a hotel in Harbin. The prosecution charged that the fire was started by a cigarette that Ondrik was smoking when he fell asleep. The stiff sentence, as well as the handling of the trial, caused concern among other foreigners doing business in China. On November 28, Chinese authorities said Ondrik had shown remorse and tried to reform. He was then released from prison.

Signs of Cultural Freedom appeared in 1985. A historical play, *Hai Jui Dismissed from Office,* was revived. An attack on that play had been one of the opening shots of the Cultural Revolution in 1965. Other banned plays also reappeared. Hu Yaobang said in February "there must be complete freedom of creation in literature and art."

Cultural contact with other countries also increased during the year. In April, the British group Wham! became the first major rock group to play in China. In November, the Alvin Ailey American Dance Theater became the first American modern dance company to perform there.

Space Plans. Astronautics Minister Li Xue announced plans to compete with Western countries in commercial satellite launching services. Rockets named Long March 2 and Long March 3 would carry the satellites into orbit.   Henry S. Bradsher

See also ASIA (Facts in Brief Table). In the Special Reports section, see CHINA AFTER MAO: CHARTING A NEW COURSE. In WORLD BOOK, see CHINA.

CHURCHES. See EASTERN ORTHODOX CHURCHES; JEWS AND JUDAISM; PROTESTANTISM; RELIGION; ROMAN CATHOLIC CHURCH.

CISKEI. See AFRICA.

CITY. The cities of the United States continued to suffer the impact of several continuing trends in 1985, including decreasing federal grants; population shifts; increasing poverty, unemployment, homelessness, and hunger; high crime rates; high tax burdens; and a loss of political influence. But urban leaders, determined to show that the United States derives its strength and vitality from its cities, labored to reverse—or at least halt—those discouraging trends.

Federal Support. In its first National Urban Policy Report, drafted in May, the U.S. Conference of Mayors noted, "Grants to state and local governments have declined from an 11.7 per cent share of the federal budget in 1978 to a 1.2 per cent share in 1985. This translates to a 1985 loss of $52.7 billion a year." Meeting in Anchorage, Alaska, from June 15 to 19, the mayors again expressed grave concern about declining federal support for urban programs.

But the mayors were not blind to the U.S. government's serious fiscal problems. In March, the conference acknowledged that the government's enormous budget deficits pose a serious threat to the economic health of the nation. The conference's executive committee adopted a resolution that endorsed a federal spending freeze for at least one year on many welfare programs. The resolution also urged the government to find ways—other than hikes in the personal income tax—to increase revenues.

Poverty. The growing number of children living in poverty became a national concern in 1985. (The poverty level in 1985 was defined as an annual income of $10,650 for a family of four.) According to a report issued in May by the Congressional Research Service and the Congressional Budget Office, children make up about 27 per cent of the U.S. population but about 39 per cent of the poor—with a total of some 13.8 million children existing in poverty. The report said the number of needy children in the United States increased by 3 million from 1968 to 1983, even though the total number of children decreased by 9 million during those same years.

Many of those impoverished children are members of the so-called *underclass*—the urban poor, mostly black and Hispanic, who are trapped in a seemingly unbreakable cycle of poverty. The news media focused special attention on the underclass in 1985. In the fall, the *Chicago Tribune* published a series of articles that identified the underclass as the main cause of urban ills and called for government policies that would bring the urban poor into the mainstream of American life. *The Boston Globe,* the *Los Angeles Times,* *The New York Times,* and the "NBC Nightly News" also devoted considerable attention to the underclass, suggesting an emerging nationwide concern about this problem.

Homelessness. Another group of urban poor—the homeless—have also aroused the nation's sympathy. A number of U.S. cities have made efforts to provide shelter for these street dwellers, and recently the homeless have begun to get their due in court. In May 1985, for instance, a suit filed in the Philadelphia Court of Common Pleas by a group supporting the rights of the homeless resulted in an agreement by the city of Philadelphia to offer shelter and health services to all city residents who have nowhere to live.

Crime Statistics compiled by the Federal Bureau of Investigation showed that although serious crimes in the United States as a whole increased by an average of 3 per cent during the first six months of 1985, crime in major cities continued a four-year decline. In the United States overall, rape and aggravated assault increased by 7 per cent, followed by motor vehicle theft, up 5 per cent; arson, up 3 per cent; and larceny, up 1 per cent. Murder showed a 2 per cent drop, and there was no change in the incidence of robbery. Crime rates for cities with more than 1 million inhabitants declined an average of 2 per cent, but the rates for midsized cities increased by 10 to 13 per cent. Crime was up 6 per cent in the South and West, held steady in the Northeast, and declined 1 per cent in the Midwest.

Mayors Win Big. Despite the increasingly difficult task that urban leaders have in satisfying the many interest groups and racial and ethnic populations they serve, several big-city mayors were reelected by large margins in 1985. Mayor Edward I. Koch of New York City was reelected to a third term in November, and in April Los Angeles Mayor Thomas Bradley breezed to a fourth term. Other mayors reelected included Andrew J. Young, Jr., of Atlanta, Ga.; Kathryn J. Whitmire of Houston; and Coleman A. Young of Detroit.

Meanwhile, San Diego Mayor Roger Hedgecock was found guilty in San Diego County Superior Court on October 9 of illegally funneling more than $360,000 into his 1983 campaign and of lying about it. He had been overwhelmingly reelected 11 months earlier despite being under indictment. Hedgecock resigned on December 10, the day he was sentenced to one year in the custody of the county sheriff and fined $1,000.

Municipal Services have eroded in a number of U.S. cities in recent years as a result of tight budgets. But some cities have begun trying to correct that problem. In New York City, for example, Mayor Koch on May 3 proposed a $20-billion budget for the 1986 fiscal year that increased spending by 10 per cent and added more than 10,000 city workers—mostly police officers, sanitation workers, and teachers—to the city's payroll. The proposed spending plan was the city's sixth consecutive balanced budget.

50 Largest Cities in the World

Rank	City	Population
1.	Shanghai	11,859,748
2.	Mexico City	9,373,353
3.	Beijing (Peking)	9,230,687
4.	Seoul, South Korea	8,364,379
5.	Tokyo	8,349,209
6.	Moscow	8,275,000
7.	Bombay, India	8,227,332
8.	Tianjin (Tientsin), China	7,764,141
9.	New York City	7,164,742
10.	São Paulo, Brazil	7,033,529
11.	London	6,608,598
12.	Jakarta, Indonesia	6,503,449
13.	Cairo, Egypt	6,133,000
14.	Hong Kong	5,664,000
15.	Karachi, Pakistan	5,208,170
16.	Bangkok, Thailand	5,153,902
17.	Rio de Janeiro, Brazil	5,093,232
18.	Delhi, India	4,884,234
19.	Teheran, Iran	4,496,159
20.	Leningrad, Soviet Union	4,295,000
21.	Santiago, Chile	4,225,299
22.	Lima, Peru	4,164,597
23.	Bogotá, Colombia	4,055,909
24.	Shenyang (Shen-yang), China	3,944,240
25.	Ho Chi Minh City, Vietnam	3,419,978
26.	Calcutta, India	3,305,006
27.	Wuhan (Wu-han), China	3,287,720
28.	Madras, India	3,276,622
29.	Madrid, Spain	3,188,297
30.	Guangzhou (Canton), China	3,181,510
31.	Pusan, South Korea	3,159,766
32.	Los Angeles	3,096,721
33.	Berlin (East and West), East and West Germany	3,038,689
34.	Chicago	2,992,472
35.	Baghdad, Iraq	2,969,000
36.	Lahore, Pakistan	2,952,689
37.	Buenos Aires, Argentina	2,908,001
38.	Sydney, Australia	2,874,415
39.	Rome	2,830,569
40.	Yokohama, Japan	2,773,822
41.	Istanbul, Turkey	2,772,708
42.	Chongqing (Ch'ung-ch'ing), China	2,673,170
43.	Osaka, Japan	2,648,158
44.	Pyongyang, North Korea	2,639,448
45.	Melbourne, Australia	2,578,527
46.	Hanoi, Vietnam	2,570,905
47.	Harbin, China	2,519,120
48.	Chengdu (Ch'eng-tu), China	2,499,000
49.	Bangalore, India	2,476,355
50.	Kinshasa, Zaire	2,443,876

Sources: 1984 Bureau of the Census estimates for cities of the United States; censuses and estimates from governments for cities of other countries.

50 Largest Cities in the United States

Rank	City	Population*	Per cent change in population since 1980	Mayor†
1.	New York City	7,164,742	+1.3	Edward I. Koch (D, 1/90)
2.	Los Angeles	3,096,721	+4.3	Thomas Bradley (NP, 6/89)
3.	Chicago	2,992,472	−0.4	Harold Washington (D, 4/87)
4.	Houston	1,705,697	+6.9	Kathryn J. Whitmire (NP, 1/88)
5.	Philadelphia	1,646,713	−2.5	W. Wilson Goode (D, 1/88)
6.	Detroit	1,088,973	−9.5	Coleman A. Young (D, 1/90)
7.	Dallas	974,234	+7.7	A. Starke Taylor (NP, 5/87)
8.	San Diego	960,452	+9.7	Ed Struiksma (R)
9.	Phoenix	853,266	+8.0	Terry Goddard (D, 12/87)
10.	San Antonio	842,779	+7.2	Henry G. Cisneros (D, 4/87)
11.	Baltimore	763,570	−2.9	William Donald Schaefer (D, 12/87)
12.	San Francisco	712,753	+5.0	Dianne Feinstein (NP, 1/88)
13.	Indianapolis	710,280	+1.4	William H. Hudnut III (R, 12/87)
14.	San Jose	686,178	+9.0	Thomas McEnery (D, 12/86)
15.	Memphis	648,399	+0.3	Dick Hackett (I, 12/87)
16.	Washington, D.C.	622,823	−2.4	Marion S. Barry, Jr. (D, 1/87)
17.	Milwaukee	620,811	−2.4	Henry W. Maier (D, 4/88)
18.	Jacksonville	577,971	+6.8	Jake M. Godbold (D, 7/87)
19.	Boston	570,719	+1.4	Raymond L. Flynn (D, 1/88)
20.	Columbus, Ohio	566,114	+0.2	Dana G. Rinehart (R, 1/88)
21.	New Orleans	559,101	+0.2	Ernest N. Dutch Morial (D, 5/86)
22.	Cleveland	546,543	−4.7	George V. Voinovich (R, 11/87)
23.	Denver	504,588	+2.4	Federico Peña (D, 6/87)
24.	Seattle	488,474	−1.1	Charles Royer (NP, 1/90)
25.	El Paso	463,809	+9.1	Jonathan W. Rogers (NP, 4/87)
26.	Nashville	462,450	+1.5	Richard H. Fulton (D, 9/87)
27.	Oklahoma City	443,172	+9.7	Andy Coats (D, 4/87)
28.	Kansas City, Mo.	443,075	−1.0	Richard L. Berkley (NP, 4/87)
29.	St. Louis	429,296	−5.2	Vincent L. Schoemehl, Jr. (D, 4/89)
30.	Atlanta	426,090	+0.3	Andrew J. Young, Jr. (D, 1/90)
31.	Fort Worth	414,562	+7.6	Bob Bolen (NP, 4/87)
32.	Pittsburgh	402,583	−5.0	Richard S. Caliguiri (D, 1/90)
33.	Austin	397,001	+14.8	Frank Cooksey (NP, 5/87)
34.	Honolulu	385,489	+5.6	Frank Fasi (R, 1/89)
35.	Long Beach	378,752	+4.8	Ernie Kell (D, 7/86)
36.	Tulsa	374,535	+3.8	Terry Young (D, 5/86)
37.	Miami	372,634	+7.4	Xavier L. Suarez (NP, 11/87)
38.	Cincinnati	370,481	−3.9	Charles J. Luken (D, 12/87)
39.	Portland, Ore.	365,861	−0.6	J. E. Clark (NP, 11/88)
40.	Tucson	365,422	+8.4	Lewis C. Murphy (R, 12/87)
41.	Minneapolis	358,335	−3.4	Donald M. Fraser (D, 1/90)
42.	Oakland	351,898	+3.7	Lionel J. Wilson (D, 7/89)
43.	Albuquerque	350,575	+5.5	Ken Schultz (NP, 12/87)
44.	Toledo	343,939	−3.0	Donna Owens (R, 12/87)
45.	Buffalo	338,982	−5.3	James D. Griffin (D, 12/89)
46.	Omaha	332,237	+1.4	Michael Boyle (NP, 6/89)
47.	Charlotte	330,838	+4.9	Harvey B. Gantt (D, 11/87)
48.	Newark	314,387	−4.5	Kenneth A. Gibson (D, 7/86)
49.	Virginia Beach	308,664	+17.7	Harold Heischober (R, 6/86)
50.	Sacramento	304,131	+10.3	Anne Rudin (NP, 12/87)

*1984 estimates (source: U.S. Bureau of the Census, except for Honolulu, which has a WORLD BOOK estimate).
†The letters in parentheses represent the mayor's party, with *D* meaning Democrat, *R* Republican, *I* Independent, and *NP* nonpartisan. The date is when the mayor's term of office ends (source: National League of Cities).

Cost of living index‡	Unemployment rate§	Revenue#	Gross debt outstanding#	Per capita income**	Sales tax rate††
140.4	6.9%	$22,568,075,000	$11,490,700,000	$13,808	8.25%
113.8	8.2	3,414,569,000	3,117,222,000	13,417	6.5
119.1 est.	8.4	2,496,280,000	1,233,316,000	13,456	8
109.2	8.4	1,206,068,000	1,821,054,000	13,655	6.125
113.9	6.0	2,527,414,000	2,295,776,000	12,700	6
107.0 est.	10.9	1,642,121,000	923,310,000	12,537	4
108.7 est.	5.2	657,135,000	630,513,000	14,222	6.125
114.7	6.0	512,200,000	167,944,000	12,272	6
104.5	5.2	595,883,000	737,611,000	11,779	6
100.7	6.7	981,602,000	1,544,614,000	10,569	5.625
106.6	5.2	1,530,637,000	1,004,825,000	12,254	5
124.8	5.2	1,832,289,000	1,103,526,000	17,875	6.5
99.8	5.6	488,073,000	404,384,000	11,858	5
113.9	6.1	412,081,000	225,946,000	15,853	6
98.6	6.7	1,340,945,000	601,793,000	10,590	7.75
120.1 est.	4.1	2,633,796,000	1,998,524,000	16,173	6
115.3 est.	6.3	514,776,000	449,815,000	13,001	5
101.5	5.9	818,794,000	770,845,000	11,149	5
122.0 est.	3.7	1,077,999,000	597,028,000	14,297	5
101.8	7.1	346,005,000	696,417,000	11,445	6
98.2	11.7	568,925,000	622,369,000	11,706	9
100.5	9.0	461,614,000	363,715,000	13,103	6.5
109.4	4.7	727,735,000	667,725,000	14,504	6.6
112.9 est.	6.5	625,621,000	692,215,000	13,955	7.9
102.2	11.9	223,792,000	193,822,000	8,290	5.125
99.7	5.1	860,311,000	817,335,000	11,058	7.75
99.5	5.8	256,061,000	343,448,000	12,427	5.25
104.6	4.5	417,490,000	295,115,000	12,654	5.225
98.1	7.4	471,002,000	247,213,000	12,710	6
104.2	5.6	534,611,000	982,431,000	12,492	4
103.3	5.6	246,748,000	280,650,000	13,103	5.375
105.5 est.	9.0	304,740,000	322,483,000	11,920	6
110.5	5.1	638,180,000	949,723,000	11,937	6.125
149.7 est.	5.0	478,892,000	242,400,000	12,697	4
113.8	8.2	542,259,000	238,781,000	13,417	6
102.7	6.5	230,231,000	174,916,000	12,381	6.25
108.4 est.	8.1	224,560,000	206,475,000	12,131	5
110.2 est.	7.8	377,262,000	188,685,000	11,777	5.5
107.9	7.8	261,741,000	459,252,000	12,268	0
100.3	5.4	271,655,000	551,167,000	10,694	7
111.6 est.	4.4	461,930,000	1,139,599,000	13,781	6
113.4 est.	7.0	324,133,000	540,775,000	14,653	6.5
103.1	7.2	295,301,000	576,227,000	11,520	4.375
101.2 est.	9.3	176,579,000	182,415,000	11,613	6
99.5	7.3	493,457,000	281,999,000	11,398	7
97.0	5.8	167,898,000	162,082,000	12,105	5
96.1	5.5	209,224,000	238,210,000	11,152	4.5
114.7	6.5	282,844,000	131,109,000	14,847	6
102.8	4.7	289,749,000	268,010,000	11,314	4
101.9	7.2	181,618,000	69,611,000	11,676	6

‡The higher the number, the higher the cost of living. Entries marked *est.* are WORLD BOOK estimates. Based on a survey done in fall 1984 (source: American Chamber of Commerce Researchers Association).
§July 1985 figures for metropolitan areas (source: U.S. Bureau of Labor Statistics).
#Figures are for fiscal year 1982-1983 (source: U.S. Bureau of the Census.)
**1983 figures for metropolitan areas (source: U.S. Bureau of Economic Analysis).
††Total sales tax rate, including state, county, city, school district, and special district taxes (source: Tax Foundation, Inc.).

New Orleans Mayor Ernest Morial, left, head of the U.S. Conference of Mayors, talks with Chicago's Harold Washington at a January meeting in Washington, D.C.

A growing number of cities, however, prodded by cuts in federal aid, have turned the operation of their jails, hospitals, mass transit systems, and other services over to private industry. "Local governments are redefining their role," Lydia D. Manchester, associate director of the Office of Information Services of the International City Management Association in Washington, D.C., said in May. "They're making a distinction between making policy and actually delivering the services."

Urban Schools have been feeling the impact of the massive influx of immigrants from Mexico and Central America. Los Angeles schools have been particularly hard-hit. After years of declining enrollment, the Los Angeles Unified School District, the second largest in the United States after New York City's, reported in October that within five years all of the district's schools may have to operate throughout the year. Hispanic children now make up 52.2 per cent of the district's enrollment.

Acquired immune deficiency syndrome (AIDS), a deadly disease that severely weakens the immune system, became an issue for several big-city school districts in 1985. In September, two community school boards in New York City's borough of Queens went to court to prevent the central board of education from permitting a 7-year-old girl with AIDS to attend regular classes. Thousands of New Yorkers kept their children home from school out of fear that the children would contract the disease. In Chicago, the city health department ruled in September that children who develop AIDS would be allowed to attend school classes. No Chicago children were then known to have AIDS.

If anyone doubted that students are better off at suburban, predominantly white schools than at black inner-city schools, a study reported in September by Johns Hopkins University in Baltimore laid those doubts to rest. The 15-year study found that poor black youths who were educated at suburban schools were more likely to attend good colleges, enter skilled occupations, and live in integrated neighborhoods than students who attended inner-city schools.

A study released in December by the Center for Urban Affairs and Policy Research at Northwestern University in Evanston, Ill., had similar findings. The study found that low-income black children who moved from Chicago to white suburbs were getting better grades and taking part in more extracurricular activities than they were in Chicago.

Revitalizing the Cities. In an effort to revive the vitality of American cities, many civic and political leaders in recent years have proposed multimillion-dollar urban projects. Two such projects died in 1985—Chicago's proposed 1992 World's Fair, and New York City's Westway, a new highway planned for the West Side of Manhattan. Both the fair and Westway were enormously expensive projects that many city leaders feared would cost even more by the time they were finally completed. Moreover, environmental impact studies indicated that the projects would be harmful to the environment.

In many cases, smaller-scale projects, seeming more suited to the spirit of the times, proved to be models for urban redevelopment. For example, in Brownsville, a section of the New York City borough of Brooklyn, a neighborhood group decided to "redo" a slum and built 900 brick town houses. Encouraged by their success and by the satisfied reactions of the tenants, the group announced on May 20 that they would next try to close local "smoke shops," stores that sell drugs to teen-agers.

Better, Not Bigger. In July, the city of San Francisco enacted a plan for controlling future construction in the downtown area. The plan, the first of its kind passed by a major U.S. city, places size and design restrictions on new buildings. Construction will be limited each year to a total of 950,000 square feet (88,300 square meters), about the size of a large office building. The plan also requires new buildings to be light in color, to have a tapering top, and to be constructed of solid materials, such as stone.   Margaret T. Gordon

See also ELECTIONS and articles on individual cities. In WORLD BOOK, see CITY.

CIVIL RIGHTS. In its annual review of human rights around the world, the United States Department of State reported on Feb. 13, 1985, that human rights abuses continued in most of the 164 countries surveyed but that there were significant improvements in Latin America. Human rights groups attacked the report for presenting a "rosy portrait" of human rights in countries friendly to the United States, such as El Salvador, Guatemala, and Honduras, and an "unrealistically grim portrait" of unfriendly countries, such as Nicaragua. In his "State of the World" message on January 12, Pope John Paul II criticized countries that defend human rights abroad but violate such rights at home and interfere in the internal affairs of other nations.

Reports on Rights. An international conference on human rights in Ottawa, Canada, ended in June with the attending countries unable to agree on a final report. The purpose of the meeting was to review how well the 35 participating nations were putting into effect the human rights provisions of the 1975 Helsinki Agreement. Western countries expressed concern over "serious violations of human rights" by the Soviet Union and its Eastern European allies. The Soviet bloc, for its part, deplored unemployment, homelessness, racism, and malnutrition in the West.

Almost half the governments of the world held political prisoners in 1984, and many tortured prisoners as part of state policy, according to a report issued in October 1985 by Amnesty International, an independent worldwide human rights organization based in London. The report, which surveyed 123 countries, also criticized Afghanistan, Iran, and Libya for condemning people in courts that the organization said did not meet international standards of fairness.

In February, 20 countries signed a United Nations (UN) treaty outlawing torture. The United States supported the agreement, but at year-end it had not been ratified by the U.S. Senate.

Europe and Asia. In Great Britain, attacks by whites on Asians and other minorities increased during 1985. In August, September, and October, a number of riots, due partly to racial tensions, broke out in areas of London, Birmingham, and Liverpool.

In July, Amnesty International reported that nearly 180,000 political prisoners had been held in Turkey since 1980. The report also charged that the torture of such prisoners continues to be "widespread and systematic." A report by the UN Commission on Human Rights, released in March, accused the Soviet Union and the Soviet-backed government of Afghanistan of "gross violations"

Coretta Scott King and two of her children are arrested in Washington, D.C., in June at a demonstration against apartheid at the South African Embassy.

of human rights in that country both before and since the Soviet invasion in 1979.

In South Korea, Kim Dae Jung, that country's leading opposition politician, was placed under house arrest at least four times in 1985. He and his supporters were roughed up at the Seoul airport when he returned from exile in the United States in February. Fearful of annoying the government, Kim refrained from public speeches.

African Problems. As struggle flamed in South Africa over apartheid, repression surfaced elsewhere on that continent. Amnesty International charged on June 11 that civilians in Uganda were unlawfully confined and systematically tortured by the army and security forces of President Milton Obote. In July, military officers seized power and overthrew Obote. On July 28, the new rulers suspended Uganda's Constitution.

On May 19, an Egyptian judge approved the government's confiscation of copies of an uncensored edition of *The Arabian Nights,* a classic collection of folk tales, because it contained what the government said were obscene passages.

Latin America. In El Salvador, President José Napoleón Duarte's Christian Democratic Party won a majority of votes in elections on March 31 for the National Assembly and municipal offices. Although Duarte's government claimed improvements in human rights, critics continued to attack that country's slow progress in that area.

In September, Americas Watch, a private human rights group, issued a report accusing the Duarte government of "gross violations" of human rights, including attacks by the armed forces on civilians, increased death-squad activity, and torture. The group also condemned the rebels fighting the Duarte government for "mounting abuses," including assassinations and kidnappings.

On March 1, Julio María Sanguinetti took office as the first civilian president of Uruguay since the 1970's. Also in March, Brazil returned to civilian rule, suspended since 1964. In November, Guatemala held elections for its first civilian government since 1966.

Bonner's Trip West. Yelena G. Bonner, wife of human rights advocate Andrei D. Sakharov of the Soviet Union, arrived in the United States on December 7 for a three-month stay for medical treatment. In 1984 and 1985, Sakharov, who won the 1975 Nobel Peace Prize, staged hunger strikes to pressure Soviet authorities to allow his wife to seek medical help abroad.

Eliminating Quotas. In the United States, the Administration of President Ronald Reagan pressed its attack on the use of quotas and timetables to increase the hiring of blacks, Hispanic Americans, and women. The Administration based its efforts on a 1984 ruling by the Supreme Court of the United States. The court ruled that judges could not interfere with a legitimate seniority system in order to protect blacks from being laid off by the Memphis Fire Department, even if the seniority system favored whites.

In April, the U.S. Department of Justice urged 56 cities, states, and counties to change their affirmative action plans to eliminate preferential racial or sexual hiring quotas. In May, San Diego agreed to do so, but a number of other cities refused. Judges generally continued to uphold affirmative action plans with quotas.

On April 29, the Justice Department filed suit in a federal court against Indianapolis, asking the court to overturn that city's quota system. On May 1, the National Association for the Advancement of Colored People (NAACP) filed suit against the Justice Department to block its efforts to eliminate hiring quotas.

Reynolds Rejected. In a move applauded by civil rights groups, the Judiciary Committee of the U.S. Senate on June 27 voted against recommending William Bradford Reynolds for the job of associate attorney general. Civil rights groups had attacked Reynolds, the assistant attorney general for civil rights, for what they said was his lax enforcement of civil rights laws.

Comparable Worth. On April 11, the U.S. Commission on Civil Rights rejected the idea of comparable worth as "profoundly flawed" and said it was not a remedy for sex discrimination in the workplace. *Comparable worth* is the idea that men and women holding jobs requiring comparable skill, effort, and knowledge should be paid the same. Women's rights groups denounced the decision. On June 18, the General Accounting Office, the investigative arm of Congress, criticized the commission's ruling, saying that it had defined comparable worth differently than did the concept's supporters.

In June, the Equal Employment Opportunity Commission ruled that unequal pay for comparable jobs was not in itself proof of sex discrimination. Supporters of comparable pay got another jolt on September 4 when the U.S. Court of Appeals in San Francisco overturned a district judge's 1983 order that the state of Washington give comparable pay for jobs of comparable worth. But on Dec. 31, 1985, Washington and the state's largest employee union agreed on a settlement that would give 35,000 state workers, most of them women, salary increases of at least 2.5 per cent.

Decade for Women. Women from at least 150 countries met in Nairobi, Kenya, in July in observance of the last year of the UN Decade for Women. The conference, which assessed the achievements and failures of the past 10 years, unanimously approved a resolution on women's goals for the next 25 years.   Louis W. Koenig

In WORLD BOOK, see CIVIL RIGHTS.

CLASSICAL MUSIC. Musical anniversaries abounded in 1985. The Baltimore Opera Company and the Canadian Opera Company celebrated their 35th year, and the Boston Pops Orchestra marked its 100th. Composer William Schuman celebrated his 75th birthday, and fellow composers Aaron Copland and Otto Luening were cheered on their 85th. Music lovers also remembered composers Jerome Kern and Alban Berg 100 years after their birth, Heinrich Schütz at 400, and Domenico Scarlatti at 300.

But it was two of Scarlatti's contemporaries—Johann Sebastian Bach and George Frideric Handel—who received most of the attention. The musical world seemed to go Bach and Handel crazy honoring the 300th anniversary of their birth.

Political boundaries fell on March 21, Bach's birthday, as his *The Passion According to St. Matthew* was broadcast by radio from Leipzig, East Germany, to West Germany and the United States. The *St. Matthew Passion* was staged, rather than just performed, in Venice and Milan, Italy, and by the Boston Symphony Orchestra at Tanglewood, Mass. Bach's passion music was done more traditionally by the Philadelphia Orchestra and the Indianapolis Symphony Orchestra. His *Mass in B minor* was performed in Boston; Cincinnati, Ohio; Milwaukee; Montreal, Canada; and Philadelphia.

The Toronto Symphony Orchestra offered a "Bachamania" concert. In June, on Portugal's Madeira Islands, 25 concerts were devoted to Bach. But Flint, Mich., outdid the Portuguese, with 40 concerts featuring Bach over four months.

Performances of Handel's *Messiah* were numerous, as usual, but Handel's operas, so long ignored and even forgotten, gained prominence during 1985. The Spoleto U.S.A. Festival in Charleston, S.C., offered *Ariodante* and *Teseo*. The Boston Symphony contributed *Acis and Galatea* and the San Francisco Opera Company did *Orlando*. Chicago's Lyric Opera Company staged *Samson*, the John F. Kennedy Center for the Performing Arts in Washington, D.C., presented *Julius Caesar*, and Milwaukee's Skylight Theater revived *Xerxes*. In New York City, the Clarion Concerts Orchestra turned to *Agrippina*, and Carnegie Hall completed its season-long tribute to Handel with *Ariodante* and *Semele*. The PepsiCo Summerfare festival in Purchase, N.Y., revived three Handel operas—*Julius Caesar*, *Teseo*, and *Tamerlane*. Even the Carmel, Calif., Bach Festival joined in—with Handel's *Imeneo*.

Dresden Opera Rebuilt. In Dresden, East Germany, not far from where both Bach and Handel grew up, there was another cause for celebration—the February reopening of the historic Sem-

George Gershwin's *Porgy and Bess* makes its debut in New York City's Metropolitan Opera House in February, 50 years after its Broadway premiere.

per Opera House. It was destroyed by Allied bombers during World War II.

In April 1985, Brisbane, Australia, celebrated the opening of a Performing Arts Complex housing a lyric theater and a concert hall. The new Ordway Music Theatre opened in St. Paul, Minn., in January, providing a new home for that city's Chamber Orchestra and the Minnesota Opera.

New Directors. Three U.S. orchestras welcomed new music directors in 1985. André Previn took over in Los Angeles, Herbert Blomstedt in San Francisco, and Semyon Bychkov in Buffalo, N.Y.

Opera Premieres. The year was rich in new operas. In March, the Virginia Opera Association in Norfolk introduced Thea Musgrave's *Harriet, The Woman Called Moses*, based on the life of Harriet Tubman, a runaway black slave who helped hundreds of her people escape to freedom in the years before the Civil War. John Eaton's *The Tempest*, based on the play by William Shakespeare, featured orchestration involving a mix of instruments from harpsichords to synthesizers.

Other opera premieres in 1985 included: *Dreyfus* by Morris Moshe Cotel (New York City) in January; *Montségur* by Marcel Landowski (Toulouse, France), *Atem* by Franco Donatoni (Milan), and *Clair de Lune* by Libby Larsen (Little Rock, Ark.) in February; and *Casanova's Homecoming* by Dominick Argento (Minneapolis, Minn.), *The Sibyl* by Vincent Persichetti (Philadelphia), and *Behold the Sun* by Alexander Goehr (Duisburg, West Germany) in April. The St. Louis (Mo.) Opera Theatre staged two new works in May and June—Minoru Miki's *Jōruri* and Stephen Paulus' *The Woodlanders*. Premiering in June were *Hedda Gabler* by Edward Harper (Glasgow, Scotland), *Thomas* by Einojuhani Rautavaara (Joensuu, Finland), and *Frederick Douglass* by Dorothy Rudd Moore (New York City). Richard Wargo's *The Seduction of a Lady* premiered in August at the Lake George Opera Festival in New York, and Elie Siegmeister's *Lady of the Lake* had its debut in New York City in October. Also in October, the Minnesota Opera premiered *Where the Wild Things Are*, a delightful operatic retelling by Oliver Knussen of Maurice Sendak's dark fantasy about a naughty boy who becomes the king of the monsters.

Symphony Premieres. Orchestras were busy with their introductions: Henry Brant's *Desert Forest* (Atlanta, Ga.); Charles Wuorinen's *Crossfire* (Baltimore); Morton Gould's Flute Concerto and David Del Tredici's *March to Tonality* (Chicago); Ira Taxin's Concerto for Brass Quintet and Orchestra and Jonathan Kramer's *Moments In and Out of Time* (Cincinnati); *Movers and Shakers* by Wuorinen (Cleveland); Contrabassoon Concerto by Donald Erb and Symphony Number 6 by Ezra Laderman (Houston); Toru Takemitsu's Piano Concerto and *Riverrun* (Los Angeles); Paulus' *Overture* and

Larsen's Symphony Number 1 (Minnesota); Gunther Schuller's Bassoon Concerto and the Pulitzer Prize-winning *Symphony, RiverRun* by Stephen Albert (Washington, D.C.); Karel Husa's Concerto for Orchestra (New York City); Siegmeister's Violin Concerto (Oakland, Calif.); Raymond Premru's *Music for Three Trombones, Tuba, and Orchestra* (Philadelphia); *An American Oratorio* by Ned Rorem and *A Joyful Noise* by David Stock (Pittsburgh, Pa.); Rorem's Organ Concerto (Portland, Me.); and Andrew Imbrie's *Elegy*, John Adams' *Harmonielehre*, Wuorinen's *Rhapsody for Orchestra*, Gordon Getty's *Plump Jack*, and Ellen Taafe Zwilich's Symphony Number 2 (San Francisco).

Special Events. In February, George Gershwin finally made it to the Met when his folk opera *Porgy and Bess*, which premiered in 1935, was presented there for the first time. Other musical events in 1985 included the India Festival of Music and Dance in New York City in September, and the New Music America 1985 celebration in Los Angeles in late October and early November. The Los Angeles presentations featured the world premiere of Bonnie Barnett's *Auto Humn*, in which the performers portray drivers who are encouraged to hum a note offered them by their car radio.   Peter P. Jacobi

In WORLD BOOK, see CLASSICAL MUSIC; OPERA.

CLOTHING. See FASHION.

COAL. The National Coal Association (NCA), the major association of coal producers, said on Sept. 16, 1985, that widespread public fear about the environmental effects of burning coal represents the single greatest threat to the future of both the United States and Canadian coal industries. Carl E. Bagge, president of the NCA, said that such fears were hindering increased use of coal, the world's most plentiful fossil fuel. Much of the concern has centered on the problem of *acid rain*, which is believed to result chiefly from sulfur dioxide and other pollutants emitted by coal-burning power plants. Bagge contended that concerns about coal burning are "misplaced" because acid rain can be controlled.

Coal Consumption. Despite such concerns, the increased use of coal to generate electricity was expected to result in record consumption of coal during 1985. The NCA forecast on June 20 that coal consumption in 1985 would reach a record 891 million short tons (808 million metric tons), an increase of 2.6 per cent from the 1984 level of 868 million short tons (787 million metric tons). Production, however, was expected to decline by about 1 per cent, to 877 million short tons (796 million metric tons), from the record 886 million short tons (804 million metric tons) mined in 1984.

The drop in production was expected because

A steam engine hauls coal cars through the mountains of West Virginia in January in an experiment to see if a cleaner coal-burning engine can be built.

electric utilities had stockpiled large quantities of coal in 1984 in anticipation of a miners' strike that never occurred. Electric utilities in 1985 were expected to consume 686 million short tons (622 million metric tons), an increase of 23 million short tons (21 million metric tons) over 1984 levels. The NCA said that exports would remain essentially unchanged during 1985, at about 80 million short tons (73 million metric tons).

Pollution Rules. Regulations issued by the U.S. Environmental Protection Agency on June 27 reducing the amount of sulfur dioxide that could be emitted by certain coal-burning electric power plants drew fire from the coal industry and environmentalists. The new rules affected power plants that use tall smokestacks—some up to 1,200 feet (370 meters) high—to disperse pollutants over a wider area and so reduce the amount of pollution deposited nearby. The regulations cut allowable emissions of sulfur dioxide by 1.7 million short tons (1.5 million metric tons) per year. The NCA criticized the regulations as unnecessary, predicting that they would cost consumers $750-million in increased electricity costs per year. Environmental groups also denounced the Environmental Protection Agency rules, claiming they would not reduce pollution.

Coal Leasing. The U.S. Department of the Interior in February proposed resuming leasing federal land in Western states to private companies for coal mining. The program was suspended in 1984 after charges that it was mismanaged by Secretary of the Interior James G. Watt, who resigned in 1983. A final decision had not been made by year-end.

British Coal Strike. A long coal strike in Great Britain ended on March 5 when miners returned to work, despite their failure to obtain key concessions from the British government, which owns the mining industry. The strike began on March 12, 1984, after the government announced plans to close 20 mines and lay off about 20,000 miners as part of a program to make the mining industry profitable. In its annual report released on July 29, the National Coal Board, which operates British mines, said it had lost a record $3.1 billion in the year ending in March 1985. The board attributed most of the loss to the strike.

Chinese Mine. China and the Occidental Petroleum Corporation on June 29 signed an agreement for the joint development of the Antaibao mine, one of the world's largest open-pit coal mines. The $650-million project, located in Shanxi (Shansi) province, is expected to produce about 41 million short tons (37 million metric tons) of coal per year. Michael Woods

See also ENERGY SUPPLY; ENVIRONMENTAL POLLUTION; MINING. In WORLD BOOK, see COAL.

COIN COLLECTING

COIN COLLECTING. On July 9, 1985, United States President Ronald Reagan signed into law the Statue of Liberty-Ellis Island Commemorative Coin Act. The act provided for the minting of a $5 gold piece, a silver dollar, and a copper-nickel half dollar commemorating the restoration of the statue and the long-unused immigration facilities on the island, both located in New York Harbor. The coins, dated 1986, were priced at $165, $22.50, and $6, respectively, as of Dec. 31, 1985. Twelve different presentation sets were available. Prices ranged from $6 for the half dollar to $439.50 for a six-coin presentation set.

United States Olympic commemorative coin sales as of March 1985 totaled $308.7 million. In the fall, the U.S. Department of the Treasury was still filling orders for the coins. The Treasury said that after all orders had been satisfied, remaining stocks of Olympic coins would be melted down.

The unpopular Susan B. Anthony dollar was selling again because of a Bureau of the Mint policy of offering the coins to investors and collectors. One 1979 coin and one 1980 coin from each of the three mints—Denver, Philadelphia, and San Francisco—formed a six-coin set priced at $10. The mint also sold the coins in large lots.

Auction Prices in 1985 made headlines with the sale of two major rarities. At a January auction in Beverly Hills, Calif., a 1913 Liberty Head nickel brought a winning bid of $385,000, and an 1804 silver dollar sold for $308,000, both record prices for those coins. In the late 1970's, a 1913 Liberty Head nickel was sold at auction for $200,000. In 1984, an 1804 silver dollar fetched $180,000. The coins at the 1985 auction were from the collection of Jerry Buss, owner of the Los Angeles Lakers basketball team. In another noteworthy sale, at a July auction in Chicago, a bidder paid $286,000 for a 1907 $20 gold proof coin. The coin was a rare type of gold piece on which the year was stamped in high-relief Roman numerals.

Gold and Silver Prices remained fairly steady in 1985. The price of silver varied from slightly more than $5 per troy ounce (31.1 grams) to about $7.50 per troy ounce. Gold prices ranged from $300 to about $360 per troy ounce.

Buyers Dump Krugerrand. South Africa's gold Krugerrand lost much of its popularity in 1985 as racial strife rocked the African nation. Sales of Krugerrands in the United States totaled just $87.5 million in the first six months of 1985, compared with $480 million in the first half of 1984. On the orders of President Reagan, the importation of Krugerrands into the United States was banned as of Oct. 11, 1985, as an economic measure directed against South Africa's discriminatory racial policies. Krugerrands already in the United States could still be bought and sold.　　Lee Martin

In WORLD BOOK, see COIN COLLECTING.

COLOMBIA. "The ash rain increased and the whole world began to scream," said a resident of Armero, describing the eruption of the Colombian volcano Nevado del Ruiz on Nov. 13, 1985. The eruption of hot ash and gases melted the snowcap atop the volcano, causing a massive mud slide that buried the town of Armero 30 miles (48 kilometers) away. Most of the 25,000 deaths from the mud slide occurred in Armero, a thriving agricultural center. It was one of the deadliest volcanic eruptions in history, comparable to the eruption of Vesuvius in Italy in A.D. 79 that buried the towns of Pompeii and Herculaneum.

The government of President Belisario Betancur came under criticism for its handling of rescue efforts following the eruption. There were conflicting reports of rescue efforts being suspended while survivors remained trapped in the mud, and rescue workers complained bitterly of inadequate assistance from the army.

Hostage Crisis. The criticisms could not have come at a worse time for Betancur, who was already under fire for his handling of a hostage crisis. On Nov. 6, 1985, members of a left wing guerrilla group known as the Movement of April 19 (M-19) took over the Palace of Justice in Bogotá, the capital, to call attention to charges that the army was violating terms of a truce with the guerrillas. Betancur refused to negotiate with M-19. On November 7, he ordered an assault on the palace that left about 100 people dead, including 11 Supreme Court justices and 35 guerrillas.

Peace Efforts. Frustrated in his efforts to achieve peace at home, Betancur also suffered setbacks in his efforts to achieve peace in Central America. As a leader of the Contadora Group, a coalition of four Latin-American nations, Betancur has sought a negotiated settlement to conflicts in that region. But during a trip to the United States in April, those efforts were undermined by Washington politics. After meeting with Betancur, U.S. President Reagan announced a "proposal for peace" that called for a cease-fire in Nicaragua and talks between the Sandinista government and the U.S.-backed *contra* rebels.

Asked for his reaction to Reagan's proposal, Betancur called it "positive," but he later charged that his words were misrepresented as all-out support for the President's position by White House aides seeking renewed assistance for the contras from the U.S. Congress. In Colombia on April 15, Betancur denied he had supported Reagan's proposal and added he had not been told the proposal included the possible resumption of military aid for the contras.　　Nathan A. Haverstock

See also LATIN AMERICA (Facts in Brief Table). In WORLD BOOK, see COLOMBIA.

COLORADO. See STATE GOVERNMENT.

COMMON MARKET. See EUROPE.

COMMUNICATIONS. In 1985, the second year after the breakup of the American Telephone and Telegraph Company (AT&T), forecasters who had predicted turmoil in the United States market place were proved to be correct. Major regulatory changes throughout 1985 continued to alter the structure of U.S. telecommunications. Japan and Great Britain followed the United States into the age of competitive telecommunications by converting their government-owned communications monopolies into private firms and opening their markets for hardware and services.

IBM vs. AT&T. International Business Machines Corporation (IBM) increased its investment in telecommunications by buying 16 per cent of MCI Communications Corporation, AT&T's main competitor in the intercity long-distance telephone business. IBM merged its Satellite Business Systems subsidiary with MCI and promised to invest $400 million more in MCI. AT&T increased its stake in the computer business, introducing powerful new machines to compete with IBM's dominant products.

The Federal Communications Commission (FCC) continued to scrap and modify regulations no longer considered to be in the public interest. During the summer, the FCC voted to begin a wide-ranging inquiry into the regulation of communications between computers. Industry observers expected the inquiry to lead to an additional relaxation of rules controlling competition between AT&T and its rivals.

The FCC remained receptive to new communications techniques, authorizing the construction of a high-capacity submarine cable between the United States and Great Britain. On July 25, the FCC approved the construction and launching of 24 communications satellites.

International Disagreements on communications satellites came to a head at a meeting held in August and September in Geneva, Switzerland. The International Telecommunication Union (ITU), a specialized agency of the United Nations, called the meeting to discuss proposals for changing the rules that determine various nations' rights to launch satellites. The conference ended inconclusively.

In July, the FCC granted three U.S. companies permission to launch satellites to compete with the International Telecommunications Satellite Organization (INTELSAT), a 109-nation consortium. INTELSAT had held a monopoly on transoceanic satellite communications since 1964. Competition for INTELSAT may not come quickly, however. The companies must prove in 1986 whether they can raise enough money to compete with INTELSAT.

Jerry Barnett, *The Indianapolis News*

Long-Distance Service. Local telephone companies were required in 1985 to begin to offer their customers equal access to the competing companies offering long-distance service. The customers choose a service that then handles their long-distance calls automatically. Almost all U.S. customers will be converted to equal access by 1987. As customers began to make their choices, the rosy economic forecasts for the long-distance business began to look too optimistic. The third largest firm in the business, GTE Corporation, was among many long-distance companies reporting layoffs and heavy losses related to the high costs of participation in the industry and a lower-than-expected share of the market.

Firms Go Private. In December 1984, the government of Great Britain sold 51 per cent of the shares of British Telecommunications PLC—the state-owned communications monopoly—to the public for $5 billion. At the same time, Mercury Communications received a license to compete with British Telecommunications.

In April 1985, Japan converted Nippon Telegraph and Telephone Public Corporation from a state-owned firm to a private business. The Ministry of Posts and Telecommunications then began to license competitors.   Jonathan Miller

In WORLD BOOK, see COMMUNICATIONS.

COMOROS. See AFRICA.

COMPUTER. The pace of technological advancement in the United States computer industry accelerated in 1985 as competition took on a more international look. The United States maintained its technological lead, but France, Great Britain, Japan, and West Germany moved closer. Japan, in turn, began to look over its shoulder as several South Korean companies, announcing their intention to join the top of the list, made impressive debuts. Three major areas of development occupied those nations' computer manufacturers—scalable computer systems supported by parallel processing, reduced-instruction-set computers, and artificial intelligence.

Scalable Computer Systems can be expanded in stages from small systems to extremely large ones without requiring changes in memory subsystems, *software* (programs), or *peripheral devices* such as printers or displays. Scalability has become possible because of the development of *microprocessors* (computers on a chip) with the computing power once available from only big mainframe computers, and of individual memory chips with the capacity of entire *memory systems*—many smaller memory chips linked together. Industry experts agree that most computer systems introduced in the next two to five years will be scalable because such systems can be expanded quickly and relatively inexpensively.

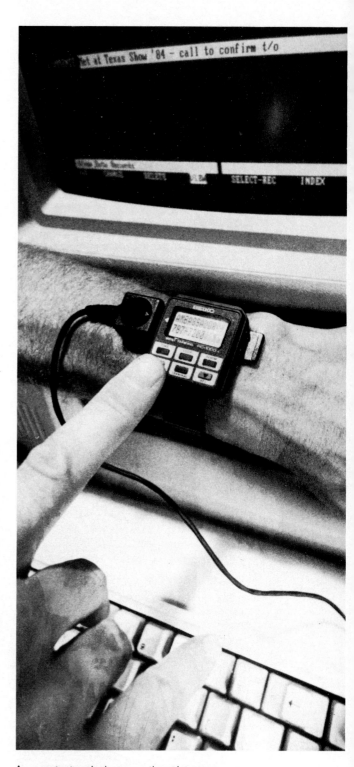

A computer terminal worn on the wrist stores about 2,000 numerals or letters in its memory for immediate recall on a two-line display.

Parallel processing—the performing of many operations simultaneously, or *in parallel*, by one computer—became more popular in 1985. A conventional computer processes data one operation at a time, or *in series*. Parallel processing—performed by many microprocessors linked together—is much faster than serial processing. The main challenge for manufacturers of computers that use parallel processing is to develop more efficient techniques for dividing up the overall task to be performed and assigning the individual parts of the task to the various microprocessors.

The Reduced-Instruction-Set Computer (RISC) needs fewer instructions from its memory than does a conventional computer, so the RISC executes a command more rapidly. A RISC needs fewer instructions from its memory because more instructions are built into its *arithmetic/logic unit* (*ALU*), which carries out all the arithmetic functions and logic processes required to solve a problem. Many manufacturers are teaming up RISC computers with parallel processors.

Artificial Intelligence activity expanded tremendously in 1985, but with few commercial results. Artificial intelligence is the ability of a computer to combine and manipulate symbols representing facts and objects in ways that imitate human thought. The field of artificial intelligence began to take on the look of a gold rush, with companies throughout the world trying for a share of the lode. With such concentration of research and development, much of it backed by government funding, the goal of "teaching" a computer to "reason" may soon be in sight.

A major trend in the area of computer memory is the increasing use of *optical storage disks*. These devices resemble phonograph records, but information is "written" on them, and played back, with a laser. The advantage of optical storage over *magnetic storage*—the technique used in conventional disks for computers—is that an optical disk holds much more information in a given area than does a magnetic disk.

IBM Earnings Decline. In spite of the encouraging advancement of computer technology, the computer industry was gloomy because of sagging profits. Even International Business Machines Corporation (IBM)—one of the most successful companies in history—reported discouraging financial figures. For example, in the nine months ending on Sept. 30, 1985, IBM's earnings were down 12.2 per cent, to $3.87 billion from $4.41-billion for the first nine months of 1984.

Network. IBM made a bid for tremendous profits on Oct. 15, 1985, introducing a *local area network*, a system for linking together up to several hundred small computers via ordinary telephone lines. This development had been the subject of speculation for several years.

The market for such networks is enormous. Companies large and small consider small computers such as IBM's PC and Apple Computer Incorporated's Macintosh to be essential equipment. In some offices, these machines are as numerous as typewriters were in the 1970's. Networks enable small computers—which are already used to process data—to transmit data as well, avoiding paperwork that slows the daily routine of doing business. Networks also eliminate the need to transport disks and other devices containing computer data from one office to another. In addition, networks enable computer users to share files and expensive peripheral equipment.

The IBM network will compete with Ethernet, a system developed by Xerox Corporation, Digital Equipment Corporation, and Intel Corporation; and with MAP (Manufacturing Automation Protocol), developed by General Motors Corporation. MAP is aimed more at product design and manufacturing than are the other two systems.

The IBM network lacked means of connection with IBM's minicomputers and its mainframes. Industry experts expected IBM to provide such means in 1986 or 1987.   Howard Wolff

See also ELECTRONICS. In the WORLD BOOK SUPPLEMENT section, see COMPUTER, PERSONAL. In WORLD BOOK, see COMPUTER.

CONGO. See AFRICA.

CONGRESS OF THE UNITED STATES. Taking the deficit bull firmly by the horns, Congress on Dec. 11, 1985, passed a bill requiring that red ink in the federal budget be reduced in each coming fiscal year and that the budget be balanced by 1991. President Ronald Reagan, who had supported the legislation—while expressing reservations about its constitutionality—signed the bill the next day.

But another fiscal issue close to the President's heart—reforming the United States income tax laws—almost died in Congress. In a move that came as a surprise to the White House, the House of Representatives voted on December 11 not to consider a Reagan-backed tax-revision bill. Nearly all of the House's Republican members voted to block the legislation. But on December 17, the House reversed itself and passed a sweeping revision of the nation's tax laws. The Senate was expected to consider the legislation in early 1986.

That near-upset for the President was typical of the entire 1985 legislative session. When Reagan began his second term in January, after winning a 49-state landslide in the November 1984 election, he had hoped to set the congressional agenda for the year. As it turned out, however, Congress had its own agenda, and time after time it forced the President to retreat on key issues or face defeat.

Dole Leads on Deficit Reduction. Senator Robert J. Dole of Kansas—who in January 1985 suc-

Congressmen Jim Wright and William Gray, at left of table, greet Senators Lawton Chiles and Pete Domenici, at right, during an August budget meeting.

ceeded retiring Senator Howard H. Baker, Jr., of Tennessee as the new Senate majority leader—launched the 99th Congress on Jan. 3, 1985, by resolving to seek more than $250 billion in spending cuts over three years. Guessing correctly that reducing the record federal deficits would emerge as the session's top priority, Dole promised to unveil a Senate Republican leadership budget for the 1986 fiscal year by February 1—three days in advance of the President's budget. Dole missed his self-imposed deadline, however, and through much of the year the senator had a frustrating time trying to reach agreement with Reagan on budgetary measures.

Dole and his Republican colleagues in the Senate thought by early summer that they had fashioned an acceptable deficit-reduction plan. Their proposal called for curbing annual increases in cost-of-living adjustments (COLA's) for social security recipients and imposing a tax of $5 per barrel on imported oil. But Reagan torpedoed the proposal on July 29, rejecting any reduction in social security payments or any kind of tax increase.

Three days of frantic Senate-House negotiations followed, and the two chambers on August 1 adopted a compromise budget resolution calling for $967.6 billion in expenditures for the fiscal year beginning Oct. 1, 1985. Congress claimed its budget blueprint would reduce deficits by $276.2-

billion over a three-year period ending Sept. 30, 1988. About half the savings, $137 billion, would come from putting the brakes on Reagan's massive defense spending. Pentagon outlays would increase no faster than inflation in fiscal 1986 and by 3 per cent after allowing for inflation in each of the two following years. Reagan had wanted an after-inflation increase of 6 per cent in fiscal 1986.

The budget preserved virtually all the programs the President wanted to eliminate, including the Job Corps, subsidies for mass transit and the Amtrak national railway system, the Small Business Administration, and grants for urban development. The budget did, however, call for the elimination of *general revenue sharing* (returning tax money to the states) after 1986, a one-year salary freeze for civil service employees, and major cuts in Medicare and farm programs.

The Biggest Budget Battle came later, after Reagan on September 10 requested that the national debt limit be increased to $2.079 trillion to cover federal spending in the coming year. That amount was more than double the debt when the President first took office in 1981. The mood of Congress was to couple a higher debt limit with action to curb, and even eliminate, future federal deficits. Taking the initiative, the Republican-controlled Senate voted 75 to 24 on October 9 for historic and sweeping budget controls aimed at eliminating the deficit by 1991. The measure was sponsored by Senators Phil Gramm (R., Tex.), Warren Rudman (R., N.H.), and Ernest F. Hollings (D., S.C.) and became known as the Gramm-Rudman bill. The legislation had such powerful bipartisan appeal that Senator Edward M. Kennedy (D., Mass.) and 26 other Democrats ignored Democratic leaders and joined an almost-solid Republican majority in supporting the bill.

The Gramm-Rudman plan required budget deficits to be reduced by $36 billion a year until red-ink spending drops to zero in 1991. If the deficit seemed likely to exceed target levels in any of those fiscal years, the President would be required to make across-the-board spending cuts in defense and domestic programs under guidelines fixed by Congress. The only items exempt from cuts would be social security, interest on the national debt, and existing government contracts, such as those for military weapons.

When the bill came up for a vote on December 11, it passed by margins of 271 to 154 in the House and 61 to 31 in the Senate. But despite its strong backing, the legislation created many doubts, both on Capitol Hill and in the White House. A number of legislators predicted that the measure would give new powers to the President. Reagan, on the other hand, expressed exactly the opposite concern. As he signed the bill into law, the President remarked that the legislation contained "constitutionally suspect provisions" providing for congressional officers to take part in budgetary procedures that he said belonged to the executive branch. Before the ink was dry on the President's signature, Representative Mike Synar (D., Okla.) filed a lawsuit challenging the constitutionality of the new law.

It was clear to most members of Congress and the Administration that the deficit-reduction law would have a tremendous impact on federal spending. As Congress labored in mid-December to pass various appropriations bills for the fiscal 1986 budget, the new law was already making itself felt, requiring $11.7 billion in spending cuts. The lawmakers tried to pass a three-year package of spending reductions but could not reach agreement before their adjournment on December 20.

Income Tax Reform. Reagan's top domestic policy goal in 1985 was enactment of a broad revision of the U.S. income tax code. On May 28, Reagan called for compressing the current 14 tax brackets into 3 and reducing the maximum personal tax rate from 50 per cent to 35 per cent. He also proposed that the maximum corporate rate be reduced from 46 per cent to 33 per cent. Altogether, the President's suggested changes would have cut personal income taxes by 7 per cent while boosting business taxes by 9 per cent.

Although Reagan stumped the country for tax reform, fellow Republicans showed scant enthusiasm for his plan, arguing that it would be harmful to business and to the economy. It therefore fell to the chairman of the House Ways and Means Committee, Representative Dan Rostenkowski (D., Ill.), to champion tax revision. Rostenkowski's committee drew up a sweeping tax-reform bill, which it formally reported out on December 3 and sent to the floor of the House. House leaders expected the bill to pass because Reagan had assured them that at least 40 Republican members of the House would vote for it. But on a December 11 resolution to present the bill for debate, only 14 Republicans—along with 188 Democrats—voted in favor of it, and the resolution was defeated 223 to 202.

In the waning days of December, Reagan rounded up more Republican votes for the tax bill, and on December 17, the House passed the bill and sent it to the Senate.

Farm Bill. Another 11th-hour battle was fought over a bill to revise federal farm policy. Early in the year, on February 22, Secretary of Agriculture John R. Block unveiled the Reagan Administration's proposed "market-oriented" farm bill, designed to drastically reduce the government's participation in agriculture. The bill called for cutting federal farm subsidies in half and encouraging lower prices for agricultural products to boost export sales. With the old farm program expiring,

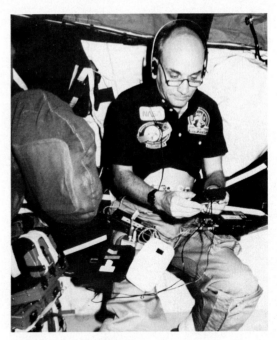

Senator E. Jacob (Jake) Garn (R., Utah), wired for medical tests on spacesickness, flies aboard the space shuttle *Discovery* in April.

both the Senate and House in the fall passed five-year farm bills. The bills cut subsidies for farmers and reduced the price-support levels that keep prices for agricultural products from dropping below a certain minimum. But total federal outlays in the bills were targeted at several billion dollars above the $50 billion sought by the Administration. Senate-House conferees hammered out a revised version of the legislation, which was approved by both houses of Congress on December 18. Reagan signed the bill on December 23.

Foreign Policy, National Security. On August 8, Reagan signed a bill authorizing $12.8 billion in foreign aid for fiscal 1986 and 1987. The measure was the first foreign aid authorization bill in four years. Issues of foreign policy and national security occupied much of Congress's time during the year. The House, for example, took an on-again off-again posture toward the controversial MX intercontinental ballistic missile. By a 217 to 210 vote on March 28, it reversed an earlier vote and released $1.5 billion, tied up since 1984, for the production of 21 MX missiles. The House's mixed feelings about the MX were underscored on October 29. On that day, the lawmakers voted 211 to 207 against appropriating any money for the missile in fiscal 1986, then changed their minds two hours later and approved $1.8 billion to build 12 MX's.

Members of the United States House of Representatives

The House of Representatives of the second session of the 99th Congress consisted of 253 Democrats and 182 Republicans (not including representatives from American Samoa, the District of Columbia, Guam, Puerto Rico, and the Virgin Islands) when it convened in January 1986, compared with 252 Democrats and 182 Republicans, with 1 seat being contested, when the first session convened. This table shows congressional district, legislator, and party affiliation. Asterisk (*) denotes those who served in the 98th Congress; dagger (†) denotes "at large."

Alabama
1. H. L. Callahan, R.
2. William L. Dickinson, R.*
3. Bill Nichols, D.*
4. Tom Bevill, D.*
5. Ronnie G. Flippo, D.*
6. Ben Erdreich, D.*
7. Richard C. Shelby, D.*

Alaska
†Donald E. Young, R.*

Arizona
1. John S. McCain III, R.*
2. Morris K. Udall, D.*
3. Bob Stump, R.*
4. Eldon D. Rudd, R.*
5. Jim Kolbe, R.

Arkansas
1. Bill Alexander, D.*
2. Tommy Robinson, D.
3. John P. Hammerschmidt, R.*
4. Beryl F. Anthony, Jr., D.*

California
1. Douglas H. Bosco, D.*
2. Eugene A. Chappie, R.*
3. Robert T. Matsui, D.*
4. Vic Fazio, D.*
5. Sala Burton, D.*
6. Barbara Boxer, D.*
7. George Miller, D.*
8. Ronald V. Dellums, D.*
9. Fortney H. (Pete) Stark, D.*
10. Don Edwards, D.*
11. Tom Lantos, D.*
12. Edwin V. W. Zschau, R.*
13. Norman Y. Mineta, D.*
14. Norman D. Shumway, R.*
15. Tony Coelho, D.*
16. Leon E. Panetta, D.*
17. Charles Pashayan, Jr., R.*
18. Richard H. Lehman, D.*
19. Robert J. Lagomarsino, R.*
20. William M. Thomas, R.*
21. Bobbi Fiedler, R.*
22. Carlos J. Moorhead, R.*
23. Anthony C. Beilenson, D.*
24. Henry A. Waxman, D.*
25. Edward R. Roybal, D.*
26. Howard L. Berman, D.*
27. Mel Levine, D.*
28. Julian C. Dixon, D.*
29. Augustus F. (Gus) Hawkins, D.*
30. Matthew G. Martinez, D.*
31. Mervyn M. Dymally, D.*
32. Glenn M. Anderson, D.*
33. David Dreier, R.*
34. Esteban E. Torres, D.*
35. Jerry Lewis, R.*
36. George E. Brown, Jr., D.*
37. Alfred A. McCandless, R.*
38. Robert K. Dornan, R.

39. William E. Dannemeyer, R.*
40. Robert E. Badham, R.*
41. William D. Lowery, R.*
42. Daniel E. Lungren, R.*
43. Ronald C. Packard, R.*
44. Jim Bates, D.*
45. Duncan L. Hunter, R.*

Colorado
1. Patricia Schroeder, D.*
2. Timothy E. Wirth, D.*
3. Michael L. Strang, R.
4. Hank Brown, R.*
5. Kenneth B. Kramer, R.*
6. Daniel Schaefer, R.*

Connecticut
1. Barbara B. Kennelly, D.*
2. Samuel Gejdenson, D.*
3. Bruce A. Morrison, D.*
4. Stewart B. McKinney, R.*
5. John G. Rowland, R.
6. Nancy L. Johnson, R.*

Delaware
†Thomas R. Carper, D.*

Florida
1. Earl Hutto, D.*
2. Don Fuqua, D.*
3. Charles E. Bennett, D.*
4. Bill Chappell, Jr., D.*
5. Bill McCollum, R.*
6. Kenneth H. (Buddy) MacKay, D.*
7. Sam M. Gibbons, D.*
8. C. W. Bill Young, R.*
9. Michael Bilirakis, R.*
10. Andy Ireland, R.*
11. Bill Nelson, D.*
12. Thomas F. Lewis, R.*
13. Connie Mack III, R.*
14. Daniel A. Mica, D.*
15. E. Clay Shaw, Jr., R.*
16. Lawrence J. Smith, D.*
17. William Lehman, D.*
18. Claude D. Pepper, D.*
19. Dante B. Fascell, D.*

Georgia
1. Lindsay Thomas, D.*
2. Charles F. Hatcher, D.*
3. Richard B. Ray, D.*
4. Pat Swindall, R.
5. Wyche Fowler, Jr., D.*
6. Newt Gingrich, R.*
7. George Darden, D.*
8. J. Roy Rowland, D.*
9. Edgar L. Jenkins, D.*
10. Doug Barnard, Jr., D.*

Hawaii
1. Cecil Heftel, D.*
2. Daniel K. Akaka, D.*

Idaho
1. Larry Craig, R.*
2. Richard Stallings, D.

Illinois
1. Charles A. Hayes, D.*
2. Gus Savage, D.*
3. Marty Russo, D.*
4. George M. O'Brien, R.*
5. William O. Lipinski, D.*
6. Henry J. Hyde, R.*
7. Cardiss Collins, D.*
8. Dan Rostenkowski, D.*
9. Sidney R. Yates, D.*
10. John Edward Porter, R.*
11. Frank Annunzio, D.*
12. Philip M. Crane, R.*
13. Harris W. Fawell, R.
14. John E. Grotberg, R.
15. Edward R. Madigan, R.*
16. Lynn M. Martin, R.*
17. Lane A. Evans, D.*
18. Robert H. Michel, R.*
19. Terry L. Bruce, D.
20. Richard J. Durbin, D.*
21. Melvin Price, D.*
22. Kenneth J. Gray, D.

Indiana
1. Peter J. Visclosky, D.
2. Philip R. Sharp, D.*
3. John Patrick Hiler, R.*
4. Dan R. Coats, R.*
5. Elwood H. Hillis, R.*
6. Danny L. Burton, R.*
7. John T. Myers, R.*
8. Frank McCloskey, D.*
9. Lee H. Hamilton, D.*
10. Andrew Jacobs, Jr., D.*

Iowa
1. Jim Leach, R.*
2. Thomas J. Tauke, R.*
3. Cooper Evans, R.*
4. Neal Smith, D.*
5. Jim Ross Lightfoot, R.
6. Berkley Bedell, D.*

Kansas
1. Pat Roberts, R.*
2. James C. Slattery, D.*
3. Jan Meyers, R.
4. Dan Glickman, D.*
5. Bob Whittaker, R.*

Kentucky
1. Carroll Hubbard, Jr., D.*
2. William H. Natcher, D.*
3. Romano L. Mazzoli, D.*
4. M. G. (Gene) Snyder, R.*
5. Harold (Hal) Rogers, R.*
6. Larry J. Hopkins, R.*
7. Carl C. (Chris) Perkins, D.

Louisiana
1. Robert L. Livingston, R*
2. Corinne C. (Lindy) Boggs, D.*
3. W. J. (Billy) Tauzin, D.*
4. Charles Roemer, D.*
5. Thomas J. (Jerry) Huckaby, D.*
6. W. Henson Moore, R.*
7. John B. Breaux, D.*
8. Cathy Long, D.

Maine
1. John R. McKernan, Jr., R.*
2. Olympia J. Snowe, R.*

Maryland
1. Roy P. Dyson, D.*
2. Helen Delich Bentley, R.
3. Barbara A. Mikulski, D.*
4. Marjorie S. Holt, R.*
5. Steny H. Hoyer, D.*
6. Beverly B. Byron, D.*
7. Parren J. Mitchell, D.*
8. Michael D. Barnes, D.*

Massachusetts
1. Silvio O. Conte, R.*
2. Edward P. Boland, D.*
3. Joseph D. Early, D.*
4. Barney Frank, D.*
5. Chester G. Atkins, D.
6. Nicholas Mavroules, D.*
7. Edward J. Markey, D.*
8. Thomas P. O'Neill, Jr., D.*
9. John Joseph Moakley, D.*
10. Gerry E. Studds, D.*
11. Brian J. Donnelly, D.*

Michigan
1. John Conyers, Jr., D.*
2. Carl D. Pursell, R.*
3. Howard E. Wolpe, D.*
4. Mark D. Siljander, R.*
5. Paul B. Henry, R.
6. Bob Carr, D.*
7. Dale E. Kildee, D.*
8. Bob Traxler, D.*
9. Guy Vander Jagt, R.*
10. Bill Schuette, R.
11. Robert W. Davis, R.*
12. David E. Bonior, D.*
13. George W. Crockett, Jr., D.*
14. Dennis M. Hertel, D.*
15. William D. Ford, D.*
16. John D. Dingell, D.*
17. Sander M. Levin, D.*
18. William S. Broomfield, R.*

Minnesota
1. Timothy J. Penny, D.*
2. Vin Weber, R.*
3. Bill Frenzel, R.*
4. Bruce F. Vento, D.*
5. Martin O. Sabo, D.*
6. Gerry Sikorski, D.*
7. Arlan Stangeland, R.*
8. James L. Oberstar, D.*

Mississippi
1. Jamie L. Whitten, D.*
2. William W. Franklin, R.*
3. G. V. (Sonny) Montgomery, D.*
4. Wayne Dowdy, D.*
5. Trent Lott, R.*

Missouri
1. William L. (Bill) Clay, D.*
2. Robert A. Young, D.*
3. Richard A. Gephardt, D.*
4. Ike Skelton, D.*
5. Alan D. Wheat, D.*
6. E. Thomas Coleman, R.*
7. Gene Taylor, R.*
8. Bill Emerson, R.*
9. Harold L. Volkmer, D.*

Montana
1. Pat Williams, D.*
2. Ron Marlenee, R.*

Nebraska
1. Doug Bereuter, R.*
2. Hal Daub, R.*
3. Virginia Smith, R.*

Nevada
1. Harry M. Reid, D.*
2. Barbara F. Vucanovich, R.*

New Hampshire
1. Robert C. Smith, R.
2. Judd Gregg, R.*

New Jersey
1. James J. Florio, D.*
2. William J. Hughes, D.*
3. James J. Howard, D.*
4. Christopher H. Smith, R.*
5. Marge Roukema, R.*
6. Bernard J. Dwyer, D.*
7. Matthew J. Rinaldo, R.*
8. Robert A. Roe, D.*
9. Robert G. Torricelli, D.*
10. Peter W. Rodino, Jr., D.*
11. Dean A. Gallo, R.
12. Jim Courter, R.*
13. H. James Saxton, R.
14. Frank J. Guarini, D.*

New Mexico
1. Manuel Lujan, Jr., R.*
2. Joe Skeen, R.*
3. William B. Richardson, D.*

New York
1. William Carney, R.*
2. Thomas J. Downey, D.*
3. Robert J. Mrazek, D.*
4. Norman F. Lent, R.*
5. Raymond J. McGrath, R.*
6. Joseph P. Addabbo, D.*
7. Gary L. Ackerman, D.*
8. James H. Scheuer, D.*
9. Thomas J. Manton, D.
10. Charles E. Schumer, D.*
11. Edolphus Towns, D.*
12. Major R. Owens, D.*
13. Stephen J. Solarz, D.*

14. Guy V. Molinari, R.*
15. Bill Green, R.*
16. Charles B. Rangel, D.*
17. Ted Weiss, D.*
18. Robert Garcia, D.*
19. Mario Biaggi, D.*
20. Joseph D. DioGuardi, R.
21. Hamilton Fish, Jr., R.*
22. Benjamin A. Gilman, R.*
23. Samuel S. Stratton, D.*
24. Gerald B. Solomon, R.*
25. Sherwood L. Boehlert, R.*
26. David O'B. Martin, R.*
27. George C. Wortley, R.*
28. Matthew F. McHugh, D.*
29. Frank Horton, R.*
30. Fred J. Eckert, R.
31. Jack Kemp, R.*
32. John J. LaFalce, D.*
33. Henry J. Nowak, D.*
34. Stan Lundine, D.*

North Carolina
1. Walter B. Jones, D.*
2. Tim Valentine, D.*
3. Charles O. Whitley, D.*
4. William W. Cobey, Jr., R.
5. Stephen L. Neal, D.*
6. Howard Coble, R.
7. Charlie Rose, D.*
8. W. G. (Bill) Hefner, D.*
9. J. Alex McMillan III, R.
10. James T. Broyhill, R.*
11. William H. Hendon, R.

North Dakota
†Byron L. Dorgan, D.*

Ohio
1. Thomas A. Luken, D.*
2. Willis D. Gradison, Jr., R.*
3. Tony P. Hall, D.*
4. Michael G. Oxley, R.*
5. Delbert L. Latta, R.*
6. Bob McEwen, R.*
7. Michael DeWine, R.*
8. Thomas N. Kindness, R.*
9. Marcy Kaptur, D.*
10. Clarence E. Miller, R.*
11. Dennis E. Eckart, D.*
12. John R. Kasich, R.*
13. Donald J. Pease, D.*
14. John F. Seiberling, D.*
15. Chalmers P. Wylie, R.*
16. Ralph Regula, R.*
17. James Traficant, Jr., D.
18. Douglas Applegate, D.*
19. Edward F. Feighan, D.*
20. Mary Rose Oakar, D.*
21. Louis Stokes, D.*

Oklahoma
1. James R. Jones, D.*
2. Mike Synar, D.*
3. Wesley W. Watkins, D.*
4. Dave McCurdy, D.*
5. Mickey Edwards, R.*
6. Glenn English, D.*

Oregon
1. Les AuCoin, D.*
2. Robert F. Smith, R.*

3. Ron Wyden, D.*
4. Jim Weaver, D.*
5. Denny Smith, R.*

Pennsylvania
1. Thomas M. Foglietta, D.*
2. William H. (Bill) Gray III, D.*
3. Robert A. Borski, Jr., D.*
4. Joseph P. Kolter, D.*
5. Richard T. Schulze, R.*
6. Gus Yatron, D.*
7. Bob Edgar, D.*
8. Peter H. Kostmayer, D.*
9. E. G. (Bud) Shuster, R.*
10. Joseph M. McDade, R.*
11. Paul E. Kanjorski, D.
12. John P. Murtha, D.*
13. Lawrence Coughlin, R.*
14. William J. Coyne, D.*
15. Don Ritter, R.*
16. Robert S. Walker, R.*
17. George W. Gekas, R.*
18. Doug Walgren, D.*
19. William F. Goodling, R.*
20. Joseph M. Gaydos, D.*
21. Thomas J. Ridge, R.*
22. Austin J. Murphy, D.*
23. William F. Clinger, Jr., R.*

Rhode Island
1. Fernand J. St Germain, D.*
2. Claudine Schneider, R.*

South Carolina
1. Thomas F. Harnett, R.*
2. Floyd Spence, R.*
3. Butler Derrick, D.*
4. Carroll A. Campbell, Jr., R.*
5. John McK. Spratt, D.*
6. Robert M. (Robin) Tallon, D.*

South Dakota
†Thomas A. Daschle, D.*

Tennessee
1. James H. Quillen, R.*
2. John J. Duncan, R.*
3. Marilyn Lloyd, D.*
4. James H. Cooper, D.*
5. William H. Boner, D.*
6. Bart Gordon, D.
7. Donald K. Sundquist, R.*
8. Ed Jones, D.*
9. Harold E. Ford, D.*

Texas
1. Jim Chapman, D.
2. Charles Wilson, D.*
3. Steve Bartlett, R.*
4. Ralph M. Hall, D.*
5. John W. Bryant, D.*
6. Joe Barton, R.
7. Bill Archer, R.*
8. Jack Fields, R.*
9. Jack Brooks, D.*
10. J. J. (Jake) Pickle, D.*
11. J. Marvin Leath, D.*
12. James C. Wright, Jr., D.*
13. Beau Boulter, R.
14. Mac Sweeney, R.
15. Eligio (Kika) de la Garza, D.*
16. Ronald Coleman, D.*
17. Charles W. Stenholm, D.*

18. Mickey Leland, D.*
19. Larry Combest, R.
20. Henry B. Gonzalez, D.*
21. Tom Loeffler, R.*
22. Tom DeLay, R.
23. Albert G. Bustamante, D.
24. Martin Frost, D.*
25. Michael A. Andrews, D.*
26. Richard Armey, R.
27. Solomon P. Ortiz, D.*

Utah
1. James V. Hansen, R.*
2. David S. Monson, R.
3. Howard C. Nielson, R.*

Vermont
†James M. Jeffords, R.*

Virginia
1. Herbert H. Bateman, R.*
2. G. William Whitehurst, R.*
3. Thomas J. (Tom) Bliley, Jr., R.*
4. Norman Sisisky, D.*
5. Dan Daniel, D.*
6. James R. Olin, D.*
7. D. French Slaughter, R.
8. Stanford E. (Stan) Parris, R.*
9. Frederick C. Boucher, D.*
10. Frank R. Wolf, R.*

Washington
1. John Miller, R.
2. Al Swift, D.*
3. Don Bonker, D.*
4. Sid Morrison, R.*
5. Thomas S. Foley, D.*
6. Norman D. Dicks, D.*
7. Mike Lowry, D.*
8. Rod Chandler, R.*

West Virginia
1. Alan B. Mollohan, D.*
2. Harley O. Staggers, Jr., D.*
3. Robert E. Wise, Jr., D.*
4. Nick J. Rahall II, D.*

Wisconsin
1. Les Aspin, D.*
2. Robert W. Kastenmeier, D.*
3. Steven Gunderson, R.*
4. Gerald D. Kleczka, D.*
5. Jim Moody, D.*
6. Thomas E. Petri, R.*
7. David R. Obey, D.*
8. Toby Roth, R.*
9. F. James Sensenbrenner, Jr., R.*

Wyoming
†Dick Cheney, R.*

Nonvoting Representatives
American Samoa
Fofo I. F. Sunia, D.*

District of Columbia
Walter E. Fauntroy, D.*

Guam
Ben Blaz, R.

Puerto Rico
Baltasar Corrada, D.*

Virgin Islands
Ron de Lugo, D.*

269

Members of the United States Senate

The Senate of the second session of the 99th Congress consisted of 53 Republicans and 47 Democrats when it convened in January 1986. Senators shown starting their term in 1985 were elected for the first time in the Nov. 6, 1984, elections. Others shown ending their current terms in 1991 were reelected to the Senate in the 1984 balloting. The second date in each listing shows when the term of a previously elected senator expires.

State	Term	State	Term	State	Term
Alabama		**Louisiana**		**Ohio**	
Howell T. Heflin, D.	1979 — 1991	Russell B. Long, D.	1948 — 1987	John H. Glenn, Jr., D.	1975 — 1987
Jeremiah Denton, R.	1981 — 1987	J. Bennett Johnston, Jr., D.	1972 — 1991	Howard M. Metzenbaum, D.	1977 — 1989
Alaska		**Maine**		**Oklahoma**	
Theodore F. Stevens, R.	1968 — 1991	William S. Cohen, R.	1979 — 1991	David L. Boren, D.	1979 — 1991
Frank H. Murkowski, R.	1981 — 1987	George J. Mitchell, D.	1980 — 1989	Don Nickles, R.	1981 — 1987
Arizona		**Maryland**		**Oregon**	
Barry Goldwater, R.	1969 — 1987	Charles McC. Mathias, Jr., R.	1969 — 1987	Mark O. Hatfield, R.	1967 — 1991
Dennis DeConcini, D.	1977 — 1989	Paul S. Sarbanes, D.	1977 — 1989	Bob Packwood, R.	1969 — 1987
Arkansas		**Massachusetts**		**Pennsylvania**	
Dale Bumpers, D.	1975 — 1987	Edward M. Kennedy, D.	1962 — 1989	John Heinz, R.	1977 — 1989
David H. Pryor, D.	1979 — 1991	John F. Kerry, D.	1985 — 1991	Arlen Specter, R.	1981 — 1987
California		**Michigan**		**Rhode Island**	
Alan Cranston, D.	1969 — 1987	Donald W. Riegle, Jr., D.	1977 — 1989	Claiborne Pell, D.	1961 — 1991
Pete Wilson, R.	1983 — 1989	Carl Levin, D.	1979 — 1991	John H. Chafee, R.	1977 — 1989
Colorado		**Minnesota**		**South Carolina**	
Gary W. Hart, D.	1975 — 1987	David F. Durenberger, R.	1978 — 1989	Strom Thurmond, R.	1956 — 1991
William L. Armstrong, R.	1979 — 1991	Rudy Boschwitz, R.	1979 — 1991	Ernest F. Hollings, D.	1966 — 1987
Connecticut		**Mississippi**		**South Dakota**	
Lowell P. Weicker, Jr., R.	1971 — 1989	John C. Stennis, D.	1947 — 1989	Larry Pressler, R.	1979 — 1991
Christopher J. Dodd, D.	1981 — 1987	Thad Cochran, R.	1979 — 1991	James Abdnor, R.	1981 — 1987
Delaware		**Missouri**		**Tennessee**	
William V. Roth, Jr., R.	1971 — 1989	Thomas F. Eagleton, D.	1968 — 1987	James R. Sasser, D.,	1977 — 1989
Joseph R. Biden, Jr., D.	1973 — 1991	John C. Danforth, R.	1977 — 1989	Albert A. Gore, Jr., D.	1985 — 1991
Florida		**Montana**		**Texas**	
Lawton Chiles, D.	1971 — 1989	John Melcher, D.	1977 — 1989	Lloyd M. Bentsen, D.	1971 — 1989
Paula Hawkins, R.	1981 — 1987	Max Baucus, D.	1979 — 1991	Phil Gramm, R.	1985 — 1991
Georgia		**Nebraska**		**Utah**	
Sam Nunn, D.	1972 — 1991	Edward Zorinsky, D.	1977 — 1989	Edwin Jacob Garn, R.	1975 — 1987
Mack Mattingly, R.	1981 — 1987	J. James Exon, D.	1979 — 1991	Orrin G. Hatch, R.	1977 — 1989
Hawaii		**Nevada**		**Vermont**	
Daniel K. Inouye, D.	1963 — 1987	Paul Laxalt, R.	1975 — 1987	Robert T. Stafford, R.	1971 — 1989
Spark M. Matsunaga, D.	1977 — 1989	Chic Hecht, R.	1983 — 1989	Patrick J. Leahy, D.	1975 — 1987
Idaho		**New Hampshire**		**Virginia**	
James A. McClure, R.	1973 — 1991	Gordon J. Humphrey, R.	1979 — 1991	John W. Warner, R.	1979 — 1991
Steve Symms, R.	1981 — 1987	Warren Rudman, R.	1981 — 1987	Paul S. Trible, Jr., R.	1983 — 1989
Illinois		**New Jersey**		**Washington**	
Alan J. Dixon, D.	1981 — 1987	Bill Bradley, D.	1979 — 1991	Slade Gorton, R.	1981 — 1987
Paul Simon, D.	1985 — 1991	Frank R. Lautenberg, D.	1983 — 1989	Daniel J. Evans, R.	1983 — 1989
Indiana		**New Mexico**		**West Virginia**	
Richard G. Lugar, R.	1977 — 1989	Pete V. Domenici, R.	1973 — 1991	Robert C. Byrd, D.	1959 — 1989
Dan Quayle, R.	1981 — 1987	Jeff Bingaman, D.	1983 — 1989	John D. Rockefeller IV, D.	1985 — 1991
Iowa		**New York**		**Wisconsin**	
Charles E. Grassley, R.	1981 — 1987	Daniel P. Moynihan, D.	1977 — 1989	William Proxmire, D.	1957 — 1989
Tom Harkin, D.	1985 — 1991	Alfonse M. D'Amato, R.	1981 — 1987	Robert W. Kasten, Jr., R.	1981 — 1987
Kansas		**North Carolina**		**Wyoming**	
Robert J. Dole, R.	1969 — 1987	Jesse A. Helms, R.	1973 — 1991	Malcolm Wallop, R.	1977 — 1989
Nancy Landon Kassebaum, R.	1979 — 1991	John P. East, R.	1981 — 1987	Alan K. Simpson, R.	1979 — 1991
Kentucky		**North Dakota**			
Wendell H. Ford, D.	1975 — 1987	Quentin N. Burdick, D.	1960 — 1989		
Mitch McConnell, R.	1985 — 1991	Mark Andrews, R.	1981 — 1987		

The House also had difficulty deciding what to do about Reagan's request for aid to the *contras*—guerrillas fighting the leftist Sandinista government of Nicaragua. After the House rejected the President's 1984 call for military aid to the contras, Reagan made an amended request for "non-lethal" aid, primarily food, clothing, and medicines. But the House on April 24 voted 215 to 213 to bar any form of assistance. The President countered with strenuous lobbying, and on June 12, 73 House Democrats deserted their leaders and joined all but 7 House Republicans in voting 248 to 184 to provide $27 million in humanitarian assistance to the contras.

In June and July, the House and Senate, by lop-sided margins, passed differing bills to impose relatively mild economic sanctions against South Africa's government. The purpose of the measures was to put pressure on South Africa to reform its repressive racial policies. When the Senate returned from its Labor Day recess on September 9, it was scheduled to vote on a compromise sanctions bill that had cleared the House on August 1 by a vote of 380 to 48. But on the day the Senate returned to work, Reagan signed an executive order imposing mild sanctions of his own. Congress then set aside its legislation.

Trade Action. Disturbed by soaring imports and a record trade deficit, Congress seemed certain in 1985 to pass protectionist trade legislation. Once again, Reagan moved first by embracing a "fair trade" program of his own. He also gave the go-ahead for an international effort to lower the value of the U.S. dollar on world markets, something he had opposed in the past. The weaker dollar made U.S. exports less expensive to buyers in other countries and imports more costly to Americans. The President's actions took much of the steam out of the protectionist drive.

Congressional Leadership. In the House, Speaker Thomas P. (Tip) O'Neill, Jr. (D., Mass.), strengthened his leadership position, overcoming the complaints of some younger Democrats who wanted a larger share of power. But O'Neill stood by his announced intention to retire after the 1986 session. On February 7, House Democratic leader James C. Wright, Jr., of Texas claimed that three-fourths of his Democratic colleagues were pledged to support him as the next Speaker. The younger generation's claim to congressional power was underscored as the House Democratic caucus voted to unseat 80-year-old Melvin Price of Illinois as chairman of the House Armed Services Committee, replacing him with 46-year-old Les Aspin of Wisconsin.   Frank Cormier and Margot Cormier

See also UNITED STATES, GOVERNMENT OF THE; PRESIDENT OF THE UNITED STATES. In WORLD BOOK, see CONGRESS OF THE UNITED STATES.

CONNECTICUT. See STATE GOVERNMENT.

CONSERVATION. The United States House of Representatives approved a three-year extension of the Endangered Species Act (ESA) of 1973 on July 29, 1985. The act gives legal protection to species listed as endangered. Environmentalists nevertheless claimed that the process of placing threatened species on the protected list was so slow that species considered eligible may become extinct while waiting to be listed. Biologists fear that the Texas Henslow's sparrow has suffered such a fate. The piping plover, a shore bird, was added to the protected list on December 11. The Senate had not reauthorized the ESA by year's end.

Ferret Failure. The black-footed ferret, a "masked" member of the weasel family, neared extinction in 1985. The ferret once ranged from Alberta and Saskatchewan in Canada to Texas, New Mexico, and Arizona. As the livestock industry exterminated prairie dogs, the ferret's primary food, the ferret population dwindled. By 1974, conservationists feared the ferret was extinct.

In September 1981, however, a colony of the ferrets was discovered near Meeteetse, Wyo. A census taken in 1984 counted 129 ferrets at the 8,000-acre (3,200-hectare) site. Private organizations sponsoring biological research on the ferrets urged that captive-breeding programs be started and that some ferrets be moved to suitable sites in other states. With all known ferrets in a single location, biologists warned, the species was especially vulnerable to catastrophe, such as an outbreak of disease. The Wyoming Game and Fish Department rejected this advice, however.

Early in the summer of 1985, fieldworkers discovered an outbreak of bubonic plague in the prairie dog population. The flea-borne disease was wiping out the ferrets' main food source. In July, federal and state agencies began dusting prairie dog burrows with insecticide to kill the fleas. But by late summer, more than 50 per cent of the ferrets had died—mostly from starvation.

In September, the Wyoming Game and Fish Department began collecting some of the rare animals for a breeding project. Twelve were captured, but several died of distemper. At year's end, the entire known population of healthy black-footed ferrets numbered six. Researchers believed that about 10 others may have been living in the wild, but neither their whereabouts nor the state of their health was known.

Illegal Wildlife Trade. Delegates from 68 nations attended the fifth meeting of the Convention on International Trade in Endangered Species of Wild Fauna and Flora (CITES) in Buenos Aires, Argentina, in April and May. Delegates added a number of species to their most-endangered list, thus prohibiting trade in these species among nations that have signed the convention. Species added to the list in 1985 were scarlet macaws, Buf-

Russell E. Train, president of World Wildlife Fund—U.S., announces in May
a $1-million fund drive to save wild primates whose habitats are threatened.

fon's macaws, jabiru storks, the North American population of gyrfalcons, and several plants.

Malawi, backed by 25 other African countries, obtained the necessary votes to permit ranching of Nile crocodiles, collecting their eggs, and killing the animals when they reach suitable size. Under a quota system, nine countries were permitted to harvest more than 11,600 Nile crocodile hides a year. Conservationists feared that the action would provide a loophole allowing the skins of crocodiles killed illegally to be sold as "approved" products.

In July, the U.S. Fish and Wildlife Service (FWS) announced plans to add 18 inspectors at U.S. ports of entry—an increase of more than 50 per cent—in an effort to intercept products made from endangered plants and animals.

On March 19, a federal court sentenced Loren Jay Ellison of Big Timber, Mont., to 15 years in prison for commercial slaughter of wildlife. The penalty was the harshest ever imposed in the United States for a wildlife offense.

Galapagos Aflame. In March and April, fire raged across the southern portion of Isabela, largest of the Galapagos Islands. The island's rare life forms helped inspire the British naturalist Charles Darwin's theory of evolution 150 years earlier. The blaze apparently started on February 26, and it eventually devastated 100,000 acres (40,000 hectares) on the island.

Greatest concern centered on the unique plants and animals on these islands, which belong to Ecuador. On March 20, Ecuadorean scientists reported that rare dwarf penguins were deserting their eggs and offspring as the blaze neared their breeding grounds. Naturalists from Ecuador's national park agency evacuated a threatened colony of giant tortoises in April. Officials concluded that the blaze had not affected major wildlife populations, but that habitat destruction caused by the blaze could hurt wildlife in the future.

National Parks. Interior Secretary Donald P. Hodel on May 1 named William Penn Mott, Jr., as director of the National Park Service. Mott had been president of the California State Park Foundation and general manager of the East Bay Zoological Society in Oakland, Calif. He is a trustee of the National Parks and Conservation Association, a nonprofit group often critical of the government's management of parklands.

In May, the chairman of the House Subcommittee on National Parks and Recreation, Representative Bruce F. Vento (D., Minn.), described air pollution as "the number-one threat to the parks." Several park superintendents described the situation as urgent, with pollution obscuring mountain ranges and killing plant life.

Water Issues. On August 8, officials of the National Clean Air Fund and the Natural Resources

Defense Council declared that acid rain, a long-standing problem in the East and Midwest, had begun to affect Western lakes and streams that lacked the natural ability to neutralize acid rainfall. They included Yosemite National Park in California and Rocky Mountain National Park in Colorado among the most vulnerable sites.

The Department of the Interior announced on April 29 that 121 of its wildlife refuges were threatened by water pollution. Waters in the refuges had been contaminated by agricultural fertilizers, pesticides, herbicides, petroleum, industrial and domestic wastes, and other toxic chemicals. The Kesterson National Wildlife Refuge in California was closed in March.

On November 26, a federal judge in Denver ruled that rivers running through federally designated wilderness areas must be preserved regardless of plans for water use upstream. His decision could restrict mining, public water projects for growing cities, and other activities that involve discharging wastewater into such rivers. Although the ruling applied only to Colorado, it could have far-reaching implications. The state of Colorado, the city of Denver, the Mountain States Legal Foundation, and the Colorado Water Congress planned to appeal the decision.   Eugene J. Walter, Jr.

See also ENVIRONMENTAL POLLUTION; WATER; ZOOLOGY. In WORLD BOOK, see CONSERVATION.

CONSTITUTION OF THE UNITED STATES. Shortly before undergoing surgery on July 13, 1985, President Ronald Reagan temporarily transferred executive power to Vice President George H. W. Bush, following the provisions of the 25th Amendment. The amendment spells out procedures for placing the Vice President in command of the executive branch of government if the President is unable to carry out the duties of office.

Although Reagan followed the procedures in the amendment, he declined to actually invoke it. In identical letters to the Senate and House of Representatives, in which he conferred presidential authority on Bush, Reagan said it was doubtful the amendment was intended for situations such as his—a few hours under anesthesia. The President said he did not want to set a precedent binding future chief executives.

No additional states in 1985 passed resolutions calling for a constitutional convention to write an amendment requiring balanced federal budgets. Missouri in 1983 became the 32nd state to pass such a resolution; 34 states must do so before a constitutional convention can be held.

A constitutional amendment that would have given the District of Columbia full voting rights in Congress died in August 1985. Only 16 states had approved the measure.   David L. Dreier

In WORLD BOOK, see CONSTITUTION OF THE U.S.

CONSUMERISM. Living costs continued to rise at a relatively slow pace in the United States in 1985. By year-end, the Consumer Price Index (CPI)—the most widely used measure of inflation—stood only 3.6 per cent higher than a year earlier. Record U.S. harvests during 1985 helped keep food prices down, and a worldwide oil glut tended to restrain prices for petroleum products.

Under such circumstances, many Americans were mystified by the fact that retail food and fuel prices continued to go up. Industry experts explained that, although farmers received less for their output, food-processing and distribution expenses continued to rise, leaving little or no room for price cuts on most items at the retail end. Also in 1985, the Organization of Petroleum Exporting Countries (OPEC) failed to prevent world oil prices from falling. Yet prices of motor fuel in September stood 4.4 per cent higher than a year earlier. Industry officials blamed the higher retail prices on area shortages, increased demand, and higher processing costs due to the growing demand for lead-free gasoline.

In the Market Place. Prices of prescription drugs continued to skyrocket, rising 56 per cent from January 1981 to June 1985—twice the increase in consumer prices overall. But several patents expired in 1985, including those for the tranquilizer Valium and the blood-pressure drug Inderal, making 8 of the 10 largest-selling medicines available in lower-priced generic versions.

Communications became more costly. First-class postage rose by 10 per cent in February, to 22 cents per ounce (28 grams). And telephone charges continued to soar. In May, a study by consumer advocate Ralph Nader's Public Interest Research Group and the Consumer Federation of America, a national advocacy group, reported that costs for residential telephone service had risen 20 per cent in one year. The report claimed that if costs kept rising at that pace, some 6 million customers might be unable to afford telephone service. A spokesperson for the United States Telephone Association, an industry trade group, acknowledged that some charges had gone up by 20 per cent but claimed that most disconnected telephone service resulted from accumulated long-distance charges, not from local service costs.

The costs of borrowing money also were perplexing. Business loans could be had for as little as 9.5 per cent—the prime interest rate that banks supposedly charge their best corporate customers. Consumer loans, however, remained much more costly. Mortgage rates stayed steady at about 3 percentage points above the prime rate. The interest rate on credit card sales reached an average of 19.8 per cent—1 percentage point higher than it was in early 1981, when the prime rate of 21.5 per cent was more than double the 1985 rate.

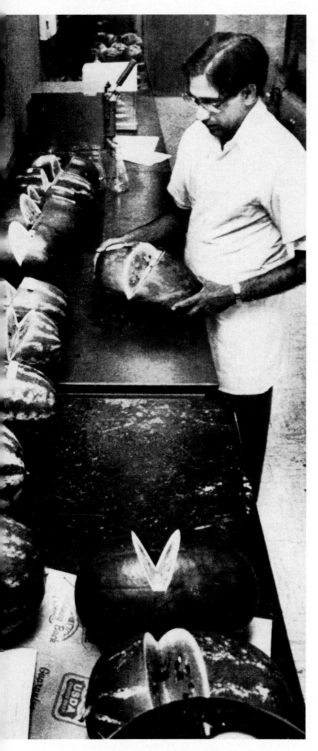

A California agricultural inspector examines watermelons after pesticide-contaminated melons were linked with a wave of illnesses in July.

There were signs, however, that consumers still had the power to influence some parts of the market. After the Coca-Cola Company announced a new formula for its popular soft drink in April, Coke fans from coast to coast put up so much resistance that the company in July resurrected the traditional formula, which it renamed Coca-Cola Classic. See FOOD (Close-Up).

The Federal Trade Commission (FTC), the government's chief agency for consumer protection, continued to soften its stance toward business practices in 1985, preferring to pursue specific cases rather than issue industrywide rules. The FTC decided to cancel proposals of the Administration of President Jimmy Carter to regulate the sale of health club memberships and hearing aids. After a decade of discussion, the agency also voted to drop a plan to police the setting of product standards by private industry.

But FTC efforts to drop an existing rule that required food stores to stock sufficient quantities of advertised sale items ran into a flood of negative comments from consumers. The agency decided instead to require retailers to provide "rain checks" if they run out of advertised sale items.

The FTC's controversial used-car rule became effective in May in all states except Wisconsin, which has a rule considered to be much stronger. Under the federal regulation, a dealer must attach a sticker to a used car stating whether it is being sold under a warranty or "as is" without a warranty. Critics claimed that the rule was useless without a rejected clause that would have required dealers to disclose any known defects of the car.

An FTC regulation that tightens consumer protection in credit matters took effect in May. The rule prohibits car dealers, department stores, and finance companies from assessing more than one late charge on an overdue payment. It also requires a warning to cosigners that they might have to pay the loan if the debtor defaults.

In July, the FTC announced that nearly 10,000 owners of automobiles manufactured by General Motors Corporation (GM) had received more than $3 million under an arbitration program set up by the FTC and run by the Council of Better Business Bureaus Incorporated (CBBB). (The CBBB is a trade organization supported by business firms, including GM.) The program grew out of a charge by the Carter Administration that GM had failed to notify consumers about serious engine problems in as many as 50 million GM vehicles. The FTC said that results in the first 10 months indicated the program was working well, even though many auto owners apparently were unaware of its existence.

Starting in October 1985, tobacco manufacturers began to make warning notices on cigarette packages more specific, as required under a 1984 law. Four different warnings about the health hazards of smoking were to rotate during a year. The first said, "Surgeon General's Warning: Smoking causes lung cancer, heart disease, emphysema, and may complicate pregnancy."

Other Government Actions. In July 1985, a federal appeals court ruled that the Department of Energy had illegally dropped energy-efficiency standards for such major home appliances as furnaces, water heaters, freezers, refrigerators, air conditioners, dryers, and ranges. The department had reasoned that the standards were no longer economically justified because of voluntary improvements made by manufacturers. A suit by the Natural Resources Defense Council, a public interest group, forced reinstatement of the goals for energy efficiency.

The Food and Drug Administration, a federal agency, proposed in April that package labels disclose any significant amount of sulfites in processed foods. Sulfites are used mainly as preservatives. The agency acted on the recommendation of a scientific panel. In addition, a consumer group, the Center for Science in the Public Interest, had reported a number of serious reactions, including several that proved fatal, in people sensitive to sulfites.   Arthur E. Rowse

In WORLD BOOK, see CONSUMERISM.

COSTA RICA. See LATIN AMERICA.

Seats for U.S. delegates are empty as the World Court in the Netherlands begins hearing a Nicaraguan grievance against the United States on September 12.

COURTS. In one of the most controversial hearings at the International Court of Justice in years, Nicaragua charged in September 1985 that the United States was conducting military operations against Nicaraguan territory without declaring war. This marked the first time the court, an agency of the United Nations often called the World Court, had been asked to rule on an armed conflict. Although the United States had long bound itself to the jurisdiction of the court, there were no American representatives at the hearing in The Hague, the Netherlands. The U.S. Department of State had announced in January that it would boycott the proceedings on the grounds that Nicaragua's lawsuit was "a misuse of the court for political and propaganda purposes." In October, the State Department said the United States was withdrawing from its pledge to honor World Court decisions.

Adding to the controversy was the presence of two Americans on Nicaragua's legal team, including Abram Chayes, once the top-ranking State Department lawyer and now a professor at Harvard Law School in Cambridge, Mass. Nicaragua's attorneys charged that *contra* guerrillas operating from neighboring countries against Nicaragua's Sandinista government were agents of the United States and that American actions supporting the contras violated international law. Responding to the United States contention that the World Court had no jurisdiction in the matter, Nicaraguan representative Carlos Arguello told the judges, "Your authority is being challenged by a superpower that wishes to set law aside in order to have a free hand for destroying a small nation." The judges had issued no opinion by the end of the year.

Judicial Misconduct was much in the news in 1985. In Rhode Island, the chief justice of the state Supreme Court, Joseph A. Bevilacqua, was censured and suspended without pay for four months for bringing his office "into serious disrepute" through his friendships with suspected mobsters. The disciplinary action was recommended even though a judicial inquiry failed to turn up any evidence that Bevilacqua's associations affected his legal rulings.

In Chicago, a federal jury on July 13 found Judge Richard F. LeFevour, the highest-ranking judge of the Cook County Circuit Court, guilty of mail fraud, racketeering, and filing false tax returns. LeFevour, the third judge convicted in the Federal Bureau of Investigation's "Operation Greylord" probe of Cook County courts, was accused of taking thousands of dollars in bribes in return for fixing parking tickets, reducing drunken driving charges, and allowing lawyers to solicit clients outside courtrooms. On August 27, LeFevour was sentenced to 12 years in prison.

In Mississippi, U.S. District Judge Walter L. Nixon, Jr., was indicted on August 29 on perjury and bribery charges. Nixon was accused of intervening on behalf of a suspect in a marijuana smuggling case after accepting shares in three oil wells from the suspect's father.

Von Bülow Acquitted. The year's most celebrated trial ended on June 10 when a jury in Providence, R.I., found New York City socialite Claus von Bülow not guilty of attempting to murder his wealthy wife, Martha (Sunny) von Bülow, by giving her injections of insulin. Martha von Bülow has been in an irreversible coma since 1980, but several physicians and drug experts testifying for the defense said they did not think her coma was caused by insulin.

In 1982, von Bülow was found guilty of the attempted murder of his wife. That conviction, however, was overturned on technical grounds by an appeals court, which ordered a retrial.

In another well-publicized trial, a federal judge in New York City on June 24 found two defendants, one of them a former reporter for *The Wall Street Journal*, guilty of selling inside information on U.S. corporations to stock traders. R. Foster Winans and his roommate David Carpenter were convicted of securities fraud for a scheme in which Winans, while writing the *Journal*'s influential "Heard on the Street" column, leaked news items from upcoming columns to stock traders. The defendants were fined and ordered to perform community service, and Winans was additionally sentenced to 18 months in prison. Two stockbrokers were also convicted in the scheme.

Protecting Workers. In a decision that could have far-reaching effects in the workplace, a Chicago judge ruled on June 14 that three local business executives were guilty of murder in the work-related death of an employee. Cook County Circuit Court Judge Ronald J. P. Banks said the 1983 cyanide poisoning death of Stefan Golab resulted from unsafe working conditions that the defendants were aware of but failed to correct.

The convicted executives—Steven O'Neil, Charles Kirschbaum, and Daniel Rodriguez—ran a now-defunct Chicago-area company that recovered silver from used photographic film. Large quantities of cyanide, which produces highly poisonous fumes, were used in processing the film. Prosecutors in the case said that although the defendants knew that workers at the plant frequently suffered from nausea and vomiting, they did nothing to improve safety conditions. The executives, who were each sentenced to 25 years in prison, planned to appeal the verdict.

Courts and the Media. In New York City, General William C. Westmoreland, commander of United States forces in Vietnam from 1964 to 1968, dropped his libel action against CBS Inc. on February 17 after the television network agreed to issue a statement expressing respect for the general's patriotism and service to the nation. Westmoreland brought the suit in 1982 to challenge a TV documentary in which he was accused of lying to his superiors and to the public about enemy troop strength in Vietnam. The general said the CBS statement amounted to an apology, but network officials denied that. They maintained that the program was accurate and fair. The statement, they said, merely declared that CBS had not intended, in the documentary, to cast doubts on Westmoreland's patriotism.

Another libel case being tried in New York City, this one between Time Incorporated and former Israeli Defense Minister Ariel Sharon, ended on Jan. 24, 1985. The jury found that a 1982 *Time* magazine article about the massacre of Palestinians in two refugee camps in West Beirut, Lebanon, had defamed Sharon. The article contained a paragraph implying that Sharon had encouraged Lebanese Christian militiamen to carry out the slaughter. Although it declared that paragraph libelous, the jury said *Time* had not printed it with the knowledge that it was false. As a result, Sharon lost the suit and received no monetary award from the verdict. David C. Beckwith

See also CRIME; SUPREME COURT OF THE UNITED STATES. In WORLD BOOK, see COURT; LAW.

CRIME. International terrorism in support of political objectives escalated during 1985. On June 14, Lebanese Shiite Muslim gunmen hijacked a Trans World Airlines jet carrying 153 people shortly after take-off from Athens, Greece. The terrorists murdered a young American sailor and held 39 other United States citizens hostage until June 30.

On June 23, an Air-India passenger jet flying from Toronto, Canada, to Bombay apparently broke apart in midair. The plane crashed into the Atlantic Ocean near Ireland, killing all 329 people on board. On November 6, Canadian authorities charged two Canadian-based Sikh extremists with planting a bomb on the plane.

On October 7, four Palestinians seized the *Achille Lauro*, an Italian cruise ship carrying more than 400 people, off Egypt. The terrorists killed an elderly American the next day and surrendered to Egyptian officials on October 9. On October 10, U.S. Navy fighter planes intercepted an Egyptian airliner carrying the four to an unknown destination and forced it down in Sigonella, Italy, near Catania. Italian authorities arrested the hijackers but allowed the alleged mastermind of the hijacking to leave Italy.

Armed Arab terrorists on December 27 staged attacks in airports in Vienna, Austria, and Rome. Nineteen people were killed, including four of the terrorists, and 121 people were wounded.

Even the Soviet Union suffered a terrorist assault in 1985. On September 30, Lebanese Muslims kidnapped four Soviets in West Beirut. One of the Soviets was found murdered two days later. The three others were released on October 30.

Espionage. United States officials charged an unusually large number of individuals with spying. In October 1984, Richard W. Miller became the first Federal Bureau of Investigation (FBI) agent ever accused of espionage. The U.S. government charged him with seven felonies, including conspiracy to commit espionage for the Soviet Union. Miller's trial ended in a mistrial on Nov. 6, 1985, after the jury reported a hopeless deadlock.

On July 11, the government accused Sharon M. Scranage, an employee of the U.S. Central Intelligence Agency (CIA) stationed in Ghana, and Michael A. Soussoudis, a Ghanaian described as her lover, of passing secrets to Ghana. On August 12, Scranage pleaded guilty to 2 counts of disclosing the identity of U.S. intelligence agents and not guilty to 16 other counts. Soussoudis pleaded not guilty to charges of espionage and receiving classified information.

Perhaps the most talked-about spy case of 1985 involved a spy ring led by former U.S. Navy officer John A. Walker, Jr., and including his brother, Arthur J. Walker, his son, Michael L. Walker, and allegedly a friend, Jerry A. Whitworth. Secretary of Defense Caspar W. Weinberger described the secrets that the Walker ring had turned over to the Soviet Union as "a serious loss."

On August 9, a jury in Norfolk, Va., found Arthur J. Walker guilty of espionage, conspiracy, and unauthorized possession of classified data. He received three life sentences. Michael and John Walker pleaded guilty on October 28. Michael received a sentence of 25 years as a result of a plea bargain. John was sentenced to life imprisonment. Whitworth's trial was pending at year-end.

On November 21, federal agents arrested Jonathan Jay Pollard, a civilian counterintelligence analyst for the Navy, and accused him of selling information to Israel. The FBI said on November 27 that Pollard had admitted his spying. Pollard's wife, Anne, was also arrested.

On November 25, Ronald W. Pelton, a former communications specialist with the National Security Agency, was charged with conspiracy to commit espionage. The FBI said on November 27 that he had admitted spying for the Soviet Union. Larry Wu-Tai Chin, a former CIA employee, was arrested on November 22 and accused of spying for China for more than 30 years.

White-Collar Crime. The U.S. Department of Justice announced on May 2 that the brokerage firm of E. F. Hutton & Company had agreed to pay $2 million in fines and restore money to banks victimized by a check-writing scheme that had

A police officer demonstrates a handheld shield adopted by the Boston Police Department in 1985. Called the Body Bunker, it can deflect bullets.

lasted from 1980 to 1982. The scheme gave Hutton the interest-free use of up to $250 million per day that the firm was not entitled to.

On October 9, San Diego Mayor Roger Hedgecock was found guilty of perjury and election-fraud conspiracy. He was convicted on charges involving $350,000 in illegal contributions during his 1983 campaign. On December 10, he was fined $1,000 and sentenced to one year in the custody of the San Diego County sheriff.

On February 28, a federal grand jury indicted Louisiana's Governor Edwin W. Edwards on 50 counts of obstruction of justice, fraud, racketeering, and bribery. The indictment pertained to Edwards' dealings with a hospital consulting firm. A U.S. district judge declared a mistrial on December 18 after the jury failed to reach a unanimous verdict in the case.

Child Abuse. The National Committee for the Prevention of Child Abuse reported on February 16 that complaints about child abuse had jumped some 35 per cent over the past year, in large part because of heightened public awareness.

Bernhard H. Goetz, who in December 1984 shot four men he said were demanding money from him in a New York City subway car, was indicted on charges of assault and attempted murder on March 27, 1985. On January 25, a grand jury had indicted Goetz on relatively minor weapons charges, rejecting charges of attempted murder and reckless endangerment. Manhattan District Attorney Robert M. Morgenthau said the jury concluded that Goetz had shot the men in self-defense. The matter was reconsidered in March after newspaper articles said Goetz reportedly told police he had examined one victim, told him "You don't look so bad," and shot him again.

Night Stalker. On August 31, after a lengthy investigation, California authorities arrested Richard Ramirez in the Night Stalker case. Police had connected the Night Stalker with 36 incidents of crime, including murder, attempted murder, rape, and battery. Most of the victims were young women in the Los Angeles area. On October 24, Ramirez pleaded not guilty to 14 counts of murder and 54 other counts.

Major Crime Reported by police departments to the FBI rose 3 per cent in the first six months of 1985, the first increase in four years. Almost all the increase occurred in the Southern and Western parts of the United States. Among violent crimes for the period, murder declined by 2 per cent, robbery remained at the 1984 level, and rape and aggravated assault were up by 7 per cent. Among property crimes, motor vehicle theft rose 5 per cent; larceny-theft, 4 per cent; arson, 3 per cent; and burglary, 1 per cent.   David C. Beckwith

In WORLD BOOK, see CRIME.

CUBA. The governments of Cuba and the United States exchanged angry words during 1985. The United States increased the volume of the exchange on May 20 by throwing the switch on Radio Martí, a broadcasting service operated by the Voice of America and aimed at Cuba.

With powerful transmitters located in the Florida Keys, the new station, named after Cuban independence hero José Martí, beamed 14½ hours of broadcasting daily at Cuba. The programming included a mix of entertainment and world news designed to inform Cubans, who live under a regime that censors the news.

Refugee Agreement. In retaliation, Cuba's President Fidel Castro revoked his 1984 agreement to take back the 2,746 Cuban criminals and mental patients who were among refugees that came to the United States during a 1980 boat lift. On June 14, 1985, the United States responded in kind by announcing that it would no longer admit Cuban immigrants, as provided by the agreement.

The Year Began on a friendlier note. In an interview with *The Washington Post* published on February 3, Castro raised the possibility of improved U.S.-Cuban relations. Castro even suggested that he would be willing to cooperate in bringing about a peaceful settlement to the civil wars in Central America. He said he would not withdraw Cuban troops from Angola in Africa, where they are

Cuban President Fidel Castro, at right, embraces Nicaraguan President-elect Daniel Ortega in Managua in January, prior to Ortega's inauguration.

helping to prop up a Marxist regime. The United States regards Cuban troop withdrawals from Africa as a precondition for improved relations.

On July 26, the 32nd anniversary of the beginning of the Cuban revolution, Castro again appeared the reasonable leader. In his annual speech, usually the occasion for an attack on "U.S. imperialism," the Cuban leader did not even mention the United States, nor did he cite Radio Martí. Instead, his remarks were concerned almost exclusively with Latin America's debt crisis.

Latin-American Relations. Castro's efforts to improve Cuba's standing with other Latin-American nations met with some success in 1985. He received a visit from the conservative president of Ecuador, León Febres-Cordero, in April. In addition, Brazil, Peru, Uruguay, and Venezuela indicated that they might soon reestablish diplomatic ties with Cuba.

Castro angered many Latin-American officials when he suggested that they not repay their foreign debts, at a time when Cuba was arranging to renegotiate its own foreign-debt payments. Latin-American leaders declined Castro's invitation to attend a conference on the debt issue in Havana from July 30 to August 3. Nathan A. Haverstock

See also LATIN AMERICA (Facts in Brief Table). In WORLD BOOK, see CUBA.

CYPRUS. See EUROPE.

CZECHOSLOVAKIA. On May 22, 1985, Gustáv Husák, 72, was reelected for his third five-year term as president of Czechoslovakia. On June 19, he stressed his regime's rejection of market-oriented economic reforms. In line with a drive for greater discipline in the Soviet Union, however, Czechoslovakia cracked down on corruption in May, arresting, firing, or transferring about 250 customs officials. The officials allegedly had been involved in international smuggling, including drug trafficking. Ladislav Kusy, head of the customs service, was sentenced to 40 years in prison. In October, there were unofficial reports that Finance Minister Leopold Lér was under arrest for alleged involvement in smuggling.

Church and State. The government continued to quarrel with the Roman Catholic Church. In January, František Cardinal Tomášek, the archbishop of Prague, wrote to all the dioceses in Czechoslovakia, urging them to carry out a 1982 Vatican decree aimed at limiting priests' political activities. The decree referred to Pacem in Terris, an association of priests who favor the government. On April 10, Tomášek read a letter from Pope John Paul II to 1,000 priests gathered at Velehrad, Czechoslovakia's most important Roman Catholic shrine. The letter called for church unity.

On April 27, the pope elevated Archbishop Jozef Tomko, a Slovak prelate living in the West,

to the rank of cardinal and named him head of the Vatican's department for evangelization. The government-controlled news media in Czechoslovakia did not report the appointment.

The government and the church also quarreled about celebrating the 1,100th anniversary of the death of Saint Methodius, a Greek-born missionary to the Slavs. He is believed to be buried in Czechoslovakia. Government authorities forbade several European cardinals to enter the country for the main celebration in Velehrad on July 6. But Agostino Cardinal Casaroli, the Vatican's secretary of state, spoke at the celebration. The crowd of about 150,000 booed Milan Klusák, Czechoslovakia's minister of culture, who emphasized the role of Saint Methodius and his brother Saint Cyril as secular educators without mentioning their sainthood.

The Economy. Harsh winter weather disrupted transportation and industry. In the first six months of 1985, industrial production grew by 2.8 per cent, compared with 4.1 per cent in the first half of 1984, and less than planned. Trade with Communist nations grew by 4.7 per cent in the first six months of 1985, compared with the same period in 1984. Trade with non-Communist countries diminished by 6.5 per cent. Chris Cviic

See also EUROPE (Facts in Brief Table). In WORLD BOOK, see CZECHOSLOVAKIA.

DANCING. In 1985, a number of once-stable ballet organizations in the United States experienced administrative and artistic ferment. Perhaps the most dramatic instance concerned Lincoln E. Kirstein, one of the founders of the New York City Ballet and School of American Ballet (SAB), considered one of the finest dance academies in the world. Kirstein is a greatly respected writer and distinguished patron of the arts in the United States.

As president of the SAB, Kirstein in late April 1985 fired Mary L. Porter, the school's director of development. His action was challenged by the SAB's board of directors, and several major donors to the school reportedly threatened to withhold further contributions unless Porter was reinstated. Some board members reportedly considered introducing a motion to dismiss Kirstein as president. The controversy ended on May 15 when the board issued a statement supporting Kirstein's action, but the affair left a residue of mistrust.

New Directors. Changes in other ballet companies reflected the passing of long-time leaders. In early 1985, the San Francisco Ballet was still embroiled in a bitter dispute that erupted in August 1984 over its artistic leadership. Some members of its board of trustees wanted Michael Smuin to continue his 12-year stint as coartistic director. Another group of trustees, however, criticized Smuin's style of choreography. The group critical

Dancers in the American Ballet Theatre use metal folding chairs as partners in David Gordon's *Field, Chair and Mountain,* which premiered in February.

of Smuin was led by the troupe's founder, Lew Christensen, until his death in late 1984. On Feb. 1, 1985, Icelandic dancer Helgi Tomasson, who had just retired as principal dancer of the New York City Ballet, was appointed to succeed Smuin.

The Boston Ballet had been in a state of upheaval since its founder, E. Virginia Williams, retired from public life and subsequently died, on May 8, 1984. In June 1984, director Violette Verdy quit. Following a period of interim leadership, Bruce Marks, who had been director of Ballet West in Salt Lake City, Utah, became director in June 1985.

***Abdallah* Revived.** Ballet West produced the most interesting new ballet production of 1985—a reconstruction of *Abdallah*, an evening-long work by the great Danish choreographer August Bournonville. Created in 1855 and last performed in 1858, *Abdallah* was thought to be a lost ballet until Marks and his Danish-born wife, former ballerina Toni Lander, found a libretto, costume designs, and choreographic notations. *Abdallah*'s revival won acclaim in Salt Lake City on Feb. 20, 1985, and received even wider attention when Ballet West performed it at the John F. Kennedy Center for the Performing Arts in Washington, D.C., in May. A sad footnote is that Lander, who was responsible for the dancers' fine performance in the difficult Bournonville style, died on May 19.

Cunningham and Taylor. In modern dance, two leaders of the older generation, Merce Cunningham and Paul Taylor, had banner years. Their companies toured the United States and performed at festivals in Europe, and they themselves were honored in June when they became the first choreographers to receive MacArthur Foundation awards. Cunningham got $300,000; Taylor, $260,000. Cunningham also received honors from the Kennedy Center on December 8.

Taylor, who marked his 30th anniversary as a choreographer in 1985, created two new works—*Last Look* and *Roses*, both premiered by the Paul Taylor Dance Company in April at the City Center Theater in New York City. With appropriately grim décor by artist Alex Katz, *Last Look* is a savage portrait of the down-and-out. *Roses*, set to music by German composer Richard Wagner—an unlikely choice for a modern dance choreographer—is an abstract dance on the theme of love. At the least, these dances attest to Taylor's versatility. The productions were also popular with the public.

Cunningham also presented new dances at the City Center. *Phrases*, which was first performed in Angers, France, in December 1984, received its U.S. debut in February 1985. *Native Green*, which was given its world premiere on March 12, was especially remarkable for the sheer vibrancy of the choreography and dancing.

Many dances by Taylor and Cunningham have also been picked up by ballet troupes. The Joffrey Ballet, for example, danced Taylor's *Arden Court* for the first time on October 23. And on September 11, the Pennsylvania Ballet in Philadelphia premiered Cunningham's *Arcade* to a score by American composer John Cage. It was the first dance created by Cunningham for a company other than his own since 1973. This marriage of ballet and modern dance was funded by an innovative program, the National Choreography Project, established in 1984.

Touring Program. Another dance program with nationwide scope, the National Performance Network, was announced on March 13, 1985. Funded by the Ford Foundation and the National Endowment for the Arts, the network was designed to subsidize tours for experimental dancers and performance artists. Fourteen American theaters noted for their interest in avant-garde performances were selected to receive financial support from the network. These theaters are in Atlanta, Ga.; Austin, Tex.; Boston; Denver; Chicago; Cincinnati, Ohio; Los Angeles; Minneapolis, Minn.; New Orleans; New York City; Philadelphia; San Francisco; Seattle; and Washington, D.C.

German Companies. Of the companies visiting the United States from abroad in 1985, the most newsworthy came from West Germany. Interpreters of the expressionist movement currently experiencing a vigorous revival, they formed the crux of the Brooklyn Academy of Music's glamorous Next Wave Festival, held from October 1 to December 8 in New York City.

Pina Bausch's Dance Theater from Wuppertal, West Germany, which created a sensation when it opened the Olympic Arts Festival in Los Angeles in June 1984, returned for a three-week season in 1985 with no less power to create controversy. One of Bausch's four productions was an interpretation of the famous musical play *Seven Deadly Sins* (1933) by Kurt Weill and Bertolt Brecht. Another of Bausch's pieces, *Arien*, featured a life-sized hippopotamus (played by two actors) that ambled about in ankle-deep water. Other events from Germany included Reinhild Hoffmann's large-scale *Callas*, based on the life of opera star Maria Callas and performed by the Dance Theater of Bremen, headed by Hoffmann.

Company Notes. The Dance Theatre of Harlem appeared for the first time at the Metropolitan Opera House in New York City in June. In January, the board of directors of the Los Angeles Ballet, citing financial problems, decided to close the company.   Nancy Goldner

In WORLD BOOK, see BALLET; DANCING.

David Parsons and Cathy McCann celebrate romantic love in *Roses*, a new dance piece by Paul Taylor that premiered in New York City in April.

DEATHS

DEATHS of notable persons in 1985 included those listed below. Those listed were Americans unless otherwise indicated. An asterisk (*) indicates the person is the subject of a biography in THE WORLD BOOK ENCYCLOPEDIA.

Abruzzo, Ben (1930-Feb. 11), balloonist who participated in the first balloon crossings of the Atlantic and Pacific oceans in 1978 and 1981, respectively.

Arends, Leslie C. (1895-July 16), Republican congressman from Illinois from 1935 to 1975.

Ashley, Laura (1925-Sept. 17), British designer who in 1953 founded the international textile company that bears her name.

Bailey, Sir Donald (1901-May 5), British engineer who invented the portable Bailey Bridge used in Allied landings during World War II.

Baxter, Anne (1923-Dec. 12), who in 1946 won an Academy Award for best supporting actress for her portrayal of Sophie in *The Razor's Edge*.

Beard, James A. (1903-Jan. 23), author of such best-selling cookbooks as *Beard on Bread* (1973) and *The New James Beard* (1981).

Beck, Julian (1925-Sept. 14), cofounder in 1947 of the avant-garde Living Theater company.

Beckwith, Robert Todd Lincoln (1904-Dec. 24), great-grandson of Abraham Lincoln and that President's last direct descendant.

Benson, Elmer A. (1895-March 13), governor of Minnesota from 1937 to 1939.

Phil Silvers, talented comedian.

Heinrich Böll, German novelist, winner of a 1972 Nobel Prize.

Marc Chagall, noted for his joyous art.

Taylor Caldwell, author of many best-selling novels.

Bessie, Alvah (1904-July 21), author, one of the Hollywood 10 imprisoned by the House Committee on Un-American Activities in the late 1940's for refusing to answer questions about alleged Communist activity in the film industry.

Blake, Eugene C. (1906-July 31), general secretary of the World Council of Churches from 1966 to 1972.

Blanding, Sarah G. (1898-March 3), president of Vassar College in Poughkeepsie, N.Y., from 1946 to 1964—the first woman to hold that post.

Blood, Johnny (John Victor McNally) (1903-Nov. 28), star National Football League halfback of the 1930's, an original member of the Pro Football Hall of Fame.

Blough, Roger M. (1904-Oct. 8), chief executive of U.S. Steel Corporation from 1955 to 1969.

Boland, Frederick (1904-Dec. 4), leading Irish diplomat, ambassador to London from 1950 to 1956.

*Böll, Heinrich (1917-July 16), German novelist, winner of the Nobel Prize for literature in 1972.

Boulting, John (1913-June 17), British filmmaker who produced and directed such comedy films as *I'm All Right, Jack* (1959) and *Heavens Above* (1963).

Boyle, William Anthony (Tony) (1904-May 31), labor union leader who headed the United Mine Workers of America from 1963 to 1972 and was convicted in 1974 of ordering the murder of union rival Joseph A. (Jock) Yablonski and members of his family.

Braudel, Fernand (1902-Nov. 28), renowned French historian whose major works included *The Mediterranean and the Mediterranean World in the Age of Philip II* (1949).

Brooks, Louise (1906-Aug. 8), silent screen actress who symbolized the 1920's flapper.

Brown, Carter (Alan Yates) (1923-May 5), British-born Australian novelist.

Bryant, Sir Arthur (1899-Jan. 22), British historian who wrote such popular sagas as *Dunkirk* (1943) and *Spirit of England* (1982).

Brynner, Yul (1920-Oct. 10), actor born on Japanese island of Sakhalin who won an Oscar for his performance as the king of Siam in the film *The King and I* (1956). He played the role on stage in 4,625 performances.

*Burnet, Sir Macfarlane (1899-Aug. 31), Australian physician and virologist who shared the 1960 Nobel Prize in physiology or medicine.

Burnham, Forbes (1923-Aug. 6), prime minister of Guyana from 1966 to 1980 and president since 1980.

Burrows, Abe (1910-May 17), Broadway writer and director who wrote such hit shows as *Guys and Dolls* (1950) and *Forty Carats* (1968).

Byrnes, John W. (1913-Jan. 12), Republican congressman from Wisconsin from 1945 to 1973.

Caldwell, Taylor (1900-Aug. 30), British-born author of many best sellers.

Calvino, Italo (1923-Sept. 19), Italian novelist and short-story writer. His best-known work was *Italian Folktales* (1980).

Campbell, Kay (1905-May 27), actress who played Kate Martin in the TV series "All My Children" since 1960.

Canaday, John (1907-July 19), noted art critic with *The New York Times* from 1959 to 1977.

*Chagall, Marc (1887-March 28), Russian-born artist whose huge, whimsical paintings and other works adorn many public buildings throughout the world.

Charlotte (1896-July 9), Grand Duchess of Luxembourg from 1919 to 1964.

Chase, James Hadley (René Raymond) (1906-Feb. 6), British-born author of nearly 100 thrillers.

*Chernenko, Konstantin U. (1911-March 10), general secretary of the Communist Party of the Soviet Union. See RUSSIA (Close-Up).

Claire, Ina (1892-Feb. 21), actress who starred in such Broadway comedies as *The Last of Mrs. Cheyney* (1925) and *Ode to Liberty* (1934).

Clarke, Kenny (Klook) (1914-Jan. 26), jazz drummer, a pioneer of bebop with the Modern Jazz Quartet.

Clements, Earle C. (1896-March 12), Democratic governor of Kentucky from 1947 to 1950. He also served as U.S. representative from 1945 to 1947 and as U.S. senator from 1950 to 1957.

Clute, Sidney (1916-Oct. 2), film and television actor best known for his performance as Detective Paul LaGuardia on the "Cagney & Lacey" TV show.

Colasanto, Nicholas (1923?-Feb. 12), actor who played Coach, the bartender in the TV series "Cheers."

Cole, Lester (1904-Aug. 15), screenwriter, one of the Hollywood 10. His screenplays include *Born Free* (1965) written under the pseudonym Gerald L. C. Copley.

Collingwood, Charles (1917-Oct. 3), CBS-TV news correspondent for more than 40 years.

Coots, J. Fred (John Frederick) (1897-April 8), composer of such 1930's songs as *Santa Claus Is Coming to Town* and *You Go to My Head.*

Cowles, Gardner, Jr. (1903-July 8), publisher who founded *Look* magazine in 1937.

Crane, Barry (Barry Cohen) (1928-July 5), film director and tournament bridge champion who won more master points than anyone else in the history of bridge.

Creston, Paul (1906-Aug. 24), musician and composer, best known for his Symphony No. 1 (1943).

Crossley, Archibald M. (1896-May 1), who pioneered in methods of public opinion polling in the 1930's.

Cushman, Robert E., Jr. (1914-Jan. 2), commandant of the U.S. Marine Corps from 1972 to 1975. He served as deputy director of the Central Intelligence Agency (CIA) from 1969 to 1972.

Dale, Edgar (1901-March 8), professor of education at Ohio State University, authority on readability, and special consultant to THE WORLD BOOK ENCYCLOPEDIA.

Davidson, Joe (1914-Sept. 22), Scottish-born Canadian labor leader, head of the Canadian Union of Postal Workers from 1974 to 1977.

Deckers, Jeanine (1933-reported April 1), Belgium's Singing Nun, best known for her hit record "Dominique" (1963). She left her religious order in 1966.

De Rivera, José (1904-March 19), sculptor, noted for his work in bronze and stainless steel.

Desmond, Johnny (1920-Sept. 6), singer who rose to fame as a vocalist with Glenn Miller's Army Air Force Band during World War II.

Dewar, James A. (1897-June 30), baking company manager who invented the Hostess Twinkie in 1930.

Diamond, Selma (1921-May 14), Canadian-born comedy writer and gravel-voiced actress who most recently appeared in the TV series "Night Court."

Douglas-Home, Charles (1937-Oct. 29), British journalist, editor of *The Times* of London since 1982.

Downey, Morton (1901-Oct. 25), popular singer of the 1930's and 1940's, known as "the Irish thrush."

D'Oyly Carte, Dame Bridget (1908-May 2), British director of the D'Oyly Carte Opera Company from 1948 until its demise in 1982.

*Dubuffet, Jean (1901-May 12), French painter noted for his primitive style and rich textures.

Eisenhower, Milton S. (1899-May 2), diplomat, adviser to six Presidents.

*Enders, John F. (1897-Sept. 1), bacteriologist, co-winner of the 1954 Nobel Prize in physiology or medicine.

Erlander, Tage F. (1901-June 21), prime minister of Sweden from 1946 to 1969.

Ervin, Sam J., Jr. (1896-April 23), Democratic senator from North Carolina from 1954 to 1975. He directed the Senate Watergate investigation.

Fetchit, Stepin (Lincoln Theodore Perry) (1902-Nov. 19), black motion-picture comedian.

Fisher, Gordon N. (1928-Aug. 8), president of Southam, Incorporated, Canada's largest newspaper chain.

Cootie Williams, trumpet player with Duke Ellington.

Samantha Smith, a messenger for peace.

Sam J. Ervin, Jr., eloquent senator from North Carolina.

James Beard, author of popular cookbooks.

Fitzgerald, Robert (1910-Jan. 16), poet, noted for his rich imagery. His bold translations of Homer's *Odyssey* (1961) and *Iliad* (1974) became classics.

Flory, Paul J. (1910-Sept. 9), chemist, winner of the 1974 Nobel Prize for chemistry.

Foster, Phil (Fivel Feldman) (1914-July 8), stand-up comic and actor who played the father of Laverne in the hit television series "Laverne and Shirley" from 1976 to 1983.

George-Brown, Lord (1914-June 2), British Labour Party politician, foreign secretary from 1966 to 1968.

Gernreich, Rudi (1922-April 21), Austrian-born fashion designer known for his avant-garde fashions.

Gilels, Emil (1916-Oct. 14), Soviet musician, one of the world's great pianists.

Gordon, Ruth (1896-Aug. 28), actress and writer whose 70-year career included an Oscar for best supporting actress for her performance in *Rosemary's Baby* (1968).

Gould, Chester (1900-May 11), cartoonist who created Dick Tracy in 1931. See Close-Up.

*Graves, Robert (1895-Dec. 7), English poet, novelist, and classical scholar whose novels included *I, Claudius* (1934).

Greene, Richard (1918-June 1), British actor best known for his starring role in the 1950's TV series "Robin Hood."

Grimes, Burleigh (1893-Dec. 6), baseball Hall of Famer and the last legal spitball pitcher in the major leagues.

Guarnieri, Johnny (1917-Jan. 7), a leading jazz pianist of the swing era.

DEATHS

Margaret Hamilton,
a bewitching actress.

Eugene Ormandy, conductor of
the Philadelphia Orchestra.

F. R. Scott, Canada's
poet-politician.

Konstantin U. Chernenko,
leader of the Soviet Union.

Hamilton, Margaret (1902-May 16), actress best known for her performance as the Wicked Witch of the West in the classic film *The Wizard of Oz* (1939).

Harlech, Lord (William David Ormsby Gore) (1918-Jan. 26), British diplomat.

*Harris, Patricia R. (1924-March 23), secretary of housing and urban development from 1977 to 1979 and secretary of health, education, and welfare from 1979 to 1981, the first black woman to hold a Cabinet post.

Hayes, Alfred (1911-Aug. 14), poet and screenwriter. His poem "Joe Hill" became a popular ballad.

Hayward, Louis (1909-Feb. 21), South African-born actor known for his swashbuckling performances.

Hecht, Harold (1908-May 25), Hollywood film producer.

Helstein, Ralph (1908-Feb. 14), labor union leader, president of the United Packinghouse Workers of America from 1946 to 1968.

Hewitt, Foster (1902-April 21), Canadian radio announcer known as the "voice of hockey."

Holland, Jerome (1916-Jan. 13), U.S. ambassador to Sweden from 1970 to 1972 and the first black member of the New York Stock Exchange.

Holt, John (1923-Sept. 14), educator whose book *How Children Fail* (1964) denounced the quality of education in U.S. schools.

Hopman, Harry (1906-Dec. 28), former Australian Davis Cup tennis coach.

Horrocks, Sir Brian G. (1895-Jan. 6), British general and military writer who served in World Wars I and II.

Hough, Henry Beetle (1896-June 6), acclaimed editor of the *Vineyard Gazette* in Edgartown, Mass., for 65 years.

*Hoxha, Enver (1908-April 11), first secretary of Albania's Communist Party since 1944.

Hudson, Rock (Roy Fitzgerald) (1925-Oct. 2), Hollywood star, a romantic idol in such films as *Giant* (1956) and in the TV series "McMillan and Wife."

Hughes, Sarah T. (1896-April 23), federal district judge who swore in President Lyndon B. Johnson after President John F. Kennedy was assassinated in 1963.

Hutchinson, Edward (1914-July 22), Republican congressman from Michigan from 1963 to 1977.

Ingersoll, Ralph McA. (1900-March 8), editor and publisher, founder of the newspaper *PM* and the first managing editor of *The New Yorker* magazine.

Jenner, William E. (1908-March 9), Republican senator from Indiana in 1944 and 1945 and from 1947 to 1959.

Johnson, Paul B. (1916-Oct. 14), Democratic governor of Mississippi from 1964 to 1968.

Jones, Jo (1911-Sept. 3), pioneering jazz drummer with Count Basie's band from 1935 to 1948.

Jones, Philly Joe (1923-Aug. 30), leading modern-jazz drummer who played with the Miles Davis quintet.

Karas, Anton (1906-Jan. 10), Austrian zither player who composed the haunting theme for the film *The Third Man* (1949).

Kelly, Charles E. (Commando Kelly) (1921-Jan. 11), U.S. Army sergeant who single-handedly fought off a German platoon in World War II.

Kertész, André (1894-Sept. 27), Hungarian-born photographer whose tender images of everyday life influenced modern photography.

Kimball, Spencer W. (1895-Nov. 5), president of the Church of Jesus Christ of Latter-day Saints since 1974.

King, Wayne (1901-July 16), bandleader and saxophonist known as The Waltz King.

*Kuznets, Simon (1901-July 8), Russian-born economist who won the 1971 Nobel Prize in economics.

Kyser, Kay (1906-July 23), bandleader whose swing-era band entertained millions on radio.

Langer, Susanne K. (1895-July 17), philosopher whose work on aesthetics profoundly affected modern thinking on psychology and social sciences.

Larkin, Philip (1922-Dec. 2), British poet whose witty, objective poems touched a universal chord.

List, Eugene (1918-March 1), concert pianist noted for his wide repertory and stylistic knowledge.

*Lodge, Henry Cabot, Jr. (1902-Feb. 27), Republican senator from Massachusetts from 1937 to 1944 and 1947 to 1953. He served as ambassador to the United Nations from 1953 to 1960.

Lodge, John D. (1903-Oct. 29), Republican governor of Connecticut from 1951 to 1955. He also served as congressman from 1947 to 1951.

London, George (1920-March 24), Canadian-born bass-baritone opera star.

Long, Gillis W. (1923-Jan. 20), Democratic congressman from Louisiana since 1973.

MacDougall, Curtis D. (1903-Nov. 10), professor of journalism at Northwestern University from 1942 to 1971 and a strong influence on American journalism. His books include *Interpretative Reporting* (1932).

MacInnes, Helen (1907-Sept. 30), Scottish-born novelist whose 21 best-selling espionage stories included *Assignment in Brittany* (1942) and *Ride a Pale Horse* (1985).

Maltz, Albert (1908-April 26), screenwriter, one of the Hollywood 10. He won Oscars in 1942 and 1945 for his documentaries.

*Maris, Roger (1934-Dec. 14), baseball player who in 1961 hit 61 home runs for the New York Yankees, breaking Babe Ruth's record of 60 in 1927.

Marks, Johnny (1909-Sept. 3), musician who wrote the song "Rudolph the Red-Nosed Reindeer" (1949).

Cartoonist on the Side of the Law

The art of the comic strip lost one of its most influential figures on May 11, 1985, with the death of Chester Gould, who created the famous police detective Dick Tracy and kept him thwarting villains for 46 years. Gould was a pioneer of realism in the comic pages. Many comic strips before his time told continuing stories, but none were based as closely on the real world as "Dick Tracy." Gould took the reader right into the squad car chasing the criminal or into the hideouts where the bad guys hatched their evil schemes. Tracy got into such suspenseful scrapes that anxious readers, too impatient to wait for the outcome of a story, sometimes smuggled the next day's comic pages out of newspaper offices.

Gould was born in Pawnee, Okla., on Nov. 20, 1900. He graduated from Northwestern University in Evanston, Ill., in 1923 and became a cartoonist for Hearst Publications the next year. He joined the *Chicago Tribune* staff in 1931, the year he created "Dick Tracy."

During his nearly five decades at the drawing board—until 1977, when he turned the strip over to his assistants—Gould compiled a "Who's Who" of criminal masterminds, including such memorable villains as Pruneface, Shakey, 88 Keyes, Spots, B-B Eyes, the Mole, and Mumbles. Another cast of characters, friendly and whimsical folks such as B.O. Plenty and his wife, Gravel Gertie, also contributed to the strip's popularity. Many readers who were not particularly interested in kidnappings and shoot-outs would search out "Dick Tracy" each day to keep up with the B.O. Plentys and their fellow eccentrics. In all, Gould created more than 250 characters who will live on in comic-strip annals.

In contrast to his numerous one-dimensional characters, Gould was a many-sided man who combined a masterful storytelling touch with a vivid imagination and a delightful sense of humor. He was also a hard worker. Even after "Dick Tracy" had gained a wide following and was syndicated in hundreds of newspapers, Gould would frequently redo a strip two or three times until it satisfied him. To inject authenticity into his stories, he sought advice from police departments and took courses in fingerprinting, firearms, and other aspects of police work.

Gould was fascinated with the modern technology used in law enforcement, and he conjured up a number of devices that were ahead of their time—each carefully pointed out to the reader with a tiny arrow and a label. Tracy's two-way wrist radio appeared in 1945, inspired by the Army's walkie-talkie. In today's strip, it is still in use, augmented by a two-way wrist television. Gould created Diet Smith, the owner of a megabucks corporation, to invent and manufacture other crime-fighting tools for Tracy: night-sights for police officers' guns, machines to identify culprits by their voiceprints, and even worldwide criminal line-ups via television.

Chester Gould and Dick Tracy came on the scene when comics that were merely funny were no longer enough to satisfy newspaper readers. Together, they brought to the comic pages the excitement of patrolling with an untouchable supersleuth who could dodge a stream of Tommy-gun bullets, or the thrill of riding in a getaway car with the likes of Stooge Viller and Littleface and Flattop. Gould fashioned a folk hero, and in so doing he made the comic strip an art form.

Dick Locher

Dick Locher, who has drawn "Dick Tracy" since 1983, created this tribute to the strip's originator, Chester Gould, shown, *right,* at work in 1965.

DEATHS

Marriott, J. Willard (1900-August 13), founder of a $3-billion hotel and catering business.

Marshall, Fred (1906-June 5), Democratic congressman from Minnesota from 1949 to 1963.

Marshall-Cornwall, Sir James (1887-Dec. 25), who became the British army's youngest general in 1934 at the age of 47.

Mayer, Sir Robert (1879-Jan. 9), British philanthropist who founded musical education programs for children.

Medici, Emilio G. (1905-Oct. 9), president of Brazil from 1969 to 1974.

Miller, Arnold R. (1923-July 12), president of the United Mine Workers of America from 1972 to 1979.

Miller, Marvin (1913-Feb. 8), actor in the 1950's TV series "The Millionaire."

Montagu, Ewen (1901-July 19), former British intelligence officer who masterminded a hoax that deceived the Nazis about Allied landings in World War II.

Mungo, Van Lingle (1912-Feb. 12), baseball pitcher who played 14 major-league seasons from 1931 to 1945.

Naipaul, Shiva (1945-Aug. 13), Trinidad-born journalist, author of such books as *North of South* (1979) and *Beyond the Dragon's Mouth* (1985).

Nash, Clarence (Ducky) (1904-Feb. 20), actor who provided the squawking voice for Walt Disney's Donald Duck since 1934.

Nelson, Ricky (Eric Hilliard Nelson) (1940-Dec. 31), who portrayed himself on the TV series "The Adventures of Ozzie and Harriet" and was a popular singer.

Nolan, Lloyd (1902-Sept. 27), actor whose 50-year career included his acclaimed performance as Captain Queeg in *The Caine Mutiny Court Martial.*

Norris, Bruce A. (1924-Dec. 31), former owner of the Detroit Red Wings and a member of the National Hockey League Hall of Fame.

O'Brien, Edmond (1915-May 9), actor who won an Oscar in 1954 for his performance in *The Barefoot Contessa.*

Oppenheimer, Frank F. (1912-Feb. 3), nuclear physicist who worked on the Manhattan Project.

*Ormandy, Eugene (1899-March 12), Hungarian-born orchestra conductor with the Philadelphia Orchestra from 1936 to 1980.

Osijchuk, Hryhorij (1898-Feb. 13), Russian-born archbishop, head of the Ukrainian Orthodox Church in the United States since 1971.

Peary, Harold (1908-March 30), actor who played Throckmorton P. Gildersleeve on "The Great Gildersleeve" radio show in the 1940's.

Porter, Rodney R. (1917-Sept. 7), British biochemist, co-winner of the 1972 Nobel Prize for physiology or medicine.

Pritikin, Nathan (1915-Feb. 21), nutritionist who advocated a strict regimen of exercise and a salt-free, low-cholesterol diet to treat heart disease.

Pullins, Albert (Runt) (1911-Oct. 19), a member of the original Harlem Globetrotters basketball team from 1929 to 1934.

Quinlan, Karen Ann (1954-June 11), young woman whose comatose condition since 1975 touched off a national debate after her parents won a court battle to remove her from a life-sustaining respirator.

Ramu (1965-Feb. 18), India's "Wolf Boy," found in the jungle in 1976 and thought to have been raised by wolves.

*Redgrave, Sir Michael (1908-March 21), British Shakespearean actor, star of such films as *The Lady Vanishes* (1938) and *The Browning Version* (1951).

Richter, Charles F. (1900-Sept. 30), seismologist who in 1935 devised the Richter scale for measuring the intensity of earthquakes.

Riddle, Nelson (1921-Oct. 6), composer and arranger who won an Oscar for his score for *The Great Gatsby* (1975).

*Romulo, Carlos Pena (1901-Dec. 15), noted Filipino diplomat and author.

Rosenstock, Joseph (1895-Oct. 17), conductor of such orchestras as the Metropolitan Opera in New York City and the Nippon Philharmonic in Tokyo.

Rothstein, Arthur (1915-Nov. 11), photojournalist, noted for his vivid pictures of the Dust Bowl during the Great Depression of the 1930's.

*Roy, Maurice Cardinal (1905-Oct. 24), Canadian religious leader, Roman Catholic primate of Canada from 1956 to 1981.

Sandman, Charles W., Jr. (1921-Aug. 26), Republican congressman from New Jersey from 1967 to 1975.

Sarkis, Elias (1924-June 27), president of Lebanon from 1976 to 1982.

Schlamme, Martha (1925-Oct. 6), Austrian-born soprano, best known for her Kurt Weill interpretations.

*Scott, F. R. (Francis Reginald) (1899-Jan. 31), Canadian politician and poet. He helped establish the New Democratic Party.

Scourby, Alexander (1913-Feb. 23), actor who narrated hundreds of records for the blind, including the entire King James version of the Bible. He also narrated TV documentaries, including "Victory at Sea" (1960).

*Sessions, Roger (1896-March 16), composer of symphonies, chamber music, and operas, including his most popular work, *The Black Maskers* (1923).

Shivers, Allan (1907-Jan. 14), Democratic governor of Texas from 1949 to 1957.

Patricia R. Harris, a Cabinet member.

Rock Hudson, romantic leading man in many Hollywood films.

Lord George-Brown, British politician.

Ruth Gordon, actress whose brilliant career ran 70 years.

Shook, Karel (1920-July 25), ballet master who cofounded the Dance Theatre of Harlem in 1968.

Shore, Eddie (1902-March 16), Canadian-born hockey player, the only defenseman to win the Hart Trophy for Most Valuable Player four times.

Signoret, Simone (1921-Sept. 30), French actress who won an Oscar in 1959 for her performance in the film *Room at the Top.*

Silvers, Phil (1912-Nov. 1), comedian of stage, screen, and television, best known as Sergeant Bilko on the 1950's TV series "The Phil Silvers Show."

Sims, Zoot (John Haley Sims) (1925-March 23), jazz saxophonist with such bands as those of Benny Goodman and Stan Kenton.

Sloane, Eric (Everard Jean Hinrichs) (1905-March 6), artist noted for his paintings of early Americana and for such skyscapes as the six-story mural at the Smithsonian Institution's National Air and Space Museum in Washington, D.C.

Smith, Samantha (1972-Aug. 25), schoolgirl whose 1983 letter to Soviet leader Yuri V. Andropov launched her on a tour of the Soviet Union to promote peace.

Snyder, John W. (1895-Oct. 9), U.S. secretary of the treasury from 1946 to 1953.

Sondergaard, Gale (1901-Aug. 14), actress who won an Oscar for her performance in *Anthony Adverse* (1936).

*****Sparkman, John J.** (1899-Nov. 16), Democratic senator from Alabama from 1947 to 1979.

Spiegel, Sam (1903-Dec. 31), Austrian-born film producer whose movies won many Academy Awards.

Springer, Axel (1912-Sept. 22), West German who headed one of Western Europe's publishing empires.

*****Stewart, Potter** (1915-Dec. 7), associate justice of the Supreme Court of the United States from 1958 to 1981.

*****Sturgeon, Theodore (Edward Hamilton Waldo)** (1918-May 8), science-fiction writer.

Surtees, Robert L. (1906-Jan. 5), Hollywood cinematographer who won Oscars for his work in *The Bad and the Beautiful* (1952), *King Solomon's Mines* (1950), and *Ben-Hur* (1959).

Tanny, Vic (1912-June 11), physical fitness buff who led in the development of health clubs in the 1930's and 1940's.

Tebelak, John-Michael (1948-April 2), playwright and director, best known for the musical *Godspell* (1971).

Terry, Luther L. (1911-March 29), surgeon general of the United States from 1961 to 1965. He was instrumental in preparing the 1964 report warning of the dangers of cigarette smoking.

Tillstrom, Burr (1917-Dec. 6), puppeteer, creator of the "Kukla, Fran, and Ollie" TV show.

Turner, Big Joe (Joseph Vernon Turner) (1911-Nov. 24), Kansas City blues singer often called "Boss of the Blues."

Visser 't Hooft, Willem A. (1900-July 4), Dutch clergyman, secretary general of the World Council of Churches from its beginning in 1948 to 1966.

Vokes, Christopher (1904-March 27), military officer who led the Canadian Army during World War II.

Wallop, (John) Douglass (1920-April 1), author whose novels included *The Year the Yankees Lost the Pennant* (1954), which became the hit musical *Damn Yankees.*

Walsh, Adam (1901-Jan. 12), football coach, once captain of the undefeated Notre Dame team that featured The Four Horsemen and The Seven Mules.

Wambsganss, Bill (William Adolph Wambsganss) (1894-Dec. 8), who became a baseball legend in 1920 when, as the Cleveland Indians second baseman, he made an unassisted triple play in the World Series against the Brooklyn Dodgers.

*****Ward, Lynd Kendall** (1905-June 28), artist who won the Caldecott Medal in 1953 for *The Biggest Bear.*

Weatherwax, Rudd (1908-Feb. 25), Hollywood dog trainer who trained the original Lassie in the film *Lassie Come Home* (1943).

Yul Brynner, actor who played the king of Siam 4,625 times.

Michael Redgrave, noted British actor.

Henry Cabot Lodge, member of the Senate and UN ambassador.

Laura Ashley, top textile designer.

Weir, Walter C. (1929-April 17), Canadian politician, Progressive Conservative premier of Manitoba from 1967 to 1969.

Welch, Robert H. W. (1899-Jan. 6), a founder of the John Birch Society in 1958.

*****Welles, Orson** (1915-Oct. 10), legendary actor and director. See MOTION PICTURES (Close-Up).

*****White, E. B. (Elwyn Brooks White)** (1899-Oct. 1), author and essayist whose style and wit helped set the tone of *The New Yorker* magazine. His classic children's books included *Charlotte's Web* (1952) and his contributions to American English usage in *The Elements of Style* influenced generations of writers and students.

Williams, Charles (Cootie) (1913-Sept. 15), trumpet player with Duke Ellington's Orchestra, 1928 to 1940.

Williams, Tex (1917-Oct. 11), country and western singer whose hits included "Smoke! Smoke! Smoke That Cigarette!" and "Texas in My Soul."

Williams, Tom (1885-July 25), Canadian aviator, a founding member of the Royal Canadian Air Force.

Wirkkala, Tapio (1915-May 19), Finnish designer, a pioneer in modern Scandinavian design.

Wolfenden, Lord (John Frederick Wolfenden) (1906-Jan. 18), British educator and social reformer.

Woodruff, Robert W. (1889-March 7), corporate leader who headed the Coca-Cola Company from 1923 to 1955.

Zimbalist, Efrem (1889-Feb. 22), Russian-born violinist, celebrated for his assured technique and sensitive interpretation. Irene B. Keller

DELAWARE. See STATE GOVERNMENT.

DEMOCRATIC PARTY. Reeling after the landslide defeat of former United States Vice President Walter F. Mondale in the November 1984 presidential election, the Democratic Party spent much of 1985 trying to regroup. Democratic leaders also worked to spruce up the party's image and revive its appeal.

New Chairman. The first order of business—the election of a new chairman of the Democratic National Committee (DNC) to succeed outgoing Chairman Charles T. Manatt—resulted in a divisive fight. There were four aspirants for the job: Paul G. Kirk, Jr., the party treasurer and a former assistant to Senator Edward M. Kennedy (D., Mass.); Terry Sanford, former governor of North Carolina; Nancy Pelosi, former California Democratic chairman; and Robert J. Keefe, a long-time Washington, D.C., political figure. Kirk had strong support from organized labor and from the party's liberal wing. Sanford had firm backing from Southern state chairmen and such prominent party moderates as Governors Charles S. Robb of Virginia and Bruce E. Babbitt of Arizona.

When the DNC met in Washington, D.C., on February 1, Pelosi withdrew and gave her support to Sanford. Keefe also stepped aside and backed Sanford.

After Sanford lost to Kirk, 151 to 203, many

Paul G. Kirk, Jr., wields the gavel at a Democratic National Committee (DNC) meeting in Washington, D.C., in February after being elected DNC chairman.

black and Southern delegates left the meeting in an angry mood. Some moderates complained that union representatives had wielded too much power on Kirk's behalf. A number of blacks were dismayed because Kirk had derailed the campaign of Richard G. Hatcher, the black mayor of Gary, Ind., for the DNC vice chairmanship. Although Hatcher had received the endorsement of the party's black caucus, Kirk engineered the election of another black, Illinois Comptroller Roland W. Burris, as vice chairman.

Kirk Goes South. Two weeks after his election, Kirk met in Atlanta, Ga., with Democratic leaders of 13 Southern states. He acknowledged that the growing number of single-issue interest groups within the party was making "diversity a weakness" but added that the party had always thrived on diversity. Noting the growing mood of conservatism among Democrats, Kirk cautioned, "We can't succeed if we turn our backs on the [traditional Democratic] coalition"—blacks, intellectuals, and wage earners.

Throughout February, the DNC chairman tried to head off a movement by Democratic officeholders in the South and West to create a Democratic Leadership Council, independent of the formal party machinery, to push the party in a more conservative direction. Kirk signaled his intent to set up a similar policy council within the DNC. But the non-DNC panel was launched on February 28 by an all-male group that included two black members of Congress, Representatives William H. (Bill) Gray III of Pennsylvania and Allan D. Wheat of Missouri. Among its principal sponsors were Governors Robb and Babbitt; Congressman James C. Wright, Jr., of Texas, the Democratic leader of the House of Representatives; Senator Sam Nunn of Georgia; and Representative Richard A. Gephardt of Missouri.

Taking Stock. Although the Democratic Party held on to its House majority in the 1984 election, party members felt compelled in 1985 to do some soul-searching. They gathered at the Greenbrier resort in White Sulphur Springs, W. Va., for a three-day retreat in early March to assess their problems. Much of the cost was financed by corporate and union lobbying groups, whose representatives were permitted to attend the closed sessions.

The Chairman Scores Points. During the spring, Kirk won the approval of many who had opposed his election when he reduced the policymaking influence of a number of special-interest groups, denounced the 1984 labor union tactic of endorsing a presidential candidate before the party primaries, and named party members from the South and West—most of them male and white—to important party posts. On May 15, Kirk announced the formation of a new group, the Democratic Policy Commission, to guide the party's quest for a new image that will lure back disillusioned voters.

Meeting in Washington, D.C., in June, the DNC heeded Kirk's advice and voted against holding a midterm convention in 1986. Such meetings had been held in each midterm election year since 1974, but Kirk argued they were a waste of time, money, and energy. The delegates also approved Kirk's nominees to a Fairness Commission to review the party's rules for nominating presidential candidates. Donald L. Fowler, former South Carolina Democratic chairman, was named chairman of the commission.

On October 18, the commission agreed with Kirk's call for only minor changes in the nominating process, with one exception: It proposed lowering from 20 to 15 per cent the minimum amount of votes a candidate must get in a state caucus or primary to qualify for a proportional share of the state's delegates to the party's national convention. A few days later, Jesse L. Jackson of Chicago, who had complained that the 20 per cent threshold had deprived him of delegates in his 1984 run for the presidency, said the 5 percentage point change was still unfair to minority candidates.   Frank Cormier and Margot Cormier

See also ELECTIONS; REPUBLICAN PARTY. In WORLD BOOK, see DEMOCRATIC PARTY.

DENMARK suffered from labor unrest and nationwide demonstrations during March and April 1985. Employers resisted union demands for a two-year wage agreement with a 4 per cent pay hike and a cut in the workweek from 40 to 38½ hours. Danes fearing a strike bought large supplies of fuels, milk, meat, bread, fruit, and beer, putting these goods in short supply.

Discussions among employers, unions, and a government arbitrator broke down on March 21. On March 24, flights and ferry services were disrupted, air mail was suspended, and schools were closed as 300,000 men and women stopped work.

The Government Acts. On March 27, Prime Minister Poul Schlüter proposed an immediate return to work, maximum pay increases of 2 per cent for 1985 and 1.5 per cent for 1986, a 39-hour workweek, and a compulsory savings plan for the highest-paid workers. But 1,500 workers blockaded Christiansborg Palace, the home of the Folketing (parliament), preventing more than half the members of that body from getting in to vote on the measure. On March 30, police escorted Schlüter through the unruly crowd and into the palace, where he managed to get his proposal passed.

Workers ignored the call for an immediate return to their jobs. On April 10, demonstrations by hundreds of thousands of workers brought the

Rioters in Copenhagen, Denmark, use a sentry box to batter the door of the prime minister's offices in April, protesting legislation to end a strike.

country to a halt. On the following day, however, workers began to drift back to their jobs.

Greenland Quits EC. Greenland withdrew from the European Community (EC or Common Market) on February 1. The EC bought fishing rights from Greenland for $20 million, as specified in the withdrawal treaty. (Greenland is a province of Denmark but has its own government responsible for internal affairs.)

Defense. Great Britain's Secretary of State for Defence Michael Heseltine, visiting Copenhagen on June 4, called on Denmark to pay its share of the cost of installing Pershing 2 and cruise missiles in North Atlantic Treaty Organization (NATO) countries. (Denmark is a member of NATO, but that organization did not plan to install any of the missiles in Denmark.) On May 14, the Folketing voted, 64 to 4, against cooperation in research connected with the United States Strategic Defense Initiative, also known as "Star Wars."

Austerity Continues. Finance Minister Palle Simonsen said on August 15 that measures designed to end Denmark's budgetary and payments deficits were likely to continue through the 1980's. He presented a budget that froze spending at $17 billion for the third year.   Kenneth Brown

See also EUROPE (Facts in Brief Table). In WORLD BOOK, see DENMARK.

DENTISTRY. Dentist Arthur Mashberg of the New Jersey College of Medicine and Dentistry in Newark, N.J., reported in July 1985 that there is no link between cancer and mouthwash. Some researchers had suggested that the alcohol in mouthwash may be a cancer risk factor. Mashberg studied 96 male patients suffering from mouth or throat cancer and compared them with a control group of cancer-free volunteers. He found that the risk of cancer was actually slightly less for the mouthwash users. The study did confirm a link between oral cancer and alcohol consumption; 71 per cent of the people in the cancer group but only 44 per cent of those in the control group drank at least 6 ounces (180 milliliters) of alcohol per day.

New Cleft Lip Clue. A long-term study carried out in Denmark indicated that cleft lip and palate, a common birth defect, might be caused by environmental as well as genetic factors. The study was reported in mid-1985 by geneticist Michael Melnick of the University of Southern California School of Dentistry in Los Angeles. "We need to identify the specific environmental factors that might be involved," said Melnick, "such as toxic wastes and drugs." Because defining environmental factors has been difficult, Melnick will concentrate on genetic factors in an ongoing study in

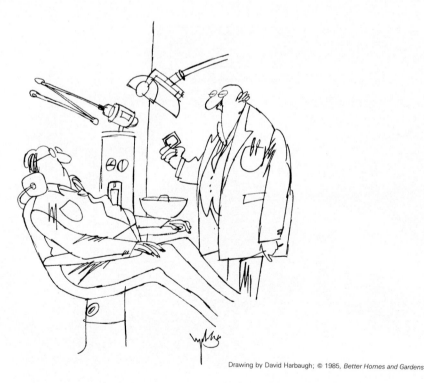

Drawing by David Harbaugh; © 1985, *Better Homes and Gardens.*

"From the looks of these x-rays you're going to have a cavity in your wallet."

China, where there is a high incidence of children born with this malformation.

The Prediction that the number of dental offices in shopping malls would multiply has not proved correct, according to an American Dental Association (ADA) survey reported in September 1985. The survey found that only 2 per cent of all dental care in the United States is actually offered in such locations. The ADA study also found that the one-dentist practice will continue to be the predominant mode of treating dental patients.

Herbs That Prevent Decay. Dental researchers in Taiwan tested herbal medicines used for thousands of years in China to treat tooth decay and gum disease. They reported in March 1985 that they have found some extracts from these plants that inhibit the growth of bacteria responsible for causing the decay and disease. The researchers are now working to find the active ingredients of these extracts, which then could be used in toothpaste or mouthwash formulas.

Christine Wu-Yuan of the Yang-Ming Medical College in Taipei told the International Association for Dental Research that she and her colleagues examined old Chinese medical books that identified about 60 herbs commonly recommended for treating dental problems.   Lou Joseph

In WORLD BOOK, see CLEFT PALATE; DENTISTRY; TEETH.

DETROIT. The United States automobile industry, based in Detroit, continued its gradual recovery in the 1985 model year, selling nearly 8.4 million cars—more than in any year since 1979. Despite that bright note, the economic picture was mixed, with three large employers shutting down local plants. Also during the year, Detroit Mayor Coleman A. Young was elected to a fourth term, and several important building projects were planned or completed.

Election. Young finished a solid first in the city's mayoral primary on September 10, and he won reelection easily over challenger Thomas Barrow, an accountant, in the November 5 general election. Young, the city's first black chief executive, took office in 1974 and is the longest-serving mayor in Detroit history.

In April, Young introduced a $1.65-billion city budget for 1985-1986 that called for the hiring of nearly 800 new police officers. But the hiring plan was threatened in June when a contract arbitrator awarded Detroit's police officers and fire fighters salary increases that would cost the city more than it had budgeted for such pay hikes. Earlier in 1985, the city rehired more than 700 officers who had been laid off in 1979 and 1980.

Building Projects. Several major developments proceeded on schedule in 1985. The Michigan legislature approved tax increases on liquor and

hotel rooms to pay for a $200-million expansion of Cobo Hall, the city's major civic center.

Among the projects completed in 1985 were a 465-acre (188.2-hectare), $1.2-billion General Motors Corporation automobile assembly plant in the city's Poletown section; the Millender Center, a $73-million hotel and apartment complex in downtown Detroit; and Trappers Alley, a $20-million "festival market place" in the city's Greektown neighborhood.

A movement to redevelop a seedy area of warehouses and factories along the Detroit River gained momentum in 1985. In April, ground was broken for a privately owned 48-acre (19.4-hectare) complex of condominiums, apartments, and retail stores that will be built around a series of lagoons leading to the river. The city made plans to erect a middle-income housing project a few blocks from the river and to construct two new parks on the riverfront. In addition, city officials encouraged local industrialists to buy and develop large blocks of land along the waterway.

New construction was also scheduled or proposed for other parts of the city. A developer announced plans to convert the 25-story J. L. Hudson department store in downtown Detroit, which closed in 1983, to office, retail, and parking space, at an estimated cost of $60 million. Another developer proposed the construction of a $400-million complex of 12 gambling casinos and luxury hotels on Belle Isle, an island in the Detroit River within the city limits. Young said he would appoint a committee to study the issue. Both the city and the state would have to approve the plan.

Economic Woes. Although redevelopment projects boomed, there were trouble spots in the city's economy. The year saw the closing of several major Detroit manufacturing facilities, including the Stroh Brewery Company's 75-year-old plant, the 71-year-old Wonder Bread bakery, and the main plant of Vernor's, Incorporated, which had bottled ginger ale in Detroit for 119 years. As a result, more than 1,500 employees lost their jobs.

People Mover. The $210-million People Mover, a 2.9-mile (4.7-kilometer) elevated train that will loop around the city's downtown area, developed dozens of serious cracks in its concrete guideway during construction in 1985. The federal government, after balking for several months at the city's plea for more money to help cover $72.5 million in cost overruns on the project, agreed to contribute another $52.6 million. The People Mover is scheduled to carry its first riders in February 1987. The financially strapped Southeastern Michigan Transportation Authority, which owns the People Mover, voted in October 1985 to turn the entire project over to the city.   David W. Kushma

See also CITY. In WORLD BOOK, see DETROIT.

DISARMAMENT. See ARMED FORCES.

DISASTERS. More people died in airplane disasters during 1985 than in any other year in history. Civil aviation accidents claimed 2,089 lives. The worst accident in history involving a single plane occurred when a Japan Air Lines jet slammed into Mount Osutaka, Japan, in August, killing 520 people.

The worst natural disasters occurred in Bangladesh, Mexico, and Colombia. A tidal wave driven by hurricane-force winds of 100 miles (160 kilometers) per hour struck Bangladesh in May. The wall of water swept over towns on the southern coast and low-lying islands in the Ganges River Delta, washing away several inhabited islands. No one knows how many people died, but estimates range from 10,000 to 40,000.

On September 19, Mexico was rocked by the most devastating earthquake ever to hit North America. The next day, a second earthquake demolished many buildings weakened by the first quake. The two quakes left more than 7,000 people dead and thousands more missing.

In November, the Nevado del Ruiz volcano in northern Colombia erupted in a roar of hot ash. The heat melted the volcano's snowcap and sent an avalanche of mud down the mountain, burying the city of Armero. The eruption, which left about 25,000 people dead, was the deadliest since the 1902 eruption of Mount Pelée in Martinique, which killed about 38,000 people.

Disasters that resulted in 45 or more deaths in 1985 included the following:

Aircraft Crashes

Jan. 21—Reno, Nev. A chartered plane returning from a weekend gambling trip slammed into a recreational vehicle dealer's lot, causing 70 deaths.

Feb. 1—Near Minsk, Soviet Union. At least 80 passengers died in the crash of a Soviet Aeroflot jetliner shortly after it took off from Minsk.

Feb. 19—Near Durango, Spain. A Spanish jetliner collided with a mountaintop television aerial and crashed, causing the deaths of all 148 people aboard.

May 3—Western Ukraine, Soviet Union. A Soviet airliner collided in midair with a small military plane, killing about 80 people.

June 23—Off Ireland. An Air-India jetliner broke apart in midair, killing all 329 people on board. Sabotage was suspected but had not been proved by year-end.

July 10—Soviet Union. A Soviet airliner carrying up to 150 passengers crashed on a flight from Karshi to Leningrad, killing everyone on board.

July 24—Near Leticia, Colombia. A Colombian air force plane crashed, killing all 81 people on board.

Aug. 2—Near Dallas. A Delta Air Lines jumbo jet crashed while trying to land in a thunderstorm at Dallas-Fort Worth International Airport, killing 137 people.

Aug. 12—Central Japan. A Japan Air Lines jumbo jet crashed into Mount Osutaka, Japan, killing 520 people.

Dec. 12—Gander, Canada. A chartered jet carrying U.S. soldiers crashed shortly after take-off, killing all 256 people aboard.

Japanese Army troops search wreckage of a Japan Air Lines jet that crashed in August, killing 520 people in the worst single-plane accident in history.

Bus Crash

Nov. 6 —Northern India. A bus swerved off a highway and plunged into a gorge in the Himalayas, killing at least 82 people.

Earthquakes

March 3 —Central Chile. A powerful earthquake rocked central Chile, killing 151 people.

Aug. 23 —Xinjiang (Sinkiang) autonomous region, China. An earthquake struck western China, causing at least 60 deaths.

Sept. 19-20 —Mexico. Two powerful earthquakes jolted western and central Mexico, including Mexico City, and left more than 7,000 people dead.

Explosions and Fires

Jan. 13 —Kushtia district, Bangladesh. Between 150 and 300 people burned in or jumped to their deaths from a train that ran for more than an hour after catching fire due to an electrical short circuit.

April—Taiyuan (T'ai-yuan), China. A fireworks factory exploded and burned, killing 82 workers.

April 26 —Buenos Aires, Argentina. A fire at a private mental hospital caused 79 deaths.

May 11 —Bradford, England. Fire engulfed a wooden grandstand at a soccer match, killing 56 spectators.

Aug. 22 —Manchester, England. An engine exploded on a British Airtours jetliner as it took off from Manchester Airport, and 55 people died.

Floods

January—Eastern Brazil. Month-long rains caused floods that killed at least 150 people in the states of Espírito Santo, Minas Gerais, and Rio de Janeiro.

April—Northeastern Brazil. More than 30 inches (76 centimeters) of rain in less than a month brought on flooding in which more than 100 people drowned.

Early June—Southeastern China. The area's worst flooding since 1908 killed at least 64 people in Hunan province and Guangxi (Kwangsi) autonomous region.

June 28-30 —Philippines. Floods and landslides brought on by heavy rains caused at least 78 deaths in Manila and outlying provinces.

Early July—Guizhou (Kweichow) and Sichuan (Szechwan) provinces, China. Torrential rains burst dams and overflowed irrigation canals, causing landslides and floods that killed about 275 people.

July 19 —Stava, Italy, near Bolzano. A dam burst, sending a flood of water and mud through a resort town and killing at least 232 people.

Late July and early August—Liaoning province, China. Two weeks of heavy rains turned the Yalu River into a raging flood that swept away two villages near Dandong (Tan-tung) and killed at least 64 people.

Late August—Northeast China. More than 180 people perished in floods, and about 220 others were missing.

Mid-October—Eastern India. Flooding set off by severe storms killed about 80 people in Orissa, West Bengal, and Uttar Pradesh states.

Nov. 5 —Eastern United States. Floods brought on by four days of heavy rains took 45 lives in Maryland, Pennsylvania, Virginia, and West Virginia.

Hurricanes, Tornadoes, and Other Storms

Jan. 18-23 —Eastern and central United States. A winter storm and cold wave caused at least 123 deaths.

March 29 —Near Pabna, Bangladesh. About 300 people died, many killed by hailstones, in a monsoon storm.

May 24-25 —Southern Bangladesh. A cyclone and tidal wave swept over coastal towns and islands off Bangladesh, killing at least 10,000 people.

May 31 —Pennsylvania and Ohio; and Ontario, Canada. A series of tornadoes killed 88 people.

July 30 —Zhejiang (Chekiang) province, China. A typhoon killed 177 people.

Aug. 23 —Fujian (Fukien) province, China. Typhoon Nelson's heavy winds and rain killed 48 people.

Oct. 7 —Ponce, Puerto Rico. A mud slide triggered by a rainstorm buried a hillside shantytown, killing as many as 150 people.

Mid-October—Vietnam. Typhoons Cecil and Dot struck central Vietnam back-to-back, destroying five villages and causing up to 600 deaths.

Oct. 18-19 —Philippines. Typhoon Dot battered the main Philippine island of Luzon, causing flash floods that left at least 63 people dead.

Mine Disasters

May 17 —Yubari, Japan. Leaking methane gas set off an explosion in a coal mine, killing 62 miners.

July 12 —Guangdong (Kwangtung) province, China. A coal-mine explosion left 53 miners dead.

Shipwrecks

Mid-January—Southeastern Nigeria. About 100 people were missing after a ferry capsized.

March 23 —Near Dhaka, Bangladesh. At least 200 and perhaps as many as 450 people drowned after a ferry capsized in the Buri Ganga River.

April 9 —Bihar state, India. Seventy-five people were believed drowned after their boat capsized in the Ganges River.

May 26 —Madhya Pradesh state, India. An overloaded boat capsized in the Chambal River, drowning at least 74 passengers.

Aug. 18 —Harbin, China. A ferry capsized in the Sungari (Songhua) River, drowning 174 people.

Oct. 5 —Near Chittagong, Bangladesh. A ferry hit a fishing trawler, broke in half, and sank in the Karnaphuli River, drowning up to 100 passengers.

Nov. 15 —Uttar Pradesh state, India. At least 60 people were feared drowned after a boat capsized in the Chambal River.

Dec. 18 —Mindoro Strait, Philippines. About 115 people were missing and feared drowned after a ferry sank.

Train Wrecks

Jan. 13 —Near Awash, Ethiopia. An express train derailed on a bridge and hurtled into a ravine, killing as many as 450 people.

Aug. 31 —Argenton-sur-Creuse, France, near Châteauroux. A passenger train derailed in the direct path of an oncoming mail train, which rammed it moments later and killed 49 people.

Sept. 11 —Nelas, Portugal, near Viseu. A head-on collision between two trains killed more than 100 people.

Other Disasters

Early to mid-January—Europe. Bitterly cold weather throughout Europe caused about 320 deaths due to freezing or weather-related accidents.

April 7 —Colcabamba, Peru. A landslide smothered this Andes mountain town in several feet of mud, killing at least 120 villagers.

Early June—Bihar state, India. A heat wave caused more than 100 deaths as temperatures soared to 115° F. (46° C) on June 5.

Aug. 13 —Bombay, India. A crowded tenement collapsed while the residents slept, killing 52.

Oct. 15 —Dhaka, Bangladesh. A roof at a university auditorium collapsed during a heavy rain, killing more than 70 students.

Nov. 13 —Colombia. A volcanic eruption triggered mud slides that took about 25,000 lives.   Sara Dreyfuss

DJIBOUTI. See AFRICA.

DOG. Judge Elsworth Howell of Darien, Conn., selected a black female Scottish terrier, Champion Braeburn's Close Encounter, as best-in-show at the Westminster Kennel Club's 109th annual show held in February 1985 at Madison Square Garden in New York City. There were 2,130 dogs in competition. The champion is owned by Sonnie and Alan Novick of Plantation Acres, Fla., near Fort Lauderdale. The Scottie has won more than 200 best-in-show awards in her career, making her the top winner in dog-show history. Among her other wins was the spring 1985 show of the International Kennel Club of Chicago, judged by R. William Taylor of Montreal, Canada.

Cocker spaniels headed the list of 1984 registrations by the American Kennel Club (AKC). Poodles remained in second place, followed by Labrador retrievers, German shepherds, golden retrievers, Doberman pinschers, beagles, miniature schnauzers, Shetland sheepdogs, and dachshunds. Golden retrievers advanced one place, while Dobermans fell two places. In late 1984 and early 1985, the AKC instituted new events designed to evaluate the hunting abilities of retrievers, pointing breeds, and spaniels.   Roberta Vesley

In WORLD BOOK, see DOG.

DOMINICAN REPUBLIC. See LATIN AMERICA.

DROUGHT. See WATER; WEATHER.

DRUG ABUSE. See CRIME; DRUGS (Close-Up).

A tiny electronic pump unveiled in May can be worn on a patient's belt and programmed to dispense drugs up to five days without refilling.

DRUGS. A number of widely used brand-name prescription drugs became available to consumers in 1985 in lower-priced generic versions after the drug patents expired. The best known of these were the blood pressure medication Inderal and the tranquilizer Valium. On July 31, the United States Food and Drug Administration (FDA) gave drug companies permission to market generic versions of Inderal. On September 4, the FDA gave its approval for generic versions of Valium. The FDA during the year also approved generic versions of the pain relievers Darvocet-N and Motrin; the popular tranquilizer Ativan; Reglan, an antiulcer drug; and Norpace, used to treat disturbances in heart rhythm. FDA Commissioner Frank E. Young said that lower-cost generic drugs have the same medical effect as brand-name products.

New Drugs. On May 10, the FDA approved the first true antihistamine capable of relieving sneezing, runny nose, and other symptoms of allergy without causing drowsiness. The new product, terfenadine, is sold by Merrell Dow Pharmaceuticals, Incorporated, of Cincinnati, Ohio, under the brand name Seldane.

The first oral gold compound for treatment of severe rheumatoid arthritis was approved by the FDA in May. The capsule contains 29 per cent gold and will be sold by SmithKline Beckman Corporation of Philadelphia under the brand name Ridaura. In March, researchers at Brigham and Women's Hospital in Boston reported that the anticancer drug methotrexate proved highly effective in treating rheumatoid arthritis.

Human Growth Hormone. In October, the FDA approved a genetically engineered human growth hormone. This was the second genetically engineered drug to receive FDA approval. The first was human insulin, in 1982.

Human growth hormone is used to treat children whose growth is hampered because of a genetic defect that prevents their bodies from producing the hormone. The federal government had been distributing natural growth hormone taken from cadavers. The distribution was halted in April 1985 because officials feared the supply had become contaminated with a virus that causes a rare but fatal brain disease. The genetically engineered version of the hormone was developed by Genentech, Incorporated, of South San Francisco, Calif., and will be marketed under the name Protropin.

Vaccines. On April 25, the U.S. Centers for Disease Control in Atlanta, Ga., declared that a shortage of the vaccine that provides protection against diphtheria, tetanus, and *pertussis* (whooping cough) had ended. The shortage developed in 1984, when two of the three vaccine manufacturers stopped production, one because of technical

Deadly Designer Drugs

"You can hold 200 grams of this stuff in your hand," said a dismayed California drug official recently. "That's the equivalent of 200 million doses when cut."

The "stuff" is synthetic heroin, up to 3,000 times more potent than the real thing. An estimated 20 per cent of the heroin sold in California in 1985 was synthetic—peddled under such names as China White, Persian White, and Mexican Brown.

The synthetic heroin is just one of several new "designer drugs"—narcotics and hallucinogenic drugs cooked up in "underground" laboratories from common chemical ingredients. These substances threaten to open a new era of drug abuse in the United States.

Federal narcotics officials have been frustrated by existing laws in their efforts to control designer drugs because each successive form of these mind-bending substances is legal. Narcotics laws identify illegal drugs by precise chemical formulas. So by making minor changes in a drug's molecular structure, a chemist can produce a compound whose effects are the same as,

or greater than, the original's, but with structural differences that make the new version lawful to manufacture and sell. Several types of synthetic heroin, for example, are slightly altered versions of a surgical anesthetic named fentanyl. The first variant of fentanyl showed up on California streets in 1979. When the U.S. Drug Enforcement Administration (DEA) finally banned that formulation, another compound took its place until it too was declared illegal. By June 1985, outlaw chemists had come up with at least 10 variations of fentanyl.

As part of the Comprehensive Crime Control Act of 1984, the DEA acquired emergency powers allowing the agency to act in just 30 days to put a one-year prohibition on a hazardous new drug. The temporary ban can later be made permanent. But because the DEA was still limited to prohibiting only specific drugs after they were introduced, it continued to play a game of catch-up with free-lance drugmakers.

Almost everyone agrees that highly potent and addictive compounds like synthetic heroin should be banned. But there were some protests in May when the DEA announced that, effective July 1, 1985, it was placing a one-year prohibition on the drug MDMA—commonly known as Ecstasy—while research continued into the drug's possible harmful effects. MDMA has gained wide popularity among college students and young professionals. The drug's advocates—including a number of psychologists and psychiatrists who use Ecstasy in treating their patients—claim that the drug breaks down emotional barriers between people while causing no harmful side effects.

Many drug researchers, however, support the DEA ban. University of Chicago researchers reported in July that animal studies indicate MDMA can cause brain damage.

While the debate over Ecstasy continued, the United States government laid plans to crack down harder on the makers of all designer drugs. On July 10, the Department of Justice announced that it had prepared legislation making it a felony to manufacture any drug that is "substantially similar" to an existing illegal drug. The bill was introduced in Congress later in the month by Senator Strom Thurmond (R., S.C.). The proposed legislation was still pending in Congress at year-end.

Until the bill is passed into law, however, underground chemists can continue, legally, to flood the streets with synthetic drugs. Because many such drugs are so powerful, a little goes a long way. According to California narcotics authorities, one chemist working an eight-hour day could produce enough synthetic heroin for every addict in the United States.   David L. Dreier

Senator Paula Hawkins (R., Fla.) holds a model of a "designer drug" molecule at a Senate hearing on such legal but lethal drugs in July.

difficulties, the other because of high insurance rates resulting from lawsuits over side effects.

The FDA in April 1985 approved a new vaccine that protects against infection with *Haemophilus influenzae* type B bacteria. This type of bacteria is the most common cause of *meningitis,* inflammation of the membrane covering the brain and spinal cord, and other diseases, such as pneumonia, that kill about 1,000 young children each year.

Drugs and the Law. Eli Lilly and Company of Indianapolis pleaded guilty on August 21 to charges that it failed to inform the FDA of serious side effects caused by the arthritis drug Oraflex. A federal judge fined the pharmaceutical firm $25,000. Lilly introduced Oraflex in the United States in April 1982 but withdrew it in August of that year. Oraflex later was linked with more than 70 deaths in the United States and Europe, and with hundreds of serious side-effects cases. The U.S. Department of Justice charged that Lilly officials knew in 1981 that Oraflex could have such adverse effects but failed to tell the FDA.

On Feb. 25, 1985, in Philadelphia, SmithKline Beckman was placed on two years probation and ordered to spend $100,000 to establish a child-abuse prevention program, for delayed reporting of side effects related to its high blood pressure drug Selacryn. The drug, prescribed from May 1979 to January 1980, was linked with 35 deaths as well as many liver and kidney problems.

On March 12, 1985, a federal jury in Cincinnati found that Bendectin, an antinausea medication manufactured by Merrell Dow, does not cause genetic defects in unborn children. Many pregnant women took Bendectin between 1956 and 1983, when Merrell Dow halted production because of mounting legal costs.

A. H. Robins Company, a pharmaceutical concern based in Richmond, Va., on April 2, 1985, established a $615-million fund to compensate women injured by its Dalkon Shield birth control device. The device, used by about 2.2 million women between 1971 and 1974, has been linked with pelvic infections, sterility, and other health problems. After realizing that the fund would be insufficient to pay all claims, the firm filed for bankruptcy in August 1985.

The U.S. Drug Enforcement Administration (DEA) on May 31 placed an emergency one-year ban—effective July 1—on use of MDMA, a hallucinogenic drug popularly known as Ecstasy. John C. Lawn, acting administrator of the agency, said the drug had become a nationwide problem because of its potential for abuse. See Close-Up.

The FDA in June approved the use of THC, the active ingredient in marijuana, in treating nausea caused by cancer chemotherapy. Michael Woods

In WORLD BOOK, see DRUG.

EARTHQUAKE. See DISASTERS.

EASTERN ORTHODOX CHURCHES. In a New Year's message ushering in 1985, Archbishop Seraphim, primate of Greece, announced that he was donating his eyes and kidneys for transplantation upon his death. His announcement reflected the growing concern of Orthodox churches with contemporary problems.

Another indication of this concern came in April, when the Ecumenical Patriarchate of Constantinople, the leading center of Eastern Orthodoxy, announced plans for a future Great and Holy Council of the Orthodox Church. Among the topics proposed for discussion at this meeting of Orthodox churches from around the world were "peace, freedom, brotherhood, and love." The subject of peace also came under scrutiny at the annual theological seminar held in June at the Orthodox Center of the Ecumenical Patriarchate in Chambésy, Switzerland, ouside Geneva.

Copts in Egypt, along with the rest of the Orthodox world, celebrated the release from house arrest of Pope Shenouda III, patriarch of the Coptic Orthodox Church, in January. Shenouda had been banished to a monastery in the desert in 1981 for alleged political activities.

Year of Saint Cyril and Saint Methodius. The Orthodox world honored the 1,100th anniversary of the death of the Greek missionary Saint Methodius in 1985. Methodius and his brother Cyril brought Christianity to the Slavs and invented the Cyrillic alphabet. On May 12, a church in honor of the brothers was consecrated in their home city of Salonika, inaugurating a three-day conference on their missionary work. Another international conference on the two saints was held in Sofia, Bulgaria, in June. On July 2, Pope John Paul II, spiritual leader of the world's Roman Catholics, praised Saints Cyril and Methodius as "the connecting links or spiritual bridge between the Eastern and Western traditions."

Other Events. The first symposium on Orthodox-Islamic relations was held in March at Holy Cross Greek Orthodox School of Theology in Brookline, Mass. In April, the Romanian Orthodox Church celebrated its 100th anniversary as an *autocephalous* (self-governing) church. The Orthodox Theological Institute of Saint Sergius in Paris observed its 60th anniversary in June. Archbishop Iakovos, primate of the Greek Orthodox Diocese of North and South America, received permission to visit his homeland, Turkey, in September. Iakovos had been prohibited from entering Turkey because of his outspoken opposition to Turkish intervention in Cyprus in 1974. Archbishop Philaret, primate of the Russian Orthodox Church Outside of Russia since 1964, died on Nov. 21, 1985, in New York City. Stanley Samuel Harakas

In WORLD BOOK, see EASTERN ORTHODOX CHURCHES.

ECONOMICS. The United States economy grew moderately in 1985. Unemployment was at its lowest level since 1979, and the rate of inflation remained low. In December 1985, the gross national product (GNP)—the total value of goods and services produced—was running at a clip that would bring it above the $4-trillion level by year's end.

The recession that many economists had predicted would begin in late 1985 did not develop, and most forecasters predicted continued moderate growth in 1986. Uncertainty was created, however, by a federal government deficit apparently out of control, a growing trade imbalance, the threatened collapse of the Farm Credit System, and continuing problems with debt repayments by many foreign countries.

The economy grew slowly in the first quarter of 1985, showing only a 0.3 per cent gain in GNP in real terms—that is, after adjusting for inflation. But GNP growth picked up sharply in the second quarter to 1.9 per cent and reached 3 per cent in the third quarter. With an expected gain of about 3.2 per cent in the fourth quarter, the total GNP growth for the year was expected to hover around 2.4 per cent. This was sharply below the 6.8 per cent growth rate of 1984, but considering that 1985 was the third year of expansion following the recession of 1981-1982, it was not a bad performance. It also compared favorably with rates of growth among other industrialized countries.

Personal consumption expenditures rose by almost 5 per cent above 1984 levels, again measured in real terms. This resulted in the lowest personal savings rate in many years. People were spending more and saving less. After fluctuating between 6.9 per cent in 1976 and 5 per cent in 1983, the personal savings rate for 1985 was only a little more than 4 per cent. With corporate savings also down from 1984, this might have led either to higher interest rates or to a sharp rise in the rate of inflation, but fortunately, neither occurred.

Inflation. The inflation rate, according to the Implicit Price Deflator—also called the Implicit Price Index or Gross National Product Deflator—was slightly below 3 per cent, barely less than that of 1984. As measured by the Consumer Price Index (CPI), the inflation rate dropped from about 4 per cent in 1984 to about 3.6 per cent in 1985. Because the GNP Deflator measures the prices of more goods than the CPI, many economists feel it is a better guide to the nation's real inflation rate.

With inflation seemingly under control in 1985, interest rates fell substantially. At year-end, the rate on three-month Treasury bills was only slightly above 7 per cent, two full percentage points below the average for 1984. Similar de-

President Ronald Reagan announces in January that his chief of staff, James Baker III, will change places with Treasury Secretary Donald Regan.

Selected Key U.S. Economic Indicators

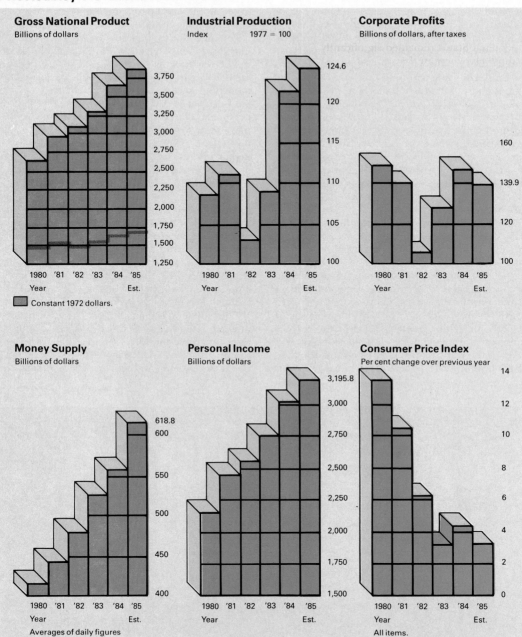

Gross National Product
Billions of dollars

3,750
3,500
3,250
3,000
2,750
2,500
2,250
2,000
1,750
1,500
1,250

1980 '81 '82 '83 '84 '85
Year   Est.

▨ Constant 1972 dollars.

Industrial Production
Index   1977 = 100

124.6
120
115
110
105
100

1980 '81 '82 '83 '84 '85
Year   Est.

Corporate Profits
Billions of dollars, after taxes

160
139.9
120
100

1980 '81 '82 '83 '84 '85
Year   Est.

Money Supply
Billions of dollars

618.8
600
550
500
450
400

1980 '81 '82 '83 '84 '85
Year   Est.

Averages of daily figures
as of December each year.

Personal Income
Billions of dollars

3,195.8
3,000
2,750
2,500
2,250
2,000
1,750
1,500

1980 '81 '82 '83 '84 '85
Year   Est.

Consumer Price Index
Per cent change over previous year

14
12
10
8
6
4
2
0

1980 '81 '82 '83 '84 '85
Year   Est.

All items.

The most comprehensive measure of the nation's total output of goods and services is the gross national product (GNP). The GNP represents the dollar value in current prices of all goods and services plus the estimated value of certain other outputs, such as the rental value of owner-occupied dwellings. Industrial production is a monthly measure of the physical output of manufacturing, mining, and utility industries. Corporate profits are quarterly profit samplings from major industries. Money supply measures the total amount of money in the economy in currency and checking account deposits. Personal income is current income received by people (including nonprofit institutions and private trust funds) before taxes. The consumer price index (CPI) is a measure of changes in the prices of selected goods and services consumed by urban families and individuals.
All 1985 figures are *Year Book* estimates.

clines appeared for government securities with longer maturities. Although these lower rates were an improvement over previous years, interest rates in the United States remained significantly higher than those elsewhere in the world.

Several elements affected interest rates and inflation in 1985. The economic climate in the United States attracted large amounts of foreign capital. Rising consumer expenditures also helped to fuel a boom in imports, which tended to hold down prices in the United States. The Federal Reserve System, which serves as the central bank of the United States, also cooperated by permitting the money supply to rise fairly rapidly. Thus, it was possible to hold down interest rates and prices in the face of increased consumer demand and substantial borrowing by the federal government.

Employment. Although the unemployment rate declined only slightly to 7.2 per cent in 1985, down from 7.4 per cent in 1984, the real story concerned other developments. Since 1982, the civilian labor force has grown by more than 5 million. The number of employed has grown by nearly 8 million for a net job creation of 3 million. During the same period, jobs in other industrialized countries, especially in Europe, decreased by nearly 10 million. Unemployment rates elsewhere were typically above those in the United States.

Also encouraging was the fact that the long-term unemployment rate—for those unemployed for 27 weeks or more—continued the decline that it began in 1984, dropping to the 1982 level of about 15.6 per cent. Not unexpectedly, the percentage of unemployed people who were out of work for less than 5 weeks rose to 42 per cent. This indicates that about 3 per cent of the work force are constantly in the process of changing jobs (a process known as *frictional unemployment*).

The remaining unemployment picture, however, represented a more serious problem. Black unemployment was 15.9 per cent in November 1985, more than double that for the population as a whole. Women who head households also experienced significantly higher rates of unemployment.

Wages Up Slowly. Average hourly earnings in 1985 grew at the slowest pace in more than a decade with an increase of about 2.9 per cent. As a result, unit labor costs in the nonfarm business sector rose by only 3 per cent, though this was still above 1983 and 1984 levels. Unit labor costs were sharply down from the more than 10 per cent levels of 1979-1980 and well below the pace that began in 1973, except for the years 1983 and 1984.

Farming Woes Increase. Farmers were among those who failed to share in the general prosperity. The net farm income dropped by nearly 20 per cent because prices for both grain and livestock were sharply lower than in 1984. The high value of the dollar and uneconomically high support prices in the United States combined to bring about a substantial reduction in farm exports.

The year 1985 saw a further decline in the price of farmland, which in many places has dropped by 40 per cent over the past three years. This, in turn, has weakened many small banks in rural areas where bank loans have been based primarily on the value of land. Many of these small rural banks were forced to close, and others, in an effort to stay in business, began foreclosures. Many farmers were forced into bankruptcy, especially in the grain-producing states of the Midwest. See FARM AND FARMING.

Stock Market Breaks Records. Corporate profits after taxes were down by 7 per cent, compared with 1984, but the growing vigor of the economy and optimistic forecasts for 1986 inspired the stock market to record-breaking levels in 1985. The most widely followed stock market index, the Dow Jones Industrial Average, rose to a record high of 1,553.10 points on December 16. During the year, the industrial average broke the 1,300 level for the first time in May, the 1,400 level in November, and then the 1,500 level in December.

Also setting new records were Standard & Poor's index of 500 stocks at 212.02, and the New York Stock Exchange Index, at 121.90. This represented an increase of more than 20 per cent over the closing levels of 1984. Among the developments contributing to this rise was an unprecedented number of *buy-backs*, in which companies with listed stocks began to purchase their own securities in the open market, thus reducing the number of securities available. In addition, a substantial number of companies *went private*—that is, their stocks were no longer sold publicly. When this occurs, wealthy investors often combine with top executives of the firm going private. They purchase all the outstanding shares held by institutions and individual investors, and the stock ceases to be listed. Mergers also contribute to this trend when the acquiring company buys all the stock of another public company and does not issue more of its own shares as payment.

The Dollar Problem. In September, the finance ministers and central bankers of France, West Germany, Japan, and Great Britain met with U.S. Secretary of the Treasury James A. Baker III in what may come to be regarded as a historic meeting in New York City. The finance specialists, who came to be known as the Group of Five for the number of nations they represented, agreed to intervene in foreign-exchange markets in an effort to drive down the value of the U.S. dollar in relation to the price of the other major foreign trading currencies. Their objective was twofold. First, they wanted to head off growing protectionist sentiment in the U.S. Congress, and second, they

"Would you mind explaining again how high interest rates and the national deficit affect my allowance?"

Earl Engleman, *The Wall Street Journal;* permission, Cartoon Features Syndicate

wanted to reduce the attractiveness of the U.S. market for foreign capital. By late September, the value of the dollar against major foreign currencies had declined 5.2 per cent.

Protectionism Threat. If the intervention succeeded and the dollar fell significantly, it was hoped that the flood of imports into the United States would be slowed and that U.S. exporters would sell more goods in other countries. In this way, the Group of Five hoped to avoid measures to impose highly protectionist trade barriers. More than 300 protectionist bills designed to increase tariffs or impose quotas had already been introduced in Congress. Economists were generally agreed that all such legislation has the net effect of reducing foreign trade. Most economists believed that protectionist bills invite retaliation by the countries affected and, more important, that they lower the standard of living in the country imposing the quotas by making it impossible to purchase low-priced foreign goods.

The interests of the industries affected by imports usually have more weight in Congress than the opinions of economists or the interests of consumers who suffer a relatively small loss, on an individual basis, as a result of their reduced opportunities. As Congress weighed the merits of the protectionist bills in 1985, however, it also had to consider the impact on countries that

would suffer from such quotas and would find it necessary to reduce their purchases of U.S. goods. Such countries might, in some instances, find it impossible to pay the interest on their foreign debts, thus jeopardizing U.S. banks that hold those debts. Few of these bills were expected to pass, and President Ronald Reagan was expected to veto any extreme measures.

Baker had hoped to go beyond the monetary agreement that was reached at the September meeting. Ideally, he had hoped that both West Germany and France would agree to stimulate their economies. For France and West Germany, this might have provided a better market for U.S. exports and increased consumption of their home-produced goods on the domestic front. Such measures, Baker thought, would have reduced pressures on those countries to export. Japan, which has an unusually low rate of consumption, might then have been expected to take the same steps. None of the countries agreed to this further move to bring down the dollar. Consequently, the long-term results of the September agreement remained to be seen.

The U.S. Government Budget Deficit, which was $202.8 billion in the 1985 fiscal year ending September 30, was a cause of substantial alarm. The congressional budgeting process was seemingly incapable of reducing federal expenditures. Some members of Congress sought alternatives that would force mandatory reductions if the budget was out of balance by more than 5 per cent.

The most popular of these alternatives was known as the Gramm-Rudman bill, after two of its sponsors, Senators Phil Gramm (R., Tex.) and Warren Rudman (R., N.H.). Gramm-Rudman would force a reduction in the deficit by $36 billion each year starting in 1987 so that, presumably, the deficit would be eliminated completely by 1991. By the time various amendments to the bill had been adopted eliminating any cuts in social security and other programs, it appeared that failure to meet the deficit-reduction targets would trigger heavy cuts in defense expenditures and equally severe across-the-board cuts in other functions of the government. Opinion was sharply divided on this approach during the year. Some regarded it as unconstitutional, and when President Reagan signed the Gramm-Rudman bill into law on December 12, a lawsuit challenging its constitutionality was filed the same day. The suit contended in part that the law violated the Constitution's separation of powers between the executive and legislative branches of government.   Warren W. Shearer

See also INTERNATIONAL TRADE; MANUFACTURING; STOCKS AND BONDS; and individual country articles. In WORLD BOOK, see ECONOMICS.

ECUADOR. See LATIN AMERICA.

EDUCATION. The drive for excellence in education in the United States continued in 1985. A series of strongly worded reports calling for reforms in public schools ignited the nationwide movement in 1983. Georgia, Illinois, Kentucky, Massachusetts, and South Dakota joined a dozen other states that since 1983 have enacted sweeping reforms in education. The Georgia package was typical. It included mandatory full-day kindergarten, a new statewide core curriculum, a career ladder for teachers, more testing of students, and a 10 per cent increase in starting salaries for teachers.

Higher Funding and Enrollments. Funding for education rose dramatically in many states during 1985. The Illinois legislature, for example, earmarked $411 million in new funds for reforms in elementary and secondary education. Overall, it hiked spending on education by 18.4 per cent. California's public schools received a 9.4 per cent boost in state aid, and Alabama increased its support for education by 20 per cent. A number of states passed new taxes to fund the increases.

Total enrollment in U.S. schools rose for the first time in 13 years. The number of students in public and private elementary and secondary schools reached 44,680,000 during the 1985-1986 school year, up 50,000 from 1984-1985. The gains took place almost entirely at the elementary school level.

Students at Risk. Reformers began to focus attention on students at risk. For a variety of reasons, such students are likely to have difficulty meeting the higher academic standards that are a key element of the excellence movement.

In January 1985, a coalition of child-advocacy groups called for more resources to be directed to the disadvantaged, the handicapped, and members of minority groups. In its report, *Barriers to Excellence: Our Children at Risk,* the coalition said that these groups had been largely ignored by the reform efforts of recent years. In March, the President's Commission on Industrial Competitiveness warned that high dropout rates, particularly among minority groups, posed a major threat to American society and industry. A report by Design for Change, a Chicago citizens group, found that 53 per cent of the students who enter public high schools in that city fail to graduate.

William J. Bennett, former chairman of the National Endowment for the Humanities, a federal agency, replaced Terrel H. Bell as secretary of education in February. Bennett promoted President Ronald Reagan's education agenda aggressively during 1985. He endorsed federal income tax credits for parents who send their children to private schools, and in November, he proposed legislation calling for federal aid to disadvantaged students to be distributed in the form of vouchers that students could use for tuition at private schools. Bennett argued that the tax-credit and voucher plans would stimulate public schools to improve and give parents more choice in where to send their children to school. Congress had rejected both plans earlier in Reagan's presidency.

The Issue of Choice—the right of parents to use tax monies to send their children to the schools they wish—received serious attention at the state level for the first time in 1985. Minnesota Governor Rudy Perpich, an advocate of public education and an opponent of tuition tax credits, proposed in January that all Minnesota 11th- and 12th-grade students be permitted to choose which public school they would attend, regardless of school district boundaries. Perpich claimed that his plan would promote better schools through competition and would build support for public education. After heavy lobbying by educators' groups, the Minnesota legislature defeated the proposal in April. But the lawmakers passed an unprecedented bill that allowed 11th- and 12th-graders to take courses at Minnesota colleges using funds from their public school districts.

"Choice" was also one of the three "C's" discussed by Bennett in a speech to the National Press Club in Washington, D.C., in March. The second was "content." Echoing a recommendation in the Education Department's widely publicized 1983 study, *A Nation at Risk,* Bennett urged that

The Growing Shortage of Teachers

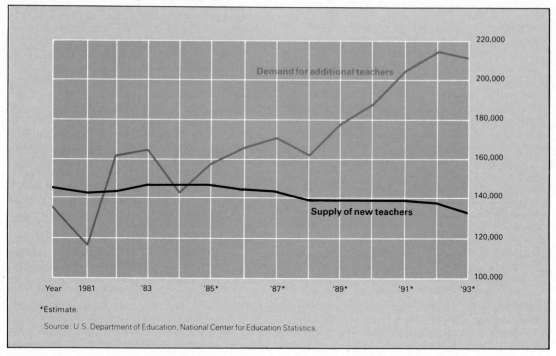

Demand for additional teachers

Supply of new teachers

220,000
200,000
180,000
160,000
140,000
120,000
100,000

Year 1981 '83 '85* '87* '89* '91* '93*

*Estimate.

Source: U.S. Department of Education, National Center for Education Statistics.

all students, whether college-bound or not, study a common core of English, history, science, and mathematics. By 1985, nearly every state had raised its high school graduation requirements in these subjects. Bennett's third "C" was "character." He said schools have a responsibility to develop the moral character of students. Kindness, honesty, respect for law, and self-discipline were among qualities he said should be stressed.

School Prayer. Bennett provoked widespread criticism when he told the National Press Club that voluntary school prayer should play a role in efforts to develop character. Reagan has repeatedly asked Congress to pass a bill permitting voluntary prayer in public schools.

In July, Bennett criticized the Supreme Court of the United States for ruling that New York City had violated constitutional guarantees of the separation of church and state by allowing public school teachers to provide remedial instruction in parochial schools. Bennett offered the legal services of the Department of Education to school systems refusing to carry out the court's decision.

In June 1985, the Supreme Court struck down an Alabama law that permitted a daily one-minute period of silence for prayer or meditation in the state's public schools (see SUPREME COURT [Close-Up]). The case was watched closely because it was the first test of the constitutionality of moment-of-

silence laws enacted in Alabama and 24 other states after a 1962 Supreme Court decision declared organized prayer in public schools unconstitutional. The Reagan Administration suffered another defeat on the issue in September 1985 when the Senate rejected an Administration-backed bill that would have stripped federal courts of jurisdiction in school-prayer cases.

Student Aid Under Fire. Bennett, a former professor, provoked perhaps the greatest controversy in higher education during the year when he said in February that federal student-aid programs could be cut because many of the students receiving aid were not making financial sacrifices to attend college. Instead, he said, they were spending money on stereos, cars, and beach vacations.

Bennett's remarks came at a time when the number of minority students attending college was decreasing. Many of these students depend on federal aid to pay for college. A report released in midyear by the American Association of State Colleges and Universities, an advocacy group, revealed that the proportion of black high school graduates entering college dropped by 11 per cent from 1975 to 1981. For Hispanics, the decrease was 18 per cent.

Attracting Teachers. Much of the education news of 1985 concerned the public school teaching profession. Increases in student enrollment, changes in graduation requirements, teacher retirements, and unattractive working conditions were expected to create a need for about 1 million new teachers by 1990. Some school systems already had to scramble to find enough people to staff classrooms. A number of systems recruited in other countries.

Many states and many city school systems raised salaries in an effort to attract teachers. The average salary for teachers nationwide stood at $23,546 in the 1984-1985 school year, up 7.3 per cent from 1983-1984. In September, New Jersey Governor Thomas H. Kean signed a law increasing starting salaries for teachers in that state from $14,900 to $18,500. The average starting salary for teachers nationwide was $14,000.

In an effort to improve teachers' working conditions, a number of states and hundreds of school systems had begun to implement career ladders for teachers by year's end. The ladders, which were recommended in a number of the reform reports published in 1983, were designed to identify outstanding teachers and reward them with higher salaries and increased authority, thereby encouraging them to stay in the profession. In Florida, a career-ladder plan withstood legal challenges and scattered boycotts in 1985 from teachers' unions that favored rewarding teachers strictly on the basis of seniority and education. The unions argued that merit pay programs, such as the career ladders, violated collective-bargaining agreements.

New Jersey schools hired their first 110 teachers under a controversial but promising program designed to bring top liberal arts graduates into the state's schools. Under the plan, the state allowed graduates who met certain requirements to by-pass traditional teacher-education programs, which have been widely criticized as mediocre. To become certified, the graduates must major in the subject they plan to teach, pass a test in that subject, and complete 80 hours of study in teaching techniques during the summer before they enter a classroom. Houston, Los Angeles, and New York City introduced similar plans.

Testing Teachers. Also controversial was an Arkansas decision to test the state's 28,000 teachers on their mastery of basic reading, writing, and arithmetic skills. In an effort to raise teaching standards, many states have begun to test those about to enter the profession. But in March, Arkansas became the first state to test current teachers. In June, the state announced that 10 per cent of its teachers had failed the basic skills test and would be dismissed if they did not pass it by 1987. The test sparked a dramatic confrontation be-

Students from J. J. Pearce High School in Richardson, Tex., show the first-place trophy their team won in the U.S. Academic Decathlon in April.

tween Arkansas Governor Bill Clinton and the Arkansas Education Association (AEA), the state's largest teachers' union. Clinton favored the test as a means of gaining public support for public education. The AEA unsuccessfully lobbied against it in the state legislature and in the courts.

In July, the 1.7-million member National Education Association (NEA), the AEA's parent organization, bowed to intense public pressure and dropped its long-standing opposition to testing teacher candidates. But the NEA reaffirmed its opposition to the testing of current teachers.

An indication of the extent of the troubles facing the teaching profession came in April when Albert Shanker, the influential president of the American Federation of Teachers, a nationwide teachers' union, shocked educators by saying, "Unless we go beyond collective bargaining . . . we will fail . . . to preserve public education in the United States." This was a radical departure for a labor leader, especially for one who had been a driving force behind the unionization of teachers and the push for collective bargaining in education during the early 1960's. In January 1985, Shanker endorsed a tough national test for all teacher candidates, similar to the bar examination for lawyers. He pledged that his union would not accept those who failed the test.   Thomas Toch

In WORLD BOOK, see EDUCATION.

EGYPT. Relations between Egypt and the United States were strained when U.S. jets intercepted an Egyptian airliner carrying the Palestinian hijackers of the Italian cruise ship *Achille Lauro* on Oct. 10, 1985. The hijackers had surrendered in Egypt to a representative of the Palestine Liberation Organization (PLO). They had also been given safe conduct out of Egypt, despite repeated U.S. requests that Egypt prosecute the terrorists for killing an American tourist on the ship or turn them over to Italy or the United States for prosecution. Egyptian President Hosni Mubarak angrily denounced the U.S. interception as an act of international piracy and demanded an apology.

Jet Hijacking. On November 23, terrorists hijacked the same Egyptian airliner on its way from Athens, Greece, to Cairo. Sixty people, including two hijackers, died, most of them when Egyptian commandos stormed the plane the next day.

Egyptian-Israeli Relations. The delicate relationship between Egypt and Israel suffered when Israeli jets raided PLO headquarters near Tunis, Tunisia, on October 1, in retaliation for the killing of three Israelis in Cyprus in September. After the raid, Egypt suspended talks with Israel involving the ownership of Taba, a resort area in the Sinai claimed by Egypt but held by Israel.

The status of the talks also was affected by the killing of seven Israelis by an Egyptian policeman

in the Sinai on October 5. On December 1, Israel agreed to resume talks after Egypt promised to submit a report on the incident.

Fundamentalist Challenge. During 1985, Mubarak came under attack from Islamic fundamentalists demanding that the People's Assembly, Egypt's legislature, revise existing laws to conform to Sharia (Islamic law). In May, the Assembly voted instead to review Egypt's legal code gradually to revise laws that contradicted Sharia.

In May, Egypt's Supreme Constitutional Court struck down a 1979 law giving women greater rights in divorce cases. But the Assembly restored most of these rights in July under pressure from moderate groups. Also in July, in a campaign to halt the growth of fundamentalism, the government arrested several religious leaders who were agitating for the restoration of Sharia. In August, an Egyptian court ordered the religious leaders released, ruling that they had been held illegally.

The Economy. With Egypt's foreign debt approaching $31 billion in September, Mubarak appointed a new cabinet headed by Prime Minister Ali Lotfy, a leading economist and former finance minister. The new government began to cut subsidies of basic commodities, starting with electricity, flour, and gasoline.   William Spencer

See also ARMED FORCES; MIDDLE EAST (Facts in Brief Table). In WORLD BOOK, see EGYPT.

ELECTIONS. Most elections held in the United States in 1985 resulted in a continuation of the status quo. Candidates of the party in power—newcomers as well as incumbents—won the vast majority of contests, which included two governorships and an array of big-city mayoral races.

State Races. In November 5 elections, Democrats scored big in Virginia, while Republicans won most of the races in New Jersey. Virginia's former Democratic attorney general, Gerald L. Baliles, was elected governor over Republican Wyatt B. Durrette, collecting 55 per cent of the vote. Other Democratic winners in Virginia included State Senator L. Douglas Wilder, elected the South's first black lieutenant governor, and State Delegate (representative) Mary Sue Terry, who won the race for attorney general, becoming the first woman ever elected to statewide office in Virginia. The Democratic sweep in Virginia owed much to the popularity of outgoing Governor Charles S. Robb, a Democratic moderate who was prohibited by state law from running again.

In New Jersey, Republican Governor Thomas H. Kean collected more than 70 per cent of the vote as he coasted to victory over Democrat Peter Shapiro. Kean, first elected in 1981 by the narrowest margin in state history, won the support in 1985 of blacks, union members, and other groups traditionally allied to the Democratic Party.

Mayoral Elections. New York City Mayor Edward I. Koch easily defeated five challengers in that city's Democratic primary in September, then won a third consecutive four-year term in November. Other Democratic mayors reelected in November included Coleman A. Young of Detroit; Donald M. Fraser of Minneapolis, Minn.; and Richard S. Caliguiri of Pittsburgh, Pa. Also reelected were Republican Mayor George V. Voinovich of Cleveland and nonpartisan mayors Kathryn J. Whitmire of Houston and Charles Royer of Seattle. Palmer DePaulis, a Democrat appointed mayor of Salt Lake City, Utah, in 1985, was elected to a regular term in office.

In a nonpartisan election on April 9, Los Angeles Mayor Thomas Bradley, a black Democrat, was reelected to a fourth term, becoming the first person ever elected to four full terms as mayor of that city. Other prominent black mayors who won reelection during the year included Andrew J. Young, Jr., of Atlanta, Ga.; Lionel J. Wilson of Oakland, Calif.; and Harvey B. Gantt of Charlotte, N.C. Miami, Fla., Mayor Maurice A. Ferre, a Puerto Rican-born Democrat, lost his bid for a seventh term to a Cuban-born independent, Xavier L. Suarez.

In April, Vincent L. Schoemehl, Jr., a Democrat, became the first St. Louis mayor in 16 years to be reelected. A. Starke Taylor won a second term as mayor of Dallas in a nonpartisan election.

Congressional Elections. Two special congressional elections were held in 1985, and both were won by Democrats. On March 30, Cathy Long won a five-person primary in Louisiana's Eighth Congressional District to succeed her husband, Gillis W. Long, who had died on January 20.

In Texas on August 3, an election was held to fill the seat of Representative Sam B. Hall, Jr., a Democrat, in the state's First Congressional District. Hall had resigned in May to become a federal judge. Republicans spent an estimated $1 million in a determined effort to win the traditionally Democratic seat in rural northeast Texas for Edd Hargett, a political beginner and onetime Texas A&M football hero. But he was defeated by Democrat Jim Chapman, a former district attorney.

House Seat Disputed. The 1984 race between U.S. Representative Frank McCloskey, a Democrat, and Republican Richard D. McIntyre in Indiana's Eighth Congressional District was not settled until well into 1985. During the November 1984 vote count, McCloskey appeared at first to have won narrowly, but adjustments to the count shifted the advantage to McIntyre. Indiana's Republican secretary of state, Edwin J. Simcox, then declared McIntyre the winner by 34 votes out of more than 233,000. The Democratic-controlled House of Representatives, however, did not accept Simcox' finding. Instead, it voted along party lines

Cathy Long, left, widow of Representative Gillis W. Long (D., La.), gets a hug from a supporter after being elected to her husband's seat in March.

against seating McIntyre, an action that left the seat vacant pending a recount.

The Republican challenger won the state-supervised recount by more than 400 votes, but Democrats claimed that some 4,800 legitimate ballots, many from predominantly black precincts, had been disallowed. The House set up a special task force of two Democrats and one Republican to supervise yet another recount, conducted by the nonpartisan General Accounting Office. On April 18, the task force—splitting 2 to 1 along party lines—declared that McCloskey had been reelected by four votes in the closest congressional election in history.

Outraged Republicans, calling for a special election to settle the dispute, threatened to disrupt House activities indefinitely. But on May 1, the House finally voted, 236 to 190, to seat McCloskey. Ten Democrats voted with the Republican minority, all of whom promptly walked out of the chamber in protest. It was the first walkout since 1890, when the Democrats staged a similar protest. But passions soon cooled, and the House returned to business.   Frank Cormier and Margot Cormier

See also DEMOCRATIC PARTY; REPUBLICAN PARTY. In WORLD BOOK, see ELECTIONS.

ELECTRIC POWER. See ENERGY SUPPLY. In the WORLD BOOK SUPPLEMENT section, see ELECTRIC POWER.

ELECTRONICS. The United States electronics industry in 1985 continued to struggle through its deepest recession in a decade, with U.S. manufacturers of *semiconductor chips* hit the hardest. A semiconductor chip is a piece of material—usually silicon—containing complete electronic circuits. A typical chip is about the size of a fingernail and contains many thousands of circuits. Industry observers blamed the recession on two major factors—increased and more aggressive competition from Japanese manufacturers of *memory chips,* semiconductor chips that store information; and plummeting sales of personal computers, a major market for semiconductor chips.

One immediate effect of the recession was an apparent decision by makers of memory chips that the market for reprogrammable chips known as *256-kilobit (256K) dynamic RAM's* had faded away. A 256K chip can hold 262,144 *bits*—the 0's and 1's of the binary numeration system.

Buyers of chips have become accustomed to increases in chip capacity every two to four years. Most personal computers made in 1984 used 64K chips, which hold 65,536 bits. Companies that built those machines looked forward to using 256K chips, which entered the market in large numbers in 1984. The computer manufacturers may have to wait, however, for the chip makers to develop the next generation of RAM's—*1-megabit* chips, each capable of holding about 1 million bits.

Consumer Electronics Designers devoted most of their energies to improving existing products. Their results included smaller, more versatile video cassette recorders (VCR's); and television sets using *liquid crystal display* (LCD) technology. Such technology—of the type used in many digital wrist watches—began to emerge as the means to the long-sought flatter TV set.

All-Electronic Photography. In 1985, researchers continued to develop equipment for tomorrow's all-electronic still cameras for the home. Equipment for cameras included *charge-coupled devices (CCD's),* which convert light that strikes them into electrical impulses. In an all-electronic camera, lenses would focus an image to be photographed onto CCD's, rather than onto film. The CCD's would react to the image by transmitting electrical impulses to a built-in computer, which would store the image in memory chips.

The all-electronic system may store large numbers of photographs on another component currently under development—the *optical disk,* on which a laser records data. An optical disk looks like a phonograph record.   Howard Wolff

See also COMPUTER. In WORLD BOOK, see ELECTRONICS.

A digital TV set, which controls the picture with computer-style circuits, draws a crowd at the Consumer Electronics Show in Chicago in June.

EL SALVADOR. During most of 1985, the six-year civil war in El Salvador had seemed to be winding down, despite the failure of meaningful negotiations between rebel and government factions in 1984. With troops trained by the United States, the government of El Salvador appeared to be gaining the upper hand militarily.

Thrown on the defensive in the countryside by bombing attacks, the guerrillas adopted new urban terrorist tactics. On June 19, terrorist rebels shot and killed 13 people eating at a sidewalk restaurant in San Salvador. The dead included 4 United States marines and 2 U.S. businessmen. The Revolutionary Party of Central American Workers, the smallest group in the rebel coalition, claimed responsibility. On August 27, El Salvador's President José Napoleon Duarte announced that three of the suspected terrorists had been arrested and a fourth killed.

Terrorist tactics again appeared on September 10 when guerrillas kidnapped Duarte's 35-year-old daughter, Inés Guadalupe Duarte Durán. A bodyguard was killed during the kidnapping.

Despite incidents such as these, the general level of violence appeared to be diminishing. On September 29, Roberto D'Aubuisson, who had been linked to far right death squads, stepped down as the head of the Nationalist Republican Alliance. Observers speculated that with the easing of El Salvador's civil war, D'Aubuisson had outlived his usefulness.

Then the rebels struck, and hard. In a raid beginning at 1:30 A.M. on October 10, guerrillas killed at least 40 government soldiers and wounded 68 others at the main government training base for recruits near La Unión. It was the first significant rebel attack since 1983. None of five U.S. military advisers at the base was hurt.

The day after the raid, the rebel high command announced a change of strategy. Henceforth, they said, their main objective would be the killing of U.S. military advisers. The U.S. Congress has limited the number of advisers in El Salvador to 55, but owing to a series of exceptions, more than 100 U.S. military advisers serve in El Salvador at any one time.

On October 24, both sides in the war observed a brief truce, during which Duarte's daughter was released unharmed along with the mayors of some 23 villages who had also been kidnapped by rebel forces. In exchange, the Salvadoran government released 22 political prisoners and provided safe passage out of the country for about 100 wounded guerrillas.   Nathan A. Haverstock

See also LATIN AMERICA (Facts in Brief Table). In WORLD BOOK, see EL SALVADOR.

EMPLOYMENT. See ECONOMICS; LABOR; SOCIAL SECURITY; WELFARE.

ENDANGERED SPECIES. See CONSERVATION.

ENERGY SUPPLY. Officials at the only full-scale synthetic fuels plant in the United States, the Great Plains coal gasification plant near Beulah, N. Dak., announced on August 1 that they were abandoning the project. They also said they would default on $1.5 billion in federal loans used to construct and operate the plant.

The default occurred only one year after the $2.1-billion project, once viewed as the flagship of the U.S. synfuels industry, began commercial operation. Designed to produce gas from coal, the plant was built by five energy firms and financed with $543 million in private capital and $1.5 billion in federal loan guarantees.

Financial problems caused by a decline in world energy prices led the plant's investors to seek an additional $720 million in government money from the Synthetic Fuels Corporation. The corporation was created by Congress in 1980 to promote technology for turning abundant domestic energy resources, such as coal and oil shale, into liquid and gas fuels. The corporation approved the request for additional money on July 17. But Secretary of Energy John S. Herrington vetoed the move on July 30, maintaining that the coal gasification project had become too expensive and uneconomical.

The Congressional Ax. Congress moved once again during 1985 to abolish the Synthetic Fuels Corporation. On July 31, the House of Representatives voted to cut $6.6 billion from the corporation's proposed $7.9-billion budget. The House gave the remaining money to the Department of Energy (DOE) for a small-scale synfuels program. In December, Congress effectively killed the corporation by eliminating its remaining funds.

Hydropower Dispute. A bitter battle between private and public utilities over who should control hundreds of U.S. hydroelectric power projects—the cheapest source of electricity—raged during 1985. The dispute involved certain provisions of the Federal Power Act of 1920. This act gave cities, states, and other public bodies preference over private utilities in obtaining licenses to build hydroelectric dams.

By 1994, licenses for 177 of the 366 hydroelectric projects built by private utilities will come up for renewal. Public utilities claimed in 1985 that the 1920 law gave them preference not just in obtaining licenses for new dams but also in obtaining renewal licenses to take over existing hydroelectric dams.

On October 22, a federal appeals court in Washington, D.C., ruled that the law does give public utilities preference in license renewals. Specifically, the court ordered Pacific Power & Light Company, a private, investor-owned utility in Portland, Ore., to turn over its Merwin Dam in southwestern Washington state to two small public

Solar collectors swivel to track the sun at SEGS I, the world's largest
solar electric generating plant, which opened in March near Daggett, Calif.

utilities in Washington. The public utilities would
have to pay only $9.4 million for the dam. Pacific
Power said it would have to spend at least $732-
million to build a coal-fired generating station to
replace the lost power and that construction costs
could raise the bills of its 665,000 customers as
much as 10 per cent. On October 23, the electric
power industry urged action by Congress, warning
that if the decision were not reversed, consumers
currently served by cheap hydroelectric power
could eventually pay up to $4.5 billion per year in
higher rates.

Canadian Power Purchase. A group of 92 electric utility companies in New England, seeking
ways to delay the construction of costly new generating stations, agreed on October 14 to import
about $3 billion of hydroelectric power from Can-
ada beginning in 1990. Hydro-Québec, a major
Canadian utility, promised lower prices than the
utilities would pay to generate the power with oil
and other fuels. The deal was expected to reduce
electric bills in the region served by the utilities by
2 to 4 per cent.

World Energy Consumption. The DOE on October 28 reported that in 1984, world energy consumption rose substantially for the first time since
1979. Energy production during 1984 rose by
about 4 per cent, to a record 293 quadrillion British thermal units (B.T.U.'s). The United States re-

mained the world's leading energy producer, followed by the Soviet Union, China, and Canada.

Nuclear Power. Americans grew increasingly dependent on electricity generated by nuclear power
plants during 1985. The DOE on March 5 reported that in 1984 nuclear energy became the
second most important source of energy in the
United States, accounting for about 14 per cent of
total U.S. electricity production. Electricity produced by coal-fired plants remained in first place.
But years of construction delays, plant cancellations, and other economic problems in the commercial nuclear power industry made nuclear
power more expensive. On September 13, the
Atomic Industrial Forum, a nuclear industry
group based in Washington, D.C., said that the average cost of nuclear electricity was higher than
that of coal during 1984 for the first time. The
group said that a kilowatt-hour of electricity generated with nuclear power cost 4.1 cents, compared with 3.4 cents for coal.

Three Mile Start-Up. The undamaged Nuclear
Unit Number 1 at Three Mile Island Nuclear
Power Station near Harrisburg, Pa., returned to
operation on Oct. 3, 1985, ending a long legal and
political battle over the plant's safety. It was shut
down in 1979, when the worst commercial nuclear
accident in history struck Unit Number 2 at the
plant.

Diablo Canyon. The Unit 1 reactor of the Diablo Canyon nuclear power plant near San Luis Obispo, Calif., began producing electricity on May 7, 1985, after years of public protest over its location near an earthquake fault. On August 1, the Nuclear Regulatory Commission granted a full-power license to the plant's Unit 2 reactor.

TVA Problems. The Tennessee Valley Authority's (TVA) $14-billion nuclear power program slowed to a virtual standstill during 1985. On August 23, the TVA closed its Sequoyah nuclear plant near Chattanooga, amid concerns about its safety. Sequoyah was the last of the TVA's operational nuclear plants. The TVA on March 28 shut down its Browns Ferry nuclear station near Athens, Ala., where a number of safety problems had occurred since a serious fire there in 1975. The agency also delayed construction on the $3.3-billion Watts Bar nuclear plant near Spring City, Tenn., on August 23 because of safety problems.

Uranium Plant Closings. Decreased demand for the enriched uranium fuel used in commercial nuclear plants forced the U.S. government to close its original uranium enrichment plant at Oak Ridge, Tenn., on June 5. The DOE also halted work on an unfinished enrichment plant at Portsmouth, Ohio, after spending $2.6 billion on construction. The department said it would adopt a newer and more economical laser technique for producing nuclear fuel in the future.

Solar Cells. The Solar Energy Research Institute near Denver on October 18 announced a $25-million program to improve the performance of a new kind of solar cell. The cells, which have no moving parts, use a material called *amorphous silicon* to convert sunlight directly into electricity. The new cells are thinner, easier to manufacture, and cheaper than conventional solar cells.

Energy Conservation. The DOE on August 2 reported a sizable increase in the use of energy conservation features in new office buildings and other commercial structures. The department said that about 75 per cent of the new commercial buildings completed in the 1980's incorporate such features, compared with only about 56 per cent of those built in the 1970's.

Soviet Synfuels Plant. The Soviet Union on October 28 announced the start-up of a new synfuels plant using what Russian officials said was a unique process. The plant, located at Tula, southwest of Moscow, converts coal into a pastelike material, then into a liquid fuel in a process requiring only a minimum of energy.   Michael Woods

See also COAL; PETROLEUM AND GAS. In the Special Reports section, see NUCLEAR POWER AT THE CROSSROADS. In the WORLD BOOK SUPPLEMENT section, see ELECTRIC POWER. In WORLD BOOK, see ENERGY SUPPLY.

ENGINEERING. See BUILDING AND CONSTRUCTION.

ENGLAND had an unusually gloomy year in 1985. In February, teachers in the country's state-run schools began striking at selected schools because of a pay dispute. By year's end, the dispute still had not been resolved. On the brighter side, after a strike lasting nearly a year, coal miners went back to work on March 5.

Liverpool barely escaped bankruptcy in November after refusing to observe spending limits and set realistic local tax rates. The local council had to use bank loans and funds from its 1986-1987 budget to pay public employees.

Urban Riots. Arson, looting, and the throwing of gasoline bombs marked clashes between police and mobs composed mainly of black youths during the autumn. Hundreds of people were injured, hundreds more were arrested, and damage to property was considerable.

In the Handsworth district of Birmingham on September 9, rioting followed a police attempt to arrest a black youth. Two Asian immigrants were burned to death in their shop during the rioting.

In London, the accidental shooting of a black woman by a policeman during a search of her home on September 28 sparked off severe rioting in the Brixton neighborhood. A press photographer who was hit on the head by a concrete slab during the disturbance later died of his injury.

The worst rioting occurred in the Tottenham area of London on October 6, following the death of a black woman who suffered a heart attack during a police search of her home. The Tottenham riot marked the first time that rioters in England used firearms against police. A police constable was stabbed to death by a mob. Later, four people, including two juvenile boys, were arrested in connection with the killing.

Soccer Tragedies. On May 11, a soccer match ended in disaster as fire swept a grandstand at a stadium in Bradford, West Yorkshire, killing 56 people. A government inquiry revealed that the fire had probably been caused by a cigarette. The report called for better safety controls and evacuation training at soccer stadiums.

On the same day as the Bradford fire, an outburst of spectator violence at a soccer match in Birmingham caused the death of a 15-year-old boy. The judge investigating the incident proposed a ban on visiting fans, the use of closed-circuit television at the grounds, and the building of fences around the field. A government ban on alcoholic beverages at soccer grounds went into effect in August, but after only a few weeks, all 92 clubs in the English League had applied for exemptions from it.

On May 29, a riot broke out at a stadium in Brussels, Belgium, between British fans of the Liverpool club and Italian fans of the Juventus team of Turin, who were competing in the European

Fire fighters hose down smoldering buildings burned in rioting, mainly by black youths, on September 9 in the Handsworth district of Birmingham.

Cup Final. In the riot, 38 people were killed and hundreds injured. This tragedy led to a ban of indefinite length on English soccer teams playing on the European mainland. On October 19, however, it was decided that the ban would not bar England's national team from playing in the 1986 World Cup finals or the 1988 European Cup Championships.

Child Abuse. In September, the National Society for the Prevention of Cruelty to Children reported that child abuse in Britain had risen by 70 per cent since 1979. The report was published amid news stories of the deaths of several children resulting from abuse by adults. These cases caused concern about the effectiveness of the monitoring of problem families by social service agencies.

Accidents. On August 22, a British Airtours Boeing 737 burst into flames on the runway at Manchester Airport, killing 55 people. A faulty combustion chamber on one of the jet's engines was blamed. On October 21, 13 people died in an 11-vehicle highway crash in Lancashire.

Cricket Triumph. On September 2, a win by England's cricket team clinched its six-match series against Australia. The win gave England an informal championship called *the Ashes*, which it had lost in 1983.   William Gould

See also GREAT BRITAIN. In WORLD BOOK, see ENGLAND.

ENVIRONMENTAL POLLUTION. The safety of the chemical industry came under intense investigation in the United States during 1985. Attention was focused on the issue in large part as a result of a December 1984 toxic chemical leak from a Union Carbide Corporation plant in Bhopal, India, that killed more than 2,500 people. On March 20, 1985, a Union Carbide representative explained that the poison gas leak had resulted from a chemical reaction caused when water was "inadvertently or deliberately" pumped into a tank storing methyl isocyanate, a highly toxic chemical.

On August 11, a toxic chemical leak at Union Carbide's plant in Institute, W. Va., sent 134 people to the hospital. The Institute plant is the only one in the United States that manufactures methyl isocyanate. On August 16, Union Carbide chairman Warren M. Anderson said that any future leak at a Union Carbide plant would be reported to surrounding communities immediately. His announcement came in response to criticism for a delay in notifying public officials after the August 11 leak at the Institute plant.

EPA Action. On June 4, the United States Environmental Protection Agency (EPA) announced its national strategy for controlling toxic air pollution. Under the plan, the EPA would regulate pollution from wood-burning stoves, dry cleaners, and gasoline stations, while state and local governments were encouraged to regulate emissions from major chemical companies. Critics of the plan, including some members of Congress, argued that the EPA was attempting to evade its legal responsibilities and that the states were ill-equipped to accept these additional duties.

Information from a report on toxic chemical accidents prepared for the EPA was released in October. The report revealed that nearly 7,000 accidents involving toxic chemicals had occurred in the United States between 1980 and 1985, killing 135 people and injuring nearly 1,500.

Toxic Wastes. The $1.6-billion government Superfund program to clean up hazardous toxic waste dumps expired on Sept. 30, 1985. Both houses of Congress in 1985 passed bills to renew the program for another five years. Congress and the Administration of President Ronald Reagan disagreed about the amount of funding for the program and the source of the funds. The House bill proposed $10 billion. The Senate bill provided for $7.5 billion and would fund the program in part by levying a tax on large chemical manufacturers and processors. The Administration, which wanted only $5.3 billion, opposed this tax and threatened to veto the bill. At year's end, differences between the House and Senate versions were being resolved in conference.

On May 20, Westinghouse Electric Corporation agreed to spend up to $100 million to clean up six dumps near Bloomington, Ind., where the company had disposed of toxic polychlorinated biphenyls (PCB's). The EPA said that this was the largest settlement in the history of the agency.

The EPA in 1985 added 64 sites to its list of waste dumps posing an immediate health hazard and thus eligible to receive Superfund money for long-term cleanup activities. This brought the number of sites on the EPA national priority list to 850. EPA officials stated that up to 2,000 sites may eventually be placed on the list.

On November 8, new EPA rules went into effect requiring all toxic-waste landfill sites to monitor the water beneath the dumps for contamination and to carry liability insurance. On December 6, the EPA said more than two-thirds of the nation's toxic-waste dumps failed to meet the requirements and must be closed.

Water Pollution. Both houses of Congress in 1985 passed legislation to renew the Clean Water Act of 1972. The Reagan Administration wanted to eliminate by 1990 government grants offered under the act to build or improve sewage-treatment plants. The House and Senate bills included funding for construction of sewage-treatment facilities, but they differed in funding levels for such grants and in a cutoff date for the construction grant program. Both houses favored creating a revolving loan program to replace such grants. At

the end of 1985, differences between the bills were being resolved in conference.

Both houses of Congress in 1985 also passed bills to renew the Safe Drinking Water Act of 1974. The bills would require the EPA to add more than 60 chemical pollutants to the list of 22 such substances that the agency already regulates. They also called for states to protect underground sources of water from pollution and for water systems to monitor their water for any contaminants. Differences in the bills were being resolved in conference at year's end.

In March, the U.S. Department of the Interior closed the Kesterson National Wildlife Refuge in California and announced the phased closing of an irrigation drainage canal emptying into the refuge. Agricultural drainage carried by the canal had resulted in high levels of toxic selenium at the refuge, leading to the death or deformity of thousands of fish and birds.

The International Joint Commission—a U.S.-Canadian agency—on June 25 added 3 Michigan waterways to its list of seriously polluted areas on the Great Lakes. This addition brought the total number of such sites to 42. Toxic-chemical contamination is the leading pollution problem of the Great Lakes. On October 9, the EPA unveiled a five-year strategy for cleaning up the Great Lakes. The plan could put the lakes "well underway to permanent recovery" by 1990, the agency said.

Acid Rain was a major topic at a March 1985 meeting of President Reagan and Canada's Prime Minister Brian Mulroney. Reagan maintained his position that further study is needed before federal government action should be taken to control acid rain. The two leaders agreed to continue high-level discussions on the problem. A committee of U.S. scientists, in a report released on October 18, challenged the position of the Reagan Administration that more research is needed before acting to control acid rain. Their conclusion was based on information contained in U.S. government studies.

The government of Ontario in December ordered four large companies to reduce emissions of sulfur dioxide about 65 per cent by 1994. Sulfur dioxide pollution is a leading cause of acid rain. The move was expected to greatly reduce acid rain in New York state and New England.

A U.S. federal court on July 26 ordered the EPA to require seven Midwestern and Southern states to reduce emissions of sulfur dioxide and nitrogen oxides—primary causes of acid rain. The states are Illinois, Indiana, Kentucky, Michigan, Ohio, Tennessee, and West Virginia.

Pesticides. In July, 10 million watermelons in California food stores were destroyed when they were found to be contaminated with the pesticide aldicarb, marketed under the brand name Temik

California's Kesterson National Wildlife Refuge was closed in March because toxic chemicals from agricultural drainage endangered wildlife living there.

by Union Carbide. About 200 people in the Western United States and Canada became ill after eating contaminated watermelons.

In July, the EPA announced that its $3.5-million experimental mobile incinerator had destroyed wastes contaminated with dioxin, a toxic by-product of the manufacture of some herbicides. The success could pave the way for cleanup of sites contaminated with the chemical. There are at least 42 such sites in Missouri alone.

Antifrost Bacteria Suit. On November 14, the EPA approved experimental field application of bacteria that have been genetically altered to reduce the formation of ice on plants, thereby decreasing frost damage. The test called for applying the bacteria to a field of strawberry plants in California. On the same day, environmentalist Jeremy Rifkin filed a suit to prevent the test, arguing that further laboratory testing was needed to ensure that the bacteria would not spread from the test area and cause environmental damage.

New EPA Administrator. On Feb. 8, 1985, Lee M. Thomas was sworn in as EPA administrator. He succeeded William D. Ruckelshaus, who retired. Thomas had been chief of the EPA's Superfund program.   Casey Bukro

See also CONSERVATION; WATER. In WORLD BOOK, see ENVIRONMENTAL POLLUTION.

EQUATORIAL GUINEA. See AFRICA.

ETHIOPIA. The government of Ethiopia in 1985 complicated relief operations aimed at helping the nation's estimated 8 million famine victims. Ethiopian officials made it difficult for food and medical supplies to be delivered, and they forced thousands of refugees to leave relief camps.

When the spring rainy season promised to end the drought that had caused the famine, the government decided to close some refugee camps and reduce the population of others. Some peasants volunteered to be resettled in areas less ravaged by drought. Others, however, were forcibly ejected from the camps. At the Ibnat camp, about 250 miles (400 kilometers) north of the capital city, Addis Ababa, Ethiopian army units in late April evicted up to 38,000 refugees and burned their shelters. On May 6, Ethiopia's head of state, Mengistu Haile-Mariam, announced that the action had been a mistake and that the evicted people would be allowed back into the camp.

Grain Rots on Docks. Relief operations were hindered by transportation problems. Because of a shortage of docking space, many relief ships were forced to wait a week or more at anchor before unloading their supplies. Furthermore, a severe shortage of trucks to deliver supplies inland caused large backlogs at the ports. In late April, United Nations officials estimated that 60 per cent of the emergency food imported since January remained at the ports. Several thousand tons of grain rotted as it lay on the docks.

Food for the Rebels. The distribution problems were particularly serious in Eritrea and Tigre, provinces in northern Ethiopia under the control of rebel forces. Since the beginning of the famine in 1984, the government had tried to prohibit international relief agencies from operating in those areas or sending supplies there except through government channels. In mid-July 1985, however, the government agreed to permit two private relief organizations from the United States—Catholic Relief Services and World Vision—to distribute food in Eritrea and Tigre.

The main Eritrean rebel movement continued operations in much of the province. On July 6, its forces captured the important town of Barentu and held it for more than two months.

Ethiopian Jews. Between November 1984 and late March 1985, about 8,000 Ethiopian Jews were secretly flown from Sudan to Israel aboard chartered Belgian airliners and U.S. Air Force transport planes. Called Falashas, the Ethiopian Jews had been living in camps in Sudan as refugees from the famine in Ethiopia. The Haile-Mariam government strongly protested their unauthorized immigration to Israel.   J. Dixon Esseks

See also AFRICA (Facts in Brief Table). In the WORLD BOOK SUPPLEMENT section, see ETHIOPIA.

EUROPE. Many European countries suffered setbacks and international embarrassments in 1985. The European Community (EC or Common Market) failed to solve its financial problems and to reduce its growing surpluses of grain, butter, and wine.

West Germany suffered an escalating spy scandal in the summer. Hans Joachim Tiedge, a senior counterintelligence officer, defected to East Germany on August 19; and three civil servants disappeared, presumably going to East Germany.

Great Britain and the Soviet Union waged a diplomatic war in the late summer. The conflict began in September with the defection of Oleg A. Gordievsky, Soviet espionage chief in Great Britain. Gordievsky had been a British and Danish counterspy for more than 16 years. On September 12, Britain announced that Gordievsky had identified 25 Soviet diplomats and journalists working in Britain as spies, and that it had asked them to leave. The Soviet Union retaliated on September 14, ordering 25 British citizens out of Russia.

New Zealand accused France of involvement in the July 10 sinking of *Rainbow Warrior*, a ship owned by Greenpeace, a pacifist and environmentalist group, in Auckland Harbor. A Portuguese-born Dutch photographer died in the explosion that sank the ship. On July 23, New Zealand authorities arrested two French secret service agents in Auckland and charged them with murder and arson. On August 26, a French commission reported that the French intelligence service had not been involved in the sinking. On September 22, however, France's Prime Minister Laurent Fabius admitted that French intelligence agents acting under orders were responsible for it. On November 4, the day on which the two agents' trial was to have begun, they pleaded guilty to arson and manslaughter. On November 22, they were sentenced to 10 years in prison.

Soccer Riot. A May 29 riot at the Heysel soccer stadium in Brussels, Belgium, killed 38 people. The riot occurred during a European Cup match between Liverpool of England and Juventus of Turin, Italy. On July 6, a Belgian commission appointed to investigate the riot said that Belgian authorities had not taken proper measures to prevent a riot. The criticism threatened to bring down the Belgian government and led to an early general election, which the governing coalition won.

Wine Scandal. Wine manufacturers in Austria were arrested for fraud following the July discovery that diethylene glycol, a chemical used in automotive antifreeze, had contaminated some Austrian wines. Many countries, including Britain and the United States, banned the sale of Austrian wine.

Labor Unrest paralyzed Denmark in the spring. In Sweden, a May strike over a wage ceiling stopped almost all public services. In Norway, an opposition campaign for more welfare spending cut the majority of the ruling rightist parties to one seat in a general election in September.

EC Expands. Portugal and Spain, after years of negotiation, became the 11th and 12th members of the EC on Jan. 1, 1986. The other 10 members are Belgium, Denmark, France, Great Britain, Greece, Ireland, Italy, Luxembourg, the Netherlands, and West Germany.

"Star Wars." United States President Ronald Reagan's call for research on technically advanced, space-based antimissile weapons met with a mixed response in Europe. In February, U.S. Secretary of Defense Caspar W. Weinberger urged West Europeans to support a $26-billion research program called the Strategic Defense Initiative (SDI), also known as "Star Wars." West German Chancellor Helmut Kohl supported the program "in principle." France's Defense Minister Charles Hernu said his country could not contribute to a new and dangerous arms race. Norway and Denmark refused to participate.

The European Commission, the executive branch of the EC government, suggested that the EC double research spending to find money for SDI technology. The rulers of the EC nations, meeting in Brussels on March 30, rejected the

Automobiles cross the border from Spain to Gibraltar shortly after the border was opened in February, for the first time since 1969.

suggestion. Britain's Prime Minister Margaret Thatcher said that the SDI was not a proper subject for the EC. Ireland threatened to veto any proposal on the subject. On December 6, however, Britain became the first U.S. ally to agree to participate in SDI research.

France proposed to create a European organization named the European Research Agency (Eureka) to improve Europe's capability in some of the advanced technologies that may be used for a space-based defense. The director of the U.S. program, James A. Abrahamson, said on May 23 that Eureka was "fully compatible" with the SDI and "not a blow to the United States at all."

The first round of Soviet-American nuclear arms talks in Geneva, Switzerland, ended on April 24 with the Soviets demanding that the United States abandon the SDI. When the second round opened on May 30, Russia made the same demand.

The Western European Union (WEU)—a defensive alliance made up of Belgium, France, Great Britain, Italy, Luxembourg, the Netherlands, and West Germany—met in Paris on July 18 to consider a response to the U.S. invitation to join SDI research. The WEU failed to agree on a response, however, mainly because of an unequivocal refusal by France.

On the same day, representatives of 17 nations, also meeting in Paris, created Eureka. The nations were the 10 members of the EC; Portugal and Spain, the prospective members; and Austria, Finland, Norway, Sweden, and Switzerland.

Bitburg. Relations between West Germany and the United States suffered a setback in the spring, when the White House announced Reagan's plans for celebrating the 40th anniversary of V-E Day—May 8, 1945—when World War II ended in Europe. Reagan planned to lay a wreath at a German military cemetery in Bitburg, West Germany. He did not, however, plan to visit a former Nazi concentration camp at Dachau, as Jewish leaders had encouraged him to do. Jewish leaders and U.S. veterans' organizations tried in vain to persuade Reagan to call off his Bitburg visit. On May 5, he visited both the Bitburg cemetery and the former Bergen-Belsen Nazi concentration camp near Hamburg.

Antagonism to the United States went a stage further on May 23, in a statement by Willy de Clercq, the EC Commission minister responsible for external trade relations. De Clercq said in Brussels that growing protectionism endangered international relations. He was concerned about a new $2-billion U.S. plan to encourage exports from the United States.

Dollar Worries. On January 14, the value of the British pound closed at $1.1110 in London trading, its lowest in many months. On January 22,

Facts in Brief on European Countries

Country	Population	Government	Monetary Unit*	Foreign Trade (million U.S. $) Exports†	Imports†
Albania	3,111,000	Communist Party First Secretary and People's Assembly Presidium Chairman Ramiz Alia; Prime Minister Adil Çarçani	lek (6.9 = $1)	no statistics available	
Andorra	42,000	The bishop of Urgel, Spain, and the president of France	French franc & Spanish peseta	no statistics available	
Austria	7,499,000	President Rudolf Kirchschläger; Chancellor Fred Sinowatz	schilling (17.6 = $1)	15,739	19,629
Belgium	9,892,000	King Baudouin I; Prime Minister Wilfried A. E. Martens	franc (51 = $1)	51,813 (includes Luxembourg)	55,400
Bulgaria	9,239,000	Communist Party General Secretary & State Council Chairman Todor Zhivkov; Prime Minister Georgi Stanchev Filipov	lev (1 = $1)	12,130	12,283
Czechoslovakia	15,700,000	Communist Party General Secretary & President Gustáv Husák; Prime Minister Lubomir Strougal	koruna (6.6 = $1)	17,173	17,070
Denmark	5,148,000	Queen Margrethe II; Prime Minister Poul Schlüter	krone (9.1 = $1)	15,966	16,614
Finland	4,900,000	President Mauno Koivisto; Prime Minister Kalevi Sorsa	markka (5.4 = $1)	13,471	12,433
France	54,780,000	President François Mitterrand; Prime Minister Laurent Fabius	franc (7.7 = $1)	97,566	103,739
Germany, East	16,547,000	Communist Party Secretary General & State Council Chairman Erich Honecker; Prime Minister Willi Stoph	mark (2.77 = $1)	24,836	22,940
Germany, West	60,967,000	President Richard von Weizsäcker; Chancellor Helmut Kohl	Deutsche mark (2.5 = $1)	171,728	153,007
Great Britain	56,442,000	Queen Elizabeth II; Prime Minister Margaret Thatcher	pound (1 = $1.49)	93,772	104,863
Greece	10,079,000	President Christos Sartzetakis; Prime Minister Andreas Papandreou	drachma (150.5 = $1)	4,811	9,435
Hungary	10,745,000	Communist Party First Secretary Janos Kadar; President Pal Losonczi; Prime Minister Gyorgy Lazar	forint (47.9 = $1)	8,563	8,091
Iceland	245,000	President Vigdis Finnbogadottir; Prime Minister Steingrimur Hermannsson	krona (41.5 = $1)	728	820
Ireland	3,632,000	President Patrick J. Hillery; Prime Minister Garret FitzGerald	pound (punt) (1 = $1.23)	9,641	9,675
Italy	56,562,000	President Francesco Cossiga; Prime Minister Bettino Craxi	lira (1,709 = $1)	73,318	84,225
Liechtenstein	28,000	Prince Franz Joseph II; Prime Minister Hans Brunhart	Swiss franc	no statistics available	
Luxembourg	368,000	Grand Duke Jean; Prime Minister Jacques Santer	franc (51 = $1)	51,813 (includes Belgium)	55,400
Malta	362,000	President Agatha Barbara; Prime Minister Karmenu Mifsud Bonnici	lira (1 = $2.37)	363	733
Monaco	29,000	Prince Rainier III	French franc	no statistics available	
Netherlands	14,568,000	Queen Beatrix; Prime Minister Ruud Lubbers	guilder (2.87 = $1)	65,863	62,295
Norway	4,162,000	King Olav V; Prime Minister Kaare Willoch	krone (7.55 = $1)	18,915	13,886
Poland	37,889,000	Communist Party First Secretary & President Wojciech Jaruzelski; Council of Ministers Chairman Zbigniew Messner	zloty (149.2 = $1)	11,408	10,324
Portugal	10,122,000	President António dos Santos Ramalho Eanes; Prime Minister Aníbal Cavaco Silva	escudo (160.9 = $1)	5,179	7,790
Romania	23,185,000	Communist Party General Secretary & President Nicolae Ceausescu; Prime Minister Constantin Dascalescu	leu (4.06 = $1)	10,719	8,161
Russia	281,057,000	Communist Party General Secretary Mikhail S. Gorbachev; Supreme Soviet Presidium Chairman Andrei A. Gromyko; Council of Ministers Chairman Nikolai I. Ryzhkov	ruble (1 = $1.31)	91,649	80,624
San Marino	24,000	2 captains regent appointed by Grand Council every 6 months	Italian lira	no statistics available	
Spain	39,322,000	King Juan Carlos I; President Felipe González Márquez	peseta (155.9 = $1)	23,561	28,831
Sweden	8,346,000	King Carl XVI Gustaf; Prime Minister Olof Palme	krona (7.6 = $1)	29,379	26,370
Switzerland	6,334,000	President Kurt Furgler	franc (2.08 = $1)	25,849	29,521
Turkey	52,387,000	President Kenan Evren; Prime Minister Turgut Ozal	lira (561 = $1)	7,134	10,735
Yugoslavia	23,392,000	President Radovan Vlajković; Prime Minister Milka Planinc	dinar (296 = $1)	10,254	11,996

*Exchange rates as of Dec. 1, 1985, or latest available data. †Latest available data.

Soviet leader Mikhail S. Gorbachev signs an extension of the 30-year-old
Warsaw Pact, the Soviet bloc's military treaty, in April in Warsaw, Poland.

European banks sold large amounts of dollars to support their currencies and curb the strength of the dollar. (Selling dollars increased the supply of dollars relative to the supply of other currencies. With more dollars available for exchange with other currencies, the value of the dollar declined.)

On February 25, the pound closed at $1.0545 in New York City trading. On February 27, European banks again sold dollars, causing the value of the pound to rise. But on March 5, it hit a low of $1.0540. The dollar then began to slide because the U.S. economy appeared to be slowing. By year's end, a pound was worth $1.45.

EC in the Red. The EC began 1985 in dire need of cash and a budget. The European Parliament—the EC's legislative branch—had thrown out the 1985 budget in December 1984. The EC did not have enough money to pay its farm bills or a $780-million rebate it had promised to Great Britain. Furthermore, Greece demanded that the EC pay Greece, France, and Italy a total of $1.56 billion to compensate for the effects of the entry of Spain and Portugal into the EC in January 1986.

Greece Relents. At the March 1985 meeting of EC leaders, Greece said it would accept a lower amount. The EC then drew up a new budget. The EC estimated that it would need $2.26 billion above the previously established budget ceiling of $20.8 billion. The European Parliament approved the revised 1985 budget and Britain's rebate on May 9.

Voting Problems. The EC leaders met on June 28 and 29 in Milan, Italy, to discuss streamlining the EC's decision-making procedures and a unified foreign policy. The talks foundered when Thatcher insisted on maintaining the right to veto certain types of decisions. Nevertheless, the leaders voted, 7 to 3, to set up a committee to review the Rome Treaties, on which the EC is founded.

On July 22, all EC members agreed to discuss amendments to the Rome Treaties. On December 4, EC leaders agreed to moderate revisions to speed up the elimination of the remaining barriers to trade among the member nations. The EC had already abolished tariffs, but safety standards and other administrative barriers remained.

The leaders also agreed to a minor strengthening of the powers of the European Parliament. And Britain and West Germany dropped their objections to a treaty revision committing the EC to the unification of the member nations' currencies.

Farm Budget. EC ministers were deeply divided in spring meetings on fixing farm prices. A price freeze that took effect on April 1 angered farmers and led to demonstrations in agricultural areas.

An EC paper on farm reform published on July 15 said that the only way to eliminate the EC's agricultural surpluses was to hold down farm prices for many years. The surpluses were crippling the EC. They included 14 million metric tons (15 million short tons) of cereal grains, vast quantities of butter, and a wine "lake" growing by 600 million gallons (2,300 million liters) a year.

Warsaw Pact Extended. Soviet leader Mikhail S. Gorbachev and colleagues from the other Warsaw Pact nations met in Warsaw, Poland, on April 26. They signed a 20-year extension of the pact, the foundation of the East European military alliance. (The Warsaw Pact nations are the Soviet Union, Bulgaria, Czechoslovakia, East Germany, Hungary, Poland, and Romania.)

COMECON Summit. Leaders of the 10 nations in the Council for Mutual Economic Assistance (COMECON), the Soviet trading bloc, met in Warsaw from June 25 to 27. The leaders supported moves to establish formal relations with the EC, but they insisted that the West must abandon the use of economic sanctions against COMECON. (The COMECON nations include the Warsaw Pact countries, plus Cuba, Mongolia, and Vietnam.)

EC and South Africa. On August 6, the EC's De Clercq warned South Africa that economic sanctions by the EC were inevitable unless that nation changed its policy of *apartheid*, or racial segregation. Three EC ministers who visited South Africa for talks in September, however, reported that sanctions would not help to end apartheid. On September 10, some EC countries imposed limited sanctions against South Africa. Britain blocked moves for sanctions by the EC, however. A sanctions bill introduced in the European Parliament lost on September 11.

Terrorism. Between mid-December 1984 and Jan. 30, 1985, terrorists made 60 attacks on military installations in Western Europe, most of them North Atlantic Treaty Organization (NATO) bases. On February 19, Britain and Italy agreed to reopen negotiations for a new extradition treaty as part of a common front against terrorism and drug trafficking. France and West Germany increased joint antiterrorist measures. Nevertheless, attacks and killing continued in Paris and Bonn, as well as in Greece, Spain, Austria, and Italy.

Missile Bases. On March 15, Belgium agreed to the installation of U.S. cruise missiles on its soil. The installation would implement a 1979 decision by NATO to deploy 572 cruise and Pershing 2 missiles in Belgium, Britain, Italy, the Netherlands, and West Germany. Belgium's decision left the Netherlands as the only country of the five that had not yet approved the installation of these missiles on its soil. On November 1, the Dutch government said it had decided to take the missiles, and on November 13, the Dutch parliament approved the missile plan in principle. Kenneth Brown

See also the various European country articles. In WORLD BOOK, see EUROPE.

EWING, PATRICK (1962-   ), was selected on June 18, 1985, as the top choice in the first round of the National Basketball Association draft by the New York Knicks. Ewing, a 7-foot (213-centimeter) center out of Georgetown University in Washington, D.C., signed a professional contract with the Knicks in September. The contract guarantees him $17 million for six years, making him the highest-paid rookie in basketball history.

Ewing was born in Kingston, Jamaica, on Aug. 5, 1962. He left Jamaica with his family at the age of 12 to settle in Cambridge, Mass. He had never played basketball until he arrived there.

Ewing gained a national reputation as a glowering, towering center known for his ability to rebound and block shots during his four years with the Georgetown team. He was a first-team all-American in 1983, 1984, and 1985. In 1984, he led Georgetown to a national championship as the team won the National Collegiate Athletic Association (NCAA) tournament, and he was named the tournament's Most Valuable Player. Ewing was also a member of the U.S. basketball team that won a gold medal at the 1984 Summer Olympics in Los Angeles. In 1985, Georgetown lost in the NCAA finals, but Ewing was named College Player of the Year as recipient of the Adolph Rupp, Eastman Kodak, and Naismith awards.   Rod Such

EXPLOSION. See DISASTERS.

FARM AND FARMING. United States farmers harvested bumper crops in 1985, but stiffening competition from abroad and a continued decline in U.S. farm exports further eroded the underpinnings of the U.S. agricultural economy.

Rallies protesting farm problems, reminiscent of those held during the Great Depression of the 1930's, drew thousands of people to Pierre, S. Dak.; Sioux City and Ames, Iowa; and St. Paul, Minn. Crisis hotlines to help farmers suffering from financial and emotional stress were started in farm states. Farmers blocked farm auctions and planted crosses to represent farmers forced out of business. A Farm Aid concert held on September 22 in Champaign, Ill., generated about $7 million for financially troubled U.S. farmers.

U.S. Production. Ideal weather in most of the United States brought record and near-record crops in 1985, and the amount of surplus crops farmers turned over to the government rose sharply. Corn production was up 14 per cent; grain sorghum, 30 per cent; soybeans, 14 per cent; and cotton, 6 per cent. Production of wheat fell almost 7 per cent; peanuts, 4 per cent; and rice, 4 per cent. United States beef and pork production remained essentially unchanged. Poultry production rose 5.5 per cent. The U.S. Department of Agriculture (USDA) reported that by the end of 1985, the United States had enough sur-

Music fans jam the University of Illinois stadium in Champaign on
September 22 for the Farm Aid concert to help financially pressed farmers.

plus grain to meet 54 per cent of an entire year's demand, compared with 31 per cent in 1984.

World Production. The world rice crop rose 1 per cent, setting a record for the sixth consecutive year. Corn production, up 4.4 per cent, also set a record. The production of coarse grains and soybeans rose 5 per cent and 8 per cent, respectively. The world wheat crop was down 2 per cent. World pork production rose 2.3 per cent, setting a record. Beef rose 1.3 per cent, and poultry was up 3.4 per cent.

Farm Aid. For four days in February, senators from farm states blocked a vote to confirm presidential counselor Edwin Meese III as attorney general of the United States in an attempt to obtain increased aid for financially strapped farmers. On March 4, Congress passed a farm-aid bill that provided emergency loans to heavily indebted farmers and subsidies to banks in order to lower interest rates on farm loans.

But on March 6, President Ronald Reagan rejected the debt-relief bill in the first veto of his second term. He said the legislation was "merely designed to convey the impression of helping farmers" and would add billions to the national deficit.

1985 Farm Bill. Members of Congress sparred most of the year about farm legislation to replace programs due to expire in 1985. A new five-year farm bill passed on December 18 was designed to help farmers recapture lost export business. Lawmakers froze or reduced the ceilings on income supports—thus lowering prices—to make U.S. farm products more competitive on world markets. Ceilings for wheat and corn were frozen for two years, those for cotton and rice for one year. During the remaining years of the bill, which will expire in 1990, subsidies were slated to fall slightly.

The new farm programs were expected to cost a record $77 billion spread over five years, though many farm experts predicted even higher outlays. Farm legislation enacted in 1981, expected to cost $11 billion over four years, actually cost a record $63 billion.

Hopes for more significant reform in U.S. farm programs in 1985 were dashed by fears that a reduction in government farm supports would aggravate the already serious problems facing many farmers. Hard-pressed farmers, however, complained that the new legislation did not provide enough help.

Soil Conservation. The most historic section of the farm bill was a sweeping soil-conservation measure that for the first time allocated payments to farmers to take up to 40 million acres (16 million hectares) of highly erodible land out of production. Farmers would be permitted to plant only erosion-resistant trees or grass on such land.

Another provision of the bill gave farmers tilling marginal cropland until 1990 to develop a soil-conservation program and until 1995 to put that program into effect. Farmers who continued to farm such land after that deadline would not be eligible for government subsidies.

Troubled Farmers. A USDA survey conducted in January 1985 showed that 214,000 of the 2.3 million U.S. farmers were in serious financial difficulty and 38,000 of them were technically bankrupt. Sixty-three per cent of the total farm debt of $211 billion was owed by farmers with a negative cash flow—expenses exceeding income—though some of those farmers had assets greater than their debts. Even more troublesome was the fact that 45 per cent of the total farm debt was owed by farmers who had both a negative cash flow and heavy debts.

Also according to the USDA, nearly one-third of the 635,000 commercial farmers who produce 90 per cent of the nation's crops and livestock had heavy debts, negative cash flow, or both. Three-fourths of the farmers in trouble were grain, dairy, or livestock producers.

A survey by the American Bankers Association released in late 1985 estimated that 4.8 per cent of the farmers in the United States went out of business in the last half of 1984 and the first half of 1985, up from 3.6 per cent during the previous 12-month period and 2 per cent in the two years before that. Farm failures for all of 1985 were at the low end of forecasts made early in the year, but bankers predicted the failure rate would increase in 1986. In August 1985, the USDA reported that the number of U.S. farms had fallen by an estimated 44,000—to 2.29 million from 2.33 million—in 1984, continuing a 50-year trend.

Farm Credit System. The deteriorating farm economy led the Farm Credit System, the nation's largest lender, to seek federal help. The Farm Credit System, a federally supervised farmer-owned system, held about one-third, or $70 billion, of the $211-billion farm debt in 1985. On December 18, Congress passed legislation to assist the system. The bill tightened federal regulation of the system and restructured it to enable stronger units in the 37-bank network to aid weaker units. Congress also provided federal backup funds to be used if the system's own resources proved insufficient.

Foreign Competition. Declining U.S. farm exports contributed significantly to the problems facing American farmers. In fiscal 1985—ending September 30—farm exports fell to $31.2 billion from $38 billion in 1984. The 1985 figure represented a 28 per cent drop from 1981's record level of $43.5 billion.

One of the clearest examples of the global competition that hurt American farmers concerned

Agricultural Statistics, 1985

World Crop Production
(million units)

Crop	Units	1984-1985*	1985-1986*†	% U.S. 1985-1986†
Corn	Metric tons	455	475	47
Wheat	Metric tons	514	505	13
Rice (rough)	Metric tons	469	466	1
Barley	Metric tons	173	179	7
Oats	Metric tons	46	48	16
Rye	Metric tons	33	31	2
Soybeans	Metric tons	91	99	59
Cotton	Bales‡	87	81	17
Coffee	Bags§	90	99	0.3
Sugar (centrifugal)	Short tons	101	98	5.5

*Crop year. †Preliminary.
‡480 pounds (217.7 kilograms) net.
§132.3 pounds (60 kilograms).

Output of Major U.S. Crops
(millions of bushels)

Crop	1962-1966*	1984-1985†	1985-1986†‡
Corn	3,876	7,656	8,717
Sorghum	595	866	1,127
Oats	912	472	537
Wheat	1,229	2,595	2,419
Soybeans	769	1,861	2,129
Rice (rough)§	742	1,370	1,315
Potatoes#	275	363	400
Cotton**	140	130	138
Tobacco††	2,126	1,727	1,526

*Average. †Crop year. ‡Preliminary.
§100,000 hundredweight (4.54 million kilograms).
#1 million hundredweight (45.4 million kilograms).
**100,000 bales (50 million pounds) (22.7 million kilograms).
††1 million pounds (454,000 kilograms).

U.S. Production of Animal Products
(millions of pounds)

	1957-1959*	1984-1985†	1985-1986†‡
Beef	13,704	23,499	22,175
Veal	1,240	493	465
Lamb and mutton	711	354	322
Pork	10,957	14,711	14,600
Eggs§	5,475	5,704	5,655
Turkey	1,382	2,813	2,985
Total milk#	1,230	1,432	1,480
Broilers	4,430	13,584	14,200

*Average. †Crop year. ‡Preliminary.
§1 million dozens.
#100 millions of pounds (45.4 million kilograms).

China, which has moved from being a customer to a competitor in the 1980's. In fiscal 1981, China bought $2.2 billion in U.S. farm products, ranking fourth among U.S. farm customers. By fiscal 1985, United States sales to China had skidded to about $500 million.

Dramatic changes in China's government policies that gave farmers financial incentives to grow crops resulted in such increases as 150 per cent more cotton, 84 per cent more oilseed crops, 58 per cent more wheat, and 27 per cent more rice than was grown in 1978. In late December 1985, however, China said that the 1985 grain harvest would be only about 354 million short tons (321 million metric tons), a 13 per cent decrease from

1984. Bad weather was cited as one reason for the drop. Severe summer floods hit several northeastern provinces, drastically reducing crops there.

In fiscal 1985, the Soviet Union bought less than 2.9 million metric tons (2.6 million short tons) of wheat, 1.1 million metric tons (1 million short tons) less than it had promised to buy in a 1983 U.S.-Soviet grain agreement. In August 1985, the Soviets agreed to purchase an additional 1.1 million metric tons of wheat to make up for the shortfall, but it did not do so.

Trade Problems. Economic pressure on U.S. farmers heightened trade friction, especially with the European Community (EC or Common Market), which subsidizes its farm exports. In retaliation for what the United States said was the EC's refusal to lift restrictions on U.S. citrus products, the Reagan Administration in June raised duties on imports of Italian pasta. The EC countered by levying tariffs on U.S. lemons and walnuts.

In May, the Reagan Administration also set up a limited program to subsidize some farm exports with government-owned surpluses to win back foreign markets lost to the Europeans. In August, the United States, in response to complaints by U.S. hog producers, imposed duties on imports of hogs from Canada.   Sonja Hillgren

See also FOOD. In WORLD BOOK, see AGRICULTURE; FARM AND FARMING.

FASHION. Diametrically different styles existed side by side in 1985, often in the same woman's wardrobe. Long hemlines appeared along with very short ones. Clingy, draped dresses were acceptable, as were oversized sweaters and jackets.

An Absence of Uniformity marked the 1985 collections. Fashion became permissive, welcoming a variety of shapes and lengths and a broad spectrum of colors. Shoulders tended to be wide and padded, but that was the only unifying element.

The world of fashion recognized at least four capitals in 1985. Paris maintained its long-standing position of leadership and supplemented ready-to-wear clothes with a revival of its *couture*, or made-to-order, business. Milan solidified its place as the center of Italian fashion, specializing in luxurious casual clothes, especially leathers and knitwear. London continued its bid to regain the reputation it enjoyed during the 1960's as the spawning ground of kicky, young clothes. New York City designers strengthened their hold on the sportswear market, branching out into lower-priced clothing to appeal to a wider audience while maintaining their top-priced flagship collections.

Only Tokyo appeared to mark time. After astonishing the world a few years ago by showing baggy, strange-looking clothes in dark colors, Japanese designers seemed to be returning to the mainstream. They added bright colors to their

Donna Karan's first collection features sophisticated separates such as this sarong skirt of gray cashmere and matching dolman-sleeved sweater.

palette and pulled their shapes in closer to the body. The revolution they promised in world fashion had not taken place.

In all five fashion centers, the better-known designers consolidated their position. In France, Emanuel Ungaro, Yves Saint Laurent, Karl Lagerfeld designing for the house of Chanel, and Hubert de Givenchy were the major forces. Italy's biggest names were Valentino and Giorgio Armani. In London, such newcomers as Betty Jackson and Sheridan Barnett joined the established houses of Zandra Rhodes and Jean Muir.

The most prestigious American designers in 1985 were Geoffrey Beene and James Galanos. Along with Adolfo and Bill Blass, they designed clothes for first lady Nancy Reagan. Their styles were traditional, and they emphasized clothes for evening. American sportswear designers showed a bolder spirit, simplifying their clothes for a more modern look. Calvin Klein, Ralph Lauren, Anne Klein, and Donna Karan set the pace.

The Success Story of the year belonged to Donna Karan. For more than a decade after the death of its founder, Karan had guided Anne Klein & Company to its highly successful position. In the middle of 1984, she unexpectedly left Anne Klein to open her own company. Karan's fall 1985 collection, the first under her own name, received wide praise for its sophisticated yet feminine approach to casual, comfortable dressing. This approach was exemplified by a sarong skirt that tied seductively around narrow pants. Karan's resort collection developed the same concept in warm-weather wear for the Sun Belt. It, too, was well received. By the time her spring 1986 collection appeared, Karan was widely acclaimed as the designer of the year. Anne Klein & Company continued to prosper under the design direction of Louis Dell'Olio, who had worked with Karan. His clothes were in the classic sportswear tradition.

Stephen Sprouse, who tried to revive the miniskirts and spare shapes of the 1960's, had been touted for several seasons as the most promising U.S. designer. But in 1985, he went out of business. So did the Coty American Fashion Critics' Awards, which for 43 years had honored the country's most creative designers. There was talk of reviving the awards under other sponsorship.

No particular designer left a strong imprint on the year 1985. Fashion dictatorship seemed a thing of the past, along with a uniform look for everyone. Women could wear skirts of any length or trousers. Shorts showed up in spring collections as an alternative to miniskirts. There was a choice of a covered or a bare look for evening. Even professional women were not restricted during daytime to severely tailored suits in somber colors. Fashion was loosening the reins.   Bernadine Morris

In WORLD BOOK, see FASHION.

FIELD, SALLY (1946-   ), won the Academy of Motion Picture Arts and Sciences Award for best actress on March 25, 1985. The award honored her performance as a determined young widow struggling to save her farm in *Places in the Heart*. Field also won an Oscar for best actress in 1980 for her portrayal of a union organizer in *Norma Rae*. With her performance in *Places in the Heart*, Field, who began her career in light comedy, strengthened her reputation as an accomplished dramatic actress.

Field was born on Nov. 6, 1946, in Pasadena, Calif. Her first starring role was in the 1965 television series "Gidget." But her career soared in 1967 with the premiere of the TV series "The Flying Nun," in which she played Sister Bertrille. In 1973, she starred in the short-lived comedy series "The Girl with Something Extra."

Field made her motion-picture debut in 1967 in *The Way West*. Her other films include *Smokey and the Bandit* (1977), *The End* (1978), *Beyond the Poseidon Adventure* (1979), and *Absence of Malice* (1981).

Field's TV credits include *Marriage: Year One* (1971) and *Bridges* (1976). The 1976 TV movie *Sybil*, in which Field starred as a tormented woman with multiple personalities, won an Emmy for best comedy or drama special. Field married producer Alan Greisman in 1984. She has two sons from a previous marriage.   Barbara A. Mayes

FINLAND. A Soviet missile flew over Norway and crashed in Finland on Dec. 28, 1984, but its wreckage was not found until January 1985. The missile crashed in remote, frozen Lake Inari, about 115 miles (185 kilometers) west of Murmansk, Russia, a Soviet submarine base. The Soviets apologized to Norway and Finland for the incident. Finnish investigators identified the object as an SN-3 target missile used for firing practice. The Soviets said that the missile had gone off course because of a technical defect.

On February 1, the Soviet Embassy in Finland asked for the return of the wreckage. Finland returned the debris—the tail section but not the engine—on February 8, along with a bill for $83,000 for recovery costs.

Finland's longest border is with the Soviet Union, and the Finns did not wish to endanger their delicate relations with their powerful neighbor over the incident. Finland interpreted Moscow's rapid apology as an attempt to defuse a touchy situation.

Stalinists Lose. The moderate Eurocommunist majority of Finland's Communist Party held a conference on March 23 without the extremist Stalinist minority, a faction backed by Moscow. At the conference, the Eurocommunists decided to establish their own organizations in the eight districts controlled by Stalinists. The Eurocommunists con-

321

trolled nine districts. On October 14, the Communists expelled the eight Stalinist groups.

Spirits Lifted. Finland celebrated May Day, May 1, enthusiastically in 1985 because it marked the end of a month-long strike over pay in shops of the state-owned liquor monopoly Alko. During the strike, alcoholic drinks had been on sale only in licensed restaurants.

Buoyant Economy. The economic growth of 1984, sustained chiefly by exports and investments, persisted in 1985. Inflation and unemployment continued to fall slowly. The government expected the 1985 growth rate to be 4 per cent in real gross domestic product, the value of all the goods and services produced within the country, after adjusting for inflation. By August, growth was on target. An expansion of 4.5 per cent in industrial output brought unemployment down to 5.2 per cent and inflation to 6 per cent.

One continuing worry was Finland's increase in imports. But exports gained, led by agricultural and forestry products, chemicals, and metal goods. Capital continued to flow into Finland. Currency reserves were $2.7 billion in August, up from $1.2 billion in 1984.　　　Kenneth Brown

See also EUROPE (Facts in Brief Table). In WORLD BOOK, see FINLAND.

FIRE. See DISASTERS; FOREST AND BRUSH FIRES.

FISHING. Jack Chancellor, a fishing-tackle manufacturer from Phenix City, Ala., won the first prize of $50,000 in the 15th annual Bass Anglers Sportsman Society Masters Classic tournament held in August 1985 on the Arkansas River near Pine Bluff, Ark. He caught 43 pounds (19.5 kilograms) of bass in three days. Tommy Martin of Hemphill, Tex., received the second-place prize of $12,000.

In November, Burma Thomas of Rainsville, Ala., won $18,750 in the ninth annual Bass N'Gal Classic at Sam Rayburn Reservoir near Jasper, Tex. Her winning catch weighed 20 pounds 6 ounces (9.24 kilograms).

On November 8 and 9, 39 competitors vied for the $100,000 first prize in the Red Man All American Bass Championship at Lake Havasu on the Colorado River in Arizona. Ricky Clunn of Montgomery, Tex., won the event with a total catch of 17 pounds 10 ounces (8.0 kilograms). Danny Walden of Columbus, Mo., won the $15,000 second-place prize.

In October, the Arizona Game and Fish Commission issued a regulation intended to restore a 15-mile (24-kilometer) stretch of the Colorado River below Lake Powell's Glen Canyon Dam to the status of a trophy trout fishery. The rule, which requires anglers to use only flies and other

Dion Gilmore, 16, of Streaky Bay, Australia, shows off a 2,068-pound (938-kilogram) white shark he landed after a 1½-hour battle in May.

artificial lures on the section of river known as Lee's Ferry, was to take effect on Jan. 1, 1986. About 10 years ago, rainbow trout of more than 10 pounds (4.5 kilograms) were common in Lee's Ferry. Recently, fish weighing 2 pounds (0.9 kilogram) have been considered trophy catches.

Family Takes Shark. Dion Gilmore, 16, of Streaky Bay, near Adelaide, Australia, landed a 2,068-pound (938-kilogram) white shark in May 1985. Gilmore's grandfather coached him during a 90-minute battle with the shark, while his father steered the boat. The all-tackle record for a white shark is 2,664 pounds (1,208 kilograms).

Funds Threatened. In early 1985, the United States Office of Management and Budget (OMB) tried to freeze spending of approximately $77 million in excise taxes and import duties paid by fishing enthusiasts and boaters on their equipment. The federal government collects the money and distributes it to states and to the U.S. Coast Guard for the improvement of fishing and boating safety. The Senate Budget Committee included a provision in its budget resolution backing the OMB effort. The sponsors of the 1984 bill providing for the collection and distribution of the money, Senator Malcolm Wallop (R., Wyo.) and Representative John B. Breaux (D., La.), prevailed on Congress to drop the provision. Tony Mandile

In WORLD BOOK, see FISHING.

FISHING INDUSTRY. Preliminary estimates in 1985 indicated that the world fish catch in 1984 could set a record of 88 million short tons (80 million metric tons). The catch had fallen to 84 million short tons (76 million metric tons) in 1983 as a result of *El Niño*, a warm-water current in the Pacific Ocean that disrupted fishing. The 1984 increase was distributed almost equally between developed and developing countries.

The United States Fish Catch in 1984 reached 6.4 billion pounds (2.9 billion kilograms) valued at $2.4 billion, according to statistics released in 1985. The figures represented an increase in quantity of 941,000 pounds (427,000 kilograms) over 1983, but a decrease in value of $5 million. Larger landings of clams, salmon, and shrimp helped to offset smaller landings of other major species, including menhaden, anchovies, flounder, and rockfish. Fishing crews received the same average price for fish—37 cents per pound (0.45 kilogram)—in 1984 as in 1983. Per capita consumption of fish and shellfish in the United States hit a record 13.6 pounds (6.1 kilograms) in 1984, up ½ pound (0.23 kilogram) from 1983.

Fleets from other countries caught 3 billion pounds (1.4 billion kilograms) of fish and shellfish within the U.S. 200-nautical-mile (370-kilometer) economic zone in 1984. Japan continued to rank as the leading foreign harvester in U.S. territorial waters. Japan's catch of 2.1 billion pounds (950 million kilograms) made up 69 per cent of the total foreign landings. South Korea ranked second, with 605 million pounds (274 million kilograms), or 20 per cent of the catch. About 97 per cent of the total foreign catch in U.S. waters came from the Gulf of Alaska and the Bering Sea.

Salmon Treaty. The United States and Canada ended a long-standing dispute in March 1985 when President Ronald Reagan and Prime Minister Brian Mulroney signed a treaty regulating salmon fishing on the west coasts of both nations. As a result, fishing crews from Alaska and British Columbia were instructed to cut their harvests of chinook salmon in 1985, kicking off a 14-year program to rebuild salmon stock.

U.S.-China Fisheries Trade, which got underway in the early 1970's, posted further growth in 1984—to about $20.8 million. China's fish imports from the United States consist mainly of herring, and its fish exports to the United States are mostly shrimp and other shellfish. Sharply reduced tariffs on China's fishery imports should spark additional gains for United States exporters in this potentially large market. Donald R. Whitaker

In WORLD BOOK, see FISHING INDUSTRY.

FLOOD. See DISASTERS.

FLORIDA. See STATE GOVERNMENT.

FLOWER. See GARDENING.

FOOD. In 1985, the news for the United States food industry was generally good. Bountiful harvests of major food crops helped to hold food prices down to a relatively low 4.1 per cent increase. The Consumer Price Index—the most widely used measure of inflation—registered only a 3.6 per cent gain. Americans continued to enjoy one of the world's lowest rates of spending on food. Only 17.2 per cent of disposable income—income left after taxes—went for food.

The good news for consumers, however, spelled disaster for many farmers. Record crops pushed farm prices down. The lower prices—combined with declining exports; a lower inflation rate, which made farmland less valuable; and an overextended farm-lending system—forced many farmers out of business.

Parts of Africa continued to experience severe famine as a result of crop failures during previous years. Altogether, abnormal food shortages were reported in 20 countries, mainly in Africa and Asia. Eleven countries experienced unfavorable crop conditions, such as floods or droughts.

Eating Out accounted for slightly more than 40 per cent of the dollars spent on food in the United States in 1985. Menu prices rose by 3.9 per cent. Sales in all eating and drinking establishments amounted to $119.8 billion, a 6.2 per cent increase over the previous year. Because restaurant costs

Long strands of spaghetti made from sweet potatoes dry in the sun at a commune in China, where spaghetti is said to have originated.

rose by just 3.9 per cent, restaurants experienced a real growth rate of 2.3 per cent. The rate of growth, however, was lower than 1984's 5 per cent, a situation attributed to greater spending by consumers on durable goods, which left less disposable income for spending on food.

Fast-food establishments led in traffic and sales gains, primarily because of the increasing popularity of their breakfast menus. Sales increased markedly in the second half of 1985 after a slow beginning. Ethnic eating establishments continued to show the fastest growth.

Grocery Store Sales increased 7.3 per cent overall for a real growth rate of 3.5 per cent. Although sales volume continued to grow, the rate of growth was lower than that in 1984, continuing a five-year downward trend.

Combination stores—stores selling both food and drugs—led all others in average weekly sales, followed by superstores, warehouse stores, and conventional grocery stores. Superstores are supermarkets with at least 30,000 square feet (2,800 square meters). Warehouse stores are usually twice that size and charge lower prices but also offer less variety than superstores and conventional grocery stores. Warehouse stores led in average sale per visit with $21.92. Distinctions between the types of stores became increasingly blurred as the stores expanded and carried more types of items.

Food prices rose by 4.1 per cent. Although retail beef prices remained up, the difference between those prices and the prices received by cattle producers hit a new high. As a result, the producers complained to Congress that food retailers were not passing on lower prices to customers and that unless they did so—and thereby encouraged sales—some producers could face disaster. Food retailers, however, denied profiting at the expense of producers and said prices reflected lower-than-expected supplies.

Consumption. In general, 1985 saw a leveling off of several food trends of previous years. As two-paycheck families increased, convenience, taste, and ease of preparation became increasingly important. Brand-name products continued to flourish, as did higher-priced products, such as imported specialty foods, expensive cuts of meat, fresh seafood, and low-calorie frozen dinners.

Advertising. The Federal Trade Commission in September began to amend its food-store advertising rule so that grocers could offer rain checks or substitutes of comparable value when they ran out of advertised items. Under the previous regulation, adopted in 1971, retail food stores had to stock enough items to meet any "reasonably anticipated" demand for an advertised item.

Irradiation Controversy. During 1985, the Food and Drug Administration (FDA) approved the use

Coke Fans Fight for "Real Thing"

Some people said it was a colossal marketing mistake. Others called it a brilliant move to boost sales. On April 23, 1985, the Coca-Cola Company retired a 99-year tradition by changing the flavor of Coke, the world's best-selling soft drink. On July 10, however, amid an uproar by die-hard Coke fans who just weren't swallowing the new product, the company announced it was bringing back the original formula. The old Coke, renamed Coca-Cola Classic, would once again take its place on grocery store shelves, alongside the new Coke.

The decision to introduce a new, sweeter version of Coke was an attempt to add fizz to Coke's flat sales by appealing to teen-agers, the largest market for sugared soft drinks. It was also an effort to beat back the challenge from Pepsi-Cola, whch in recent years had made inroads in Coke's sales.

The results of extensive consumer tests of new Coke convinced Coca-Cola Company executives that they had a sure thing as well as "the real thing." In nearly 200,000 taste tests, 55 per cent of consumers said they preferred the sweeter taste of the new Coke to the more acid taste of the old.

Confident company executives introduced the new Coke with fanfare. The news spread quickly. According to Coca-Cola surveys, 81 per cent of Americans knew about the change within 24 hours. This figure was higher than the percentage of Americans who were aware, within the same period, of the first walk on the moon by astronaut Neil A. Armstrong in 1969. What Coke's taste tests apparently failed to reveal, however, was the psychological effect of tampering with a 99-year American tradition.

Company executives were prepared for a certain amount of resistance by some Coke fans, but they figured it would fade after a few months. They were not prepared for outrage. In the six weeks following the introduction of new Coke, Coca-Cola's headquarters in Atlanta, Ga., were besieged by angry telegrams and letters and nearly 40,000 telephone calls. One disgruntled Coke fan likened the change to "spitting on the flag." Furious old-Coke loyalists claimed that not only did new Coke taste worse than old Coke but it also lacked old Coke's zing, despite the company's insistence that new Coke had just as much carbonation. One newspaper columnist called new Coke "a Coke for wimps."

Some Cokaholics began to stockpile supplies of old Coke. The owner of a wine shop in Beverly Hills, Calif., sold 500 cases of old Coke for at least $30 each, three times the normal price.

Old-Coke clubs sprang up across the United States. Perhaps the most active of these was the Old Cola Drinkers of America, founded in Seattle by a 50-year Coke drinker named Gay Mullin. Mullin spent at least $30,000 of his own money to lobby for the return of the old favorite.

All this consumer pressure—and the extensive coverage it received in the media—had an effect. Less than three months after launching new Coke, Coca-Cola executives held another press conference to admit their mistake. Saying they had misjudged the "deep and abiding emotional attachment" Americans had to old Coke, they announced the product's return.

Another, perhaps more significant, factor in their decision involved sales figures for new Coke. Although new Coke went down reasonably well in most areas of the United States, sales dropped in the South, traditionally Coke's strongest market. Also worrisome was the 14 per cent jump in June in sales of all the soft drink brands made by Pepsi-Cola Company U.S.A., the largest monthly spurt in that company's 87-year history.

Some observers charged that the whole episode was a calculated maneuver to increase sales, pointing out that the controversy brought the company millions of dollars in free publicity. Donald R. Keough, president and chief operating officer of Coca-Cola, denied the charge, however. "Some critics say Coca-Cola made a marketing mistake," he said. "Some cynics say we planned the whole thing. The truth is we are not that dumb and we are not that smart. It's been a humbling experience." Barbara A. Mayes

The Old Cola Drinkers of America celebrate victory in July after Coca-Cola announced the return of original-formula Coke.

of irradiation on a variety of food products. In irradiation, foods are subjected to low levels of radioactive energy. The process kills insects and microbes and prolongs shelf life. The decision caused controversy in Congress, which introduced legislation to restrict the use of the process. No action had been taken by year's end.

Sulfite Ban. In August, the FDA announced a limited ban on the use of six sulfite preservatives by food markets and restaurants to keep fresh vegetables and fruit from turning brown. The ban did not apply to the more common use of the chemicals in packaged foods and in some drugs.

Sweetener Controversy. In September, the United States Circuit Court of Appeals in Washington, D.C., ruled that the FDA had adequately tested aspartame, a low-calorie sugar substitute, before approving its use by the public. The court also ruled that studies had disproved claims that the sweetener could cause brain seizures, birth defects, and other problems.

Nevertheless, consumer groups pointed to new studies published in 1985 that reported a link between aspartame and such problems. In November, the General Accounting Office, the investigative arm of Congress, launched a probe into the FDA's 1981 approval of the sweetener.   Bob Gatty

See also FARM AND FARMING; NUTRITION. In WORLD BOOK, see FOOD; FOOD SUPPLY.

FOOTBALL. The Chicago Bears, professional football's dominant team in the early 1940's, returned to form in 1985, winning 15 of their 16 regular-season games. In Super Bowl XX in New Orleans, the Bears defeated the New England Patriots. The University of Oklahoma gained near-unanimous acclaim as the best team in college football, and the three-year-old United States Football League (USFL) struggled to survive.

USFL. As in its previous seasons, the USFL played in the spring. On April 20, however, the USFL club owners reaffirmed their decision to move to a fall season in 1986, playing head-to-head against the established National Football League (NFL).

The American Broadcasting Companies (ABC), which had televised the USFL's first three seasons, opposed the move. The network said it would not televise USFL games in the fall because it did not need such programming then.

When the USFL could not find an over-the-air network to carry its 1986 games, it turned to satellite syndication. It also added to charges in its $1.32-billion antitrust suit against the NFL, accusing it of conspiring to monopolize pro football since 1945. The suit contended that by showing its games on all three major networks—CBS Inc., the National Broadcasting Company (NBC), and ABC—the NFL sought to eliminate competition.

Meanwhile, the USFL, which had 18 teams in 1984 and 14 in 1985, planned to play the 1986 season with 9—Arizona; Baltimore; Birmingham, Ala.; Jacksonville; Memphis; New Jersey; Orlando and Tampa Bay, Fla.; and Portland, Ore.

Each USFL team had been receiving about $1.3-million a year from television, compared with $14-million for each NFL team. The USFL estimated that it had lost $150 million in its three-year history.

In the 1985 season, the USFL teams played 18 games each from February to June. The Birmingham Stallions (13-5) and the Oakland Invaders (13-4-1) won the division titles and led eight teams into the play-offs. In the USFL championship game, which was played on July 14 in East Rutherford, N.J., the Baltimore Stars defeated Oakland, 28-24.

After the season, several USFL players signed with NFL teams, including such stars as running backs Mike Rozier and Gary Anderson, quarterback Steve Young, and receiver Anthony Carter. Some players paid their USFL teams as much as $1.1 million to buy out their contracts.

NFL. The NFL's 28 teams played 16 games each from September to December. The division winners were the Bears (15-1), the Los Angeles Rams (11-5), and the Dallas Cowboys (10-6) in the National Conference and the Miami Dolphins (12-4), the Los Angeles Raiders (12-4), and the Cleveland Browns (8-8) in the American Conference.

The most exciting team was the Bears, who won their first 12 games before losing to Miami, 38-24, on December 2. The Bears led the league in rushing offense, rushing defense, and total defense. They had the league's most visible player in William (the Refrigerator) Perry, a 308-pound (140-kilogram) rookie defensive tackle, who became celebrated for his occasional offensive running, blocking, and pass receiving near the opposing goal line.

Play-Offs. The six division winners qualified for the play-offs along with four wild-card teams—the New York Jets (11-5), the Patriots (11-5), the New York Giants (10-6), and the San Francisco 49ers (10-6). The tie-breaking rules kept the Denver Broncos (11-5) and the Washington Redskins (10-6) out of the play-offs.

The National Conference play-offs began on December 29 with the wild-card game at East Rutherford. The Giants defeated the 49ers, the defending Super Bowl champions, 17-3, as running back Joe Morris rushed for 141 yards (129 meters).

In the conference semifinals, the Rams routed Dallas, 20-0, on Jan. 4, 1986, in Anaheim, Calif., as running back Eric Dickerson ran for 248 yards (227 meters), a play-off record. On January 5 in Chicago, the Bears whipped the Giants, 21-0, as

National Football League Final Standings

American Conference

Eastern Division
	W.	L.	T.	Pct.
Miami Dolphins	12	4	0	.750
New England Patriots	11	5	0	.688
New York Jets	11	5	0	.688
Indianapolis Colts	5	11	0	.313
Buffalo Bills	2	14	0	.125

Central Division
	W.	L.	T.	Pct.
Cleveland Browns	8	8	0	.500
Cincinnati Bengals	7	9	0	.438
Pittsburgh Steelers	7	9	0	.438
Houston Oilers	5	11	0	.313

Western Division
	W.	L.	T.	Pct.
Los Angeles Raiders	12	4	0	.750
Denver Broncos	11	5	0	.688
Seattle Seahawks	8	8	0	.500
San Diego Chargers	8	8	0	.500
Kansas City Chiefs	6	10	0	.375

National Conference

Eastern Division
	W.	L.	T.	Pct.
Dallas Cowboys	10	6	0	.625
New York Giants	10	6	0	.625
Washington Redskins	10	6	0	.625
Philadelphia Eagles	7	9	0	.438
St. Louis Cardinals	5	11	0	.313

Central Division
	W.	L.	T.	Pct.
Chicago Bears	15	1	0	.938
Green Bay Packers	8	8	0	.500
Detroit Lions	7	9	0	.438
Minnesota Vikings	7	9	0	.438
Tampa Bay Buccaneers	2	14	0	.125

Western Division
	W.	L.	T.	Pct.
Los Angeles Rams	11	5	0	.688
San Francisco 49ers	10	6	0	.625
New Orleans Saints	5	11	0	.313
Atlanta Falcons	4	12	0	.250

Individual Statistics

Leading Scorers, Touchdowns
	TDs.	Rush.	Rec.	Ret.	Pts.
Louis Lipps, Pittsburgh	15	1	12	2	90
Marcus Allen, L.A. Raiders	14	11	3	0	84
Ron Davenport, Miami	13	11	2	0	78
Daryl Turner, Seattle	13	0	13	0	78
James Brooks, Cincinnati	12	7	5	0	72
Earnest Byner, Cleveland	10	8	2	0	60

Leading Scorers, Kicking
	PAT	FG	Longest	Pts.
Gary Anderson, Pittsburgh	40-40	33-42	52	139
Pat Leahy, N.Y. Jets	43-45	26-34	55	121
Jim Breech, Cincinnati	48-50	24-33	53	120
Fuad Reveiz, Miami	50-52	22-27	49	116
Tony Franklin, New England	40-41	24-30	50	112

Leading Quarterbacks
	Att.	Comp.	Yds.	TDs.	Int.
Ken O'Brien, N.Y. Jets	488	297	3,888	25	8
Boomer Esiason, Cincinnati	431	251	3,443	27	12
Dan Fouts, San Diego	430	254	3,638	27	20
Dan Marino, Miami	567	336	4,137	30	21

Leading Receivers
	No. Caught	Total Yds.	Avg. Gain	TDs.
Lionel James, San Diego	86	1,027	11.9	6
Todd Christensen, L.A. Raiders	82	987	12.0	6
Butch Woolfolk, Houston	80	814	10.2	4
Steve Largent, Seattle	79	1,287	16.3	6

Leading Rushers
	No.	Yds.	Avg.	TDs.
Marcus Allen, L.A. Raiders	380	1,759	4.6	11
Freeman McNeil, N.Y. Jets	294	1,331	4.5	3
Craig James, New England	263	1,227	4.7	5
Kevin Mack, Cleveland	222	1,104	5.0	7

Leading Punters
	No.	Yds.	Avg.	Longest
Rohn Stark, Indianapolis	78	3,584	45.9	68
Reggie Roby, Miami	59	2,576	43.7	63
Rich Camarillo, New England	92	3,953	43.0	75
Ralf Mojsiejenko, San Diego	68	2,881	42.4	67

Individual Statistics

Leading Scorers, Touchdowns
	TDs.	Rush.	Rec.	Ret.	Pts.
Joe Morris, N.Y. Giants	21	21	0	0	126
Roger Craig, San Francisco	15	9	6	0	90
Eric Dickerson, L.A. Rams	12	12	0	0	72
Walter Payton, Chicago	11	9	2	0	66
Mike Quick, Philadelphia	11	0	11	0	66
Ted Brown, Minnesota	10	7	3	0	60

Leading Scorers, Kicking
	PAT	FG	Longest	Pts.
Kevin Butler, Chicago	51-51	31-37	46	144
Morten Andersen, New Orleans	27-29	31-35	55	120
Ed Murray, Detroit	31-33	26-31	51	109
Mike Lansford, L.A. Rams	38-39	22-29	52	104
Paul McFadden, Philadelphia	29-29	25-30	52	104

Leading Quarterbacks
	Att.	Comp.	Yds.	TDs.	Int.
Joe Montana, San Francisco	494	303	3,653	27	13
Jim McMahon, Chicago	313	178	2,392	15	11
Dieter Brock, L.A. Rams	365	218	2,658	16	13
Danny White, Dallas	450	267	3,157	21	17

Leading Receivers
	No. Caught	Total Yds.	Avg. Gain	TDs.
Roger Craig, San Francisco	92	1,016	11.0	6
Art Monk, Washington	91	1,226	13.5	2
Tony Hill, Dallas	74	1,113	15.0	7
Mike Quick, Philadelphia	73	1,247	17.1	11

Leading Rushers
	No.	Yds.	Avg.	TDs.
Gerald Riggs, Atlanta	397	1,719	4.3	10
Walter Payton, Chicago	324	1,551	4.8	9
Joe Morris, N.Y. Giants	294	1,336	4.5	21
Tony Dorsett, Dallas	305	1,307	4.3	7

Leading Punters
	No.	Yds.	Avg.	Longest
Rick Donnelly, Atlanta	59	2,574	43.6	68
Dale Hatcher, L.A. Rams	87	3,761	43.2	67
Sean Landeta, N.Y. Giants	81	3,472	42.9	68
Greg Coleman, Minnesota	67	2,867	42.8	62

United States Football League Final Standings

Eastern Conference
	W.	L.	T.	Pct.
Birmingham Stallions	13	5	0	.722
New Jersey Generals	11	7	0	.611
Memphis Showboats	11	7	0	.611
Baltimore Stars	10	7	1	.583
Tampa Bay Bandits	10	8	0	.556
Jacksonville Bulls	9	9	0	.550
Orlando Renegades	5	13	0	.278

Western Conference
	W.	L.	T.	Pct.
Oakland Invaders	13	4	1	.750
Denver Gold	11	7	0	.611
Houston Gamblers	10	8	0	.556
Arizona Wranglers	8	10	0	.444
Portland Breakers	6	12	0	.333
San Antonio Gunslingers	5	13	0	.278
Los Angeles Express	3	15	0	.167

Individual Statistics

Leading Scorers
	TDs.	FG	Att.	1XP	Att.	Pts.
Herschel Walker, New Jersey	22	0	0	0	0	132
Jim Smith, Birmingham	21	0	0	0	0	126
Toni Fritsch, Houston	0	21	24	59	62	122
Gary Anderson, Tampa Bay	20	0	0	0	0	120

Leading Quarterbacks
	Atts.	Comp.	Yds.	TDs.	Int.
Jim Kelly, Houston	567	360	4,623	39	19
Cliff Stoudt, Birmingham	444	266	3,358	34	19
Bobby Hebert, Oakland	456	244	3,811	30	19
Chuck Fusina, Baltimore	496	303	3,496	20	14

Leading Receivers
	No. Caught	Total Yds.	Avg. Gain	TDs.
Richard Johnson, Houston	103	1,384	13.4	14
Leonard Harris, Denver	101	1,432	14.2	8
Jim Smith, Birmingham	87	1,322	15.2	20
Clarence Verdin, Houston	84	1,004	12.0	9

Leading Rushers
	No.	Yds.	Avg. Gain	TDs.
Herschel Walker, New Jersey	438	2,411	5.5	21
Mike Rozier, Jacksonville	320	1,361	4.3	12
Bill Johnson, Denver	212	1,261	6.0	15
Gary Anderson, Tampa Bay	276	1,207	4.4	16
Kelvin Bryant, Baltimore	238	1,207	5.1	12

Leading Punters
	No.	Yds.	Avg.	Longest
Stan Talley, Oakland	66	2,922	44.3	76
Case deBruijn, Arizona	65	2,765	42.5	79
Greg Cater, Orlando	87	3,685	42.4	64
Jeff Gossett, Portland	74	3,120	42.2	56

The 1985 College Football Season

1985 College Conference Champions

Conference	School
Atlantic Coast	Maryland
Big Eight	Oklahoma
Big Sky	Idaho—Nevada-Reno (tie)
Big Ten	Iowa
Ivy League	Pennsylvania
Mid-American	Bowling Green
Missouri Valley	Tulsa
Ohio Valley	Middle Tennessee
Pacific Coast	Fresno State
Pacific Ten	UCLA
Southeastern	Florida—Tennessee (tie)
Southland	Arkansas State
Southwest	Texas A & M
Southwestern	Grambling—Jackson State (tie)
Western Athletic	Air Force—Brigham Young (tie)
Yankee	Rhode Island

Major Bowl Games

Bowl	Winner	Loser
All-American	Georgia Tech 17	Michigan State 14
Aloha	Alabama 24	Southern California 3
Amos Alonzo Stagg (Div. III)	Augustana (Ill.) 20	Ithaca (N.Y.) 7
Bluebonnet	Air Force 24	Texas 16
Blue-Gray	Blue 27	Gray 20
California	Fresno State 51	Bowling Green 7
Cherry	Maryland 35	Syracuse 18
Cotton	Texas A & M 36	Auburn 16
Fiesta	Michigan 27	Nebraska 23
Florida Citrus	Ohio State 10	Brigham Young 7
Freedom	Washington 20	Colorado 17
Gator	Florida State 34	Oklahoma State 23
Holiday	Arkansas 18	Arizona State 17
Hula	West 23	East 10
Independence	Minnesota 20	Clemson 13
Liberty	Baylor 21	Louisiana State 7
Orange	Oklahoma 25	Penn State 10
Palm (Div. II)	North Dakota State 35	North Alabama 7
Peach	Army 31	Illinois 29
Rose	UCLA 45	Iowa 28
Senior	North 31	South 17
Sugar	Tennessee 35	Miami (Fla.) 7
Sun	Arizona 13 (tie)	Georgia 13 (tie)
NCAA Div. I-AA	Georgia Southern 44	Furman (S.C.) 42
NAIA Div. I	Central Arkansas 10 (tie)	Hillsdale (Mich.) 10 (tie)
NAIA Div. II	Wisconsin-La Crosse 24	Pacific Lutheran (Wash.) 7

All-American Team (as picked by AP)

Offense

Tight end—Willie Smith, Miami (Fla.)
Wide receivers—Tim McGee, Tennessee; David Williams, Illinois
Tackles—Jim Dombrowski, Virginia; Brian Jozwiak, West Virginia
Guards—Jeff Bregel, Southern California; John Rienstra, Temple
Center—Pete Anderson, Georgia
Quarterback—Chuck Long, Iowa
Running backs—Bo Jackson, Auburn; Lorenzo White, Michigan State
Place kicker—John Lee, UCLA

Defense

Linemen—Tony Casillas, Oklahoma; Tim Green, Syracuse; Mike Hammerstein, Michigan; Leslie O'Neal, Oklahoma State
Linebackers—Brian Bosworth, Oklahoma; Michael Brooks, Louisiana State; Johnny Holland, Texas A & M; Larry Station, Iowa
Defensive backs—Thomas Everett, Baylor; David Fulcher, Arizona State; Mark Moore, Oklahoma State
Punter—Barry Helton, Colorado

Player Awards

Heisman Trophy (best player)—Bo Jackson, Auburn
Lombardi Award (best lineman)—Tony Casillas, Oklahoma
Outland Award (best interior lineman)—Mike Ruth, Boston College

their fired-up defense shut down Morris' running and quarterback Phil Simms's passing.

The National Conference championship game on January 12 matched the Bears against the Rams in Chicago. The Bears won, 21-0.

In the American Conference wild-card game on Dec. 28, 1985, in East Rutherford, New England defeated the Jets, 26-14, by stopping the Jets' running game and leaving quarterback Ken O'Brien with a concussion. The conference semifinals began on Jan. 4, 1986, in Miami, Fla., where the Dolphins rallied from an 18-point deficit to defeat Cleveland, 24-21. On January 5 in Los Angeles, New England upset the Raiders, 27-20, making the most of three interceptions and three fumble recoveries.

That set up the American Conference championship game on January 12 with New England against the Dolphins in Miami. The Patriots won, 31-14.

In the Super Bowl on January 26, the Bears beat the Patriots, 46-10, in the most one-sided game in Super Bowl history.

Other Pro Football. NFL attendance averaged 59,568, and television ratings increased 16 per cent on ABC, 10 per cent on CBS, and 4 per cent on NBC. In the Grey Cup game for the Canadian Football League championship, the British Columbia Lions defeated the Hamilton Tiger-Cats, 37-24, on November 24 in Montreal, Que. In 1985, a panel of sportswriters and broadcasters elected quarterbacks Joe Namath and Roger Staubach, running back O. J. Simpson, center Frank Gatski, and NFL Commissioner Pete Rozelle to the Pro Football Hall of Fame in Canton, Ohio.

College. The major-college teams with the best regular-season records were Penn State (11-0), Bowling Green (11-0), Fresno State (10-0-1), Air Force Academy (11-1), Oklahoma (10-1), Miami of Florida (10-1), Iowa (10-1), Michigan (9-1-1), Florida (9-1-1), Louisiana State (9-1-1), and Tennessee (8-1-2).

After the regular season, the Associated Press (AP) poll of sportswriters and broadcasters ranked Penn State first in the nation, Miami second, Oklahoma third, Iowa fourth, and Michigan fifth. The United Press International (UPI) board of coaches ranked Penn State first, Oklahoma second, Iowa third, Miami fourth, and Michigan fifth.

The unofficial national championship was to be decided in the New Year's Day 1986 bowl games. If Penn State defeated Oklahoma in the Orange Bowl in Miami, it seemed sure to be named national champion. If Oklahoma won, it had a chance to become champion. Miami also had a chance if it beat Tennessee impressively in the Sugar Bowl in New Orleans. Iowa had an outside chance if it won impressively over UCLA in the Rose Bowl in Pasadena, Calif.

Heisman Trophy winner Bo Jackson of Auburn, a tailback, rushes for yardage during a game against Florida in November.

Penn State saw its opportunity vanish. It lost to Oklahoma, 25-10, as Oklahoma, ranked first in the nation in defense, took advantage of five turnovers—four interceptions and a fumbled punt.

Tennessee upset Miami, 35-7. Tennessee's blitzing defense sacked quarterback Vinny Testaverde eight times, intercepted him three times, and forced him to fumble three times.

UCLA trounced Iowa, 45-28, after forcing Iowa tailback Ronnie Harmon to fumble away the ball four times in the first half. Eric Ball, UCLA's second-string tailback, ran for 227 yards (208 meters) and four touchdowns.

The day after the bowl games, Oklahoma was named national champion. The AP poll placed Oklahoma first, Michigan second, Penn State third, Tennessee fourth, and Florida fifth. The UPI had the same rankings except that the Air Force Academy was fifth.

Bo Jackson, the Auburn tailback, was voted the Heisman Trophy as the nation's outstanding college player in the closest voting ever. Jackson received 1,509 points to 1,464 for Chuck Long, the Iowa quarterback.

Gerry Faust resigned after the 1985 season as the head football coach at Notre Dame. He was replaced by Lou Holtz, who had been the Minnesota coach the last two years.   Frank Litsky

In WORLD BOOK, see FOOTBALL.

FORD, GERALD RUDOLPH (1913-   ), the 38th President of the United States, took part in April 1985 in an unusual five-day gathering of more than 50 specialists in U.S.-Soviet relations, including former President Jimmy Carter and Soviet Ambassador Anatoly Dobrynin. The conference, held at Emory University in Atlanta, Ga., marked the continuation of a special relationship between Ford and Carter, who defeated him in the 1976 presidential election. They made two appearances together in 1984. On Feb. 12, 1985, they were both in Washington, D.C., for meetings with King Fahd of Saudi Arabia.

The wives of the two former chief executives, Betty Ford and Rosalynn Carter, appeared in January at American University in Washington, D.C., where they participated in a program on "Women in a Changing World." Betty Ford expressed strong support for the idea of a woman as U.S. Vice President and said she expected the Republican Party to nominate a woman as running mate to the 1988 presidential candidate.

Former President Ford continued during the year to serve on the boards of directors of several major corporations and made a number of appearances at televised celebrity pro-am golf tournaments. His golf game was hampered somewhat by an old knee injury.   Frank Cormier and Margot Cormier

In WORLD BOOK, see FORD, GERALD R.

Fire fighters in British Columbia in July carry water by helicopter to battle one of many forest and brush fires throughout western North America.

FOREST AND BRUSH FIRES, spread in most cases by unusually dry weather, burned millions of acres throughout the world in 1985. More than 200 brush fires raged across southern Australia in mid-January. The fires killed three people and destroyed at least 50,000 acres (20,000 hectares) of farmland.

Brush and timber fires charred more than 120,000 acres (48,600 hectares) in Florida in January and early February. The largest blaze scorched about 50,000 acres of uninhabited grassland in the Florida Everglades.

Rare Habitat Burned. In March and April, brush fires swept across southern Isabela Island, the largest of Ecuador's Galapagos Islands, which are famous for their unusual wildlife. The fires blackened about 100,000 acres (40,000 hectares), including the habitats of numerous rare animals. When the fire approached, rare dwarf penguins fled their breeding grounds, leaving eggs and chicks behind. In an unusual rescue operation, naturalists from Ecuador's national park service evacuated dozens of giant Galapagos tortoises to safe areas.

Fires in the Southeast. In April, fires blackened vast areas of brush and woodland in the Southeastern United States, which had suffered extremely dry weather during the year. The largest fires burned in North and South Carolina, where more than 150,000 acres (60,000 hectares) were charred. Major fires also struck Alabama, Georgia, Kentucky, Tennessee, Virginia, and West Virginia.

The worst brush fires in Florida's history raged throughout the state in mid-May. Fanned by strong winds, the blazes charred some 175,000 acres (70,800 hectares), destroyed about 200 homes, and killed two fire fighters.

The Blazing West. In July, the largest crew of fire fighters in United States history—nearly 17,000 men and women—battled brush and timber fires throughout the Western states. Major fires also burned in Alberta, British Columbia, and Manitoba, Canada. Altogether, the fires scorched more than 1,500,000 acres (607,000 hectares) in the United States and Canada. Lightning started most of the blazes by igniting tinder-dry foliage. But officials blamed arsonists for several fires, including one in Los Angeles that killed three people and destroyed more than 50 homes.

Twenty brush fires blackened about 100,000 acres (40,000 hectares) in southern California in mid-October. The state's hot, dry Santa Ana winds fanned the flames, which destroyed 21 homes before fire fighters controlled the last blaze on October 21. One man died of a heart attack while fighting to save his house from fire.   Sara Dreyfuss

FOUR-H CLUBS. See YOUTH ORGANIZATIONS.

FRANCE drew heavy criticism on Sept. 22, 1985, when Prime Minister Laurent Fabius admitted that French security forces had been involved in the sinking of a ship owned by an environmentalist organization on July 10. French agents sank the ship, *Rainbow Warrior*, while it was anchored in Auckland Harbor, New Zealand. The organization, Greenpeace, was going to use the ship to monitor French nuclear tests on Mururoa, an atoll in the Pacific Ocean. A Portuguese-born Dutch photographer, Fernando Periera, was killed in the explosion that sank the ship.

On July 23, New Zealand police arrested two French army officers and secret agents, Captain Dominique Prieur and Major Alain Mafart, in Auckland. They were charged with murder and arson, and warrants were issued for four other French agents. On August 26, a committee led by Bernard Tricot, a member of the Gaullist Party, reported that the French government and intelligence service had no knowledge of the sinking. New Zealand's Prime Minister David R. Lange called the report a "whitewash," and French media were skeptical. On August 27, Fabius ordered an inquiry into "important shortcomings" in the running of the French foreign intelligence service. On September 17, the French newspaper *Le Monde* (*The World*) charged that a team of military advisers had sunk the ship with the approval of Defense Minister Charles Hernu. Hernu resigned on September 20. Shortly afterward, Fabius announced the firing of Pierre Lacoste, chief of the French secret service.

On September 25, Fabius blamed Hernu for the sinking of *Rainbow Warrior*. Fabius also promised that France would compensate Periera's family. He did not mention an apology to New Zealand, however.

On November 4, Mafart and Prieur pleaded guilty to arson and to a reduced charge of manslaughter. On November 22, they were sentenced to prison terms of 10 years.

Quarrel with United States. France's President François Mitterrand came into conflict with United States President Ronald Reagan on two issues—the U.S. Strategic Defense Initiative, also called the "Star Wars" program, and plans for a new round of trade talks in 1986. At an economic summit held in Bonn, the West German capital, from May 2 to 4, Mitterrand bluntly refused to accept Reagan's invitation to take part in American space defense research and blocked plans for talks on the General Agreement on Tariffs and Trade (GATT), the chief international world trade pact. The first nations signed the GATT in 1947. "Europe must mobilize itself around a great project that is truly European," Mitterrand said concerning his objection to "Star Wars" participation. Mitterrand's motives for blocking the trade

French steelworkers burn a picture of President François Mitterrand during a protest against France's high rate of unemployment.

talks were a desire to protect France's agriculture and his anxiety about the 1986 French general election.

Election Setback. In regional elections on March 10 and 17, the Socialist and Communist parties suffered severe defeats in many areas. The balloting left these parties in control of only one-fourth of the councils of the nation's metropolitan departments. (Mainland France and the island of Corsica are divided into 96 such departments.) The result strengthened Mitterrand's support for plans, announced in April, to replace France's *two-round majority system* of voting with *proportional representation*. Under France's majority system, a candidate must receive at least 50 per cent of the vote to be elected. If no candidate receives 50 per cent, the top two candidates face each other in a runoff election. In proportional representation, seats are assigned to political parties according to their shares of the vote. France will use proportional representation in the 1986 elections. Mitterrand and other Socialist leaders expect their party to do better under this system.   Kenneth Brown

See also EUROPE (Facts in Brief Table). In WORLD BOOK, see FRANCE.

FUTURE FARMERS OF AMERICA (FFA). See YOUTH ORGANIZATIONS.

GABON. See AFRICA.

GAMBIA. See AFRICA.

GAMES AND TOYS. Retail sales of toys in the United States were expected to be 10 to 15 per cent higher in 1985 than in 1984. The industry's biggest business news, however, came from indications that sales, traditionally heaviest in the fourth quarter of the year, have begun to spread out. In 1975, 70 per cent of all sales took place in the fourth quarter. By 1984, fourth-quarter sales had fallen to 60 per cent of the annual total, and they were expected to drop to 55 per cent in 1985.

Big Hits. The first new toy to become a big seller in 1985 was the Bubble Mower from Fisher-Price Toys. This child-sized lawn mower that blows bubbles hit the stores in January and quickly became a favorite of preschoolers. Among the most popular toys in 1985 were Tonka Corporation's Pound Puppies, stuffed animals that came with adoption papers.

Dolls introduced in 1985 included Real Baby, a realistic-looking doll weighted to feel like an actual baby, and My Buddy, a toddler boy doll that was also weighted. Both dolls were made by Hasbro Incorporated. Two companies introduced female action figures. She-Ra, the Princess of Power, joined her brother, He-Man, in the Masters of the Universe collection by Mattel, Incorporated. Golden Girl, the other female action figure, was made by Lewis Galoob Toys, Incorporated.

The Cabbage Patch of Coleco Industries, Incorporated, sprouted Twins, a two-doll set, and World Travelers, dolls that brought along a suitcase filled with costumes from different countries. Oscar de la Renta, a well-known fashion designer, created four evening gowns for Mattel's Barbie doll. LJN Toys Limited created action figures based on such wrestling superstars as Hulk Hogan, Andre the Giant, and Jimmy Super-Fly Snuka.

Programmed Toys. Several manufacturers found new ways to incorporate microprocessors in toys, especially in cuddly stuffed animals. Teddy Ruxpin from Worlds of Wonder, Incorporated, became the first animated talking teddy bear. Its eyes and mouth moved along with the voice on a storybook tape cassette inside the bear. Chatter Animals from R. Dakin and Company and A. G. Bear from Axlon Incorporated talked back to their owners.

Monopoly, first produced by Parker Brothers in 1935, celebrated its golden anniversary in 1985. A World Monopoly Championship held in Atlantic City, N. J., marked the occasion. The new champion, 25-year-old Jason Bunn of Great Britain, won $15,140—the equivalent of the play money in a Monopoly set.   Donna M. Datre

In WORLD BOOK, see DOLL; GAME; TOY.

Stuffed animals called Wuzzles come with their own storybook, as manufacturers in 1985 marketed not only the toy but also the make-believe world it inhabits.

GARCÍA PÉREZ, ALAN (1949-   ), began a five-year term as president of Peru on July 28, 1985, succeeding Fernando Belaúnde Terry. García, the candidate of the left-of-center American Popular Revolutionary Alliance (APRA), wasted no time in establishing himself as a bold and controversial figure. In his inaugural address, García said his government would limit Peru's payments on its $14-billion foreign debt, linking them to the country's export earnings, a move described as the most daring challenge to bank creditors since the Latin-American debt crisis began. See PERU.

García was born on May 23, 1949, in Lima, Peru's capital. He graduated from the University of San Marcos in that city, earning his law degree, and continued postgraduate studies in law and sociology at universities in Madrid, Spain, and in Paris. Returning to Peru in 1978, García was elected to the Constituent Assembly that drafted Peru's current Constitution.

In 1980, he was elected to the 180-member Chamber of Deputies, one of Peru's two legislative houses. In 1984, García received APRA's nomination for president of Peru. In elections held on April 14, 1985, he led all candidates with 45.7 per cent of the vote. After his closest rival withdrew, García was named president-elect on June 1.

García is married to Pilar Nores and has four daughters. _Rod Such_

GARDENING. In 1985, the American Horticultural Society presented the first Wildflower Rediscovery Awards. The awards went to 10 people who discovered populations of American plants thought to have been extinct in the wild. One of the rediscovered plants is running buffalo clover (_Trifolium stoloniferum_), recently found in West Virginia after not having been seen since 1940. In addition, mat-forming water hyssop (_Bacopa stragula_), last seen in 1941, was rediscovered in Virginia; and _Amsinckia carinata_, which had not been seen since 1896, was found in Oregon.

Many of North America's native plants are endangered by land development and other threats. Botanists estimate that 10 per cent of the plant species in the continental United States and 40 to 50 per cent of the plants native to Hawaii are threatened with extinction.

New Essential Mineral. Scientists at the United States Department of Agriculture (USDA) Plant, Soil, and Nutrition Laboratory at Cornell University in Ithaca, N.Y., have discovered that soybeans, cowpeas, and possibly most other plants require tiny amounts of nickel for proper growth. It is the first chemical element shown to be essential to plants since scientists discovered in 1954 that chlorine is necessary for _photosynthesis_, the process by which plants use light to convert water and carbon dioxide into food.

Anniversary Celebrated. The Brooklyn Botanic Garden in New York City celebrated its 75th anniversary in 1985. The garden was founded in 1910 and was built on a rocky site, part of which had been used as a dump. Today, it is recognized as one of the world's most beautiful gardens.

Biological Control. In 1985, scientists at the USDA's Agricultural Research Service announced that they had identified several compounds in the spike rush plant that may be useful in natural weed control. The compounds, called _allelochemicals_, are released from the roots of the spike rush plant, injuring aquatic weeds growing nearby. Scientists at the USDA also discovered a chemical scent that attracts spined soldier bugs. This chemical can be used to lure soldier bugs to fields to feed on crop-destroying insects. After the pests have been eliminated, the soldier bugs can be lured to another area.

Home and Community Gardening. The National Gardening Association reported that there were more than 12,000 community gardens in the United States in 1985. Home and community gardens occupied about 1.3 million acres (526,000 hectares) of land and grew about $12 billion worth of produce. _Barbara W. Ellis_

In WORLD BOOK, see FLOWER; GARDENING.

GAS AND GASOLINE. See ENERGY SUPPLY; PETROLEUM AND GAS.

GEOLOGY. On Nov. 13, 1985, a volcano in northern Colombia that had not erupted in nearly 400 years exploded, causing floods of water and mud that killed at least 25,000 people (see COLOMBIA). Other major geologic events in 1985 included earthquakes in Mexico, more evidence of the importance of meteorite impacts in Earth's history, and the discovery of an ancient boundary.

Mexican Quake. On September 19 and 20, two powerful earthquakes struck Mexico. They were not unexpected. In May, geophysicists L. Victoria LeFevre of the California Institute of Technology in Pasadena and Karen C. McNally of the University of California, Santa Cruz, reported on their study of earthquake activity along the southwestern coast of Mexico and Guatemala, where one _tectonic plate_ (one of the huge segments of crust that make up Earth's outer surface) is being _subducted_ (thrust under) another.

LeFevre and McNally called attention to two _seismic gaps_—areas along the plate boundary where earthquakes had not occurred for a long time. They suggested these gaps were either areas where subduction was taking place without earthquakes or areas where earthquakes would take place. The second suggestion was in agreement with a widely accepted theory that major earthquakes are likely to occur at seismic gaps.

The September earthquakes and their aftershocks effectively filled one of the gaps. The major quake on September 19, which measured 8.1 on the Richter scale, was located approximately 40 kilometers (25 miles) below the surface at a point along the Pacific Coast near the border between the Mexican states of Michoacán and Guerrero.

Damage from the earthquake was most extensive in Mexico City, much of which sits on an old lake bed of loosely packed sediments. These sediments amplified seismic waves traveling near the surface with a frequency of about 2 cycles per second. The amplified waves particularly affected buildings between 7 and 20 stories high with similar vibration cycles. Shorter or taller buildings, with, respectively, shorter or longer vibration cycles, generally escaped damage because they did not absorb energy from the amplified waves.

The Sudbury Meteorite. In October 1985, a team headed by geologist Asish R. Basu of the University of Rochester in New York published evidence supporting the theory that the Sudbury Igneous Complex in Ontario, Canada, was formed by a meteorite impact.

The Sudbury structure, an elliptical formation about 60 kilometers (37 miles) long and 27 kilometers (17 miles) wide, contains the world's largest deposit of nickel ore. Basu's team analyzed the concentrations of specific *isotopes* (forms) of neodymium and samarium, two rare-earth elements, from each type of rock at the site. Because of their atomic structure, these elements are useful for determining whether rocks were formed in the crust or from magma from the mantle that moved up through the crust. The scientists found that the rocks in the Sudbury structure formed from the melting of crustal rocks by a meteorite impact about 1.84 billion years ago.

Ancient Boundary. In June, a team of scientists headed by geologist Douglas Nelson of Cornell University in Ithaca, N.Y., reported finding the buried boundary where a region that is now part of Georgia and Florida became joined to North America about 250 million years ago. About that time, North America collided with Africa, to which these regions belonged. For nearly 20 years, scientists have suspected that when the two continents broke apart about 50 million years later, southern Georgia and Florida were left behind as part of North America. But the scientists were unsure about the location of the boundary.

The scientists traced the boundary by setting up tremors in the earth with huge vibrators mounted on trucks. By analyzing the echoes of the sound waves, the scientists identified the underground structures marking the boundary.   Eldridge M. Moores

In the Special Reports section, see DOOMSDAY FOR THE DINOSAURS. In WORLD BOOK, see GEOLOGY.

GEORGIA. See STATE GOVERNMENT.

GERMANY, EAST. Hopes grew in 1985 that Communist Party Secretary General and State Council Chairman Erich Honecker would schedule a visit to West Germany. He had canceled a 1984 visit at the insistence of the Soviet Union. On March 12, 1985, while in Moscow to attend the funeral of Soviet leader Konstantin U. Chernenko, Honecker met with West German Chancellor Helmut Kohl. After two hours of cordial talks, Kohl and Honecker issued a communiqué emphasizing their desire to improve their countries' relationship while respecting the sovereignty of all European nations.

A Honecker visit became even more likely after an April 19 trip to Bonn, West Germany, by Günter Mittag, a member of the Political Bureau of East Germany's Communist Party. The Political Bureau establishes policy for East Germany, and Mittag is the member responsible for economics. Mittag discussed financial and economic issues with Kohl and Martin Bangemann, West Germany's economics minister. Political observers saw the visit as part of an effort by the two Germanys to show that they are on better terms.

East Germany was disappointed, however, by Kohl's decision not to send representatives to V-E Day celebrations in East Germany on May 8, the 40th anniversary of the Allied victory in Europe in World War II.

Honecker in Italy. On April 24, Honecker met with Pope John Paul II at the Vatican. They spoke in German, chiefly about East-West relations and the treatment of East Germany's 1½ million Roman Catholics. Honecker also met with Italy's President Sandro Pertini and Prime Minister Bettino Craxi. The visit was regarded as important in improving East Germany's relationship with the West.

Booming Economy. Annual economic figures issued on January 19 confirmed that East Germany's economy was one of the strongest among Eastern European countries. The nation's farmers harvested a record 11.5 million metric tons (12.7 million short tons) of grain. Produced national income rose 5.5 per cent, and labor productivity was up 5 per cent. Trade with the Soviet Union grew by 10 per cent. East Germany used scarce raw materials sparingly, following restrictive laws passed in 1981.

Mystery Credit. On July 10, East Germany received $600 million in credits from 100 banks in Western countries. East Germany did not reveal its reasons for obtaining the credits, but some observers said that East Germany would use them to modernize its aging industry. Others claimed, however, that East Germany would use the credits to aid the Soviet Union.   Kenneth Brown

See also EUROPE (Facts in Brief Table). In WORLD BOOK, see GERMANY.

GERMANY, WEST. A spy scandal shook Chancellor Helmut Kohl's government in the summer of 1985. On August 6, Sonja Lüneburg, a personal aide to Economics Minister Martin Bangemann, disappeared. A police search of her apartment turned up equipment that could be used to photograph documents. On August 16, another woman, Ursula Richter, vanished and was suspected of espionage. Richter worked for the League of Expellees, which represents Germans expelled from territory lost to Poland, the Soviet Union, and Czechoslovakia after World War II.

Investigators said that both women had fled to East Germany. A third suspected agent vanished on August 19. This suspect, a man identified as Lorenz Betzing, was a messenger at an army administrative center in Bonn, West Germany.

Spies Defect. On August 22, West Germany's counterintelligence service announced that a senior official, Hans Joachim Tiedge, had been missing since August 19. He was one of West Germany's top spy hunters, with responsibility for combating East German espionage networks. On August 23, East Germany reported that Tiedge was seeking asylum in East Berlin. The West German federal prosecutor, Kurt Rebmann, said that Tiedge knew virtually all the secrets of West Germany's intelligence service.

Kohl called the defection "catastrophic" and ordered a review of West Germany's security services. The scandal damaged North Atlantic Treaty Organization (NATO) security and put Bonn's relations with the United States in jeopardy.

On August 28, Kohl fired Heribert Hellenbroich, head of the secret service. Hellenbroich admitted that he knew Tiedge had "serious drink and debt problems that had made him a security risk" but said that removing him "could have made him a greater risk."

On September 17, Herta-Astrid Willner, a secretary in Kohl's office, defected to East Germany with her husband. She had worked in the chancellery since 1973.

Bitburg. Commemoration on May 8 of the 40th anniversary of V-E Day, celebrating the Allied victory in Europe in World War II, was another embarrassment for Kohl. After much agonizing by politicians on the role of a defeated nation in the celebration, Kohl told the Bundestag on February 27 that Germans should use the anniversary to reflect on the "precious value of freedom and the responsibility for preservation of freedom and peace."

But what had been intended as a symbolic gesture of reconciliation between two former foes turned sour. United States President Ronald Rea-

West Germany's Chancellor Helmut Kohl, second from left, plays host to Japan's Prime Minister Yasuhiro Nakasone and his wife in April.

gan had planned to commemorate V-E Day during a trip to Europe for a multinational summit meeting on economics. Jewish leaders had encouraged Reagan to include a stop at the former Nazi concentration camp at Dachau. On January 24, the White House announced that Reagan would not go to Dachau. And on April 11, the United States said that Reagan would lay a wreath at a German military cemetery in Bitburg. It was quickly reported that members of the Waffen SS—a Nazi elite military unit—are among the German soldiers buried at Bitburg. Jewish leaders in the United States and Europe as well as U.S. veterans' organizations tried in vain to persuade Reagan not to visit Bitburg. On April 19, the White House said Reagan would also visit the former Nazi concentration camp of Bergen-Belsen, near Hamburg. He made both visits on May 5.

Election Defeat. On May 12, Kohl's Christian Democratic Union suffered a heavy defeat in state elections in North Rhine-Westphalia. The Social Democratic Party won 52.1 per cent of the vote. Two issues dominated the election: Kohl's indecision on whether to support the U.S. Strategic Defense Initiative, also known as "Star Wars"; and West Germany's rising unemployment rate, which reached 10.6 per cent in February.   Kenneth Brown

See also EUROPE (Facts in Brief Table). In WORLD BOOK, see GERMANY.

GETTY, DONALD ROSS (1933-   ), was sworn in as Alberta's 11th premier on Nov. 1, 1985. On October 13, he had won election for the leadership of Alberta's Progressive Conservative Party (PC). He thereby succeeded retiring premier and party leader Peter Lougheed. During his political career, Getty has earned a reputation for being a tough negotiator and a staunch defender of Alberta's interests.

Getty was born on Aug. 30, 1933, in Montreal, Que. He grew up in Montreal and in Ottawa and Toronto, Ont. In 1955, he received a bachelor's degree in business from the University of Western Ontario in London. From 1955 to 1965, Getty played professional football as a quarterback for the Edmonton Eskimos.

Getty was first elected to Alberta's Legislative Assembly in 1967 as the member for the Strathcona West area of south Edmonton. He served as minister of intergovernmental affairs from 1971 to 1975 and as minister of energy from 1975 to 1979. Getty left politics in 1979 to work in the oil industry, becoming chief executive officer of Nortek Energy Corporation, an oil-field service company. He returned to politics in the summer of 1985 to enter the Alberta PC leadership race.

Getty and the former Margaret Mitchell married in 1955. They have four sons.   Robie Liscomb

See also ALBERTA.

GHANA. The economy of Ghana, which began showing signs of growth in 1984 after many years of decline, continued to improve in 1985. Minister of Finance Kwesi Botchway announced on April 18 that the nation's economic output had increased by 7.6 per cent in 1984 and that a growth rate of more than 5 per cent was feasible for 1985.

Higher amounts of rainfall enabled farmers to expand agricultural production. And because more water was available for generating hydroelectric power, the government was able to restore 24-hour electrical service to factories and other businesses.

Unemployment, however, remained high and worsened after some 300,000 Ghanaians who had gone to Nigeria in search of work were ordered by the Nigerian government to leave by May 10.

Ghana's relations with the United States were shaken in 1985 by a spy scandal. In July, Federal Bureau of Investigation (FBI) agents in Virginia arrested a Ghanaian, Michael A. Soussoudis, and an employee of the U.S. Central Intelligence Agency (CIA), Sharon M. Scranage. The FBI accused Scranage of giving Soussoudis details of CIA operations in Ghana. See CRIME.   J. Dixon Esseks

See also AFRICA (Facts in Brief Table). In WORLD BOOK, see GHANA.

GIRL SCOUTS. See YOUTH ORGANIZATIONS.

GIRLS CLUBS. See YOUTH ORGANIZATIONS.

GOLF. In the first three Grand Slam tournaments of 1985, four players—Curtis Strange in the Masters, Tze-Chung Chen in the United States Open, and Bernhard Langer and David Graham in the British Open—held leads going into the final rounds. All four fell back, and the respective winners with come-from-behind victories were Langer of West Germany, Andy North of the United States, and Sandy Lyle of England.

In the Masters tournament, held from April 11 to 14 in Augusta, Ga., Strange led by 4 strokes with nine holes to play. Then he bogeyed the two par-5 holes and took a 38 on the final nine. Langer, who started the final round 4 strokes behind Strange, rallied with a 68 for the last 18 holes. He won with a 72-hole score of 282. Strange, Severiano (Seve) Ballesteros of Spain, and Ray Floyd tied for second at 284.

In the U.S. Open, held from June 13 to 16 in Birmingham, Mich., Chen of Taiwan led by 4 strokes with 14 holes remaining. Then, on the fifth hole of the last round, he accidentally struck his ball twice on a sand-wedge shot out of high grass. That cost him a 1-stroke penalty, and he took a 4-over-par 8 on the hole. He bogeyed the next two holes and finished with a 77.

North had problems in the final round, landing in eight bunkers and reaching only 11 greens in regulation figures. Still, he shot a 74 for 279 and

Golfer Scott Verplank became the first amateur in 29 years to win a PGA Tour event by capturing the Western Open in August.

gained his first tournament victory since the 1978 U.S. Open. North finished a stroke ahead of Chen, Dave Barr of Canada, and Denis Watson of South Africa.

In the British Open, played from July 18 to 21 in Sandwich, England, Langer and Graham of Australia started the final round 3 strokes ahead of Lyle and three others. Langer and Graham finished with 75's. Lyle rallied for a 70, despite a bogey on the last hole, and won with 282. He beat Payne Stewart of the United States by a stroke and became the first Briton to win the tournament since Tony Jacklin in 1969.

PGA Tournament. The other Grand Slam tournament was the Professional Golfers' Association of America (PGA) championship, held from August 8 to 11 in Denver. Starting the final round, Hubert Green led Lee Trevino, the defending champion, by 3 strokes. On the last day, Trevino had four 3-putt greens for a 71. Green, helped by a 35-foot (11-meter) sand wedge into the cup, shot a 72 for a 278 and beat Trevino by 2 strokes.

Tours. The PGA Tour comprised 46 tournaments with more than $22 million in prize money. The Ladies Professional Golf Association (LPGA) tour had 35 major tournaments worth $9 million.

On the PGA Tour, Strange and Lanny Wadkins won three tournaments each. They also led in prize money—$542,321 for Strange and $444,893

for Wadkins, who was named Player of the Year. Scott Verplank—an Oklahoma State University student and the U.S. amateur champion—became the first amateur in 29 years to win on the tour when he captured the Western Open on August 4 in Oak Brook, Ill.

The star of the LPGA tour was Nancy Lopez, who won five tournaments. Alice Miller won four, and Pat Bradley and Amy Alcott won three each. Lopez also led in earnings with a record $416,472 to $384,376 for Bradley.

The winners of the major tournaments were Miller in the Nabisco Dinah Shore tournament from April 4 to 7 in Rancho Mirage, Calif.; Lopez in the LPGA championship from May 30 to June 2 in Mason, Ohio; Kathy Baker in the U.S. Open from July 11 to 14 in Springfield, N.J.; and Bradley in the Du Maurier Classic from July 25 to 28 in Montreal, Canada. Baker's victory was her first in two years on the tour.

Seniors. On the PGA seniors tour for professionals 50 and older, Peter Thomson of Australia won nine tournaments, Don January and Miller Barber won five each, and Lee Elder won four. In the major seniors tournaments, Barber won the U.S. Open, Thomson won the Tournament of Champions, and Arnold Palmer took the Tournament Players Championship. Frank Litsky

In WORLD BOOK, see GOLF.

GORBACHEV, MIKHAIL SERGEEVICH (1931-   ), was elected to the Soviet Union's most powerful position, general secretary of the Communist Party's Central Committee, on March 11, 1985. He succeeded Konstantin U. Chernenko, who died on March 10. See RUSSIA.

Gorbachev (pronounced *gawr baht CHAWF*) was born on March 2, 1931, in the district of Stavropol, an agricultural region between the Black and Caspian seas. As a young man, he worked on a collective farm in his native region.

Gorbachev obtained a law degree at Moscow State University in 1955 and returned to Stavropol, where he held a series of posts in the Young Communist League and became a Communist Party organizer for collective and state farms. In 1967, he obtained a degree in agriculture from Stavropol Agricultural Institute. In 1970, Gorbachev became first secretary of the regional Communist Party.

In 1978, Gorbachev went to Moscow to take the Central Committee post of secretary for agriculture. In 1979, he became a nonvoting member of the Politburo, the party's policymaking body. He became a full member in 1980.

Gorbachev's wife, Raisa, has lectured on Marxist-Leninist theory at Moscow State University. The Gorbachevs have a grown daughter and a granddaughter. Jay Myers

337

GREAT BRITAIN. The mood of the country appeared to be shifting against the ruling Conservative Party government of Prime Minister Margaret Thatcher during 1985. Thatcher's personal style was the subject of intense political debate among Tories—members of the Conservative Party. Her strong leadership qualities and unbending dedication to tough policies had enabled her to trounce Labour Party opposition in the 1983 general election. These same traits, however, were seen as liabilities in 1985 as unemployment stubbornly continued to rise and government spending on health, welfare, and education services was cut.

The first indication that voters were turning against the Conservatives came on May 2 when candidates of the allied Liberal Party and Social Democratic Party (SDP) scored widespread gains in local elections. The alliance gained the balance of power in 27 of 47 counties and deprived the Tories of majorities they had come to expect in 10 major rural areas.

A special election to fill a vacant seat in Parliament in the Welsh district of Brecon and Radnor on July 4 was won by the Liberal-SDP candidate, with the Labour Party candidate a close second. The Conservative Party candidate had won the seat with ease in 1983.

In the face of these setbacks, some Tory members of Parliament (MP's) began to clamor for policy changes, arguing that Thatcher should increase government spending in order to stimulate the economy and create jobs. On May 12, Francis Pym, a former defense minister and foreign secretary, announced the formation of Conservative Centre Forward, a group of Tory MP's seeking to persuade the government to show more concern for the unfortunates of society.

Others blamed the government's style for the Conservatives' drop in popularity. Thatcher's powerful public speaking voice, which had seemed to denote appropriate leadership qualities during the Falklands conflict in 1982, now sounded harsh and domineering to many people. Thatcher reacted by deliberately softening and lowering her voice in her speeches.

Cabinet Changes. On September 2, Thatcher revealed details of a Cabinet reshuffle, apparently aimed in large part at reducing unemployment, which stood at 13.2 per cent. The new team would fight the next general election, she said, which is expected in 1987 or 1988. Three ministers were dropped from the Cabinet. A member of the House of Lords, Lord Young of Graffham, was made minister for employment. Opposition leaders ridiculed Thatcher's choice on the grounds that Lord Young was a nonelected, wealthy aristocrat who was out of touch with the people. Another important move was that of Norman Tebbit from secretary of state for trade and industry to

Prince William, son of Prince Charles and Princess Diana, arrives at a London kindergarten on September 24 for his first day of school.

chairman of the Conservative Party, a key post in the forthcoming election campaign. Tebbit, a former Royal Air Force and civil airline pilot, was joined by Jeffrey Archer as deputy chairman of the party. Archer is a former Tory MP and an author of best-selling novels.

Britain's Labour Party in 1985 recovered much of the ground it had lost in the Tory landslide of 1983. At Labour's annual conference in early October, party leader Neil G. Kinnock made a determined bid to woo back middle-of-the-road voters who had been alienated by Labour's lunge to the left. He clashed with Arthur Scargill, left wing leader of the National Union of Mineworkers (NUM), who had led a disastrous coal strike that lasted almost a year, ending in March 1985. By a narrow vote, Scargill and his supporters committed any future Labour government to repay more than $1 million in fines levied on the union during the strike. But in a tough speech widely heralded as a triumph, Kinnock said he would ignore the decision.

Local Government. A number of local councils controlled by the Labour Party in economically depressed areas refused to reduce their spending to bring it within limits set by the government. The number of rebel councils soon dropped to two: Liverpool and Lambeth, an area of London. The Liverpool council, which had been controlled by left wing militants since May 1983, refused to fix legal *rates* (local property taxes) in accordance with government guidelines. This plunged Liverpool more than $35 million in the red. With bankruptcy looming, 31,000 public employees faced dismissal. To meet the payroll and maintain services, the council had to borrow money from a bank and use funds from its 1986-1987 budget.

Labor. Britain's labor unions had a bad year. The marathon coal strike, which began on March 12, 1984, collapsed when miners went back to work on March 5, 1985. As soon as the strike ended, the state-run National Coal Board began to close unprofitable mines. The strike had been called to prevent such closings. The miners' union appeared to be heading for a permanent split in October when miners in Nottinghamshire, South Derbyshire, and parts of Durham voted to break from the NUM and create a new Union of Democratic Mineworkers.

The Trades Union Congress (TUC), to which nearly all unions belong, was split over whether unions should accept government funds to pay postal charges for union balloting. The TUC policy was to reject the money, and it threatened to expel the Amalgamated Union of Engineering Workers because its leaders had accepted government funds. A temporary compromise was reached on September 4.

The National Union of Teachers, in a pay dispute, called out teachers on selective strikes beginning on February 26. At year's end, a settlement still had not been reached.

Espionage. On April 18, the government announced it was expelling two Soviet diplomats for spying. On April 22, the Soviets expelled three British diplomats, so Britain expelled three more Soviets.

On September 12, the government revealed that Oleg A. Gordievsky, a high officer in the KGB—the Soviet intelligence agency—had been a double agent working for the British for nearly 20 years. Gordievsky, a counselor at the Soviet Embassy in London, had been granted political asylum. Acting on information provided by Gordievsky, Britain expelled 25 Soviets for spying. The Russians retaliated by expelling the same number of Britons from Moscow. Britain then expelled six more Soviets on September 16, and Moscow responded by expelling six more Britons.

Urban Riots. Tensions between police and blacks in inner city areas led to serious rioting in 1985. In the Handsworth district of Birmingham, rioting erupted on September 9 after police attempted to arrest a black youth. Police battled with youths who looted and set fire to shops, causing the deaths of two Asian immigrants.

Rioting in the Brixton area of London on September 28 followed the accidental shooting of a

Britain's Prime Minister Thatcher addresses the U.S. Congress on February 20 in the first such speech since Winston Churchill's in 1952.

339

Union president Arthur Scargill, in a light-colored coat, leads British coal miners back to work on March 5, ending a bitter strike lasting nearly a year.

black woman by police. She was shot as police raided her house looking for her son, who was wanted on a firearms charge. The woman was permanently paralyzed. Black anger had been aroused by an earlier incident on August 25, when police accidentally shot dead a 5-year-old boy during another raid. On October 6, a policeman was stabbed to death in the Tottenham area of London during rioting that broke out when a black woman died of a heart attack during a police search of her home.

Soccer Tragedies. On May 11, 56 people died when a wooden stand caught fire during a soccer game at Bradford stadium in West Yorkshire. Thirty-eight people were killed and hundreds injured on May 29 when part of a stadium in Brussels, Belgium, collapsed during violent clashes between fans of a British soccer team from Liverpool and those of the Italian team Juventus from Turin playing in the European Cup final. British fans were largely to blame, and all English clubs were temporarily banned from playing on the European mainland.

Other Developments. British police announced on June 24 that they had foiled a major plot by the Irish Republican Army (IRA) to plant bombs in hotels in London and 12 resort towns as part of a campaign of economic sabotage. Only one bomb was found—on June 23 at a London hotel. On July 1, police charged Patrick Joseph Magee, 34, of Belfast, with bombing the Grand Hotel in Brighton on Oct. 2, 1984, killing five senior Conservative Party members. On Nov. 15, 1985, Prime Minister Thatcher and Prime Minister Garret FitzGerald of Ireland signed a landmark agreement giving Ireland an advisory role in governing Northern Ireland (see NORTHERN IRELAND).

A furor arose over the publication in April of the fact that the father of Princess Michael of Kent, wife of a cousin of Queen Elizabeth II, had been a Nazi during World War II (1939-1945). The London *Daily Mirror* revealed that Baron Günther von Reibnitz had joined the Nazi Party in 1930 and the SS—a select military unit—in 1933. Princess Michael said these facts were "a deep shame" to her.

Prince Charles and Diana, Princess of Wales, visited Australia in late October and the United States in early November. In Washington, D.C., they visited the National Gallery of Art and viewed the exhibition "The Treasure Houses of Britain: Five Hundred Years of Private Patronage and Art Collecting." They also traveled to Palm Beach, Fla., where Prince Charles participated in a polo match, playing for the Palm Beach All Stars.   Ian J. Mather

See also ENGLAND; IRELAND; SCOTLAND; WALES. In WORLD BOOK, see GREAT BRITAIN.

GREECE was stunned on March 9, 1985, when Socialist Prime Minister Andreas Papandreou withdrew his support for the reelection of President Constantine Karamanlis, a member of the conservative New Democracy Party, and backed Christos Sartzetakis, a Supreme Court judge. Karamanlis said Papandreou had "double-crossed" him. At the same time, Papandreou announced that he was seeking to curtail the president's powers. Karamanlis resigned on March 10. A quickly created alliance with the Communists gave the Socialists every chance of success in the election.

On March 29, Sartzetakis polled the required three-fifths majority—180 votes out of 300—in a tumultuous session of Parliament. He was sworn in on March 30. The election plunged Greece into a new constitutional crisis. Opposition parties challenged the validity of the election and refused to acknowledge Sartzetakis as head of state.

Early Election. Papandreou moved toward an early general election in a bid to end the crisis. On May 7, Parliament was dissolved after approving the constitutional reforms Papandreou had sought. The new laws deprive the president of the right to dissolve Parliament, dismiss the prime minister, or proclaim a state of siege.

Papandreou's Panhellenic Socialist Movement (PASOK) won 161 of the 300 seats in Parliament in the elections held on June 2. Papandreou said he wished to improve relations with the United States but confirmed that the government will close American bases in Greece when its agreement with the United States expires in 1988. He ruled out a dialogue with neighboring Turkey until it "withdrew its last soldier" from Cyprus.

Cyprus Failure. Repeated efforts during the year to reunify Cyprus failed. (Cyprus has been divided between Greeks and Turks since 1974. In November 1983, the Turkish Cypriots declared their part of the island an independent nation, the Turkish Republic of Northern Cyprus.) On Jan. 17, 1985, Cyprus' President Spyros Kyprianou met Rauf R. Denktaş, the Turkish Cypriot leader, at United Nations (UN) Headquarters in New York City. The meeting collapsed in wrangling over procedures, however.

Denktaş had accepted a settlement proposed by UN Secretary-General Javier Pérez de Cuéllar, but the Greeks spurned it. Denktaş promptly announced general elections in the Turkish sector, dashing hopes of a settlement. On April 18, Kyprianou said he would accept a revamped UN package for reunification of the island. Denktaş produced a new constitution, however, and on June 9 was elected president of the Turkish Republic of Northern Cyprus. Kenneth Brown

See also EUROPE (Facts in Brief Table). In WORLD BOOK, see GREECE.

GRENADA. See LATIN AMERICA.

GROMYKO, ANDREI ANDREYEVICH (1909-   ), on July 2, 1985, became the Soviet Union's head of state as chairman of the Presidium of the Supreme Soviet, the national legislature. The Presidium handles legislation between sessions of the Supreme Soviet. See RUSSIA.

Gromyko had long been a powerful figure in the Soviet Union, having served as foreign minister since 1957. The Presidium chairmanship is largely a ceremonial post, so political observers were not sure how Gromyko's change in position affected his standing among Soviet leaders. He retained great power, however, through his membership in the Politburo, the Communist Party's policymaking body, which he joined in 1973.

Gromyko was born on July 18, 1909, near Minsk. He began his career in 1936 as a research economist. He joined the Soviet diplomatic service in 1939. In 1943, he became ambassador to the United States.

From 1946 to 1948, Gromyko represented the Soviet Union in the United Nations Security Council. He was deputy foreign minister from 1947 to 1952, ambassador to Great Britain in 1952 and 1953, and first deputy foreign minister from 1953 to 1957. He joined the Communist Party Central Committee in 1952.

Gromyko and his wife, Lidiya, have a son and a daughter. Jay Myers

GUATEMALA. Marco Vinicio Cerezo Arévalo won a landslide victory in a runoff election on Dec. 8, 1985, for the Guatemalan presidency. The Christian Democrat, a left-of-center candidate, won 68 per cent of the vote in the runoff against Jorge Carpio Nicolle of the conservative National Union of the Center. Cerezo's inauguration was set for Jan. 14, 1986.

President-elect Cerezo pledged to make necessary reforms without unduly alarming Guatemala's entrenched aristocracy. Before taking office, he toured Central America, including Mexico and Nicaragua; Europe; the United States; and Venezuela. In Mexico and Venezuela, Cerezo pleaded for easy terms on Guatemala's oil purchases. In Europe and the United States, he sought reassurances that Guatemala will receive scheduled payments of $300 million in foreign aid.

As the new president prepared to take office in 1986, Guatemala experienced its worst depression in 50 years. Inflation ran at more than 50 per cent, and unemployment was estimated at 45 per cent. Nathan A. Haverstock

See also LATIN AMERICA (Facts in Brief Table). In WORLD BOOK, see GUATEMALA.

GUINEA. See AFRICA.

GUINEA-BISSAU. See AFRICA.

GUYANA. See LATIN AMERICA.

HAITI. See LATIN AMERICA.

Handicapped runner Steve Fonyo in May nears the end of his east-to-west run across Canada to raise funds for the Canadian Cancer Society.

HANDICAPPED. There is a large wage gap between handicapped and other workers in the United States, according to a study released in August 1985 by researchers at Syracuse University in Syracuse, N.Y., and Union College in Schenectady, N.Y. The study found that handicapped men earn 15 per cent less than their nonhandicapped counterparts. Handicapped women earn 30 per cent less than other women. The study, based on a 1972 survey of 5,000 disabled workers, was the first to document such pay discrimination.

Disabled Rights Issues. The Supreme Court of the United States on January 9 ruled unanimously that a state could be liable even for unintentional discrimination against disabled persons under provisions of the federal Rehabilitation Act of 1973. The case involved a suit by a group of handicapped people against Tennessee for eliminating some of their Medicaid health benefits as part of a larger cutback program. The high court ruling stated that the law was intended to protect the disabled against "thoughtlessness and indifference" as well as intentional neglect.

On June 19, the Canadian Human Rights Commission found that Canada's Department of National Defence discriminated against the handicapped. A requirement that military recruits be able to perform full combat duties, the commission said, prevented men with minor disabilities from enlisting.

A U.S. Appeals Court ruled in January that major airlines as well as small airlines are covered by a law prohibiting discrimination against the handicapped by any airline receiving federal funds. The court said major airlines are covered because they receive federal subsidies in the form of airport services, air-traffic controllers, and tax breaks.

Benefits Review. On December 5, Secretary of Health and Human Services Margaret M. Heckler announced that a review of social security disability requirements would resume in January 1986. The review of 2.6 million disabled workers under age 65 had begun in March 1981. But it was halted in April 1984 after complaints that thousands of deserving persons had been cut from the benefit roles. Heckler said that when the review resumed, it would be conducted under more equitable procedures, calling for substantial proof of medical improvement before a person's disability benefits could be taken away.

Infant Care. On July 25, the National Conference of Catholic Bishops and the American Jewish Congress issued a statement on the treatment of severely handicapped infants. They said medical treatment should be withheld only if treatment would prolong a child's dying.   Darlene R. Stille

In WORLD BOOK, see HANDICAPPED.
HARNESS RACING. See HORSE RACING.
HAWAII. See STATE GOVERNMENT.

HEALTH AND DISEASE. Public health officials grew concerned in 1985 about an "epidemic of fear" surrounding acquired immune deficiency syndrome (AIDS), a viral disease that cripples the body's disease-fighting immune system. Concern about AIDS intensified on July 25 when a spokeswoman for Rock Hudson disclosed that the actor was under treatment for AIDS. Hudson died of the disease on October 2.

AIDS Prevention Plans. On September 19, officials responsible for United States AIDS research efforts reassured the public that AIDS is not easily transmitted from person to person and issued recommendations on how individuals could reduce their risk of becoming infected with the AIDS virus. Scientists have found that the virus is transmitted mainly by sexual contact with an AIDS victim and by the sharing of contaminated hypodermic needles by intravenous drug abusers.

The government health officials said that most cases of AIDS had occurred among promiscuous male homosexuals and intravenous drug abusers. Only 1 per cent of all AIDS cases had occurred among heterosexuals, many of whom had been sexual partners of prostitutes or drug abusers. By year's end, about 15,000 AIDS cases had been reported in the United States.

On September 30, the U.S. Public Health Serv-

ice published a long-range plan designed to eliminate the spread of AIDS by the year 2000. The plan acknowledged that AIDS would probably continue to spread until at least 1990, the earliest date by which a vaccine or cure would be available. Therefore, the plan calls for early emphasis on educational programs designed to reduce transmission of AIDS from person to person.

At the start of the 1985-1986 school year, there was debate over whether schoolchildren with AIDS should be allowed to attend regular classes. The U.S. Centers for Disease Control (CDC) in Atlanta, Ga., in August recommended that most older children with AIDS be admitted without restriction. The CDC said there was no evidence that such children posed a threat to classmates. But the agency recommended greater caution with younger or neurologically handicapped children who are unable to control body fluids or who might bite other children.

The United States Food and Drug Administration (FDA) said on July 31 that a new test had succeeded in eliminating the AIDS virus from the national supply of blood used for transfusions. The agency had approved the first AIDS blood test in March.

Weighty Concerns. A panel of experts at the National Institutes of Health (NIH) in Bethesda,

Health and Human Services Secretary Margaret M. Heckler reports on March 22 that lung cancer now kills more women than does breast cancer.

Workers dismantle milk pipes at an Illinois dairy in April to test for salmonella bacteria that caused more than 18,000 poisoning cases.

Md., on February 13 concluded that obesity is "a killer disease" that deserves the same attention from doctors as other health hazards. The panel cautioned that people who are even 5 pounds (2.3 kilograms) above their desirable weight should reduce. But the panel urged doctors to begin treating obesity in patients whose weight is 20 per cent or more above desirable levels. The NIH estimated that 34 million Americans fall into that category. Of these, 11 million are severely obese and face increased risks of high blood pressure, diabetes, cancer, and other ailments.

Fish and Health. Two studies published in the May 9 issue of *The New England Journal of Medicine* showed a connection between eating fish and reduced risk of heart attack. One study, conducted by researchers at the State University of Leiden in the Netherlands, found that men who ate no fish were twice as likely to die of a heart attack as men who ate at least 30 grams (1 ounce) of fish a day. The Dutch researchers recommended that people eat one or two fish dishes per week to guard against heart disease. The other study, conducted at the Oregon Health Sciences University in Portland, found that a diet rich in fish oils was far more beneficial in reducing fat and cholesterol levels in blood than a vegetable-oil-enriched diet.

Sulfites and Salads. A growing number of allergic reactions to sulfites led the FDA on August 9 to propose a ban against use of these preservatives in supermarket and restaurant salad bars. Sulfites have long been used to preserve dried fruit and other processed foods. But they only recently became widely used in salad bars to keep fresh fruits and vegetables from turning brown. The FDA linked sulfites with hives, nausea and diarrhea, and other allergic reactions in some people.

Pregnancy Issues. Several groups of medical researchers reported in April that use of an intrauterine device (IUD) for birth control doubles a woman's risk of permanent infertility. Their studies found that women using IUD's face a higher risk of pelvic inflammatory disease, which can damage the Fallopian tubes and result in infertility. Scientists at Brigham and Women's Hospital in Boston and the University of Washington in Seattle advised women who have never had a child to use some form of contraception other than an IUD.

Margaret M. Heckler, U.S. secretary of health and human services, in July urged gynecologists to encourage their patients to quit smoking during pregnancy. Heckler cited evidence that smoking contributes to infant mortality.　Michael Woods

See also MEDICINE; MENTAL ILLNESS; NUTRITION; PSYCHOLOGY; PUBLIC HEALTH. In WORLD BOOK, see HEALTH; DISEASE.

HERNÁNDEZ COLÓN, RAFAEL (1936-　), became governor of Puerto Rico for the second time on Jan. 2, 1985. Hernández Colón, who was first elected governor in 1972, defeated incumbent Carlos Romero Barceló, who had beaten him in the 1976 and 1980 campaigns for the governorship. See PUERTO RICO.

At his inauguration, Hernández Colón pledged to reduce Puerto Rico's high unemployment rate. He also promised to abandon efforts to win more self-government for Puerto Rico, which is a United States commonwealth.

Hernández Colón was born in Ponce, Puerto Rico, on Oct. 24, 1936. He earned a bachelor's degree in 1956 from Johns Hopkins University in Baltimore and a law degree in 1959 from the University of Puerto Rico. While a student, he wrote a thesis on the political relationship between the United States and Puerto Rico that attracted the attention of Luis Muñoz Marín, then governor of Puerto Rico. In 1960, Muñoz Marín appointed him to Puerto Rico's Public Service Commission.

From 1965 to 1967, Hernández Colón served as secretary of justice. In 1968, he was elected to Puerto Rico's Senate. The following year, he became president of the Senate and leader of the Popular Democratic Party.

Hernández Colón married Lila Mayoral in 1959. They have four children.　Barbara A. Mayes

HERRINGTON, JOHN STEWART (1939-   ), became United States secretary of energy on Feb. 7, 1985, replacing Donald P. Hodel, who became secretary of the interior. Herrington was considered an unlikely choice for the position because he had no background in the energy field, having served as White House personnel director. Political analysts speculated that his main function as energy chief would be to carry out President Ronald Reagan's desire to dismantle the department.

Herrington was born on May 31, 1939, in Los Angeles. He graduated from Stanford University in California in 1961 and earned a law degree at the University of California in San Francisco in 1964. He was an attorney and businessman in the Los Angeles area from 1967 to 1981.

In 1981, Reagan appointed Herrington deputy personnel chief of the White House. Soon afterward, Herrington moved to the Pentagon as assistant secretary of the Navy in charge of manpower. In 1983, he returned to the White House as a consultant on improving staff organization and effectiveness and later was made director of personnel.

Herrington's wife, Lois, is an assistant attorney general at the Justice Department. The Herringtons have two daughters.   David L. Dreier

See also CABINET, UNITED STATES.

HOBBIES. See COIN COLLECTING; GAMES AND TOYS; STAMP COLLECTING.

HOCKEY. The Edmonton Oilers and the Philadelphia Flyers dominated the National Hockey League's (NHL) 1984-1985 season. The Oilers won the Stanley Cup play-offs for the second consecutive year.

The 21 NHL teams played 80 regular-season games from October 1984 to April 1985. Division winners were Philadelphia (113 points), Edmonton (109), the Montreal Canadiens (94), and the St. Louis Blues (86). As a result of the play-offs, Edmonton and Philadelphia reached the finals.

The Stanley Cup finals matched Edmonton's aggressive, high-scoring offense against Philadelphia's conservative defense. Philadelphia won the first game of the best-of-seven-game play-off finals by a score of 4-1. But Edmonton won the next three games, 3-1, 4-3, 5-3, and then clinched the title by winning the fifth game, 8-3, on May 30. In Edmonton's 18 play-off games, center Wayne Gretzky set play-off records with 17 goals, 30 assists, and 47 points. He won the Smythe Trophy as Most Valuable Player in the play-offs.

The Oilers began the season with 15 consecutive victories, an NHL season-opening record. Gretzky won a record sixth straight Hart Trophy as the regular-season's Most Valuable Player and his fifth straight Ross Trophy as scoring champion, with 73 goals and a record 135 assists for 208 points. Paul Coffey of Edmonton won the Norris Trophy as

National Hockey League Standings

Prince of Wales Conference

Lester Patrick Division

	W.	L.	T.	Pts.
Philadelphia Flyers	53	20	7	113
Washington Capitals	46	25	9	101
New York Islanders	40	34	6	86
New York Rangers	26	44	10	62
New Jersey Devils	22	48	10	54
Pittsburgh Penguins	24	51	5	53

Charles F. Adams Division

Montreal Canadiens	41	27	12	94
Quebec Nordiques	41	30	9	91
Buffalo Sabres	38	28	14	90
Boston Bruins	36	34	10	82
Hartford Whalers	30	41	9	69

Clarence Campbell Conference

James Norris Division

	W.	L.	T.	Pts.
St. Louis Blues	37	31	12	86
Chicago Black Hawks	38	35	7	83
Detroit Red Wings	27	41	12	66
Minnesota North Stars	25	43	12	62
Toronto Maple Leafs	20	52	8	48

Conn Smythe Division

Edmonton Oilers	49	20	11	109
Winnipeg Jets	43	27	10	96
Calgary Flames	41	27	12	94
Los Angeles Kings	34	32	14	82
Vancouver Canucks	25	46	9	59

Scoring Leaders

	Games	Goals	Assists	Points
Wayne Gretzky, Edmonton	80	73	135	208
Jari Kurri, Edmonton	73	71	64	135
Dale Hawerchuk, Winnipeg	80	53	77	130
Marcel Dionne, Los Angeles	80	46	80	126
Paul Coffey, Edmonton	80	37	84	121
Mike Bossy, New York Islanders	76	58	59	117
John Ogrodnick, Detroit	79	55	50	105
Denis Savard, Chicago	79	38	67	105
Bernie Federko, St. Louis	76	30	73	103
Mike Gartner, Washington	80	50	52	102
Brent Sutter, N.Y. Islanders	72	42	60	102

Leading Goalies (25 or more games)

	Games	Goals against	Avg.
Tom Barrasso, Buffalo	54	144	2.66
Pat Riggin, Washington	57	168	2.98
Pelle Lindbergh, Philadelphia	65	194	3.02
Steve Penney, Montreal	54	167	3.08
Warren Skorodenski, Chicago	27	75	3.22

Awards

Calder Trophy (best rookie) — Mario Lemieux, Pittsburgh

Hart Trophy (most valuable player) — Wayne Gretzky, Edmonton

Lady Byng Trophy (sportsmanship) — Jari Kurri, Edmonton

Masterton Trophy (perseverance, dedication to hockey) — Anders Hedberg, New York Rangers

Norris Trophy (best defenseman) — Paul Coffey, Edmonton

Ross Trophy (leading scorer) — Wayne Gretzky, Edmonton

Selke Trophy (best defensive forward) — Craig Ramsay, Buffalo

Smythe Trophy (most valuable player in Stanley Cup) — Wayne Gretzky, Edmonton

Vezina Trophy (most valuable goalie) — Pelle Lindbergh, Philadelphia

The Edmonton Oilers defend their goal in a clash with the Philadelphia Flyers during Stanley Cup play-offs in May, which Edmonton went on to win.

the league's best defenseman. Right wing Jari Kurri of Edmonton won the Lady Byng Trophy for sportsmanship, Pelle Lindbergh of Philadelphia the Vezina Trophy for best goalie, and Craig Ramsay of the Buffalo Sabres the Selke Trophy as best defensive forward.

Fatal Crash. Tragedy struck on November 10 when the 26-year-old Lindbergh crashed his red Porsche in Somerdale, N.J. Philadelphia's most valuable player died two days later.

World Championship. Eight nations played in the world championship from April 17 to May 3 in Prague, Czechoslovakia. The Soviet Union swept its seven games in the preliminary round robin and advanced to the medal round with Czechoslovakia, Canada, and the United States. The surprising U.S. team—of 10 NHL players and 11 college players—upset Sweden, Canada, and Czechoslovakia in preliminary games.

In the first game of the round-robin medal round, Czechoslovakia upset the Soviet Union, 2-1. That ended the Soviet Union's seven-year unbeaten streak in world championship games. On May 3, in the game for the gold and silver medals, Czechoslovakia defeated Canada, 5-3. The Soviet Union defeated the United States, 10-3, for the bronze medal, the third straight loss for the U.S. team in the medal round. Frank Litsky

In WORLD BOOK, see HOCKEY.

HODEL, DONALD PAUL (1935-   ), former United States secretary of energy, was sworn in as secretary of the interior on Feb. 7, 1985. Disappointed conservationists said Hodel's appointment marked a return to the proindustry days of former interior chief James G. Watt, under whom Hodel served until 1982. The new secretary quickly surprised many people, however, by siding with environmentalists on several issues, and he became increasingly unpopular with the energy industry.

Hodel was born in Portland, Ore., on May 23, 1935. He received a bachelor's degree in 1957 from Harvard University in Cambridge, Mass., and a law degree in 1960 from the University of Oregon in Eugene.

After practicing law in Portland, Hodel in 1969 became deputy administrator of the Bonneville Power Administration, a giant electric transmission system in the Northwest. He served as the utility's administrator from 1972 to 1977 and was often at odds with environmental groups for his advocacy of nuclear power and apparent lack of interest in conservation. From 1978 to 1980, Hodel was president of the National Electric Reliability Council in Princeton, N.J., an organization of electric utility companies. Hodel and his wife, Barbara, have one son. David L. Dreier

See also CABINET, UNITED STATES.

HONDURAS. A bizarre series of events in March 1985 set the conditions for a disputed presidential election in Honduras in November. At year's end, it was unclear just who would be sworn in as Honduras' new president on Jan. 27, 1986.

In March, a constitutional crisis erupted when President Roberto Suazo Córdova, a member of the Liberal Party, ordered troops to surround the Supreme Court building in the capital, Tegucigalpa, to prevent five newly appointed justices from taking office. In Honduras, the Supreme Court's nine justices are appointed by the National Assembly. On March 28, the Assembly voted to replace five justices who were members of the Liberal Party, charging that they were bending electoral laws to favor Suazo's hand-picked candidate for president in the forthcoming election.

Declaring that the Assembly had attempted "a technical coup d'état," Suazo issued warrants for the arrest of the five new justices. Four went into hiding, and the new president of the Supreme Court was jailed, charged with treason. In April, 53 members of the Assembly who voted for the five new justices also faced treason charges.

In May, a compromise was reached when the Assembly passed a new electoral law, which declared that the winner of November's presidential election would be the leading candidate of the party with the most votes. This appeared to give all the groups in the faction-ridden Liberal Party a chance to run their own candidates.

When the ballots were counted following the November 24 election, a new dilemma arose. The most popular vote-getter was Rafael Leonardo Callejas of the opposition National Party, who won 41 per cent of the total vote. The next highest was José Azcona Hoyo of the Liberal Party with 25 per cent. A field of four Liberal Party candidates, however, outpolled the National Party candidates by 51 to 45 per cent, and under the new electoral law, the winner of the election was Azcona, the leading candidate of the leading party. This result raised questions about the validity of the new law, however, because the Constitution states that the president must be elected directly by a majority vote. Azcona's apparent victory was expected to be challenged in the Supreme Court, but the Liberal Party appeared to have the upper hand by virtue of its support from the military.

Contras. No matter who won the election, the policy of providing bases in Honduras for some 15,000 *contras*—rebels fighting to overthrow the Sandinista regime in Nicaragua—was unlikely to change. On May 15, however, the government ordered the contras to abandon three bases bordering Nicaragua after they became frequent targets of Sandinista raids. Nathan A. Haverstock

See also LATIN AMERICA (Facts in Brief Table). In WORLD BOOK, see HONDURAS.

HORSE RACING. The second Breeders' Cup Series, held on Nov. 2, 1985, attracted many of the best horses in the United States and Europe. The seven races, offering total purses of $10 million, were run at Aqueduct Race Track near New York City. Proud Truth won the $3-million Classic. Pebbles, a 4-year-old filly from England, beat males in the $2-million Turf.

Owner Eugene V. Klein and his trainer, D. Wayne Lukas, won two of the high-paying races—the Juvenile Fillies with Twilight Ridge and the Distaff with Life's Magic. These victories put Lukas over $10 million in purses earned in 1985 by horses he trained, far exceeding his previous $5.8-million record, set in 1984.

Absent from Breeders' Cup competition were two 3-year-olds, Spend a Buck and Mom's Command. Both retired earlier in the year due to injuries. Spend a Buck went to stud on Sept. 14, 1985, with earnings of $4,220,689, the second highest in history. His total included a $2-million bonus for winning the Cherry Hill Handicap, Garden State Stakes, Kentucky Derby, and Jersey Derby. The bonus was paid by Garden State Park in New Jersey, where all but the Kentucky Derby were run.

Mom's Command became the sixth winner of the New York Filly Triple Crown, which includes

Major Horse Races of 1985

Race	Winner	Value to Winner
Belmont Stakes	Creme Fraiche	$307,740
Breeders' Cup Juvenile	Tasso	450,000
Breeders' Cup Juvenile Fillies	Twilight Ridge	450,000
Breeders' Cup Sprint	Precisionist	450,000
Breeders' Cup Mile	Cozzene	450,000
Breeders' Cup Distaff	Life's Magic	450,000
Breeders' Cup Turf	Pebbles	900,000
Breeders' Cup Classic	Proud Truth	1,350,000
Budweiser-Arlington Million	Teleprompter	600,000
Epsom Derby (England)	Slip Anchor	257,303
Grand National Steeplechase (England)	Last Suspect	67,349
Jersey Derby	Spend a Buck	600,000
Kentucky Derby	Spend a Buck	406,800
Marlboro Cup Handicap	Chief's Crown	300,000
Preakness Stakes	Tank's Prospect	423,200
Prix de l'Arc de Triomphe (France)	Rainbow Quest	312,000
Rothmans International (Canada)	Nassipour	262,800

Major U.S. Harness Races of 1985

Race	Winner	Value to Winner
Cane Pace	Chairmanoftheboard	$210,000
Hambletonian	Prakas	636,000
Little Brown Jug	Nihilator	129,770
Meadowlands Pace	Nihilator	509,000
Messenger Stakes	Pershing Square	145,068
Roosevelt International	Lutin d'Isigny	125,000
Woodrow Wilson Pace	Grade One	672,000

Smoke billows from the flaming grandstand of Arlington Park Race Track near Chicago in July, as fire totally destroys the 58-year-old facility.

the Acorn, Mother Goose, and Coaching Club American Oaks races. Mom's Command also won the Alabama Stakes.

Another notable retirement came in July when the career of thoroughbred racing's record money-winner, John Henry, ended because of a tendon injury. The 10-year-old gelding earned $6,597,947 while winning 39 of his 83 races. Thirty of his wins were in *stakes* (well-known races in which owners add to the purse).

Despite a fire on July 31 that destroyed the grandstand and clubhouse, Arlington Park near Chicago presented the Budweiser-Arlington Million on August 25 with temporary facilities for the 35,651 fans who attended. Teleprompter, a long shot from Great Britain, won the race.

Harness Racing. Nihilator dominated his sport as a 3-year-old, winning 23 of his first 25 races in 1985 and retiring with record career earnings of $3.2 million. Nihilator paced the fastest mile ever in a harness race with a time of 1 minute 49⅗ seconds on August 3 at the Meadowlands in East Rutherford, N.J. His sire, Niatross, paced a faster mile, but in a time trial, not a race.

Quarter Horse. Mr. Trucka Jet won $1 million by taking the All-American Futurity on September 2 at Ruidoso Downs, N. Mex.   Jane Goldstein

In WORLD BOOK, see HARNESS RACING; HORSE RACING.

HOSPITAL. Hospitals throughout the United States during 1985 continued to feel the effects of stricter government reimbursement policies for Medicare patients and other efforts by private industry and health insurance firms to control the high costs of hospital care. The American Hospital Association said in April that hospital costs during 1984 had risen by 4.5 per cent, the smallest increase since 1963. About 1.3 million fewer patients were admitted to hospitals in 1984 than in 1983. The association said on July 16, 1985, that this trend toward fewer admissions continued into the first three months of the year. The lower admission rate indicated that only the sickest patients were being admitted to hospitals.

Medicare Concerns. Trustees of the Hospital Insurance Trust Fund, which pays hospital bills through Medicare for about 30 million elderly and disabled Americans, said on March 28 that it would have enough money to remain solvent until 1998. Previous calculations had indicated that the Medicare fund would become bankrupt by 1991 or sooner. The Medicare fund trustees credited stricter government reimbursement policies, which pay hospitals at a fixed rate set in advance, with keeping the fund financially sound.

The Administration of President Ronald Reagan on May 28, 1985, proposed a one-year freeze on Medicare hospital payment rates to save $1.8-

billion. The Department of Health and Human Services, however, to comply with a federal court order, on July 1 authorized higher Medicare payment rates for hospitals serving large numbers of poor people. This was intended to compensate for the high costs of treating patients who have more serious illnesses because of a lack of routine care.

Major Merger. Hospital Corporation of America, based in Nashville, Tenn., and American Hospital Supply Corporation of Evanston, Ill., on March 31 announced plans to merge. Hospital Corporation is the largest U.S. chain of *proprietary* hospitals—private hospitals operated like businesses to make a profit. American Hospital Supply is the biggest U.S. distributor of hospital medical supplies. The proposed merger, if approved by the U.S. Department of Justice, would be one of the largest in corporate history.

A study reported in July by researchers at Johns Hopkins School of Public Health in Baltimore cautioned that the sale of large teaching hospitals to private chains could decrease the medical research they perform and the amount of free care they provide to the poor as well as hamper medical education. On October 15, a study group recommended that teaching hospitals be subsidized by taxes.   Michael Woods

In WORLD BOOK, see HOSPITAL.

HOUSING. See BUILDING AND CONSTRUCTION.

HOUSTON Mayor Kathryn J. Whitmire was elected to a third term on Nov. 5, 1985, after a campaign marked by discord over homosexuals and their civil rights. The controversy began in 1984, when the City Council passed ordinances barring discrimination against homosexuals in municipal jobs. But a petition circulated by conservative and religious groups forced a voter referendum on Jan. 19, 1985, and the laws were overturned by a 4 to 1 margin.

Whitmire was opposed in the November election by former Mayor Louie Welch, who held the office from 1964 to 1974. Welch blamed Whitmire for the growing number of sex-oriented businesses in Houston and for a local increase in acquired immune deficiency syndrome (AIDS), a disease that strikes mainly homosexuals and severely weakens the immune system.

Two weeks before the election, Welch, unaware that his microphone was on, quipped on television that one way to halt AIDS was to shoot homosexuals. The gaffe damaged Welch's already faltering campaign, and Whitmire defeated him easily at the polls, collecting almost 60 per cent of the vote. A conservative, antihomosexual "Straight Slate" ran for 6 of 14 City Council seats, but none of those candidates was elected.

The Economy of Houston, a center of the oil industry, continued to be depressed by low world-wide petroleum prices. The sluggish economy was reflected in one of the highest office and residential vacancy rates in the United States. In February, a University of Houston study found that there were 200,000 unoccupied residential units in the city. A national survey in August showed Houston to be third in the nation in office vacancies, behind Chicago and Dallas.

Houston's unemployment rate was about the same as the national average until October, when it rose to 8.1 per cent, 1 percentage point above the national figure.

Education. Teachers were one group of workers with no unemployment problem. The Houston Independent School District averted a 2,000-teacher shortage for the 1985-1986 school year only by making major changes in its recruiting policies. The district hired teachers from other countries, including Canada and Mexico. It also started a program that allowed college graduates without education degrees to teach while preparing to take a proficiency test for certification. In other actions, district officials imposed tougher standards for passing pupils on to the next grade.

Fire Chief Resigns. On April 12, Fire Chief Robert Swartout rocked the Whitmire administration by resigning less than four months after taking the post, complaining that he had too little authority. Swartout, the former fire chief of Seattle, had been hired after a lengthy nationwide search. He was succeeded by Assistant Chief Robert Clayton.

Crime. At midyear, Houston police statistics showed that major crime in the city had risen 0.2 per cent over 1984, reversing a two-year downturn. That increase was far less than the 9.9 per cent statewide jump in serious crime. In late March, however, state figures showed that the Houston police had solved only 12 per cent of all the crimes they investigated in 1984, well under the Texas average of 21 per cent.

Medical Care for Houston's needy became a controversial issue during the year. In January, the Hermann Hospital Estate, a 60-year-old nonprofit institution established to care for the poor, was found to be using less than 3 per cent of its budget for charitable work. The disclosure led to the resignation of four members of the estate's board of trustees and the indictment of four people on charges of theft and mismanagement. The remaining board members agreed to devote more of the estate's resources to charity.

In 1985, broad opposition arose to the Harris County Hospital District's plan to close its two charity hospitals and build two new ones. Critics said the board would better serve the poor—and the taxpayers—by renovating the old buildings. The issue had still not been resolved by the end of the year.   Charles Reinken

See also CITY. In WORLD BOOK, see HOUSTON.

HUNGARY continued to reform its economy but suffered some political strains in 1985. In March, delegates at the Communist Party congress re-elected 73-year-old Janos Kadar as leader for another five years. The delegates also elected three individuals to the Politburo, the party's policymaking body: Karoly Grosz, Csaba Hamori, and Istvan Szabo. Lajos Mehes lost his membership in the Politburo.

On June 8, Hungary held its first elections under new rules requiring at least two candidates for each contested seat in the National Assembly. A reported 93 per cent of the registered voters cast ballots, compared with 97 per cent in the most recent election, held in 1980. The June 8, 1985, elections failed to fill 42 seats. For the first time since the establishment of Communist rule in the late 1940's, no candidate for those seats received the required 50 per cent of the vote. A special election held on June 22 filled the seats.

From October 15 to November 25, Hungary was host to the Cultural Forum, held in accordance with the Helsinki Agreement of 1975, a pact that pledged increased cooperation between the nations of Eastern and Western Europe. During the 1985 forum, Hungarian authorities forbade dissidents from Hungary and other East European nations from holding an unofficial conference. The government did allow meetings to take place in apartments belonging to Hungarian dissidents, however.

Economic Reform. The main changes in Hungary's economic system in 1985 included a further push to eliminate subsidies granted to manufacturers of consumer goods; the introduction of competition into bank financing of business enterprises; an increase in competition among Hungarian companies in foreign trade; the establishment of business-management councils with worker participation; and a reduction in the tax on profits.

Industrial Output in the first half of 1985 was about equal to that in the first six months of 1984. Construction was down 13.3 per cent. The grain harvest reached the planned output of 15.4 million metric tons (16.9 million short tons). Severe energy shortages occurred in the early months of 1985 and toward the end of the year.

Exports to the West increased by 2 per cent in the first nine months of 1985, compared with the corresponding period in 1984. Exports to other members of the Soviet bloc rose by 11 per cent. In April, Hungary joined two United Nations agencies—the International Finance Corporation (IFC), an investment organization owned and financed by about 110 countries; and the International Development Association (IDA), which loans countries money on easy terms.   Chris Cviic

See also EUROPE (Facts in Brief Table). In WORLD BOOK, see HUNGARY.

HUNTING. On Sept. 20, 1985, Mike O'Haco shot what may be a world record pronghorn on his ranch near Winslow, Ariz. At that time, the Boone and Crockett Club, the organization that compiles the records for North American big game, was evaluating another pronghorn as a possible world record. Susan Whitaker of Wellton, Ariz., killed that animal in September 1984 near Seligman, Ariz. Preliminary measurements showed that the horns of Whitaker's animal were larger than those of one shot in Arizona in 1975 by Edwin L. Wetzler, the current recordholder. According to the Arizona Game and Fish Department, both Whitaker's and O'Haco's pronghorns should displace Wetzler's.

Ducks Down. The United States Fish and Wildlife Service's 1985 waterfowl survey, conducted throughout the United States and Canada in May, showed that about 62 million ducks would fly south in the fall, a 22 per cent decline from 1984. Biologists for the service said that only 1 of 10 species listed in the survey, the green-winged teal, showed a slight increase from 1984 to 1985. The numbers of all species were lower than the averages compiled since the survey began in 1969. Reasons cited for the drop include loss of habitat and possible overhunting.

Steel Shot. On Oct. 3, 1985, the United States Ninth Circuit Court of Appeals in San Francisco upheld an order issued by Federal District Judge Edward Garcia on August 26 requiring the use of steel shot for waterfowl hunting in parts of California, Illinois, Missouri, Oklahoma, and Oregon. Garcia's order resulted from a suit filed by the National Wildlife Federation against the U.S. Department of the Interior to protect the bald eagle from lead poisoning, a consequence of the bird's feeding on the remains of waterfowl killed with lead shot.

Both the National Rifle Association of America and the Wildlife Legislative Fund of America attempted to overturn the order. The Interior Department did not join these organizations in their appeal.

Illegal Grizzly. The Flathead County Justice Court in Kalispell, Mont., fined Gordon L. Pouliot $500 and revoked his hunting and fishing privileges for 2½ years for killing a grizzly bear illegally. Pouliot killed the bear behind his home near West Glacier one day after officials closed the season. The officials ended the season early because hunters had killed five of a quota of six female grizzlies. The court suspended the penalties because Pouliot had a permit to hunt grizzlies, and because he turned himself in to the authorities. Pouliot claimed that he did not know the season had ended when he killed the bear and that he turned himself in when he found out.   Tony Mandile

In WORLD BOOK, see HUNTING.

ICE SKATING. The Soviet Union took three of the four titles in the 1985 world figure-skating championships. In speed skating, the major world championships were won by Dutch and Soviet men and East German women.

The Figure-Skating Championships were held from March 4 to 9 in Tokyo with 119 athletes from 24 nations competing. The winners were Katarina Witt of East Germany in women's singles and the Soviet Union's Aleksandr Fadeev in men's singles, Elena Valova and Oleg Vasiliev in pairs, and Natalya Bestemianova and Andrei Bukin in dance. United States skaters won three bronze medals—Tiffany Chin of Toluca Lake, Calif., in women's; Brian Boitano of Sunnyvale, Calif., in men's; and Judy Blumberg of Tarzana, Calif., and Michael Seibert of Washington, Pa., in dance.

The surprise performer of the championships was 17-year-old Debi Thomas of San Jose in her first world championships. Despite a pinched nerve in her back and two falls in free skating, she finished fifth. She was the first black skater ever to represent the United States in international competition.

The United States Championships were held from January 29 to February 3 in Kansas City, Mo. Blumberg and Seibert won the dance for the fifth consecutive year. The other winners, all for the first time, were Chin, Boitano, and the pairs team of Jill Watson of Bloomington, Ind., and Peter Oppegard of Hacienda Heights, Calif.

Speed Skating. The most significant speed-skating championships were held on three consecutive weekends in February in Hamar, Norway; Sarajevo, Yugoslavia; and Heerenveen, the Netherlands. The winners were Hein Vergeer of the Netherlands in men's overall, Andrea Schöne of East Germany in women's overall, Igor Dhelezovski of the Soviet Union in men's sprint, and Christa Rothenburger of East Germany in women's sprint.

The Americans, who won no speed-skating medals in the 1984 Olympics, did better this time. Dave Silk of Butte, Mont., took the silver medal in the 10,000-meter race and placed sixth in the final standing. Dan Jansen of West Allis, Wis., finished third, and Nick Thometz of Minnetonka, Minn., was fourth in the men's sprint championship. Bonnie Blair of Champaign, Ill., placed second to Eiko Shishii of Japan in the world indoor short-course championships held from March 15 to 17 in Amsterdam, the Netherlands.   Frank Litsky

In WORLD BOOK, see ICE SKATING.

ICELAND. See EUROPE.

IDAHO. See STATE GOVERNMENT.

ILLINOIS. See CHICAGO; STATE GOVERNMENT.

Katarina Witt of East Germany displays the poise that won her the singles title in the world figure-skating championships in March.

IMMIGRATION

IMMIGRATION. For the third time in four years, the United States Senate voted in 1985 for a landmark revision of the nation's immigration laws, a congressional objective since the late 1970's. The Senate passed a sweeping measure by a vote of 69 to 30 on September 19 as a subcommittee of the House of Representatives Judiciary Committee began hearings on its own version of the legislation. House Democratic Leader James C. Wright, Jr., of Texas predicted the immigration bill would reach the House floor in early 1986. Both the Senate and House passed immigration bills in 1984 but adjourned without taking final action.

The Senate's 1985 bill would grant amnesty to aliens who illegally entered the United States before Jan. 1, 1980, and would provide for criminal and civil penalties against employers who knowingly hire illegal aliens. One provision—perhaps the most controversial part of the bill—would temporarily admit up to 350,000 agricultural workers each year from 1986 through 1988.

The Status of Aliens from Latin America was the dominant immigration issue in the United States during 1985. On January 14, the Department of Justice announced the indictment of 16 people, including a Protestant minister, 2 Roman Catholic priests, and 3 nuns, on a charge of harboring illegal immigrants. The trial began on November 15. The action was part of a nationwide crackdown on a "sanctuary" movement that provided a haven for people said to be political refugees from Central America. In addition, more than 60 illegal aliens were arrested. The Justice Department said that the aliens had fled their home countries to escape poverty, not political oppression.

Cubans Deported. On February 21, the U.S. government began putting into effect a December 1984 agreement with the Cuban government aimed at restoring normal immigration between the two countries. United States officials deported 23 Cuban criminals to Havana. The Cubans had been jailed in Atlanta, Ga., since coming to the United States in 1980 as part of a refugee boat lift from the Cuban port of Mariel. They were the first of 2,746 "excludable" Cubans, mainly criminals or mental patients, that the Cuban government had agreed to accept.

The deportations had been expected to clear the way for 20,000 to 30,000 Cubans to enter the United States each year. The U.S.-Cuban accord was suspended, however, by Cuban President Fidel Castro after Radio Martí, a U.S. government radio station, began Spanish-language broadcasts to Cuba on May 20. Castro termed them a "barefaced provocation." Frank Cormier and Margot Cormier

In the Special Reports section, see THE NEW NEW AMERICANS. In WORLD BOOK, see IMMIGRATION.

INCOME TAX. See TAXATION.

INDIA. Prime Minister Rajiv Gandhi moved in 1985 to solve some of India's long-standing problems. He sought solutions to complaints in Punjab and Assam states, initiated political reforms, and loosened government controls on the economy.

Punjab Peace Efforts. Violence in the Punjab—which had led to the assassination of Prime Minister Indira Gandhi, Rajiv's mother, on Oct. 31, 1984—continued into 1985. Extremists in the Sikh religious community, which makes up a majority of the Punjab's population, used terrorism to press their demands for control of the state. A wave of bombings on May 10 and 11 killed 85 people. On May 13, the U.S. Federal Bureau of Investigation announced that it had foiled a plot by Sikh extremists to assassinate Gandhi when he visited the United States in June. In July and September, two of Gandhi's political allies accused of stirring up anti-Sikh riots after his mother's murder were themselves assassinated.

Gandhi reached an agreement with the main Sikh political party, Akali Dal, on July 24 that met many Sikh demands that his mother had rejected. He signed a pact with Harchand Singh Longowal, a moderate leader of Akali Dal. Sikh extremists denounced the agreement, however, and Longowal was assassinated on August 20.

Despite the murder, Gandhi went ahead with voting on September 25 to elect an assembly for the Punjab, which had been ruled by the federal government since 1983, and to fill the state's seats in Parliament. Extremists called for an election boycott, but some 60 per cent of the voters turned out. The moderate Akali Dal won 73 of the 115 assembly seats, upsetting Gandhi's Congress-I Party, which got only 32 seats. Akali Dal also won 7 of 13 places in Parliament to Congress-I's 6.

An Air-India jumbo jet apparently disintegrated in midair and fell into the Atlantic Ocean on June 23, killing all 329 people aboard. Two Sikh groups claimed they had planted a bomb on the plane, as did a group seeking freedom from India for Jammu and Kashmir state. There was no immediate proof that the plane had been bombed. The same day, a piece of luggage awaiting an Air-India flight exploded in Tokyo, killing two people.

Assam Solution. Leaders of a Hindu student movement in Assam met with Gandhi on August 15 and then announced that they would call off violent agitation that had taken thousands of lives in six years. Assamese Hindus had been agitating since 1979 for the expulsion of Bengali Muslim immigrants, many of whom moved to Assam from Bangladesh. Under the 1985 agreement, immigrants who had arrived in Assam between Jan. 1, 1966, and March 24, 1971, could stay but could not vote for 10 years. Those who arrived after 1971 had to leave. Where they would go was unclear. President Hussain Muhammad Ershad of

Indian security troops stand guard in the background as the body of assassinated Sikh leader Harchand Singh Longowal is cremated in August.

Bangladesh said the immigrants were not Bangalees and were India's problem. In state elections on Dec. 16, 1985, the Assam People's Front, which called for the expulsion of immigrants, defeated Gandhi's Congress-I Party.

Gujarat Strife. Scattered violence took hundreds of lives in Gujarat state in 1985. The trouble began in February, after Gujarat's Congress-I Party government made election promises to increase from 10 to 28 per cent the quota of university places and from 31 to 49 per cent the share of government jobs reserved for lower-caste Hindus and those outside the caste system. The upper castes reacted with anger. Rioting, looting, and vandalism broke out on numerous occasions, and the army had to be called in twice to restore order. The trouble subsided when a new party leader withdrew the proposed quota changes.

Political Reforms. Gandhi tried during 1985 to reform a political system that had become corrupt and inefficient because of his mother's preference for supporters chosen more for their loyalty to her than for their honesty and competence. He had the Congress-I Party drop more than 1,000 incumbent state legislators and 70 ministers from the list of party candidates for March elections. In the voting, which chose assemblies in 11 states and 1 territory, the Congress-I Party won control of 7 states. Its share of seats in the 12 areas, which had been 84 per cent in December 1984 elections, dropped to 56.3 per cent. But Gandhi's overall political dominance remained unquestioned.

A new law initiated by Gandhi and passed by Parliament in January said members of Parliament or state assemblies would lose their seats if they failed to vote with the party for which they had been elected. Indian politics had long been chaotic because legislators frequently switched sides for money or other favors.

Spy Scandal. Government agents made a series of arrests, beginning on January 17, that revealed what was called India's biggest spy scandal since independence in 1947. The government charged that Indian businessmen had bribed government officials and staff to permit the photocopying of secret documents. The businessmen allegedly sold copies to French, Polish, and Soviet diplomats.

Economic Changes. The budget for the fiscal year that began on April 1, 1985, introduced major changes intended to reduce the government's control of the economy. Personal and corporate taxes were cut. Licensing requirements were abolished in 25 industries. To stimulate foreign trade, the government dropped export taxes on most items, increased some export incentives, and reduced import restrictions.   Henry S. Bradsher

See also ASIA (Facts in Brief Table). In WORLD BOOK, see INDIA.

INDIAN, AMERICAN. Canada's Parliament on June 28, 1985, struck down provisions in the 114-year-old Indian Act that denied rights associated with native status to many Indians living in Canada. According to the provisions struck down, any Indian woman who married a non-Indian lost her native status. The law had also denied native status to any Indian who became a member of the clergy, registered to vote, worked outside a reserve, joined the armed forces, or sent his or her children to a non-Indian school. In losing native status, Indians lost the right to live on reserves, participate in tribal affairs, and receive certain government benefits. Parliament's action could restore rights to an estimated 76,000 Indians. Some Indian groups objected to Parliament's action, arguing that it was not the government's business to decide who was or was not an Indian.

Meetings. The National Tribal Chairmen's Association, a group of Indian leaders in the United States, met in Reno, Nev., in January. The group voted to reject proposals made by the Presidential Commission on Indian Reservation Economies in November 1984. The commission's proposals included abolishing the Bureau of Indian Affairs, shifting ownership of Indian businesses from tribes to individuals, increasing outside investment in reservations, and giving federal courts jurisdic-

tion in certain Indian affairs. In rejecting the proposals, the Indian leaders said that they threatened the special status and sovereignty of Indian tribes.

Reuben Snake, chairman of the Winnebago tribe of Nebraska and Iowa, was elected president of the National Congress of American Indians at its 42nd annual meeting, held in Tulsa, Okla., in October. Snake said that he intended to block state government efforts to regulate bingo on Indian reservations. Courts have ruled that reservations are not subject to state laws limiting bingo jackpots. In December, a federal judge in Oklahoma ruled that the state has no authority to tax bingo games held by the Muskogee Creek Indian Nation. Bingo is economically important for many reservations.

Other Indian Leaders. In December, Ross O. Swimmer resigned as principal chief of the Cherokees to become assistant secretary of the interior for Indian affairs. His successor as principal chief of the Cherokees was Wilma P. Mankiller, his deputy principal chief. She became the first woman to serve as chief of a large American Indian tribe. At least 29 other women lead smaller tribes.

Land Settlements. In February, the U.S. government agreed to pay about $5.5 million to Wyandotte Indians in Kansas and Oklahoma. The payment settles a 143-year-old debt incurred when the government bought 9 million acres (3.6 million hectares) of land from the Indians but paid only half of what it was worth.

On March 4, the Supreme Court of the United States upheld the right of the Oneida Indian Nation to sue two New York counties for damages incurred when, in 1795, the state bought Indian land without the federal government's approval. The case, involving 900 acres (360 hectares) owned by the counties, was a test of Indian claims to about 100,000 acres (40,000 hectares).

The Narragansett tribe in October 1985 received 900 acres taken from their ancestors by the Rhode Island General Assembly in 1880. The land is part of a settlement reached between the Narragansett and federal, state, and local officials. Earlier in 1985, the U.S. government had given the tribe another 900 acres bought from private owners.

Misurasata Struggle. In November, Russell Means and two other leaders of the American Indian Movement announced that they would join Misurasata—a group of Indians fighting for self-determination against the Sandinista government of Nicaragua. The Sandinistas had promised the Indians a degree of autonomy, but Misurasata leaders feared that the government would keep its power over the Indians.   Robie Liscomb

In WORLD BOOK, see INDIAN, AMERICAN.

INDIANA. See STATE GOVERNMENT.

Navajo Indians meet in May to support members of their tribe refusing to move from land in Arizona awarded to Hopi Indians in a 1974 land settlement.

INDONESIA experienced political troubles and slower economic growth in 1985. In January, bombs damaged a magnificent Buddhist temple dating from the 800's at Borobudur in central Java, and fire ravaged a royal Javanese palace. These and other incidents were generally attributed to Islamic militants who opposed President Suharto's policy of making religious traditions secondary to a vague doctrine known as Pancasila.

Trials and Sentences. Trials of 10 men accused of bombing Chinese-owned businesses in October 1984 took place in 1985. Evidence brought out at the trials showed that Islamic religious leaders had encouraged reactions against the army's handling of clashes between Muslims and security forces in Jakarta's port district on Sept. 12 and 13, 1984. Some critics charged that the army had killed as many as 100 people and that the government had covered up its actions. A Muslim former Cabinet minister, H. M. Sanusi, was convicted of masterminding and financing the bombings and sentenced on May 15, 1985, to 19 years in prison. Other defendants got 10- to 17-year sentences.

Sanusi was a member of the Group of 50, an opposition organization. Since 1980, the group, which included a number of important former officials, had accused Suharto of corrupting the original principles of Indonesian democracy. Two other members, who had been held since they challenged the official account of the September 1984 troubles, were put on trial in August 1985 for trying to overthrow the government. One of them was Hartono R. Dharsono, a retired army lieutenant general who had been secretary-general of the Association of Southeast Asian Nations. He said his writings were meant not to undermine but to uphold the initial principles of the New Order that Suharto had promised during the early years of his administration in the late 1960's.

A member of a fundamentalist Islamic sect was executed in February 1985, and four others were sentenced to death. In May, the former head of a pro-Communist labor union, who had been imprisoned since 1968, was executed. Three other leaders of the outlawed Indonesian Communist movement, also imprisoned for 17 years, were executed in August 1985. Diplomats in Jakarta thought the government was trying to show that it was evenhanded with both the right and the left.

The Economy suffered from a worldwide drop in prices for oil, which with natural gas continued to account for 60 to 70 per cent of Indonesia's foreign earnings despite efforts to diversify. Attacking corruption, Suharto replaced half the country's customs officials with Swiss inspectors. He also moved to reduce red tape at Indonesia's ports.   Henry S. Bradsher

See also ASIA (Facts in Brief Table). In WORLD BOOK, see INDONESIA.

INSURANCE. As 1985 drew to a close, top insurance industry executives expressed optimism about the recovery of United States property and casualty insurers after 1984's disastrous results. In 1984, property and casualty insurers suffered a $3.8-billion net loss, their worst loss ever, as a result of higher payments on claims and declining investment income. Even securities analysts specializing in the insurance field became optimistic in late 1985.

This confidence may have seemed misplaced in view of the financial results for 1985, including an estimated operating loss of $5.5 billion and a pretax loss of $25.2 billion from *underwriting* (insuring against financial loss). This was $3.7 billion more than 1984's underwriting loss.

Positive signs, however, included a 20.9 per cent gain in net written premiums, which went from $117.7 billion in 1984 to $142.3 billion in 1985. Another improvement was an 11.3 per cent rise in net investment income, from $17.7 billion for 1984 to $19.7 billion for 1985. The industry also reported a $5-billion rise in surplus funds, which meant more insurance could be sold. (An insurance company generally writes premiums equal to three times its surplus.)

Peter Lardner, president of the American Insurance Association, an industry trade group, said in mid-November, "I think most of us can say we've weathered the worst of the storm." Also in November, a survey of 170 leading insurance executives found agreement that "the industry is basically healthy and growing." Investor confidence in the industry was another indicator. During the stock market rally of late September and early October, Standard & Poor's Corporation, an investment research service, listed property and casualty insurers fifth among the best-performing industries. Their stocks registered a gain of 17.4 per cent.

The Flip Side of the Coin, however, was the skyrocketing increase in the cost of insurance for businesses and government agencies. Even more disturbing were the exceptionally large number of midterm cancellations of insurance policies and the equally large number of policyholders who were refused renewal. These actions resulted from underwriters' fears about certain kinds of liability risks faced by—among others—day-care centers, manufacturers of consumer products, and local governments and such government agencies as transit systems and schools. Among those whose policies were canceled in midterm were the state of Colorado and, just before the start of the school year, nearly all U.S. school-bus companies.

The insurance industry blamed the cancellations and nonrenewals on a broadened definition of liability by U.S. courts and on the multimillion-dollar damage awards in recent years. In addition, *reinsurance*—that is, the coverage insurance companies buy to protect themselves—became more expensive and, in some cases, unavailable.

With large numbers of former policyholders forced to go "bare"—that is, without insurance—state legislatures and state insurance regulators began to look for solutions. The problem also attracted attention from Congress and from federal agencies. In August, consumer advocate Ralph Nader and Robert Hunter, president of the National Insurance Consumer Organization, charged that there was an insurance industry conspiracy aimed at forcing rates up. They called for an investigation by the Department of Justice.

States reacted in a variety of ways to the sudden unavailability of liability insurance. Responses included the formation of market assistance programs to put buyers of insurance in touch with sellers, and regulations that barred midterm cancellations and limited the reasons for nonrenewal.

There were also calls for joint underwriting associations to assign difficult risks to insurers. This approach would require legislation.

In Other News, losses from 34 catastrophes—hurricanes, tornadoes, and other natural disasters—in 1985 resulted in $2.8 billion in paid claims. This made 1985 the industry's worst catastrophe year.   Emanuel Levy

In WORLD BOOK, see INSURANCE.

INTERNATIONAL TRADE. World economic growth in 1985 slowed to about 3 per cent, largely because of an unexpectedly sharp decline in the United States growth rate to about 2.4 per cent. Japan's economy also grew more slowly than in 1984, while countries in Western Europe again achieved only modest growth, about 2.3 per cent.

Despite the slower growth, unemployment rates in the United States, Canada, and Japan fell slightly. The number of jobless in Western Europe, however, edged past 11 per cent of the work force, double the unemployment rate in 1979.

The economies of the developing countries, which rely heavily on sales to industrial nations, also grew more slowly in 1985. Still, their estimated growth rate of about 4 per cent exceeded their average annual growth in 1981-1984.

Inflation in the industrial nations again declined, to slightly under 4 per cent. It remained below 4 per cent in the United States and under 1 per cent in Japan. In Western Europe, it fell to about 5.5 per cent, the lowest in more than a decade. Inflation in the developing countries averaged about 40 per cent, the highest rate ever recorded.

The Foreign Debt Problems of many developing countries remained a concern in the international economy. By year's end, the overall debt of the developing nations was estimated at $865 billion.

The stagnating export revenue of the develop-

ing countries, due largely to falling commodity prices, aggravated the debt problem. Moreover, international banks further reduced their lending to highly indebted developing countries.

The two biggest debtors—Brazil and Mexico—failed to meet promised economic goals. As a result, the International Monetary Fund (IMF)—an agency of the United Nations (UN) that assists countries with large international payment deficits—suspended loan installments to these nations.

Aid to Developing Nations. Reacting to the rising concerns over the debt problems of the developing nations, the United States proposed two plans to boost loans to these countries at the annual meeting of the World Bank—another UN agency—and the IMF, held from October 7 to 11, in Seoul, South Korea.

Under one plan, commercial banks in the United States, many European nations, Japan, and Canada would lend an additional $20 billion and the World Bank and the Inter-American Development Bank would lend an additional $9 billion over the next three years to 15 heavily indebted developing countries. In return, these countries would have to agree to "growth-oriented" economic reforms, such as encouraging savings.

In a second proposal, the United States urged the establishment of a $2.7-billion lending pool for

President Ronald Reagan and Prime Minister Yasuhiro Nakasone of Japan discuss trade relations at a Los Angeles meeting in January.

A broker on the Paris Stock Exchange writes the quotation of the United States dollar as it hits a new high against other currencies on January 7.

loans to the world's poorest nations between 1986 and 1991. The proposal, designed chiefly to assist African nations, was widely endorsed. In return for the loans, the borrowing countries would be required to undertake economic reforms. Finance ministers at the World Bank-IMF meeting also agreed to the establishment of an agency to promote foreign investment in developing countries by insuring investors against political risks.

Summit Meeting. At an economic summit meeting in Bonn, West Germany, held from May 2 to 4, the leaders of seven major industrial nations—Canada, France, Great Britain, Italy, Japan, the United States, and West Germany—concluded that "world economic conditions are better than they have been for a considerable time." The seven leaders acknowledged, however, that the debt problems of the developing countries were "far from solved."

U.S. Trade Deficit. In June, the Organization for Economic Cooperation and Development (OECD)—an association of 24 industrial nations—issued a report warning that the U.S. merchandise trade deficit might reach "unmanageable proportions" and threaten world economic recovery. To avoid such problems, the OECD urged the United States to reduce its federal budget deficit. A smaller budget deficit, the organization said, would help to lower U.S. interest rates, bring down the dollar's value, and, eventually, reduce the U.S. trade deficit.

By September 1985, the growing deficit—which was expected to reach a record $145 billion in 1985—began to threaten an outbreak of protectionist legislation in Congress. In response, on September 22, Secretary of the Treasury James A. Baker III and the finance ministers of France, Great Britain, Japan, and West Germany announced they would work to reduce the dollar's value. A reduced dollar would make imported goods sold in the United States more expensive and make American goods sold abroad cheaper.

Almost immediately, the dollar's value fell by more than 5 per cent. By late December, it was down about 14 per cent from its February peak.

Concern over the U.S. trade deficit mounted in September when the United States became a net debtor in its international accounts for the first time since 1914. Foreign financial claims on the United States, in the form of loans and investment, exceeded U.S. claims on other countries.

World Trade Volume in 1985 grew by about 3 per cent, about one-third the rate of growth in 1984. Almost all the growth was in trade among the industrial nations and the more advanced developing countries that export manufactured goods. The biggest factor in the rise was a large jump in imports into the United States.

"Made in U.S.A." tags were required for all American-produced clothing and home furnishings beginning in September, to encourage consumers to buy U.S. goods.

Free-Trade Issues. Despite the huge United States trade deficit, President Ronald Reagan sought to maintain a "free-trade" policy. He rejected a proposal to impose import quotas on footwear in August, and he notified Japan in March that he would not ask it to continue limiting its car exports to the United States. Japan responded by raising the number of cars shipped to the United States by about 24 per cent.

The Reagan Administration, however, tightened controls on steel imports. By December, it concluded agreements with the European Community and 16 other countries under which those countries promised to restrain steel exports to the United States through September 1989.

Japan, whose trade accounted for almost one-third of the total U.S. deficit, announced on July 30 a new series of measures to ease restrictions on U.S. exports. Some of the steps, however, would not be fully implemented for three years.

Free-Trade Agreement. On September 1, the United States and Israel implemented the first stage of a free-trade agreement, the first such pact in United States history. The agreement, which was to be fully implemented by 1995, would permit the two countries to exempt each other's goods from import duties.   Richard Lawrence

In WORLD BOOK, see INTERNATIONAL TRADE.

IOWA. See STATE GOVERNMENT.

IRAN. President Ali Khamenei was reelected to a second four-year term on Aug. 16, 1985, receiving 12.2 million of the 14.2 million votes cast. He was opposed by two relatively unknown candidates.

Seventeen other potential candidates were disqualified by the ruling Council of Guardians headed by Ayatollah Ruhollah Khomeini. They included former Prime Minister Mehdi Bazargan, the leader of the Freedom Movement, Iran's token opposition party. The council rejected Bazargan's candidacy because of his opposition to the war with Iraq. But there was some popular support for Bazargan's position. Khamenei's closest challenger in the election, who also opposed the war, received 1.4 million votes, far more than expected.

New Leaders. On October 27, Khamenei formed a cabinet again headed by Prime Minister Hosein Musavi-Khamenei (no relation to the president). Musavi was opposed by many religious leaders who argued that his economic policies were too liberal. But Ayatollah Khomeini backed the prime minister. On October 28, the Majlis (parliament) approved 22 of the 24 cabinet ministers nominated by Khamenei, including Musavi.

Relaxation, Backlash. The absence of organized opposition encouraged the government to modify some of the stricter features of its Islamic system. In February, the revolutionary prosecutor in Teheran—who had become a symbol of the mass jailings and executions of the early years of the regime—was removed from office. The government also announced an amnesty in March for Iran's 10,000 to 20,000 political prisoners.

Some loosening of the strict Islamic dress and behavior code prescribed for women was allowed early in 1985. But this led to violent demonstrations by young fundamentalists, mostly from the poorer classes, who are the government's main supporters. In April and May, gangs of motorcyclists roamed the streets of Teheran, attacking women and couples who they said were not conforming to Islamic morality. About 300 of these young fundamentalists, called *Hezbollahis* (Servants of God), were arrested. Nevertheless, the regime felt obliged to reimpose the strict provisions of the code, especially after a counterdemonstration by middle-class youths wearing suits and ties embarrassed the regime by creating massive traffic jams in Teheran.

War with Iraq. Despite high casualties and the heavy cost of arms purchases—estimated at $4.2-billion since 1980—the war with Iraq was generally supported by the Iranian people. The Iraqi bombing of Iranian cities in early 1985 whipped up popular feeling against Iraq. On June 14, several million people joined in a massive rally in Teheran to urge a continuation of the war.

Iranian ground forces were unable to make any

significant progress against Iraqi defenses during 1985, however. A major Iranian assault in March in the Huweiza marshes in southern Iraq was beaten back.

Foreign Departures. One result of the Iraqi raids on civilian areas was the abrupt departure of thousands of foreign technicians who had been working on development projects. The Soviet Union withdrew its technical advisers in March, and other countries followed suit. The departure of the technicians brought to a halt work on such projects as a steel mill in Isfahan.

The Economy. Despite the costs of war and Iraqi attacks on oil facilities, the Iranian economy showed surprising resiliency. The Musavi government held inflation to 5.5 per cent, the lowest in a decade. Iraqi raids on Kharg Island, Iran's chief oil terminal, cut oil exports. But temporary export terminals at Sirri Island and Bandar-e Abbas took up most of the slack.

Land Reform. In May, the Majlis approved a land reform bill that gave ownership of the estates of 5,300 landlords, most of whom had fled the country or had their estates seized, to the peasants and squatters farming the land. About 600,000 peasants received title to about 1.5 million acres (607,000 hectares).   William Spencer

See also IRAQ; MIDDLE EAST (Facts in Brief Table). In WORLD BOOK, see IRAN.

IRAQ sharply escalated its war with Iran on March 4, 1985, by raiding Iranian cities and bombing civilian targets. On March 12, the Iranians launched a major ground attack through the Huweiza marshes north of Al Basrah, Iraq's second largest city. The Iranians crossed the Tigris River for the first time and briefly cut the vital Al Basrah-Baghdad road before they were thrown back with an estimated 15,000 casualties.

The Iraqi air attacks caused extensive damage and about 600 casualties in Iran. Iran retaliated with air and rocket attacks on Baghdad, Al Basrah, and other Iraqi cities. On June 14, Iraq unilaterally halted the raids to give Iran an opportunity to consider a peace agreement. After Iran refused the offer, the attacks resumed but on a more limited scale.

War on Oil Production. In August, Iraq changed its strategy and began bombing Kharg Island, Iran's principal oil export terminal, in the Persian Gulf. The attacks succeeded in putting from 40 to 60 per cent of the terminal's facilities out of commission. But this strategy also failed to force Iran to the conference table as Iran continued to export oil from a temporary terminal at Sirri Island, about 300 miles (480 kilometers) south of Kharg Island and out of range of Iraqi jets.

The sticking point was Iran's insistence on huge reparations for war damage and the ouster of the

An Iraqi soldier piles up Iranian ammunition captured during an unsuccessful Iranian assault on the Huweiza marshes in southern Iraq in March.

Baath regime of Iraq's President Saddam Hussein. The only progress made by outside negotiators in mediating the conflict was the return of 30 disabled Iranian prisoners of war arranged by the International Committee of the Red Cross in April. The United Nations also arranged for improved prison camp conditions for the estimated 50,000 Iraqi prisoners in Iran and the 9,000 Iranian prisoners in Iraq.

Internal Affairs. Popular support for the war and Hussein's personal popularity remained high. In February, the president offered an amnesty to all members of *al-Dawa al-Islamiya* (Islamic Call Organization), a Shiite group that has been his principal opposition, and invited those members of the group in exile to return to Iraq.

Arab Support. Other Arab states and most powers outside the Middle East continued to support Iraq in the Gulf War, with both money and weapons. Egypt provided $100 million in arms in June. In August, the United States agreed to sell Iraq 24 530-F flight-training helicopters and 45 214ST helicopters, worth $250 million. The United States also purchased large amounts of Iraqi oil, averaging 309,000 barrels per day (bpd) during April and May.

Foreign Debt. Despite its strong position in relation to Iran, Iraq faced serious financial problems, chiefly a foreign debt of $40 billion, most of it for military supplies and payments to foreign contractors. The war, which cost $15 million per day in 1985, cut deeply into the country's financial reserves, already stretched because of interest payments on the debt. In March, France—which is one of Iraq's main arms suppliers—agreed to reschedule $300 million in debts over a three-year period.

The Economy. The completion of a pipeline stretching from Iraqi oil fields to the Saudi Arabian port of Yanbu on the Red Sea not only diverted oil exports away from the dangerous sea route through the Persian Gulf but also provided a much-needed boost to Iraq's oil exports. The pipeline, which opened on September 30, was expected to carry 500,000 bpd. This new capacity, the increased capacity of another pipeline running across Turkey, and shipments trucked across the Syrian Desert to the Jordanian port of Al Aqabah enabled Iraq to increase its oil exports to 3.1 million bpd by year's end.

Cement production from new plants reached 20 million metric tons (22 million short tons) in 1985, enough to meet domestic needs. Iraq's first fish-hatchery complex opened on January 13 in Baghdad. In other good news, in June, Iraq's oil and gas reserves were reported at 145 billion barrels, much higher than earlier reports. William Spencer

See also IRAN; MIDDLE EAST (Facts in Brief Table). In WORLD BOOK, see IRAQ.

IRELAND. Local elections on June 22, 1985, indicated the unpopularity of the coalition government of the Labour Party and Fine Gael (Gaelic People), headed by Prime Minister Garret Fitz-Gerald. The opposition Fianna Fáil (Soldiers of Destiny) won in many areas and, had it been a general election, would have swept to a landslide national victory.

Fine Gael strategists recommended cutting personal taxes to boost the party's popularity before the next general election, due in 1987. It would be difficult, however, to cut taxes without adding to the budget deficit and huge foreign debt. The government's austere economic policies had reduced inflation to below 6 per cent—the lowest level in 16 years—but had failed to cut unemployment, which had risen to about 17 per cent.

Prime Minister FitzGerald and Great Britain's Prime Minister Margaret Thatcher on November 15 signed an agreement to create a joint commission that gives the Republic of Ireland an advisory role in governing Northern Ireland. It was widely hoped that this would be a first step in solving the political problems of Northern Ireland.

Taxes. On April 19, the government published the names of 800 tax-dodgers. Officials said that similar lists would follow and estimated that the money owed in delinquent taxes could fund the entire national health service for a year.

Funds Seized. The Irish Parliament on February 19 hurriedly passed a bill allowing government seizure of money thought to belong to subversive organizations. The following day, the High Court seized $1.64 million from a bank account suspected of belonging to the outlawed Irish Republican Army (IRA).

Church and State. On March 7, despite strong opposition from the Roman Catholic Church, the Irish Parliament passed a bill making birth control aids available without a doctor's prescription to anyone over 18. This was the first time Parliament had passed a measure directly opposed by the Catholic Church. Another clash occurred when the Department of Health decided, in spite of church objections, that public hospitals should continue to offer surgical sterilization to women.

Religious Phenomena. On February 14, a group of children said they saw a statue of the Virgin Mary in Asdee, County Kerry, move its eyes and hands. By midsummer, 15 statues of the Virgin Mary in Ireland were said to have moved. Skeptics argued that the observations, which had all happened after dark, were optical illusions. The Catholic Church took no official stand on the matter. People flocked to see the statues, however, stimulating a lively tourist trade. Ian J. Mather

See also NORTHERN IRELAND. In WORLD BOOK, see IRELAND.

IRON AND STEEL. See STEEL INDUSTRY.

ISRAEL completed the withdrawal of all of its forces from Lebanon on June 10, 1985, ending a three-year occupation. The operation had been undertaken to destroy Palestine Liberation Organization (PLO) bases in Lebanon and help establish a Lebanese government friendly to Israel. But the campaign polarized Israeli society, caused political turmoil, produced high casualties, and seriously damaged Israel's economy.

Shiite Conflict. The Israeli pullout, originally scheduled for late in 1985, was accelerated because of attacks by the southern Lebanon Shiite population. Shiite animosity was fueled by Israeli retaliation against Shiite villages suspected of aiding or harboring terrorists. When the Israelis withdrew, they took with them more than 700 Shiite prisoners. The prisoners were to serve as hostages to guarantee the good behavior of the southern Lebanon Shiite population. Other nations criticized the action.

The status of the prisoners became an international issue on June 14 when Lebanese Shiites hijacked a United States airliner. After killing 1 American, the hijackers demanded the release of the prisoners in exchange for freeing 39 other Americans on the flight. The Americans were freed on June 30. In July, August, and September, Israel released the Shiites in groups, though the government insisted the releases were unconnected to the hijacking.

Prisoner Exchange. Earlier in 1985, on May 20, the government ignored its policy of never dealing with terrorists and exchanged 1,150 Arab prisoners for 3 Israeli soldiers held by the PLO. Many Israelis feared the exchange would lead to an increase in terrorism.

Jewish Terrorism. Israel was also divided over Jewish terrorism against Arabs on the West Bank. The 13-month trial of 15 Israelis charged with acts of violence against Arabs from 1980 to 1984 ended in July with 3 of the defendants receiving life sentences. The remaining defendants were given sentences ranging from 3 to 10 years. Massive protest demonstrations by supporters of the defendants followed the sentencing.

Right Wing Challenge. Israel's political system was severely tested in 1985 by Meir Kahane, who was elected to the Knesset (parliament) in 1984 as the lone representative of the Kach party, which advocates the expulsion of all Arabs from Israel. Kahane used the immunity granted him by his position in the Knesset to make inflammatory speeches in Arab villages. On July 30, the Knesset passed a bill banning from parliamentary elections any party advocating racism or trying to undermine the democratic character of Israel.

Five of the 8,000 Ethiopian Jews airlifted to Israel from refugee camps in Sudan in a secret rescue operation await relocation in January.

West Bank Tensions increased noticeably during 1985. By October, 12 Jews had been killed on or near the West Bank, allegedly by Palestinians. Analysts attributed the upsurge in violence to a number of factors, including Arab success against Israeli forces in Lebanon and the loss of Israeli intelligence agents in Lebanon. Drastic security measures, including detention without trial and deportation, which had been suspended, were reintroduced in August.

During 1985, Israel continued to consolidate its hold on the West Bank. The West Bank Data Base Project, an independent research organization, reported in April that since 1967, Israel had seized direct or indirect control over 51.6 per cent of all West Bank land. In November, the organization reported that the number of Jewish settlers on the West Bank grew to 51,600 in 1985, a 21.5 per cent increase over the Jewish population in 1984.

The Economy. Increased public support enabled Prime Minister Shimon Peres to initiate a long-overdue restructuring of Israel's economy. The United States continued to provide strong financial support, with Congress in June 1985 adding $1.5 billion to the $2.6 billion allocated to Israel in 1985 and the $3 billion allocated for 1986. The Administration of President Ronald Reagan warned, however, that the funds might be held up unless Israel enacted economic reforms.

In May, Peres had introduced an austerity program that included a three-month wage freeze for civil servants, a 17 per cent increase in the value-added tax—a type of sales tax—and a doubling of the tax Israelis must pay to travel abroad.

Additional austerity measures were approved by the Cabinet on July 1. They included a 30 per cent wage reduction for government employees, sharp decreases in government subsidies for basic goods, a three-month wage freeze for all employees, a three-month price freeze, and the elimination of more than 9,000 government jobs.

On July 2, 1.5 million Israelis went on strike to protest the measures. On July 16, the government reached an agreement with the Histadrut, the Israeli labor federation, under which the government dropped its plans to fire the 9,000 workers and agreed to pay higher-than-expected cost-of-living allowances to ease the impact of the wage freeze.

U.S. Relations. In April, the United States and Israel signed a free-trade agreement, the first ever for the United States. The pact allows the two countries to exempt each other's goods from import duties. Relations between the two countries were strained in November when an American working for the U.S. Navy was arrested for spying for Israel (see ARMED FORCES). William Spencer

See also MIDDLE EAST (Facts in Brief Table). In WORLD BOOK, see ISRAEL.

ITALY. The hijacking of the Italian cruise ship *Achille Lauro* on Oct. 7, 1985, temporarily brought down the coalition government of Socialist Prime Minister Bettino Craxi. Four Palestinian terrorists seized the ship off the coast of Egypt and, on October 8, murdered Leon Klinghoffer, 69, a United States citizen. On October 9, they surrendered in Egypt in exchange for a pledge of safe-conduct out of the country. An Egyptian jet carried the hijackers out of Egypt on October 10, but U.S. fighters forced the plane to land in Italy.

Italian police then arrested the hijackers. The United States issued a warrant for the arrest of a fifth Palestinian, Muhammad Abbas, suspected by U.S. authorities of having masterminded the hijacking. The Italian government, however, allowed him to leave the country. This move drew criticism from the United States and from political circles within Italy. On October 16, Italy's Republican Party withdrew from the coalition to protest Abbas' release. Craxi resigned the next day, and his government continued to serve in a caretaker role. On October 30, he announced that the five coalition partners had resolved their differences and would remain in power.

On November 18, an Italian court sentenced the four hijackers to prison terms ranging from four to nine years. They had been found guilty of illegal possession of firearms and explosives and still faced charges of kidnapping and murder.

On December 27, Palestinian terrorists staged an attack at a Rome airport. Fifteen people were killed, including three of the gunmen.

Wage Referendum. In June, the Craxi government had survived the Communist Party's attempt to repeal a section of a wage law passed in 1984. The section altered a formula for adjusting wages to compensate for inflation. A repeal would have restored $13 per month to workers' wages.

The Communists organized a *referendum*, or direct vote, on the proposal. In balloting on June 8 and 9, 1985, the Communist proposal lost, 54.3 to 45.7 per cent. A repeal would have been inflationary—a severe blow for Italy's already weakening currency, the lira.

Lira Devalued. On July 19, the value of the lira plunged from 1,840 to 2,200 to U.S. $1. The monetary crisis coincided with the release of foreign trade figures for the first five months of 1985. The trade deficit stood at $7.5 billion, compared with $4.7 billion for the same period in 1984.

On July 20, European Community (EC or Common Market) officials and representatives of member nations' central banks agreed to adjust exchange rates because of the weakness of the lira. The adjustment decreased the value of the lira by 7.8 per cent relative to the seven other currencies in the European Monetary System, a structure that eight nations set up in 1979 to stabilize their exchange rates. The change made Italian goods cheaper in the other seven countries.

The government immediately introduced emergency measures to fight inflation by cutting public spending. The measures included a cut in government contributions to Italy's social security program, and another change in the system that increases wages to compensate for inflation. Beginning in the fall of 1985, wages were to go up every six months instead of quarterly.

Communist Setbacks. Failure to win the June referendum was not the first setback to Italy's Communist Party in 1985. In local elections in May, 58.1 per cent of the electorate voted for candidates of the coalition parties. The Communists gained only 30.2 per cent of the vote. The Communists lost control of major cities—including Rome—they had ruled for a decade.

New President. On June 24, Parliament elected Christian Democrat Francesco Cossiga president, succeeding Sandro Pertini, a Socialist. Pertini had announced that he would not seek reelection after the Christian Democrats said they did not want Socialists to hold the top two posts in the government.
Kenneth Brown

See also EUROPE (Facts in Brief Table). In WORLD BOOK, see ITALY.

IVORY COAST. See AFRICA.

JAMAICA. See LATIN AMERICA.

JAPAN faced increasing tension in its relations with its trading partners, especially the United States, during 1985. The tension was caused by Japan's huge trade surplus, which reached a record $44.2 billion in 1984. Efforts by other countries to erect trade barriers against Japanese exports caused growing concern in Japan, which has few natural resources and depends on foreign trade for its prosperity.

Japan's trade surplus with the United States was its single most serious foreign-trade problem. In 1984, the surplus totaled $37 billion and was expected to rise to $50 billion in 1985. The result was mounting pressure in the United States for tariffs, import quotas, and other measures to protect American industries against Japanese competition. The two governments consulted throughout the year on ways to reduce the surplus.

Easing Trade Tension. Japan's Prime Minister Yasuhiro Nakasone urged the Japanese public to "buy foreign" in an unusual personal appeal televised nationwide on April 9. He declared that if Japan did not reduce its trade surplus, the resulting friction "could threaten Japan's very existence in the future." He said Japan must relax its restrictions on imports to prevent retaliation against its exports. He urged each Japanese citizen to spend $100 on foreign goods, which would result in a $12-billion increase in imports.

In another move to prevent retaliation against its exports, Japan announced on July 30 a comprehensive program to open its own markets to more imports. Included in the program were the reduction or elimination of tariffs on about 1,800 items, the relaxation of standards that imported goods must meet before they may be sold in Japan, and simplification and speeding up of import procedures.

Foreign business leaders were skeptical of the program's effectiveness because it was to be phased in over three years. In addition, the program would do nothing to lower informal trade barriers, such as Japan's complex distribution system, which makes it difficult for outsiders to move their goods to customers.

In a major step to deal with the trade crisis, Japan joined France, Great Britain, the United States, and West Germany to lower the value of the U.S. dollar measured against other currencies. The five nations announced their plan on September 22 in New York City. Lowering the dollar's value would make U.S. goods cheaper for other countries to buy and would make imported goods more expensive for Americans to buy. One result would be fewer imports from Japan and more exports to it, decreasing Japan's trade surplus. Within a week after the announcement, the dollar plunged more than 5 per cent against other major currencies.

Dumping Charged. In November, the U.S. International Trade Commission (ITC) ruled that Japanese manufacturers of microchips were guilty of an unfair trade practice called *dumping*. Dumping involves selling goods below the cost of production to drive other manufacturers out of a market. The ITC ruling sent the case to the U.S. Department of Commerce for further investigation. If the Commerce Department also finds evidence of dumping, it will increase the duty on Japanese microchips, the highly miniaturized circuits that are basic to electronic products. The American microchip industry also charged that the Japanese were using restrictive practices to keep American microchips out of the Japanese market.

End of a Monopoly. The government-operated Nippon Telegraph and Telephone Public Corporation became on April 1 a private company called the Nippon Telegraph and Telephone Corporation (NTT) and lost its monopoly on telecommunications services. The end of the monopoly permitted other private corporations, including foreign firms, to enter Japan's telecommunications market. Two U.S. firms, International Business Machines Corporation (IBM) and American Telephone and Telegraph Company (AT&T), reached agreements with NTT in September giving them greater access to Japan, a long-held objective. IBM and NTT announced a joint venture to build a

The pavilions of Expo '85, a science fair held from March to September, give a futuristic look to Tsukuba Science City, a community near Tokyo.

computer network in Japan. AT&T and the Japanese company agreed to exchange information.

Japan's Estimated Economic Growth for 1985 was 4.6 per cent with an unemployment rate of 2.7 per cent. Some economists argued for a higher rate of growth as a way of shrinking Japan's trade surplus. The more the economy grows, the more money consumers would have available to spend on imports. On October 15, the government announced a number of measures to stimulate the economy, including cheaper housing loans and changes making it easier to buy on credit.

Prime Minister Nakasone used personal diplomacy to ease the trade crisis throughout the year. On January 2, he met with U.S. President Ronald Reagan in Los Angeles. In Japanese eyes, this trip was unusual because it meant Nakasone's absence during the important New Year holiday period. Later in January, he traveled to Fiji, Papua New Guinea, Australia, and New Zealand. From July 10 to 21, he visited France, Italy, Vatican City, and Belgium. Trade problems dominated discussions on these trips.

On October 23, Nakasone addressed the United Nations General Assembly in New York City. He urged the delegates to promote free trade.

Militarism Reborn? In 1985, 40 years after Japan's defeat in World War II, the government took a number of actions that both domestic and foreign critics described as a revival of the old nationalism and militarism that led Japan into the war. On February 11, a Japanese holiday called National Foundation Day, Nakasone and his Cabinet took part in a ceremony observing the mythical enthronement of the first Japanese emperor. On August 15, to observe the anniversary of the end of the war, he and his Cabinet paid a formal visit to Yasukuni Shrine, a Shinto shrine in Tokyo where the souls of Japan's modern war dead are believed to rest.

On September 18, the Japanese government approved a five-year budget of $76.3 billion for its defense program. Unless Japan's economy expands much more than is expected, the annual military budget will by 1990 exceed 1 per cent of the gross national product. The Japanese government imposed the 1 per cent limit on military spending in 1976, and public opinion has strongly supported it.

Air Disaster. The worst single-plane accident in history occurred on August 12 when a Japan Air Lines (JAL) Boeing jumbo jet crashed northwest of Tokyo after flying out of control for more than 30 minutes. The crash killed 520 passengers and crew members. Only 4 passengers survived.

Investigation revealed that the tail of the plane had disintegrated, causing the pilot to lose control. The Boeing Company admitted that it had made faulty repairs to the jet in 1978 but said it was not clear that the poor repairs caused the crash. Nevertheless, JAL announced in October that it and Boeing would make compensation payments of about $200 million to families of the victims.

Rail Sabotage. On November 29, saboteurs cut railroad communication lines and set fires on rail lines in Tokyo and Osaka, knocking out commuter trains during the morning rush hour. The sabotage occurred during a 24-hour strike by railway workers protesting government plans to put the national railway in private hands, eliminating an estimated 100,000 jobs. Japanese police arrested 48 people in connection with the sabotage, most of them members of a left wing group called Chukakuha.

The Poison-Candy Gang made another series of attempts to obtain money from candy companies early in the year by threatening to place poisoned candy on store shelves. In late February, several of the companies received letters announcing an "armistice" signed by "the mystery man with 21 faces," the name used by the group. The candy gang made its threats for nearly a year without receiving any payments, and no one ate any poisoned candy. Despite massive efforts, the police failed to solve the case. John M. Maki

See also ASIA (Facts in Brief Table). In WORLD BOOK, see JAPAN.

In the first bar mitzvah held in Poland in more than 20 years, Eric Strom of Scarsdale, N.Y., reads from the Torah in a Kraków synagogue on September 7.

JEWS AND JUDAISM. The attention of the world Jewish community was focused in early 1985 on the plight of Ethiopian Jews, who are known as Falashas. In the wake of the famine that has afflicted millions of Ethiopians in recent years, this ancient community of black Jews experienced particular isolation and persecution. Several thousand Falashas had fled to refugee camps in Sudan, only to meet with further deprivation and harassment.

In an effort to rescue Falashas in Sudanese camps, the Israeli government launched a secret airlift in November 1984. The rescue mission, which was dubbed "Operation Moses," succeeded in moving about 8,000 Ethiopian Jews to Israel. After news of the airlift was leaked to the world press by Israeli sources in early January 1985, however, the government of Sudan ordered a halt to the flights. Sudan apparently feared reprisals from other Arab governments. The news leak and the cancellation of the rescue mission stirred controversy in Israel and around the world. In March, the United States government was able to evacuate to Israel about 800 Jews who remained in the Sudanese camps.

Numerous problems of adjustment faced the Ethiopian refugees in Israel as they began their integration into a society that differed greatly from the simple village life to which they were accustomed. Yet they were gradually taking their

place alongside the many different ethnic groups that make up Israeli society.

At year's end, an estimated 7,000 Jews remained in the Gondar region of northern Ethiopia. They continued to suffer from starvation, disease, and religious persecution. Although the Ethiopian government prevented further evacuation of Jews, Jewish organizations around the world continued to send aid and supplies to Ethiopia. One of the most active groups, the American Association for Ethiopian Jews, independently rescued about 100 Jews in 1985. The organization also led efforts to encourage the U.S. government to negotiate a family reunification program with the government of Ethiopia. Such a program would enable the remaining Falashas to join their relatives in Israel.

Soviet Jewry. Concern continued to mount over the ongoing repression of the approximately 2½ million Jews who live in the Soviet Union. From 1970 to 1980, thousands of Jews were allowed to leave the Soviet Union, following years of discrimination and the suppression of Jewish religious life in that country. Most of the emigrants settled in Israel or the United States. After a peak emigration of 51,000 in 1979, the Soviet government severely limited the number of exit visas it granted. In 1985, fewer than 800 Soviet Jews were permitted to leave Russia.

The government also continued to arrest activists who attempted to develop Jewish religious and cultural life in the Soviet Union. The most famous of these "prisoners of conscience," Anatoly Shcharansky, remained in prison on charges of treason. His wife, Avital, who lives in Israel, was a leading figure in worldwide efforts to gain emigration rights for Soviet Jews. An estimated 400,000 Soviet Jews have applied for exit visas.

As reports have reached the West of the growing problems faced by Soviet citizens of other faiths, particularly by Pentecostal Christians, Jews and Christians in the United States have joined together in interfaith coalitions established to aid and to free all religious and political dissidents imprisoned in the Soviet Union.

Religious Developments. Following 10 years of intense debate, the Conservative branch of American Judaism ordained its first woman rabbi on May 12, 1985. The new rabbi, Amy Eilberg, graduated from the Jewish Theological Seminary of America in New York City. The action created dissension among the more traditional factions of Conservative Judaism, which claimed that the ordination of women went against Jewish law. Eilberg joined the approximately 80 women who have already been ordained as rabbis by Reform and Reconstructionist seminaries in the United States over the past 10 years. Howard A. Berman

In WORLD BOOK, see JEWS; JUDAISM.

JORDAN. King Hussein I took a bold step toward revitalizing the Middle Eastern peace process in February 1985. The king reached an agreement with Yasir Arafat, leader of the Palestine Liberation Organization (PLO), that called for a joint Jordanian-Palestinian delegation to represent the Arabs in talks with Israel. The agreement called for such talks to take place at an international conference. The proposal seemed to imply that the PLO would recognize Israel's right to exist. But Arafat refused to promise such recognition.

Syrian Talks. On December 30 and 31, Hussein traveled to Syria for talks with Syrian President Hafiz al-Assad, who opposed his agreement with Arafat. It was the first meeting between the leaders of Jordan and Syria since 1979.

U.S. Arms. Hussein's peace initiative was linked to his desire to strengthen the Jordanian armed forces through United States arms purchases. In September, the Administration of President Ronald Reagan approved a $1.5-billion to $1.9-billion arms sale to Jordan. But in October, the Senate voted to block the sale until March 1, 1986, unless Hussein began direct talks with Israel.

PLO Return. The Hussein-Arafat agreement signaled the return of the PLO to Jordan in strength 15 years after it had been driven out of that country by the Jordanian army. The PLO opened offices in Amman, Jordan's capital, in the spring.

But the Jordanian government imposed strict regulations on PLO activities. Members of the PLO were forbidden to carry personal weapons, and a limit was set on the number of PLO members allowed to enter the country.

The Economy slowed down in 1985 after two decades of rapid growth. The gross domestic product (GDP)—the value of all goods and services produced within the country—grew only 3.5 per cent after averaging 8.4 per cent annually from 1976 to 1984. Financial aid from other countries in 1985 dropped from that of previous years.

Exports of phosphate, Jordan's major natural resource, increased to 9 million metric tons (10 million short tons), mainly through the development of new reserves at Shidiya. In March, reserves of 1.5 million metric tons (1.7 million short tons) of gypsum were discovered at Tafilah, enough to meet domestic needs for the next decade. The increased phosphate exports, plus the $1.5 million sent home by Jordanians working abroad, helped keep the balance of payments for 1985 in the black, though the cumulative trade deficit remained at $2 billion. William Spencer

See also MIDDLE EAST (Facts in Brief Table). In WORLD BOOK, see JORDAN.

JUDAISM. See JEWS AND JUDAISM.

JUNIOR ACHIEVEMENT (JA). See YOUTH ORGANIZATIONS.

KAMPUCHEA. Political changes occurred during 1985 on both sides in the continuing war in Kampuchea (formerly known as Cambodia). The prime minister of Kampuchea's Vietnamese-backed regime, Chan Si, died in late December 1984. On Jan. 14, 1985, the National Assembly named as his successor Hun Sen, who also kept the post of foreign minister.

The People's Revolutionary Party of Kampuchea, the Communist organization that controls the government, held its fifth congress from October 13 to 16. Council of State President Heng Samrin was unanimously reelected as the party's secretary general.

Prince Norodom Sihanouk, Kampuchea's former chief of state, remained head of a loose coalition of both Communists and non-Communists opposing the Heng Samrin regime by guerrilla warfare. But he threatened several times to resign. One such threat, in April, was to protest inadequate Chinese support for his group in the coalition. Another on June 10 came after reports that the Communists in his coalition, the Khmer Rouge, had killed 38 of their non-Communist allies.

Sihanouk was important to the coalition because many Kampucheans considered him their true ruler. In addition, his political respectability offset the brutal reputation of the Khmer Rouge and enabled the coalition to gain international support.

Civilians from Ampil, Kampuchea, flee to Thailand in January before Vietnamese forces seize their village, headquarters of anti-Communist rebels.

The Khmer Rouge, led by Pol Pot, had ruled Kampuchea from 1975 until the Vietnamese overthrew them and installed a puppet regime in 1979. During their rule, they killed hundreds of thousands of people.

The Khmer Rouge announced on Sept. 2, 1985, that Pol Pot would retire from command of the Khmer Rouge army. Sihanouk and Vietnam both denounced the announcement as a trick.

The Vietnamese Army, each year since it occupied Kampuchea in 1979, has launched fierce attacks against the guerrillas during the dry season, which runs from December to May. The 1984-1985 dry season offensive began earlier than ever—in November 1984—and was the largest so far. Vietnam sought to destroy the numerous camps used by both guerrillas and refugees. On Jan. 8, 1985, Vietnamese troops captured Ampil, headquarters of the main non-Communist guerrilla force in Sihanouk's coalition. In February, the Khmer Rouge stronghold of Phnom Malai fell.

Continued Poor Harvests, blamed on both the war and bad weather, caused food shortages. A drought during the summer destroyed rice crops in several provinces. Henry S. Bradsher

See also Asia (Facts in Brief Table). In World Book, see Cambodia or Kampuchea.

KANSAS. See State Government.

KENTUCKY. See State Government.

KENYA. The drought broke earlier in Kenya in 1985 than in most other African countries. Precipitation in the rainy season—March through May—was better than average, raising expectations that Kenya's agriculture would rebound considerably from 1984 levels. The drought caused a 40 per cent reduction in the 1984 corn harvest.

Increased food production is especially important in Kenya because of the nation's extraordinarily high rate of population growth—estimated at 4 per cent in 1985. If that growth rate is not reduced, Kenya's population will almost double by the year 2000.

Protests at the University of Nairobi from February 10 to 14 resulted in the death of at least one student, the jailing of five others, and the closing of the university until April 23. Although the students claimed to be protesting university policies, some students used the demonstrations to criticize the government of Daniel T. arap Moi.

Kenya's only legal political party, the Kenya African National Union (KANU), held its party elections on July 2, the first since 1978. The nation's two top leaders, President Moi and Vice President Mwai Kibaki, were reelected to those same posts in the party, but KANU's secretary-general and party chairman were replaced. J. Dixon Esseks

See also Africa (Facts in Brief Table). In World Book, see Kenya.

KING, STEPHEN (1947-   ), had three books on United States best-seller lists in 1985, demonstrating convincingly that his horror fiction gives readers something they want and cannot get enough of. The three works were *The Talisman*, a novel co-written with Peter Straub; *Skeleton Crew*, a collection of macabre short stories; and *Thinner*, a novel written under the pen name Richard Bachman. Since the appearance of his first novel, *Carrie* (1974), King has produced at least one best seller per year. Many of his scary tales have been turned into motion pictures.

King has been praised as a masterful storyteller who deftly leads readers from the familiar to the terrifying against a backdrop of contemporary American popular culture. King describes his work as "plain fiction for plain folks, the literary equivalent of a Big Mac and a large fries from McDonald's." He sees the function of horror fiction as basically reassuring. According to King, we all face a world out of control. But, as his books show, things could be a lot worse.

Stephen Edwin King was born on Sept. 21, 1947, in Portland, Me. He graduated from the University of Maine in 1970 and married Tabitha Spruce, a poet, in 1971. The Kings live with their three children in Bangor, Me. King calls himself "just an ordinary person" who likes baseball, rock music, and being with his family.   Karin C. Rosenberg

KOREA, NORTH. Communist North Korea developed closer relations with the Soviet Union during 1985. The Soviets had rejected North Korea's requests for new, improved armaments for more than a decade. But in April 1985, the Soviets delivered the first of an estimated 50 MIG-23 jet fighters to North Korea. The new planes improved North Korea's air force while air defenses of neighboring South Korea, which is strongly anti-Communist, were being upgraded with the help of the United States.

A Soviet squadron of MIG-23's visited North Korea from May 8 to 10. On August 13, three warships began the first Soviet naval visit to a North Korean port. Amid these signs of closer military cooperation, Japanese defense officials reported detecting Soviet military flights over North Korea that enabled the Soviets to watch China.

President Kim Il-song met with Hu Yaobang, general secretary of China's Communist Party, from May 4 to 6 on the Chinese border. China had long been North Korea's closest ally, and Pyongyang's ties to Moscow apparently worried China, which has tense relations with the Soviets.

Every voter in North Korea reportedly voted by noon on February 24 for official candidates in provincial and local elections.   Henry S. Bradsher

See also ASIA (Facts in Brief Table); KOREA, SOUTH. In WORLD BOOK, see KOREA.

KOREA, SOUTH. After decades of dictatorship, South Korea took a major step toward a two-party system as a result of National Assembly elections on Feb. 12, 1985. President Chun Doo Hwan allowed opposition candidates virtually free rein to criticize his administration.

Growing Opposition. Chun's Democratic Justice Party (DJP) got 35 per cent of the votes and won 87 Assembly seats in the election. The New Korea Democratic Party (NKDP), formed on January 18 by a number of opposition leaders, eclipsed other opposition parties by winning 29 per cent of the votes and 50 seats. The new party outpolled the DJP by a wide margin in urban areas, but rural areas followed tradition by backing the ruling party.

Less than a week after the NKDP's unexpectedly strong showing, on February 18, Chun made the 14th cabinet shakeup in five years. He named a career diplomat, Shinyong Lho, as prime minister. Roh Tae Woo, a retired army general, became DJP chairman a few days later.

The opposition Democratic Korea Party almost disintegrated in early April when 29 of its newly elected Assembly members joined the more outspoken NKDP. This and other changes gave the new party more than a third of the seats in the Assembly, enough to block constitutional changes and to convene the Assembly. The NKDP thus became capable of subjecting the government to unaccustomed parliamentary challenges.

The new party was steered by two politicians who remained outside of it—Kim Dae Jung and Kim Young Sam. The two old rivals, who were South Korea's most prominent opposition leaders, had begun cooperating in June 1984. On March 6, 1985, Chun lifted a ban on political activities by the two leaders. Kim Dae Jung's actions were limited, however, because he remained under a 20-year suspended sentence for trying to overthrow the government. He had returned to Korea from exile in the United States on February 8. American human rights activists who accompanied him accused the police of roughing him up at the airport—which they denied—before rushing him off to house arrest.

Cracking Down on Dissent. A United States Information Service building in Seoul, South Korea's capital, was stormed and held from May 23 to 26 by a group of about 70 students. They condemned the United States for its support of Chun. The Korean government put 21 leaders of the student protest on trial. They were sentenced to prison terms of three to seven years.

The trial was part of a new crackdown on dissent. Predawn raids on nine university campuses in July resulted in 56 arrests. In August, the government proposed legislation to send leftist radical students to camps for six months of "guidance and enlightenment." The bill was withdrawn after a public furor. Also in August, security police beat three journalists after their newspaper published an article of which the government disapproved. Several judges were banished to small provincial posts after showing leniency to demonstrators.

Economic Slowdown. Officials predicted 5 per cent economic growth in 1985. Declining exports had slowed the rate of growth, but they began to level off. Exports in the first nine months of 1985 were down by only 1.3 per cent from 1984, compared with a 4.1 per cent drop from 1983 to 1984.

Relations with North Korea. Negotiations between South Korea, which is strongly anti-Communist, and Communist North Korea during 1985 made progress toward overcoming decades of hostile separation. Some 10 million people were separated from family members when the Korean Peninsula was divided into Soviet and American sectors in 1945. On Sept. 21, 1985, 50 people from each side who crossed the demilitarized zone dividing North and South met relatives under Red Cross supervision. It was the first exchange of family members since the Korean War ended in 1953. The two countries also exchanged song and dance troupes.   Henry S. Bradsher

See also ASIA (Facts in Brief Table). In WORLD BOOK, see KOREA.

KUWAIT. See MIDDLE EAST.

LABOR. Job growth, a major concern of United States workers, continued to surge in 1985. From December 1984 to December 1985, 2 million civilian jobs were added to the U.S. economy. Unemployment held steady at about 7.3 per cent of the civilian labor force for the first seven months of the year. For the year, the civilian jobless rate averaged 7.2 per cent.

Wage and benefit gains remained moderate in 1985. The U.S. Bureau of Labor Statistics reported a 4.2 per cent increase over the first nine months of 1985 in its *Employment Cost Index*, which measures the change in wages and benefits for all workers except those employed by the federal government. Collective bargaining settlements during the same period resulted in wage increases averaging 2.9 per cent. Workers continued to make concessions to hard-pressed employers. In exchange, they sought shares in company ownership and improved job security.

Trucking Along. On March 31, the Teamsters Union reached agreement with two bargaining groups that represented management. The three-year contract, known as the National Master Freight Agreement, provided a two-tier wage scale. Veteran drivers received increases in wages and benefits totaling $1.50 an hour over the term of the contract. But new drivers were to receive less than the current wage during their first three

Changes in the United States Labor Force

	1984	1985
Total labor force	**115,241,000**	**117,695,000**
Armed forces	1,697,000	2,234,000
Civilian labor force	113,544,000	115,461,000
Total employment	106,702,000	107,150,000
Unemployment	8,539,000	8,312,000
Civilian unemployment rate	7.4%	7.2%
Change in real earnings of production and nonsupervisory workers (private nonfarm sector)*	No change	+0.3%
Change in output per employee hour (private nonfarm sector)†	+2.7%	+0.4%

*Constant (1977) dollars; 1984 change from December 1983 to December 1984; 1985 change from September 1984 to September 1985 (preliminary data).
†Annual data for 1984; for 1985, change is from third quarter 1984 to third quarter 1985 (preliminary data).
Source: U.S. Bureau of Labor Statistics.

years. A cost-of-living adjustment (COLA) stayed in the contract but was not to take effect. Union members narrowly approved the pact, 62,296, or 53.2 per cent of those voting, to 54,873.

On July 26, 21,000 teamsters in the automobile-hauling industry went out on strike after voting down the contract they were offered. A settlement was reached on August 14. The pact called for an hourly increase of 60 cents for veteran haulers, lower pay for workers in storage yards, and restrictions on COLA's. In addition, management dropped plans to cut by 50 per cent the rate paid to car haulers on return trips.

Electrical Connection. Just before 1985 contract negotiations got underway in the electrical industry, Westinghouse Electric Corporation expressed its intention to bargain separately, thus breaking from the pattern of industrywide bargaining. Since the last contract negotiations in 1983, the work force had dropped sharply, from 105,000 to 80,000 at General Electric Company (GE) and from 41,500 to 34,500 at Westinghouse. For this reason, the 13-union coalition that usually bargains with GE and Westinghouse sought greater job security and improved pensions.

On June 30, some 56,000 employees at GE accepted a three-year contract that provided a 3 per cent bonus in the first year and 3 per cent salary increases in the next two years. Despite its earlier

A strike by Wheeling-Pittsburgh steelworkers—the steel industry's first major strike since 1959—shuts down an Allenport, Pa., plant from July to October.

intention, Westinghouse agreed on July 22 to a three-year contract that closely followed GE's.

Rubber Elasticity. In April, the bargaining committee of the United Rubber Workers (URW) deadlocked over whether to accept a contract offered by Goodyear Tire & Rubber Company, the world's largest tire maker. The URW then shifted bargaining efforts to B. F. Goodrich Company in an attempt to achieve the best possible settlement and set a pattern for the industry before contracts expired on April 20. The settlement, which was reached without a strike, provided hourly wage increases of 25 cents in the first year, 10 cents in the second, and 8 cents in the third. Wages would also be adjusted for inflation. The contract boosted monthly pensions for future retirees from $16.50 per year of service to $20. Current retirees were to receive a monthly increase of 50 cents per year of service. In May, Goodyear and the URW agreed to similar terms.

Airsickness. Collective bargaining in the airline industry in 1985 was both cooperative and troubled as large airlines struggled to remain competitive in the wake of the 1978 deregulation of the industry. To help Eastern Airlines avoid technical default on its long-term debt, several unions agreed in spring to extend pay cuts of 18 to 22 per cent, which they had accepted in 1984. The unions involved were the Air Line Pilots Associa-

tion (ALPA), the International Association of Machinists and Aerospace Workers, and the Transport Workers Union of America. The pay cuts were reduced, however, to 13 per cent in 1985, and transport workers were to receive increases. In addition, flying time was reduced for pilots.

A strike by the Transport Workers Union shut down Pan American World Airways (PanAm) on February 28. In early March, however, pilots and flight engineers began to cross the picket lines of striking workers, and PanAm restored operations to half their normal level. On March 27, workers approved a new contract that included cuts in benefits and changes in work rules.

About 5,000 pilots who belong to ALPA struck United Airlines, the largest U.S. air carrier, from mid-May to mid-June. At issue was a two-tier wage system under which new pilots would work for wages substantially below those of pilots hired under the previous contract. A compromise reached early in the strike provided a five-year trial period for the two-tier scale. But pilots continued to strike over United's insistence that nonstriking pilots receive preference over strikers in future cockpit assignments. United and ALPA finally asked a federal judge to decide this and other issues, including the disposition of more than 500 newly trained pilots who had refused to cross picket lines during the strike. The airline claimed that the union could not force it to hire the new pilots. In August, Judge Nicholas J. Bua of Chicago ordered United to put the new pilots on flight duty. He also struck down United's plan to give preferential treatment to nonstrikers.

In the oddest "negotiations" of 1985, unions representing pilots, flight attendants, and machinists met in June to try to head off a take-over of Trans World Airlines (TWA). The take-over bid came from Texas Air Corporation, which had canceled labor contracts after gaining control of Continental Airlines in 1983. The unions decided to ally themselves with investor Carl C. Icahn and offered substantial wage concessions if he took over TWA. As a result, Icahn was able to persuade TWA directors to accept his offer, and he became chairman of TWA on Jan. 3, 1986.

In October 1985, ALPA ended its 25-month strike against Continental. The two parties agreed on back-to-work terms, severance pay of $4,000 for each year of service for pilots who chose not to return to Continental, and an end to ALPA suits against the airline. Machinists and flight attendants had called off their strikes against Continental earlier in the year.

Automobile Accord. In fall bargaining with Chrysler Corporation, the United Automobile Workers (UAW) expressed its determination to achieve wages and benefits equal to those of workers at General Motors Corporation (GM) and Ford Motor Company. (GM and Ford workers signed new contracts in 1984.) After negotiations failed to produce an agreement, Chrysler workers in the United States and Canada went on strike on Oct. 16, 1985. Canadian workers went back to work on October 21 and U.S. workers on October 28. The settlement substantially met union goals.

In other automobile industry developments, GM announced plans for a plant to produce its new Saturn car, developed to compete with Japanese cars. GM stressed its intention to involve workers in plant management. GM also agreed to draw staff as much as possible from UAW membership and to offer wages and benefits comparable to those in its other plants. The New United Motor Manufacturing, Incorporated, of Fremont, Calif.—a joint venture between GM and Japan's Toyota Motor Corporation—settled on a contract with the UAW in June. It was the UAW's first contract with a Japanese firm.

Steel Doldrums. Although contracts in the U.S. steel industry were not to expire until 1986, the parties involved began maneuvering in 1985. In January, the troubled Kaiser Aluminum & Chemical Corporation met with the United Steelworkers of America (USWA) to discuss renegotiating contracts. In March, the union agreed to accept pay and benefit cuts in exchange for shares of company stock.

In May, five major steel companies—U.S. Steel Corporation, LTV Steel Company, Bethlehem Steel Corporation, Inland Steel Company, and Armco, Incorporated—dissolved their joint bargaining committee. The companies had bargained jointly with the USWA for nearly 30 years. Dissolution of the committee was a sign of troubled times and of management's determination to cut labor costs to compete with foreign steel producers. Since the last negotiations in 1983, total employment at the five companies dropped from 250,000 workers to just over 136,000 workers.

Steelworkers at the Wheeling-Pittsburgh Steel Corporation went on strike on July 21, 1985, after a judge ruled that the company could cancel its labor contracts under 1984 amendments to the U.S. Bankruptcy Code. (Wheeling-Pittsburgh filed for bankruptcy in April 1985.) In October, union members voted 5,924 to 789 to accept a contract only slightly better than the one they rejected in July. Under the pact, the company's labor costs dropped from $21.40 an hour to $18, and average pay went from $10 an hour to $8; the pension plan was eliminated (though pensions of present employees were protected); and two union members were to become directors of the company.

Baseball Strikes Out. Members of the Major League Baseball Players Association went on strike on Aug. 6 and 7, 1985, in a dispute with team owners over contract terms. The strike ended with a compromise. Owners abandoned their demand for a lid on salaries, and players agreed to changes in rules governing salary arbitration.

Government Policies. In accordance with its belief in free trade, the Administration of President Ronald Reagan in early March declined to extend quotas on imports of automobiles from Japan. In August, the Administration rejected a recommendation from the U.S. International Trade Commission, an independent government agency, favoring import quotas on shoes to relieve the hard-hit domestic shoe industry. The Administration also worked in 1985 to end affirmative action plans that used goals and timetables to encourage employment of women and minorities.

Secretary of Labor Raymond J. Donovan stepped down on March 15, after a New York City judge ruled that he had to stand trial on fraud and larceny charges. The charges stemmed from a construction contract Donovan had been involved in before taking office. William E. Brock III, the U.S. trade representative, was named to succeed Donovan. He assumed office on April 29. Brock enjoyed cordial relations with organized labor, unlike Donovan, with whom many labor leaders refused to meet. See BROCK, WILLIAM EMERSON, III.   Robert W. Fisher

See also ECONOMICS. In WORLD BOOK, see LABOR FORCE; LABOR MOVEMENT.

LAOS

LAOS improved relations with both the Soviet Union and the United States during 1985 while remaining closely tied to Vietnam and feuding with Thailand. Laotian Prime Minister Kayson Phomvihan—also general secretary of the Lao People's Revolutionary Party, the Communist organization that runs Laos with Vietnamese advice—visited Moscow from Aug. 25 to 28, 1985. A joint statement issued during his visit reported that "the Soviet Union will expand its economic and technical assistance" during Laos' second five-year economic development plan, for 1986-1990. The statement also announced that Laos would deliver more goods to the Soviet Union so that trade would be less unbalanced.

The 25th anniversary of the establishment of diplomatic relations between Laos and the Soviet Union was celebrated in Vientiane, the Laotian capital, on Oct. 7, 1985. Deputy Prime Minister Phoumi Vongvichit told a rally that development of Laos' economy was "absolutely dependent on socialist countries, in particular the Soviet Union."

Vietnam, which might view the Soviets as competitors for power in Laos, continued to have great influence there. The government of Thailand warned, "The presence of 40,000 Vietnamese troops in Laos in addition to hundreds of Vietnamese advisers points clearly to Hanoi's long-standing aim to dominate Laos." Some Thai press reports blamed Vietnamese influence for the continuing purges of Laotian officials who were not considered strongly pro-Vietnamese.

Laos and Thailand argued throughout 1985 over three small border villages—Klang, Mai, and Sawang. Thai troops had briefly seized the villages in 1984 but then withdrew from them. Despite this, 90 per cent of Laos' foreign earnings came from selling hydroelectric power to Thailand.

Friendlier U.S. Relations. For the first time, Laos allowed a United States team to search for American servicemen missing since the Vietnam War. In February 1985, the team recovered the bodies of 13 men killed in 1972 when their plane crashed near Pakse in southern Laos.

Laotian Deputy Foreign Minister Soulivong Prasithdeth became on Sept. 24, 1985, the first high-ranking Indochinese Communist to visit the U.S. Department of State for talks. Laotian Foreign Minister Phoune Sipraseuth met in New York City on September 30 with the third-ranked State Department official, Undersecretary for Political Affairs Michael H. Armacost.

New Five-Year Plan. The Central Committee of the Lao People's Revolutionary Party and the cabinet met jointly from September 20 to October 4. They approved an outline of the 1986-1990 economic development plan.   Henry S. Bradsher

See also ASIA (Facts in Brief Table). In WORLD BOOK, see LAOS.

LATIN AMERICA

Latin-American nations drew renewed attention during 1985 to their inability to make scheduled payments on an estimated $400 billion in foreign debts that had accumulated over the last 10 years. In the mid-1970's, world economic conditions had appeared to favor investment in Latin America, and banks had been eager to lend to Latin-American nations seeking to develop their resources.

By 1985, those loans, made more costly by increasingly high interest rates, were coming due

faster than the debtor nations could repay them. Throughout Latin America, the debt crisis became the leading political and economic concern.

Latin America's 11 major debtor nations, known as the Cartagena Group after the city in Colombia where the first meeting on the debt crisis was held in 1984, could not agree on how to resolve the crisis. The 11 nations—Argentina, Bolivia, Brazil, Chile, Colombia, the Dominican Republic, Ecuador, Mexico, Peru, Uruguay, and Venezuela—agreed emphatically on the causes of the debt crisis. But it became apparent at a meeting held in Santo Domingo, capital of the Dominican Republic, on February 7 and 8 that the nations were too diverse to agree on a course of action.

Red Cross workers try to free a body from the mud slide that killed about 25,000 people in Colombia in November after a volcano erupted.

Mexico began to take a more active role in the debt-crisis deliberations when it hosted a secret meeting at the resort town of Oaxtepec from July 12 to 14. Representatives from about 10 nations discussed ways of pressuring the industrialized nations to help relieve the mounting debt problem. Cuba's President Fidel Castro, seeking the limelight on the debt issue, hosted a meeting of his own in Havana, Cuba's capital, from July 30 to August 3. The Cuban leader urged Latin-Ameri-

373

Pope John Paul II presides as Argentina and Chile sign a peace treaty in the Vatican on May 2, ending a 200-year-old dispute over the Beagle Channel.

can nations to renounce their debt payments. Castro suggested that the United States or other industrialized nations should pay whatever was owed. The meeting was largely ignored by Latin-American governments, many of which noted that Cuba itself had worked hard to renegotiate its own foreign debts prior to the meeting.

UN Speeches. Several Latin-American leaders expressed themselves on the debt issue at the United Nations (UN) General Assembly in late September. Brazil's President José Sarney urged increased economic productivity and growth as the way out of the debt dilemma. "Brazil will not pay its foreign debt with recession, nor with unemployment, nor with hunger," he told the Assembly.

The economies of several Latin-American nations were ravaged during 1985 by shortfalls in earnings from oil, nickel, tin, and such important exports as coffee, cocoa, and sugar. Speaking for those nations, Mexico's Foreign Minister Bernardo Sepúlveda Amor asserted in his UN speech that "the foreign debt problem of Latin-American and other developing countries cannot be definitely solved through the rescheduling [of debts] that grants only temporary relief to the debtor countries and to the international community."

Peru's charismatic new President Alan García Pérez had boldly defied the existing international

system by vowing when he took office in July to limit payments on Peru's foreign debt to 10 per cent of export earnings over the next year. At the UN session, García explained, "We are faced with a dramatic choice: It is either debt or democracy." The statement reflected feelings in Peru, where the economy has long been in the doldrums; further damaging it to make the payments could endanger democracy, which has yet to take firm root.

U.S. Proposal. Reacting to these and other statements, United States Secretary of the Treasury James A. Baker III in October signaled a change in the attitude of the Administration of U.S. President Ronald Reagan. Baker was reportedly impressed with the viewpoint of Latin-American leaders who argued that measures to stimulate economic growth would enable Latin America to repay its debts more effectively than austerity measures imposed by the International Monetary Fund (IMF). Baker unveiled a U.S. plan on world debt on October 8 at the annual joint meeting of the IMF and the World Bank in Seoul, South Korea. (Both the IMF and the World Bank are UN agencies.) Under the proposal, commercial banks would provide up to $20 billion to Latin America over the next three years on easy terms. The Latin-American countries would agree to adhere to policies that promote foreign investment and

Facts in Brief on Latin American Political Units

Country	Population	Government	Monetary Unit*	Foreign Trade (million U.S. $) Exports†	Imports†
Antigua and Barbuda	82,000	Governor General Sir Wilfred Ebenezer Jacobs; Prime Minister Vere C. Bird	dollar (2.7 = $1)	34	138
Argentina	31,065,000	President Raúl Alfonsín	austral (1 = $1.27)	7,836	4,504
Bahamas	237,000	Governor General Sir Gerald C. Cash; Prime Minister Lynden O. Pindling	dollar (1 = $1)	2,346	3,024
Barbados	264,000	Governor General Sir Hugh Springer; Prime Minister Bernard St. John	dollar (2 = $1)	391	659
Belize	165,000	Governor General Minita Gordon; Prime Minister Manuel Esquivel	dollar (2 = $1)	78	113
Bolivia	6,527,000	President Víctor Paz Estenssoro	peso (1,149,425 = $1)	773	631
Brazil	138,820,000	President José Sarney	cruzeiro (9,091 = $1)	27,005	15,210
Chile	12,237,000	President Augusto Pinochet Ugarte	peso (176 = $1)	3,657	3,191
Colombia	29,303,000	President Belisario Betancur	peso (160 = $1)	3,462	4,498
Costa Rica	2,667,000	President Luis Alberto Monge Alvarez	colón (52.9 = $1)	941	1,121
Cuba	10,086,000	President Fidel Castro	peso (1 = $1.11)	6,172	8,144
Dominica	74,000	President Clarence Seignoret; Prime Minister Mary Eugenia Charles	dollar (2.7 = $1)	29	43
Dominican Republic	6,385,000	President Salvador Jorge Blanco	peso (3 = $1)	785	1,279
Ecuador	9,662,000	President León Febres-Cordero	sucre (95 = $1)	2,583	1,716
El Salvador	5,286,000	President José Napoleón Duarte	colón (2.5 = $1)	735	892
Grenada	116,000	Governor General Sir Paul Godwin Scoon; Prime Minister Herbert A. Blaize	dollar (2.7 = $1)	19	59
Guatemala	6,973,000	Head of State Oscar Humberto Mejía Víctores	quetzal (1 = $1)	1,159	1,135
Guyana	844,000	President Hugh Desmond Hoyte; Prime Minister Hamilton Green	dollar (4.1 = $1)	91	601
Haiti	5,033,000	President Jean-Claude Duvalier	gourde (5 = $1)	187	314
Honduras	4,525,000	President Roberto Suazo Córdova	lempira (2 = $1)	692	767
Jamaica	2,437,000	Governor General Sir Florizel Glasspole; Prime Minister Edward Seaga	dollar (5.5 = $1)	714	1,130
Mexico	81,098,000	President Miguel de la Madrid Hurtado	peso (476 = $1)	24,407	11,267
Nicaragua	3,145,000	President Daniel Ortega	córdoba (10 = $1)	393	808
Panama	2,225,000	President Eric Arturó Delvalle	balboa (1 = $1)	256	1,423
Paraguay	3,772,000	President Alfredo Stroessner	guaraní (240 = $1)	284	506
Peru	20,208,000	President Alan García Pérez; Prime Minister Luis Alva Castro	sol (13,889 = $1)	3,147	2,212
Puerto Rico	3,188,000	Governor Rafael Hernández Colón	U.S. $	9,146	9,529
St. Christopher and Nevis	44,000	Governor General Clement Arrindell; Prime Minister Kennedy Alphonse Simmonds	dollar (2.7 = $1)	31	47
St. Lucia	123,000	Governor General Sir Allen Montgomery Lewis; Prime Minister John Compton	dollar (2.7 = $1)	42	111
St. Vincent and the Grenadines	147,000	Governor General Joseph Lambert Eustace; Prime Minister James Mitchell	dollar (2.7 = $1)	33	62
Suriname	382,000	Commander of the National Army Desire D. Bouterse; Acting President L. F. Ramdat-Misier; Prime Minister Wim Udenhout	guilder (1.8 = $1)	345	446
Trinidad and Tobago	1,206,000	President Ellis Emmanuel Innocent Clarke; Prime Minister George Chambers	dollar (2.3 = $1)	2,162	1,902
Uruguay	3,008,000	President Julio María Sanguinetti	peso (122 = $1)	925	769
Venezuela	19,014,000	President Jaime Lusinchi	bolívar (14.6 = $1)	13,417	7,373

*Exchange rates as of Dec. 1, 1985, or latest available data. †Latest available data.

encourage private enterprise in those countries where the economies are presently state-dominated. Although no action was taken on Baker's proposal, the plan was expected to aid future discussions.

Conflict. The civil war in El Salvador heated up in the last quarter of 1985, despite earlier hopes that the violence was tapering off. Anti-Sandinista rebels known as *contras*, operating from Honduras and Costa Rica, succeeded in keeping the Marxist Sandinista government of Nicaragua off balance. United States support for the contras, whom President Reagan called "freedom fighters," included humanitarian aid, advice on how to raise funds from supporters in the United States, and advice on military strategy. United States military forces staged nearly continuous maneuvers during 1985—on land in Honduras, and at sea off both coasts of Nicaragua.

U.S. Strategy. The Reagan Administration's policy in Latin America continued to place heavy emphasis on measures designed to contain what the Administration saw as Communist-sponsored expansionism. The United States stepped up its military assistance to the government of El Salvador headed by José Napoleón Duarte in an effort to end the six-year civil war. In May, Reagan placed a trade embargo on Nicaragua. Most of Latin America opposed the embargo. At a meeting of the Latin American Economic System in Caracas, Venezuela, on May 15, 24 Latin-American nations called for an end to the trade sanctions.

In an ironic twist, one of the largest beneficiaries of U.S. efforts to contain Communism in Central America was tiny, democratic Costa Rica on Nicaragua's southern border. Costa Rica received $198 million in U.S. aid in 1985 alone—a sum equal to the total U.S. aid to Costa Rica over the previous 18 years. With a population of only about 2.7 million, Costa Rica was the second highest per capita recipient of U.S. foreign aid in 1985, after Israel. "Our best industry is Sandinistas," quipped Roberto de la Ossa, executive director of the Central American Institute for International Affairs in San José, Costa Rica's capital.

Easing of Tensions. Elsewhere, Latin Americans witnessed the easing of tensions between nations. The Chilean government in April ratified a treaty with Argentina, negotiated by Pope John Paul II, ending a dispute over maritime rights and ownership of islands in the Beagle Channel off the southern tip of the two countries. Argentina's Congress had previously ratified the treaty.

In the wake of another conflict, Great Britain lifted its ban on trade with Argentina in July. The ban had been in effect since the 1982 war between

Julio María Sanguinetti waves to supporters in Montevideo following his inauguration in March as Uruguay's first civilian president since the mid-1970's.

Argentina and Great Britain over the Falkland Islands. Great Britain—the victor in the war—still refused to enter into negotiations on the future of the islands it controls.

Grenada was also returning to normalcy after the U.S. invasion of 1983. The last U.S. occupation forces left Grenada in June 1985.

Human Rights. Few events of 1985 could equal the drama played out in Argentina. The Argentine generals who headed three previous governments between 1976 and 1983 found themselves on trial, along with some of their subordinates. They were charged with violations of human rights during a crackdown on left wing guerrillas in the late 1970's. In December, five of the defendants were found guilty, including former President Jorge Rafael Videla, who was given the maximum sentence of life in prison. Videla was found guilty on 16 counts of aggravated murder, 50 counts of murder, 91 counts of torture, and 306 counts of kidnapping.

In Chile, a brave judge, José Cánovas Robles, won national acclaim for his investigation of the assassination of three Communists. The judge's actions awakened hopes among some Chileans that, as in neighboring Argentina, their military leaders would eventually be brought to justice for their brutality in stifling dissent.

In Panama, the mere hint of an investigation into the torture and beheading of Hugo Spadafora, an outspoken foe of the nation's all-powerful military, led to the forced resignation of the first civilian head of state since 1968. President Nicolás Ardito Barletta Vallarina resigned on Sept. 28, 1985, and was replaced by Eric Arturo Delvalle. Brazil and Uruguay returned to civilian rule in 1985; Brazil for the first time since 1964 and Uruguay for the first time since the mid-1970's. Uruguay's new president was Julio María Sanguinetti, and Brazil's new president was José Sarney. See SANGUINETTI, JULIO MARÍA; SARNEY, JOSÉ.

Mengele's Remains. On June 21, a team of forensic scientists announced in São Paulo, Brazil, that a skeleton removed from a grave was that of the notorious Nazi Josef Mengele. Mengele, a war criminal wanted for the torture and murder of inmates at the infamous Auschwitz concentration camp in Poland during World War II, had been the object of a worldwide manhunt. He was long rumored to be hiding out in South America. See MENGELE, JOSEF.

Natural Disasters. Earthquakes in Mexico and the eruption of a volcano in Colombia brought a tragic loss of life in 1985. These natural disasters also had political and economic consequences for the two countries.

On November 13, the eruption of the Nevado del Ruiz volcano in Colombia triggered a mud slide that killed about 25,000 people, mostly in the

The Spread of Civilian Government

Civilian governments elected before 1979

Civilian governments elected since 1979

Other types of government

agricultural town of Armero, which was buried underneath a river of mud. About 60,000 people were left homeless in one of the worst volcanic disasters in history. Controversy over rescue efforts and whether the government issued adequate warnings compounded political problems for Colombia's President Belisario Betancur, who was already under attack for his handling of a hostage crisis on November 7.

On September 19 and 20, two major earthquakes jolted western and central Mexico, causing the greatest damage in Mexico City, the world's largest metropolitan area, with a population unofficially estimated to be as high as 18 million people. Some 7,000 people died in the earthquakes, which leveled many office and apartment buildings in the city's center.

In October, Mexico's finance minister, Jesús Silva Herzog, issued a report that put the quakes' economic impact at $700 million. The report said that Mexico's dollar reserves would fall drastically due to reduced tourism, the cost of rescue efforts, and the cost of rebuilding. The report pleaded with foreign creditors for a deferment on loan payments so that Mexico could avoid a worsening of its debt burden, which, at $96 billion, is among the highest in Latin America.

Mexico's Economic Plight led to a wave of illegal immigration, according to U.S. immigration officials. They reported that in one border area—San Diego County in California—arrests of illegal immigrants from Mexico were up 20 per cent for the nine-month period ending Sept. 30, 1985, compared with the same period in 1984. Illegal immigration from other Latin-American countries also increased during the first nine months of 1985, with illegal entries from Guatemala reported to be up 30 per cent; from Nicaragua, up 58 per cent; and from Colombia, up 89 per cent.

Hispanics. The immigrant inflow was changing the social structure of several U.S. cities. Miami, Fla., was 60 per cent Hispanic in 1985, and in November, the city's Puerto Rican-born mayor was replaced by a Cuban-born challenger. In Los Angeles, where hundreds of thousands of immigrants from Central America have settled, candidates for local office have found it necessary to take positions on such foreign policy issues as Castro's Cuba, the Sandinistas of Nicaragua, and the rebellion in El Salvador in order to respond to the interests of an increasingly Hispanic electorate. In the Special Reports section, see THE NEW NEW AMERICANS. Nathan A. Haverstock

See also articles on the various Latin-American countries. In WORLD BOOK, see LATIN AMERICA and articles on the individual countries.

LAW. See CIVIL RIGHTS; COURTS; CRIME; SUPREME COURT OF THE UNITED STATES.

LEBANON. The withdrawal of the last Israeli forces from Lebanon in June 1985 briefly raised hopes that the various Lebanese factions could finally unite behind the "government of national unity" of President Amin Gemayel. But the most violent civil strife in several years engulfed the country in a new blood bath. Hopes were again raised on December 28 when the leaders of Lebanon's most powerful militias signed a Syrian-sponsored peace accord that called for an immediate cease-fire in Lebanon's civil war and the restructuring of the Lebanese government to give the country's Muslims more political power. The accord, signed by the leaders of the country's main Christian, Shiite Muslim, and Druse militias, in essence gave Syria control over Lebanon's foreign policy. It also called for an enlarged cabinet and parliament, which was to be divided equally between Christians and Muslims.

The Israeli Withdrawal took place in stages, beginning with a pullout from the Sidon area in February. In April, Israeli forces pulled back from the eastern Bekaa Valley to a security zone 8 to 10 miles (13 to 16 kilometers) deep along the Israeli-Lebanese border. The Israelis pulled back sooner than planned because of an escalation in attacks by the southern Lebanese Shiite population, who were angered by what they contended was Israeli mistreatment and by Israeli reprisals against their

villages. On June 10, the last Israeli troops withdrew from the security zone.

Civil Strife. The Israeli departure left a power vacuum that various factions fought to fill. The Israelis had expected that the South Lebanon Army (SLA), an Israeli-trained and Israeli-financed militia, would be able to control the border zone and thus protect Israel's northern settlements. But the SLA was even more detested by the southern Lebanese than the Israelis had been, mainly because SLA troops were mostly Christian. The Amal (Hope) militia, the largest Shiite faction in Lebanon, drove SLA units into a few Christian strongholds in a series of bloody clashes during the summer. In August, rocket attacks into northern Israel brought Israeli forces back across the Lebanese border. They destroyed three Shiite Muslim villages in retaliation for the attacks.

Christian Split. A major split in the Christian community developed in mid-March. Samir Geagea, commander of the Lebanese Forces, a Maronite Christian militia, broke with Gemayel, accusing him of selling out to Syrian interests. Geagea said his forces would oppose any Syrian-sponsored peace plan. Although Geagea was replaced in May by Elie Hobeika, both Muslim and Druse leaders refused to discuss a peace settlement with Maronite leaders. They objected to Hobeika's involvement in the September 1982 massacre of Palestinians in two refugee camps in West Beirut.

Factional conflict seemed endless during the spring and summer as one cease-fire after another broke down. In April, Amal fighters defeated the Sunni Mourabitoun militia, giving them temporary control of West Beirut. In May, Amal militiamen surrounded Palestinian refugee camps in West Beirut, causing more than 2,000 casualties as Palestinians and their Sunni Muslim allies fought desperately to defend their positions.

Syrian Intervention. Syria, which had kept 30,000 troops in eastern Lebanon after the Israeli withdrawal, began to intervene directly in the conflict in July. A Syrian-sponsored National Unity Front of about 100 Muslim, Druse, and moderate Christian leaders hostile to Gemayel was formed in August. Syrian efforts to end the blood bath bore fruit in late September, when Syrian troops intervened to halt anarchy in West Beirut and end a 13-day power struggle between Shiite and Palestinian groups in Tripoli (also called Tarabulus). The December accord was also a measure of Syria's influence as a regional power broker.

Attacks on Gemayel. The embattled Lebanese president was shaken by several blows during 1985. He narrowly escaped death on May 29 when the presidential palace was shelled by what the government said were Muslim gunners, and again on December 31 when gunmen ambushed his car.

A woman and her children are led to safety in Beirut after they flee from a Palestinian refugee camp being attacked by Shiite Muslims in May.

Prime Minister Rashid Karami and Education Minister Selim al-Hoss, both Sunni Muslims and long-time allies, began a boycott of Cabinet meetings in early April to protest Gemayel's handling of Muslim-Christian fighting in Sidon. The entire Cabinet resigned on April 17, though on April 24, Karami withdrew his resignation and agreed to remain as head of a caretaker government.

The Economy remained in a state of near-paralysis due to the civil war. Customs receipts, one of Lebanon's few remaining sources of revenue, were only $13 million for the first six months of 1985, less than 10 per cent of the amount anticipated. Various militias controlling Lebanese ports diverted the revenues for their own use. The port of Beirut, once the busiest in the Mideast, shut when the company running it went out of business.

Lebanon's currency, which had been stable even during the worst years of the civil war, dropped from 6 pounds = U.S.$1 in January to 17.5 pounds = U.S.$1 at year-end. Annual per capita income, which had been $1,300 in 1982, was estimated at $200 at midyear. With debts of $2.4 billion and an anticipated 1985 budget deficit of $1-billion, the only hope for Lebanon was massive foreign aid for reconstruction. 　William Spencer

See also ISRAEL; MIDDLE EAST (Facts in Brief Table). In WORLD BOOK, see LEBANON.

LESOTHO. See AFRICA.

LIBERIA. On Oct. 15, 1985, Liberia held its first national election since 1980, when a military coup toppled the civilian regime. Samuel K. Doe, the head of state and leader of the 1980 coup, was elected president with 51 per cent of the vote. His National Democratic Party of Liberia gained large majorities in both houses of the legislature.

The election marked two historic firsts for the West African nation, which was founded in 1822 as a home for freed slaves from the United States. It was Liberia's first multiparty election and the first election in which all adults—not just wealthy landowners—were permitted to vote.

Despite those reforms, many Liberians were unhappy with the election. Opposition politicians claimed that Doe's government rigged the results in various ways, such as by barring two potentially strong presidential candidates and evicting voters from polling places.

On April 1, the deputy commander of the presidential guard, Lieutenant Colonel Moses Flanzamaton, tried to assassinate Doe. Flanzamaton was executed on April 8.

On November 12, rebel troops led by a former military commander attempted to overthrow Doe's government, but they were defeated by soldiers loyal to Doe. 　J. Dixon Esseks

See also AFRICA (Facts in Brief Table). In WORLD BOOK, see LIBERIA.

LIBRARY. Libraries in the United States sharpened their promotional skills in 1985 in an effort to combat illiteracy. United States media donated nearly $6 million in print space and television and radio time to a campaign designed to increase public awareness of functional illiteracy and to recruit volunteer tutors. The campaign, launched in late 1984, was sponsored by the Coalition for Literacy, a group of 11 organizations founded by the American Library Association (ALA).

Libraries in 49 states held photography contests on the theme "A Nation of Readers" during National Library Week in April 1985. Winning entries were exhibited at the Library of Congress in Washington, D.C. The National Endowment for the Humanities awarded grants to 15 state library groups for reading and discussion programs in libraries.

Technology. Beginning in January, the New York City Public Library replaced its card catalog, which consisted of 10 million cards, with a computerized catalog system as part of its $45-million restoration program. In July, the Westminster (Colo.) Public Library bookmobile became the first to operate a computerized card catalog by radio.

Intellectual Freedom. Reports issued in 1985 by the ALA and Harvard University in Cambridge, Mass., pointed to a continuing pattern of restric-

tions on the flow of government information to the public. The ALA report, *Less Access to Less Information by and About the U.S. Government*, detailed actions taken since President Ronald Reagan declared a moratorium on new government publications in April 1981. The Harvard report asserted that federal agencies have expanded efforts to review research before publication and to censor technical papers at scientific meetings.

In July, the House of Representatives eliminated *Playboy* magazine from a Library of Congress program that makes magazines available in braille to the blind. It was the first time Congress had interfered with the library's selection policy.

Funding. During 1985, spending by U.S. public libraries jumped 11.5 per cent. Circulation rose 1.9 per cent. Despite greater state and private support, the Reagan Administration in its fiscal 1986 budget requested no money for the Library Services and Construction Act, through which public libraries receive funds for improvements. The Administration also attempted to eliminate the National Commission on Libraries and Information Science, a board that develops plans for coordinating information services. In October, Congress approved funds for these programs.   Peggy Barber

See also AMERICAN LIBRARY ASSOCIATION; CANADIAN LIBRARY ASSOCIATION. In WORLD BOOK, see LIBRARY.

Actor Bill Cosby and friends promote reading in a poster celebrating National Library Week, which was held from April 14 to 20, 1985.

LIBYA. Leader of the Revolution Muammar Muhammad al-Qadhafi continued to play the role of an agitator in Middle Eastern and international affairs in 1985. For example, in February, he spoke by satellite to a meeting of the Nation of Islam (Black Muslims) in Chicago, urging those attending to revolt against the United States government and to establish a separate black nation. In April, he presided over the first meeting of the Pan-Arab Command for Leading the Arab Revolutionary Forces, an international group formed to carry out acts of violence against the United States, other Western countries, and moderate Arab governments.

In May, Qadhafi called for a crusade to topple the government of Zaire. Also that month, Egypt said it had uncovered an alleged Libyan-financed plot to bomb the U.S. Embassy in Cairo. Then in August, Libya expelled about 21,000 Tunisian workers, bringing those two countries close to war.

Yet some actions of the changeable Libyan leader brought positive results for Libya. Diplomatic relations were established or restored with Burundi, Mauritania, and Somalia. In April, after the overthrow of President and Prime Minister Gaafar Mohamed Nimeiri of Sudan, Libya promptly recognized the new government there and in July signed a military agreement with Sudanese leaders.

Arab Affairs. The Libyan leader was less successful in his efforts to build Arab unity. Iraq broke off relations in June after Libya signed a friendship pact with Iran, which has been at war with Iraq since 1980. Qadhafi accused Iraq's President Saddam Hussein of being an agent of imperialism and Zionism. Relations with Egypt soured after Egypt foiled a plot to assassinate a Libyan opponent of Qadhafi's living in exile in Egypt and after Egypt blamed Libya for the November hijacking of an Egyptian airliner.

Internal Opposition to Qadhafi surfaced in the armed forces. In April, there were two attempts by army officers to overthrow him, both thwarted by his East German bodyguards and loyal Libyan officers. As many as 75 officers were executed in a purge of the army. Libyan pilots mutinied in August after Qadhafi ordered them to fly over Tunisia during the dispute over the expulsion of Tunisian workers.

The Economy continued a slow downturn. The budget, approved by the General People's Congress (GPC) in March, set expenditures at $4.9 billion, a 25 per cent drop from 1984. The GPC also canceled 300 "nonessential" foreign contracts and banned imports of luxury goods.   William Spencer

See also AFRICA (Facts in Brief Table). In WORLD BOOK, see LIBYA.

LIECHTENSTEIN. See EUROPE.

LITERATURE. Although no extraordinary novels were published in the United States in 1985, the year was commendable for the number of younger fiction writers who added to their reputation. Conventional realism was the order of the day, though some notable fantasies also appeared.

Short-story writer and radio-show host Garrison Keillor suprised the literary world with *Lake Wobegon Days*, a comic novel about rural Minnesota that quickly became a best seller. Denis Johnson came out with *Fiskadoro*, a surrealistic novel set 60 years after global nuclear destruction.

Short-story writer Bobbie Ann Mason portrayed the effects of the Vietnam War on life in western Kentucky in her first novel, *In Country*. Another splendid first novel was Nancy Willard's *Things Invisible to See*. Good first novels also came from Carolyn Chute, Fernanda Eberstadt, Annie Greene, Mary-Ann Tirone Smith, and Ira Wood.

Several respected novelists in their 30's or 40's enhanced their reputations in 1985. Most notable was Anne Tyler, who explored happiness and unhappiness in a Baltimore family in *The Accidental Tourist*. Mary Gordon investigated the problem of loving the unlovely in *Men and Angels*.

Ann Beattie's *Love Always* was a cool and controlled comic novel that captured the self-obsession of the generation now in their 30's. John Irving's *The Cider House Rules* was a best-selling novel

about a Maine abortionist of the early 1900's. Don DeLillo's ironic and grimly funny novel, *White Noise*, told of the evacuation of a town after an industrial accident. American history provided material for two fine books. Texas writer Larry McMurtry produced a Western novel of high quality in *Lonesome Dove*, the story of a cattle drive in the late 1800's. Hugh Nissenson's *The Tree of Life* was an affecting novel in journal form about life on the Ohio frontier in 1811 and 1812.

Several veteran novelists also turned out first-rate work. William Gaddis' *Carpenter's Gothic* was a difficult and brilliant experimental tale. Philip Roth added *The Prague Orgy*, a short novel that celebrated the outrageous, to his comic trilogy, *Zuckerman Bound*. John Hersey added to his distinguished career with *The Call*, the story of a missionary in China. *Stanley Elkin's The Magic Kingdom* confirmed that author's reputation as one of the most profound comic novelists in the United States. E. L. Doctorow's *World's Fair* was a lyrical exploration of childhood memories.

Commendable novels also were published by Russell Banks, John Calvin Batchelor, Peter De Vries, Gail Godwin, Francine du Plessix Gray, Barry Hannah, John Hawkes, Alice Hoffman, Ursula K. Le Guin, Julius Lester, Cormac McCarthy, Brian Moore, Joyce Carol Oates, Susan Fromberg Schaeffer, Lore Segal, and Ntozake Shange.

Nobel Prize winner Isaac Bashevis Singer's *The Image and Other Stories*, which explored the little madnesses of daily life, was the year's most notable collection of short stories. Other important collections were Grace Paley's *Later the Same Day* and Peter Taylor's *The Old Forest and Other Stories*. Distinguished books of stories came also from Alice Adams, Carol Bly, T. Coraghessan Boyle, Susan Engberg, Amy Hempel, and William Humphrey.

Fiction from Other Countries. Great Britain produced much noteworthy fiction in 1985. These works included Kingsley Amis' *Stanley and the Women*, Julian Barnes's *Flaubert's Parrot*, Anita Brookner's *Family and Friends*, John Fowles's *A Maggot*, Doris Lessing's *The Good Terrorist*, and Jonathan Raban's first novel, *Foreign Land*.

Benedict Kiely's powerful *Nothing Happened in Carmincross* led new novels from Ireland. R. K. Narayan, India's noted English-language novelist, produced *Under the Banyan Tree*, a masterly collection of short stories.

France's leading contribution was Marguerite Duras's *The Lover*, and West Germany provided Martin Walser's *The Inner Man*. Italo Calvino's last novel, *Mr. Palomar*, appeared just after the death of the distinguished Italian novelist in September.

Mexico contributed Carlos Fuentes' *The Old Gringo* and Arturo Azuela's *Shadows of Silence*. From Chile came Isabel Allende's powerful and disturbing *The House of the Spirits*.

Biography and Autobiography. Most notable in this genre were two superb efforts to rehabilitate Ernest Hemingway's literary reputation, which declined after his death in 1961. They were Peter Griffin's *Along with Youth: Hemingway, the Early Years*, the first volume of a projected three-volume biography, and Jeffrey Meyers' *Hemingway*. Among other literary lives, *Wallace Stevens: A Mythology of Self* was Milton J. Bates's perceptive biography of the poet. David Castronovo's *Edmund Wilson* provided a lively portrait of the critic.

Popular political lives included *FDR*, Ted Morgan's biography of President Franklin D. Roosevelt, and Philip Ziegler's *Mountbatten*, which highlighted the achievements of Great Britain's Earl Mountbatten of Burma.

Two biographies of a distinguished actor and director appeared shortly before his death in October: Barbara Leaming's *Orson Welles* and Charles Higham's *Orson Welles: The Rise and Fall of an American Genius*. David Robinson's *Chaplin: His Life and Art* was a highly readable biography of another great actor and director.

A variety of interesting autobiographies appeared during 1985. *Ansel Adams: An Autobiography* was the great photographer's final professional testament. *The Inman Diary* was a fascinating journal by Arthur Crew Inman, an obscure writer who

died by suicide in 1963. Whittled down from 17 million words to 1,661 pages by Daniel Aaron, the journal provided a record of sexual obsession. Wright Morris' *A Cloak of Light*, his third volume of memoirs, was the year's most notable autobiography by a U.S. literary figure.

The remarkable story of Milovan Djilas, who was once a close aide of Yugoslav leader Josip Broz Tito, continued in *Rise and Fall*. Arkady N. Shevchenko, a high-ranking Soviet diplomat who defected to the United States in 1978, told of life in the Soviet foreign service in the revealing *Breaking with Moscow*.

Essays, Criticism, and Letters. The year's most important critical work was the fifth edition of *The Oxford Companion to English Literature*, which was ably edited by British novelist Margaret Drabble. William H. Gass's *Habitations of the Word* was a collection of essays rich in antic wordplay. *Plausible Prejudices* gathered Joseph Epstein's brilliant, acerbic essays on American writing. *The Price of the Ticket* collected James Baldwin's acute observations about the United States.

Among collections of correspondence, *Darlinghissima* was a stately and passionate book of letters from the late *New Yorker* magazine correspondent Janet Flanner to her beloved friend Natalia Danesi Murray. *Bernard Shaw: Collected Letters, 1911-1925*,

Storyteller Garrison Keillor signs copies of his best seller, *Lake Wobegon Days*, a humorous celebration of life in an imaginary Minnesota town.

Peruvian writer Mario Vargas Llosa wins the new Ritz Paris Hemingway Award in March. With him are Ernest Hemingway's granddaughters Margaux, left, and Mariel.

demonstrated the great Irish playwright's wit and seriousness. *Randall Jarrell's Letters* provided insights into the personality of the strongly opinionated critic and poet. *The Correspondence of Charles Darwin* spanned the years 1821 to 1836.

History. Forty years after the first atomic bomb was dropped on Japan, three important books looked at the aftermath of that event. Rodney Barker's *The Hiroshima Maidens* told the story of several young Japanese women brought to the United States in 1955 for plastic surgery on their radiation burns. Roger Rosenblatt's *Witness: The World Since Hiroshima* reviewed changing attitudes about the morality of nuclear war. John Hersey reissued *Hiroshima*, his classic 1946 account of the lives of six survivors, with a lengthy postscript.

The 10th anniversary of the end of the Vietnam War occasioned a number of books. Most notable was David Butler's *The Fall of Saigon*, a detailed recreation of the last 55 days of the war. Michael Schaller investigated the origins of the Cold War in Asia in *The American Occupation of Japan*. Harrison E. Salisbury told the story of Mao Zedong's (Mao Tse-tung's) 6,000-mile (9,700-kilometer) trek with his Communist army to the hinterlands of China in 1934 and 1935 in *The Long March*. James MacGregor Burns's *The Workshop of Democracy*, the second in his planned three-volume history of the United States, moved from the end of the Civil

War to the early years of the Great Depression. Walter A. McDougall's *. . .The Heavens and the Earth* explored the politics of the race into space.

The rise of the influential Church of Jesus Christ of Latter-day Saints was tracked in three books: Richard L. Bushman's *Joseph Smith and the Beginnings of Mormonism*, Leonard J. Arrington's *Brigham Young: American Moses*, and Jan Shipps's *Mormonism: The Story of a New Religious Tradition*.

Contemporary Affairs. It was an exceptional year for this genre. The powerful and disturbing book *Common Ground*, by distinguished reporter J. Anthony Lukas, followed the lives of three families in an account of Boston's racial tensions during the decade from 1968 to 1978. Charles E. Silberman concluded in *A Certain People* that Jews had successfully assimilated into U.S. society while retaining their cultural and religious identity.

The agonies of South Africa occupied the attention of several distinguished writers in 1985. Joseph Lelyveld's *Move Your Shadow* vividly described the ordeals of blacks in that troubled country. James North's *Freedom Rising* told of that reporter's travels and conversations throughout the country. Vincent Crapanzano's *Waiting* examined the lives and thoughts of South Africa's increasingly beleaguered white minority.

Roy Mottahedeh's *The Mantle of the Prophet* reflected on how wrath and impatience have replaced the tradition of tolerance in Iran's politics. Ryszard Kapuscinski's fine study, *Shah of Shahs*, provided a riveting account of the downfall of Iran's monarch, Mohammad Reza Pahlavi, in 1979. Another important book on Iran was Gary Sick's *All Fall Down*, which assessed U.S. foreign policy during the last months of the shah's regime.

Shirley Christian produced the year's best book on Central American conflicts, *Nicaragua: Revolution in the Family*, which told how that country's Sandinista regime came to power and suggested ways in which the United States might better have dealt with it. William J. Broad's *Star Warriors* contended that the scientists at work on the U.S. Strategic Defense Initiative, known as "Star Wars," are unimaginative and hampered by careerism.

One of the year's most fascinating books, Tracy Kidder's *House*, explored the complex relationships that developed during the building of a single-family dwelling. *Funny Money*, by Mark Singer, delved into the failure of Oklahoma's Penn Square Bank, which had arranged huge energy loans that were less than credit-worthy.

Science and Natural History. Daniel J. Kevles' *In the Name of Eugenics* studied the history of the eugenics movement, which believed that behavioral traits were inherited. Stephen Jay Gould's fourth collection of essays, *The Flamingo's Smile*, was as memorable as its forerunners. Frank Gonzalez-Crussi, a pathologist, reflected on his medical specialty in the fascinating *Notes of an Anatomist. Crime and Human Nature* by James Q. Wilson and Richard J. Herrnstein was a controversial study of the causes of crime that applied the latest theories of behavioral psychology.

Best Sellers in hardcover were *Iacocca*, by Lee A. Iacocca with William Novak; *Loving Each Other*, by Leo Buscaglia; *Family Album*, by Danielle Steel; *Thinner*, by Stephen King writing under the pen name Richard Bachman; *The Frugal Gourmet*, by Jeff Smith; *Smart Women, Foolish Choices*, by Connell Cowan and Melvyn Kinder; *Lake Wobegon Days*, by Garrison Keillor; *Skeleton Crew*, by King; *Yeager*, by Charles E. (Chuck) Yeager; and *Elvis and Me* by Priscilla Beaulieu Presley.

Top-selling paperbacks of 1985 were *Love and War*, by John Jakes; *Out on a Limb*, by Shirley MacLaine; *The Hunt for Red October*, by Tom Clancy; *Crescent City*, by Belva Plain; *Heaven*, by V. C. Andrews; *The Talisman*, by King and Peter Straub; *Thinner*, by King writing under the name Bachman; *Iacocca*, by David Abodaher; and the *Rand McNally Road Atlas*.   Henry Kisor

See also AWARDS AND PRIZES (Literature Awards); CANADIAN LITERATURE; KING, STEPHEN; LITERATURE FOR CHILDREN; POETRY; PUBLISHING. In WORLD BOOK, see LITERATURE.

LITERATURE, CANADIAN. See CANADIAN LIBRARY ASSOCIATION; CANADIAN LITERATURE.

LITERATURE FOR CHILDREN. Historical fiction that revolved around family life appeared with greater frequency in 1985 than in previous years. Fewer books of poetry were published, but fantasy, realism, and informational books of all kinds abounded. Picture books were available in great variety. Some outstanding books of 1985 were:

Picture Books

Fergus and Bridey, by Olivier Dunrea (Holiday House). Fergus and his dog, Bridey, hunt for treasure in this delightful story. Ages 4 to 8.

The Troublesome Pig, by Priscilla Lamont (Crown). An old tale is amusingly retold and illustrated. Ages 3 to 7.

Washday on Noah's Ark, by Glen Rounds (Holiday House). Noah's wife finds an imaginative substitute for a clothesline in this wonderfully illustrated, comical tale. All ages.

Tog the Ribber, or Granny's Tale, by Paul Coltman, illustrated by Gillian McClure (Farrar, Straus, & Giroux). Eerie paintings accompany this marvelous, nonsensical poem. All ages.

Look-Alikes, by Henrik Drescher (Lothrop, Lee & Shepard Bks.). Imaginative illustrations and events should enthrall readers. Ages 4 to 8.

The Nightingale, by Hans Christian Andersen, adapted by Alan Benjamin, illustrated by Beni Montresor (Crown). A favorite Andersen tale is beautifully rendered in glowing colors. All ages.

Dad's Back, Reading, Messy Baby, and *Sleeping,* by Jan Ormerod (Lothrop, Lee & Shepard Bks.). Four books delightfully depict the interaction between father and baby. Ages 1 to 4.

Maria Theresa, by Petra Mathers (Harper & Row). A talented chicken becomes a circus star, but her former owner misses her. Ages 4 to 8.

First Comes Spring, by Anne Rockwell (Crowell). The reader is asked to spot what is happening during each season. Answers appear on the following page. Ages 3 to 6.

Annie and the Wild Animals, by Jan Brett (Houghton Mifflin). Annie wants a replacement for Taffy, her missing cat. Border illustrations show the absent Taffy's activities. Ages 4 to 8.

Pancake Pie, by Sven Nordqvist (Morrow). Farmer Festus prepares a birthday celebration in this droll tale. Ages 5 to 8.

How Much Is a Million?, by David Schwartz, illustrated by Steven Kellogg (Lothrop, Lee & Shepard Bks.). Exuberant illustrations accompany an informative book about numbers. Ages 5 and up.

Brother to the Wind, by Mildred Pitts Walter, illustrated by Diane and Leo Dillon (Lothrop, Lee & Shepard Bks.). Fine paintings enhance a West African tale about a boy's desire to fly. Ages 7 to 10.

The Very Worst Monster, by Pat Hutchins (Greenwillow Bks.). Hazel is ignored when a new baby comes, but she finds a solution. Ages 4 to 8.

What's That Noise?, by Michele Lemieux (Morrow). Beautiful paintings highlight Bear's search for the source of a strange sound. Ages 3 to 7.

Rabbit's Morning, by Nancy Tafuri (Greenwillow Bks.). Large, realistic paintings reveal what a rabbit sees on its way home. Ages 2 to 5.

Big World, Small World, by Jeanne Titherington (Greenwillow Bks.). Anna and her mother react differently in the same situations. Ages 3 to 6.

An Evening at Alfie's, by Shirley Hughes (Lothrop, Lee & Shepard Bks.). Maureen is baby-sitting with Alfie when a pipe bursts. Ages 3 to 6.

The Quilt Story, by Tony Johnston, illustrated by Tomie de Paola (Putnam). A warmly illustrated tale about the love for a handmade quilt in two generations. Ages 4 to 8.

Gorilla, by Anthony Browne (Knopf). Hannah, ignored by her father, dreams of an adventure with a friendly gorilla. Ages 5 to 8.

A Country Tale, by Diane Stanley (Four Winds Press). One of two friends has her head turned by wealth and elegance in this well-told and richly illustrated story. Ages 5 to 8.

The Sign in Mendel's Window, by Mildred Phillips, illustrated by Margot Zemach (Macmillan). A stranger tries to swindle the butcher in a tiny Polish town, with unexpected results. Ages 5 to 9.

The Relatives Came, by Cynthia Rylant, illustrated by Stephen Gammell (Bradbury Press). Humorous illustrations accompany a loving account of a summer visit from relatives. Ages 4 to 7.

Benjamin Rabbit and the Stranger Danger, by Irene Keller, illustrated by Dick Keller (Dodd, Mead). A blend of fact and fiction shows how young people can gain confidence in their ability to handle potentially dangerous situations. Ages 4 to 8.

Poetry and Songs

Celebrations, by Myra Cohn Livingston, illustrated by Leonard Everett Fisher (Holiday House). Sixteen special days from New Year's Eve to Christmas Eve are celebrated in poetry and paintings. All ages.

Inside Turtle's Shell and Other Poems of the Field, by Joanne Ryder, drawings by Susan Bonners (Macmillan). Poems about small animals combine the everyday and the surprising. Ages 7 to 10.

Tomie de Paola's Mother Goose, by Tomie de Paola (Putnam). Familiar favorites plus less well-known rhymes are glowingly illustrated in this large, well-arranged collection. All ages.

Blackberry Ink, by Eve Merriam, illustrated by Hans Wilhelm (Morrow). The mostly humorous verses are gaily illustrated. Ages 4 to 9.

Whiskers & Rhymes, by Arnold Lobel (Greenwillow Bks.). Fanciful paintings of cats illustrate Lobel's delightful rhymes. Ages 3 to 8.

Thanksgiving Poems, selected by Myra Cohn Livingston, illustrated by Stephen Gammell (Holiday

Robin McKinley's *The Hero and the Crown* won the 1985 Newbery Medal for the "most distinguished contribution to American literature for children."

House). This varied collection is beautifully illustrated in water color. All ages.

Fantasy

Amy's Eyes, by Richard Kennedy, illustrated by Richard Egielski (Harper & Row). A doll becomes human and a child becomes a doll in this fascinating tale of a search for gold. All ages.

All of Our Noses Are Here, and Other Noodle Tales, retold by Alvin Schwartz, illustrated by Karen Ann Weinhaus (Harper & Row). Five entertaining stories tell of one family's antics. Ages 4 to 8.

Babe, the Gallant Pig, by Dick King-Smith, illustrated by Mary Rayner (Crown). A pig becomes a sheepherder, or "sheep-pig," in this delightful tale. Ages 8 and up.

Dragon Steel, by Lawrence Yep (Harper & Row). Thorn and the dragon seek to restore the Inland Sea in this engrossing tale. Ages 12 and up.

Tales for the Perfect Child, by Florence Parry Heide, illustrated by Victoria Chess (Lothrop, Lee & Shepard Bks.). Parents may cringe, but young readers will delight in the antics of the children in these seven tales. Ages 7 to 10.

The Changing Maze, by Zilpha Keatly Snyder, illustrated by Charles Mikolaycak (Macmillan). A boy struggles with an evil maze when he goes in search of his pet lamb. The illustrations capture the mood perfectly. Ages 8 to 12.

Saint George and the Dragon retold by Margaret Hodges and illustrated by Trina Schart Hyman won the 1985 Caldecott Medal for children's picture books.

Jackaroo, by Cynthia Voigt (Atheneum Pubs.). Gwyn, an innkeeper's daughter, brings a legend to life during troubled times. Ages 12 and up.

The People Could Fly: American Black Folktales, by Virginia Hamilton, illustrated by Leo and Diane Dillon (Knopf). Informative annotations and fine illustrations enhance this excellent, varied collection. Ages 8 and up.

Seasons of Splendor: Tales, Myths, and Legends from India, by Madhur Jaffrey, illustrated by Michael Foreman (Atheneum Pubs.). This fine collection of tales about the triumph of cleverness, goodness, and other virtues delights the eye and ear. The author's memories introduce each section. Ages 8 and up.

Fiction

Encyclopedia Brown and the Case of the Mysterious Handprints, by Donald J. Sobol, illustrated by Gail Owens (Morrow). Readers can match wits with a young detective. Ages 8 to 12.

Sarah, Plain and Tall, by Patricia MacLachlan (Harper & Row). This excellent story tells of a mail-order bride's trial period with her new family. Ages 8 to 10.

One Special Year, by N. A. Perez (Houghton Mifflin). A family is viewed through the eyes of a 14-year-old girl in the year 1900. Ages 12 and up.

Sirens and Spies, by Janet Taylor Lisle (Bradbury Press). An attack upon a violin teacher draws two sisters into a mystery. Ages 12 and up.

Angel in Charge, by Judy Delton, illustrated by Leslie Morrill (Houghton Mifflin). Angel takes over when her sitter breaks a leg. Ages 8 to 10.

Dogsong, by Gary Paulsen (Bradbury Press). An Eskimo looks back at the hardships and indomitable spirit of the old days. Ages 12 and up.

Blackberries in the Dark, by Mavis Jukes, illustrated by Thomas B. Allen (Knopf). With the help of his grandmother, a boy overcomes his grief about the death of his grandfather. Ages 6 to 9.

Anastasia on Her Own, by Lois Lowry (Houghton Mifflin). Anastasia takes charge in her mother's absence, with disastrous results. Ages 8 to 12.

Animals, People, Places, and Projects

Town and Country, by Alice and Martin Provensen (Crown). Detailed paintings accompany interesting information about town and country. All ages.

The Comet and You, by E. C. Krupp, illustrated by Robin Rector Krupp (Macmillan). Halley's Comet and other features of the solar system are explained in a readable style. Ages 7 to 10.

How Life Begins: A Look at Birth and Care in the Animal World, by Chrissy Rankin, photographs by Oxford Scientific Films (Putnam). Excellent photographs and a clear text make this book a winner. All ages.

Germs Make Me Sick!, by Melvin Berger, illustrated by Marylin Hafner (Crowell). Humorous color illustrations accompany a readable, informative text. Ages 4 to 8.

The Big Book of Animal Records, by Annette Tison and Talus Taylor (Putnam Pub. Group). This oversized book is filled with fascinating facts and colorful pictures. All ages.

Volcanoes, by Franklyn M. Branley, illustrated by Marc Simont (Crowell). Color illustrations enhance a fine book about volcanoes. Ages 4 to 8.

How to Talk to Your Computer and *Meet the Computer*, by Seymour Simon, illustrated by Barbara and Ed Emberly (Crowell). The first book shows that computers must be told every step of a process. The second provides additional information. Both have bright, amusing illustrations. Ages 5 to 9.

Statue of Liberty, by Charles Mercer (Putnam). This book about the statue's creation has fascinating photographs and drawings. Ages 11 and up.

Puppeteer, by Kathryn Lasky, photographs by Christopher G. Knight (Macmillan). Readers are shown behind-the-scenes preparations for a puppet show. Ages 8 to 12.

Fill It Up: All About Service Stations, by Gail Gibbons (Crowell). This well-designed book presents information clearly. Ages 5 to 9.

Large As Life: Daytime Animals Life Size, by Joanna Cole, illustrated by Kenneth Lilly (Knopf). Gorgeous paintings highlight a simple text. All ages.

Guinea Pigs Don't Read Books, by Colleen Stanley Bare (Dodd, Mead). Beautiful photographs and a simple text tell all about guinea pigs. Ages 3 to 7.

Elephants Can't Jump & Other Freaky Facts About Animals, by Barbara Seuling (Lodestar Bks.). Fascinating facts about animals and amusing pen-and-ink illustrations fill this book. All ages.

Logging Machines in the Forest, by Janet Chiefari (Dodd, Mead). This fine book explains what specialized logging machines can do. Ages 7 to 11.

The Milk Makers, by Gail Gibbons (Macmillan). Bright illustrations and clear text tell how cows produce milk and what happens to milk afterward. Ages 5 to 8.

Awards in 1985 included:

The Newbery Medal for "the most distinguished contribution to American literature for children" was awarded to Robin McKinley for *The Hero and the Crown*. The Caldecott Medal for "the most distinguished American picture book for children" went to Trina Schart Hyman for *Saint George and the Dragon*. The Mildred L. Batchelder Award cited Houghton Mifflin for its publication of *The Island on Bird Street* by Uri Orlev.   Marilyn Fain Apseloff

In WORLD BOOK, see CALDECOTT MEDAL; LITERATURE FOR CHILDREN; NEWBERY MEDAL.

LIVESTOCK. See FARM AND FARMING.

LOS ANGELES in 1985 took a stand against the racial policies of South Africa, agreed to raise the pay of female city employees, and adopted a landmark ordinance banning discrimination against victims of acquired immune deficiency syndrome (AIDS). Mayor Thomas Bradley swept to a fourth term in office, and it appeared that construction would finally begin on a long-awaited subway.

South Africa. At the urging of the mayor and City Council, the Los Angeles Board of Police and Fire Commissioners on August 16 agreed to gradually rid its investment portfolio of $350 million in stocks and bonds from companies that do business with South Africa. The move was part of a city protest against South Africa's policy of *apartheid* (racial segregation).

AIDS Law. The Los Angeles City Council on August 14 unanimously adopted a law prohibiting discrimination against victims of AIDS, a deadly disease that destroys the body's immune system. The ordinance allows the city attorney to sue employers who fire or refuse to hire AIDS victims, restaurants that bar customers with the disease, and landlords who evict tenants or turn down prospective renters because of AIDS. The ordinance also prohibits schools from barring AIDS victims or their brothers and sisters.

Elections. On April 9, Bradley—a liberal Democrat—became the first Los Angeles mayor elected to four full terms in office. And with 68 per cent of the vote to his main opponent's 30 per cent, Bradley's margin of victory was believed to be the largest of any mayoral contest in the city's history.

Bradley made history in 1973 when he became the city's first black mayor. In the June 4 runoff election, Michael Woo became the first person of Asian heritage to be elected to the Los Angeles City Council. Woo, 33, was elected to represent an area of the city that includes Hollywood. On December 10, Richard Alatorre, a Democrat, became the only Hispanic council member when he was elected to fill the unexpired term of a member who had resigned in September. On November 26, the U.S. Department of Justice filed suit to overturn Los Angeles' 1982 redistricting plan, claiming that it violates the voting rights of Hispanics.

Subway. Plans for the long-awaited Metro Rail, a subway to run for 18.6 miles (29.9 kilometers) from downtown Los Angeles to the San Fernando Valley, received a boost on December 19 when President Ronald Reagan signed a federal spending bill that provided $429 million in additional funding for the $3.3-billion rail line. The Southern California Rapid Transit District, which will build and operate the subway, hopes to begin construction on the first 4.4 miles (7.1 kilometers) of the project in 1986.

Equal Pay. The City Council on May 10 approved a union contract raising the salaries of

Thomas Bradley flashes the victory sign on April 9 after becoming the first Los Angeles mayor to win a fourth full term in office.

more than 3,000 women clerks and librarians to the same level as those of men performing different, but comparable, city services. The contract resulted from lengthy negotiations between the city and the American Federation of State, County, and Municipal Employees (AFSCME), the union to which most city employees belong. A study by AFSCME found that fewer than 20 per cent of the city's female employees earned more than $25,000 a year, while more than 65 per cent of male employees made salaries above that figure.

Murder Suspect Charged. Los Angeles residents breathed a sigh of relief on August 31 when a man suspected of being the so-called Night Stalker who had murdered at least 14 people over a 13-month period was apprehended by the police. The suspect, Richard Ramirez, a 25-year-old drifter from El Paso, Tex., was arrested after being chased and subdued by people who had seen him attack a woman as she entered her car. On October 24, Ramirez pleaded not guilty to 14 charges of murder and to charges that he had also committed a series of robberies, rapes, and other crimes. Victor Merina

See also CITY. In WORLD BOOK, see LOS ANGELES.

LOUISIANA. See STATE GOVERNMENT.
LUXEMBOURG. See EUROPE.
MADAGASCAR. See AFRICA.

MADONNA (1959-   ), a flashy singer with a steamy appeal, became one of popular music's hottest superstars in 1985. Madonna's trademarks include cross-shaped earrings and midriff-baring costumes, many of which incorporate black, lacy lingerie. During 1985, sellout crowds flocked to her 28-city concert tour. In addition, she received favorable reviews for her performance as a free-thinking vagabond in the 1985 motion picture *Desperately Seeking Susan.*

Madonna Louise Ciccone was born on Aug. 16, 1959, in Bay City, Mich. She originally intended to pursue a career in dance, which she began to study in grade school. After graduating from high school in 1976, she attended the University of Michigan in Ann Arbor on a dance scholarship. In 1977, however, she quit school and moved to New York City. While trying to establish a dance career, she worked as a model and musician. Eventually, she turned to singing.

Madonna got her break in 1982, when a disk jockey at Danceteria, a New York City disco, played a song that she had recorded on a demonstration tape. In 1983, Madonna signed with Sire Records, which produced her first album, *Madonna.* Her second album, *Like a Virgin,* was released in 1984. A series of provocative music videos boosted her popularity. She married actor Sean Penn on Aug. 16, 1985. Barbara A. Mayes

MAGAZINE advertising revenues in the United States increased in 1985 by about 6 per cent over 1984's record high, reaching nearly $4.8 billion, and the number of pages of advertising grew by about 1 per cent. The combined circulation per issue of all consumer magazines surveyed by the Audit Bureau of Circulations (ABC) in the United States climbed to a record high of 321.4 million during the first six months of 1985, up 3 per cent over the same period in 1984. The ABC is an independent organization that issues circulation figures, verified by auditors, for magazines and other publications.

An annual survey conducted by the Magazine Publishers Association (MPA) and Price Waterhouse indicated that U.S. magazines were more profitable in 1984 than in 1983. In 1984, magazines showed a pretax operating profit of 11.3 per cent.

According to a survey conducted in the spring of 1985 by Mediamark Research, Incorporated, 94 per cent of all U.S. adults read magazines, and these people read 9.9 issues per month. The survey indicated the typical magazine reader is about 37 years old with at least a high school education, is married, lives in a household of three or more people, owns a home in a major metropolitan area, and has a household income of $30,978, 13 per cent above the national average.

Israel's former Defense Minister Ariel Sharon, center, meets the press after losing a libel case against *Time* magazine in January.

Awards. The MPA named S. I. Newhouse, Jr., chairman of Advance Publications, Incorporated, as the 1985 recipient of the Henry Johnson Fisher Award, the industry's most prestigious honor. The American Society of Magazine Editors presented its National Magazine Awards in April. Among the winning publications were *The Washingtonian* for public service, *Forbes* for design, *Playboy* for fiction, *Texas Monthly* for reporting, *Boston* for essays and criticism, *American Heritage* for single-topic issue, *The Washingtonian* for service to the individual, and *Life* for photography.

In the category of general excellence, which is presented in four groups according to circulation size, the winners were *Manhattan, inc.* (less than 100,000); *American Heritage* (100,000 to 400,000); *American Health* (400,000 to 1,000,000); and *Time* (more than 1 million).

New Magazines. Among the magazines introduced in 1985 was *EM Ebony Man*, intended for the upwardly mobile black man. The publication covers fashion, fitness, and personal finance. Johnson Publishing Company introduced the magazine in November.

Southern Progress Corporation, publisher of *Southern Living*, *Creative Ideas for Living*, and *Progressive Farmer* magazines and the nation's largest publisher of regional magazines, introduced *Southern Living Classics* in September 1985. The magazine is for affluent Southerners interested in art, interior design, and travel.

Changes. Advance Publications, Incorporated, publisher of *Vogue*, *Vanity Fair*, and *Glamour*, purchased *The New Yorker* on May 7. Advance, which already owned 17 per cent of the magazine, paid various stockholders approximately $142 million for the remainder.

Time Incorporated broke its long-standing tradition of starting new magazines rather than purchasing them. The company announced in February that it had bought Southern Progress Corporation. The reported purchase price was $480 million.

In May, *Rolling Stone* and Telepictures Corporation purchased *US* magazine from MacFadden Holdings, Incorporated, and the publishing division of Warner Communications, Incorporated, for an estimated $29 million. Family Media, Incorporated, bought *World Tennis* from CBS Magazines in January. Terms of the purchases were not disclosed. In November, Family Media agreed to sell the *Ladies' Home Journal* to Meredith Corporation, publisher of *Better Homes and Gardens*, for $96 million. Annmaria B. DiCesare

See also PUBLISHING. In WORLD BOOK, see MAGAZINE.

MAINE. See STATE GOVERNMENT.
MALAWI. See AFRICA.

MALAYSIA diversified its economy during 1985. The country had grown prosperous by Asian standards from its exports of petroleum, rubber, palm oil, and other commodities, but it sought to expand its manufacturing industries, particularly those that produced heavy goods.

Economic Policy. A factory to manufacture cars with Japanese help opened on July 9 in Shah Alam, near Kuala Lumpur, Malaysia's capital. The $230-million project was designed to produce 120,000 cars a year by 1994. As part of an industrial plan costing more than $3 billion, the government was also building two iron-processing plants, a paper mill, a cement factory, and a plant to produce methyl alcohol—a fuel and solvent.

On July 6, 1985, Finance Minister Daim Zainuddin announced steps to encourage foreign investment in industries where new technology was needed. The official New Economic Policy, a program adopted in 1971 to encourage more business ownership by Malays, had tried to limit foreign investment to 30 per cent of any one venture. Under the new rules, however, the proportion of a company's output that was exported would determine the percentage of foreign ownership allowed.

Part of the government's economic policy was to encourage an increase in the average family size from two or three children to five. Prime Minister Mahathir bin Mohamed set a goal of raising the population of Malaysia from about 15.9 million in 1985 to 70 million by the year 2100. He contended that Malaysia would need a larger domestic market to support its industries in a world that might have more restrictive trade policies.

Dress Code. The government, though committed to greater adherence to Islamic principles, issued regulations in March 1985 forbidding women civil servants and students from wearing traditional Middle Eastern clothing that completely covered their bodies. A modified costume that showed only the face was acceptable. Officials were reported to be worried that Islamic fundamentalism might conflict with economic progress.

Death Penalty Debate. The scheduled execution on August 14 of Sim Kie Chon was postponed amid controversy over whether security or drug offenses deserved death. Sim, a 28-year-old factory worker, had been sentenced in 1983 to die for possession of a revolver and five rounds of ammunition. Henry S. Bradsher

See also ASIA (Facts in Brief Table). In WORLD BOOK, see MALAYSIA.

MALDIVES. See ASIA.
MALI. See AFRICA.
MALTA. See EUROPE.

Malaysian soldiers keep watch on a road near Betong, Thailand, to guard Malaysia's northern border against smugglers and Communist guerrillas.

MANITOBA. In a historic decision on June 13, 1985, the Supreme Court of Canada ruled that almost all laws in Manitoba "are and always have been invalid and of no force or effect." The decision was based on the fact that the laws were written in English only and therefore not in conformity with the 1870 Manitoba Act, which brought the province into Canada and required that all laws be written in French as well as English. Manitoba suspended French as an official language in 1890, and the June 1985 ruling covered about 4,500 statutes and countless regulations passed since then. The Supreme Court stated that the laws would be retained temporarily to prevent chaos. But it ordered Manitoba to submit a reasonable schedule for the translation of its laws. In November, the court endorsed a three-year period for carrying out the task.

Premier Howard Pawley announced he was prepared to live with the decision. He said that his New Democratic Party government would continue to improve services for Manitoba's 60,000 French-speaking residents, but it would not reintroduce a controversial bill to restore French-language rights. The Progressive Conservative Party blocked passage of the bill in the provincial legislature in 1984.   David M. L. Farr

See also CANADA. In WORLD BOOK, see MANITOBA.

MANUFACTURING. In 1985, the United States economy continued to experience greater growth in service industries than in manufacturing. During the year, leading economists and industrialists debated the significance of this apparent shift toward a largely service-oriented economy.

Many experts warned that U.S. manufacturing was in grave danger. They argued that the United States has shifted too heavily to a service-oriented economy. Some industry experts, including Donald H. Trautlein, chairman and chief executive officer of Bethlehem Steel Corporation, proposed government action to aid U.S. manufacturers. "A dollar spent in manufacturing provides a lift to the rest of the economy," Trautlein argued. "It creates an additional $1.34 in domestic spending. Contrast that with a dollar in services, which adds only 72 cents to the rest of the economy. Financial services, insurance, and real estate provide even less. They add only 60 cents."

Other experts, however, such as economist Robert Z. Lawrence of the Brookings Institution in Washington, D.C., argued that the U.S. economy was basically unchanged. Lawrence said that the United States was "in no imminent danger of vanishing as a manufacturing power. Judged by the volume of production, America is no more a service economy today than it was in 1960," he said. Lawrence pointed to figures showing that the output of goods was 45.6 per cent of the gross national product—the total goods and services produced—in 1960, 45.8 per cent in 1979, and 45.3 per cent in the final quarter of 1983.

Another observer, journalist James Fallows, concluded that "because the service sector is already so large and manufacturing so small, the prospects for a dramatic swing in employment are remote. Many of the jobs that are going to disappear from manufacturing have already disappeared."

Manufacturing Jobs. Nevertheless, most of the new jobs that were created in 1985 were in the service industries. Manufacturing employment declined by 325,000 jobs between January and September 1985. In 1985, 17.5 million people were employed in manufacturing, down from 20.6 million in 1980.

The largest manufacturing employer in 1985 was the electronics industry, which led the automobile, steel, and textile industries. The electronics industry gained 200,000 new jobs in 1984, making it the largest employer in the manufacturing sector, with 2.6 million jobs.

Foreign Imports. Two major factors made 1985 a troubled year for manufacturing—the crippling effect of the overvalued dollar and increasing foreign competition. The overvalued dollar made goods from other countries cheaper and U.S. exports more expensive. Imports of steel, automobiles, apparel, machine tools, consumer electronics, and other products were expected to result in a $145-billion U.S. trade deficit in 1985. This compared with the previous year's record trade deficit of $123.3 billion. The wave of foreign imports resulted in lower sales for U.S. manufacturers and in layoffs.

There Was Light at the end of the tunnel, however. The dollar dropped 14 per cent in value between February and late December 1985 after active intervention in foreign exchange markets by the United States and four other major trading nations. In November, employment figures showed there had been an increase of 100,000 manufacturing jobs.

Business Inventories. The U.S. business climate in 1985 reflected guarded optimism. Inventories climbed 0.5 per cent in October to $582-billion. The inventory-to-sales ratio—indicating the amount of unsold goods on retail shelves or in warehouses—was 1.37 in October, a historically low figure. Businesses clearly remained cautious about the outlook for the economy. Merchants reduced inventories before placing new orders, slowing production and growth.

New Factory Orders, on the rise throughout 1984, fell 1.1 per cent in October 1985, the third decline in four months, to $195.1 billion. Demand for manufactured goods decreased in 1985. Factory orders were up a healthy 10.6 per cent in

1984, but they were up only 2.1 per cent in the first 10 months of 1985.

The biggest drop in factory orders was in the volatile military category, which plunged 21.1 per cent in September and 26.3 per cent in October. Orders for nonmilitary capital goods, a closely watched indicator of industry expansion, fell 7.1 per cent.

Orders for durable goods—items expected to last three or more years—fell 2.1 per cent in October to $104.4 billion. For the first 10 months of 1985, durable goods orders rose at an annual rate of 3.7 per cent, after a 14.8 per cent gain in 1984.

Capital Spending slowed considerably during the year. Spending on plants and equipment had gone up 15 per cent in 1984. Much of this money went for computer-related equipment. But in 1985, the increase in capital spending was only 6 per cent, which was one reason why the computer industry slumped so badly.

U.S. Factories ran at 80.1 per cent of capacity in November, close to the level for the entire year. Factory output for October 1985 was just 1.8 per cent above the figure for October 1984, reflecting a stagnant production picture. Imports hurt. They accounted for 10.5 per cent of the U.S. market for manufactured goods, up from 9.7 per cent in 1984 and 6.8 per cent in 1980.

Research and Development (R & D) remained a bright spot, however. Total U.S. expenditures in 1985 were expected to be an estimated $107.3 billion, up 10.6 per cent over 1984, according to the National Science Foundation (NSF) and Battelle Columbus Laboratories, an independent research concern. Federal government funding accounted for 45.4 per cent of R & D outlays, and private industry accounted for 51.3 per cent.

Since 1980, R & D expenditures have increased 55 per cent. According to the NSF, 370,400 scientists and 631,400 engineers were employed in R & D activities in 1982, the last year for which employment figures were available. This reflected a 3 per cent annual increase between 1972 and 1982.

The commitment of the Administration of President Ronald Reagan to the Strategic Defense Initiative, a space-based missile defense system commonly known as "Star Wars," along with a continuing military build-up, ensured that R & D expenditures would remain high.

High-Technology Slump. The high-flying high-technology industries, which grew at tremendous rates in 1983 and 1984, slumped in 1985. Life in the fast lane came to a screeching halt, according to Michael W. Kubiak, a specialist on the semiconductor industry. Japanese competition and price

Japanese workers in March autograph the first car built at the Smyrna, Tenn., manufacturing plant owned by Nissan, Japan's second-largest automaker.

Selected United States Manufacturing Statistics

	Sales or Production		
Product	1984	1985	Per cent change
Machine tools	$2.9 billion	$2.6 billion	− 11.5
Paper and paperboard	68.5 million short tons (62.1 million metric tons)	66.9 million short tons (60.7 million metric tons)	− 2.4
Semiconductors	$11.6 billion	$8 billion*	n.a.
Tires (bus and truck)	36.4 million units	31.1 million units*	− 7.9[†]
Tires (passenger)	172.9 million units	151.1 million units*	− 5.5[†]

n.a. = not available.

*From January to November 1985.

[†]Per cent change for comparable 1984 period.

Source: Various industry associations.

Robotics. The use of robots in manufacturing continued to increase in 1985. An estimated 20,000 industrial robots were in use in the United States in 1985, according to the Robotic Industries Association. More than half of these machines were used on automobile assembly lines. The use of robots was expected to increase as innovations in technology improve the precision of arm movements and electronic vision systems in robots.

Factory Automation became increasingly important in 1985. General Motors Corporation (GM) awarded Digital Equipment Corporation a five-year contract for factory automation equipment as part of a $40-billion factory-modernization program. Ford Motor Company and the Pratt & Whitney Aircraft Group of United Technologies Corporation also made factory-modernization plans.

GM acquired Hughes Aircraft Company in June for $5.1 billion. The purpose of the acquisition was, in part, to use Hughes's technology and expertise to build better cars and to help design the auto factory of the future. Ronald Kolgraf

In WORLD BOOK, see MANUFACTURING.

MARINE CORPS, U.S. See ARMED FORCES.

MARYLAND. See STATE GOVERNMENT.

MASSACHUSETTS. See STATE GOVERNMENT.

MAURITANIA. See AFRICA.

MAURITIUS. See AFRICA.

cutting hurt U.S. manufacturers. For example, 256K random access memory chips that sold for $20 two years ago sold for $3 to $4 in 1985. Japan's share of the U.S. semiconductor market increased from 12 to 17 per cent in 1985.

The Machine Tool Industry continued to climb out of its long slump in 1985, though orders were down 19 per cent in November from the previous month, according to the National Machine Tool Builders' Association, and down by 12.2 per cent compared with November 1984. Machine tools are used by the automobile, aerospace, and manufacturing industries to cut and shape metal.

Total machine tool orders for 1985 were estimated at $2.6 billion, down from 1984's $2.9 billion, but higher than the $1.6-billion low point in 1982-1983. In 1980, at their peak, orders totaled $4.8 billion. Japanese imports accounted for 45 per cent of the U.S. market in 1985.

The key to keeping this industry competitive, according to many experts, is high technology. For example, McDonnell Douglas Corporation in 1985 awarded Cincinnati Milacron Incorporated, a leading machine tool builder, a $20-million order for machines that cut structural parts for aircraft. Many machine tool makers have begun a shift to this type of new high-technology equipment and have moved away from basic machine tools, where foreign imports have made strong inroads.

MEDICINE. Use of the Jarvik-7 artificial heart continued during 1985, but enthusiasm for the device diminished because so many recipients suffered strokes and related complications following surgery. Nevertheless, some artificial-heart recipients survived. On March 13, William J. Schroeder, the second artificial-heart recipient, surpassed the 112-day survival record set by Barney B. Clark, who received the first implant of a permanent artificial heart in December 1982. Schroeder underwent the implant surgery on Nov. 25, 1984, then suffered a series of paralyzing strokes. By April 6, 1985, he had recovered sufficiently to leave Humana Hospital Audubon in Louisville, Ky., for a specially equipped apartment nearby. He was readmitted to the hospital following another stroke on May 6, then released again on August 11.

Humana surgeon William C. DeVries implanted the third artificial heart on February 17 in Murray P. Haydon, a 58-year-old plumber. On June 3, Haydon also suffered a stroke. The fourth recipient of the Jarvik-7 heart, Jack C. Burcham, a 62-year-old retired engineer, died on April 24 at Humana Hospital 10 days after the operation. His death was associated with internal bleeding caused by drugs designed to prevent blood clots.

Other Heart "Firsts." Leif Stenberg, a 52-year-old Swedish businessman, on April 7 became the first person outside the United States to receive the Jarvik-7. He, too, suffered a stroke after surgery, and he died on November 21.

Surgeons at the University of Arizona in Tucson on August 29 temporarily implanted the Jarvik-7 in Michael Drummond, age 25. The mechanical heart was replaced with a human heart on September 7. In October, 47-year-old Thomas J. Gaidosh survived for four days with a Jarvik-7 before he received a human heart at Presbyterian-University Hospital in Pittsburgh, Pa.

On March 14, the U.S. Food and Drug Administration (FDA) approved a second type of mechanical heart for experimental use in human beings. The device, developed at Pennsylvania State University's Hershey Medical Center in Hershey, Pa., was approved for temporary use in keeping critically ill patients alive until a human heart transplant could be performed. The Penn State heart was first used in a patient, 44-year-old Anthony Mandia, on October 18. Mandia died on November 14.

On December 19, 40-year-old Mary Lund became the first woman recipient of an artificial heart. Surgeons at Abbott Northwestern Hospital in Minneapolis, Minn., gave her a new, smaller version of the Jarvik-7.

Controversy Flared on March 6 after surgeons at the University of Arizona implanted a mechanical device called the "Phoenix heart" in 33-year-old Thomas Creighton, who had rejected a transplanted human heart. The device had not been approved by the FDA. Surgeons replaced the artificial heart 11 hours later with another human heart, but Creighton died on March 8.

High Blood Pressure Estimates. The American Heart Association (AHA) on September 18 substantially increased its estimates of the number of people who suffer from high blood pressure, or hypertension. By applying a new statistical yardstick, the association concluded that hypertension now affects 57.7 million people in the United States, almost 20 million more than was previously believed. The revised estimates resulted from a lowering of the threshold for diagnosing hypertension—based on new medical evidence—to a reading of 140/90 on the instrument used for measuring blood pressure. The first number is the blood pressure when the heart contracts; the second, when it relaxes. The AHA had previously accepted a definition of high blood pressure as readings consistently at or above 160/95. The AHA said that new medical findings indicate that blood pressure readings previously considered in the normal range actually can pose a health threat.

Cancer Developments. The American Cancer Society (ACS) reported a dramatic increase in

Miniaturized blood-analysis equipment, unveiled in June, may allow many tests to be done in the doctor's office rather than in an outside lab.

public interest about early detection of colorectal cancer after U.S. President Ronald Reagan underwent surgery for removal of a cancerous growth in his intestine on July 13. Cancer surgeon Arthur I. Holleb, ACS senior vice president for medical affairs, said that early detection through tests for blood in the feces and examinations of the large intestine could result in a major reduction in deaths from colorectal cancer. The disease strikes about 138,000 Americans each year and kills almost 60,000.

Cancer researchers at Johns Hopkins University in Baltimore on August 13 announced development of the first effective treatment for liver cancer that is too advanced for surgery and therefore usually fatal. Radiation oncologist Stanley E. Order said the treatment reduced tumors in almost 50 per cent of the patients treated. The treatment involves injecting disease-fighting molecules called antibodies that have been tagged with a radioactive substance. Like "magic bullets," the antibodies seek out and destroy the cancer cells.

A major new study reported on March 13 endorsed the use of less extensive surgery to treat some forms of breast cancer. Vincent T. DeVita, Jr., director of the National Cancer Institute in Bethesda, Md., said that about 60,000 of the 119,000 women who develop breast cancer each year might qualify for the limited surgery, popularly known as a *lumpectomy*. It involves removal of the tumor and a small amount of surrounding tissue. In the past, doctors treated breast cancer with more extensive surgery in the belief that this improved the chances for survival. But DeVita said that a new study, conducted at 89 medical institutions since 1976, found that women with small tumors who had a lumpectomy live as long and remain free of cancer for as long as women who had surgery to remove the entire breast. Researchers cautioned, however, about the need for additional time to verify the long-term effectiveness of the lumpectomy.

On September 11, a panel convened by the National Institutes of Health in Bethesda recommended hormone treatment for most older women with breast cancer. Studies had shown that a hormonal preparation called tamoxifen was more effective than toxic drugs in preventing breast cancer recurrences. The panel therefore recommended tamoxifen for breast cancer victims over 50 years old whose tumors involved the lymph nodes and whose cancer cells were shown by tests to have structures called estrogen receptors on their surfaces.

The ACS in February reported that in 1985 lung cancer would overtake breast cancer as the leading cause of cancer death among U.S. women. The U.S. Office of Technology Assessment (OTA) estimated on September 26 that the treatment of

A researcher displays a synthetic red blood cell substitute undergoing testing in 1985 at Chicago's Rush-Presbyterian-St. Luke's Medical Center.

all diseases associated with cigarette smoking would cost between $27 billion and $61 billion during 1985. The OTA, an advisory agency of Congress, said total costs for smoking-related diseases far exceed the $4.6 billion generated each year by the federal cigarette tax.

A New Experimental Treatment for cancer was announced on December 4 by researchers working at the National Cancer Institute. The experimental therapy involves treating white blood cells removed from the patient with a genetically engineered substance called *interleukin-2*. The white cells, which are then reinjected into the patient, attack the cancerous cells.

Medical Costs. On July 31, the Department of Health and Human Services issued the most recent available data on the costs of medical care in the United States. The agency reported that health-care costs in 1984 rose by 9.4 per cent, the smallest increase since 1965. Americans spent $387.4 billion for health care in 1984—about $1,580 for every person in the country. The total included $158 billion for hospital care; $75.4 billion for doctors' bills; $32 billion for nursing homes; and $25.8 billion for drugs.   Michael Woods

See also DRUGS; HEALTH AND DISEASE; PUBLIC HEALTH. In the Special Reports section, see HOW SCIENCE IS SAVING SIGHT. In WORLD BOOK, see MEDICINE.

MEESE, EDWIN, III (1931-   ) became United States attorney general on Feb. 25, 1985. Meese had received Senate confirmation, 63 to 31, two days earlier—more than a year after President Ronald Reagan first nominated him for the post. Meese's confirmation had been held up while an independent investigator looked into a variety of matters, including charges that Meese had been guilty of financial misconduct while serving as presidential counselor since 1981.

Meese was born Dec. 2, 1931, in Oakland, Calif. He graduated from Yale University in New Haven, Conn., in 1953 and earned a law degree at the University of California at Berkeley in 1958.

After serving as deputy district attorney of Alameda County, California, Meese in 1966 was hired by Reagan—then governor-elect of California—to be his legal affairs secretary. From 1970 to 1974, Meese was Reagan's chief of staff.

In 1975 and 1976, Meese was a vice president of Rohr Industries of Chula Vista, Calif., an aerospace and transportation company. He later taught law at the University of San Diego.

During Reagan's first presidential campaign, in 1980, Meese served as chief of staff for the Reagan-Bush Committee. At the White House, Meese was popular with conservatives for his efforts to reshape the U.S. Commission on Civil Rights and the Legal Services Corporation.   David L. Dreier

MENGELE, JOSEF (1911-1979). On June 21, 1985, a team of medical experts in São Paulo, Brazil, identified a skeleton as that of Josef Mengele, the Nazi "Angel of Death." He had been wanted for the torture and murder of inmates at the German concentration camp in Auschwitz (now Oświęcim), Poland, during World War II.

The medical experts said that a skeleton dug up by investigators on June 6, 1985, was Mengele's. They said he had been using an assumed name and had been buried after drowning on Feb. 7, 1979, near São Paulo.

Mengele was born on March 16, 1911, in Günzburg, in what is now West Germany. He received a medical degree in the mid-1930's and was chief medical officer at Auschwitz from 1943 until Russian troops captured the camp in 1944.

Mengele is believed to have hidden in Germany after the war. About 1949, he fled to Argentina, where he obtained citizenship in 1954. He became a citizen of Paraguay in 1959. Mengele lived in Brazil from 1961 until his death.

The trail that led to Mengele's bones began in Günzburg, where West German officials searched the home of a family friend and business associate on May 31, 1985. A date book discovered there led investigators to an Austrian-born couple in São Paulo. The woman revealed she had buried Mengele, and directed police to his grave.   Jay Myers

MENTAL ILLNESS. Electroshock therapy, the most controversial treatment for mental illness, received a cautious endorsement on June 29, 1985, from a panel of experts appointed to evaluate the procedure by the National Institutes of Health (NIH) in Bethesda, Md. The 14-member panel found that electroshock therapy can be effective in treating patients with severe forms of mental illness that do not respond to drugs or other treatment. The panel said that electroshock therapy can even save the lives of severely depressed patients who are at high risk of committing suicide.

Electroshock therapy was introduced in the 1930's and involves administering a brief surge of electric current to the patient's skull. The shock causes a seizure or a convulsion. The NIH panel indicated that much of today's concern about electroshock stems from its overuse in the 1940's and 1950's. Critics have charged that electroshock is still overused and represents an abusive form of therapy because it can cause memory loss and other side effects. The panel recommended that patients should be free to accept or refuse electroshock therapy after being fully informed about its effects and side effects; that standards be developed for therapists who administer electroshock; and that more research be conducted into how the procedure alleviates severe mental illness.

TV Violence. The American Psychological Association (APA) on Feb. 22, 1985, recommended that parents monitor and control the number of violent television programs viewed by their children. The APA, which is based in Washington, D.C., and represents more than 60,000 psychologists, emphasized that televised violence does not harm all children who watch it. But the APA cited research conducted since 1960 that has established a relationship between televised violence and aggressive behavior in children.

The association pointed out that many children's programs include some form of violence, and that many children imitate the violent behavior and attitudes they see on television. In addition, the APA called upon the television industry to reduce the amount of violence in children's programs, including cartoons. The APA also said that it would encourage action by Congress to reduce the amount of violence on television.

Patient Care and Treatment. A Senate investigation concluded on April 1, 1985, that widespread patient neglect and abuse exists in state institutions for the mentally ill and the mentally retarded. The study, conducted in 12 states by a Senate subcommittee, found that patients in some state institutions live "in a climate of fear and intimidation." The investigation also found that some patients are kept in unsanitary conditions and often receive no treatment except for medications to sedate them.

George Dole, *The Wall Street Journal;* permission Cartoon Features Syndicate.

"Well, we can rule out stress."

The American Psychiatric Association on August 5 called upon psychiatrists to be more cautious in prescribing medications used to treat severe mental disorders called psychoses. The association, which is based in Washington, D.C., told its 31,000 members that antipsychotic medications are effective in relieving the symptoms of disabling mental disorders. But it reminded psychiatrists of the potentially serious side effects associated with these medications. The association specifically cited *tardive dyskinesia*, a side effect that causes involuntary muscle movements that can be so severe that the patient is almost disabled.

On June 3, the Supreme Court of the United States upheld a Massachusetts law requiring employer-sponsored health insurance policies and employee benefit programs to provide at least $500 in outpatient benefits and 60 days of inpatient care for mental health problems.

On February 26, the Supreme Court ruled that states must provide free psychiatric assistance to needy defendants who plead not guilty to crimes by reason of insanity. Under the ruling, defendants unable to pay for a psychiatrist themselves would be entitled to free psychiatric examinations and psychiatric help in preparing, evaluating, and presenting their insanity defense. Michael Woods

See also PSYCHOLOGY. In WORLD BOOK, see MENTAL ILLNESS.

MEXICO. A devastating earthquake, measuring 8.1 on the Richter scale, struck Mexico at 7:18 A.M. on Sept. 19, 1985, toppling buildings and wreaking havoc in Mexico City. A second quake, or aftershock, followed on September 20 and measured 7.3 on the Richter scale. The quakes left some 7,000 Mexicans dead, most of them buried under tons of rubble. More than 100 tourists from foreign countries were among the fatalities. Nightly television reports around the world showed the search in the debris for survivors, particularly those victims trapped in a collapsed hospital.

Many Mexicans were angry at what they considered their government's slow response to the disaster. The first government employees to hit the streets were not rescue squads but soldiers with orders to prevent looting. For 36 hours after the first quake, the government, headed by President Miguel de la Madrid Hurtado, maintained that Mexico could handle rescue efforts on its own, despite offers of assistance from other nations.

In the aftermath of the earthquakes, rescue efforts also appeared to uncover wrongdoing in the office of Mexico's attorney general. The bodies of four Colombians and several Mexicans, bearing signs of torture, turned up in the ruins of a building that housed the attorney general's offices. Many Mexicans were outraged when their Congress turned down a request for an investigation.

Rescue workers remove an injured victim of Mexico's first earthquake in September from a collapsed building in downtown Mexico City.

Economic Plight. The earthquake devastation seemed likely to worsen Mexico's economic plight. Increasing numbers of Mexico's wealthy citizens have reportedly joined the tide of immigration to the United States, taking their wealth with them. Mexico's Central Bank estimated that at least $33-billion flowed out of the country between 1977 and 1984, though other economists put the figure closer to $60 billion. The flight of capital from Mexico was the largest among the debtor nations of the Third World. The World Bank, an agency of the United Nations, reported that much of the money Mexico borrowed from creditors in a number of other nations found its way back into investments in those same foreign nations. The World Bank report called this situation "a recipe for disaster."

Pessimism about Mexico's future fed the flow of intellectuals, professionals, and business managers out of Mexico. In addition, devaluation of the peso has so eroded the value of their insurance policies that Mexicans have even begun buying their insurance in the United States. For example, Mexicans accounted for 25 per cent of the insurance policies sold in San Antonio, Tex., where Mexican nationals in 1985 held about 20 per cent of the $30 million on deposit at a First City Bank branch.

Museum Theft. On December 25, more than 140 rare and exquisite pieces of Maya and Aztec treasures and other ancient objects made of gold were discovered missing from the National Museum of Anthropology in Mexico City. Officials speculated that the theft was the work of an international ring of art thieves.

Oil Prices. On July 10, Mexico decided to go it alone in cutting the price of its oil to levels below those set by the squabbling members of the Organization of Petroleum Exporting Countries (OPEC). Although Mexico does not belong to OPEC, it had followed OPEC price levels over the previous two years. The price cuts were seen as an effort to recover sales lost because of the higher prices.

Mexico's action followed fierce debates within Petróleos Mexicanos (PEMEX), the state-owned oil company. The problems at PEMEX seemed to mirror those of the nation as a whole. During 1985, the former director of PEMEX, 64-year-old Jorge Díaz Serrano, languished in jail, where he has been since July 1983, awaiting the outcome of his trial on corruption charges. Ironically, Díaz Serrano aroused considerable public sympathy, as more and more Mexicans came to view him as a scapegoat for hundreds, perhaps thousands, of corrupt PEMEX employees.   Nathan A. Haverstock

See also LATIN AMERICA (Facts in Brief Table). In WORLD BOOK, see MEXICO.

MICHIGAN. See DETROIT; STATE GOVERNMENT.

MIDDLE EAST. Conflict continued to plague the Middle East in 1985 with little hope of resolution. The five-year war between Iran and Iraq remained stalemated, despite a sharp escalation in the fighting. Talks aimed at a political settlement to end the struggle in Afghanistan between the government and its Soviet allies and Afghan *mujahedeen* (fighters for the faith) got nowhere. Israel's withdrawal from Lebanon in June led to the most violent civil strife in that country in several years. And an upsurge of terrorism and counterterrorism threatened to trigger another war between Arab states and Israel. Neither the United States nor the Soviet Union seemed able to influence any Middle East conflict to an appreciable degree.

The Arab-Israeli Conflict returned to center stage with a vengeance in 1985, partly because of an upsurge in terrorism and partly because of the efforts of Arab and Israeli leaders to revive peace talks. On February 11, King Hussein I of Jordan and Yasir Arafat, chairman of the Palestine Liberation Organization (PLO), agreed to form a joint Jordanian-Palestinian delegation to negotiate with Israel. The terms of the agreement, while similar to those advanced many times before by Arab leaders, had several important differences. By agreeing to negotiate jointly with Jordan, the PLO bound itself to eventually recognize Israel's right to exist, which it had previously refused to do. The PLO also seemed to abandon its long-held goal of establishing an independent Palestinian state on the West Bank, agreeing instead to a Jordanian-Palestinian confederation.

Hussein and Arafat even agreed on a negotiating team made up of Jordanians, Palestinians from the West Bank, and PLO members. But Israel categorically refused to deal with any PLO members unless the PLO recognized Israel's right to exist and renounced terrorism. In addition, strong opposition by the U.S. Congress to the PLO members caused the Administration of President Ronald Reagan to cancel scheduled meetings with the negotiating team.

Another sticking point was PLO demands that negotiations be conducted at a conference held under United Nations (UN) auspices that would include participation by the Soviet Union. Both Israel and the United States had long opposed a Soviet role in talks on the Middle East. Israel insisted that the Soviets must first reestablish diplomatic relations with Israel—broken in 1967—and lift restrictions on the emigration of Soviet Jews.

Israeli Withdrawal. Israeli forces withdrew completely from Lebanon by June 10, 1985. The pullout ended an invasion begun optimistically three years earlier in the expectation of the quick destruction of the PLO and the establishment of a strong Christian government friendly to Israel.

Iraqi soldiers guard Iranian prisoners who were captured during an unsuccessful Iranian offensive in southern Iraq in March.

But the Israelis left behind them a country still racked by civil war, with PLO units filtering back to participate in the Lebanese power struggle.

When they withdrew, Israeli forces took with them more than 700 Shiite Muslim prisoners, who were to serve as hostages to guarantee the good behavior of southern Lebanon's Shiite population. Many countries denounced the action as a violation of international law.

TWA Hijacking. On June 14, Lebanese Shiite terrorists hijacked a TWA jet en route from Athens, Greece, to Rome. The hijackers diverted the plane to Beirut, Lebanon, where they killed an American passenger—U.S. Navy diver Robert D. Stethem—and held 39 other American passengers hostage. The hijackers demanded that Israel release the Shiite prisoners as the price of freedom for the hostages. Several days later, the Americans were transferred to the control of Amal (Hope), the largest Shiite militia in Lebanon.

Both the United States and Israel refused to bargain with Amal. But on June 24, Israel released 31 of the Shiite prisoners. The Israelis denied, however, that the release was connected with the hijacking. On June 30, the hostages were freed, unharmed. In July, August, and September, Israel freed the rest of the Shiite prisoners.

Increased Kidnappings. The TWA hijacking underlined the difficulties the United States and

Facts in Brief on Middle Eastern Countries

Country	Population	Government	Monetary Unit*	Foreign Trade (million U.S. $) Exports†	Imports†
Bahrain	447,000	Amir Isa bin Sulman Al-Khalifa; Prime Minister Khalifa bin Sulman Al-Khalifa	dinar (1 = $2.65)	3,139	3,531
Cyprus	674,000	President Spyros Kyprianou (Turkish Republic of Northern Cyprus: Acting President Rauf R. Denktaş)	pound (1 = $1.83)	575	1,364
Egypt	47,968,000	President Hosni Mubarak; Prime Minister Ali Lotfy	pound (1 = $1.23)	3,215	10,274
Iran	46,466,000	President Ali Khamenei; Prime Minister Hosein Musavi-Khamenei	rial (84.7 = $1)	19,414	11,539
Iraq	16,175,000	President Saddam Hussein	dinar (1 = $3.22)	10,300	13,700
Israel	4,094,000	President Chaim Herzog; Prime Minister Shimon Peres	shekel (1,471 = $1)	5,804	9,889
Jordan	3,629,000	King Hussein I; Prime Minister Zaid Rifai	dinar (1 = $2.81)	752	2,784
Kuwait	1,888,000	Amir Jabir al-Ahmad al-Sabah; Prime Minister & Crown Prince Saad Al-Abdullah Al-Sabah	dinar (1 = $3.46)	10,861	8,283
Lebanon	2,663,000	President Amin Gemayel; Prime Minister Rashid Karami	pound (17.5 = $1)	690	3,300
Oman	1,255,000	Sultan Qaboos bin Said	rial (1 = $2.89)	4,421	2,640
Qatar	296,000	Amir & Prime Minister Khalifa bin Hamad Al-Thani	riyal (3.62 = $1)	3,384	1,402
Saudi Arabia	11,550,000	King & Prime Minister Fahd ibn Abd al-Aziz Al Saud	riyal (3.64 = $1)	46,941	39,206
Sudan	22,177,000	Transitional Military Council Chairman Abdul Rahman Mohamed el Hassan Suwar El-Dahab; Prime Minister Jazzuli Dafalla	pound (2.5 = $1)	790	1,800
Syria	10,894,000	President Hafiz al-Assad; Prime Minister Abd al Ra'uf al-Kassem	pound (3.9 = $1)	1,853	4,114
Turkey	52,387,000	President Kenan Evren; Prime Minister Turgut Ozal	lira (561 = $1)	7,089	10,817
United Arab Emirates	1,407,000	President Zayid bin Sultan Al-Nahayyan; Prime Minister Rashid ibn Said al-Maktum	dirham (3.64 = $1)	15,300	8,300
Yemen (Aden)	2,275,000	Supreme People's Council Presidium Chairman & Council of Ministers Chairman Ali Nasir Muhammad	dinar (1 = $2.91)	40	768
Yemen (Sana)	6,677,000	President Ali Abdallah Salih; Prime Minister Abdel Aziz Abdel Ghani	rial (7.54 = $1)	39	1,521

*Exchange rates as of Dec. 1, 1985, or latest available data. †Latest available data.

other nations faced when dealing with terrorism. One factor behind the violence was the exclusion of important minority Muslim groups, chiefly the Shiites, from power and political representation in most Middle Eastern countries. The Shiite Islamic Jihad (Holy War) organization in Lebanon was especially active in taking hostages to bolster its demand for greater power for Shiites. Islamic Jihad during 1985 held hostages from the United States, Great Britain, France, and the Soviet Union.

One American hostage, Benjamin Weir, a Presbyterian minister, was released unexpectedly on September 14 after 16 months in captivity. Another hostage, William Buckley, reportedly was murdered in early October. At year-end, at least six Americans were still being held hostage in Lebanon. The kidnappers hinted that they might free the captives if Kuwait released Shiites jailed there for the 1983 bombings of foreign embassies. But Kuwait refused.

In 1985, for the first time, Soviet citizens became the target of Middle East terrorism. On September 30, three Soviet diplomats and a doctor were kidnapped in West Beirut by an Islamic fundamentalist group. One of the hostages was killed several days later. The kidnappers threatened to kill the remaining hostages unless the Soviet Union pressured Syria to halt an offensive against an Islamic fundamentalist militia in Tripoli (also called Tarabulus), Lebanon. In early October,

Iran arranged a cease-fire in Tripoli. On October 30, the three Soviet hostages were released.

Attacks and Counterattacks. During 1985, the possibility that PLO factions loyal to Arafat would arrange a settlement with Israel spurred anti-Arafat factions to increase the level of violence against Israelis. At least 12 Israeli civilians were murdered on the West Bank. On September 25, 3 Israelis were killed by PLO gunmen in Larnaca, Cyprus. Israel retaliated by bombing Arafat's headquarters near Tunis, Tunisia, on October 1, killing at least 73 people, including 12 Tunisians.

The Israeli raid was strongly criticized by Arab governments as well as many friendly Western governments. On October 4, the UN Security Council condemned the action by a 14-0 vote, with the United States abstaining. President Reagan first characterized the raid as a legitimate response to terrorist violence. But after criticism by Arab countries, especially pro-Western Tunisia, he shifted his position, calling the attack understandable but not to be condoned.

***Achille Lauro* Affair.** Only a few days later, on October 7, members of the Palestine Liberation Front, a splinter PLO faction loyal to Arafat, hijacked the Italian cruise ship *Achille Lauro* off the coast of Egypt. The hijackers demanded the release of PLO members recently jailed in Israel and murdered 69-year-old Leon Klinghoffer, a Jewish American tourist confined to a wheelchair, to dramatize their demand.

On October 9, Egyptian authorities negotiated the hijackers' surrender at Port Said. Egypt agreed to turn them over to the PLO for disciplinary action—Arafat claimed he had not authorized the hijacking—despite U.S. demands that the hijackers be prosecuted. On October 10, U.S. jets intercepted the Egyptian plane carrying the hijackers and forced it down in Sigonella, Italy, where the terrorists were turned over to Italian authorities. On November 18, the hijackers were convicted of illegal possession of explosives. They were also held over for trial for hijacking and murder.

The United States strongly protested Italy's decision to free Muhammad Abbas, a PLO official arrested with the hijackers. Abbas quickly left Italy for Yugoslavia. The United States claimed that Abbas had masterminded the hijacking. The *Achille Lauro* affair severely damaged Arafat's credibility and the PLO's claim to be an organization committed to negotiations for peace.

Airport Assaults. On December 27, Arab terrorists attacked airports at Rome and Vienna, Austria. Nineteen people were killed and more than 120 wounded. The dead included four of the gunmen.

Peace Process. The effort to establish a framework for Arab-Israeli peace lurched along. In an address to the UN on October 21, Israel's Prime

Israeli tanks in April pull out of Nabatiye, a Shiite Muslim village in southern Lebanon, as part of their complete withdrawal from that country.

Minister Shimon Peres called for an end to the state of war between Israel and Jordan and offered to go to Jordan for peace talks. Peres also reversed a long-standing Israeli position and said his country might be willing to participate in an international conference on the Middle East.

Jordan's King Hussein, for his part, forced a limited concession from Arafat. The PLO leader stated his opposition to all violence against unarmed civilians anywhere in the world. But he later refused to renounce violence in Israel or in Israeli-occupied territory, such as the West Bank.

The Iran-Iraq War marked its fifth anniversary in September with no progress toward a solution. Efforts by the UN and other mediating agencies were stymied by Iran's refusal to accept a cease-fire or to negotiate until Iraq's President Saddam Hussein was ousted. Iran also insisted that Iraq pay billions of dollars in war reparations.

In fierce ground attacks early in 1985—the first in nearly three years—the Iranians overran about 2,500 square miles (6,500 square kilometers) of marsh and mountain territory in southern Iraq. Iraq, with its vast air superiority, concentrated on air strikes against urban and industrial targets in Iran. Iraqi ground forces pursued a strategy of using artillery fire to limit Iranian land advances and inflict as many casualties as possible.

In March, Iraqi planes escalated the air war by

Flanked by an armed terrorist, the captain of a TWA airliner hijacked on
June 14 answers reporters' questions at Beirut airport in Lebanon.

stepping up raids on Iranian cities in the hope
that heavy civilian casualties would encourage Iran
to negotiate. But the strategy backfired, and the
attacks whipped Iranian patriotism to new heights.

Iraq's attempts to force Iran to the conference
table by disrupting Iranian oil exports also failed.
Iraq used sophisticated laser-guided missiles to
make attacks on the main Iranian oil export terminal at Kharg Island. Although the raids cut Iranian oil exports from 4 million barrels per day
(bpd) to 1.6 million bpd, they failed to put the terminal out of commission. Iran recouped to some
extent by shipping oil from two smaller terminals
out of range of Iraqi jets. In addition, the exports
remained in line with Iranian production quotas
set by the Organization of Petroleum Exporting
Countries (OPEC) and were sufficient to maintain
Iran's economy on a wartime footing.

The War in Afghanistan proved equally unyielding. Soviet occupation forces and their Afghan allies made important gains, capturing most of the
strategic Panjshir Valley in July and sealing off
parts of the Afghanistan-Pakistan border to the
mujahedeens' weapons and supplies. But government forces were unable to wrest control over the
Afghan countryside from the mujahedeen.

The mujahedeen improved their bargaining position in April when various factions united to
form an Islamic Alliance for the Liberation of Af-

ghanistan. The group's status was enhanced in
August when it arranged the first prisoner exchange since the 1979 Soviet occupation.

Other Developments. One major change in the
Arab world in 1985 was the overthrow of Sudan's
President Gaafar Mohamed Nimeiri after 16 years
in power. Nimeiri's mismanagement of the nation's economy and his efforts to impose Islamic
law throughout the country—particularly resented
in the non-Muslim South—finally turned the majority of the Sudanese people against him.

Other Arab leaders were more fortunate. Libya's leader Muammar Muhammad al-Qadhafi survived at least two coup attempts, and Syria's President Hafiz al-Assad was reelected for a third
seven-year term in February with 99.97 per cent
of the vote.

Amid the political upheavals, some Middle East
countries continued to diversify and strengthen
their economies. Yemen (Sana) entered the ranks
of Arab oil-producing countries with the discovery
of important oil and gas deposits. Oman marked
the 15th anniversary of Sultan Qaboos bin Said's
rule with a celebration befitting a country that has
risen from poverty to an $8,000 per capita annual
income in 15 years.   William Spencer

See also articles on the various Middle Eastern
countries. In WORLD BOOK, see MIDDLE EAST and
individual Middle Eastern country articles.

MINING. The severe economic problems affecting the United States uranium mining and milling industry led the federal government on Sept. 26, 1985, to declare the entire industry incapable of surviving without outside assistance for the first time in 30 years. The determination was made by Secretary of Energy John S. Herrington based on a review of the industry's performance during 1984.

The government analysis noted that U.S. uranium production in 1984 fell to the lowest level since the mid-1950's, while exploration and development of new uranium mines dropped to the lowest level since the mid-1960's. In addition, the number of operating mines dropped from 362 in 1979 to 50 in 1984, and employment dwindled to the equivalent of 3,400 full-time workers. The industry had lost money since 1980.

Herrington cited lower-than-expected demand for uranium by the nuclear power industry and imports of uranium from other countries as the chief reasons for the industry's problems. He requested a review of U.S. policy on imports and took action to boost sales of domestic uranium.

Copper Problems. Similar economic problems continued to plague the beleaguered U.S. copper-mining industry. On April 4, Phelps Dodge Corporation, the second largest U.S. copper producer, closed its copper smelter at Ajo, Ariz., rather than invest $5 million in pollution-control equipment as required by the government. About 200 workers were laid off. In March, 32 members of Congress from copper-producing states formed a "copper caucus" to seek emergency action they said was necessary to save the industry.

Mining Regulations Withdrawn. The Department of the Interior on Feb. 25, 1985, issued new regulations that would have made it easier for mining firms to explore and develop mineral deposits in wilderness areas. Previously, holders of mineral rights in wilderness areas had to demonstrate that the mineral deposits were valuable before taking any steps toward developing the deposits. Under the new regulations, developers would have had to show only that there were "exposed" minerals at the site and would not have had to determine the value of those minerals. But in March, the Interior Department withdrew the new regulations following sharp criticism from environmental groups.

Titanium Find. On June 28, the Interior Department announced the discovery of a potentially important deposit of titanium-rich minerals on the floor of the Atlantic Ocean off the coasts of Virginia and Georgia. Titanium is a light but extremely strong metal that is highly resistant to heat and corrosion. It has important uses in the aerospace and chemical industries and is used in paints and other coatings. The deposits consisted of a ti-tanium-bearing mineral called ilmenite. The Interior Department said the discovery could lead to the first ocean-floor mining off the East Coast of the United States.

Cobalt, Manganese Extraction. Scientists at Argonne National Laboratory near Chicago reported on March 26 the discovery of a new method for extracting cobalt and manganese from low- and medium-grade ores mined chiefly for other metals. The scientists said the method was cheaper than conventional extraction and could decrease U.S. reliance on imported cobalt and manganese. It involves the use of a molten salt that dissolves more than 90 per cent of the cobalt or manganese in the ore. The United States imports 90 per cent of its supply of the two metals, vital for the production of high-strength alloys with a variety of military and industrial uses.

Australian Ore Deal. Hancock Prospecting Proprietary Limited, a large Australian mining firm, agreed on April 15 to supply Romania with 48 million metric tons (53 million short tons) of iron ore over a 15-year period. Michael Woods

In WORLD BOOK, see MINING.

MINNESOTA. See STATE GOVERNMENT.
MISSISSIPPI. See STATE GOVERNMENT.
MISSOURI. See STATE GOVERNMENT.
MONGOLIA. See ASIA.
MONTANA. See STATE GOVERNMENT.

MONTREAL. Results of a general election held on Dec. 2, 1985, in the province of Quebec were expected to have profound effects on Montreal. In the elections, the Parti Québécois (PQ), led by Pierre Marc Johnson, was swept from power. The Liberal Party won the election, returning Robert Bourassa as prime minister of Quebec—the office he had lost to the PQ in 1976 elections.

The voters' disenchantment with the PQ reflected several economic factors. The PQ's intention to have Quebec secede from the Canadian federation had been blamed for the fact that many businesses had moved from Montreal during the PQ's nine years in office. Business leaders complained that the city had become isolated because of restrictions on the use of languages other than French. The PQ had supported these restrictions in an effort to promote French culture. During the election campaign, Bourassa promised that his government would remove many such restrictions.

On another issue of great importance to Montreal—that of free trade—Bourassa was noncommittal. Montreal industrialists estimated that more than 15,000 people would lose their jobs in the city's large footwear and textile industries if all tariff barriers with the United States were removed. In late November 1985, federal authorities agreed to give provincial premiers a voice in free-trade negotiations.

Montreal Mayor Jean Drapeau and Shanghai Mayor Wang Daohan plant a Canadian maple in Shanghai, China, after signing a friendship agreement in May.

Building Boom. Montreal experienced a major construction boom in 1985. Building permits for a record $313 million in construction were issued during the first six months of the year. (All monetary amounts in this article are Canadian dollars, with $1 = U.S. 72 cents as of Dec. 31, 1985.) Among large new projects that were scheduled to begin in 1986 were a $125-million office and retail complex and a $100-million office complex to be built in the downtown area. Also scheduled were a $30-million symphony hall for the city's east end and the conversion of the Windsor Hotel into offices.

Growing Tourism. The lower value of the Canadian dollar plus a number of special art exhibits brought a record 1.2 million visitors to Montreal from the United States in 1985. About 1 million Canadians from other provinces and 250,000 tourists from countries outside North America also visited the city. Preliminary estimates indicated that revenue from tourism increased by about 20 per cent over 1984 levels—surpassing $1-billion for the first time.

The Port of Montreal in 1985 experienced a drop in shipping traffic of about 9 per cent from 1984 levels. One reason for the port's poor economic performance was the closing of the St. Lawrence Seaway twice during 1985 due to accidents and bad weather.

Budget and Taxation. In September, the ruling Civic Party presented a special three-year capital spending budget to the City Council. It included $553 million for such items as industrial revitalization, street repair, and lighting. Estimates for such services as snow removal and road and sidewalk maintenance for 1986 rose sharply.

Montreal continued to be the most heavily taxed city in North America in 1985. In November, the administration of Mayor Jean Drapeau raised the tax valuation on all types of dwellings—in some cases by as much as 20 per cent.

Other News. A dispute over social services arose between the English-speaking and French-speaking communities in Montreal in 1985. English-speaking and French-speaking social workers had served their respective communities until September, when the government started to integrate social services. As a result, some English-speaking citizens complained that they could not communicate with the social workers assigned to them.

In May, Thomas Brigham, a mentally disturbed United States citizen from Rochester, N.Y., was found guilty of first-degree murder in the September 1984 bombing of Montreal's Central Station, which left three people dead. He was sentenced to life imprisonment.   Kendal Windeyer

See also BOURASSA, ROBERT; CANADA; QUEBEC. In WORLD BOOK, see MONTREAL.

MOROCCO. King Hassan II marked the 24th anniversary of his rule in 1985 with renewed efforts to end the war in Western Sahara with Polisario Front guerrillas, who have been fighting for independence since Morocco annexed the area in 1976. In March 1985, Hassan made his first visit to El Aiún, the capital of the Saharan province. He pledged $1 billion to modernize the armies defending the territory and to develop the provincial economy. He also told the newly elected Saharan Consultative Assembly that Morocco's claim to Western Sahara was not subject to negotiation.

Cease-Fire. On October 23, Hassan declared a unilateral cease-fire in the Saharan war. He also said that Morocco was ready to hold a *referendum* (direct vote) in Western Sahara in January 1986 to determine whether the people of the region want to remain part of Morocco or become independent. Hassan ruled out direct talks with the Polisario Front, however.

Regional Affairs. The king also pressed his campaign to gain support from other African countries for the annexation. He signed cooperation treaties with the leaders of Mauritania in April and Chad in July.

There was little progress toward putting Morocco's 1984 federation agreement with Libya into effect, though Libya withdrew its support for the Polisario Front as called for in the pact. The first meeting of the Moroccan-Libyan joint legislature, scheduled for June 30 in Rabat, was canceled after Libya signed an alliance earlier that month with Iran against Iraq. Hassan angrily criticized the action as hostile to Arab interests.

The Economy. The Saharan conflict, which was costing Morocco $1.5 million per day, continued to aggravate the country's economic problems. In January, Morocco's major foreign creditors agreed to provide $3 billion annually through 1987 to cover interest on the country's foreign debt. In March, some $535 million owed to 200 foreign banks was rescheduled for payment over an eight-year period.

The willingness of creditors to support the Moroccan economy stemmed from the success of the 1983 economic recovery plan set up with the help of the World Bank, an agency of the United Nations (UN) that provides loans to countries for development projects, and the International Monetary Fund, another UN agency. During 1984-1985, exports increased 7 per cent. Production of citrus fruits and phosphates increased significantly, as did the amount of money sent home by Moroccans working abroad. The government's decision to increase basic food prices 11 to 40 per cent in September was accepted without protest. Price hikes in 1984 had set off riots.   William Spencer

See also AFRICA (Facts in Brief Table). In WORLD BOOK, see MOROCCO.

MOTION PICTURES in the United States sank in 1985 to what most critics considered one of the lowest levels of quality in many years. And 1985 was also one of the worst financial years for Hollywood in recent memory. Gross box-office receipts during the summer, the film industry's most important season, were down 14 per cent from 1984. Ticket sales for September were the lowest since 1968, with the box-office gross at its lowest since 1980.

Teen Movie Glut. A major problem, in the opinion of many critics, was the studios' tendency to aim many feature-length films toward a teen-aged audience. The problem was compounded by Hollywood's habitual underestimation of the teen audience it sought to win. At least 10 films released during the summer dealt with oversexed teenagers involved in dating rituals, sexual adventures, and science projects. None of the films was well received by audiences of any age.

The only successful teen-oriented film was John Hughes's *The Breakfast Club*, which won a loyal following by presenting teens as reasonable facsimiles of real human beings. The film depicted its young characters as alternately peevish and passionate, trying to cope with the pressures exerted by their parents, their peers, and the inflexible caste system that defines much of teen-aged social life.

Spring Releases. By the end of spring, only two other films seemed worthy of note. One was Woody Allen's *The Purple Rose of Cairo*, a bittersweet fantasy in which Mia Farrow played a Depression-era waitress who lives a dream life through the movies. The film won critical praise but failed to attract large audiences outside major metropolitan areas, where Allen's unique wit traditionally finds the greatest response.

Far more popular with moviegoers was Peter Weir's *Witness*, the story of a streetwise urban cop hiding from corrupt fellow officers in an Amish community in Pennsylvania. The film contained elements easily recognizable from older movies, including *High Noon* (1952) and *Friendly Persuasion* (1956). But it was expertly directed and well acted, winning star Harrison Ford the best reviews of his career. *Witness* also offered moviegoers a bona fide love story, something of a novelty in a romantically bleak year.

Prizzi's Honor, a dark comedy by veteran director John Huston, also helped bring adults back to the movie theaters. In the film, a Mafia enforcer, played by Jack Nicholson, marries a free-lance hit woman, played by Kathleen Turner.

The Most Controversial Success of 1985 was *Rambo: First Blood, Part II*. The film presented Sylvester Stallone as a Vietnam War veteran who frees American prisoners of war in Indochina despite U.S. government indifference. Superficially, *Rambo* resembled a John Wayne 1940's action film.

On closer inspection, some viewers felt it presented a dangerously revisionist view of the Vietnam War. The film's spectacular box-office success, both in the United States and abroad, fueled editorials questioning its prowar viewpoint.

Nevertheless, the movie's influence on popular culture could not be ignored. Rambo became an instant folk hero, and Rambo merchandise, including toy guns and knives, flooded the market.

Science Fiction with a Heart, a new genre started by Steven Spielberg in 1977 with *Close Encounters of the Third Kind*, produced two of the summer's best movies. One of them, *Back to the Future*, emerged as the clear winner of the year, with critical endorsement matched by gross box-office receipts that ultimately surpassed those of *Rambo*. *Back to the Future* sold about $190 million worth of tickets, compared with *Rambo*'s approximately $150 million. *Back to the Future*, directed by Robert Zemeckis, was a lightweight but hugely entertaining time-travel fantasy that combined elements of Frank Capra's 1946 *It's a Wonderful Life* with modern technology. Only *Cocoon*, the second success of director Ron Howard, came close to matching the critical and public acceptance of *Back to the Future*. *Cocoon*, a fantasy in which a swimming pool becomes a fountain of youth, represented the apex of science fiction with heart appeal.

Sylvester Stallone stars in *Rambo: First Blood, Part II*, an adventure film set in Vietnam that was one of 1985's biggest commercial successes.

Among the Disappointments of 1985 was Michael Cimino's *Year of the Dragon*. An overblown and operatic look at gang warfare in New York City's Chinatown, the film did little to resurrect Cimino's reputation following the disaster of 1980's *Heaven's Gate*. Equally disappointing was William Friedkin's *To Live and Die in L.A.*, a technically efficient but emotionally cold look at the uncovering of a counterfeiting ring.

Other renowned directors were similarly unlucky. Arthur Penn, director of *Bonnie and Clyde* (1967) and *Little Big Man* (1970), failed in 1985 with *Target*, an attempt at slick international intrigue. Bruce Beresford, whose previous credits included *Breaker Morant* (1981) and *Tender Mercies* (1983), fulfilled a long-time ambition by filming *King David*, with Richard Gere as the Biblical leader. But the subject proved too vast for a two-hour film. Fred Schepisi's *Plenty* gave Meryl Streep the worst reviews of her career. Another disappointment was Louis Malle's *Alamo Bay*, the story of the conflict between native-born Americans and Vietnamese immigrants on the Texas Gulf Coast. The film was a comedown for the director of *Pretty Baby* (1978) and *Atlantic City* (1981).

The Western, the most respected and typically American film genre, was expected to make a comeback in 1985 with the release of Clint Eastwood's *Pale Rider* and Lawrence Kasdan's *Silverado*. Neither film made a strong impression, however, either critically or commercially, and major studios planned no new Westerns.

By the End of 1985, movie buffs' hopes were pinned on *Out of Africa*, which became the second success in a row for director Sydney Pollack, whose last picture was the 1982 hit *Tootsie*. *Out of Africa* told the story of Danish author Isak Dinesen, who owned a coffee plantation in Africa. Meryl Streep, rising from the disappointment of *Plenty*, played the writer, and Robert Redford played her adventurer lover.

The film version of Alice Walker's Pulitzer Prize-winning novel *The Color Purple* was 1985's most eagerly awaited film and also its most secret project. Steven Spielberg, who had received mild disdain from critics after the June release of *The Goonies*, which he wrote, chose to direct *The Color Purple* as his first serious dramatic film.

The motion picture dealt with the struggle for independence of a black girl, played by Whoopi Goldberg, suffering from various forms of emotional dependency. By the end of November, no one except those involved in the production had seen any footage of the film, which opened on December 18 to generally good reviews.

Young Sherlock Holmes, a clever, romantic action-comedy about the fictional detective's formative years at an English boys' school, seemed assured of winning large audiences. So did *The Jewel of the*

Citizen Welles (1915-1985)

The death of Orson Welles on Oct. 10, 1985, reinforced one of the sad ironies of motion-picture history. A "boy genius," Welles stunned the world with his creations twice before he was 26 years old. But he never fully evolved into a mature genius. In 1938, his realistic radio production of *The War of the Worlds* convinced many listeners that Martians had landed in New Jersey. Three years later, he produced, directed, co-wrote, and starred in *Citizen Kane*, possibly the best and certainly the most influential American film ever made. Yet at the time of his death, the actor-director-writer-producer was probably best known for appearing in television commercials advertising wine.

Welles remained a mass of contradictions. He liked his reputation as a Hollywood rebel, yet he had a regular table at Ma Maison, the most "in" of Hollywood restaurants. He dismissed the traditional Hollywood notion of glamour, while having widely publicized romances with such glamorous actresses as Dolores Del Rio and Rita Hayworth, who in 1943 became the second of his three wives.

George Orson Welles was born May 6, 1915, in Kenosha, Wis. His father, Richard Head Welles, was an inventor and manufacturer. His mother, Beatrice, was a concert pianist. Welles wrote poetry and had cartoons published before he was 10 years old.

Welles's early experience in the theater revolved around William Shakespeare, the greatest of English playwrights. At the age of 21,

Orson Welles stars, with Dorothy Comingore playing his second wife, in *Citizen Kane* (1941), which he also produced, directed, and co-wrote.

Welles staged an all-black version of Shakespeare's *Macbeth* in New York City's Harlem. In 1937, he and American producer John Houseman formed the Mercury Theatre and presented *Julius Caesar* in modern dress as its first production. The following year, *The War of the Worlds* made Welles a household name. It also won him a Hollywood contract, with *Citizen Kane*—a thinly disguised portrait of publisher William Randolph Hearst—as his first film.

So many articles have been written about *Kane* and so many film professors have dissected it in class that seeing the film has come to seem like doing homework. Nevertheless, *Kane* remains a remarkably entertaining movie.

Aided immeasurably by cinematographer Gregg Toland, Welles employed a new bag of cinematic tricks in *Kane*. He showed ceilings for the first time in Hollywood moviemaking, creating a pressing sense of the characters' surroundings. He used dramatic lighting that cast deep shadows over much of the screen. He moved the camera with new grace, constantly shifting focus to highlight an important incident or gesture.

Despite rave reviews, *Kane* attracted small audiences. Welles's follow-up film, *The Magnificent Ambersons*, brilliantly portrayed the disintegration of a prominent Midwestern family. The studio released the film in 1942 in a severely cut form that failed at the box office. On stage, Welles attempted an extravagant musical in 1946 based on French novelist Jules Verne's *Around the World in 80 Days* that became one of Broadway's biggest flops. His commercial failures—more than his reputation for being a difficult director who insisted on artistic independence—scared away backers. Welles went into voluntary exile in Europe, where he spent most of his life after the late 1940's. Still, many of his post-*Kane* films are admirable. His stylish thrillers *The Lady from Shanghai* (1948) and *Touch of Evil* (1958) have grown in reputation.

Welles constantly talked of raising enough money to make a comeback picture, a film that would answer the critics who felt he had declined sadly since *Kane*. For financial reasons, he took acting jobs, ranging from the distinguished—*The Third Man* (1949)—to the purely commercial—*The Muppet Movie* (1979)—to the ridiculous—*Butterfly* (1982) with Pia Zadora. Yet Welles never lost his enthusiasm. In 1981, he said of moviemaking, "It's a love you never cure yourself of."

Whatever criticism may be leveled at the ultimate shape and scope of Welles's career, his name remains synonymous with *Citizen Kane*. For film scholars and movie fans, that is achievement enough.   Philip Wuntch

Nile, a sequel to 1984's smash hit *Romancing the Stone.*

The long-planned film version of the Broadway hit *A Chorus Line* finally became a motion-picture reality. The film, the first directed by Sir Richard Attenborough since 1982's *Gandhi,* received respectful but not overwhelming reviews.

The newest of the Rocky movies, *Rocky IV,* in which the boxing champion defended the honor of the United States against a contender from the Soviet Union, got the worst reviews of any of the films in the Rocky series. Critics longed for the simpler days when Rocky Balboa just wanted "to go the distance." Despite the bad reviews, *Rocky IV* got off to a record-breaking box-office start. It sold $31.8 million in tickets during its first five days, the best nonsummer opening in motion-picture history.

The World Market continued to be dominated by American films. *Ghostbusters,* the top-grossing U.S. film of 1984, became the third most popular film in Japanese history and the most successful comedy ever to play in Japan. By the end of 1985, *Rambo* looked likely to attract an equal number of filmgoers. Ironically, *Ran,* a new film by the great Japanese director Akira Kurosawa, did only modest business in its homeland. But the film, a version of William Shakespeare's *King Lear* set in Ja-

pan, promised to be a major import on the art-house circuit in the United States.

Although many films made in other countries failed to stir much interest on their home ground, even some American films that did poorly in the United States did exceptionally well abroad. For example, Francis Ford Coppola's *The Cotton Club,* a disappointment in the United States in 1984, made an honorable showing in its overseas engagements. When *Rambo* opened in Paris, it drastically outsold the opening week of *Hold-Up,* starring long-time French box-office champion Jean-Paul Belmondo. So extreme was the difference between the commercial performances of French and American films that French Minister for Cultural Affairs Jack Lang hinted he might seek an import quota on American films.

Latin-American Films emerged as a genuine force in motion pictures with the success of Argentine-born director Hector Babenco's *Kiss of the Spider Woman,* filmed in Brazil. *Kiss,* adapted from a novel by Argentine author Manuel Puig, dealt with the relationship between an imprisoned political radical, played by Puerto Rican actor Raul Julia, and a homosexual serving time on a morals charge, played by American actor William Hurt.

The British Film Industry enjoyed a minor renaissance during 1985. *A Private Function,* a comedy

Michael J. Fox, right, plays a teen-aged time traveler in *Back to the Future,* the film that made the most money at the box office in 1985.

that alternated broad slapstick with traditional English drollery, was a major art-house success. The film won praise for the performances of Maggie Smith and Michael Palin as a pair of social climbers who abduct a pig that is to be served at an elite party celebrating the marriage of Princess Elizabeth and Prince Philip. The British export *Dance with a Stranger* also proved popular with audiences. The film was a cold and dour account of Ruth Ellis, who in 1955 became the last woman to be hanged in Great Britain. *Dance* brought considerable attention to its star, Miranda Richardson.

Godard Film Controversy. French filmmaker Jean-Luc Godard released his most controversial film yet with *Hail Mary*, a contemporary version of the story of Mary and Joseph in which Mary is a service station attendant and Joseph is a cab driver. The film, which was denounced by Pope John Paul II, shows the virgin birth in detail. Myriem Roussel, the actress playing Mary, appears nude on several occasions. When Godard's film had its American debut at the New York Film Festival in October, approximately 4,000 demonstrators protested the showing. Other demonstrations, some resulting in violence, met the film's opening in France, Italy, and Spain.   Philip Wuntch

See also ABRAHAM, F. MURRAY; AWARDS AND PRIZES (Arts Awards); FIELD, SALLY. In WORLD BOOK, see MOTION PICTURES.

MOZAMBIQUE. A cease-fire negotiated in October 1984 between the central government and a rebel force, the Mozambique National Resistance (MNR), ended in 1985. In January, units of the MNR killed three British travelers, cut power lines leading to the capital city, Maputo, and committed other acts of sabotage. Throughout the rest of the year, the rebels staged attacks in all 10 of Mozambique's provinces. One of the worst incidents took place on June 27, when MNR guerrillas ambushed a convoy of buses 30 miles (48 kilometers) north of Maputo, killing 37 people and wounding 62.

Machel Accuses South Africa. Mozambique's President Samora Moisés Machel accused the government of South Africa's State President Pieter Willem Botha of violating a March 1984 agreement. Under the terms of that pact, South Africa pledged not to aid the MNR in exchange for Mozambique's assurance that it would not help black nationalist groups from South Africa.

In late April, Mozambique and South Africa agreed to join forces on their border to stop the flow of military goods to the MNR. On September 16, however, after a raid on a rebel camp had turned up weapons and other supplies of South African origin, Machel said South Africa was still aiding the MNR. Later that month, Botha's government admitted that it had been supplying guerrillas in both Mozambique and Angola.

Mozambique and the United States strengthened their ties in 1985. In response to Machel's request for military aid to help cope with the MNR rebellion, the U.S. Congress voted $3 million in "nonlethal" assistance, such as transportation and communications equipment.

President Ronald Reagan invited Machel to Washington, D.C., for an official five-day visit from September 17 to 21, including talks at the White House on September 19. Among the issues discussed by Machel and Reagan was the continuation of U.S. famine aid. Although most of Africa experienced better rains and harvests in 1985, the United Nations Food and Agriculture Organization predicted that Mozambique would continue to need large donations of food in 1986.

New Policies. In May, to stimulate agricultural production, Machel's government instituted a new policy that allowed farmers to charge higher prices for their crops. Under the previous policy of price controls, farmers received so little money for their produce that many of them did not bother taking it to market. On June 25, the 10th anniversary of Mozambique's independence, Machel launched a program of economic reform that included policies to end laziness and theft in state-run enterprises.   J. Dixon Esseks

See also AFRICA (Facts in Brief Table). In WORLD BOOK, see MOZAMBIQUE.

MULRONEY, M. BRIAN (1939-   ), completed his first year as prime minister of Canada on Sept. 17, 1985. On September 4, the first anniversary of his Progressive Conservative Party's landslide electoral victory, his wife, Mila, gave birth to a son—their fourth child.

Mulroney sought to centralize control of government operations in his office and the Privy Council Office, which coordinates policy. His party commanded a massive majority in Parliament, but to many Canadians, the prime minister seemed indecisive, and the popularity of his government slipped during the year. On controversial measures, he retreated. On patronage, which he had made an issue in the 1984 campaign, he failed to effect genuine reform.

Mulroney's strength was as a mediator. His Atlantic and Western accords resolved long-standing resource disputes with Newfoundland and with Western oil-producing provinces. At the Heads of Government meeting of the Commonwealth in October, Mulroney was instrumental in working out a common position on sanctions against South Africa and its government policy of racial segregation.   David M. L. Farr

See also CANADA. In WORLD BOOK, see MULRONEY, MARTIN BRIAN.

MUSIC, CLASSICAL. See CLASSICAL MUSIC.
MUSIC, POPULAR. See POPULAR MUSIC.

NAMIBIA. South Africa, which has administered Namibia—formerly called South West Africa—as a territory since 1920, established an interim government on June 17, 1985, that was charged with governing Namibia's internal, nonmilitary affairs until the territory becomes independent.

The new government consisted of a 62-member National Assembly and an 8-person Cabinet, whose chairmanship was to rotate among the leaders of six parties joined in an alliance called the Multiparty Conference. Five of the six parties represented nonwhites. The Namibian political organization with the largest popular following, the South West Africa People's Organization (SWAPO), was not invited to participate.

The United Nations (UN) Security Council on June 19 denounced the interim government and reaffirmed a 1978 resolution calling for UN-supervised elections in Namibia. The United States government favored the UN plan but supported South Africa's insistence that it would not withdraw from Namibia while some 25,000 Cuban troops were in neighboring Angola. A U.S. proposal for the phased withdrawal of the Cubans fell through in May when Angola captured South African commandos who were apparently intending to blow up an oil installation.   J. Dixon Esseks

See also AFRICA (Facts in Brief Table); ANGOLA. In WORLD BOOK, see NAMIBIA.

NATIONAL PTA membership climbed to more than 5.6 million in 1985, the third straight year of increase in membership. At the National PTA convention in June in Washington, D.C., new President Ann Kahn said the theme of her two years in office would be "The National PTA: Advocates for America's Children." Kahn said the PTA has a responsibility to make sure the "doors to education and opportunity remain wide open for all children, now and in the future." The PTA in May sponsored Teacher Appreciation Week for the second consecutive year.

Concerned about the problems of drug use and drinking by young people in the United States, the National PTA in March sponsored Drug and Alcohol Awareness Week. Among other National PTA activities, more than 330,000 children throughout the United States and on American military bases in Europe participated in the PTA arts program, "Reflections." The children, in kindergarten through grade 12, competed for prizes by creating works of art in three categories: visual arts, literature, and music.   Joan Kuersten

In WORLD BOOK, see NATIONAL CONGRESS OF PARENTS AND TEACHERS; PARENT-TEACHER ORGANIZATIONS.

NAVY. See ARMED FORCES.

NEBRASKA. See STATE GOVERNMENT.

NEPAL. See ASIA.

NETHERLANDS. The Dutch government agonized in 1985 over whether to install United States nuclear cruise missiles on its soil. In 1979, the North Atlantic Treaty Organization (NATO) had decided to place 572 nuclear-armed Pershing 2 ballistic and cruise missiles in five European countries—Belgium, Great Britain, Italy, the Netherlands, and West Germany. As 1985 began, only Belgium and the Netherlands had not yet agreed to take the missiles.

In March 1985, Belgium finally decided to accept the missiles. The Netherlands' defense minister, Jacob de Ruiter, said that Belgium's decision would not influence either the Dutch government or public opinion. He said his government would make a final decision in November 1985, based on "objective criteria." On September 17, Queen Beatrix said in her Speech from the Throne—an annual statement of government policy—that if the Soviet Union did not cut the number of SS-20 missiles aimed at Western Europe by November 1, her country would take the U.S. missiles. On November 1, the administration of Prime Minister Ruud Lubbers said it had decided to take the missiles, and that it would ask the Dutch parliament to approve a U.S.-Netherlands treaty covering their installation and use.

Visit by Pope. The crisis in relations between Dutch Roman Catholics and the Vatican was highlighted when Pope John Paul II visited the Netherlands in May. In recent years, radical Dutch Catholics have shocked Rome by demanding that the church allow priests to marry, permit Catholics to use artificial methods of birth control, and ease its policy of not granting the sacrament of Holy Communion to certain people who have been divorced and remarried.

Radical Catholics demonstrated during the pope's visit, and on May 13, 50 women went to municipal authorities in The Hague to cancel their membership in the church. The pope did not meet with dissident groups, but on the last day of his visit, May 14, he delivered a stern lecture on sexual morality and the vices of the consumer society. He declared the church's opposition to sexual promiscuity, homosexuality, artificial methods of birth control, and abortion "for all time." He made it clear that he would not allow women to become priests.

The Economy. The unemployment rate in the Netherlands, almost 15 per cent, was one of the highest in Europe. The 1986 budget, presented on September 17, decreased public spending by $2.6 billion. The cuts were deep in the areas of wages for public employees, social security payments, and health-care benefits.   Kenneth Brown

See also EUROPE (Facts in Brief Table). In WORLD BOOK, see NETHERLANDS.

NEVADA. See STATE GOVERNMENT.

NEW BRUNSWICK. Premier Richard B. Hatfield, in power since 1970 and Canada's longest-serving premier, found himself at the center of a political storm during 1985. On January 29, Hatfield was acquitted of a charge of drug possession. In 1984, the Royal Canadian Mounted Police (RCMP) had seized 35 grams (1.2 ounces) of marijuana from an outside pocket in Hatfield's baggage. The judge ruled that there was no firm evidence to show that the premier had the marijuana in his personal possession. Hatfield later charged that political enemies within the RCMP were anxious to discredit him.

An internal RCMP report released on May 24 maintained that there was no evidence of a conspiracy within the federal police organization to bring down Hatfield's Progressive Conservative Party (PC) government. These events produced rumblings in the PC, however, regarding Hatfield's continuing leadership. The voters of a riding, or electoral district, near the capital of Fredericton showed their disapproval on April 29 by electing a Liberal to the legislature after having voted for the PC for 32 years. The defeat left Hatfield's PC government with 38 supporters in the legislature facing 18 Liberals and 2 New Democratic Party members.   David M. L. Farr

See also CANADA. In WORLD BOOK, see NEW BRUNSWICK.

NEW CALEDONIA. Melanesians eager to end 132 years of French rule gave the Kanak Socialist National Liberation Front control of three out of the four newly created regional councils in elections held on Sept. 29, 1985. The fourth region, containing Nouméa, the capital, was won by French and pro-French settlers who oppose independence. Voters opposed to independence won about 60 per cent of the total vote and 31 of the 47 seats in the regional councils. The councils together form a new territorial Congress and Consultative Council. The election attracted 80 to 90 per cent of eligible voters. Despite more than 20 deaths in politically inspired unrest over the previous 10 months, no violence occurred during the election. More than 3,000 police had been flown in from France to maintain order.

Despite the Melanesians' victories, many observers felt the poll had further polarized the territory's population, two-fifths of whom are Melanesians. The election was the first step toward a referendum on territorial independence planned to be held before the end of 1987.   Robert Langdon

See also PACIFIC ISLANDS. In WORLD BOOK, see NEW CALEDONIA.

NEW HAMPSHIRE. See STATE GOVERNMENT.

NEW JERSEY. See STATE GOVERNMENT.

NEW MEXICO. See STATE GOVERNMENT.

NEW YORK. See NEW YORK CITY; STATE GOV'T.

New Caledonia: Seeking Independence

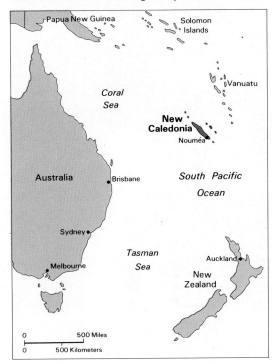

NEW YORK CITY. Mayor Edward I. Koch won a decisive victory in the Nov. 5, 1985, mayoral election, collecting more than 75 per cent of the votes cast. Koch became the third mayor in New York City history—along with Fiorello H. La Guardia and Robert F. Wagner—to be elected to three consecutive terms. Koch, a Democrat, defeated two female challengers—City Council President Carol Bellamy, running as the Liberal Party candidate, and Diane McGrath, a member of the state Crime Victims Board, who was the candidate of the Republican and Conservative parties.

Healthy Economy. The city's continued strong economy and sound fiscal condition were key factors in Koch's reelection. City Controller Harrison Jay Goldin reported on November 1 that the city ended the 1985 fiscal year with a $570-million surplus, the fifth straight year with a surplus.

In October, the Port Authority of New York and New Jersey reported that the metropolitan area, paced by New York City, had gained 147,000 new jobs during the first six months of 1985 and was expected to add another 80,000 before the end of the year. The service, trade, construction, and tourism industries experienced the greatest growth.

Westway. Mayor Koch and New York Governor Mario M. Cuomo announced on September 19 that the city was abandoning a 14-year campaign

411

Mayor Koch exulted after winning the mayoral primary election in September, then went on to capture a third term in the November election.

to build the $2.3-billion Westway highway and development project along 4.2 miles (6.8 kilometers) of the Hudson River waterfront on Manhattan's West Side. The project's demise came after a United States district judge refused to permit the U.S. Army Corps of Engineers to dredge the river. Environmentalists had argued that the landfill project threatened the striped bass, an endangered species. But the deciding factor in the city's decision was the opposition of New Jersey political leaders, who feared the project would jeopardize development on the New Jersey side of the Hudson.

Tallest Building? On November 18, the flamboyant and controversial real estate developer Donald J. Trump announced plans for constructing the world's tallest building in New York City. The 150-story skyscraper—40 stories higher than the current recordholder, the Sears Tower in Chicago—would be the centerpiece of Television City, a city-within-a-city that would occupy 100 acres (40 hectares) of a former railroad yard on Manhattan's West Side. Trump also proposed building seven other towers on the same site, as well as a shopping mall and studio space for television and motion-picture production. The project faces an uncertain fate because of the zoning changes that will be required before it can be built.

City authorities reached an agreement with Bos-

ton Properties, headed by developer Mortimer B. Zuckerman, on July 11 for the sale of the New York Coliseum site for $455 million, a record for a real estate transaction in New York City. Zuckerman said he plans to build two towers of 56 and 72 stories containing offices, a 300-room hotel, and 300 luxury condominiums. The Coliseum has been the city's main exhibition hall since 1953. It was scheduled to close on April 1, 1986, when the Jacob Javits Convention Center was to open.

Water. New York City residents had to cut back on their use of water in 1985 as the city coped with one of the worst droughts in years. City reservoirs were less than half full in the fall.

New Yorkers coped with a different sort of water problem in July and August, when tiny amounts of plutonium, a radioactive element that is also a deadly poison, were found in the municipal water supply. City officials had received an anonymous letter in April threatening to contaminate the water supply with plutonium unless charges were dropped against Bernhard H. Goetz—the so-called Subway Vigilante who shot four black youths aboard a New York City subway train in December 1984. Koch insisted that the city's water was still safe, but many New Yorkers reportedly switched to bottled water.   Owen Moritz

See also CITY. In WORLD BOOK, see NEW YORK CITY.

NEW ZEALAND. The Labour Party government headed by Prime Minister David R. Lange in 1985 continued its domestic policy of economic conservatism and its antinuclear foreign policy. Relations with the United States were strained during the year due to New Zealand's refusal to allow nuclear-armed or nuclear-powered warships to enter its ports. The U.S. government refuses to acknowledge whether particular ships carry nuclear arms. Because of this deadlock, the U.S. government considered its obligations to New Zealand under the 1952 ANZUS (Australia, New Zealand, United States) mutual defense treaty to be no longer operative. On Dec. 10, 1985, the Lange government introduced legislation to give its antinuclear policy the force of law.

New Zealand's antinuclear stand was also reflected in government protests against French nuclear tests at Mururoa Atoll in the South Pacific Ocean. Relations between France and New Zealand deteriorated with the July 10 bombing of the Greenpeace environmental group's ship *Rainbow Warrior* in Auckland Harbor, which caused the death of a Greenpeace photographer. The ship had been about to sail to Mururoa Atoll to protest French nuclear tests. Two French secret service agents were arrested and pleaded guilty to manslaughter in the case. On November 22, they were sentenced to 10 years in prison.

The Greenpeace environmental group's ship *Rainbow Warrior* lists in Auckland (New Zealand) Harbor after it was bombed by French agents in July.

NEWFOUNDLAND. On Feb. 11, 1985, Canada's Prime Minister Brian Mulroney and Newfoundland Premier Brian Peckford signed an agreement that gave the province control of offshore oil and natural gas resources jointly with the federal government. The agreement allows Newfoundland to tax the resources as if they were on land and to have a say in their development.

In elections on April 2, Peckford's Progressive Conservative (PC) Party won 36 of the Legislative Assembly's 52 seats—down from the 44 it had held before the election. The Liberal Party won 15 seats, and the remaining seat was won by a New Democratic Party member. A wage freeze for government employees and tough labor legislation approved by the Peckford government undoubtedly hurt the PC at the polls.

The 1985-1986 provincial budget forecast economic growth of only about 3 per cent. The public debt was expected to continue growing.

Newfoundland's fishing catch was down about 40 per cent during the summer. The federal government in December granted a Nova Scotia company a license to operate factory freezer-trawlers off Newfoundland's coast. Newfoundland feared such floating fish factories would deplete northern cod stocks and lead to the loss of jobs at shore-based fish processing plants.   David M. L. Farr

In WORLD BOOK, see NEWFOUNDLAND.

NEWSMAKERS OF 1985 included the following:

An American Dream. The winning combination of numbers was picked by an immigrant from Paraguay. The winning ticket was purchased by a native of Hong Kong. And the prize—one-third of a New York state lottery jackpot of $41 million—was won in August by a group of 21 men, many of them recent immigrants, representing nearly every American ethnic, racial, and religious group. The men, employees of Hantscho, Incorporated, in Mount Vernon, N.Y., each ended up with about $650,000 from the largest lottery jackpot in U.S. history. Two other tickets also had the winning numbers. The 21 workers had chipped in to buy lottery tickets, then signed an agreement to share any winnings.

A New Citizen. Walter Polovchak, who as a 12-year-old sought political asylum in the United States when his parents tried to take him back to the Soviet Union, became a U.S. citizen in October after turning 18. Walter and his family moved to Chicago from the Ukraine in 1980. After a few months, Walter's parents decided to return to their homeland, but Walter decided to stay. He was granted political asylum, and in 1981, the Polovchaks left for the Soviet Union without him. In numerous court hearings after that, Walter claimed that he would be persecuted if forced to return. The American Civil Liberties Union,

Economy. New Zealand's Labour Party government abolished various controls on financial institutions, overseas investments, and imports during the year. The New Zealand dollar was allowed to float on the international market starting on March 4 and showed unexpected strength. This strength, however, created difficulties for the country's export drive.

The government introduced a new 10 per cent sales tax, effective in 1986, to be accompanied by substantial cuts in income tax. The budget for the fiscal year ending in March 1986 provided for a significant reduction in the deficit, made possible partly by large reductions in agricultural and export subsidies. At year's end, inflation stood at about 18 per cent, the rate of economic growth remained low, and record high interest rates were hampering business.

Politics. A June election in the South Island district of Timaru resulted in the Labour Party losing a seat in Parliament that it had held for 57 years. The National Party candidate won.

Archbishop of the Anglican Church of New Zealand Sir Paul Reeves became governor general of New Zealand on November 20. He is the first person of Maori (native Polynesian) ancestry to hold this largely ceremonial post.   David A. Shand

See also ASIA (Facts in Brief Table); REEVES, PAUL. In WORLD BOOK, see NEW ZEALAND.

Las Vegas pedestrians flee a fugitive ostrich that escaped while being transported to a zoo in Minnesota in February. It was soon captured unharmed.

which represented Walter's parents, argued that the parents had the right to decide where their son should live. On his 18th birthday, Walter automatically left his parents' custody and so became entitled to live where he chooses.

Applauding a Master. Gene Kelly, 72, who created a more masculine, athletic style of dancing in motion pictures, received the American Film Institute's 13th Life Achievement Award in March. The award is given annually to someone whose work in film has "stood the test of time." Kelly, whose dancing partners included a mop and bucket and an animated mouse as well as glamorous actresses, starred in such film classics as *An American in Paris* (1951) and *Singin' in the Rain* (1952). On receiving the award, Kelly blushed and confessed that he "never wanted to be a dancer. My whole ambition was to play shortstop for the Pittsburgh Pirates."

Spelling Champ. Balu Natarjan, 13, of Bolingbrook, Ill., won the 1985 National Spelling Bee on June 6. He bested Kate Lingley, 13, of Dover-Foxcroft, Me., by correctly spelling the word *milieu*, which means *environment* or *surroundings*.

Seven for the Record Books. Patricia Ann, Stephen Earl, and Richard Charles Frustaci were the only survivors of seven babies born on May 21 in Orange, Calif., the largest multiple birth on record in the United States. The babies' mother, Pa-

tricia J. Frustaci, 30, had taken a fertility drug. She and her husband, Samuel, 32, already had an 18-month-old son. The septuplets were born by Caesarean section and 12 weeks premature. One of them, a girl, was stillborn. Three others, two boys and a girl, died within days of their birth.

A New Court Jester. The newest member of the Harlem Globetrotters basketball team holds the career-scoring record at the University of Kansas in Lawrence (besting Wilt Chamberlain and Jo Jo White) and helped the United States win a gold medal in basketball at the 1984 Olympics. The newest Globetrotter is also a woman, the first on the team. Lynette Woodard, 26, was chosen in October 1985. The 5-foot 11-inch (180-centimeter) Woodard beat out 22 other women for the spot.

Belated Peace. When the ancient Romans captured the city of Carthage in northern Africa in 146 B.C., they took a terrible revenge for a Roman defeat 70 years earlier by the Carthaginian general Hannibal. The Roman soldiers killed four-fifths of Carthage's population, sold the rest into slavery, leveled the city, and sowed the surrounding area with salt so crops could not be grown. Eventually—it took 2,131 years—the mayor of Carthage, now a suburb of Tunis, Tunisia, and the mayor of Rome decided to let bygones be bygones and signed a peace treaty in February 1985 officially ending the Third Punic War.

Long Shot. It was Marshall University of Huntington, W. Va., against Appalachian State University of Boone, N.C., and the basketball action was hot. With just three seconds left in the first half, Marshall guard Bruce Morris grabbed the ball near Appalachian State's basket. As the buzzer sounded, the Deerfield, Ill., senior hurled the ball down the court. To everyone's surprise, including his, the ball swished cleanly through the net, setting a record for the longest field goal in basketball history. Morris' miraculous shot on Feb. 8, 1985, traveled 89 feet 10 inches (27.38 meters), beating the previous record by 7 inches (18 centimeters). Marshall beat Appalachian State 93-82.

Old Man of the Mountain. Richard Bass, 55, a geologist, cattle rancher, and ski-resort developer from Dallas, on April 30 became the oldest person to climb Mount Everest. By scaling the world's tallest mountain, located on the Tibet-Nepal border, Bass also became the first person to reach the highest points on all seven continents.

The Lone Ranger Rides Again, Masked. In January, actor Clayton Moore, who portrayed the Lone Ranger in television and movies in the 1950's and in many public appearances since then, won the right to don his famous black mask once again. Moore had been reduced to wearing dark sunglasses by a 1979 court order issued at the request of the Wrather Corporation of Beverly Hills, Calif., which owns the rights to the Lone Ranger character. The company said it filed suit against Moore because he continued to make appearances while another actor was being promoted for the 1981 movie *The Legend of the Lone Ranger*. In January 1985, a Los Angeles court notified Moore it had dismissed Wrather's suit. Said an elated Moore, "The mask will never be taken off again."

Winning Musher. By plunging into a blinding blizzard that kept her competitors indoors, Libby Riddles, 28, of Teller, Alaska, gained the edge she needed to become the first woman to win Alaska's grueling Iditarod Trail Sled Dog Race. The first-place *musher*—sled dog driver—finished the rugged 1,135-mile (1,827-kilometer) course from Anchorage to Nome in 18 days 20 minutes 17 seconds, earning a $50,000 prize. The weather was so bad that officials twice halted the race, and 21 of the 61 contestants were unable to finish.

First Teacher in Space. In September, Sharon Christa McAuliffe, 36, a social studies teacher from Concord, N.H., began training to become the first citizen observer on a U.S. space flight. McAuliffe, a mother of two, was chosen from more than 11,000 teachers who had applied for the coveted berth. She was scheduled to blast off aboard the space shuttle *Challenger* on Jan. 24, 1986. The idea of selecting a teacher as the first private shuttle passenger was proposed by President Ronald Reagan in August 1984.

An elaborate sand castle, said to be the world's tallest, towers 40 feet (12 meters) above the beach near San Diego in September.

Furious Author. A simple apology wasn't enough for Farley Mowat, the well-known Canadian author of *Never Cry Wolf* (1963), when he was denied entry into the United States in April. Officials of the U.S. Immigration and Naturalization Service (INS) blocked his visit because of what they said were past or current associations with "Communists or anarchists." Mowat, who was planning a tour of the United States to promote his book *Sea of Slaughter*, not only denied the charges but also demanded a written apology from the INS to be delivered on *Air Force One*, the jet used by the President of the United States. Several days later, the INS relented and offered Mowat a onetime visit. But Mowat, who cooled off enough to drop his demand for the apology, refused the offer, saying he would settle for nothing less than "free and open" entry into the United States.

Three Little Kittens. In May, Koko, the 14-year-old lowland gorilla who can communicate in sign language, finally got the pet she wanted so badly. In the summer of 1984, after repeated requests, Koko was given a Manx kitten—which she named All Ball. Unfortunately, All Ball died just a few days before Christmas, apparently the victim of a traffic accident. In March 1985, Koko, who had cried when told of All Ball's death, received a second Manx. But Michael, another gorilla at the Gorilla Foundation in Woodside, Calif., where Koko

Saying good-by in 1985 were Marlin Perkins, who stepped down as host of TV's "Wild Kingdom," and Leontyne Price, who gave her final opera performance.

lives, decided to claim that kitten for his own. So to prevent gorilla warfare, Koko's trainers in May presented her with a third kitten, a gray part-Manx cat that Koko appropriately named Smoky.

The Name Is the Game. Remembering names was no problem for a group of picnickers who met in a New York City park in July. That's because they all had the same name—Bob Joseph. The picnic was sponsored by a New York City advertising executive, who got the idea while looking through a telephone book to see if he could find enough other Bob Josephs to invite to a dinner party. News of the picnic spread, and 36 Bob Josephs from around the United States showed up—including one whose name was really Roberta. Among the day's events were bobbing for apples and a guitar rendition of "I Wanna Be Bobby's Girl."

Independence Day. Sun Myung Moon, 65, the spiritual leader of the Unification Church, celebrated the Fourth of July in 1985 by leaving the federal prison in Danbury, Conn., where he had served nearly 12 months for income-tax evasion. Convicted in 1982, Moon had remained free until May 1984, when the Supreme Court of the United States refused to hear his appeal. Moon maintained his innocence throughout his court fight, claiming he was the victim of religious prejudice. Released six months early for good behavior,

Moon was required to spend 1½ months at an inmate rehabilitation center in New York City.

The Last Fugitive. After 40 years on the run, escaped World War II prisoner of war Georg Gaertner surrendered to U.S. authorities in September. A sergeant in German Field Marshal Erwin Rommel's Afrika Korps, Gaertner was captured in 1943. He escaped from Fort Deming, N. Mex., on Sept. 21, 1945, one of 2,000 POW's to break out of U.S. camps during the war. By 1963, all but Gaertner had been recaptured. Gaertner's surrender coincided with the publication of his book, *Hitler's Last Soldier in America*, the story of his years as a fugitive. An immigration official said Gaertner probably could remain in the United States because his wife is a U.S. citizen.

Math Wizard. Ruth Lawrence, a 13-year-old from Huddersfield, England, became in July the youngest person ever to graduate from Oxford University. She was awarded a first-class degree (equivalent to a bachelor of arts degree with honors) in mathematics. Lawrence, who won a scholarship to the university when she was 10, completed her degree in two years instead of the usual three. Her father, a computer analyst, quit his job in 1977 to concentrate on educating Ruth and her younger sister, Rebecca.

Mount Adams. For more than 50 years, Ansel Adams' dramatic photographs captured the splendor of Western landscapes, so it seemed only natural that a mountain in Yosemite National Park in California be named after him. The 11,900-foot (3,600-meter) peak, named Mount Ansel Adams, was dedicated in August to honor the photographer and environmentalist, who died in 1984.

Teacher of the Year. Therese Knecht Dozier, a 32-year-old history teacher who was abandoned as a child in Vietnam, won the 1985 National Teacher of the Year award in April. Dozier, who teaches at Irmo High School in Columbia, S.C., was sold by her German father after her Vietnamese mother died. Later placed in an orphanage, she and a younger brother were brought to the United States in 1954 after being adopted by a U.S. Army adviser and his wife.

Fast Track. John Patrick Buellesfeld, 20, of Wellington, Kans., earned a master of arts degree in business administration from Webster University in St. Louis, Mo., in October 1985, just one year after receiving his bachelor's degree and 2½ years after graduating from high school. Buellesfeld managed his academic feat by taking college classes while still in high school and carrying double the normal class load.

Love's Labor's Lost—and Found. A 32-year-old Shakespeare scholar from Topeka, Kans., made the discovery of a lifetime in November—what may be a previously unrecognized poem by William Shakespeare. Gary Taylor found the 90-line love poem in a collection of verse that had been in the Bodleian Library at Oxford University for the past 230 years. If the poem is authentic—and some experts say it is not—it would be the first "new" work by the Bard of Avon found in more than 200 years.

Tale of a Whale and Vice Versa. Humphrey the humpback whale finally swam back into the Pacific Ocean on November 4, after a 24-day excursion that took the giant animal 70 miles (110 kilometers) inland into California's Sacramento and San Joaquin rivers. Scientists tried to scare Humphrey back to the ocean by playing unfriendly killer whale sounds underwater. But neither that nor an attempt by parapsychologists to create a mental "force field" worked. Finally, scientists serenaded Humphrey with friendly humpback whale sounds, and to the applause of spectators aboard a fleet of more than 35 boats, the wayward whale passed beneath San Francisco's Golden Gate Bridge and into history.

Piggott's Last Ride. Lester Piggott, 50, who won more horse races in Great Britain (4,349) than any other jockey except Sir Gordon Richards (4,870), retired in late 1985 after nearly 40 years on the turf. Piggott planned a new career as a horse trainer.   Barbara A. Mayes

NEWSPAPER. A wave of mergers and big-money take-overs swept through the United States newspaper industry during 1985. Gannett Company, the chain that owns *USA Today*, made the two biggest buys. On January 31, Gannett bought *The Des Moines* (Iowa) *Register*, which had a circulation of about 240,000 and had been owned by the Cowles family of Iowa since 1903. Gannett paid $200 million for the *Register*, the *Jackson* (Tenn.) *Sun*, and two Iowa weekly newspapers.

On September 7, Gannett spent $717 million and won a bidding war among several of the largest U.S. media firms to buy another family-owned newspaper and broadcasting concern, the Evening News Association (ENA). Newspaper legend James E. Scripps established the ENA in 1873. The ENA publishes *The Detroit News*, which has a circulation of about 650,000, and four other dailies. The ENA also owns five television stations and two radio stations.

The circulations of the biggest U.S. dailies increased for the third year in a row in 1985. The top 10 newspapers had a combined circulation of 9,775,111.

Hard Times. Despite these increases, most newspaper companies reported a lackluster year financially. The *St. Louis Globe-Democrat* filed for Chapter 11 bankruptcy protection from creditors on September 26 and suspended publication on De-

Walter Polovchak, who refused to return to the Soviet Union with his parents in 1980, flashes his new U.S. citizenship papers in October 1985.

cember 6. On December 30, a federal bankruptcy judge approved the proposed sale of the newspaper to the Veritas Corporation, a new firm headed by two local businessmen. Also on December 30, the *Columbus* (Ohio) *Citizen-Journal* announced that it would cease publication the next day.

United Press International (UPI), the country's second-biggest news service, filed for bankruptcy on April 28 after its debts ballooned to more than $40 million. On November 12, Mexican publisher Mario Vázquez Reña bid a reported $40 million for UPI.

Credibility. Louis D. Boccardi, president of the Associated Press (AP) wire service, warned editors in February that the U.S. public thinks journalists are "arrogant" and out of touch with readers' concerns. And a study released on April 12 by the American Society of Newspaper Editors indicated that 68 per cent of those surveyed thought television did a more reliable job of presenting national and international news than newspapers did.

Foreign Reporting remained dangerous for U.S. journalists in 1985. In March, Terry A. Anderson, chief Middle East correspondent for the AP, was kidnapped in Beirut, Lebanon. At year's end, he had not been released. Phoenix *Arizona Republic* reporter Charles Thornton was killed on September 19 while working in Afghanistan.   Mark Fitzgerald

In WORLD BOOK, see NEWSPAPER.

Nicaragua's President Daniel Ortega waves to supporters at his inauguration ceremony in the capital city, Managua, in January.

NICARAGUA. Nicaragua's President Daniel Ortega told the United Nations (UN) General Assembly on Oct. 21, 1985, that Nicaragua had suffered 11,000 killed, 5,000 wounded, 5,000 kidnapped, and the relocation of 250,000 people since the Sandinistas' ruling junta was established in 1981. Ortega laid the blame on the Administration of United States President Ronald Reagan because of its support for anti-Sandinista rebels known as *contras*, who are based in the neighboring countries of Honduras and Costa Rica. Had the United States suffered similar losses—proportional to its much larger population—those losses would have been three times greater than the casualties the United States sustained during World War II, Ortega calculated. He said the United States was trying "to deny the existence of a nonaligned Nicaragua in the Central American region."

Curbs on Civil Rights. For supporters of U.S. policy, it appeared that United States support for the contras was successfully keeping the Sandinista regime on the defensive. On October 15, the Sandinistas imposed strict curbs on civil rights, citing an "extraordinary situation" created by contra attacks. The curbs included the suspension of constitutional provisions guaranteeing freedom of speech, assembly, and travel; the right of workers to strike; and the right of *habeas corpus*, which guarantees a prisoner's right to a court hearing. In addition, the Sandinista regime clamped even tighter controls on the press, requiring journalists to submit material for government scrutiny before publication or broadcast.

Earlier, on October 12, the Sandinista regime further widened its split with the Roman Catholic Church in Nicaragua by shutting down a church-sponsored newspaper named *Iglesia* (*Church*). The Nicaraguan government claimed that the offending newspaper was "not religious, but highly political." The Reagan Administration immediately condemned the regime's actions, saying it was yet another step toward creating a totalitarian Communist system.

U.S. Aid to Contras. On August 8, the Reagan Administration acknowledged that National Security Council officials had provided advice on military operations to the contras. Some members of the U.S. Congress argued that such advice violated Congress's intent when it passed legislation in June granting $27 million in nonmilitary aid to the contras. The legislation stipulated that the Central Intelligence Agency (CIA) and the Department of Defense could not provide direct military assistance to the rebels. The use of the National Security Council—which is part of the President's Executive Office—seemed to be a way of getting around that stipulation, some Congress members complained.

Trade Embargo. In May, the Reagan Administration resorted to economic warfare against Nicaragua, declaring an embargo on trade and banning Nicaraguan ships and aircraft from the United States. The move was roundly criticized by U.S. allies in Europe and Latin America. It appeared likely that a number of Western European and Latin-American nations would step up their aid to Nicaragua in the wake of the United States embargo.

Other Developments. Hard pressed by the Reagan Administration, Nicaragua drew closer in 1985 to governments unfriendly to the United States. Following a visit to Nicaragua by Iran's Prime Minister Hosein Musavi-Khamenei from January 23 to 25, Iran reportedly agreed to supply Nicaragua with oil.

In an attempt to sway public opinion in the United States, the Sandinistas allowed a television crew from the program "60 Minutes" to film Nicaragua's preparations to counter a possible U.S. invasion. The film, aired at midyear, showed Sandinista forces equipped with arms from the Soviet Union. Nathan A. Haverstock

See also COURTS; LATIN AMERICA (Facts in Brief Table); ORTEGA, DANIEL. In WORLD BOOK, see NICARAGUA.

NIGER. See AFRICA.

NIGERIA. On Aug. 27, 1985, Nigeria experienced its fifth military coup since gaining political independence from Great Britain in 1960. Members of the ruling Supreme Military Council (SMC) deposed the nation's head of state, Major General Muhammadu Buhari, and the council's second most important leader, Major General Tunde Idiagbon. Buhari was arrested, but Idiagbon was in Saudi Arabia and so escaped arrest. Apparently, no blood was spilled, and the dusk-to-dawn curfew imposed in Nigeria's major cities was lifted after only two days.

Buhari and the SMC had come to power just 20 months before, in December 1983, in a coup against an elected civilian regime. The leaders of the 1985 coup retained the SMC as Nigeria's chief ruling body, replacing Buhari with Major General Ibrahim Babangida, who had been army chief of staff.

Babangida charged that Buhari had violated human rights and failed to revive the country's economy. One of Babangida's first acts was to repeal a Buhari decree authorizing the jailing of journalists and others for criticizing the government. Babangida also appointed a special committee to review government policies on human rights. The Buhari regime had shocked many Nigerians by imposing harsh penalties to deter crime.

Illegal aliens, ordered out of Nigeria by the government, collect at a customs post on the Benin border in May as the departure deadline nears.

Economic Crisis Declared. On October 1, the 25th anniversary of Nigeria's independence, Babangida announced a 15-month state of economic emergency. To cope with the trade deficit, he imposed a ban on importing rice and corn. Nigeria's oil industry, the source of more than 90 per cent of the nation's export earnings, continued to be depressed because of a worldwide glut of crude oil. Nigeria was also deeply in debt to foreign banks. As the new government looked for other ways to ease the economic situation, it considered borrowing $2.4 billion from the International Monetary Fund (IMF), an agency of the United Nations. In the fall, many people became discontented with the new regime.

On December 20, a government spokesman said a group of military officers had been arrested for plotting another coup.

Alien Workers Expelled. In the spring, the Buhari government expelled some 200,000 illegal aliens, primarily to reduce unemployment in Nigeria. The government announced on April 15 that illegal aliens—mostly people from neighboring countries who had come in search of work—had to obtain a residency permit or leave the country by May 10. J. Dixon Esseks

See also AFRICA (Facts in Brief Table). In WORLD BOOK, see NIGERIA.

NIXON, RICHARD MILHOUS (1913-   ), the 37th President of the United States, had a new book published in January 1985—*No More Vietnams*. In it, he took a veiled swipe at the Administration of President Ronald Reagan for not striking back more strongly against Middle East terrorists.

Despite a painful attack of *shingles*, a viral disease that causes skin eruptions along certain nerves, Nixon went to Washington, D.C., on January 8 to discuss plans for a presidential library bearing his name. But a day later, the illness confined him to his home in Saddle River, N.J., as he celebrated his 72nd birthday.

The former President traveled to Beijing (Peking), China, in September. He spent six days in China and also visited Japan, South Korea, and several other countries.

On February 8, Nixon notified the U.S. Department of the Treasury that to save the government some $3 million a year, he would begin using private security guards instead of the Secret Service agents provided by law to all former Presidents. In October, Nixon acted as arbitrator in a dispute between the owners of major-league baseball teams and major-league umpires over what pay umpires should receive for officiating at championship games. Frank Cormier and Margot Cormier

In WORLD BOOK, see NIXON, RICHARD M.

Visiting China in September, former President Richard M. Nixon plays the piano to entertain children at a Beijing (Peking) commune.

NOBEL PRIZES in peace, literature, economics, and the sciences were awarded in 1985 by the Norwegian Storting (parliament) in Oslo and by the Royal Academy of Science, the Caroline Institute, and the Swedish Academy of Literature, which are in Stockholm, Sweden.

The Peace Prize was awarded to the International Physicians for the Prevention of Nuclear War, a worldwide organization based in Boston. The award was accepted by the two cofounders of the group: Bernard Lown, a professor of cardiology at Harvard University's School of Public Health in Boston, and Yevgeny I. Chazov, a deputy minister of health in the Soviet Union and a personal physician to top Soviet leaders. The Nobel committee said it chose the group for the peace award because it had "performed a considerable service to mankind by spreading authoritative information and by creating an awareness of the catastrophic consequences of atomic warfare."

Human rights activists demonstrated against Chazov because he was among 40 Soviet scientists who signed a letter attacking Russian dissident Andrei D. Sakharov, winner of the 1975 Nobel Prize for peace. In addition, the U.S. and West German ambassadors to Norway stayed away from the Nobel ceremony, apparently because of Chazov's attack on Sakharov.

The Literature Prize went to novelist Claude Simon, 72, of France, a leading pioneer of the *nouveau roman* (new novel), a literary trend of the 1950's and 1960's that disdained traditional plot and character development. Born in Madagascar to French parents but raised in the south of France, Simon began writing during World War II. Many of his novels, such as *The Flanders Road* (1961) and *The Palace* (1963), concern his experiences with the French resistance during that war and with the Loyalists during the Spanish Civil War in the 1930's. The new novel trend reached the height of its influence in the 1960's.

The Chemistry Prize was shared by Herbert A. Hauptman, 68, research director and vice president of the Medical Foundation of Buffalo, N.Y., and Jerome Karle, 67, a chief scientist at the United States Naval Research Laboratory in Washington, D.C. The two men, experts in the field of X-ray crystallography, developed new mathematical equations to describe the three-dimensional structure of a crystallized molecule. Due to their formula, more than 45,000 molecules have been analyzed, and the process, which once took years, now takes days. Their method of studying crystals, used routinely by chemists with the aid of computers, led to the development of new antibiotics, painkilling drugs, and vaccines.

The Economics Prize was given to Franco Modigliani, 67, a professor of economics at the Massachusetts Institute of Technology in Cambridge, for his *life-cycle* theory of why and when people save money. His theory provided a useful tool for analyzing national pension plans, such as the social security system in the United States. The Nobel committee also cited his studies of how the market value of a company's stock is determined. Modigliani determined that expectation of future profitability is most important in determining the value of a stock and that the amount of company debt has little influence. The Italian-born Modigliani became a U.S. citizen in 1946.

The Physics Prize went to Klaus von Klitzing, 42, of West Germany, director of the Max Planck Institute for Solid State Research in Stuttgart. Von Klitzing used the theory of quantum mechanics to measure with great accuracy how voltage changes when a magnetic field is applied perpendicularly to the flow of an electric current. Von Klitzing's discovery in 1980 was based on work first done by American physicist Edwin H. Hall in 1879.

The Physiology or Medicine Prize was shared by Michael S. Brown, 44, and Joseph L. Goldstein, 45, both professors of molecular genetics at the University of Texas Health Science Center in Dallas. The Nobel committee credited the two medical researchers with having "revolutionized our knowledge" of cholesterol and how it can accumulate in arteries, causing strokes and heart attacks. Brown and Goldstein discovered how certain receptors in human cells trap and absorb bloodstream particles, known as low-density lipoproteins (LDL), that contain cholesterol, a fatty substance. They showed how a diet that is too rich in cholesterol lowers the number of these receptors and thereby increases a person's chances of heart disease, while a low-cholesterol diet raises the number of LDL receptors, helping to prevent heart disease. They also discovered that some people inherit a low number of LDL receptors and are therefore more prone to heart disease. This discovery, which occurred in 1973, opened the door to new research into possible drug treatments that could reduce cholesterol levels.

1984 Winners. The winners of Nobel Prizes in 1984 were Bishop Desmond Tutu of South Africa for peace, Jaroslav Seifert of Czechoslovakia for literature, R. Bruce Merrifield of the United States for chemistry, Sir Richard Stone of Great Britain for economics, Carlo Rubbia of Italy and Simon van der Meer of the Netherlands for physics, and Argentine-born César Milstein of Great Britain, Georges J. F. Köhler of West Germany, and Niels K. Jerne of Denmark for physiology or medicine.   Rod Such

In WORLD BOOK, see NOBEL PRIZES.

NORTH ATLANTIC TREATY ORGANIZATION (NATO). See EUROPE.

NORTH CAROLINA. See STATE GOVERNMENT.

NORTH DAKOTA. See STATE GOVERNMENT.

NORTHERN IRELAND. On Nov. 15, 1985, Prime Ministers Margaret Thatcher of Great Britain and Garret FitzGerald of the Republic of Ireland signed an agreement giving the Irish republic an advisory role in the affairs of Northern Ireland. The agreement established an intergovernmental conference of British and Irish Cabinet ministers that would meet frequently to discuss political, security, and legal matters affecting Northern Ireland. Both governments pledged not to change the status of Northern Ireland without the consent of a majority of voters there.

The first meeting of the intergovernmental conference was held on November 11 in Belfast, Northern Ireland. Improving security cooperation between north and south and allowing judges from the republic to participate in court cases along with judges in Northern Ireland were on the agenda. To encourage the Roman Catholic minority in the north, the conference allowed the flag of the Republic of Ireland to be flown in Northern Ireland and allowed street names in Gaelic as well as in English.

Unionist Reaction. The agreement provoked loud and angry opposition from Protestant unionist political parties in Northern Ireland who opposed giving the republic a voice in the affairs of Northern Ireland. On November 15, Ian Gow,

Britain's minister of state at the treasury, resigned office because of his objections to the agreement.

By late November, both the Irish and British parliaments had approved the agreement. Fifteen members of Britain's House of Commons from Northern Ireland resigned their seats in protest. They objected to the fact that the people of Northern Ireland had not been allowed to vote on the arrangement. They planned to make their reelection fight, with voting scheduled for Jan. 23, 1986, an unofficial referendum on the agreement.

Elections. On May 15, 1985, Sinn Féin (Ourselves Alone), the political wing of the outlawed Irish Republican Army (IRA), fielded candidates in local elections in Northern Ireland for the first time. They won 59 of 566 seats on local councils with about 12 per cent of the vote. The presence of Sinn Féin councilors proved too much for many unionists. Craigavon Council in County Armagh sought to freeze its two Sinn Féin councilors out by excluding them from a special committee that would conduct all council business. This action was invalidated by the courts in June.

British Cabinet Replacement. On September 2, Thatcher replaced Douglas Hurd, who had been secretary of state for Northern Ireland for less than a year, with Tom King. King had served as secretary of employment.   Ian J. Mather

In WORLD BOOK, see NORTHERN IRELAND.

Gerry Adams, president of Sinn Féin, campaigns as his party runs candidates for the first time in local elections in Northern Ireland in May.

NORTHWEST TERRITORIES. The controversy increased during 1985 over the proposed division of the Northwest Territories into two regions for administrative purposes. Canada's Minister of Indian Affairs and Northern Development David E. Crombie urged a division by 1987. In January 1985, two constitutional forums representing the western and eastern Arctic regions proposed a tentative boundary line. This boundary would start north of the Saskatchewan border and run northwest to the delta of the Mackenzie River on the Beaufort Sea. The division would create two political jurisdictions—an ethnic homeland for the Inuit (Eskimo) population of the eastern Arctic and another for the mixture of Dene (Indians), *métis* (persons of mixed white and Indian descent), Inuit, and whites living in the oil- and gas-bearing lands to the west.

Of the 50,900 people in the Northwest Territories, two-thirds live in the west. Four Inuit communities in the central Arctic were unhappy with the proposal, finding themselves pulled by sentiment to the east but by economic ties to the west.

On October 21, the 24 members of the territorial legislative assembly elected Nick Sibbeston leader of the territorial cabinet. Sibbeston, 42, was a métis lawyer from Fort Simpson.   David M. L. Farr

See also CANADA. In WORLD BOOK, see NORTHWEST TERRITORIES.

NORWAY. Prime Minister Kaare Willoch's Conservative-led coalition government held on by one seat in general elections on Sept. 8 and 9, 1985. The Labor Party increased its share of the vote by 4 per cent, a triumph for its leader, Gro Harlem Brundtland. Labor had campaigned vigorously, especially in rural areas that did not benefit from the North Sea oil boom. Labor candidates attacked Willoch's record on health and social services, calling him "uncaring."

Willoch admitted after the election that his policy of curbing welfare benefits cost him votes. His coalition partners, the Center and Christian People's parties, said that they would press for less restraint on government spending on health and welfare.

Willoch, who became prime minister in 1981, campaigned on his record of having cut personal taxation and of reducing inflation from 12 to 5.5 per cent. He promised that by the end of 1985, Norway would have zero unemployment among workers under 20 years of age.

Soviet Missile. On Dec. 28, 1984, a Soviet missile, believed to be an SN-3, a type the Soviets use for target practice, flew over Norway and crashed in Finland. On Jan. 4, 1985, Norway and Finland announced that they had received apologies from the Soviet Union. The incident led Norway to reappraise its air defense.

Gas Plan Fails. A $30-billion deal to export gas from Norway's Sleipner field in the North Sea to Great Britain in the 1990's fell through on February 11, when the British government rejected it. Britain said that its own gas reserves were adequate.

On January 14, Norway defied the Organization of Petroleum Exporting Countries (OPEC) by abandoning fixed prices for its North Sea oil and moving to a system linked to *spot*, or noncontract, markets. This effectively cut the oil price from the OPEC figure of $28.65 per barrel to $27.20.

Spy Trial. Norway's biggest spy trial opened on February 25 when a former Labor Party politician and diplomat, Arne Treholt, was charged with working for the Soviet Union. On June 20, he was found guilty and sentenced to 20 years in prison. The court also confiscated $52,000 from a Swiss bank account and an additional $81,000 that Treholt had received from the Soviets.

Stable Economy. In January, the 24-nation Organization for Economic Cooperation and Development (OECD) praised Norway's management of its economy. The OECD said the rapid growth of Norway's oil revenues had enabled the government to subsidize businesses to support employment without creating problems with the balance of payments or national debt.   Kenneth Brown

See also EUROPE (Facts in Brief Table). In WORLD BOOK, see NORWAY.

NOVA SCOTIA felt the harsh effects of the Canadian government's cost-cutting measures in 1985. On May 23, federal budget cuts were announced. They included the immediate closing of two government-owned plants on Cape Breton Island that made *heavy water* (a chemical compound used in some nuclear reactors as a coolant and to help control the energy of a nuclear reaction). The two plants had employed more than 600 people on the impoverished island, plagued by an unemployment rate of 27 per cent. The plants had required huge federal subsidies for years.

The federal government in May offered companies starting new businesses on Cape Breton Island a 10-year exemption from federal income taxes. The government also provided grants to rebuild a burned-out fish-processing plant, improve a pulp and paper mill, and excavate a new tunnel in a Cape Breton coal mine. Premier John Buchanan on March 29 signed a tentative agreement for the developers of a natural gas field off Sable Island, Nova Scotia, to supply the Northeastern United States with about 300 million cubic feet (8.5 million cubic meters) of natural gas per day within five years.   David M. L. Farr

In WORLD BOOK, see NOVA SCOTIA.

NUCLEAR ENERGY. See ENERGY SUPPLY. In the Special Reports section, see NUCLEAR POWER AT THE CROSSROADS.

NUTRITION. A panel of United States medical experts reported in April 1985 that high blood cholesterol is a major cause of heart disease and that diet should be considered the primary means of both treating and preventing heart disease. The panel had been convened in December 1984 by the National Institutes of Health (NIH) in Bethesda, Md., to study the evidence and reach a consensus about blood cholesterol and heart disease, a focal point of much research and controversy over the years. In the United States, heart disease causes more than 500,000 deaths each year.

The consensus statement adopted by the panel was published in the April 12, 1985, issue of *The Journal of the American Medical Association*. It asserted that blood cholesterol levels of most Americans are undesirably high. The federal advisory panel recommended a diet lower in total fat, saturated fat, and cholesterol for everyone except infants under 2 years old—not just for those people whose higher blood cholesterol levels put them at greater risk of heart disease.

Their specific dietary recommendations were to reduce total fat intake from about 40 per cent of total calories to 30 per cent and restrict cholesterol intake to 250 to 300 milligrams a day. To comply with these guidelines, most people would have to eat more vegetables, fruits, and starches; fewer

Food scientists concerned with reducing salt in food try a low-sodium hot dog recipe at a U.S. government laboratory in Philadelphia.

fatty meats, whole milk dairy products, and egg yolks; and less of all types of fat.

The NIH panel urged people to have their blood cholesterol levels checked by their physicians and to ask for the results. The recommended levels are approximately 180 milligrams of cholesterol per deciliter of blood for adults under age 30, and 200 milligrams of cholesterol for those 30 and older.

In addition, the panel urged the food industry to develop and market more-healthful foods; offer foods lower in fat and cholesterol in restaurants and fast-food outlets; and specify fat and cholesterol content more clearly on food labels.

Hazards of Obesity. Obesity is a killing disease that causes chronic illnesses and premature death, according to a 14-member panel of experts at an NIH meeting in February. The researchers noted that in addition to creating a psychological burden, obesity is clearly associated with high blood pressure, high blood cholesterol, diabetes, certain cancers, and other medical problems.

Using Metropolitan Life Insurance Company tables as guidelines for desirable weight, the panel cited studies indicating that people most likely to live longest are slightly below the desirable weight for their age and height. The experts concluded that any amount of overweight, even 5 to 10 pounds (2.3 to 4.5 kilograms), may be hazardous,

and that people who are 20 per cent or more overweight should try to reduce. Panel Chairman Jules Hirsch, an obesity researcher at Rockefeller University in New York City, said the evidence indicates that adverse health effects decline when obese people lose weight.

Dietary Guidelines and Allowances. A new version of *The Dietary Guidelines* was released in September 1985 by the U.S. Department of Agriculture and the Department of Health and Human Services. It was almost identical to the edition published in 1980. The new guidelines urged Americans to eat a variety of foods; maintain desirable weight; avoid too much fat, saturated fat, cholesterol, sugar, and sodium; eat foods with adequate starch and fiber; and drink alcoholic beverages only in moderation, if at all.

A revision of the 1980 Recommended Dietary Allowances (RDA's) of nutrients, such as vitamins and minerals, had been expected in 1985. RDA's are widely used in public food programs and in the food industry and need approval by the National Academy of Sciences before they become official. The scientists charged with proposing and reviewing the RDA's could not reach agreement on new standards, and in October the RDA revision was postponed indefinitely.   Jean Weininger

See also FOOD. In WORLD BOOK, see DIET; FOOD; NUTRITION.

OCEAN. The Ocean Drilling Program (ODP), a 10-year scientific research project, began its first expedition in January 1985. A new drill ship, the *JOIDES Resolution* (officially registered as *Sedco/BP 471*), will drill sites chosen by JOIDES (*Joint Oceanographic Institutions for Deep Earth Sampling*), an international scientific organization. The purpose of the ODP is to answer questions about the ages and origins of the ocean basins.

A spring cruise made by the *Resolution* in the Atlantic Ocean provided evidence that Europe, Africa, and North America were once a single continent. About 110 million years ago, the area between Spain and Newfoundland began to tear apart, creating what is now the Atlantic Ocean.

To learn more about this tear, scientists aboard the *Resolution* drilled 12 holes off the coast of Spain. The deepest hole reached 1,600 feet (500 meters) below the sea floor, which is under 15,500 feet (4,700 meters) of water. Cores of sediment and rock taken from the holes revealed that a shallow, muddy sea flooded the area 150 million years ago. Oysters, small snails, and corals thrived for 10 million years. As they died, their shells became embedded in limestone on the sea floor.

Some 140 million years ago, the upper part of Earth's crust stretched, thinned, and broke. Enormous faults formed under the sea. The sea floor sank to great depths along these faults. Huge

Finding the Legendary *Titanic*

The team of United States and French oceanic researchers had wanted to keep their find a secret until returning to port. But within hours, the world had heard the news: On Sept. 1, 1985, the group discovered the hulk of the British luxury liner *Titanic*, unseen since the night in 1912 when it sank into the icy depths of the North Atlantic Ocean.

The huge ship was located by a sophisticated new remote-control submarine, the *Argo*. The automobile-sized vessel, equipped with video and still cameras, is owned by the U.S. Navy and operated by Woods Hole Oceanographic Institution in Massachusetts. When the Navy asked Woods Hole scientists to test the *Argo*, researchers decided to use the cable-towed craft to search for the *Titanic*. French scientists agreed to participate in the quest.

The ocean liner—which struck an iceberg on the night of April 14-15, 1912, during its first voyage, from England to New York City—was known to have sunk somewhere south of Newfoundland. The exact location was not known, though, because the distress signal radioed from the *Titanic* on the fateful night gave inexact geographic information.

The research team sailed to the North Atlantic in mid-August 1985 aboard the Woods Hole research vessel *Knorr*, the *Argo*'s mother ship. The investigators towed the *Argo* in an area where the French scientists, who earlier had combed the sea floor with sonar, believed they had found the *Titanic*. On September 1, the researchers hit the jackpot. Pictures taken by the *Argo* showed the nearly intact liner sitting upright on the ocean floor about 12,000 feet (3,660 meters) below the surface.

The *Argo* and an older remote-control craft, the *Angus*, took hundreds of feet of videotape and more than 12,000 color photographs of the wreck. The pictures revealed that the stern of the *Titanic* broke off when the ship went down. Other images showed the ocean floor littered with cargo, luggage, wine bottles, and other items, most likely blown out of the hull when the boilers exploded. Of the approximately 1,500 people who perished with the ship, there was no sign.

The finding of the *Titanic* renewed speculation about salvaging the riches that supposedly rest inside the hulk. Many of the passengers were wealthy, and the ship's safe held diamonds and other valuables worth millions of dollars. Some historians, however, think that most such items were hurriedly retrieved by their owners as the vessel began to sink.

The director of the discovery team, Woods Hole oceanographer Robert D. Ballard, said the extreme depth of the wreck would make it all but impossible to carry out a successful salvage operation. Besides, he said, it would be more fitting for the *Titanic* to be left in peace as a memorial to its victims.

David L. Dreier

Anchor chains are clearly visible on the *Titanic*'s bow section as it lies on the floor of the North Atlantic Ocean.

Mel Fisher, left, toasts his son, Kane—holding a bar of silver—after discovering a fabulous sunken treasure off the coast of Florida in July.

masses of sand and mud, some containing fragments of plants, slid off the edge of the continent, burying the limestone.

The sea floor sank rapidly for about 25 million years. During the past 110 million years, the floor has sunk much more slowly and has accumulated sediment and ooze formed by the skeletons of microscopic organisms that live near the surface.

Link with Atmosphere. On Jan. 1, 1985, researchers began the Tropical Ocean and Global Atmosphere (TOGA) project, one of the largest international scientific experiments ever. For 10 years, scientists will study how the behavior of the tropical oceans is linked to that of the atmosphere.

***Titanic* Found.** An expedition of French and United States scientists led by marine geologist and geophysicist Robert D. Ballard of Woods Hole Oceanographic Institution in Massachusetts announced in September 1985 that it had found the luxury liner *Titanic*. The supposedly unsinkable ship struck an iceberg just before midnight on April 14, 1912, and sank 2½ hours later. More than 1,500 people died.

The French research ship *Suroit* and the U.S. craft *Knorr* found the wreck in waters about 12,000 feet (3,700 meters) deep about 560 miles (900 kilometers) off the coast of Newfoundland. The *Suroit* used a device called a side-scanning sonar, which bounces sound waves off underwater objects. The *Knorr* employed an unpiloted submarine equipped with stroboscopic lights and television cameras. See Close-Up.

Sunken Treasure. An extraordinary adventurer, 62-year-old Mel Fisher, ended his 16-year quest for the wreckage of the Spanish galleon *Nuestra Señora de Atocha* on July 20. On that day, in waters only 54 feet (16 meters) deep, 40 miles (64 kilometers) west of Key West, Fla., his diving team discovered what may be the most valuable sunken treasure ever found—gold, silver, and jewels worth perhaps $400 million. The *Atocha* was headed from Havana, Cuba, to Cadiz, Spain, when it sank during a hurricane in 1622.

Still in IOC. The United States in January 1985 quit the United Nations Educational, Scientific and Cultural Organization (UNESCO), the parent body of the Intergovernmental Oceanographic Commission (IOC). The United States maintained its membership in the IOC, however. At the IOC General Assembly in March 1985, the United States announced that it expected to give the IOC the same amount of money the IOC would have received from a normal U.S. contribution to UNESCO.   Arthur G. Alexiou

In WORLD BOOK, see OCEAN.

OHIO. See STATE GOVERNMENT.

OKLAHOMA. See STATE GOVERNMENT.

OLD AGE. See SOCIAL SECURITY.

OLYMPIC GAMES. The National Broadcasting Company (NBC) in 1985 won the United States television rights to the 1988 Summer Olympic Games to be held in Seoul, South Korea. In October 1985, NBC agreed to pay at least $300 million and up to $500 million to the Olympic organizing committee.

The organizing committee had hoped that the rights would bring from $500 million to $750 million. Instead, NBC originally offered $325 million; CBS Inc., $300 million; and American Broadcasting Companies (ABC), $225 million. The committee rejected these bids and reopened the bidding. NBC reduced its guarantee to $300-million, but it won the rights when it promised the committee an additional sum of up to $200 million from ad revenues. The networks were apprehensive because the 14-hour time difference between Seoul and New York City will prevent many important events from being shown during prime evening hours in the United States.

In February 1985, the executive board of the International Olympic Committee voted to allow professional athletes in tennis, ice hockey, and soccer under the age of 23 to compete for the first time in the Olympic Games, beginning with the 1988 Winter Games.   Frank Litsky

In WORLD BOOK, see OLYMPIC GAMES.

OMAN. See MIDDLE EAST.

ONTARIO. Canada's most populous province saw dramatic political change in 1985. After almost 42 years of uninterrupted power, the Progressive Conservative (PC) Party was swept out of office by an alliance between the Liberal and New Democratic parties. David Peterson, Liberal Party leader since 1982, became the new premier on June 26 (see PETERSON, DAVID).

Conservatives' Downfall. The trigger for this overthrow was the resignation of William Davis, PC premier for 14 years. On January 26, the Conservatives chose Frank Miller to succeed Davis. Miller, a veteran government minister who had served under Davis, was sworn in as premier on February 8. Miller's right wing position on economic and social questions did not sit well with all sections of the party. Hampered by disunity, the Conservatives went into a general election on May 2 and lost 20 seats and their majority in the 125-seat Legislative Assembly, retaining only 52 seats. The Liberals gained 20 seats for a total of 48, and the New Democratic Party (NDP) had 25.

After the election, the Liberals and NDP joined forces in the Assembly to defeat the Miller government. The NDP promised not to call a no-confidence vote against a Liberal government for two years, and the Liberals agreed not to seek another election for the same period. The two parties then defeated the Miller government in a no-confi-

dence vote on June 18. Peterson formed a Liberal government, and was sworn in as Ontario's 20th premier on June 26.

Miller announced in August that he would resign as PC leader. On November 16, Larry Grossman, education minister under Miller, was elected to replace him as party leader.

Catholic School Funding. Peterson's Liberal government continued efforts begun by PC Premier Davis to extend government financing to the upper grades of Roman Catholic secondary schools. The schools received their first government checks in December. Meanwhile, the government had asked the courts to rule whether the funding violated Canada's Charter of Rights and Freedoms.

Other Developments. Prime Minister Brian Mulroney in September appointed Lincoln MacCauley Alexander to be Ontario's 24th lieutenant governor. Alexander, a lawyer and former labor minister, became the first black to hold the post of lieutenant governor—Ontario's constitutional representative of the monarch.

In the worst natural disaster in Ontario since 1954, tornadoes hit the south-central part of the province on May 31. The twisters killed 12 people and injured about 400.   David M. L. Farr

In WORLD BOOK, see ONTARIO.

OPERA. See CLASSICAL MUSIC.

OREGON. See STATE GOVERNMENT.

ORTEGA, DANIEL (1945-   ), took office as president of Nicaragua on Jan. 10, 1985. Cuban President Fidel Castro was the only head of state to attend the inauguration, a reflection of Nicaragua's growing isolation in Latin America, according to some observers. See NICARAGUA.

Ortega was born on Nov. 11, 1945, in the town of La Libertad, 110 miles (180 kilometers) northwest of Nicaragua's capital city, Managua. His parents were middle-class merchants.

The new president's political activism began at the age of 15 when he was arrested as a member of a group that called for revolution against the dictatorship of Nicaragua's Somoza family. In the early 1960's, Ortega attended Central American University in Managua and was jailed several times for leading student protests.

In the mid-1960's, Ortega joined the Sandinista National Liberation Front and became an urban guerrilla, robbing banks to raise money for his cause. In 1967, he was arrested for bank robbery and was jailed for seven years. He was released in December 1974 in exchange for hostages seized by a Sandinista group. When the Sandinistas overthrew President Anastasio Somoza Debayle in 1979, Ortega emerged as a national leader.

Ortega's brother Humberto is minister of defense. Another brother, Camilo, was killed by Somoza's National Guard in 1978.   Rod Such

PACIFIC ISLANDS continued to grapple with issues concerning nuclear weapons in 1985. Nuclear testing by France at Mururoa Atoll in French Polynesia, a sore point with island nations since the tests began in 1966, held the spotlight through much of the year. On July 10, bombs ripped through the *Rainbow Warrior*, a ship owned by the Greenpeace environmental group that was about to sail from Auckland, New Zealand, to Mururoa to protest the tests. Two French secret service agents were later found to be involved in the bombing, which killed a Greenpeace photographer. See FRANCE.

On August 6, 8 of the 13 member-nations of the South Pacific Forum signed a treaty declaring the South Pacific a nuclear-free zone. France continued nuclear testing at Mururoa, however. Greenpeace protests continued also.

On March 13, the Administration of United States President Ronald Reagan agreed to clean up Bikini Atoll, in the Marshall Islands, which had been contaminated by radioactivity from U.S. nuclear bomb tests made between 1946 and 1958. The agreement, which lacked congressional approval at year's end, was part of the settlement of a lawsuit brought against the United States by residents of Bikini who had been evacuated from the atoll in 1946 and wished to return home.

Papua New Guinea got a new government on November 21 when Paias Wingti replaced Prime Minister Michael Thomas Somare. The change of government came as a result of Somare's loss of a parliamentary no-confidence vote. Wingti, a 34-year-old New Guinea highlander, inherited a shaky economy, a rising foreign debt, and a severe law-and-order problem in Port Moresby, the capital. He also faced the vexing issue of about 10,000 Melanesian refugees living in camps just inside his country's border with Irian Jaya, the western half of New Guinea ruled by Indonesia. Most of the refugees had fled Irian Jaya after an unsuccessful revolt against Indonesian rule in 1984. Wingti promised to cut government spending, reduce the bureaucracy, and limit ministerial travel and allowances.

Local Political Developments. President Haruo I. Remeliik of Belau (formerly Palau) was shot and killed on June 30. No motive for the slaying was apparent. Four men arrested in connection with the murder were later released for lack of evidence. Vice President Alfonso R. Oiterong took over as acting president. In elections held on August 28, Senator Lazarus Salii was elected president of Belau.

In Western Samoa, the Human Rights Protection Party of Prime Minister Tofilau Eti Alesana retained power in elections held on February 23.

Demonstrators in New Caledonia use a wrecked car as a barricade during clashes in January between groups demanding and opposing independence from France.

Facts in Brief on Pacific Island Countries

Country	Population	Government	Monetary Unit*	Foreign Trade (million U.S. $) Exports†	Imports†
Australia	15,924,000	Governor General Sir Ninian Martin Stephen; Prime Minister Robert Hawke	dollar (1.5 = $1)	23,774	26,468
Fiji	697,000	Governor General Sir Penaia Ganilau; Prime Minister Sir Kamisese Mara	dollar (1.1 = $1)	256	450
Kiribati	63,000	President Ieremia Tabai	Australian dollar	3	14
Nauru	8,000	President Hammer DeRoburt	Australian dollar	75	11
New Zealand	3,315,000	Governor General Sir Paul Reeves; Prime Minister David R. Lange	dollar (1.7 = $1)	5,517	6,195
Papua New Guinea	3,506,000	Governor General Sir Kingsford Dibela; Prime Minister Paias Wingti	kina (1 = $1.01)	915	966
Solomon Islands	283,000	Governor General Sir Baddeley Devesi; Prime Minister Sir Peter Kenilorea	dollar (1.56 = $1)	61	61
Tonga	110,000	King Taufa'ahau Tupou IV; Prime Minister Prince Fatafehi Tu'ipelehake	pa'anga (1.47 = $1)	6	38
Tuvalu	8,000	Governor General Sir Fiatau Penitala Teo; Prime Minister Tomasi Puapua	Australian dollar	0.3	2.8
Vanuatu	137,000	President Ati George Sokomanu; Prime Minister Walter H. Lini	vatu (104 = $1)	44	67
Western Samoa	164,000	Head of State Malietoa Tanumafili II; Prime Minister Va'ai Kolone	tala (2.17 = $1)	20	50

*Exchange rates as of Dec. 1, 1985, or latest available data.   †Latest available data.

Alesana's party emerged with a majority of 15 seats in the 47-seat Legislative Assembly.

In the Cook Islands, a self-governing dependency of New Zealand, the coalition government of Prime Minister Sir Thomas Davis of the Democratic Party was weakened in August when four of the eight Cook Islands Party members in the government withdrew their support. The leader of the four, Geoffrey A. Henry, was replaced as deputy prime minister by Terepai Maoate, also of the Cook Islands Party.

Soviet Fishing Agreement. Despite strong protests by Australia, New Zealand, and the United States, the House of Assembly (parliament) of Kiribati ratified an agreement signed on August 18 giving the Soviet Union fishing rights in Kiribati waters for an annual fee of $1.5 million. The agreement allows 16 Soviet vessels to operate in the 200-nautical-mile (370-kilometer) zone surrounding the Gilbert, Phoenix, and Line islands. The Soviets will not be allowed to enter the 12-nautical-mile (22.2-kilometer) territorial zone surrounding the islands. It was widely assumed that the Soviet fishing boats would also be used for intelligence gathering. The government of Kiribati President Ieremia Tabai survived a no-confidence vote on the agreement in late August.

Sovereignty Agreement. In 1985, the U.S. Congress approved and President Reagan signed an agreement—called the Compact of Free Association—that would end United States trusteeship of the Federated States of Micronesia and the Marshall Islands. The compact recognizes the islands' rights to self-government but provides for continued United States control of military affairs. It also includes an estimated $2.4 billion in economic aid for the islands, certain tax and trade preferences, and a 30-year continuation of the United States lease of a missile-testing range on Kwajalein Atoll in the Marshall Islands. The lease had been a point of contention between the United States and local landowners who wanted to raise rents.

Before the compact goes into effect, it must be endorsed by island governments and the United Nations. Micronesian government representatives had signed a draft compact in 1982. Island leaders were angered in 1985, however, by amendments that were added by the U.S. House of Representatives that would limit the islands' control of fishing rights in their territorial waters. The Reagan Administration and Congress were hopeful, however, that island governments would endorse the compact in its final form.   Robert Langdon

See also NEW CALEDONIA; NEW ZEALAND. In WORLD BOOK, see PACIFIC ISLANDS; PACIFIC ISLANDS, TRUST TERRITORY OF THE.

PAINTING. See VISUAL ARTS.

PAKISTAN elected a National Assembly on Feb. 25, 1985. The military government of President M. Zia-ul-Haq barred political parties from campaigning. Opposition groups called the election a sham and urged a boycott, but the government claimed that 52 per cent of the voters turned out. The voters showed their independence and their disapproval of Zia's administration, however, by defeating six Cabinet ministers and many members of the old Federal Advisory Council, a consultant group hand-picked by Zia. The voters also unseated a number of Islamic fundamentalists.

Governmental Changes. On March 2, Zia announced amendments to the 1973 Constitution, which had made Pakistan a parliamentary democracy. The amendments increased presidential power and reduced the authority of the prime minister to handling routine administration.

At an inaugural session of the National Assembly on March 23, Zia was sworn in as a civilian president, instead of martial law ruler. He named Mohammed Khan Junejo as prime minister. The Assembly rejected Zia's choice for speaker, instead naming Fakr Imam.

Junejo and a nonpartisan group of about two-thirds of the Assembly members presented a bill validating Zia's constitutional changes. The bill was to ensure that a civilian government could not punish Zia for any of his martial law actions since he seized power in 1977. An independent group in the Assembly opposed the bill, leading to extensive debate. After modifying it, the Assembly passed the bill unanimously on Oct. 16, 1985.

Addressing the Assembly on October 17, Zia repeated his intention to give Pakistan an Islamic system of government based on the Koran, the holy book of Islam. The Assembly weakened a number of Islamic measures, however.

On December 30, Zia announced an end to martial law. He retained great power as president and army chief of staff, however.

Karachi Riots. An estimated 100 people died in six days of riots in Karachi, Pakistan's largest city, on April 15. Touched off by a traffic accident, the riots expressed economic and social tensions among the city's 5 million people. Bangalee and Afghan refugees clashed with each other, the area's original inhabitants, and Punjabis.

The Economy slowed during 1985. Drought hurt wheat crops, and exports lagged. Money sent home by Pakistanis working in the Persian Gulf region declined because of a recession there. A steel plant built with Soviet aid opened on January 15 near Karachi, but its output cost 40 per cent more than imported steel.   Henry S. Bradsher

See also ASIA (Facts in Brief Table). In WORLD BOOK, see PAKISTAN.

Pakistan's President M. Zia-ul-Haq casts his vote in Rawalpindi, Pakistan, on February 25 in elections for a new National Assembly.

PALEONTOLOGY. In October 1985, chemists from the University of Chicago reported that a vast fire storm ignited by the impact of a meteorite may have swept across Earth 65 million years ago, contributing to the mass extinction of dinosaurs and many other groups of animals. The scientists—Wendy S. Wolbach, Roy S. Lewis, and Edward Anders—based their conclusions on the discovery of soot particles in 65-million-year-old sediment from Spain, Denmark, and New Zealand. The discovery provides support for the theory that a mass extinction 65 million years ago was caused by the collision of a giant comet or asteroid with Earth.

The scientists theorized that the soot particles did not come from the meteorite itself. Instead, they believe it is more likely that heat generated by the impact ignited wildfires that swept across the continents. Even if the meteorite fell into the sea, the scientists said, the heat would have been great enough to set off fires on land hundreds of miles away. In the Special Reports section, see DOOMSDAY FOR THE DINOSAURS.

Dinosaur Finds. The discovery of the skeleton of what is believed to be the oldest known dinosaur was reported in May 1985 by a team of scientists from the University of California, Berkeley. Found in the Painted Desert of Arizona, the skeleton is believed to be about 225 million years old, 3 million to 4 million years older than any other dinosaur fossil ever discovered. The animal, which weighed about 200 pounds (91 kilograms), was about 7 to 8 feet (2 to 2.4 meters) long.

The discovery in Texas of a large deposit of fossil bones from dinosaurs that lived more than 100 million years ago was announced in July by paleontologists Louis Jacobs of Southern Methodist University in Dallas and Phillip Murray of Tarleton State University in Stephenville, Tex. Few dinosaur fossils from this period have been found.

Tarsier Fossil Found. In February, a team of scientists headed by paleontologist Elwyn L. Simons of Duke University in Durham, N.C., reported finding a fragment of the lower jaw of a tarsier—a small, nocturnal primate about the size of a chipmunk—believed to be from 30 million to 40 million years old. The fossil, found near Cairo, Egypt, was the first tarsier fossil discovered in Africa. Tarsier fossils of that age had previously been found in North America, Europe, and Asia. The Egyptian tarsier fossil is expected to provide scientists with new information about the origin and spread of these primitive primates.

Largest Known Cambrian Animal. In May, paleontologists Harold B. Whittington of Cambridge University in England and Derek E. G. Briggs of the University of London published the first detailed description of *Anomalocaris*, the largest known animal from the Cambrian Period, a geological period that ended about 550 million years ago. *Anomalocaris*, which measured about 20 inches (50 centimeters) long, is one of the few known predators of that time. Whittington and Briggs reported that *Anomalocaris* cannot be placed in any known animal phylum, though in some ways it resembles *arthropods*—a group of animals that includes spiders, beetles, and crabs.

Soft-Bodied Animals. The discovery of a rare collection of fossils of soft-bodied animals near Milwaukee was reported in May by a team of paleontologists headed by Donald G. Mikulic of the Illinois State Geological Survey in Champaign. The scientists found the fossils, which represent many types of soft-bodied marine animals, in rocks about 430 million years old. Because soft tissue usually decays rapidly, only a few fossils of soft-bodied animals have been found.

One of the fossils may be that of an early relative of the horseshoe crab. Another has a round leechlike sucker and may be that of the earliest known leech. The scientists also reported finding the fossil of a conodont animal, a small animal with an eel-shaped body. Although the teeth of conodont animals are common in rocks from 190 million to 500 million years old, only one fossil of the entire animal had been found previously, near Edinburgh, Scotland.   Ida Thompson

In WORLD BOOK, see DINOSAUR; PALEONTOLOGY.

PANAMA. A bizarre chapter in Panama's history unfolded at 2:30 A.M. on Sept. 28, 1985, when Nicolás Ardito Barletta Vallarina, the country's first elected president since 1968, announced his resignation after less than a year in office.

He was succeeded by First Vice President Eric Arturo Delvalle, who was sworn in later that same day. The 48-year-old Delvalle is a leading member of Panama's right wing Republican Party, comprised mainly of business people.

Ardito Barletta had run afoul of Panama's all-powerful armed forces by hinting that he might appoint a commission to investigate the brutal killing of Hugo Spadafora, an outspoken critic of the military. The tortured and decapitated body of Spadafora, a physician and political activist, was found on September 14 in Costa Rica. Strong circumstantial evidence pointed to Panama's army.

General Manuel Antonio Noriega, army commander and Panama's strongman, was reportedly incensed that Ardito Barletta might investigate a crime in which Panama's military was likely to be involved. Ardito Barletta reportedly resisted resigning at first but gave in after 14 hours of confinement and threats.   Nathan A. Haverstock

See also LATIN AMERICA (Facts in Brief Table). In WORLD BOOK, see PANAMA.

PAPUA NEW GUINEA. See ASIA; PACIFIC ISLANDS.

PARAGUAY. See LATIN AMERICA.

PAZ ESTENSSORO, VÍCTOR (1907-   ), became president of Bolivia for the fourth time on Aug. 5, 1985. Bolivia's Congress selected Paz Estenssoro to succeed Hernán Siles Zuazo after none of the 18 candidates in a July general election captured a majority of the popular vote.

Paz Estenssoro was born into a landowning family on Oct. 2, 1907, in Tarija in south-central Bolivia. He studied law and economics at the Higher Bolivian University of San Andrés in La Paz, Bolivia's capital, and became a professor of economic history at La Paz University in 1939. In 1942, along with Siles Zuazo and labor leader Juan Lechín, he founded a political party called the National Revolutionary Movement. In 1952, the party overthrew Bolivia's military rulers, and Paz Estenssoro returned from exile in Argentina to be president. During his first term, the government took ownership of the largest tin mines and broke up large estates, distributing the land to farmers. Paz Estenssoro was reelected in 1960 and 1964, but his third term was cut short by a coup.

During his long career, Paz Estenssoro was forced into exile three times. He taught economics in Peru in the late 1960's, and during another period of exile in the United States in the late 1970's, he taught history at universities in California and New Mexico.   Rod Such

PENNSYLVANIA. See PHILADELPHIA; STATE GOV'T.

PERU. On July 28, 1985, Alan García Pérez, the charismatic 36-year-old leader of the left-of-center American Popular Revolutionary Alliance, took office as president of Peru. At his inaugural, García issued a challenge to the existing world economic system, declaring that Peru would limit payments on its staggering $14-billion foreign debt to 10 per cent of its export earnings over the next 12 months. García said that in renegotiating its debt, Peru would deal directly with its creditors without consulting the International Monetary Fund (IMF), an agency of the United Nations. The new Peruvian president characterized the IMF as an "accomplice" in his nation's acute financial predicament.

"Alan García has been elected by 20 million Peruvians," he told a crowd in Lima, the capital, "and not by international bank officials. Peru has one overwhelming creditor: It is our own people."

As García took office, Peru's unemployment rate was running at 50 per cent in many areas. The value of wages was so eroded by inflation that the average worker's buying power was down 60 per cent from 1975 levels. Frequent strikes paralyzed the economy.

Economic Reforms. The new chief executive promised governmental reform to help solve Peru's economic woes. To trim the cost of government, he reduced the salaries of top officials, including his own. The salary of the head of the government-owned oil company was slashed from $10,000 per month to $1,000. To bring in sorely needed dollars, García put up for sale diplomatic sites that Peru owns in the United States. He also cut back Peru's order for Mirage fighter planes from France. He vowed a campaign against corruption, particularly in the police force, and fired 37 police generals. He also pledged to work with neighboring Colombia to end trade in illegal drugs.

Guerrilla Campaign. The new president also faced serious obstacles from left wing guerrillas. In an effort to end a five-year guerrilla war, he announced during his inaugural speech that he would seek negotiations with the Maoist guerrilla group Sendero Luminoso (Shining Path). He held out the promise of pardon for those "who return to democracy."

Although the terrorist group ignored the peace offer, García followed through on a pledge to end the human rights abuses that marked the previous government's campaign against the guerrillas. On September 18, two generals were removed after an investigation showed that government soldiers killed about 40 peasants in August in an area where guerrillas were active.   Nathan A. Haverstock

See also GARCÍA PÉREZ, ALAN; LATIN AMERICA (Facts in Brief Table). In WORLD BOOK, see PERU.
PET. See CAT; DOG.

PETERSON, DAVID ROBERT (1943-   ), leader of Ontario's Liberal Party, was sworn in as the province's 20th premier on June 26, 1985. He succeeded Frank Miller of the Progressive Conservative Party (PC). Peterson came to power after Liberal and New Democratic Party members of Ontario's Legislative Assembly joined in a vote of no confidence on June 18. The vote forced Miller's government to resign, ending nearly 42 consecutive years of PC rule in Ontario. See ONTARIO.

Peterson was born in Toronto on Dec. 29, 1943, and grew up in London, Ont. He received a bachelor's degree in philosophy and political science from the University of Western Ontario in 1964 and a law degree from the University of Toronto in 1967. While attending law school, Peterson served as director of a volunteer legal aid service in Toronto. After graduation, he ran his father's electronics business in London.

Peterson was first elected to Ontario's legislature in 1975 as member for London Centre. He was reelected in 1977 and 1981. In 1982, Peterson was elected leader of Ontario's Liberal Party.

Peterson comes from a political family. His father served as an alderman in London. His brother, Jim, is a former Liberal Party member of the federal House of Commons. Peterson married actress Shelley Christine Matthews in 1974. They have three children.   Robie Liscomb

PETROLEUM AND GAS. Sharp disagreement among members of the Organization of Petroleum Exporting Countries (OPEC) in 1985 forced the 13-nation oil cartel to loosen its economic stranglehold on the world's oil supply. OPEC members failed several times during the year to agree on new quotas that would have reduced production in member states.

Saudi Arabia urged such a reduction to help end a persistent world oversupply of oil and to shore up sliding oil prices. Instead, OPEC members—faced with severe budget problems due to plunging oil revenues—moved to establish their own individual production and pricing policies. The actions ended the uniform-pricing policy, in which members sold oil at a predetermined price.

At an OPEC meeting held from July 5 to 7 in Vienna, Austria, Saudi Arabia announced that it would no longer serve as the cartel's "swing producer," the country willing to reduce its oil production to support prices fixed by the cartel. During 1985, Saudi Arabia had cut its oil output to 2.5 million barrels per day (bpd), the lowest level since 1965, in an effort to maintain prices at the level set by OPEC. At another OPEC meeting, held on October 3 and 4, Saudi Oil Minister Sheik Ahmed Zaki Yamani acknowledged that his country had begun offering price discounts on crude oil in violation of the cartel's rules.

Saudi Arabia in September began a steep increase in oil production aimed at raising oil output by perhaps 1.5 million bpd. Oil industry analysts said that a major share of the increase, perhaps 850,000 bpd, was to be sold to United States oil companies at a price substantially below the official OPEC price of $28 per barrel.

On December 8, OPEC oil ministers meeting in Geneva, Switzerland, agreed to abandon the cartel's official price of $28 per barrel. They announced that the cartel would instead seek to protect a fixed share of the oil market by matching the lower prices charged by other oil exporters. OPEC called on Great Britain and other non-OPEC oil exporters to reduce their output or risk a price war. On December 10, Great Britain formally refused the OPEC request, increasing the possibility of a worldwide price war in 1986.

U.S. Reserves. The U.S. Department of Energy (DOE) reported on September 4 that proven reserves of crude oil in the United States increased during 1984 for the first time since 1970. According to the DOE, crude oil reserves stood at 28.4 billion barrels, an increase of 711 million barrels, or 2.6 per cent, from 1984. The increase was primarily due to the introduction of enhanced oil-recovery techniques that allow greater production of oil from existing fields. New offshore discoveries in California added 131 million barrels to the total. The last increase in crude oil reserves, in 1970, occurred as a result of discoveries in Alaska's Prudhoe Bay oil field, the largest in North America.

The DOE also said that in 1984 natural gas reserves declined by 1.4 per cent, or about 2.8 trillion cubic feet (79 billion cubic meters), reaching their lowest level since 1976. Natural gas reserves in 1984 totaled 197.5 trillion cubic feet (5.6 trillion cubic meters). The amount of new natural gas discovered in 1984 increased by 18.1 per cent, or 13.5 trillion cubic feet (382 billion cubic meters), but it was insufficient to offset increased use.

Court Action. A federal appeals court on July 1 upheld a 1983 ruling ordering Exxon Corporation to pay about $1.9 billion for overcharging customers who bought oil produced from 1975 through 1980 at an Exxon field near Tyler, Tex. The judgment resulted from charges brought against Exxon by the DOE. The agency accused Exxon of violating the complex system of government price controls that were in effect until January 1981. Similar charges were pending in about 450 other cases. Citing the difficulty in identifying each person overcharged by Exxon, the court ordered that the government collect the fine and distribute it to the states to fund energy-conservation programs and help poor people pay energy bills.

On Nov. 19, 1985, a Texas state court jury ordered Texaco Incorporated to pay $10.53 billion to the Pennzoil Company for inducing Getty Oil

Saudi Oil Minister Sheik Ahmed Zaki Yamani, at left, is welcomed by an OPEC staff member at an OPEC meeting in Vienna, Austria, in October.

Company to back out of a merger agreement with Pennzoil by offering more favorable terms. The award was the largest civil judgment in U.S. history. The jury ruled that Pennzoil had a binding agreement to buy Getty even though Getty's directors had not signed a definite contract. A state judge upheld the judgment on December 10.

Leasing Program Faulted. The General Accounting Office (GAO), the investigative arm of Congress, said on July 25 that the U.S. government had lost $7 billion in revenue as a result of the accelerated offshore oil and gas leasing program instituted in 1981 by then Secretary of the Interior James G. Watt. The GAO found that during the first 18 months of the program, 265 million acres (107 million hectares) of the outer continental shelf were offered to the oil and gas industry, which took leases on 13 million acres (5.3 million hectares). The GAO said the rapid pace of leasing under Watt significantly reduced bidding and government revenues for the leases.

Leasing Battle. Members of Congress from California and Secretary of the Interior Donald P. Hodel reached a preliminary agreement in July 1985 that would have prohibited oil exploration off most of the California coast through 1999. Under the agreement, all but 150 of the offshore tracts would be off-limits for oil and gas exploration and thus protected against potential environ-

433

Little Relief at the Gas Pump

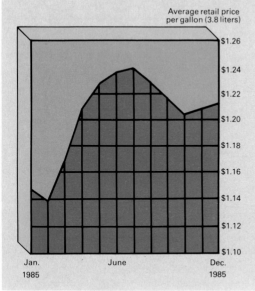

Although the price of crude oil fell worldwide during 1985, the cost of gasoline rose in the United States. The average retail price for all grades of gas jumped from $1.14 in February to $1.24 in July.

Average retail price
per gallon (3.8 liters)

$1.26
$1.24
$1.22
$1.20
$1.18
$1.16
$1.14
$1.12
$1.10

Jan.   June   Dec.
1985   1985

Source: *Lundberg Letter.*

mental problems resulting from drilling and production. But the agreement broke down on September 10, when Hodel proposed substituting tracts with a higher potential for oil and gas strikes for the tracts previously named.

New Regulations. The Federal Energy Regulatory Commission on October 9 approved new regulations for the natural gas industry that were expected to result in lower prices for consumers. The new regulations, which went into effect on November 1, required greater uniformity in the way pipeline companies transport gas. Pipeline companies usually buy gas from producers and transport it for distribution to residential, industrial, and business customers. Sometimes, however, large industrial users are able to purchase cheaper gas themselves. Pipeline companies have agreed to transport that gas, rather than risk losing the customer. Under the new regulations, pipeline companies that transport privately purchased gas for one customer must do it for other, smaller customers. The Energy Department estimated that the new regulations would save consumers up to $4.9 billion over the next 11 years.

But the commission took no action on a proposed regulation that would have resulted in immediate consumer savings of $5 billion per year by giving consumers greater access to cheap natural gas still subject to government price controls. The

natural gas industry argued that the measure would have caused it serious financial problems and discouraged exploration.

Strategic Reserve Test. On December 11, the DOE began delivering to U.S. refiners the first crude oil ever sold from the strategic petroleum reserve, the underground stockpile intended to protect the United States from possible future foreign oil embargoes. The DOE sold 1 million barrels of oil for $28.9 million to test the bidding and sales procedures that would be used to tap the reserve during a disruption in foreign oil deliveries. By the end of December, the reserve contained more than 490 million barrels of oil, enough to replace more than 100 days of oil imports.

Canada Deregulates. Canada on June 1 ended its program of government controls—in effect since 1974—on the price that refiners pay for crude oil. The action resulted in a decrease in oil prices and an increase in the production of oil for export. Alberta, which produces 90 per cent of Canada's oil, decreased its royalty charges on the oil and gas industry on June 24. The 5 per cent decrease, intended to stimulate energy production, was expected to save the oil industry about $1 billion (U.S. dollars) per year. On October 31, Canada began deregulating the price of natural gas for both domestic use and export. Michael Woods

In WORLD BOOK, see GAS; PETROLEUM.

PHILADELPHIA was preoccupied during much of 1985 with the aftereffects of a disaster that occurred on May 13. A dispute between city officials and a radical group called MOVE ended that day when police bombed a West Philadelphia house where members of the group lived and had barricaded themselves. A massive fire, triggered by the bomb, raged through the neighborhood of row houses, destroying 61 houses, damaging 82, and leaving about 250 people homeless. The fire took at least 11 lives, all of them inside the MOVE house.

The confrontation began on May 12 when the police tried to evict members of MOVE—a group that calls itself a back-to-nature movement and preaches armed resistance to authority—from the house. On the morning of May 13, MOVE members began firing at the police, and a heated gun battle broke out. At 5:30 P.M., in an attempt to destroy a fortified defensive structure on the roof of the house, a state police helicopter dropped an explosive device on the roof. The device blew up about 30 seconds later, igniting a fire. Flames spread from house to house for six hours before finally being subdued.

Philadelphia Mayor W. Wilson Goode appointed a commission to investigate the events leading up to the incident. The commission held hearings from October 8 to November 6. The tes-

Row houses in a Philadelphia neighborhood lie in ruins after being swept
by a fire stemming from a May 13 battle between police and a radical group.

timony of the 88 witnesses who appeared pointed to one overall conclusion: No one was really in control of events on May 13. On November 13, Police Commissioner Gregore J. Sambor, who directed the bombing of the MOVE house, resigned. Goode announced on December 18 that Kevin M. Tucker, a former United States Secret Service agent, would succeed Sambor.

Goode committed the city to spend about $10-million to help victims of the fire, providing free repairs for damaged houses and constructing $110,000 homes to replace those burned down. That work was to be completed by early 1986.

Racial Strife. On Nov. 22, 1985, Mayor Goode declared a state of emergency in a neighborhood where white residents had been protesting noisily outside the homes of blacks. The demonstrators had been demanding that the blacks move out of the neighborhood. Goode issued an order prohibiting people from gathering in groups larger than four, except to wait for transportation or take part in religious or recreational activities. He lifted the state of emergency on Jan. 3, 1986.

Live Aid. On July 13, 1985, Philadelphia hosted the American segment of Live Aid, an all-star rock concert organized to raise relief funds for famine-stricken areas of Africa. Another segment was held in London, and the entire concert was broadcast worldwide. See POPULAR MUSIC.

Police Corruption. An ongoing four-year federal probe of the Philadelphia Police Department had, by October, resulted in confessions or convictions on extortion and bribery charges by 26 officers, ranging from patrol officers to a deputy commissioner. On August 23, Assistant United States Attorney Howard B. Klein, chief of the corruption section of the U.S. Attorney's office, told a federal judge that the investigation would continue.

Changing Skyline. On May 13, ground was broken in downtown Philadelphia for One Liberty Place, a 60-story, $230-million office building. The skyscraper, scheduled for completion in 1987, will shatter a long-standing Philadelphia tradition by rising higher than the statue of William Penn, founder of Pennsylvania, atop City Hall. It will be 935 feet (285 meters) high.

Newspaper Strike. The city's two major newspapers, *The Philadelphia Inquirer* and the *Philadelphia Daily News*, shut down on September 7 after nine unions struck the publisher, Philadelphia Newspapers Incorporated, a subsidiary of Knight-Ridder Newspapers Incorporated. The unions were striking for both higher pay and improved working conditions. The strike ended on October 22, when the two sides agreed on the provisions of a new four-year contract.   Howard S. Shapiro

See also CITY. In WORLD BOOK, see PHILADELPHIA.

PHILIPPINES President Ferdinand E. Marcos signed on Dec. 2, 1985, a National Assembly bill calling an election for president on Feb. 7, 1986. The unusual election, a year ahead of schedule, was Marcos' response to increasing domestic pressure caused by an expanding Communist rebel movement and a declining economy.

The Pressure on Marcos was intensified by the concern of the United States, which has its largest overseas military bases—Clark Air Base and Subic Bay Naval Station—in the Philippines. United States President Ronald Reagan urged Marcos to make economic and military reforms and to move toward more democratic politics. On October 16 and 17, a close friend of Reagan's, Senator Paul Laxalt (R., Nev.), met with Marcos in Manila to convey U.S. worry over deteriorating conditions in the islands.

Aquino Verdict. On December 2, the same day that Marcos signed the election bill, a special court acquitted 26 people accused of a role in the 1983 murder of opposition leader Benigno S. Aquino, Jr. The Supreme Court had on Aug. 31, 1985, barred some of the prosecution's strongest evidence. The prosecution argued that Rogelio Moreno of the Manila police had shot Aquino as part of a conspiracy that included General Fabian C. Ver, the chief of staff of the Philippine armed forces. The court upheld the armed forces' contention that Aquino had been shot by a man who probably acted on orders of the New People's Army (NPA), the Communist rebel organization.

The Campaign Begins. Aquino's widow, Corazon C. Aquino, decided after the verdict to run for president. Jaime Cardinal Sin, the Roman Catholic archbishop of Manila and a frequent Marcos critic, arranged for her to become the candidate of a 12-party opposition coalition, the United Nationalist Democratic Organization. Its head, Salvador H. Laurel, agreed to run for vice president on her ticket. Laurel had earlier threatened to run separately for president, dividing the anti-Marcos vote.

Marcos chose as his running mate National Assembly member Arturo M. Tolentino, one of the most popular vote-getters of the ruling New Society Movement, Marcos' party. Tolentino had been fired from the post of foreign minister on March 4 for criticizing Marcos for continuing to make laws by personal decree despite the end of martial law in 1981. Before Marcos chose him, Tolentino had opposed the special election as unconstitutional. The Philippine Supreme Court held hearings on its constitutionality. The court on December 19 ruled, 7 to 5, that the issue was political, not constitutional, and the election therefore could be held.

Videotape of the 1983 murder of Philippine leader Benigno S. Aquino, Jr., is shown in March 1985 during the trial of 26 men accused of the crime.

NPA Growth. Beginning his election campaign on December 14, Marcos said that in 1985 10,000 "innocent civilians" had been killed by NPA guerrillas. In September, a military leader had said that incidents of guerrilla violence had increased 30 per cent.

The goverment issued an official report in May saying the NPA had between 10,000 and 12,000 regular fighters, only two-thirds of them armed. The Communists claimed 30,000 guerrillas. A U.S. Department of Defense officer said in March that the guerrillas would achieve military equality with Philippine government forces within five years. This estimate was later cut to three years. Abuses of power by soldiers and rural police were blamed for much of the appeal of the Communists, who offered to protect villagers against official mistreatment. But the guerrillas shot many people who challenged their control.

Economic Distress also alienated many people from the government. The collapse of world prices for sugar and coconuts cut farmers' income. Mining and other industries suffered a recession. Average income declined 6.8 per cent from the first half of 1984 to the same period of 1985. Overall national productivity dropped about 10 per cent in 1984 and 1985 combined.   Henry S. Bradsher

See also ASIA (Facts in Brief Table). In WORLD BOOK, see PHILIPPINES.

PHOTOGRAPHY. In January 1985, Minolta Camera Company transformed the market for single-lens reflex (SLR) 35-millimeter (mm) cameras with the introduction of the automatic-focusing Maxxum 7000. The Maxxum's sophisticated autofocus system, which couples automatically to a new line of lenses, made this electronic camera such an immediate success that Canon Incorporated rushed to introduce its own autofocus SLR—the T80—in March. In November, Canon brought out an improved model, the T90, a highly automated, professional quality SLR with a motorized film advance. In August, Minolta followed up the Maxxum 7000 with the Maxxum 9000 Professional. This model offers even faster focusing and film advance, higher shutter speeds, and sturdier construction than the original.

New Film, Paper. In November, Fuji Photo Film Company introduced the world's fastest color film, Fujichrome P1600 Professional. Fuji claimed the film, rated at ISO 1,600, would—with extended "push" developing—produce high-quality color slides at film speeds up to ISO 4,800, making it more than twice as sensitive as any existing film. Fuji also introduced an ISO 1,600 color-slide film in 1984, but it could not be "pushed" as much.

Four major manufacturers—Agfa-Gevaert of West Germany, Eastman Kodak Company of the United States, and Fuji and Konica of Japan—announced breakthroughs in the quality of printing paper for amateur and professional color prints. Although most color prints tend to fade or change color over time, the new papers promise to hold their color well into the next century.

Home-Video moviemakers had a much wider choice of equipment in 1985, as electronics manufacturers introduced a variety of new "camcorder"—camera-plus-recorder—systems. The smallest of these was the Sony Mini 8 camcorder, a 2.2-pound (1-kilogram) record-only unit that uses the increasingly popular 8-mm video format. Sony also came out with a more sophisticated and somewhat larger 8-mm camcorder, as did Canon, Kodak, and several other companies. Kodak's entry, called the Modular Video System (MVS), is manufactured in Japan by Matsushita Electric Industrial Company. It features digital sound recording in high-fidelity stereo and a small video cassette recorder that can be detached from the camera and "docked" with another component to record from a television set.

In September, Kodak unveiled a prototype still-video system that it said would be tested in several parts of the United States in 1986. The system will enable processing laboratories to transfer ordinary 35-mm color negatives onto video floppy disks. With the aid of a special unit, the images can be displayed on a home television screen.

Other Kodak Plans. Kodak also made plans to get back into one kind of photography and out of another. In March, Kodak announced an agreement with Chinon Industries of Japan to produce a 35-mm camera that will be introduced in 1986 and sold under the Kodak name. Kodak last marketed a 35-mm camera in 1974. In October, a federal judge in Boston ruled that Kodak's line of instant-photography cameras and films infringed on patents held by the Polaroid Corporation. The judge ordered Kodak to stop selling those products by Jan. 9, 1986. Kodak said if it could not get a reversal of the ruling, it would abandon the instant-photography business.

Record Price for Print. In March, a photograph of President Abraham Lincoln and his son Tad, signed by Lincoln, sold for $104,500 at a Sotheby Parke Bernet auction in New York City. It was the highest auction price ever paid for a photograph.

Deaths. Pioneering photojournalist André Kertész died on September 27 in New York City at the age of 91. Kertész was renowned for his warm images of his native Hungary in the early 1900's as well as for avant-garde work in Paris in the 1920's and 1930's.

Arthur Rothstein, a photojournalist and editor best known for his stark pictures of the Dust Bowl during the 1930's, died on November 11 in New Rochelle, N.Y. He was 70.   Steve Pollock

In WORLD BOOK, see CAMERA; PHOTOGRAPHY.

437

PHYSICS. Scientists who study the structure of solid substances attempted in 1985 to explain an astonishing discovery made in late 1984 by an international team of physicists at the National Bureau of Standards (NBS) laboratory in Gaithersburg, Md. The NBS researchers found that atoms in certain solids are arranged in an unexpected way. Scientists classify solids into two groups according to the positioning of their atoms. In an *amorphous solid* such as glass, the atoms are not positioned in any pattern. A *crystal*, on the other hand, is made up of identical *unit cells*—groups of atoms arranged in a certain pattern—aligned regularly throughout the three-dimensional structure of the crystal. A two-dimensional structure analogous to a crystal is a tiled floor, all the tiles of which are alike. The tiles are the floor's "unit cells."

Scientists Have Known for decades that only a few patterns of atoms can produce the regular three-dimensional structure of crystals, just as only a few patterns of tiles can fit together to cover a floor without leaving spaces between tiles. A group of square tiles, for example, can cover a rectangular floor completely, as can a group of hexagonal tiles. But a group of tiles in the shape of a regular pentagon cannot do so. One class of atomic groups that cannot form crystals are those

exhibiting *five-fold symmetry*—a certain characteristic of their shapes.

When the NBS researchers examined a certain *alloy* (solid mixture) of aluminum and manganese through an electron microscope, they saw clear, sharp pictures that are characteristic of unit cells arranged regularly, as in a crystal. Yet, the picture also indicated the presence of five-fold symmetry in the alloy.

One possible explanation for this strange result under consideration in 1985 is that the alloy is made up of a combination of several kinds of unit cells. Certain such combinations can form shapes that produce five-fold symmetry at special places in a material.

Theorists have developed an understanding of how a combination might yield sharp pictures under the electron microscope, even though the unit cells cannot be arranged in a regular pattern. Physicists still must do a great deal of work to determine the atoms' positions in the alloy. The information available at the end of 1985 suggested that the NBS researchers discovered a new class of solids—*quasicrystals*, possessing neither the order of crystals nor the disorder of amorphous solids.

Superstrings. A vast amount of experimental and theoretical research in physics has been motivated by the prospect of developing a theory de-

A technician at Lawrence Livermore National Laboratory in California checks Nova, the world's largest laser, which was dedicated in April.

scribing all types of matter and all the forces acting on matter. In 1985, physicists examined many theories that seemed to point the way toward this long-sought goal.

An especially promising group of theories are known as *supersymmetric theories* for technical reasons having to do with relationships among *elementary particles* (subatomic objects that are not made up of smaller parts). Many supersymmetric theories that are sound mathematically have failed in at least one of two fundamental ways to describe physical reality, however. Either they give infinite answers to mathematical problems known to have finite answers, or they cannot provide a consistent account of the known properties of elementary particles.

In December 1984, physicists Michael B. Green of Queen Mary College in London and John H. Schwartz of the California Institute of Technology in Pasadena announced that a certain form of supersymmetric theory does give the necessary consistent account of particle properties. And in January 1985, they reported that this form of theory does not give nonsensical infinite answers. Theories of this form are called *superstring* theories, because they treat elementary particles as objects somewhat like pieces of string. Conventional theories treat such particles as points.   Thomas O. White

In WORLD BOOK, see PHYSICS.

POETRY. Perhaps the biggest poetry news of 1985 came from the past. What may be a previously unrecognized poem by William Shakespeare, "Shall I die? Shall I fly," written in the late 1500's, was discovered in November 1985 at Oxford University (see NEWSMAKERS OF 1985).

Several eminent poets issued collections of their work in 1985. Robert Penn Warren's *New and Selected Poems* updated his *Selected Poems* (1976). Derek Walcott gathered his work together for the first time since 1964 in his new *Collected Poems.* Other notable collections included John Ashbery's *Selected Poems;* Donald Davie's *Selected Poems;* Louis Simpson's *People Live Here: Selected Poems;* Dave Smith's *The Roundhouse Voices: Selected and New Poems;* and Philip Levine's *Selected Poems.* Levine also brought out a volume of new work, *Sweet Will.* The *Collected Poems of Paul Blackburn* came out 14 years after his death in 1971.

Among Other Volumes of interest were *Next-to-Last Things: New Poems and Essays* by Stanley Kunitz and Seamus Heaney's *Station Island,* named for its title poem. Maxine Kumin's *The Long Approach* spanned a wide range from domestic poetry to re-flections on nuclear war. As the title suggests, many of the poems in James Merrill's *Late Settings* were concerned with the approach of old age. The third and fourth sections of Thomas McGrath's sequence, *Letters to an Imaginary Friend,* were politi-cally involved and complex in historical references. Marge Piercy's *My Mother's Body* revealed the sexual politics present in everyday life.

Amy Clampitt, whose first book, *The Kingfisher* (1983), was widely praised, followed with a second, *What the Light Was Like.* Gjertrud Schnackenberg's second book, *The Lamplit Answer,* brought her national prominence. Both poets at times used traditional forms and frequently referred to earlier literature. Louise Glück extended her range in *The Triumph of Achilles,* which was less intensely private than her previous work and more at ease with a leisurely narrative pace. And Raymond Carver, best known as a writer of fiction, published his first book of poems, *Where Water Comes Together with Other Water.* As might be expected, Carver's poems were often narrative, as if he sought to condense short stories into verse.

Younger or Less Well-Known Poets also produced books worth noting. Brendan Galvin in *Seals in the Harbor* displayed a quiet wit often missing in other nature poets. W. S. Di Piero's *Early Light* combined moral intelligence with a lyric gift. Andrew Hudgins' *Saints and Strangers* was distinguished by its colloquial ease in blank verse and its fullness of detail. Bruce Smith's *Silver and Information* revealed a style distinguished for its intelligence and its richness to the ear.   Paul Breslin

In WORLD BOOK, see POETRY.

POLAND. Communist Party First Secretary Wojciech Jaruzelski consolidated his position during 1985. The nation's financial situation remained shaky, however, and there was little sign that economic reforms promised by Jaruzelski would get underway soon.

On October 13, Poland held the first elections for the Sejm (parliament) since 1980. According to government reports, 78.88 per cent of all registered voters cast ballots, compared with 98.77 per cent in 1980. Representatives of the outlawed labor union Solidarity claimed the true figure for 1985 was even lower—about 68 per cent.

On November 6, Jaruzelski resigned as Poland's head of government—officially as chairman of the Council of Ministers—and took up the post of head of state as chairman of the Council of State, a largely ceremonial position. He remained leader of the Communist Party. Interpretations of this move varied. According to some observers, Jaruzelski changed jobs because he believed the unrest that propelled him to the leadership of the party and the government in 1981 had diminished so much that powers could be divided more normally. Other observers said he wanted to distance himself from Poland's economic problems.

Jaruzelski succeeded Henryk Jablonski as head of state. Zbigniew Messner, an economist, became Council of Ministers chairman.

439

These changes marked the beginning of a shakeup that resulted in the replacement of 13 of Poland's 30 ministers. Stefan Olszowski resigned as foreign minister "on health grounds." He also left the Politburo—the policymaking body of the Communist Party. Marian Orzechowski succeeded him as foreign minister.

Mieczyslaw Rakowski lost his job as deputy prime minister, a position he had held since 1981, even though he was thought to be close to Jaruzelski. He received a minor post in the Sejm.

Murder Trial. On Dec. 27, 1984, four members of the secret police went on trial for the October 1984 kidnapping and murder of Jerzy Popieluszko, a Roman Catholic priest who supported Solidarity. The trial, held in Torun, ended on Feb. 7, 1985, with all four defendants declared guilty. Adam Pietruszka, deputy head of the secret police department that monitored the Roman Catholic Church, was sentenced to 25 years in prison as the instigator of the crime. Grzegorz Piotrowski, the organizer of the crime, was also sentenced to 25 years. Two other officers received sentences of 15 and 14 years. On May 14, Miroslaw Milewski, who had been in charge of the police and security services, resigned from the Politburo and the Central Committee.

The Church. The government's relations with the Roman Catholic Church remained cool throughout 1985. The government tried to gain church support for the October elections, but Jozef Cardinal Glemp, head of the church in Poland, insisted on absolute impartiality. No Polish bishop voted in the October 13 election.

Foreign Relations. The foreign ministers of Great Britain, Italy, and Japan visited Poland in the first half of 1985. Jaruzelski visited Yugoslavia in July, and Cuba and the United States in September. He attended the 40th anniversary session of the United Nations General Assembly in New York City in September. While in the United States, however, he did not meet with any representative of the United States government. On December 4, Jaruzelski met in Paris with France's President François Mitterrand. The Polish leader's visit drew many expressions of outrage, and Prime Minister Laurent Fabius said the meeting "troubled" him.

Debt. In July, Western banks to which Poland owes money agreed to a new schedule of payments for $12 billion that had fallen due in 1982, 1983, and 1984. In November, Poland signed a rescheduling agreement with Western nations to which it owes money. The agreement covered $1.4 billion due in 1985. Poland is to pay this money over the next 10 years.   Chris Cviic

See also EUROPE (Facts in Brief Table). In WORLD BOOK, see POLAND.

POLLUTION. See ENVIRONMENTAL POLLUTION.

POPULAR MUSIC. The United States popular music business prospered and grew in 1985. There were 46 per cent more *platinum* (million-seller) albums in the first half of 1985 than in the same period in 1984. Manufacturers of compact disks (CD's) and CD players rushed to fill orders.

Humanitarian Efforts by recording artists continued on a large scale in 1985. An American group called USA for Africa recorded "We Are the World" in January 1985 to raise funds to feed famine victims in Africa. The song was written by Michael Jackson and Lionel Richie, produced by Quincy Jones, and sung by 46 rock and pop singers. It was a number-one single, and the album and video also went to the top of the charts.

These efforts culminated in the greatest one-day event in rock history—Live Aid—on July 13, 1985. Over 60 rock and pop artists performed at London's Wembley Stadium and Philadelphia's John F. Kennedy Stadium. The shows were broadcast live on radio and television to more than 1½ billion people in 152 countries. The benefit was organized by Bob Geldof of Ireland's Boomtown Rats, who was later nominated for a Nobel Prize for his efforts. By October, popular music artists had raised $100 million for famine relief.

Farm Aid, a 14-hour televised benefit concert for American farmers, was held in Champaign, Ill., on September 22. The concert was organized by Willie Nelson and included 50 rock and country acts. The event raised about $7 million.

Steve Van Zandt, formerly of Bruce Springsteen's E Street Band, rounded up dozens of punk, funk, rap, and rock musicians in 1985 to record "Sun City," a song critical of *apartheid*, South Africa's policy of racial segregation. The single and its associated album and video were released in October. Money from record sales was to aid families of political prisoners in South Africa and to support antiapartheid efforts.

Rating Lyrics. Concern grew in the United States in 1985 over the issue of song lyrics that seem to promote sex, drugs, violence, or the occult. The National PTA and a group from Washington, D.C., called the Parents' Music Resource Center tried to persuade the music industry to adopt a rating system for recordings similar to that used for motion pictures. In Senate hearings in September, many musicians and music industry executives spoke against the proposed rating system. The Recording Industry Association of America rejected the system, but encouraged its members to label some records "Explicit Lyrics—Parental Advisory." In November, the parents' group announced that 22 record companies, including some of the largest, had agreed to print warning labels or song lyrics on the covers of albums.

Black Music continued its growth and renewal in 1985. In January, Motown Records opened a full

Pop music fans jam Philadelphia's John F. Kennedy Stadium on July 13 for the Live Aid concert to raise funds for African famine relief efforts.

creative office in New York City for the first time in 10 years.

At the American Music Awards in January, Lionel Richie was the big winner with six awards, and Prince received three. At the Grammys in February, Tina Turner received three awards, including record of the year for "What's Love Got to Do With It?" Other winners were Richie, Prince, the Pointer Sisters, and Ray Parker, Jr. An album by Ray Charles even reached number one on the country charts. Veteran soulster Aretha Franklin made a big comeback with the album *Who's Zoomin' Who* and its hit single "Freeway of Love."

Dance Music showed a dramatic increase in sales of long-playing 12-inch (30-centimeter) singles, an active dance-club scene, and expanded radio play. Performers with dance remixes—rock songs remixed in a recording studio to emphasize the beat—included Sting, Paul Young, Wham!, Pat Benatar, Turner, Huey Lewis and the News, and Tears for Fears. Some of the most popular dance-club hits were by Madonna, Paul Hardcastle, Franklin, Billy Ocean, and Patti LaBelle.

Rock Music in 1985 was dominated by Bruce Springsteen. His 1984 album *Born in the U.S.A.* had sold more than 13 million copies by the fall of 1985, and his 15-month concert tour that ended in October drew an estimated 5 million fans. He won six major categories in *Rolling Stone* maga-

zine's readers' poll, and his hit single "Dancing in the Dark" received awards at the American Music Awards and the Grammys.

Daryl Hall and John Oates won favorite duo or group in the American Music Awards for the third year. In February, they tied the Everly Brothers' record of 15 top-10 singles by a duo.

British musicians stormed the United States in 1985 with four acts scoring simultaneous number-one singles and albums—Phil Collins, Tears for Fears, Wham!, and Dire Straits.

Bob Dylan's 29th album, *Empire Burlesque*, combined hot rock and roll with humanitarian and spiritual values. Dylan also released a five-record set, *Biograph*, featuring most of his well-known songs, 18 previously unreleased recordings, and a booklet containing his explanations of each song.

Oldies. In early 1985, Verve/Polydor released *V.U.*, a previously unreleased album by the Velvet Underground recorded in the late 1960's at the height of their popularity. MCA Home Video released a 65-minute video of Jim Morrison and the Doors. Fifties-style vocals and modern rap were combined and called "hip-hop doo-wop" by New York City's Force-M.D.'s in their album *Love Letters*. Johnny Cash, Jerry Lee Lewis, Carl Perkins, and Roy Orbison, all of whom recorded in the 1950's at Sun Records in Memphis, returned to the studio and recorded an upcoming album.

Rocker Bruce Springsteen plays to 70,000 delighted fans in Chicago's Soldier Field on August 9 during his 15-month international concert tour.

Women continued to be a big part of rock and pop. Madonna's *Like a Virgin* became the first album by a woman to sell 5 million copies. Cyndi Lauper won two awards in the American Music Awards and one—best new artist—in the Grammys. Sheena Easton became the first artist to score top-five hits in *Billboard*'s five major charts—pop, black, country, dance, and adult contemporary. Aimee Mann of the new band 'til Tuesday was named best new artist in MTV's Music Video Awards in September.

Music Video showed signs of continued growth. Industry giant RCA/Columbia Home Video created a music video line. The new International Music Video Festival was held in London in October. *Billboard* added a music video chart, and in September videos by Prince, Tina Turner, Duran Duran, and USA for Africa were certified platinum. MTV Network made great financial gains, and its 24-hour cable channel for the 25 to 54 age group began in January.

Jazz Was Alive and Well, and the 16th Annual New Orleans Jazz and Heritage Festival drew a record crowd of more than 200,000 in April. Performers included Miles Davis, Wynton Marsalis, Spyro Gyra, and Allen Toussaint. The 10th North Sea Jazz Festival in July at The Hague, the Netherlands, had a record turnout of 36,000 and featured such diverse artists as Davis, B. B. King, Os-

car Peterson, Ray Charles, and Dizzy Gillespie. Sting, already popular in rock and pop, issued a jazz-oriented album, *Dream of the Blue Turtles*. The revival of historically important Blue Note Records was celebrated on February 28 at New York City's Town Hall Theatre.

Country Music business executives spent a large part of 1985 trying to reverse a slump in record sales and concert attendance. Festival turnout was up, however. In July, Jamboree in the Hills drew a record crowd of 60,000 country music fans to St. Clairsville, Ohio. Performers included Earl Thomas Conley, Brenda Lee, Ronnie McDowell, Crystal Gayle, Exile, Glen Campbell, and Louise Mandrell. The Charlie Daniels Band's 11th Annual Volunteer Jam in February reached a pay-TV audience of 200,000. The Society for the Preservation of Bluegrass Music in America convention at Nashville's Opryland Hotel in January drew 4,500 fans—double 1984's attendance. The superstar group Alabama dominated the 20th Annual Academy of Country Music Awards Show in May at Knott's Berry Farm, Los Angeles. They were named favorite country group in the American Music Awards. Jerry M. Grigadean

See also AWARDS AND PRIZES (Arts Awards); MADONNA; SPRINGSTEEN, BRUCE; TURNER, TINA. In WORLD BOOK, see COUNTRY MUSIC; JAZZ; POPULAR MUSIC; ROCK MUSIC.

POPULATION. World population in 1985 exceeded 4.8 billion—about 30 per cent more people than in 1970 and 60 per cent more than in 1960, according to the United States Bureau of the Census. The current rate of annual increase in worldwide population is about 1.7 per cent. If this rate continues, the population of the world will double in about 40 years. The rate of increase has been declining slowly—it was about 2.2 per cent in the mid-1970's—so world population is expected to stabilize at about 10 billion by the year 2110.

Growth Rates. The population of the industrialized nations, which now makes up less than 25 per cent of the world's population, has increased at the relatively low rate of 0.6 per cent annually in recent years. The annual growth rate of developing nations will probably stabilize soon at about 2 per cent, but at that rate their populations will double in size in about 33 years. By the year 2000, those nations will probably have more than 80 per cent of the world's population.

The fastest-growing nations are in Africa, where the average annual rate of increase is nearly 3 per cent per year—a rate that will double the population in 24 years—and the total population is 562 million. Latin America, with a population of 412 million and a growth rate of 2.4 per cent, is also growing more rapidly than the world as a whole, as is Asia, with 3 billion people and a growth rate

How State Populations Will Change Between 1980 and 2000

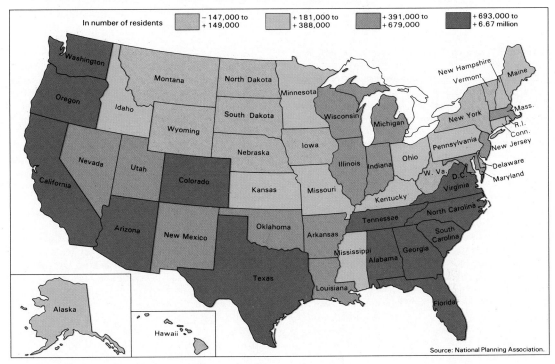

In number of residents

| | −147,000 to +149,000 | +181,000 to +388,000 | +391,000 to +679,000 | +693,000 to +6.67 million |

Source: National Planning Association.

of 1.8 per cent. The slow growth rates of North America (0.7 per cent) and Europe (0.3 per cent) indicate that their shares of world population will continue to decline. By the turn of the century, population experts predict, North America will have only 5 per cent, and Europe only 7 per cent, of the world's people.

China, the world's most populous country, had more than 1 billion people in 1985, but its growth rate—1.1 per cent—was lower than that of the world as a whole. India, with the second-highest population—778 million—continued to grow by more than 2 per cent per year, so that by the year 2050, its population may exceed that of China. The Soviet Union, with 281 million people, and the United States with 241 million, ranked third and fourth in population size. Both nations have growth rates below the world average—1 per cent and 0.7 per cent, respectively.

Life Expectancy continued to increase in most countries in 1985, and death rates, particularly infant mortality rates, continued to decrease. Life expectancy at birth was 75 years or more in Australia, Iceland, the Netherlands, Norway, Sweden, and Switzerland. On the other hand, life expectancy in some areas of Africa was little more than half that long. People in Chad and Ethiopia had a life expectancy of only 41 years.   Jeanne C. Biggar

In WORLD BOOK, see POPULATION.

PORTUGAL. Social Democrat Aníbal Cavaco Silva became prime minister of Portugal on Nov. 6, 1985, succeeding Mário Soares, a Socialist. Soares had headed a coalition government of Socialists and Social Democrats. See CAVACO SILVA, ANÍBAL.

The two parties had disagreed over labor and agricultural policies in June, causing the Social Democrats to withdraw from the coalition. On July 12, President António dos Santos Ramalho Eanes dissolved Parliament and scheduled general elections for October 6.

The Social Democrats defeated the Socialists in the elections, but both parties fell short of a majority in Parliament. The Social Democrats won 85 of the 250 seats. The Socialists won 55; and the Democratic Renewal Party, a new party backed by Eanes, won 45.

Soares stepped down immediately, delegating his power to Deputy Prime Minister Rui Machete, a Social Democrat. But Eanes told Soares that only the president can relieve a prime minister of his responsiblities, and Soares agreed to rule as the head of a caretaker government until a new government was sworn in.

Only 75 per cent of the electorate voted. The turnout was the lowest since the 1974 revolution that restored democracy to Portugal.

Presidential Campaign. Soares was eager to leave Parliament immediately after the election to begin a campaign for president. Portuguese voters were scheduled to cast their ballots in January 1986 to replace Eanes, who is required by law to step down. Soares had two opponents in the presidential campaign: Diogo Freitas do Amaral, a Conservative; and Maria de Lurdes Pintassilgo, a left wing Roman Catholic activist.

EC Entry. On June 12, Soares signed treaties of entry into the European Community (EC or Common Market). Portugal and Spain were scheduled to join the EC on Jan. 1, 1986.

Unpaid Workers. At least 100,000 employees of state-owned firms went without pay for several months in 1985, helping to cut Portugal's *current account deficit*, an imbalance in the basic flow of goods into and out of the nation. This deficit, which stood at $3.3 billion in 1982, was only $500-million on Sept. 1, 1985. An official report published on January 24 said Portugal would have to spend $3.4 billion to ensure the survival of the 18 poorest state-owned companies.

Reagan Snubbed. Thirty-five Communist members of Parliament walked out when United States President Ronald Reagan addressed Portugal's Parliament on May 9. They objected to Reagan's praise of Portugal as a democracy and to United States policy in Nicaragua.   Kenneth Brown

See also EUROPE (Facts in Brief Table). In WORLD BOOK, see PORTUGAL.

POSTAL SERVICE, UNITED STATES. The Postal Service increased first-class mail rates on Feb. 17, 1985, for the first time since 1981. The first-class rate for the first ounce (28 grams) rose to 22 cents from 20 cents. In addition, the post-card rate rose to 14 cents from 13 cents, and the basic international rate for a ½-ounce (14-gram) airmail letter jumped to 44 cents from 40 cents. The increases were expected to add about $2 billion to Postal Service revenues.

Despite the higher postal rates and a heavier volume of mail, Postmaster General Paul N. Carlin said on December 3 that the Postal Service had a deficit of $251.4 million in the 1985 fiscal year, ending September 30. The service had completed several years of break-even or profitable operations and had a surplus of $117 million in fiscal 1984.

Carlin said part of the red ink was caused by an increase in personnel, to 740,000 from 702,000, at the start of the fiscal year in fall 1984. He said that to cut costs, the salaries of 34 top Postal Service officials would be reduced by 3.5 per cent and a 3.14 per cent pay increase for more than 700 other managers would be delayed. The postmaster predicted that the belt-tightening moves would save $2 million a year.

Outlook Brightens. On September 18, Carlin gave a more optimistic report on the fiscal outlook, saying that cost-cutting moves plus a further

increase in mail volume promised to pare the deficit to "less than half" of the $500-million minimum predicted just two months earlier. Some Postal Service officials went so far as to predict a return to break-even status in fiscal 1986.

Because of the brighter outlook, a Postal Service spokesman said first-class mail rates were unlikely to increase again until 1987 at the earliest. He said the service had no plans to seek a rate hike in the near future.

With just one member disagreeing, the nine-member Board of Governors of the Postal Service voted in September 1985 to borrow money, rather than use existing assets, to pay for new facilities and equipment. The dissenting board member, Ruth O. Peters, a retired postal employee, contended the decision reflected "the inability of the Board of Governors . . . to operate this institution within its budget." The service announced it would borrow $1 billion initially to help finance a five-year, $5-billion improvement program.

Woman Named Deputy Postmaster. On January 8, Carlin named Jackie Anderson Strange, former head of the Postal Service's 11-state southern region, as deputy postmaster general, the agency's second-ranking job and its highest position ever filled by a woman.   Frank Cormier and Margot Cormier

In WORLD BOOK, see POST OFFICE; POSTAL SERVICE, UNITED STATES.

PRESIDENT OF THE UNITED STATES Ronald Reagan, after four years of lambasting the Soviet Union as "the evil empire," made what he termed "a fresh start" in 1985 in dealings with Moscow. Reagan's year was capped, in the foreign policy area, by a November 19-20 summit in Geneva, Switzerland, with the new general secretary of the Soviet Communist Party, Mikhail S. Gorbachev. "I can't claim we had a meeting of the minds on such fundamentals as ideology or national purpose," Reagan told a joint session of Congress on November 21, "but we understand each other better."

Some observers were disappointed that Reagan and Gorbachev had reached no major agreements on arms control and other areas of discord between the United States and the Soviet Union. But the two leaders agreed to work for progress on arms reduction, and they planned to continue their dialogue at summits in Washington, D.C., and Moscow. Gorbachev was expected to visit the United States in 1986.

Reagan's Popularity Remains High. Reagan threw his political critics off-balance not only by meeting with Gorbachev but also by transforming a series of threatened international policy defeats into compromise victories. Although many U.S. Presidents experience a second-term slump, Reagan's popularity remained extraordinarily high. Low inflation and relative prosperity at home, coupled with the November summit and the seizure in October of four Palestinian terrorists who had killed an American during a cruise ship hijacking, did much to bolster the President's standing with the public.

During the year, Reagan persuaded Congress to provide production money for the MX intercontinental ballistic missile, though not as much as he wanted, and to extend nonmilitary aid to antigovernment guerrillas in Nicaragua. The President also staved off a congressional drive to vote economic sanctions against South Africa in protest of that nation's racial policies, and a move to enact strongly protectionist trade bills. Reagan headed off Congress by hastily ordering sanctions of his own against South Africa and by embracing a less restrictive "fair trade" program. And in May, during a trip to Western Europe, Reagan shrugged off criticism of his decision to visit a military cemetery at Bitburg, West Germany, where about 30 Nazi SS soldiers are buried.

Health Problem. Reagan was sidetracked for a while by an unexpected health problem. On July 13, after doctors discovered a possibly cancerous growth in his lower intestine, Reagan underwent abdominal surgery. The growth was malignant, but the President's physicians said there was a good chance that the cancer had not spread.

Before being operated on, Reagan transferred executive power to Vice President George H. W. Bush under the provisions of the 25th Amendment to the Constitution. Bush in effect became acting President for about eight hours.

Prelude to the Summit. No foreign policy initiative in 1985 attracted so much attention as the Geneva talks, which marked the first softening of hostility between the two superpowers since the 1979 Soviet invasion of Afghanistan. The road to the summit began on Jan. 8, 1985, when the two nations announced they would resume arms reduction talks in Geneva. The Soviets had broken off negotiations in late 1983 when the North Atlantic Treaty Organization (NATO) began installing a new generation of missiles in Western Europe. The negotiations were resumed in March 1985 after the United States agreed that Geneva could provide a forum for discussion of Reagan's Strategic Defense Initiative (SDI)—the so-called "Star Wars" missile defense plan—which the Soviets had denounced as a move to launch a new arms race in space. Reagan appointed Democrat Max M. Kampelman, a Washington, D.C., lawyer, to head the negotiating team.

The months prior to the summit were marked by a flurry of propaganda moves and proposals by both Gorbachev and Reagan. Moscow welcomed

President Reagan makes a point to Soviet leader Mikhail S. Gorbachev during their summit conference in Geneva, Switzerland, in November.

During a May trip to West Germany, President Reagan visits Bergen-Belsen concentration camp, *left*, and a military cemetery in Bitburg.

Reagan's announcement on June 10 that the United States would abide, at least temporarily, by provisions of the never-ratified Strategic Arms Limitation Talks (SALT II) treaty of 1979. Foreign Minister Andrei A. Gromyko was named president of the Soviet Union on July 2. In September, Gorbachev sent Gromyko's successor, Eduard A. Shevardnadze, to the White House with a Soviet offer. Shevardnadze said the Soviet Union would reduce its arsenal of nuclear arms by 50 per cent in return for curbs on Reagan's SDI plan. On October 24, addressing the United Nations (UN) General Assembly during the UN's 40th anniversary celebration, Reagan said the Soviet proposal was unacceptable but that it contained "certain positive seeds we wish to nurture."

A few hours after making his speech, the President met for an hour in New York City with the heads of government of Canada, Great Britain, Italy, Japan, and West Germany. They publicly offered Reagan their "full support" for his meeting with Gorbachev, while pressing him in private to make a new arms control offer in response to the Soviet leader's September initiative. Reagan agreed, and on November 1 American negotiators in Geneva outlined a renewed U.S. offer. Like the Soviet proposal, the Reagan-endorsed plan would involve big cuts in nuclear arsenals, limiting each superpower to 6,000 "charges"—a term referring

to warheads and bombs. But the two sides remained far apart on what to include in the 6,000 charges, and the Soviets continued to insist on a trade-off that Reagan rejected: arms cuts in exchange for abandonment of the SDI.

On November 4, the Moscow newspaper *Izvestia* (*News*) published an interview with Reagan that had been conducted at the White House four days earlier by five Soviet journalists. Reagan's remarks about Soviet actions in Afghanistan, the Soviet military presence in Eastern Europe, and Soviet secrecy about its own space-based defenses against missiles were deleted from the *Izvestia* account.

Defector Incidents. News of the interview was eclipsed in the United States by a stunning disclosure on November 4 that a Soviet spy who had been hailed as a major defector was returning to Moscow. The spy, Vitaly Yurchenko, a top official of the KGB, the Soviet intelligence agency, claimed that agents of the Central Intelligence Agency (CIA) had kidnapped him in Rome three months earlier and kept him drugged on a Virginia estate. Although U.S. intelligence officials denied Yurchenko's story, the puzzling affair was a major embarrassment to the CIA.

The presummit period also was marked by two other bizarre episodes in which Soviet citizens made apparent efforts to seek American sanctuary. On October 31, a Soviet enlisted man in Afghanistan went to the U.S. Embassy in Kabul and indicated he was homesick. American diplomats turned the soldier over to the Soviet ambassador after receiving assurances the young man would not be harmed.

More disturbing to many Americans was the case of Miroslav Medved, a Soviet seaman who twice jumped into the Mississippi River on October 24 in an apparent attempt to defect from his ship, a grain carrier anchored near New Orleans. After telling U.S. officials that he wished to go back to the Soviet Union, Medved was returned to the ship. Reagan wondered aloud whether the three cases were a Soviet ploy.

Low Hopes for Summit. On November 5, Secretary of State George P. Shultz, in Moscow for pre-summit discussions with Gorbachev and other Soviet leaders, gave a decidedly downbeat assessment of summit prospects. And on November 9, when Reagan made a 10-minute radio broadcast to the Soviet Union on the Voice of America (VOA), the Soviets jammed most of the VOA frequencies.

But the summit seemed friendly by all accounts, despite sharp exchanges between Reagan and Gorbachev. The two leaders spent five hours alone, with only interpreters present. After Reagan briefed NATO leaders in Brussels, Belgium, on the way home, Italy's Prime Minister Bettino Craxi said the U.S. President had reported finding Gorbachev "more flexible and more reasonable" than he had expected. But Gorbachev won no concessions from Reagan on the SDI, despite warning that significant arms cuts would be possible only if "the door to the arms race in space is closed and tightly shut." The summit did, however, produce minor accords on cultural exchanges, safety for air routes over the North Pacific Ocean, the opening of new U.S. and Soviet consulates, and several other matters.

Middle East Terrorists continued to plague Reagan in 1985. On June 14, two Shiite Muslim gunmen hijacked a Trans World Airlines jet after its take-off from Athens, Greece, and, after murdering a U.S. Navy enlisted man and freeing more than 100 other passengers, held 39 Americans hostage in Beirut, Lebanon. The hostages were freed on June 30 after Syria intervened. The hijackers also went free. Reagan threatened to retaliate for the hijacking but found no acceptable options for doing so.

Reagan faced a new terrorist crisis on October 7 when four Palestinian gunmen seized the Italian cruise ship *Achille Lauro* with more than 400 passengers and crew in the Mediterranean Sea off the coast of Egypt. On October 9, representatives of Egypt and the Palestine Liberation Organization (PLO) arranged for the surrender of the terrorists, who were members of a PLO splinter group. The gunmen had murdered a stroke-disabled American, Leon Klinghoffer, 69, of New York City and thrown his body and his wheelchair into the sea.

American officials expressed outrage when Egypt announced that the hijackers were being released to the PLO. But the drama reached an unexpected climax on the night of October 10 when an Egyptian airliner carrying the hijackers was intercepted near Crete by U.S. Navy planes and forced to land at an air base in Sicily. Italian authorities took the four hijackers into custody but released another passenger, Muhammad Abbas, despite a request by the United States that he be held as the mastermind of the hijacking.

The seizure severely strained diplomatic ties between the United States and Egypt, and the Italian government temporarily collapsed because of disputes over the release of Abbas. Attorney General of the United States Edwin Meese III promised a worldwide effort to capture Abbas, saying military means might be used to apprehend him. Meanwhile, most Americans were jubilant over the capture of the hijackers, and Reagan's popularity continued to soar.   Frank Cormier and Margot Cormier

See also CABINET, UNITED STATES; CONSTITUTION OF THE UNITED STATES; CONGRESS OF THE UNITED STATES; REAGAN, RONALD WILSON; UNITED STATES, GOVERNMENT OF THE. In WORLD BOOK, see PRESIDENT OF THE UNITED STATES.

PRINCE EDWARD ISLAND. The Progressive Conservative (PC) administration of this island province's Premier James M. Lee was shaken temporarily by the resignation of one of its supporters early in 1985. On February 7, Peter Pope, a representative from Summerside, the province's second largest town, left the PC caucus. He claimed that not enough was being done to promote economic development in his community.

In August, Pope rejoined the party, as minister of transportation and public works in Lee's cabinet. Pope's return gave the PC 20 seats in the Legislative Assembly to 12 for the Liberals.

The government's statement at the opening of the Assembly session emphasized a desire to enhance farming, fishing, and tourism as the main industries of the chiefly agricultural province. The government offered financial assistance for projects in each of these fields.

Finance Minister Lloyd MacPhail introduced a new budget on March 5. It was $11.5 million less than the previous year's, totaling $481.1 million (Canadian dollars, with $1 = U.S. 72 cents as of Dec. 31, 1985). On August 1, MacPhail, a veteran of many ministerial posts since his first election in 1961, was sworn in as lieutenant governor of the province.   David M. L. Farr

See also CANADA. In WORLD BOOK, see PRINCE EDWARD ISLAND.

PRISON. The population of prisons in the United States hit record high levels during 1985. A survey by the Bureau of Justice Statistics, a unit of the U.S. Department of Justice, revealed that 490,041 inmates were housed in state and federal prisons at midyear, a 5.6 per cent increase over the previous record of 463,858 at the end of 1984.

Although the U.S. crime rate continued to drop, federal and state prisons were overcrowded at the end of 1985. Justice officials predicted that the prison population would continue to rise because of hardening public attitudes toward crime.

Overcrowding. Thirty-four states and the District of Columbia were under court orders to relieve overcrowding in prisons. Citing "foot-dragging, ignorance, and indifference" on the part of state officials, U.S. District Court Judge Thomas A. Higgins on October 23 barred new admissions to Tennessee's prisons until the inmate population was reduced by 10 per cent. Under the order, the second such statewide judicial directive in U.S. history, only such "severe security risks" as psychopaths and inmates sentenced to death were exempted. The state put new convicts in hard-pressed local jails.

Tennessee Governor Lamar Alexander on December 11 signed into law six bills designed to improve conditions in the state's prisons, including an early-release program for many prisoners and funding for prison renovation.

Riots. Prisoners at four Tennessee facilities rebelled on July 1 and 2 after being ordered to wear new striped uniforms instead of civilian clothes. The disturbances left one inmate dead and caused about $11 million in damage. Inmates in a state prison in Odenville, Ala., rioted for 10 hours on April 15, seizing 22 hostages and demanding an end to late-night searches and protection from homosexual assaults. The incident ended with 10 injuries but no deaths.

Executions failed to keep pace with death sentences in 1985. More than 200 murderers received death sentences, but only 18 were executed, leaving some 1,630 inmates awaiting execution. The executions brought to 50 the number put to death since the Supreme Court of the United States authorized resumption of capital punishment in 1976.

Escape. The most notorious prison escape of 1985 was that of Bernard C. Welch, Jr., a burglar convicted in the 1980 slaying of cardiologist Michael J. Halberstam. Welch persuaded officials to transfer him to Chicago's barless Metropolitan Correctional Center by promising to inform on other prisoners and then escaped on May 15, 1985. He was recaptured on August 7 in Greensburg, Pa.   David C. Beckwith

In WORLD BOOK, see PRISON.

PRIZES. See AWARDS AND PRIZES; NOBEL PRIZES.

PROTESTANTISM. Protestants around the world focused much of their attention on South Africa in 1985. Support for the government's *apartheid* policy of racial segregation has long come from South Africa's Dutch Reformed Church. In 1985, however, South African churches provided much of the leadership for reform and change.

The most visible and best-known leader of church opposition in South Africa was Desmond Tutu, the Anglican bishop of Johannesburg and winner of the 1984 Nobel Peace Prize (in the WORLD BOOK SUPPLEMENT section, see TUTU, DESMOND). Tutu regularly expressed regret over policies of the United States government, which he felt reinforced the rule of South Africa's State President Pieter Willem Botha. Botha remained virtually unyielding in the face of demands for change.

During the course of 1985, a second South African clergyman came to the fore as an opposition leader. Allan Boesak, president of the World Alliance of Reformed Churches, an international organization of Congregational and Presbyterian churches, was arrested in August and held without formal charges. After nearly a month, he was charged with subversion and released on bail. Among white religious leaders, Afrikaner dissident C. F. Beyers Naudé, a pastor of the Dutch Reformed Church, remained an eloquent witness at the side of black leadership.

United States evangelist Jerry Falwell, after a brief visit to South Africa in August, called for support for Botha's government and for what he claimed were Botha's reformist policies. Falwell was widely criticized for his remarks and apologized for personal attacks on Tutu. But he continued to stand behind Botha.

Issues Among U.S. Denominations. Many Protestant denominations debated at their annual conventions whether to sell their investments in companies that do business in South Africa. The denominations increasingly made such sales a matter of individual conscience, but most stopped short of taking consistent action.

Also attracting support from Protestants was the movement to provide sanctuary for Central Americans who had fled their home countries, many of them because they feared persecution. The number of churches identified with the movement—about 180 at the start of 1985—grew throughout the year. As the Immigration and Naturalization Service of the Department of Justice stepped up efforts to quell the illegal activity, it drew increased resistance from advocates of sanctuary.

In January, the Justice Department indicted 16 Arizona sanctuary workers on charges of conspiracy and transporting and harboring illegal aliens. Among those arrested was John Fife, a Presbyterian minister from Tucson. Fife had started the

Fundamentalists maintain control of the 14.3-million-member Southern Baptist Convention as the denomination elects a new president in Dallas in June.

sanctuary movement in March 1982 by offering asylum to Central American refugees in his church. A number of religious groups jointly filed suit in May 1985 to stop the government from prosecuting church workers.

Protestants moved to center stage in an international hostage drama in September, when Presbyterian missionary Benjamin Weir was released by Shiite militants in Lebanon. Weir, who had been kidnapped in May 1984, was critical of the Middle East policies of the Administration of President Ronald Reagan and of what he thought were inadequate efforts to gain the release of six other Americans still held hostage in Lebanon. Weir, in turn, drew criticism from those who advocated a policy of "no dealing" with terrorists and from those who found his Middle East position not sufficiently favorable to Israel.

Less easily defined but extremely troubling was the issue of church attitudes toward acquired immune deficiency syndrome (AIDS). Some fundamentalists saw AIDS as God's punishment of homosexuals, the group hardest hit by the disease. The Episcopal bishop of California, William E. Swing, wrote a pastoral letter on the question of whether the AIDS virus could be transmitted through the chalice passed from lip to lip during Holy Communion. Swing urged parishes to be understanding toward those who chose not to drink from a common cup during the period of fear and uncertainty.

Conventions and Actions. The largest Protestant denomination in the United States, the 14.3-million-member Southern Baptist Convention, attracted 45,431 delegates to its annual meeting in Dallas in June. At the convention, moderates and conservatives continued their struggle for power, and the fundamentalist faction remained in control for another year. Conservatives reelected fundamentalist Pastor Charles F. Stanley of Atlanta, Ga., as president. But the convention then showed its divided mind by electing moderate W. Winfred Moore from Amarillo, Tex., as first vice president. Moderate church seminaries feared Stanley's powers to make appointments to their boards of trustees. Before concluding, the convention established a "peace committee" to moderate disputes.

The Presbyterian Church (U.S.A.) at its annual convention in Indianapolis in June gave evidence that it was responding to efforts to introduce more conservative policies into the denomination's mainstream. A caucus called Presbyterians United for Biblical Concerns worked to reverse the church's support for a woman's right to an abortion. Although the General Assembly voted down challenges to its stand on abortion, it did change the wording in a 1983 statement to strengthen its opposition to abortion as a means of birth control.

449

Three Lutheran denominations—the Lutheran Church in America (LCA), the American Lutheran Church, and the Association of Evangelical Lutheran Churches—worked to bring about their merger scheduled to take place on Jan. 1, 1988. But many Lutherans were distracted from these efforts by the attention paid to D. Douglas Roth, former pastor of the Trinity Lutheran Church in Clairton, Pa. In March 1985, Roth was removed from the ministry by the Western Pennsylvania-West Virginia Synod of the LCA.

Both civil and church courts had earlier faulted Roth and his colleagues in the Denominational Ministry Strategy, a group of activist ministers, for disrupting church services attended by local business leaders and for other acts of civil disobedience. Roth blamed these business leaders for the hard times and unemployment in the steel-mill towns around Pittsburgh. The LCA finally removed Roth from the ordained ministry for his refusal to obey church authorities.

The Episcopal Church held its General Convention in Anaheim, Calif., in September. After the controversies at its conventions in recent years, the denomination devoted itself in 1985 to electing a new presiding bishop and chief pastor—an activity that takes place only once every 12 years. The chosen leader was Edmond Lee Browning of Hawaii. Although Browning was described by the media as a liberal on social issues, he evidently drew broad support from across the church body.

The President of the Church of Jesus Christ of Latter-day Saints (Mormon Church), Spencer W. Kimball, died in November at the age of 90. Ezra Taft Benson, former secretary of agriculture under President Dwight D. Eisenhower, replaced him as head of the church.

Revivalist Forms of Protestantism made news at times in 1985 when they received challenges. For example, Richard Yao, a former Wall Street lawyer, drew attention when he and some associates organized a group called Fundamentalists Anonymous. The group was intended to address the consciences of former fundamentalists who found themselves unable to adhere to fundamentalist systems of belief but lacked moral support after they changed their beliefs.

Statistics. Overall, the news on North American church life was relatively positive during the year, according to the 1985 *Yearbook of American and Canadian Churches*. The Episcopal Church and the Lutheran Church—Missouri Synod showed small gains in membership, while the Assemblies of God and the Church of Jesus Christ of Latter-day Saints posted hearty gains of 6 per cent and 2.3 per cent, respectively. Martin E. Marty

See also RELIGION. In WORLD BOOK, see PROTESTANTISM and articles on Protestant denominations.

PSYCHOLOGY. The idea that states of mind can affect health gained respect among scientists during 1985. A new discipline called *psychoneuroimmunology* or *behavioral immunology* emerged. Research in this discipline focused on links between mental states, hormones, the nervous system, and the body's disease-fighting immune system.

A relationship involving the immune system, food, and moodiness was reported by University of Chicago researchers in September. The researchers studied 23 psychiatric patients who complained of food sensitivity and also 12 *controls*, volunteers with neither psychiatric nor food-sensitivity complaints. All of the people in the study ate capsules that contained wheat, milk, chocolate, or a *placebo* (a substance with no active ingredients). Their blood was tested twice a day.

When they were fed wheat or milk capsules, 16 of the psychiatric patients and 1 of the controls experienced increased anxiety, irritability, or depression. The blood tests revealed changes in their immune systems similar to the changes that occur during allergic reactions or infections.

Animal Language. The study of chimpanzee language skills continued at Yerkes Primate Research Center in Atlanta, Ga., in 1985. A 4-year-old pygmy chimp named Kanzi emerged as a star performer. According to psychologist E. Sue Savage-Rumbaugh of Georgia State University, who administers the Yerkes ape-language program, Kanzi showed clear signs of comprehending spoken English. He also learned sign language readily, without the intensive training given to other chimps in the study.

Savage-Rumbaugh's work led toward a reconciliation between competing views of researchers in the ape-language field. Psychologist Herbert S. Terrace of Columbia University in New York City in 1980 had criticized researchers who claimed chimps could "talk." Terrace pointed out that chimps lack the ability to create new, meaningful grammatical expressions. In the September 1985 issue of *American Psychologist*, however, he praised the work of such researchers as Savage-Rumbaugh, saying they have demonstrated that chimps are capable of "naming" objects.

Education and Psychology. The growing emphasis on improving the quality of schools in the United States during 1985 brought a new flurry of advice from psychologists concerned with education. Much of the advice was contradictory.

One focus of concern centered on the ideal environment for learning. Many educational reformers pushed for more discipline, stricter dress codes, and tighter control over student life. Psychology Professor Edward L. Deci of the University of Rochester in New York argued in March 1985, however, that this type of atmosphere discourages both teachers and students. According to

© Sidney Harris

"Then, as you can see, we give them some multiple choice tests."

Deci, a helpful learning atmosphere is one that encourages involvement and deep thinking rather than conformity in dress and behavior.

Cultivation of "critical thinking" skills—popular in the early 1950's—was making a comeback in 1985. The American Federation of Teachers in July announced a "Critical Thinking Project" designed to encourage students to learn how to reason rather than simply to memorize facts.

Not everyone, however, agreed that "thinking skills" can be taught in isolation from specific detailed knowledge. A panel advising U.S. Secretary of Education William J. Bennett said during the year that teachers should stress specific facts. Bennett also expressed skepticism of courses that claim to teach "higher-order cognitive processes."

Even the idea of pushing for "educational excellence" had its critics. A panel of five psychologists at the American Orthopsychiatric Association meeting held in New York City in March and April criticized the new stress on educational excellence. They said today's "strident rhetoric" suffers from two misconceptions—that existing schools are inadequate, and that children benefit from being pushed to accomplish more in early grades. The panel contended that most schools are good and that most young schoolchildren do not benefit from pressure.   Russell A. Dewey

In WORLD BOOK, see PSYCHOLOGY.

PUBLIC HEALTH. Representatives of 33 North and South American nations on Aug. 9, 1985, urged the World Health Organization (WHO) and the Food and Agriculture Organization, both agencies of the United Nations, to support a massive effort to improve public health through higher standards for food protection. The delegates, meeting at the International Conference on Food Protection in Washington, D.C., emphasized the crucial link between food safety and public health. They said, for example, that contaminated food is responsible for more than 1 billion cases of acute diarrhea among the world's children each year. Acute diarrhea causes more than 5 million deaths annually, mostly in developing areas of the world.

Food Poisoning. An outbreak of salmonella food poisoning, believed to be the largest in United States history, struck six Midwestern states during March and April. Illinois public health authorities said that there were two deaths directly caused by salmonella and more than 18,000 confirmed cases of the illness. Most of the cases occurred in Illinois, but some were reported in Indiana, Iowa, Michigan, Minnesota, and Wisconsin. The epidemic was traced to contaminated milk packaged at a dairy in Melrose Park, a suburb of Chicago. A task force investigating the outbreak concluded on September 14 that faulty valves at the dairy had allowed raw milk, tainted with salmonella bacteria, to mix with pasteurized milk ready for packaging.

More than 60 deaths and stillbirths in California and several other states were linked to cheese contaminated with bacteria that cause a rare form of meningitis called listeriosis. State health officials in California recalled the cheese on June 13.

An illness involving dizziness, nausea, and tremors struck about 200 people in California, Oregon, Washington, and British Columbia, Canada, during the year. The illness was linked to watermelons contaminated with the pesticide aldicarb. California officials on July 8 ordered the destruction of about 10 million tainted watermelons.

The Injury Toll. Injuries are the principal public health problem in the United States, according to a report by the National Research Council (NRC) released in May. The NRC found that injuries cause the loss of more working years than heart disease and cancer combined. The report estimated that injuries cost the economy $75 billion to $100 billion annually.

According to the report, injuries are the leading cause of death among Americans under age 44. Some 143,000 deaths result from injuries yearly, including deaths due to accidents, suicides, and homicides. Motor vehicle accidents take the highest toll, followed by shootings, falls and jumps, drownings, poisonings, and fires and burns.

The NRC urged aggressive new efforts to prevent and treat injuries and to rehabilitate victims.

Health and Human Services Secretary Margaret M. Heckler on March 2 announces approval of an AIDS-virus test for screening donated blood.

The NRC said that many injuries could be avoided through efforts to change human behavior, such as mandatory seat-belt laws and measures that discourage drunken driving. Likewise, the NRC said that a well-coordinated system of emergency medical care and rehabilitation could both save lives and reduce long-term disability from injuries.

An Intensified Immunization Program for six childhood diseases saves the lives of an estimated 800,000 infants in developing countries each year, according to a WHO report on August 23. The program, begun in 1974, encourages full immunization against measles, polio, diphtheria, *pertussis* (whooping cough), tetanus, and tuberculosis. Nevertheless, WHO emphasized that the continuing lack of adequate immunization programs in many developing countries continues to result in deaths from illnesses considered minor in industrialized nations. For example, WHO pointed out that 2 million deaths from measles still occur each year in developing nations.

Public health officials reported on July 31, 1985, that they believed the U.S. blood supply was then apparently free of the virus that causes acquired immune deficiency syndrome (AIDS). This was the result of a test for the likely presence of the virus.   Michael Woods

See also HEALTH AND DISEASE; MEDICINE. In WORLD BOOK, see PUBLIC HEALTH.

PUBLISHING. Book sales in the United States were mixed in 1985. In the first six months of the year, sales of hard-cover books aimed at adults were up 8.1 per cent compared with the first half of 1984. Sales of *mass market* paperbacks, the type displayed in drugstores and bookstore racks, were down 4 per cent.

Two long-time publishers of books fell victim to the harsh economy of the industry. In April, Macmillan Publishing Company absorbed Bobbs-Merrill, which had been in business for 147 years. In the fall, Doubleday Publishing Company disbanded the 61-year-old Dial Press.

Fiction Best-Seller Lists reflected an increased taste for lighter reading throughout 1985. Stephen King, best known for his horror stories, placed three books on the lists: *Skeleton Crew*, *The Talisman* (with coauthor Peter Straub), and *Thinner* (written under the pen name Richard Bachman). Romances also were popular, with *Lucky* by Jackie Collins and *Family Album* by Danielle Steel being particularly big sellers. See KING, STEPHEN.

Nonfiction Best-Seller Lists reflected Americans' continuing fascination with celebrities, business, and health. *Iacocca: An Autobiography* by automaker Lee Iacocca was the top seller in the first half of 1985. It was displaced by *Yeager: An Autobiography*, the story of test pilot Charles E. (Chuck) Yeager; then by *Elvis and Me* by Priscilla Beaulieu Presley, former wife of singer Elvis Presley, who died in 1977. *What They Don't Teach You at Harvard Business School: Notes from a Street-Smart Executive* by Mark H. McCormack and *Dr. Berger's Immune Power Diet* by Stuart M. Berger were also huge sellers.

Courts. On May 20, the Supreme Court of the United States ruled that *The Nation* magazine infringed the copyright of *A Time to Heal*, the memoirs of former President Gerald R. Ford, by publishing unauthorized quotations from the book several weeks before its 1979 publication date. Most publishing houses hailed the decision, saying it added needed protection to an author's right of expression.

Book publishers also hailed an April decision by a three-judge panel of the Second Circuit United States Court of Appeals overturning a $20,005 libel judgment against a French-language restaurant guide, *Gault & Millau Guide New York*. Mr. Chow, a restaurant, had sued over a 1981 review that was highly critical of its food and service. The appeals judges ruled that such a review is protected by the First Amendment.

Beyond Books. Several publishers in 1985 brought out *electronic novels*, adventure stories in a computer-game format. The reader can affect the course of a story by typing commands on a keyboard.   Mark Fitzgerald

In WORLD BOOK, see PUBLISHING.

PUERTO RICO. Disaster struck at 2:15 A.M. on Oct. 7, 1985, when a wall of mud and rock from surrounding hills buried Mameyes, a slum community just north of Ponce on Puerto Rico's south coast. Governor Rafael Hernández Colón called it "the worst tragedy to ever strike the island." About 150 people died in the mud slide following a three-day rainstorm. The tragedy underscored the precarious plight of more than 200,000 people who live in substandard housing in communities that ring Puerto Rico's cities.

On March 28, a jury convicted 10 police officers of lying to two federal grand juries investigating the 1978 murders of Carlos Soto Arriví and Arnaldo Darío Rosado, who were radical advocates of independence for Puerto Rico. The case was a major issue during the 1984 elections. Hernández Colón had vowed to bring the guilty to justice.

On September 7, the Federal Bureau of Investigation announced that with 17 arrests it was close to breaking up a terrorist organization of Puerto Rican origin. The 17 arrested included 11 Puerto Ricans wanted in connection with the theft of $7-million in 1983 from a Wells Fargo depot in West Hartford, Conn.   Nathan A. Haverstock

See also HERNÁNDEZ COLÓN, RAFAEL; LATIN AMERICA (Facts in Brief Table). In WORLD BOOK, see PUERTO RICO.

PULITZER PRIZES. See AWARDS AND PRIZES.

Robert Bourassa basks in his Liberal Party's December 2 election victory that ousted the Parti Québécois and brought him the prime ministership of Quebec.

QUEBEC. The Liberal Party, led by Robert Bourassa, roundly defeated the Parti Québécois (PQ), under Prime Minister Pierre Marc Johnson, in general elections on Dec. 2, 1985. Johnson had served as prime minister for only two months, having succeeded retiring Prime Minister René Lévesque on October 3. Bourassa was sworn into office on December 12. See BOURASSA, ROBERT.

PQ Troubles. The PQ, which had long sought independence for Quebec from the Canadian federation, voted at a convention in Montreal on January 19 not to fight the next election on the issue of independence. Hard-line proponents of independence walked out of the convention hall, and several PQ ministers resigned from the cabinet and, in some cases, from Quebec's National Assembly. Lévesque narrowly survived several votes in the Assembly, as the PQ dissidents voted with the Liberals against the government.

Lévesque suffered another blow on June 3 when his party lost by-elections in four legislative districts to the Liberals. In one race, Liberal Party leader Bourassa, whose administration Lévesque had replaced in 1976, won election to the Assembly. Conscious that the PQ was slipping in the polls and exhausted by his party's internal strife over the independence issue, Lévesque submitted his resignation as leader on June 20. He had led the party for almost 17 years.

Johnson was chosen to succeed Lévesque as party leader in a unique direct polling of 90,000 party members at a convention on Sept. 29, 1985. Johnson, a moderate who distanced himself from the question of independence, served as a cabinet minister under Lévesque and is the son of a former Quebec prime minister. As leader of the governing party, Johnson automatically became prime minister.

Language Rights. On January 2, Quebec's superior court declared that a law forbidding the use of languages other than French on commercial signs was invalid. The court held that the government could demand French on signs but could not forbid the use of other languages without violating the province's human rights charter.

Budget. Quebec's 1985-1986 budget, announced on April 23, called for $27.2 billion in spending (Canadian dollars; $1 = U.S. 72 cents as of Dec. 31, 1985), with a deficit of about $3 billion, slightly less than in 1984. It included a new tax on insurance premiums but abolished gift and inheritance taxes. In December, the Liberal government said it would exempt personal life, sickness, and accident insurance from the tax and review a budget provision to sell government-owned liquor stores.   David M. L. Farr

See also CANADA; MONTREAL. In WORLD BOOK, see QUEBEC.

RADIO. The most unusual event on United States radio during 1985 may have taken place at noon on April 5. At that time, an estimated 8,000 U.S. radio stations simultaneously played "We Are the World," an anthemlike song that cried out against the famine afflicting Ethiopia and other African nations. The recording had been made a few months earlier by a group of prominent rock musicians, who organized under the banner USA for Africa. The musicians donated revenue from record sales to famine relief efforts in Africa. Among those listening to the broadcast was U.S. President Ronald Reagan, who was flying to his southern California ranch at the time and asked that a radio signal be piped into his plane.

On July 13, in another event associated with famine relief, hundreds of stations aired the 14-hour Live Aid concert that began in London and continued in Philadelphia. The concert was sponsored by an international group of rock musicians. During the concert, radio and television audiences were encourged to telephone in donation pledges. An estimated $50 million was raised.

Rock Lyrics Controversy. The positive publicity that radio reaped from famine-aid efforts may have been offset by a controversy concerning the lyrics of rock songs. Starting in spring, a group called Parents' Music Resource Center (PMRC) spearheaded a drive to create a rating system for rock lyrics. The group was led by Susan Baker, wife of Secretary of the Treasury James A. Baker III. Its lobbying efforts eventually led to a Senate hearing on rock lyrics. The PMRC also put pressure on some radio stations that played rock records with sexually explicit lyrics or with lyrics that seemed to glorify violence or drug use.

In November, the PMRC and the Recording Industry Association of America (RIAA), an industry trade organization, reached an agreement on voluntary warnings for some record jackets. The warning, "Explicit Lyrics—Parental Advisory," was to identify albums with songs containing lyrics that dealt with "explicit sex, explicit violence or explicit substance abuse." The RIAA said that 22 of its member companies had agreed to affix the warning to albums. Some companies said they might print the lyrics on the back of the album instead.

Radio Remains Local. Otherwise, radio remained a medium of local impact. Although national radio networks thrived, each city also had its own cast of local radio personalities and formats. In general, rock stations dominated the airwaves. An unusual attempt to broadcast game shows on radio failed in San Francisco. But Minneapolis, Minn., supported an all-weather station, and a Los Angeles station broadcast only traffic problems in that clogged city. P. J. Bednarski

See also POPULAR MUSIC. In WORLD BOOK, see RADIO.

RAILROAD companies in the United States suffered a drop in earnings and traffic in 1985. The Association of American Railroads reported that U.S. railroads earned about $1.06 billion during the first half of 1985, down from $1.40 billion for the same period in 1984. Rail freight traffic through Oct. 5, 1985, totaled 680.1 billion ton-miles, down from 718.1 billion ton-miles in the same period in 1984. On National Railroad Passenger Corporation (Amtrak) trains, ridership was up about 4 per cent from 1984 levels.

Railroad Sales and Mergers. The U.S. Department of Transportation (DOT) on February 8 announced its intention to sell the Consolidated Rail Corporation (Conrail), the big federally owned railroad serving the Northeast and Midwest, to the Norfolk Southern Corporation. The plan generated strong opposition from other railroads, unions, and some legislators. Congress must approve the sale. Critics contended that the $1.2-billion price tag was too low and that the sale would greatly reduce rail competition. In an attempt to head off the sale, a group of investors, including CSX Corporation, which owns the Chessie Systems, Incorporated, and the Seaboard Coast Line railroad, offered in May to purchase the government's stock in Conrail and then sell it to the public. Congress had not acted on the sale by year's end.

In February, the Soo Line Railroad completed its purchase of the bankrupt Milwaukee Road. The Interstate Commerce Commission (ICC) had chosen the Soo Line offer over a more generous offer by the Chicago & North Western Transportation Company to preserve a greater measure of rail competition.

The ICC also completed hearings in August on the proposed merger of the Atchison, Topeka & Santa Fe Railway with the Southern Pacific Transportation Company. A final ICC decision was expected in 1986.

Labor Issues. In October, U.S. railroads and the United Transportation Union agreed on a new labor contract. The pact calls for the eventual elimination of firemen from locomotive crews and the establishment of a two-tier pay scale with lower wages for newly hired employees.

In September, Canadian National Railways announced planned layoffs of more than 1,300 employees. It cited declining freight traffic and financial losses as reasons for the layoffs.

Regulations. Coal and electric power companies complained to Congress and the ICC that railroads were unfairly raising freight rates for companies that depend exclusively on rail shipping. In July, the ICC approved new guidelines that would determine if rate increases for shipping coal should be allowed. David M. Cawthorne

In WORLD BOOK, see RAILROAD.

REAGAN, RONALD WILSON (1911-   ), the 40th President of the United States, underwent surgery for intestinal cancer on July 13, 1985. The surgery went well, and Reagan's doctors said he would probably not have a recurrence of the disease.

Reagan, at 74 the oldest President in U.S. history, had had his annual physical examination on March 8 at the Naval Medical Command Center in Bethesda, Md. For the second straight year, a benign polyp was found in his large intestine, and, more worrisome, there was evidence of blood in stool samples.

Reagan returned to the hospital on July 12 to have the polyp removed. During the procedure, doctors found a potentially cancerous intestinal growth, and a decision was made to remove it the next day. Five surgeons, working for 2 hours and 53 minutes, removed a 2-foot (61-centimeter) section of Reagan's large intestine containing a growth about 2 inches (5 centimeters) in diameter.

On July 15, the President's physicians announced that the growth was cancerous, but they said there was no evidence that the disease had spread beyond the area removed. Steven A. Rosenberg, chief of surgery at the National Cancer Institute in Bethesda, said the President's chances of living out his normal life span were "certainly greater than 50 per cent."

Reagan left the hospital on July 20, after making what his doctors described as a remarkable recovery. On August 11, he and his wife, Nancy, went to their ranch near Santa Barbara, Calif., where the President recuperated for 23 days.

Other Health Problems. Before the California trip, on July 30, a doctor removed a small blemish from the right side of Reagan's nose. Several days later, Reagan said laboratory tests had found the piece of skin to be cancerous. On October 10, another small patch of skin, containing additional cancer cells, was removed from the same area of the President's nose. The following day, Reagan said doctors had assured him that "my nose is clean." The skin cancer was diagnosed as a relatively harmless type of cancer that is often caused by exposure to the sun.

Reagan continued to cope with impaired hearing—his only other known health problem. In March, he began wearing a hearing aid in his "good" left ear to balance one he had been wearing in his right ear since 1983. Doctors hoped it would help him distinguish the direction of sounds.

Nancy Reagan had a physical examination in October, including a colonoscopy to detect any sign of intestinal cancer. "She's just fine," said Elaine Crispen, the first lady's press secretary.

Reagan and his wife, Nancy, wave to well-wishers from his room at the Naval Medical Center in Bethesda, Md., in July as he recovers from cancer surgery.

The President's Top Staff underwent a broad shakeup. On January 8, Reagan made a surprise announcement that Secretary of the Treasury Donald T. Regan would become White House chief of staff, succeeding James A. Baker III. Baker, in turn, took Regan's position at the treasury. Regan quickly asserted his new authority and appointed three new aides, including conservative journalist Patrick J. Buchanan as director of communications. Michael K. Deaver, Reagan's deputy chief of staff, announced his resignation in January. In December, national security adviser Robert C. McFarlane resigned, and Reagan appointed John M. Poindexter to replace him.

Reagans Report Taxes. On April 12, the Reagans disclosed that they paid $147,826 in federal income taxes on a reported 1984 income of $440,657. The Reagans listed charitable contributions of $20,616.

The Reagan Children. In July, Maureen Reagan, the President's daughter by his first wife, actress Jane Wyman, headed the U.S. delegation to the closing conference of the United Nations Decade for Women, held in Nairobi, Kenya. Also in July, son Ronald P. Reagan was hired by the American Broadcasting Companies as an entertainment industry reporter.   Frank Cormier and Margot Cormier

See also PRESIDENT OF THE UNITED STATES. In WORLD BOOK, see REAGAN, RONALD WILSON.

REEVES, PAUL (1932-   ), was sworn in as New Zealand's 15th governor general on Nov. 20, 1985. He succeeded Sir David Stuart Beattie in the largely ceremonial post as representative of the monarch, Queen Elizabeth II, in New Zealand. Before assuming his duties as governor general, Reeves served as archbishop of the Anglican Church of New Zealand. He is the first clergyman and the first person of Maori ancestry to hold the office of governor general.

Reeves was born on Dec. 6, 1932, in Wellington, New Zealand. He earned a bachelor's degree and a master's degree from Victoria University of Wellington. He also received a graduate degree in theology from St. John's Theological College in Auckland and a master's degree from Oxford University in England.

Reeves became an Anglican deacon in 1958 and a priest in 1960. From 1958 to 1966, he served in several parishes. He taught church history at St. John's Theological College from 1966 to 1969 and was director of Christian education for the diocese of Auckland from 1969 to 1971. Reeves was made a bishop in 1971 and became archbishop of New Zealand in May 1980. He was knighted in August 1985. He will not serve as archbishop during his term as governor general.

Reeves married Beverley Watkins in 1959. They have three daughters.   Robie Liscomb

RELIGION made world news again in 1985, chiefly when religious groups met up with political or military forces. Thus, news stories spotlighted the continued tensions between Sikhs and Hindus in India's Punjab state, where members of the Sikh religion had assassinated India's Prime Minister Indira Gandhi in 1984. Some Sikhs continued to protest certain Indian government policies, which they claimed repressed Sikh people and denied them their rights.

More widely publicized were Islamic brotherhood and Shiite Muslim organizations in the Middle East. As some of these groups carried out terrorist activities, it became important for non-Muslims to learn about the faith and policy of militant groups acting in the name of Allah.

Public Religion in the United States. While keeping an eye on the world scene, Americans increasingly became drawn into debate about their own nation's public faith, its loose collection of beliefs, rites, and ceremonies—not all of them religious—which scholars called its "civil religion." Such debate had been passionate but often confusing during the presidential election campaigns of 1980 and 1984. In a widely appreciated book, *Habits of the Heart* (1985), a team of social philosophers led by Californian Robert N. Bellah traced the spiritual roots of American life to two sources.

Pope John Paul II, televised on a stadium scoreboard, winds up an August visit to Africa by addressing a crowd of Muslims in Casablanca, Morocco.

One source was the human-centered moral philosophy, or "natural religion," of the nation's founders, including Thomas Jefferson, James Madison, and George Washington. Although ever respectful of religion, most of the Founding Fathers did not want to see an established church or a legally privileged religion in the United States, nor did they want nonbelievers penalized by law.

The second source was the tradition of Bible-oriented thought that had animated the Puritans and other early U.S. settlers and had once played a prominent part in American education. This tradition—usually promoted not by law but by voluntary support—has found aggressive spokespersons in recent years.

Among them was U.S. President Ronald Reagan, who repeatedly criticized the Supreme Court of the United States for rulings that he thought "kept God out" of the schools. While the President evoked nostalgic images of a more religious nation, Attorney General Edwin Meese III made headlines for attacks on the court and the schools.

Secretary of Education William J. Bennett was an articulate advocate of the Biblical theme. He argued that "the fate of our democracy is intimately intertwined . . . with the vitality of the Judeo-Christian tradition." Bennett called the Supreme Court's decisions regarding church and state "misguided."

Meanwhile, the Supreme Court continued on the course Bennett termed "misguided." After its 1984 session, in which some rulings seemed to erode lines between church and state, the session ending in spring 1985 found those lines redrawn. In June, for example, the high court struck down an Alabama law that permitted a one-minute period of silence for meditation or prayer in the public schools. See SUPREME COURT OF THE UNITED STATES (Close-Up).

Trouble in Rajneeshpuram, a commune in Oregon run by Indian religious leader Bhagwan Shree Rajneesh, came to public attention in September 1985. At that time, the Bhagwan's top aide, Ma Anand Sheela, and 20 of her allies denounced the leader for fraud and repression. In October, an Oregon grand jury indicted Rajneesh on 35 counts, many of them dealing with immigration fraud—namely, the arrangement of sham marriages between U.S. citizens and illegal aliens to get around U.S. immigration laws. Rajneesh was arrested on October 28 in Charlotte, N.C., while allegedly trying to flee the country. Ma Anand Sheela was arrested that same day in West Germany. Rajneesh pleaded guilty on November 14 and received a five-year suspended sentence. He also agreed to pay a fine and to leave the United States immediately. At year's end, the commune was being disbanded.   Martin E. Marty

In WORLD BOOK, see RELIGION.

U.S. Membership Reported for Religious Groups with 150,000 or More Members*

African Methodist Episcopal Church	2,210,000
African Methodist Episcopal Zion Church	1,202,229
American Baptist Association	225,000
American Baptist Churches in the U.S.A.	1,620,153
American Lutheran Church	2,339,946
Antiochian Orthodox Christian Archdiocese of North America	280,000
Armenian Apostolic Church of America	225,000
Armenian Church of America, Diocese of the	450,000
Assemblies of God	2,036,453
Baptist Bible Fellowship, International	1,400,900
Baptist Missionary Association of America	228,868
Christian and Missionary Alliance	223,141
Christian Church (Disciples of Christ)	1,132,510
Christian Churches and Churches of Christ	1,043,642
Christian Methodist Episcopal Church	718,922
Christian Reformed Church in North America	224,764
Church of God (Anderson, Ind.)	185,404
Church of God (Cleveland, Tenn.)	505,775
Church of God in Christ	3,709,661
Church of God in Christ, International	200,000
Church of Jesus Christ of Latter-day Saints	3,602,000
Church of the Brethren	161,824
Church of the Nazarene	516,020
Churches of Christ	1,600,500
Conservative Baptist Association of America	225,000
Episcopal Church	2,775,424
Free Will Baptists	212,527
General Association of Regular Baptist Churches	300,834
Greek Orthodox Archdiocese of North and South America	1,950,000
International Church of the Foursquare Gospel	171,928
International Council of Community Churches	185,000
Jehovah's Witnesses	697,660
Jews	5,817,000
Lutheran Church in America	2,910,281
Lutheran Church-Missouri Synod	2,628,133
National Baptist Convention of America	2,668,799
National Baptist Convention, U.S.A., Inc.	5,500,000
National Primitive Baptist Convention	250,000
Orthodox Church in America	1,000,000
Polish National Catholic Church of America	282,411
Presbyterian Church in America	168,239
Presbyterian Church (U.S.A)	3,092,151
Progressive National Baptist Convention, Inc.	521,692
Reformed Church in America	341,866
Reorganized Church of Jesus Christ of Latter Day Saints	192,445
Roman Catholic Church	52,286,043
Salvation Army	420,971
Seventh-day Adventists	638,929
Southern Baptist Convention	14,341,822
Unitarian Universalist Association	170,510
United Church of Christ	1,696,107
United Methodist Church	9,291,936
United Pentecostal Church, International	475,000
Wisconsin Evangelical Lutheran Synod	415,630

*A majority of the figures are for the years 1984 and 1985.
Source: National Council of the Churches of Christ in the U.S.A., *Yearbook of American and Canadian Churches* for 1986.

REPUBLICAN PARTY. The national leadership of the Republican Party (GOP) was kept intact in 1985, thanks largely to President Ronald Reagan, whose personal influence was high in the months following his 1984 landslide reelection. Meeting in Washington, D.C., on Jan. 18, 1985, the 162 members of the Republican National Committee (RNC) unanimously reelected Senator Paul Laxalt of Nevada, a long-time friend of the President's, as RNC general chairman; Frank J. Fahrenkopf, Jr., as national chairman; and Betty Heitman as cochairman. Reagan had endorsed all three officers.

Party morale, already high, was lifted further by a report released on January 8 by the Committee for the Study of the American Electorate, a political research organization in Washington, D.C. The report disclosed that the percentage of eligible voters who were registered to vote increased in 1984 for the first time in 20 years. The committee said the number of registered voters rose by 12 million to 127 million—73 per cent of the eligible total—between 1980 and 1984. The information that especially delighted Republicans, however, was the revelation that 61 per cent of the newly registered voters cast their ballots for Reagan, while only 32 per cent voted for his Democratic opponent, former Vice President Walter F. Mondale. The new voters favored Republican congressional candidates by a margin of 45 to 39 per cent.

Switching to the GOP. In one of the most striking political developments of 1985, a number of prominent Democrats shifted their loyalty to the Republican Party. Jeane J. Kirkpatrick, who had served as U.S. representative to the United Nations during Reagan's first term, formally announced on April 3 that she was switching to the GOP. On May 3, former Representative Kent R. Hance of Texas, long a conservative Democrat, said he was becoming a Republican so that "my personal political philosophy will no longer be in conflict with my party."

Political ambitions may have prompted other party switches. On May 8, William Lucas, one of the most popular black Democrats in Michigan, announced he was becoming a Republican. Lucas, chief executive of Wayne County, which includes predominantly black Detroit, was considered a possible candidate for governor in 1986. Another party switcher was Edward J. King, a former governor of Massachusetts who had often been called Reagan's favorite Democrat. King announced on June 3 that he was changing parties, a move that many political analysts thought was a prelude to another run for governor.

The party switching came as the GOP on May 7

Former UN representative Jeane J. Kirkpatrick talks with Republican Party Chairman Frank Fahrenkopf, Jr., in April after switching her allegiance to the GOP.

launched a drive to recruit 100,000 disenchanted Democratic voters and officeholders in 100 days. Although precise numbers were hard to come by, the "Operation Open Door" campaign apparently met with considerable success.

But shifting political loyalties did not always favor the Republicans. On April 5, for example, Nebraska State Senator James Pappas returned to the Democratic Party after nine years as a Republican. His switch, coupled with earlier shifts by three colleagues, put Democrats on an equal footing with Republicans in Nebraska's one-chamber legislature. Because tie-breaking votes in the Nebraska legislature are cast by the lieutenant governor, who is a Democrat, the Pappas move gave Democrats possible control of Nebraska's legislature for the first time since it began operation in 1937, replacing the previous two-house legislature.

Little Support Among Blacks. The GOP continued to have difficulty attracting black voters and party workers. *The Washington Post* reported on Jan. 28, 1985, that Vice President George H. W. Bush, meeting with black Republican leaders, was bombarded with grievances. The black leaders complained that their suggestions had been ignored in party councils and their loyalty had not been rewarded.

On April 4, LeGree Daniels, cochairperson of the National Black Republican Council, announced she was resigning that position—in part, she said, because the party had promised blacks more than it was willing to deliver. Daniels, however, remained a member of the RNC executive board.

Looking Ahead to the 1986 congressional elections, Republicans had cause for worry because they must defend 22 of the 34 Senate seats to be contested. The GOP's prospects looked even shakier when three Republican incumbents in the Senate—Laxalt, Charles McC. Mathias, Jr., of Maryland, and John P. East of North Carolina—announced they would not seek reelection. The three had been considered heavy favorites to retain their seats.

Some Republicans were looking further ahead, to the 1988 presidential campaign. When party workers from 14 states gathered in Grand Rapids, Mich., in June for the Republican Midwest Leadership Conference, presidential hopefuls besieged them with appeals for support. Prospective candidates included Vice President Bush, Representative Jack Kemp of New York, Senator Robert J. Dole of Kansas, and former Delaware Governor Pierre S. du Pont.   Frank Cormier and Margot Cormier

See also DEMOCRATIC PARTY; ELECTIONS. In WORLD BOOK, see REPUBLICAN PARTY.

RHODE ISLAND. See STATE GOVERNMENT.

RHODESIA. See ZIMBABWE.

ROADS. See TRANSPORTATION.

ROMAN CATHOLIC CHURCH. An extraordinary synod of Roman Catholic bishops, called by Pope John Paul II, met in Rome from Nov. 24 to Dec. 8, 1985. The purpose of the synod, an advisory body, was to celebrate the 20th anniversary of the conclusion of Vatican Council II, held from 1962 to 1965, and to assess the council's impact.

At the synod's conclusion, the bishops presented a message to Catholics praising Vatican II and calling for renewed commitment to religion, social justice, and peace. To the pope, the bishops delivered more specific recommendations. They urged the Vatican to publish a new *catechism*, a detailed statement of Catholic belief, which would serve as a guide for local churches. They encouraged the church to restore a sense of mystery to Catholic practices and to stress the importance of the crucifixion of Jesus Christ. They requested strengthened concern for the education of priests and continued dialogues with other Christians and with non-Christians. They asked for a "preferential option for the poor" and applauded efforts to end poverty and oppression but added that material needs could never be met without a recognition of spiritual needs. The synod also requested a study of the role of local conferences of bishops in church government.

Questions of Church Teaching—or the interpretation of church teaching—came to the fore several times in 1985. In 1984, the Sacred Congregation for the Doctrine of the Faith, a Vatican body that safeguards faith and morals, had summoned Leonardo Boff, a Franciscan friar and theologian from Brazil, to Rome to discuss his religious teachings. Boff is a leading advocate of *liberation theology*, which focuses on the church's mission to fight against poverty and social injustice. At times, it uses the theories of Karl Marx, the founder of Communism.

On March 11, 1985, the Sacred Congregation condemned several positions taken by Boff in his book *Church: Charism and Power* (1985). In particular, the Vatican criticized two views put forth by Boff: (1) that the One True Church established by Jesus Christ and His 12 apostles can exist outside the visible form of the Roman Catholic Church, and (2) that *dogma*, or official and precise church teaching, can change from time to time.

The criticism of Boff, at first, was limited to his book. In response, Boff said that he would accept the Vatican's view: "I would prefer to walk with my church than to walk alone with my theology."

On May 9, however, the Vatican announced that it had directed Boff to maintain "a period of respectful silence, which will permit Father Boff serious reflection." The Vatican forbade the Brazilian friar to write, to continue his work on a Brazilian theological journal, or to speak at conferences. The Vatican's statement noted that Boff

Pope John Paul II, in white, joins prayers during a synod of bishops that met in the Vatican from November 24 to December 8 to review Vatican Council II.

criticized interpretations of morality stating that nothing is good or bad in itself and that moral judgments arise from weighing various goods or evils under specific circumstances. The cardinal claimed that such views were more prevalent in the United States than anywhere else. He blamed American theologians for "blurring" traditional values but mentioned no one by name.

Ratzinger also criticized nuns in the United States. "A certain feminist mentality" was found in too many communities of American nuns, he insisted in his press conference. The cardinal said that this mentality had created in those communities "lacerating problems of identity and the loss of sufficient motivation for many."

Ratzinger's book and his remarks at the press conference were publicized widely, as were reactions to them. On June 26, Gerald O'Collins, an Australian Jesuit and dean of theology at Rome's Pontifical Gregorian University, reported that many people in the Vatican were "sad" about Ratzinger's views. Those views, O'Collins said at a press conference in New York City, were "not what you hear from the pope."

Pope John Paul II, meeting with reporters accompanying him to Africa in August, said that Ratzinger's views were the cardinal's own. The pope said that he himself believed that Vatican II was a positive influence on the church.

Another Vatican Disciplinary Action that received wide attention in 1985 was an order directed at Catholics who had signed an advertisement that ran in *The New York Times* on Oct. 7, 1984. The advertisement, which was sponsored by a group called Catholics for a Free Choice, stated that American Catholics held a variety of views about abortion and that not all Catholics condemned abortion in all circumstances. It appeared during the 1984 presidential race, when Democratic vice presidential candidate Geraldine A. Ferraro and other prominent Catholic politicians stated that they would not let their private views about the wrongfulness of abortion influence their public decisions.

On Nov. 30, 1984, the Vatican's Congregation for Religious and Secular Institutes, which has authority over Catholic religious orders, insisted that only one correct position about abortion exists. It ordered the signers to retract their statement or face expulsion from the religious community. The order was signed by Jean Jérôme Cardinal Hamer, the head of the congregation.

In reaction to Hamer's order, more than 30 members of religious orders who had signed the advertisement met in Chicago in January 1985 and announced that they would prepare a "counteroffensive." In the March 1 issue of *The National Catholic Reporter*, a weekly newspaper, 800 Catholics signed another advertisement supporting

had accepted this directive "with religious spirit." The statement was signed by Joseph Cardinal Ratzinger, a West German theologian who heads the Sacred Congregation.

Another Franciscan from Brazil, Paulo Evaristo Cardinal Arns, called the Vatican's action in silencing Boff "curious" and "surprising." Arns was speaking at the annual convention of the United States Catholic Press Association in Orlando, Fla., on May 16. The cardinal, who is archbishop of São Paulo—the largest diocese in the world—once taught Boff and accompanied him to Rome for his 1984 meeting with Vatican officials.

A Conservative Catholic Viewpoint came from Cardinal Ratzinger himself. An interview with Ratzinger on the state of the Roman Catholic Church after Vatican II was published in book form in the United States as *The Ratzinger Report* in 1985. In the book, he stated that the Catholic Church had moved from "self-criticism to self-destruction" in the 20 years following the council. Ratzinger also rebuked a "progressive process of decadence which has developed in large measure under the slogan of a so-called 'spirit of the council.'" The cardinal made clear that the book expressed his own thoughts and "in no way implicated the institutions of the Holy See."

In a press conference in Rome on May 30, Ratzinger explained some of the views in his book. He

those whose signatures had appeared in *The New York Times* on the grounds that "unanimity cannot be imposed." As 1985 progressed, the dispute continued, but neither the Vatican nor any religious superior took public action. Positions were not abandoned, however.

John J. Cardinal O'Connor of New York City won a court case in June when a New York Court of Appeals invalidated part of a 1980 executive order by New York City Mayor Edward I. Koch that banned discrimination against homosexuals by agencies doing business with the city. O'Connor took exception to this order, which could force the New York archdiocese to hire practicing homosexuals. He threatened to run church social service agencies without government funds rather than submit to the order. In its decision, the court focused on the issue of mayoral authority rather than on that of discrimination.

In Other News, three U.S. citizens officially became cardinals on May 25, 1985. They were Archbishops O'Connor of New York City and Bernard F. Law of Boston and Archbishop Myroslav Lubachivsky, spiritual leader of Ukrainian Catholics, who became a U.S. citizen in 1952. The pope visited Latin America in January and February 1985; the Netherlands, Belgium, and Luxembourg in May; and Africa in August.   Owen F. Campion

In WORLD BOOK, see ROMAN CATHOLIC CHURCH.

ROMANIA suffered economically and politically in 1985. In 1984, industrial output had grown 7 per cent, compared with rates of up to 3 per cent from 1981 through 1983. But severe weather during the winter of 1984-1985 stopped many kinds of economic activity for weeks. Domestic and public heating systems broke down in many places, and the government banned the use of private cars. Extra oil had to be imported. In March, the government stepped up coal and oil production.

A Long Drought caused a sharp drop in output from hydroelectric power plants later in 1985. In October, the government placed all the country's power stations under military supervision and fired Deputy Prime Minister Ioan Avram for failures in the management of the country's energy program. In addition, Ion Licu replaced Nicolae Busui as electric power minister, and Ilie Verdet replaced Marin Stefanache as minister of mining. Verdet had been prime minister from 1979 to 1982. In November 1985, Ilie Vaduca replaced Stefan Andrei as foreign minister. Later, Andrei advanced to the position of secretary of the Communist Party Central Committee.

Parliamentary Elections took place on March 17. A reported 97.8 per cent of registered voters cast ballots in the lowest turnout since establishment of the Communist government in the 1940's.

President Nicolae Ceausescu was reelected president on March 27, 1985. He showed signs of serious illness during the year. Newspapers touched up his picture to make him look healthier. And his son Nicu, leader of the official youth organization, played a more public role. Nevertheless, President Ceausescu visited Canada in April and China in November.

Religious Repression increased in Romania during 1985. Among the targets of repression were members of small sects, and *Uniats*, Roman Catholics who acknowledge the supremacy of the pope but have their own liturgy. But in September, the government permitted United States Protestant evangelist Billy Graham to preach in a number of cities. Graham drew crowds of up to 150,000 people. Political observers thought the government let Graham preach to appease critics in the West—in the United States in particular—who objected to the Western policy of support for Ceausescu. The West provides this limited support because Ceausescu's foreign policy has been somewhat independent of the Soviet Union's.

In April, Romania signed a 20-year extension of the Warsaw Pact, the treaty that established the Soviet bloc's military alliance in 1955. But Ceausescu made it clear that he would have preferred a shorter extension.   Chris Cviic

See also EUROPE (Facts in Brief Table). In WORLD BOOK, see ROMANIA.

ROSE, PETE (1941-   ), lined a single to left-center field on Sept. 11, 1985, for his 4,192nd career hit, breaking one of baseball's most enduring records—the 4,191 career-hit total of Ty Cobb. Rose got his record-breaking hit for the Cincinnati Reds off San Diego Padres pitcher Eric Show in the first inning of a game at Riverfront Stadium in Cincinnati, Ohio, exactly 57 years after Cobb made his last appearance at the plate.

Peter Edward Rose was born on April 14, 1941, in Cincinnati, the son of LaVerne and Harry (Pete) Rose. He spent his first 16 years in the major leagues with the Reds, beginning in 1963. He played for the Philadelphia Phillies from 1979 to 1983. After playing with the Montreal Expos for part of the 1984 season, he returned to the Reds as player-manager.

During his career, Rose has set 35 major and National League records. He set a major-league record for having 10 seasons with 200 or more hits, and in 1978, he tied a National League record by hitting safely in 44 consecutive games. He won the National League batting title three times. Rose is known for a style of play that earned him the nickname "Charlie Hustle."

Rose has married twice and has two sons, Peter and Tyler, and a daughter, Fawn.   Rod Such

In WORLD BOOK, see ROSE, PETE.

ROWING. See SPORTS.

RUSSIA in 1985 changed its top leader for the third time in four years. The new government put new stress on economic efficiency and discipline. The Soviets became friendlier toward China, and chilly relations with the United States thawed enough to allow a summit meeting to be held.

Many Changes. Soviet leader Konstantin U. Chernenko died on March 10, after only 13 months in office. On March 11, Mikhail S. Gorbachev succeeded him as general secretary of the Communist Party Central Committee—the top Soviet post. See Close-Up.

On April 23, three close associates of Gorbachev's—Yegor K. Ligachev, Viktor M. Chebrikov, and Nikolai I. Ryzhkov—became full members of the Politburo, the policymaking body of the Communist Party. On July 1, Grigoriy V. Romanov, who had been a rival of Gorbachev's, resigned on "health grounds" from the Politburo and from his post as a secretary of the Central Committee.

On July 2, the long-serving foreign minister, Andrei A. Gromyko, became chairman of the Presidium of the Supreme Soviet, the national legislature. The Presidium handles legislation between sessions of the Supreme Soviet. The Presidium chairman is the Soviet Union's head of state, a largely ceremonial post. Chernenko had been chairman, but Gorbachev chose not to take the post (see GROMYKO, ANDREI A.). Eduard A. Shevardnadze, first secretary of the Communist Party in the Georgian Soviet Socialist Republic, succeeded Gromyko as foreign minister and was elevated to full membership in the Politburo.

On August 1, the Communist Party disclosed that, upon becoming party leader, Gorbachev had also become chairman of the National Defense Council. That group directs the Soviet Union's armed forces.

On September 27, Nikolay A. Tikhonov retired as the Soviet Union's formal head of government, chairman of the Council of Ministers. Ryzhkov succeeded him. The Central Committee confirmed on October 15 that Tikhonov had retired from the Politburo.

Domestic Policy. Gorbachev embarked on a program of local visits and tours not pursued by top Soviet leaders since the days of Nikita S. Khrushchev in the late 1950's and early 1960's. Gorbachev also resumed the campaign of Chernenko's predecessor, Yuri V. Andropov, for greater discipline at work and cracked down on corruption, as Andropov had. On May 16, 1985, the government issued regulations aimed at combating alcoholism.

Industrial Output grew by 3.1 per cent in the first six months of 1985, compared with the first half of 1984. This was less than the planned 3.9 per cent increase, however, and less than the growth in the first half of 1984. Oil production was down 4 per cent. Soviet agricultural officials predicted a grain harvest of 190 million metric tons (209 million short tons) in 1985, compared with 170 million metric tons (187 million short tons) in 1984.

U.S. Relations. On March 12, 1985, Soviet and United States negotiators began arms talks in Geneva, Switzerland. The Soviets had broken off the previous round of talks in 1983 because the North Atlantic Treaty Organization (NATO) had begun to install U.S. Pershing 2 and cruise nuclear missiles in Western Europe.

Russia attacked U.S. President Ronald Reagan's plan for a Strategic Defense Initiative (SDI), also known as "Star Wars"—intended to lead to the development of technologically advanced antimissile and antisatellite weapons, many of which would be based in outer space. The Soviets tried to provoke opposition to the SDI in Western Europe.

The Summit Meeting between Gorbachev and Reagan, announced in July 1985, took place in Geneva on November 19 and 20. The main points of a joint statement issued after the meeting included an agreement to accelerate the arms talks in Geneva, with a goal of a 50 per cent reduction in both countries' nuclear arsenals; an expansion of cultural, scientific, and technical exchanges; and an exchange of mutual visits, with Gorbachev to visit the United States in 1986 and Reagan to travel to the Soviet Union in 1987.

Other Foreign Relations. China and the Soviet Union held talks in April 1985 aimed at the normalization of their relations. During a July visit to Moscow, China's Deputy Prime Minister Yao Yilin signed two agreements with the Soviets. One pact called for a doubling of the trade between the two countries during the period from 1986 through 1990. The other provided for Soviet technical and financial aid.

In July, the Soviets announced that their economic aid to Vietnam would double during the period from 1986 through 1990, and that Vietnam's payments on its debt to the Soviet Union would be delayed.

On Sept. 30, 1985, Muslim extremists in Beirut, Lebanon, kidnapped three Soviet diplomats and a physician who was stationed at the Soviet Embassy. One of the four men was killed, and the three others were released at the end of October.

The Soviet Union continued to support Nicaragua. Nicaragua's President Daniel Ortega visited Moscow in May and obtained promises of help.

In Eastern Europe, the Soviet Union emphasized the need for unity among the seven Warsaw Pact nations. In April, these nations signed a 20-year extension of the pact.

Relations with Great Britain soured. On September 12, Great Britain announced that Oleg A. Gordievsky—an officer of the KGB, the Soviet intelligence agency—had defected. The British said

The Kremlin Opts for Youth and Change

On March 11, 1985, Mikhail S. Gorbachev became the leader of the Soviet Union at the age of 54. Many political observers saw the accession of Gorbachev as an indication that Soviet ruling circles no longer could stand the tension and uncertainty of having frail, elderly individuals at the top. Gorbachev's predecessor, Konstantin U. Chernenko, was 73 when he died after only 13 months in office. Chernenko succeeded Yuri V. Andropov, who died at the age of 69 after ruling the Soviet Union for 15 months. Andropov's predecessor, Leonid I. Brezhnev, was 75 when he died in office.

But why did the men in the Kremlin select the elderly Andropov after Brezhnev died? And why was Andropov followed by the even older Chernenko?

During Leonid Brezhnev's last years, industrial growth slowed, a series of agricultural disasters occurred, and corruption and other types of crime increased. Andropov succeeded Brezhnev because a major segment of the country's ruling group believed that the Soviet Union needed to be revitalized and that, in spite of his age, Yuri Andropov was best qualified to revitalize it.

Once in power, Andropov moved quickly, firing high officials of the government and the Communist Party and promoting Gorbachev and other younger, reform-minded individuals. He urged the Soviet people to work harder and called for more discipline on the job.

In his dealings with the West, Andropov stepped back from détente, the easing of tensions that had been a major element of Brezhnev's foreign policy. In November 1983, for example, Andropov broke off arms talks with the United States.

After Andropov died, power shifted to Soviet leaders who had viewed Andropov as a threat to their positions and their ways of doing things. Their choice for the top position—Chernenko—stuck to Andropov's domestic agenda officially, but the fight against corruption proceeded more slowly.

Chernenko agreed to resume the arms dialogue with the United States. The arms issue got him into trouble with some of the Soviet Union's allies in Eastern Europe, however. East Germany, Hungary, and Romania opposed Soviet attempts to make them cut economic links with the West as part of a campaign to halt the installation of intermediate-range missiles in Western Europe.

After Chernenko's death, the Kremlin swung back to the Andropov approach. They chose Gorbachev because of his youth and because his policies were similar to Andropov's.

There were still strong forces opposing change in the Soviet Union, and Gorbachev dealt successfully with them in 1985. In 1986 and beyond, he can use his power to hire and fire to strengthen his support in the government and the Communist Party. Unlike Andropov, Gorbachev has time on his side.   Chris Cviic

Soldiers and mourners follow the wagon-borne coffin of Soviet leader Konstantin U. Chernenko to Moscow's Red Square for burial in March.

Soviet leader Mikhail S. Gorbachev and his wife, Raisa, wearing neckerchiefs, celebrate the 60th anniversary of a Soviet youth organization.

that, acting on information supplied by Gordievsky, they were expelling 25 Soviet trade and diplomatic officials as well as some nondiplomatic personnel for spying. Russia retaliated by expelling 25 Britons from Moscow. A further British expulsion of six Soviet citizens was followed by a similar Soviet expulsion of six British people.

Three Turn Back. United States sources said on September 26 that Vitaly Yurchenko, identified as a high-ranking officer of the KGB, had defected to the West after disappearing in Rome in July. But in a November 4 press conference in the Soviet Embassy in Washington, D.C., Yurchenko claimed that U.S. agents had kidnapped, drugged, and interrogated him. Yurchenko said that he had escaped from the Americans and was returning to the Soviet Union. The U.S. Department of State said Yurchenko had defected "of his own volition" and had "willingly cooperated" with the U.S. Central Intelligence Agency (CIA) and the Federal Bureau of Investigation (FBI).

On October 24, a Soviet seaman, Miroslav Medved, jumped from a Soviet freighter near New Orleans, swam ashore, and was picked up by police, who turned him over to the U.S. Border Patrol. The Border Patrol officials, unable to speak Russian, assumed that Medved was a stowaway and not a defector and were returning him to the freighter when he jumped into the water.

Other Soviet seamen captured him and took him on board the ship.

After negotiations between U.S. and Soviet officials, Medved was removed from the ship and interviewed by U.S. authorities. The next day, the Americans became convinced that Medved wanted to go back to the Soviet Union, and returned him to the freighter.

Before the vessel left on November 9, the U.S. Senate, two U.S. courts, three justices of the Supreme Court of the United States, and the White House became involved in the case. The Soviets ignored a Senate subpoena for Medved, the courts and the justices refused to intervene in the case, and, on November 8, White House spokesman Larry Speakes said Reagan believed "the executive branch has carried out its responsibilities."

On October 31, Aleksandr V. Sukhanov, a 19-year-old Soviet soldier stationed in Afghanistan, entered the U.S. Embassy in Kabul and said that he wanted to go home. On November 4, a U.S. official told Sukhanov that he would try to secure a grant of asylum if Sukhanov wanted it. But on the same day, Sukhanov signed a statement that he wished to return to the Soviet Union, and he left with the Soviet ambassador.   Chris Cviic

See also EUROPE (Facts in Brief Table). In WORLD BOOK, see RUSSIA.

RWANDA. See AFRICA.

SAFETY. Transportation hazards became a major safety concern in the United States in 1985. As a result, there were calls for new government controls over industries that had only recently won various degrees of deregulation.

Commercial Airlines experienced their worst year, with a record 2,089 fatalities. Airplane disasters in August alone accounted for more than 700 deaths, due largely to a few spectacular accidents involving Delta Air Lines, Japan Air Lines, and British Airtours.

The string of disasters not only fanned public fears but also stirred criticism from Congress. In the House of Representatives, a subcommittee of the Public Works and Transportation Committee charged in September that the Administration of President Ronald Reagan had allowed the number of air-traffic controllers to fall below the level needed to run an effective system. There were about 14,000 air controllers at work in 1985, compared with more than 16,000 in 1981, before Reagan fired 11,500 striking controllers.

Later in September 1985, Secretary of Transportation Elizabeth Hanford Dole announced plans to hire nearly 1,000 controllers over the next two years and 500 safety inspectors over three years. She denied that her actions were related to the rash of accidents or the House report.

A task force set up earlier by Dole reported that the Federal Aviation Administration, a regulatory agency under Department of Transportation (DOT) jurisdiction, had been deficient in identifying and correcting serious safety problems. Dole responded by cracking down on several airlines— ordering changes in maintenance practices and probes of certain parts. But investigators found no problems common to the major crashes.

A Series of Railroad Accidents led the DOT to authorize railroads to test and fire employees for alcohol and drug abuse. Since 1975, there have been at least 48 alcohol- or drug-related accidents, resulting in 37 deaths. On Jan. 3, 1986, a federal appeals court in San Francisco delayed the start of the tests.

Automobile Seat Belts continued to be a major safety issue in 1985. In October, Massachusetts became the 16th state to pass a law requiring the use of safety belts. The Massachusetts law extended state seat-belt laws to more than half the nation's population. In some states, however, the statutes did not appear to meet federal requirements.

Nevertheless, the new seat-belt laws seemed to have had an immediate effect on traffic casualties. In the first five months after a New York law took effect on Jan. 1, 1985, for example, automobile deaths in that state dropped by 24 per cent.

Beginning in September, all new cars were required to have a high-mounted rear brake light. This was one of the few safety regulations enacted

Accidental Deaths in the United States

	1983-1984* Number	1983-1984* Rate†	1984-1985* Number	1984-1985* Rate†
Motor Vehicle	45,100	19.2	46,100	19.4
Home	20,500	8.7	19,700	8.3
Public	19,200	8.2	18,100	7.6
Work	11,500	4.9	11,400	4.8
Total‡	92,300	39.3	91,000	38.4

*For 12-month period ending June 30.
†Deaths per 100,000 U.S. population.
‡The total does not equal the sum of the four classes because *Motor Vehicle* includes some deaths also included in *Work* and *Home.*

Source: National Safety Council estimates.

by the Reagan Administration, which estimated the device would eliminate some 40,000 personal injuries and $434 million in property damage due to rear-end collisions.

Consumer Products. The chief government watchdog on product hazards, the Consumer Product Safety Commission (CPSC), became involved in controversy when its acting chairman, Terrence M. Scanlon, was accused by a consumer group of relaying CPSC plans to companies that were targets of potential investigations by the commission. He was also charged with using government facilities to help an antiabortion group. Scanlon denied the accusations at Senate hearings on his nomination, but at year's end, he had not been confirmed as CPSC chairman.

The CPSC voted in August to drop a long-pending standard for chain saws after determining that a voluntary standard covered nearly all saws on the market. The commission also held hearings on the safety of three-wheel all-terrain vehicles (ATV's). In the first four months of 1985, the rate of injuries due to ATV accidents was reported to be 80 per cent higher than the year before. In three years, 128,000 injuries and 161 deaths resulted from ATV's, according to the agency. Most victims were teen-agers. Arthur E. Rowse

In WORLD BOOK, see SAFETY.

SAILING. See BOATING.

SANGUINETTI, JULIO MARÍA (1936-   ), a lawyer and journalist and the head of Uruguay's centrist Colorado Party, took office as president of that country on March 1, 1985. He defeated two other candidates in November 1984 elections—Uruguay's first national election since the military took control of the government in 1973. Sanguinetti was widely credited with persuading the military regime to hold the election, which returned Uruguay to civilian rule. The new president succeeded General Gregorio C. Alvarez.

Sanguinetti was born Jan. 6, 1936, in Montevideo, Uruguay, and received a law degree there from the University of the Republic in 1961. He soon embarked upon a career in politics, entering Congress in 1963 and winning reelection in 1966 and 1971. Sanguinetti was appointed minister of industry and commerce in 1970 and minister of education and culture in 1972. But he resigned the latter post after six months to protest the interference of the armed forces in Uruguay's government. From 1973 to 1981, he served as political editor and columnist for his party's newspaper, *El Día* (*The Day*). In 1982, the military rulers permitted elections for party leaders, and Sanguinetti became secretary-general of the Colorados.

Sanguinetti is known as an ardent supporter of the arts. He and his wife, the former Marta Canessa, have two children.   Karin C. Rosenberg

SARNEY, JOSÉ (1930-   ), became president of Brazil on April 21, 1985, when President-elect Tancredo Neves died following surgery. Sarney, who had been elected vice president, thus became Brazil's first civilian president since 1964, but he was a reluctant officeholder. He told Brazilians at his swearing-in ceremony: "Here I stand, with the weight of a moment that I did not request and did not desire." See BRAZIL.

Sarney was born on April 24, 1930, in Pinheiro in the northern state of Maranhão. He earned a law degree in 1953 from Maranhão Law School in São Luís and soon after began a long political career. He was elected to the lower house of Brazil's Congress in 1958 and 1962 and was elected governor of Maranhão in 1965. He was elected to the Senate in 1970 and 1979.

Sarney switched political loyalties often. In 1984, he defected from the military-backed Social Democratic Party to the Party of the Brazilian Democratic Movement led by Neves. Angered, many military leaders called him a traitor. The outgoing president, General João Baptista de Oliveira Figueiredo, refused to place the presidential sash on Sarney, a traditional gesture.

Although known best as a politician, Sarney is also a published novelist, poet, and storywriter. In 1952, he married Marly Macieira. They have three children and three grandchildren.   Rod Such

SASKATCHEWAN. A special election was held on March 28, 1985, to fill the seat in Saskatchewan's Legislative Assembly made vacant by the expulsion in 1984 of Progressive Conservative Party (PC) politician Wilbert Colin Thatcher. Thatcher had been convicted of the 1983 murder of his former wife. Another PC member, Rick Swenson, won the election. Bill Sveinson, the sole Liberal Party legislator, was kicked out of the party on January 12 for trying to block action to expel Thatcher. The New Democratic Party (NDP) picked up a seat from the PC in an election in November, and in December, a PC legislator defected to the Western Canada Concept Party. This left Premier Grant Devine's PC government with 53 seats, the NDP with 9, and the Western Canada Concept Party with 1. There was 1 independent.

The government's 1985-1986 budget called for a 1 per cent surtax on net personal income higher than $10,000. (All monetary amounts in this article are in Canadian dollars, with $1 = U.S. 72 cents as of Dec. 31, 1985.) Total spending was up 5.7 per cent at $3.46 billion, with an expected deficit of $291 million.

Devine announced a program on January 30 to step up uranium exploration. A $10.7-million contract with France, Great Britain, and West Germany helped fund the program.   David M. L. Farr

In WORLD BOOK, see SASKATCHEWAN.

SAUDI ARABIA. King and Prime Minister Fahd ibn Abd al-Aziz Al Saud met with President Ronald Reagan in Washington, D.C., on Feb. 11 and 12, 1985, in the first U.S. visit by a Saudi leader in 14 years. Questions about United States efforts to mediate a Middle East peace settlement and U.S. willingness to pressure Israel to offer concessions dominated discussions between the two leaders.

Although Fahd was not completely satisfied with the answers he received, relations between the United States and Saudi Arabia remained cordial. Following the visit, the Saudi government awarded U.S. defense firms $1.1 billion in contracts for the Saudi "Peace Shield" program, a technologically advanced, computerized air defense and communications system. The system was to be coordinated with U.S. AWACS (Airborne Warning and Control System) reconnaissance aircraft sold to Saudi Arabia in 1981. The AWACS were to be linked with 5 underground command centers and 17 long-range radar stations. The system was scheduled to be fully operational by 1992.

An attempt by Saudi Arabia to purchase U.S. F-15 fighters in 1985, however, was delayed by the U.S. Congress because Israel objected. As a result, the Saudis in September ordered 132 aircraft and an air defense system from Great Britain. The $4.2-billion export order was the largest ever negotiated by a British firm.

The President and Nancy Reagan greet King Fahd on his visit to the United States in February, the first such visit by a Saudi leader in 14 years.

Saudi Arabia continued to maintain a low profile in its relations with other Middle Eastern countries. The government aided reconstruction efforts in Lebanon and provided assistance to Jordan as a front-line state in the conflict with Israel.

The Economy. Declining oil revenues and sharply reduced oil production caused a cutback in Saudi development programs. During 1985, oil production averaged about 3.4 million barrels per day. The fiscal 1985 budget, approved in March, was set at $55 billion. The budget, which was balanced for the first time in three years, reflected a 6 per cent cut in government spending from 1984 levels. To balance the budget, the government reduced defense expenditures 20 per cent to $17.75 billion and canceled several large-scale projects, including two major refineries.

Five new petrochemical plants at Al Jubayl and Yanbu went into production in 1985. With $4 billion in revenues generated annually by petrochemical exports, Saudi Arabia was expected to supplant the United States as the world's second largest petrochemical supplier after Canada.

Saudi Astronaut. In June, Prince Sultan Salman al-Saud, nephew of King Fahd, flew aboard the U.S. space shuttle *Discovery*. He became the first Arab astronaut in space.   William Spencer

See also MIDDLE EAST (Facts in Brief Table). In WORLD BOOK, see SAUDI ARABIA.

SAUVÉ, JEANNE M. (1922-   ), spent a busy year in 1985 as Canada's 23rd governor general. As the representative in Canada of the head of state, Queen Elizabeth II, Sauvé visited each of Canada's 10 provinces and the Yukon Territory during the year. She also traveled abroad, inspecting Canada's North Atlantic Treaty Organization (NATO) bases at Lahr and Baden in West Germany in late July.

Among notable events of the year, the governor general on June 28 reviewed a fleet of 35 naval vessels from Canada and other countries at the Atlantic Naval Assembly in the harbor at Halifax, Nova Scotia. The event commemorated the 75th anniversary of the Canadian naval service. She also entertained, on May 16, more than 50 Canadian athletes who had won medals in the 1984 Olympic Games, plus their coaches.

Among royal guests welcomed to Canada by Governor General Sauvé during the year were the Queen Mother, Prince Philip, and his son Prince Andrew. Other notable visitors to Rideau Hall, the governor general's official residence in Ottawa, Ont., included Romania's President Nicolae Ceausescu, Secretary-General of the United Nations Javier Pérez de Cuéllar, and Chief Justice of the United States Warren E. Burger.   David M. L. Farr

In WORLD BOOK, see CANADA, GOVERNMENT OF.

SCHOOL. See CIVIL RIGHTS; EDUCATION.

SCOTLAND. Coal miners in Scotland ended their strike on March 7, 1985—two days after most miners in the rest of Great Britain went back to work. The Scottish miners delayed returning to work in hopes of gaining the reinstatement of 206 miners fired for activities during the strike. By October, however, only 9 of the miners had been rehired. The strike, which lasted nearly a year, had been called in an effort to prevent the National Coal Board from closing mines. Two coal mines in Scotland were closed during 1985, however.

Unemployment continued to rise in 1985. In November, the unemployment rate was 15.6 per cent. It ranged from 25.9 per cent in the west coast town of Irvine to 5.9 per cent in the North Sea oil city of Aberdeen.

Taxes. A storm of protest followed the March revaluation of property on which the *rate* (property tax) is based. In March, the Edinburgh District Council defied the secretary of state for Scotland by setting an illegal property tax rate. In August, however, the council was forced to revise the rate and adjust its budget accordingly.

Industry. The British Steel Corporation in August revealed plans to close its steel rolling mill in Motherwell. The company also announced that it would not invest in new coke ovens needed at its steel plant in nearby Ravenscraig. Despite government promises that steelmaking would continue for at least three years at Ravenscraig, many believed that British Steel's decisions meant the end of steel production in Scotland.

In February, Govan Shipbuilders, near Glasgow, received an order from the Royal Group to build the world's largest passenger-car ferry. It will operate in the North Sea between the English port of Hull and Rotterdam in the Netherlands.

In April, Trafalgar House Offshore revealed plans to use its Scott Lithgow shipyard near Glasgow as a base for Europe's largest offshore construction group. In September, however, Scott Lithgow announced that one-third of its 2,500 workers would be laid off by year's end.

Digital Equipment Corporation in August said it planned to build a new silicon chip factory near its electronics plant in Ayr. In September, Esso Chemicals opened its huge new petrochemical refinery at Mossmorran in Fife.

Environmental Controversies. In March, the Development Corporation of Livingston New Town, near Edinburgh, rejected a proposal by Union Carbide Corporation to build a large chemical plant in the town. Citizens were concerned about the safety of the proposed plant because a gas leak from a Union Carbide plant in Bhopal, India, in 1984 killed about 2,500 people.

In August 1985, conservationists protested plans by Scottish Malt Distillers, Limited, to cut peat in Duich Moss on the island of Islay in the Inner Hebrides. The protesters were worried about the effects on rare Greenland white-fronted geese, which winter in the moss. Many islanders, eager to protect their jobs at the distillery, which uses peat in the making of Scotch whisky, resented the protests. Environmental groups also protested a proposal to build a plant to reprocess nuclear fuel at Dounreay, in northern Scotland. Their efforts led on September 19 to the establishment of a local public board to investigate the matter.

Sports. Jock Stein, Scotland's most famous soccer manager, died suddenly of a heart attack after watching his team tie Wales in a World Cup match on September 10.

On September 15, Scotland's Sam Torrance won his Ryder Cup golf match with Andy North of the United States to give the European team their first victory in 28 years. The Ryder Cup competition is played every two years between male professionals from the United States and Europe.

On September 1, a village cricket team from Freuchie in Fife won the Village Cricket Championship. They captured the title by beating an English team at Lord's, in London.   Doreen Taylor

See also GREAT BRITAIN. In WORLD BOOK, see SCOTLAND.

SCULPTURE. See VISUAL ARTS.

SENEGAL. See AFRICA.

SEYCHELLES. See AFRICA.

SHIP AND SHIPPING. Overcapacity continued to plague the world's shipping industry in 1985 as major new container ships came into service. United States Lines, Incorporated, introduced vessels that can each hold more than 4,000 large, standard containers, spawning drastic cuts in freight rates.

Some steamship companies attempted to reduce capacity by offering joint service. By providing service jointly—selling space on the same ship—carriers can reduce the number of ships on a particular route. In this way, they can ensure relatively frequent service without requiring customers to pay for unused space on a ship.

The year also saw a major bankruptcy. In August, Sanko Steamship Company, Limited, the world's largest operator of tankers, sought financial protection under Japanese law.

A wave of loan defaults began in 1985 as shipping companies were unable to repay U.S. government loans used to finance ship construction. Increasing U.S. dependence on foreign oil in the early 1970's had led to a sharp increase in the number of tankers financed with U.S. government loans. With the decline in the oil business in the mid-1980's, however, some companies were unable to repay the loans. In 1985, the U.S. government had to use general funds for the first time to cover losses from this loan program.

Shipbuilding was depressed worldwide in 1985. The Maritime Administration of the U.S. Department of Transportation (DOT) reported that ships being built in the United States were valued at $818.7 million as of August 1. American shipyards were almost totally dependent on U.S. Navy orders to stay in business. This dependence was expected to continue as U.S. shipyards lose orders to builders in countries where construction costs are lower.

Canal Blocked. Part of the concrete wall of a lock in the Welland Canal in the St. Lawrence Seaway collapsed on October 14. This accident, at the height of the shipping season, blocked traffic between Lake Ontario and Lake Erie until the canal was repaired on November 7. A shipwreck and high winds also blocked seaway traffic for several days in late November and early December.

Government Policy. On May 3, the DOT announced that U.S. tankers built with government subsidies will be allowed to carry oil from Alaska to other states if their owners repay the subsidy within one year. Previously, a regulation prevented ships built with government subsidies from making domestic runs.   David M. Cawthorne

In WORLD BOOK, see SHIP.

SHOOTING. See HUNTING; SPORTS.

SIERRA LEONE. See AFRICA.

SINGAPORE. See ASIA.

SKATING. See HOCKEY; ICE SKATING; SPORTS.

SKIING. Switzerland, led by Pirmin Zurbriggen, took the major honors in the 1985 World Alpine Skiing Championships. The biggest surprise was the victory of 17-year-old Diann Roffe of Williamson, N.Y., on February 6 in the women's giant slalom. She became the first woman from the United States to win a gold medal in these competitions.

The championships were held from January 30 to February 10 in Bormio and Santa Caterina Valfurva in the Italian Alps. Of the 24 medals, Switzerland won 8, Austria won 5, and the United States won 4. Bronze medals went to Eva Twardokens of Squaw Valley, Calif., in the women's giant slalom; Tamara McKinney of Squaw Valley in the women's combined, and Doug Lewis of Salisbury, Vt., in the men's downhill.

Roffe, who started skiing at age 3, was a 12th-grade, straight-A student. This was her first year of international competition.

Lewis had never finished higher than eighth in an international downhill. In 1981, he broke his back when he skied into a lift tower during a race.

Zurbriggen won the men's downhill and the combined event and took second place in the giant slalom behind Marcus Washeier of West Germany. The other winners were Jonas Nilsson of Sweden in the men's slalom, Perrine Pelen of France in the women's slalom, Michela Figini of Switzerland in the women's downhill, and Erika Hess of Switzerland in the women's combined.

World Cup. The World Cup season ran from December 1984 to March 1985. The most successful cup skier was Marc Girardelli of Luxembourg, who won the men's overall, slalom, and giant slalom titles. Girardelli captured seven slaloms and four giant slaloms in totaling 262 points to 244 for the second-place Zurbriggen.

Among the women, Figini won seven races in a three-week period and became overall champion with 259 points to 218 for Brigitte Oertli of Switzerland. The leading American was McKinney, who was ranked eighth with 139 points. The only individual victories by American men or women during 1985 were by McKinney in slaloms on January 5 in Maribor, Yugoslavia, and on March 16 in Waterville Valley, N.H., and by Roffe in a giant slalom on March 13 in Lake Placid, N.Y.

Nordic. The World Nordic Skiing Championships for cross-country and jumping in 1985 were conducted from January 18 to 27 in Seefeld, Austria. Of the 39 medals, Norway won 15, and Finland won 9. Gunde Svan of Sweden led the men with two gold medals and a bronze, and Anette Boe of Norway led the women with two golds, a silver, and a bronze. Frank Litsky

In WORLD BOOK, see SKIING.

Erika Hess of Switzerland races toward a first-place finish in the women's combined during the World Alpine Skiing Championships in February in Italy.

SOCCER

SOCCER had a disastrous year in 1985 in much of the world, especially in Europe and North America. Internationally, more than 100 soccer spectators were killed in riots and a fire. In the United States and Canada, the North American Soccer League (NASL) collapsed.

The sport suffered four major incidents in May 1985. A fire swept through a soccer stadium in Bradford, England, on May 11, killing 56 spectators. A Chinese crowd in Beijing (Peking), China's capital, rioted and attacked foreigners on May 19 after its team was eliminated from the World Cup preliminaries. A Mexican crowd stormed a sold-out stadium in Mexico City on May 26, and 10 people were trampled to death.

In many ways the worst incident happened on May 29 in Brussels, Belgium, before the European Champions Cup final between Liverpool of England and Juventus of Turin, Italy. Liverpool fans charged into a group of Juventus supporters, and a wall collapsed. In all, 38 spectators were killed. The game was played, and Juventus won, 1-0.

In response to the behavior of the Liverpool fans, the Union of European Football Associations banned the 92 English League teams indefinitely from European competition. The Fédération Internationale de Football Association, soccer's world governing body, also banned English professional teams indefinitely from competition in other European countries.

NASL. The NASL, formed in 1968, reached its peak when 24 teams competed from 1978 to 1980. Only nine teams remained in 1984. In March 1985, when only the Toronto Blizzard and Minnesota Strikers posted letters of credit indicating that they had sufficient funds in a bank deposit to cover debts, the league suspended operations. So did the New York Cosmos, the team that inspired the North American soccer boom in 1975 by signing the aging Brazilian superstar, Pelé. In June 1985, the Cosmos suspended operations.

MISL. The demise of the NASL meant that the Major Indoor Soccer League (MISL) was the only remaining professional soccer league in the United States or Canada. In the MISL play-off series, the San Diego Sockers won the championship on May 28 with a 5-3 victory over the defending champion Baltimore Blast. The Sockers took the best-of-seven series, 4 games to 1.

International. In England, Manchester United won the English Football Association Cup, defeating Everton of Liverpool, the league champion and the winner of the European Cup Winners Cup. Norwich won the English Milk Cup, and Celtic won the Scottish Football Association Cup. Aberdeen was the top team in the Scottish Premier League. Shrewsbury repeated as winner of the Welsh Cup. Frank Litsky

In WORLD BOOK, see SOCCER.

SOCIAL SECURITY. Republican Party leaders in the United States Senate proposed curbing the annual cost-of-living adjustment (COLA) in social security benefits as part of a 1985 drive to reduce federal budget deficits. Senate Republicans, led by Majority Leader Robert J. Dole (R., Kans.), announced on February 7 they would propose a one-year elimination of the COLA. But on April 4, the Senate leaders and President Ronald Reagan seemingly agreed to a three-year reduction of the COLA. Under the new proposal, benefit increases based on living costs would be held to 2 per cent per year, plus any amount by which the inflation rate exceeded 4 per cent. The restrictions, to apply from 1986 through 1988, would save the government an estimated $22 billion.

On April 29, 1985, White House spokesman Larry Speakes said Reagan—who had promised during the 1984 presidential campaign not to cut social security benefits—opposed any move to reduce the COLA increases. Senate Republicans expressed outrage at what they saw as Reagan's backing out of a firm agreement. On May 1, 1985, the Republican-controlled Senate voted 65 to 34 against the COLA-reduction plan. The Democratic-controlled House on May 23 adopted a budget resolution preserving full COLA's. The Senate later adopted the same position.

Following the COLA Fight, strong sentiment developed in both houses of Congress to remove the social security Old-Age and Survivors Insurance Trust Fund and the Disability Insurance Trust Fund from the federal budget. The thinking was that there would be less temptation to alter social security benefits to make the federal deficit look smaller if these funds were not part of the budget. The two trust funds currently produce surpluses.

Also under congressional fire was a plan initiated by the Office of Management and Budget (OMB) to cut 17,000 workers from the Social Security Administration payroll by 1990. OMB spokesman Edwin L. Dale, Jr., said the cutback, which might also include closing some local offices, was based on an assumption of "really significant" management and computer improvements.

Payroll Deductions. Effective Jan. 1, 1986, earnings subject to social security payroll taxes were to increase to $42,000, up from $39,600 in 1985, in line with an increase in average wages during the year. The tax rate was to increase to 7.15 per cent from 7.05 per cent. The maximum per-worker tax was to rise to $3,003 in 1986, from $2,791.80 in 1985. Also to take effect on Jan. 1, 1986, was a 3.1 per cent COLA increase in social security benefits, the smallest increase since such adjustments began in 1975. Frank Cormier and Margot Cormier

In WORLD BOOK, see SOCIAL SECURITY.

SOCIAL WELFARE. See WELFARE.

SOMALIA. See AFRICA.

SOUTH AFRICA in 1985 was shaken by angry and often bloody protests by blacks against the white-imposed system of racial discrimination. South Africa's racial policies are summed up by the Afrikaans term *apartheid*, which literally means *apartness*. As applied by the white power elite, apartheid has resulted in racially separate residential areas, schools, and other facilities; most of the best farmland and the best-paying jobs reserved for whites; white control of all branches of government; and security forces that are permitted to use harsh measures, including detention without trial, to protect white privileges.

Protests and Violence. The current series of protests began in September 1984 in the Johannesburg-area township of Sharpeville, one of the segregated communities in which blacks are forced to live. The violence spread quickly to other black townships, and by the end of 1984, an estimated 149 blacks had been killed in the disturbances. By the end of 1985, the number of deaths was nearing 1,000. Virtually all of the victims were black. Although most were killed by security forces, some were killed by other blacks, who viewed them as traitors collaborating with the government by serving in the police force or in the township governments.

The widening protests were directed against a wide variety of black grievances: overpriced ramshackle housing; inadequate schooling; low wages; high prices charged by white retailers; the pass laws, which require that all blacks carry identification documents showing that they have received government permission to move from a rural black "homeland" to an urban township; laws forbidding blacks to own real estate in urban areas; alleged police brutality; and the continuing exclusion of blacks from participation in the central government.

One goal that many protesters had in common was the release of Nelson Mandela, the leader of the banned African National Congress, who has been in prison since 1962 for plotting sabotage against the government. The government offered on Jan. 31, 1985, to release him if he renounced the use of violence as a political tool. Mandela refused to submit to this condition and remained in prison, despite poor health. Mandela's wife, Winnie, emerged in 1985 as a leader of the antiapartheid movement. The government followed her movements closely, and she was detained temporarily several times in December for defying a government order banning her from the black township of Soweto, near Johannesburg.

Boycotts, Confrontations. In mid-July 1985, black consumers in Port Elizabeth began a boycott

Police and soldiers guard a road near Uitenhage, South Africa, in March before a funeral for black activists slain by police during protests.

against white-owned retail outlets that by early November had spread to many of the country's other urban areas. And in October, some 500,000 students stayed away from school to challenge the government's education policies. Most protests during the year, however, involved street confrontations between blacks and police or army units. When such confrontations turned violent—as many did—numerous observers blamed the security forces, saying that they had provoked the demonstrators. In other instances, government forces allegedly opened fire on crowds with little or no warning.

Government Declares Emergency. To cope with the widespread unrest, the government on July 20 declared a state of emergency in three major areas: the eastern part of Cape Province, black townships east of Johannesburg, and Johannesburg itself. The emergency conditions allowed police to impose curfews, detain people without trial, and search homes and other buildings without search warrants. On October 25, Cape Town and seven surrounding districts were also designated crisis areas. And on December 13, the government gave the army police powers—allowing the army to arrest suspects, search buildings, and disperse illegal meetings.

Economic Sanctions. Public opinion in the United States and other countries supported the use of economic sanctions to pressure the South African government to end apartheid. On September 9, U.S. President Ronald Reagan ordered the imposition of sanctions against South Africa, and 11 Western European nations followed suit the next day. On October 22, Great Britain and 48 other members of the Commonwealth—the former British Empire—agreed to a similar set of sanctions.

Government Proposes Reforms. In an effort to defuse the racial crisis, the government, led by State President Pieter Willem Botha, proposed significant reforms. On September 12, a committee appointed by Botha recommended the abolition of the pass laws. The panel said that blacks should be allowed unrestricted access to black townships—though not that they be allowed to live in white areas. In a speech on September 30, Botha offered a plan for bringing blacks into the political system. President Botha's proposals, however, were short on specifics and long on implications that whites intended to maintain their iron grip on the government.   J. Dixon Esseks

See also AFRICA (Facts in Brief Table). In WORLD BOOK, see SOUTH AFRICA.

SOUTH AMERICA. See LATIN AMERICA and articles on Latin-American countries.

SOUTH CAROLINA. See STATE GOVERNMENT.

SOUTH DAKOTA. See STATE GOVERNMENT.

SOUTH WEST AFRICA. See NAMIBIA.

SPACE EXPLORATION. The United States completed nine space shuttle missions in 1985. In the first flight, the shuttle *Discovery* rocketed aloft from Cape Canaveral, Fla., on January 24 on a military mission about which the National Aeronautics and Space Administration (NASA) released little information. The five-man crew, all military astronauts, landed at Cape Canaveral on January 27.

Discovery went into orbit again on April 12 after weather and equipment malfunctions delayed the launch five times. The crew of seven included Senator E. Jacob (Jake) Garn (R., Utah), chairman of a Senate subcommittee that oversees the funding of the civilian space program. Garn was the first member of Congress to fly in space.

The crew launched *Anik C-1*, a Canadian communications satellite, successfully, but a *Syncom 3* military communications satellite they released failed to reach proper orbit. The crew tried unsuccessfully to repair it during a spacewalk that extended the flight two days beyond schedule. Bad weather delayed the landing further. On April 19, a rough touchdown at Cape Canaveral damaged a wing, heat shield tiles, and two tires.

Spacelab Mission. On April 29, only 10 days after *Discovery* landed, *Challenger* lifted 7 human beings, 2 monkeys, and 24 rats into orbit. In its cargo bay, the shuttle carried a European-built Spacelab, in which astronauts can work without wearing space suits. The crew released a satellite designed to provide a standard of measurement for radar screens used in air traffic control. A second satellite failed to leave the cargo bay. *Challenger* landed at Edwards Air Force Base in California on May 6.

International Mission. *Discovery* rocketed aloft again on June 17 on an international mission with a crew of seven that included Prince Sultan Salman al-Saud of Saudi Arabia and Patrick Baudry of France. The astronauts launched *Morelos-A*, Mexico's first communications satellite; *Arabsat-1B*, a communications satellite owned by 22 Arab nations; *Telstar 3-D*, a U.S. commercial communications satellite; and six smaller satellites, three owned by West Germany. Then the crew launched and retrieved *Spartan*, a platform holding instruments that recorded X rays from deep space. The mission ended with a landing at Cape Canaveral on June 24.

Troubled Flight. *Challenger* started into space again on July 29, but minutes after liftoff one of the shuttle's three main engines shut down. An on-board computer shut down the engine when faulty sensors indicated that the engine was overheating. After determining that the seven crew members were in no danger, flight controllers went ahead with a mission in a lower orbit than planned.

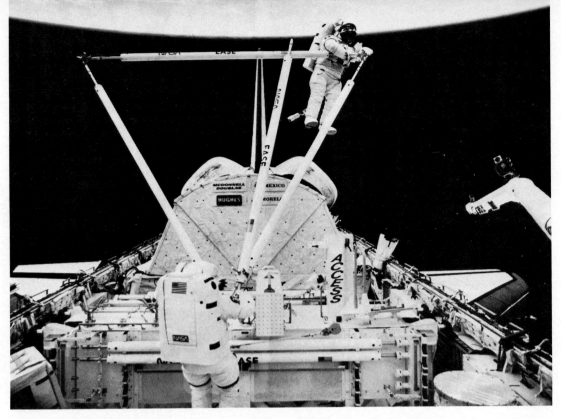

Atlantis astronauts in November test techniques that will be used to assemble permanent space stations and other large structures in orbit.

The mission continued to be troubled with instrument problems, and flight controllers extended it for an extra day so the crew could make scheduled scientific observations. *Challenger* landed at Edwards on August 6.

After two delays within three days, one caused by weather and the other by a computer failure, *Discovery* returned to orbit on August 27. The crew orbited three satellites. *Discovery* then rendezvoused with the crippled *Syncom 3* satellite launched from *Discovery* in April. On August 31 and September 1, James D. van Hoften and William F. Fisher took spacewalks on which they captured the satellite with the shuttle's robot arm, repaired it, and relaunched it. The long salvage job forced the crew to make a rare predawn landing at Edwards on September 3.

A New Space Shuttle, *Atlantis,* made its maiden flight on October 3 to 7. It carried a payload for the U.S. Department of Defense.

Eight Aboard. *Challenger* returned to orbit on October 30, carrying the largest shuttle crew to date—five Americans, two West Germans, and one Dutchman. West Germany was in charge of the flight—the first manned mission managed by a nation other than the United States or Soviet Union. The flight was devoted entirely to studies conducted on-board a Spacelab. *Challenger* landed on November 6.

Construction in Space. On November 26, *Atlantis* blasted off from Cape Canaveral. The seven-member crew included mission specialist Rodolfo Neri Vela, the first Mexican to ride a shuttle. Astronauts Sherwood C. Spring and Jerry L. Ross took spacewalks during which they practiced assembling and disassembling two types of structures that may be used in building a large space station. The crew also launched three communications satellites. *Atlantis* returned to Earth on December 3.

Soviet Activity. In the first Soviet manned space flight since October 1984, cosmonauts Vladimir Dzhanibekov and Viktor Savinykh lifted off in a *Soyuz T-13* spacecraft on June 6. They docked with *Salyut 7,* a space station put in orbit in April 1982. Dzhanibekov said later that they worked in darkness and subzero temperatures to reactivate the station, which had been shut down by failure of its solar-charged batteries. A crewless *Progress 24* supply ship docked with *Salyut 7* and refueled it on June 23. The next robot visitor was *Cosmos 1169,* a new type of unmanned platform carrying scientific equipment, which docked with *Salyut 7* on July 21. *Progress 24* separated from *Salyut 7* on July 15, and the platform left the space station on August 29. Both *Progress 24* and *Cosmos 1169* were destroyed as they reentered Earth's atmosphere.

On September 17, a *Soyuz T-14* spaceship carrying Vladimir V. Vasyutin, Georgi M. Grechko, and Aleksandr A. Volkov docked with the station. A week later, Dzhanibekov and Grechko left *Salyut 7* in the *Soyuz T-13*. They landed safely on September 26. The others returned to Earth on November 21 because Vasyutin needed medical attention.

Comet Encounters. Two unmanned Soviet spacecraft, *Vega 1* and *Vega 2*, left Earth on Dec. 15 and 24, 1984, respectively. Both reached Venus in June 1985. Each released landing craft that recorded data as they descended and while on the surface. *Vega 1* and *Vega 2* then headed for a March 1986 rendezvous with Halley's Comet. On July 2, the European Space Agency launched the *Giotto* spacecraft, which also was targeted to intercept Halley's Comet.

On September 11, the *International Cometary Explorer* (*ICE*), a U.S. space probe, made the first flight through the tail of a comet. Flight controllers maneuvered *ICE* to a meeting with Comet Giacobini-Zinner as it passed about 71 million kilometers (44 million miles) from Earth. Instruments aboard *ICE* supported the theory that comets are "dirty snowballs" made of dust and ordinary ice. William J. Cromie

See also ASTRONOMY; ASTRONOMY (Close-Up). In the Special Reports section, see A NEW ERA IN SPACE. In WORLD BOOK, see SPACE TRAVEL.

U.S. President Ronald Reagan chats with Spain's President Felipe González Márquez in Madrid's historic El Pardo Palace in May.

SPAIN. On June 12, 1985, Spain signed treaties to bring it into the European Community (EC or Common Market) on Jan. 1, 1986. Before signing the treaties, Spain had to reach a trade agreement with Portugal, which also was to join the EC in January 1986. Spain agreed to accept a limitation on its use of Portuguese fishing waters, while Portugal accepted Spain's import quotas on Portuguese textiles, cork, and some petrochemicals.

NATO Vote. Spain scheduled for February 1986 a *referendum* (direct vote of the people) on whether to remain in the North Atlantic Treaty Organization (NATO). Defense Minister Narcis Serra Serra warned on Jan. 20, 1985, that Spain would display "a historic sense of irresponsibility" by voting to leave the alliance. On May 14, President Felipe González Márquez indicated that he would ignore a vote in favor of leaving NATO.

Gibraltar Opens. On February 5, Spain opened its frontier gates to Gibraltar, a British dependency on the southern coast of Spain. The gates had been closed since 1969, after Spain and Great Britain disagreed on whether Gibraltar could become independent if Britain wanted to give up control over the dependency. In 1985, Spain and Britain agreed to cooperate in economic and social matters pertaining to Gibraltar. Britain's Prime Minister Margaret Thatcher told the British House of Commons, however, that Britain would never hand Gibraltar to Spain against the wishes of the people of the dependency.

U.S. Bases. Left wing groups demonstrated in Spanish cities on May 5, the day before a visit by United States President Ronald Reagan. Reagan agreed to Spain's request for early talks on the future of U.S. military bases in Spain. González believed that a reduction in U.S. bases would help him to win the NATO referendum.

Government Crisis. On July 4, Economy, Finance, and Commerce Minister Miguel Boyer resigned because González overruled him in a cabinet reshuffle. On July 3, González had replaced Foreign Minister Fernando Morán with Francisco Fernández Ordóñez, described as a "convinced Atlantist"—one who favors close relations between Western Europe and the United States. Boyer objected to the removal of Morán. Carlos Solchaga replaced Boyer, and there were four other cabinet changes. The disagreement and the departure of Boyer led to sharp drops on the stock exchange.

Abortion Defiance. On August 7, a law authorizing abortion in certain circumstances went into effect. Doctors and some local government bodies resisted the law. On August 12, the first woman to take advantage of it was excommunicated from the Roman Catholic Church. Kenneth Brown

See also EUROPE (Facts in Brief Table). In WORLD BOOK, see SPAIN.

SPORTS. College and university athletic programs came under tighter control in 1985. The National Collegiate Athletic Association (NCAA), the major governing body for intercollegiate sports, found several member institutions guilty of violating rules governing recruiting, academic standards, and ethics. Other colleges reportedly were being investigated.

College and university presidents took a broader role in the NCAA and called an NCAA special convention on June 20 and 21 in New Orleans. Almost unanimously, the NCAA approved the strongest penalties ever. One penalty allowed a team to be suspended from competition and barred from giving athletic scholarships for up to two years if found guilty of major rule violations twice within five years.

The convention also agreed that penalties should include the suspension or dismissal of any coach involved in major violations and suspension of the college's right to recruit athletes in the sport.

Probations. Since 1980, the NCAA had placed at least 20 university teams on probation for serious violations. Among them were such major universities as Arizona, Arizona State, Florida, Illinois, Kansas, Southern California, Southern Methodist, and UCLA. The violations included giving cash, automobiles, apartments, and jobs to athletes, changing classroom transcripts, and accepting fake classroom credits.

In August 1985, the NCAA penalized Southern Methodist University (SMU) of Dallas by revoking all 30 of its football scholarships for freshmen entering for the 1986 season and 15 scholarships for the 1987 season. SMU *boosters* (alumni and friends of the university) were accused of having offered high school athletes money, automobiles, and jobs for relatives if they enrolled at SMU.

Texas Christian University in Fort Worth, SMU's traditional athletic rival, also had problems because of boosters. Seven Texas Christian football players admitted they had accepted cash payments from boosters in violation of NCAA rules. One of the players was Heisman Trophy candidate Kenneth Davis, an all-America running back. In September, Texas Christian officials suspended the seven players from the team, though it meant a setback for a promising football season.

A basketball point-shaving scandal erupted in April 1985 at Tulane University in New Orleans. Three players accused of taking $23,000 from gamblers to shave points in two games in February were indicted, along with five other people. Two other players were implicated, but they were granted immunity from prosecution. As a result of the scandal, Tulane University President Eamon Kelly ended the university's basketball program. Charges were dropped against the best-known player, John (Hot Rod) Williams, after a mistrial was declared on August 13. On November 13, however, a state appeals court ruled that the charges should not have been dismissed, clearing the way for a retrial.

At Vanderbilt University in Nashville, strength coach E. J. (Doc) Kreis resigned after he was linked to illegal sales of anabolic steroids to athletes at Vanderbilt and at Clemson University in Clemson, S.C. In November, he pleaded guilty to a charge of illegally distributing the drugs and was sentenced to a year's probation. (Anabolic steroids help build muscles but have dangerous side effects.) In a separate but related inquiry, Stan Narewski and Sam Colson, former Clemson coaches, pleaded guilty in March to possession and distribution of steroids. Clemson President William Atchley said he tried to make changes in the athletic department but could not get approval from the university trustees. Atchley resigned on March 1.

The Sullivan Award, given annually by the Amateur Athletic Union to the outstanding amateur athlete in the United States, went to Greg Louganis of Mission Viejo, Calif. Louganis won the two diving gold medals for men in the 1984 Summer Olympic Games in Los Angeles. He was a Sullivan Award finalist for a record sixth consecutive year. The other amateur athletes named as finalists were Mary Lou Retton and Bart Conner (gymnastics), Valerie Brisco-Hooks and Joan Benoit Samuelson (track and field), Ambrose (Rowdy) Gaines IV (swimming), Bill Johnson (skiing), Tracie Ruiz (synchronized swimming), Joe Fargis (equestrian), and Steven Fraser (wrestling).

Among the Winners in 1985 were the following:
Diving. Michele Mitchell of Mission Viejo, Calif., won the women's platform title in the Fédération Internationale de Natation Amateur (FINA or International Amateur Swimming Federation) Cup competition. The three other titles went to Chinese athletes—Li Qiaoxian in women's springboard, Tan Liangde in men's springboard, and Li Kongzeng in men's platform.
Fencing. West Germany won three gold medals and Italy won two in the world championships held from July 11 to 21 in Barcelona, Spain. The individual champions were Mauro Numa of Italy in men's foil, Gyoergy Nebald of Hungary in sabre, Philippe Boisse of France in epee, and Cornelia Hanisch of West Germany in women's foil.
Gymnastics. The Soviet Union won both team titles and both all-around titles in the world championships held from November 4 to 10 in Montreal, Canada.
Marathon. World records were set by Carlos Lopes of Portugal among the men (2 hours 7 minutes 12 seconds on April 20 in Rotterdam, the Netherlands) and Ingrid Kristiansen of Norway among the women (2:21.06 on April 21 in London). The World Cup winners were Ahmed Saleh of Djibouti and Katrin Doerre of East Germany.
Rowing. East German women won four gold medals, and Soviet and Italian men won three each in the world championships held from August 26 to September 1 in Belgium. The Soviet Union won the men's and the wom-

en's eight-oared competition. The eight-oared crew of Harvard University in Cambridge, Mass., won the United States college title and the Henley Grand Challenge Cup.

Wrestling. The Soviet Union won the team titles in the world championships in freestyle in October in Budapest, Hungary, and in the Greco-Roman events in August in Norway. Three Americans won titles—Mark Schultz of Palo Alto, Calif., in 180.5-pound freestyle; Bill Scherr of Bloomington, Ind., in 198-pound freestyle; and Michael Houck of Robbinsdale, Minn., in 198-pound Greco-Roman.

Other Champions

Archery, world champions: men, Rick McKinney, Glendale, Ariz.; women, Irina Soldatova, Soviet Union.

Badminton, world champions: men, Han Jian, China; women, Han Aiping, China.

Bandy ball, world champion: Soviet Union.

Biathlon, world champions: men's 10-kilometer, Frank-Peter Rötsch, East Germany; men's 20-kilometer, Yuri Kashkarov, Soviet Union; women's 5-kilometer, Sanna Groemlid, Norway; women's 10-kilometer, Kaya Parve, Soviet Union.

Billiards, world three-cushion champion: Raymond Ceulemans, Belgium.

Boardsailing, U.S. heavyweight champion: Peter Johnson, Oyster Bay, N.Y.

Bobsledding, world champions: two-man, Wolfgang Hoppe, East Germany; four-man, Bernhard Lehmann, East Germany; World Cup, Jeff Jost, Burke, N.Y.

Canoeing, world champions: 10,000-meter kayak, Greg Barton, Homer, Mich.; slalom, David Hearn, Bethesda, Md.

Casting, U.S. all-around champion: Steve Rajeff, Poulsbo, Wash.

Cyclists race through the Place de la Concorde in Paris in July in the final stage of the annual Tour de France competition.

Court tennis, world champion: Chris Ronaldson, Great Britain.

Cross-country, world champions: men, Carlos Lopes, Portugal; women, Zola Budd, Great Britain.

Curling, world champions: men, Al Hackner, Canada; women, Linda Moore, Canada.

Cycling, world women's pursuit champion: Rebecca Twigg, Tacoma, Wash.; Tour de France champion: Bernard Hinault, France.

Darts, North American champions: men, Joe Lowe, Great Britain; women, Sonya Ralphs, Great Britain.

Equestrian, World Cup jumping champion: Conrad Homfeld, Petersburg, Va.

Field hockey, U.S. college women's champion: Old Dominion.

Frisbee, U.S. open champions: men, Scott Zimmerman, Arcadia, Calif.; women, Judy Horowitz, Forest Hills, N.Y.

Handball, U.S. four-wall champions: men, Naty Alvarado, Hesperia, Calif.; women, Peanut Motal, Martinez, Calif.

Hang gliding, world champion: John Pendry, Great Britain.

Horseshoe pitching, world champions: men, Walter Ray Williams, Jr., Chino, Calif.; women, Debbie Michaud, Raynham, Mass.

Iceboating, world DN Class champion: Jan Gougeon, Bay City, Mich.

Judo, world open champion: Yoshimi Masaki, Japan.

Lacrosse, U.S. college champion: Johns Hopkins University.

Lawn bowling, national open champions: men, John Johnson, Seattle; women, Dorothy Macy, Seattle.

Luge, world champions: men, Michael Walter, East Germany; women, Steffi Martin, East Germany.

Modern pentathlon, world champion: Attila Mizner, Hungary.

Motorcycle racing, world 250-cc and 500-cc champion: Freddie Spencer, Shreveport, La.

Orienteering, world champions: men, Kari Sallinen, Finland; women, Annichen Kringstad, Sweden.

Paddle tennis, U.S. champions: men, Mark Rifenbark, Los Angeles; women, Kathy May Paben, Santa Monica, Calif.

Parachute jumping, U.S. overall champions: men, Cliff Jones, Fort Bragg, N.C.; women, Cheryl Stearns, Salisbury, Md.

Platform tennis, U.S. doubles champions: men, Steve Baird, Harrison, N.Y., and Rich Maier, Nyack, N.Y.; women, Robin Fulton, Darien, Conn., and Linda Wolf, New Canaan, Conn.

Polo, Gold Cup champion: Chasqui, Argentina.

Racquetball, U.S. champions: DP men's nationals, Gregg Peck, Austin, Tex.; Ektelon men's nationals, Cliff Swain, Braintree, Mass.; women, Lynn Adams, Costa Mesa, Calif.

Racquets, world champion: William Boone, Britain.

Rhythmic gymnastics, world all-around champion: Diliana Gueorguieva, Bulgaria.

Rodeo, U.S. all-around champion: Lewis Feild, Elk Ridge, Utah.

Roller skating, world champions: men's free skating, Scott Cohen, New Brunswick, N.J.; women's free skating, Chiara Sartori, Italy; men's 20-kilometer speed, Bobby Kaiser, High Point, N.C.; women's 10-kilometer speed, Darlene Kessinger, New Albany, Ind.

Rugby, U.S. champion: Milwaukee.

Shooting, world skeet champion: Charlie Martin, Roswell, N.Mex.

Skateboarding, Capitola Classic champion: Tommy Guerrero, San Francisco.

Sled dog racing, world champion: Chuck Erhart, Tanana, Alaska.

Softball, U.S. fast-pitch champions: men, Pay 'n Pak, Bellevue, Wash.; women, Hi-Ho Brakettes, Stratford, Conn.

Squash racquets, North American men's champion: Jahangir Khan, Pakistan; U.S. women's champion: Alicia McConnell, New York City.

Squash tennis, U.S. champion: Gary Squires, Rowayton, Conn.

Surfing, Ocean Pacific pro champions: men, Mark Occhilupo, Australia; women, Pam Burridge, Australia.

Synchronized swimming, FINA Cup champion: Carolyn Waldo, Canada.

Table tennis, world champions: men, Jiang Jialiang, China; women, Cao Yanhua, China.

Tae kwon do, women's world heavyweight champion: Lynnette Love, Detroit.

Team handball, U.S. champions: men, California Heat, Hayward, Calif.; women, Washington, D.C., Panthers.

Triathlon, U.S. series champions: men, Scott Molina, Del Mar, Calif.; women, Linda Buchanan, San Diego.

Tumbling, World Cup champions: men, Igor Brikman, Soviet Union; women, tie between Huang Ruisen and Yao Zhihua, both of China.

Volleyball, U.S. champions: men, Molten, Torrance, Calif.; women, Merrill Lynch, Albuquerque, N. Mex.

Water polo, U.S. outdoor champions: men, Newport, Newport Beach, Calif.; women, Hackers, Orange County, California.

Water skiing, world overall champions: men, Sammy Duvall, Windermere, Fla.; women, Karen Neville, Australia.

Weight lifting, world super heavyweight champion: Antonio Krastev, Bulgaria. Frank Litsky

See also articles on the various sports. In WORLD BOOK, see articles on the various sports.

SPRINGSTEEN, BRUCE (1949-   ), an American singer, songwriter, and musician, is one of the most popular performers in rock music. In October 1985, Springsteen and his group, the E Street Band, completed a 15-month international concert tour that drew record crowds.

Springsteen, known as "The Boss," performs for nearly four hours at his concerts. Many of his songs deal with the problems and broken dreams of ordinary people. See POPULAR MUSIC.

Springsteen was born in Freehold, N.J., on Sept. 23, 1949. He became a professional musician after graduating from high school and briefly attending a community college.

Springsteen's first album, *Greetings from Asbury Park, N.J.*, was released in 1973. He gained nationwide fame with his third album, *Born to Run* (1975). *Born in the U.S.A.*, his seventh, was released in 1984 and remained near the top of the bestseller charts for more than a year. It had sold more than 13 million copies worldwide by the fall of 1985. A song from that album, "Dancing in the Dark," won a Grammy Award as best male rock performance from the National Academy of Recording Arts and Sciences on Feb. 26, 1984. Despite Springsteen's many hits, the award was his first Grammy.

Springsteen married Julianne Phillips, an actress and model, on May 13, 1985. Sara Dreyfuss

SRI LANKA. Negotiations between the government and representatives of Sri Lanka's Tamil ethnic minority began on July 8, 1985, in an effort to end years of bloodshed. At year's end, however, the talks had produced little result.

Tamil Separatists. Five main Tamil groups with some 7,500 guerrillas fought to win a separate state—which they called Eelam—for the Tamil Hindus. The Tamils are a minority in Sri Lanka, an island nation dominated by Sinhalese Buddhists. Most of the fighting between the guerrillas and government forces occurred in the predominantly Tamil-inhabited north and in the east, where a Muslim minority was also involved. Each side accused the other of atrocities.

Some 40 Tamils disguised as soldiers carried the conflict into Anuradhapura, a city sacred to the Buddhists, on May 14. The Tamils killed about 145 people and wounded another 100, including many nuns, other women, and children.

The Anuradhapura attack and the general deterioration of security led President J. R. Jayewardene to fly to New Delhi, India's capital, on June 2 to appeal to India's Prime Minister Rajiv Gandhi to help end the conflict. The guerrillas drew support from India's Tamil Nadu state, a Tamil-inhabited southern state close to Sri Lanka. Gandhi gave his cooperation by threatening to close guerrilla bases in India and to arrest guerrilla leaders if they refused to seek a peaceful solution.

Peace Efforts. Indian officials helped arrange a cease-fire beginning on June 18 and the start of negotiations at Thimphu, Bhutan. After two rounds, the negotiations broke down on August 17 when Tamil representatives walked out, charging governmental genocide—that is, the systematic extermination of their people.

India got new talks going in New Delhi that led to an August 31 proposal for elected councils to assume some power in Tamil areas of Sri Lanka. On September 3, unidentified guerrilla elements murdered two leading Tamil moderates in an apparent effort to block any compromise.

Scattered bloodshed continued despite the cease-fire. India worked out an October agreement on a multiethnic committee of Sri Lankans to investigate charges of cease-fire violations.

Jayewardene was widely criticized as indecisive in handling the Tamil problem. On September 12, however, his United National Party won a special election in the Sinhalese south to fill a vacant seat in Parliament. The candidates fought the campaign primarily over policy toward Tamils.

The Economy was not badly damaged by the conflict, though it cut the tourist trade. Tight fiscal policies and good harvests of tea, coconuts, and rice controlled inflation. Henry S. Bradsher

See also ASIA (Facts in Brief Table). In WORLD BOOK, see SRI LANKA.

STAMP COLLECTING. The United States Postal Service raised the cost of mailing a first-class letter from 20 cents to 22 cents on Feb. 17, 1985. Despite the rate increase, the Postal Service by July was faced with a projected deficit of $500 million. To cope with the red ink, the service instituted several cost-cutting measures, including dropping a planned 14-cent stamp for holiday post cards.

New Stamps. The Postal Service in 1985 issued 22-cent commemorative stamps to honor U.S. composer Jerome Kern (1885-1945); American veterans of World War I and Korea; and AMERIPEX '86, an international stamp exhibition scheduled to be held in Chicago from May 22 to June 1, 1986. Other new U.S. issues in 1985 included a striking block of four jumbo-sized 22-cent stamps picturing American breeds of horses—the quarter horse, the Morgan, the saddlebred, and the Appaloosa—as well as a 33-cent international airmail postal card featuring a "clipper"-type passenger seaplane that made flights across the Pacific Ocean prior to World War II. A 36-cent *aerogramme* (air letter) released on December 4 commemorated the reappearance of Halley's Comet and the 150th anniversary of the birth of the American writer Mark Twain (Samuel Clemens). The dual theme was selected because the years of Twain's birth and death—1835 and 1910—coincided with appearances of the comet.

Stamps from Other Countries. New Zealand issued a set of six stamps depicting old-time public transportation. The series pictures an 1862 horse-drawn streetcar, an 1871 steam-powered streetcar, an 1881 cable car, and three types of electric streetcars introduced between 1902 and 1905.

Bermuda issued a set of four stamps commemorating the 200th anniversary of the birth of the American naturalist and artist John James Audubon (1785-1851). The stamps reproduce four of Audubon's bird illustrations. Great Britain released a set of five stamps honoring British Film Year. The stamps feature black-and-white color-tinted portraits of screen actor David Niven, comedians Peter Sellers and Charlie Chaplin, actress Vivien Leigh, and director Alfred Hitchcock.

Auction Sales. The first of several special auction sales was held on March 16 in Wiesbaden, West Germany, to sell the old German states stamp collection of John R. Boker, Jr., a prominent New York City collector. The most valuable piece in this exceptionally fine collection was one of three known copies of a stamp called the 1851 Baden 9-kreuzer—also spelled kreutzer—black numeral design on blue-green paper error. (The kreuzer was a German coin.) The 9-kreuzer stamp was normally printed on rose-lilac colored paper, while blue-green paper was used for a similar stamp costing 6 kreuzer. The Boker stamp sold for 2,645,000 Deutsche marks (about $808,000),

and the entire 272-lot sale brought more than 7.6 million Deutsche marks (about $2.3 million).

On April 20, at the annual Robert A. Siegel Auction Galleries' Rarities of the World Sale in New York City, a mint block of eight U.S. 1893 $5 stamps commemorating the Columbian Exposition in Chicago sold for $99,000. Only three or four of these blocks, which include the printer's imprint and plate number, are known to exist. Also at the Siegel sale, a block of four 1962 4-cent stamps issued in the Panama Canal Zone sold for $28,600. The 1962 stamps ordinarily picture the Thatcher Ferry Bridge over the canal. The block of stamps sold at the Siegel auction, however, contain a printing error that omitted the bridge.

Electronic Stamp Design. Among other commemorative stamps issued by the U.S. Postal Service in 1985 was a 22-cent stamp depicting Frédéric Auguste Bartholdi (1834-1904), the French sculptor who designed the Statue of Liberty. The stamp was the first that the Postal Service designed with the aid of a computer. Postal Service artists fed into a computer's memory a portrait of Bartholdi, a painting of the Statue of Liberty and New York Harbor, and the type for the stamp's lettering. The artists then combined the elements on a video screen, eliminating some details and altering others.   Paul A. Larsen

In WORLD BOOK, see STAMP COLLECTING.

STATE GOVERNMENT. The legislatures of all 50 states met in 1985. Kentucky held a special session but not a regular session.

The Financial Picture. Except for those that rely heavily on energy and agriculture, states were better off financially than they had been in 1984 and much better off than in 1983, when many had budget problems. Only Vermont ended fiscal year 1985 with a deficit. (June 30 ends the fiscal year in every state except Alabama, Michigan, New York, and Texas.) Ending balances were thin in many states, however. Only 23 states had balances of 5 per cent or more. (The percentage is figured by dividing the balance by the amount of money spent.) Financial analysts regard a 5 per cent balance as the minimum advisable figure. Total state balances at the end of fiscal 1985 amounted to $8.9 billion, or 4.5 per cent of total state spending.

Taxes. A dozen states reduced income taxes, with the cuts totaling $1.6 billion for the first year. The largest decrease was New York's three-year phased cut, scheduled to reach $1.7 billion annually by fiscal year 1988.

Oklahoma raised its sales tax from 3 per cent to 3.25 per cent, while Oregon voters overwhelmingly again rejected a proposal to adopt a sales tax. Sixteen states raised motor fuel taxes (mostly earmarked for roads), 23 states called for higher cigarette taxes, and 7 raised taxes on alcoholic beverages. Overall, 25 states raised taxes and 20 states lowered them for a net reduction of $1.1 billion.

Education. Spending for elementary and secondary education rose by 9.8 per cent nationwide, compared with a hike of 6.8 per cent in overall state spending. In 30 states, the percentage increase in funding for higher education was higher than the percentage increase in overall spending.

Legislatures in more than half the states boosted teacher salaries. Maine, Missouri, New Jersey, and Ohio set minimum levels for teachers' salaries. By the end of 1985, at least half the states had started or planned career-ladder programs for teachers. These programs provide for raises and promotions for teachers who perform well in the classroom and who increase their subject knowledge.

Kentucky joined other Southern states in emphasizing education by calling a special session to enact school improvements. The Kentucky legislature increased taxes to pay for increases in teachers' salaries, merit bonuses, and reductions in class sizes.

At least 45 states now require new and prospective teachers to take competency tests. Illinois became one of them in 1985, as it passed record funding for education. Illinois also made the formal evaluation of teachers mandatory. Arkansas teachers took a state-required competency test in March, and a new law in Nevada requires annual evaluation of teachers and administrators hired after June 30, 1985.

Louisiana established an education trust fund that is to use oil and gas revenues obtained from leases in the outer continental shelf. Nebraska approved the consolidation of small school districts in rural areas over four years.

Child Protection. Many states passed laws designed to curb child abuse, child abduction, and child pornography. Nearly every state at least considered child-abuse legislation. Proposals included allowing children in abuse cases to testify on videotape rather than in the courtroom, and requiring that employees of child-care facilities submit to fingerprinting and background checks.

By the end of 1985, more than 30 states had children's trust funds—most of them established in the past two years—to finance child-protection services. Income tax checkoffs financed funds in 11 states, while 16 states imposed surcharges—7 on birth certificates and 9 on marriage licenses.

Illinois, Indiana, Iowa, Kentucky, Missouri, and Wisconsin formed a missing children's network for the pooling and transmission of information. Several states established centers or improved laws to speed searches for missing children.

States also strengthened efforts to collect child-support payments. As a result, judges in Connecticut, Mississippi, New Jersey, New York, Tennessee, and Texas will be required to have payments deducted from the wages of parents ordered to pay child support. Many other states already required judges to do this. A new sex-education law in Wisconsin makes grandparents responsible—under certain circumstances—for the costs of raising children their minor children have.

Health and Welfare. The New York legislature passed a comprehensive medical malpractice insurance law, decreasing the premiums that doctors and other health-care personnel pay for such insurance. Malpractice laws also passed in other states, including Florida, Illinois, and Nevada.

To hold down health-care costs, several states passed laws to set hospital rates and promote competition in health care. Many states studied methods of providing care to the *medically indigent* (people too poor to pay their medical and hospital bills). At least four states created indigent-care programs.

Legislatures in 13 states enacted so-called *right-to-die*, or *living will*, bills, bringing the total to 36 states with such provisions. These bills allow a person to specify, in advance of a terminal illness, a limit on the measures to be taken to prolong his or her life.

More than 20 states considered legislation related to acquired immune deficiency syndrome (AIDS). California enacted a $20-million program

Ohio's Governor Celeste goes on the radio in March to answer questions about the health of state-insured savings and loan associations.

Selected Statistics on State Governments

State	Resident population*	Governor†	House (D)	House (R)	Senate (D)	Senate (R)	State tax revenue‡	Tax revenue per capita‡	Public school expenditures per pupil§
Alabama	3,990,000	George C. Wallace (D)	88	12#	28	4#	$2,704,000,000	678	$2,055
Alaska	500,000	Bill Sheffield (D)	21	18**	9	11	1,973,000,000	3,947	8,627
Arizona	3,053,000	Bruce E. Babbitt (D)	22	38**	12	18	2,526,000,000	827	2,751
Arkansas	2,349,000	Bill Clinton (D)	90	10	31	4	1,541,000,000	656	2,235
California	25,622,000	George Deukmejian (R)	47	33	25	15	25,618,000,000	1,000	2,963
Colorado	3,178,000	Richard D. Lamm (D)	18	47	11	24	2,133,000,000	671	3,373
Connecticut	3,154,000	William A. O'Neill (D)	64	87	12	24	3,086,000,000	978	4,023
Delaware	613,000	Michael Castle (R)	19	22	13	8	713,000,000	1,162	3,849
Florida	10,976,000	Bob Graham (D)	78	42	32	8	7,329,000,000	668	2,932
Georgia	5,837,000	Joe Frank Harris (D)	154	26	47	9	3,955,000,000	678	2,352
Hawaii	1,039,000	George R. Ariyoshi (D)	40	11	21	4	1,248,000,000	1,201	3,334
Idaho	1,001,000	John V. Evans (D)	17	67	14	28	687,000,000	687	2,181
Illinois	11,511,000	James R. Thompson (R)	67	51	31	28	8,701,000,000	756	3,298
Indiana	5,498,000	Robert D. Orr (R)	39	61	20	30	4,043,000,000	735	2,725
Iowa	2,910,000	Terry E. Branstad (R)	60	40	29	21	2,242,000,000	770	3,274
Kansas	2,438,000	John W. Carlin (D)	49	76	16	24	1,790,000,000	734	3,284
Kentucky	3,723,000	Martha Layne Collins (D)	74	26	28	10	2,799,000,000	752	2,311
Louisiana	4,462,000	Edwin W. Edwards (D)	89	16	38	1	3,132,000,000	702	2,670
Maine	1,156,000	Joseph E. Brennan (D)	85	66	24	11	920,000,000	796	2,700
Maryland	4,349,000	Harry R. Hughes (D)	124	17	41	6	3,947,000,000	908	3,858
Massachusetts	5,798,000	Michael S. Dukakis (D)	126	34	32	8	5,839,000,000	1,007	3,595
Michigan	9,075,000	James J. Blanchard (D)	57	53	18	20	8,569,000,000	944	3,605
Minnesota	4,162,000	Rudy Perpich (DFL)	65	69	42	25	5,077,000,000	1,220	3,395
Mississippi	2,598,000	Bill Allain (D)	116	6	49	3	1,741,000,000	670	2,080
Missouri	5,008,000	John Ashcroft (R)	108	55	22	12	3,053,000,000	610	2,748
Montana	824,000	Ted Schwinden (D)	50	50	28	22	583,000,000	708	3,604
Nebraska	1,606,000	Robert Kerrey (D)	49	(unicameral, nonpartisan)			1,069,000,000	665	3,221
Nevada	911,000	Richard H. Bryan (D)	17	25	13	8	861,000,000	945	2,690
New Hampshire	977,000	John H. Sununu (R)	102	298	6	18	423,000,000	433	2,980
New Jersey	7,515,000	Thomas H. Kean (R)	30	50	23	17	7,137,000,000	950	4,483
New Mexico	1,424,000	Toney Anaya (D)	43	27	21	21	1,377,000,000	967	2,928
New York	17,735,000	Mario M. Cuomo (D)	94	56	26	35	18,818,000,000	1,061	5,117
North Carolina	6,165,000	James G. Martin (R)	83	37	38	12	4,636,000,000	752	2,303
North Dakota	686,000	George Sinner (D)	41	65	24	29	684,000,000	998	3,028
Ohio	10,752,000	Richard F. Celeste (D)	59	40	15	18	7,985,000,000	743	2,982
Oklahoma	3,298,000	George P. Nigh (D)	69	32	34	14	2,662,000,000	807	2,880
Oregon	2,674,000	Victor G. Atiyeh (R)	34	26	18	12	1,851,000,000	692	3,677
Pennsylvania	11,901,000	Dick Thornburgh (R)	103	100	23	27	9,600,000,000	807	3,648
Rhode Island	962,000	Edward D. DiPrete (R)	78	22	39	11	810,000,000	842	3,938
South Carolina	3,300,000	Richard W. Riley (D)	97	27	37	9	2,385,000,000	723	2,183
South Dakota	706,000	William J. Janklow (R)	13	57	10	25	359,000,000	508	2,685
Tennessee	4,717,000	Lamar Alexander (R)	62	37	23	10	2,512,000,000	532	2,100
Texas	15,989,000	Mark White (D)	97	53	25	6	9,829,000,000	615	2,784
Utah	1,652,000	Norman H. Bangerter (R)	16	59	6	23	1,197,000,000	724	2,053
Vermont	530,000	Madeleine M. Kunin (D)	72	78	18	22	413,000,000	779	3,147
Virginia	5,636,000	Gerald L. Baliles (D)	65	33††	32	8††	4,064,000,000	721	2,878
Washington	4,349,000	W. Booth Gardner (D)	53	45	27	22	4,542,000,000	1,044	3,465
West Virginia	1,952,000	Arch A. Moore, Jr. (R)	76	24	29	5	1,714,000,000	878	2,879
Wisconsin	4,766,000	Anthony S. Earl (D)	52	47	19	14	5,116,000,000	1,073	3,513
Wyoming	511,000	Ed Herschler (D)	18	46	11	19	802,000,000	1,569	4,523

*1984 estimates (source: U.S. Bureau of the Census).
†As of November 1985 (source: Council of State Governments; National Conference of State Legislatures).
‡1984 figures (source: U.S. Bureau of the Census).
§1983-1984 per pupil in average daily attendance (source: National Center for Education Statistics).
#5 Independents in the House, 3 in the Senate.
**1 Libertarian in the House.
††1 Independent in the House, 1 in the Senate.

involving education, emotional counseling, and sociological research. Florida, Illinois, New Jersey, New York, and Wisconsin launched public-education programs. And California, Florida, and Wisconsin placed limits on the use of blood tests for insurance and employment purposes. (Blood testing can reveal whether an individual has been exposed to the virus that causes AIDS.)

Commerce and Labor. Laws allowing interstate banking passed in 12 states. Other states expanded the services that banks may provide.

The major banking issue in the Midwest was tied to the farm-credit crisis. Midwestern states enacted or expanded farm operating loan programs to help financially strapped farmers. Iowa placed a moratorium on foreclosure of farm mortgages. Other states provided financial and emotional counseling for farmers. Ohio and Maryland dealt with problems caused by the collapse of privately insured savings and loan institutions. See BANK.

Law and Public Safety. Federally inspired campaigns to require the use of seat belts and raise the drinking age made progress in many states. At least 16 states had approved laws requiring automobile and truck drivers and their passengers to buckle up. Acting under the threatened loss of federal highway funds, all but 13 states had acted to raise their drinking age to 21 by the federal deadline of Oct. 1, 1986.

Prison overcrowding remained a major problem for state governments. Tennessee's legislature met in a special session to draft a comprehensive plan to deal with prison conditions that had been declared unconstitutional because of violence and overcrowding. On December 1, Tennessee Governor Lamar Alexander signed into law six bills designed to improve prison conditions. Major features include the provision of funds for prison renovation and the establishment of an early-release program for many state prisoners. Tennessee and Kentucky considered proposals to turn prisons over to private operators. Kentucky and other states adopted programs that placed prisoners under arrest in their own homes—in some cases, under supervision via electronic devices.

Other Measures. Several states passed right-to-know laws on toxic substances in the workplace. Companies whose operations involve such substances must provide information about the substances to workers who might be endangered by them, and to neighboring communities. Other new laws were intended to protect ground water from toxic substances, including oil and other fluids stored in underground tanks.

California, Iowa, and Oregon started lotteries in 1985. Missouri and West Virginia scheduled lotteries to begin in 1986.   Elaine Stuart Knapp

See also ELECTIONS. In WORLD BOOK, see STATE GOVERNMENT and articles on the individual states.

STEEL INDUSTRY. The United States steel industry continued to struggle with foreign competition and financial problems that left almost one-third of U.S. steelmaking capacity idle during the first half of 1985. Steel production during the first nine months of the year totaled 66.2 million short tons (60.0 million metric tons), down from the 72.1 million short tons (65.4 million metric tons) produced during the same period in 1984. The American Iron and Steel Institute (AISI), the chief association of U.S. steel producers, reported on Aug. 13, 1985, that employment in the industry had dropped by more than 50 per cent since 1979. On Sept. 11, 1985, the AISI said that the number of U.S. steelmaking jobs had fallen to 207,300, the lowest level since the group began compiling statistics in 1933.

On September 25, the AISI said U.S. steelmakers reported a small profit during the second quarter of 1985. But the gain was not enough to offset the losses in the first quarter.

Import Problems Agreements. The AISI blamed the situation largely on a continued surge of cheap imported steel into the United States. Steel imports reached a record 12.9 million short tons (11.7 million metric tons) during the first half of 1985, up from 12.4 million short tons (11.2 million metric tons) during the same period in 1984. Imports accounted for 26.2 per cent of the U.S. market through mid-1985, up from 24.2 per cent in 1984. In addition, the number of countries exporting steel to the United States increased from 50 during the first half of 1984 to 76 by mid-1985.

By November, steel imports had reached a level 40 per cent above the targets set in an import-restraint program announced in September 1984 by U.S. President Ronald Reagan. On Oct. 31, 1985, the steel industry urged an embargo or other strong action to control imports.

Recommendations. A study conducted by the National Academy of Engineering (NAE), an agency of the National Academy of Sciences in Washington, D.C., was released on April 30. The NAE study said that the steel industry, by becoming more efficient and by modernizing its equipment, could become profitable again. But the NAE found that even under the best of conditions, a reduction of the industry was inevitable because of competition from other countries and increasing substitution of other materials for steel.

Wheeling-Pittsburgh Woes. Wheeling-Pittsburgh Steel Corporation, the seventh largest steel producer in the United States, filed for bankruptcy in Pittsburgh, Pa., on April 16. The company became the largest steelmaker ever to do so. Company officials said the firm would remain in operation while attempting to repay its creditors.

On July 21, about 8,500 workers at Wheeling-Pittsburgh went on strike. It was the first major strike in the steel industry since 1959. The strike followed a court-approved move by the company to cancel its contract with the United Steelworkers of America (USWA) and cut wages by 18 per cent. The strike ended on October 28, after USWA members accepted a new contract that reduced wages and benefits by 16 per cent.

U.S. Steel Buy. The United States Steel Corporation on October 30 agreed to acquire Texas Oil & Gas Corporation for about $3.6 billion, continuing its expansion in the energy field. In 1982, U.S. Steel bought Marathon Oil Company.

Contract Negotiations. The five major steel companies in the United States announced on May 2 that they would no longer negotiate contracts with the USWA as a group. The firms—U.S. Steel; Bethlehem Steel Corporation; Inland Steel Company; Armco, Incorporated; and LTV Steel Corporation—planned to bargain separately. The existing national contract expires on July 31, 1986.

EC Agreement. Ministers of the European Community (EC or Common Market), meeting in Brussels, Belgium, on March 27, 1985, approved a request by Italy, France, Belgium, and Luxembourg to increase government subsidies to their steel industries. In return, the four countries agreed to consider reducing their production capacity.   Michael Woods

In WORLD BOOK, see IRON AND STEEL.

STOCKS AND BONDS. The United States economy slowed in 1985, but stock markets around the world took off in anticipation of good times. The Dow Jones Industrial Average (the Dow), the most widely watched index of stock prices, began the year at 1,198.87, hit its low for 1985 on January 4 at 1,184.96, and then started the first of several rallies. Rising quickly in January, it hovered between 1,280 and 1,299 through the beginning of March. In March, it remained between 1,240 and 1,290 until it closed above 1,300 for the first time on May 20. June through August saw the Dow fluctuate between 1,300 and 1,360. In mid-September, the Dow briefly slipped below 1,300 before beginning the year's major rise.

From September 20 to December 16, the Dow zoomed more than 250 points, from just below 1,300 to a peak of 1,553.10 at the close on December 16. In the process, the Dow closed above 1,400 for the first time in history on November 6 and above 1,500 for the first time on December 11. In late December, the Dow lost a little ground, ending the year at 1,546.67.

That year-end figure represented a 27.7 per cent increase from the beginning of 1985. Adding back dividends paid during the year would raise an investor's total return to 33.6 per cent during a year when the inflation rate was only 3.6 per cent. This performance represented a big improvement

The Dow Zooms in 1985

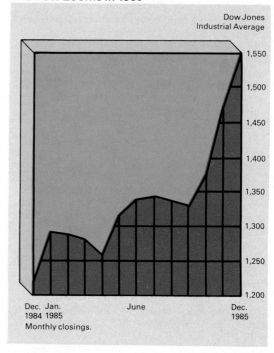

Dow Jones Industrial Average

1,550
1,500
1,450
1,400
1,350
1,300
1,250
1,200

Dec. Jan.
1984 1985   June   Dec.
                                        1985
Monthly closings.

on 1984's inflation-adjusted return of 2.2 per cent.

The Broader Market moved with the Dow. The Standard & Poor's 500 Index, which tracks 500 stocks representing more than 90 per cent of the dollar volume on the New York Stock Exchange (NYSE), began the year at 165.37. It also hit its low for the year on January 4 at 163.68 and by February was in the 180 to 185 range. It broke 190 for the first time on June 4, 200 on November 21, and peaked at 212.02 on December 16, finishing 1985 at 211.28.

Analysts were divided about the cause of the fall stock rally. Some cited lower long-term interest rates, which made bonds less attractive than stocks. Others pointed to the prospect of lower tax rates as Congress wrestled with a tax-reform bill. Still others looked to the Federal Reserve Board's new policy of making more credit available. Other explanations included worldwide economic improvement and the boost to exports provided by the decline of the dollar by more than 20 per cent.

Foreign Stocks. The U.S. boom was more than matched by the performance of stocks elsewhere. The Capital International SA World Index rose by 31 per cent in the first 10 months of 1985, and the last six weeks of the year saw records set in a number of countries, including Belgium, France, South Africa, and Canada.

Bond Market. Long-term corporate AAA bonds—the highest rated bonds—opened the year yielding 12.1 per cent, dipped below 12 per cent briefly in early February, and peaked at 12.6 per cent in the third week of March. They held at about 11 per cent until the beginning of November, when they began to slide again during the autumn stock rally, ending the year at 9.9 per cent.

Long-term Treasury bonds for the most part yielded 0.5 to 1 percentage point less than corporate bonds until fall. On November 19, the new issue of 30-year Treasury bonds yielded less than 10 per cent for the first time since 1980.

Municipal bonds (muni's), whose interest payments are not taxed by the federal government, paralleled ordinary bond rates at a lower level, as usual. They began the year at 9.9 per cent, then peaked at 9.8 per cent in the first week of March. They slid to 8.7 per cent in early June, climbed to 9.4 per cent in late September, then dropped to 8.4 per cent at year-end.

Volume. No new trading records were set on the NYSE despite the fall rally. New issues, however, did rise as they usually do when prices climb. New stock issues rose from $1.88 billion per month in 1984 to $2.67 billion per month during the first half of 1985.   Donald W. Swanton

In WORLD BOOK, see BOND; INVESTMENT; STOCK, CAPITAL.

SUDAN. After 16 years in power, President and Prime Minister Gaafar Mohamed Nimeiri, who had survived numerous coup attempts, was overthrown by his own military commanders on April 6, 1985. They acted while he was in the United States seeking aid for the hard-pressed Sudanese economy. General Abdul Rahman Mohamed el Hassan Suwar El-Dahab, Nimeiri's minister of defense, led the coup, forming a 15-member Transitional Military Council to run the country.

Nimeiri's downfall was the result of economic mismanagement; the imposition of Islamic law, a policy particularly resented in the non-Muslim southern Sudan; corruption; and the repressive policies of his security forces. Finally, the cutoff of government subsidies for basic foodstuffs united the country against him.

New Government. Suwar El-Dahab said elections would be held within a year to reestablish civilian rule. Nimeiri's Sudanese Socialist Union, the country's only legal political party, was abolished, and new political parties were permitted to organize. By July, 38 parties had been formed.

On April 22, the new leaders also named a civilian Council of Ministers. On September 29, the government said it had foiled an attempted coup.

Civil Strife. The major political problem facing the new government was the status of the South. The leader of the rebel Sudanese People's Libera-

tion Army (SPLA), John Garang, refused to accept the new government.

In April, Suwar El-Dahab said the government was reuniting the South, reversing an unpopular 1983 decision by Nimeiri to divide the South into three semi-independent provinces. In addition, the government formed a transitional cabinet to administer the South under the terms of a 1972 self-rule agreement Nimeiri had abandoned in an effort to bring all Sudan under central control. But Garang rejected the arrangement.

Some outside support for the SPLA disappeared after Sudan signed a military agreement with Libya in August. Among other things, Libya agreed to withdraw its backing from the SPLA.

Continuing Problems. Nimeiri's successors faced the same staggering economic problems that had daunted him. The most urgent problem was famine. By mid-April, drought spreading across the Sahara had brought hundreds of thousands of refugees from Ethiopia, Chad, and other neighboring countries into Sudan. Before the rains finally came in July, 2 million Sudanese had died or become seriously malnourished. Relief supplies poured in, but Sudan's transportation system was inadequate to deliver the food.   William Spencer

See also AFRICA (Facts in Brief Table); SUWAR EL-DAHAB, ABDUL RAHMAN. In WORLD BOOK, see SUDAN.

SUPREME COURT OF THE UNITED STATES. A year after making a sharply conservative shift in civil rights cases, the Supreme Court of the United States edged back toward a more moderate stance during the term ending in 1985. The justices supported, to a surprising extent, the rights of the individual against the government. In a series of unexpected decisions, the court rejected attempts by church groups, supported by the Administration of President Ronald Reagan, to permit more government involvement in the practice of religion. Those rulings reinforced the wall of separation between church and state (see Close-Up).

The court also dealt a heavy blow to the Reagan Administration's states' rights, or "new federalism," concept by ruling that local governments must obey federal laws such as minimum wage and overtime pay statutes. ("New federalism" advocates hold that the Constitution sets limits on the federal government's power to interfere in state affairs.) The court's 5 to 4 ruling on February 19 reversed a decision issued just nine years earlier. The difference was the vote of Associate Justice Harry A. Blackmun, who changed his mind on the issue of states' rights.

Individual Rights. In an important discrimination case, the court on July 1 rejected an attempt by the city of Cleburne, Tex., to use city zoning laws to ban a group home for the mentally re-

More Mortar for a Wall of Separation

"The greatest achievement ever made in the cause of human progress," declared Justice Stephen J. Field of the Supreme Court of the United States about 100 years ago, "is the total and final separation of church and state." Field's sentiments, however, turned out to be, at best, premature.

Since his time, various American courts and legislatures have become involved in a series of increasingly difficult decisions on the subject, gradually allowing more government involvement in religious matters. In 1985, the United States Supreme Court decided seven cases on church-state relations, more than in any other year in its history. One observer called 1985 "the year of religion" at the Supreme Court.

When the dust had cleared, the court had apparently rebuilt and shored up a "wall of separation" that had been noticeably crumbling in recent years. But the narrow margins involved—5 to 4 votes in some cases—left open the possibility that the long-term trend toward more government-religion entanglement would reassert itself.

The First Amendment to the United States Constitution simply declares that "Congress shall make no law respecting an establishment of religion, or prohibiting the free exercise thereof. . . ." Even though many settlers came to colonial America to escape religious persecution, an *established* (government-sponsored) church or religion developed in at least 11 of the original 13 colonies. After the Revolutionary War in America, however, many leaders of the fledgling democracy came to believe that religious freedom was at the heart of freedom generally.

An upsurge of separationist sentiment helped James Madison push the First Amendment through the constitutional convention of 1787. In 1802, President Thomas Jefferson coined the phrase that now symbolizes the discussion. In a letter to Baptists in Danbury, Conn., Jefferson declared, "I contemplate with sovereign reverence" the First Amendment's "wall of separation between church and state."

The wall has never been free of assault, however. Attacks intensified as tax-supported public schools replaced private and church-sponsored institutions in the 1800's as the dominant method of education. The Supreme Court was forced to decide whether the First Amendment allowed states to provide financial support to *parochial* (church) schools, permit Bible reading and prayers in public schools, release public school pupils for religious education, or establish special rights to accommodate believers of a particular religion. Although the court flatly ruled in 1962 that a state-sponsored program of prayers in public schools is unconstitutional, the court in 1983 allowed state income tax deductions for parochial school tuition and in 1984

Public school students take advantage of a moment of silence, but in 1985 the legality of such a practice came into question.

allowed construction of Christmas Nativity scenes on government property, among other exceptions to the strict doctrine of church-state separation. Going into the 1984-1985 Supreme Court term, Secretary of Education William J. Bennett remarked that Jefferson's wall of separation had become a "pile of rocks."

In 1985, the court put the wall back together again. In an 8 to 1 vote on June 26, the justices knocked down a Connecticut state law granting workers "an absolute and unqualified right" to refuse to work on their chosen Sabbath. In a 6 to 3 decision on June 4, the court struck down an Alabama law permitting a daily one-minute period of silence "for meditation or voluntary prayer" in public schools, saying it violated the 23-year-old ban on government-sponsored prayer in public schools. And on July 1, the justices ruled 5 to 4 against government programs in Michigan and New York that paid for remedial and enrichment instruction in parochial schools, even though there was no religious content to the instruction. The government programs, wrote Justice William J. Brennan, Jr., in the majority decision, created a "symbolic union of church and state."

The "voluntary prayer" decision was not completely unexpected. The majority found a clear intent by the Alabama legislature to evade the court's 1962 decision and to promote religion. The justices concluded that by inserting the words "voluntary prayer" into a law that already permitted silent reflection, the legislators revealed that their intent was to promote religion and prayer in public schools. "Such an endorsement," wrote Justice John Paul Stevens in the majority opinion, "is not consistent with the established principle that the government must pursue a course of complete neutrality toward religion." Justice Stevens also indicated, however, that the court might consider different approaches to "moment of silence" laws, such as those that have been passed in more than 20 states. The decision appeared to leave room for such state authorized moments of silence—for prayer, meditation, or reflection—as long as government authorities and school officials do not suggest that students use the time for religious purposes.

The problem with Alabama's law, according to Justice Sandra Day O'Connor, who voted with the majority but wrote her own separate opinion, was that it had "intentionally crossed the line between creating a quiet moment during which those so inclined may pray and affirmatively endorsing the particular religious practice of prayer. This line may be a fine one, but our precedents and the principles of religious liberty require that we draw it."

The cases concerning aid to parochial schools were, in contrast, bitterly divisive. To determine the constitutionality of government programs in major church-state cases, the court uses a three-part test first set out in the 1971 decision *Lemon v. Kurtzman*. The justices ask if the programs have secular purpose, if they significantly advance or inhibit religion, and if they foster excessive government entanglement with religion. The wrong answer to any of the three questions—"no" to the first one and "yes" to the other two—is sufficient to invalidate the law, and the parochial aid plans in Michigan and New York were determined to promote religion. "Providing for education of schoolchildren is surely a praiseworthy purpose," wrote Brennan for the majority, "but our cases have consistently recognized that even such a praiseworthy, secular purpose cannot validate government aid to parochial schools when the aid has the effect of promoting a single religion or religion generally." The programs promoted religion, in part, wrote Brennan in the majority opinion, because they conveyed "a message of state support for religion to students and to the general public."

That opinion provoked a sarcastic dissent from Chief Justice Warren E. Burger and rebukes from the Administration of President Ronald Reagan. The programs in question posed no threat of a government establishment of religion, wrote Burger. "Federal programs designed to prevent a generation of children from growing up without being able to read effectively are not remotely steps in that direction," he said. United States Attorney General Edwin Meese III complained that the objectives of the nation's Founding Fathers were being distorted in a "bizarre" manner. "Their purpose was to prohibit religious tyranny, not to undermine religion generally," Meese complained. Education Secretary Bennett said the decisions by the court demonstrated a "fastidious disdain for religion."

Although separationists claimed landmark victories in these Supreme Court decisions, the newly rebuilt wall between church and state remained vulnerable to assault. The court continued to accept new cases involving religion controversies; at least four others were to be decided in 1986. More important, the court's proseparation faction was aging. Four of the five justices in the parochial aid majority decision passed their 77th birthdays in 1985. If President Reagan can appoint one or more new justices with an outlook on church-state issues reflecting the President's philosophy, the court's wall of separation may again become Bennett's "pile of rocks."

David C. Beckwith

Demonstrators protesting legal abortions march in front of the U.S. Supreme Court Building in Washington, D.C., in January.

tarded. Legal experts said the 9 to 0 decision would make it difficult for government agencies to justify laws that treat some groups, such as the retarded, differently from others.

The court also upheld the rights of individuals in two workplace controversies. In June, the court ruled that airlines cannot automatically retire flight engineers before age 70. The court also prohibited unions from imposing fines or other punishment on members who resign from the union during a strike and then return to work.

The Rights of Criminal Suspects were bolstered by several important Supreme Court rulings during the year. On March 27, the justices declared, 6 to 3, that police have no right to shoot to kill an unarmed, fleeing suspected felon unless the suspect's escape would threaten public safety. The case arose from the death of an unarmed 15-year-old burglary suspect in Memphis who was shot in the back by a policeman as the youth climbed a fence. In another landmark criminal-rights ruling, the court held in January that *indigent* (needy) convicts appealing their conviction are entitled to a court-appointed lawyer.

Not all the court's 1985 rulings sided with criminal suspects, however. In a 6 to 3 decision on March 4, the court declared that police may obtain a second confession from a suspect if the initial confession is legally unusable because police failed to advise the suspect of his or her right to a lawyer. In other decisions, the court in January made it easier for prosecutors to eliminate from capital punishment cases potential jurors who have doubts about the death penalty, and it declared that public-school officials may lawfully search students if there are "reasonable grounds" for believing that the search will turn up evidence of a violation of a law or school regulations.

Press Rights. The court's 1985 decisions on the rights of the press were mixed. On June 10, it ruled that independent financial newsletters were not subject to regulation by the federal Securities and Exchange Commission. On June 26, however, in another case, the court made it easier for people who believe they have been libeled but who are not public figures to sue publishers for damages.

Other Important Decisions included:

■ A 6 to 3 ruling, on June 28, upholding a 123-year-old law that set a $10 limit on legal fees paid by veterans in disability and pension disputes with the Veterans Administration.

■ A 9 to 0 ruling, on March 20, upholding a Food and Drug Administration refusal to review the safety and effectiveness of lethal drugs used by several states to execute criminals.

■ A 4 to 4 decision, on March 26, upholding a federal appeals court decision that rejected an Oklahoma law ordering the dismissal of any public-school teacher who advocated homosexual rights. Because the vote was a tie, it automatically upheld the lower court's decision, but the ruling will not serve as a *precedent* (guide) in similar future cases. It was one of a record eight tie votes during the term resulting from the 11-week absence of Associate Justice Lewis F. Powell, Jr., who underwent surgery in January for prostate cancer.

Meese Criticizes Court. On July 9, in an address to the American Bar Association in Washington, D.C., U.S. Attorney General Edwin Meese III said the Supreme Court should follow "a jurisprudence of original intention." He said the justices should try to decide issues as the framers of the Constitution would have decided them, rather than injecting personal preferences into their rulings. Meese expressed particular displeasure with 1985 decisions on religion and states' rights.

Responding to the attorney general's comments, Associate Justice William J. Brennan, Jr., said that present-day justices cannot "pretend that from our vantage we can gauge accurately the intent of the framers on application of principle to specific, contemporary questions. We current justices read the Constitution in the only way that we can: As 20th-century Americans."   David C. Beckwith

See also COURTS. In WORLD BOOK, see SUPREME COURT OF THE UNITED STATES.

SURINAME. See LATIN AMERICA.

SUWAR EL-DAHAB, ABDUL RAHMAN (1934-   ), a career soldier, seized power in Sudan on April 6, 1985, three weeks after he was appointed minister of defense. He deposed President and Prime Minister Gaafar Mohamed Nimeiri, who had governed since 1969. Suwar El-Dahab, who became chairman of a 15-member military council, promised to hold free elections within one year.

Abdul Rahman Mohamed el Hassan Suwar El-Dahab was born in 1934 in Omdurman, near the Sudanese capital of Khartoum. He graduated from Sudan's military academy in 1958 and received further training at military academies in Great Britain, Egypt, and Jordan.

After serving as a colonel in the police force of the Persian Gulf country of Qatar, Suwar El-Dahab became a brigadier general in Qatar's army. In 1975, he became commander of Sudan's armed forces supply department. He was promoted to chief of the southern command and later served as chief of the northern command.

Suwar El-Dahab is a member of the Khatemia Islamic sect, known for its pro-Egypt leanings. Although deeply religious, he is reportedly a moderate who did not approve of Nimeiri's 1983 decision to impose strict Islamic law.

Suwar El-Dahab is married. He has two sons and three daughters.   Barbara A. Mayes

SWAZILAND. See AFRICA.

SWEDEN. Social Democrat Prime Minister Olof Palme won a hollow victory in a general election on Sept. 15, 1985, losing his three-seat majority over Sweden's three non-Socialist parties and forcing him to rely on Communist support to remain in power. The Social Democratic Party lost seven seats. The biggest gainer in the election was the Liberal Party, which picked up 30 seats. Palme blamed his party's loss on the Liberals' criticism of Sweden's welfare state, which Palme described as "the most humane and civilized social system ever created." In local government elections held at the same time, the Social Democrats lost control of Sweden's three main cities, Stockholm, Göteborg, and Malmö.

Strike. On May 2, 20,000 civil servants struck, demanding a 3.1 per cent pay increase above the government's 5 per cent ceiling on wage hikes. The strike almost brought Sweden to a halt. Exports and imports were at a standstill, and airports closed as air-traffic controllers and customs officials stopped work. A government-inspired lockout on May 10 affected 80,000 workers. Schools and post offices closed, and some food items—notably fruit and vegetables—were almost unobtainable. Icebreakers in the Baltic Sea stopped work, leaving many ships frozen fast.

The strike ended with a compromise agreement

Sweden's Prime Minister Olof Palme signs an autograph for a taxi driver after being elected for a fourth term in September.

on May 20. All public workers received a 2 per cent raise starting in December 1985.

Palme arranged the compromise in secret meetings with union leaders. He told the officials that they were causing enormous economic damage.

Nuclear Weapons. A political scandal began in April with revelations that the government had been prepared to acquire nuclear weapons from the United States or Great Britain. Palme denied that he had been a member of a group of Social Democrats who considered permitting research on nuclear weapons in Sweden. The nation's leading weekly technical publication, *Ny Teknik*, had claimed that such a research program had continued for 18 years after the Riksdag (parliament) voted against it in 1957. Palme said Swedish nuclear research had been "only protective."

Acid Rain. Palme blamed Britain for much of the air pollution affecting Scandinavia. On March 4, he criticized Britain's refusal to join 20 other European countries committed to cutting the emission of sulfur compounds from burning coal. The countries agreed to cut their emissions by 30 per cent by 1993. Earlier in 1985, Sweden had refused a $330,000 grant from Britain to study the effects of acid rain. Swedish scientists said Britain was trying to "buy time."   Kenneth Brown

See also EUROPE (Facts in Brief Table). In WORLD BOOK, see SWEDEN.

SWIMMING. When Matt Biondi won a gold medal during the 1984 Summer Olympics in Los Angeles, many observers of the sport were surprised. He had little experience swimming at the national level, let alone in the Olympics.

In 1985, the 6-foot 6-inch (198-centimeter) 19-year-old from Moraga, Calif., proved that he belonged. He broke world and United States freestyle sprint records held by Ambrose (Rowdy) Gaines IV of Winter Haven, Fla., in 25-yard (22.9-meter) short-course pools indoors and 50-meter (54.7-yard) long-course pools outdoors.

Biondi's major achievement came on August 6 in the United States Long Course Championships in Mission Viejo, Calif. He broke the world record twice that day in the 100-meter freestyle, swimming 49.24 seconds in the preliminaries and 48.95 seconds in the final.

Biondi went on to star during the Pan Pacific Swimming Championships held from August 15 to 18 in Tokyo. There, he anchored United States teams to world records in the 400-meter freestyle relay (3 minutes 17.08 seconds on August 17) and the 400-meter medley relay (3:38.28 on August 18). The United States dominated the Pan Pacific competition, winning 24 of the 32 events. A week later, Biondi went to Kobe, Japan, for the World University Games, where he won two gold and two silver medals in individual events.

Biondi's 1985 success began in the National Collegiate Athletic Association championships, held from March 28 to 30 in Austin, Tex. He set U.S. short-course records for the 100-yard (41.87) and 200-yard (1:33.22) freestyles. Neither of these times qualified as world records, however, because they were set on a 25-yard course, rather than a 50-meter course.

In Europe, the best swimmer during 1985 was Michael Gross of West Germany. He broke world records in two events—the 400-meter freestyle (3:47.80 on June 27 in Remscheid, West Germany) and the 200-meter butterfly (1:56.65 on August 10 in Sofia, Bulgaria).

It was a quiet year for world records. Igor Poliansky of the Soviet Union set the only other men's record, in the 200-meter backstroke (1:58.14 on March 3 in Erfurt, East Germany). Silke Hörner of East Germany set the only women's world record, in the 200-meter breaststroke (2:28.33 on June 5 in Leipzig, East Germany).

United States Swimming remained strong. Among the members of the 1984 Olympic team who won major titles nationally and internationally in 1985 were Pablo Morales, John Moffet, Rick Carey, Michael O'Brien, Mary T. Meagher, Tiffany Cohen, and Mary Wayte.   Frank Litsky

See also SPORTS. In WORLD BOOK, see SWIMMING.

SWITZERLAND. The Swiss government decided in February 1985 to submit the question of whether to seek United Nations (UN) membership to a *referendum*, or direct vote of the people, in March 1986. Switzerland already is represented on several UN bodies, and the UN's European Headquarters are in Geneva.

The Swiss government wants UN membership to give the nation a voice in debates and decisions on leading world issues. Both houses of the Federal Assembly voted in 1984 in favor of entry.

Bank Secrecy. Switzerland dissociated itself from a 1985 report by the Organization for Economic Cooperation and Development (OECD), of which it is a member. The report recommended a loosening of Switzerland's bank-secrecy rules. The change would give other OECD countries' tax collectors greater access to Swiss bank records.

Buoyant Economy. Switzerland expected its economic growth, which began in 1983, to continue through 1986. The continuing strength of the United States dollar helped the Swiss economy in 1985. A strong U.S. dollar makes Swiss products less expensive in the United States and therefore easier to sell in that country. The United States is Switzerland's second-largest trading partner after West Germany.   Kenneth Brown

See also EUROPE (Facts in Brief Table). In WORLD BOOK, see SWITZERLAND.

SYRIA. President Hafiz al-Assad was reelected for a third seven-year term in a national *referendum* (direct vote) held on Feb. 11, 1985, receiving 99.97 per cent of the 6.52 million votes cast, with only 376 Syrians casting "No" votes. The referendum followed the first congress held by the ruling Baath Party since 1980. At the congress, party leaders gave Assad new powers that enabled him to control appointments to both the party's Regional Command—its overall governing body—and to the party's Central Committee, which is responsible for internal affairs.

New Cabinet. In April, Assad appointed a new cabinet headed by Prime Minister Abd al Ra'uf al-Kassem. The major change was a number of new appointments to economic ministries.

Brotherhood Amnesty. There was little internal opposition to Assad's regime during the year. In January, the president announced an amnesty for some members of the Muslim Brotherhood, an underground organization of fundamentalist Sunni Muslims that has been the main focus of opposition to Assad. He said the Brotherhood would no longer be "the tool of Syria's enemies."

Lebanese Tangle. On April 24, a Syrian-sponsored peace agreement between the various Lebanese factions and the government of President Amin Gemayel revived Lebanon's "government of national unity," which had collapsed on April 17. But unity quickly broke down as Palestinian guerrillas and Syrian-backed Shiite Muslim militias clashed in Tripoli (also called Tarabulus) and other Lebanese cities. Syrian mediators arranged cease-fire agreements in July and August, but these too broke down. On December 28, the three main Lebanese militias signed a Syrian-sponsored peace treaty that would gradually give Lebanon's Muslims more political power.

A by-product of Syria's "Lebanese problem" was a disagreement with Libya, a Palestinian ally. Angered by the siege of Palestinian refugee camps in West Beirut in May and June by Amal (Hope), the Syrian-supported Shiite militia, Libya expelled about 20,000 Syrian workers.

The Economy was also affected by inter-Arab conflicts. In June, Kuwait's National Assembly (parliament) voted to cancel $334 million in aid pledged to Syria under a 1978 agreement providing aid to front-line Arab states in the struggle with Israel. The action made it more difficult for Syria to meet its high defense costs. The 1986 budget, approved in August, set total expenditures at $11 billion, of which 50 per cent was slated for defense.   William Spencer

See also MIDDLE EAST (Facts in Brief Table). In WORLD BOOK, see SYRIA.

Syria's President Hafiz al-Assad, at right, greets Lebanon's President Amin Gemayel at a summit meeting held in Damascus in August.

TAIWAN experienced scandals and economic troubles in 1985. The Ministry of National Defense disclosed on Jan. 15, 1985, that Taiwanese officials had been involved in a 1984 murder in California. Henry Liu, a Chinese-American author who had criticized Taiwan's leaders, was killed by members of the Bamboo Union, Taiwan's most powerful underworld gang. A civilian court sentenced two gang members on April 9, 1985, to life imprisonment for the murder. The government said the gang had been recruited by Taiwan's military intelligence bureau. The head of the bureau, Vice Admiral Wong Hsi-ling, was convicted of the murder on April 19 by a military court and sentenced to life in prison. California police and the U.S. Federal Bureau of Investigation reportedly provided the information that led to the trials.

Journalist Arrested. Lee Ya-ping, the publisher of a Chinese-American newspaper in southern California, was arrested in Taiwan on September 17. She was accused of sedition because her paper supported a Chinese proposal for exchanges of letters and telephone calls between Taiwan and China. She was released on September 26.

Economic Woes. The worst financial scandal in Taiwan's history developed from the collapse in February of the country's largest savings and loan institution. Two cabinet ministers resigned after disclosures that government officials had tolerated some $190 million in improper loans by the savings and loan to companies affiliated with it.

The banking scandal compounded public concern about slowing economic growth. For two decades, Taiwan had averaged a remarkable 9 per cent growth per year. In 1984, the growth rate was 10.9 per cent. In 1985, it dropped to 4.5 per cent—good by most countries' standards, but worrisome in Taiwan. Declining investment in factories and machinery was partly to blame.

Despite this slower growth, Taiwan's foreign trade surplus was estimated at $9.5 billion for 1985 because costs of the raw materials it imported fell while its manufactured exports rose in price. In trade with the United States alone, Taiwan ran a $10-billion surplus. As a result, the United States pressured Taiwan to open its markets more to U.S. goods. In trade talks in Washington, D.C., from October 7 to 9, Taiwan promised to lower tariffs on 192 items by 20 per cent and to drop some other trade restrictions.

Local Elections. The Kuomintang, Taiwan's ruling party, won 146 out of 191 local elections on November 16. Independent candidates, who were not allowed to form opposition political parties, did well in the capital, Taipei, but got only 29 per cent of the vote nationwide.   Henry S. Bradsher

See also ASIA (Facts in Brief Table). In WORLD BOOK, see TAIWAN.

TANZANIA. See AFRICA.

TAXATION. President Ronald Reagan made revision of the United States tax code his chief domestic objective in 1985, but the year ended without final action on tax reform. In a May 28 television address, Reagan called the current tax system "unwise, unwanted, and unfair." He proposed to cut the number of income tax brackets for individuals from 14 to 3, reduce the maximum tax rate for individuals from 50 to 35 per cent, and boost the minimum rate from 11 to 15 per cent. He asked Congress to increase personal exemptions from $1,080 to $2,000 and to raise the standard deduction to $2,900 for an individual and $4,000 for a couple. He also called for cutting the maximum corporate tax from 46 to 33 per cent.

On November 23, the House Ways and Means Committee, chaired by Representative Dan Rostenkowski (D., Ill.), completed work on a tax reform bill that would cut the top individual tax rate to 38 per cent and the maximum corporate rate to 36 per cent. The full House passed the bill by a voice vote on December 17 after Reagan lobbied strongly to round up support from Republicans opposed to it. The Senate was expected to take action on the bill in early 1986.

Overseas Profits Tax. In October, the Reagan Administration backed legislation that would forbid states to tax the overseas earnings of multi-

© Sidney Harris

"Why didn't you use the short form?"

national corporations. Alaska, California, Idaho, Montana, New Hampshire, and North Dakota already imposed such taxes. Great Britain had threatened to retaliate against these taxes by denying tax benefits to subsidiaries of U.S. companies in Britain.

Compliance Down. In fiscal year 1985, which ended on Sept. 30, 1985, the Internal Revenue Service (IRS) collected $17.5 billion in delinquent tax debts, up from $16.4 billion for the previous year. But uncollected debts increased from $8.5-billion for fiscal 1984 to $9 billion for fiscal 1985.

Bad Year. In 1985, the IRS performed what may have been its worst job yet of processing income tax returns. The IRS was late in processing hundreds of thousands of returns, and it accidentally destroyed thousands of letters from taxpayers at several processing centers. In at least one instance, the IRS shredded returns.

State Legislatures reduced taxes by more than $1 billion during their 1985 sessions, the National Conference of State Legislatures reported in August. During the year, 25 states raised taxes by $1.1 billion, but the increases were more than offset by cuts of $2.2 billion in 19 other states. Minnesota, New York, and Ohio made the sharpest cuts.   Frank Cormier and Margot Cormier

See also STATE GOVERNMENT. In WORLD BOOK, see INCOME TAX; TAXATION.

TELEVISION. In business terms, 1985 was easily the most turbulent year in the history of United States television. All three major networks—American Broadcasting Companies (ABC), CBS Inc., and the National Broadcasting Company (NBC)—became the object of acquisition bids. ABC was the first major network to change hands. In March, ABC agreed to a $3.5-billion buy-out by Capital Cities Communications, Incorporated. At the time, this was the largest transaction in broadcasting history. It was surpassed, however, in December, when General Electric Company announced plans to buy NBC's parent company, RCA Corporation, for more than $6 billion.

CBS successfully defended itself early in the year against an unwanted take-over by Turner Broadcasting Systems, owned by cable-television entrepreneur Ted Turner of Atlanta, Ga. CBS also fought off a less-organized take-over attempt by a conservative group called Fairness in Media. The group hoped to end what it termed a "liberal bias in news reporting" at CBS by buying up the company's stock and becoming "Dan Rather's boss." Rather is the popular anchorman of "CBS Evening News." Although both take-over efforts failed, CBS was wounded financially from the fight. To maintain control of the company, CBS bought back nearly $1 billion of its stock from shareholders and had to enact cutbacks as a result.

In Other Buy-Out News, Australian-born publisher Rupert Murdoch announced in July that he would purchase six big-city television stations from Metromedia, Incorporated. In March, he had purchased a 50 per cent share of a financially troubled motion-picture studio, 20th Century-Fox Film Corporation. Murdoch boasted that by combining the movie studio facilities and the television stations he could put together something akin to a fourth major network.

Prime-Time Programs. The fall 1985 television season was characterized to some extent more by the old than by the new. Showtime, a movie channel on cable TV, made a splash by buying rights to 75 recently discovered episodes of "The Honeymooners," a classic comedy routine starring Jackie Gleason. The sketches had not been broadcast since their original airing in the 1950's.

NBC revived another old favorite, "Alfred Hitchcock Presents," which first appeared on CBS in 1955. The episodes were remade versions of dramas from the original series, but they began with the familiar Hitchcock introduction. A relatively new computerized process gave the once black-and-white introductions a color tint.

In a similar vein, CBS brought back "The Twilight Zone," at least in name. The stories, however, did not come from the old Rod Serling series on

Top-Rated Television Series

The following were the most-watched television series for the 31-week regular season—Sept. 23, 1984, through April 21, 1985—as determined by the A. C. Nielsen Company.

1. "Dynasty" (ABC)
2. "Dallas" (CBS)
3. "The Cosby Show" (NBC)
4. "60 Minutes" (CBS)
5. "Family Ties" (NBC)
6. (tie) "Simon & Simon" (CBS)
       "The A-Team" (NBC)
8. "Knots Landing" (CBS)
9. "Murder, She Wrote" (CBS)
10. (tie) "Crazy Like a Fox" (CBS)
        "Falcon Crest" (CBS)
12. "Hotel" (ABC)
13. "Cheers" (NBC)
14. "Riptide" (NBC)
15. "Magnum, P.I." (CBS)
16. "Hail to the Chief" (ABC)
17. "Newhart" (CBS)
18. "Kate & Allie" (CBS)
19. "NBC Monday Night Movies" (NBC)
20. "Highway to Heaven" (NBC)

Betty White, left, and Beatrice Arthur—two of the stars of NBC's new fall hit "The Golden Girls"—play women over 50 who share a house in Miami, Fla.

CBS but were said to be "inspired" by that classic series. CBS also tried out the "George Burns Comedy Week," hosted by the veteran comedian, but at year-end planned to shelve it.

These shows represented the return of anthology programs to the prime-time schedule. Anthologies—TV shows without continuing characters or story lines—flourished during the 1950's and early 1960's. None of the 1985 anthologies was more heavily promoted or eagerly anticipated than "Amazing Stories," a half-hour drama produced by noted filmmaker Steven Spielberg. But the series had only modest success in its first weeks.

The year turned out to be a good one for television programs set in Miami, Fla. "Miami Vice," a violent detective story, premiered on NBC to generally low ratings but critical applause in the fall of 1984. It became a genuine hit in spring 1985 and had an even larger following by the fall. The series used film techniques borrowed from rock videos and starred Don Johnson and Philip Michael Thomas.

At the other end of the spectrum was NBC's "The Golden Girls," a situation comedy also set in Miami. Its trio of stars—Beatrice Arthur, Betty White, and Rue McClanahan—played middle-aged women who share a house. The program seemed to overcome television's long-time aversion to showcasing older actresses.

NBC's "The Cosby Show," starring comedian Bill Cosby, became television's most popular program, lauded—almost sanctified—by critics and viewers for its wholesomeness. At the start of the 1985 season, "The Cosby Show" helped keep NBC at the top of weekly ratings of television viewership. ABC, which had programmed several flops in the 1984-1985 season, was still trying to dig itself out of last place. CBS, the ratings winner in 1984-1985, lagged behind NBC during the early part of the 1985-1986 season.

The most notable series in the fall of 1985 included ABC's "Moonlighting," a comedy about a detective team, starring Cybill Shepherd and Bruce Willis; CBS' "The Equalizer," starring Edward Woodward as a former intelligence agent; and "The Colbys," a spin-off from the successful ABC series "Dynasty." The popular CBS program "Cagney & Lacey" created a stir when its two female detectives endorsed a prochoice attitude toward abortion in an unusual departure for a series. Such programs usually steer a cautious middle course on controversial topics.

Several made-for-television movies also focused on controversial topics during the year. NBC aired "An Early Frost," television's first drama about acquired immune deficiency syndrome (AIDS), a disease whose victims have been primarily homosexuals and intravenous drug users. ABC pre-

A Slambang Success

The return of professional wrestling as a national attraction in the United States was one of television's top success stories of 1985. Wrestling programs were among the highest-rated shows on cable television. Grapplers Hulk Hogan, Rowdy Roddy Piper, and The Road Warriors approached household-word status. Professional wrestlers even experienced *crossover*—a show-business term for the movement of performers from one field of entertainment to another. Rock singer Cyndi Lauper, for example, turned up as the manager of Wendi Richter, one of the top women wrestlers. Flamboyant piano player Liberace appeared as a guest timekeeper on a wrestling show. Baseball manager Billy Martin served as a ring announcer.

Several wrestlers played in motion pictures, and a large group of grapplers made a successful video. A wrestling promoter built a TV talk show around himself and his wrestlers. And there were wrestler dolls, wrestler T-shirts, and wrestler cartoons.

Professional wrestling is in its second wave of success as a national TV attraction. The first wave occurred during the early 1950's, with prime-time shows on two networks. The show format would be familiar to today's wrestling fan. Men and women of all sizes and shapes wrestled. Many combatants assumed roles like parts in a play. Some of the characters were outrageous—most notably "Gorgeous George" Wagner, a golden-haired, magnificently robed individual who disdained to step into a ring until it had been perfumed by his valet, Jeffrey.

Most bouts pitted a "hero" against a "villain." The villains "broke the rules." Referees seemed not to notice most of the violations, and when officials did take notice, they most often merely warned the offenders.

Popular as pro wrestling was, it failed to win the respect enjoyed by other forms of TV entertainment such as the Western and the situation comedy. Professional wrestling was considered to be a degenerate form of a legitimate sport—the type of wrestling that appears on TV whenever the Olympic Games roll around. Critics said that pro wrestling was degenerate because the matches were "fixed" and seemed to be excessively violent.

Eventually, the interest in pro wrestling waned. The grapplers lost their prime-time network slots but remained fairly popular as local and regional entertainment.

Then regional promoters improved the format. More wrestlers assumed roles, and the roles became more colorful. The promoters elevated the promotional interview to a form of entertainment in its own right. They developed elaborate story lines for interviews involving grudges, unfair treatment in the ring, cowardly refusal of challenges, and, of course, predictions of what was going to happen in forthcoming matches. It was soap opera with sweat.

Vince McMahon, head of the World Wrestling Federation (WWF), which promoted wrestling in the northeastern part of the United States, used the old and the new techniques extremely well. WWF wrestling was not a "sport," but it did not have to be. It was drama. It was excitement. It was fun.

McMahon put shows on national cable television in late 1983 and early 1984. Pro wrestling has been gaining in popularity ever since, with the WWF at the forefront.

Critics still claim that pro wrestling matches are fixed. Are the critics correct? In the words of a *Newsweek* writer, "How could wrestling be fixed when it's never been broken?" Jay Myers

Hulk Hogan prepares to slam Rowdy Roddy Piper to the mat in March during a wrestling extravaganza in New York City's Madison Square Garden.

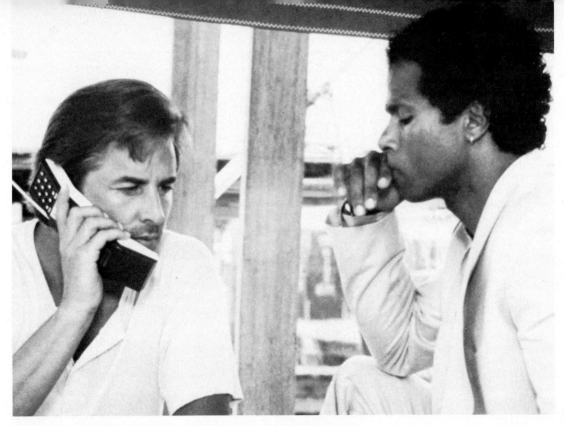

"Miami Vice" helped keep NBC on top of the ratings at the start of the 1985-1986 television season. It featured hip cops, rock music, and trendy clothes.

sented "Consenting Adult," a drama about a young man who tells his parents he is homosexual. CBS presented "The Atlanta Child Murders," a controversial docudrama about events leading to the arrest and 1982 conviction of Wayne B. Williams for two killings.

The Public Broadcasting Service (PBS) completed its presentation of "The Jewel in the Crown," a highly acclaimed 14-part saga based on *The Raj Quartet* by British author Paul Scott. In December, it began another much-touted series, "Bleak House," taken from the classic work by British novelist Charles Dickens.

Network News. CBS produced the most-watched evening newscast on U.S. networks. But layoffs and a seeming change of direction disturbed some CBS veterans, who thought that the news division, once the pride of the company, had become just another source of profit under CBS Chairman Thomas H. Wyman and CBS News President Edward M. Joyce. In December, Van Gordon Sauter, a senior vice president of CBS, replaced Joyce as head of CBS News.

In October, Roone Arledge, president of ABC News, personally canceled a segment on the network's weekly news magazine, "20/20." According to its producers, the segment proved conclusively that President John F. Kennedy and his brother Robert F. Kennedy had affairs with motion-pic-

ture actress Marilyn Monroe. Arledge said that the allegations had not been adequately substantiated.

On February 17, General William C. Westmoreland dropped a $120-million libel suit against CBS Inc. Westmoreland, commander of United States forces in Vietnam from 1964 to 1968, brought the suit in 1982 to challenge a TV documentary in which he was accused of lying about enemy troop strength in Vietnam. See COURTS.

The Video Cassette Recorder (VCR) remained at the forefront of new trends in TV viewing. With a VCR, viewers could tape a TV program when it aired and watch it at a more convenient time. Or, they could forsake over-the-air television and buy or rent a movie. Vigorous VCR sales created fears among commercial networks about the erosion of their viewership. VCR's seemed to be hurting the cable television industry, too. Although VCR's had come down in price since 1980, further reductions in 1985 proved irresistible to customers. By October 1985, VCR sales had jumped 55 per cent from the year before, bringing the total number of VCR's in U.S. homes to about 25 million. Manufacturers predicted that by early 1986, one-third of U.S. homes with a TV set would also have a VCR.
P. J. Bednarski

See also AWARDS AND PRIZES. In WORLD BOOK, see TELEVISION.

TENNESSEE. See STATE GOVERNMENT.

TENNIS. Boris Becker, an exuberant, 17-year-old West German, created the greatest tennis excitement in 1985. He became the youngest man ever to win the men's singles title at Wimbledon and the first unseeded player to win the hallowed English tournament. See BECKER, BORIS.

Women's competition again was dominated by Martina Navratilova of Dallas and Chris Evert Lloyd of Amelia Island, Fla. Navratilova won her sixth Wimbledon championship and her eighth Virginia Slims series final. Lloyd won her sixth French Open, eighth Family Circle Cup, and fourth Canadian Open title.

Record prize money was paid in 1985 by the United States Open, with $3,073,500, and Wimbledon, with $2,440,000. The Nabisco Grand Prix circuit for men, encompassing 78 tournaments in 25 nations, paid $16 million in prize money plus a $4-million bonus pool. The Virginia Slims tour for women—60 tournaments with $50,000 or more in prize money—awarded $12 million in purses.

Men. South African-born Kevin Curren of Austin, Tex., who became a U.S. citizen in April, shared attention with Becker at Wimbledon. In the quarterfinal round on July 3, Curren defeated defending champion John McEnroe of Douglaston, N.Y., who was seeded first, 6-2, 6-2, 6-4. In the semifinals, Curren swept by Jimmy Connors of Belleville, Ill., 6-2, 6-2, 6-1, with 17 service aces and 20 service winners.

Meanwhile, Becker, ranked 20th in the world, also moved toward the final. Few people gave him a chance to win, even though he had won the Queen's Club tournament in London, which, like Wimbledon, is played on grass, on June 16. Wimbledon's July 7 final was a battle of big servers, with Becker scoring 21 aces and Curren 19. Becker won in four sets, 6-3, 6-7, 7-6, 6-4.

Two months later, in the U.S. Open in Flushing Meadow, N.Y., there was great anticipation of a quarterfinal match between McEnroe, the defending champion and top seed, and the eighth-seeded Becker. The match never took place because Becker was eliminated by Joakim Nystrom of Sweden, 6-3, 6-4, 4-6, 6-4, in the round before the quarterfinals.

McEnroe, seeking his fifth U.S. Open title, reached the final against Ivan Lendl of Czechoslovakia. Lendl lost the final to Connors in 1982 and 1983 and to McEnroe in 1984. This time, on September 8, he defeated McEnroe, 7-6, 6-3, 6-4.

It was a disappointing year for McEnroe, who also lost to Mats Wilander of Sweden in the French Open semifinals. Wilander won the final on June 9, beating Lendl, 3-6, 6-4, 6-2, 6-2.

Women. The Navratilova-Lloyd battles included the June 8 women's final of the French Open. The 30-year-old Lloyd defeated the 28-year-old Navratilova, 6-3, 6-7, 7-5. Lloyd's sixth title tied her with

Boris Becker, 17, of West Germany, shows the form that in July helped him become the youngest player ever to win the Wimbledon men's singles title.

Suzanne Lenglen, who won six French Opens between 1920 and 1926.

Four weeks later, Navratilova and Lloyd shared first-seed ranking at Wimbledon. On July 6, Navratilova beat Lloyd, 4-6, 6-3, 6-2, for her fourth straight Wimbledon title and her fifth victory over Lloyd in five Wimbledon finals.

The expected meeting between Navratilova and Lloyd for the U.S. Open title did not materialize because of Hana Mandlikova of Czechoslovakia. In the semifinals on September 6, Mandlikova upset Lloyd, 4-6, 6-2, 6-3. In a spectacular final on September 7, Mandlikova upset Navratilova, 7-6, 1-6, 7-6, foiling Navratilova's bid for a third consecutive U.S. Open title. Years before, Mandlikova had been a ball girl for Navratilova's matches in Czechoslovakia.

Davis Cup. The United States was eliminated from Davis Cup competition when it lost to West Germany for the first time ever, 3 matches to 2, from August 2 to 4 in Hamburg, West Germany. Becker led the West Germans with victories over Eliot Teltscher of Rancho Palos Verdes, Calif., and Aaron Krickstein of Grosse Pointe, Mich. Sweden and West Germany met in the final, held from December 20 to 22 in West Germany. Sweden won, 3 matches to 2.   Frank Litsky

In WORLD BOOK, see TENNIS.

TEXAS. See HOUSTON; STATE GOVERNMENT.

THAILAND. Before dawn on Sept. 9, 1985, some 500 soldiers seized the headquarters of Thailand's supreme military command and sent 22 tanks into downtown Bangkok, the capital, in an unsuccessful attempt to overthrow the government. It was Thailand's 16th coup attempt, and the 8th to fail, since the government changed from an absolute monarchy to a constitutional monarchy in 1932.

The Uprising was led by Colonel Manoon Roopkachorn, a former tank regiment commander. He had been dismissed from the army for leading an unsuccessful coup attempt in 1981. Officials said Manoon and his brother, an air force wing commander, apparently hoped other troops would join the 1985 uprising. But loyal forces were rallied by generals acting for Prime Minister Prem Tinsulanonda, who was in Indonesia, and for the supreme military commander, General Arthit Kamlang-ek, who was in Sweden. After gunfire that killed at least 5 people and wounded 59, the coup attempt collapsed. Manoon and his brother fled the country.

The motives for the attempt were left unclear. On October 25, 40 people were charged with conspiracy to commit insurrection, a crime punishable by life imprisonment or death. The 40 included former Prime Minister Kriangsak Chamanan and former supreme military commander Serm Nanakorn. All 40 denied the charges, and a lengthy trial was expected. The trial began on December 4 but was immediately adjourned until Jan. 8, 1986.

Relations with Other Countries. Thailand accused Vietnam of 10 "serious acts of violation" of its border during late 1984 and early 1985. The Vietnamese army, which has occupied Kampuchea (formerly Cambodia) since 1979, was trying to destroy Kampuchean guerrilla bases near the border. Thai troops fought several battles with the Vietnamese in 1985 in an effort to drive them out of Thai territory.

United States troops participated in joint training exercises with Thai forces in July. The annual exercises were larger than ever, signifying American support for Thailand. On October 3, Prem and U.S. Secretary of Defense Caspar W. Weinberger signed an agreement in Washington, D.C., providing material support to Thai armed forces. The agreement gave Thailand direct and immediate access to U.S. military supply systems in time of crisis, as well as long-term help in producing armaments.

Economic Growth for 1985 was estimated at 4.8 per cent, a low rate for Thailand. Devaluation of Thailand's currency in 1984 failed to increase exports or cut imports as much as hoped, leaving a large trade imbalance. Farmers suffered from low prices for rice, their main export.   Henry S. Bradsher

See also ASIA (Facts in Brief Table); KAMPUCHEA; LAOS. In WORLD BOOK, see THAILAND.

THEATER. When the musical *Big River* opened on Broadway on April 25, 1985, it pulled the New York City theater season out of a big slump. This heart-warming musical version of Mark Twain's classic novel *The Adventures of Huckleberry Finn* featured Daniel H. Jenkins as the adventure-loving Huck and Ron Richardson as Jim, the runaway black slave who accompanies him on his exciting raft trip down the Mississippi River. In June, the show captured seven Antoinette Perry (Tony) Awards, including honors for best musical and for best score, book, direction, and scenic design.

Lackluster Musical Season. Before *Big River* rolled in, Broadway was dangerously low on new musicals. Harold Prince's *Grind*, a flashy musical about black and white performers working in a Chicago burlesque house during the 1930's, had only a thin story that failed to win audiences. It closed quickly. So did *Leader of the Pack*, a nostalgic tribute to the 1960's rock 'n' roll music of songwriter Ellie Greenwich.

So modest, in fact, was 1985's showing of new American musicals that, for the first time in the 38-year history of the Tony Awards, no presentation of honors was made in three categories—choreography, leading actor in a musical, and leading actress in a musical.

Broadway's hunger for a hit musical probably

Army recruit Eugene Morris (Matthew Broderick) learns about love from Daisy Hannigan (Penelope Ann Miller) in Neil Simon's *Biloxi Blues*.

Huck Finn (Daniel H. Jenkins) and Jim (Ron Richardson), the runaway slave, pole down the Mississippi River in the hit Broadway musical *Big River*.

explains the survival of two shows produced in 1985. Hopes ran high for *Singin' in the Rain*, a remake of the classic 1952 motion picture, which starred Gene Kelly. But Twyla Tharp, the avant-garde choreographer who made her Broadway directing debut with the production, showed little invention and less fun in her approach to the material. Another minor musical entry, *Song & Dance*, had a sweet score by Andrew Lloyd Webber, the British composer of such glossy musicals as *Cats* and *Evita*, but was insubstantial. It survived on the basis of a stunning solo performance by Bernadette Peters, who played a British waif who comes to the United States and gets tangled up in several disastrous love affairs.

The musical bounced back to life with *The Mystery of Edwin Drood*, a clever and light-hearted treatment of the Charles Dickens novel. Rupert Holmes's music-hall version of this Victorian mystery, a New York Shakespeare Festival production that moved to Broadway in December, let audiences vote on the play's ending.

Coincidentally, another musical that opened late in 1985, *Poppy*, by Great Britain's Royal Shakespeare Company, was also based on an old British theater tradition. The show used the conventions of the British pantomime—a mixture of music and vaudeville comedy—to spoof Victorian England's imperialism in China.

Drama. Broadway's infatuation with British musical influences did not extend to drama during the year. Glenda Jackson created a stir in an imported five-hour version of *Strange Interlude*, a rarely performed 1928 psychodrama by American playwright Eugene O'Neill. But new plays by British writers David Hare—*A Map of the World*—and Hugh Whitemore—*Pack of Lies*—were received without enthusiasm, though respectfully.

Broadway audiences seemed to prefer American plays on American subjects in 1985. Neil Simon won the Tony for best play for *Biloxi Blues*, which starred Matthew Broderick as a young New Yorker who finds himself out of his depth during Army basic training in 1943. Audiences also loved *The Search for Signs of Intelligent Life in the Universe*, a one-woman play starring Lily Tomlin as several characters.

Two dramas that won special attention were William M. Hoffman's *As Is* and Larry Kramer's *The Normal Heart*, which dealt sensitively with the subject of acquired immune deficiency syndrome (AIDS). Critics also praised Lyle Kessler's *Orphans*, a moody drama about two violent brothers in North Philadelphia who kidnap a Chicago mobster to serve as a father figure.

Regional Influence. Many Broadway and off-Broadway productions made their way to New York City from regional theater companies, which have

497

become an important source for new theater in the United States. For the first time, the New York theater formally acknowledged its debt by inviting three companies to showcase plays at a special festival. The Alley Theater in Houston, the Mark Taper Forum in Los Angeles, and the Yale Repertory Theater in New Haven, Conn., all presented plays at the Joyce Theater in New York City.

The importance of regional theater was underlined in April when Gregory Mosher left his position as the artistic director of Chicago's Goodman Theatre to become the new artistic director of the Lincoln Center Theater Company. Robert Falls, artistic director of Chicago's Wisdom Bridge Theatre, succeeded Mosher at the Goodman. On December 20, two new plays by Chicago playwright David Mamet—*The Shawl* and *Prairie du Chien*—reopened the Mitzi E. Newhouse Theater at Lincoln Center, which had been closed since 1981.

Financial Problems. The financial picture for both Broadway and regional theaters was troubling in 1984-1985. *Variety*, the show-business newspaper, reported that during the 1984-1985 season, box-office income on Broadway fell $15-million from 1983-1984 levels, to $208 million. Attendance also dropped, to 7.5 million from 7.9 million. Analysts blamed the slump on the scarcity of new shows, especially musicals. In March, the Theater Communications Group, an organization representing 230 nonprofit off-Broadway and regional theaters, reported that losses by 37 of its largest and most important member theaters doubled in 1984, to $1.4 million, despite record attendance and box-office income.

German Controversy. A major theatrical controversy erupted in Frankfurt, West Germany, over plans to stage *Garbage, the City and Death* by German playwright and filmmaker Rainer Werner Fassbinder, who died in 1982. Written in 1975, the play had never been produced, despite four previous attempts.

On Oct. 31, 1985, the world premiere of the play at the Kammerspiel theater in Frankfurt was halted by groups of Jewish protesters who said the portrayal of one of the play's major characters, a corrupt Jewish real estate speculator, was anti-Semitic. The protesters also prevented the play from opening on November 6.

On November 10, Frankfurt Mayor Walter Wallmann appeared at a local synagogue to apologize officially for the play's content and to urge Günter Rühle, the manager of the theater, to withdraw the production. The next day, Rühle agreed to do so.   Marilyn Stasio

See also AWARDS AND PRIZES (Arts Awards). In WORLD BOOK, see DRAMA; THEATER.

TIMOR. See ASIA.

TOGO. See AFRICA.

TORNADO. See DISASTERS; WEATHER.

TORONTO, Canada's largest metropolitan area and its main commercial and financial center, appeared in 1985 to be heading into an era of unprecedented growth and development. Wrecking companies tore down old buildings throughout the city core, and spindly boom cranes towered over rising concrete and glass structures. Planned construction projects extended to the year 2000 and beyond.

Helped by the construction activity, Toronto's unemployment rate was below 7 per cent in 1985—lower than that of any other major Canadian city. The new surge of prosperity, however, brought back some familiar problems for city administrators. Toronto suffered from an acute shortage of rental housing in 1985. Other problems included traffic congestion and rising prices for homes.

Municipal Elections on November 12 centered on development issues. The debate involved whether the city should stress the development of commercial business or private housing and whether more money should be spent on building roads or on improving public transportation. In the contest for mayor of the City of Toronto, incumbent Arthur Eggleton was challenged by veteran City Council member Anne Johnston. Eggleton was the business-oriented candidate, and he won, as did most prodevelopment office seekers in the five boroughs that, along with the City of Toronto, make up the Municipality of Metropolitan Toronto.

Building Boom. Curiously, it was baseball that gave development plans in Toronto a big boost during the summer and fall of 1985. The Toronto Blue Jays almost made it to the World Series but were eliminated after losing to the Kansas City Royals, 4 games to 3, in the American League play-offs in October. The excitement generated by the Blue Jays effectively quelled opposition to a $225-million project to build a new domed stadium for professional sporting events and concerts in Toronto. (All monetary amounts in this article are Canadian dollars, with $1 = U.S. 72 cents as of Dec. 31, 1985.) Critics of the project argued that it was wrong to spend so much money on a sports palace at a time when the money could better be spent on badly needed housing construction. They also claimed that the proposed $60-million subsidy of the project from the city and province placed an unnecessary burden on taxpayers. The critics' voices were lost among the cheers of the baseball fans, however.

Toronto's role as the cultural center for English-speaking Canada was strengthened by final approval in October of plans for the construction of a $530-million headquarters building for the publicly owned Canadian Broadcasting Corporation (CBC). Also given final approval in 1985 was a $2-

Thousands of baseball fans gather in Toronto in October to celebrate the Blue Jays' winning the American League Eastern Division championship.

TRACK AND FIELD. Steve Cram of Great Britain and Said Aouita of Morocco, both 24 years old, took turns in 1985 breaking world records for middle-distance and long-distance runs. Perhaps because they ran so often, however, they suffered hamstring injuries that kept them out of two climactic competitions—the Grand Prix final on September 7 in Rome and the World Cup, held from October 4 to 6 in Canberra, Australia.

In the 1984 Summer Olympic Games in Los Angeles, Aouita won the gold medal in the 5,000-meter event, and Cram won the silver medal in the 1,500 meters. In 1985, Cram set three world records in 20 days—for 1,500 meters (3 minutes 29.67 seconds on July 16 in Nice, France), for 1 mile (3 minutes 46.31 seconds on July 27 in Oslo, Norway), and for 2,000 meters (4 minutes 51.39 seconds on August 4 in Budapest, Hungary). Aouita bettered the world record for 5,000 meters with a time of 13 minutes 0.40 second on July 27 in Oslo and then broke Cram's record for the 1,500 meters with a time of 3 minutes 29.45 seconds on August 23 in West Berlin.

Jumpers from the Soviet Union reached one milestone and approached another during 1985. On July 13 in Paris, Sergei Bubka set a world pole vault record of 19 feet 8¼ inches, exactly 6 meters. In the high jump, the goal of reaching 8 feet

billion development project for a 200-acre (80-hectare) waterfront area of abandoned railroad yards and maintenance shops. Plans call for building 15 million square feet (1.4 million square meters) of commercial office space and nearly 6,000 housing units over the next 20 years.

The Toronto Transit Commission in October announced a $2.7-billion plan to expand the city's network of subway, bus, and streetcar lines over the next 28 years. Public hearings on the plan were set for early 1986. The plan includes spending about $100 million a year.

Waterfront Decline. Toronto's harbor on Lake Ontario continued its decline in 1985. Once a thriving shipping center, the port of Toronto has become less competitive because large container ships are too big to pass through the locks of the St. Lawrence Seaway.

The city's developers continued dumping landfill in 1985 to create a narrow point of land reaching into Lake Ontario. The project was planned in the mid-1960's to expand port facilities. Since an enlarged port is no longer needed, debate in 1985 centered on whether to use the land for marinas and parks or as a nature preserve. In 1985, the point was home to the world's largest population of ring-billed gulls. Robert R. Duffy

In WORLD BOOK, see TORONTO.
TOYS. See GAMES AND TOYS.

Steve Cram of Great Britain crosses the finish line in a 2,000-meter race in August in Budapest, Hungary, setting a world record.

World Track and Field Records Established in 1985

Men

Event	Holder	Country	Where Set	Date	Record
1,500 meters	Said Aouita	Morocco	West Berlin	Aug. 23	3:29.45
1 mile	Steve Cram	Great Britain	Oslo, Norway	July 27	3:46.31
2,000 meters	Steve Cram	Great Britain	Budapest, Hungary	Aug. 4	4:51.39
5,000 meters	Said Aouita	Morocco	Oslo, Norway	July 27	13:00.40
Marathon	Carlos Lopes	Portugal	Rotterdam, Netherlands	April 20	2:07:12*
30-kilometer walk	Maurizio Damilano	Italy	San Donato Milanese, Italy	May 5	2:06:27
High jump	Igor Paklin	U.S.S.R.	Kobe, Japan	Sept. 4	7 ft. 10¾ in. (2.41 m)
Pole vault	Sergei Bubka	U.S.S.R.	Paris	July 13	19 ft. 8¼ in. (6.00 m)
Triple jump	Willie Banks	U.S.A.	Indianapolis	June 16	58 ft. 11½ in. (17.97 m)
Shot-put	Ulf Timmermann	E. Germany	East Berlin	Sept. 22	74 ft. 1¾ in. (22.60 m)

Women

Event	Holder	Country	Where Set	Date	Record
400 meters	Marita Koch	E. Germany	Canberra, Australia	Oct. 6	:47.60
1 mile	Mary Decker Slaney	U.S.A.	Zurich, Switzerland	Aug. 21	4:16.71
5,000 meters	Zola Budd	Great Britain	London	Aug. 26	14:48.07
10,000 meters	Ingrid Kristiansen	Norway	Oslo, Norway	July 27	30:59.42
Marathon	Ingrid Kristiansen	Norway	London	April 21	2:21:06*
400-meter hurdles	Sabine Busch	E. Germany	East Berlin	Sept. 22	:53.56
400-meter relay	Silke Gladisch Sabine Rieger Ingrid Auerswald Marlies Göhr	E. Germany	Canberra, Australia	Oct. 6	:41.37
Long jump	Heike Drechsler	E. Germany	East Berlin	Sept. 22	24 ft. 5 in. (7.44 m)
Triple jump	Wendy Brown	U.S.A.	Austin, Tex.	May 30	44 ft. 6¾ in. (13.58 m)*
Javelin throw	Petra Falke	E. Germany	Schwerin, E. Germany	June 4	247 ft. 4 in. (75.40 m)

m = meters; *unofficial record.

(2.44 meters) came nearer when Rudolf Povarnitsin set a world record of 7 feet 10½ inches (2.40 meters) on August 11 in Donetsk, Soviet Union. Igor Paklin's mark of 7 feet 10¾ inches (2.41 meters) bettered it on September 4 in Kobe, Japan.

Women. Mary Decker Slaney of Eugene, Ore., Maricica Puica of Romania, and Zola Budd of Great Britain—the central figures in the controversial 3,000-meter final in the 1984 Summer Olympics—met three times in three weeks in 1985. Each time, Slaney finished first, Puica second, and Budd third.

In their Olympic race, Slaney collided with Budd, fell with a hip injury, and was out of the race. Puica, who avoided the collision, won the gold medal. In 1985, Slaney defeated these rivals during the one-mile race (4 minutes 16.71 seconds, a world record, on August 21 in Zurich, Switzerland); the 1,500 meters (3 minutes 57.24 seconds, the year's fastest time, on August 30 in Brussels, Belgium); and the 3,000 meters (8 minutes 25.83 seconds, the second fastest ever, on September 7 in Rome). The 27-year-old Slaney finished the 1985 track season with 14 victories in 14 races.

Other Americans. The year was wonderful for Willie Banks, mixed for Carl Lewis, and empty for Edwin Moses. The 29-year-old Banks said he had forgotten the disappointment over his sixth-place finish in the 1984 Olympic triple jump. He thought only of breaking the world record, and he did it on June 16 in Indianapolis by jumping 58 feet 11½ inches (17.97 meters).

Lewis, the winner of four Olympic gold medals in Los Angeles in 1984, strained a hamstring during a long-jump competition in Los Angeles on May 18, 1985. Nevertheless, he won that competition for his 42nd consecutive victory, a record for this event. After the injury, Lewis did not compete for a month.

Moses, the world champion in the 400-meter hurdles and a two-time Olympic champion, ran only one race during 1985, a 400-meter dash. He injured a knee ligament during a workout on a wet track, and the injury wiped out the rest of his season.

Slaney and Banks were the only Americans who broke world records during the year. Sydney Maree established U.S. records for 1,500 meters (3 minutes 29.77 seconds); 2,000 meters (4 minutes 54.20 seconds); and 5,000 meters (13 minutes 1.15 seconds). Joe Dial raised the U.S. outdoor record in the pole vault, first to 19 feet 1½ inches (5.83 meters) and then to 19 feet 2½ inches (5.85 meters). Jim Howard high-jumped 7 feet 8½ inches (2.35 meters) indoors and the same height outdoors, both U.S. records.

Frank Litsky

In WORLD BOOK, see TRACK AND FIELD.

TRANSIT systems in United States cities had ridership increases in 1985 for the third consecutive year. According to the American Public Transit Association (APTA), a Washington, D.C.-based trade association that represents public mass-transit systems, ridership from January to August 1985 ran 1.3 per cent above 1984 levels. Some cities showed even greater increases. For example, the Washington Area Metropolitan Transit Authority in Washington, D.C., reported that its April 1985 ridership averaged more than 400,000 per day, 31,000 above the previous record. Atlanta, Ga., had an 18.6 per cent increase, and total passengers in Houston rose 11 per cent. Ridership in Los Angeles was up 3.4 per cent.

Some systems showed ridership declines. For example, ridership in New York City was down 0.2 per cent. The number of passengers in Minneapolis, Minn., and Milwaukee dropped by 1.7 and 4.4 per cent, respectively. The Cincinnati, Ohio, system had a 5.6 per cent decline in riders, according to the APTA report.

Fare Increases took effect in several cities during the year. Buffalo, N.Y., fares increased from 60 to 75 cents, for example. Fares in Philadelphia went from 75 to 85 cents and then to 90 cents. The base fare for Houston riders increased from 50 to 55 cents. In Orange County, California—which includes several suburbs of Los Angeles—transit users saw their fares increase from 60 to 75 cents. In December, the Metropolitan Transit Authority raised New York City's fare from 90 cents to $1, effective Jan. 1, 1986.

Extensions of Transit Systems were completed in several U.S. cities during the year. In May, a 6.4-mile (10.3-kilometer) segment of *light rail*—electrically powered railroad passenger lines—opened in Buffalo. The second half of a 20.5-mile (33-kilometer) rapid transit system began service in Miami, Fla., on May 19. A 9.5-mile (15.3-kilometer) commuter railroad line to and from the Philadelphia airport began operation in April. And a new subway tunnel segment of the light-rail system in Pittsburgh, Pa., opened in July.

Seoul, South Korea—which was preparing to host the 1988 Olympic Games—had expanded its subway system by nearly 72 miles (116 kilometers) by the end of 1985.

Private Firms Take Over. As a result of prodding from the Administration of President Ronald Reagan, a growing number of cities turned to private industry to provide transit services. For example, Dallas Area Rapid Transit contracted with the Trailways Bus System to provide commuter service. Other towns hired van or taxi companies to provide rides for the elderly or handicapped, or to furnish Sunday or late-night service.

Controversies over Funding for mass-transit projects continued in Congress during 1985. In

To accommodate higher fares, new electronic fareboxes installed on Chicago Transit Authority buses beginning in March accept both coins and $1 bills.

January, the Reagan Administration proposed that federal funding for such projects be eliminated, but Congress refused to cooperate. There also were disputes over the Administration's refusal to approve some new projects. In December, however, Reagan signed a federal spending bill that included $429 million to help build a $3.3-billion subway system for Los Angeles.

The Office of Management and Budget (OMB), a U.S. government agency that helps prepare the federal budget, at year's end was proposing major changes in highway funding that could affect mass-transit funding. The OMB proposal would establish a block-grant program, under which states would receive a lump sum of money for highway and transit projects. The states then would be free to decide whether to spend the money on roads or on transit projects. Advocates of the change contend that the states know their own needs better than the federal government does and that the block-grant program would give more flexibility to the states and cities in how they use their money. But any such change must be approved by Congress and undoubtedly would be strongly opposed by the trucking and highway lobbies. David M. Cawthorne

In WORLD BOOK, see BUS; ELECTRIC RAILROAD; SUBWAY; TRANSPORTATION.

TRANSKEI. See AFRICA.

TRANSPORTATION

TRANSPORTATION companies in the United States saw sharp drops in earnings and traffic during 1985. Railroad freight traffic for the first 40 weeks of the year was 5.3 per cent below 1984 levels. Trucking industry earnings also showed a sharp drop. Surplus capacity and lagging demand continued to plague shipping lines, though companies moved to reduce their overcapacity. Only mass transit systems had increased business—more riders—during the year.

Frank Smith of Transportation Policy Associates, a consulting firm, estimated U.S. transportation revenue at $280 billion for 1985, up 2 per cent from 1984. Intercity freight on the United States mainland, measured in ton-miles, fell 3 per cent, with railroad freight down about 4.1 per cent, truck freight down 1 per cent, air freight down 5.8 per cent, and pipeline volume down 1 per cent. Great Lakes shipping traffic dipped 10 to 15 per cent, while river and canal traffic increased 6 to 10 per cent.

Highway Funds. Congress in March passed legislation releasing $7.2 billion in federal highway construction funds due the states. The money had been collected as federal gasoline, diesel fuel, and truck taxes and was earmarked for interstate highways. It was held up for nearly two years while Congress argued about a number of road projects that various members sought to add to the bill. During that time, more than 40 states had been forced to use general revenues to finance their highway programs.

The Regulators. Funding problems forced the Interstate Commerce Commission, the federal agency that regulates the railroad and trucking industries, to go on a four-day workweek from April to June 1985. The agency's decisions continued to favor deregulation.

The Federal Maritime Commission, the U.S. government agency that administers shipping laws, kept busy throughout 1985 carrying out new legislation. The new legislation included many changes in the government's powers to supervise rates and to enforce antitrust measures in the shipping industry.

In September, the Administration of United States President Ronald Reagan sent a trucking deregulation bill to Congress. The Administration also attempted to head off attempts to reregulate the railroad industry during the year.

Transportation Policy Associates reported in March that, for the first time in 50 years, more than half the freight moving in the United States was not regulated. That fact reflected the reduction in government rate controls resulting from legislation enacted in 1978, 1980, and 1984.

A barge moves along the Tennessee-Tombigbee Waterway, a system of canals dedicated in June that links the Tennessee River with the Gulf of Mexico.

The Department of Transportation (DOT) fought drug abuse in the transportation industry through three of its major agencies in 1985. The DOT's Federal Aviation Administration in June adopted new rules barring aircraft crew members from working under the influence of mind-altering substances. The Federal Railroad Administration in July adopted similar regulations covering railroad employees. In October, the Federal Highway Administration proposed new rules prohibiting truck drivers from using dangerous or habit-forming drugs.

Waterway Opened. The Tennessee-Tombigbee Waterway, a 234-mile (377-kilometer) system of canals and locks in Alabama and Mississippi, was officially dedicated in June. By linking the Tennessee and Tombigbee rivers, the waterway—nicknamed the Tenn-Tom—gives ships a more direct route to the Gulf of Mexico, cutting the distance by about 800 miles (1,300 kilometers). After construction began in 1971, the Tenn-Tom drew much criticism from members of Congress and the public. Many questioned whether the waterway would produce sufficient economic benefits to justify its $2-billion cost.   David M. Cawthorne

See also AUTOMOBILE; AVIATION; RAILROAD; SHIP AND SHIPPING; TRANSIT; TRUCK AND TRUCKING. In WORLD BOOK, see TRANSPORTATION.

TRINIDAD AND TOBAGO. See LATIN AMERICA.

TRUCK AND TRUCKING. Earnings for the trucking industry in the United States dropped sharply in 1985. Net income for the first six months of 1985 was down about 33 per cent from 1984 levels. Revenues were up by about 3 per cent, but this gain was more than offset by higher expenses.

Insurance costs, in particular, rose drastically for the carriers, with some companies facing increases of up to 600 per cent in insurance premiums. In November, the Interstate Commerce Commission (ICC)—the federal government agency that regulates interstate trucking—voted to investigate skyrocketing insurance costs.

Deregulation. In September, the Administration of President Ronald Reagan sent its long-awaited trucking deregulation bill to Congress. The bill would end ICC regulation of the trucking industry and eliminate protection of trucking firms from antitrust prosecution when they jointly set freight rates. Responsibility for trucking safety would be transferred to the Department of Transportation, and supervision of household goods moving would be assumed by the Federal Trade Commission.

Labor. On May 17, the members of the Teamsters Union ratified a new three-year labor contract that had been negotiated with representatives of trucking management. The contract includes modest wage increases but establishes a two-tier

wage structure under which newly hired drivers will be paid at a lower rate.

On July 26, truckers who haul new cars to dealers went out on strike. A major issue involved management's desire to greatly reduce wages for the time drivers spend returning empty after delivery. The strike ended on August 18 with union leaders announcing an agreement that maintained full pay levels for drivers returning empty.

The Department of Justice in July decided not to pursue further a four-year investigation of Teamsters Union President Jackie Presser. Department of Labor investigators had recommended that Presser be indicted for padding the payroll of a Teamster local in Cleveland. Reports concerning the investigation indicated that Presser had for several years worked as an informant on organized crime for the Federal Bureau of Investigation.

Highway Funds. President Reagan on March 13 signed into law a bill releasing $7.2 billion for interstate highway construction. The funds had been held up for two years because of disputes over a series of highway projects that some legislators wanted attached to the bill. The final bill, however, contained none of these controversial highway projects.   David M. Cawthorne

See also TRANSPORTATION. In WORLD BOOK, see TRUCK.

TRUDEAU, PIERRE ELLIOTT (1919-   ), kept mainly out of public attention during 1985. He had stepped down as prime minister of Canada in June 1984 after 15 years in that office. Trudeau worked as a senior counsel in a large law firm in Montreal, Que., and furthered his often-stated desire to improve East-West relations by spending a month in the Soviet Union in late June and July. The Soviet Union's Institute for the Study of the United States and Canada had invited him to Moscow. During his stay in the Soviet Union, Trudeau met with Soviet leader Mikhail S. Gorbachev on July 5.

In late October, after the Commonwealth Heads of Government meeting in Nassau, the Bahamas, Canada's new Prime Minister Brian Mulroney asked Trudeau to participate in a Commonwealth committee of "eminent persons" to encourage talks between the South African government and black leaders. But Trudeau declined Mulroney's invitation in November.

On October 30, at a ceremony in Ottawa, Ont., Canada's Governor General Jeanne M. Sauvé conferred the honor of Companion of the Order of Canada, the nation's highest award, on Trudeau. The citation praised his accomplishments as prime minister, lawyer, professor, author, and defender of human rights.   David M. L. Farr

In WORLD BOOK, see TRUDEAU, PIERRE E.

TUNISIA. The bombing of Palestine Liberation Organization (PLO) headquarters in a suburb of Tunis by Israeli jets on Oct. 1, 1985, brought this small North African country squarely into the mainstream of the Middle East conflict. At least 73 people were killed and more than 100 injured in the raid, which the Israeli government said was carried out in revenge for the September 25 murder of 3 Israelis in Cyprus by Palestinian terrorists. The PLO denied involvement in the killings.

The Israeli attack was a considerable embarrassment to the United States because the United States had played a role in persuading Tunisia to take in the PLO after the PLO was routed from Lebanon in 1982. In addition, the Tunisian government is normally pro-Western, though it supports Palestinian efforts to establish a separate homeland. On Oct. 4, 1985, the United States abstained on, instead of vetoing, a United Nations Security Council resolution condemning Israel for the raid, thus avoiding a break in diplomatic relations with Tunisia.

Tensions with Libya. Tunisia's relations with Libya reached a crisis point in August, when Libya expelled about 21,000 Tunisian workers after they refused to accept Libyan citizenship. Libya said that Libyans should have the jobs. But most observers believed the move was the result of falling oil revenues, which required cost-cutting measures. Tunisia responded by expelling 283 Libyans, including 30 diplomats. It also placed its armed forces on alert after Libya threatened to use force to stop an anti-Libyan campaign in the Tunisian press. Most of the Tunisian workers were later given jobs in Iraq, which has good relations with Tunisia.

Elections. The ruling Socialist Destour Party (PSD) had some success in its effort to broaden the base of political participation and develop a multiparty system without surrendering too much power. Local and municipal elections were held in May. The three legal opposition parties and the Islamic Tendency Movement, an outlawed fundamentalist organization, boycotted the elections. Nevertheless, a record 92.8 per cent of the voters participated. Some 3,540 candidates, including 478 women, all screened by the PSD, were elected to office.

The Economy improved with a record grain harvest and increased exports of textiles and crude oil. The trade deficit was reduced by 11.9 per cent. In October, Tunisia's creditors agreed to reschedule $800 million in debts over a seven-year period as a mark of confidence.   William Spencer

See also AFRICA (Facts in Brief Table). In WORLD BOOK, see TUNISIA.

The mayors of Rome and Carthage (now a suburb of Tunis, Tunisia) sign a treaty ending the Third Punic War in February 1985—2,131 years after the fighting stopped.

TURKEY in 1985 continued its steady progress toward the full restoration of civilian rule. In February, the founder and 23 leaders of the outlawed National Salvation Party, an Islamic fundamentalist party, were acquitted by a Turkish court of trying to overthrow the Constitution.

In July, Turkey's two major leftist parties, the Populist Party and the Social Democracy Party, merged to form a single opposition party, the Social Democratic Populist Party. In November, Rahsan Ecevit, the wife of former Prime Minister Bülent Ecevit, organized a new political party, the Democratic Left Party. Her husband has been banned from politics since being ousted in a 1980 military coup.

Police Act. One stumbling block to the restoration of civil liberties was the Police Duties and Powers Act, passed in June 1985 by the Grand National Assembly, Turkey's parliament, under military prodding. The law gave the police emergency powers to search homes without warrants and to make arrests on grounds of suspicion. The law also made the police the "moral and ethical guardians" of the state. Opponents criticized the law for being vague and for giving police the authority to determine acceptable public behavior. After a policeman killed a street vendor in September for alleged immorality, opponents said they would file suit to have the law repealed.

Rebel Activity. Martial law was lifted in six provinces in July and in eight others in November. Only the turbulent eastern region, where the population is mainly Kurdish, remained under military control.

In August, the government announced the results of "Operation Sun," a yearlong campaign against Kurdish guerrillas. The report stated that 309 guerrillas had been captured and 272 detained for trial. But clashes continued. In September, the government closed Mount Ararat in eastern Turkey to mountaineering expeditions because of the unrest.

Rights Violations. In July, Amnesty International, an independent human rights organization, reported that nearly 180,000 political prisoners had been held in Turkey since 1980. The group's report also charged that the torture of such prisoners continued to be "widespread and systematic."

The Economy. Talks between the government and the International Monetary Fund (IMF), an agency of the United Nations, on rescheduling Turkey's foreign debts broke down in May. The IMF refused to provide even stand-by credits until Turkey, which was $638 million over budget for the period from January to July 1985, put its financial house in order.   William Spencer

See also MIDDLE EAST (Facts in Brief Table). In WORLD BOOK, see TURKEY.

TURNER, TINA (1939-   ), remained hot on the comeback trail in 1985 as she wailed, screamed, stomped, and shimmied her way across North America. Before sellout crowds in 86 cities, the sultry singer displayed the explosive style that has made her famous. In February, she won three Grammy Awards, including the record of the year award for "What's Love Got to Do with It?" She also co-starred in the motion-picture thriller *Mad Max Beyond Thunderdome*.

Turner worked hard for this success. She was born Anna Mae Bullock on Nov. 26, 1939, in Nutbush, Tenn., near Brownsville. As a child, she worked in the cotton fields with her family. In the mid-1950's, she moved to St. Louis, Mo., and in 1956 met her future husband, bandleader Ike Turner, who was performing there with his Kings of Rhythm. She began singing with the group. After they recorded the hit single "Fool in Love" in 1959, Ike named her "Tina" and reorganized the act around her. They performed as the Ike and Tina Turner Revue and enjoyed their greatest success in Europe, where they toured in 1966 with the British rock group the Rolling Stones.

In 1976, after 14 years of marriage, Turner left Ike and the revue. Their divorce in 1978 left her penniless, and she began slowly to build a career on her own.   Karin C. Rosenberg

See also POPULAR MUSIC.

UGANDA. On July 27, 1985, military units led by Brigadier Basilio Olara Okello deposed the civilian government of President Milton Obote. On July 29, the chief of staff of Uganda's armed forces, Lieutenant General Tito Okello Lutwa—no relation to Brigadier Okello—was sworn in as head of state. Brigadier Okello justified the coup by accusing Obote of favoritism toward members of Obote's ethnic group, the Langi, and of brutally repressing groups that opposed him.

Resentments Lead to Violence. Brigadier Okello and the other officers leading the coup belong to the Acholi people, and they resented the favored treatment of Langis in the army. On July 7, pitched battles had broken out in the capital city, Kampala, between Acholi and Langi soldiers. Brigadier Okello and his fellow Acholi officers then returned to their ethnic homeland in northern Uganda, where many Acholi soldiers were stationed. Those soldiers rallied to the side of the rebel officers, and together they marched on Kampala. Warned of the revolt, Obote fled to neighboring Kenya on July 27.

Military Council. Okello named a nine-member military council to rule the country until elections are held. The nine positions were to include a post for Salim Saleh Rufulla, military commander of the National Resistance Army (NRA), the largest of three anti-Obote guerrilla forces. But the NRA refused Okello's initial invitation to join the government. The group objected to the domination of the ruling council by northerners and to the appointment of Paulo Muwanga as Uganda's new prime minister. Although a member of a southern ethnic group, the Baganda, Muwanga had been a close aide of Obote's and was suspected of helping to rig the 1980 elections in his favor. To appease rebel leaders, the military government dismissed Muwanga on August 25.

Rebel Attacks. Throughout the year, the NRA mounted hit-and-run attacks against government forces in southwestern Uganda. On July 22, the NRA captured the town of Fort Portal near the border with Zaire, and in early August NRA troops seized control of Masaka.

By August 10, the two smaller guerrilla armies had declared cease-fires in their struggles with government forces. Uganda's new leaders asked the NRA to also cease hostilities and continued to seek its participation in the military council. On December 17, the NRA and the government signed a peace agreement that called for the NRA to share national power.   J. Dixon Esseks

See also AFRICA (Facts in Brief Table). In WORLD BOOK, see UGANDA.

UNEMPLOYMENT. See ECONOMICS; LABOR.
UNION OF SOVIET SOCIALIST REPUBLICS (U.S.S.R.). See RUSSIA.

UNITED NATIONS (UN) commemorated its 40th anniversary during 1985. The UN General Assembly's 40th regular fall session began on September 17, with the election of Jaime de Piniés of Spain as president.

Commemoration Ceremonies took place during General Assembly meetings between October 14 and 24. Member nations sent high government officials to the UN's New York City Headquarters. More than 200 speakers addressed the General Assembly, including prime ministers, presidents, and one king—Moshoeshoe II of Lesotho in southern Africa. Also among the notables visiting UN Headquarters were Prime Ministers Margaret Thatcher of Great Britain, Brian Mulroney of Canada, Rajiv Gandhi of India, Zhao Ziyang of China, and David R. Lange of New Zealand and President Amin Gemayel of Lebanon.

Anniversary Disagreements. The General Assembly's commemoration program called for adoption of a universal declaration of purpose on October 24, but none was issued. The committee drafting the declaration disagreed over proposals concerning Palestine. An Arab and Indian group wanted a call for Palestinian self-determination and for withdrawal of occupying Israeli forces from the West Bank and Gaza. The United States wanted a more general call for peace in the Middle East, and Western Europeans proposed a ver-

sion that did not even mention Palestinians. This was not acceptable to the Arabs, and the committee, hopelessly divided, finally gave up.

Faced with such disagreements, the best the full Assembly could do on October 24 was proclaim an "International Year of Peace" in a resolution promoted by Costa Rica, cosponsored by 52 other countries, and adopted by unanimous consent.

Arms Control. United States President Ronald Reagan addressed the Assembly on October 24, 40 years to the day since the UN Charter took effect. Reagan promised that at the upcoming summit meeting in Geneva, Switzerland, in November, he would discuss with Soviet leader Mikhail S. Gorbachev verifiable reductions in nuclear weapons because a nuclear war "cannot be won and must never be fought." Reagan added that the Soviet Union need not fear U.S. research on a space-based defense against intercontinental ballistic missiles—the so-called Star Wars—because such a system would threaten only missiles, not people.

Soviet Foreign Minister Eduard A. Shevardnadze, later that day, read the Assembly a message from Gorbachev that called for "ending the arms race on Earth and preventing it in space." Shevardnadze gave the UN some credit for the fact that there had been no world war in the last 40 years, but he added that small wars had inflicted enormous suffering in the Middle East, southern Africa, Afghanistan, and Nicaragua. He called for a world "without weapons in space" in which the Soviet Union and the United States would, as an example to other nuclear powers, stop developing new nuclear weapons, freeze their arsenals, and ban orbiting antisatellite systems.

On November 18, the General Assembly voted 76-0, with 12 abstentions, to adopt a resolution expressing hope that the U.S.-Soviet summit meeting would produce early agreements to stop the nuclear arms race on Earth and prevent one from developing in space. The Soviet Union voted for the resolution. The United States abstained.

Middle East Issues. Israel's Prime Minister Shimon Peres, in the General Assembly on October 21, called for peace negotiations between Israel and Arab countries, particularly Jordan. He suggested that the state of war between Israel and Jordan end at once. Jordanian reaction was noncommittal.

Western pressure sidetracked a bid to invite Chairman Yasir Arafat of the Palestine Liberation Organization (PLO) to the October commemorative session. On October 9, India, Nigeria, Senegal, Iraq, Kuwait, and Yemen (Sana) introduced a resolution to invite Arafat and Sam Nujoma, leader of the South West Africa People's Organization, to participate as UN observers. After the hijacking of the Italian cruise ship *Achille Lauro* in October and the killing of an American passenger by members of a Palestinian faction, U.S. diplomats spread the word that if Arafat showed up, Reagan might not attend. As a result, on October 14 when the commemorative session began, the sponsors of the Arafat-Nujoma invitation said they would not press the resolution to a vote, thus averting a crisis in the ceremonies.

On March 31, UN Secretary-General Javier Pérez de Cuéllar began a visit to several Persian Gulf nations in the hope of bringing about talks to end the war between Iran and Iraq. After visiting Bahrain, Iran, Iraq, Oman, Qatar, and Saudi Arabia, Pérez concluded on April 9 that the gap between Iran and Iraq was as wide as ever and that no peace was in sight.

Security Council Vetoes. During the year, there were a number of vetoes by the United States in the 15-member UN Security Council. A "no" vote—or veto—by any one of the five permanent Security Council members defeats a measure. On March 12, on a vote of 11-1 with 3 abstentions, the United States vetoed a resolution condemning Israeli practices against civilians in Lebanon. On September 13, it vetoed another resolution accusing Israel of oppressing Palestinians.

On May 10, the United States vetoed part of a resolution calling for a U.S.-Nicaraguan dialogue because the paragraphs involved condemned the U.S. trade embargo against Nicaragua.

South Africa Condemned. In a number of moves during the year, the United Nations showed its disapproval of the South African government's policy of *apartheid*, or racial separation, and its efforts to suppress black protest. On May 12, the Security Council condemned the killing of 18 black protesters.

In June, the Security Council passed three resolutions against South Africa—for a military strike against guerrillas in Angola, for failing to establish an independent Namibia, and for a raid into Botswana that killed 16 people.

On July 26, 13 members of the Security Council approved a resolution calling on South Africa to end its state of emergency and release all political prisoners. The resolution also called for economic sanctions against South Africa. The United States and Great Britain, opposing economic sanctions, abstained. On October 7, the Council again condemned South Africa for an air raid on Angola that killed 65 people.

Beginning with the 40th session's opening of debate on September 23, dignitaries from dozens of nations in addresses before the General Assembly called for an end to South Africa's apartheid and the extension of full civil and political rights to all that nation's black and mixed-race citizens. See SOUTH AFRICA.

A Women's Conference marking the end of the UN Decade for Women was held in Nairobi,

Women from more than 150 countries meet in Nairobi, Kenya, in July at the conclusion of the United Nations Decade for Women.

Kenya, in July. There were 2,200 official delegates from more than 150 nations, and an additional 10,000 women gathered for unofficial meetings at the University of Nairobi.

Despite flare-ups of political disputes involving the Middle East and other matters, the delegates unanimously adopted a nonbinding document, "Forward-Looking Strategies," mapping out women's goals until the year 2000. Concerns included working conditions, pay, and child care.

New U.S. Ambassador. Vernon A. Walters, a former U.S. Army general, became U.S. representative to the United Nations on May 22. He replaced Jeane J. Kirkpatrick, who returned to a teaching post as professor of government at Georgetown University. See WALTERS, VERNON A.

Other UN Actions. The General Assembly unanimously adopted two resolutions urging emergency relief for UN members stricken by natural disasters. One was aimed at helping Mexico, which had been hit by two earthquakes in September (see MEXICO). The other resolution was for the benefit of Colombia, which had been ravaged by mud slides caused by the eruption of a volcano in November (see COLOMBIA).

On October 4, the Security Council on a vote of 14-0, with the United States abstaining, condemned an Israeli air raid on PLO headquarters in Tunisia.

On October 9, the Council issued a unanimous statement condemning the hijacking of the *Achille Lauro* and "other acts of terrorism, including hostage-taking." On December 18, the Council adopted a unanimous resolution condemning "all acts of hostage-taking and abduction" and calling for the safe release of all hostages.

On November 13, the General Assembly on a vote of 122-19 with 12 abstentions passed a resolution calling for the withdrawal of foreign troops from Afghanistan. It was similar to other resolutions passed each year since Soviet troops invaded Afghanistan in December 1979.

On December 9, the General Assembly unanimously adopted a resolution condemning terrorism as criminal. The vote was significant because it was the first time that Assembly delegates were able to agree on a broad condemnation of acts of terrorism.

Five new nonpermanent member nations were elected to two-year terms on the Security Council on October 17—Bulgaria, Congo, Ghana, United Arab Emirates, and Venezuela.

On December 5, Britain confirmed that it would withdraw from the United Nations Educational, Scientific and Cultural Organization at the end of the year on the grounds that the organization had become "harmfully politicized."   William N. Oatis

In WORLD BOOK, see UNITED NATIONS.

UNITED STATES, GOVERNMENT OF THE. More than ever in 1985, the United States government's agenda was dominated by the subject of money: how to raise more of it, how to spend less of it, and how to get the most for what it does spend.

The federal budget for the 1985 fiscal year, which ended on September 30, had a record deficit of $202.8 billion. With massive deficits on the verge of becoming an annual tradition, Congress on December 11 passed a bill requiring that red-ink spending be reduced in each coming fiscal year and drop to zero by 1991. President Ronald Reagan signed the legislation into law the following day. The President and Congress then began thinking about how to chop $11.7 billion out of the budget for fiscal 1986, already underway, and $50 billion out of the still-unwritten 1987 budget.

Although Congress had favored limited tax increases—including a $5-a-barrel tariff on imported oil—to increase federal revenues, Reagan rejected the idea of new taxes. That meant that deficits would have to be brought down with spending cuts. Throughout the year, the President conferred with his Cabinet on ways to reduce federal expenditures. On April 8, the Cabinet approved a plan for cutting 80,000 jobs from the government payroll over a three-year period.

Defense Contractors. Secretary of Defense Caspar W. Weinberger frequently angered Congress by his unyielding insistence—in which he was usually backed up by Reagan—that the Pentagon budget should be spared from cost-cutting measures. But Weinberger was forced to come down on the side of economy in perhaps the biggest government controversy of 1985—a furor involving the nation's largest military suppliers and their financial dealings with the Defense Department.

On March 5, Weinberger announced a crackdown on defense contractors. On March 28, two days after a federal grand jury in Philadelphia indicted General Electric Company (GE) for fraud in relation to the manufacture of missile warheads for the Air Force, the Pentagon asked GE and the Pratt & Whitney Division of the United Technologies Corporation to refund $208 million in alleged excess profits on spare parts for jet engines. A week later, the Defense Department accused the General Dynamics Corporation of overcharging the government a total of $244 million since 1973. General Dynamics, GE, Rockwell International Corporation, and several other companies were temporarily barred from receiving new contracts. GE pleaded guilty on May 13, 1985, to defrauding the government on the missile contract and was fined $1.04 million.

Taxpayers were particularly angered by disclosure of the high prices charged by military suppliers for everyday items classified as "spare parts and equipment." The Boeing Company, criticized for charging $748 apiece for duckbill pliers, lowered the price to $80 but added a charge of $143,000 for "support equipment management," leaving the contract total unchanged. Lockheed Aircraft Corporation had charged the Navy $640.09 each for toilet seats. And Grumman Aerospace Corporation had billed the Navy $659 apiece for customized ashtrays and $404.25 for socket wrenches.

On June 20, the Defense Department announced that 9 of the nation's 10 largest defense contractors were under criminal investigation. Reagan signed an executive order on July 15 creating a 15-member Commission on Defense Management, headed by David Packard, chairman of Hewlett-Packard Company, to study Pentagon procurement procedures.

Committee Urges Military Revamp. While critics hammered away at the Pentagon's policies for obtaining weapons, spare parts, and supplies, the Senate Armed Services Committee was conducting its own study of the military command structure. On October 16, in a staff report that was strongly backed by Chairman Barry Goldwater (R., Ariz.) and ranking Democratic member Sam Nunn of Georgia—both outspoken advocates of a strong defense program—the committee recommended a major reorganization of the nation's military establishment. The report, criticizing interservice rival-

Federal Spending

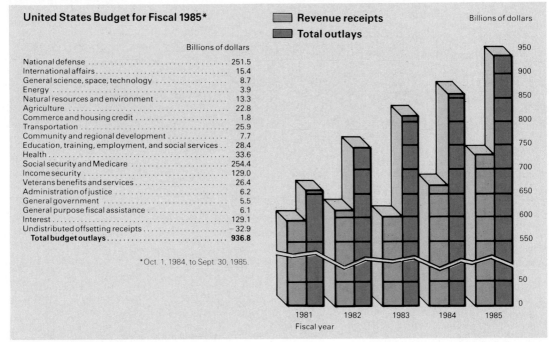

United States Budget for Fiscal 1985*

	Billions of dollars
National defense	251.5
International affairs	15.4
General science, space, technology	8.7
Energy	3.9
Natural resources and environment	13.3
Agriculture	22.8
Commerce and housing credit	1.8
Transportation	25.9
Community and regional development	7.7
Education, training, employment, and social services	28.4
Health	33.6
Social security and Medicare	254.4
Income security	129.0
Veterans benefits and services	26.4
Administration of justice	6.2
General government	5.5
General purpose fiscal assistance	6.1
Interest	129.1
Undistributed offsetting receipts	−32.9
Total budget outlays	**936.8**

*Oct. 1, 1984, to Sept. 30, 1985.

U.S. Income and Outlays

Revenue receipts
Total outlays

Billions of dollars

Fiscal year: 1981, 1982, 1983, 1984, 1985

Source: U.S. Department of the Treasury.

ries, poor Pentagon management, and congressional meddling in defense matters, urged that the Joint Chiefs of Staff be replaced by a more independent council of senior military advisers. It also recommended combining the civilian and military staffs within each service (see ARMED FORCES).

Federal Insurers Hard-Hit. Although most of the federal government's money problems were its own doing, some were directly related to failures in the private sector. On April 23, federal regulators took over the insolvent Beverly Hills (Calif.) Savings and Loan. The collapse equaled the largest savings and loan failure in U.S. history, that of Fidelity Savings and Loan of San Francisco in 1982. The growing problems of thrift institutions threatened in 1985 to deplete the resources of the Federal Savings and Loan Insurance Corporation (FSLIC), which insures accounts up to $100,000. But the FSLIC's problems did not match those of the federal Farm Credit System, which told Congress on October 30 that it needed $5 billion to $6 billion to remain solvent. The system had made about a third of the nation's $211 billion in farm loans (see FARM AND FARMING).

Domestic Spies. Not all of the government's woes in 1985 centered on money. A major problem that came into the limelight during the year was the growing number of American citizens who were arrested on charges of spying for other na-

tions. The year's biggest spy scandal involved four present or former members of the Navy who were arrested in late spring and charged with being agents for the Soviet Union. Two of the four—John A. Walker, Jr., a onetime Navy communications specialist, who pleaded guilty in October, and his brother, retired Lieutenant Commander Arthur J. Walker, who was convicted in August—were sentenced to life in prison. John Walker's son, Seaman Michael L. Walker, pleaded guilty in October and received a 25-year sentence. Trial of the fourth defendant, Jerry A. Whitworth, a retired senior chief petty officer, was set for 1986.

In other cases, past and present employees of the Central Intelligence Agency (CIA) were accused of spying for China and Ghana, and a Navy civilian was charged with providing secrets to a foreign government—Israel. See CRIME.

To combat domestic spying, Congress approved an amendment to the fiscal 1986 military authorization bill allowing the death penalty for military personnel convicted of peacetime espionage. President Reagan signed the bill on November 8.

Meese vs. Supreme Court. On July 9, U.S. Attorney General Edwin Meese III made an unusual attack on the Supreme Court of the United States. Speaking at the annual meeting of the American Bar Association in Washington, D.C., Meese charged that the high court justices made "policy

Major Agencies and Bureaus of the U.S. Government*

Executive Office of the President

President, Ronald Reagan
  Vice President, George H. W. Bush
  White House Chief of Staff, Donald T. Regan
  Presidential Press Secretary, James S. Brady
  Assistant to the President for National Security Affairs, John M. Poindexter
  Central Intelligence Agency—William J. Casey, Director
  Council of Economic Advisers—Beryl W. Sprinkel, Chairman
  Council on Environmental Quality—A. Alan Hill, Chairman
  Office of Management and Budget—James C. Miller III, Director
  Office of Science and Technology Policy—Director, vacant
  U.S. Trade Representative, Clayton K. Yeutter

The Supreme Court of the United States

Chief Justice of the United States, Warren E. Burger
  Associate Justices

William J. Brennan, Jr.	Lewis F. Powell, Jr.
Byron R. White	William H. Rehnquist
Thurgood Marshall	John Paul Stevens
Harry A. Blackmun	Sandra Day O'Connor

Department of State

Secretary of State, George P. Shultz
  U.S. Representative to the United Nations—Vernon A. Walters

Department of the Treasury

Secretary of the Treasury, James A. Baker III
  Bureau of Alcohol, Tobacco and Firearms—Stephen E. Higgins, Director
  Bureau of Engraving and Printing—Robert J. Leuver, Director
  Bureau of the Mint—Donna Pope, Director
  Comptroller of the Currency—Robert L. Clarke
  Internal Revenue Service—Roscoe L. Egger, Jr., Commissioner
  Treasurer of the United States—Katherine Davalos Ortega
  U.S. Customs Service—William von Raab, Commissioner
  U.S. Secret Service—John R. Simpson, Director

Department of Commerce

Secretary of Commerce, Malcolm Baldrige
  Bureau of the Census—John G. Keane, Director
  Economic Development Administration—Orson G. Swindle III, Administrator
  National Bureau of Standards—Ernest Ambler, Director
  National Oceanic and Atmospheric Administration—Anthony J. Calio, Acting Administrator
  Minority Business Development Agency—James H. Richardson Gonzales, Director
  Patent and Trademark Office—Donald J. Quigg, Acting Commissioner

Department of Labor

Secretary of Labor, William E. Brock III
  Bureau of Labor Statistics—Janet L. Norwood, Commissioner
  Employment and Training Administration—Roger D. Semerad, Administrator
  Employment Standards Administration—Susan R. Meisinger, Administrator
  Mine Safety and Health Administration—David A. Zegeer, Administrator
  Occupational Safety and Health Administration—John A. Pendergrass†, Administrator
  Women's Bureau—Lenora Cole-Alexander, Director

Department of Health and Human Services

Secretary of Health and Human Services, Otis R. Bowen
  Administration for Children, Youth and Families—Dodie Truman Livingston, Commissioner
  Administration on Aging—Carol Fraser Fisk, Acting Commissioner
  Alcohol, Drug Abuse, and Mental Health Administration—Donald Ian Macdonald, Administrator
  Centers for Disease Control—James O. Mason, Director
  Food and Drug Administration—Frank E. Young, Commissioner
  Health Care Financing Administration—C. McClain Haddow, Acting Administrator
  Health Resources and Services Administration—Robert Graham, Administrator

National Institutes of Health—James B. Wyngaarden, Director
Office of Consumer Affairs—Virginia Knauer, Director
Public Health Service—C. Everett Koop, Director
Social Security Administration—Martha A. McSteen, Acting Commissioner

Department of Defense

Secretary of Defense, Caspar W. Weinberger
  Joint Chiefs of Staff—William J. Crowe, Jr., Chairman
  Secretary of the Air Force—Russell A. Rourke
  Secretary of the Army—John O. Marsh, Jr.
  Secretary of the Navy—John F. Lehman, Jr.

Department of Justice

Attorney General, Edwin Meese III
  Bureau of Prisons—Norman A. Carlson, Director
  Drug Enforcement Administration—John C. Lawn, Administrator
  Federal Bureau of Investigation—William H. Webster, Director
  Immigration and Naturalization Service—Alan C. Nelson, Commissioner
  Solicitor General—Charles Fried

Department of the Interior

Secretary of the Interior, Donald P. Hodel
  Assistant Secretary for Indian Affairs—Ross O. Swimmer
  Bureau of Land Management—Robert F. Burford, Director
  Bureau of Mines—Robert C. Horton, Director
  Bureau of Reclamation—Robert Olson, Acting Commissioner
  Geological Survey—Dallas L. Peck, Director
  National Park Service—William Penn Mott, Jr., Director
  Office of Territorial and International Affairs—Richard T. Montoya, Director
  U.S. Fish and Wildlife Service—Robert A. Jantzen, Director

Department of Agriculture

Secretary of Agriculture, John R. Block
  Agricultural Economics—William Gene Lesher, Director
  Agricultural Marketing Service—Vern Highley, Administrator
  Agricultural Stabilization and Conservation Service—Everett G. Rank, Administrator
  Farmers Home Administration—Vance L. Clark, Administrator
  Federal Crop Insurance Corporation—Merritt Sprague, Manager
  Food and Consumer Services—John W. Bode, Administrator
  Food and Nutrition Service—Robert Leard, Administrator
  Forest Service—R. Max Peterson, Chief
  Rural Electrification Administration—Harold V. Hunter, Administrator
  Soil Conservation Service—Wilson Scaling, Chief

Department of Housing and Urban Development

Secretary of Housing and Urban Development, Samuel R. Pierce, Jr.
  Community Planning and Development—Alfred C. Moran, Administrator
  Federal Housing Commissioner—vacant
  Government National Mortgage Association—Glenn R. Wilson, President

Department of Transportation

Secretary of Transportation, Elizabeth Hanford Dole
  Federal Aviation Administration—Donald D. Engen, Administrator
  Federal Highway Administration—Ray A. Barnhart, Administrator
  Federal Railroad Administration—John H. Riley, Administrator
  Maritime Administration—John A. Gaughan, Administrator
  National Highway Traffic Safety Administration—Diane K. Steed, Administrator
  U.S. Coast Guard—Admiral James S. Gracey, Commandant
  Urban Mass Transportation Administration—Ralph L. Stanley, Administrator

Department of Energy

Secretary of Energy, John S. Herrington
  Economic Regulatory Administration—Marshall Staunton, Administrator
  Energy Information Administration—Helmut A. Merklein, Administrator

Federal Energy Regulatory Commission—
  Raymond J. O'Connor, Chairman
Office of Energy Research—Alvin W. Trivelpiece, Director

Department of Education
Secretary of Education, William J. Bennett

Congressional Officials
President of the Senate pro tempore—Strom Thurmond
Senate Majority Leader—Robert J. Dole
Senate Minority Leader—Robert C. Byrd
Speaker of the House—Thomas P. O'Neill, Jr.
House Minority Leader—Robert H. Michel
Architect of the Capitol—George M. White
Comptroller General of the U.S.—Charles A. Bowsher
Congressional Budget Office—Rudolph G. Penner, Director
Librarian of Congress—Daniel J. Boorstin
Office of Technology Assessment—John H. Gibbons, Director
Public Printer of the U.S.—Ralph E. Kennickell, Jr.

Independent Agencies
ACTION—Donna M. Alvarado, Director
Commodity Futures Trading Commission—Susan M. Phillips,
  Chairman
Consumer Product Safety Commission—
  Terrence M. Scanlon, Chairman
Environmental Protection Agency—Lee M. Thomas,
  Administrator
Equal Employment Opportunity Commission—Clarence Thomas,
  Chairman
Export-Import Bank—William H. Draper III, President
Farm Credit Administration—Donald E. Wilkinson, Governor
Federal Communications Commission—Mark S. Fowler, Chairman
Federal Deposit Insurance Corporation—William Seidman,
  Chairman
Federal Election Commission—John Warren McGarry, Chairman
Federal Emergency Management Agency—Julius W. Becton, Jr.,
  Director
Federal Home Loan Bank Board—Edwin J. Gray, Chairman
Federal Maritime Commission—Edward V. Hickey, Jr., Chairman
Federal Mediation and Conciliation Service—Kay McMurray,
  Director
Federal Reserve System—Paul A. Volcker,
  Board of Governors Chairman
Federal Trade Commission—Daniel Olivert, Chairman
General Services Administration—Terence C. Golden,
  Administrator
Interstate Commerce Commission—Heather J. Gradison,
  Chairman
National Aeronautics and Space Administration—
  William R. Graham, Acting Administrator
National Endowment for the Arts—Francis S. M. Hodsoll, Chairman
National Endowment for the Humanities—John Agresto, Acting
  Chairman
National Labor Relations Board—Donald L. Dotson, Chairman
National Mediation Board—Walter C. Wallace, Chairman
National Railroad Passenger Corporation (Amtrak)—
  W. Graham Claytor, Jr., President
National Science Foundation—Erich Bloch, Director
National Transportation Safety Board—James E. Burnett, Jr.,
  Chairman
Nuclear Regulatory Commission—Nunzio J. Palladino, Chairman
Occupational Safety and Health Review Commission—
  E. Ross Buckley, Chairman
Office of Personnel Management—Constance J. Horner, Director
Peace Corps—Loret Miller Ruppe, Director
Securities and Exchange Commission—John S. R. Shad,
  Chairman
Small Business Administration—James C. Sanders, Administrator
Smithsonian Institution—Robert McC. Adams, Secretary
Synthetic Fuels Corporation—Edward E. Noble, Chairman
Tennessee Valley Authority—Charles H. Dean, Jr., Chairman
U.S. Arms Control and Disarmament Agency—
  Kenneth L. Adelman, Director
U.S. Commission on Civil Rights—
  Clarence M. Pendleton, Jr., Chairman
U.S. Information Agency—Charles Z. Wick, Director
U.S. International Development Cooperation Agency—
  M. Peter McPherson, Acting Director
U.S. International Trade Commission—Paula Stern, Chair
U.S. Postal Service—Paul N. Carlin, Postmaster General
Veterans Administration—Harry N. Walters, Administrator

*As of Jan. 1, 1986.   †Nominated but not yet confirmed.

choices" instead of hewing to "constitutional principles." He speculated that the Founding Fathers would find the court's position in requiring "strict [government] neutrality" toward religion "somewhat bizarre." Responding to the attorney general's comments, Supreme Court Justice William J. Brennan, Jr., said that Meese's complaints were politically motivated and mirrored the views of "persons who have no familiarity with the historical record."

The new attorney general's choice for associate attorney general, William Bradford Reynolds, was scuttled on June 27 when the Senate Judiciary Committee voted 10 to 8 against recommending his confirmation. Reynolds was criticized for what some senators saw as his lax enforcement of civil rights laws as assistant attorney general for civil rights, a post he kept.　　Frank Cormier and Margot Cormier

See also CABINET, UNITED STATES; CONGRESS OF THE UNITED STATES; PRESIDENT OF THE UNITED STATES. In WORLD BOOK, see UNITED STATES, GOVERNMENT OF THE.

UNITED STATES CONSTITUTION. See CONSTITUTION OF THE UNITED STATES.

UPPER VOLTA (BURKINA FASO). See AFRICA.

URUGUAY. See LATIN AMERICA.

UTAH. See STATE GOVERNMENT.

VANUATU. See PACIFIC ISLANDS.

VENDA. See AFRICA.

VENEZUELA. Pope John Paul II drew huge crowds on a visit to Venezuela from Jan. 26 to 29, 1985, the first ever by a Roman Catholic pope. The pope hoped to reinvigorate faith among the people of a country that is about 90 per cent Roman Catholic, but where only about 10 per cent of the church members attend services regularly.

City Blues. More than 1 million people attended an outdoor Mass in Caracas, the capital, on January 27. Overpopulated with people who flocked to Caracas during the 1970's oil boom, the city—like Venezuela as a whole—has fallen on hard times. With the country's oil reserves running out and the price of world oil in decline, Caracas has lost much of its luster. The city's dream of becoming the financial hub of the Caribbean has dimmed before the competition of Miami, Fla., which offers Latin Americans the safe haven of U.S. banks and investment opportunities.

The pope also offered Mass at Mérida in the Venezuelan Andes for an estimated 100,000 people on January 28. There, the pope's message concerned piety, adherence to the traditional Catholic faith, obedience to the church's pastors, and acceptance of its teachings.

Debt Action. Without its oil earnings, the administration of President Jaime Lusinchi was hard put to make its peace with foreign creditors. On May 17, Venezuela's 13-member bank advisory committee announced that agreement had finally been reached with foreign creditors on a plan to restructure $21.2 billion of the Venezuelan government's $35-billion foreign debt. Agreement in principle on the restructuring of the debt had been reached in September 1984. But the negotiations had then been suspended at the insistence of foreign commercial banks. The foreign banks were unhappy with the Venezuelan government's failure to remove obstacles to the repayment of overdue interest owed by the country's private sector. Under pressure from these banks, the Venezuelan government hurried the registration of private foreign debt. This step allowed private borrowers to buy foreign exchange at preferential rates so that they could pay their overdue interest.

Under the terms of the May agreement, Venezuelan debts due between 1983 and 1988 will now become due over a period ending in 1997. Venezuela was required to make a $750-million down payment on its debt and report periodically on its economy to its creditors abroad. The International Monetary Fund, an agency of the United Nations, was charged with monitoring the country's economic performance and compliance with the agreement.　　　　　　　　　Nathan A. Haverstock

See also LATIN AMERICA (Facts in Brief Table). In WORLD BOOK, see VENEZUELA.

VERMONT. See STATE GOVERNMENT.

VETERANS. On Jan. 7, 1985, United States District Judge Jack B. Weinstein in New York City formally approved a $180-million settlement of a class-action suit brought by 16,000 Vietnam War veterans and their families against seven makers of Agent Orange, a herbicide used to defoliate Vietnamese jungles. The veterans claimed various health problems, including cancer, had resulted from exposure to Agent Orange. The manufacturers agreed to pay benefits to the veterans but denied that the herbicide had caused them injury. A May ruling set the maximum award for an individual at $12,800, payable over 10 years. Weinstein also dismissed all remaining lawsuits against the manufacturers of Agent Orange by veterans who chose not to join the class-action suit.

The Veterans Administration (VA) reported that the 10th anniversary of the fall of Saigon (now Ho Chi Minh City), at the end of the Vietnam War, produced a flood of phone calls to the VA Readjustment Counseling Center from veterans who said they suffered from nightmares, anxiety, and depression. The April 30 anniversary received enormous attention from the United States media.　　　　　　　　Frank Cormier and Margot Cormier

In WORLD BOOK, see VETERANS ADMINISTRATION; VETERANS' ORGANIZATIONS.

VICE PRESIDENT OF THE UNITED STATES. See BUSH, GEORGE H. W.

VIETNAM tried to improve relations with the United States in 1985 by cooperating in the search for the more than 1,800 Americans missing since the Vietnam War, which ended in 1975. Contacts between the two countries from 1975 until mid-1985 had yielded the remains of only 99 people.

Finding the Missing. On July 6, 1985, Vietnam told U.S. officials visiting Hanoi, the capital, that it would allow a U.S. team to search for further remains at a nearby site where a B-52 bomber crashed in 1972. At the same time, Vietnamese Foreign Minister Nguyen Co Thach said in a letter to Southeast Asian foreign ministers that his country would provide a full accounting for missing Americans and resolve the problem within two years. Vietnam returned the remains of 26 Americans on August 14 and those of another 7 on December 4.

A four-member U.S. team met with Vietnamese officials in Hanoi on August 28 and 29. The Vietnamese denied that they were holding any living Americans but agreed to investigate reports that such prisoners had been sighted. Under a two-year plan for seeking remains, 11 Americans and 10 Vietnamese completed excavation of the B-52 crash site on December 1. They found a number of bone fragments but said there was little hope of identifying missing servicemen from the remains.

Executives of more than 30 large American corporations visited Vietnam on October 31 and November 1. They met Prime Minister Pham Van Dong and Foreign Minister Thach. The visit—the most important such contact since the war—indicated Vietnam's desire for trade.

Nothing came of discussions about a 1984 United States offer to accept political prisoners from Vietnamese "reeducation camps" if Vietnam would release them.

Soviet Ties. Vietnam's top leader, Communist Party General Secretary Le Duan, visited the Soviet Union from June 26 to July 1, 1985. The Soviets promised him more economic aid. In return, Vietnam pledged to try harder to send rubber, other raw materials, and light industrial goods to the Soviet Union.

Economic Changes. Vietnam devalued its currency, the dong, on September 14. The government exchanged money at the rate of 1 new dong for 10 old ones. The change was intended to reduce illegal private currency trading and speculation, giving the government tighter control of the economy.

The Communist Party Central Committee, made up of party leaders, decided in June to reduce state subsidies. It also called for a reduction in "bureaucratic centralism."　　　　Henry S. Bradsher

See also ASIA (Facts in Brief Table); KAMPUCHEA. In WORLD BOOK, see VIETNAM.

VIRGINIA. See STATE GOVERNMENT.

VISUAL ARTS. Corporate business in the United States continued its close connection to the art world during 1985. The Whitney Museum of American Art in New York City opened its fourth branch museum, and the third donated by business firms, in the lobby of Equitable Center, the new Equitable Life Assurance Society building, completed in October. The International Museum of Photography in Rochester, N.Y., also received corporate help in 1985. The photography collection had outgrown its original building, George Eastman House, the former home of the founder of the Eastman Kodak Company. Kodak provided substantial funds to sustain the museum during a $7.2-million fund-raising drive for a new building.

Museum Building Activity continued strong throughout the United States. In May, the Whitney Museum announced plans for a $37.5-million, 10-story expansion designed by American architect Michael Graves. The addition, scheduled to open in 1990, would surround the Whitney's present building, designed by Hungarian-born architect Marcel Breuer and completed in 1966.

Another New York City landmark, the Solomon R. Guggenheim Museum, will build an 11-story, $12-million extension scheduled for completion in 1987. The New York City firm of Gwathmey Siegel & Associates designed the extension in a style

sympathetic to the Guggenheim's famous 1960 structure, created by Frank Lloyd Wright, the greatest figure in modern American architecture.

Other new museum buildings designed by leading architects included the Arthur M. Sackler Museum by British architect James Stirling, which opened in October at Harvard University in Cambridge, Mass., and the $7-million Hood Museum of Art by American architect Charles W. Moore, completed in September at Dartmouth College in Hanover, N.H. In addition, the Des Moines (Iowa) Art Center in May added a large, $7.2-million annex by American architect Richard Meier.

A museum devoted to the Spanish-born artist Pablo Picasso opened in Paris in a renovated 1656 mansion, the Hôtel Sale. The works displayed include 229 paintings and 3,000 prints and drawings by Picasso, who lived most of his life in France. The government accepted them in place of estate taxes after the artist's death in 1973.

The Decorative Arts—that is, the design of useful objects such as furniture and tableware—received increased emphasis from museums in 1985. The Whitney Museum presented "High Styles: 20th Century American Design," an exhibit of well-designed appliances, dishes, furniture, and other goods, that ran from September 1985 to February 1986. The $17-million Dewitt Wallace

The Pont Neuf, the oldest bridge in Paris, takes on a new look in September under wrappings designed by Bulgarian-born artist Christo.

Gallery opened in Williamsburg, Va., displaying 8,000 items of American decorative arts. In Richmond, Va., a new $22-million West Wing at the Virginia Museum of Fine Arts will house not only paintings but also about 600 household objects.

The Dallas Museum of Art in November unveiled its new Decorative Arts Wing, a $5-million rooftop addition. The wing was built to house the Reves Collection of porcelain, silver, and other decorative objects donated by Wendy Reves, widow of Hungarian-born publisher Emery Reves.

Sculpture News. At Stanford University in California, banker B. Gerald Cantor dedicated a sculpture garden for the display of 19 large works by Auguste Rodin, a French sculptor of the 1800's, which Cantor donated. The Isamu Noguchi Garden Museum opened in May in New York City, endowed by the American sculptor Noguchi. The museum features his sculptures in landscaped settings he designed. An exhibition reviewing 25 years of works by the modern American sculptor Mark di Suvero was held from May to October to celebrate the 25th anniversary of Storm King Art Center in Mountainville, N.Y., near Newburgh.

Large-Scale Art. In September, the Bulgarian-born artist Christo wrapped the oldest bridge in Paris, the Pont Neuf over the Seine River, with 47,680 square yards (39,870 square meters) of beige nylon. The project cost $2.6 million.

A four-year controversy prompted the U.S. General Services Administration (GSA) to announce in May 1985 that it would consider moving a sculpture called *Tilted Arc* by American artist Richard Serra. The sculpture, a steel wall 12 feet (3.66 meters) high and 120 feet (36.6 meters) long, cuts across the plaza of the Jacob K. Javits Federal Building in New York City. After *Tilted Arc* was installed in 1981, more than 7,000 residents and workers in the area signed petitions to have the wall removed. They claimed that it hindered foot traffic and blocked their view. The GSA said it would appoint a panel of artists and community representatives to consider a new site. Serra opposed any move, claiming the work could exist only in the space for which it was made.

Photography Exhibitions throughout the United States honored important photographers. The Philadelphia Museum of Art displayed "W. Eugene Smith: Let Truth Be the Prejudice" from October 1985 to January 1986. The Art Institute of Chicago, together with the Metropolitan Museum of Art in New York City, organized "Kertész: Of Paris and New York," devoted to the work of Hungarian-born photographer André Kertész, who died in September. In Washington, D.C., the National Gallery of Art showed "Ansel Adams: Classic Images," from October 1985 to January 1986, reviewing the career of Adams, an American photographer known for his landscapes.

The federal government agreed in May to consider moving *Tilted Arc*, a controversial sculpture in New York City by American artist Richard Serra.

Festival of India. There was wide-ranging participation during 1985 in the 18-month Festival of India. Among the major shows was "India! Art and Culture, 1300-1900," a survey of India's art at the Metropolitan Museum of Art in New York City from September 1985 to January 1986. Other exhibitions included "Kushan Sculpture: Images from Early India" at the Cleveland Museum of Art from November 1985 to January 1986 and "The Sculpture of India, 300 B.C.—1300 A.D.," with many objects seen for the first time outside India, at the National Gallery of Art from May to September 1985.

Older European Art. "The Treasury of San Marco," which opened at the Metropolitan Museum of Art and toured cross-country, surveyed medieval Christian art. The Metropolitan also organized an exhibition called "The Age of Caravaggio," which ran from February to April. It featured works by the Italian painter Caravaggio and his contemporaries of the 1500's and 1600's.

Great Britain's Prince Charles and Diana, Princess of Wales, visited Washington, D.C., in November for the opening week of "The Treasure Houses of Britain: Five Hundred Years of Private Patronage and Art Collecting" at the National Gallery of Art. The show, an exhibition of paintings and furnishings from English country houses, was scheduled to run through March 1986.

Pioneers of Modern Art were seen in several large exhibitions. The Boston Museum of Fine Arts presented paintings of French impressionist Pierre Auguste Renoir from October 1985 to January 1986. The Philadelphia Museum of Art prepared a show of the fanciful paintings of Russian-born artist Marc Chagall, who died in March 1985. The show appeared from May to July.

In New York City, the Museum of Modern Art (MOMA) held several significant exhibitions. Museum visitors could see the collage-based art of Germany's Kurt Schwitters, who worked by gluing bits of paper and other materials to canvas, at MOMA from June to October. A MOMA exhibition from November 1985 to January 1986 surveyed the lithographs and posters of French artist Henri de Toulouse-Lautrec. Working together with the Réunion des Musées Nationaux of France, MOMA displayed from February to June the first complete show of the works of Henri Rousseau, a French painter of the late 1800's.

In Canada, the Montreal Museum of Fine Arts presented 82 works from Picasso's own collection, selected by his widow, Jacqueline. The exhibition, which ran from June to November, was called "Picasso: Meeting in Montreal."

American Artists. The American Museum of Natural History in New York City celebrated the 200th anniversary of the birth of American wildlife painter John James Audubon with an exhibition of his works. Other large exhibitions featuring American artists included "Red Grooms: Retrospective, 1956-1984," at the Pennsylvania Academy of the Fine Arts in Philadelphia from June to September and—featuring a leading artist of the 1800's—"George Inness: American Landscape Painter" at the Metropolitan from April to June.

Sky-High Art Prices continued to be reached at auction in 1985. At a January auction, for instance, a record $682,000 was paid for a portrait done in the 1830's by the American folk painter Ammi Phillips. The world's richest museum, the J. Paul Getty Museum in Malibu, Calif., spent $10.4 million—the most ever paid for a work of art—at an April auction for a painting by Italian master Andrea Mantegna, *Adoration of the Magi* (about 1500).

Vincent van Gogh's *Landscape with Rising Sun* (1889) sold in April for $9.9 million, the most ever paid for that Dutch-born painter's work. In December, the United States National Gallery of Art paid $4.07 million for Rembrandt Peale's 1801 portrait of his brother, the highest price ever paid at auction for an American painting.

Perhaps most striking of all was the $4.3 million paid by a private collector for a single page from a scrapbook compiled by Giorgio Vasari, an Italian artist and historian of the 1500's. The page contained drawings by Italian Renaissance painters Sandro Botticelli and Filippino Lippi.

A giant red toothpaste tube created by sculptor Claes Oldenburg stands in a park in Düsseldorf, West Germany, in August.

Museum Gains and Losses. In June, oil billionaire J. Paul Getty II announced a gift of $62.5 million to the National Gallery in London. Getty said he was giving the money to prevent works that might otherwise be sold abroad from leaving Great Britain.

On October 27, an armed gang stole nine impressionist paintings, including two by Renoir and five by Claude Monet, from the Marmottan Museum in Paris. One of the stolen paintings was Monet's *Impression: Sunrise* (1872), from which the impressionist movement got its name.

In November, art experts announced that *The Man with the Golden Helmet* was not by the Dutch master Rembrandt, as once thought. Stylistic analysis showed that the painting, in West Germany's National Gallery in West Berlin, was by an unknown Dutch painter of the 1600's.

On December 24, thieves stole more than 140 priceless Aztec, Maya, and other Indian art objects from the National Museum of Anthropology in Mexico City. Officials called it one of the biggest art thefts in history.   Joshua B. Kind

In the Special Reports section, see ARCHITECTURE'S NEW LOOK. In WORLD BOOK, see ART AND THE ARTS; PAINTING; SCULPTURE.

VITAL STATISTICS. See CENSUS; POPULATION.

WALES. On March 5, 1985, South Wales coal miners, like other coal miners throughout Great Britain, returned to work after a strike that had lasted nearly a year. The South Wales miners had strongly supported the strike through most of the year. At one stage, every miner in South Wales had been on strike. Later, however, Welsh miners decided to end the action before a formal settlement had been reached. The strike had been called in March 1984 in an attempt to prevent the National Coal Board from closing 20 mines. Following the end of the strike, 7 coal mines in South Wales were shut down. This left only 20 coal mines operating. The number of miners working in 1985 fell below 18,000, compared with more than 100,000 in the 1950's.

On May 16, 1985, Reginald Dean Hancock and Russell Shankland, two miners, were sentenced to life imprisonment for the murder of David Wilkie, a taxi driver. Wilkie had been driving a working miner to his job during the strike when he was killed by a concrete block thrown at his car. The guilty verdict against Hancock and Shankland brought protests from their supporters. On October 31, the Court of Appeal changed the charge to manslaughter and sentenced the men to eight years in prison.

Unemployment. The unemployment rate in Wales continued to rise in 1985, reaching 17.6 per cent in October. This was the highest level of unemployment since 1936.

Politics. A parliamentary by-election in the Brecon and Radnor area on July 4 brought a remarkable victory for the Liberal Party, running in alliance with the Social Democratic Party. The election had been called to fill the vacancy left by the death of Tom Hooson, who had won the seat for the Conservative Party in 1979. Although Hooson's majority in the previous general election had been more than 8,000 votes, the Conservative candidate finished in third place in 1985—more than 3,000 votes behind the Liberal winner, Richard Livsey.

John Stradling Thomas, who had been minister of state at the Welsh Office since 1983, was replaced in that position as a result of a government reshuffle in September. He was succeeded by Mark Robinson, who had been the member of Parliament for Newport West since June 1983.

Saunders Lewis, one of the founders of Plaid Cymru, the Welsh nationalist party, died on Sept. 1, 1985, at the age of 91. He had helped found the party in 1926. In 1936, he and two other nationalists were tried for setting fire to a Royal Air Force base in northern Wales. After a jury in Wales had failed to agree on a verdict, the defendants were tried in London and imprisoned for nine months. Lewis was the leading Welsh-language playwright of his day. A radio lecture he gave in 1956 led to the founding of Cymdeithas yr Iaith Gymraeg—the Welsh Language Society—which led many campaigns to promote the Welsh language.

Other Developments. The Royal National Eisteddfod of Wales—a festival promoting Welsh culture—was held near Rhyl in northern Wales in August 1985. The chair—the principal poetry prize—was won by Robat Powel, a university lecturer who had not learned Welsh until he was an adult.

Scotland's soccer team tied Wales in Cardiff on September 10. The result kept the Welsh team from reaching the finals of the World Cup Championship. In cricket, Gregory Thomas, the Glamorgan fast bowler, was a surprise choice for membership in the English team that will tour the West Indies in 1986.

In rugby, the Welsh team won two and lost two of their matches in the 1985 home international championship. In August, the Crawshay's XV rugby team went on a six-match tour that included South Africa. Crawshay's is a renowned team that is formed occasionally and whose members are invited to play. Sir William Crawshay, the team's president, resigned because he objected to the decision to tour South Africa.   Patrick Hannan

See also GREAT BRITAIN. In WORLD BOOK, see WALES.

WALTERS, VERNON ANTHONY (1917-   ), became United States permanent representative to the United Nations on May 22, 1985, succeeding Jeane J. Kirkpatrick, who resigned. As U.S. ambassador-at-large since 1981, Walters was a leading troubleshooter for the Department of State. In his new position, he also serves in the U.S. Cabinet.

Walters was born on Jan. 3, 1917, in New York City, where he lived until 1923, when his family moved to Europe. He attended schools in France and England but dropped out at the age of 16 to work in his father's insurance business.

Walters enlisted in the U.S. Army in 1941. He rose through the ranks rapidly, largely because of his linguistic skills—he speaks seven languages besides English. During World War II, he was a liaison officer with Brazilian troops fighting in Italy and an aide to U.S. General Mark W. Clark.

After the war, Walters helped W. Averell Harriman manage the European Recovery Program, popularly known as the Marshall Plan. Walters later served as a military attaché and as an aide and interpreter for three U.S. Presidents.

From 1972 to 1976, Walters was deputy director of the Central Intelligence Agency. In 1976, he retired from the Army with the rank of lieutenant general. He rejoined the government in 1981 as senior adviser to the secretary of state.   Jay Myers

WASHINGTON. See STATE GOVERNMENT.

WASHINGTON, D.C., in 1985 celebrated the 10th anniversary of home rule. The system, which was approved by Congress in 1973 but did not go into effect until 1975, gave Washington the authority to pass its own local laws, subject to congressional review and veto.

The city had also hoped to obtain full voting representation in Congress, but that dream died in 1985. On August 22, time ran out for a proposed constitutional amendment that would have allowed District of Columbia residents to send two senators and one representative to Congress. (The district has had a nonvoting delegate since 1971.) Only 16 of the required 38 states had approved the amendment.

New Prison. In early 1985, District of Columbia Mayor Marion S. Barry, Jr., endorsed the construction of a new prison to relieve serious overcrowding at the city's existing correctional facility. In December, Congress approved a $30-million appropriation to enable the district to start constructing the prison. At year-end, the City Council was still debating where to build the facility, and some council members opposed the whole idea.

Bombings. An abortion clinic in southeast Washington was bombed shortly after midnight on January 1. The blast—one of a series of abortion-center bombings in the Washington area that began in February 1984—caused extensive damage to the clinic and broke more than 300 windows in two nearby apartment buildings. An investigation of the bombings by the United States Bureau of Alcohol, Tobacco and Firearms resulted in the arrest on Jan. 19, 1985, of three Maryland men. The three were convicted and sentenced to prison terms of 2, 10, and 15 years.

Cable TV. District Cablevision Incorporated, a local company, signed a 15-year agreement with the city in February to build a $130-million citywide cable television system. The company promised to provide 78 channels and an institutional network for communications between businesses, hospitals, schools, and government offices. In July, however, District Cablevision said it could not get financing for a system that size. At the company's urging, the City Council in September approved modifications to the agreement, including a reduction in the number of channels to 54 and a postponement of the institutional network.

Drug Probe. On April 4, 1985, U.S. Attorney Joseph E. diGenova announced the end of a two-year federal investigation into drug use by district employees. The probe involved Mayor Barry in 1984 when Karen K. Johnson, a lower-level city employee and a friend of the mayor's, was convicted of selling cocaine. Barry denied throughout the investigation that he had bought or used cocaine, and Johnson refused to testify before a grand jury. She was sentenced to eight months in jail for contempt of court and to an additional four months on the drug charge.

Rent Control. The City Council in April narrowly passed a revised rent control law that treated landlords more leniently than the existing law, which was due to expire. The new law would have allowed property owners unrestricted rent increases in four categories of apartment buildings, including buildings with 80 per cent of the units vacant and certain "distressed," or rundown, properties. But a group of tenants opposed to the measure succeeded in getting parts of it overturned. The group collected enough signatures on a petition to get a referendum on some provisions of the new law put on the November ballot, and city voters rejected the rent control revisions by 50.8 to 49.1 per cent. This was the first time the referendum process was used in the district to overturn a City Council action.

Shelter to Close. A U.S. Court of Appeals on December 10 upheld the federal government's authority to close a shelter for the homeless. President Ronald Reagan had promised in 1984 to renovate the shelter after a 51-day hunger strike by its director, Mitch Snyder. But Snyder and the Reagan Administration could not agree on how much renovation was needed. Sandra Evans

See also CITY. In WORLD BOOK, see WASHINGTON, D.C.

WATER. There was disagreement during 1985 between the Congress of the United States and the Administration of President Ronald Reagan over funding for water-treatment plants. On June 13, the Senate voted unanimously to renew and strengthen the Clean Water Act of 1972, which had expired at the end of 1981. The Senate bill allocated $18 billion to assist communities in building wastewater treatment plants and sewer systems over a nine-year period. The House of Representatives' clean water bill was approved overwhelmingly on July 23 and authorized spending of $21 billion. The two bills were sent to a joint committee to work out differences, where the bills remained at year-end. Despite strong congressional support, the legislation faced presidential opposition. The Administration proposed that only $6 billion be allocated for wastewater treatment and that federal funding be phased out entirely by 1990.

Major Water Projects. The House on November 13 passed a bill providing $20 billion for major water projects, including dams, harbors, hydroelectric plants, and inland waterways. To help finance the projects, the bill called for a new tax on cargo moving through U.S. ports and set up a formula for sharing the costs of the projects with the local governments involved. Nevertheless, the bill was opposed by the Reagan Administration.

New York City's Mayor Edward I. Koch looks on as a New York state
official in April describes a water shortage that led to restrictions in use.

A more modest water-projects bill that was
passed by the Senate in June did have the approval of the Reagan Administration. The Senate
bill budgeted $14 billion for water projects and
also contained a cost-sharing formula.

The Central Arizona Project, designed to divert
water from the Colorado River, delivered its first
irrigation water to farms in May and its first drinking water to Phoenix on November 15. The project carries water through a concrete canal that,
when completed, will stretch 335 miles (539 kilometers) southeast from Parker Dam on the California border to Tucson.

"Water marketing," or selling water to the highest bidder, is beginning to emerge as a means of
allocating water supplies. For example, in June,
the Imperial Irrigation District in California announced the start of a water-conservation project
designed to save up to 500,000 acre-feet (620 million cubic meters) of water now being wasted
through overirrigation and seepage from canals.
An acre-foot is the amount of water covering a 1-
acre (0.4-hectare) area to a depth of 1 foot (30
centimeters). Water conserved by the project
would be sold, most likely to the Metropolitan Water District of Southern California.

Refuge Pollution. A simmering controversy over
polluted agricultural runoff water draining into a
reservoir at the Kesterson National Wildlife Refuge, 110 miles (177 kilometers) southeast of San
Francisco, boiled over on March 15 when the U.S.
Department of the Interior announced it was ending deliveries of irrigation water from the Central
Valley Project to the 42,000 acres (17,000 hectares) of farmland that produce the polluted
drainage water. Since 1982, biologists have observed a high rate of birth defects in waterfowl at
Kesterson. The problem was attributed to high
concentrations of selenium in runoff water from
farms. The soil in this area contains unusually
large amounts of this mineral. Concern also arose
that selenium and other minerals would affect the
San Joaquin River and municipal water supplies.

The irrigation cutoff shocked valley farmers,
who predicted loss of the year's crops and severe
economic impact throughout the region. Then on
March 28, Interior Secretary Donald P. Hodel announced that an agreement had been reached
with the farmers. The federal government would
continue to supply irrigation water if the region's
Westlands Water District would gradually stop the
polluted water from draining into the refuge
through a canal 82 miles (132 kilometers) long. All
such drainage was to cease by June 1986. In the
meantime, the threat to waterfowl was being min-
imized through a "hazing" program to drive birds
from the refuge.   Iris Priestaf

In WORLD BOOK, see WATER.

WEATHER. The coldest weather in the United States during 1985 occurred in the second half of January after an arctic high-pressure center developed near the northern fringe of North America. On January 20, Chicago recorded a record low of −27°F. (−33°C). Between January 21 and 24, the cold set low-temperature records at numerous places in eastern North America, including Knoxville, Tenn., with −24°F. (−31°C); Nashville, Tenn., with −17°F. (−27°C); and Asheville, N.C., with −16°F. (−27°C). During this period, Alaska had unusually warm weather.

Drought in the East. By April, it was apparent that a severe drought prevailed on the East Coast from Maine to Virginia. New Jersey was typical, with abnormally low precipitation every month since August 1984. A water emergency was declared for New York City and remained in effect until November 29.

Throughout May, severe weather and heavy rain plagued the Midwest. Baseball-sized hailstones fell in Dallas on May 7. Flash floods raged in southern Texas on May 15. During the last 10 days of the month, a heat wave developed in the Central and Eastern states, while in the Far West, the weather was much colder than normal.

On May 31, one of the worst strings of tornadoes in North American history occurred in Ohio, Pennsylvania, and New York and in Ontario, Canada. The combined paths of the 41 twisters stretched for 685 miles (1,100 kilometers). Winds of up to 300 miles per hour (mph), or 480 kilometers per hour (kph), cut a swath as wide as 2.1 miles (3.4 kilometers). The tornadoes claimed 88 lives.

The Last Half of June saw a reversal of May's temperature pattern. Cold weather moved into the Northeastern states. A large warm *anticyclone*—a system of winds rotating clockwise in the Northern Hemisphere—became established over the Great Basin, a large desert region in Nevada, Utah, and other Western states. Dry winds from this area brought hot, dry weather to California, setting the stage for a rash of destructive forest fires there in July.

Temperature Extremes. In the Southeast, temperatures during September, October, and November were the second highest on record for those months. In the Northwest, the temperatures were the coldest in 55 years of record keeping. On November 21, a record 6-inch (15-centimeter) snowfall blanketed Seattle. The 10°F. (−12°C) temperature the next morning was the second coldest ever recorded there.

Hurricanes. An unusually large number of hurricanes reached the shores of the United States in

A tornado approaches an Ohio town during a series of twisters that stormed through the Northeastern United States and Ontario, Canada, in June.

1985. The first of these was Danny, a mild hurricane that crossed the coast of the Gulf of Mexico near New Orleans on August 15. Two weeks later, Hurricane Elena entered the Gulf of Mexico with winds up to 125 mph (200 kph). Watched closely by radar, satellite, and aircraft, the storm wandered along an erratic course, striking Florida, Alabama, Mississippi, and Louisiana. On September 1, Governor Bob Graham of Florida ordered the evacuation of coastal areas threatened by the storm. More than 500,000 people responded in one of the largest evacuations in history. The hurricane killed four people, one of them at sea. Insured property losses, which reflect only part of the total property loss, were about $543 million.

The third major hurricane, Gloria, crossed Cape Hatteras, North Carolina, on the morning of September 27 with winds of 130 mph (210 kph). Much of the expected damage and loss of life was avoided because the storm moved rapidly northward just off the coast.

About 1 P.M. on September 27, Gloria crossed Long Island and moved into Connecticut and New Hampshire, where it exhausted its energy. Early estimates of the damage in New York, New Jersey, and Connecticut totaled more than $400 million. Most of the damage occurred in eastern Long Island and southern Connecticut.

On October 27, an unusually late hurricane, Juan, came out of the Gulf of Mexico. The storm developed rapidly, toppling two oil-drilling platforms and swamping a ship that was being towed. After a number of erratic changes of direction, the storm moved across the coast of Louisiana, causing tides 5 to 8 feet (1.5 to 2.4 meters) above normal and flooding wide areas. Eight people were known to have lost their lives in the storm, and another seven were missing. Property damage was estimated at more than $1 billion. More than 200,000 people left their homes, and Louisiana's Governor Edwin W. Edwards declared a state of emergency in 21 *parishes* (counties).

The remnants of Hurricane Juan proceeded north, lashing North Carolina, Virginia, West Virginia, Maryland, and Pennsylvania. Rivers roared over their banks on November 5. Floods killed at least 44 people.

Still another late hurricane, Kate, struck Florida, Georgia, and South Carolina on November 21-22. The storm caused seven deaths.

A Snowstorm that hit the upper Midwest in late November was blamed for at least 25 deaths. Minnesota received about 18 inches (46 centimeters) of snow. International Falls, Minn., registered a record low temperature of −27°F. (−33°C) on December 3.   Alfred K. Blackadar

In WORLD BOOK, see HURRICANE; METEOROLOGY; TORNADO; WEATHER.

WEIGHT LIFTING. See SPORTS.

WELFARE. In his proposed budget for the 1986 fiscal year beginning Oct. 1, 1985, United States President Ronald Reagan called for reductions in social welfare spending to partially offset a hike of $31.2 billion in defense spending. The budget resolution passed by Congress in August, however, rejected deep cuts in welfare programs.

Poverty. In his annual economic report to Congress, Reagan noted that the national poverty rate remained "stubbornly high despite a strong recovery and a continued increase in government assistance." But in August, the Bureau of the Census reported a decline in the poverty rate after five years of sharp increases.

According to Census Bureau figures, the number of Americans living in poverty fell in 1984 to 14.4 per cent of the population, down from 15.3 per cent in 1983. The poverty level was defined in 1984 as an annual cash income of $10,609 for a family of four. The Census Bureau also reported that in 1984 the median family income rose 3.3 per cent, after adjustment for inflation, to $26,430 for the largest one-year rise since 1972.

The Census Bureau attributed the drop in poverty to the strong economic recovery of 1983 and 1984 and to a decline in the average unemployment rate from 9.6 per cent in 1983 to 7.5 per cent in 1984. In a statement issued from his vacation headquarters near Santa Barbara, Calif., Reagan hailed the numbers as "further proof that the greatest enemy of poverty is the free enterprise system." Critics of the Administration charged, however, that the gap between rich and poor had widened under Reagan and that the percentage of Americans living in poverty remained higher than at any time during the 15 years before he took office.

In September, the Census Bureau issued a clarification of its report, noting that part of the sharp drop in the poverty rate had resulted from a new method of calculating interest income. Had the same method been used in 1983, the poverty rate would then have stood at a slightly lower 15.2 per cent. By the same token, the 1983 median income would have been $25,724, yielding a 1984 increase of 2.8 per cent instead of the 3.3 per cent increase reported earlier.

Poverty Among Children. While the Census Bureau pointed to an overall drop in poverty in the United States, other government agencies drew attention to a rise in poverty among U.S. children. The Congressional Budget Office and the Congressional Research Service reported in May that the number of poor children in the nation had increased 54 per cent from 1973 to 1983, even though the total number of U.S. children had decreased during that time. The two agencies found that 13.8 million children, or 22.2 per cent of Americans under age 18, lived in families with incomes below the poverty level in 1983. Despite an increase of 83 per cent in federal spending on welfare programs during the decade from 1973 to 1983, spending directed at children had decreased by 6 per cent.

Poverty-Related Issues dominated other reports. A private panel of physicians and health officials warned in a report released in February 1985 that hunger in the United States had reached "epidemic proportions." The study was prepared by the Physician Task Force on Hunger in America under the sponsorship of the Harvard School of Public Health in Boston. It contended that the problem "can be traced in substantial measure to clear and conscious policies of the federal government." The report contrasted markedly with a study issued in 1984 by a presidential advisory committee that found widespread hunger was not a significant problem in the United States.

Secretary of Health and Human Services Margaret M. Heckler resigned from the Cabinet on October 1 and accepted the post of ambassador to Ireland. Reagan nominated former Indiana Governor Otis R. Bowen, a physician and a professor at the Indiana University School of Medicine, to succeed Heckler.   Frank Cormier and Margot Cormier

See also BOWEN, OTIS R. In WORLD BOOK, see WELFARE.

WEST INDIES. The Caribbean region was relatively peaceful during 1985. On June 12, the United States withdrew the last of its troops from Grenada, almost two years after the United States invaded the island nation. On October 9, Great Britain's Queen Elizabeth II began a four-week, 10-nation Caribbean tour. She presided over a meeting of Commonwealth heads of government held in the Bahamas and the opening of parliament in Grenada on October 31.

Netherlands Antilles. The economies of Curaçao and Aruba, two of the most heavily populated islands in the Netherlands Antilles, experienced hard times following the closing in March of an Exxon Corporation oil refinery on Aruba. The refinery produced half of the island's income. The Shell Oil Company in mid-September sold its refinery on Curaçao to the Netherlands Antilles government for the token amount of one Dutch florin (about half a U.S. cent), writing off the refinery as a tax loss. The government, in turn, leased the refinery to Venezuela's state-owned oil company, which promised to keep the refinery operating for five years.

Haiti. On July 22, the government of Jean-Claude Duvalier, lifetime president of Haiti, declared that in a *referendum* (direct vote), 99.9 per cent of Haiti's voters had approved four amend-

A soldier patrols a street in Jamaica's capital, Kingston, in January after a riot that broke out over an increase in fuel prices.

ments to the Constitution. The amendments ratify the president's life term and allow for the formation of opposition parties only if they pledge support for the president's life term. Another amendment permits the president to name his successor, paving the way for Duvalier's son to succeed him.

Informed observers noted that President Duvalier arranged the referendum to assure the U.S. Congress that Haiti was making progress toward democracy. The referendum, however, had no legal impact on the amendments. United States assistance to Haiti, which was running at a level of $50 million a year in 1985, depends on assurances that Haiti is moving toward democracy.

Guadeloupe. On March 13, a bomb exploded in a downtown restaurant in Point-à-Pitre, killing the daughter of the president of Guadeloupe's Chamber of Commerce and injuring 11 others. The incident was attributed to proindependence factions on the French colony. It horrified local residents because it marked a violent turn in the struggle for independence. Nathan A. Haverstock

See also LATIN AMERICA (Facts in Brief Table). In WORLD BOOK, see WEST INDIES.

WEST VIRGINIA. See STATE GOVERNMENT.

WISCONSIN. See STATE GOVERNMENT.

WYOMING. See STATE GOVERNMENT.

YEMEN (ADEN). See MIDDLE EAST.

YEMEN (SANA). See MIDDLE EAST.

Elizabeth Brinton, 13, of Falls Church, Va., became the Girl Scout cookie-selling champion of 1985 after peddling 11,200 boxes.

YOUTH ORGANIZATIONS. The Boy Scouts of America (BSA) celebrated its 75th anniversary in 1985. As part of the celebration, beginning in May, a Heritage Campfire Caravan made up chiefly of Scout leaders crossed the United States by automobile, stopping at most state capitals. At each stop, local Scouts and Scout leaders joined members of the caravan at a campfire. The caravan carried ashes from the fires to the national Scout Jamboree, held in July at Fort A. P. Hill, near Fredericksburg, Va. There, Scouts added the ashes to a campfire, symbolizing the enduring spirit of Scouting.

In January, the BSA introduced 14 sports to the Cub Scout program. The activities are designed to acquaint Cub Scouts with a variety of individual and team sports and to help improve their performance in sports they already know.

Boys Clubs of America (BCA) in 1985 celebrated the 125th anniversary of the founding of the first Boys Club in Hartford, Conn. Also during the year, the BCA established a special task group to educate local clubs about the problem of sexual abuse of children.

In May, the BCA held its annual national conference in San Juan, Puerto Rico. More than 1,400 volunteer and professional leaders attended. In September, Carlos Romo of La Habra, Calif., was named 1985-1986 National Youth of the Year.

Camp Fire celebrated its 75th anniversary in 1985. The theme of the anniversary was "Celebrate Friendship, Celebrate Camp Fire." March 23 was declared "Camp Fire Friendship Day" by mayors and other local officials throughout the United States. Among the day's activities was a massive balloon launch, during which the organization's 300 local councils released thousands of balloons carrying friendship messages. In November, Camp Fire members at the organization's national congress in Kansas City, Mo., got their first look at the new Camp Fire uniforms, which will be worn beginning in 1986.

4-H Clubs in 1985 launched a five-year leadership training program called "Volunteers for the Future." Under the program, state 4-H councils receive grants for pilot projects designed to increase the effectiveness of 4-H volunteer leaders. In fall 1985, 4-H Clubs premiered a three-part television series called "Blue Sky Below My Feet: Adventures in Space Technology." Produced in cooperation with the National Aeronautics and Space Administration, the films focus on advances and discoveries in the space program involving fibers and clothing, food and fitness, and computers.

During National 4-H Week, held from October 6 to 12, 4-H Clubs hosted an Inter-American Rural Youth Conference at the National 4-H Center in Chevy Chase, Md. Rural youth workers from 50 nations attended the meeting. About 1,700 4-H members attended the 63rd National 4-H Congress, held in Chicago from November 30 to December 5.

Future Farmers of America (FFA) held its 58th annual national convention in Kansas City, Mo., from November 14 to 16. At the convention, which was attended by nearly 22,000 FFA members and supporters, Mike Arends, 21, of Willmar, Minn., was named Star Farmer of America. Scott Cochran, 21, of Lavonia, Ga., was named Star Agribusinessman.

Girl Scouts of the United States of America (GSUSA) in 1985 expanded its commitment to meeting the needs of girls aged 6 to 12. In January, at a GSUSA conference on middle childhood, experts in child development, middle childhood, and social research examined the roles society and family play in the development of girls in this stage of life. The conference marked the beginning of an effort by the GSUSA to reassess its current program for Brownie and Junior Girl Scouts. As part of this effort, the GSUSA in January introduced a new uniform for Junior Girl Scouts.

Girls Clubs of America (GCA) celebrated its 40th anniversary in 1985. As part of its celebration, the GCA held a conference in New York City in April to focus attention on the needs of girls in the United States. At the conference, the organization released an information packet called *Action Agenda for Equalizing Girls' Options*. It describes 50 ways to improve the social and economic status of girls and girls' programs in the family, school, community, workplace, and nation.

The GCA also introduced several new programs in 1985. "Girl Power: Health Power" is a health promotion program designed to teach preteen girls good lifelong health habits. Operation S.M.A.R.T. (*S*cience, *M*ath, *A*nd *R*elevant Technology) is designed to encourage girls aged 6 through 18 from low-income backgrounds to pursue careers in traditionally male-dominated fields.

Junior Achievement (JA) reported that 691,800 students participated in JA programs during the 1984-1985 school year, a 12.5 per cent increase over the previous year. The organization held its 11th annual National Business Leadership Conference and Business Hall of Fame induction ceremony in Cleveland on April 3, 1985. About 2,000 business executives attended. At the National Junior Achievers Conference, held in Bloomington, Ind., in August, Marla McFadden of Dubuque, Iowa, was named Outstanding Young Businesswoman. Scott Kleinberg of San Jose was named Outstanding Young Businessman. Diversified Interests of San Jose was recognized as the JA Company of the Year.   Barbara A. Mayes

In WORLD BOOK, see entries on the individual organizations.

YUGOSLAVIA continued to struggle with economic and political problems in 1985. In 1984, Yugoslavia had begun to negotiate with Western banks to reschedule payments on $19.5 billion owed to the West. The negotiations ended in September 1985 with an agreement to reschedule $3.5 billion in payments due from 1985 to 1988. This cleared the way for the International Monetary Fund, a United Nations agency, to issue the first installment of a loan negotiated previously.

Yugoslavia hoped to increase its exports to the West by 15 per cent for the first half of 1985 to earn more Western currency to pay off the debt. But exports to the West were up only 2 per cent in the first six months of 1985, compared with the first half of 1984. Exports to other Eastern European nations were up by 15 per cent for the first six months of the year. Industrial output was up 2.9 per cent, half the planned increase. The 1985 grain harvest was 20 per cent lower than that of 1984 because of a long drought.

Inflation climbed to 80 per cent in the second half of 1985. Unemployment exceeded 15 per cent. About 77 per cent of the unemployed were under 30 years old.

Bills Fail. In July, two finance bills failed to get the necessary two-thirds majority at a joint session of the two houses of Yugoslavia's federal legisla-

Yugoslavia's Prime Minister Milka Planinc, right, visits Laurent Fabius, the prime minister of France, in Paris in January.

ture. The bills would have affected the spending of Western currency earned by businesses in the six republics that make up Yugoslavia. Under present laws, the federal government receives part of this money and the remainder stays in the republics in which it is earned. The proposed bills would have increased the federal share of the money. Critics of the bills argued that the proposed changes would hamper Yugoslavia's drive to hike its exports because Slovenia and Croatia—the two major earners of Western currency—would have less incentive to promote export business. A compromise bill passed in December.

New Leaders. On May 15, Radovan Vlajković of Serbia became president of the nine-member Presidency, the country's chief policymaking body. Members take turns serving one-year terms as president. Vidoje Žarković of Montenegro became leader of the Communist Party Presidium, a 23-member council that directs the party's operations.

Kosovo Tensions. Most residents of Kosovo—a self-governing province of Serbia—are ethnic Albanians. Many of them want to upgrade Kosovo to the status of a republic. In 1985, the government jailed many ethnic Albanians for agitating in favor of a republic.   Chris Cviic

See also EUROPE (Facts in Brief Table). In WORLD BOOK, see YUGOSLAVIA.

YUKON TERRITORY. Christopher Pearson, government leader and Progressive Conservative Party leader in the Yukon since 1978, retired in March 1985. Succeeding him in both posts was Willard Phelps, who had served as the Yukon's land claims negotiator. Phelps called elections for May 13. The elections resulted in victory for the New Democratic Party (NDP), which won 8 of the 16 seats in the territory's Legislative Assembly. The Conservatives won 6 seats, and the Liberal Party won 2. The new NDP government leader was Antony Penikett, who had served on the staff of the leader of the federal NDP.

Since 1982, about 3,000 Yukoners have lost their jobs due to mine closings. This has resulted in an unemployment rate of about 20 per cent. Plans were made to reopen the Cyprus Anvil zinc-lead mine at Faro in 1986. The mine, which was closed in 1982, had once accounted for 14 per cent of the jobs in the Yukon. On October 29, the Yukon legislature approved federal and territorial financial incentives to help the mine reopen. Curragh Resources Corporation of Toronto, Ont., will purchase the mine from Dome Petroleum Limited of Calgary, Alta.   David M. L. Farr

See also CANADA. In WORLD BOOK, see YUKON TERRITORY.

ZAIRE. See AFRICA.

ZAMBIA. See AFRICA.

ZIMBABWE. The Zimbabwe African National Union-Patriotic Front (ZANU-PF), the party of Prime Minister Robert Gabriel Mugabe, won national elections in 1985. Whites and blacks voted separately, whites on June 27 and blacks on July 1 and 2. ZANU-PF took 63 of the 80 regular seats reserved for blacks in the lower house of Parliament, 6 more than it won in the 1980 elections. An additional 20 seats are reserved under Zimbabwe's Constitution for representatives of the nation's white minority, but candidates sympathetic to ZANU-PF gained only 5. The other 15 seats were won by the Conservative Alliance of Zimbabwe, led by former Prime Minister Ian Smith.

Mugabe Dissatisfied. Although the 1985 elections increased ZANU-PF's majority in Parliament, Mugabe was dissatisfied on at least two grounds. First, he was unhappy with the white vote. In a post-election speech, he said he regarded the strong showing of Smith's party as a rejection of his government's policy of improving relations with whites, who make up only 2 per cent of Zimbabwe's population. Secondly, Mugabe had expected to do better against his black opposition, but the Zimbabwe African People's Union (ZAPU) held onto 15 of its 19 seats in Parliament. All of the winning ZAPU candidates were from Matabeleland province, home of the Matabele people. The Matabele are long-standing rivals of Mugabe's Mashona people, Zimbabwe's majority ethnic group. ZANU-PF had hoped to win at least 5 of the Matabele seats but had to content itself with capturing the 4 ZAPU seats outside Matabeleland.

ZAPU Denounces Government. ZAPU leaders charged that Mugabe's government severely hindered their election campaign. They said government security forces permitted ZANU-PF militants to break up ZAPU rallies. ZAPU also contended that the Central Intelligence Organization, an agency attached to the prime minister's office, abducted dozens of ZAPU officials from rural areas.

Toward One-Party Rule. The continued opposition of the Matabele people obstructed Mugabe's plans for establishing a one-party socialist state. The Matabele people were too large a minority—about 18 per cent of the population—and their homeland too economically important for their opposition to be ignored. Also, to legislate a one-party state into being before 1990, Mugabe needed some of the ZAPU votes in Parliament. Under the Constitution, a major change in the structure of the government must be supported by 100 per cent of the members of Parliament from 1980 to 1987 and by at least 70 per cent from 1987 to 1990. After that, a simple majority would do. After the 1985 elections, ZANU-PF and ZAPU discussed a merger.   J. Dixon Esseks

See also AFRICA (Facts in Brief Table). In WORLD BOOK, see ZIMBABWE.

ZOOLOGY. In December 1985, only six wild California condors remained alive, the last survivors of a species that once ranged from Los Angeles to San Francisco. Urban development in southern California has destroyed vast tracts of land used by condors for hunting food and for nesting. Lead poisoning seems to be killing the last survivors. Condors feed on the remains of dead animals, and a number of the birds appear to have died after ingesting toxic levels of lead from deer and other animals killed by hunters using lead shot.

During the year, intense debate developed over the best strategy for saving the mammoth birds, which have a wingspan of 8 to 9½ feet (2.4 to 2.9 meters). In June, the California Fish and Game Commission proposed trapping wild condors and placing them temporarily in zoos. The birds could then breed over several years, and the new condors could eventually be released back into the wild to repopulate the area. Captive breeding of condors has been quite successful—12 condors had been born in captivity by November 1985. The plan received support from biologists with the American Ornithologists' Union and from a group of geneticists affiliated with the California Condor Recovery Team, a conservation group composed of federal and state agencies.

The United States Fish and Wildlife Service and the National Audubon Society, however, voiced strong objections to the trapping program. They argued that condors raised in zoos would have a hard time adjusting to life in the wild unless some native birds were left to show them traditional nesting, feeding, and roosting sites.

A Dilemma and a Compromise. The proposed removal of all the remaining wild birds posed another dilemma. Lands now protected from developers because of the presence of the endangered birds would become open to development, according to some local officials. The mere proposal to capture the birds sidetracked the federal government's planned purchase of the 13,800-acre (5,580-hectare) Hudson Ranch near Santa Barbara, Calif., as a safe area for condors. In July, the U.S. Department of the Interior proposed that the purchase be postponed because the land would be unnecessary if the birds were placed in zoos.

On December 17, the Fish and Wildlife Service proposed—"with great reluctance"—that the last remaining wild condors be captured immediately and put in zoos. The service said that one of the remaining birds showed signs of lead poisoning and needed treatment and that two of the birds showed signs of courtship and possible breeding. The service said it wanted the breeding pair in captivity, because there are very few breeding pairs. The Audubon Society said, however, that removal of the remaining condors from the wild "is not biologically justified."

Quagga Genes. In June 1985, scientists at the University of California, Berkeley, reported the first extraction of genetic material from the pelt of an extinct animal, the quagga. The last quagga died in 1883. This mammal lived in South Africa and had a striped front end like a zebra and a rear end like a horse. Just how closely the quagga was related to modern horses and living zebra species had been a matter of debate.

Zoologists Allan C. Wilson and Russell Higuchi of Berkeley attempted to resolve the debate by removing muscle tissue from a 140-year-old quagga pelt found in a museum. They were able to extract two fragments of the still-intact genetic material—deoxyribonucleic acid (DNA). Each fragment was composed of more than 100 molecules called *base pairs*. The scientists inserted the DNA into dividing bacteria that made multiple copies, or clones, of the quagga's genetic material.

When the Berkeley scientists compared the quagga DNA with DNA from a mountain zebra, they found a difference of only 12 base pairs. Such similarities suggested the two animals had a common ancestor about 3 million years ago. Early tests indicated that the Burchell's zebra may be a close relative to the quagga, while the horse is more distant.   Clyde Freeman Herreid II

See also PALEONTOLOGY; ZOOS. In WORLD BOOK, see ZOOLOGY.

ZOOS and aquariums in North America opened a number of notable new exhibits in 1985 that focused on a specific geographic region or a particular animal family. The largest and most elaborate of these was JungleWorld at the New York Zoological Park (Bronx Zoo), which re-created indoors the tropical forests of southern Asia.

Visitors to JungleWorld journey through a variety of habitats. A scrub forest, for example, is inhabited by giant monitor lizards, mugger crocodiles, snow-white myna birds from Bali, and a variety of other birds. In a mangrove swamp, proboscis monkeys frolic in trees, and small-clawed otters swoop through the water. In rain forests, visitors view silver-leaf monkeys, Malayan tapirs, black leopards, gibbons, fruit bats, hornbills and other birds, and relatives of the crocodile called *gavials* or *gharials*. Other galleries give visitors close-up views of small tropical creatures.

In addition to 70 species of animals, JungleWorld contains more than 100 species of tropical plants. Water circulates continuously through five waterfalls and a network of pools and streams. Dense mists produced by a machine float over the treetops. Streams, ravines, and cliffs—rather than bars—separate the animals from visitors.

In Junglelab, a classroom in the treetops made to resemble a research station, students are introduced to field biology, shown how to gather data

New York City's Bronx Zoo re-creates a tropical rain forest and other habitats of southern Asia in its JungleWorld, which opened on June 22.

freshwater gallery. Six exhibits focus on the Amazon River and feature piranhas, anacondas, poison-arrow frogs, and other inhabitants of the river. A 4,000-gallon (15,000-liter) tank demonstrates the impact of a six-month rainy season on lowland forests. Exhibits of brook trout, Atlantic salmon, and New England pond dwellers highlight the Connecticut River system and offer comparisons with the mighty Amazon.

Visitors to the Metro Toronto Zoo in Canada began touring a Grizzly Trail in spring. They followed the paw prints of a bear to encounters with various North American animals, including musk oxen, Canada lynx, mountain lions, bobcats, bison, pronghorns, elk, waterfowl, and, of course, grizzly bears. The Washington Park Zoo in Portland, Ore., on March 16 opened a re-creation of the treeless arctic tundra of Alaska. Inhabiting these frosty environs are wolves, musk oxen, lemmings, snowy owls, waterfowl, and grizzly bears.

Koala Crossing, which opened at the San Francisco Zoo on August 22, is modeled after a ranch in Australia's *outback* (open country). California has the only zoos in North America that display these marsupials because eucalyptus leaves—the koalas' food—grow in abundance there.

Children Act Like the Animals. The Philadelphia Zoological Gardens' Treehouse, which opened on May 1, provides children with insights into animal life through participation in six environments. Youngsters can climb inside an oversized model of a beaver lodge to grasp the construction of this aquatic architecture. Children can also view their surroundings through the compound eye of a honeybee, and they can sniff the bee-luring smell of honey when they enter a giant model of a bee. They can even share the sensory experiences of a *hadrosaur*, a species of dinosaur.

Rare Births. The year saw reproductive advances among several species that had never before bred in a zoo and some that had rarely done so. The first zoo-bred Papuan pythons hatched in the Knoxville (Tenn.) Zoological Park in February. Also in February, Sea World in San Diego recorded the first birth in captivity of a Commerson's dolphin. In August, the Audubon Park and Zoological Garden in New Orleans announced the hatching of rhinoceros hornbills, the first of these birds ever bred in a zoo. Four Madagascar ground boas hatched on August 17 at the Fresno (Calif.) Zoo in the first breeding of this snake north of the equator.

Public interest in zoo breeding, as usual, centered on giant pandas in 1985. Late in June, in Chapultepec Zoo in Mexico City, the panda Ying-Ying gave birth to twins, one of which soon died. It was the third successful pregnancy for Ying-Ying and her mate, Pei-Pei.　Eugene J. Walter, Jr.

In WORLD BOOK, see ZOO.

on animal behavior, and taught to use equipment that tests soil and atmospheric conditions.

Primates and Predators. On April 27, the San Francisco Zoological Gardens opened its new Primate Discovery Center. This spacious multilevel structure permits close viewing of 16 species of primates—the group of mammals that includes apes, monkeys, and human beings. Patas monkeys forage for insects and seeds, and romp playfully in an environment that resembles African grasslands. In a replica of a West African forest, a group of female mandrills, ruled by a vividly colored male, provides insights into the social organization of this monkey species.

The Topeka (Kans.) Zoological Park on May 12 opened Gorilla Encounter, the first walk-through gorilla exhibit. Trees, meadow, streams, and a waterfall make up the gorillas' territory. Visitors, however, are safely "caged" in a glass tunnel, which the apes climb over and around, frequently coming close enough for nose-to-nose interaction.

A new building at the Cincinnati (Ohio) Zoo houses 18 species of the cat family in environments that duplicate forests, deserts, and jungles. A jaguar, for example, searches for prey in a setting designed to look like a Central American jungle complete with ancient Indian ruins.

Regional Specialties. In mid-October, the New England Aquarium in Boston completed its new

Answers to the Quiz

1. Search them.

2. President Reagan transferred his powers to Bush while Reagan underwent surgery to remove a cancerous tumor from his large intestine.

3. She was chosen to become the first private citizen observer on the space shuttle.

4. Pete Rose of the Cincinnati Reds, who got his 4,192nd career hit to break the record set by Ty Cobb in 1928.

5. Bangladesh.

6. *Atlantis*.

7. Bernhard Langer won the Masters Tournament of golf in April, and Boris Becker won the Wimbledon men's singles tennis championship in July.

8. Attorney general of the United States.

9. To attend the conference on the conclusion of the United Nations Decade for Women.

10. Chess. Gary Kasparov was the winner.

11. **b.**

12. He was hospitalized for an intestinal ailment hours before his scheduled inauguration and died in April after undergoing a series of operations.

13. Spying for the Soviet Union.

14. Israel.

15. Brazil.

16. The milk was contaminated by salmonella bacteria and caused an outbreak of food poisoning.

17. It was the closest congressional election in history. After a recount, McCloskey won by only four votes.

18. A United States government radio service that began broadcasting to Cuba in May.

19. The Warsaw Pact.

20. New Caledonia (island in South Pacific); Tsukuba (research center in Japan); Johannesburg (city in South Africa); Bitburg (town in West Germany); Punjab (state in India).

21. Because of the violent behavior of British soccer fans, who stormed Italian fans at a match in Brussels, Belgium, on May 29, setting off a riot in which 38 people died.

22. U.S. fighter planes intercepted an Egyptian airliner carrying four suspected Palestinian hijackers and forced it to land in Italy.

23. A bomb dropped by Philadelphia police on a house occupied by a group called MOVE.

24. The wife of Soviet dissident Andrei D. Sakharov. He staged three hunger strikes to win permission for her to leave the Soviet Union for medical treatment in December.

25. "The Refrigerator," nickname of William Perry of the Chicago Bears football team.

26. The Third Punic War between Rome and Carthage (149-146 B.C.).

27. The wine is suspected of being contaminated with diethylene glycol, a poisonous chemical used in automobile antifreeze.

28. The new monetary unit of Argentina, which replaced the peso in June.

29. *Back to the Future*.

30. The court overturned all four laws.

31. Los Angeles.

32. He flew on the space shuttle *Discovery*, becoming the first political leader to ride on a space shuttle.

33. He said that Peru will limit repayment of its foreign debt to no more than 10 per cent of its export earnings for the next year.

34. Rock Hudson.

35. San Francisco.

36. Former U.S. President Jimmy Carter.

37. Prince Charles and Diana, Princess of Wales.

38. July 1986.

39. She marched too close to the South African Embassy in Washington, D.C., during a demonstration against apartheid.

40. A run on deposits.

41. The Coca-Cola Company changed the taste of Coke.

42. Leontyne Price.

43. The Soviet Union.

44. Mexico.

45. Tiny plastic beads, perfectly round and of uniform size.

46. The European Community (EC or Common Market).

47. Fuel-price increases triggered riots on Jamaica. On New Caledonia, there were clashes between islanders seeking independence and French settlers.

48. Former Israeli Defense Minister Ariel Sharon lost his libel suit against *Time* magazine in January, and United States General William C. Westmoreland dropped his libel suit against CBS Inc. in February.

49. General Motors Corporation; an automobile.

50. Divers found the wreck of a Spanish ship that sank off Florida in 1622 carrying hundreds of silver bars and other treasure.

World Book Supplement

1981
1982
1983
1984
1985

To help WORLD BOOK owners keep their encyclopedias up to date, the following new or revised articles are reprinted from the 1986 edition of the encyclopedia.

See "Burma," page 546.

Culver

Goodyear

The Uses of Airships have changed through the years. During the 1920's and 1930's, the U.S. Navy's *Los Angeles, left,* performed such military tasks as escorting ships and patrolling coastal waters. Today, the Goodyear blimp *America, right,* serves mainly as an advertising craft.

AIRSHIP is a lighter-than-air aircraft. An airship has a huge main body that contains a lighter-than-air gas. The gas raises the craft and keeps it aloft in the same way a gas balloon is lifted. However, airships, unlike balloons, have engines that move them through the air and nearly all have equipment for steering. Balloons are moved by the wind, and cannot be steered. They thus travel in the direction the wind blows. Airships also differ from helicopters and airplanes, which are heavier than air. Helicopters and airplanes use their engines and blades or wings to lift them and keep them aloft.

Airships were introduced in the 1800's as the first manned flying machines capable of prolonged flight and of being steered. This feature of these craft led to their being called *dirigibles,* which comes from the Latin word *dirigere,* meaning *to direct.* In World War I (1914-1918), airships were used as bombers, for protecting ships against submarine attack, and for other duties. Before and after the war, they were used to carry passengers. Airship passenger services reached their height in the 1930's, but a series of disastrous crashes and the increasing popularity and long-range capability of the airplane brought airship passenger services to an end. Today, several countries have shown a renewed interest in airships for use in such operations as surveillance, offshore patrol, advertising, and lifting bulky cargoes.

Types of Airships

There are three main types of airships: (1) nonrigid airships, (2) rigid airships, (3) semirigid airships.

Nonrigid Airships were the first airships and some are flown today. They have no major internal structures and no framework for the outer skin. The gas pressure causes this skin, called the *envelope,* to keep its shape. Modern envelopes are made of synthetic fabrics.

The smallest airships have been nonrigid craft. Some have measured less than 100 feet (30 meters) long. The largest nonrigid airships were the United States Navy's ZPG-3W airships. These craft were flown from 1958 to 1962 and were used for airborne early-warning duties. Each ZPG-3W measured about 403 feet (123 meters) long. Today's nonrigid airships average about 200 feet

(60 meters) in length. They cruise at approximately 35 to 40 miles (56 to 65 kilometers) per hour at heights reaching about 7,500 feet (2,300 meters).

The U.S. Navy's B-class nonrigid airships, built in 1917, gave rise to the term *blimp* for nonrigid craft. The term came from *B-nonrigid,* or *B-limp.*

Rigid Airships, the largest airships, are no longer flown. Engineers designed large airships because carrying capacity increased with size. The main body of rigid airships was called the *hull.* The most famous rigid airships had a hull consisting of a wooden or metal framework that supported the outer skin. Such airships became known as *Zeppelins,* after Count Ferdinand von Zeppelin, a German airship pioneer.

Zeppelins were cigar-shaped and ranged from about 400 feet (120 meters) to over 800 feet (240 meters) long. Advanced models could reach speeds of about 80 miles (130 kilometers) per hour. Inside the hulls were several compartments, called *gas cells,* that held the lifting gas. Many hulls contained corridors along which cargo, crew quarters, and the fuel tanks were located. Envelope materials ranged from weatherproof cotton to aluminum alloy.

Semirigid Airships became fairly common in the early 1900's. They often resembled nonrigid ships, except that a support ran along most of the length of the envelope and helped maintain its shape and distribute loads. Semirigid airships were often larger than nonrigid craft, but they faded in the 1920's because of the increased capabilities of nonrigid and rigid models.

How Airships Fly

Lift is the force that raises an airship off the ground and keeps it aloft. Airships generate lift because the gas they contain has a lower density than the air outside the craft. Airships hold enough of this lighter-than-air gas to overcome their own weight and rise from the ground.

Early airships contained hydrogen, the lightest of all gases. But hydrogen is highly flammable, and this property of the gas was an important factor in a number of airship disasters. As a result, helium eventually replaced hydrogen for use in airships.

Thrust is the force that moves an airship through the air. Most airships use engines and propellers to obtain thrust. On large rigid airships, the engines and propellers were located in *gondolas* (cars) attached to the hull. Such craft had separate gondolas for the passengers and crew. On most nonrigid airships, engines have been mounted on a gondola that also holds the crew and passengers.

Control. Most airships have tail structures that include *fins*, *rudders*, and *elevators*. Fins are large, flat-looking, fixed surfaces. Typically, four fins are arranged equally distant from one another around the ship's *stern* (rear). The smaller, movable rudders and elevators are surfaces attached to the fins. The pilot moves the rudders to steer and the elevators to raise or lower the ship's nose.

For improved control, rigid airships contained *ballast*. Ballast was usually water. When released, the water helped the craft gain height by making it lighter. Rain or other weather conditions that made the craft heavier during flight often required the pilot to release ballast to lighten the craft to maintain its altitude.

Ballonets are air-filled bags or compartments inside nonrigid and semirigid pressure craft. One ballonet lies in the *bow* (front) of the envelope, and another lies in the stern. Ballonets help maintain the shape of the envelope. For example, if the gas pressure in the envelope decreases, air is pumped into the ballonets so that the envelope will not sag.

Storage. Early airships were kept in huge hangars or sheds, but moving the craft in and out of these shelters sometimes proved disastrous. Engineers partly solved the problem when they developed the *mooring mast*, a

high, stable tower to which an airship could be anchored without touching the ground. The bow of the airship was secured to the tower. Mooring masts allowed airships a limited amount of movement to help them survive high winds. To enter rigid craft, the crew and passengers passed up a staircase within the mast.

Low mooring masts secure nonrigid airships close to the ground. The crew and passengers can board these craft by a short ladder leading into the gondola.

History

The First Airships evolved from balloons. Henri Giffard, a French engineer, built and piloted the first powered and manned airship. As with many balloons, ropes covered the envelope and hung down to support an open gondola. But unlike the ball-shaped balloons, Giffard's airship was cigar-shaped, and the gondola supported a 3-horsepower (2.2-kilowatt) steam engine. A saillike rudder was carried in the gondola.

On Sept. 24, 1852, Giffard flew his craft about 17 miles (27 kilometers) from Paris to Trappes, near Versailles, at an average speed of 5 miles (8 kilometers) per hour. The small rudder and engine enabled him to alter his course, but the craft was not properly steerable.

In 1884, Charles Renard and Arthur Krebs, two French inventors, completed *La France*. This airship had a battery-powered electric motor that produced about 9 horsepower (7 kilowatts). It also had an efficient rudder and elevator. Renard and Krebs flew *La France* around a 5-mile (8-kilometer) circular course near Paris at

Kinds of Airships There are three main types of airships. A *nonrigid airship* has no framework supporting its gas-filled *envelope* (outer skin). In a *semirigid airship,* metal supports brace the craft's gas-filled bag. An extensive inner framework of wood or metal supports the gas bags of a *rigid airship.*

WORLD BOOK illustrations by Tony Gibbons, Linden Artists Ltd.

Gas bag

Fins

Nonrigid Airship

Envelope

Ballonet

Bracing supports

Main frame   Gondola

Fins

Engine gondolas

Semirigid Airship

Engines   Gondola

Outer framing

Fins

Main frame   Gas bag

Wire supports   Engine   Stores   Cabins   Ladder   Control gondola

Catwalk

Rigid Airship

speeds over 14 miles (23 kilometers) per hour. In 1901, the Brazilian-born inventor Alberto Santos-Dumont completed a controlled journey around the Eiffel Tower in Paris. His adventures won him great popularity.

David Schwarz of Austria designed the first truly rigid airship. His craft flew on Nov. 3, 1897. But due to windy conditions, mechanical problems, and an inexperienced pilot, the craft crashed.

The Zeppelins. In 1900, Count Ferdinand von Zeppelin flew his first airship, the LZ-1. It was 420 feet (128 meters) long and could reach a top speed of about 17 miles (27 kilometers) per hour. It made only three flights because it was underpowered and lacked proper control. Zeppelin completed the LZ-2 in 1905, and he launched the LZ-3 in 1906. The German Army later made the LZ-3 the first military Zeppelin.

In 1909, Zeppelin helped establish the world's first commercial airline, known as DELAG. The *Deutschland*, DELAG's first airship, was over 485 feet (148 meters) long and had three 120-horsepower (90-kilowatt) engines. From 1910 to 1914, over 10,000 passengers paid to fly by Zeppelin airships on DELAG flights.

World War I. During World War I, Germany used Zeppelins and other airships to patrol the North Sea and scout enemy craft and positions. In addition, Germany was the only country to make large-scale use of rigid airships for strategic bombing. But the frequent raids over England caused little damage.

The largest user of rigid airships during the war was the German Naval Airship Division. It received about 70 Zeppelin and Schütte-Lanz craft. Due to accidents, bad weather, and enemy fire, 53 of these airships were lost. The capabilities of Zeppelins, however, improved dramatically. For example, the L-59 once flew 4,200 miles (6,800 kilometers) nonstop. It had five engines, which could produce speeds of over 60 miles (95 kilometers) per hour.

Great Britain built and operated a large number of nonrigid airships during the war. British airships primarily protected ships from submarine attack. The United States used nonrigid airships for some overwater patrol duties and antisubmarine warfare. Other countries that used airships during the war included France and Italy.

Between World Wars. After World War I, airships became bigger, faster, and stronger. For example, in 1919, Britain's rigid R-34 made the first transatlantic crossing by an airship. In 1926, the Italian-built semirigid *Norge* became the first airship to fly over the North Pole. The replacement of hydrogen with helium to prevent airship disasters began in the 1920's, on U.S. craft.

In the 1920's and 1930's, the Navy experimented with giant rigid airships. The *Akron*, launched in 1931, and the *Macon*, launched in 1933, carried fighter airplanes. While in flight, these airships could launch and receive the planes. In April 1933, the *Akron* went down in a storm off the coast of New Jersey, killing 73 people. In February 1935, bad weather forced the *Macon* into the sea off the coast of California, killing two people and ending U.S. construction of rigid airships.

The most successful rigid airship ever built was the German LZ-127 *Graf Zeppelin*. Between 1928 and 1937, it flew more than 1 million miles (1.6 million kilometers) and carried over 13,000 passengers, many of them over-

News Syndicate Co., Inc.

The *Hindenburg*'s Crash marked the end of the use of airships for regular passenger service. One of the largest airships ever built, this German craft burst into flames while approaching its dock in Lakehurst, N.J., in 1937. The ship's hydrogen gas had somehow ignited. Thirty-five persons died in the disaster.

seas. The *Graf Zeppelin* ranks among the fastest rigid airships ever flown. It could reach a maximum speed of about 80 miles (130 kilometers) per hour.

The *Hindenburg*. Construction and operation of rigid airships in Germany came to a swift end following the destruction of the *Hindenburg*. One of the largest airships ever built, the *Hindenburg* was about 804 feet (245 meters) long and 135 feet (41 meters) wide. It had a volume of 7,062,100 cubic feet (199,980 cubic meters) and cruised at 78 miles (126 kilometers) per hour. On May 6, 1937, while approaching its docking in Lakehurst, N.J., the *Hindenburg* exploded. Of the 97 people on board, 35 were killed. In addition, one member of the ground crew was killed. The ship's hydrogen gas had somehow ignited. The *Hindenburg* disaster marked the end of the use of airships for regular passenger services. In addition, development of rigid airships ended.

World War II to the Present. The evolution of the airplane contributed greatly to the decreased use of the military nonrigid airship during World War II (1939-1945). The U.S. Navy made the only significant use of nonrigid airships during the war, flying mainly its K-class airships. Most of these craft patrolled U.S. coastal waters and escorted surface ships there.

In the late 1950's, the Navy introduced its ZPG-3W nonrigid airships. One of the ZPG-3W craft crashed at sea in 1960, killing nearly everyone on board. This crash contributed to ending the use of nonrigid airships for military operations.

Today, there has been a limited revival of nonrigid airships. A few are used for advertising purposes and as airborne platforms for television cameras. In the future, new nonrigid models might perform patrol and early-warning duties, rescue missions, and other similar military roles. The future for airships may also lie in commercial heavy-lift operations.   MICHAEL J. H. TAYLOR

Related Articles in WORLD BOOK include:
Balloon   Blimp

Shostal

Algiers, the capital and largest city of Algeria, is often called *Algiers the White* because of its many white buildings. The city has an excellent harbor on the Mediterranean Sea. Most Algerians live in cities in the country's narrow Mediterranean coastal region.

ALGERIA

ALGERIA, *al JEER ee uh*, is a large country in northern Africa. It is more than three times as big as Texas. Among the countries of Africa, only Sudan is larger.

Northern Algeria stretches along the Mediterranean Sea. The country's narrow Mediterranean region has a warm climate and rich farmland. Almost all Algerians live in this region. Algiers, the country's capital and largest city, lies on the Mediterranean. To the south, the sun-scorched wastes of the Sahara cover more than four-fifths of Algeria. Beneath the surface of this desert area lie huge deposits of natural gas and petroleum.

Most Algerians are of mixed Arab and Berber descent. However, the people form two distinct cultural groups—Arab and Berber. Each group has its own customs and language. But nearly all Algerians are Muslims and are thus united by their religion, Islam.

For about 130 years, Algeria belonged to France. In 1962, it gained independence following a bloody revolution in which more than 250,000 French and Algerians died. Algerians then formed a socialist government that began a program of rapid industrial development. The program has been financed chiefly by income from Algeria's government-owned natural gas and petroleum industries. But industry has not grown fast enough to eliminate poverty and widespread unemployment.

Government

Algeria's Constitution, adopted in 1976, established the Front de Libération Nationale (FLN)—or National

Kenneth J. Perkins, the contributor of this article, is Associate Professor of History at the University of South Carolina.

Liberation Front—as the country's only political party. The FLN, which is committed to socialism, nominates all candidates for political office. Algerian citizens who are 19 years of age or older may vote in national and local elections.

National Government. The Algerian government is headed by a powerful president, who also serves as head

Facts in Brief

Capital: Algiers.

Official Language: Arabic.

Official Name: Al-Jumhuriyah al-Jaz'iriyah ad Dimuqratiyah wa ash-Sha'biyah (Democratic and Popular Republic of Algeria).

Form of Government: Republic.

Area: 919,595 sq. mi. (2,381,741 km²). *Greatest Distances*—east-west, 1,500 mi. (2,400 km); north-south, 1,300 mi. (2,100 km). *Coastline*—750 mi. (1,200 km).

Elevation: *Highest*—Mount Tahat, 9,573 ft. (2,918 m) above sea level. *Lowest*—Chott Melrhir, 102 ft. (31 m) below sea level.

Population: *Estimated 1986 Population*—22,611,000; density, 23 persons per sq. mi. (9 per km²); distribution, 67 per cent urban, 33 per cent rural. *1977 Census*—16,948,000. *Estimated 1991 Population*—26,340,000.

Chief Products: *Agriculture*—wheat, barley, milk, potatoes, citrus fruits, grapes, dates, meat, olives, cork. *Manufacturing*—liquid natural gas, refined petroleum products, iron and steel, transport vehicles, construction materials, textiles. *Mining*—natural gas, petroleum, iron ore, phosphate rock, mercury, zinc, lead.

National Anthem: "Kassaman" ("We Pledge").

Money: *Basic Unit*—dinar. One hundred centimes equal one dinar. For the price of the dinar in U.S. dollars, see MONEY (table: Exchange Rates). See also DINAR.

533

of the FLN. The president makes all government policies, serves as commander in chief of the armed forces, and heads the Supreme Court. The president also appoints the Council of Ministers, a cabinet whose members supervise the various government departments. Algeria's national legislature, called the Popular National Assembly, consists of 261 members. The people elect the Assembly members and Algeria's president to five-year terms.

Local Government. Algeria is divided into 48 provinces called *wilayas*. Each wilaya has an elected assembly and a *wali* (governor), who is appointed by Algeria's president.

Courts. The Supreme Court is Algeria's highest court. It reviews cases from 48 wilaya courts. Wilaya courts hear appeals from lower courts called *tribunals*.

Armed Forces. About 130,000 men serve in Algeria's army, air force, and navy. About 85 per cent of them serve in the army. Algerian men 19 years or older may be drafted for two years of military duty. Members of the armed forces also work on the construction of highways and other public works projects.

People

Population. Algeria has about 23 million people. Its population growth rate, which is about 3 per cent a year, ranks among the world's highest. Nearly 70 per cent of all Algerians live in cities. The rest live in rural areas. More than $1\frac{1}{2}$ million people live in Algiers, the nation's capital and largest city by far.

Ancestry. Most of Algeria's people are of mixed Arab and Berber ancestry. Berbers lived in what is now Algeria at least 5,000 years ago. Arabs began to arrive from the Arabian Peninsula during the A.D. 600's. Through the years, Arabs and Berbers intermarried so extensively that it is now difficult to separate the groups by ancestry. Less than 1 per cent of the country's people are of European descent.

Language. A large majority of Algerians speak Arabic, the country's official language. In addition to Arabic, many Algerians speak French. About a fifth of the people speak dialects of the Berber language.

Way of Life. Since Algeria gained its independence in 1962, the government has worked to rid the country of French cultural influences. For example, it requires that legal proceedings be in Arabic rather than French. Arabic has also replaced French as the language used to teach elementary and high school students. In addition, many Algerians have called for stricter observance of Islamic teachings, which regulate family and community relationships and many other aspects of daily life.

Rural Life. Rural Algerians typically live in large family groups made up of several generations. Most houses are built of mud and straw or of stone and have flat tile or tin roofs. The majority of rural Algerians make a living raising livestock or farming small plots.

City Life. The architecture of Algeria's larger cities reflects Islamic and European influences. *Mosques* (Islamic houses of worship) and open-air markets are common. Older sections of the cities are called *casbahs*. In these sections, shops and houses are crowded along narrow streets. Newer sections have broad boulevards and tall office and apartment buildings.

In Algeria's cities, many men work in factories or offices. The typical household consists of only a father and mother and their children. City people have much more contact with Western ideas than do rural Algerians. As a result, some city dwellers follow Western customs.

Since Algeria gained independence, large numbers of poor rural people have moved to cities to seek factory work. But many of them have not been able to find jobs. The migration and a severe housing shortage in urban areas have resulted in the growth of large slums in many cities.

Clothing. Many Algerians, especially in rural areas, wear traditional clothing. For example, a woman may wear a long, white cotton outer garment called a *haik*. It covers the head and the lower part of the face and extends downward as far as the feet. Traditional clothing for men includes a long, hooded cloak called a *burnoose*. Many urban people wear Western-style clothing.

Foods made from such grains as wheat and barley form the chief part of the diet of most Algerians. The national dish is *couscous*. It consists of steamed wheat served with meat, vegetables, and a souplike sauce. Many city dwellers eat Western-style dishes.

Recreation. Soccer is the most popular sport in Algeria. Many Algerians enjoy playing the game or watching soccer matches. A favorite pastime in the cities is

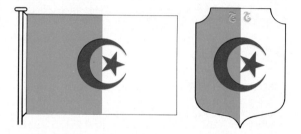

Algeria's Flag and Coat of Arms display a star and crescent, symbols of Islam, partly against a background of green, a traditional Islamic color. The flag was officially adopted in 1962, when Algeria gained its independence from France. The Arabic letter *djim*, which appears twice at the top of the coat of arms, is an abbreviation for an old Arabic form of the country's name.

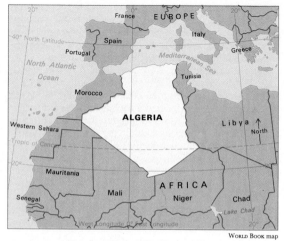

WORLD BOOK map

Algeria is a large country in northern Africa. It borders seven other countries and the Mediterranean Sea.

going to the movies. Algerians celebrate several national holidays, including their country's independence day on July 5. They also enjoy a number of religious festivals.

Religion. Algeria's Constitution declares Islam to be the country's official religion. About 99 per cent of the people are Muslims. The Algerian government strongly supports Islam and pays for the maintenance of mosques and for the training of mosque officials.

Education. Although the government has spent much money to improve and expand education, only about 45 per cent of all Algerians aged 15 or older can read and write. Algerian law requires all children from 6 to 15 years old to attend school. More than 90 per cent of all children attend elementary school. But only about a third of them go on to high school. The University of

Algiers, with about 17,000 students, is the country's largest university.

The Arts. Many of Algeria's finest works of art reflect the influence of Islam. Outstanding examples are the beautiful domed mosques found throughout the country. Algerians are also known for their superb jewelry, pottery, rugs, and other handicrafts in which they use distinct Islamic designs and traditional techniques.

Algerian painters and writers were strongly influenced by French culture during the period when Algeria belonged to France. Since then, they have increasingly drawn upon their Arabic, Berber, and Islamic cultural roots. Today, many Algerian painters use traditional Ar-

Algeria

Legend:
International boundary
Road
Railroad
Oil pipeline
Seasonal stream
⊛ National capital
• Other city or town
+ Elevation above sea level

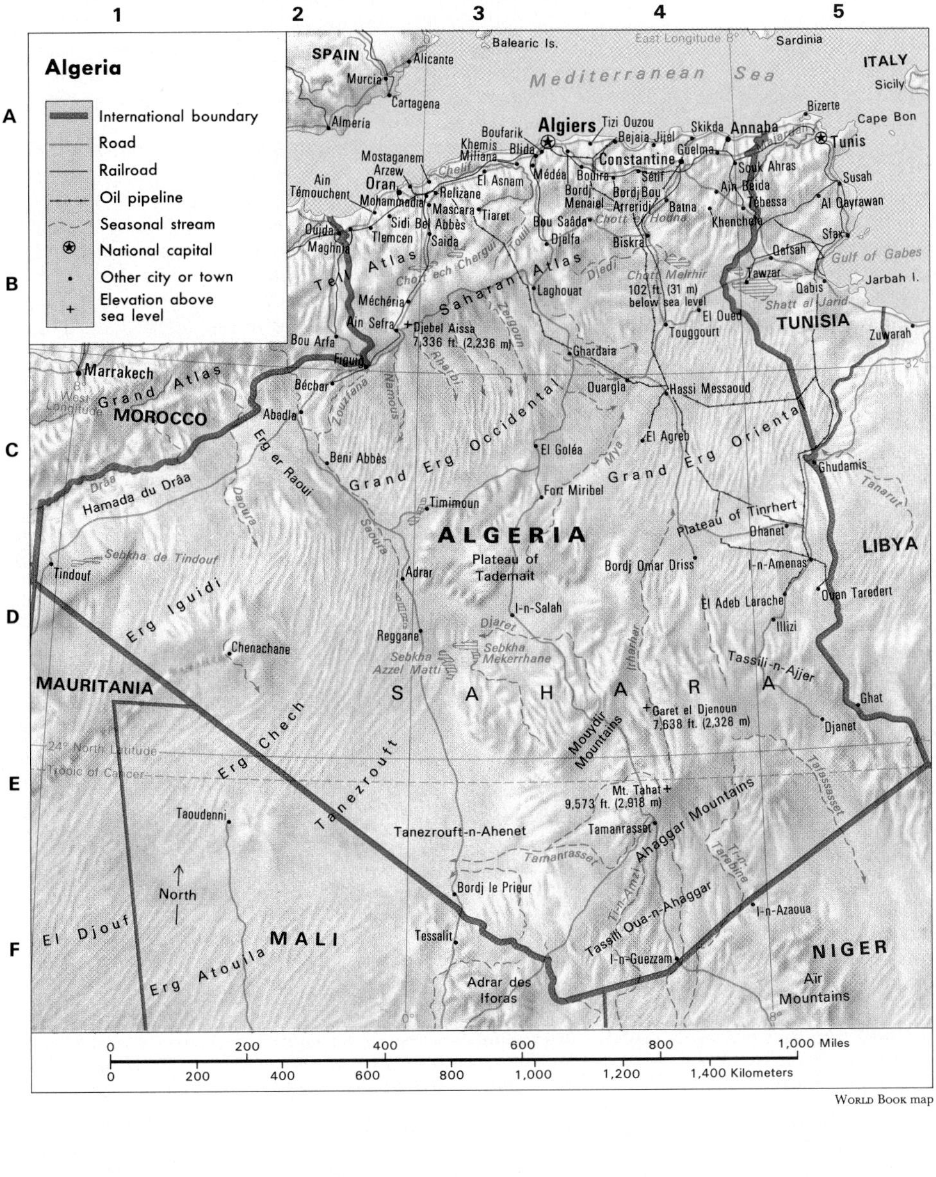

WORLD BOOK map

Algerian Townspeople in Timimoun, in the country's Sahara region, wear either traditional or Western-style clothing. The group at the right includes schoolchildren.

abic or Berber designs. Numerous authors now write novels and plays in Arabic instead of in French.

The Land and Climate

Algeria has three major land regions. They are, from north to south: (1) the Tell, (2) the High Plateaus, and (3) the Sahara.

The Tell stretches about 750 miles (1,200 kilometers) along the Mediterranean coast. The region is from about 80 to 200 miles (130 to 320 kilometers) wide. It consists chiefly of coastal plains and gently rolling hills. The word *Tell* is an Arabic term meaning *hill.* Much of Algeria's best farmland lies in the western and central parts of the region. Rugged mountains cover most of the eastern Tell. Many Aleppo pine, juniper, and cork oak trees grow on the mountain slopes. The Tell Atlas Mountains rise along the region's southern edge. Over 90 per cent of Algeria's people live in the Tell.

Near the sea, temperatures in the Tell average 77° F. (25° C) in summer and 52° F. (11° C) in winter. Annual rainfall averages 16 inches (41 centimeters) in the west and 27 inches (69 centimeters) in the east.

The High Plateaus lie south of the Tell Atlas Mountains and range from about 1,300 to 4,300 feet (400 to 1,300 meters) above sea level. Herders graze cattle, sheep, and goats on the grasses and shrubs that cover much of the region. During rainy periods, shallow salt lakes called *chotts* form on the plateaus. About 7 per cent of the Algerian people live in the region.

Average temperatures on the High Plateaus range from 81° F. (27° C) in summer to 41° F. (5° C) in winter. The region receives less than 16 inches (41 centimeters) of rain a year.

The Sahara. The Saharan Atlas Mountains form the northern border of the Algerian Sahara. This vast desert region occupies more than 80 per cent of the country. Sand dunes cover much of the northern Sahara. Other parts of the region consist of bare rock, boulders, and stones. A wealth of natural gas and oil lies under the eastern part of the wasteland. In the southeast, the Ahaggar Mountains tower above the desert floor. The range includes Algeria's highest peak, Mount Tahat, which rises 9,573 feet (2,918 meters) above sea level.

Daytime temperatures in the Algerian Sahara sometimes soar above 120° F. (49° C). During the summer, a very hot, dusty wind called the *sirocco* blows northward across the region. The sirocco parches the High Plateaus about 40 days each summer and the Tell about 20 days.

Less than 3 per cent of all Algerians live in the Sahara. Many of the region's people live on oases and rely on underground springs to water such crops as dates and citrus fruits. Nomads travel between grazing areas with their camels, sheep, and other livestock.

The High Plateaus Region stretches across northern Algeria. The region's grasses and shrubs provide feed for herds of livestock. This shepherd is grazing a flock of sheep near Tiaret.

The Sahara, a hot desert region, covers over four-fifths of Algeria. Date palm trees, such as the ones shown above, grow on oases, where they are watered by underground springs.

Algeria has a developing economy based largely on income from natural gas and petroleum production. The government controls the nation's key industries, including the production of natural gas and petroleum and the manufacture of construction materials, textiles, and iron and steel. However, most farms and small factories and service industries are privately owned.

Service Industries account for about 34 per cent of the total value of Algeria's economic production and employ about 35 per cent of all workers. These industries—which include banks, government agencies, hospitals, insurance companies, and schools—provide business, community, or personal services.

Mining accounts for about 30 per cent of the value of Algeria's economic production and employs about 2 per cent of the nation's workers. Algeria produces large quantities of natural gas and petroleum, chiefly from fields in the northeastern part of the Sahara region. Other important minerals produced in Algeria include iron ore, lead, mercury, phosphate rock, and zinc.

Manufacturing and Construction account for about 25 per cent of the value of Algeria's economic production and employ about 30 per cent of all workers. The nation's chief manufactured products include construction materials, iron and steel, refined petroleum products, liquid natural gas, and textiles. Almost all Algerian factories are on or near the Mediterranean coast in such cities as Algiers, Annaba, Arzew, Constantine, and Skikda.

The government has poured much money into the construction of factories. But the construction and man-ufacturing industries have not grown fast enough to provide jobs for all workers. Thus, hundreds of thousands of Algerians work in foreign countries, especially France.

Agriculture provides a living for about 30 per cent of Algeria's workers, but it generates only about 6 per cent of the value of the country's economic production. The great majority of farmers own small plots on which they produce only enough to feed their families. Other farmers work on large government farms. Grains, especially wheat and barley, are Algeria's chief crops. Other major crops include dates, grapes, olives, potatoes, and citrus fruits. Dairy products and meat come from cattle, goats, and sheep.

Trade. Natural gas, petroleum, and refined petroleum products account for about 90 per cent of the total value of Algeria's exports. Algeria belongs to the Organization of Petroleum Exporting Countries (OPEC). OPEC promotes the interests of member countries, whose economies depend heavily on oil exports. Other Algerian exports include citrus fruits, dates, iron ore, mercury, phosphate rock, and wine. Algeria imports large amounts of machinery and raw materials and more than a third of its food. Its main trading partners include France, Italy, the United States, and West Germany.

Transportation and Communication. Algeria has about 50,000 miles (80,000 kilometers) of roads and about 2,500 miles (4,000 kilometers) of railroad track. Nearly all the roads and railroad track lie north of the Sahara. Camel caravans still cross the Algerian Sahara, as they have for hundreds of years. However, aircraft, jeeps, and trucks are also used to move goods and people across the desert. Algeria's chief international airports are in Algiers, Constantine, and Oran. Algiers and Oran are the main seaports.

The government controls the country's four daily newspapers. It also operates all radio and television stations. About 16 per cent of the people own a radio, and about 6 per cent have a TV set. Most of these people live in or near urban areas. In numerous rural areas, one radio serves many people, and few ever see TV.

History

People have lived in what is now Algeria for at least 40,000 years. By about 3000 B.C., nomadic Berbers had begun migrating to the region. They probably came from Europe or Asia. During the 1100's B.C., the Phoenicians, who lived along the eastern shore of the Mediterranean Sea, established trading posts on the Algerian coast.

About 200 B.C., the Romans helped a Berber chieftain named Massinissa form and become ruler of the Kingdom of Numidia in northern Algeria. From 46 B.C. to the A.D. 600's, the area was controlled, in turn, by the Romans, the Vandals, and the Byzantines.

Arab Conquest. During the A.D. 600's, Arabs from the Arabian Peninsula began to invade much of northern Africa, including Algeria. This invasion resulted in the spread of Arabic culture throughout northern Africa and into what is now Spain. In Algeria, most Berbers adopted Islam—the religion of the Arabs—and, in time, the Arabic language. In addition, many Arabs and Berbers intermarried.

Ottoman Rule. During the early 1500's, Spanish

© Daniel Simon, Gamma/Liaison

A Gas-Processing Plant in Arzew, *above*, changes natural gas into a liquid so that it can be shipped overseas. Natural gas is one of Algeria's most valuable exports.

ALGERIA

Christians captured Algiers and other Algerian coastal cities. But in 1518, Barbarossa, a Turkish sea captain, gained control of Algiers. He later helped drive the Spanish from most other Algerian coastal areas. Barbarossa joined the areas under his control to the Ottoman Empire, an Islamic empire based in what is now Turkey. Algeria remained a part of the empire until the early 1800's. During that time, ships in the Mediterranean Sea were attacked by private warships under the command of *corsairs* from Algeria and other countries. Raids by Algerian corsairs on the ships of other nations became Algeria's chief source of income.

French Rule. In 1830, France invaded and gained control of northern Algeria. The French king, Charles X, hoped an overseas military victory would strengthen his rule in France. The French governed Algeria as part of France. Many French and other Europeans settled in Algeria. These settlers became known as *colons*. Non-French colons were given French citizenship. However, France made it very difficult for Muslims to become French citizens, even though Muslims made up the great majority of the Algerian population. France gave the colons large amounts of Algerian tribal land, and the colons soon controlled Algeria's economy and government. Many native Algerians fought against French rule. In 1847, the French defeated powerful rebel forces led by Abd al-Qadir, a Muslim religious leader. By 1914, France controlled all of what is now Algeria.

As part of France, Algeria fought on the side of the Allies during World War I (1914-1918). During World War II (1939-1945), Algeria became a battleground. In 1940, France surrendered to invading German forces. French officials, cooperating with Germany, formed a government at Vichy, a town in central France. The Vichy government ruled Algeria until 1942, when Great Britain, the United States, and other Allied countries invaded and occupied Algeria (see WORLD WAR II [The North African Campaign]). After the war, the Allies returned control of Algeria to France.

The Algerian Revolution. After both world wars, native Algerians demanded greater political power. But each time, the colons blocked all reforms that would have given the native Algerians an equal voice in the government. As a result, many native Algerians began to call for freedom from French rule.

In 1954, native Algerians formed an organization to fight for independence—the Front de Libération Nationale (FLN), or National Liberation Front. The FLN launched a revolution on November 1. It carried out ambushes, assassinations, and bombing raids against the colons and the French forces in Algeria. In response, the French army destroyed orchards and cropland belonging to native Algerians, forced millions of native Algerians into concentration camps, and tortured rebel leaders. By the late 1950's, the army's tactics had aroused strong opposition in France. Peace talks began in 1961. On July 3, 1962, France finally granted Algeria independence. By that time, more than 250,000 French and Algerians had died in the fighting. For more information on the Algerian revolution, see FRANCE (History).

Independence. Most colons—about a million of them—fled Algeria during or soon after the revolution. In 1963, one of the rebel leaders, Ahmed Ben Bella, be-

came Algeria's first president. Ben Bella proclaimed Algeria a socialist state and urged Algerian workers to take over and manage businesses and farms abandoned by colons.

In 1965, Houari Boumedienne, the army commander, overthrew Ben Bella. Boumedienne began a program of rapid economic development based on government ownership and control of Algerian industry. He used income from natural gas and petroleum production to build fertilizer plants, steel mills, oil refineries, and other factories.

Boumedienne died in 1978. In 1979, Chadli Bendjedid, Algeria's defense minister, was elected president. Bendjedid slowed the pace of industrial development to devote more resources to the production of agricultural and consumer goods. Bendjedid was reelected in 1984.

Algeria Today ranks as a leader among the developing nations and often speaks on their behalf. It also supports various independence movements around the world. These movements include the Palestine Liberation Organization (PLO) and the Polisario Front. The PLO seeks to establish a state in Palestine for Palestinian Arabs. The Polisario Front is fighting Morocco for control of Western Sahara, an area that borders Algeria on the west.   KENNETH J. PERKINS

Related Articles in WORLD BOOK include:

Outline

Questions

How did the Arab invasion of Algeria during the 600's influence most Berbers?

How have literature and painting changed in Algeria since the country became independent?

What French army tactics aroused strong opposition in France during the Algerian revolution?

How do Algerians on oases water their crops?

What is the *sirocco*?

How does the Algerian government support Islam?

Why have large numbers of rural Algerians moved to urban areas?

Why did France invade Algeria in 1830?

In which land region do more than 90 per cent of Algeria's people live?

Who nominates candidates for political office in Algeria?

Stock Cars whip around a curve during the annual Daytona 500 race in Daytona Beach, Fla. Stock car racing is the most popular kind of automobile racing in the United States.

AUTOMOBILE RACING

AUTOMOBILE RACING is a thrilling sport that tests the speed and performance of automobiles and the skill and daring of drivers. Each year, millions of spectators around the world attend a wide variety of automobile races. One of the most famous races is the Indianapolis 500, which attracts about 300,000 spectators annually.

Much of automobile racing's popularity lies in the great variety of racing cars and racing events. The cars range in size from small, open karts (formerly called *go-karts*) to large, closed sedans. However, all racing cars can be divided into two major groups: (1) production cars and (2) cars built specifically for racing. Production cars are factory-made passenger cars converted into racing cars. Most cars built only for racing are not designed to carry passengers. Automobile races range from ¼-mile (0.4-kilometer) *drag races* that last only seconds to *rallies* that may cover great distances and last weeks.

Most automobile races are held on either *oval tracks* or *road-racing courses*. Oval tracks vary from less than ¼ mile (0.4 kilometer) to more than 2½ miles (4 kilometers) long. They have straightaways and banked curves. Most oval tracks have an asphalt surface, but many others have a dirt surface. Road-racing courses resemble country roads. The courses have straightaways, hills, and a variety of turns. Many turns are described by their names, such as *hairpin*, *dogleg*, and *ess*. Some courses include sections of public roads or are combined with oval

tracks. Races are faster on oval tracks than on road courses because cars can maintain higher speeds on banked curves than on sharp, irregularly shaped turns. Road courses in the United States range from less than 2 miles (3.2 kilometers) to almost 5 miles (8 kilometers) long.

Events called *street races* or *round-the-houses races* have become increasingly popular in automobile racing. Such a race is run on a temporary course on city streets. The most famous street race is the one held annually in Monaco. Street races have also been held in such cities as Dallas; Detroit; Long Beach, Calif.; Miami, Fla.; and Montreal, Canada.

Alongside both oval tracks and road-racing courses are special areas called *pits*, where drivers make refueling stops during a race. In the pits, a skilled crew may also have to change tires and make minor adjustments and repairs. The pit stops often take only seconds to complete. A delay in the pits can lose the race for a driver. Pit crews are part of large professional racing teams. Such teams also include car designers, builders, mechanics, and timekeepers, as well as the car owners and the drivers themselves.

Safety Measures

Automobile racing is a highly dangerous sport, but many steps have been taken over the years to make it as safe as possible for both spectators and drivers. Strong guardrails and heavy fencing protect spectators from cars that have gone out of control. A driver's most important piece of safety gear is a racing helmet. Such a helmet has a hard outer shell made of fiberglass or carbon fiber and a foam-cushioned lining. Drivers also wear flame-resistant clothing from head to toe, including a special face mask.

Sylvia Wilkinson, the contributor of this article, is the author of numerous books on automobile racing, including the series World of Racing. *She is also a contributing editor to* Autoweek *magazine.*

Kinds of Automobile Racing Courses and Tracks

Most automobile races are held on *oval tracks* or *road-racing courses*. Oval tracks have banked curves. Road-racing courses have sharp, unbanked curves. On a combined road course and oval track, races may be run on the combined course or only the oval track. *Drag strips* are straight tracks.

WORLD BOOK diagram

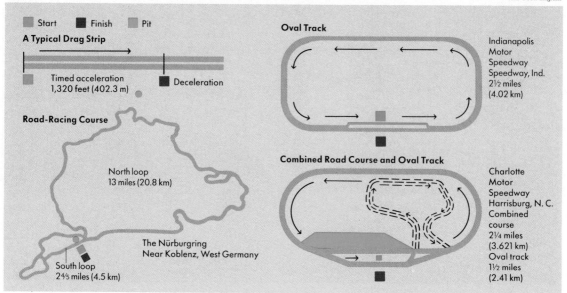

■ Start ■ Finish ■ Pit

A Typical Drag Strip

Timed acceleration
1,320 feet (402.3 m)

Deceleration

Road-Racing Course

North loop
13 miles (20.8 km)

The Nürburgring
Near Koblenz, West Germany

South loop
2⅘ miles (4.5 km)

Oval Track

Indianapolis
Motor
Speedway
Speedway, Ind.
2½ miles
(4.02 km)

Combined Road Course and Oval Track

Charlotte
Motor
Speedway
Harrisburg, N. C.
Combined
course
2¼ miles
(3.621 km)
Oval track
1½ miles
(2.41 km)

Lap and shoulder belts are standard safety equipment on racing cars. Every car also has a built-in structure to help protect a driver's upper body if the car rolls over. A racing car with an *open cockpit*—that is, without a roof—has a *roll bar*, a dome-shaped metal bar that arches over the driver's head. A car with a roof has a *roll cage*, a structure of steel tubes that prevents the roof of an overturned car from collapsing.

A racing car carries fuel in a leak-resistant *fuel cell* within a metal or plastic fuel tank. A fuel cell consists of a strong, rubberlike bladder filled with a spongy material. The "cells" of the spongy material absorb the fuel and help keep it from spraying in case of a crash. A fuel cell also prevents fuel from sloshing around in the tank during a race, which makes a car harder to control.

Many race sites have medical facilities to provide emergency treatment to injured drivers in the event of a crash. In some cases, helicopters rush injured drivers to nearby hospitals.

Sponsorship

The cost of building or buying a racing car and keeping it in top condition makes automobile racing one of the most expensive sports. For this reason, all professional racing teams have sponsors. A sponsor may be a wealthy person or a manufacturing company, such as a major automobile maker or a tobacco company. In return for their financial support, manufacturers advertise their products on the racing cars and on the uniforms of the drivers and crew.

Racing Organizations

The Fédération Internationale de l'Automobile (FIA) regulates organized automobile racing in about 90 countries throughout the world. The FIA has its headquarters in Paris. The United States has five national racing organizations represented in the FIA. They are the National Association for Stock Car Auto Racing (NASCAR), the Sports Car Club of America (SCCA), the United States Auto Club (USAC), the International Motor Sports Association (IMSA), and the National Hot Rod Association (NHRA). Another major American racing organization is Championship Auto Racing Teams (CART). These groups plan and supervise certain kinds of races. Each group establishes *classes* (divisions) of races for the type of racing it governs and specifies the cars in a class. Canada has about 100

Bob Waterman, West Light

An *Ess* Turn on a Road-Racing Course challenges drivers, who must reduce their speed to navigate the curves. Most road courses include straightaways, hills, and a variety of turns.

organizations represented in the FIA through the Canadian Automobile Sports Club (CASC).

Kinds of Automobile Racing

There are five major kinds of automobile racing: (1) Formula One racing, (2) sports car racing, (3) Indy car racing, (4) stock car racing, and (5) drag racing.

Formula One Racing features the most expensive racing cars. Each Formula One car is designed and manufactured individually. The cars are built according to a *formula* (set of specifications) drawn up by the FIA. The formula limits the engine size and determines overall body design. Formula One cars are also called *Grand Prix* (pronounced *grahn PREE*) cars. The French term *Grand Prix* means *large prize* and is the name of the series of races in which the cars compete.

Formula One cars are designed on some of the same principles as airplanes. Like the *fuselage* (body) of an airplane, a Formula One car has a monocoque (*maw naw KAWK* or *MAHN uh kohk*) construction. In this type of construction, the car's central structure is a tube-shaped shell made of aluminum, carbon fiber, or other durable, lightweight material. This structure, sometimes called the *tub*, provides the connecting point for the engine, suspension system, and other parts of the car and bears the mechanical stresses. A Formula One car has front and rear wings. The flow of air over and under the wings produces a downward force that presses the car to the ground. This *downforce* holds the car to the road, which enables it to go faster on turns.

Formula One cars have only one seat, an open cockpit, and *open wheels*—that is, no fenders. The engine is in the rear. All Formula One cars have a *turbocharged* engine. Turbocharging increases the power of a small engine by using the energy from the engine's exhaust gases to spin a windmill-like pump. The pump forces a large volume of a fuel and air mixture into the engine's *combustion chamber*, where the mixture is burned. The greater the volume of the fuel-air mixture in the combustion chamber, the more power is released and the more energy is converted into the car's speed.

The Grand Prix races are the most famous international series of racing events held on road courses. The series consists of about 15 races held in Canada, France, Monaco, the United States, and other countries. The

Thomas Zimmermann, FPG

Formula One Racing features cars with one seat, a rear engine, and front and rear wings. They do not have a roof or fenders. The wings produce a *downforce* that presses the cars to the ground.

races are governed by the FIA representative in each country. In the United States, the representative is the Automobile Competition Committee for the United States FIA (ACCUS). ACCUS, in turn, authorizes the SCCA to organize U.S. Grand Prix events. In Canada, the races are governed by the CASC.

Grand Prix races are held on exceptionally challenging courses. The races range from about 150 to 200 miles (240 to 320 kilometers) long. Cars reach speeds of more than 200 miles (320 kilometers) per hour on straightaways and may go as slow as 30 miles (48 kilometers) per hour around sharp curves. The first driver to finish the required number of laps around the course wins. The top six drivers receive points. The driver who earns the most points in Grand Prix races in a year wins the World Drivers' Championship.

Sports Car Racing consists of events for both production sports cars and specially built *sports-racing cars*. Most sports car races are held on road courses or on combined road courses and oval tracks. The SCCA governs two major series of races for sports cars: (1) the Trans-American (Trans-Am) Championship and (2) the Canadian-American (Can-Am) Challenge Cup. Sports

P. Boisvert, FPG

Endurance Races are among the most popular sports car events. Such a race may last from 3 to 24 hours. The cars shown are competing in the 24-hour event held in Daytona Beach, Fla.

Sports-Racing Cars, which are built especially for sports car racing, navigate a sharp turn during a race in Miami. The cars shown here have rear engines, rear wings, and enclosed cockpits.

During a Pit Stop at the Indianapolis 500, crew members refuel a car and change its tires. Pit stops must be made in seconds. A delay in the pits can lose the race for a driver.

cars are also driven in endurance races.

The Trans-Am Championship consists of a series of road races in the United States and Canada that feature top American and foreign production sports cars. Such American cars as the Mercury Capri, Chevrolet Camaro and Corvette, and Pontiac Firebird compete against such foreign models as the Japanese Nissan 300ZX Turbo and the West German Porsche Carrera Turbo.

A Trans-Am car has the same shape as the original production model and retains such features as doors, fenders, and windshield. However, the spare tire, headlights, and certain other parts are removed to make the car lighter. The Trans-Am series uses a *power-to-weight formula* to help make the races more competitive. According to the formula, cars with less potential horsepower may weigh less than cars with more powerful engines. Some Trans-Am cars have turbocharged engines.

The Trans-Am series involves about 14 to 16 races, each about 100 miles (160 kilometers) long. The winner and runners-up in each race earn points. The driver who earns the most points becomes the Trans-Am champion.

The Can-Am Challenge Cup features specially designed sports-racing cars. A Can-Am car has a monocoque tub covered by a wide body. It is called an *envelope-body car* because the body of the car *envelops* (surrounds) all the car's moving parts. A Can-Am car has a rear engine, open cockpit, and large rear wing.

Can-Am races are held on major road courses in the United States and Canada, such as those in Lime Rock, Conn., and Trois-Rivières, Que. Most races range from about 100 to 150 miles (160 to 240 kilometers) long. The winner and runners-up are awarded points that count toward winning the Can-Am Challenge Cup.

Endurance Races are among the most popular sports car events. Such races last from 3 to 24 hours. The winner is the driver who completes the most laps within the specified time or becomes the first to cover the required distance. During an endurance race, cars make regular pit stops to refuel, change tires, and alternate drivers. Two or three drivers usually take turns driving the car. Famous endurance races include the 24-hour events held in Daytona Beach, Fla., and Le Mans, France. IMSA governs most U.S. endurance races.

Indy Car Racing. Indy cars, named after the Indianapolis 500, resemble Formula One cars. They have one seat, an open cockpit, open wheels, and a monocoque tub covered by a fiberglass body. To provide downforce, an Indy car has front and rear wings plus two structures called *sidepods*, one on each side of the cockpit. Each sidepod has a curved *ground-effects panel* on its underside. The ground-effects panels direct the flow of air moving under the car so that a low-pressure area, or partial vacuum, is created beneath the car. The resulting suction helps hold the car to the track. Indy cars are also called *Championship* or *Champ* cars.

Indy cars have turbocharged engines that burn a form of alcohol called *methanol*. Methanol provides maximum horsepower without overheating the engine. In addition, methanol does not ignite as easily as gasoline, reducing the risk of fire in case of a crash. Indy car races are held on oval asphalt tracks, such as the Pocono International Raceway in Long Pond, Pa., and on road courses, such as Road America in Elkhart Lake, Wis. Races range from 150 to 500 miles (240 to 805 kilometers) long. Indy cars can average more than 200 miles (320 kilometers) per hour on oval tracks.

The Indianapolis 500 is the most popular race for Indy cars. It takes place on the 2½-mile (4.02-kilometer) Indianapolis Motor Speedway. There are 33 starting positions. Drivers with the highest average speeds in four qualifying laps earn the chance to race. The first driver to complete 200 laps around the track—a distance of 500 miles (805 kilometers)—wins the race. All the participants share in the largest *purse* (amount of prize money) in automobile racing—over $3 million. First prize is more than $500,000.

The Indianapolis 500 is governed by the USAC. CART controls all other Indy car races.

Stock Car Racing is the most popular kind of automobile racing in the United States, especially in the South, where the races originated. Stock car racing is the only major form of track racing that has always been restricted to American-made automobiles. The chief stock car races are restricted to large, late-model sedans like those car dealers have in stock. The cars are altered to increase their speed and power, but they still look like ordinary passenger cars. They have a front engine, fenders, doors, and a windshield. Drivers sit in the usual upright position. Stock cars have steel bodies and are therefore much heavier than many other kinds of racing cars. Stock cars that are raced in the Grand National series weigh 3,700 pounds (1,700 kilograms), compared with about 1,500 pounds (680 kilograms) for an Indy car. However, a stock car's large, powerful engine enables it to reach speeds of 200 miles (320 kilometers) per hour.

Most major stock car races are held on oval asphalt tracks. The distance around the tracks ranges from about $\frac{1}{5}$ mile (0.32 kilometer) to $2\frac{2}{3}$ miles (4.29 kilometers) for *superspeedways*, such as the one in Talladega, Ala. A superspeedway has wide, high-banked corners that enable many cars to make the curves at speeds up to 200 miles (320 kilometers) per hour.

Most stock car races are held in Canada and the United States. NASCAR governs the major races, including the Grand National series. Grand National races are held only in the United States and range from 100 to 600 miles (160 to 960 kilometers) long. Highlights of this series of some 30 races include the Daytona 500 in Daytona Beach, the Southern 500 in Darlington, S.C., and the Winston 500 in Talladega.

Drag Racing. A drag race is a high-speed event held on a straight paved track called a *drag strip*. Most drag races are $\frac{1}{4}$ mile (0.4 kilometer) long, and many cars cross the finish line in less than six seconds. The fastest cars reach speeds of more than 260 miles (420 kilometers) per hour. Such cars use a parachute at the rear to help come to a stop.

Drag-racing cars range from mass-produced passenger cars to strange-looking models built for racing only. The three most important types of drag-racing cars are (1) Pro Stock cars; (2) Top Fuel, or AA Fuel, cars; and (3) Funny Cars. Pro Stock cars are production cars that have been altered for racing. A Pro Stock car burns gasoline and must use the car manufacturer's engine. For example, a Ford body must use a Ford engine. Top Fuel cars, also called *dragsters*, and Funny Cars burn a mixture of nitromethane and alcohol. Top Fuel cars may be built in any way the designer wishes. Most of the cars have a rear engine, one seat, and a long, slender frame. They have small front tires and large rear tires because most of the weight of the cars shifts to the rear during acceleration. Funny Cars must have a fiberglass copy of a

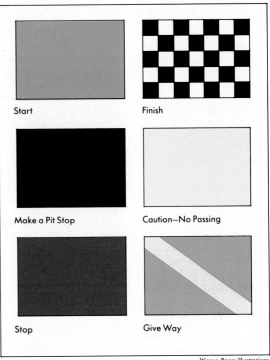

Start   Finish

Make a Pit Stop   Caution—No Passing

Stop   Give Way

WORLD BOOK illustrations

Automobile-Racing Flags signal the start and finish of a race. During a race, other flags tell drivers to make a pit stop, to drive with caution and not to pass because of an accident on the course, to stop, or to give way to a faster car.

passenger car body and meet restrictions on the *wheelbase* (distance between front and rear axles).

Hundreds of dragsters may race in a *drag meet*. The cars race two at a time, accelerating from a standing start. The losing car is eliminated from the competition, and the winner advances to race against another car. The elimination continues until only two cars are left. The winner of the last round is the meet champion.

The NHRA supervises the major drag races in the United States and Canada. Each year, it conducts a series of races in which the drivers earn points toward the Winston World Championship. Important races in the series include the Gator Nationals in Gainesville, Fla., the U.S. Nationals in Indianapolis, and the Winternationals in Pomona, Calif.

Other Kinds of Racing. Many race drivers begin their careers in karting. A kart is the smallest racing vehicle. Children as young as 8 years old—and many adults—compete in kart races on short asphalt or dirt tracks. Road-racing courses are restricted to drivers at least 16 years old. See GO-KART.

A *midget car* is slightly larger than a kart. It has open wheels and an open cockpit. Midget cars race on oval dirt or asphalt tracks. The distance around the tracks is usually $\frac{1}{4}$ mile (0.4 kilometer) or $\frac{1}{2}$ mile (0.8 kilometer). Midget races generally are no longer than 25 miles (40.2 kilometers). The fastest midget cars reach speeds of about 115 miles (185 kilometers) per hour on steeply banked tracks. A *sprint car* is bigger than a midget car. It has a tall, narrow shape, a powerful front engine, and

R. Mackson, FPG

At the Start of a Drag Race, a car's front wheels lift up as the driver quickly accelerates the car from a standing position. The fastest cars top 260 miles (420 kilometers) per hour.

AUTOMOBILE RACING

open wheels. The cars race on oval dirt or asphalt tracks and can reach speeds of about 115 miles (185 kilometers) per hour. Sprint car races generally cover the same distance as midget car races.

A *Super Vee* looks like a small Formula One or Indy car. The car has front and rear wings and a Volkswagen engine, from which it gets its name. Super Vees race on oval asphalt tracks and on road-racing courses. They can go as fast as 160 miles (260 kilometers) per hour. Super Vee racing is popular in the United States as a stepping stone for young drivers who hope to move up to Formula One or Indy car racing.

Two rugged forms of racing are *off-road races* and *rallies*. Popular vehicles for off-road races include small trucks produced by such manufacturers as Nissan, Toyota, and Mazda. Most off-road races are long-distance events run on rough, desert terrain.

Most rally cars are production models, some of which have four-wheel drive. The chief kinds of rallies are *road rallies* and *pro-rallies*. Road rallies are held on public roads and feature some of the longest automobile races. Pro-rallies are held on rugged back roads. The SCCA governs the major U.S. rallies.

The world's fastest cars are rocket-powered vehicles that look like missiles. These cars do not race against other cars but against the clock to break the world land speed record. Most speed trials consist of two 1-mile (1.6-kilometer) runs on the hard, level surface of the Bonneville Salt Flats in Utah. The current land speed record of 633.468 miles (1,019.47 kilometers) per hour was set in 1983 by Richard Noble, a British driver.

History

The sport of automobile racing began in the 1890's. The first races were run on *open-road courses*, which consisted of public roads between towns. Many of the courses were hilly, sharply winding dirt roads. Drivers often lost control of their cars and crashed, sometimes injuring spectators standing along the road.

Growth of Organized Automobile Racing. The world's first organized automobile-racing organization, the Automobile Club of France, was established in 1895. Later that year, it supervised the first actual automobile race—a 732-mile (1,178-kilometer) round trip between Paris and Bordeaux, France. Twenty-two drivers started in the race, but only nine finished. The winners averaged 15 miles (24 kilometers) per hour. That same year in the United States, J. Frank Duryea, a pio-

Grand Prix World Champions

Year	Driver	Country	Year	Driver	Country	Year	Driver	Country
1950	Giuseppe Farina	Italy	1962	Graham Hill	Great Britain	1974	Emerson Fittipaldi	Brazil
1951	Juan M. Fangio	Argentina	1963	Jim Clark	Great Britain	1975	Niki Lauda	Austria
1952	Alberto Ascari	Italy	1964	John Surtees	Great Britain	1976	James Hunt	Great Britain
1953	Alberto Ascari	Italy	1965	Jim Clark	Great Britain	1977	Niki Lauda	Austria
1954	Juan M. Fangio	Argentina	1966	Jack Brabham	Australia	1978	Mario Andretti	United States
1955	Juan M. Fangio	Argentina	1967	Denis Hulme	New Zealand	1979	Jody Scheckter	South Africa
1956	Juan M. Fangio	Argentina	1968	Graham Hill	Great Britain	1980	Alan Jones	Australia
1957	Juan M. Fangio	Argentina	1969	Jackie Stewart	Great Britain	1981	Nelson Piquet	Brazil
1958	Mike Hawthorn	Great Britain	1970	Jochen Rindt	Austria	1982	Keke Rosberg	Finland
1959	Jack Brabham	Australia	1971	Jackie Stewart	Great Britain	1983	Nelson Piquet	Brazil
1960	Jack Brabham	Australia	1972	Emerson Fittipaldi	Brazil	1984	Niki Lauda	Austria
1961	Phil Hill	United States	1973	Jackie Stewart	Great Britain	1985	Alain Prost	France

Indianapolis 500 Winners

Year	Driver	MPH	KPH	Year	Driver	MPH	KPH	Year	Driver	MPH	KPH
1911	Ray Harroun	74.59	120.04	1936	Louis Meyer	109.07	175.53	1963	Parnelli Jones	143.14	230.36
1912	Joe Dawson	78.72	126.69	1937	Wilbur Shaw	113.58	182.79	1964	A. J. Foyt	147.35	237.14
1913	Jules Goux	75.93	122.20	1938	Floyd Roberts	117.20	188.62	1965	Jim Clark	150.69	242.51
1914	Rene Thomas	82.47	132.72	1939	Wilbur Shaw	115.04	185.14	1966	Graham Hill	144.32	232.26
1915	Ralph De Palma	89.84	144.58	1940	Wilbur Shaw	114.28	183.92	1967	A. J. Foyt	151.21	243.35
1916	Dario Resta	84.00	135.18	1941	Mauri Rose and			1968	Bobby Unser	152.88	246.04
1919	Howdy Wilcox	88.05	141.70		Floyd Davis	115.12	185.27	1969	Mario Andretti	156.87	252.46
1920	Gaston Chevrolet	88.62	142.62	1946	George Robson	114.82	184.78	1970	Al Unser	155.75	250.66
1921	Tommy Milton	89.62	144.23	1947	Mauri Rose	116.34	187.23	1971	Al Unser	157.74	253.86
1922	Jimmy Murphy	94.48	152.05	1948	Mauri Rose	119.81	192.82	1972	Mark Donohue	162.96	262.26
1923	Tommy Milton	90.95	146.37	1949	William Holland	121.33	195.26	1973	Gordon Johncock	159.04	255.95
1924	L. L. Corum and			1950	Johnny Parsons	124.00	199.56	1974	Johnny Rutherford	158.59	255.22
	Joe Boyer	98.23	158.09	1951	Lee Wallard	126.24	203.16	1975	Bobby Unser	149.21	240.13
1925	Peter De Paolo	101.13	162.75	1952	Troy Ruttman	128.92	207.48	1976	Johnny Rutherford	148.73	239.36
1926	Frank Lockhart	95.90	154.34	1953	Bill Vukovich	128.74	207.19	1977	A. J. Foyt	161.33	259.64
1927	George Souders	97.55	156.99	1954	Bill Vukovich	130.84	210.57	1978	Al Unser	161.36	259.68
1928	Louis Meyer	99.48	160.10	1955	Bob Sweikert	128.21	206.33	1979	Rick Mears	158.90	255.72
1929	Ray Keech	97.59	157.06	1956	Pat Flaherty	128.49	206.78	1980	Johnny Rutherford	142.86	229.87
1930	Billy Arnold	100.45	161.66	1957	Sam Hanks	135.60	218.23	1981	Bobby Unser	139.08	223.83
1931	Louis Schneider	96.63	155.51	1958	Jimmy Bryan	133.79	215.31	1982	Gordon Johncock	162.03	260.76
1932	Frederick Frame	104.14	167.60	1959	Rodger Ward	135.86	218.65	1983	Tom Sneva	162.12	260.90
1933	Louis Meyer	104.16	167.63	1960	Jim Rathmann	138.77	223.33	1984	Rick Mears	163.61	263.30
1934	Bill Cummings	104.86	168.76	1961	A. J. Foyt	139.13	223.91	1985	Danny Sullivan	152.98	246.20
1935	Kelly Petillo	106.24	170.98	1962	Rodger Ward	140.29	225.77				

Year	Driver	Year	Driver
1949	Red Byron	1968	David Pearson
1950	Bill Rexford	1969	David Pearson
1951	Herb Thomas	1970	Bobby Isaac
1952	Tim Flock	1971	Richard Petty
1953	Herb Thomas	1972	Richard Petty
1954	Lee Petty	1973	Benny Parsons
1955	Tim Flock	1974	Richard Petty
1956	Buck Baker	1975	Richard Petty
1957	Buck Baker	1976	Cale Yarborough
1958	Lee Petty	1977	Cale Yarborough
1959	Lee Petty	1978	Cale Yarborough
1960	Rex White	1979	Richard Petty
1961	Ned Jarrett	1980	Dale Earnhardt
1962	Joe Weatherly	1981	Darrell Waltrip
1963	Joe Weatherly	1982	Darrell Waltrip
1964	Richard Petty	1983	Bobby Allison
1965	Ned Jarrett	1984	Terry Labonte
1966	David Pearson		
1967	Richard Petty		

neer automobile maker, beat five other drivers in a race between Chicago and Evanston, Ill.

The most famous open-road races in the United States, the Vanderbilt Cup races, began on Long Island in New York in 1904. But the crowds along the road were difficult to control, and so the races were held in several other places around the country after 1910. In 1916, the races were discontinued. In time, more and more races in Europe and the United States were run on tracks designed specifically for automobile racing.

The first Grand Prix race took place on a large course near Le Mans, France, in 1906. The race was supervised by the Fédération Internationale de l'Automobile (FIA), which was established in Hamburg, Germany, in 1904 to govern international automobile racing. The Indianapolis Motor Speedway opened in 1909, and the first Indianapolis 500 was run in 1911.

The Grand Prix series began in 1920. The first 24-hour endurance race for sports cars was held in Le Mans, France, in 1923. Organized stock car racing began in 1936 in Daytona Beach. Many of the first stock cars were *bootleg* cars that raced during the day and hauled illegal whiskey at night. The first Grand National race for stock cars took place in Charlotte, N.C., in 1949. In 1950, the FIA established the World Drivers' Championship for Grand Prix drivers.

Development of Racing Cars. The earliest racing cars were simply the first automobiles. These heavy, open vehicles had poor brakes and were hard to steer. The main way to increase a car's power for racing was to make its engine bigger. However, technological advances during World War I (1914-1918) enabled car designers to produce more power from a smaller engine. Racing cars thus became trimmer and faster in the 1920's and 1930's. Competition among carmakers also hastened the development of racing cars.

The major automobile races were canceled during World War II (1939-1945). After the war, racing cars became faster than ever. The development of the rear-engined racing car in the mid-1950's revolutionized the sport. Drivers no longer had to sit upright to see over the front engine. Instead, they could lean back and so conform to a car's streamlined body. Placing the engine behind the driver also improved the car's weight distribu-

tion and provided better traction. By the early 1960's, rear-engined vehicles had almost completely replaced front-engined cars in Formula One and Indy racing. In 1962, an English racing car designer named Colin Chapman introduced the monocoque construction to Formula One cars. Wings appeared on racing cars in the mid-1960's. In 1978, Chapman introduced the Lotus 79 ground-effects car.

Automobile Racing Today. Racing car designers are constantly seeking new ways to make cars run faster. At the same time, some racing organizations are changing their rules for safety reasons. In the early 1980's, for example, Grand Prix racing teams approved rule changes that banned ground-effects panels on Formula One cars.

Most professional drivers today compete in many kinds of races. Outstanding drivers of the 1970's and 1980's included Brazil's Emerson Fittipaldi and Nelson Piquet, Keke Rosberg of Finland, Niki Lauda of Austria, and Alan Jones of Australia. Leading American drivers included Mario Andretti, Bill Elliott, A. J. Foyt, Don Garlits, Al Holbert, Rick Mears, Richard Petty, Don Prudhomme, Danny Sullivan, Al Unser, Darrell Waltrip, and Cale Yarborough.

Several women have also achieved success in automobile racing. In 1977, Janet Guthrie of the United States became the first woman to race in the Indianapolis 500. She placed ninth in the race in 1978. Shirley Muldowney, an American drag racer, won the Top Fuel Winston World Championship three times—in 1977, 1980, and 1982.   SYLVIA WILKINSON

Related Articles in WORLD BOOK include:

Andretti, Mario	Hill, Graham	Oldfield, Barney
Breedlove, Craig	Hot Rod	Petty, Richard
Chevrolet, Louis	Indiana (pictures)	Rickenbacker, Eddie
Daytona Beach	Le Mans	Soap Box Derby

Outline

I. **Safety Measures**
II. **Sponsorship**
III. **Racing Organizations**
IV. **Kinds of Automobile Racing**
    A. Formula One Racing   D. Stock Car Racing
    B. Sports Car Racing   E. Drag Racing
    C. Indy Car Racing   F. Other Kinds of Racing
V. **History**

Questions

How is the winner of a drag meet determined?
How does a *fuel cell* help keep fuel from spraying in a crash?
Why is a Can-Am car called an *envelope-body car*?
When and where was the first actual automobile race held?
How long do *endurance races* last?
What purpose does a *roll bar* or *roll cage* serve?
How do wings enable racing cars to go faster on turns?
What are the smallest racing vehicles?
What major form of track racing has always been restricted to American-made automobiles?
Why are automobile races faster on oval tracks than on road courses?

Additional Resources

BODDY, WILLIAM. *The History of Motor Racing.* Putnam, 1977.
CHAPIN, KIM. *Fast as White Lightning: The Story of Stock Car Racing.* Dial, 1981.
MURPHY, JIM. *The Indy 500.* Ticknor & Fields, 1983. For younger readers.
OLNEY, ROSS R. *Illustrated Auto Racing Dictionary for Young People.* Prentice-Hall, 1981. *Super Champions of Auto Racing.* Ticknor & Fields, 1984.

The Magnificent Shwe Dagon Pagoda is the most famous of Burma's thousands of Buddhist temples. The pagoda is in Rangoon, the country's capital and largest city.

BURMA

BURMA, *BUR muh,* is a country in Southeast Asia. It lies along the Bay of Bengal. The country is about as large as Texas but has almost three times as many people. Mountains border Burma on the west, north, and east. They enclose the Irrawaddy River Valley. The Irrawaddy River empties into the Bay of Bengal through many mouths, forming a fertile delta. Rangoon, Burma's capital and largest city, lies on the delta.

The people of Burma are called *Burmese.* The great majority of them are Buddhists and live in villages on the delta and in the Irrawaddy Valley. They make a bare living farming the land.

People have lived in what is now Burma since prehistoric times. Several kingdoms arose and fell in Burma from the A.D. 1000's to the 1800's, when Great Britain conquered the country. Burma won its independence in 1948. Today, Burma is a socialist republic ruled by one political party. It is one of the most politically independent countries in the world.

Government

The government of Burma is controlled by the Burma Socialist Programme Party (BSPP). Nearly all party leaders are or were military officers. Since its creation in 1962, the BSPP has been the only party allowed in Burma. The head of the BSPP is the nation's most pow-

---

James F. Guyot, the contributor of this article, is Professor of Political Science and Public Administration at the City University of New York.

erful person. The BSPP controls all levels of government. It runs the national government through governmental bodies set up under the 1974 Constitution.

National Government. The highest governmental body in Burma is a one-house legislature called the People's Assembly. The people elect the 475 Assembly members to four-year terms. Only candidates approved by the BSPP may run for election. All citizens 18 years of age or older may vote. The People's Assembly elects from its members the Council of Ministers, Burma's cabinet. The Council of Ministers supervises the various de-

Facts in Brief

Capital: Rangoon.

Official Language: Burmese.

Official Name: Pyidaungzu Soshalit Thamada Myanma Nainggandaw (Socialist Republic of the Union of Burma).

Form of Government: Socialist republic.

Area: 261,218 sq. mi. (676,552 km²). *Greatest Distances*—north-south, 1,300 mi. (2,090 km); east-west, 580 mi. (930 km). *Coastline*—1,650 mi. (2,655 km).

Elevation: *Highest*—Hkakabo Razi, 19,296 ft. (5,881 m) above sea level. *Lowest*—sea level.

Population: *Estimated 1986 Population*—40,069,000; density, 153 persons per sq. mi. (59 per km²); distribution, 70 per cent rural, 30 per cent urban. *1983 Census*—35,313,905. *Estimated 1991 Population*—44,239,000.

Chief Products: *Agriculture*—rice, vegetables and fruits, sugar cane, peanuts, sesame seeds, corn, wheat, millet, tobacco, jute, cotton, rubber. *Forestry*—teak. *Manufacturing*—fertilizer, processed foods. *Mining*—coal, natural gas, petroleum, zinc, lead, tin, tungsten, silver, jade, rubies, sapphires.

National Anthem: "Kaba Makye" ("Our Free Homeland").

Money: *Basic Unit*—kyat. See MONEY (table).

partments of government. It is headed by a prime minister. Burma's president heads the State Council, which directs the work of all governmental bodies.

Local Government. Burma is divided into 14 large administrative units. They consist of 7 *divisions* and 7 *states*. The divisions are inhabited chiefly by Burma's largest ethnic group, the Burmans. People of other ethnic groups live mainly in the states. The divisions and states are further divided into many smaller units. Each unit of local government has a People's Council elected by the voters.

Courts. Burma's highest court is the nine-member Council of People's Justices. For each unit of local government, the People's Council sets up a committee that serves as the court.

Armed Forces. Burma's army, navy, and air force have about 180,000 members. About 90 per cent of them serve in the army. Most members of the armed forces belong to the BSPP. Service is voluntary. Burma has a national police force of about 73,000 members.

People

Population and Ancestry. Burma has about 40 million people. About 70 per cent of them live in rural areas. The rest live in cities. The country has an average of 153 persons per square mile (59 per square kilometer)—nearly twice the world average. However, Burma is less crowded than most other Asian countries.

Most Burmese are descendants of various peoples who moved into the region from central Asia. The Burmans, Burma's largest ethnic group, make up about two-thirds of the population. Other ethnic groups include the Karen, Shan, Arakanese, Chin, Kachin, Mon, Naga, and Wa. Most members of these groups live in the hills and mountains bordering Burma. Each of these *hill peoples* seeks to preserve its own culture. Since 1948, several groups have been in armed rebellion against the government to obtain more rights or to form separate countries.

Languages. Burmese is the official language of Burma. It is related to Tibetan. Nearly all the people speak Burmese, and many also speak English. In addition, many hill peoples have languages of their own.

Religion. About 85 per cent of Burma's people are members of the Theravada school of Buddhism (see BUDDHISM). Buddhism, which teaches that people can find happiness by freeing themselves of worldly desires, strongly influences family and community life. Other religious groups include Christians, Hindus, and Muslims.

Way of Life. The majority of Burmese people live in farm villages. Most villages consist of about 50 to 100 bamboo houses with thatch roofs. The houses are built on poles above the ground for protection against floods and wild animals. Most villages have a Buddhist monastery, which is the center of much social as well as religious activity. Boys spend from a few days to several months in the monastery after an adulthood ceremony called *shin-pyu*. In the ceremony, the boys' heads are shaved to symbolize their temporary rejection of the world. Girls mark their entry into adulthood with an earlobe-piercing ceremony called *nahtwin*, after which they receive their first pair of earrings.

In the cities, many people live in small brick or concrete buildings and work for the government or in industry. City life offers more recreational and cultural activities than country life and moves at a faster pace. But most city people keep close ties to their family and ethnic group, and religion remains important to them.

In both rural and urban areas, men and women usually wear a *longyi*, a long, tightly wrapped skirt made from a cylinder of cotton cloth. Women's longyis have bright colors and patterns and are bound at the side. Men's longyis often have a checked pattern and are bound in front. With the longyi, women wear a thin blouse, and men wear a shirt. Many women wear their hair in a knot on top of the head. On special occasions, men may wear a silk jacket and a *gaungbaung*, a small headdress made of cloth wrapped around a wicker frame. For pictures of other Burmese clothing, see CLOTHING (Traditional Costumes).

Burmese women have more rights than do women in some other Asian countries. A Burmese woman keeps her name after marriage and owns property equally with her husband. In most families, the mother manages finances and runs the household. Many women work outside the home, and some own or manage a business.

Food. The Burmese eat rice with almost every meal. The rice is often flavored with chili peppers. Fish or vegetables may also be added. The Burmese like fish, shrimp, and chicken but rarely eat beef or other red meats. Seafood and meat seasonings include onions, gar-

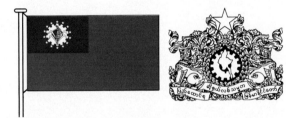

Symbols of Burma. The official flag of Burma's government was adopted in 1974. The cogwheel and rice plant stand for industry and agriculture, and the 14 stars represent Burma's 7 states and 7 divisions. Blue symbolizes peace, and red courage. The coat of arms features a map of Burma in the center, with the country's name in Burmese script below. The star stands for independence.

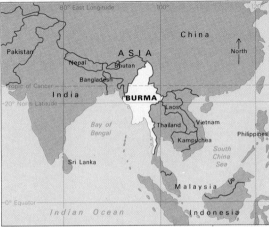

WORLD BOOK map

Burma lies on the mainland of Southeast Asia along the Bay of Bengal. It borders Bangladesh, India, China, Laos, and Thailand.

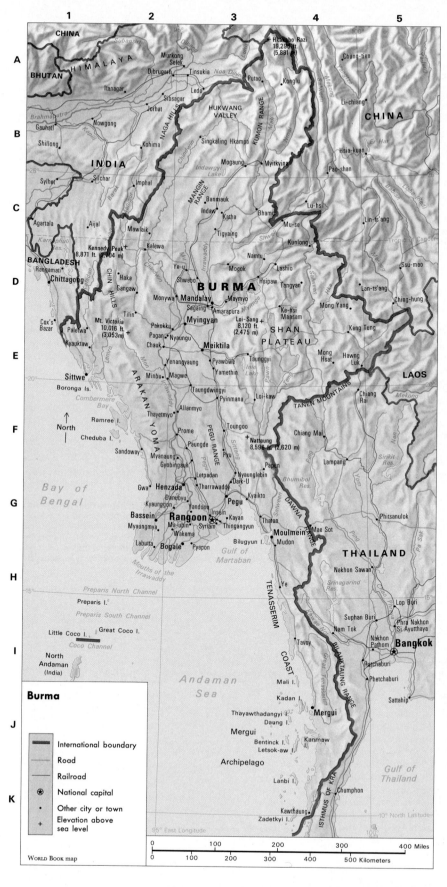

Burma
Map Index

Cities and Towns

Akyab, see Sittwe
Allanmyo . . . .149,297. .F 2
Amarapura . .120,196. .D 3
Bassein . . . .380,020. .G 2
Bhamo . . . . .74,040. .C 3
Bogale . . . .262,078. .H 2
Chauk . . . .175,256. .E 2
Daik-U . . . .140,972. .G 3
Danubyu . . . .155,455. .G 2
Gyobin-
  gauk . . . .104,484. .F 3
Henzada . . . .321,214. .G 2
Insein . . . . . . .183,931. .G 3
Kamayut* . . . .76,128. .G 3
Kayan . . . .118,208. .G 3
Kyaikto . . . .94,661. .G 3
Labutta . . . .195,457. .H 2
Letpadan . . . .157,230. .G 3
Magwe . . . .198,735. .E 2
Mandalay . .472,512. .D 3
Ma-ubin . . . .233,580. .G 3
Maymyo . . . .114,184. .D 3
Meiktila . . . .259,949. .E 3
Mergui . . . .226,298. .J 4
Monywa . . . .221,854. .D 2
Moulmein . . . .229,840. .G 4
Mudon . . . .175,310. .H 4
Myanaung . . . .207,447. .F 2
Myaung-
  mya . . . . . .250,688. .G 2
Myingyan . . . .249,274. .E 2
Myitkyina . . .116,892. .B 3
Nyaung-
  lebin . . . .156,005. .G 3
Nyaungu . . . .184,688. .E 2
Pakokku . . . .240,760. .E 2
Paungde . . . .118,507. .F 2
Pegu . . . .2₹8,491. .G 3
Prome . . . .167,734. .F 2
Pyapon . . . .152,885. .H 2
Pyawbwe . . . .191,495. .E 3
Pye, see Prome
Pyinmana . . .195,551. .F 3
Pyu . . . . . .185,736. .F 3
Rangoon . . 1,315,964
  . . . . . . .2,452,881†. .G 3
Sagaing . . . .215,247. .D 3
Shwebo . . . .189,131. .D 3
Sittwe . . . . . .162,177. .E 1
Syriam . . . .102,218. .G 3
Taungdwin-
  gyi . . . . . .176,440. .E 3
Taunggyi . . . .107,907. .E 3
Tavoy . . . .114,979. .I 4
Tharra-
  waddy . . . .133,167. .G 3
Thaton . . . .174,048. .G 3
Thayetmyo . . .87,570. .F 2
Thing-
  angyun . . . .160,005. .G 3
Thongwa* . . . .113,687. .G 3
Toungoo . . . .162,882. .F 3
Wakema . . . .228,294. .G 2
Yamethin . . . .163,847. .E 3
Yandoon . . . .152,987. .G 3
Ye . . . . .151,388. .H 4
Yenangya-
  ung . . . . . .145,003. .E 2

Physical Features

Andaman Sea . . . . .I 3
Arakan Yoma . . . . .F 2
Bay of Bengal . . . . .G 1
Cheduba Island . . . . .F 2
Chindwin River . . . . .D 2
Combermere Bay . . . . . .F 1
Daung Island . . . . .J 4
Great Tenas-
  serim River . . . . .I 4
Gulf of Martaban . . . . . .H 3
Gulf of Thailand . . . . . . .K 5
Hkakabo Razi
  (Mountain) . . . . .A 3
Indawgyi Lake . . . . .B 3
Irrawaddy River . . . . . . .F 2
Kadan Island . . . . .J 4
Kaladan River . . . . .E 1
Lanbi Island . . . . .K 4
Letsok-aw Island . . . . . .J 4
Mali Island . . . . .I 4
Mergui Archipelago . . . .J 4
Mount Victoria . . . . .E 2
Mouths of
  the Irrawaddy . . . . . . .H 2
Myitnge River . . . . .D 3
Nattaung (Mountain) . .F 3
Nmai River . . . . .B 4
Pegu Range . . . . .F 3
Ramree Island . . . . .F 2
Salween River . . . . .G 4
Shan Plateau . . . . .E 4
Sittang River . . . . .F 3
Tenasserim Coast . . . . .I 4
Zadetkyi Island . . . . . . .K 4

*Not on map; key shows general
location.
†Population of metropolitan area,
including suburbs.
Source: 1979 official estimates.

lic, ginger, and *ngapi*, a sharp paste made from preserved fish or shrimp. Favorite fruits include bananas, citrus fruits, and Southeast Asian fruits called *durians*.

Recreation. Popular spectator sports in Burma include soccer and a form of boxing that allows hitting with any part of the body. The favorite participant sport is *chinlon*. In this game, a ball of woven cane is passed among players by hitting it with the feet, knees, or head.

The Burmese enjoy many festivals. The most popular festival is held for three days before the Buddhist New Year begins, usually in April during the hot, dry season. People dump water on one another in a rowdy celebration that leaves everyone soaked. The New Year festival and many other celebrations include a *pwe*, an all-night performance by actors, dancers, singers, and clowns.

Education. About 70 per cent of Burma's people aged 15 or older can read and write. Burmese law requires children from 5 through 9 years old to attend school. The government offers free education from kindergarten through the university level. However, education beyond elementary school is available only in the larger towns and cities. Burma's major universities are in Rangoon and Mandalay. The country also has many colleges and technical schools.

The Arts. The best-known Burmese works of art are the thousands of *pagodas* (towerlike temples) found throughout the country. The most famous pagoda is the Shwe Dagon Pagoda in Rangoon. The golden-domed structure rises 326 feet (99 meters) above a marble platform on a hilltop. The ancient city of Pagan has hundreds of pagodas. Burmese craftworkers are known for their woodcarving, lacquer ware, and jewelry.

The Land and Climate

Land Regions. Burma has three main land regions. They are (1) the Eastern Mountain System, (2) the Western Mountain Belt, and (3) the Central Belt.

The Eastern Mountain System separates Burma from Thailand, Laos, and China. The region includes the long, narrow Tenasserim Coast bordering the Andaman Sea and the the hilly Shan Plateau to the north. Some of the world's finest rubies and best jade come from the region. It also has deposits of silver, lead, and zinc.

The Western Mountain Belt is a region of thick forests along the border between Burma and India. A group of low mountains called the Arakan Yoma forms the southern part of the region and extends to the Bay of Bengal. A narrow plain of rich farmland borders the bay.

The Central Belt lies between the eastern and western mountain regions. It includes Burma's highest mountains in the far north. Hkakabo Razi, the country's tallest peak, rises 19,296 feet (5,881 meters) above sea level. The Central Belt consists chiefly of the Irrawaddy and Sittang river valleys. The Irrawaddy River flows about 1,250 miles (2,010 kilometers) down the middle of the country to the Bay of Bengal. It is Burma's major transportation route. The 350-mile (563-kilometer) long Sittang River lies east of the Irrawaddy. Farmers use water from the rivers to irrigate their rice fields.

Climate. Most of Burma has a tropical climate. Temperatures in Mandalay, in central Burma, average 68° F. (20° C) in January and 85° F. (29° C) in July. Temperatures in Rangoon, on the delta, average 77° F. (25° C) in January and 80° F. (27° C) in July. Burma has three seasons: (1) rainy, (2) cool, and (3) hot.

The Rainy Season, during which Burma receives nearly all its rain, lasts from late May to October. Rainfall varies greatly in each region. For example, the Mandalay area gets only about 30 inches (76 centimeters) of rain a year. But the Tenasserim Coast is drenched with over 200 inches (510 centimeters) of rain. The heavy rainfall is brought by seasonal winds called *monsoons*, which sweep northeastward from the Indian Ocean.

The Cool Season lasts from late October to mid-February. Temperatures are lowest at this time, though the climate remains tropical throughout most of Burma.

The Hot Season lasts from late February to about mid-May. During this season, temperatures often top 100° F. (38° C) in many parts of Burma.

Economy

Burma has a developing economy based mainly on agriculture, which employs about two-thirds of the country's workers. The government owns all the land.

© Fred Ward, Black Star

A "Floating Market" is a colorful tradition on Inle Lake in central Burma. Farmers, craftworkers, and other people in the area gather in boats every five days to trade their specialties, such as rice cakes, fish, fruits and vegetables, farm tools, and silk.

Rice Fields surround a village in the Irrawaddy River Valley. Most Burmese live in villages like the one shown here and grow rice, the country's chief crop. The spire of a pagoda rises in the foreground.

© John Elk III, Bruce Coleman Inc.

Government factories produce about half the nation's industrial output.

Agriculture, Forestry, and Fishing. Rice is Burma's chief crop, and rice fields cover about half the farmland. Much of the rice is exported. Other important crops include vegetables and fruits, sugar cane, peanuts, sesame seeds, corn, wheat, millet, tobacco, jute, cotton, and rubber. Most crops are raised on small family farms.

Forests cover about half of Burma. They contain about 80 per cent of the world's teakwood. Fish and shellfish are caught in Burma's rivers and coastal waters. Many Burmese also raise fish in village ponds.

Manufacturing employs less than a tenth of Burma's workers. Most manufactured goods are produced for local use. They include processed foods, textiles, and fertilizer. Rangoon is the nation's chief industrial center.

Mining employs less than 1 per cent of Burma's workers. The country has a wealth of minerals, including zinc, lead, tin, tungsten, and silver. It is also rich in jade and such precious stones as rubies and sapphires. However, much of Burma's mineral wealth is undeveloped.

Energy Sources. Burma produces barely enough oil and natural gas to meet its needs. Hydroelectric plants supply more than half the country's electricity. Oil, gas, and coal produce the rest.

Service Industries employ about a fourth of Burma's workers. Numerous service industries workers are government administrators. Others work for schools, hospitals, and other institutions that provide community services. Service industries workers also include people employed in trade, transportation, and communication.

Trade. Rice and teak account for about two-thirds of Burma's export income. Other Asian countries buy most of Burma's exports. The nation's leading imports include machinery, transportation equipment, fertilizer, and chemicals. Many of Burma's imports come from Japan. Strict government controls on trade and a severe shortage of consumer goods have resulted in a widespread *black market* in Burma. Such items as transistor radios, television sets, and clothing are smuggled into the country in exchange for teak, rice, gems, and opium.

Transportation. Most freight travels by riverboats on Burma's more than 5,000 miles (8,000 kilometers) of inland waterways. Freight is also carried by trucks and railroads. Burma has about 17,000 miles (27,000 kilometers) of all-weather roads and about 2,700 miles (4,300 kilometers) of railroad track. Most riverboat and truck operations are privately owned, but the government owns the railroads. Few Burmese own an automobile. Many people travel between cities on riverboats. Oxcarts are common in rural areas. Burma's chief seaports are Rangoon, Bassein, Moulmein, and Sittwe. Mandalay is a major inland port and transportation center. Rangoon has an international airport.

Communication. The Burmese government controls mass communication. It publishes six daily newspapers, four in Burmese and two in English. Government radio programs are broadcast in Burmese, English, and local languages. Only about 4 per cent of the people own a radio. Government TV broadcasts began in 1980.

History

Early Days. The first known people to live in what is now Burma were the Mon. They moved into the region as early as 3000 B.C. and settled near the mouths of the Salween and Sittang rivers. The Mon, like the peoples who came later, migrated from an area in central Asia that is now southwestern China. The Pyu arrived in the A.D. 600's. The Burmans, Chin, Kachin, Karen, and Shan came during the 800's. Most of these peoples lived apart from one another and kept their own cultures.

In 1044, a Burman ruler named Anawrahta united the region and founded a kingdom that lasted nearly 250 years. The kingdom's capital, Pagan, lay on the Irrawaddy River in central Burma. The Burmans adopted features of the Mon and Pyu cultures, including Theravada Buddhism. Mongol invaders led by Kublai Khan captured Pagan in 1287, shattering the kingdom. A new Burman kingdom arose at Toungoo during the 1500's. It was brought down by a Mon rebellion in 1752.

British Conquest and Rule. The last Burman kingdom was founded by Alaungpaya, a Burman leader, after the Mon rebellion. Three wars with the British—triggered by Burmese resistance to Great Britain's commercial and territorial ambitions—led to the kingdom's collapse. The first war was fought from 1824 to 1826, the second in 1852, and the third in 1885. In these wars, the British gradually conquered all Burma.

After the third war with Britain, Burma became a province of India, which the British ruled. Under British control, Burma's population and economy grew rapidly. But educated Burmese called for Burma's separation from India and eventual independence. The Burmese protests led Britain to set up a legislature in the 1920's that gave the people a small role in the government.

Protests against British rule continued, however. During the early 1930's, a former Buddhist monk named Saya San led thousands of peasants in an unsuccessful rebellion. At the same time, university students founded the All-Burma Students' Union to work for independence. The students called one another *Thakin* (Master), a title of respect that had been used before only in addressing the British. Leaders of the movement included Thakin Nu and Thakin Aung San. They organized a student strike in 1936. Britain separated Burma from India in 1937 and gave the Burmese partial self-government. But the struggle for full independence continued.

World War II (1939-1945). In 1942, Japan invaded Burma. The Thakins formed the Burma Independence Army, which helped the Japanese drive the British out of Burma. The Japanese declared Burma independent in 1943, but they actually controlled the government. The Burmese disliked Japanese rule even more than British rule. To fight the Japanese, the Thakins formed the Anti-Fascist People's Freedom League (AFPFL), led by General Aung San. The AFPFL helped Britain and other Allied powers regain Burma in 1945.

Independence. Following Japan's defeat, the British returned to power in Burma. However, the AFPFL had become a strong political party and challenged British control. The British could not govern the country without AFPFL support. They decided in 1947 to name AFPFL President Aung San prime minister of Burma, but he was assassinated before independence came. AFPFL Vice President U Nu became president of the party, and the British appointed him prime minister. Burma won full independence on Jan. 4, 1948.

The new Burmese government faced many problems. Some Communists rebelled against the government in 1948. Various ethnic groups also fought the new government. However, U Nu's leadership won the support of most Burmese. The AFPFL overwhelmingly won elections in 1951 and 1956, though Communist and rebel ethnic groups continued to fight the government.

In 1958, a split developed between U Nu's followers and another AFPFL *faction* (group). The split threatened to plunge Burma into a deeper civil war. U Nu asked General Ne Win to set up a military government temporarily. Ne Win restored order and promoted economic growth. He ruled until elections were held in 1960. U Nu's faction won a landslide victory, and he again became prime minister. But he could not control the political and ethnic disputes. To hold Burma together, Ne Win seized the government in a bloodless take-over in March 1962. He suspended the Constitution and set up a Revolutionary Council to rule Burma.

Socialist Republic. Ne Win and his Revolutionary Council wanted to make Burma a socialist nation. They explained their ideas in *The Burmese Way to Socialism*, a document that has guided many of the government's plans. In July 1962, Ne Win and the council founded the Burma Socialist Programme Party (BSPP). It became the only political party allowed in Burma. The

government began to take strict control of the economy. For several years thereafter, farm production fell, and consumer goods disappeared into the black market. The government rejected most foreign aid and restricted visits by foreign reporters and tourists. It also closed or took over all privately owned newspapers and schools. Student strikes were ended by army gunfire. Revolts by the Shan, Kachin, and other ethnic groups flared openly.

On March 2, 1974, the country adopted a new Constitution that officially created the Socialist Republic of the Union of Burma, with U Ne Win as president. The Constitution reestablished elections, but the BSPP still held all power. The government removed some restrictions on agriculture and began to accept more foreign aid. These actions improved the economy. U Ne Win resigned as president in 1981, but he remained head of the BSPP. U San Yu became president.

Burma Today remains a developing nation. However, Burma's great wealth of natural resources could provide for economic growth if those resources were used more fully. The country has been politically stable for more than 20 years. Although the Burmese army continues to fight rebel groups in the mountains, Burma has remained uninvolved in foreign conflicts. It has thus avoided the wars that have torn other countries in Southeast Asia.

JAMES F. GUYOT

Related Articles in WORLD BOOK include:

Asia	Elephant	Rangoon
Bamboo	Irrawaddy River	Teak
Bay of Bengal	Jade	Thant, U
Buddhism	Mandalay	World War II (The
Burma Road	Monsoon	War in Asia)
Colombo Plan	Pagoda	

Outline

I. Government
  A. National Government
  B. Local Government
  C. Courts
  D. Armed Forces

II. People
  A. Population and Ancestry
  B. Languages
  C. Religion
  D. Way of Life
  E. Food
  F. Recreation
  G. Education
  H. The Arts

III. The Land and Climate
  A. Land Regions
  B. Climate

IV. Economy
  A. Agriculture, Forestry, and Fishing
  B. Manufacturing
  C. Mining
  D. Energy Sources
  E. Service Industries
  F. Trade
  G. Transportation
  H. Communication

V. History

Questions

What is Burma's chief crop?
Who was Anawrahta?
What is the religion of most Burmese people?
Why does a widespread black market operate in Burma?
How does most freight travel in Burma?
What is the center of much social as well as religious activity in most Burmese villages?
What is a *pwe*?
When does Burma receive nearly all its rain?
What are the best-known Burmese works of art?
What organization controls the government of Burma?

Additional Resources

CADY, JOHN F. *The United States and Burma*. Harvard, 1976.
STEINBERG, DAVID I. *Burma: A Socialist Nation of Southeast Asia*. Westview, 1982.

Chess Tournament Games are played within a certain time limit. The time used by each player is recorded on a special chess clock, which can be seen next to the chessboard in this picture. After making a move, a player presses a button that stops the player's clock and starts the opponent's clock.

CHESS is a game of skill in which two players move objects called *men* on a board divided into squares. Players try to *checkmate* (trap) the opponent's principal man, the king, while protecting their own king.

The Board and the Men. There is no standard size for chessboards, but most boards fit easily on a table. The board is divided into 64 squares arranged in 8 rows of 8 squares each. The squares are alternately light and dark in color. The rows of squares that run across the board are called *ranks*. The rows that run up and down are called *files*. The slanting rows are called *diagonals*. Players sit at opposite ends of the board, each with a light-colored square at the right-hand corner.

Each player uses a set of 16 men. One set is light-colored, and the other set is dark-colored. The player who uses the light-colored set is called *White*. The player with the dark-colored set is *Black*. Each player's set includes eight identical men called *pawns*. The other eight men are called *pieces*. The pieces consist of a *king*, a *queen*, two *rooks*, two *bishops*, and two *knights*.

Before a game begins, players arrange their pieces on the rank nearest them. They also place their pawns on the rank in front of the pieces. The rooks occupy the corner squares. The knights stand next to them, and the bishops stand beside the knights. The queen occupies the central square of its own color, and the king stands next to the queen.

The Moves. Each chessman moves in a specific way and, except for the king, is assigned a value according to its degree of mobility. The men, in order of assigned value from greatest to least, are the queen, rook, bishop, knight, and pawn. A man's value may increase or de-

The Chessboard and Chessmen
The diagram at the left shows the three types of rows on a chessboard. The six kinds of chessmen appear below the board. The position of the men at the beginning of a game is shown at the right.

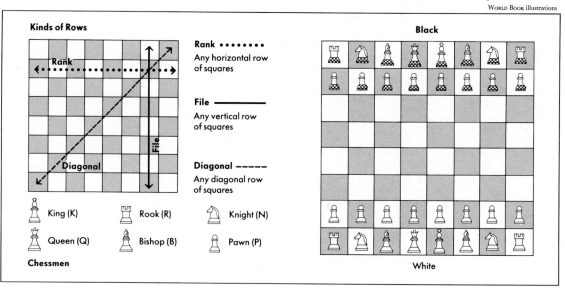

Kinds of Rows

Rank • • • • • • • •
Any horizontal row of squares

File ————
Any vertical row of squares

Diagonal — — — —
Any diagonal row of squares

King (K)   Rook (R)   Knight (N)

Queen (Q)   Bishop (B)   Pawn (P)

Chessmen

Black

White

crease during a game, depending on its position in relation to the other men.

The queen is the most powerful chessman because it can move in any direction along any rank, file, or diagonal until its path is blocked by another man. The king moves the same way the queen does, but it can move only one square at a time. However, players cannot make any move that would expose their king to capture.

A rook can move along any rank or file as far as its path is clear. A bishop can move as far as its path is clear along any diagonal but stays on either a light square or a dark square. Knights are the only men that can leap over men in their paths. A knight moves in an L shape—one rank up or down and two files left or right, or two ranks up or down and one file left or right. A pawn can move forward only one space at a time, except on its first move, when it can advance either one or two squares.

A piece may *capture* any opposing man that stops its progress. A player makes a *capture* by moving a man to a space occupied by an enemy man. The player removes the captured man from the board and replaces it on the space with his or her capturing man. A piece can only capture men in its path.

A pawn is the only man that does not capture men straight in its path. Instead, it normally captures a man one square to the left or right of the square in front of the pawn. A pawn may also capture *en passant* (French for "in passing"). This special rule applies only if a player has a pawn on the fifth rank. If an enemy pawn on a neighboring file advances two squares, it can be captured as if it had moved only one square, but it must be captured on the player's next move.

When a pawn reaches the rank farthest from its player, it is *promoted* (exchanged) for any piece other than a king. Because players usually exchange pawns for queens, this is often called *queening the pawn*.

How Chess Is Played. White always moves first in a chess game. The players then alternate moves.

Most chess games are played in three stages—(1) the opening, (2) the middle game, and (3) the end game. During the opening, players move their men to positions where they can attack opposing men or hamper their movements. Chess experts generally advise beginning players to move each piece only once or twice until they have moved them all.

Players often *castle* during the opening to protect the king. This is the only move during which a player can move two men at the same time. To castle, a player moves the king two squares toward either rook, and places the rook on the square the king passed over. A player can castle only if the king and rook have not been moved and no men stand between them. In addition, neither the king nor the squares it passes over can be under attack.

Much of the excitement in a game occurs during the middle game. Players try to gain an advantage in the position or number of their men in preparation for an attack on the enemy king. The kings generally stay well protected, because many men are still on the board.

During the end game, each player concentrates on queening a pawn. Players may use the king as an aggressor during the end game.

A player who attacks the enemy king traditionally gives notice by saying "check," though this is not required. A player whose king is in check must move only

How Chessmen Move

WORLD BOOK illustrations

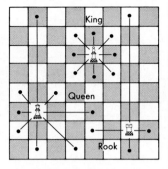

The queen and king may both move in any direction. The queen may move any number of squares, but the king can move only one square at a time. The rook may move any number of squares, but only along a rank or file.

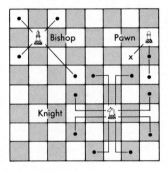

The bishop can move any number of squares, but only along diagonals. The knight moves in an L-shaped route. The pawn can move forward one or two squares on its first move and after that only one square at a time. It captures men by moving diagonally.

to rescue the king. The player may capture the attacking man or move the king to a square that is not under attack. A player can also place a man between the king and the attacking man, called *interposition*. If none of these moves is possible, the game ends in a checkmate and the attacking player wins. A player can *resign* (surrender) before checkmate if the position is hopeless.

A chess game may also end in a tie, called a *draw*. Players may agree to a draw if neither one has an advantage that could lead to a victory. Sometimes, players repeat the same sequence of moves. They declare a draw when they have repeated the sequence three times in a row. Players also draw if each has made 50 consecutive moves without moving a pawn or capturing a man. A kind of draw called a *stalemate* occurs when a player's only move would put his or her king in check.

Chess Notation. Most chess players in English-speaking nations use *descriptive notation*, also called *English notation*, to keep a written record of their games. In this system, the pieces beside the king are called the *king's men*, and those beside the queen are called the *queen's men*. Pawns are named for the pieces they stand in front of at the beginning of the game. Players using descriptive notation record moves by naming the men and the squares they move to. The squares in each file are named for the piece that occupies the first square in that file at the beginning of the game. For example, the squares in the center files are called the *king's squares* and the *queen's squares*. Players number the ranks from one through eight starting from the ranks nearest them.

Letters represent the men. *K* stands for *King*, *KB* for *King's Bishop*, *KN* for *King's Knight*, and *KR* for *King's*

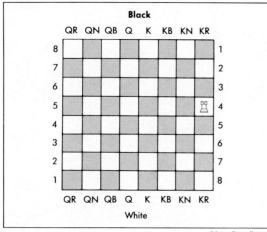

Black

	QR	QN	QB	Q	K	KB	KN	KR	
8									1
7									2
6									3
5									4
4									5
3									6
2									7
1									8

QR QN QB Q K KB KN KR

White

WORLD BOOK diagram

In Descriptive Notation, each file is named for the piece on the first square of that file at the start of the game. The ranks are numbered from 1 to 8, beginning with the rank nearest each player. The rook shown above is on White's *KR5* and on Black's *KR4*.

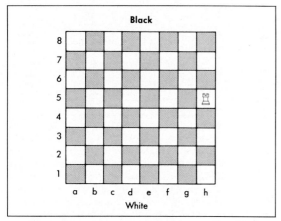

Black

	a	b	c	d	e	f	g	h
8								
7								
6								
5								
4								
3								
2								
1								

White

WORLD BOOK diagram

In Algebraic Notation, files are lettered a to h. Ranks are numbered 1 to 8, beginning with White's first rank. Every square has a name consisting of its file letter and its rank number. In the diagram above, the rook stands on square *h5*.

Rook. The queen's men are indicated in the same way, using *Q* for *Queen. P* stands for *Pawn.* Other symbols used in descriptive notation include *x* for *captures,* — for *moves to,* and *ch* for *check.*

Today, players use *algebraic notation* in most countries. In this system, the letters *a* through *h* indicate the files, beginning from White's left. The numbers one through eight indicate the ranks, beginning from the rank nearest White. Players record moves of pieces by naming the pieces and the squares they move them to. They record pawn moves by naming only the square the pawn moves to.

Tournament Competition. The Fédération Internationale des Échecs (FIDE) governs chess internationally. FIDE holds a match every two years to determine the world chess champion. A challenger to the champion is determined in preliminary rounds of competition. In the championship series, the first player to win six games wins the world title.

World Chess Champions

1866-1894	William Steinitz, Austria
1894-1921	Emanuel Lasker, Germany
1921-1927	José R. Capablanca, Cuba
1927-1935	Alexander A. Alekhine, Russia
1935-1937	Max Euwe, The Netherlands
1937-1946	Alexander A. Alekhine, Russia
1948-1956	Mikhail Botvinnik, Russia
1957-1958	Vassily Smyslov, Russia
1958-1960	Mikhail Botvinnik, Russia
1960-1961	Mikhail Tal, Russia
1961-1963	Mikhail Botvinnik, Russia
1963-1969	Tigran Petrosian, Russia
1969-1972	Boris Spassky, Russia
1972-1975	Bobby Fischer, United States
1975-1985	Anatoly Karpov, Russia
1985-	Gary Kasparov, Russia

United States Chess Champions

1857-1871	Paul Morphy
1871-1876	George Mackenzie
1876-1880	James Mason
1880-1889	George Mackenzie
1889-1890	S. Lipschütz
1890-	Jackson Showalter
1890-1891	Max Judd
1891-1892	Jackson Showalter
1892-1894	S. Lipschütz
1894-	Jackson Showalter
1894-1895	Albert Hodges
1895-1897	Jackson Showalter
1897-1906	Harry Pillsbury
1906-1909	Open (Pillsbury died in 1906)
1909-1936	Frank Marshall*
1936-1944	Samuel Reshevsky
1944-1946	Arnold Denker
1946-1948	Samuel Reshevsky
1948-1951	Herman Steiner
1951-1954	Larry Evans
1954-1958	Arthur Bisguier
1958-1962	Bobby Fischer
1962-1963	Larry Evans
1963-1968	Bobby Fischer
1968-1969	Larry Evans
1969-1972	Samuel Reshevsky
1972-1973	Robert Byrne
1973-1974	John Grefe and Lubomir Kavalek (tie)
1974-1978	Walter Browne
1978-1980	Lubomir Kavalek
1980-1981	Walter Browne, Larry Christiansen, and Larry Evans (tie)
1981-1983	Walter Browne and Yasser Seirawan (tie)
1983-	Walter Browne, Larry Christiansen, and Roman Dzindzichashvili (tie)
1984-	Lev Alburt

*Until 1936, the United States had a series of unofficial champions. Since that time, tournaments have been held periodically to determine the U.S. champion. The U.S. Chess Federation selects the players that take part in the tournaments.
Source: U.S. Chess Federation.

History. Historians do not agree on how old chess is or who invented it. They believe it originated in India in the A.D. 600's, perhaps earlier, and spread to Persia. Knowledge of the game spread from Persia to nearby countries after the Arabs conquered Persia in the 640's. Muslim invaders brought chess to Spain in the early 700's. By 1000, the game had probably spread through Europe as far north as Scandinavia.

The modern era of chess dates from the 1500's, when the moves of the game began to take their present form. In 1972, Bobby Fischer became the first American to win the official world chess championship. FIDE took away Fischer's title in 1975 after he refused to play challenger Anatoly Karpov of the Soviet Union under federation rules. Karpov therefore became the world champion by default.   LARRY EVANS

A Personal Computer System

A personal computer system has many uses in small businesses and in the home. The parts that make up such a system vary according to the needs of the user. The illustration below shows some of the hardware in a basic personal computer system.

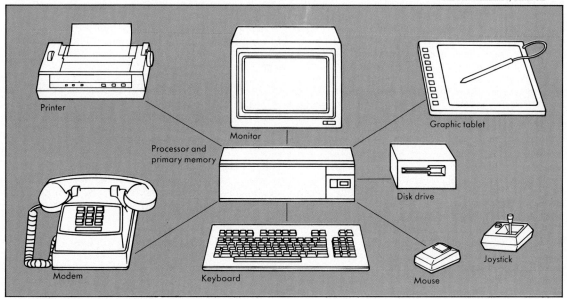

Printer

Monitor

Graphic tablet

Processor and primary memory

Disk drive

Modem

Keyboard

Mouse

Joystick

COMPUTER, PERSONAL, is a desk-top or handheld computer designed for general-purpose use. Personal computers are used by individuals, families, schools, or small companies for such purposes as keeping records, writing reports, learning a new subject, playing games, programming, or even running household appliances.

All computers store and handle information. Many large businesses use large, expensive computers that must be shared by a number of people to be economical. Personal computers, however, are smaller than such business computers, because they are equipped with a *microprocessor*. Microprocessors, which were introduced in 1971, are miniature electronic devices that can handle many of the same tasks as a large computer, though more slowly and with smaller amounts of information. The development of microprocessors led to a reduction in the cost of computers and thus made it possible for computers to be purchased by individuals, schools, and small companies.

Uses of a Personal Computer

Like other computers, personal computers can be instructed to perform a variety of individual functions. A set of instructions that tells a computer what to do is called a *program*. Today, more than 10,000 application programs are available for use on personal computers. They include such popular programs as *word processing programs, spreadsheet programs, database programs*, and *communication programs*.

Word processing programs are used to type, correct, rearrange, or delete text in letters, memos, reports, and school papers. Spreadsheet programs enable individuals to easily prepare tables. The users of such programs establish rules for handling large groups of numbers. For example, using a spreadsheet program, a person can enter some numbers into a table and the program will

calculate and fill in the rest of the table. When the user changes one number in the table, the other numbers will change according to the rules established by that user. Spreadsheets may be used for preparing budgets and financial plans, balancing a checkbook, or keeping track of personal investments.

Database programs allow a computer to store large amounts of *data* (information) in a systematic way. Such data might include the name, address, telephone number, salary, and hiring date of every employee in a company. The computer could then be asked to produce a list of all employees who receive a certain salary.

Communication programs connect a personal computer to other computers. People can thereby exchange information with one another via their personal computers. In addition, communication programs enable people to link their personal computers with *databanks*. Databanks are huge collections of information stored in large centralized computers. News, financial and travel information, and other data of interest to many users can be obtained from a databank.

Other programs include recreational and educational programs for playing games, composing and hearing music, and learning a variety of subjects. Programs have also been written that turn household appliances on and off. A number of people also develop their own programs for personal computers to meet needs not covered by commercially prepared programs. Others buy personal computers mainly to learn about computers and how to program them.

Hardware

The physical equipment that makes up a computer system is called *hardware*. The two most important pieces of hardware are the *primary memory* and the *processor*. The primary memory, sometimes called the *main memory*, stores information and programs in the computer. The processor in a personal computer is a microprocessor. It carries out programs and transforms information. Adding or subtracting numbers, arranging text, and producing pictures and sounds are all ways the processor transforms data. A processor works very fast. It can carry out 1 million additions in a single second.

Equipment other than the processor and primary memory is called *peripheral hardware*, and the individual devices are sometimes called *peripherals*. Peripheral hardware includes *input devices, output devices, secondary memories*, and *modems*.

Input devices are used for entering data and programs into the computer. A keyboard for typing words and numbers—and thus entering them into the computer—is one of the most common input devices. A *mouse* can also be used to give commands to a computer. When this handheld box is moved on a flat surface, it causes a pointer to point at a specific instruction or other data displayed on a computer screen. Clicking a button on the mouse causes the indicated instruction to be carried out or the data to be selected for use elsewhere. Other input devices include a *joystick* for moving figures about on a screen and a *graphic tablet* consisting of a pad and a "wired" pen for producing illustrations.

Output devices allow a person to receive information from the computer. They include a *monitor* (TV screen) for showing text and pictures, a *printer* for producing data on paper, and a speaker for producing sounds.

A secondary memory, also called an *auxiliary memory*, is used for storing data and programs for long periods of time. Secondary memories are generally bigger and less expensive—but slower—than the main memory, which is built into the computer itself (see COMPUTER [Parts of a Digital Computer]). The two chief kinds of secondary memory are cassette tapes and magnetic disks. Some disks, called *floppy disks* or *diskettes*, are made of flexible material and can be removed from the *disk drives* that operate them. Diskettes can store several hundred thousand *characters* (letters or numbers). Other disks, called *hard disks*, hold millions of characters and generally are not removable. Hard disks are more expensive than floppy disks, but they are faster and more convenient. All the computer's programs and other data can be kept on a hard disk so that they can all be used without the user's having to change disks.

Modems connect a computer to a telephone. They enable a computer to transmit data to other computers via telephone lines or other communications networks, and to receive data from distant computers.

Software

The programs that tell various parts of a computer what to do are called *software*. A program is made up of many instructions that direct a variety of activities. For example, some tell the processor to move data from one part of the computer to another, such as from the keyboard to the primary or secondary memory. Others control how the computer transforms information. In addition, they tell the computer to remember as a single new instruction or procedure a program made up of many old instructions. Whenever the new instruction is used in a program, all the old instructions are carried out.

The instructions used to write a program make up a *programming language*. There are several levels of increasingly complicated programming languages, from *machine language* through *assembly language* to *higher level languages*.

Like all computers, personal computers become easier to use through higher level languages. These languages allow the user to give the computer such commands as *draw a circle, move this paragraph*, or *print this letter*.

How to Choose a Personal Computer

The chief factors involved in the selection of a personal computer are the buyer's needs and budget. For example, before choosing a personal computer, you need to know whether you plan to use it mainly for one purpose—such as word processing—or for many different purposes. Different software is available for different types of computers, and so the types of functions a particular computer can perform vary. In addition, the amount of memory in the computer determines the length of a program that a computer can handle as well as the speed with which the computer will work. If you wish to run useful programs, you will need a computer with a memory of at least 64K. Such a computer is able to store more than 64,000 characters in primary memory. For more specialized programs, you may need as many as 100,000 characters in primary memory.

Needs and budget also influence the selection of the peripheral hardware. A computer system that uses a home television screen will be less expensive than one with its own monitor screen. A television screen, however, may not be as clear or show as much text as a monitor. Also, if you want to draw pictures or graphs, you should choose a computer and screen that can handle graphics and perhaps color.

To get a paper copy of work done by the computer, you will need a printer. Inexpensive printers are slow, printing about 30 characters per second. The printed copy may also be hard to read. Letter-quality printers can be faster and can produce better-quality copy than other printers, but are more expensive.

If you plan to write long reports or wish to handle a lot of data, you should have a two-diskette secondary memory system. Copying information and programs from one diskette to another is much easier and faster with this arrangement. Or, you may decide to buy a hard disk for handling large amounts of data.

To send electronic mail to other computer users or to use information from databanks, you will need a modem. Modems vary in communication speed and cost. They can transmit as few as 30 characters per second or as many as 120 characters per second.

History. During the 1940's, scientists developed the *transistor*, a tiny device that controls electronic signals. By the early 1960's, researchers had succeeded in building integrated circuits by arranging thousands of transistors and other electronic parts on tiny slices of silicon called *silicon chips*. The first microprocessors were produced in 1971. The development of microprocessors made small, inexpensive *microcomputers* such as personal computers possible.

Electronic games played with a television set provided one of the first popular uses for microcomputer technology. During the early 1970's, manufacturers began selling personal computers.   MICHAEL L. DERTOUZOS

The Nile River Was the Lifeblood of Ancient Egypt. Its floodwaters deposited rich, black soil on the land year after year, enabling farmers to grow huge supplies of food. The Nile also provided water for irrigation and served as ancient Egypt's main transportation route.

ANCIENT EGYPT

EGYPT, ANCIENT, was the birthplace of one of the world's first civilizations. This advanced culture arose about 5,000 years ago in the Nile River Valley in northeastern Africa. It thrived for over 2,000 years and so became one of the longest lasting civilizations in history.

The mighty Nile River was the lifeblood of ancient Egypt. Every year, it overflowed and deposited a strip of rich, black soil along each bank. The fertile soil enabled farmers to raise a huge supply of food. The ancient Egyptians called their country *Kemet,* meaning *Black Land,* after the dark soil. The Nile also provided water for irrigation and was Egypt's main transportation route. For all these reasons, the ancient Greek historian Herodotus called Egypt "the gift of the Nile."

The ancient Egyptians made outstanding contributions to the development of civilization. They created the world's first national government, basic forms of arithmetic, and a 365-day calendar. They invented a form of picture writing called *hieroglyphics.* They also invented *papyrus,* a paperlike writing material made from the stems of papyrus plants. The Egyptians developed

---

Leonard H. Lesko, the contributor of this article, is Wilbour Professor of Egyptology at Brown University.

one of the first religions to emphasize life after death. They built great cities in which many skilled architects, doctors, engineers, painters, and sculptors worked.

The best-known achievements of the ancient Egyptians, however, are the pyramids they built as tombs for their rulers. The most famous pyramids stand at Giza. These gigantic stone structures—marvels of architectural and engineering skills—have been preserved by the country's dry climate for about 4,500 years. They serve as spectacular reminders of the glory of ancient Egypt.

The Egyptian World

The Land. Ancient Egypt was a long, narrow country through which the Nile River flowed. Deserts bordered the country on the east, south, and west. The Mediterranean Sea lay to the north. The Nile River, which began in central Africa, flowed northward to the Mediterranean through the heart of the Egyptian desert. The Egyptians called the desert *Deshret,* meaning *Red Land.* The course of the Nile through ancient Egypt was about 600 miles (1,000 kilometers). The river split into several channels north of what is now Cairo, forming the Nile Delta. Gently rolling desert land lay west of the Nile Valley, and mountains rose to the east.

The Nile River flooded its banks each year. The flooding started in July, when the rainy season began in central Africa. The rains raised the water level of the river as the Nile flowed northward. The floodwaters usu-

557

Ancient Egypt

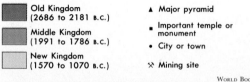

- Old Kingdom (2686 to 2181 B.C.)
- Middle Kingdom (1991 to 1786 B.C.)
- New Kingdom (1570 to 1070 B.C.)

- ▲ Major pyramid
- ■ Important temple or monument
- ● City or town
- ⚒ Mining site

WORLD BOOK map

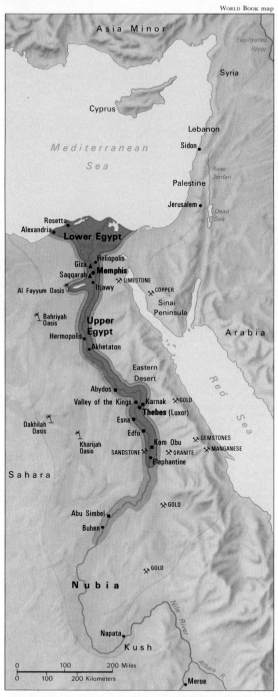

This map shows the extent of ancient Egypt during three important periods, known as the Old Kingdom, Middle Kingdom, and New Kingdom. Also shown are the major cities and historic sites.

ally went down in September, leaving a strip of fertile land that averaged about 6 miles (10 kilometers) wide on each side of the river. Farmers plowed and seeded the rich soil as soon as the floodwaters retreated. The Egyptians also depended on the Nile as their chief transportation route. Memphis and Thebes—the main capitals of ancient Egypt—and many other cities developed along the river because of its importance to farming and transportation.

The People. Most people of ancient Egypt lived in the Nile River Valley. Scholars believe the valley had from about 1 million to 4 million people at various times during ancient Egypt's history. The rest of the population lived in the delta and on oases west of the river.

The ancient Egyptians had dark skin and dark hair. They spoke a language that was related both to the Semitic languages of southwestern Asia and to certain languages of northern Africa. The Egyptian language was written in hieroglyphics, a system of picture symbols that stood for ideas and sounds. The Egyptians began to use this system about 3000 B.C. It consisted of over 700 picture symbols. The Egyptians used hieroglyphics to inscribe monuments and temples and to record official texts. For everyday use, they developed simpler hieroglyphic forms called *hieratic* and *demotic*.

Ancient Egypt had three main social classes—upper, middle, and lower. The upper class consisted of the royal family, rich landowners, government officials, high-ranking priests and army officers, and doctors. The middle class was made up chiefly of merchants, manufacturers, and craftworkers. The lower class, the largest class by far, consisted of unskilled laborers. Most of these laborers worked on farms. Prisoners captured in foreign wars became slaves and formed a separate class.

Ancient Egypt's class system was not rigid. People in the lower or middle class could move to a higher position. They improved their status mainly through marriage or success in their jobs. Even slaves had rights. They could own personal items, get married, and inherit land. They could also be given their freedom.

Life of the People

Family Life. The father headed the family in ancient Egypt. Upon his death, his oldest son became the head. Women had almost as many rights as men. They could own and inherit property, buy and sell goods, and make a will. A wife could obtain a divorce. Few other ancient civilizations gave women all these rights.

Kings commonly had several wives at the same time. In many cases, a king's chief wife was a member of the royal family, such as his sister or half sister.

Children played with dolls, tops, and stuffed leather balls. They had board games with moves determined by the throw of dice. They also had several kinds of pets, including cats, dogs, monkeys, baboons, and birds.

Education. Only a small percentage of boys and girls went to school in ancient Egypt, and most of them came from upper-class families. These students attended schools for scribes. Scribes made written records for government offices, temples, and other institutions. They also read and wrote letters for the large numbers of Egyptians who could not read and write.

The king's palace, government departments, and temples operated the scribal schools. All the schools prepared the students to become scribes or to follow other careers. The main subjects were reading, literature, geography, mathematics, and writing. The students learned writing by copying literature, letters, and business accounts. They used papyrus, the world's first paperlike material, and wrote with brushes made of reeds whose ends were softened and shaped. The Egyptians made ink by mixing water and *soot*, a black powder formed in the burning of wood or other substances.

Most Egyptian boys followed their fathers' occupations and were taught by their fathers. Some boys thus learned a trade, but the majority became farmers. Many parents placed their sons with master craftsmen, who taught carpentry, pottery making, or other skills. Boys who wanted to become doctors probably went to work with a doctor after finishing their basic schooling. Most girls were trained for the roles of wife and mother. Their mothers taught them cooking, sewing, and other skills.

Ancient Egypt had many libraries. A famous library in Alexandria had over 400,000 papyrus scrolls, which dealt with astronomy, geography, and many other subjects. Alexandria also had an outstanding museum.

Food, Clothing, and Shelter. Bread was the chief food in the diet of most ancient Egyptians, and beer was the favorite beverage. The bread was made from wheat, and the beer from barley. Many Egyptians also enjoyed a variety of vegetables and fruits, fish, milk, cheese, butter, and meat from ducks and geese. Wealthy Egyptians regularly ate beef, antelope and gazelle meat, and fancy cakes and other baked goods. They drank grape, date, and palm wine. The people ate with their fingers.

The Egyptians generally dressed in white linen garments. Women wore robes or tight dresses with shoulder straps. Men wore skirts or robes. The Egyptians often wore colored, shoulder-length headdresses. Rich Egyptians wore wigs, partly for protection against the sun. Wealthy Egyptians also wore leather sandals. The common people usually went barefoot. Young children rarely wore any clothes.

The ancient Egyptians liked to use cosmetics and wear jewelry. Women wore red lip powder, dyed their hair, and painted their fingernails. They outlined their eyes and colored their eyebrows with gray, black, or green paint. Men also outlined their eyes and often wore as much makeup as women. Both sexes used perfume and wore necklaces, rings, and bracelets. Combs, mirrors, and razors were common grooming aids.

The Egyptians built their houses with bricks of dried mud. They used trunks of palm trees to support the flat roofs. Many city houses were narrow buildings with three or more floors. Most poor Egyptians lived in one-room huts. The typical middle-class Egyptian lived in a one- or two-story house with at least 3 rooms. Many rich Egyptians had houses with as many as 70 rooms. Some of these homes were country estates with orchards, pools, and large gardens. Egyptian houses had small windows placed high in the walls to help keep out the sun. The people spread wet mats on the floors to help cool the air inside their houses. On hot nights, they often slept on the roof, where it was cooler.

Ancient Egyptian furniture included wooden stools, chairs, beds, and chests. People used pottery to store, cook, and serve food. They cooked food in clay ovens or over fires and used charcoal and wood for fuel. Candles and lamps provided lighting. The lamps had flax or cotton wicks and burned oil in jars or hollowed-out stones.

Recreation. The ancient Egyptians enjoyed numerous leisure activities. They fished and swam in the Nile River. Sailing on the Nile was a popular family activity. Adventurous Egyptians hunted crocodiles, lions, hippopotamuses, and wild cattle with bows and arrows or spears. Many Egyptians liked to watch wrestling matches. At home, the Egyptians played *senet*, a board game similar to backgammon.

Religion

Gods and Goddesses. The ancient Egyptians believed that various *deities* (gods and goddesses) influenced every aspect of nature and every human activity. They therefore worshiped many deities. The main god was the sun god Re. The Egyptians relied on Re and the goddess Rennutet for good harvests. The most important goddess was Isis. She represented the devoted mother and wife. Her husband and brother, Osiris, ruled over vegetation and the dead. Horus, son of Isis and Osiris, was god of the sky. He was called the lord of heaven and was often pictured with the head of a falcon.

In each city and town of ancient Egypt, the people worshiped their own special god in addition to the major deities. For example, the people of Thebes worshiped Amon, a sun god. Amon was later identified with Re and called Amon-Re. Amon-Re in time became the chief deity. Other important local deities and their main centers of worship included Ptah, the creator god of Memphis; Thoth, the god of wisdom and writing in Hermopolis; and Khnum, the creator god of Elephantine. Many deities were pictured with human bodies and the heads of animals. Such a head suggested a real or imagined quality of the animal and made identification of the deity easy.

Most ancient Egyptians prayed at home because the temples did not offer regular services for people. Each temple was either regarded as the home of a certain deity or dedicated to a dead king. A temple built in honor of Amon-Re at Karnak was the country's largest temple. It had more than 130 columns that rose about 80 feet (24 meters). Brilliantly colored paintings decorated the columns and walls in the temple's Great Hall, which still ranks as the largest columned hall ever built.

The priests' main job was to serve the deity or king, who was represented by a statue in the temple. The king reigning at the time was considered the chief priest of Egypt. Each day, he or other local priests washed and dressed the statue and brought it food. Priests also offered prayers requested by individuals.

The Afterlife. The ancient Egyptians believed that they could enjoy life after death. This belief in an *afterlife* sometimes led to much preparation for death and burial. It resulted, for example, in the construction of the pyramids and other great tombs for kings and queens. Other Egyptians had smaller tombs.

The Egyptians believed that the bodies of the dead had to be preserved for the next life, and so they *mummified* (embalmed and dried) corpses to prevent them from decaying. After a body was mummified, it was wrapped in layers of linen strips and placed in a coffin. The mummy was then put in a tomb. Some Egyptians mummified pets, including cats and monkeys. A number of Egyptian mummies have survived to the present day.

A Typical Country Estate in Ancient Egypt had a shallow pool enclosed in a courtyard. The pool served as a decoration but also was stocked with fish. Wealthy families had a number of servants and owned at least one dog and several cats. Girls played with dolls and often wore their hair in pigtails. Boys had their heads shaved, except for a braided lock on one side.

The Egyptians filled their tombs with items for use in the afterlife. These items included clothing, wigs, food, cosmetics, and jewelry. The tombs of rich Egyptians also had statues representing servants who would care for them in the next world. Scenes of daily life were painted on walls inside the tombs. The Egyptians believed that certain prayers said by priests would make Osiris bring the scenes as well as the dead to life.

Many Egyptians bought texts containing prayers, hymns, spells, and other information to guide souls through the afterlife, protect them from evil, and provide for their needs. Egyptians had passages from such texts carved or written on walls inside their tombs or had a copy of a text placed in their tombs. Collections of these texts are known as the Book of the Dead.

Work of the People

The fertile Nile Valley made agriculture the chief industry in ancient Egypt, and most of the workers were farm laborers. Great harvests year after year helped make Egypt rich. Many other people made their living in manufacturing, mining, transportation, or trade.

The Egyptians did not have a money system. Instead, they traded goods or services directly for other goods or services. Under this *barter* system, workers were often paid in wheat and barley. They used any extra quantities they got to trade for needed goods.

Agriculture. Most farm laborers in ancient Egypt worked on the large estates of the royal family, the temples, or other wealthy landowners. They received small amounts of crops as pay for their hard work, partly because landowners had to turn over a large percentage of all farm production in taxes. Some farmers were able to rent fields from rich landowners.

Ancient Egypt was a hot country in which almost no rain fell. But farmers grew crops most of the year by irrigating their land. They built canals that carried water from the Nile to their fields. Farmers used wooden plows pulled by oxen to prepare the fields for planting.

Wheat and barley were the main crops of ancient Egypt. Other crops included lettuce, beans, onions, figs, dates, grapes, melons, and cucumbers. Parts of the date and grape crops were crushed to make wine. Many farmers grew flax, which was used to make linen. The Egyptians raised dairy and beef cattle, goats, ducks, geese, and donkeys. Some people kept bees for honey.

Manufacturing and Mining. Craftsmen who operated small shops made most of the manufactured goods in ancient Egypt. The production of linen clothing and linen textiles ranked among the chief industries. Other important products included pottery, bricks, tools, glass, weapons, furniture, jewelry, and perfume. The Egyptians also made many products from plants, including rope, baskets, mats, and sheets of writing material.

Ancient Egypt had rich supplies of minerals. Miners produced large quantities of limestone, sandstone, and granite for the construction of pyramids and monuments. They also mined copper, gold, and manganese and such gems as turquoises and amethysts. Much of Egypt's gold came from the hills east of the Nile.

Trade and Transportation. Ancient Egyptian traders sailed to lands bordering the Aegean, Mediterranean, and Red seas. They acquired silver, iron, horses, and cedar logs from Syria, Lebanon, and other areas of southwestern Asia. They got ivory, leopard skins, copper, cattle, and spices from Nubia, a country south of Egypt. For these goods, the Egyptians bartered gold, other minerals, wheat, barley, and papyrus sheets.

Transportation within ancient Egypt was chiefly by boats and barges on the Nile River. The earliest Egyptian boats were made of papyrus reeds. Moved by poles at first, they later were powered by rowers with oars. By about 3200 B.C., the Egyptians had invented sails and begun to rely on the wind for power. About 3000 B.C., they started to use wooden planks to build ships.

During ancient Egypt's early history, most people walked when they traveled by land. Wealthy Egyptians were carried on special chairs. During the 1600's B.C., the Egyptians began to ride in horse-drawn chariots.

Crafts and Professions. The royal family and the temples of ancient Egypt employed many skilled architects, engineers, carpenters, artists, and sculptors. They also hired bakers, butchers, teachers, scribes, accountants, musicians, butlers, and shoemakers. The Egyptians' belief that their bodies had to be preserved for the afterlife made embalming a highly skilled profession. Many Egyptians served in the army and navy. Others worked on cargo ships or fishing boats.

Arts and Sciences

Architecture. Ancient Egypt's pyramids are the oldest and largest stone structures in the world. The ruins of 35 major pyramids still stand along the Nile. Three huge pyramids at Giza rank as one of the Seven Wonders of the Ancient World, a list of notable things to see that was made up by travelers during ancient times. The first Egyptian pyramids were built about 4,500 years ago. The largest one, the Great Pyramid at Giza, stands about 450 feet (140 meters) high. Its base covers about 13 acres (5 hectares). This pyramid was built with more than 2 million limestone blocks, each weighing an average of $2\frac{1}{2}$ short tons (2.3 metric tons).

The ancient Egyptians also built temples of limestone. They designed parts of the temples to resemble plants. For example, some temples had columns carved to look like palm trees or papyrus reeds. The temples had three main sections—a small shrine, a large hall with many columns, and an open courtyard.

Painting and Sculpture. Many of ancient Egypt's finest paintings and other works of art were produced for tombs and temples. Artists covered the walls of tombs with bright, imaginative scenes of daily life and pictorial guides to the afterlife. The tomb paintings were not simply decorations. They reflected the Egyptians' belief that the scenes could come to life in the next world. The tomb owners therefore had themselves pictured not only as young and attractive but also in highly pleasant settings that they wished to enjoy in the afterlife.

Ancient Egyptian sculptors decorated temples with carvings showing festivals, military victories, and other important events. Sculptors also carved large stone sphinxes. These statues were supposed to represent Egyptian kings or gods and were used to guard temples and tombs. The Great Sphinx, for example, is believed to represent either King Khafre or the god Re-Harakhte. This magnificent statue has a human head and the body of a lion. It is 240 feet (73 meters) long and about 66 feet (20 meters) high. The Great Sphinx, which is near the Great Pyramid at Giza, was carved about 4,500 years ago. Sculptors also created small figures from wood, ivory, alabaster, bronze, gold, and turquoise. Favorite subjects for small sculptures included cats, which the Egyptians considered sacred and valued for protecting their grain supplies from mice.

Music and Literature. The ancient Egyptians enjoyed music and singing. They used harps, lutes, and other string instruments to accompany their singing. Egyptian love songs were poetic and passionate.

Writers created many stories that featured imaginary characters, settings, or events and were clearly meant to entertain. Other writings included essays on good living called "Instructions."

Sciences. The ancient Egyptians made observations in the fields of astronomy and geography that helped them develop a calendar of 365 days a year. The calendar was based on the annual flooding of the Nile River. The flooding began soon after the star Sirius reappeared on the eastern horizon after months of being out of sight. This reappearance occurred about June 20 each year. The calendar enabled the Egyptians to date much of their history. The dated material from ancient Egypt has helped scholars date events in other parts of the ancient world.

The ancient Egyptians could measure areas, volumes, distances, lengths, and weights. They used geometry to determine farm boundaries. Mathematics was based on a system of counting by tens, but the system had no zeros.

Ancient Egyptian doctors were the first physicians to study the human body scientifically. They studied the structure of the brain and knew that the pulse was in some way connected with the heart. They could set broken bones, care for wounds, and treat many illnesses. Some doctors specialized in a particular field of medicine, such as eye defects or stomach disorders.

Government

Kings ruled ancient Egypt throughout most of its history. Sometime between 1570 and 1293 B.C., the people began to call the king *pharaoh*. The word *pharaoh* comes from words that meant *great house* in Egyptian. The Egyptians believed that each of their kings was the god Horus in human form. This belief helped strengthen the authority of the kings.

The position of king was inherited. It passed to the eldest son of the king's chief wife. Many Egyptian kings had several other wives, called *lesser wives*, at the same time. Some chief wives gave birth to daughters but no sons, and several of those daughters claimed the right to the throne. At least four women became rulers.

Officials called *viziers* helped the king govern ancient Egypt. By the 1400's B.C., the king appointed two of

RELIGION OF ANCIENT EGYPT

The ancient Egyptians worshiped many *deities* (gods and goddesses) and built huge temples to honor the major ones. The Egyptians also believed they would experience life after death in an *afterlife* and sometimes made elaborate preparations for death and burial. For example, the Egyptians *mummified* (embalmed and dried) corpses to prevent the bodies from decaying and to preserve them for the afterlife. The mummy was then wrapped in linen bandages, placed in a coffin, and put in a tomb.

Important Deities of Ancient Egypt

WORLD BOOK illustration by Linden Artists Ltd.

Amon-Re   Re   Osiris   Isis   Horus   Ptah

Gigantic Pyramids, built as tombs for Egyptian rulers, were used to hide the rulers' mummies and protect their souls. Some pyramids are about 4,500 years old.

Paintings Inside Tombs of many ancient Egyptians show the tomb owner as young and attractive in pleasant settings, *left.* The Egyptians believed certain prayers said by priests would make the god Osiris bring the scenes as well as the dead to life in the next world.

© Brian Brake, Photo Researchers

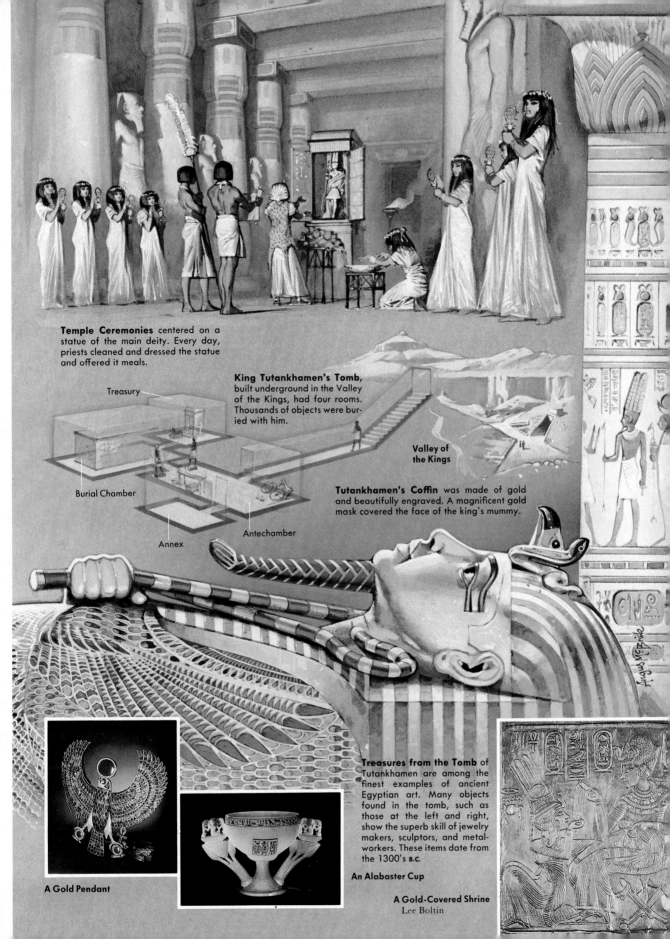

Temple Ceremonies centered on a statue of the main deity. Every day, priests cleaned and dressed the statue and offered it meals.

King Tutankhamen's Tomb, built underground in the Valley of the Kings, had four rooms. Thousands of objects were buried with him.

Treasury

Burial Chamber

Annex

Antechamber

Valley of the Kings

Tutankhamen's Coffin was made of gold and beautifully engraved. A magnificent gold mask covered the face of the king's mummy.

Treasures from the Tomb of Tutankhamen are among the finest examples of ancient Egyptian art. Many objects found in the tomb, such as those at the left and right, show the superb skill of jewelry makers, sculptors, and metalworkers. These items date from the 1300's B.C.

An Alabaster Cup

A Gold Pendant

A Gold-Covered Shrine
Lee Boltin

EGYPT, ANCIENT

them. One vizier administered the Nile Delta area, and the other one managed the region to the south. The viziers acted as mayors, tax collectors, and judges, and some even controlled temple treasuries. Other high officials included a treasurer and army commander. The government collected taxes from farmers in the form of crops. Skilled workers paid taxes in the goods or services they produced. The treasuries of kings and temples were thus actually warehouses consisting largely of crops and various manufactured goods. The government also levied a *corvée* (tax paid in the form of labor) to obtain troops and government workers.

For purposes of local government, ancient Egypt was divided into 42 provinces called *nomes*. The king appointed an official known as a *nomarch* to govern each province. There were courts in each nome and a high court in the capital. Viziers judged most cases. Kings decided cases involving crimes punishable by death.

In its early days, ancient Egypt had a small army of foot soldiers equipped with spears. During the 1500's B.C., Egypt built up a large army. The army included soldiers who were trained to shoot arrows from their bows accurately while riding in fast-moving, horse-drawn chariots. Egypt had a large navy consisting of long ships called *galleys*. Galleys were powered chiefly by oarsmen, though most vessels also had sails.

History

Beginnings. The earliest known communities in ancient Egypt were villages established over 5,000 years ago. In time, the villages became part of two kingdoms.

One of these kingdoms controlled the villages that lay on the Nile Delta, and the other controlled the villages south of the delta. The delta area was known as Lower Egypt. The southern region was called Upper Egypt.

Egyptian civilization began about 3100 B.C. According to tradition, King Menes of Upper Egypt conquered Lower Egypt at that time. He then united the country and formed the world's first national government. Menes founded Memphis as his capital near the site of present-day Cairo. He also established the first Egyptian *dynasty* (series of rulers in the same family). More than 30 other dynasties ruled ancient Egypt.

The Early Period of ancient Egyptian history covered Dynasties I and II, which ruled for about 400 years. During this period, the kings built a temple to Ptah, the chief god of Memphis, and erected several palaces near the temple. The Egyptians also developed irrigation systems, invented ox-drawn plows, and began to use hieroglyphic writing during the first two dynasties.

The Old Kingdom. Dynasty III began in 2686 B.C. By that time, Egypt had a strong central government. The next 500 years became known for the construction of Egypt's gigantic pyramids. The period is called the Old Kingdom or the Pyramid Age.

The first known Egyptian pyramid was built for King Zoser at Saqqarah about 2650 B.C. The tomb rises about 200 feet (60 meters) in six giant steps and is called the Step Pyramid. During Dynasty IV, workers built the Great Pyramid and other pyramids at Giza. The Great Pyramid was built for King Khufu. Huge pyramids were built nearby for his son, King Khafre, and for King Menkaure. Farm laborers worked on the pyramids when floodwaters of the Nile covered their fields.

Important Dates in Ancient Egypt's History

	The Old Kingdom was a period known for the construction of great pyramids.		Hyksos rulers formed a dynasty that ruled Egypt for about 100 years.	
◯ c. 3100 B.C.	◯ 2686-2181 B.C.	◯ 1991 B.C.	◯ c. 1670 B.C.	◯ 1490-1436 B.C.
Egyptian civilization began with the union of Lower and Upper Egypt.		King Amenemhet founded Dynasty XII, which greatly increased Egypt's power.		The Egyptian empire reached its height during the reign of King Thutmose III.

Hirmer Fotoarchiv

King Menes, *center,* was a legendary ruler who united Lower and Upper Egypt and set up the world's first national government.

© M. Timothy O'Keefe, Bruce Coleman Inc.

The First Pyramid in ancient Egypt was built for King Zoser about 2650 B.C. It rises about 200 feet (60 meters) and is called the Step Pyramid.

© John G. Ross, Robert Harding Associates

King Thutmose III led military campaigns into southwestern Asia almost yearly for 20 years and brought Palestine and Syria into the Egyptian empire.

By Dynasty V, the king's authority began to weaken as high priests and government officials fought for power. The Old Kingdom lasted until 2181 B.C., when Dynasty VI ended. Most of the next five dynasties had weak rulers.

The Middle Kingdom was the period in ancient Egyptian history during which Dynasty XII ruled. The dynasty was founded in 1991 B.C., when Amenemhet, a vizier in southern Egypt, seized the throne. He moved the capital to Itjawy, near Memphis. Amenemhet and his strong successors, including Senusret I, Amenemhet III, and Senusret III, helped restore Egypt's wealth and power. During Dynasty XII, Egypt conquered Nubia and promoted trade with Palestine and Syria in southwestern Asia. Architecture, literature, and other arts flourished under this dynasty. The Middle Kingdom ended in 1786 B.C.

Weak kings led the next several dynasties. Settlers from Asia gradually spread throughout the Nile Delta, and they seized control of Egypt about 1670 B.C. During the fighting, the immigrants used horse-drawn chariots, improved bows, and other tools of war unknown to the native Egyptians. The immigrants' leaders, called the Hyksos kings, ruled Egypt for about 100 years.

The New Kingdom was a 500-year period in which ancient Egypt became the world's strongest power. The period began in 1570 B.C., with Dynasty XVIII. During this dynasty, native Egyptians drove the Hyksos forces out of Egypt, and Thebes regained its importance. Amon, a god worshiped mainly in Thebes, was increasingly identified with the god Re and called Amon-Re.

At the beginning of Dynasty XVIII, Egypt developed a permanent army that used horse-drawn chariots

and other advanced military techniques introduced during the Hyksos period. The dynasty's early rulers led military forces into southwestern Asia. Thutmose I apparently reached the Euphrates River. Queen Hatshepsut, his daughter, also led armies in battle. Egypt developed a great empire and reached the height of its power during the 1400's B.C., under King Thutmose III. He led military campaigns into Asia almost yearly for 20 years and brought Palestine and Syria into the Egyptian empire. Thutmose also reestablished Egyptian control over Nubia and nearby Kush, which were valuable sources of slaves, copper, gold, ivory, and ebony. As a result of these victories, Egypt became the strongest and wealthiest nation in the Middle East.

The course of Egyptian history changed unexpectedly after Amenhotep IV came to the throne in 1367 B.C. He devoted himself to a sun god called the Aton. The Aton was represented as the disk of the sun. Amenhotep changed his own name to Akhenaton and declared that the Aton had replaced Amon and all other gods except Re. He believed that Re was part of the sunlight that came from the Aton. The king also moved the capital to a new city, Akhetaton, about 300 miles (500 kilometers) north of Thebes. Ruins of the city lie near what is now Tell el Amarna. Akhenaton's religious reforms, which historians call the Amarna Revolution, led to an outpouring of art and sculpture that glorified the Aton. But the changes angered many Egyptians.

Akhenaton's immediate successors ended the unrest. King Tutankhaton removed -aton from his name and became Tutankhamen. He restored the old state reli-

Akhenaton became king of Egypt and introduced major religious reforms.		Alexander the Great added Egypt to his empire and founded the city of Alexandria.		Muslims from Arabia seized Alexandria and completed their conquest of Egypt.
○ 1367 B.C.	○ c. 1070 B.C.	○ 332 B.C.	○ 31 B.C.	○ A.D. 642
	Dynasty XX ended, and Egypt began to decline rapidly as a strong nation.		A Roman fleet crushed an Egyptian force in the Battle of Actium, leading to Rome's take-over of Egypt in 30 B.C.	

© Erich Lessing, Magnum

King Akhenaton, *left,* started the Amarna Revolution during the 1300's B.C. He urged the Egyptians to worship a sun god called the Aton.

Detail of a mosaic *Alexander the Great at the Battle of Isso* (150 B.C.); National Museum of Naples, Italy (SCALA/Art Resource)

Alexander the Great, king of Macedonia, ended Persia's control of Egypt. Ptolemy, one of Alexander's generals, later founded a dynasty in Egypt.

Roger Viollet

Queen Cleopatra VII was the last ruler of Egypt's Ptolemaic dynasty. After she died in 30 B.C., Egypt became a province of Rome.

565

gion, allowing the worship of the old deities as well as the Aton. Horemheb, the last Dynasty XVIII king, completely rejected Akhenaton's religious beliefs. Dynasty XIX kings erected temples to many gods throughout Egypt. Two of the kings, Seti I and his son, Ramses II, also regained Asian territories lost after the reign of Thutmose III.

Ancient Egypt began to decline during Dynasty XX. Increasingly bitter struggles for royal power by priests and nobles broke the country into small states. Egypt lost its territories abroad, and its weakness attracted a series of invaders.

The Periods of Foreign Control. Ancient Egypt's decline accelerated rapidly after about 1070 B.C., when Dynasty XX ended. During the next 700 years, more than 10 dynasties ruled Egypt. Most of them were formed by Nubian, Assyrian, and Persian rulers. In 332 B.C., the Macedonian conqueror Alexander the Great added Egypt to his empire. That same year, Alexander founded the city of Alexandria in the delta.

The Ptolemies. Alexander died in 323 B.C., and his generals divided his empire. Ptolemy, one of the generals, gained control of Egypt. About 305 B.C., he took the title of king and founded a dynasty known as the Ptolemies. The dynasty's early rulers spread Greek culture in Egypt. They also built temples to Egyptian gods, developed Egypt's natural resources, and increased foreign trade. Alexandria became Egypt's capital, and its magnificent library and museum helped make the city one of the greatest cultural centers of ancient times.

Roman Rule. In 37 B.C., Queen Cleopatra VII of the Ptolemies married Mark Antony, a co-ruler of Rome. Antony wanted to rule the vast Roman lands by himself. He combined his and Cleopatra's military forces to fight forces led by Octavian, another co-ruler of Rome. But the navy of Antony and Cleopatra lost the vital Battle of Actium to Octavian's fleet in 31 B.C. The couple committed suicide the next year, and Octavian then made Egypt a province of Rome. Rome's control of Egypt gradually weakened after A.D. 395, when the Roman Empire split into eastern and western parts. By A.D. 642, Muslims from Arabia had conquered Egypt. For the story of Egypt after 642, see EGYPT (History).

Learning About Ancient Egypt

The study of ancient Egypt is called *Egyptology*, and experts in the field are *Egyptologists*. Much of their knowledge comes from studying the architecture and other arts of ancient Egypt. Ruins of magnificent temples stand at Abydos, Kom Ombo, Edfu, Esna, Luxor, and Karnak. Excavations of pharaohs' tombs, such as those in a burial ground called the Valley of the Kings, near Luxor, have yielded superb paintings. Tutankhamen's tomb was filled with stunning examples of the ancient Egyptians' skill in woodworking and metalworking.

Information about ancient Egypt also comes from written records made by the Egyptians themselves and by such ancient Greek writers as Herodotus and Strabo. The Egyptians used hieroglyphics until sometime after they came under Roman rule. The ability of anyone to read Egyptian hieroglyphics was then quickly lost.

For over 1,000 years, scholars tried but failed to decipher the writing system of ancient Egypt. Then, in 1799, a rock slab with ancient Greek and Egyptian writing was found outside Rosetta, a city near Alexandria. A French scholar named Jean François Champollion began to compare the Greek and Egyptian words on the so-called Rosetta Stone. By 1822, he had deciphered the hieroglyphics. Dictionaries developed since then have helped scholars translate the writings on many monuments and in temples and tombs.   LEONARD H. LESKO

Related Articles in WORLD BOOK include:

BIOGRAPHIES

Akhenaton	Cleopatra	Nefertiti	Seti I
Alexander the Great	Imhotep	Ptolemy I	Thutmose III
	Khufu	Ramses II	Tutankhamen

CONTRIBUTIONS TO CIVILIZATION

Architecture (Egyptian)	Obelisk
Bread (History)	Painting (Egyptian Painting)
Calendar	
Clothing (Ancient Times)	Papyrus
Dancing (Ancient Times)	Pyramids
Furniture (Ancient Egypt)	Sculpture (The Beginnings)
Geometry (History)	Ship (Egyptian Ships)
Glass (History)	Sphinx
Hieroglyphics	Surveying
Irrigation	Textile (History)
Mythology (Egyptian Mythology)	

GODS AND GODDESSES

Amon	Horus	Osiris	Set
Anubis	Isis	Re	Thoth

OTHER RELATED ARTICLES

Abu Simbel, Temples of	Animal Worship Asp	Hyskos Kush	Pharaoh Rosetta Stone
Agriculture (picture)	Bed (picture)	Lotus	Scarab
Alexandria	Bronze (picture)	Memphis	Thebes (Egypt)
Alexandrian Library	Cat (History) Cleopatra's Needles	Mummy Nile River Nubia	Valley of the Kings

Outline

I. The Egyptian World
 A. The Land
 B. The People

II. Life of the People
 A. Family Life
 B. Education
 C. Food, Clothing, and Shelter
 D. Recreation

III. Religion
 A. Gods and Goddesses
 B. The Afterlife

IV. Work of the People
 A. Agriculture
 B. Manufacturing and Mining
 C. Trade and Transportation
 D. Crafts and Professions

V. Arts and Sciences
 A. Architecture
 B. Painting and Sculpture
 C. Music and Literature
 D. Sciences

VI. Government

VII. History

VIII. Learning About Ancient Egypt

Questions

Why did the ancient Greek historian Herodotus call Egypt "the gift of the Nile"?

What were some achievements of the ancient Egyptians?

Why did the ancient Egyptians make mummies?

What was the Amarna Revolution?

Why did the Egyptians build pyramids?

What discovery led to the deciphering of the ancient Egyptian hieroglyphics in modern times?

When did ancient Egypt reach the height of its power?

What did the ancient Egyptians call their country? Why?

From where does our knowledge of ancient Egypt come?

What was the chief industry in ancient Egypt?

Reading and Study Guide
See *Egypt, Ancient*, in the RESEARCH GUIDE/INDEX, Volume 22, for a *Reading and Study Guide*.

Additional Resources

ALDRED, CYRIL. *The Egyptians*. Rev. ed. Thames & Hudson, 1984.

CARTER, HOWARD. *The Tomb of Tutankhamen*. Dutton, 1972.

MERTZ, BARBARA. *Red Land, Black Land: Daily Life in Ancient Egypt*. Rev. ed. Dodd, 1978.

MILLARD, ANNE, and others. *Ancient Egypt*. Watts, 1979. For younger readers.

PAYNE, ELIZABETH. *The Pharaohs of Ancient Egypt*. Random House, 1981. For younger readers.

ROMER, JOHN. *People of the Nile: Everyday Life in Ancient Egypt*. Crown, 1983.

STEINDORFF, GEORGE, and SEELE, K. C. *When Egypt Ruled the East*. Rev. ed. Univ. of Chicago Press, 1957.

TUTANKHAMEN, *TOOT ahngk AH muhn,* served as king of Egypt from about 1347 B.C. until his death in 1339 B.C. His name is also spelled *Tutankhamun* or *Tutankhamon*. His reign was unimportant. But interest in Tutankhamen began in 1922, when the British archaeologist Howard Carter discovered his tomb. The tomb had not been opened since ancient times and still contained most of its treasures. It is the only tomb of an ancient Egyptian king to be discovered almost completely undamaged. See CARTER, HOWARD.

Tutankhamen became king at about the age of 9. He probably received much assistance from Ay, his *vizier* (minister of state). Scholars disagree on who Tutankhamen's relatives were. Some believe the king was a son-in-law of King Akhenaton. Others think Tutankhamen was the son of Akhenaton and the grandson of King Amenhotep III. Still others argue that Tutankhamen and Akhenaton were brothers. Tutankhamen's original name was *Tutankhaton,* meaning *the living image of Aton* or *the life of Aton is pleasing*. Akhenaton had made Aton the sole god of Egypt. He wanted Egyptians to stop worshiping the chief sun god Amon and other traditional gods. But many Egyptians, including the powerful priests devoted to Amon, rejected the worship of Aton. Thus, about four years after he became king, Tutankha-

ton took the name Tutankhamen and restored Egypt's old religion. See AKHENATON.

Historians believe Tutankhamen died at about the age of 18, but they are unsure about the cause of his death. Ay succeeded Tutankhamen as king and held his funeral in the Valley of the Kings, a burial center at Thebes. Horemheb, a leading general, later succeeded Ay as king. Horemheb and his successors destroyed or removed all monuments built by or in honor of Tutankhamen and others who had accepted Aton as Egypt's chief god.

Carter searched for Tutankhamen's tomb for about 10 years. He finally discovered that its entrance had been hidden by debris from digging at the entrance of the nearby tomb of King Ramses VI. Tutankhamen's four-room tomb contained more than 5,000 objects, including many beautiful carved and gold-covered items. A magnificent lifelike gold mask of Tutankhamen covered the head and shoulders of the royal mummy.

Among the items discovered were luxurious chests, thrones, beds, linens, clothing, necklaces, bracelets, rings, and earrings. Carter also found chariots, bows and arrows, swords, daggers, shields, ostrich feather fans, trumpets, statues of Tutankhamen and many Egyptian gods, figures of animals, models of ships, toys, games, and storage jars containing precious oils. The ancient Egyptians believed in a life after death, called the *afterlife*. They had their favorite possessions and practical objects buried with them for later use in the afterlife. Most of the items found in Tutankhamen's tomb are now displayed in the Egyptian Museum in Cairo.

One of the most informative items in the tomb was a note on the handle of the king's fan. The note indicated that the young Tutankhamen hunted at Heliopolis, near modern Cairo. Wine-jar labels indicated the length of Tutankhamen's reign. Several objects included scenes that show Tutankhamen slaying foreign enemies in battle. But scholars doubt that these scenes pictured actual events.

LEONARD H. LESKO

Robert Harding Associates

Ronald Sheridan

© Lee Boltin

© Lee Boltin

Beautiful Treasures of Tutankhamen were found inside the young king's tomb in 1922. The most exquisite items included, *left to right,* a throne, a necklace honoring the sun, a gold death mask, and a small alabaster boat and pedestal.

Distribution Substation

Coal-Burning Electric Power Plant

Typical Uses of Electric Power

An Electric Power System begins with power plants, which produce large amounts of electricity. Wires carry high-voltage electric current from the power plants to substations, where the voltage is reduced. The electricity is then distributed for use in homes, offices, businesses, and factories.

ELECTRIC POWER

ELECTRIC POWER is the use of electric energy to do work. It lights, heats, and cools many homes. Electricity also provides power for television sets, refrigerators, vacuum cleaners, and many other home appliances. Electric power runs machinery in factories. Escalators, elevators, and computers and other business machines in stores and offices use electric power. Electricity drives many trains and subway systems. On farms, electric machinery performs such tasks as pumping water, milking cows, and drying hay.

Huge electric generators in power plants produce almost all the world's electricity. The majority of these plants burn coal, oil, or natural gas to run the generators. Most other plants drive the generators by means of nuclear energy or the force of falling water. Wires carry the electricity from power plants to the cities or other areas where it is needed. The electricity is then distributed to individual consumers.

Electric power is measured in units called *watts*. For example, it takes 100 watts of electric power to operate a 100-watt light bulb. Ten 100-watt bulbs require 1,000 watts, or 1 *kilowatt*. The amount of power used is ex-

M. E. El-Hawary, the contributor of this article, is Professor of Electrical Engineering at the Technical University of Nova Scotia and the author of Electric Power Systems: Design and Analysis.

pressed in *kilowatt-hours*. A kilowatt-hour equals the amount of work done by 1 kilowatt in one hour. If you burn ten 100-watt bulbs for one hour or one 100-watt bulb for 10 hours, you use 1 kilowatt-hour of electric power.

The world's electric power plants can produce more than $2\frac{1}{4}$ billion kilowatts of electricity at any given time. The United States leads all other countries in generating capacity. American power plants can generate as much as 672 million kilowatts. Canadian plants can produce about 96 million kilowatts.

Sources of Electric Power

Large electric power plants supply nearly all the electricity that people use. The power plants first create mechanical energy by harnessing the pressure of steam or flowing water to turn the shaft of a device called a *turbine*. The turning shaft drives an electric generator, which converts the mechanical energy into electricity.

An electric generator has a stationary part called a *stator* and a rotating part called a *rotor*. In the huge electric generators used in power plants, the stator consists of hundreds of windings of wire. The rotor is a large electromagnet that receives electricity from a small separate generator called an *exciter*. An external source of mechanical energy turns the rotor. The magnetic field created by the rotor turns as the rotor turns. As the magnetic field rotates, it produces an electric charge in the windings of the stator. This charge can then be transmitted as electric current. See ELECTRIC GENERATOR.

The major types of electric power plants are (1) fossil-fueled steam electric power plants, (2) hydroelectric power plants, and (3) nuclear power plants. Various other kinds of power plants produce smaller amounts of electricity.

Fossil-Fueled Steam Electric Power Plants generate about 67 per cent of the world's electric power and about 70 per cent of the electric power produced in the United States. Such plants burn coal, oil, or natural gas. These substances are called *fossil fuels* because they developed from *fossils* (the remains of prehistoric plants and animals). The fuel is burned in a *combustion chamber* to produce heat. The heat, in turn, is used to convert water to steam in a boiler. The steam then flows through a set of tubes in a device called a *superheater*. Hot combustion gases surround the steam-filled tubes in the superheater, increasing the temperature and pressure of the steam in the tubes.

The superheated, high-pressure steam is used to drive a huge steam turbine. A steam turbine has a series of wheels, each with many fanlike blades, mounted on a shaft. As the steam rushes through the turbine, it pushes against the blades, causing both the wheels and the turbine shaft to spin. The spinning shaft turns the rotor of the electric generator, thereby producing electricity. See TURBINE (Steam Turbines).

After the steam has passed through the turbine, it en-

ters a *condenser*. In the condenser, the steam passes around pipes carrying cool water. The water in the pipes absorbs heat from the steam. As the steam cools, it *condenses* into water. This water is then pumped back to the boiler to be turned into steam again.

At many power plants, the water in the condenser pipes, which has absorbed heat from the steam, is pumped to a *spray pond* or a *cooling tower* to be cooled. At a spray pond, the heated water is sent through nozzles that form a spray of droplets. The spray increases the surface area of the water that is exposed to the air, quickly cooling the water. A cooling tower has a series of decks. The heated water spills down from one deck to another, cooling as it comes into contact with the air. The cooled water is recycled through the condenser or discharged into a lake, river, or other body of water.

Fossil-fueled steam electric power plants are efficient and reliable. But they can cause pollution. Some power plants do not use cooling towers or spray ponds. Instead, they release heated water into lakes, ponds, rivers, or streams. Such *thermal pollution* may harm plant and animal life in these bodies of water. In many areas, laws limit the discharge of heated water by power plants.

The smoke from burning fossil fuels contains chemicals and tiny particles that cause air pollution if they are

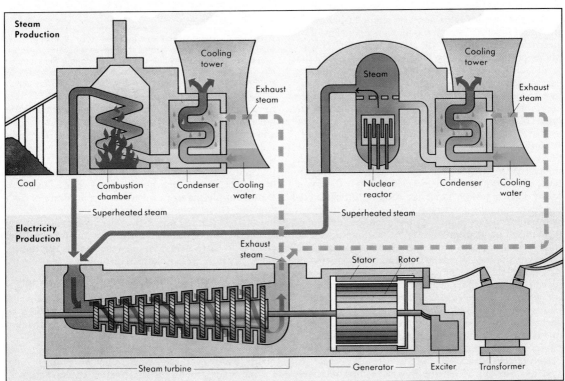

WORLD BOOK illustration by Oxford Illustrators Limited

Steam Electric Power Plants create steam by heating water in a nuclear reactor or in a combustion chamber, where coal, oil, or gas is burned. The steam turns a turbine that runs a generator. The generator has a rotating electromagnet called a *rotor* and a stationary part called a *stator*. A separate generator called an *exciter* powers the rotor, creating a magnetic field that produces an electric charge in the stator. The charge is transmitted as electricity. A transformer boosts the voltage. Exhaust steam passes cool water pipes in a condenser and turns back to water for reheating. The water that has absorbed the steam's heat in the condenser is piped to a cooling tower to be cooled.

released into the atmosphere. Most power plants that burn these fuels use pollution control equipment to limit the release of pollutants. However, the use of such equipment has not fully eliminated the air pollution created by plants that burn fossil fuels.

Hydroelectric Power Plants generate about 22 per cent of the world's electric power and about 15 per cent of the electricity produced in the United States. Such plants convert the energy of falling water into electric energy. A hydroelectric plant uses water that is stored in a reservoir behind a dam. The water flows through a tunnel or pipe to the plant's *water turbine*, or *hydraulic turbine*. As the water rushes through the turbine, it spins the turbine shaft, which drives the electric generator. See WATER POWER; TURBINE (Water Turbines).

Hydroelectric power plants called *pumped-storage hydroelectric plants* can store energy by operating in reverse. When the demand for electricity is low, such plants can use their generators as motors to turn the turbines. The turbines then function as pumps, raising water to the reservoir. The water can be used at a later time to produce electricity.

Hydroelectric power plants cost less to operate than fossil-fueled plants and do not pollute the air. The number of hydroelectric power plants is limited, however, by the availability of water power and suitable locations for dams and reservoirs.

Nuclear Power Plants generate about 11 per cent of the world's electric power and about 15 per cent of the electricity generated in the United States. Nuclear plants produce electricity in much the same way that fossil-fueled plants do. But instead of a fuel-burning combustion chamber, a nuclear power plant has a device called a *nuclear reactor*. A nuclear reactor produces enormous amounts of heat by *fissioning* (splitting) the nuclei of atoms of a heavy element. Most nuclear plants use the element uranium as the fuel in their reactors.

Heat from the nuclear fission is used to convert water into steam. The steam drives the steam turbine that runs the electric generator. After the steam has left the turbine, it is condensed and recycled through the plant. Many nuclear power plants use cooling towers to cool the water from the condenser pipes.

A nuclear power plant requires much less fuel than a fossil-fueled plant to produce an equal amount of electricity. Nuclear plants also cause much less air pollution. However, they contain dangerous radioactive materials. As a result, the plants must install special safety systems to help prevent and quickly deal with accidents that could cause the release of radiation. Nuclear power plants cost more to build than fossil-fueled plants, partly because of the expense of the safety systems. Nuclear plants also create radioactive wastes that remain hazardous for thousands of years and must be disposed of safely. See NUCLEAR ENERGY.

Other Sources of Electric Power produce relatively small amounts of electricity. *Geothermal power plants* use steam from the depths of the earth to run turbines that drive electric generators. Some power plants harness wind energy by using windmills to drive electric generators. A number of power plants use the energy of the ocean tides to turn turbines that run generators. A few power plants convert the sun's energy into electricity by

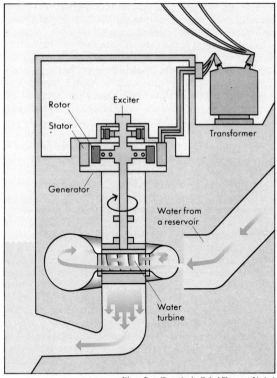

WORLD BOOK illustration by Oxford Illustrators Limited

A Hydroelectric Power Plant uses the force of falling water from a reservoir to turn a turbine that drives a generator. An exciter powers the rotor. As the rotor and its magnetic field turn, an electric charge is created in the stator. A transformer increases the voltage of the current coming from the stator.

means of devices called *solar cells*. Producing electric power with solar cells is expensive. However, scientists and engineers are studying ways to improve solar cells in order to produce large quantities of electric power more economically. See SOLAR ENERGY.

A number of electric power plants have gas turbines or diesel engines to drive auxiliary generators. Such generators supply the extra power needed in times of high demand. Diesel engines are also used to drive generators in isolated areas not served by power companies. Many hospitals, factories, and apartment buildings have diesel engines to drive generators in case the distribution of electricity from power plants is disrupted.

Transmitting and Distributing Electric Power

The electricity generated by power plants is transmitted to cities or other areas. It is then distributed to houses, factories, farms, offices, and other individual consumers.

Transmission. Most electricity travels from power plants along overhead wires called *transmission lines*. Laying underground or underwater cables generally costs more than stringing overhead wires. Cables are thus used far less frequently than overhead wires.

As electric current moves along transmission lines, the lines resist the current flow. The resistance causes the current to lose energy. Power plants limit energy losses by transmitting electricity at high voltages. As voltage is increased, the amount of current needed to transmit a particular amount of electric power decreases. Because less current is used, there is less resistance, and so less energy is lost.

Electric current may be either *direct current* (DC) or *alternating current* (AC). Direct current flows in only one direction. Alternating current reverses direction many times each second. It is easier to boost the voltage of alternating current than that of direct current. Alternating current is therefore easier to transmit than direct current. For this reason, electric power plants generate alternating current.

The typical power plant generator can produce about 1 million kilowatts of electric power at up to 22,000 volts. Devices called *step-up transformers* then boost this voltage as high as 765,000 volts for transmission.

Distribution. Some large industries require high-voltage current and receive it directly from transmission lines. But high-voltages are unsafe in homes, offices, and most factories. The voltage must therefore be decreased before electricity is distributed to them.

High-voltage electricity is carried by the transmission lines to *subtransmission substations* near the area where the power will be used. These substations have devices called *step-down transformers* that reduce the voltage to 12,500 to 138,000 volts. The voltage is then further reduced at *distribution substations* to 2,000 to 34,500 volts. *Distribution lines* may carry this medium-voltage current directly to commercial, industrial, or institutional users. Distribution lines also carry electric power to *distribution*

transformers on poles, on the ground, or in underground vaults. Distribution transformers reduce the voltage to the levels needed by most users. Wires from the transformers run to homes, stores, offices, and other users. Nearly all such consumers in the United States and Canada receive electric power at about 110 or 220 volts.

Providing Reliable Service. Equipment failures or damage caused by storms or accidents can interrupt local service of electric power. Such interruptions are known as *power blackouts*. Engineers called *load dispatchers* keep track of the flow of current through the transmission network. When a blackout occurs, the load dispatcher may restore service to the affected area by rerouting current along usable lines.

The demand for electricity often varies greatly from hour to hour. For example, sudden, dark storm clouds will increase demand for power because many lights will be turned on. The load dispatcher forecasts changes in demand and adjusts the generation and transmission of power accordingly. When demand exceeds the generating capacity of a power plant, the load dispatcher may reduce the voltage to prevent a blackout. Such a situation is called a *brownout*. A brownout may damage electrical equipment or cause it to operate less efficiently.

The transmission networks of most electric companies are interconnected, forming a *power pool*. Power pools enable companies to receive additional power from one

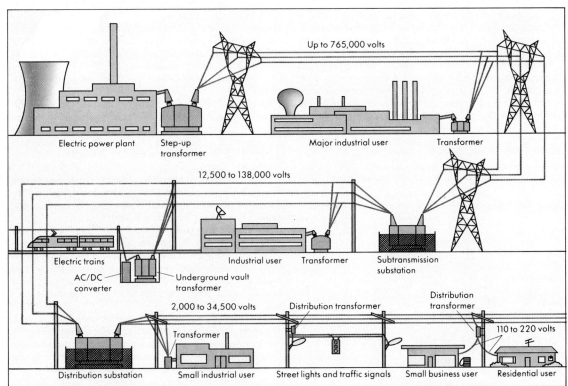

WORLD BOOK illustration by Oxford Illustrators Limited

An Electric Power Delivery System has power lines to carry current and transformers to change its voltage. Step-up transformers at power plants boost voltages so that current can be transmitted long distances. Substations and transformers reduce voltages to levels needed by consumers. Some industrial users and transportation systems that require high voltages have their own transformers.

ELECTRIC POWER

another in an emergency. Electric companies use computers to control the supply and flow of electricity through transmission networks.

The Electric Power Industry

Organizations that generate, transmit, or distribute electric power are called *electric utilities*. Nearly every electric utility is the sole supplier of electricity in a particular area. Government agencies regulate electric utilities to ensure that they serve the needs of the public. In some countries, the government owns all electric utilities. In other countries, stockholders or cooperatives as well as the government may own electric utilities.

In the United States, there are about 3,300 electric utilities. Stockholders own about 200 of them. These stockholder-owned electric companies account for about 75 per cent of the nation's generating capacity. City governments own about 1,900 electric utilities. The remaining utilities are owned by cooperatives, public power districts, or state or federal government organizations. Most cooperatives were established to supply electricity to rural areas not served by other electric utilities. Public power districts consist of several counties that jointly produce and distribute electricity.

One of the largest federal power projects is the Tennessee Valley Authority (TVA). The TVA's power plants generate more than 32 million kilowatts of power, which is distributed to several Southern states.

Local and state utility commissions set the rates that electric utilities charge their customers. A number of federal agencies govern the design and licensing of power plants, regulate the interstate sale of electric power, and set and enforce pollution control standards.

In Canada, the governments of the various provinces own most major electric utilities. However, stockholders own large electric utilities in Alberta and Prince Edward Island. Provincial public utility boards regulate Canada's electric utilities. The federal Atomic Energy Control Board oversees the nation's nuclear energy industry. The National Utility Board controls the export of electric power. About 9 per cent of the electricity generated in Canada is sold in the United States.

History

Early Developments. One of the earliest practical uses of electric power was to light the lamps of lighthouses. In 1858, South Foreland Lighthouse near Dover, England, became the first electric lighthouse. Its generator powered an *arc lamp*. An arc lamp produces bright light by means of an electric arc (see ELECTRIC ARC). Beginning in the 1870's, arc lamps illuminated such places as railroad stations, factories, and public squares in major cities in Europe and the United States.

In 1879, the California Electric Light Company in San Francisco began operating the world's first central power plant that sold electricity to private customers. Also in 1879, the American inventor Thomas A. Edison perfected a lamp that glowed and gave off light when a filament in the lamp was heated by an electric current. Edison's *incandescent* lamp burned much longer than an arc lamp, and it quickly created a growing demand for electricity. In 1882, Edison opened the Pearl Street Station, a steam electric power plant, in New York City. Shortly after it opened, the plant was providing direct current to light more than 1,000 incandescent lamps. In 1895, hydroelectric generators at Niagara Falls began providing industries in the area with electric power.

Growth of the Electric Power Industry. By the end of the 1800's, there were over 3,600 electric utilities in the United States. However, they did not all provide electricity at the same voltages. Studies conducted by electrical engineers in 1891 resulted in the standardization of voltages. Utilities could then form power pools by interconnecting their transmission lines.

By the early 1930's, electric utilities served about two-thirds of the U.S. population. But only about 10 per cent of U.S. farms had electricity. President Franklin D. Roosevelt established the Rural Electrification Administration (REA) in 1935 to expand electric service in rural areas. Today, nearly all American farms have electricity. Half the farms are served by REA-financed electric power systems.

The first full-scale nuclear power plant began operation in 1956 at Calder Hall in northwestern England. In 1966, the world's first tidal power plant opened on the Rance River near St.-Malo, France.

Electric Power Today. The demand for electric power continues to grow. Power companies must plan carefully for expansion to meet the ever-increasing demand. However, construction of new power plants is costly and takes several years. Many planned nuclear power plants in the United States have been canceled because of soaring construction costs.

The supply of fossil fuels will eventually run out. However, many scientists believe that energy from the earth, sun, wind, and oceans can be used more extensively to produce electric power cheaply and efficiently in the future. Some utilities have already begun to use solar, geothermal, tidal, or wind power in addition to regular energy sources to generate electricity. The utilities have thereby increased their generating capacity while avoiding some environmental hazards created by fossil-fueled and nuclear plants.　　　　M. E. EL-HAWARY

Leading Electric Power Producing Countries

Kilowatt-hours of electric power produced each year

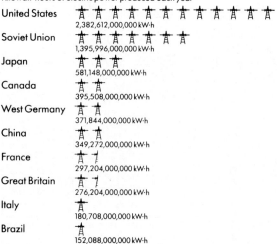

United States	2,382,612,000,000 kW·h
Soviet Union	1,395,996,000,000 kW·h
Japan	581,148,000,000 kW·h
Canada	395,508,000,000 kW·h
West Germany	371,844,000,000 kW·h
China	349,272,000,000 kW·h
France	297,204,000,000 kW·h
Great Britain	276,204,000,000 kW·h
Italy	180,708,000,000 kW·h
Brazil	152,088,000,000 kW·h

Source: Monthly Bulletin of Statistics, October 1984, UN. Figures are for 1983; 1982 for Japan and Brazil.

A. Tessore, Shostal

Members of the Ethiopian Orthodox Church, the country's chief Christian faith, take part in Timkat—an annual religious festival. Most Ethiopians are either Christians or Muslims.

ETHIOPIA is a country in northeastern Africa. It borders the Red Sea in the north. Southern and western Ethiopia extend far into the interior of Africa.

The name *Ethiopia* comes from a Greek word meaning *sunburned faces.* The ancient Greeks applied the word to people living south of Egypt—including in Ethiopia—because the people had darker skin than the Greeks did. Ethiopia was formerly often called *Abyssinia.* Some people think this name came from an Arabic word meaning *mixed,* a reference to the fact that many ethnic groups make up Ethiopia's population. Other people believe it came from the name of an early Ethiopian tribe. Most Ethiopians are classified into one of two large groups—Semites and Cushites—depending on the language they speak.

Much of Ethiopia consists of rugged mountains and a high, fertile plateau. The country's Red Sea coast ranks among the hottest places in the world. Droughts have occurred in Ethiopia from time to time. In the mid-1970's and mid-1980's, droughts helped cause severe famines, which led to large numbers of deaths.

Ethiopia is one of the oldest African nations. According to tradition, the first emperor of Ethiopia, Menelik I, was the son of the Biblical Queen of Sheba and King Solomon of Israel. Many later Ethiopian rulers claimed descent from Solomon and Sheba. Emperors or kings ruled Ethiopia for about 2,000 years. In 1974, Ethiopian military leaders overthrew Emperor Haile Selassie and took control of the government.

Government

Ethiopia operates under military rule. The country has no legislature.

National Government of Ethiopia is headed by the chairman of a committee of military leaders. This group is called the Provisional Military Administrative Council, or *Dergue* (also spelled *Derg*). A Council of Ministers appointed by the Dergue carries out government policies. Some of the ministers are also military leaders. The

Workers' Party of Ethiopia, which is controlled by the Dergue, is Ethiopia's only legal political party. The chairman of the Dergue heads the party and also heads the armed forces. A number of illegal parties operate in various parts of the country.

Local Government. Ethiopia is divided into 14 administrative regions for purposes of local government. A governor heads each region. Most of the governors are members of the Dergue and are appointed by that body. Peasants' and urban dwellers' associations play important roles in Ethiopian local government. The associations help preserve law and order.

Courts. The Supreme Court is Ethiopia's highest court. It hears appeals from the High Court, the second highest court. The peasants' and urban dwellers' associations serve as courts for a variety of minor civil and criminal cases.

Armed Forces. About 306,000 people serve in Ethiopia's armed forces. The armed forces include a large army, a small navy, and a small air force. The army consists of a regular force and a *militia* (group of citizen soldiers). Citizens from 18 to 30 years of age may be drafted to serve in the armed forces.

People

Population, Ancestry, and Languages. Ethiopia has a population of about 44 million. Among Africa's nations, only Nigeria and Egypt have more people. About four-fifths of Ethiopia's people live in rural areas and about one-fifth in urban areas. Addis Ababa, Ethiopia's largest city, has about 1,413,000 people.

Ethiopians are descended chiefly from three groups of people. These groups are brown-skinned people who resembled Europeans, black Africans, and people from the Arabian Peninsula. Today, most Ethiopians have brown skin and physical features that range from European to black African.

Most Ethiopians are classified into two large groups based on the languages they speak. The groups are the

Facts in Brief

Capital: Addis Ababa.

Official Language: Amharic.

Form of Government: Military rule.

Area: 471,800 sq. mi. (1,221,900 km²). *Greatest Distances*—north-south, 1,020 mi. (1,642 km); east-west, 1,035 mi. (1,666 km). *Coastline*—628 mi. (1,011 km).

Elevation: *Highest*—Ras Dashen, 15,158 ft. (4,620 m) above sea level. *Lowest*—Denakil Depression, 381 ft. (116 m) below sea level.

Population: *Estimated 1986 Population*—44,233,000; distribution, 82 per cent rural, 18 per cent urban; density, 94 persons per sq. mi. (36 per km²). *1984 Census*—42,019,418. *Estimated 1991 Population*—51,627,000.

Chief Products: *Agriculture*—coffee, corn, oilseeds, sorghum, sugar cane, teff, wheat. *Manufacturing*—cement, cigarettes, processed food, refined petroleum products, shoes, textiles.

National Anthem: "Whedefit Gesgeshi Woude Henate Ethiopia" ("March Forward, Dear Mother Ethiopia, Bloom and Flourish").

Flag: Three horizontal stripes—green, yellow, and red (top to bottom). See FLAG (picture: Flags of Africa).

Money: *Basic Unit*—Birr. See MONEY (table: Exchange Rates).

ETHIOPIA

Semites (people who speak Semitic languages) and the *Cushites* (people who speak Cushitic languages). The Semites live mainly in northern and central Ethiopia. They include the Amhara, Tigre, and Gurage. The Cushites live chiefly in southern and eastern Ethiopia. They include the Afar (also called Danakil), Somali, and Oromo (also called Galla).

People of mostly black African ancestry live along Ethiopia's western border. They speak languages of the Nilo-Saharan family and make up about 5 per cent of Ethiopia's population. The population also includes several thousand Ethiopian Jews known as *Falashas* or *Beta Israel*. These people are sometimes called *Black Jews* because, like other Ethiopians, they have dark skin. They formerly spoke a Cushitic language, but now speak Semitic ones.

More than 70 languages and 200 dialects are spoken in Ethiopia. Amharic, a Semitic language, is the country's official language. Amharic is spoken by about half of the people. Many Ethiopians speak English or Arabic in addition to their own languages. Ge'ez (also called Ethiopic) is an ancient Ethiopian language. In the past, all Ethiopian Bibles were written in it. Ge'ez is still used in ceremonies of the Ethiopian Orthodox Church.

Way of Life. Most rural Ethiopians live in villages or isolated homesteads. Their lives differ little from those led by their ancestors hundreds of years ago. The majority of the rural people are farmers who work the land with wooden plows pulled by oxen. The rural population also includes nomads, who make their living chiefly by raising livestock.

Poverty is widespread in Ethiopia's rural areas. Each year, large numbers of rural people move to urban areas to try to find jobs. Poverty also exists in the urban areas. But in general the urban people are better off economically than the rural people. Also, schools, medical care, and such modern living comforts as electricity are more widely available in the urban areas.

Most Ethiopians live in round huts that have walls made of wooden frames plastered with mud. The huts have cone-shaped roofs of thatched straw or, occasionally, metal sheeting. Many people in areas where stone is plentiful live in rectangular stone houses. In addition to traditional housing, Ethiopian towns and cities have many modern buildings. Addis Ababa has a number of modern apartment buildings and several skyscrapers.

Many Ethiopian men and women wear one-piece cloths called *shammas*. Most shammas are made of a thin, white cotton fabric. Some people in southern Ethiopia wear leather clothing. Many Ethiopians—especially urban people—wear Western-style clothing.

A thick and spicy stew called *wat* is a popular food

Ethiopia

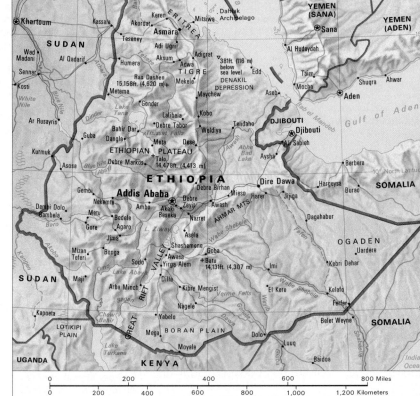

International boundary
Road
Railroad
Seasonal stream
Swamp
⊛ National capital
• Other city or town
+ Elevation above sea level

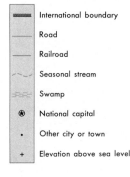

WORLD BOOK map

574

among Ethiopians. The people make wat from meat and vegetables and often add eggs to it. They usually eat wat by picking it up with pieces of slightly sour pancake-shaped bread called *injera*. Popular beverages include beer, coffee, and tea.

Favorite sports in Ethiopia include soccer, tennis, and volleyball. Ethiopians also enjoy playing card games, and a type of chess and other board games. Many people hold special feasts to celebrate such events as baptisms, weddings, and religious holidays.

Religion. As many as 50 per cent of Ethiopia's people belong to the Ethiopian Orthodox Church, a Christian faith. About 40 per cent of the people are Muslims. The Beta Israel practice a form of Judaism. Most of the rest of the people practice traditional African religions.

Education. Ethiopian children are not required by law to attend school. About 46 per cent of the children attend elementary school, but only about 12 per cent attend high school. Ethiopia has two universities. They are the University of Addis Ababa—which has branches in several towns—and the University of Asmara.

The Arts. Much of the country's art is related to the Ethiopian Orthodox religion. In the past, many artists painted church walls with Biblical scenes and pictures of saints. Artists also illustrated religious manuscripts with elaborate decorations. Writers created religious poetry and other sacred works in the Ge'ez language.

Since the early 1900's, Ethiopian writers have produced novels, plays, and poetry in Amharic and other modern Ethiopian languages. Modern artists have created murals, paintings, and stained-glass windows that incorporate Western styles.

Land and Climate

Ethiopia has an area of about 471,800 square miles (1,221,900 square kilometers). The Ethiopian Plateau covers much of the western and central parts of the country. Lowlands surround the plateau.

The Ethiopian Plateau spreads out over about two-thirds of the country. It lies between 6,000 and 10,000 feet (1,800 and 3,000 meters) above sea level. Most of

Ethiopia's people live on the plateau, which has the country's best agricultural land. Most of the plateau receives more than 40 inches (102 centimeters) of rain annually. Average temperatures range from about 72° F. (22° C) in areas below 8,000 feet (2,400 meters) to less than 60° F. (16° C) at higher altitudes.

The Great Rift Valley, which runs north and south through eastern Africa, divides the plateau into two large sections. The sections are further divided by deep, spectacular river gorges and high mountain ranges. Ethiopia's highest mountain, Ras Dashen, rises 15,158 feet (4,620 meters) above sea level on the plateau.

The Lowlands. The Ethiopian Plateau slopes downward in all directions toward lowland regions. Most of the lowland areas have an average temperature of about 80° F. (27° C) and receive less than 20 inches (51 centimeters) of rain a year. Scorching hot deserts lie in the lowlands of northeastern Ethiopia. Temperatures sometimes rise above 120° F. (49° C) there. The lowlands are thinly populated because of the hot, dry climate and because the soil is poor for farming.

Rivers and Lakes. Ethiopia's chief rivers include the Awash, Baro, Blue Nile (called Abay in Ethiopia), Genale, Omo, and Wabe Shebele. Lake Tana, the country's largest lake, lies in the northwest. A series of lakes extends through southern Ethiopia along the Great Rift Valley. The lakes include Abaya and Ziway.

Animal Life and Vegetation. A wide variety of wild animals live in Ethiopia. The animals include antelope, elephants, giraffes, lions, monkeys, and rhinoceroses. Grasslands spread out over much of the Ethiopian Plateau, as well as many lowland areas in the south and east. Tropical rain forests cover parts of southwestern Ethiopia. Coffee bushes also grow wild in highland forests of the southwest.

Economy

Ethiopia has a developing economy. Agriculture is the chief economic activity. But many farmers struggle

E. Streichan, Shostal

Addis Ababa, the capital and largest city of Ethiopia, has many modern buildings. An important Ethiopian economic center, the city also hosts many international African conferences.

Zweli, Gamma/Liaison

Rural Ethiopians live in villages or isolated homesteads. The people above live in the Bale region of southern Ethiopia. The round huts, *background,* are typical rural Ethiopian dwellings.

just to raise enough food for their families. Droughts occur from time to time and sometimes result in famine. Agriculture employs about 85 per cent of the country's workers. About 5 per cent of the workers have jobs in manufacturing, and about 10 per cent in service industries, such as banking, government, insurance, and tourism. Mining and fishing are minor economic activities. The government has much control over the economy.

Agriculture. Most Ethiopian farmers produce goods chiefly for their own use. The main crops include wheat, corn, sorghum, and a kind of grain called teff. Many farmers in the southwest produce coffee for sale. Other crops grown for sale include oilseeds and sugar cane. Most Ethiopian farmers also raise cattle, goats, sheep, and chickens. The Ethiopian government owns all farmland in the country and limits each farm family to no more than 25 acres (10 hectares) of land. The government also operates large state farms.

Farmers make use of only a small part of the land suitable for agriculture in Ethiopia. Improvements in farming equipment and methods, marketing, and transportation are needed to increase agricultural output.

Manufacturing. The production of textiles ranks as Ethiopia's chief manufacturing activity. Other products include cement, cigarettes, processed foods, and shoes. A refinery in the coastal town of Aseb refines petroleum produced in other countries. Most of the largest factories are owned by the Ethiopian government.

Foreign Trade. Coffee, hides and skins, and oilseeds rank among Ethiopia's chief exports. Imports include chemicals, crude petroleum, and machinery. Ethiopia's chief trading partners include Italy, Japan, the United States, West Germany, and the Soviet Union.

Transportation and Communication. Ethiopia has about 25,000 miles (40,000 kilometers) of roads, most of which are unpaved. The country has two railroads. One helps connect Addis Ababa with the foreign port city of Djibouti. The other links the cities of Keren and Asmara with the Red Sea port of Mitsiwa. International airports operate at Addis Ababa and Asmara. Aseb and Mitsiwa are Ethiopia's seaports. But much of the country's foreign trade takes place through Djibouti.

There are about 3 million radios and about 40,000 television sets in Ethiopia. Three daily newspapers are published in the country, two in Amharic and one in English.

History

Early Days. Some of the oldest fossil fragments of human beings have been found in Ethiopia. They date from about 2 million years ago. By the 400's B.C., two major groups—the Cushites and the Semites—inhabited the area. The Cushites were farmers or nomadic shepherds. The Semites were farmers or traders.

The Aksum Kingdom was the first important state in what is now Ethiopia. It was well established by the A.D. 200's, and had its capital at the city of Aksum. The Aksum Kingdom gained much wealth through trade with Arabia, Egypt, Greece, India, Persia, and Rome. The Aksumites exported gold, ivory, and spices.

Aksum reached its height of power in the 300's under King Ezana. Ezana made Christianity the official religion of Aksum. In the 600's, Aksum's power declined sharply after Muslims gained control of Arabia, the Red Sea, and the coast of northern Africa. The Muslims, religious enemies of Christian Aksum, put an end to the kingdom's foreign trade.

The Zagwé Dynasty. In 1137, the Zagwé *dynasty* (series of rulers) rose to power on the Ethiopian Plateau. The Zagwé rulers had their capital at Roha—now called Lalibela. During the reign of the Zagwé emperors, 11 magnificent churches were carved out of solid rock at Roha. The churches still stand. In 1270, Yekuno Amlak overthrew the Zagwé dynasty. After the 1500's, the Ethiopian Empire broke up into a number of small kingdoms.

Menelik II, who became emperor in 1889, reunified the Ethiopian Empire by gaining control of many of the small kingdoms. In 1896, at the Battle of Adwa, Menelik defeated an Italian army that had occupied part of

© Karl Muller, Woodfin Camp, Inc.

The Spectacular Tisissat Falls is formed by waters of the Blue Nile River. The falls is on the Ethiopian Plateau, about 20 miles (32 kilometers) southeast of Lake Tana.

Zweli, Gamma/Liaison

Rural Ethiopians Use Camels to carry supplies home from market, *above.* Many people must travel long distances on foot to get to and from their market.

Farm Workers tend a crop of young coffee plants. Many farmers in the southwest produce coffee, which ranks among Ethiopia's chief exports.

Louise Grubb, Gamma/Liaison

Ethiopia. This victory earned him much respect and helped increase his power in Ethiopia. Menelik made Addis Ababa the capital and began the construction of a railway that, when completed, linked Addis Ababa to Djibouti. He also established the first modern schools and hospitals in Ethiopia.

In 1913, Lij Iyasu, Menelik's grandson, became emperor of Ethiopia. An unpopular ruler, Iyasu was removed from power in 1916 by Ethiopians with the help of Great Britain, France, and Italy. These countries opposed Iyasu because he sided against them in World War I, which began in 1914. Zauditu, Menelik's daughter, then became empress of Ethiopia. She ruled with the help of Ras Tafari, the son of Menelik's cousin. Tafari was named heir to the throne.

Haile Selassie. Zauditu died in 1930. Tafari then became emperor and took the title Haile Selassie I. He continued Menelik's policy of modernizing Ethiopia. In 1931, he gave the country its first written constitution.

Italy invaded Ethiopia in 1935 in an attempt to expand its colonies in Africa. In 1936, the Italians conquered Addis Ababa and Haile Selassie fled to Great Britain. In 1941, during World War II, British troops helped the Ethiopians drive the Italians out of Ethiopia. Haile Selassie then returned to the throne.

Eritrea, an Ethiopian area along the Red Sea, had been captured by Italy in the late 1800's. In 1952, Ethiopia regained control of the area. In the early 1960's, Eritrean rebels demanded independence for Eritrea. The Ethiopian government rejected the demand, and civil war broke out between the rebels and Ethiopian government troops. The Ogaden region of southeastern Ethiopia also became a trouble spot in the 1960's. The government of neighboring Somalia claimed the region. Large numbers of Somali people live there, and they revolted against Ethiopian rule. Troops from Somalia invaded Ethiopia in the late 1970's, but they were driven back.

Military Take-Over. In the 1960's, many Ethiopians became dissatisfied with Haile Selassie's government. They demanded better living conditions for the poor and an end to government corruption. In the early 1970's, severe drought led to famine in northeastern Ethiopia. Haile Selassie's critics claimed that the government did not give enough aid to victims of the famine. In 1974, Ethiopian military leaders took control of the government and removed Haile Selassie from power.

The military government adopted socialist policies and established close relations with the Soviet Union. The military leaders killed many of their Ethiopian opponents. In the early 1980's, heavy fighting broke out between the Ethiopian government and rebels in the Tigre region of northern Ethiopia.

Ethiopia Today. The military government continues to face rebellions in many areas of the country, including the Eritrea and Tigre regions. In 1984, the government established a party called the Workers' Party of Ethiopia and made it the country's only legal political party.

In the mid-1980's, severe famine again struck Ethiopia. It led to widespread starvation, malnutrition, and disease. Hundreds of thousands of Ethiopians died as a result of the famine.   RICHARD PANKHURST

Related Articles in WORLD BOOK include:

Addis Ababa	Eritrea
Africa (picture: Islam and Christianity)	Great Rift Valley
	Haile Selassie I
Aksum	Hamites
Asmara	Helmet
Clothing (picture: Traditional Costumes)	Italo-Ethiopian War
	Lake Tana
Culture (picture: Different Cultures Have Different Customs)	Prester John
	Semites

Additional Resources

AMERICAN UNIVERSITY. *Ethiopia: A Country Study*. U.S. Government Printing Office, 1981.

ULLENDORF, EDWARD. *The Ethiopians: An Introduction to Country and People*. 3rd ed. Oxford, 1973.

CUOMO, MARIO MATTHEW

CUOMO, *KWOH moh,* **MARIO MATTHEW** (1932-   ), gained national attention as the governor of New York. Cuomo, a Democrat, was elected to the governorship in 1982. He was the first Italian-American elected to that office. A powerful orator, Cuomo established himself as a potential presidential candidate when he delivered a stirring address at the 1984 Democratic National Convention.

State of New York

Mario Cuomo

Cuomo was born in New York City. He received a bachelor's degree in 1953 from St. John's College (now St. John's University). In 1956, Cuomo received a law degree from St. John's. From 1956 to 1958, he served as a legal assistant to Judge Adrian Burke of New York's Court of Appeals, the state's highest court. Cuomo then entered private law practice.

Cuomo first attracted public attention in 1972, when he settled a bitter housing dispute between blacks and Jews in Queens, N.Y. Governor Hugh L. Carey of New York appointed him secretary of state in 1975. Cuomo won election as lieutenant governor of New York in 1978. Four years later, he defeated Republican Lewis Lehrman to become governor.   GERALD BENJAMIN

DINE, JIM (1935-   ), is an American artist. Dine is sometimes associated with the pop art movement, which emerged in the United States during the 1960's.

Like the pop artists, Dine has painted realistic pictures of familiar everyday objects, such as articles of clothing and gardening equipment. But Dine's style tends to be more personal than theirs. Sometimes he has added actual objects to his paintings or placed real objects in front of his paintings. For example, in *Black Bathroom No. 2* (1962), Dine attached a sink to a canvas painted black to represent a bathroom wall. Dine repeats certain images in many of his works. These images include a bathrobe and a necktie. In some paintings, he features the tools and equipment of professional house painters, such as brushes and color paint charts.

James Dine was born in Cincinnati, Ohio. In 1959, he moved to New York City, where he began to exhibit his paintings. Dine has also gained recognition as a printmaker, especially in the fields of lithography and silkscreen printing. In addition, he has created sculptures, collages, and book illustrations, and has designed sets and costumes for plays.   ANN LEE MORGAN

DE NIRO, *duh NEER oh,* **ROBERT** (1943-   ), is an American motion-picture actor. He is best known for his portrayals of intense, psychologically troubled characters. He received the 1980 Academy Award as best actor for his portrayal of boxer Jake LaMotta in *Raging Bull.* He also won the 1974 Academy Award as best supporting actor for his performance as gangster boss Vito Corleone in *The Godfather, Part II.* De Niro received Academy Award nominations as best actor for his roles as a Vietnam War veteran in *The Deer Hunter* (1979), and as a mentally disturbed killer in *Taxi Driver* (1976).

Paramount Pictures Corporation

Robert De Niro

De Niro was born in New York City. He studied under the famous acting teachers Lee Strasberg and Stella Adler, and appeared in several plays in New York City before making his film debut in 1968 in *Greetings.* De Niro's other films include *Mean Streets* (1973), *Bang the Drum Slowly* (1973), *The King of Comedy* (1983), and *Falling in Love* (1984).   JOHN F. MARIANI

GARNEAU, *gar NOH,* **MARC** (1949-   ), was the first Canadian to travel in space. Garneau, a commander in the Royal Canadian Navy, accompanied six American astronauts on a mission aboard the United States space shuttle *Challenger* from Oct. 5 to 13, 1984. He conducted 10 scientific experiments for the Canadian government on the flight.

Garneau was born in Quebec City, Que. His father, André Garneau, made a career of the Canadian armed forces and became a general. At the age of 16, Marc Garneau enrolled at the Collège militaire royal de Saint-Jean. Garneau received a bachelor's degree in engineering physics from the Royal Military College of Canada and a doctor's degree in electrical engineering from the Imperial College of Science and Technology in London. Garneau began his naval career in 1965. He be-

NASA

Marc Garneau

black bathroom #2

Art Gallery of Ontario, Toronto, Gift of Mr. and Mrs. M. H. Rapp, 1966

Jim Dine's *Black Bathroom No. 2* consists of a bathroom sink projecting from a partially painted canvas. Many of Dine's works combine everyday objects with painting.

came a leading authority on naval communications and warfare systems. Garneau was selected as one of six Canadian astronauts in 1983. Kendal Windeyer

GLASS, PHILIP (1937-), is an American composer. His works combine elements of rock music, the music of Africa and India, and classical Western music. In the late 1960's, Glass and fellow American composers Steve Reich, La Monte Young, and Terry Riley began to compose in a musical style called *minimalism*. Minimalism often uses repeated short patterns of music with complex rhythmic variations but simple harmonies.

Glass formed a chamber music group called the Philip Glass Ensemble to perform his compositions. The ensemble, which began performing in 1968, consists of amplified instruments. Glass himself performs on electronic keyboards.

Glass frequently collaborates with artists in dance and drama. With playwright and director Robert Wilson, he created the opera *Einstein on the Beach* (1976). The opera is loosely based on the life of scientist Albert Einstein. *Akhnaten* (1984), another Glass opera, deals with an Egyptian pharaoh and religious reformer of the 1300's B.C. He has also collaborated with a number of famous choreographers, including Jerome Robbins and Twyla Tharp.

Glass was born in Baltimore. As a child, he studied the flute at the Peabody Conservatory of Music. He later attended the University of Chicago and the Juilliard School of Music. In Paris, Glass worked briefly with the Indian musician Ravi Shankar, who strongly influenced his music. Vincent McDermott

HUGHES, TED (1930-), is an English poet known for his violent and symbolic nature poems. Hughes was appointed poet laureate of England in 1984.

Hughes's first collection of poetry, *The Hawk in the Rain* (1957), portrays in powerful and descriptive language the beauty and brutality he saw in nature. Hughes's reputation increased after he published a long cycle of lyrics dominated by a menacing bird called Crow. The bird is a composite symbol taken from several mythical and religious traditions. The Crow poems were published in five volumes in 1970 and 1971. The best-known work in the cycle is *Crow: From the Life and Songs of the Crow* (1970). Hughes continued his mythical themes in *Cave Birds* (1975). Hughes's later nature poems, beginning with *Moortown* (1980), carry a note of hope and affirmation absent from his previous work.

Edward James Hughes was born in Mytholmroyd in West Yorkshire. The birds and other animals Hughes observed on the moors near his home strongly influenced the content and imagery of his poetry. Hughes was married to the American poet Sylvia Plath from 1956 until her suicide in 1963. Elmer Borklund

IACOCCA, *eye uh KOH kuh*, **LEE** (1924-), is an American automobile executive. As chairman of the board of the Chrysler Corporation, Iacocca helped save the company from bankruptcy. He reduced company spending and helped persuade the United States government in 1980 to guarantee 1\frac{1}{2}$ billion in private loans to Chrysler. Chrysler repaid the loans in 1983.

Iacocca began his career in 1946 with the Ford Motor Company. He joined Ford as an engineer, but soon switched to sales. In 1960, he became a general manager and vice president. Iacocca headed the team of engineers and designers who developed the Ford Mustang.

Chrysler Corporation
Lee Iacocca

The Mustang was introduced in 1964 and it quickly became one of the most popular cars ever made. In 1965, Iacocca was named vice president of Ford's corporate car and truck group. From 1970 to 1978, he served as president of the company. In 1978, Iacocca became president of Chrysler Corporation, and in 1979, he was named Chrysler's chairman and chief executive officer.

Iacocca was born in Allentown, Pa., and was christened Lido Anthony. He received a B.S. degree from Lehigh University in 1945 and an M.S. degree from Princeton University in 1946. William H. Becker

LANG, FRITZ (1890?-1976), was a motion-picture director who made classic horror and suspense films in both Germany and the United States. Lang first gained recognition in Germany for his silent films about the corruption of society by criminals and mad scientists. The most important of these movies were *Dr. Mabuse, the Gambler* (1922), *Metropolis* (1926), and *Spies* (1928). Lang's first sound film, *M* (1931), describes the search for an insane killer of children.

Lang fled Germany in 1933 rather than direct motion pictures for the Nazis, and he settled in the United States. His best American films all concern a man being pursued by an evil force that drives him to desperation. For example, *Fury* (1936), Lang's first American film, deals with a man threatened by a lynch mob. *The Big Heat* (1953) portrays a man's battle against gangsters. Lang's other American movies include *You Only Live Once* (1937), *The Return of Frank James* (1940), *Man Hunt* (1941), *The Ministry of Fear* (1944), *The Woman in the Window* (1945), and *Rancho Notorious* (1952).

Lang was born in Vienna. He directed his first motion picture in 1919. John F. Mariani

LEAN, SIR DAVID (1908-) is a highly acclaimed English motion-picture director. He won Academy Awards as best director for *The Bridge on the River Kwai* (1957) and *Lawrence of Arabia* (1962).

Lean was born in Croydon. He began his motion-picture career in London at the age of 19. He performed a variety of duties before becoming a successful film editor in the mid-1930's. Lean made his debut as a director in *In Which We Serve* (1942), which he co-directed with English playwright Sir Noel Coward. The movie won praise for its portrayal of the heroism of British sailors during World War II (1939-1945).

Lean directed two movies adapted from the novels of Charles Dickens, *Great Expectations* (1946) and *Oliver Twist* (1948). He also directed the comedy fantasy *Blithe Spirit* (1945), the love stories *Brief Encounter* (1945) and *Summertime* (1955), the Russian historical epic *Dr. Zhivago* (1965), and the Asian drama *A Passage to India* (1984). Lean produced and directed *The Sound Barrier* (1952), an exciting aviation drama. He was knighted by Queen Elizabeth II in 1984. John F. Mariani

James Levine

LEVINE, *leh VYN,* **JAMES** (1943-   ), is an American conductor and pianist. He became principal conductor of the Metropolitan Opera in New York City in 1973 and the company's music director in 1976. He was scheduled to become artistic director in 1986.

Levine was born in Cincinnati and began piano lessons at the age of 4. He made his debut as a soloist at the age of 10, performing with the Cincinnati Symphony Orchestra. From 1964 to 1970, he was apprentice conductor and then assistant conductor of the Cleveland Orchestra. Levine made his Metropolitan Opera debut in 1971. Since 1973, he has been music director of the summer Ravinia Festival near Chicago. He also conducts at the annual Bayreuth Festival in West Germany and the Salzburg Festival in Austria. Levine has been a guest conductor of the Berlin Philharmonic and the London Symphony Orchestra.   LEONARD W. VAN CAMP

ROSENQUIST, *ROH zuhn kwihst,* **JAMES ALBERT** (1933-   ), an American painter and sculptor, gained fame as a leader of the pop art movement during the 1960's. Rosenquist is best known for the extremely large canvases he painted using the style of billboard and outdoor sign art. This style includes the use of bright colors and magnified but realistic images of everyday scenes and objects.

Rosenquist's most famous work, *F-111* (1965), is a mural 86 feet (26 meters) long. It includes realistic images of an F-111 fighter airplane, a little girl under a hairdrier, a light bulb, a mass of spaghetti, and an umbrella. In many of his sculptures, Rosenquist combines realistic painted images with actual objects in unusual ways, but the subjects remain recognizable. He also mixes a number of materials in his sculptures. For example, *Capillary Action II* (1963) consists of metal, neon, paint, plastic, and wood.

Rosenquist was born in Grand Forks, N. Dak. During the 1950's, he was a commercial artist, painting gas tanks and billboards.   ANN LEE MORGAN

See also POP ART.

RUDOLPH, PAUL (1918-   ), is an American architect. He is best known for his dramatic and complex designs, especially for urban and academic environments. Rudolph's imaginative use of concrete and the absence of ornamentation in his exteriors show the influence of the modern French architect Le Corbusier (see LE CORBUSIER).

Rudolph served as chairman of the architecture department at Yale University in New Haven, Conn., from 1958 to 1965. Several of his important buildings are in New Haven. His most controversial work is the Art and Architecture Building (1963) at Yale, a complicated, 9-story building with 36 interior levels. The Temple Street parking garage (1963) is an example of his skill in integrating structures into urban settings. It is also an attempt to turn a simple, functional building

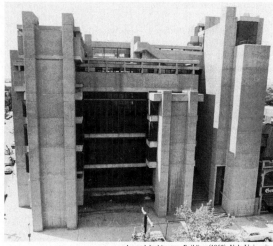

A Building by Paul Rudolph serves as the home of the schools of art and architecture at Yale University. The building features an exterior of glass and roughly textured concrete. The absence of ornamentation is typical of the architect's designs.

into an object of beauty. In the 1960's, Rudolph began to design low-cost, prefabricated residential buildings, such as Crawford Manor (1966) in New Haven. Rudolph was born in Elkton, Ky.   NICHOLAS ADAMS

TUTU, *TOO too,* **DESMOND** (1931-   ), is a South African civil rights leader and Anglican bishop. He has worked to end South Africa's strict racial segregation policy, known as *apartheid*. This policy prohibits blacks from mixing with whites in most activities, including education, employment, housing, and politics. Tutu has threatened to ask other nations to limit trade and investment activities in South Africa unless the government eliminates apartheid. He won the 1984 Nobel Peace Prize for his nonviolent campaign against apartheid. Also in 1984, Tutu became the first black to be elected Anglican bishop of Johannesburg, South Africa.

Tutu was born in Klerksdorp, South Africa. In 1961, he was ordained an Anglican priest. During the mid-1960's, Tutu received degrees in divinity and theology from King's College in London. He

Desmond Tutu

worked as an educator during the early 1970's. In 1975, he became Anglican dean of Johannesburg. From 1976 to 1978, Tutu served as bishop of Lesotho, a small country surrounded by South Africa. From 1978 to 1984, he was general secretary of the South African Council of Churches.   ROBERT I. ROTBERG

Dictionary
Supplement

1985

This section lists important words from the 1986 edition of THE WORLD BOOK DICTIONARY. This dictionary, first published in 1963, keeps abreast of our living language with a program of continuous editorial revision. The following supplement has been prepared under the direction of the editors of THE WORLD BOOK ENCYCLOPEDIA and Clarence L. Barnhart, editor in chief of THE WORLD BOOK DICTIONARY. It is presented as a service to owners of the dictionary and as an informative feature to subscribers to THE WORLD BOOK YEAR BOOK.

A a

anchor[1], **5** *U.S.* a department store, convention center, or other project large enough to make a shopping or business area around it safe for investment: *With the confidence provided by the anchor, the neighborhood often flourishes* (New Yorker). *The anchor tenant also acts as a magnet to others and in the larger centres two, three or more department stores may be attracted to a particular site* (Geographical). *The regional center . . . had two anchor stores and from 50 to 75 stores* (Isadore Barmash).

ax·i·on (ak′sē on), *n.* a hypothetical elementary particle having neutral charge and zero spin, and a mass of less than one-thousandth of a proton: *If the axion is found not to exist then the theory of quantum chromodynamics will lose much of its attractiveness* (London Times). *The search . . . is thus increasingly turning to different types of hypothetical particles with names like gravitinos . . . and axions* (New York Times). [perhaps < Greek *áxios* worthy + English -*on*]

A·za·ni·an (ə zā′nē ən), *n., adj.* —*n.* a native or inhabitant of Azania, the African nationalist name of South Africa: *He began to take the . . . position that it might be all right for American companies already in South Africa to remain there, provided they share their profits with the majority of the South African people—which was, of course, black Azanians* (New Yorker). —*adj.* of or having to do with Azania or Azanians: *. . . a new militant black organization, the Azanian People's Organization* (Manchester Guardian Weekly).

B b

ban·jax (ban′jaks), *v.t. Slang.* to hit, beat, or overcome: *So she ups and banjaxed the old man one night with a broken spade handle* (Ted Walker). *"Well, I'm banjaxed!" cries Vanya . . .* (Maclean's). [apparently < dialectal Irish *banjax*]

black knight, *U.S. Finance.* a company that makes a tender offer to forcibly gain control of another company: *But that didn't mean he had to sell to Lance, the hostile "black knight." He figured he could do what Microdot did when that manufacturer of electrical connectors was under siege by General Cable. Microdot went out and found Northwest Industries, who played the role of a "white knight"* (Milton Moskowitz).

C c

calorific, *adj.* **3** *Figurative.* showing feeling or emotion; warm: *In "Critique of Political Reason," he argues that the cold scrutinies of "scientific Marxism" should be replaced by more calorific interpretations* (New York Times Book Review).

cell, *n.* **11** a small geographical area in which a group of radiotelephones can communicate through a single radio transmitter: *As a vehicle in which a telephone call is in progress on a particular channel moves from one cell to another, the call is automatically transferred to the neighboring cell* (Duane L. Huff).

cellular phone or **telephone**, a mobile telephone unit, especially in a motor vehi-

cle, capable of extending communication over a wide geographical area by means of low-power radio transmitters linking many smaller areas called cells: *The cellular telephone . . . promises to turn your car into a 55-mph phone booth* (Money). *This man can enjoy eating outdoors and still attend to important business calls with his hand-held cellular phone* (Technology Review).

chron·o·ther·a·py (kron′ə ther′ə pē), *n.* a treatment for insomnia by adjusting the patient's rhythm of sleeping and waking: *Here's how "chronotherapy" works: For each of six days, the person is kept up three hours longer than the previous day. If he normally can't get to sleep until 3 A.M., he goes to bed on one day of chronotherapy at 6 A.M.; day two at 9, etc.* (Modern Maturity).

Com·ex or **com·ex** (kom′əks), *n.* = commodity exchange: *Gold futures on the Comex fell $2.20 to $2.30 an ounce* (New York Times).

compact object, any of a class of very dense astronomical bodies, including neutron stars, quasars, and X-ray bursters: *Scientists are still theorizing about what the mystery star could be. . . . Some suggest that it may be a neutron star, an enormously compact object with intense magnetic fields* (Newsweek). *The story of the discovery of compact objects—white dwarfs, neutron stars, and (still controversial) black holes—has been widely recounted in astronomical texts and popular books* (Science).

con·trar·i·an (kən trãr′ē ən), *n. U.S.* a contrary person, especially a stock speculator who does not follow the popular trends in buying and selling stock: *Like all other investors, contrarians follow the obvious credo of buy low, sell high. But they avoid buying or selling at obvious times. They also avoid securities heavily favored by analysts, the ones that most investors buy* (Time).

cy·clo·spor·in (sī′klə spôr′in, -spôr′-), *n.* = cyclosporine: *Cyclosporin . . . seems to be able to eliminate the T cells that attack foreign tissue while leaving other immune cells intact* (Paul Katz).

cy·clo·spor·ine (sī′klə spôr′ēn, -spôr′-), *n.* an immunosuppressive drug derived from certain brown algae, effective in stopping the rejection of transplanted tissue without destroying the body's immune system: *The immune suppressant cyclosporine produces 80% first-year survival rates in heart transplant recipients . . . Cyclosporine was also being given to patients receiving kidney, liver, bone marrow, and heart-lung transplants* (Susan V. Lawrence). [< New Latin *Cyclosporinae* the class of brown algae]

D d

digital, *adj.* **5** of or having to do with the recording of sound by means of electrical signals coded into binary digits: *digital recording, digital sound.*

dis·flu·en·cy (dis flü′ən sē), *n.* **1** a stutter: *Himself a stutterer who simply seemed to outgrow the problem, he "found the Iowa approach to 'disfluency' faintly depressing"* (Christopher Lehmann-Haupt). **2** *pl.* **-cies.** an instance of stuttering: *These normal childhood "disfluencies" occur on the average of fifty times for every thousand words spoken* (Gerald Jonas).

dits·y or **dits·ey** (dit′sē), *adj. U.S. Slang.* haughty; snobbish: *She got rid of most of her furniture and filled the place with color. The acid-green bedroom and the magenta living room are virtually furniture-free. "I love it," she says. "It's dynamic without being ditsy"* (New York Times Magazine). *He thinks women who want equality are ditsey . . . monsters who take men's jobs away from them* (Pauline Kael). [perhaps alteration of *dicty*]

dock·a·min·i·um (dok′ə min′ē əm), *n. U.S.* a berth for a boat or ship sold as a piece of real estate: *The complex includes a boating clubhouse and more than 140 boat slips or "dockaminiums" which property owners can purchase at prices beginning at $20,000* (Daily Argus). [< *dock*[1] + (condo)*minium*]

E e

e·co·to·pi·an or **E·co·to·pi·an** (ē′kə tō′pē ən), *adj., n. Informal.* —*adj.* of or having to do with an ecologically ideal society: *The desire to preserve the landscape was popularized in a 1975 novel, "Ecotopia," in which a new nation is shut off from the U.S. because of its radical environmental laws. "The long-term trend, especially in the Northwest, is still toward Ecotopian ways," says author Ernest Callenback* (Christian Science Monitor).

—*n.* a person who adopts an ecotopian way of life: *Whether we call them dropouts or ecotopians, it is clear that they are . . . a new generation of pioneers creating their own environment beyond the physical frontier* (Tom Hayden). [< *eco-* + (u)*topian*]

eth·no·ar·chae·ol·o·gy or **eth·no·ar·che·ol·o·gy** (eth′nō är′kē ol′ə jē), *n.* a branch of archaeology dealing with the tools, artifacts, and other resources of existing cultures and societies: *Ethnoarchaeology [is] seeking some methodological stability in an effort to link human behavior and material residues within the context of living societies* (Scientific American). *Ethnoarcheology . . is another new endeavor based largely on the new paradigm, one in which archeologists in increasing numbers are doing fieldwork in living societies* (Science). —**eth·no·ar·chae·ol·o·gist** or **eth·no·ar·che·ol·o·gist**, *n.*

e·tho·gram (ē′thə gram), *n.* a detailed description of the behavior of an animal: *This "looking away" gesture of the gull is only one of many in its total "ethogram" of postures and gestures which are as much a part of its genetic endowment as feathers and wings* (Robin Fox).

F f

fat-mouth (fat′mouth′), *v.i. U.S. Slang.* to talk excessively, especially without taking action: *They have to do something, have to move, where they can no longer sit back and fat-mouth about it, because the country will be on fire* (Eldridge Cleaver).

fave rave, *British Slang.* an infatuation with a popular performer, especially a singer: *As soon as he was seen on the* screen he was snatched by the American fan magazine market, always at the ready to replace a current fave rave (London Times).

feel|good (fēl′gŏd′), n., adj. U.S. Slang. —n. 1 Also, **Feelgood.** a quack doctor: The best way to guard against Feelgoods and charlatans is for the medical profession to keep its own house in order (Newsweek). 2 a blissful state; perfect contentment: The chief exponents of psychic feelgood tend to come from . . . the psychological sciences (Russell Baker). —adj. providing well-being or contentment: Some critics . . . dismiss him as a "feelgood" director whose style reeks of old-fashioned 1950's-style seamless sleekness (New York Times Magazine).

flex|i|place (flek′sē plās′), n. a workplace at home connected by a computer to an office: In experimental projects across the U.S. several hundred clerical and professional workers have agreed to abandon the office and work at home on computer terminals electronically linked to their firms' office computers. In management jargon they are "telecommuting" and work at "flexiplaces" (Time). [< flexi(ble) + (work)place]

G g

grade creep, U.S. a steady increase in the classification level of civil-service jobs, resulting in automatic promotions: The action in the department is part of a long-time Government-wide attempt by the Civil Service Commission to control "grade creep"—the growing, sometimes unmerited, promotion of Federal employees (New York Times).

graph|i|ca|cy (graf′ə kə sē), n. skill in the graphic arts: It seems that the individual who excels in literacy, numeracy and graphicacy (all needed in good measure by the first-class geographers) is indeed rare (London Times).

green|mail (grēn′māl′), n., v. U.S. n. 1 the practice by a speculator of buying a large share of a company's stocks to prompt fear of a take-over so that the stock will be bought back by the threatened company at a higher price than the speculator paid for it: Shareholders in other firms are up in arms about the recent rash of corporate "greenmail." In case after case, a marauding investor has bought a sizable block of a company's stock and threatened a takeover (Newsweek). 2 the profit made by a speculator using greenmail: The St. Regis Corporation . . . is now facing the third takeover attempt in six months, and some analysts say stockholders will not allow the company to pay "greenmail" to escape, as it has done twice before (New York Times). —v.t. to subject to greenmail: St. Regis has been greenmailed twice (Time). [< green(back) + (black)mail]

H h

Hei|sen|berg effect (hī′zən bėrg), a change in a subject under investigation due to the effect of the investigative process: No one does or can do—the same things on stage that he does unobserved.

It's the popularized Heisenberg effect: The act of observing inevitably changes the process under observation (Richard Reeves). Second, there is the possibility of a Heisenberg effect: the act of trying to outguess market psychology itself becomes a factor in the psychology and may invalidate the conclusion (London Times). [< Heisenberg uncertainty principle]

I i

in|tra|pre|neur (in′trə prə nėr′), n. a corporation executive empowered to act as an entrepreneur in undertaking new ventures: Intrapreneurs, the people who start new businesses inside established companies, will soon be as big a catchword as entrepreneurs. This is because the business recovery in America and much of the rest of the world is being sustained not only by changes in management techniques for starting up new companies but also in ways of spawning fresh ideas and products inside old ones (The Economist). [blend of intra- and entrepreneur] —**in′tra|pre|neur′ship**, n.

J j

jel|lies (jel′ēz), n.pl. = jelly bean shoes: The exhibit includes everything from "jellies" (transparent, rubbery shoes) to petroleum products (Newsweek).

jelly bean shoes, **jelly shoes**, or **jelly sandals**, shoes or sandals made of glossy, molded rubber or plastic in a variety of bright colors, especially for women and girls: Jelly shoes . . . come in such shimmering shades as wine, grape, root beer and cherry red (Ron Alexander). Also, **jellies.**

jumping gene, Informal. = transposon: Jumping genes have already been found to play a role in the transference of antibiotic resistance among bacteria (Barbara Tchabovsky). Transposons . . . are also called jumping genes because they can change their position from one place to another on the chromosomes (Daniel L. Hartl).

L l

LIPS or **lips**[2] (lips), n. logical inferences per second (a measure of the speed with which a computer solves a problem): They will be so much more powerful that where today's machines can handle 10,000 to 100,000 logical inferences per second, or LIPS, the next-generation computer will be capable of 100 million to 1,000 million LIPS (New York Times). Simulated program runs indicate that this machine might be capable of executing 400,000 lips at peak capacity (Science News).

low-tech (lō′tek′), adj., n. —adj. of or having to do with conventional or unsophisticated technology, especially that limited to the production of basic commodities: The stocks Putnam likes are those of low-priced, low-tech companies (Forbes).

—n. a style of design or interior decoration typical or imitative of early technology: Late-50's low-tech, the décor in her public rooms was harsh, metallic, and fluorescent (New York Times Magazine).

M m

mag|con (mag′kon), n. a concentration of magnetic material on the surface of a moon or planet: Magnetic concentrations ("magcons") in the lunar surface could, if of sufficient extent and field strength, interact locally with the solar wind when the magcons are on the daytime lunar side (Nature). [< mag(netic) con(centration)]

mi|cro|cas|sette (mī′krō ka set′), n. a very small cassette of tape recording: A "microcassette" which offers three hours of recording time in a module measuring just $33.5 \times 50 \times 8$ mm (New Scientist). Personal portables . . . may have Dolby B or DBX noise reduction and take metal tape or microcassettes (Washington Post).

N n

naff (naf), v.i. **naff off**, British Slang. go away; beat it; disappear: The Queen, via her press staff, gave editors a short, sharp and public "request" to tell the scribes and telephoto lens artists who had been plaguing the royals at Sandringham to naff off (The Economist). [< earlier British slang naffy shirking, avoiding work < NAAFI]

number cruncher 2 Usually, **numbers cruncher.** a researcher, financial analyst, pollster, or the like, who does complex calculations or exaggerates the importance of numerical data: For 18½ years he was a research analyst covering "smokestack" industries and a portfolio manager. The only partner with no management experience, Taggart nonetheless is more than a numbers cruncher (Intercorp).

O o

opportunistic infection, an infection which develops in people with a deficiency of the immune system, especially with such conditions as AIDS or SCID: AIDS is characterized by a disorder of the immune system that makes victims susceptible to a wide variety of so-called opportunistic infections. Such infections result from organisms that rarely cause disease in people whose immune systems are working normally (Lawrence K. Altman).

Pronunciation Key: hat, āge, câre, fär; let, ēqual, tėrm; it, īce; hot, ōpen, ôrder; oil, out; cup, pút, rüle; child; long; thin; ŦHen; zh, measure; ə represents **a** in about, **e** in taken, **i** in pencil, **o** in lemon, **u** in circus.

out|source (out'sôrs', -sōrs'), *v.i., v.t.,* **-sourced, -sourc|ing.** to acquire (a product or parts) from an outside source: *Ford now buys its valves from a non-union Eaton corporation plant in Nebraska, and . . . this "outsourcing of parts . . . will be a leading topic of debate when the union leaders discuss contract reopeners"* (New Yorker). *Outsourcing is auto-industry jargon for purchasing components or whole cars from suppliers outside the company and usually applies to areas where costs are lower* (New York Times).

P p

proactive, *adj.* **2** active in advance; anticipating trends and working to promote their development: *Keeping up with technological developments requires a new kind of management able to take risks, become more cosmopolitan, manage change, and be more proactive* (Christopher Lorenz).

producer price index, = wholesale price index: *There now comes a tough period in which unemployment will likely rise while the presumed trade-off, a slowing of inflation, will likely remain elusive. Hints of this prospect were evident in the Producer (formerly wholesale) Price Index, which was up 1.2 percent in August for the largest monthly increase since January* (New York Times).

punctuated equilibrium, a modification of the Darwinian theory of evolution which maintains that natural selection acts on a species to keep it stable rather than to alter it, and that the emergence of a new species is a separate event that points up the general equilibrium in nature: *Punctuated equilibrium provides a model for the "small" level of speciation and its consequences* (Stephen Jay Gould). *Many paleontologists favoured the model of punctuated equilibrium. In this view species normally evolve slowly, and most changes occur when small populations diverge rapidly into new forms during short intervals of time* (Peter John Wyllie).

R r

rainmaker, *n.* **2** *U.S. Slang.* a business executive, especially a partner in a law firm, who has political connections and promises to use them to bring in business: *[The] awards, to six of 18 competing airlines, had left Washington seething with charges of high-altitude politicking and string-pulling by "rainmakers"* (Time). *In legal parlance, a "rainmaker" is a business-getter* (New York Times).

rap music, a style of rock music with a very pronounced rhythmical beat and vocal accompaniment in a recitative rather than melodic style, popular in break dancing: *In the latter days of The Jam, Mr. Weller began embracing American black music, and "My Ever Changing Moods" shows that he has assimilated Motown and Philadelphia soul styles, but not rap and funk music* (Stephen Holden).

reverse annuity mortgage or **reverse mortgage**, *U.S. and Canada.* the transfer of a homeowner's mortgage to a bank, lending company, or the like, in return for a regular annuity: *The reverse annuity mortgage is designed to help the elderly who have a great deal of equity in their homes* (Edgar J. McDougall, Jr.). *In theory, a reverse mortgage allows homeowners with little cash to tap the equity in their homes. Typically they are used by retired couples who have paid off their mortgage and no longer benefit from the mortgage interest tax deduction* (American Banker). *Abbr:* RAM

S s

SCID (no periods), severe combined immunodeficiency, a disease similar to AIDS: *At least six other children with SCID have received marrow transplants [which] produce the immune-system cells that SCID victims lack* (Jenny Tesar).

Sherpa, *n.* **3** Also, **sherpa.** a representative of a head of state who is charged with the preparations for a summit meeting: *"There should be a summit where there would be no proclamation of the leader in advance," said Canadian Prime Minister Pierre Trudeau. "Unstructured, without a precise agenda, and, most important, without a lengthy communiqué which had been written over the period of weeks and months by our 'Sherpas'—that we would be meeting at summit level to, kind of, justify that we covered all these subjects"* (Christian Science Monitor).

sky-clad (skī'klad'), *adj.* unclothed: *She is sensibly shod and amply skirted . . .; not, I am glad to say, naked, or as the Californian suntan-loving neopagans here disporting prefer to call it, "sky-clad"* (Sunday Times). [translation of Sanskrit *digambara*]

smart card, a small plastic card embedded with a microprocessor and memory chip that can function as a miniature computer: *Because the microprocessor chip can generate its own code to communicate with computers, the smart card offers a highly secure system for access not only to banking transactions but to data bases and buildings* (Fortune).

T t

tech|ie (tek'ē), *n. Informal.* **1** a student at a technical institute: *Just as the spread of "aggie" schools throughout the Middle West in the 19th century increased the productivity of farms, so too would the spread of new "techie" schools revitalize middle America* (New York Times). **2** a technician, especially in the computer field: *I think everyone else in the company was a little afraid of me because I knew about computers and they didn't. They saw me as that techie in shirt-sleeves down in the basement* (Computerworld).

tech|no|pop (tek'nō pop'), *n.* popular music played on synthesizers and other electronic devices: *The technology has spawned pop bands—hence the phrase technopop—whose songs are heavy on perfect syncopation* (New York Daily News).

tel|e|com|mute (tel'ə kəm myüt'), *v.i. Informal.* to work at home while communicating with one's office by computer: *Eventually workers will telecommute from their homes, but meanwhile telecommuting from neighbourhood work centres will begin* (Economist).

trans|pu|ter (trans pyü'tər), *n.* a very high-speed computer used especially in complex data processing and artificial intelligence: *A system for scheduling tasks is wired into the transputer; this allows it to switch quickly between jobs* (Economist).

U u

upstream, *adv., adj.* **2** in, of, or toward the extractive, manufacturing, or production end of an industry: *Until now most of the oil companies' profits have been upstream* (Auckland Star). **3** *Molecular Biology.* in or toward the starting point of a genetic segment or transcription: *In the DNA stretch just "upstream" of each globin gene, scientists have found the same two short sequences . . . The sequences are thought to play some role in starting the process in which a gene acts as a template for production of messenger RNA* (Science News).

V v

vee|jay (vē'jā), *n. Slang.* video jockey: *A recent development is the video bar, with "video jockeys" or "veejays" programming the mix of [video] clips* (Peter Rauch).

video jockey, an announcer for a television show, night club, or the like, who presents and comments on music videos: *Kids dance to . . . music videos by performers like Michael Jackson, Culture Club and Prince. In some clubs there are video jockeys* (Aljean Harmetz). *Abbr:* VJ, V.J., or v.j.

W w

white-bread (hwīt'bred'), *adj. Figurative, Informal.* of, belonging to, or reflecting the values of the affluent white society: *The contrast between his white-bread liberalism and the boys' ghetto wit is the basis of all the comedy in Diff'rent Strokes* (TV Guide). *"This cast! A real Canadian mosaic. Four blondes, five WASPs, all white-bread"* (Maclean's). *"I loved the groove, but to me they were white-bread Madison Avenue songs, infected by white culture"* (Sunday Times).

white knight 2 *U.S. Finance.* a friendly bidder sought out by a company to outbid a hostile company that has made a tender offer for its control: *Mr. Johnstone denied . . . that Morgan Stanley had found a number of "white knights" willing to outbid American Express* (New York Times).

Z z

zap|ping (zap'ing), *n. U.S.* the practice of switching off commercials from a television set by using a remote control unit or by fast-forwarding a program that had been taped on a video cassette: *Of course, even before remote control, viewers could get up for a trip to the refrigerator, but zapping is regarded as a more serious situation. "During the average commercial break, there's a tune-out factor of maybe 40%," says John Jacobs, a Grey Advertising executive who studied zapping* (Fortune).

Index

1981
1982
1983
1984
1985

How to Use the Index

This index covers the contents of the 1984, 1985, and 1986 editions of THE WORLD BOOK YEAR BOOK.

Each index entry is followed by the edition year and the page number, as:

BOTANY, 86-228, 85-221, 84-223.
See also **GARDENING.**

This means that information about botany begins on page 228 in the 1986 edition of THE YEAR BOOK.

An index entry that is the title of an article appearing in THE YEAR BOOK is printed in capital letters, as:

NEWSPAPER. An entry that is not an article title, but a subject discussed in an article of some other title, is printed: **Jarvik-7 artificial heart.**

The "See" and "See also" cross-references are to other entries within the index. Clue words or phrases are used when two or more references to the same subject appear in the same edition of THE YEAR BOOK. These make it easy to locate the material on the page, since they refer to an article title or article subsection in which the reference appears, as:

Statue of Liberty: building, 85-226; conservation, 85-264, 84-267; Special Report, 86-51

The indication "il." means that the reference is to an illustration only. An index entry in capital letters followed by "WBE" refers to a new or revised WORLD BOOK ENCYCLOPEDIA article in the supplement section, as:

AIRSHIP: WBE, 86-530

Q

R

Acknowledgments

The publishers acknowledge the following sources for illustrations. Credits read from top to bottom, left to right, on their respective pages. An asterisk (*) denotes illustrations and photographs that are the exclusive property of THE YEAR BOOK. All maps, charts, and diagrams were prepared by THE YEAR BOOK staff unless otherwise noted.

3	Susan Greenwood, Gamma/Liaison; Yvonne Hemsey, Gamma/Liaison
9	Dirck Halstead, *Time* Magazine
10	© 1985 Susan Phillips, LGI
13	Allan Tannenbaum, Sygma; Dirck Halstead, *Time* Magazine
14	Gamma/Liaison; Bernard Bisson, Sygma
15	Stuart Franklin, Sygma; Louise Gubb, JB Pictures
16	Susan Meiselas, Magnum; © 1985 Carol Guzy, *The Miami Herald* from Black Star
17	Gamma/Liaison
18	Bill Smith, *Time* Magazine; Ken Regan, Camera 5
19	Rob Nelson, Picture Group; Copyright © 1985 by Universal Pictures, a division of Universal City Studios, Inc. Courtesy of MCA Publishing Rights, a division of MCA Inc.; Nancy Moran, Sygma
20	Reuters/Bettmann Newsphotos; © John Ficara, Woodfin Camp, Inc.; AP/Wide World
21	© Dennis Brack, Black Star; Polska Agencia Interpress; UPI/Bettmann Newsphotos
22	© John Ficara, Woodfin Camp, Inc.; © J. C. Francolon, Gamma/Liaison
23	Chris Walker, *Chicago Tribune;* © Rich Frishman, Picture Group; Richard Mackson, *Sports Illustrated,* © Time Inc.
24	UPI/Bettmann Newsphotos; © Gamma/Liaison; Reuters/Bettmann Newsphotos
25	© David Burnett, Contact; Reuters/Bettmann Newsphotos; AP/Wide World
26	Reuters/Bettmann Newsphotos; © Rick McCawley, *The Miami Herald;* Bill Fitz-Patrick, The White House
27	© Yamaguchi, Gamma/Liaison; AP/Wide World
28	AP/Wide World; © Paul Conklin
29	UPI/Bettmann Newsphotos; © Gary Williams, Gamma/Liaison
30	© Sloan, Gamma/Liaison; © Carraro, Rex Features; © Gamma/Liaison
31	NASA
33	© Dan Cornish, ESTO
34	Martin Marietta Corporation
37-38	NASA
40	Dale Gustafson, © National Geographic Society; NASA
41	NASA
42	European Space Agency
43	Sovfoto
44	Roberta Polfus*
47	NASA
48	© James Hervat
50	Icon Communications from FPG
53	Musée Bartholdi, Colmar, France
54	*World Book* map; P. Gridley, FPG
56	*World Book* illustration by Tony Gibbons, Linden Artists Ltd.
58-59	© Dan Cornish, ESTO
60	© Dan Cornish, ESTO; © Dan Cornish, ESTO; Swanke Hayden Connell Architects
62	© Andy Levin, Black Star
63	© Dan Cornish, ESTO
64	Kurt Scholz, Shostal from Colour Library International
66	Culver; Bettmann Archive; © Michael George
67	© Stephanie Maze, Woodfin Camp, Inc.; Phil Huber, Black Star; C. Harris, Gamma/Liaison; Susan Greenwood, Gamma/Liaison
71	Culver
72	Mark Tiberi*
74	Dirck Halstead, Gamma/Liaison
75	Jim Mendenhall, Gamma/Liaison
76	Mike Keza, Gamma/Liaison
77	Shahn Kermani, Gamma/Liaison; Owen Franken, Stock, Boston
78	© Stephanie Maze, Woodfin Camp, Inc.
79	© Joe McNally, Wheeler Pictures; Robin Mover, Gamma/Liaison; Jim Pozarik, Gamma/Liaison
80	Ralph Brunke*
82	Owen Franken, Sygma
85	Gary L. Kieffer, *U.S. News & World Report*
87-89	George V. Kelvin*
92	George V. Kelvin*; Alain Nogues; U.S. Department of Energy; U.S. Department of Energy
95	George V. Kelvin*
98-102	Roberta Polfus*; © Roger Ressmeyer, Wheeler Pictures
104	G. A. Izett, U.S. Geological Survey; Alessandro Montanari; University of Chicago
105	David J. Roddy, U.S. Geological Survey
106	Erle Kauffman; Charles C. Smith
107	Richard Faverty, © *Discover* Magazine, Time Inc.; Roberta Polfus*
110	© Thomas Hopker, Woodfin Camp, Inc.
114	© Paolo Koch, Photo Researchers
115	Diego Goldberg, Sygma
117	Eric Brissaud, Gamma/Liaison; Jonathan Wright, Gamma/Liaison
118	Matt Brown, West Stock; Doug Wilson, West Stock
120	© Wally McNamee, Woodfin Camp, Inc.
121	R. Tomkins, Gamma/Liaison; Richard and Sally Greenhill, Black Star
122	J. P. Laffont, Sygma; Matt Brown, West Stock
124	© Paolo Koch, Photo Researchers
126	© Wolfgang Hoyt, ESTO
129	© Ezra Stoller, ESTO; © Ezra Stoller, ESTO; Ronald Sheridan
130	Venturi, Rauch and Scott Brown; Virginia State Library
131	Robert A. M. Stern Architects
132	Reproduced with permission of AT&T
133	SCALA/Art Resource; © Peter Aaron, ESTO
134	© Peter Aaron, ESTO
136	Timothy Hursley, © The Arkansas Office
137	Ralph Brunke*
138-139	James Steinkamp, Murphy/Jahn
140	Timothy Hursley, © The Arkansas Office; Michael Moran
141	© Wolfgang Hoyt, ESTO; Jessica Ehlers, Bruce Coleman Inc.
142	Atelier Hans Hollein
145	F. Robert Masini, Phototake
148	Scott Thorn Barrows*
150	Scott Thorn Barrows*; Margaret C. Cubberly, Phototake; © Chet Szymecki, Phototake
151	© Bob Hahn, Taurus
152	F. Robert Masini, Phototake; Scott Thorn Barrows*
153	Scott Thorn Barrows*
155	George O. Waring, III, M.D., F.A.C.S., Emory University School of Medicine, Atlanta; Scott Thorn Barrows*
159	Newberry Library, Chicago
160	Kristin Nelson*; AT&T Information Systems; Culver
161	Bettmann Archive
162	Kristin Nelson*; Bettmann Archive
163	Kristin Nelson*; BBC Hulton Library from Bettmann Archive
164	Kristin Nelson*; Newberry Library, Chicago; Newberry Library, Chicago; Newberry Library, Chicago
165	Canadian Pacific Railroad; Newberry Library, Chicago
166	Kristin Nelson*; Culver; Bettmann Archive; Pierpont Morgan Library
167	Kristin Nelson*; Brown Bros.
168	Kristin Nelson*
170	Kristin Nelson*; Circus World Museum
173	AP/Wide World
174	UPI/Bettmann Newsphotos; AP/Wide World
175	AP/Wide World
176	The Advertising Council
178-180	Reuters/Bettmann Newsphotos
181	Pictorial Parade
185	Canapress
186	J. L. Atlan, Sygma
188	Poly-Press
189	Russell L. Ciochon
190	University of Chicago
191	National Park Service
193	Atelier Hans Hollein
194	© Enrique Shore, Woodfin Camp, Inc.
195	AP/Wide World
196	John Trever, *Albuquerque Journal*
197	Terrence McCarthy, NYT Pictures
198	Narunart Prapanya, *Time* Magazine
201	Jim Wilson, NYT Pictures
203	*Time* Magazine
206	News Ltd.

208 AP/Wide World
209 UPI/Bettmann Newsphotos
210 AP/Wide World
211 UPI/Bettmann Newsphotos
213 Barton Silverman, NYT Pictures
215-220 AP/Wide World
221 UPI/Bettmann Newsphotos
224 Focus on Sports
225 AP/Wide World
227 Melissa Priest, *U.S. News & World Report*
228 Chuck Berman, *Chicago Tribune*
231 Claudio Edinger, Gamma/Liaison
234 Reuters/Bettmann Newsphotos
236 Agence France-Presse
237 *The Globe and Mail*, Toronto
241 Canapress
243 Bill Decker, Canapress
244 AP/Wide World
247 Reuters/Bettmann Newsphotos
248-256 AP/Wide World
257 UPI/Bettmann Newsphotos
259 Martha Swope
261 Owen Rayner, NYT Pictures
263 Jerry Barnett, *The Indianapolis News*
264 AP/Wide World
266 George Tames, NYT Pictures
267 NASA
272-274 AP/Wide World
275 Agence France-Presse
277 AP/Wide World
278 Reuters/Bettmann Newsphotos
280 © 1985 Martha Swope
281 Johan Elbers, *Time* Magazine
282 AP/Wide World; Botti, Sygma; AP/Wide World; AP/Wide World
283 AP/Wide World; UPI/Bettmann Newsphotos; AP/Wide World; Dan Wynn, *Time* Magazine
284 UPI/Bettmann Newsphotos; Canapress; AP/Wide World; AP/Wide World
285 Tribune Media Services, reprinted by permission
286 AP/Wide World
287 AP/Wide World; AP/Wide World; UPI/Bettmann Newsphotos; Peter Marlow, Magnum
288 Wally McNamee, *Newsweek*
289 Reuters/Bettmann Newsphotos
290 © 1985, *Better Homes and Gardens*
292 Reuters/Bettmann Newsphotos
294 Abbott Laboratories
295 Linda L. Creighton, *U.S. News & World Report*
297 Reuters/Bettmann Newsphotos
300 From *The Wall Street Journal*—Permission, Cartoon Features Syndicate
303 *World Book* photo
305 AP/Wide World
306 Electronics Industries Association
308 © Georg Gerster, Photo Researchers
310 AP/Wide World
312 Terrence McCarthy, NYT Pictures
314 Cover, Gamma/Liaison
316-324 AP/Wide World
325 Philip Amdal, *Time* Magazine
329 AP/Wide World
330 David Ekren, *Seattle Post-Intelligencer*
331 Alain Nogues, Sygma
332 Hasbro, Inc.
335-339 AP/Wide World
340 Canapress
342 UPI/Bettmann Newsphotos
343-344 AP/Wide World
346 Focus on Sports
348 By permission of *The Daily and Sunday Herald*
351 Focus on Sports
353 AP/Wide World
354 Dan Budnik, NYT Pictures
356 UPI/Bettmann Newsphotos
357 AP/Wide World
358 UPI/Bettmann Newsphotos
359 Agence France-Presse
361 Micha Bar-Am, NYT Pictures
364 Kaku Kurita, Gamma/Liaison
365 AP/Wide World
367 Reuters/Bettmann Newsphotos
370-374 AP/Wide World
376-379 Reuters/Bettmann Newsphotos

380 AP/Wide World
382 Steve Liss, *Time* Magazine
383 AP/Wide World
385 Dan Miller*
386 From *Saint George and the Dragon* retold by Margaret Hodges, illustrated by Trina Schart Hyman. Illustration copyright © 1984 by Trina Schart Hyman. Reprinted by permission of Little, Brown and Company
388 AP/Wide World
389 Carl Andon
390 Reuters/Bettmann Newsphotos
392 AP/Wide World
394 Abbott Laboratories
395 Rush-Presbyterian-St. Luke's Medical Center
397 From *The Wall Street Journal*—Permission, Cartoon Features Syndicate
398 AP/Wide World
399 Agence France-Presse
401 Reuters/Bettmann Newsphotos
402 Agence France-Presse
404 Canapress
406 Nancy Moran, Sygma
407 Bettmann Archive
408 Copyright © 1985 Universal Pictures, a division of Universal City Studios, Inc. Courtesy of MCA Publishing Rights, a division of MCA Inc.
412-413 AP/Wide World
414 Don Ploke, *Las Vegas Sun*
415 UPI/Bettmann Newsphotos
416 UPI/Bettmann Newsphotos; AP/Wide World
417 AP/Wide World
418 Reuters/Bettmann Newsphotos
419 D. Lainé, Agence France-Presse
420-422 AP/Wide World
424 U.S. Department of Agriculture
425 Woods Hole Oceanographic Institution
426-433 AP/Wide World
435 UPI/Bettmann Newsphotos
436 Reuters/Bettmann Newsphotos
438 Lawrence Livermore National Laboratory
441 © 1985 Ken Regan, Camera 5
442 Val Mazzenga, *Chicago Tribune*
445 AP/Wide World
446 Reuters/Bettmann Newsphotos; Paul Hosefros, NYT Pictures
449 Jim Wright, *Time* Magazine
451 © Sidney Harris
452 AP/Wide World
453 Canapress
455 Paul Hosefros, NYT Pictures
456-460 AP/Wide World
463-464 Tass from Sovfoto
467 Paul Hosefros, NYT Pictures
469 Steve Powell, Duomo
471 © Allan Tannenbaum, Sygma
473 NASA
474 AP/Wide World
476 Reuters/Bettmann Newsphotos
479 AP/Wide World
484 © Yvonne Hemsey, Gamma/Liaison
486 George Tames, NYT Pictures
487-489 AP/Wide World
490 © Sidney Harris
492 National Broadcasting Company
493 AP/Wide World
494 National Broadcasting Company
495 AP/Wide World
496 Jay Thompson
497 © 1985 Martha Swope
499 John McNeill, *The Globe and Mail*, Toronto; AP/Wide World
501 José Moré, *Chicago Tribune*
502 Greg Campbell, *The Clarion-Ledger*, Jackson, Miss.
504 AP/Wide World
507 United Nations
513 AP/Wide World
514 Jack Manning, NYT Pictures
515 Reuters/Bettmann Newsphotos
518 Ruby Washington, NYT Pictures
519 Mary Circelli, *Columbus Dispatch*
521 Reuters/Bettmann Newsphotos
522 Ray Lustig, *The Washington Post*
523 Pictorial Parade
526 © N.Y. Zoological Society
529 © Terry Madison, The Image Bank

A Preview of 1986

January

				1	2	3	4
5	6	7	8	9	10	11
12	13	14	15	16	17	18
19	20	21	22	23	24	25
26	27	28	29	30	31

1 **New Year's Day.**

5 **Twelfth Night,** traditional end of Christmas festivities during the Middle Ages.

6 **Epiphany,** 12th day of Christmas, celebrates the visit of the Three Wise Men to the infant Jesus.

20 **Martin Luther King, Jr.'s Birthday,** honoring the slain civil rights leader, is celebrated on the third Monday in January, according to law. The actual anniversary is January 15.

25 **Tu B'Shebat,** Jewish arbor festival, observed by donating trees to Israel.

26 **Super Bowl XX,** the National Football League's championship game, in New Orleans.

27 **Australia Day** marks Captain Arthur Phillip's landing in 1788 where Sydney now stands. The actual anniversary is January 26.

February

						1
2	3	4	5	6	7	8
9	10	11	12	13	14	15
16	17	18	19	20	21	22
23	24	25	26	27	28

1 **Black History Month** through February 28.

2 **Ground-Hog Day.** Legend says six weeks of winter weather will follow if the ground hog sees its shadow.
Candlemas, Roman Catholic holy day, marks the presentation of infant Jesus in the Temple.

8 **Boy Scouts of America Birthday Anniversary** marks the founding of the organization in 1910.

9 **Chinese New Year** begins year 4684, the Year of the Tiger, on the ancient Chinese calendar.

11 **Mardi Gras,** celebrated in New Orleans and many Roman Catholic countries, is the last merrymaking before Lent.

12 **Abraham Lincoln's Birthday,** observed in most states.
Ash Wednesday, first day of Lent for Christians, begins the period of repentance that precedes Easter.

14 **Valentine's Day,** festival of romance and affection.

17 **George Washington's Birthday,** according to law, is celebrated on the third Monday in February. The actual anniversary is February 22.

March

						1
2	3	4	5	6	7	8
9	10	11	12	13	14	15
16	17	18	19	20	21	22
23	24	25	26	27	28	29
30	31

1-31 **Red Cross Month.**

9-15 **Girl Scout Week** marks the group's 74th birthday.

6-22 **Camp Fire Birthday Week** marks the 76th anniversary of the group.

17 **St. Patrick's Day,** honoring the patron saint of Ireland.

20 **First Day of Spring,** 5:03 P.M. E.S.T.

23 **Palm Sunday** marks Jesus Christ's last entry into Jerusalem, where people covered His path with palm branches.

24 **Academy Awards Night,** when the Academy of Motion Picture Arts and Sciences presents the Oscars.

25 **Purim,** Jewish festival commemorating how Esther saved the Jews from the tyrant Haman.

27 **Maundy Thursday,** Christian celebration of Christ's commandment to love others.

28 **Good Friday** marks the death of Jesus on the cross. It is a public holiday in many countries and several states of the United States.

30 **Easter Sunday,** commemorating the Resurrection of Jesus Christ.

April

		1	2	3	4	5
6	7	8	9	10	11	12
13	14	15	16	17	18	19
20	21	22	23	24	25	26
27	28	29	30

1 **April Fool's Day,** a traditional day for jokes and tricks.

6-12 **National Library Week.**

11 **Halley's Comet** passes closest to Earth and acquires its greatest brightness.

15 **Income Tax Day** in the United States.

23 **Professional Secretaries Day** acknowledges the contributions of secretaries in business, government, and other fields.

24 **Passover,** Jewish festival that celebrates the exodus of the Jews from bondage in Egypt.

27 **Daylight-Saving Time** begins at 2 A.M.

28 **Confederate Memorial Day,** honoring Confederate soldiers who died in the Civil War, observed on this date in Alabama and Mississippi and on other dates in other Southern states.

May

				1	2	3
4	5	6	7	8	9	10
11	12	13	14	15	16	17
18	19	20	21	22	23	24
25	26	27	28	29	30	31

1 **May Day,** observed as a festival of spring in many countries and as a holiday honoring workers in socialist and Communist countries.
Law Day U.S.A.

2 **Expo 86,** world's fair devoted to transportation, through October 13 in Vancouver, Canada.

8 **Ascension Day,** or Holy Thursday, 40 days after Easter, celebrates the ascent of Jesus Christ into heaven.

10 **First Day of Ramadan,** the Islamic holy month, observed by fasting.

11 **Mother's Day.**

17 **Armed Forces Day** honors all branches of the armed forces in the United States.

18 **Pentecost,** or Whitsunday, the seventh Sunday after Easter, commemorates the descent of the Holy Spirit upon the 12 disciples.

19 **Victoria Day,** in Canada, marks the official birthday of the reigning monarch.

26 **Memorial Day,** by law, is the last Monday in May.
Stratford Festival, drama and music, through October 13 in Stratford, Canada.

June

1	2	3	4	5	6	7
8	9	10	11	12	13	14
15	16	17	18	19	20	21
22	23	24	25	26	27	28
29	30

6 **D-Day** commemorates the Allied landing in Normandy in 1944, during World War II.

13 **Shavuot,** Jewish Feast of Weeks, marks the revealing of the Ten Commandments to Moses on Mount Sinai.

14 **Flag Day.**

15 **Father's Day.**

17-20 **Royal Ascot,** famous series of thoroughbred horse races in Ascot, England.

21 **First Day of Summer,** 12:30 P.M. E.D.T.

23 **Midsummer Day,** summer celebration in many European countries.
All-England (Wimbledon) Tennis Championship, through July 6 in Wimbledon, near London.

29 **World Cup** professional soccer title match, Mexico City.

July

	1	2	3	4	5
6	7	8	9	10	11	12
13	14	15	16	17	18	19
20	21	22	23	24	25	26
27	28	29	30	31		

1 **Canada Day,** in Canada, celebrates the Confederation of the provinces in 1867.

2 **Halfway Point of 1986,** when the year is half over.

4 **Independence Day,** in the United States, the anniversary of the day on which the Continental Congress adopted the Declaration of Independence in 1776.

8 **Baseball All-Star Game,** Houston.

14 **Bastille Day,** in France, commemorates the uprising of the people of Paris against King Louis XVI in 1789 and their seizure of the Bastille, a hated Paris prison.

15 **St. Swithin's Day.** According to legend, if it rains on this day, it will rain for 40 more.

24 **Commonwealth Games,** amateur sports festival in Edinburgh, Scotland, through August 2.

25 **Puerto Rico Constitution Day.**

August

					1	2
3	4	5	6	7	8	9
10	11	12	13	14	15	16
17	18	19	20	21	22	23
24	25	26	27	28	29	30
31						

6 **Hiroshima Day,** memorial observance for victims of the first atomic bombing, in Hiroshima, Japan, in 1945.

7-10 **Professional Golfers' Association of America Championship,** Toledo, Ohio.

11-13 **Perseid Meteor Shower.**

14 **Tishah B'Ab,** Jewish holy day, marks the destruction of the first and second temples in Jerusalem in 587 B.C. and A.D. 70.

15 **Feast of the Assumption,** Roman Catholic and Eastern Orthodox holy day, celebrates the ascent of the Virgin Mary into heaven.

19 **National Aviation Day** commemorates the birthday of pioneer pilot Orville Wright in 1871.

26 **Women's Equality Day** commemorates the enactment of the 19th Amendment in 1920 giving women the vote.

26 **United States Open Tennis Championship** through September 7 in Flushing Meadow, N.Y.

September

	1	2	3	4	5	6
7	8	9	10	11	12	13
14	15	16	17	18	19	20
21	22	23	24	25	26	27
28	29	30				

1 **Labor Day** in the United States and Canada.

7 **National Grandparents Day** honors grandfathers and grandmothers.

17 **Citizenship Day** celebrates the rights and duties of U.S. citizens.

23 **First Day of Fall,** 3:59 A.M. E.D.T.

26 **Native American Day** honors American Indians.

28 **Gold Star Mother's Day** honors mothers who lost sons in World Wars I and II, the Korean War, and the Vietnam War.

30 **End of the Fiscal Year** for the United States government.

October

		1	2	3	4
5	6	7	8	9	10	11
12	13	14	15	16	17	18
19	20	21	22	23	24	25
26	27	28	29	30	31	

4 **Rosh Ha-Shanah,** or Jewish New Year, beginning the year 5747 according to the Jewish calendar.

5-11 **National 4-H Week. Fire Prevention Week. National Employ the Handicapped Week.**

13 **Yom Kippur,** or Day of Atonement, the most solemn day in the Jewish calendar.
Columbus Day commemorates Christopher Columbus' landing in America in 1492. Celebrated in Latin-American countries on October 12, the actual anniversary.
Thanksgiving Day in Canada.

18 **Sukkot,** or Feast of Tabernacles, begins—Jewish festival for the harvest season.
Sweetest Day, when sweethearts exchange cards and gifts.

24 **United Nations (UN) Day** commemorates the founding of the UN in 1945.

26 **Simhat Torah,** Jewish festival of rejoicing in God's law, marks the end of the annual cycle of Scripture readings.
Standard Time Resumes at 2 A.M.

31 **Halloween.**
United Nations Children's Fund (UNICEF) Day.
Reformation Day, celebrated by Protestants, marks the day in 1517 when Reformation leader Martin Luther posted his Ninety-Five Theses.

November

							1
2	3	4	5	6	7	8
9	10	11	12	13	14	15
16	17	18	19	20	21	22
23	24	25	26	27	28	29
30						

1 **All Saints' Day,** observed by the Roman Catholic Church.

4 **Election Day** in the United States.

5 **Guy Fawkes Day,** in Great Britain, marks the failure of a plot to blow up King James I and Parliament in 1605.

11 **Veterans Day** in the United States.
Remembrance Day in Canada.

15-21 **American Education Week.**

17-23 **Children's Book Week.**

23-30 **National Bible Week,** an interfaith drive to promote reading and study of the Bible.

27 **Thanksgiving Day** in the United States.

30 **Advent** begins, first of the four Sundays in the season before Christmas.
St. Andrew's Day, feast day of the patron saint of Scotland.

December

	1	2	3	4	5	6
7	8	9	10	11	12	13
14	15	16	17	18	19	20
21	22	23	24	25	26	27
28	29	30	31			

6 **St. Nicholas Day,** when children in many European countries receive gifts.

10 **Human Rights Day** marks the anniversary of the adoption of the Universal Declaration of Human Rights in 1948.

13 **St. Lucia Day,** in Sweden, celebrates the return of light after the darkest time of the year.

15 **Bill of Rights Day** in the United States marks the ratification of that document in 1791.

21 **First Day of Winter,** 11:02 P.M. E.S.T.

24 **Christmas Eve.**

25 **Christmas Day.**

26 **Kwanzaa,** black American holiday based on a traditional African harvest festival, through January 1.
Boxing Day, holiday in Canada and Great Britain when mail carriers and others who perform services receive Christmas boxes.

27 **Hanukkah,** or Feast of Lights, eight-day Jewish festival that celebrates the defeat of the Syrian tyrant King Antiochus IV in 165 B.C., through Jan. 3, 1987.

31 **New Year's Eve.**

World Book Encyclopedia, Inc., offers a line of related products including The Letter People, a reading readiness program for preschoolers, and an attractive wooden bookrack for displaying *The World Book Encyclopedia*. For further information, write WORLD BOOK ENCYCLOPEDIA, INC., P.O. Box 3405, Chicago, Illinois 60654.